MW00668185

The Whole Works of Xenophon

XENOPHON'S WORKS.

F. Schofield

Collegio SS Paulat

F. Schofld.

Trin. Coll

1954

Toronto

XENOPHON.

Engraved by S. Freeman, from the

ANTIQUE BUST

THE

WHOLE WORKS

OF

XENOPHON,

TRANSLATED

BY ASHLEY COOPER, SPELMAN, SMITH, FIELDING,

AND OTHERS.

COMPLETE IN ONE VOLUME.

LONDON:

PUBLISHED BY JONES & CO.

TEMPLE OF THE MUSES, (LATE LACKINGTON's,) FINSBURY SQUARE.

MDCCCXXXII.

gx 7.637

HARVARD COLLEGE LIBRARY
GIFT OF
FRANCIS PEABODY MAGOUN, Jr.
7 Oct. 1924

O

CONTENTS.

XENOPHON

ON THE

INSTITUTION OF CYRUS.

BOOK I.

CONTENTS of BOOK I.

INSTITUTION OF CYRUS.

BOOK I.

1. I HAVE heretofore considered how many popular governments have been dissolved by men who chose to live under any other sort of government rather than the popular; and how many monarchies, and how many oligarchies, have been destroyed by the people; and how many of those who have attempted tyrannies have, some of them, been instantly and entirely destroyed; and others, if they have continued reigning but for any time, have been admired as able, wise, and happy men. And I thought I observed many masters, in their own private houses, some possessing more servants, some but very few, who yet were not able to preserve those few entirely obedient to their commands. I considered withal that keepers of oxen, and keepers of horses are, as it were, the magistrates and rulers of those oxen and horses; and, in general, all those called pastors or herdsmen may be properly accounted the magistrates of the animals they rule. I saw, I thought, all these several herds more willing to obey their pastors, than men their magistrates; for these herds go the way that their keepers direct them; they feed on those lands on which their keepers place them; they abstain from those from which their keepers drive them; they suffer their keepers to make what use they please of the fruits and profits that arise from them. Besides, I never did perceive a herd conspiring against its keepers, either so as not to obey them, or so as not to allow them the use of the fruits arising from them. Herds are rather more refractory towards any others than they are towards their rulers, and those who make profit of them; but men conspire against none sooner than against those whom they perceive undertaking the government of them. When these things were in my mind, I came to this judgment on them; that to man it was easier to rule every other sort of creature than to rule man. But when I considered that there was the Persian Cyrus, who had rendered many men, many cities, and many nations, obedient to himself, I was necessitated to change my opinion, and to think that the government of men was not amongst the things that were impossible, nor amongst the things that are difficult, if one undertook it with understanding and skill. I knew there were those that willingly obeyed Cyrus, who were many days' journey distant from him; those who were months; those who had never seen him; and those who knew very well that they never should see him; yet would they submit to his government: for he so far excelled all other kings, both those that received their dominion by succession, as well as those that acquired it themselves, that the Scythian, for example, though his people be very numerous, has not been able to obtain the dominion of any other nation, but rests satisfied if he hold but the rule of his *own*; the Thracian the same; the Illyrian the same; and other nations, as I have heard, the same: for the nations of Europe are said to be sovereign and independent of each other. But Cyrus, finding in like manner the nations of Asia sovereign and independent, and setting forward with a little army of Persians, obtained the dominion of the Medes by their own choice and voluntary submission; of the Hyrcanians the same. He conquered the Syrians, Assyrians, Arabs, Cappadocians, both Phrygias, the Lydians, Carians, Phœnicians, and Babylonians. He ruled the Bactrians, Indians, and Cilicians; in like manner the Sacians, Paphlagonians, and Megudinians, and

1 *Xenophon's Cyropædia* or *Institution of Cyrus,* from external evidence and because it contradicts other historians, is not considered as an authentic history, but rather as an historical romance, showing what should be the conduct of a wise and virtuous monarch.

A

many other nations, whose names one cannot enumerate. He ruled the Greeks that were settled in Asia; and descending to the sea, the Cyprians and Egyptians. These nations he ruled, though their languages differed from his own and from each other; and yet was he able to extend the fear of himself over so great a part of the world as to astonish all, and that no one attempted any thing against him. He was able to inspire all with so great a desire of pleasing him, that they ever desired to be governed by his opinion and will. He connected together so many nations as it would be a labour to enumerate, to whatsoever point one undertook to direct one's course, whether it were east, west, north, or south, setting out from his palace and seat of empire. With respect therefore to this man, as worthy of admiration, I have inquired by what birth, with what natural disposition, and under what discipline and education bred, he so much excelled in the art of governing men. And whatever I have learned, or think I know concerning him, I shall endeavour to relate.

II. Cyrus is said to be descended from Cambyses, king of the Persians, as his father.[1] Cambyses was of the race of the Perseidæ, who were so called from Perseus. It is agreed that he was born of a mother called Mandane; and Mandane was the daughter of Astyages, king of the Medes.[1] Cyrus is said to have had by nature a most beautiful person, and a mind of the greatest benignity and love to mankind, most desirous of knowledge, and most ambitious of glory, so as to bear any pain, and undergo any danger, for the sake of praise; and he is yet celebrated as such among the barbarians. Such is he recorded to have been with respect to his mind and person; and he was educated under the institutions and laws of the Persians.

These laws seem to begin with a provident care of the common good; not where those of most other governments begin; for most other governments, giving to all a liberty of educating their children as they please, and to the ad-

vanced in age a liberty of living as they please, do then enjoin their people not to steal, not to plunder, not to enter a house by violence, not to strike unjustly, not to be adulterous, not to disobey the magistrates, and other things in like manner; and, if any transgress, they impose punishments on them: but the Persian laws, taking things higher, are careful, from the beginning, to provide that their citizens shall not be such as to be capable of meddling with any action that is base and vile. And that care they take in this manner: they have a public place, called from the name of liberty, where the king's palace and the other courts and houses of magistrates are built; all things that are bought and sold, and the dealers in them, their noise and low disingenuous manners, are banished hence to another place, that the rout of these may not mix and interfere with the decent order of those who are under the ingenuous discipline. This place, near the public courts, is divided into four parts: one is allotted to the boys, one to the youth, one to the full-grown men, and one to those who exceed the years of military service. Each of these orders, according to the law, attend in their several parts; the boys and full-grown men as soon as it is day; the elders when they think convenient, except on appointed days when they are obliged to be present; the youth take up their rest round the courts, in their light arms, all but such as are married; these are not required to do it, unless beforehand ordered to attend; nor is it decent for them to be absent often. Over each of the orders there are twelve rulers, for the Persians are divided into twelve tribes. Those over the boys are chosen from amongst the elders, and such as are thought to make them the best boys; those over the youth are chosen from amongst the full-grown men, and such as are thought to make the best youth; and over the full-grown men, such as are thought to render them the most ready to perform their appointed parts, and to execute the orders they receive from the chief magistrate. There are likewise chosen presidents over the elders, who take care that these also perform their duty. And, that it may appear what means they use to make their citizens prove the best, I shall now relate what part is appointed for each degree.

The boys, who frequent the public places of instruction, pass their time in learning justice; and tell you that they go for that purpose, as

---

1 According to Herodotus, Cambyses was a Persian of obscure origin, to whom Astyages gave his daughter in marriage. The king had been terrified by dreams which threatened the loss of his crown by the hand of his daughter's son,—a calamity which he hoped to avert by this means; but he was eventually dethroned by Cyrus. Astyages' deposition is stated to have been occasioned by his cruelty and oppression.

those with us, who go to learn letters, tell you they go for this purpose. Their rulers, for the most part of the day, continue dispensing justice among them; for as amongst the men, so the boys have against each other their accusations for theft, robbery, violence, deceit, and calumny, and other such things as naturally occur; and when they find any acting unjustly, in any of these ways, they punish them; they punish likewise such as they find guilty of false accusation; they appeal to justice also in the case of a crime for which men hate one another excessively, but never bring to the bar of justice, that is, ingratitude; and whomsoever they find able to return a benefit, and refusing to do it, they punish severely: for they are of opinion that the ungrateful are careless and neglectful both of the gods, of their parents, of their country, and of their friends; and ingratitude seems to be certainly attended by impudence; and this seems to be the principal conductor of mankind into all things that are vile. They instil into the boys a modest and discreet temper of mind; and it contributes much towards establishing this temper in them, that they see every day their elders behaving themselves in that discreet and modest manner. They teach them obedience to their rulers; and it contributes much to their instruction in this, that they see their elders zealously obedient to their rulers. They teach them temperance with respect to eating and drinking; and it contributes much to this their temperance, to see that their elders do not quit their stations for the service of their bellies before the magistrates dismiss them; and that the boys do not eat with their mothers, but with their teachers, and when the magistrates give the signal. They bring from home with them bread for their food, and a sort of herb, much in use with them, to eat with it. And they bring a cup to drink in, that if any are thirsty, they may take from the river. They learn, besides, to shoot with the bow, and to throw the javelin. These things the boys practise till they are sixteen or seventeen years of age; then they enter the order of youth. The youth pass their time thus: for ten years after they pass from the order of boys, they take their rests around the courts, as is said before, both for the security and guard of the city, and to preserve in them a modesty and governableness of temper; for this age seems the most to need care. In the day time they chiefly give themselves up to be made

use of by their magistrates, in case they want them for any public service; and when it is necessary they all attend about the courts. But when the king goes out to hunt he takes half the guard off with him; and this he does several times every month. Those that go must have their bow and quiver, a smaller sort of sword in its proper scabbard, a shield, and two javelins; one to throw, and the other, if necessary, to use at hand. They are careful to keep up these public huntings; and the king, as in war, is in this their leader, hunts himself, and takes care that others do so; because it seems to be the truest method of practising all such things as relate to war. It accustoms them to rise early in the morning, and to bear heat and cold; it exercises them in long marches, and in running; it necessitates them to use their bow against the beast they hunt, and to throw their javelin if he fall in their way: their courage must, of necessity, be often sharpened in the hunt, when any of the strong and vigorous beasts oppose themselves; they must come to blows with the beast, if he comes up with them, and must be on their guard as he comes on them. So that it is no easy matter to find what one thing there is that is practised in war, and is not so in their hunting. They attend this hunting, being provided with a dinner, larger, indeed, as is but fit, than that of the boys, but in all other respects the same; and during the hunt sometimes, perhaps, they shall not eat it; either waiting for the beast, if it be necessary, or choosing to spend more time at the work: so they make their supper of that dinner; hunt again the next day, until the time of supper; and reckon these two days as but one, because they have ate the food but of one day. This they do to accustom themselves, that in case it may be necessary for them in war, they may be able to do it. They of this degree have what they catch for meat with their bread. If they catch nothing, then they have their usual herb. And if any one think that they eat without pleasure, when they have this herb only for food with their bread, and that they drink without pleasure when they drink water, let him recollect how pleasant it is to one who is hungry to eat plain cake or bread; and how pleasant to one who is thirsty to drink water. The tribes that remain at home pass their time in practising the things they learned while they were boys, in shooting with the bow, and throwing the javelin. These they continue exercising in emulation one against another: and there are public games, in these kinds, and prizes set; and in whichsoever of the tribes there are the most found who exceed in skill, in courage, and in obedience, the citizens applaud and honour, not only the present ruler of them, but also the person who had the instruction of them while boys. The magistrates likewise make use of the remaining youth, if they want them, to keep guard on any occasion, or to search for criminal persons, to pursue robbers, or for any other business that requires strength and agility. These things the youth practise, and when they have completed ten years they enter into the order of full-grown men. These, from the time they leave the order of youth, pass five-and-twenty years in this manner. First, as the youth, they give themselves up to be made use of by the magistrates, on any occasion that may occur for the service of the public, and that requires the service of such as have discretion, and are yet in vigour. If some military expedition be necessary to be undertaken, they who are under this degree of discipline do not engage in it with bows and javelins, but with what they call arms for close fight, a corselet about the breast, a shield in the left hand, such as the Persians are painted with, and in the right a larger sort of sword. All the magistrates are chosen from amongst these, except the teachers of the boys; and when they have completed five-and-twenty years in this order they are then something upwards of fifty years of age, and pass into the order of such as are elders, and are so called. These elders are not obliged to attend any military service abroad, but remaining at home, have the distribution of public and private justice; have judgment of life and death, and the choice of all magistrates; and if any of the youth or full-grown men fail in any thing enjoined by the laws, the phylarchs, or magistrates of the tribes, or any one that will make discovery of it, the elders hear the cause, and give judgment on it; and the person so judged and condemned remains infamous for the rest of his life.

That the whole Persian form of government may the more plainly appear, I return a little back; for, by means of what has been already said it may now be laid open in a very few words. The Persians are said to be in number about twelve myriads, or a hundred and twenty thousand; of these none are by law excluded from honours and magistracies, but all are at liberty to send their boys to the public schools of justice. They who are able to maintain their children idle, and without labour, send them to these schools; they who are not able, do not send them. They who are thus educated under the public teachers are at liberty to pass through the order of youth; they who are not so educated have not that liberty. They who pass through the youth, fully discharging all things enjoined by the law, are allowed to be incorporated amongst the full-grown men, and to partake of all honours and magistracies; but they who do not complete their course through the order of boys, and through that of the youth, do not pass into the order of the full-grown men. They who make their progress through the order of the full-grown men unexceptionable become then the elders; so the order of elders stands composed of men who have made their way through all things good and excellent. And this is the form of government, by the use of which, they think, they become the best men. There yet remain things that bear testimony to the spare diet used among the Persians, and to their carrying it off by exercise; for it is even yet shameful among them to be seen either to spit or to blow the nose, or any such matter; and these things could not possibly be unless they used a very temperate diet, and spent the moisture by exercise, making it pass some other way.

These things I had to say concerning the Persians in general. I will now relate the actions of Cyrus, on whose account this discourse was undertaken, beginning from his being a boy.

III. Cyrus, till twelve years of age, or little more, was educated under this discipline, and appeared to excel all his equals, both in his quick learning of what was proper, and in his performing every thing in a manly way. At that time Astyages sent for his daughter and her son; for he was desirous to see him, having heard that he was an excellent and lovely child. Mandane therefore came to her father, and brought her son with her. As soon as they arrived, and Cyrus knew Astyages to be his mother's father, he instantly, as being a boy of great good-nature, embraced him, just as if he had been bred under him, and had long had an affection for him: and observing him set out and adorned, with his eyes and complexion painted, and with false hair, hings that are allowed amongst the Medes (for he purple coat, the rich habit called candys, ollars about the neck, and bracelets about the ands, all belonging to the Medes; but amongst the inhabitants of Persia, even at this day, their abits are much coarser, and their diet much lainer)—observing this dress of his grandfather, and looking at him, he said: "O mother, ow handsome is my grandfather!" And his other then asking him which he thought the andsomer, either his father or his grandfather, Cyrus answered: "Of the Persians, mother, ny father is much the handsomest; and of all he Medes that I have seen, either on the road x within the city, this grandfather of mine is much the handsomest." Astyages, then embracing Cyrus, in return put on him a fine obe, honoured him, and set him out with collars and bracelets; and, whenever he went abroad, carried him with him, mounted on a orse with a bridle of gold, and such as he used aimself to appear abroad on. Cyrus being a boy much in love with what was fine and honourable, was pleased with the robe, and extremely delighted with learning to ride; for amongst the Persians, it being difficult to breed horses, and even difficult to ride, the country being mountainous, it is a rare thing to see a horse. But Astyages being at table with his daughter, and with Cyrus, and being desirous to treat the boy with all possible delight and pleasure, that he might the less miss what he enjoyed at home, set before him several dishes, with sauces and meats of all kinds; on which Cyrus is reported to have said: "What a deal of business and trouble, grandfather, have you at your meals, if you must reach out your hands to all these several dishes, and taste of all these kinds of meats!" "What, then," said Astyages, "do not you think this entertainment much finer than what you have in Persia?" Cyrus is said to have replied: "No, grandfather; with us we have a much plainer and readier way to get satisfied than you have; for plain bread and meat suffices for our meal; but you, in order to the same end, have a deal of business on your hands; and, wandering up and down through many mazes, you at last scarce arrive where we have got long before you." "But, child," said Astyages, "it is not with pain that we wander through these mazes; taste," said he, "and you will find that these things are pleasant." "Well, but, grandfather," said Cyrus, "I see that you yourself have an aversion to these sauces and

things." "What ground," replied Astyages, "have you to say so!" "Because," said he, "when you touch your bread, I see you do not wipe your hands on any thing; but, when you meddle with any of these, you presently clean your hands on your napkin, as if you were very uneasy to have them daubed with them." To this Astyages is said to have answered: "Well, child, if this be your opinion, eat heartily of plain meats, that you may return young and healthy home;" and at the same time he is said to have presented to him various meats, both of the tame and wild kinds. Cyrus, when he saw this variety of meats, is reported to have said: "And do you give me all these meats, grandfather, to do with them as I think fit?" "Yes, truly, I do," said Astyages: then Cyrus, taking of the several meats, is said to have distributed around to the servants about his grandfather, saying to one, "this for you, because you take pains to teach me to ride: this for you, because you gave me a javelin; for I have it at this time: this for you, because you serve my grandfather well: this for you, because you honour my mother:" and that thus he did till he distributed away all he had received. Astyages is then reported to have said: "And do you give nothing to this Sacian, my cup-bearer, that I favour above all?" This Sacian was a very beautiful person, and had the honour to introduce to Astyages any that had business with him, and was to hinder those that he did not think it seasonable to introduce. Cyrus to this is said to have answered, in a pert manner, as a boy not yet struck with the sense of shame; "For what reason is it, grandfather, that you favour this Sacian so much?" Astyages replied, in a jesting way: "Do not you see," said he, "how handsomely and neatly he pours me my wine?" For these cup-bearers to kings perform their business very cleverly; they pour out their wine very neatly, and give the cup, bearing it along with three fingers, and present it in such a manner, as it may best be received by the person who is to drink. "Grandfather," said Cyrus, "bid the Sacian give me the cup, that pouring you your wine to drink, I may gain your favour if I can." Astyages bade the Sacian give him the cup; and Cyrus taking it, is said to have washed the cup as he had observed the Sacian to do; and settling his countenance in a serious and decent manner, brought and presented the cup to his grandfather in such a manner as afforded much laughter to his mother and to Astyages. Then Cyrus, laughing out, leaped up to his grandfather, and kissing him, cried out: "O Sacian, you are undone! I will turn you out of your office: I will do the business better than you, and not drink the wine myself." For these cup-bearers, when they have given the cup, dip with a dish and take a little out, which, pouring into their left hand, they swallow; and this they do, that, in case they mix poison in the cup, it may be of no advantage to themselves. On this Astyages, in a jesting way, said: "And why, Cyrus, since you have imitated the Sacian in every thing else, did not you swallow some of the wine?" "Because, truly," said he, "I was afraid there had been poison mixed in the cup; for when you feasted your friends on your birthday, I plainly found that he had poured you all poison." "And how, child," said he, "did you know this?" "Truly," said he, "because I saw you all disordered in body and mind: for, first, what you do not allow us boys to do, that you did yourselves; for you all bawled together, and could learn nothing of each other: then you fell to singing very ridiculously; and without attending to the singer, you swore he sung admirably: then every one telling stories of his own strength, you rose up and fell to dancing; but without all rule or measure, for you could not so much as keep yourselves upright: then you all entirely forgot yourselves; you, that you were king, and they, that you were their governor; and then, for the first time, I discovered that you were celebrating a festival, where all were allowed to talk with equal liberty; for you never ceased talking." Astyages then said: "Does your father, child, never drink till he gets drunk?" "No, truly," said he? "What does he then." "Why, he quenches his thirst, and gets no further harm; for, as I take it, grandfather," said he, "it is no Sacian that officiates as cup-bearer about him." His mother then said: "But why, child, do you make war thus on the Sacian?" Cyrus to this is said to reply: "Why, truly, because I hate him; for very often, when I am desirous to run to my grandfather, this nasty fellow hinders me. Pray, grandfather," said he, "let me but have the government of him but for three days." "How would you govern him?" said Astyages. Cyrus replied: "Why, standing as he does, just at the entrance, when he had a mind to go in to dinner, then would I tell him that he could not possibly have his dinner yet, because: "he was busy with certain people"

then, when he came to supper, I wo him that 'he was bathing:' and if he v pressing for his victuals, I would tell l 'he was with the women:' and so on, t tormented him as he torments me w keeps me from you." Such like sul mirth did he afford them at meals: i times of the day, if he perceived his gra or his mother's brother in want of any was a difficult matter for any one to be hand with him in doing it: for Cyrus tremely delighted to gratify them in ai that lay in his power. But when M was preparing to return home to her h Astyages desired her to leave Cyrus wi She made answer that she was willing t her father in every thing; but to le child against his will she thought har this occasion Astyages said to Cyrus: ' if you will stay with me, in the first pl Sacian shall not have the command (access to me; but, whenever you come, be in your own power; and the ofter will come," said he, "the more I sha myself obliged to you. Then you sh the use of all my horses, and of as man as you please; and, when you go aw shall take as many of them as you plea you: then, at meals, you shall take wl you please to get satisfied in what you : temperate way: then all the several cr that are now in the park I give you; a besides collect more of all kinds, th may pursue them when you have le ride, and with your bow and javelin la prostrate on the ground, as grown m Boys I will furnish you with for playfe and whatever else you would have, do l me, and you shall not go without." Whe tyages had said this, Cyrus' mother aske whether he would go or stay. He did all hesitate, but presently said that he stay. And being asked by his mother th son why, it is said that he made answer: cause, mother, that at home, both at th and javelin, I am superior to all of equ with me, and am so reckoned; but here, know that in horsemanship I am their in and be it known to you, mother, this g me very much. But if you leave me her I learn to be a horseman, then I recko when I am in Persia I shall easily maste there, who are so good at all exercises on and when I come amongst the Medes I deavour to be an assistant and a support to my grandfather, making myself the most skilful amongst those who excel in horsemanship." His mother is then reported to have said: 'But how, child, will you be instructed here in the knowledge of justice, when your teachers are there?' "O mother!" said Cyrus, "that I understand exactly already." "How so?" said Mandane. "Because my teacher," said he, "appointed me judge over others, as being very exact in the knowledge of justice myself. But yet," said he, "I had some stripes given me, as not determining right in one judgment that I gave. The case was this: a bigger boy, who had a little coat, stripping a less boy, who had a larger, put on the little boy the coat that was his own, and put on himself the coat that was the little boy's. I therefore passing judgment on them, decreed that it was best that each should keep the coat that best fitted him. On this my teacher thrashed me, and told me that when I should be constituted judge of what fitted best, I should determine in this manner: but when I was to judge whose the coat was, then, said he, it must be inquired what right possession is; whether he that took a thing by force should have it, or whether he who made it or purchased it should possess it: and then he told me what was according to law was just, and that what was contrary to law was violent. He bid me take notice, therefore, that a judge ought to give his opinion with the law. So, mother," said he, "I understand what is just in all cases very exactly; or, if any thing be wanting to me, my grandfather here will teach it me." "But, child," said she, "the same things are not accounted just with your grandfather here, and yonder in Persia; for among the Medes your grandfather has made himself lord and master of all; but amongst the Persians it is accounted just that all should be equally dealt by; and your father is the first to execute the orders imposed on the whole state, and receives those orders himself: his own humour is not his rule and measure, but it is the law that is so. How then can you avoid being beat to death at home, when you come home your grandfather instructed not in kingly arts, but in the arts and manner of tyranny; one of which is, to think that power and ascendant over all is your due?" "O mother," said Cyrus, "your father is much better able to teach one to submit than to take the ascendant. Do you not see," said he, "that he has taught all the Medes to submit to him? So well assured that your father will not dismiss me, nor any one from about him, instructed how to gain power and ascendency over others."

IV. Many such kind of discourses did Cyrus hold. At last his mother went away: he stayed, and was there brought up. He immediately joined himself to those that were his equals in age, so as to be on a very familiar and friendly footing with them; and he presently gained their fathers, both by visiting them, and by giving evidence of his affection for their sons. So that if they had any business with the king, they bid their boys ask Cyrus to do it; and Cyrus, such was his benignity and love of esteem and praise, did his utmost to accomplish it for them: and Astyages had it not in his power to refuse gratifying Cyrus in whatever he asked of him; for Cyrus, when his grandfather fell ill, never quitted him; never ceased from tears; and made it evident to all that he was in the utmost fear of his dying. And in the night, if Astyages wanted any thing, Cyrus was the first to perceive it, and started up the nimblest of any to serve him in any thing that he thought pleasing to him; so that he entirely gained Astyages. Cyrus was perhaps a little over-talkative; but this he had partly from his education, his teacher obliging him to give a reason for every thing that he did, and to hearken to it from others, when he was to give his opinion in judgment: and besides, being very eager after knowledge, he was always asking those about him abundance of questions, how such and such things were; and on whatever subject he was questioned by others, being of a very quick and ready apprehension, he instantly made his answers: so that, from all these things, he contracted an over-talkativeness. But, as in the persons of very young people, who have shot up suddenly, so as to be very tall, there yet appears something childish that betrays their youth; so in Cyrus, it was not an impudence and boldness that appeared through that talkativeness, but a simplicity and good nature; so that one was desirous rather to hear yet more from him, than to be with him while he held his tongue.

But as years added to his growth, and brought him on towards the time of his becoming a youth, he then used fewer words and a softer voice; he became full of shame, so as to blush when he came into the company of men of years; and that playful pertness, in bluntly accosting every one, did not continue with him as before. So he became more soft and gentle, but, in his conversation, extremely agreeable; for in all the exercises that he and his equals used in emulation of each other, he did not challenge his companions to those in which he knew himself superior, but such as he well knew himself to be inferior in, those he set on foot, declaring that he would do them better than they. Accordingly, he would begin vaulting the horse, throwing the javelin, or shooting with the bow on horseback, while he was yet scarce well able to sit on a horse; and when he was outdone he was the first to laugh at himself: and as, on the account of being baffled, he did not fly off and meddle no more with the things he was so baffled in, but continued repeating his endeavours to do better, he presently became equal to his companions in horsemanship, and, by his love of the work, quickly left them behind. He then presently applied himself to the taking of the beasts in the park, pursuing, throwing at them, and killing them; so that Astyages could no longer supply him with them. And Cyrus, perceiving that he could not furnish him with these creatures, though very desirous to do it, often said to him: "What need you take so much pains, grandfather, to find me out these creatures? If you will but send me out to hunt with my uncle, I shall reckon that all the beasts I see are creatures that you maintain for me." But though he was very desirous to go out to hunt, yet he could not now be pressing and importunate, as when he was a boy: he became very backward in going to his grandfather; and what he blamed in the Sacian for not admitting him to his grandfather, he became in this a Sacian to himself; for he never went in, unless he knew beforehand that it was seasonable; and begged the Sacian by all means, to signify to him when it was seasonable, and when not; so that the Sacian now loved him extremely, as all the rest did.

When Astyages therefore knew that he was extremely desirous to hunt abroad and at large, he sent him out with his uncle, and sent some elderly men on horseback with him, as guards to him, to take care of him in rough and rocky parts of the country, and in case any beasts of the savage kind appeared. Cyrus therefore was very earnest in inquiring of those that attended him what beasts he was not to approach, and which those were that he might confidently pursue. They told him that bears had destroyed many that had ventured to approach them; and that lions, wild boars, and leopards had done the same; but that stags, wild goats, wild sheep, and wild asses were harmless things. They told him likewise that rough and rocky places were not less to be dreaded than the beasts; for that many, both men and horses, had fallen headlong down precipices. Cyrus took all these instructions very eagerly; but as soon as he saw a stag roused, forgetting all that he had heard, he pursued, and looked at nothing but at that which he followed; and his horse taking a leap with him, fell on his knees, and wanted but little of throwing him quite over his neck. However, Cyrus, though with difficulty, kept on his back, and the horse sprang up. When they got into the plain he struck the stag with his javelin, and brought him to the ground: a large, noble creature it was, and he was most highly delighted. But his guardians coming up with him, chid and reproved him; told him what danger he had run into; and said that they would tell it to his grandfather. Cyrus, having alighted from his horse, stood and heard this with much uneasiness; but hearing a halloo, he mounted his horse at a leap, as in a sort of enthusiasm, and as soon as he saw a boar rushing forward over against him, he rushed on him, and, aiming right with his javelin, struck the boar in the forehead: and here his uncle, seeing his boldness, reproved him: he, while his uncle was reproving him, begged that he would allow him to carry off the beasts that he had taken, and to give them to his grandfather. To this, they say, his uncle replied: "But if he discover that it is you that have pursued and taken them, he will not only reprove you, but me, for allowing you to do it." "Let him beat me," said he, "if he will, when I have given them to him: and do you, if you will, uncle," said he, "correct me as you please; do but gratify me in this." Cyaxares at last said: "Well, do as you please, for it is you that seems now to be our king."

So Cyrus, carrying off the beasts, presented them to his grandfather, and told him that he himself had taken them for him. The javelins he did not show him, but laid them down all bloody, where he thought that he certainly would see them. Astyages said: "Child, I receive with pleasure whatever you give me;

bet I am not in such want of any of these things as to run you into danger for them." "If you do not want them, grandfather," said Cyrus, "pray give them me, that I may distribute them to my companions." "Child," said Astyages, "take them, and distribute them to whom you please, and of every thing else whatever you will." Cyrus, taking the beasts, gave them to the boys; and withal told them: "Boys," said he, "what very triflers were we when we hunted in the park! In my opinion it was as if one had tied the creatures by the leg and hunted them; for, first, we were within a narrow compass of ground; then the creatures were poor, slender, scabby things: one was lame, another maimed: but the beasts in the mountains and marshes, how fine, how large, and how sleek they appear! The stags, as if they had wings, leap to the very heavens; the boars, as they say brave men do, attack one hand to hand, and their bulk is such that it is impossible to miss them. These, even when they are dead," said he, "are, in my opinion, finer than those other walled-up things when alive. But," said he, "would your father, think you, send you out to hunt?" "Yes, very readily," said they, "if Astyages ordered it." Cyrus then said: "Who is there amongst you therefore that would mention it to Astyages?" "Who more able," said they, "to persuade him than yourself?" "But, truly," said he, "for my part, I know not what kind of creature I am become; for I am neither able to speak, nor can I any longer so much as meet my grandfather's eyes; and, if I go on in this way so fast, I fear," said he, "I shall become a mere blockhead and fool; yet when I was a little boy I was thought a notable talker." The boys then said: "You tell us a sad piece of news, if you can do nothing for us in case of need, but that we must beg that of another that is in your power to effect."

Cyrus, hearing this, was nettled; and retiring without saying a word, he stirred himself up to boldness; and having contrived how to speak to his grandfather in the least offensive manner, and to obtain for himself and the boys what they desired, he went in. Thus then he began: "Tell me," said he, "grandfather, if one of your domestic servants should ran away, and you should take him again, what would you do with him?" "Why," said he, "what should I do but put him in chains, and force him to work?" "But if a runaway should of himself return to you, what would you do?" "What else," said he, "but have him whipped, that he may do so no more, then make use of him as before?" "It is time therefore," said Cyrus, "to prepare yourself to bestow a whipping on me, as having contrived to run away, and take my companions with me a-hunting." "Then," said Astyages, "you have done very well to tell it me beforehand; for henceforward, I order you not to stir. It is a fine thing, indeed," said he, "if, for the sake of a little venison, I shall send out my daughter's son to ramble at his pleasure."

Cyrus, hearing this, obeyed, and stayed at home much afflicted, carrying a melancholy countenance, and remaining silent. Astyages, when he found that he was so extremely afflicted, being willing to please him, carried him out to hunt; and, assembling abundance of people, both foot and horse, and likewise the boys, and driving the beasts out into the champaign country, he made a great hunt; and being himself present, royally attended, he gave orders that none should throw till Cyrus was satisfied and had enough of the exercise. But Cyrus would not let him hinder them. "If you have a mind, grandfather," said he, "that I should hunt with pleasure, let all those about me pursue and engage in the fray, and do the best." Astyages then gave them his leave, and, taking a station, saw them engaged amongst the beasts, striving to out-do each other, pursuing and throwing their javelins. He was delighted with Cyrus, who, in transports of joy, could not hold his tongue, but, like a young generous dog that opens when he approaches the beast he pursues, encouraged every one, calling on them by name. He was pleased to see him laughing at one: and another he observed him to praise cordially, and without the least emotion of envy. At last Astyages, having taken abundance of game, retired; but was so pleased with that hunt, that he always went out with Cyrus, whenever he was able, taking abundance of people with him, and the boys, for the sake of Cyrus. Thus, for the most part, did Cyrus pass his time, doing service and pleasure to all, and hurt to none.

But when he was about fifteen or sixteen years of age the king of Assyria's son, being to celebrate his nuptials, had a mind at that time to hunt; and hearing that there was plenty of game on the borders of the Assyrians and Medes, they having not been hunted, because of the war between the nations, hither he desir-

B

ed to go. That he might hunt therefore securely, he took with him a body of horse and another of light-armed foot, who were to drive the beasts out of their fastnesses into the open, cultivated country. Being come therefore to the place where their garrisons were, and a guard always attending, here he supped, as intending to hunt the next day early in the morning: but that evening a guard of horse and foot arrived from the city to relieve those who were there before. He therefore thought that he had now a handsome army with him, consisting of a double guard, besides a considerable number, both of horse and foot, that had attended on himself. He judged it best therefore to undertake a plunder of the Median territory; that this would be a nobler exploit than a hunt; and he thought he should procure great store of beasts for sacrifice. So rising early in the morning, he led his army forwards. The foot he left in close order on the borders: he himself advanced with the horse up to the Median garrisons; and, keeping the best of them and the greatest number with himself, he halted there, that the Medes in garrison might not march and charge those who were to scour the country; and such as were proper he sent out in parties, some to run one way and some another; and ordered them to surround and seize all that they met with, and bring all off to him. These did as they were ordered. But notice being given to Astyages that the enemy was got into the country, he marched with what forces he had at hand to the borders. His son did so, in like manner, with some horse that were at hand; and he signified to all his other forces to march after to support him. When they came up, and saw a great number of Assyrians in close order, and their horses standing quietly and still, the Medes likewise halted and stood.

Cyrus, seeing other people marching on all sides to support their friends, set forward himself, putting on his arms for the first time; never imagining that he should be so soon armed with them in the manner he desired; for they were very fine, and fitted him very well, being such as his grandfather had ordered to be made to fit his body. So, being thus completely armed, he set out on horseback. Astyages, getting sight of him, wondered by whose order and encouragement he came: however, he bid him keep by him. Cyrus, when he saw a great number of horsemen fronting him, asked · " Grandfather," said he, " are these men enemies that sit quietly there on horseback ?" " They are enemies," said he. " And are those so too that are scouring the country ?" " Yes, and those too." " By Jove, then, grandfather !" said he, " methinks these that are thus plundering us are wretched fellows, and mounted on wretched horses : and must not some of us march against them ?" " Do not you see, child," said he, " what a body of horse stands there in close order, and who, if we advance against the others, will intercept us ? And we have not yet our full strength with us." " But," said Cyrus, " if you wait here, and collect those that are marching to join us, these of our enemies that are here will be under apprehension, and will not stir; and the plunderers, when they see any men marching against them, will presently drop their booty." On his saying this, Astyages thought there was something in what he said, and wondering at his sagacity and vigilance, ordered his son to take a squadron of horse and march against the plunderers. " I," said he, " will bear down on these men that are here, if they offer to move towards you; so that they shall be obliged to be intent on us."

Cyaxares taking of the strongest and best, both of men and horses, marched; and Cyrus seeing these put forward, joined and pushed on with them, and presently got at the head of them. Cyaxares followed, and the rest were not left behind. As soon as the plunderers saw them approaching, then quitting their booty, they fled. They that were with Cyrus intercepted them, and flew to blows with such as they could come up with, and Cyrus was the first at the work. Those who, by turning aside escaped them, they pursued in the rear, and did not give over, but met with several of them. Like a generous dog that has no experience, and that runs headlong without caution on a boar, so ran Cyrus, minding only to deal his blows where any came within his reach, without farther foresight or consideration. The enemy, when they saw their people in distress, moved their main body, judging that the pursuit would cease as soon as they should be seen to advance : Cyrus, notwithstanding, did not give over, but calling out to his uncle for joy, pursued, and pressing continually on, put the enemy to an entire route. Cyaxares followed, (perhaps being in awe of his father,) and the rest followed after, who thought, perhaps, they would not have shown themselves very brave against men that had opposed them, yet were on this occasion more than ordinarily eager in pursuing. Astyages, when he saw these men so incautiously pursuing, and the enemy in a close body marching towards them, fearing for his son and for Cyrus, lest they in disorder and confusion should fall in with the enemy, prepared to receive them, and suffer damage, be presently led on towards the enemy. The enemy, as soon as they saw the Medes move forward, halted ; presenting some their javelins, and some their bows, in order to stop them, when they came within bow-shot, as their general practice is. For when they are near, they push each other at a certain distance, and so frequently skirmish on till evening. But when they saw their own men in full rout flying towards them, and those with Cyrus following close behind them, and Astyages, with his horse, already within bow-shot, they gave way and fled. The Medes, in a body, pursuing, killed several in the first charge, and whoever they came up with they fell on, whether man or horse, and whoever fell they killed. Nor did the stop till they came up with the Assyrian foot, and there they gave over, fearing lest some greater force than appeared might lie in ambuscade to receive them. Astyages on this retreated in much joy at this victory obtained by his cavalry, but knew not what to say to Cyrus, for he knew him to be the author of the action, and saw him wrought up to such a degree of boldness as amounted almost to madness ; for while the rest were retiring home, he alone, by himself, did nothing but ride round and view those that had fallen in the action. And they who had it in charge, dragging him with difficulty away, brought him to Astyages, while he put his conductors forward before him, because he saw the countenance of his grandfather look dissatisfied on seeing him.

These things passed among the Medes, and all people had Cyrus in their mouths, both in their discourses and songs. But Astyages, who before had a great esteem for him, was now quite astonished and struck with him. Cambyses, the father of Cyrus, was pleased to hear these things of him ; but when he heard that Cyrus begun to perform acts of manhood, he called him home, that he might complete his institution among the Persians, according to the rules of his country. And on this occasion Cyrus is reported to have said, " That he would return, lest his father should be uneasy and his country blame him." Astyages therefore seemed to be under a necessity of parting with him : so he sent him away, but first presented him with such horses as he desired to have, and furnishing him with other things of all kinds, both because of the affection he had for him, and because he had great assurance and hopes that he would prove a man thoroughly able to do service to his friends, and mischief to his enemies.

All people waited on Cyrus at his departure attending him part of his way on horseback, both boys, youth, men, and those in years ; so likewise did Astyages himself. And they say that not one turned back at parting with him without tears ; and it is said that Cyrus himself shed many tears at parting ; that he gave many presents to his companions and equals in age out of what Astyages had given him ; and that, at last, taking off the Median robe he had on, he gave it to a certain youth, declaring by this that he loved that youth the most of any. It is said that they who had taken and accepted of these presents returned them to Astyages, and that Astyages sent them to Cyrus, but that he sent them back again to the Medes, and sent word thus : " O grandfather! if you would have me return hither again with pleasure, and not with shame, let every one keep what I have given him :" and that Astyages hearing this, did as Cyrus had begged him by his message to do.

But if I may be allowed to relate a sportive affair, it is said that when Cyrus went away, and that he and his relations parted, they took their leave, and dismissed him with a kiss, according to the Persian custom ; for the Persians practise it to this day ; and that a certain Mede, a very excellent person, had been long struck with the beauty of Cyrus ; that when he saw Cyrus' relations kiss him, he stayed behind, and when the rest were gone, accosted Cyrus, and said to him : " And am I, Cyrus, the only one of all your relations that you do not know ?" " What !" said Cyrus, " and are you a relation ?" " Yes," said he. " This was the reason then," said Cyrus, " that you used to gaze at me ; for I think I recollect that you frequently did so." " I was very desirous," said he, " to salute you, but I was always ashamed to do it." " But," said Cyrus, " you that are a relation ought not to have been so." So, coming up to him, he kissed him. The

Mede having received the kiss, is said to have asked this question: "And is it a custom among the Persians to kiss relations?" "It is so," said Cyrus, "when they see one another at some distance of time, or when they part." "Then," said the Mede, "it seems now to be time for you to kiss me again; for, as you see, I am just going away." So Cyrus, kissing him again, dismissed him, and went his way. They had not gone very far before the Mede came up with him again, with his horse all over in a sweat; and Cyrus, getting sight of him, said, "What, have you forgot any thing that you had a mind to say to me?" "No, by Jove!" said he, "but I am come again at a distance of time." "Dear relation!" said he, "it is a very short one." "How a short one?" said the Mede, "do you not know, Cyrus," said he, "that the very twinkling of my eyes is a long time to be without seeing you, you who are so lovely?" Here Cyrus, from being in tears, broke out into laughter, bid him "go his way, and take courage; that in a little time he would be with them again; and that then he would be at liberty to look at him, if he pleased, with steady eyes, and without twinkling."

V. Cyrus, returning thus into Persia, is said to have continued a year longer amongst the boys. At first they made their jests on him, as being now come home, instructed amongst the Medes in luxury and pleasure. But when they saw that he clothed himself as they did; that he drank as they did, and with pleasure; and that in festivals, when they had a little more than ordinary plenty, they perceived him more ready to give his share away than desirous to have it himself; and besides, when they saw him in all other respects much superior to themselves, they were then astonished at him. Then having passed through the discipline of these years, and entering the order of youth, he here again appeared superior to the rest, both in executing what was proper, in undergoing every thing that was his part so to do, in his respects to his elders, and in his obedience to his rulers.

In progress of time Astyages died, and his son Cyaxares, brother to Cyrus' mother, took on him the government of the Medes. And the king of Assyria, having overthrown all the Syrians, who were no small nation, and having subjected the king of the Arabs, and holding the Hyrcanians under his dominion, and being at that time at war with the Bactrians, con-

sidered that if he could break the power of the Medes he should easily obtain the dominion of all around him; for the Medes seemed to be the strongest of all the neighbouring nations. So he sent round to all those that were subject to himself; he sent to Croesus, king of Lydia, to the king of Cappadocia, to both the Phrygias, to the Carians, Paphlagonians, Indians, and Cilicians, loading the Medes and Persians with calumny and reproach; telling them how great, how powerful, and how united in interest these two nations were by means of several intermarriages; that they would unite into one; and if he did not prevent them, and break their power, they would run a risk, by attacking each nation severally, to overturn all. Some being persuaded by these arguments, entered into a confederacy with him; others were prevailed with by money and presents, for in these he abounded.

Cyaxares, the son of Astyages, when he perceived this design, and these united preparations against him, did himself immediately make the utmost preparations that he was able to oppose them; and he sent to the Persians, both to the public council and to Cambyses, who was married to his sister, and was king of Persia. He sent likewise to Cyrus, desiring him to endeavour to come as commander of the forces, if the public council of the Persians should send any; for Cyrus by this time had completed ten years amongst the youth, and was now of the full grown men.

So Cyrus accepting it, the elders in council chose him commander of the expedition into Media. They gave him power to choose two hundred from amongst those who were equally entitled to all honours, and to each of these they gave power to choose four of their own order. These, altogether, made a thousand. Again, to each of these thousands they gave a power to choose from amongst the common people of Persia ten targeteers, ten slingers, and ten archers. Thus there were ten thousand archers, ten thousand targeteers, and ten thousand slingers, and the thousand besides. So great was the army that was given to Cyrus: and as soon as he was chosen he began by making application to the gods; and having sacrificed happily and successfully, he then chose the two hundred; and when these had afterwards chosen each their four, he assembled them together, and made his first discourse to them thus:

" Friends, I have chosen you, not as having now for the first time had proof of your worth, but as having seen you, from boys, performing with ardour all things that the city judges excellent and noble, and avoiding entirely whatever it reckons mean and base. I would now lay before you on what account it is that I, not unwillingly, am placed in this station, and that I have called you together. I have thought that our forefathers were nowise inferior to ourselves; for they passed their days in the continual exercise and practice of such things as are thought actions of virtue; but what with this their virtue they have acquired, either for the public of Persia, or for themselves, I cannot yet discover. Yet, in my opinion, men practise no virtue, but that by it they may gain the advantage of the vicious. They who abstain from pleasures at present, do not do it that they may never have delight; but they do it that, by means of that temperance at present, they may in future time have returns of delight manifold. They who are desirous to be powerful in speaking, do not exercise themselves in it that they may never give over discoursing; but they do it in hopes, that, prevailing on numbers of men by the power of their eloquence, they may effect many things, and those of great consequence.

" They who exercise themselves in martial affairs do not take pains in it that they may never cease fighting; but they judge, that by making themselves able in military affairs, they shall acquire great riches, great happiness, and great honours, to themselves and to their country. And if any have taken pains to acquire ability and skill in these affairs, and without reaping any fruits from them, have neglected themselves till they have been disabled by old age, in my opinion they have undergone the same fate as one who was desirous to be a good husbandman would do, who, sowing and planting with skill, when the time came for gathering the fruits, should let them fall ungathered to the ground again: and as a wrestler, who, after much pains bestowed, and becoming qualified for victory, should pass his days without entering the lists; and in my opinion such a one could not justly be freed from the imputation of folly. Let not us, friends, submit to such a fate; but, since we are conscious to ourselves that, from boys, we are exercised in all great and noble things, let us march against these enemies of ours, that I,

an eye-witness, well know to be poor, insignificant men, as antagonists to you: for such men are not very dangerous antagonists, who, though they may be skilful at their bow, and at their javelin, and in horsemanship, yet when they are to undergo toil and labour, sink under it: and these men, with respect to pains and labour, are mean and poor. Nor are such men dangerous antagonists, who, when they are to watch and deny themselves their usual rest, are quite broken by it: and in this respect likewise these men are mean and poor. Nor are such dangerous antagonists, who, though able in all these respects, yet are ignorant how to deal either with allies or with enemies: and these men are evidently ignorant and unpractised in the noblest arts. But you can make use of the night, as others of the day; you reckon that toil and pains must conduct you to a life of pleasure; you can use hunger to relish your food, as others do the daintiest meats; you, even with more ease than lions, can bear the drinking of plain water; and you carry within your minds the noblest and most warlike quality in the world; for praise is what you are pleased with above all things, and they that are lovers of praise do of course undergo all toil, and all danger, with pleasure. If I say these things of you, and know otherwise, I abuse myself; for whatever falls short of this in your conduct, the deficiency will fall on me. But I trust to my own experience, to your good-will towards me, and to the folly of our enemies, that these good hopes will not fail me. Let us set forward with confidence, since we are far from appearing to be taken with an unjust desire of what belongs to others; for our enemies are coming on us, being themselves the aggressors in wrong. Our friends call us to their assistance; what therefore is more just than to repel injuries? what more noble than to help our friends? Besides, methinks it ought not to be one of the least grounds of your confidence in this case, that I do not set out on this expedition with the neglect of the gods; for you, who have conversed much with me, know that I have endeavoured to begin not great affairs only, but even little ones, with application to the gods. To conclude," said he, " what farther shall I say? Do you make choice of your men, and take them under your care: and making all things else ready, march to the Medes; I, first returning back to my father, will go before you, that I may learn, as soon as possible, the condition of the enemy, and prepare things for you as well as I can, that with the assistance of the gods, we may carry on this war in the noblest manner." These men did as Cyrus required.

VI. Cyrus, returning home, and having made his supplications to Vesta, and to Jove Paternal, and to the other deities, set out on this expedition, and his father attended him on his way. As soon as they were out of the house, it is said, that it thundered and lightened in a happy manner. On which they went on without farther augury, as if no one could be ignorant what these signals of the most powerful god imported. As Cyrus proceeded on his journey, his father began a discourse with him in this manner:

"That the gods send you out on this expedition propitiously and favourably is evident, child, both from the sacrifices and from the signals from heaven: and you yourself know it to be so; for I have purposely taught you these things, that you might not come to the knowledge of what the gods advise and direct you to by means of other interpreters; but that you yourself, seeing what is to be seen, and hearing what is to be heard, may understand, and not be at the mercy of diviners, who, if they please, may deceive you, and tell you different things from what the gods really signify to you; and that, in case you are without a diviner, you may not be at a loss what use to make of the divine signals, but, by your knowledge in divination, understanding the advices given you by the gods, you may comply with them." "Father," said Cyrus, "I will always continue using my utmost care, according to your instruction, to render the gods propitious to us, and willing to give us their advice and direction; for I remember to have heard it from you, that, as from men, so likewise from the gods, the most likely person to obtain his suit is not he who, when he is in distress, flatters servilely, but he who, in his most happy circumstances, is most mindful of the gods. And you used to say that it was in the same manner that one ought to cultivate friends." "Therefore, child," said he, "on account of this your care, you now apply to the gods, and make your requests to them with the more pleasure, and you have the better hopes to obtain what you ask, appearing to yourself conscious that you have never neglected them."

"Truly, father," said he, "I am for that reason . · such a temper of mind, with respect to the gods, as to reckon them my friends." "Well, child," said he, "do you remember those other opinions that we heretofore agreed in? as that, in all things that the gods bestow, such men as have acquired skill and knowledge in them act and succeed better than they who are ignorant in them; that the laborious succeed better than the idle; that the diligent and the careful live with more security than the negligent and careless; and that, therefore, first rendering ourselves such as we ought to be, we then should make our prayers to the gods for their blessings." "Yes, indeed," said Cyrus, "I do remember to have heard these things from you; and I was forced to submit to your reasoning: for I know you used to say that it was downright impiety for such as had never learned to ride, to supplicate the gods for victory in engagements of horse: or for such as had never learned the use of the bow, to ask the superiority, at this very weapon, over those who understood it: or for such as knew not how to steer, to pray that they might preserve ships in quality of pilots; or for such as have not sown wheat, to pray that they might have a good crop of it; or for such as are not watchful in war, to pray that they may be preserved in safety; for that all such things were contrary to the settled laws of the gods: and you said that such as made impious prayers would probably meet with disappointments from the gods: as such would fail of success with men, who should desire things contrary to all human laws."

"And have you forgot, child," said he, "those other matters that you and I have heretofore discoursed on? as, that it was a great and noble work for a man to be able to approve himself a good and excellent man, and to find means to supply himself and his family with plenty of all things necessary. And this being thus allowed to be a great work, that to understand how to govern other men, so as to supply them with all things necessary, and in abundance, and so as to render them such as they ought to be; this we thought was an astonishing work!" "Yes, truly, father," said he, "I remember to have heard you say this, and I was of opinion with you, that to govern well was a work of the highest nature. And it now appears to me to be so," said he, "when I consider it with respect to government itself; but when I consider it with respect to other men, what kind of men these governors are, and what kind of men they are who are to be our antagonists, I think it very mean to be terrified with such people, and to be unwilling to march and engage them. Men," said he, " who, to begin with these friends of ours, I find are of opinion that a governor ought to distinguish himself from those that he governs, by his eating more sumptuously, by having more gold in his house, by sleeping longer, and by living, in all respects, more at ease than those that be governs. But my opinion is," said he, " that a governor ought to differ from the governed, not by a life of ease and luxury, but by care and circumspection, and by his readiness to undergo toil and labour." " But, child," said he, " there are some matters wherein you are not to contend with men, but with things ; and to have these plentifully at command is no easy matter. You readily know, that if the army have not necessaries, your command is immediately dissolved and falls to pieces." " Father," said he, " therefore Cyaxares says, that he will afford them to all that go from hence, however great the number may be." " You go then, child," said he, " trusting in these matters entirely to Cyaxares' riches ?" " I do," said Cyrus. " Well," said he, " but do you know what these riches are ?" " No, truly," said Cyrus, " I do not." " Yet," said he, " to those things, that you are thus in the dark about, do you trust. Do you not know that you will be in want of abundance of things, and that now you must of necessity spend abundance ?" " I do know it," said Cyrus. " If therefore," said he, " the supply of this expense fail him, or that he purposely deal falsely by you, how will the affairs of the army then stand ? It is plain, not very well." " Then, father," said he, " if you know any means of obtaining a supply, and such as may depend on myself, whilst I am yet on friendly ground, pray tell it me." " Do you ask, child," said he, " if there be any means of supply depending on yourself ? And on whom are these things more likely to depend than on one who has power in his hands ? You go from hence with such a body of foot, as I very well know you would not exchange for any other, though many times their number ; and you will have the Median cavalry, who are the best, and who will be with you as your allies and friends. What nation is there then, of all around, that you think will not serve you, both out of a

desire to gain your favour, and for fear of receiving harm ? These matters you ought to concert with Cyaxares, that nothing of what is necessary for you may be wanting ; and, on account of the continual expense, you ought to secure a revenue and supply that may be always accruing. But above all things remember this, never to delay the procuring your supply till want presses you to it ; but while you have the greatest plenty, and before you come to want, then labour the most to make sure of it ; for you will succeed the better with those from whom you demand it when you seem not to be in want ; and your men will have nothing to blame you for. By these means, likewise, you will have more respect paid you by others : and if by means of your forces you have a mind to do service or prejudice to any, while your men are supplied with all that they want they will do you better service. And be assured that your words will carry greater weight with them, when you can show that you have it in your power to do service or to do hurt." " I am satisfied, father," said he, " that you are right in all this, both for other reasons, as well as particularly because there are none of the soldiers that will pay me thanks for what they are now to receive ; for they know on what terms Cyaxares takes them as his allies : but whatever any of them shall receive over and above what is agreed, this they will reckon favour, and will pay the greatest gratitude to the bestower of it. And indeed for one who has a force, by whose means he may receive advantages in return of service done to friends, and may endeavour to make conquests on enemies ; for such a one to be careless in securing himself supplies, can one think this," said he, " to be less reproachful, than it would be in a man who had lands, and had servants to cultivate them, and who, after all, should let those lands lie fallow and useless ? Depend on it, therefore," said he, " that, both in the territory of friends and of enemies, I will not be sparing of my care to supply my men with all things fitting."

" Well, child," said he, " and do you remember certain other things that we heretofore agreed it was necessary not to neglect ?" " Yes," said he ; " for I remember, that when I came to you for money to give a man, who pretended to have taught me the art of commanding an army, as you gave me the money you asked me : ' Child,' said you, ' did this man, that you carry this reward to, ever, amongst the arts and business of a general, mention any thing of economy to you? for soldiers in an army are not less in want of things necessary than are domestics in a family:' and when, telling you the truth, I said that he had not made the least mention of it, you asked me again—' Whether he had spoken to me concerning the health and strength of my men? As that a general ought to mind these things, as well as the leading and managing of them in action:' when I told you no, you again asked me—' Whether he had taught me how to take care to make my men the most able at all warlike exercises ?' and when I denied this too, you inquired again—' Whether he had given me any instruction how I might raise spirit and courage in an army? for,' you said, ' that in every action, there were vast odds between an army's being in spirit and out of heart.' When I denied this too, you inquired again—' Whether he held any discourse to teach me how one might best bring an army to ready obedience ?' When you found that this had not been in the least spoken of, you at last inquired—' What it was he had taught me then, that he could say he had taught me the art of commanding an army ?' Here I replied, and told you the tactics, or the art of forming and moving in order. You, laughing at this, ran over each particular; asking me what use there was in generalship of tactics without necessaries; what without health; what without skill in the arts that have been invented for the use of war; what without obedience. So you made it evident to me that this tactic art was but a small part of generalship. And when I asked you, whether you were able to teach me any of these matters, you bid me go my ways, and discourse with men that were reputed knowing in military affairs, and inquire from them how these matters stood. On this I conversed with such as I had heard were most knowing in these matters. And with respect to health, having heard and observed that cities that want health get physicians; and that commanders, for the sake of their men, take physicians with them; so when I was placed in this station I presently took care of this: and I believe, father," said he, " that I have men with me who are very able in the art of physic." To this the father replied : " But, child," said he, " these men that you speak of are like menders of torn clothes; so

when people are sick, physicians cure them but your care of health is to be of a noble kind : to prevent the army's becoming sick is what you ought to take care of."

" And which way, father," said he, " shall I be able to do this ?" " Why, if you are to stay some time in a place, you ought not to be careless in your choice of a healthy camp : and in this you will not be deceived, provided you are but careful; for men are continually talking of healthy and unhealthy places, and on the places themselves there are sure witnesses to give their testimony either way, both by their persons and complexions. But then it will not suffice you to consider places only, but pray recollect what course you have taken yourself, in your endeavours to preserve your health." Cyrus then said : " In the first place, I endeavour not to over-fill myself, for it is a very burdensome thing; and then what I take down I work off by exercise. By this means I think that I preserve health and acquire vigour." " In the same manner, therefore, child," said he, " you must take care of others." " And shall we have leisure," said he, "father, to exercise the soldiers in this manner ?" " You will not only have leisure," said the father, " but necessity will oblige you to it; for an army that will do its duty must never be at rest, but employed either in distressing the enemy or making advantage to themselves. It is a difficult matter for a single man to be maintained idle, and yet more difficult for a family; but most difficult of all to maintain an army idle : for in an army, from the lowest to the highest, there are many mouths, and what they get they spend very lavishly; so that it is never fit for an army to be idle." " You seem to me, father," said he, " to say, that as an idle husbandman is good for nothing, so is an idle general good for nothing. But, unless some god blast my endeavours, I take it on me to show you a diligent and active general, and soldiers well supplied with all things necessary, and to take care that their bodies shall be in the best condition. But with respect to the several military arts, father," said he, " in my opinion, he that should establish games in the several kinds, and propose certain rewards to such as should excel in them, would make them be best practised, so as to have them ready for use on occasion." " Child," said he, " you say very well; for by doing this you will see the several orders and divisions of your men, like sets of dancers, always performing their proper parts."

" But then," said Cyrus, " with respect to the raising of courage and spirit amongst the soldiers ; I think nothing more effectual than to give the men great hopes of advantage." " But, child," said he, " this expedient is just as if any one in hunting should always encourage the dogs in the same manner that is used when the beast is in view ; for one that should do thus would have them very eager and ready at his encouragement at first, but, if he often deceived them, they would at last give no attention to his encouragement when the beast was really in his view. It is the same with respect to these hopes ; if any one should balk men often, after having raised them to mighty expectations, he would not at last be able to prevail with them, though he talked to them of hopes ever so real and well grounded. But, child," said he, " you must be very cautious in saying any thing that you do not very well know ; the same thing, sometimes, said by others, may do the business ; your own encouragement you must with the utmost care preserve in credit for the greatest occasions.'

" Indeed, father," said Cyrus, " in my opinion you say perfectly well, and this way is to me much the more agreeable.

" But, in the matter of rendering the soldiers obedient, I take myself, father, not to be unskilled ; for presently, from a boy, you took me under discipline, and obliged me to be obedient to you ; then you gave me up to my teachers, and they did the same thing. Then, again, when I became one of the youth, our ruler took effectual care in this matter ; and there are many laws that, in my opinion, tend chiefly to the teaching of these two things, how to govern, and how to obey ; and, on considering them, I think I find that the most proper means to enforce obedience is to praise and recompense the obedient, and to disgrace and punish the disobedient." " Indeed, child," said he, " to a forced obedience this is the way ; but to a willing obedience, which is much the better, there is another way, and a readier ; for, whoever men take to be more knowing than themselves in what is for their interest and advantage, such a one they obey with pleasure. This you may know to be true in many other cases, as well as particularly in that of sick people, who are mighty ready and zealous in sending for such as may prescribe what is fit for them to do : so at sea, the people that are on board are very ready and zealous to obey their pilots ; and travellers are extremely averse to part with such as they think know the roads better than themselves : but when men think that they shall be injured by their obedience, they will neither yield to punishments nor be raised by rewards ; for no one willingly takes a reward to his own prejudice." " You say, father," said he, " that nothing more effectually procures one obedience than to appear to have more wisdom and knowledge than those that one rules." " I do say so," said he. " And how, father," said he, " shall one be best able to raise such an opinion of one's self ?" " Child," said he, " there is no readier way to appear wise and knowing in things wherein you desire to appear so, than to be in reality knowing in those things ; and considering the things in particular, you will find that what I say is true : for if you would appear a good husbandman, a good horseman, a good physician, a good player on the flute, or any other artist whatever, when you really are not so, consider how many contrivances you must use in order to appear so. And if you can prevail with a great many people to commend you, that you may gain a reputation, and if you purchase fine instruments, and furniture belonging to each of the arts, you are then an impostor. And soon after, when you come to give proof of your skill, you would be convicted, and would appear an arrogant boaster. But with respect to future time, and to what may or may not turn to advantage in the consequence, what is the way to make one's self in this really wise and knowing ? It is plain, child," said he, " by learning every thing that one can acquire the knowledge of by learning, as you have learnt the tactic art ; but with respect to what is not to be learnt from men, nor attained to by human foresight, consulting the gods in such cases, by divination, you will make yourself more knowing than others : and what you find most proper to be done, you are to take care that it be done ; for to see to the execution of what is proper is more the part of a man of prudence than to neglect it."

" But then," said Cyrus, " as to the being beloved by those that one rules, which is amongst the things that I take to be of the greatest importance, it is evident that the way is the same as it is to gain the love of friends : for I know very well that one ought to be seen

C

doing them service." "But, child," said he, "it is a matter of great difficulty to be always able to serve those that one has a mind to serve; but to be observed to rejoice with them when any good fortune befalls them, and to grieve with them when any thing ill; to appear zealous to assist them in their distresses; afraid lest they should miscarry in any thing; and to endeavour to prevent this by care and circumspection; these are things that you ought rather to concur with them in. And in point of action, the commander ought to be observed to undergo more heat in the summer, and in the winter more cold, and in great fatigues more labour and pain than others; for all these things contribute to the being beloved by those that are under one's government." "You say, father," said he, "that a commander ought, in all respects, to undergo more than those that he commands." "I do say it," said he; "and be of good courage, child; for be assured that bodies being alike, the same labours do not fall equally heavy on the commander and the private man: for glory makes those labours lighter to the commander, and the being conscious to himself that, in whatever he does, he does not lie concealed."

"But then, father, when the soldiers are supplied with all things necessary; when they are in health and able to undergo labour; when they are skilful and well exercised in all the military arts; when they are ambitious to appear brave men; when obedience is more pleasing to them than the contrary; would you not think a man wise who should then desire, on the first opportunity, to bring them to an engagement with the enemy?" "Yes, truly," said he, "provided that he had the enemy at a proper advantage: but if otherwise, the better I thought of myself, and the better I thought of my men, the more on my guard would I be; and, as in other things that we think of greatest value to us, so in these we should endeavour to have them secured in the strongest manner."

"And what is the best way, father, to take advantage of the enemy?" "Truly, child," said he, "this is no contemptible nor simple business that you inquire about. But be it known to you, that he who is to do this must be full of wiles, a dissembler, crafty, deceitful, a thief, and a robber, and must take advantage of his enemy in all manner of ways." Cyrus, laughing at this, cried out: "O Hercules! what a man, father, do you say that I must be!"

"Such a one, child," said he, "as may yet have the strictest regard to law and justice." "Why, then," said he, "while we were boys, and while we were youths, did you teach us the direct contrary?" "And so truly we do still," said he, "with respect to friends and fellow-citizens. But do you not know, that in order to injure enemies, you have learnt a great many mischievous arts?" "Not I, father," said he. "To what end then," said he, "did you learn the use of the bow, and to throw the javelin? To what end did you learn to deceive wild boars with toils and trenches, and stags with snares and gins? What is the reason that in your encountering lions, bears, and leopards, you did not put yourself on an even footing with them, but endeavour to take all advantages in engaging them? Do you not know that these are all mischievous artifices, deceits, subtleties, and takings of advantage?" "Yes, truly," said Cyrus, "against beasts; but if I was discovered intending to deceive a man, I got a good many stripes for it." "Nor did we, I think," said he, "allow you to shoot with the bow, or shoot a javelin at a man; but we taught you to throw at a mark, that you might not, at that time, do mischief to your friends, but that in case of war, you might be able to take your aim at men. And we instructed you to practise deceits, and to take advantages, not of men, but of beasts, that you might not hurt your friends by these means, but that in case a war should happen you might not be unpractised in them." "Therefore," said he, "father, if it be of use to know, both how to do men good, and how to do them harm, it ought to have been taught us how to practise both on men." "Child," said he, "in the time of our forefathers, there is said to have been a certain teacher of youth, who, just as you desire, taught the boys both to deal justly and unjustly; to be true and to be false; to deceive and not to deceive; to practise calumny and not to practise it; to take advantage and not to take advantage. And he distinguished what was to be practised towards friends, and what towards enemies; and proceeding yet farther, he taught that it was just even to deceive friends, if it were done for their good; and just to play the thief, and to steal from friends what belonged to them, if it were done for their good. And this teacher was obliged to exercise the boys one against another in the practice of these things, as they say the Greeks teach to deceive in wrestling, and exercise the boys in it one against another, that they may know how to put it in practice. Some therefore having so natural an aptness to deceive and take advantage, and perhaps no unnatural unaptness to make profit and advantage to themselves, did not refrain from using their endeavours to take advantages of friends. On this, therefore, a decree was made, which is yet in force among us, to teach the boys, simply and directly, as we teach our servants in their behaviour towards us, to tell truth, not to deceive, not to steal, not to take advantage; and if they transgress in these things, to punish them, that being so accustomed to these manners, they might become more mild and tractable citizens. But when they come to the age that you now are at, to teach them what is lawful with respect to enemies seemed what might be done securely; for it did not seem probable that being bred together with a reverence for each other, you should afterwards break out so as to become wild and savage citizens; just as we avoid discoursing concerning the affairs of the beautiful goddess before very young people, lest a freedom from restraint being added to a vehement desire, they should fall into great excess in their dealing that way." "To me, therefore," said he, "father, as being a very late learner of these artifices, do not refuse to teach them, if you know any, that I may take advantage of the enemy." "Do all, then," said he, "that is in your power, with your own men in the best order, to take the enemy in disorder; the enemy unarmed, with your own men armed; the enemy sleeping, with your own men waking; the enemy open and exposed to you, yourself being concealed and in the dark to them; to fall on them while engaged in difficult places, yourself being master of a place of strength." "And how," said he, "can one possibly catch the enemy making such mistakes as these?" "Because, child," said he, "both the enemy and yourselves are obliged, by necessity, to undergo many things of this kind: for you must both get provisions; you must both necessarily have rest; and in your marches you must make use of such roads as you find, whatever they are: considering all these things, in whatever part you know yourself to be the weakest, in that you must be the most watchful; and in whatever part you observe the enemy to be most exposed, in that you must attack him."

"Is it in these things only," said Cyrus, "that advantages are to be taken, or may it be done in others?" "It may be done in others, child," said he, "and more effectually; for in these cases men for the most-part place strong guards, knowing full well that they are necessary. They that would deceive the enemy may possibly, by raising in them a confidence and security, surprise them unguarded; or, by letting themselves be pursued, may bring the enemy into disorder, and enticing them on by their flight into a disadvantageous post, may there attack them. But you, child, who are fond of skill in all these affairs, must not make use of such things only as you have been informed of; you must be yourself the contriver of some stratagems to put in practice against the enemy: for as musicians do not only deal in such songs as they have been taught, but endeavour to compose others; and as in music such pieces as are new, and as one may say in flower, meet with success and approbation, so, in affairs of war, new contrivances are best approved, for they are most capable of deceiving the enemy. But, child," said he, "if you do no more than transfer to men those contrivances that you have used to ensnare little animals, do you not think," said he, "you will go a great way in the art of taking advantage of your enemy? for, in order to catch birds, you used to rise and go out in the night, in the hardest winter, and before the birds were stirring you had your nets ready laid for them; and a moveable foundation was disguised, and made like an immoveable one; you had birds ready taught to serve your ends, and to deceive those of their own kind; you yourself lay hid, but so as to see them, and not to be seen by them; and you watched your opportunity to draw your nets, and to prevent the birds escaping. Then, with respect to the hare, because she feeds in the dusk, and makes away to her form by day, you keep dogs; some of them to find her by the scent; and because she takes to her heels as soon as she is discovered, you have other dogs that are proper to take her at her course; and if she escapes these, then, having before discovered the meshes, and to what part the hare chooses to run, in these places you lay nets that are hardly to be seen, that in the eagerness of her course, throwing herself into the net, she may be hampered; and that she may not escape this snare, you set people to watch what passes; and these, from some places near, are presently on her; you yourself follow her, you astonish and amaze her with clamour and noise, that never quits her, so that in this distraction she is taken; and you make those that are set to watch lie concealed, with instructions beforehand to be perfectly still and silent. As I said before, therefore, if you would form some such contrivances against men, I do not know that you would leave one enemy alive. But if there is a necessity to fight on even terms with respect to situation, openly, and both parties prepared and armed, in such a case, child, those advantages that you have been long before provided with are of great weight; I mean those when the bodies of your men are duly exercised, their minds keen, and all the soldiers' arts well practised. Besides, it is very necessary that you should know, that whoever they are that you desire should be obedient to you, they, on their part, will desire you to be provident and careful of them; therefore never be remiss, but consider at night what your men shall do when it is day; and consider in the day how matters may be on the best footing with respect to the passing of the night. But as to the forming your army for battle; the marching them, either by day or by night, through narrow or through open ways, through mountains or plains; how to encamp; how to place your guards and watches both by night and day; how to lead towards the enemy; how to retreat from them; how to march by a city belonging to the enemy; how to march up to a rampart, and to retreat from it; how to pass woods or rivers; how to be on the guard, either against horse or against men armed with javelin or bow: and if, when you are marching by way of either wing, the enemy should appear, how to form a front against them; and if you are marching by your front, and that the enemy appear in another part and not in front; how to lead against them; how to get the best intelligence of the enemy's affairs, and how best to conceal your own from them. In all these matters, what can I say to you? You have often heard from me all that I knew of them; and, besides, whoever you have thought knowing in any of these affairs, you have not neglected to take their information, nor are you unskilled in them; therefore, according to the several occurrences, you must always make use of these things as they appear to be to your advantage And take my instruction, child," said he, "likewise in these things, and which are of the greatest importance: Never engage either yourself or the army in any thing contrary to the sacrifices and auguries; reflecting how men have chosen to engage in certain actions at hazard, and without knowing at all on which side of the choice they should meet with their advantage. This you may be convinced of by things that often happen: there are many instances of men, and they such as have been thought the wisest, who have persuaded some to begin a war against others, who have destroyed those that had been persuaded to be the aggressors. There are instances of many who have raised both cities and private men, and have suffered the greatest misfortunes at the hand of those they had so raised. There are instances of many who, when they might have used others as their friends in a mutual intercourse of good offices, and who, choosing to hold them rather as slaves than as friends, have met with revenge and punishment at their hands. Many, who not liking to live contentedly, possessing a part, and affecting to be lords of all, have by this means lost what was their own: and many who have acquired the much-wished-for metal, gold, have been destroyed by it. So human wisdom knows no more how to choose the best, than one who should determine to act as chance and the lot should decide. The gods, child, who are eternal, know all things that have been, all things that are, and all that shall happen in consequence of every thing; and when men consult them, they signify to those that they are propitious to what they ought to do, and what not. And if they will not give advice to all, it is nowise wonderful; for they are not under any necessity to take care of those of whom they are not willing to take care."

XENOPHON

ON THE

INSTITUTION OF CYRUS.

———

BOOK II.

CONTENTS of BOOK II.

INSTITUTION OF CYRUS.

BOOK II.

I. DISCOURSING in this manner, they arrived at the borders of Persia, when an eagle appearing to the right, led the way before them. And when they had made their supplications to the gods and heroes, guardians of Persia, to dismiss them favourably and propitiously, they passed the borders. When they had passed them they again made supplication to the gods, guardians of Media, to receive them propitiously and favourably; and having done this, and embraced each other, as usual, the father returned into Persia, and Cyrus marched on into Media to Cyaxares.¹

When Cyrus came to Cyaxares in Media, they first embraced each other, as usual, and Cyaxares afterwards asked Cyrus, "What force he was to bring him." He replied, "Thirty thousand of such as have been before with you, and served for their pay; but there are others coming, who have never yet served out of their own country, and are of the order of those that are free, and equally entitled to all honours." "And how many of these?" said Cyaxares. "The number of them," replied Cyrus, "will not please you, when you hear it: but consider," said he, "that those who are called the alike-honoured, though but few, rule with ease the rest of the Persians, who are very numerous. But," said he, "are you in any real want of these men, or are you under a vain alarm, and the enemy not coming?" "Indeed they are," said he, "and in

great numbers." "How does this appear?" "Why, a great many people who come from thence, some by one means and some by another, all say the same thing; then engage with these men we must: we must of necessity," said he. "Well, then," said Cyrus, "why do you not tell me whether you know what these forces are that are coming on us, and what we have of our own, that being apprised of both, we may afterwards consult how to carry on the war in the best manner?" "Attend, then," said Cyaxares: "Crœsus, the Lydian, is said to bring with him ten thousand horse; targeteers and archers upwards of forty thousand. They say that Arsamas, who governs the Greater Phrygia, brings eight thousand horse; targeteers and lance-men not less than forty thousand. That Aribæus, king of the Cappadocians, brings six thousand horse; archers and targeteers not less than thirty thousand. The Arabian Maragdus, ten thousand horse, one hundred chariots, and of slingers a very considerable body. As to the Greeks that are settled in Asia, there is nothing said of certain whether they attend the expedition or no. They say that Gabæus, who rules those that inhabit the country that extends from Phrygia on the Hellespont to the plain of Cayster, contributes six thousand horse, and ten thousand targeteers. The Carians, Cilicians, and Paphlagonians, though invited, they say do not attend the expedition. The Assyrians, who possess Babylon, and the rest of Assyria, will, as I judge, bring no less than twenty thousand horse; chariots, as I know very well, not more than two hundred; but I believe a vast body of foot; for so he is accustomed to do when he falls in on us." "The enemy then," said Cyrus, "you say, amount to sixty thousand horse, and to more than two hundred thousand targeteers and

---

1 This was the second prince of that name, supposed to be the same with the Darius of Scripture. He was descended from Cyaxares the First, king of Media and Persia, in whose reign the Scythians, who had held possession of a great portion of his territories for thirty years, were destroyed by stratagem. The Scythians are said to have been invited to a feast, and slain when in a state of intoxication. This latter prince also conquered and destroyed the city of Nineveh, in conjunction with Nebuchadnezzar.

archers. To proceed, then, what do you say is the number of your own forces?" "The Median horse are above ten thousand : and of targeteers and archers there may be, perhaps, in our own territories, about sixty thousand ; and of the Armenians, our neighbours, we shall have four thousand horse and twenty thousand foot." "You say, then," said Cyrus, "that we shall have in horse less than a third part of the enemy's force of that sort, and scarce half the number of their foot." "What !" said Cyaxares, "do you think those Persians, that you say you bring, are but an inconsiderable number?" "We will take another time," said Cyrus, "to consider whether we want men or no : at present, pray tell me what is the method of fighting that is in use with those several people." "They almost all," said Cyaxares, "use the same : some of their men, as well as of our own, use the bow, and others the javelin." "Then," said Cyrus, "since such are their arms, they must necessarily engage at a distance." "Necessarily," said Cyaxares. "In this case, therefore," said Cyrus, "the victory falls to the greater number; for the few, wounded by those weapons, are much sooner destroyed by the many, than the many by the few." "If it be so, Cyrus," said he, "what way can one find better than to send to the Persians, acquaint them that if the Medes sustain any loss the misfortune will reach to themselves, and, at the same time, to require from them a greater force?" "Be assured," said Cyrus, "that if all the Persians should come, we should not exceed the enemy in numbers." "What have you in view then that is better?" "Why," said Cyrus, "if I were you, I would immediately make for all the Persians that are coming ·such arms as those men, that are called the alike-honoured, come provided with ; and these are, a corslet about the breast, a shield for the left hand, and a sword, or cutlass, for the right. If you provide these arms, you will make it the safest way for us to come to close fight with the enemy ; and better for the enemy to fly than to stand their ground. For our own station," said he, "we appoint against those that stand their ground ; and those that fly we allot to you and to your horse, that they may not have time to make their escape or to turn again." Thus Cyrus spoke. Cyaxares was of opinion that he said very right, and he thought no longer of sending for more men, but applied him-

self to the providing of the arms before tioned ; and they were scarce got ready b the Persian gentlemen, or alike-honoured rived, bringing the Persian army with the

On this Cyrus is said to have called the tlemen together, and to have spoken to thus : " Friends ! I, who saw that your pe were armed, and your minds prepared for fight with your enemy, and knew that the sians who attend you were armed in such ner as to engage only at a distance, was that, being but few in number, and des of others to support you, when you fell in the great number of the enemy, you might by some misfortune. Now, therefore," he, "that you are come, and bring with men whose bodies are not contemptible, who are to be supplied with arms like our to raise their minds is now your part. is the business of a commander not only himself brave, but to take such care of that he rules, that they may be made as as is possible." Thus he said.

They were all much pleased, imagining should now engage the enemy with mo assist and support them. And one of spoke to this effect : "Perhaps," said he, shall be thought to talk strangely, if I a Cyrus, instead of us, to say something to men, who are to be our supports and fel combatants, when they receive their arms I know," said he, "that the words of t who have the most power to do service do hurt, sink deeper into the minds of hearers. And the presents that such make, though they happen to be less than men may receive from others like themse yet the receivers value them more. So n said he, "the Persians will be much pleased if they receive an exhortation Cyrus, than if they receive it from us. when they are placed in the degree of the a honoured, they will think themselves strongly confirmed in it, if done by the so our king, and by our commander-in-chief, if they are introduced to it by us. Nor o our endeavours to be wanting ; but we sh use all possible means to excite and raise courage of these men ; for how much so they become braver and better men, it wil so much the more to our advantage."

So Cyrus, setting down the arms in a exposed to view, and calling together all Persian soldiers spoke to this effect : "]

of Persia! you were born and bred in the same country that we were; you have bodies that are nowise inferior to ours, and you ought to have souls too not inferior to ours. And yet, though such you are in yourselves, in our own country you were not on an equal footing with us. Not that you were excluded from it by us, but by the necessity you were under of providing yourselves with necessaries. Now, with the help of the gods, it shall be my care that you shall be supplied with these. And even though you may be in any sort inferior to us, yet by accepting these arms, that are such as we have ourselves, it is in your power, if you will, to run the same hazards with us; and, if any thing great and advantageous happen to us on it, to be thought worthy of like advantages with ourselves. Heretofore you have used the bow and the javelin; we have done the same: and if you are inferior to us in the practice of these, it is not at all wonderful; for you have not had the leisure that we have had to exercise yourselves in them. But, in this sort of arms, we have no advantage above you, for every one will have a corslet fitted to his breast, for the left hand a shield which you are all accustomed to wear; and, for the right, a sword or cutlass, which you are to use against the enemy; not needing to be mindful of any thing but how not to miss your blow. Under these arms, therefore, what difference can there be between one and another amongst us, unless it be in boldness, in which you ought not to be inferior to us? How should it be our part more than yours to be desirous of victory, by which all things great and advantageous are acquired and preserved? How can superiority of arms be less necessary to you than to us, when it is by this that all the conquered possess becomes yielded to the victors?" In conclusion, he said: "You have heard all these things; you, all of you, see your arms; he that thinks fit, let him take them, and enlist himself under his officer into the same order and degree with us. He that thinks it enough for him to be in the station of a mercenary, let him continue under servile arms." Thus he said. The Persians who heard him were of opinion, that if, when they were invited to an equal share of all advantages, by sharing in like labours, they should not agree to it, they should then justly pass all their days in a mean and low condition. So they were all enlisted, and all took the arms.

During the time that the enemy was said to be approaching, but did not actually come, Cyrus endeavoured to exercise the bodies of his men, in order to give them strength and vigour; to teach them how to form themselves, and to move in proper order, and to raise their minds to warlike affairs. And, in the first place, being supplied with servants by Cyaxares, he ordered them to supply all the soldiers with every thing, ready-made, that they wanted. And having provided for this, he left them nothing to do but to practise such things as related to war, seeming to have learned this maxim, that those men were best at any thing who, taking off their minds from application to many things, apply themselves to one business singly. And of affairs that relate to war, cutting them off from the practice of the bow and javelin, he left them only this one thing to do, which was to fight with sword, shield, and corslet. So that he presently brought their minds to this state, that they found they were either to engage their enemy hand to hand, or to confess that they were very worthless supports and fellow-combatants. And this was a difficult thing to be owned by such as knew they were maintained for nothing else but to fight for those that maintained them. Besides, having considered that, whatever the things are wherein men are raised to an emulation one against another, those are the things they are most willing to exercise themselves in, he appointed them to contend and vie with each other in all those kinds of things that he knew were fit to be exercised and practised by the soldiers.

The things he so appointed were these: to the private man, to make himself a good soldier, obedient to his commanders; ready to undergo labour; to be enterprising in dangers, but consistently with good order; to be skilful in the military exercises; fond of having his arms beautiful and in good condition; and in all such matters desirous of praise. To the leader of five, to make himself such as it became the private man to be; and to do his utmost to make his five likewise such. To the leader of ten, to make his ten such. To the captain to do the same for his company; the colonel for his regiment; and in the same manner, to the rest of the commanding officers, to render themselves unexceptionable and blameless; and to take care that those who were under their command should, in their several stations, make those under them ready to do their duties. The rewards he proposed in this contention were these: to the colonels, who, by their care, appeared to have made themselves the best regiments, to be made commanders of a thousand; to the captains, who appeared to have made themselves the best companies, to be made colonels; to the leaders of ten, that approved themselves the best, to be advanced to the degree of captains; and to the leaders of five, in like manner to be advanced to the degree of leaders of ten: and to the private men that behaved best, to be advanced to the degree of leaders of five. In the first place, therefore, all these officers were well served by those they commanded, and then all those other honours, suitable to every one, attended them. He likewise gave greater hopes to those who deserved praise, in case any more than ordinary advantage should on occasion fall in their way. He proposed also certain rewards of victory to whole regiments and companies. So likewise to whole tens and fives, if they appeared to be the most obedient to their commanders, and to perform the things beforementioned with the greatest ardour and readiness; and the rewards to these were such as were the most proper to be bestowed in common on a number of men. These were the things that were proposed to the army, and exercised amongst them.

Tents he likewise provided for them, as many in number as were the colonels, and of a size such as was sufficient for each regiment; and a regiment consisted of a hundred men. Thus they were quartered in tents by regiments. And it seemed to him to be of use to his men, in the war that was coming on, that, by thus inhabiting together, they saw each other maintained alike; and there was no pretence of lying under a disadvantage, so as to allow any one to be remiss, or one to be worse than another, in acting against the enemy. It seemed to him likewise that this joint habitation was of use to them with respect to their knowing one another; for, by being known, he thought that a sense of shame and reproach took more place on all; for they who are unknown seem to act with less caution and restraint, as men do who are in the dark. And this cohabitation seemed to him to be of great service to his men with respect to exactness in their orders; for thus the colonels had their several regiments in order under them in their

sleep, just as when a regiment is in a bo[ ] the march; so the captains their compa[ ] the commanders of tens their tens; an[ ] commanders of five their five: and this [ ] ness in their orders seemed to him to [ ] great service, both to prevent their bein[ ] into disorder, and, if disordered, to settle [ ] selves more readily into order again: just the case of stones and pieces of wood th[ ] to be fitted together, which, if they have c[ ] marks to make it evident to what place e[ ] them belongs, one may with ease fit tog[ ] again, into whatever irregular form they have been thrown. And their being thus [ ] tained together, he thought, was of serv[ ] them, in order to make them less ready [ ] sert each other; because he observed beasts that had their maintenance togethe[ ] in great pain if separated by any one.

Cyrus also took care that they should go to their dinner or supper without a s[ ] for he either led them out to hunt, and them a sweat that way, or he contrived sports for them as would put them into or if any business happened that was done, he so managed it that they shoul[ ] return without sweating; for this he judg[ ] be of service, in order to make them eat pleasure, and to make them healthy, a make them able to undergo labour: and [ ] he judged to be of use in making them gentle one towards another, because horses, that labour jointly together, stand wise more gently and tamely together. they, who are conscious to themselves of duly exercised, are inspired with more b[ ] and courage against the enemy.

Cyrus likewise provided himself with [ ] sufficient to contain those that he invit[ ] sup with him: he invited, for the most such of the colonels as he thought proper he sometimes invited some of the cap[ ] some of the commanders of ten, and sor[ ] the commanders of five; sometimes sor[ ] the soldiers, and sometimes a whole f[ ] whole ten, a whole company, or a whole ment together. He invited them likewise rewarded those that he saw practise any thing as he desired all the others should im And the things that were set before hi[ ] and before those that he invited to supper always alike. He always made the serva[ ] the army likewise equal sharers in all th for he thought it was not less becoming h reward those who served in the concerns of the army, than to reward heralds and ambassadors; for he was of opinion that they ought to be faithful, skilled in military affairs, and intelligent, as well as zealous in their business, quick of despatch, diligent, and orderly. Besides, whatever good quality they had, who were accounted the better sort, that Cyrus thought the servants ought to be possessed of; and that it was their duty to bring themselves, by practice, to refuse no work, but to think it becoming them to do all things whatever that their commanders should enjoin.

II. And Cyrus always took care that while he entertained any of them in his tent, the most agreeable subjects of discourse, and such as might excite them to good, should be thrown in amongst them. On a certain occasion, therefore, he began this discourse: "Friends!" said he, "are other men, think you, any ways inferior to us, by reason of their not being disciplined in the same manner as we are? or will they prove not to differ from us at all, either in their converse with each other, or in action against the enemy?" Hystaspes, in answer to him, said: "What they may prove to be in action against the enemy I do not yet know; but, by the gods! some of them seem already to be very perverse and churlish in their conversation; for yesterday," said he, "Cyaxares sent certain victims to every regiment; and we had every one of us three portions or more, that were carried and distributed around. Our cook began his first distribution by me, when the person who was to make the second distribution entered; I bade him begin with the last man, and carry round the contrary way. One, therefore, from the middle of the circle of soldiers as they lay, cried out: 'By Jove!' said he, 'there's no manner of equality or fairness in this, unless somebody begin from us here in the middle.' I, hearing this, was uneasy that any of them should think they lay under a disadvantage, and I presently bade him come to me; in this he, in a very orderly manner, obeyed me: but when the portions that were distributing came to us, who were to take last, they were the least that were left; he then plainly discovered himself to be very much afflicted, and said to himself, 'Oh, ill fortune! that I should happen to be called hither!' I then said to him, 'Do not be disturbed; it will begin presently by us, and you shall take first the biggest portion.' At the third going about,

which was the last turn, he took the next after me; but as soon as the third person had taken, he fancied that this man had taken a larger portion than himself, and he threw back that that he had taken, intending to take another; but the cook, thinking that he wanted no more meat, moved on, distributing around, before he took another portion. Here he bore so ill the misfortune of losing the portion he had taken, that being struck and in wrath at his ill fortune, he misplaced and overturned some sauce he had remaining. A captain who was the nearest us, seeing this, clapped his hands, and laughed out, much delighted; I," said Hystaspes, "made as if I coughed, for I was not able to hold from laughing. Cyrus," said he, "such a one do I show you one of our companions to be." On this, as was natural, they laughed.

Another of the colonels then spoke. "Cyrus," said he, "this Hystaspes, it seems, has met with one of a very perverse temper; but as you instructed us in the order and discipline we were to observe, and dismissed us with commands to instruct every one his regiment in the things he had learned from you; so I, as others did, came to a certain company, and was teaching them; and placing the captain first, and then a young man in order after him, and so the rest, as I thought proper; and then, standing before them, and looking on the company, when I thought it proper time, I gave the command to advance. This young man, advancing before the captain, marched first; I, seeing him do thus, said to him: 'Friend, what are you doing?' The man said: 'Why, I advance as you command me.' 'But,' said I, 'I did not command only you to advance, but all;' then, turning to his companions: 'Do not you hear,' said he, 'that the colonel commands you all to advance?' Then all of them passing the captain by, came up to me; but when the captain made them retire back they were offended, and said, 'Whom are we to obey? for now one bids us to advance, and another will not suffer us to do it.' Bearing all this contentedly, and placing them as at first, I told them that none of those behind should move till he that was before him led the way, but that they should all mind only to follow their leading man. In the meantime there came to me a certain person that was going to Persia, and he bade me give him the letter I had written home; now the captain knew where the letter lay: I bade him therefore run and fetch this letter. He ran his way: the young man, armed as he was, with corslet and sword, followed after his captain; the rest of his company, seeing him run, ran off with him; and all of them came back again, and brought me the letter. Thus," said he, " is this company of mine mighty exact in executing all the instructions they receive from you." The rest, as was natural, laughed at this guard and attendance on the letter: but Cyrus said: " O Jove, and all you gods! what men have we for our companions! They are so easily served, that many of them might be made one's friends for a little portion of meat; and they are so obedient, that they obey before they understand what they are ordered to do. For my part, I do not know what sort of men we should wish the soldiers to be, unless it be just such!" And Cyrus thus, in laughing, praised the soldiers.

There happened at that time to be in the tent a certain colonel, his name was Aglaitadas, a churlish and austere sort of man in his manners; and he spoke thus: " Do you think, now, Cyrus," said he, " that these men tell you the truth?" " Why, what end," said Cyrus, " have they in lying?" " What else," said he, " but to make you laugh? and, for this reason, they tell you these stories in a vain arrogant way." " Good words, pray!" said Cyrus: " do not say that they are vain and arrogant; for the word *arrogant* seems to me to lie on such as feign themselves richer or braver than they really are, and pretend to do what they are not able to do; and that plainly act thus, in order to get something, and make profit to themselves. They that move their companions to laughter, and do it neither for their own gain nor to the hearer's prejudice, nor with intent to do any manner of harm, why may not such be called polite and agreeable, much rather than arrogant?" " Thus did Cyrus apologise for such as afforded matter of laughter. The colonel, then, who had told the pleasant story of the company of soldiers, said: " If we endeavoured, Aglaitadas, to make you cry, would you not blame us very much? as there are some who, in songs and discourses, uttering certain melancholy notes and things, endeavour to move people by tears. But now, though you yourself know that we are desirous to give you pleasure, and not in the least to hurt you, yet you hold us thus in great disgrace!" " By Jove!" said Aglaitadas, " I do, and justly; because, in my opinion, he that makes his friend

laugh does a much more worthless and insignificant thing than he who makes him cry: and you will find, if you reckon right, that I say true. Fathers bring their sons to a discreet and modest temper of mind, and teachers their youth to all good learning, by tears; and it is by affliction and tears that the laws influence citizens to justice in their conduct. But can you possibly say that your movers of laughter either do any service to the bodies of men, or form their minds to a better sense of their duty, with respect to their private families, or to the public?" On this, Hystaspes spoke in this manner: " Aglaitadas," said he, " if you will follow my advice, you shall boldly lay out this very valuable thing on our enemies, and you shall endeavour to set them crying; but that worthless thing, laughter, you shall spend on us," said he, " here, amongst your friends. I know you have a great deal of it that lies by you in store; for you neither use nor spend it yourself, nor do you willingly afford laughter either to your friends or to strangers: so that you have no manner of pretence to refuse bestowing it on us." " Then," said Aglaitadas, " do you endeavour to get it out of me." And the leader of the company said: " By Jove, then, he is a fool indeed! for I believe one may strike fire out of you more easily than draw laughter from you." At this the others laughed, knowing the temper of the man; and Aglaitadas himself smiled at it: Cyrus, seeing him pleased, said. " Indeed, captain, you are in the wrong to corrupt the most serious man we have, by tempting him to laugh; and, to do this," said he, " to one who is so great an enemy to laughter!" Here ended this subject of discourse.

After this Chrysantas spoke thus: " But, Cyrus," said he, " I, and all that are here present, consider that there are come hither with us men, who have some of them more merit and some less; and, if any advantage fall in our way, they will all think themselves entitled to an equal share of it: but, for my part, I do not think that any thing can be more unequal amongst men, than that the good and the bad should be entitled to equal advantages." Cyrus to this said: " By the gods, then, friends! it were best for us to give this out, and propose it to be debated in the army, whether they think it proper, if in consequence of our labours the gods give us any advantage, that all should share alike in it; or that, examining the actions of every one, we should give to each rewards proportionable?" "But why," said Chrysantas, "should you give this out to be discoursed on, and not declare that you will have it so? Did not you declare," said he, " what the soldiers should contend and vie with each other in, and what the rewards of the contention should be?" "But, by Jove!" said Cyrus, " these matters and those are not alike: for what they shall acquire by their service, that, I believe, they will reckon common to all; but the command of the army they take to be mine, even from the first setting out: so that in appointing officers, I believe, they think I do them no wrong." "And do you think," said Chrysantas, "that the multitude assembled will ever decree that every one shall not have his equal share, but that the best shall have the advantage in profits and honours?" "I do think it," said Cyrus; "partly because of your assistance in it, and partly because it is infamous to assert, that he who labours most for the public, and does it most service, is not entitled to the greatest rewards; and, I believe, that the very worst of our men will think it of service to them that the best should have the advantage."

Cyrus had a mind that this should be publicly decreed, even on account of the alike-honoured; for he thought that they would be yet better men, if they knew that they themselves were to be judged by their actions, and rewarded accordingly. This therefore seemed to him to be the proper opportunity to put it to the vote, whilst the alike-honoured were dissatisfied with the claim of the multitude to equality of shares. So it was the current opinion of those in the tent to give out the discourse on the subject; and they said that every one who thought it his part to act like a man ought to give his assistance in it. On this one of the colonels laughed, and said: "I know," said he, " a man, one of the common people, who will help to justify this opinion, that this equality of shares, without distinction, ought not to be." Another asked him, "Whom he meant?" He replied: "Truly, he is one of my own tent, and is on every occasion seeking to get the advantage and upper hand of others." Another then asked: "And does he seek it in labour and taking pains?" "No, by Jove!" said he, "not in that; but here you have caught me in a lie, for, with respect to labour and things of that kind, he always contentedly

allows any one to get the upper hand of him that will."

"Friends," said Cyrus, "my judgment is, that such men as this person speaks of ought to be weeded out of the army, if we intend to preserve it in its virtue and vigour, and to render the soldiers obedient; for the soldiers seem to me to be such as will follow where any one shall lead them the way: good and excellent men certainly endeavour to lead to things good and excellent, vicious men to things vicious, and corrupt men have often more abettors than the sober and industrious: for vice, that takes its course through present pleasures, has these pleasures to assist in persuading the multitude to abet it; but virtue, that moves upwards, has not strength enough in present occasions to draw men without distinction after it, especially if there are others in opposition to it that exhort men to follow the prone and easy track. They therefore who are faulty on account of sloth and indolence, these I reckon, like drones, are burdensome to their companions only by the expense of maintaining them; but active associates in vice, who prosecute their interest with industry and impudence, these are the leaders of men to vicious courses; for they often have it in their power to show them that vice will be serviceable to their interest; so that such men must be entirely weeded out. Then, pray, do not consider how to recruit your regiments with your own countrymen; but, as in horses, you look for those that are the best, and not for those that are of your own country, so of men, take such as you think will most contribute to your strength and good order. And that it will be to our advantage to do so, this will bear me testimony, that neither is a chariot swift, if it have but slow horses; nor is it true, if joined to vicious and unmanageable ones: nor can a family be well regulated that uses vicious servants; but a family that wants servants is less injured than one that is confounded by unjust ones. And be it known to you, friends, that the turning out of the vicious will not only be of advantage to you in their being out of the way, but of those that remain; they who have had vice instilled into them will discharge themselves of it again; and the good, seeing the vicious punished, will adhere to virtue with much more warmth and zeal." Thus he said. All his friends were of opinion with him, and did accordingly.

After this Cyrus began again to set jest and

merriment on foot; for observing that one of the captains had brought with him a fellow-guest, and had placed him next to himself, that the man was excessively rough and hairy, and very ugly, he called the captain by his name, and spoke thus; "Sambaulas," said he, "that young man that lies next to you, do you carry him about with you, according to the Greek custom, because he is handsome?" "No, by Jove!" said Sambaulas; "but I am pleased with his conversation, and even with looking at him." They that were present in the tent, on hearing this, looked at the man, and when they saw that his face was excessively ugly, they all laughed; and one of them said: "In the name of all the gods, Sambaulas, by what piece of service has this man so tied himself to you?" He said: "By Jove! friends, I will tell you: whenever I have called on him, either by night or by day, he never pretended want of leisure, never obeyed lazily, but always ran to his business with the utmost despatch: as often as I have ordered him to do a thing, I never saw him execute it without putting himself into a heat; and he has made the whole twelve such as himself, not showing them in word, but in action, what they ought to be." Then somebody said: "Since he is such an extraordinary man, do you not embrace him as you do relations?" And to this the homely person replied: "No, by Jove!" said he, "for he is not one of those that are fond of labour and pains; and to embrace me would be as much to him as if he underwent the greatest toil."

III. Such kind of discourse and things, both merry and serious, passed amongst them in the tent. And having at last performed the third libation, and made their prayers to the gods for their blessings, they broke up their company in the tent, in order to go to rest.

The next day Cyrus assembled all the soldiers, and spoke to them to this effect: "Friends! the conflict is at hand, for the enemies are approaching; the rewards of our victory, if we conquer, it is evident, are our enemies themselves, and their fortunes. On the other hand, if we are conquered (for this ought always to be mentioned,) thus likewise do the fortunes of the conquered stand exposed as the rewards of the conquerors. Therefore, thus," said he, "you ought to determine with yourselves, that when men are united as associates in war, if every one within himself makes account that nothing will be as it ought to be, unless every one be inspired with zeal and ardour, they then presently perform things great and noble; for nothing of what is proper to be done is, in this case, neglected. But when every one imagines that another is to fight and act, though he himself play the drone, be it known to you," said he, "that with such the success of things will be unhappy to them all. The gods have so established it; to those who will not impose on themselves the task of labouring for their own advantage, they give other task-masters. Now, therefore," said he, "let some one stand up, and speak to this point; whether he think that virtue will be the better practised amongst us, if he, who chooses to undergo the greatest toil and run the greatest hazards, obtain the greatest rewards? or if we all see that the worthless man lies under no disadvantage, but that all of us are to share alike?"

Here Chrysantas, one of the alike-honoured, one who was neither tall in his person, nor whose looks bespoke either courage or spirit, but a man of excellent understanding, rose up and spoke thus: "In truth, Cyrus," said he, "my opinion is, that you do not propose this to our debate, as judging it fit that the worthless should stand on a footing of equal advantage with the deserving; but to try whether there be such a man amongst us, that will venture to discover himself to be of opinion, that he who performs nothing that is great and noble should share equally of those advantages that are gained by the virtue and bravery of others. I am," said he, "neither swift of foot, nor have I great strength and vigour in my hands and arms; and by what I can perform with my person, I reckon I cannot be judged to be the first man, nor yet the second, I believe not the thousandth; perhaps not the ten thousandth; but this I very well know, that if they who are men of strength set their hands vigorously to the work, I shall have my share in some advantage or other, and as much as is justly due to me; but if mean and worthless men shall do nothing, and men of bravery and vigour shall be quite out of heart, I am afraid I shall have my share in something else rather than advantage, and such a share as will be greater than I desire." Thus spoke Chrysantas.

After him rose Pheraulas, a Persian, one of the common people; a man intimately known to Cyrus, and much in his favour whilst they were yet in Persia, one whose person was not uncomely, and who, with respect to his mind, was not like one of the mean and ignoble; and he spoke to this effect: " I, Cyrus," said he, "and all the Persians here present, reckon ourselves now entered in the lists of virtue, and setting forward in its career on an equal footing; for I see that our bodies are all exercised alike, and nourished with like food; that like company and conversation is vouchsafed to us all; and that the same honourable actions lie before us: for obedience to our commanders lies before us in common, and whoever is found sincerely to practise it, that man, I see, obtains rewards and honours at the hands of Cyrus: then to act with bravery against the enemy is not a thing that is becoming to one, and is otherwise to another, but stands recommended as great and noble to us all. And I take on me to say, that our method of fighting is now plainly taught us. I see that all men naturally know it; as every other animal naturally knows a certain method of fighting, and this without learning it from any other than from nature; as the bull attacks with his horn, the horse with his hoof, the dog with his mouth, the boar with his tooth; and all of them know," said he, "by what means best to defend themselves against the attack of others; and these things proceed not from the instruction of any master in these arts. I understood presently, from a child, how to interpose something between myself and the person who offered to strike me; and if I had nothing else, I endeavoured, as well as I was able, by holding up my hands, to hinder and oppose the person that assaulted me; and this I did not only without being taught it, but even though I were beaten for defending myself. When I was a child, wherever I saw a sword, I presently seized it; nor was I taught how to handle it by any one, but, as I say, by nature. This therefore I did, not only untaught, but even crossed and hindered in it; as there are many other things that I have been necessarily prompted by nature to do, though controlled and checked in them both by my father and mother. Then, by Jove! with this sword I hacked and hewed whatever came in my way, when I could do it privately and unseen; for it was not only natural to me, like walking and running, but, besides its being natural, I thought it a pleasure to do it. Since, therefore," said he, "that fighting is the thing now left us to

do, and that it is a work that requires courage rather than art, how can it be other than a pleasure to us to enter the lists with these noble persons the alike-honoured, when the rewards of virtue lie equally before us, and we of the people do not run an equal risk? They have at stake a life of honour, which is the most agreeable, and the only one that can be called a life; we only a laborious and ignoble one, which in my opinion is but painful and unhappy. Then this, friends, greatly animates me to enter the lists against these men—that Cyrus is to be our judge: he who judges not partially and invidiously, but, I aver, and swear it by the gods, that I think Cyrus loves those that he finds to be deserving not less than he does himself. Accordingly, I observe that he bestows what he has on such men with more pleasure than he takes in his own possession of it. Besides," said he, "these men are greatly elevated with their having been disciplined to bear hunger, thirst, and cold; not knowing that we have been disciplined in the same things, under a much abler teacher than they have been; for there is none a more effectual teacher of these things than necessity, that has taught them us in the completest manner. These men have exercised themselves in the labour of bearing arms, that have been so contrived by all men as to be worn with the greatest ease; but we," said he, "have been obliged, by necessity, to walk and run under heavy burdens; so that the arms we now bear seem to me not to be like burdens, but rather like wings. So count on me," said he, " Cyrus, as one that will engage in this dispute, and who desires, whatever degree I am in, to be rewarded according to my desert. And I exhort you, my friends of the people, to embark in this military contention, against these men of discipline; for they are now drawn in, and caught in this popular dispute." So spoke Pheraulas; and many others stood up to support them both in their opinions. It was thought therefore that every one should be rewarded according to his desert, and that Cyrus should be the judge.

Thus did these things proceed; and Cyrus took an occasion to invite an entire regiment, together with their colonel, to sup with him. This he did, on having seen the man forming half the men of his regiment against the other half, in order to attack each other: they had all of them their corslets on, and in their left hands their shields : but to one half he had given good large sticks for their right hands, and the others he had ordered to gather clods to throw. When they stood thus, ready prepared, he gave them the signal to engage : then these fell on with their clods; some chanced to fall on the corslets of the opposite party; some on their shields : some hit a thigh, some a leg : but, when they came to close, they who had the sticks applied their blows on the thighs, hands, and legs of their adversaries, as well as on the necks and backs of such as stooped for their clods; and, at last, they that were armed with the sticks put the others to the rout, laying them on with much laughter and diversion. Then the others, in their turn, taking the sticks, did the same thing to those who took their turn in throwing the clods. Cyrus was much taken with these things; both with the contrivance of the officer, the obedience of the men, that they were at the same time both exercised and diverted, and that those men gained the victory who were armed in the manner that resembled the Persians. Being pleased with these things, he invited them to supper; and observing some of them with their shins bound up, and some with their hands in the same condition, he asked them what harm they had got. They said they had been struck with the clods. He then asked them again, whether it was when they were close together, or while they were at a distance. They said, while they were at a distance ; but that, when they closed it was the finest sport imaginable for those that were armed with the sticks; but then, again, they that were wounded by the sticks cried out they did not at all think it a diversion to be threshed in that close way. They showed the blows they received from those that held the sticks, both on their hands and neck, and some in their faces : and then, as was natural, they laughed at one another. The next day the whole field was full of people imitating these men; and whenever they had nothing of more serious business to do, they made use of this diversion.

And Cyrus observing another colonel on a certain occasion leading his men from the river, one by one, to their dinner; and when he thought it proper, ordering the second, third, and fourth company to advance in front; and when the captains were all in front, ordering each company to double their files, on which the commanders of tens advanced in front; and that then, when he thought proper, he ordered each company to bring themselves to be four in front; thus the commanders of five advanced, that the company might march four in front; and that, when they arrived at the door of the tent, commanding them to enter, one by one, he introduced the first company, ordering the second to follow them in the rear, and the third and fourth in like manner, and so led them all in : and that, introducing them in this manner, he sat them all down to their meat, in the order as they entered : he, being much taken with this man for his good temper, instruction, and care, invited the whole regiment to sup with him, together with the colonel. But another colonel, who had not been invited, being present at the time, spoke thus : " But my regiment, Cyrus," said he, " you do not invite to your tent ; yet when they go to their dinner, they perform all these things; and when the business in the tent is over, the rear leader of the last company leads out that company with the last men ranged first in order for battle : then the rear leader of the next company follows after these ; so the third and fourth in the same manner ; that when it is proper to lead off from the enemy, they may know how to retreat. And when we get into the course, we there move about; when we march to the east, I lead the way, and the first company moves first, the second in its order; so the third and fourth, and the tens and fives of the several companies, in the proper course, as long as I give orders accordingly : but," said he, " when we march to the west, the rear leader and the last man lead the way, and yet obey me who march last, that they may be accustomed both to follow and to lead with equal obedience." " And do you always do thus ?" said Cyrus. " As often," said he, " as we take our meals." " I will invite you, therefore," said he, " because you practise your exercise both in advancing and retreating, by day and night, and both exercise your bodies by the motion, and profit your minds by the discipline. And since you do all these things double, it is but just that I should give you double good entertainment." " By Jove!" said the colonel, " not in one day, unless you give us double stomachs too!" Thus they made an end of that conversation in the tent. And the next day Cyrus invited this regiment, as he said he would, and did the same again the day following; the rest, perceiving this, all imitated those men for the future.

IV. But as Cyrus, on a certain occasion,

was making a general muster and review of his men under arms, there came a messenger from Cyaxares, acquainting him that an Indian embassy was arrived. "Cyaxares," said the messenger, "desires that you will come as soon as possible, and from him I bring you a beautiful robe; for he has a mind that you should appear in the handsomest and most splendid manner, the Indians being to see the manner of your approach." Cyrus hearing this, gave command to the colonel who stood first in order to place himself in front, bringing his men into one line behind him, and to keep himself to the right. He commanded him to transmit the same orders to the second, and so to deliver them down through the whole. These men, in obedience to Cyrus, presently delivered down the orders, and put them in execution. In a very little time they formed a front of three hundred, for that was the number of the colonels, and they were a hundred in depth. When they stood thus, he commanded them to follow as he should lead them, and, beginning presently to run, he led them the way. But when he perceived the avenue that led to the palace straiter than to allow them all to move on in line, he commanded the first thousand to follow in the situation and order they were in, and the next to follow in the rear of this, and so in like manner throughout the whole. He himself led on without stopping. The other thousands followed, each in the rear of those that went before. And he sent two servants to the opening of the avenue, to give information of what was to be done, in case any should be ignorant of it. When they came to Cyaxares' gates, he commanded the first colonel to form his regiment to twelve in depth, and to range the commanders of twelves in front around the palace: he commanded him likewise to transmit these orders to the second, and so throughout the whole. They did accordingly. He himself went in to Cyaxares, in a plain Persian robe, undisguised with foreign ornaments. Cyaxares seeing him, was pleased with his despatch, but offended at the meanness of his robe, and said: "What have you done, Cyrus, in appearing thus before the Indians? I had a mind," said he, "that you should appear in the most splendid manner; and it had been an ornament to me, for you, who are my sister's son, to have appeared the most magnificent that was possible." Cyrus to this said: "Which way, Cyaxares, had I been

the greater ornament to you; whether, if clothing myself in purple, putting on bracelets, and encompassing my neck with a collar, I had obeyed you in a loitering manner? or now that, with so great and so good a force, I obey you with such despatch, having in honour of you adorned myself with diligence, and adorning you, by showing the rest to be so obedient to your orders?" Cyrus thus spoke.

Cyaxares, judging that he said right, gave orders to introduce the Indians. The Indians, having come in, said: "That the king of the Indians had sent them, and had commanded them to ask what was the cause of the war between the Medes and Assyrians? and, when we had heard you," said they, "he commanded us to go to the Assyrian, and ask him the same question; and, in the end, to tell you both that the king of the Indians does declare that, after having informed himself of the justice of the cause, he will take part with the injured." Cyaxares to this said: "You hear me therefore declare that we have done no injury to the Assyrians; go then and inquire from him what he says to it." Cyrus being present, asked Cyaxares this question: "And may I," said he, "say what I think proper on this occasion?" Cyaxares bade him do so. "Do you therefore," said he, "acquaint the king of the Indians thus (unless Cyaxares judge otherwise): that if the Assyrian say he has been any wise injured by us, we declare that we choose the king of the Indians himself to be our judge." These men hearing this went their way.

When the Indians were gone. Cyrus began a discourse with Cyaxares, to this effect: "I came from home, Cyaxares, without having abundance of treasure of my own; and, whatever it was, I have but very little of it left; for I have spent it," said he, "on the soldiers. This perhaps you will wonder at, since it is you that maintain them. But be it known to you," said he, "that it has gone in nothing else but in rewards and gratifications to the soldiers, whenever I have been pleased with any of them. For, in my opinion," said he, "it is a much pleasanter thing to encourage all those that one has a mind to make diligent and good fellow-labourers with one in any business, of whatever kind it be, by speaking them fair, and doing them good, than to do it by severe usage and by force. But those that one would have to be zealous fellow-labourers in the business of war, these, I think, ought absolutely to be courted to it both by good words and good deeds; for such as are to be hearty and sincere fellow-combatants, who shall neither envy their commander in prosperity, nor betray him in adversity, ought to be friends, and not enemies. Having determined thus with myself in these matters, I think myself in want of money. And yet to have my eye on every occasion on you, when I see you are already engaged in very great expenses, seems to me unreasonable. But I think it proper, that you and I should jointly consider what means to use that treasure may not fail you; for if you have plenty, I know that I may take it whenever I want; especially if I take for such a purpose as will make it more to your advantage that the treasure should be so spent. I remember therefore on some occasion lately to have heard you say, that the Armenian is now grown to contemn you, because he hears that the enemy is coming on us; and, besides, that he neither sends you the forces, nor pays you the tribute that is due." "Indeed, Cyrus," said he, "these things he really does, so that I am in doubt whether it be better for me to make war on him, and force him to comply, or whether it be most for our interest to let it pass for the present, lest we add him to the number of our enemies." Cyrus then asked: "Are their habitations in places of strength, or in such as are accessible with ease?" Cyaxares said: "Their habitations are in places that are not very strong, for I was not negligent in that affair; but there are mountains, whether he may immediately retire, and be in safety, so as neither to be himself exposed, nor any thing else that may possibly be carried off thither, unless one sit down and besiege him there, as my father once did." On this Cyrus said thus: "But if you will send me with such a number of horse as may be thought sufficient, I believe, with the assistance of the gods, I can make him send you forces, and pay you tribute. And besides, I even hope that he will be yet more our friend than he is now." Cyaxares then said: "And I have hopes that he will sooner come to you than he will to us: for I have heard that some of his children were your fellow-huntsmen; so that perhaps they may come to you again. And if some of them once come to be in our power, every thing will succeed to our desire." "Is it not your opinion, then," said Cyrus, "that it will be for our advantage to conceal this contrivance between us?" "By this means," said

Cyaxares, "some or other of them may the more easily fall into our hands; or if one fall on them, they may be taken the more unprepared." "Hear, then," said Cyrus, "if you think what I am going to say may be of any moment: I have often hunted on the borders of your territory and that of the Armenians, with all the Persians that were with me; and I went thither, taking likewise from hence several horsemen from amongst my companions here." "Therefore," said Cyaxares, "by doing just the same things now, you may pass unsuspected; but if a much greater force should appear than what you used to have with you in hunting, this would presently give suspicion." "But," said Cyrus, "one may frame a very plausible pretence in this case: and that is, if care be taken that somebody give them an account yonder, in Armenia, that I intend to undertake a great hunt; then," said he, "I would openly desire from you a body of horse." "You say very well," said Cyaxares; "but I shall consent to give you but a few, as intending to march myself to our garrisons that lie towards Assyria. And in reality," said he, "I do intend to go thither, in order to strengthen them as much as possible. But when you are got before with the force you have, and have hunted for a day or two following, I may send you a sufficient force, both of horse and foot, out of those that have rendezvoused under me. With these you may immediately fall on, and I with the other forces may endeavour to keep not far from you, that if there be occasion I may likewise appear."

Accordingly, Cyaxares presently formed a body of horse at the garrisons, and sent waggons with provisions before by the road that led that way. Cyrus presently made a sacrifice for his intended march; and at the same time sent and begged of Cyaxares some of his cavalry, and such as were of the younger sort. He, though there were multitudes that would have attended Cyrus, granted him not very many. Cyaxares being now gone before with forces, both horse and foot, on the road towards the garrisons, it happened that Cyrus' sacrifice, on his design against the Armenian, succeeded happily: so he set forward as prepared for a hunt. As he was marching, a hare started immediately in the first field, and an eagle of happy omen flying towards them, caught sight of the hare as it ran, and, bearing down on it, struck it; then, snatching it up, raised it aloft and bearing it away to an eminence not far off, did there what it thought fit with its prey. Cyrus therefore seeing this signal, paid his adoration to Jove, sovereign of the gods, and said to those that were present: "Friends, our hunt, if it please the gods, will be a noble one!'"

When they came to the borders, he hunted after his usual manner. The greater number of his horse and foot opened themselves in front, in order to rouse the beasts as they moved down on them. The best of his men, both horse and foot, stood here and there dispersed, received the beasts as they were roused, and pursued them; and they took abundance both of swine, stags, goats, and wild asses; for there are yet abundance of wild asses in those parts at this day. When they had finished the hunt, and he had brought them close up to the Armenian borders, he ordered them to supper; and the next day hunted again, advancing to those mountains that he had desired to be master of. And when he had again ended his sport he took his supper. But as soon as he found that the forces from Cyaxares were advancing, he sent privately to them, and ordered them to take their supper at about the distance of two parasangs from him, foreseeing that this would contribute to the concealing the affair. When they had supped, he ordered their commander to march and join him. After supper was over, he summoned the colonels to him, and when they were come he spoke to them thus:

"Friends! the Armenian has been heretofore both an ally and subject of Cyaxares; but now that he finds the enemy coming on him, he contemns him, and neither sends him forces nor pays him tribute. It is he therefore that we must now hunt, and catch if we can. Thus, therefore," said he, "in my opinion we must do. Do you, Chrysantas, when you have had a little time to sleep, take half the Persians that are with us, march by the hill, and make yourself master of those mountains, whither they say the Armenian flies when he finds himself in danger, and I will give you guides. They say these mountains are full of woods, so that there are hopes you will not be discovered. However, if you send before the rest of your army some light men equipped for expedition, who, both by their number and habit, may look like plunderers, these men, if they meet with any of the Ar-

menians, will prevent those that they can take from giving an account of things; and, by driving away those they cannot take, will hinder them from seeing the whole army, and will make them provide for themselves only as against a band of thieves." Do you, said he, "do thus: I, at break of day, with half the foot and all the horse will march directly to the palace of the Armenian by the plain. If he make head against us, it is plain we must fight: if he retire, and quit the plain, it is evident we must hasten after in pursuit of him. If he fly to the mountains, then," said he, "it is your business not to allow any of those that come to escape you; but reckon, as in hunting, that we are to be the finders, and that you stand at the nets. Remember, therefore, this—that the passages must be first stopped before the beast is roused; and that they who are appointed to that station ought to keep concealed, if they have not a mind to turn off every thing that takes its course towards them. And do not act now," said he, "Chrysantas, as the love of hunting has sometimes made you do; for you have often been employed the whole night, and have not slept at all; but you should now allow your men to lie down a while, that they may get a little sleep. And because you used to wander through the mountains without taking men for your guides, but pursued wherever the beasts led the way, do not march therefore now through such difficult places, but bid your guides lead you the easiest way, unless there be one that is abundantly the shorter; for to an army the easiest way is the quickest. And because you used to pass the mountains running, do not therefore now lead on at full speed, but with middling despatch, in such sort that the army may follow you. And it is of great use that some of the most vigorous and hearty should halt sometimes, and encourage the rest; and when the whole wing is passed, it animates the others' despatch to see these running beside them, and passing them by as they themselves move on in their gentle pace."

Chrysantas hearing this, and being transported with the orders Cyrus had given him, took his guides and went his way; and, having given the proper directions to those that were to attend in his march, he went to rest. When they had had a moderate time for rest, he marched to the mountains.

Cyrus, as soon as it was day, despatched a

messenger to the Armenian, and bade him say thus: " Prince of Armenia, Cyrus sends you these directions, that you would come away as soon as possible, and bring with you your tribute and your forces. If he asks you where I am, tell him the truth, that I am on the borders. If he ask whether I am advancing towards him, tell him the truth here too, that you do not know. If he inquire how many we are in number, bid him send somebody back with you to learn." Having given the messenger these orders, he despatched him away, thinking it more friendly to do thus than to march without sending word. And having formed his men into the best order, both for despatch in marching and for engagement in case of need, he began the march; first commanding his men to injure no one; and if any of them met with an Armenian, to bid him be of good heart; and to order every one that had a mind to sell either meat or drink to come and make his market wherever they were.

XENOPHON

ON THE

INSTITUTION OF CYRUS.

—

BOOK III.

CONTENTS of BOOK III.

INSTITUTION OF CYRUS.

·

BOOK III.

I. Cyrus was taken up in these affairs; but the Armenian, as soon as he heard from the messenger what Cyrus sent to tell him, was struck with it, considering that he had acted unjustly, both in failing to pay his tribute, and in not sending his forces. And the thing he principally feared was, lest he should be discovered to have begun fortifying the place of his residence in such sort as to render it defensible. Being at a loss on all these accounts, he sent around to assemble his forces. At the same time he sent his younger son Sabaris, his own wife, his son's wife, and his own daughters away to the mountains, and sent with them all his most valuable apparel and furniture, appointing them a force to conduct them. And at the same time he sent out scouts to discover what Cyrus was doing, and mustered all the Armenians he had present with him; when immediately there arrived others, who told him that Cyrus was just behind them; and not having courage enough on this occasion to come to action, he retired.

The Armenians, when they saw him act in this manner, ran every one to their own affairs with intent to put all their effects out of the way. Cyrus, when he saw the whole country full of people, running up and down, and driving all off, sent them word that he would be an enemy to none that remained at home; but if he caught any one making his escape, he declared he would treat him as an enemy. So the major part remained; some there were who went off with the king.

But when they who conducted the women fell in among those who were in the mountains, they presently set up a cry, and betaking themselves to flight, many of them were taken; and at last the son of the Armenian, the two wives, and the daughters, were likewise taken, as well as all the rich effects they were carrying off

with them. As soon as the king perceived what had passed, being at a loss which way to turn himself, he fled to a certain eminence. Cyrus seeing this, surrounded the eminence with the army that he had with him, and sending to Chrysantas, ordered him to leave a guard on the mountains, and to come away. The army then joined under Cyrus; and he, sending a herald to the Armenian, put the question to him in this manner: "Tell me," said he, "Armenian, whether it is your choice, staying there, to combat and struggle with thirst and hunger, or to come down on fair ground and fight us?" The Armenian answered, "That he did not choose to engage in either of these ways." Cyrus sending again to him, asked him this question: "Why then sit you there, and do not come down?" "I am at a loss," said he, "what I ought to do." "But you ought not to be at a loss about it," said Cyrus, "for you are at liberty to come down and have your cause tried." "And who," said he, "shall be the judge?" "He, without doubt, to whom the gods have given power to deal with you as he pleases without a trial." Here the Armenian, seeing the necessity, came down; and Cyrus taking him, and all that belonged to him, into the midst of them, encamped around, having his whole force with him.

Just at this time Tigranes, the eldest son of the Armenian, returned from a journey he had taken abroad; he who had been heretofore a fellow-huntsman with Cyrus. When he heard what had happened, he went directly to Cyrus, just as he was, and when he saw his father and mother, his brother, his sisters, and wife prisoners, he wept, as was natural for him to do. Cyrus, on seeing him, gave him no other mark of respect or friendship, but said to him, "You are come very opportunely, that you may be present, and hear the trial and determination of your father's cause." He then presently summoned all the commanders of the Persians and Medes, and invited all such of the Armenians there as were men of note and quality; and the women who were there present in their chariots, he sent, not away, but allowed them to hear.

When all was ready and in order, he began the discourse. " Armenians," said he, " first of all I advise you, in this trial of your cause, to speak the truth, that you may be free from one crime at least, which is a most hateful one: for be assured, that to be found false is the greatest bar that can lie in men's way to the obtaining of pardon. Then," said he, " these children and wives of yours, and all the Armenians present, are apprised of all that you have done; and if they perceive that you say things contrary to what has passed, they will think, if I discover the truth, that you condemn yourself to the extremity of punishment." " Ask me," said he, " Cyrus, what you will, as being resolved to tell you truth, happen what will in consequence of it." " Tell me then," said he, " did you some time ago make war with Astyages, my mother's father, and with the rest of the Medes?" " I did," said he. " And when you were conquered by him, did you agree that you would pay him tribute? that you would join your forces to his wherever he should direct? and that you would have no fortifications?" " These things were as you say." " Now, therefore, why have you neither brought your tribute, nor sent your forces, but were building your fortifications?" He replied: " I was desirous of liberty; for I thought it a noble thing, both to be free myself, and to leave liberty to my children." " It is indeed noble," said Cyrus, " to fight, in order not to be made a slave: but if a man be conquered in war, or by other means be reduced to servitude, and be found attempting to throw off his masters, do you yourself first pronounce whether you reward and honour such a one as an honest man, and as one that does noble things? or, if you take him, do you punish him as one that acts unjustly?" " I punish him," said he: " you do not suffer me to falsify." " Tell me therefore plainly," said Cyrus, " and in particular thus: if a man be a governor and transgress, do you suffer him to continue in his government, or do you constitute another in his stead?" " I constitute another," said he. " If he is a master of great riches, do you suffer him to con-

tinue rich, or do you reduce him to poverty?" " I take from him," said he, " all that he has." " If you find him revolting to the enemy, what do you do?" " I put him to death," said he; " for why should I die convicted of falsehood, rather than die telling the truth."

Here his son, as soon as he heard these things, threw off his turban, and rent his clothes. The women set up a lamentable cry, and tore themselves as if their father had expired, and themselves lost and undone. Cyrus bade them be silent, and again spoke. " Be it so, Armenian, that these determinations of yours are just, what do you advise us to do on it?" The Armenian was silent, being at a loss whether he should advise Cyrus to put him to death, or direct him to act just contrary to what he had said he would do himself.

His son Tigranes then asked Cyrus— " Tell me," said he, " Cyrus, since my father seems to be at a loss whether I shall advise you what I think best for you to do in this case?" And Cyrus, well remembering that when Tigranes used to hunt with him, there was a certain sage, very conversant with him, and much admired by him, was very desirous to hear what he would say, and joyfully bade him speak his opinion: " Then," said Tigranes, " if you approve all the measures that my father has concerted, and all that he has done, I advise you by all means to imitate him; but if you are of opinion that he has transgressed in all, my advice is that you should not imitate him." " Then," said Cyrus, " by doing justice, I shall be the farthest from an imitation of the person transgressing." " It is so," said he. " According to your own reasoning, then, your father should be punished, if it be just to punish one who acts unjustly." " But whether do you think it best, Cyrus, to inflict your punishments for your own advantage, or to your own prejudice?" " Why, this way," said he, " I should punish myself." " And truly you would be highly punished," said Tigranes, " if you put to death those that belonged to you at the time that they would be of the greatest service to you to preserve." " But how," said Cyrus, " can men be so highly serviceable and useful when found to have acted unjustly?" " Why, truly, if they become considerate and humble; for in my judgment, Cyrus, things stand thus: —there is no virtue useful and profitable without a discreet and sober sense of things: for," said he, " what use can be made of a man who has strength and bravery without discretion and modesty? What use of one skilled in horsemanship; or of one abounding in riches, or powerful in his country? But with discretion and modesty, every friend is useful, and every servant good." "This therefore," said he, "you assert, that your father, from insolent and haughty, is become discreet and humble, in this one day's time?" "I do," said he. "Then this discreet and modest state of mind you pronounce to be a passion of the soul, as grief is; and not a matter of knowledge and science? For if it be necessary that he who becomes discreet and modest should be wise and knowing, he cannot then, from insolent and haughty, become in an instant discreet and modest." "But, Cyrus," said he, "did you never observe a man, out of pride and insolence, attempt fighting with another more powerful than himself, and when conquered presently fall from that insolence? Again," said he, "have you never seen one city engaged in war with another, and when conquered, immediately, by this means, become willing to obey, instead of continuing the war?" "And what conquest over your father," said Cyrus, "is this you speak of, and that thus forcibly brings him to a discreet and humble sense of things?" "Why, truly, the being conscious to himself, that while he has affected liberty, he has become yet more a slave than ever; and that of all the things he thought to have effected, by privacy, by artifice, or by force, he has not been able to effect one: but he has seen you deceive him, in every thing you intended to deceive him in, as effectually as one might deceive the blind, or the deaf, or men of no understanding at all. He knows you have kept yourself so concealed from him, where you thought it proper so to do, that the places he thought the most secure to him, these, by concealed preparations, you have made yourself master of; and you have so far exceeded him in despatch, that you are come on him with a very considerable army, from afar, before he had assembled his forces, that were just at hand." "Are you of opinion, then," said Cyrus, "that such a conquest is sufficient to give men so much consideration and modesty, as to think others better than themselves?" "Much more," said Tigranes, "than if a man were conquered in battle; for he who is subdued by force may think that by exercising his body he may be enabled to renew the combat; and cities that have been taken,

imagine that by gaining allies they may renew the war. But men often voluntarily submit to those whom they judge better than themselves, though under no necessity of doing it." "You seem," said he, "not to be of opinion that the proud and insolent can have any sense that there are any more modest and considerate than themselves; or thieves, that there are any who are not thieves; or false men, that there are any observers of truth; or unjust men, that there are any who act with justice. Do you not know," said he, "that your father has at this time dealt falsely, and not stood to his agreements with us, though he knew very well that we had not transgressed in any sort what Astyages had stipulated?" "Nor do I say, that the knowledge alone of others being better than ourselves makes men considerate and modest, unless they receive punishment, at the hands of those their betters, as my father has now done." "But your father," said Cyrus, "has yet suffered no sort of ill. I know very well that he is afraid, indeed, of the highest punishments." "Do you think, therefore," said Tigranes, "that any thing oppresses men more than violent fear? Do you not know that they who are oppressed with the sword, which is reckoned the severest correction, will recur again to arms against the same enemy? but those that they are thoroughly afraid of, they are not able so much as to look at, when they do but confer with them." "Do you say," said he, "that fear is a heavier punishment on men than real misfortune?" "You know yourself," said he, "that what I say is true: you know that they who are in fear of being banished their country, or that are in dread of being beaten in an approaching engagement, are in a most dejected condition. They that are at sea, and that dread shipwreck, and they that fear servitude and chains, are neither able to eat nor sleep for their fear; but they who are already under banishment, who are already conquered and already slaves, are often in a condition to eat and sleep better than the fortunate themselves. And how great a burden fear is, is yet more evident by this; that some, in dread that death would follow their captivity, have died beforehand by means of that dread; some throwing themselves headlong, some hanging themselves, and some dying by the sword. So that of all things terrible, fear strikes deepest into the minds of men. In what state of mind, then," said he, "do you

F

take my father to be ; he who fears not only for his own liberty, but for mine, for that of his wife, and that of all his children ?" Then Cyrus said : " It does not seem at all improbable to me that your father is at this time affected in this manner ; but it belongs to the same man to be insolent and injurious in prosperity, and when broken in his fortune, to be dejected and sunk ; and when re-established in his affairs, to become insolent again, and again to create disturbance." " Truly, Cyrus," said he, " our transgressions give you cause to distrust us : but you are at liberty to build fortresses, to keep possession of our places of strength, and to take whatever other pledge you please ; and yet," said he, " you will not find us very uneasy under these sufferings ; for we shall remember that we ourselves were the cause of them. But if by giving up our government to any of those who are free from guilt, you appear distrustful of us ; look to it, lest at the same time you should be a benefactor to them, they shall think you no friend. And if, in caution against their enmity, you do not impose a yoke on them to prevent their injuries ; look to it, that you come not under a greater necessity of reducing them to be considerate and humble, than you are now under of acting that part towards us." " By the gods !" said he, " it is, methinks, with displeasure that I make use of such servants as I know serve me by necessity and force ; but those that I judge to act their parts in concert with me, out of friendship and good-will, these, I think, I can more easily bear with when they transgress, than with those that hate me, and who by force discharge their duty the most completely." Tigranes to this said : " And with whom can you ever acquire so great a friendship as you may with us ?" " With those, as I take it, who have never been so much at enmity with us, provided I would be that friend and benefactor to them that you now desire me to be to you." " And can you possibly find, Cyrus," said he, " at this time any one whom it is in your power to gratify in so high a degree as you may my father ? First," said he, " if you grant their lives to those who never did you any injury, what thanks will they pay you for it, think you ? If you leave a man his wife and children, who can have greater friendship for you, on this score, than he who thinks they may be justly taken from him ? Do you know any one that will be more afflicted than ourselves if the kingdom of Armenia be

not given them ? And it is evident that he who is most afflicted that he is not king, when he receives the regal power will be the most grateful to you for it. And in case," said he, " you are any-wise concerned that things should be left here in the least confusion and disorder, when you quit us, consider whether things are likely to be on a quieter footing under a new government, than if the old-accustomed government continue. If it be of any concern to you to draw from hence the greatest number of forces possible, who do you think will levy them better than he who has often made use of them ? And if you want money, who do you reckon will better raise it than he who knows all, and is in possession of all ? Good Cyrus," said he, " be careful, lest by rejecting us, you do yourself more mischief than my father has been able to do you." To this effect he spoke.

And Cyrus was extremely pleased to hear him, thinking that he should be able to effect all that he had promised Cyaxares to do ; for he remembered to have told him that he thought he should make the Armenian yet more his friend than before. On this, then, he inquired thus of the Armenian : " And if I comply with you in these things, tell me," said he, " what force will you send with me ; and what money will you contribute to the war ?" To this the Armenian said : " Cyrus," said he, " I have no reply to make more plain or more just than to expose to you all the forces I have, that, viewing the whole, you may take with you whatever you will, and leave what you will for the guard of the country. In like manner with respect to our riches, it is just that I should discover to you all that I have, that, being apprised of all, you may carry off what you will of it and leave what you please of it." Then Cyrus said : " Proceed, then, and show me what forces you have, and tell me what your riches amount to." Here the Armenian replied : " The horse of the Armenians are eight thousand, and their foot forty thousand. Our riches, including the treasure my father left and reckoned in money, amount to more than three thousand talents." Then Cyrus, without hesitation said : " Since therefore," said he, " the Chaldeans that border on you are at war with you, send me half of your forces ; and of your treasure, instead of fifty talents, which was the tribute you were to pay, give Cyaxares double that sum for your defect in the payment. Then lend me," said he, " a hundred more; and I promise you, that if the gods enable me, I will, in return of what you lend me, either do you such services as shall be of greater value; or, if I am able, will count you down the money again; if I am not able to do it, I may then appear unable, but unjust I cannot be justly accounted." Then the Armenian said : " I conjure you by the gods, Cyrus, not to talk in that manner; if you do you will afflict me; but rather reckon," said he, " that what you leave behind is not less yours than what you carry off with you." " Be it so," said Cyrus ; " but, to have your wife again, what money will you give me ?" " All that I am able," said he. " What for your children ?" " And for these too," said he, " all that I am able." " Here is then," said Cyrus, " already as much again as you have. And you, Tigranes," said he, " at what rate would you purchase the regaining of your wife ?" Now he happened to be but lately married, and had a very great love for his wife. " Cyrus," said he, " to save her from servitude I would ransom her at the expense of my life." " Take then your own to yourself," said he, " I cannot reckon that she is properly our captive ; for you never fled from us. And do you, Armenian, take your wife and children without paying any thing for them, that they may know they come free to you. And now," said he, " pray take supper with us ; and when that is over, go your ways wherever you please." So they stayed.

While they were together in the tent, Cyrus inquired thus : " Tell me," said he, " Tigranes, where is that man that used to hunt with us, and that you seemed much to admire ?" " Oh !" said he, " and has not this father of mine put him to death ?" " And what crime did he discover him committing ?" " He said that he corrupted me : and yet, Cyrus, so good and so excellent a man he was, that when he was going to die he sent for me and told me : " Tigranes," said he, " do not bear ill-will to your father for putting me to death ; for he does it not out of malice, but out of ignorance. And whatever errors men fall into by ignorance, I reckon all such involuntary." Cyrus on this said : " Alas ! good man !" The Armenian then spoke thus . " They, Cyrus, who find strangers engaged in familiar commerce with their wives do not put them to death, and charge them as endeavouring to make their wives more discreet and modest ; but they are of opinion that these men destroy that affection and love their wives

have for them, and for this reason they treat them as enemies. And I," said he, " bore hatred and ill-will to this man because I thought he made my son respect and admire him more than myself." Cyrus then said : " By the gods !" said he, " Armenian, I think you faulty, but in such a manner as human nature is often liable to be. And do you, Tigranes, forgive your father." Having at that time discoursed in this manner, and having treated each other with great kindness and friendship, as is natural on a reconciliation, they mounted their chariots in company with the women, and drove away well pleased.

When they came home one talked of Cyrus' wisdom, another of his patience and resolution; another of his mildness : one spoke of his beauty and the tallness of his person; and on that Tigranes asked his wife : " And do you," said he, " Armenian dame, think Cyrus handsome ?" " Truly," said she, " I did not look at him." " At whom then did you look ?" said Tigranes. " At him who said that, to save me from servitude, he would ransom me at the expense of his own life." And after some entertainment of this kind, as was usual, they went together to rest.

The next day the Armenian sent presents of friendship to Cyrus, and to the whole army : he sent orders to those of his people that were to serve in this expedition to attend on the third day ; and he paid down double the sum of money that Cyrus had mentioned. Cyrus, accepting the sum he had expressed, sent the rest back, and asked : " Which of them would command the army, whether his son or himself ?" They both spoke together, and the father said : " Either of us that you shall order." The son said : " I assure you, Cyrus, that I will not leave you, though I serve in the army as a slave." Cyrus, laughing at this, said : " What would one give," said he, " that your wife heard you were to carry baggage !" " There is no need," said he, " that she should hear, for I will carry her with me ; and by that means she may see what I do." " But it is full time," said he, " that you had all things ready to attend us." " Count on it," said he, " that we will be present at the time with all things ready that my father affords us." When the soldiers had been all thus entertained, and treated as friends, they went to rest.

II. The next day Cyrus, taking Tigranes with him, and the best of the Median horse, together with as many of his own friends as he thought proper, marched round, viewing the country, and examining where to build a fortress. When they came to a certain eminence he asked Tigranes which were the mountains from whence the Chaldeans made their incursions to plunder the country. Tigranes showed them to him. He then inquired again: "And are these mountains entirely desert?" "No, truly," said he; "but they have always certain scouts there, who give notice to the rest of whatever they observe." "And what do they do," said he, "when they have this notice?" "They all then run to the eminences to defend themselves, every one as fast as he can." Cyrus gave attention to these things; and, viewing around, he observed a great part of the Armenian territory to be desert and uncultivated by reason of the war. They then retired to the camp; and, taking their supper, went to rest.

The next day Tigranes, with all things ready provided, joined him; having four thousand horse, ten thousand archers, and as many targeteers with him. Cyrus at the time they joined him made a sacrifice. When the victims appeared to portend things fortunate and happy, he summoned the leaders of the Persians and Medes; and, when they were together, he spoke to them to this effect: "Friends! those mountains that we see belong to the Chaldeans; if we can seize them, and have a fortress on the summit, both Armenians and Chaldeans will be obliged to act with modesty and submission towards us. Our sacrifice promises us success; and in the execution of a design nothing favours the inclinations of men so much as despatch. If we prevent the enemy and gain the mountains before they assemble, we may either take the summit entirely without a blow, or shall have but few and weak enemies to deal with. Of all labours, therefore, there is none more easy or more free from danger than resolutely to bear the fatigue of despatch. Haste, then, to arms! and do you, Medes, march on our left; and of you, Armenians, let half march on our right, and the other half lead on in front before us; and do you, the horse, follow in the rear, exhorting us, and pushing us up before you; and if any one acts remissly, do not you suffer him to do so."

Cyrus having said this led on, drawing the several companies into single files. The Chaldeans, as soon as they perceived that their heights were going to be attacked, gave their signal to their people, hallooed out to each other, and ran together. Cyrus then gave out orders in this manner; "Men of Persia! they give us the signal of despatch; if we prevent them in gaining the heights, the efforts of the enemy will be of no significance." The Chaldeans had every one his shield and two javelins: they are said to be the most warlike people of all in that part of the world. Where they are wanted they serve for hire, being a warlike people and poor: for their country is mountainous, and but little of it fertile and rich. As Cyrus' men approached the heights, Tigranes, marching with Cyrus, spoke to him thus: "Cyrus," said he, "do you know that we must presently come to action, and that the Armenians will not stand the attack of the enemy?" Cyrus, telling him that he knew it, made it presently be declared to the Persians that they should hold themselves in readiness, as being presently to fall on; and to pursue, as soon as the flying Armenians drew the enemy down so as to be near them. So the Armenians led on: the Chaldeans, who were on the place, immediately on the approach of the Armenians set up a cry; and, according to their custom, ran on them: the Armenians, according to their custom, did not stand to them. When the pursuing Chaldeans saw swordsmen fronting them, and marching up, they some of them came up close, and were presently killed; some fled, and some were taken; and the heights were immediately gained. As soon as Cyrus' men had gained the heights, they saw the habitations of the Chaldeans, and perceived them flying from such of those habitations as were near. Cyrus, as soon as the army was got together, ordered them to dinner. When dinner was over, having got information of the place where the Chaldeans planted their watch, he undertook the building of a fortress, that was very strong, and well supplied with water. He ordered Tigranes to send to his father, and bid him come away with all the carpenters and builders he could get. The messenger went his way to the Armenian. Cyrus applied himself to the building, with all the workmen he had at that time with him.

Meanwhile they brought Cyrus the prisoners, some bound, and some wounded. As soon as he saw them he ordered those that were bound to be loosed; and, sending for the physicians, he ordered them to take care of the wounded.

He then told the Chaldeans that he was not come either with a desire to destroy them, or with inclination to make war on them; but with intention to make peace between the Armenians and Chaldeans. "Before we got possession of your mountains, I know you had no desire of peace: your own concerns were in safety; the effects of the Armenians you plundered at your pleasure. But now you see the condition you are in. Those of you therefore that have been taken, I dismiss to your homes, and allow you, together with the rest of the Chaldeans, to consult amongst yourselves, whether you incline to make war with us, or to be our friends: if war be your choice, come no more hither without arms, if you are wise: if you think peace for your turn, come without arms. And, if you are friends, it shall be my care that your affairs shall be established on the best footing." The Chaldeans having heard these things, after many praises bestowed on Cyrus, and many assurances of friendship and trust given him, went home.

The Armenian, as soon as he heard what Cyrus had done, and the request he made him, took carpenters with him, and all things else that he thought necessary, and came to Cyrus with all possible despatch. As soon as he saw Cyrus he said to him: "O Cyrus! how few things in futurity are men able to foresee! and how many projects do we undertake! I have endeavoured on this occasion to obtain liberty, and I became more a slave than ever: and, after having been made captive, and thinking our destruction certain, we now again appear to be in a condition of greater safety and security than ever: for these men never ceased doing us all manner of mischief; and I now find them just in the condition I wished. And be it known to you," said he, "Cyrus, that to have so driven the Chaldeans from these heights, I would have given many times the money you received from me; and the services you promised to do us when you took the money you have now so fully performed, that we appear to be brought under new obligations to you, which, if we are not very bad men, we shall be ashamed not to discharge; and whatever returns we make, we shall not be found to have done so much as such a benefactor deserves." Thus spoke the Armenian.

The Chaldeans came back, begging of Cyrus to make peace with them. Then Cyrus asked them: "Chaldeans!" said he, "is it on any other consideration that you desire peace, or is it only because you think you shall live with more security in peace than if you continue the war, since we ourselves told you so?" "We have other considerations," said the Chaldeans. "And what," said he, "if there are still other advantages that may accrue to you by peace?" "We shall be still the more pleased," said they. "Do you think, therefore," said he, "that your being a poor and needy people is caused by any thing else but by the want of good land." They agreed with him in this. "Well, then," said Cyrus, "would you willingly be at liberty to cultivate as much of the Armenian territory as you pleased, paying the same for it that the Armenians do?" "Yes," said they, "if we could be secure that we should not be injured." "What say you, then, Armenian?" said he, "would you be willing to have your waste land cultivated on terms that the farmers of it shall pay you the settled dues?" The Armenian said he would give a great deal to have it so; for his revenue would be much improved by it. "And you," said he, "Chaldeans, since you have mountains that are fertile, would you consent that the Armenians should use them for pasture, on condition that they who make use of them shall pay what is just and reasonable?" The Chaldeans said that they would; for it would be a considerable profit to them, without any labour. "And you, Armenian," said he, "would you make use of the pastures of these men, if by allowing a small profit to the Chaldeans, you might make a much greater profit by it yourselves?" "Readily," said he, "if I thought I might do it securely." "And securely you might do it," said he, "if the summits were in the hands of your friends." The Armenian agreed: "But, truly," said the Chaldeans, "we should not be able to cultivate securely, neither the lands of these people, nor our own, if they are in possession of the summits." "But suppose," said he, "the summits are possessed by such as are friends to you." "Thus, indeed," said they, "things might do very well." "But, indeed," said the Armenian, "things will not be well with us if these men come to be again possessed of the summits; especially when they are fortified." Then Cyrus said: "Thus therefore I will do: I will give up the summits to neither of you, but we will keep them ourselves: and if either of you injure the other, we will take part with the injured." When they heard this they both of them gave their applause, and said: "Thus only can the peace be firm and stable." On this they gave and received, mutually, assurances of friendship and trust, and stipulated to be both of them free and independent of each other; to intermarry, to cultivate, and feed each other's lands reciprocally, and to be common allies and supporters of each other against whosoever should injure either of them. Thus were these matters then transacted: and these agreements, then made beween the Chaldeans and the possessor of Armenia, subsist still to this day. When the agreements were made they both presently applied themselves with zeal to the building of this fortress, as a common guard; and they jointly furnished all things necessary towards it.

When evening came on he took both parties to sup with him, as being now friends. As they were at supper, one of the Chaldeans said: " That these things were such as all the rest of them wished for; but that there were some of the Chaldeans who lived by plunder, and who neither knew how to apply themselves to work, nor were able to do it, being accustomed to live by war: for they were always employed on plunder, or hired out on some service; frequently to the king of the Indians; for he is one, said they, "that abounds in gold; and frequently to Astyages." Then Cyrus said: " And why do they not engage themselves to me? for I will give them as much as any other ever gave." They consented, and said: " That there would be a great many that would willingly engage in his service." These things were accordingly agreed.

Cyrus, as soon as he heard that the Chaldeans frequently went to serve under the Indian, and remembering that there were certain persons that came from him to the Medes, to apprise themselves of the Median affairs, and went thence to the enemy, to get an insight likewise into their affairs, he was desirous that the Indian should be informed of what he had done: he therefore began a discourse to this effect: " Tell me," said he, "Armenian, and you, Chaldeans, if I should send one of my people to the Indian, would you send with him some of yours, who should direct him in his way, and act in concert with him to obtain from the Indian the things that I desire? for I would procure some further addition to my treasure, that I may have what will fully suffice

to discharge the pay of those to whom it comes due, and to honour and reward suc my fellow-soldiers as are deserving. On t accounts I would have plenty of treasur think I want it; and to spare you would pleasure to me; for I now reckon you friends. But from the Indian I would g accept something, if he would give it me. messenger therefore that I desire you to guides and assistants to, when he gets th shall say thus: ' Prince of India, Cyrus sent me to you: he says that he is in wai money, expecting another army from P (and in reality I do expect it, said he): if send him therefore as much as you can veniently, he assures you that, if the gods a happy issue to his affairs, he will do endeavours to make you think that you taken a happy a step in gratifying him.' he shall say from me. Do you on the c hand send him word by your people that think it will be of advantage to you. Ai we get any thing from him," said he, "we have all things in great plenty: if we nothing, we shall know that we owe hin thanks, and that as to him, we shall b liberty to regulate all our affairs as best our own interests." Thus said Cyrus, co ing on it, that those of the Armenians Chaldeans that went on this message w say such things of him, as he himself des all men should say and hear concerning Then at the proper time they broke up company in the tent, and went to rest.

III. The next day Cyrus sent away messenger, charging him with all that he before expressed. The Armenian and Chaldeans sent with him such men as judged most proper to act in concert with and to relate such things concerning Cyru were just and worthy of him.

After this, Cyrus having supplied the for with a sufficient garrison, and with all th necessary, and leaving as governor a cei Mede, one that he judged would be i agreeable to Cyaxares, marched away, ta with him both the army that he came v and that which he had from the Armeniai well as the men he had from the Chalde who amounted to about four thousand, thought themselves better than all the rest

When he came down into the inhai country, not one of the Armenians, nei man nor woman, kept within doors, but went out and met him, being overjoyed at the peace, and running out with whatever they had of greatest value. The Armenian was not at all uneasy at these things, thinking that Cyrus, by means of these honours that were thus paid him by all, would be the better pleased. At last, likewise, the wife of the Armenian met him, having her daughters with her, and her younger son; and, together with other presents, she brought that treasure that Cyrus had before refused. Cyrus, when he saw her, said: " You shall not make me such a sort of man as to run up and down the world bestowing my services for money!—Go your ways, woman, and keep all this treasure that you bring, and do not give it to the Armenian again to bury; but equip your son with it, in the handsomest manner, and send him to the wars; and out of the remainder supply yourself, your husband, your daughters, and your sons, with every thing, whether for use or ornament, that may make you pass your days in the most agreeable and handsome manner: let it suffice us to lay our bodies under ground, every one of us when we die." Having said this he marched on; the Armenian attended on him, as all the rest likewise did, calling him, aloud, " their benefactor, and an excellent man!" Thus they did till they had conducted him out of their territory. The Armenian sent a greater force with him, being now at peace at home. So Cyrus went away, not only enriched with the treasure he had received, but by means of his conduct he had laid up a much greater store, and could supply himself whenever he wanted. They then encamped on the borders. The next day he sent the army and treasure to Cyaxares, who was at hand, as he had said he would be. He with Tigranes, and the principal Persians, hunted where they met with game, and diverted themselves.

When he came into Media he distributed money to his centurions, as much as he thought sufficient for each of them, and that they might have wherewithal to reward such of their men under them as they might happen to be particularly pleased with: for he thought that if every one rendered his part of the army praise-worthy, the whole would be set right to his hands. And if he any where observed any thing that might contribute to the beauty of the army, he purchased it, and gave it to the most deserving; reckoning that whatever his

men were possessed of that was beautiful and noble, it was all an ornament to himself.

When he had made a distribution amongst them out of what he had received, then, in an assembly of centurions, captains, and all others that he particularly esteemed, he spoke to this effect: " Friends! a particular pleasure and satisfaction seems now to attend us, both because we have plenty, and that we are in possession of what enables us to bestow rewards where we desire, and to be rewarded every one according to his merit. But then we ought by all means to remember what the things are that have procured us these advantages, and on examination you will find them to be these: our being watchful on the proper occasions, our being laborious, our despatch, and our not giving way to the enemy. It is our part therefore to continue thus brave men for the future; determining with ourselves that obedience and resolution, labours and hazard, on the proper occasions, are things that produce great pleasures and great advantages."

But Cyrus considering how well the bodies of his men stood with respect to their being able to undergo all military labours, how well their minds were disposed with respect to a contempt of the enemy, how skilful they were in all things fitting, each in their several sorts of arms, and he saw that they were all well disposed with respect to obedience to their commanders; from all this therefore he now desired to come to action with the enemy, knowing that by delay some part or other of a noble preparation comes to change and fail in the commander's hands. And besides, observing that from a contention in things wherein men are ambitious to exceed, the soldiers had contracted envy and ill-will to each other; he was for this reason desirous to lead them as soon as possible out into the enemy's country; knowing that common dangers make friends, and fellow-combatants keep in a friendly disposition one towards another; and that in this circumstance, they neither envy those that are finely armed, nor those that are ambitious of glory; but that even such men themselves rather applaud and esteem others that are like them, accounting them their fellow-labourers in the public service. So, in the first place, he completely armed them all, and formed them into the best and most beautiful order that was possible. He then summoned the commanders of ten thousands, the commanders of thousands, the centurions, and captains ; for these were exempt from being reckoned of the number of those that constituted the military rank ; and when they were to execute any orders from the commander-in-chief, or to transmit any particular directions to others ; yet thus there was nothing left confused and without rule, but the remainder of the men were preserved in order by the commanders of twelves and sixes. When the proper persons were assembled, he conducted them about with him, and showed them all that was right and in proper order, and taught them in what consisted the strength of every ally. And when he had raised in these men a desire of doing something, he bade them go to their several distinct bodies, teach them what he had taught themselves, and endeavour to inspire them all with a desire of action, that they might set forward with all possible ardour. And he bade them in the morning attend at Cyaxares' door. They then retired, and did as they were ordered.

The next morning, as soon as it was day, the proper persons attended at the doors ; and Cyrus, entering in with them to Cyaxares, began a discourse to this effect : " I know, Cyaxares," said he, " that what I am going to say is not less your opinion than it is our own, but perhaps you may be unwilling to express it, lest you should seem to put us in mind of marching away, as if the maintaining of us were burdensome and uneasy to you. Therefore, since you are silent, I will speak both for you and for ourselves.—Since we are prepared and ready, it is the opinion of us all, not to delay engaging the enemy till after they have broken in on your country, and not to sit down, and wait here in the territory of our friends ; but to march with all possible despatch into the enemy's country. For now that we are in your territory, we are forced, against our wills, to injure you many ways ; but if we march into the enemy's country, we shall, with pleasure, do them mischief. Then it is you that now maintain us, and at a great expense. If we carry the war abroad, we shall be maintained on the enemy's country. But then, indeed, if our danger was to be greater there than it is here, perhaps the safest course should be taken ; but they will be the same men, whether we wait here for them, or march into their own country, ' meet them. And we shall be the same, r we receive them here, as they come

on us, or march up to them and attack them. But we shall have the minds of our men in better condition, and more animated, if we march to the enemy, and seem not to get sight of them against our wills. They will have a much greater terror of us when they shall hear that we do not sit at home in dread, and terrified with them ; but that, as soon as we perceive them advancing, we march and meet them, in order to close with them as soon as possible ; and that we do not wait till our own country is distressed by them ; but that we prevent them, and lay their lands waste. And then," said he, " if we strike terror into them, and raise courage in ourselves, I take this to be a very great advantage to us. Thus I reckon the danger to be much less to us, and much greater to the enemy. And my father always said, you yourself say, and all others agree, that battles are decided rather by the courage and spirits of men, than by the strength of their bodies." Thus he spoke, and Cyaxares replied : " O Cyrus ! and you the rest of the Persians, do not imagine that the maintaining you is burdensome and uneasy to me. But, indeed, the marching into the enemy's country seems now to me to be the better course." " Since, therefore," said Cyrus, " we agree in opinion, let us make all things ready, and if our sacred rites signify the approbation of the gods, let us depart as soon as possible."

On this, giving orders to the soldiers to make all things ready, Cyrus made a sacrifice, first to Regal Jove, then to the other deities ; and prayed that they would vouchsafe to be conductors to the army, good and gracious assistants and friends, and direct them in all happy courses ! He invoked likewise the heroes, inhabitants and guardians of the land of Media. When he had sacrificed happily, and the whole army was formed on the borders, meeting with happy auguries, he fell into the enemy's country. As soon as he had passed the borders, he performed propitiatory rites to the earth by libations, to the gods by sacrifice ; and implored the favour of the heroes, inhabitants of Assyria. And having done this, he again sacrificed to Paternal Jove ; and whatever other deity occurred to him, he neglected none.

When these things were duly performed, making the foot advance at a small distance forward, they encamped ; and making excursions around with the horse, they furnished themselves with great quantities of all kinds f booty. Then changing their encampments, ad being provided with all things necessary in bundance, and laying the country waste, they mited for the enemy. When they were said , be advancing, and not to be at the distance f above two days' march, then Cyrus said: Now, Cyaxares, is the time for us to march ad meet them, and not to appear, either to the memy or to our own people, afraid of advancing paint them; but let us make it evident that re do not come to a battle with them against ur wills." When Cyaxares had agreed, they dvanced towards the enemy, keeping always a order, and marching each day as far as they bought it proper: they took their supper by ay-light, and made no fires in their camp by aght, but made them before the front of the amp, that by means of these fires they might erceive if any people approached in the night, ad might not be seen themselves by the approachers; and they frequently made their fires rehind the camp, in order to deceive the enemy; so that the enemy's people that were sent ut for intelligence sometimes fell in with the dvanced guards, thinking themselves to be still t a distance from the camp, because the fires rere behind.

The Assyrians then, and those that attended bem, as soon as the armies were near to each ther, threw up an entrenchment round themelves; a thing that the barbarian kings practise o this day when they encamp, and they do it rith ease by means of their multitude of hands; or they know that an army of horse in the right is confused and unwieldy, especially if hey are barbarian: for they have their horses ied down to their mangers, and if they are attacked, it is troublesome in the night to loose the horses, to bridle them, and to put on them their breastplates and other furniture; and when they have mounted their horses, it is absolutely impossible to march them through the camp. On all these accounts, both they and others of them throw up an entrenchment round themselves; and they imagine that their being entrenched ruts it in their power, as long as they please, to avoid fighting. And doing thus, they approached each other.

When they were advanced to about the distance of a parasang, the Assyrians encamped in the manner before expressed, in a post entrenched, but exposed to view; Cyrus, in a place the most concealed that was possible, with villages and rising grounds before him,

reckoning that all things hostile that discover themselves on a sudden, are the more terrible to the opposite party. And both parties that night, posting advanced guards, as was proper, went to rest.

The next day the Assyrian, and Croesus, and the other leaders, gave their armies rest in their strong camp. Cyrus and Cyaxares waited in order of battle, as intending to fight, if the enemy advanced. When it appeared that the enemy would not stir out of their entrenchment, nor come to a battle that day, Cyaxares summoned Cyrus, and all the other proper persons to him, and spoke to this effect: "It is my opinion, friends," said he, "that we should march, in the order we are in, up to the entrenchment of these men, and show them that we are desirous to come to a battle; for by this means," said he, "if they do not come out to us, our men will act with the more courage against them; and the enemy, observing our boldness, will be the more terrified." This was his opinion: but Cyrus said: "By the gods! Cyaxares, we must by no means act in this manner; for if we now discover ourselves, and march as you desire, the enemy will see us advancing towards them, and will be in no manner of fear of us, knowing themselves to be in a situation secure from any danger; and after having made this march, when we shall retreat, then again, seeing our number much inferior to theirs, they will have a contempt for us, and to-morrow will march out with minds more firm and resolute. But now," said he, "that they know we are at hand, without seeing us, be assured they do not contemn us, but are solicitous to know how things stand; and are, I know very well, continually taken up in debating about us. But when they march out, then ought we, at once, to make our appearance, march instantly, and close with them, taking them at the advantage we have heretofore desired." Cyrus having spoken thus, Cyaxares and the rest agreed in opinion with him. Then, having taken their suppers, placed their guards, and made many fires in the front, before those guards, they went to rest.

The next day, early in the morning, Cyrus, with a crown on his head, made a sacrifice; and ordered the rest of the alike-honoured to attend the holy rites with crowns. When the sacrifice was over Cyrus called them together, and said: "The gods, friends, as the diviners say, and as I myself think, do foretell that there

G

. will be a battle. They give us victory, and promise us safety by the victims. I ought perhaps to be ashamed to direct what sort of men you ought to show yourselves on such an occasion; for I know you understand those things as well as I do; that you have practised and learned, and continue to learn, all the same things that I have done; so that you may justly instruct others in them: but if, perhaps, you may not have taken exact notice of them, pray hear: Those men that we have lately admitted as our fellow-combatants, and have endeavoured to make like ourselves, it is your part to put them in mind for what purposes we are all maintained by Cyaxares; what the things are that we practise, and have invited them to, and wherein they said they would joyfully be our rivals: and put them in mind likewise of this, that this day will show what every one deserves; for, in things where men have been late learners, it is no wonder that some of them have need of a monitor. One ought to be contented if they can make themselves good and useful men on admonition; then in doing this you will make trial of yourselves; for he that on such an occasion is able to make others better men, must be justly conscious of being himself completely good. But he who bears these things in mind to himself only, and rests satisfied with that, should in justice account himself but half complete. The reason why I do not speak to these men myself, but bid you do it, is, because they may endeavour to please you; for you are immediately conversant with them, every one of you in his particular part. And be assured, that while you show yourselves to be in courage and heart, you will teach courage to these men, and to many more, not by word, but by deed." In conclusion, he bade them go, crowned as they were, to their dinners; and when they had performed their libations to come crowned to their ranks.

When these men were gone, he summoned the rear-leaders to him, and spoke to them to this effect: " You, likewise, men of Persia, are become part of the alike-honoured; and have been chosen, as men who appear to be equal, in all other respects, to the bravest, but, by your age, to excel in discretion. You have therefore a station assigned you, which is not less honourable than that of the file-leaders; for being placed in the rear, and observing the brave and encouraging them, you make them still the better men; and, if any one acts re-

missly, you do not suffer him to do so. If victory be of advantage to any, it is so to you, both by reason of your age and the weight of your military habit. If they therefore who are before, call out to you and exhort you to follow, comply with them; and that you may not be outdone by them in this, do you exhort them, in return, to lead with more despatch to the enemy. Go, then," said he, "and when you have taken your dinners, come crowned, with the rest, to your ranks." Cyrus' men were thus employed.

The Assyrians, when they had dined, marched boldly out, and formed themselves with a great deal of resolution. The king himself formed them, driving round in his chariot; and he made them an exhortation in this manner: " Men of Assyria! now is the time for you to be brave men, for now is your trial for your lives, for the country where you were born, for the houses where you were bred, for your wives and children, and for all things valuable that you possess. If you conquer, you will remain masters of all these as before; if you are defeated, be assured you give them all up to the enemy. Therefore, as you value victory, stand firm and fight; for it is folly for those that desire conquest to turn the blind, unarmed, and handless parts of their bodies to the enemy by flight. He is a fool, who, for love of life, should attempt flying, when he knows that the conquerors are safe, and that run-aways meet their death more certainly than they who stand their ground. And he is a fool, who, out of love to his money, submits to a defeat; for who is there that does not know that conquerors save all that belongs to themselves, and acquire, besides, all that belongs to the defeated enemy? but they who are defeated throw both themselves and all that belongs to them away." Thus was the Assyrian employed.

But Cyaxares, sending to Cyrus, told him that now was the opportunity of leading to the enemy; " For," said he, " if there are yet but few that are got out of the entrenchment, by the time we arrive there will be great numbers of them. Therefore, let us not wait till they are more numerous than ourselves; but let us march whilst we think we may yet easily master them." Cyrus replied: " Unless those, Cyaxares, that we shall defeat, amount to above half the number of the enemy, be assured they will say that we were afraid of their numbers, and therefore attacked but a few of them.

hey will not take themselves to be defeated; d it will be necessary for you to come to other battle, when perhaps they will contrive tter than they do now, that they give themlves up to us to parcel out and engage as any of them as we please." The messengers ving heard this went their way.

On this came Chrysantas the Persian, and hers of the alike-honoured, bringing with em certain deserters. Cyrus, as usual, reired from these deserters an account of the emy. They told him that they were already arching out in arms; that the king was come t, and was forming them; and that, continuly, as they marched out, he made them many arm and vigorous exhortations, as the hear-s, they said, reported. Here Chrysantas oke: " Cyrus," said he, " what, therefore, if u should call the soldiers together while you e yet at liberty to make them an exhortation, order to make them braver and better men?" hen Cyrus said: " O Chrysantas! let not e exhortations of the Assyrians disturb you; r no exhortation whatever, though ever so ble, can, at the instant, make the hearers rave if they were not so before; nor can it ake them skilful at the bow, unless they have efore practised it; nor skilful at the javelin, or horsemen; nor can it give them bodies spable of labour unless they have been before nured to it." Chrysantas then said: " But it enough, if you can make their minds better y your exhortation." " And can a word," aid Cyrus, " spoken at the instant inspire the minds of the hearers with a sense of shame, or inder them from doing things mean and base? Can it influence them effectually to undergo all abours, and run all hazards, to gain praise? Can it establish this sentiment firmly in their minds, that to die fighting is rather to be chosen than to be saved by flying? And if such sentiments," said he, " are to be instilled into men, and to be made lasting, ought there not, in the first place, to be such laws established whereby a life with honour and liberty should be provided for the brave? and such a course of life traced out and laid before the vicious, as should be abject and painful, and not worth living out? Then there ought to be teachers and governors in these affairs, who should direct men right, should teach and accustom them to practise these things, till they come to determine with themselves, that the brave and the renowned are, in reality, the

happiest of all; and to judge that the vicious and the infamous are of all the most miserable; for thus ought those to stand affected who are to make their institution and discipline overrule their fear of the enemy. But if, just at the time that men are marching in arms to the enemy, when many are hurried out of all their former learning and knowledge, it were in any one's power, by putting together a set form of words, to make men in the instant soldiers, then were it the easiest thing in the world both to learn and to teach the greatest virtue that belongs to men. Nor could I be secure that the men we now have, and that have been exercised under us, would remain firm, unless I saw you here present with them, who will be examples to them in their behaviour, and will be able to remind them if they are at a loss in any thing. I should very much wonder," said he, " Chrysantas, if a discourse, ever so finely spoken, should be able to teach bravery to men wholly undisciplined in virtue, any more than a song well sung could teach music to such as were wholly uninstructed in it." In this manner they discoursed.

And Cyaxares sent word again to Cyrus, that he was much in the wrong to spend time, and not march immediately to the enemy. Cyrus made answer to the messengers: " Let him be assured," said he, " that there are not yet come out so many of them as there ought to be; and tell him this, openly, before all; but since it is his opinion, I will lead out this instant." Having said this, and having made his supplications to the gods, he led the army out. As soon as he began to put forward with more despatch, he led the way, and they followed; and they did it in a very orderly manner, because they understood how to march in order, and had been exercised in it; they did it with vigour and resolution, by means of their emulation of each other, by having inured their bodies to labour, and having all their officers at the head of them; and they did it with pleasure, because they were wise; for they knew, and had long since learned, that it was their safest and easiest course to close with the enemy, especially when consisting of archers, of men armed with javelins, and of horse. While they were yet out of reach of the enemy's weapons, Cyrus gave out the word, which was this, " Jove, our assistant and leader!" When the word came about to him again, he began the usual hymn to the youths of Jove, Castor and Pollux. They all, with great devotion, accompanied him, with a loud voice; for, in such a circumstance, they who fear the deities are the less in fear of men. When the hymn was over, the alike-honoured, marching with alacrity and perfect good discipline, and at the same time looking round at each other, calling by their names those that were on each hand of them, and those that were the next behind them, and frequently crying out, "Come on, friends! come on, brave men!" they exhorted each other to follow: they that were behind, hearing this, exhorted the foremost, in return, to lead on with vigour and resolution. And Cyrus had an army full of spirit and of ardour in the pursuit of honour; full of vigour, boldness, mutual exhortation, discretion, and obedience, which I think the most terrible to an enemy.

Those of the Assyrians who fought from their chariots, in front, before the rest, as soon as the Persian body was near, and ready to close in with them, mounted their chariots, and retreated to their own body. Their archers, and their men armed with the javelin, and their slingers, made the discharge of their weapons a good while before they could reach their enemy. As soon as the Persians came up on these weapons that had been thus discharged, Cyrus cried aloud, "Now, my brave men, let somebody distinguish himself, and march quicker on, and transmit this order to the rest." They accordingly transmitted it; and some, out of zeal and ardour, and out of desire to close with the enemy, began to run. The whole phalanx followed running; Cyrus himself, forgetting his slower pace, led them on running, and cried out at the same time, "Who follows? who is brave? who will first prostrate his man?" They, hearing this, cried out in the same manner; and as he first gave it out, so it ran through them all, "Who will follow? who is brave?" In this disposition did the Persians close with the enemy.

The enemy were no longer able to stand them, but turned and fled to the intrenchment: the Persians, following up to the entrances of the intrenchment, laid many of them on the ground, as they were pressing on each other, and leaping in after those that fell into the ditch, they killed them, both men and horses, promiscuously; for some of the chariots of the enemy were forced on, in their flight, and fell in amongst the rest. The Median horse, observing these things, charged the enemy's horse; and they gave way before them. Then followed a pursuit of both horses and men, and a mighty slaughter of both. They who were within the Syrian intrenchment, and were posted at the top of it, by reason of the dreadful spectacle before them, and of their terror, had neither ability nor skill to do execution with their arrows and javelins on those that were making destruction of their people. And learning, presently after, that some of the Persians had cut their way through at the entrances of the intrenchment, they turned away and fled from the top of it. The Assyrian women, and those of their allies, some of them, such as had children, and some that were of the younger sort, seeing that they already began to fly in the camp, set up a clamour, and ran up and down in consternation, rending their clothes and tearing themselves, and begging of every one they met not to fly and abandon them, but to stand by their children, by them, and by each other. Here the princes themselves, with those they chiefly confided in, standing at the entrances of the intrenchment, and mounting to the top of it, fought themselves, and encouraged the rest. As soon as Cyrus knew how things stood, being afraid lest, being but few, they should be but ill treated by the great multitude of the enemy, if they forced their way in, he gave out orders to retreat out of the reach of the enemy's weapons, and required their obedience in so doing. Here one might distinguish the alike-honoured, and such as were formed to due discipline; for they instantly obeyed, and transmitted the orders to the rest. When they were out of the reach of the enemy's weapons they stood in their several stations, much more regularly than a set of dancers; every one knowing with great exactness where he was to be.

XENOPHON

ON THE

INSTITUTION OF CYRUS.

———

BOOK IV.

CONTENTS of BOOK IV.

INSTITUTION OF CYRUS.

BOOK IV.

I. CYRUS, waiting there for some considerable time with the army, and having made it appear that they were ready to fight, if any would come out against them, since nobody stirred, led off to the distance he thought proper, and they encamped.

Then having placed his guards, and sent out his scouts, he placed himself in the midst, and calling his soldiers together, he spoke to this effect: "Men of Persia! I do, in the first place, give all possible praise to the gods; I believe you all do the same; for we have obtained conquest and safety. Out of what we possess therefore it is our duty to make the gods our presents of gratitude and thanks, in return for these things. After this, I give praise to you all; for the action that is passed has been performed by you all. When I have made my inquiry from the proper persons what each man deserves, I will endeavour, both in word and in deed, to pay every man his due. With respect to Chrysantas, indeed, who was the nearest centurion to me, I need not inquire of others, but I know myself how well he behaved; for he performed all those other acts that I believed you all did; and when I gave out orders to retreat, calling on him particularly by name, he, who had his sword held up to give his enemy a stroke, obeyed me in the instant, and, forbearing to do what he was about, performed my command. For he retreated himself, and transmitted the order with the greatest despatch to others; so that he got his century out of weapon's cast before the enemy perceived that that we were retreating, before they extended their bows, or threw their javelins; so that he was himself unhurt, and kept his men unhurt by this obedience. But there are others," said he, "that I see wounded; and when I have examined at what time it was that they were wounded, I will then declare my opinion con-cerning them. Chrysantas I now reward with the command of a thousand, as a man vigorous in action, prudent, and able both to obey and command. And when the gods shall grant us any farther advantage, neither will I then forget him. And I am desirous too," said he, "to give you all an advice; that you would never lose the remembrance and the consideration of what you now see by this battle; that you may always have it settled in your minds, whether it is flight, or virtue rather, that preserves the lives of men; whether they who readily engage in action come off the better, or they who are backward and unwilling; and that you may judge how great a pleasure it is that victory affords. You may now the better make a judgment of these things, having had experience of them, and the affair having been so lately transacted. And," said he, "by having the consideration of these things always present in your minds, you will become the better men. Now, like discreet and worthy men, favoured of heaven, take your suppers, make your libations to the gods, begin your hymn, and be observant of the word of command."

This said, he mounted on his horse and rode off. Then coming to Cyaxares, and having congratulated with him, as was proper, having seen how things stood there, and having inquired whether Cyaxares had any farther need of him, he rode back to his own army. Cyrus' men, having taken their suppers and placed their guards, as was proper, went to rest.

The Assyrians, on their prince being killed, and together with him all the bravest of their men, were all in a desponding condition, and many of them fled from the camp in the night. On seeing these things, Crœsus, and their other allies, lost all courage, for they were surrounded with difficulties on all sides. And what chiefly sunk the courage of them all, was, that the principal nation of all that were in the army were entirely confounded in their opinions. So they quitted the camp, and went off in the night.

As soon as it was day, and that the camp appeared to be entirely abandoned, Cyrus immediately made the Persians march first into it. Great numbers of sheep and oxen had been left there by the enemy, and many waggons full of abundance of valuable things. After this, the Medes with Cyaxares marched in, and there took their dinners. When they had dined, Cyrus called his centurions together, and spoke to this effect: " Friends! how many valuable things have we, in my opinion, perfectly thrown away, when the gods had delivered them into our hands! for you yourselves see that the enemy are flying for fear of us. And how can any body think that they who, when possessed of an intrenched post, quitted it and fled, can stand and look us in the face on fair ground? They who did not stand before they had made trial of us, how should such men stand after they are beaten, and have been so ill treated by us? How should the worst of those men incline to fight us, of whom the best have been destroyed?" On this somebody said: " Why do we not immediately pursue, when the advantages we have are so evident?" Cyrus replied: " Why, because we want horse. And the best of the enemy, and such as it is most for our purpose to take or to destroy, are retiring on horseback. And those that, with the help of the gods, we are able to put to flight, we are not able to take in the pursuit." " Why, then," said they, " do you not go to Cyaxares and tell him these things?" To this he said: " Come therefore all of you along with me, that he may see we are all of us of this opinion." On this they all followed him, and said what they thought was proper concerning the things they desired.

Cyaxares, partly out of a sort of envy, because they had begun the discourse on the subject, and partly, perhaps, because he thought it best for him not to hazard another battle, for he was indulging himself in pleasure, and observed that many of the Medes were doing the same thing, spoke therefore in this manner: " I am convinced, Cyrus, by the testimony both of my eyes and ears, that you Persians, of all mankind, study the most how to keep yourselves from being impotent and insatiable in any kind

of pleasure: but my opinion is, that it is by much the most advantageous thing to be master of one's self in the greatest pleasure of all. And what is there that gives men greater pleasure than the good fortune that has now befallen us? Therefore, since we have that good fortune, if we take care to preserve it with discretion and temper, perhaps we may, without hazard, grow old in happiness. But if we use it greedily and insatiably, and endeavour to pursue one piece of good fortune after another, take care lest we suffer the same fate that they say many people do at sea, who, by means of their having been once fortunate, will never cease repeating their voyages till they are lost. And as they say many do, who, having obtained one victory, and aiming at more, have lost the first. If, indeed, the enemy who are fled were fewer than we, perhaps we might pursue those with safety; but consider what part of them it was that our whole number fought and conquered, the rest were out of the action, and unless we force them to fight, are going their ways, meanly and ignorantly, without knowing their own strength or ours. If they shall find that they are not less in danger in retreating than they are in standing to us, how can it happen otherwise than that we shall force them, even against their will, to be brave? for be assured, that you are not more desirous to seize their wives and children than they are to preserve them. And consider even swine, that they, though many in number, betake themselves to flight, together with their young, as soon as they are discovered; but if any man pursue one of their little ones, the sow, though she be single, does not continue her flight, but attacks the pursuer that attempts to take it. Now these men, on this late occasion, had shut themselves up in an intrenchment, and let themselves be parcelled out by us in such a manner, as put it into our power to engage as many of them as we pleased. But if we march up to them in an open country, and they shall have learned to divide and extend themselves, so that part of them shall oppose us in front, part on one wing, and part on another, and some in our rear; do you then take care lest we, every one of us, stand in need of many more hands and arms than we have. Besides," said he, " now that I observe the Medes to be enjoying themselves, I should be very unwilling to rouse them from their pleasures, and compel them to throw themselves into danger."

Then Cyrus in reply said : " You shall compel no one : do but allow those to follow me that are willing to do it. Perhaps we may come back, and bring you, and every one of these friends of yours, what you will all be pleased with. We will not pursue the main body of the enemy ; for how should we be able to lay our hands on them ? But if we meet with any thing straggling from the rest of the army, or left behind, we will come and bring it to you. Consider then," said he, " that when you wanted us, we came a long journey to do you pleasure ; it were but just therefore that you should gratify us in return, that we may go home possessed of something, and not all of us have our eye to your treasure." Here Cyaxares said : " If any one, indeed, would attend you of his own accord, I should think myself obliged to you." " Send with me then one of these credible persons who shall tell your message." " Come," said he, " take which of them you please." And there happened to be that person present who had called himself his relation, and that he had kissed ; Cyrus therefore immediately said : " I am contented with this man." " Let him therefore," said he, " attend you ; and do you," said he, " declare that any one who is willing may go with Cyrus." So, taking this man with him, he went out. As soon as he came out, Cyrus presently said to him, " Now you will make it appear whether you spoke truth, when you said you were delighted with the sight of me." " When you propose this matter," said the Mede, " I will not abandon you." " And will you not," said Cyrus, " yourself espouse it, and propose it to others ?" Then, with an oath, " By Jove !" said he, " I will ; and that till I make you delighted with the sight of me." Then did this messenger of Cyaxares discharge himself with zeal, in all respects, by declaring his message to the Medes ; and added this of himself : " That, for his part, he would not desert this best and most excellent of men ; and, what was above all, this man who derived his origin from the gods !"

II. While Cyrus was transacting these affairs there came messengers from the Hyrcanians, as if by divine appointment. The Hyrcanians are borderers on the Assyrians ; they are no great nation, and therefore subject to the Assyrians ; they at that time, it seems, consisted of horse, and do so at this day : the Assyrians therefore used them as the Lacedæmonians do the people of Sciros, not sparing them in fatigues and dangers ; and they at that time had commanded them to make the rear-guard, being a thousand horse, that in case any danger pressed on them in the rear, these men might have it fall on them before it reached themselves. The Hyrcanians, being to march behind all, had their waggons and domestics in the rear : for most of the inhabitants of Asia are attended in their military expeditions by those that they live with at home. And the Hyrcanians at that time attended the service in that manner. Considering therefore with themselves what they suffered under the Assyrians ; that their prince was now dead, and they beaten ; that the army was now under great terror ; that their allies were in a desponding condition, and were quitting them ; on these considerations, this appeared to them to be a noble opportunity to revolt, if Cyrus' men would but fall on the enemy in conjunction with them. Accordingly, they sent messengers to Cyrus ; for, since the battle, his fame was grown to the greatest height.

The men that were sent told Cyrus—" That they had a just hatred to the Assyrians ; that if he would now march up to them, they themselves would be his assistants, and lead him the way." They gave him likewise accounts of the circumstances of the enemy, as men who were extremely desirous to animate him to this expedition. Then Cyrus asked them—" Do you think," said he, " that we can get up with them before they get into their fortresses ? For," said he, " we take it to be a very great misfortune that they fled without our knowledge." This he said with intention to raise in them the greatest confidence possible in himself and his people. They replied, " That if he and his men, setting out early in the morning, marched with expedition, they might come up with them, even the next day ; for by reason of their multitude, and the number of their carriages, they marched very slowly. And besides," said they, " having had no rest the night before, they marched but a little way, and are now encamped." Then Cyrus said : " Have you any pledge therefore to give us of the truth of what you say ?" " We will go," said they, " this instant, and bring you hostages to-night. Do you only give us the security of your taking the gods to witness on your part, and give us your right hand, that what we ourselves thus receive from you we may carry to the rest of our people." On this he gave them the testi-

H

monials of his faith, that "If they accomplished what they said, he would treat them as faithful men and friends; and that they should not be of less consideration with him than the Persians or Medes." And at this day it may be observed, that the Hyrcanians are employed in considerable trusts, and are possessed of governments, as those of the Persians and Medes are that appear worthy of them.

When they had supped he led out the army, while it was yet day, and he ordered the Hyrcanians to stay, that they might go with him. All the Persians, as one may naturally suppose, were immediately out. Tigranes, likewise, with his army, was the same. But of the Medes, some marched out, because, while they were yet boys, they had been friends to Cyrus while a boy; some because, by conversing with him in his huntings, they were much taken with his temper and manners; some out of gratitude, because they thought him the man who had relieved them when they were under very great terror; some, by his appearing already to be a man of great dignity and worth, had hopes that he would still grow farther so, as to be prodigiously fortunate and great; some, because they were desirous to return him that friendship and service that he had done them while he lived among the Medes; for out of his good-nature he had performed several services with his grandfather for many of them: but most part of them, when they saw the Hyrcanians, and that it was discoursed abroad that they were to lead the way to mighty advantages, marched out in order to get something. So almost all the Medes marched, except those that were in the tent with Cyaxares. These remained, and the men that were under their command. The rest hastened out with zeal and pleasure, as not going by restraint, but voluntarily, and with design to oblige. When they were out he went to the Medes. He first commended them, and prayed—"That the gods, being propitious both to them, to himself, and to his people, would vouchsafe to conduct them! and then that he himself might be enabled to make them grateful returns for this their zeal!" In the last place, he told them that the foot should lead the way, and bade them follow with their horse; and wherever they rested, or suspended their march, he ordered them to send off some people to him, that they might be informed of what was proper on every occasion. On this he ordered the Hyrca-

nians to lead the way, and they asked him this question: "Why," said they, "do you not stay till we bring our hostages, that you may march with the pledges of our fidelity in your hands?" He is said to have replied thus: "Why," said he, "I consider that we have all of us pledges of your fidelity in our own hearts and hands; for we take ourselves to be so well provided, that if you tell us truth, we are in a condition to do you service; and if you deceive us, we reckon that we stand on such a footing as not to be ourselves in your power, but rather, if the gods so please, that you will be in ours. Since then," said he, "O Hyrcanians! you say that your people march the hindermost, as soon as you see them signify to us that they are your people, that we may spare them." The Hyrcanians, hearing these things, led the way as he ordered. They admired his firmness of mind, and were no longer in fear either of Assyrians, the Lydians, or their allies; but only lest Cyrus should be convinced that, whether they were present or absent, they were of little significance.

While they were on the march, and night was come on, a clear light from heaven is said to have appeared to Cyrus and to the army; so that all were seized with a shivering at the divine appearance, but inspired with boldness against the enemy. As they marched without incumbrance and with despatch, they probably moved over much ground, and at the dawn of day they were near the Hyrcanian army. As soon as the messengers discovered them, they told Cyrus that these were their people: they said "They knew them by their being the hindermost, and by their multitude of fires." On this he sent one of the two messengers to them, ordering him to tell them: "If they were friends, immediately to meet him, holding out their right hands." He sent some of his own people with them, and bade them tell the Hyrcanians: "That when he and his people saw them advancing, they themselves would do the same thing." So one of the messengers stayed with Cyrus, the other rode off to the Hyrcanians. While Cyrus was observing what the Hyrcanians would do, he made the army halt; and the chief of the Medes and Tigranes rode up to him, and asked him what they were to do. He told them thus: "This body that is near us is that of the Hyrcanians. One of their messengers is going to them, and some of our people with him, to tell them, if they are friends, to meet us with their right hands held out; therefore if they come in this manner, do you, every one in your several stations, receive them with your right hands as they come, and encourage them. If they take to their arms, or attempt to fly, do you endeavour to let none of those that we first meet with escape." He gave these orders; and the Hyrcanians having heard the report of the messengers, were in great joy, and mounting their horses at a leap, came up, as was told them, with their right hands extended. The Medes and Persians, on their side, received them with their right hands, and encouraged them. On this Cyrus said: "Hyrcanians, we now trust to you. It is your part to be in the same disposition towards us: but, in the first place," said he, "tell us this—how far from hence is the place where the enemy's commanders are, and their main body?" They said, in answer, "That it was little more than a parasang."

On this occasion Cyrus said: "Come on, then," said he, "men of Persia, Medes, and you, Hyrcanians, for to you I now speak, as to confederates and sharers with us in all things. You ought now all to be assured, that we are in such a circumstance as must bring on us the greatest severities of fortune, if we act in it remissly and faintly; for the enemy know for what purposes we come. If we march to the enemy with vigour and spirit, and charge home, you will see them like slaves that have run away and are discovered, some supplicating for mercy, some flying, and some without presence of mind enough to do either; for, beaten as they are, they will see us come on them, and thinking of our coming, will be surprised, without order, and without being prepared to fight. If therefore we desire, henceforward, to take our meals, to pass our nights, and to spend the rest of our lives with pleasure, do not let us give them leisure to contrive or execute any thing that may be for their own service; nor to know so much as that we are men; but let them fancy that all is shields, swords, cutlasses, and blows that fall on them. And do you, Hyrcanians," said he, "extending yourselves in front before us, march first, that by the appearance of your arms we may keep concealed as long as possible. When I get up with the enemy's army, do you, each of you, leave with me a troop of horse that I may make use of them, in case of need, remaining in the camp. Do you, commanders, and your

men of most years, if you are wise, march together in close order, lest, meeting perhaps with a close body, you be repulsed. Send out your younger men to pursue; let these despatch the enemy, for it is our safest course at this time to leave as few of the enemy alive as we can. But lest, what has happened to many victors, a turn of fortune befall us, we ought strictly to guard against turning to plunder; and as he that does it can no longer be reckoned a man, but a mere bearer of baggage, so any one that will, is free to use him as a slave. You ought to be sensible that there is nothing more gainful than victory, for the victor sweeps all away with him, both men, women, and treasure, together with the whole country. Keep your eye therefore intent only on the preservation of victory, for even the plunderer himself is comprehended in it. And remember this too, in your pursuit, that you return again to me while it is yet day; for after it is dark we will give admittance to none."

Having said this, he dismissed them, every one to his own century, and ordered them withal to go their ways, and signify these things, every one to his chiefs of ten; for the chiefs of tens were all in front, so as to be able to hear; and he bade them order the chiefs of tens to give these directions, each to his own ten. On this the Hyrcanians led the way: he himself marched with the Persians in the centre, and formed the horse, as usual, on each wing. As soon as his army appeared, some of the enemy were astonished at the sight; some already discovered what it was; some told it about; some set up a clamour; some loosed their horses; some packed up their effects; some threw the arms from off the beasts of burden, and some armed themselves; some mounted their horses; some bridled them; some helped the women up on the waggons; some laid hold of what they had of greatest value to save it; and some were found burying such kind of things; but most of them betook themselves to flight. It must needs be thought that they were taken up with these things, and many more of various kinds, excepting only that nobody fought, but that they were destroyed without making any opposition. Croesus, the king of the Lydians, it being the summer season, had sent away his women in the night, in chariots, before, that they might travel with the more ease in the cool, and he himself with his horse had followed after. The Phrygian, they say, who was prince of that Phrygia that lies on the Hellespont, did the same. But as soon as they perceived the runaways, and that some of them came up with them, having got information of what had happened, they fled in the utmost haste. The kings of the Cappadocians, and of the Arabians that were at hand, and without their corslets, thinking themselves secure, the Hyrcanians killed.— But the greatest number of those that died on this occasion were Assyrians and Arabs; for being in their own country, they were most remiss in marching off. The Medes and Hyrcanians performed such things in the pursuit as are usual for men that have gained the victory. But Cyrus ordered the horse, that had been left with him, to ride round the camp, and kill all such as they saw going off with their arms; and to those that remained he ordered it to be proclaimed, " That all soldiers of the enemy whatever, whether horsemen, targeteers, or archers, should bring their arms, all bound up together, away to him, and leave their horses at their tents; and that if any refused to do thus, he should immediately lose his head.' Some with their swords drawn stood round in order; they who had arms brought them away, and threw them down on the place that he appointed them; and they that he ordered for that service burnt them.

But Cyrus then reflecting that they were come without either meat or drink, and that without these it was impossible to carry on a war, or do any thing else; considering therefore how he might be supplied with these things the soonest, and in the best manner, it came into his mind that it was absolutely necessary for all men that were engaged in military service to have some certain person to take care of the tent, and who should provide all things necessary for the soldiers when they came in. He judged therefore, that of all people in the camp, these were the most likely to be left behind, because of their being employed in packing up the baggage; so he ordered proclamation to be made, that all the officers of this kind should come to him, and where there was no such officer, that the oldest man of that tent should attend: he denounced all manner of severity to him that should disobey. But they all paid obedience instantly, having seen their masters do it before them. When they were present, he commanded all such as had necessaries in their tents for two months and up-

wards to sit down. When he had observed these, he again commanded all such as were provided for one month to do the same. On this almost all of them sat. When he found this, he spoke to them thus: " Come, then, good people, all those of you who would avoid evil, and desire to obtain any good from us, do you with readiness and zeal take care that in each tent there be prepared double the portion of meat and drink that you used to provide each day for your masters and their domestics; and have all things else ready that will contribute to furnish out a handsome entertainment; taking it for granted that the party conquering will be presently with you, and will require to have all things necessary provided for them in plenty. Know therefore that it may be of service to you to receive these men in the most unexceptionable manner." Having heard these things, they executed the orders with the greatest diligence. And having called the centurions together, he spoke to this effect:—

" We know, friends, that it is now in our power to take our dinners first, before our allies, who are absent, and to apply the most exquisite meats and drinks to our own use; but in my opinion this dinner will not do us so much service as our making it appear that we are careful of our allies. Nor will this good entertainment add more to our own strength, than we shall gain by making our confederates zealous and hearty in our interest. If we appear so negligent of those that are pursuing and destroying our enemies, and fighting in case there are any that oppose them, that they find we have dined before we know what they are doing; how can it happen otherwise, than that we shall appear vile in their sight, and lose our strength by losing our allies? But to be careful that they who are engaged in fatigues and dangers may have all necessaries ready for them when they come in; this, I say, is the treat that should more delight you than the present gratification of your bellies. And consider," said he, " that if we were to act without any respect to our friends, yet to cram with meat and drink is not at all proper with regard to ourselves; for we have a great many enemies in the camp loose and unconfined; it is our business to be on our guard against them, and to keep a guard on them, that we may have people to do all necessary things for us. Our horse are absent, and give us cause to be in some concern and doubt where they are, whether they are to come back to us, or whether they are to stay. So that in my opinion, friends, the meat and drink, the most for our purpose at present, ought to be what one can imagine of most use to preserve us from being drowsy and remiss. Yet farther, I know that there are great treasures in the camp; and I am not ignorant that it is in our power to appropriate to ourselves what we please of these things, that belong in common to all that were jointly concerned with us in taking them: but I am of opinion, that our taking them to ourselves cannot be a greater gain to us, than by making ourselves appear to these men to be just and honest, to purchase by that means still a greater share in their affection than we have yet obtained. And I am of opinion," said he, " to give up the distribution of these treasures to the Medes, Hyrcanians, and Tigranes, when they come; and even to reckon it an advantage, if they allot us the smallest share; for by means of their profit, they will with the more pleasure remain with us. And the taking a present advantage may indeed afford us short-lived riches, but they that give up this, acquire by it in return those things from whence riches flow. And in my opinion this may procure much more lasting riches to us and ours. It was for this end, I think, that we practised at home that continence and command over ourselves in the concerns of the belly, and in matters of unseasonable profit, that we might be able, when occasion served, to make use of these qualities for our advantage. And on what greater occasion than the present one we can show the virtue of our institution, I do not see."

Thus he spoke, and Hystaspes, a Persian, and one of the alike-honoured, spoke in favour of his opinion in this manner: " It were indeed a sad case, Cyrus, if in hunting we can continually master ourselves, and abstain from food in order to get possession of some beast, and perhaps of very little value; and, when we are in pursuit of all that is valuable in the world, we should not think it very unbecoming us to suffer ourselves to be stopped in our course by any of those things that have the command indeed of mean men, but are inferior and subservient to the deserving." Thus spoke Hystaspes in support of Cyrus' opinion; the rest approved it. Then Cyrus said: " Well, then, since we agree in these matters, do you send out five men of each company;

and such as are the most diligent and careful, let these march round, and those whom they find employed in providing the necessaries let them commend; those whom they find negligent, let them chastise, without sparing them, any more than if they themselves were their masters. These men executed their orders.

III. By this time some of the Medes drove up several waggons that had set out before from the camp, and that they had taken and turned back, laden with things that the army was in want of. Some of them brought chariots that they had taken; some full of the most considerable women, who were some of them of the legitimate sort; others of them courtesans, that were conveyed up and down by those people on account of their beauty; for to this day all the inhabitants of Asia in time of war attend the service accompanied with what they value the most: and say that they fight the better when the things that are most dear to them are present: for they say that they must of necessity defend these with zeal and ardour. Perhaps indeed it is so; but perhaps they do it only for their pleasure.

Cyrus, observing the things that were performed by the Medes and Hyrcanians, was almost angry with himself and with those that were with him; for the others seemed to outshine them at that time, and to be continually making some advantage or other, while they themselves stood quiet in an idle station: for they that brought the prizes, after showing them to Cyrus, rode off again in pursuit of others; for they said that they were ordered so to do by their commanders. Cyrus, though nettled at this, yet ordered the things away to a particular station; then calling the centurions again together, and standing in a place where what he said might be heard, he spoke thus: " I believe, friends, we are all convinced that if we had had the taking of these things that have just now appeared before us, all the Persians in general would have been great gainers, and we probably the greatest, who had been personally concerned in the action. But how we, who are not able of ourselves to acquire these things, can possibly get them into our possession, I do not yet see, unless the Persians procure a body of horse of their own. For you observe," said he," " that we Persians are possessed of arms that are proper to repel enemies that will close with us; but when they are once repulsed, what horsemen, archers, targeteers, or dartsmen, while we are without horse, can we possibly take or destroy in their flight? who would fear to annoy us, whether archers, dartsmen, or horse, when they know very well that there is no more danger of receiving any hurt from us, than from trees that grow fixed in the ground? If these things are thus, is it not plain that the horsemen now with us reckon all things that fall into our hands not less theirs than ours? Nay, perhaps, even more. On this footing therefore do things now necessarily stand. But if we get a body of horse not inferior to themselves, is it not evident to you all that we shall be able without them to perform the same things against the enemy that we now do with them? and that we shall have them in a more humble disposition towards us? for when they have a mind either to go or stay, it will be of less concern to us, if we are of ourselves sufficient without them. But be this as it will, yet no one, I believe, will be of a contrary opinion to me in this, that for the Persians to have a body of horse of their own, is not a matter that is entirely indifferent. But then, perhaps, you are considering how this can be brought about. Supposing then that we incline to constitute a body of horse, let us examine what it is we have, and what it is we want. Here are horses in great number that are left in the camp, and there are bridles to manage them, and all other things that are proper for the use of such as keep horses; and we have likewise the things that are proper for the use of a horseman himself; corslets for the defence of his body, and lances, that we may either use in throwing or by hand. What then remains? It is plain we must have men; and these we have more certainly than any thing, for there is nothing so much belongs to us as we do to ourselves. But perhaps somebody will say that we do not understand it: nor, by Jove! have any of those who understand it now attained the skill before they learned it. But they learned it, somebody may say, when they were boys. And have boys the better faculty to learn things that are told them, or shown them; or have men? And when they have once learned, which of them have bodies the most able to undergo labour, boys or men? Then we have that leisure for learning that neither boys have, nor other men; for we have neither the use of the bow to learn, as boys have, for we know it already; nor throwing of

the javelin, for we know that too; nor have we that continual employment that other men have, some in agriculture, some in trades, and some in other particular affairs. We have not only leisure to practise military affairs, but we are under a necessity of doing it. Nor is this, as many other military matters are, a thing of difficulty, as well as of use; for is it not pleasanter on the road to be on horseback, than to travel on foot? And where despatch is required, is it not a pleasure to get quickly to a friend, when there is occasion, or readily to overtake either a man or a beast in the pursuit? And is it not a convenience that whatsoever arms are to be carried, the horse helps to carry them? for to have arms and to carry them is the same thing. And as to what one may have most reason to fear, that we may perhaps be obliged to come to action on horseback, before we are yet well skilled in the work, and that we may become neither able footmen nor able horsemen; even this is not a difficulty that is unconquerable; for whenever we please we are immediately at liberty to fight on foot; nor shall we unlearn any thing of our skill as footmen by learning to ride."

Thus Cyrus spoke; and Chrysantas, speaking in favour of the same opinion, said thus: "I am," said he, "so desirous of learning to ride, that I reckon, were I a horseman, I should be a flying man. As matters now stand, were I to run a race with a man, I should be contented if I got but by the head before him; or if I saw a beast running by, I would be contented if on the stretch, I could contrive to reach him with my bow or javelin before he got at a great distance from me. But if I become a horseman I shall be able to kill any man, though at as great a distance as I can see; and in the pursuit of beasts, some I shall be able to come up with, and to strike them by hand, others I shall be able to reach with my javelin, as well as if they stood still; for if two creatures are swift alike, they continue as near to each other as if they stood still. Of all creatures, they that I think raise my envy and emulation the most, are the centaurs, if there ever were any;—creatures that, with the understanding of man, are capable of contrivance and forecast; who with their hands can effect what is proper to be done, and have the swiftness and strength of the horse, so as to overtake what flies from them, and overturn what opposes them. So when I am a horseman, all

hese powers do I carry with me: I shall be
ble to contrive things with my understanding,
a man; my arms I shall carry in my hands;
ith my horse I shall pursue, and by my horse's
strength overturn what opposes me. But then
shall not be bound down and grow to him,
ke the centaurs; and this is certainly better
an to be incorporated with him; for centaurs,
fancy, must be at a loss both how to use se-
eral conveniences discovered by men, and how
) enjoy several pleasures natural to horses.
kat I, when I have learned to ride, and am
mounted on horseback, shall perform the part
f a centaur; and when I dismount I shall
ake my meals, clothe myself, and take my rest,
s other men do. So that what am I but a
rentaur, free and separable when I please; and
hen, when I please, of a piece again? Be-
ides, I have this advantage over the centaur,"
said he, " that he saw but with two eyes and
eard but with two ears, but I shall see with
four eyes, and receive notices of things by
means of four ears; for the horse they say dis-
overs to men many things that he beforehand
ees with his own eyes, and gives them notice
f many things that he beforehand hears with
his own ears. Write me down therefore as one
of those that are desirous to serve on horseback." " And us too," said all the others. On
this Cyrus said: " Since, then," said he, " we
are so much of this opinion, what if we should
make it a law, that it should be scandalous for
any of those amongst us that I furnish with
horses to be seen travelling on foot, let the way
be it to go be little or great, that men may
imagine we are entirely centaurs?" This proposal he made them, and they all gave their
consent. So that at this day the Persians still
put it in practice; and none of the considerable
men among the Persians are ever to be seen
travelling on foot of their own good-will.

IV. These men were employed in these discourses: but when the middle of the day was
past, the Median horse and the Hyrcanians
rode up, and brought with them both horses
and men that they had taken; for as many as
delivered their arms they did not kill. When
they rode up, Cyrus first asked them whether
they were all come safe? When they said that
they were, he then asked them what they had
done, and they related the things that they had
performed, and gave magnificent accounts how
manfully they had acted in every particular.
He hearkened with pleasure to all that they had

a mind to tell him, and then commended them
thus: " It is apparent how well you have behaved, for you are now in appearance taller,
more beautiful, and more terrible than before."
He then asked them how far they had gone,
and whether the country was inhabited. They
told him, " They had gone a great way; that
the whole country was inhabited, and full of
sheep, goats, oxen, and horses, corn, and all
valuable things." " There are two things,
then," said he, " that we are to take care of;
how to subject the people that are the possessors of these things; and how to make them
remain on the place: for a country well inhabited is a very valuable acquisition; but one
destitute of men is destitute of every thing that
is good. All those that stood to their defence,"
said he, " I know you have killed; and you did
right; for this is of the greatest importance for
the maintaining of a victory. Those that delivered their arms you have taken; and if we
dismiss them, we should do what I say would
turn to our advantage; for, first, we shall not
be under a necessity of being on our guard
against them, nor of keeping a guard on them,
nor of furnishing them with provisions; for
certainly we should not be for starving them.
Then, by dismissing them, we shall have the
greater number of captives; for if we conquer
the country, all will be our captives that inhabit
it; and the rest, when they see these living and
set at liberty, will the more readily remain, and
rather choose to submit than to continue in war.
This is my judgment; but if any other person
sees what is better, let him say it." But they,
having heard these things, agreed to act accordingly.

So Cyrus, having called for the prisoners,
spoke thus: " Friends!" said he, " by your
present submission you have preserved your
lives; and, for the future, if you behave in the
same manner, no ill whatever shall befall you,
unless it be that the same person will not govern you that governed you before; but you
shall inhabit the same houses, and you shall
cultivate the same territory; and you shall live
with the same wives, and you shall rule your
children as you do now; but you shall neither
make war on us, nor on any one else; and if
any other injure you, we will fight for you.
And that nobody may order you out on military service, bring your arms to us. And to
those that bring them, peace! and what I promise shall be made good to them without fraud.

But we will make war on those that refuse to lay their arms aside. But then if any of you shall come to us, and shall appear to do any action, or to give any information, in friendship and good-will to us, him will we treat as a benefactor and a friend, not as a slave. Let these things therefore be known to you, and do you tell them to the rest. And if there are any that will not comply with us in these things that we require, do you lead us the way to them, that we may make ourselves masters of them, and they not masters of us." Thus he spoke. They paid him their adoration, and said that they would perform what he enjoined them.

V. When they were gone, Cyrus said: " It is time, O Medes and Armenians! for all of us to take our suppers : and all things proper have been made ready for you in the best manner that we are able. Go your ways, then, and send us half the bread that has been made ; for there has been enough made for us both : but send us neither meat with it, nor any thing to drink, for of these we have enough with us already provided. And do you," said he, " O Hyrcanians ! conduct them to the tents ; the commanders to the greatest, (for you know which they are,) and the others as you think most proper. And do you, likewise, take your suppers where it is most agreeable to you ; for the tents are untouched, and all things are provided there for you, as well as for the others. But let this be known to you both, that we undertake to keep the night-watch without. Do you look to what passes in the tents, and place your arms within ; for they who are in the tents are not yet our friends."

The Medes then, and Tigranes' people, bathed themselves, (for all matters for that purpose had been provided,) and, having changed their clothes, took their suppers ; and their horses were provided with all necessaries. Half their bread they sent to the Persians, but sent no meat with it, nor wine ; thinking that Cyrus' people were provided with those things, because he had said that they had them in plenty. But what Cyrus meant was, that the meat they had with their bread was hunger, and their drink was the water of a stream that ran by. Cyrus therefore having given the Persians their supper, sent many of them out, as soon as it was dark, in fives and tens, and commanded them to march round the camp privately ; judging that they would be a guard to it, if any enemy came on them from without ;

and that if any one ran off with treasure of any kind they might take him. And it happened so ; for there were many that ran away, and many were taken. Cyrus allowed the treasures to those that seized them, but ordered them to kill the men. So that afterwards, even though one desired it, one could not easily meet with a man that was going any where in the night. And thus the Persians employed themselves ; but the Medes drank and feasted, entertained themselves with the music of flutes, and indulged themselves in all kinds of delights and pleasure ; for a multitude of things of that sort had been taken. So that they who were on the watch were in no want of work.

But Cyaxares, king of the Medes, that night that Cyrus marched away, was drunk himself, as well as those that were of his company in the tent, it being on an occasion of happy success. And he thought that the rest of the Medes, excepting only some few, were still remaining in the camp, because he heard a mighty noise and uproar ; for the servants of the Medes, on their masters being gone, drank without ceasing, and were very tumultuous : and the more, because they had taken from the Assyrian army great quantities of wine, and abundance of other such things. As soon as the day came, and that nobody attended at his doors, but they that had supped with him ; and that he heard that the camp was left empty by the Medes and by their horse ; and that he himself when he went out saw that this was really the case ; he then broke out into a rage at their going away and leaving him destitute. And as he is said to have been very violent and rash, he immediately commanded one of those about him to take some horse with him, and march with the utmost despatch to the army that was with Cyrus, and to say thus : " I was of opinion, Cyrus, that even you would not have engaged in councils so imprudent and bad for me ; or if Cyrus might have thought fit to do so, I did not think that you, Medes, would have consented to leave me thus destitute. Now, therefore, whether Cyrus will or will not do you come away to me with the utmost despatch." This message he sent them ; but he that received these orders to march said : " But how, O sovereign, shall I be able to find them ?" " And how should Cyrus," said he " find those that he marched after ?" " Truly because," said he, " as I hear, certain Hyrcanians who belonged to the enemy, and who had revolted and came hither, went and led them the way." Cyaxares hearing this, was in a much greater rage at Cyrus for not having told it him ; and he sent in much more haste to the Medes that he might strip him of his forces : he ordered them back with more vehemence than before, and with threats. The messenger likewise he threatened, in case he did not discharge himself with vigour in the delivery of his message.

The person that was thus sent marched with about a hundred of his own horse, and was grieved that he himself had not gone with Cyrus. As they proceeded in their march, the roads dividing, they lost their way in a beaten track, and could not get to Cyrus' army, till meeting with some Assyrians that were retiring, they forced them to be their guides ; and by this means getting sight of their fires, they got up with them about midnight. When they were got to the army, the guards, as was ordered them by Cyrus, did not admit them before day.

And when day appeared, Cyrus, calling to him the magi, commanded them to choose out what was due to the gods on the occasion of such advantages as they had obtained. These men employed themselves accordingly. He having summoned the alike-honoured, spoke to them thus : " My friends, the gods are pleased to lay many advantages before us ; but we, O Persians ! are at present but few in number to secure to ourselves the possession of them ; for the things that we have already gained, unless we secure them by a guard, will fall again into the power of others ; and if we leave some of ourselves as guards to secure the things that are already in our power, we shall immediately be found to have no manner of strength remaining. My opinion is, therefore, that some one among you should go as soon as possible to the Persians, acquaint them with what I say, and bid them send an army as soon as they possibly can, if the Persians desire that the dominion of Asia, and the revenues that arise from it, should belong to them. Go therefore," said he, " you who are the oldest man, and when you arrive, say thus : that whatever soldiers they send, when they come to me, it shall be my care to maintain. You see all the advantages that we have gained ; conceal no part of them. What part of these things it will be handsome and just for me to send to the gods, ask of my father ; what to the public, ask of the magistrates. Let them send people to see what we do, and to acquaint them with what we desire from them. Do you," said he, " make yourself ready, and take your company to attend you."

After this he called the Medes, and with them Cyaxares' messenger appeared, and before all declared Cyaxares' anger to Cyrus, and his threats to the Medes ; and in conclusion said : " That he commanded the Medes to come away though Cyrus should incline to stay." The Medes, on hearing the messenger, were silent, not knowing how they should disobey his summons, and yet in fear how they should yield obedience to him on his threats, especially knowing the violence of the man. But Cyrus then spoke : " I do not at all wonder," said he, " O messenger, and you Medes, that Cyaxares, who had then seen a multitude of enemies, and knew not what we were doing, should be under concern both for us and for himself. But when he knows that a great many of the enemy are destroyed, and that they are all driven away before us, he will first cease to fear ; and will then be convinced that he is not destitute at this time, when his friends are destroying his enemies. But how is it possible that we can deserve reproach for doing him service, and that not of our own heads neither ? for I prevailed with him to allow me to march, and to take you with me. It was not you that, from any desire of your own to march, begged his leave to do it, and so came hither ; but it was on orders from himself to go, given to every one of you that was not averse to it. I am therefore very well satisfied that this anger of his will be allayed by our successes, and, when his fear ceases, will quite vanish. Now therefore do you messenger, take a little rest, since you have undergone a great deal of fatigue. Let us, O Persians ! since we expect the enemy to be with us, either to fight or to submit themselves, keep ourselves in the best order ; for while we are observed to be so, it is probable we shall succeed the better in what we desire. And do you," said he, " prince of the Hyrcanians, attend here, after you have commanded the leaders of your men to call them to arms."

When the Hyrcanians had done this, and came to him, Cyrus said : " It is a pleasure to me, O Hyrcanian ! not only to perceive that you attend here, after having given us marks of your friendship, but that you appear to me to be a man of great ability. It is evident that the

I

same things are now alike advantageous to us both; · for the Assyrians are enemies to me, and are now more at enmity with you than with myself. We must both of us therefore consult how to prevent any of our allies that are at present with us from falling off from us, and if we can, how to acquire others. You have heard the Mede deliver his orders to recall their cavalry. If they leave us, how can we that are foot remain alone? Your and I therefore must contrive that this messenger who recalls them shall himself desire to stay with us. Do you therefore find out for him, and give him a tent where he may pass his time in the handsomest manner, and with all things convenient about him. I will endeavour to employ him on some business that will be more agreeable to him to do, than it will be to leave us. Do you discourse to him on the many advantages we hope all our friends will make, in case we are well supplied with every thing necessary. And when you have done this, come again to me." The Hyrcanian went, and conducted the Mede to a tent.

And he that was going to the Persians attended ready prepared. Cyrus directed him to tell the Persians the things he had before mentioned in his discourse to him, and to deliver to Cyaxares a letter. " But," said he, " I have a mind to read to you what I write, that being apprised of the matter, you may own it, if any body ask you about it." The contents of the letter were thus :

CYRUS TO CYAXARES.

" Joy and happiness! We have neither left you destitute, (for nobody, while they conquer their enemies, can be destitute of friends,) nor, when we left you, did we imagine that we brought you into danger; but at the greater distance we were from you, so much the more security did we reckon we procured you; for they that sit themselves down the nearest to their friends are not the men that best afford their friends security; but they that drive their enemies to the greatest distance are the men that put their friends the most out of danger. Consider then what your conduct has been to me, in return of what mine has been to you, that you can yet blame me. I brought you friends and allies; not as many as you could persuade, but as many as I was able. You gave me, while I was yet on friendly ground, as many as I could persuade to follow me; and

now that I am in the enemy's territory, yo recall not every one that is willing to be gon but all. At that time, therefore, I thoug' myself obliged both to yourself and them ; b now you force me to leave you out, and to e deavour to make all my returns of gratitud and thanks to those that followed me. A yet I cannot act like you; but am now sendi to the Persians for an army, and give orde that whatever numbers are sent me, if yo should be in any want of them before they rea us, you are free to use them, not according their liking, but as you yourself please. A though I am the younger man, yet I advise yo not to take away what you have once give lest you meet with ill-will instead of thank and when you would have any one to con quickly to you, not to send for him with threat and when you talk of being destitute, not threaten a multitude, lest you teach them n to mind you. We will endeavour to atte you, as soon as we have effected the things th we judge to be of advantage both to you a us.—Health attend you !"

" Deliver him this letter, and whatever l asks you on the subject of these affairs, do yo answer conformable to what is here writter for with respect to the Persians, I give yo such orders as are expressed in the letter."

Having said thus to him, and given him tl letter, he dismissed him ; enjoining him with to use diligence ; as taking it for granted th it would be of great advantage to him to quickly back again.

After this he observed all the Hyrcania and Tigranes' men already armed; and t Persians were likewise armed; at which tir some of the neighbouring people brought horses and arms. Such of the javelins as th were not themselves in want of, he order them to throw on the place where he had dered others before; and those whose busine it was, he ordered to burn them. But he co manded those who brought horses to stay a look to them till he signified his intentions them. Then calling to him the commande of the horse and those of the Hyrcanians, spoke in this manner : " My friends and alli do not wonder," said he, " that I call you fi quently together; for our present circumstanc are new to us ; many things are yet in disc der ; and things that are in disorder must necessity give us trouble till they are settled their proper places. We have now in o

...ower many treasures, as well as men captive; and by our not knowing which of these belong to each of us, and by their not knowing who is to each of them severally master, there are not many of them that we see performing their proper parts; but almost all of them are at a loss what to do. That things therefore may not continue thus, do you distribute them. Whoever is in possession of a tent fully supplied with provisions of meat and drink, with servants, carpets, and apparel, and with all other things that a tent well accommodated for military service is furnished with; here there is nothing farther necessary than that the possessor should understand that it is his part to take care of these things as his own property. But where any one is possessed of a tent, where those things are wanting, after you have discovered it, on examination, do you supply what falls short; for I know there will be of many things more than enough; because the enemy was possessed of every thing in greater proportion than suits our numbers. Besides, there have been with me certain stewards belonging to the Assyrian king, and their other great men, who have told me that they had by them sums of gold in coin, arising, as they said, from certain tributary payments. Make proclamation therefore that these things be brought to you where you sit: and denounce terror and punishments to whosoever does not execute what you command them. Do you receive these things, and distribute them; to the horsemen, double payments; to the foot, single; that in case you want any thing, you may have wherewithal to buy. And have it presently proclaimed that nobody injure the camp-market; but that the sutlers and tradesmen sell what each of them has for sale; and when they have disposed of these, that they fetch more, that the camp may be supplied."

They immediately had these things proclaimed. But the Medes and Hyrcanians spoke in this manner: "And how can we," said they, "distribute these things without you and your people?" Cyrus to this question replied thus: "Is this then, friends," said he, "your opinion, that whatever is to be done, we must all of us attend on it? and shall not I be thought sufficient by you to transact any thing for you that may be proper, nor you sufficient to transact for us? By what other means can we possibly create ourselves more trouble, and do less business than by acting thus? But you see," said

he, "that we have been the guards that have kept these things for you; and you have reposed a confidence in us that they have been well and faithfully guarded. Do you on the other hand distribute these things, and we will repose a confidence in you, that they have been well and justly distributed. And on other occasions we will endeavour to perform some other public service. And now, in the first place, you observe how many horses we have at present, and that others are continually brought to us; if we leave these without riders, they will be of no manner of use to us, and will give us trouble to take care of them; but if we set horsemen on them, we shall be freed from the trouble, and shall add to our strength. If you have others that you would give them to, with whom it would be more pleasing to you to act with on any occasion in war than with us, give them the horses; but if you would rather have us for supporters and assistants, give them to us; for when you pushed on before us in the late service, without us, you put us under great apprehension lest you should come by some misfortune; and you made us ashamed that we were not at hand wherever you were. But if we once get horses we will follow you; and if it be thought of most service to engage on horseback, in concert with you, we shall lose nothing of our ardour and zeal; but if it be thought most proper to support you on foot, then to alight will be obvious and easy to us; we shall be ready at your hands on foot, and will contrive to find people to deliver our horses to."

Thus he spoke; and they replied: "We have neither men to mount on these horses, nor, if we had, would we come to any other determination, since you would have it thus. Take, then," said they, "the horses, and do as you think best." "I receive them," said he, "and may good fortune attend on our becoming horsemen! Do you divide the things that are in common; but first take out for the gods whatever the magi shall direct; and then take such things for Cyaxares as you think most acceptable to him." They laughed, and, said, that beautiful women, then, were what should be chosen for him. "Choose women, then," said he, "and whatever else you think proper: and when you have chosen for him, then do you, Hyrcanians, do all you can to give entire content to all these men that have voluntarily followed me. And you, O Medes! reward these, our first allies, in such a manner as may convince them that they took a right resolution when they became our friends. And out of the whole, give a share to the messenger that is come from Cyaxares, both to himself and the men that are with him, and exhort him to stay with us, as being my opinion, jointly with yours, that by means of his being better informed of every particular he may represent to Cyaxares a full state of things : for the Persians," said he, " that are with me, let what remains over and above, after you are all well provided for, be sufficient; for," said he, " we have not been brought up in a nice delicate way, but in a coarse, rustic manner ; so that perhaps you may laugh at us, if there should happen to be any thing fine and magnificent left for our share : as I know very well," said he, " we shall give you a great deal of laughter and diversion when we are set on horseback ; and so we shall do, I believe," said he, " when we are thrown from off our horses to the ground." On this they went their ways to the distribution, laughing heartily at this new body of horse.

But he, calling the centurions to him, ordered them to take the horses, the horse-furniture, and the men that were to take care of them ; and, after having numbered them, and drawn lots by centuries, to take each of them a like number. Cyrus himself ordered them to make proclamation, that whatever slave there might be, either in the Assyrian, Syrian, or Arabian armies, whether he were Mede, Persian, Bactrian, Carian, Cilician, or Greek, or of any other country, forced to serve, that he should appear. These men, hearing the proclamation, appeared joyfully before him in great numbers. And he, having chosen from amongst them the most personable and sightly men, told them that they should now become free, and bear such arms as he would give them. To supply them with all necessaries, he said, should be his care ; and, bringing them immediately to the centurions, be put them under their care, and commanded them to give them shields and a smaller sort of swords, that being thus equipped they might attend the horse ; that they should take all necessaries for these men as well as for the Persians that were with him ; that they themselves, with their corslets and lances, should always march on horseback ; and he began it himself : and that over the foot of the alike-honoured they should, each of them, out

of the number of the alike-honoured, appoint a commander in his own stead. In these affairs were these men employed.

VI. Meanwhile Gobryas, an Assyrian, and a man in years, arrived on horseback, attended by some cavalry, consisting of his own dependents ; and they were all provided with arms proper for horse. They that had been appointed to receive the arms bade them deliver their lances that they might burn them, as they had done others before ; but Gobryas said that he desired first to see Cyrus. Then they that attended this service left the other horsemen behind, and conducted Gobryas to Cyrus ; and, as soon as he saw Cyrus, he spoke thus : " My sovereign lord, I am by birth an Assyrian ; I have a strong fortress in my possession, and have the command of a large territory : I furnished the Assyrian king with a thousand horse, and was very much his friend : but since he, who was an excellent man, has lost his life in the war against you, and that his son, who is my greatest enemy, now possesses the government, I come and throw myself at your feet as a supplicant, and give myself to you as a servant and assistant in the war. I beg you to be my revenger : I make you my son as far as it is possible. With respect to male issue, I am childless ; for he, O sovereign ! that was my only one, an excellent youth, who loved and honoured me to as great a degree as son could do to make a father happy ; him did the present king (the late king, the father of the present, having sent for my son, as intending to give him his daughter, and I sent him away, proud that I should see my son married to the daughter of the king) invite to hunt with him, as a friend ; and, on a bear appearing in view, they both pursued. The present king having thrown his javelin, missed his aim. O that it had not happened so ! and my son making his throw— unhappy thing !—brought the bear to the ground. He was then enraged, but kept his envy concealed ; but then again a lion falling in their way, he again missed ; and that it should happen so to him I do not think at all wonderful ; but my son again hitting his mark, killed the lion, and said, ' I have twice thrown single javelins, and brought the beasts both times to the ground.' On this the impious wretch contained his malice no longer, but, snatching a lance from one of his followers, struck it into his breast, and took away the life of my dear and only son ! Then I, miserable man ! brought him away a corpse instead of a bridegroom ; and I, who am of these years, buried him, my excellent and beloved son, a youth just bearded. His murderer, as if he had destroyed an enemy, has never yet appeared to have had any remorse ; nor has he, in amends for the vile action, ever vouchsafed to pay any honour to him, who is now under the ground. His father, indeed, had compassion, and plainly appeared to join in affliction with me at this misfortune ; therefore, had he lived, I had never applied to you to his prejudice ; for I had received a great many instances of friendship from him, and I served him. But since the government has fallen to the murderer of my son, I can never possibly bear him the least good-will ; nor can he, I know very well, ever reckon me his friend ; for he knows how I stand affected towards him ; how I, who lived with that joy and satisfaction before, must now stand in this destitute condition, passing my old age in sorrow. If you receive me, therefore, and that I can have hopes of obtaining, by your means, a revenge for my dear son, I shall think I arise again to new life ; I shall neither be ashamed to live, nor, if I die, do I think that I shall end my days with grief."

Thus he spoke. And Cyrus replied : "If you make it appear, Gobryas, that you really are in that disposition towards us that you express, I receive you as our supplicant, and, with the help of the gods, I promise to revenge you on the murderer. But tell me," said he, "if we effect these things for you, and allow you to hold your fortress, your territory, and your arms, and the power that you had before, what service will you do for us in return for these things ?" He then said : "My fortress I will yield you for your habitation whenever you please ; the same tribute for my territory, that I used to pay to him, I will pay to you ; wherever you shall make war I will attend you in the service, with the forces of my territory ; and I have besides," said he, "a maiden daughter, that I tenderly love, just of an age for marriage ; one that I formerly reckoned I brought up as a wife for the person now reigning ; but she herself has now begged me, with many tears and sighs, not to give her to the murderer of her brother ; and I join with her

in opinion. I here give you leave to deal with her as I appear to deal by you." Then Cyrus said : "On these terms," said he, "with truth and sincerity do I give you my right hand, and accept of yours. Let the gods be witnesses between us !" When these things had passed, he bade Gobryas go, and keep his arms : and he asked him at what distance his habitation was, it being his intention to go thither. He then said ; "If you march to-morrow morning you may quarter with us the next day. So Gobryas went away and left a guide.

The Medes then came, after having delivered to the magi such things as they had said were to be chosen for the gods. And they had chosen for Cyrus a most beautiful tent ; a Susian woman, that was said to have been the most beautiful woman of all Asia ; and two other women that were the finest singers. And they chose the same things over again for Cyaxares. They had fully supplied themselves with all such things as they wanted, that they might be in want of nothing in the course of their service in the war ; for there were all things in great abundance. The Hyrcanians took likewise whatever they wanted ; and they made Cyaxares' messenger an equal sharer with them. As many tents as were remaining over and above, they gave to Cyrus, that the Persians might have them ; the money, they said, they would divide as soon as it was collected ; and they divided it accordingly. These things did these men do and say : but Cyrus ordered such men to take and keep the things that belonged to Cyaxares as he knew to be most intimate with him. "And all that you give me,' said he, "I accept with pleasure ; but be among you," said he, "that is the most in want of them shall have the use of them." A certain Mede, who was a lover of music, then said, "In the evening, Cyrus, I heard those singers that you now have, and I heard them with pleasure : if you would give me one of them, I believe it will be a greater pleasure to me to attend the service of the war than to stay at home." Then Cyrus said : "I give her to you, and I think myself more obliged to you for asking her of me, than you are to me for having her ; so very desirous am I to please you all." So he then took her away.

XENOPHON

ON THE

INSTITUTION OF CYRUS.

———

BOOK V.

CONTENTS of BOOK V.

INSTITUTION OF CYRUS.

BOOK V.

I. Cyrus then calling to him Araspes the Mede, (he that had been his companion from a boy, to whom he gave the Median robe, that he himself put off when he left Astyages, and departed for Persia,) commanded him to keep the woman and tent for him. This woman was wife of Abradatas, king of the Susians. And when the camp of the Assyrians was taken, her husband was not in the camp, but was gone on an embassy to the king of the Bactrians. The Assyrians had sent him to treat of an alliance between them; for he happened to have contracted a friendship with the king of the Bactrians. This woman therefore he ordered Araspes to keep till such time as he took her himself. But Araspes, having received his command, asked him this question:

"Cyrus," said he, "have you seen this woman that you bid me keep?" "No, by Jove!" said he, "I have not." "But I did," said he, "when we chose her for you. Indeed, when we first entered her tent we did not know her; for she was sitting on the ground, with all her women servants round her, and was dressed in the same manner as her servants were; but when we looked around, being desirous to know which was the mistress, she immediately appeared to excel all the others, though she was sitting with a veil over her, and looking down on the ground. When we bade her rise, she, and all the servants round her, rose. Here then she excelled first in stature, then in strength, and grace, and beautiful shape, though she was standing in a dejected posture, and tears appeared to have fallen from her eyes, some on her clothes, and some at her feet. As soon as the eldest among us had said to her, "Take courage, woman; we have heard that your husband is indeed an excellent man, but we now choose you out for a man that, be it known to you, is not inferior to him, either in person, in understanding, or in power: but, as we think, if there be a man in the world that deserves admiration, Cyrus does, and to him henceforward you shall belong." As soon as the woman heard this she tore down her robe, and set up a lamentable cry, and her servants cried out at the same time with her. On this most part of her face discovered itself, and her neck and hands appeared. And be it known to you, Cyrus," said he, "that I, and the rest that saw her, all thought that never yet was produced, or born of mortals, such a woman, throughout all Asia. And by all means," said he, "you likewise shall see her."

Then Cyrus said: "No, by Jove! not I; and much the less, if she be such a one as you say." "Why so?" said the young man. "Because," said he, "if on hearing now from you that she is handsome, I am persuaded to go and see her at a time that I have not much leisure, I am afraid that she will much more easily persuade me to go and see her again; and after that perhaps I may neglect what I am to do, and sit gazing at her." The young man then laughed, and said: "And do you think, Cyrus, that the beauty of a human creature can necessitate one against his will, to act contrary to what is best?" "If this were naturally so," said he, "we should be all under the same necessity. You see how fire burns all people alike; for such is the nature of it. But of beauties, some inspire people with love, and some do not; one loves one, and another another; for it is a voluntary thing, and every one loves those that he pleases. A brother does not fall in love with a sister, but somebody else does; nor is a father in love with a daughter, but some other person is. Fear and the law are a sufficient bar to love. If, indeed," said he, "the law should enjoin that they who did not eat should not be hungry, and that they who

K

did not drink should not be thirsty; that men should not be cold in the winter, nor hot in the summer; no law in the world could make men submit to these decisions, for by nature they are subject to these things. But love is a voluntary thing, and every one loves those that suit him, just as he does his clothes or his shoes." "How comes it to pass then," said Cyrus, "if to love be a voluntary thing, that we cannot give it over when we will? For I have seen people," said he, "in tears for grief, on account of love; slaves to those they were in love with, and yet thought slavery a very great evil before they were in love; giving away many things that they were never the better for parting with; wishing to be rid of love, as they would of any other distemper, and yet not able to get rid of it; but bound down by it, as by a stronger tie of necessity, than if they were bound in iron chains! they give themselves up therefore to those they love, to serve them in many odd and unaccountable ways: yet, with all their sufferings, they never attempt making their escape, but keep continual watch on their loves, lest they should escape from them."

The young man to this said: "There are people, indeed, that do these things; but," said he, "they are miserable wretches; and this I believe is the reason why they are always wishing themselves dead, as being wretched and unhappy; and though there are ten thousand ways of parting with life, yet they do not part with it. Just such wretches as these are they that attempt thefts, and will not abstain from what belongs to others; but when they have plundered or stolen any thing, you see," said he, "that you are the first that accuse the thief and the plunderer, as reckoning theft to be no such fatal necessary thing, and you do not pardon, but punish it. So people that are beautiful do not necessitate others to love them, nor to covet what they ought not; but mean wretched men are impotent, I know, in all their passions, and then they accuse love. Men, excellent and worthy, though they have inclinations both for gold, fine horses, and beautiful women, can yet with ease abstain from any of them, so as not to touch them contrary to right: I, therefore," said he, "who have seen this woman, and think her very beautiful, yet I am here attending on you, and I am abroad on horseback, and in all other respects I discharge my duty."

"But, by Jove!" said Cyrus, "perhaps you retired before the time that love naturally lays hold of a man. It is the nature of fire not immediately to burn the man that touches it, and wood does not immediately blaze out; yet still I am not willing either to meddle with fire, or to look at beautiful persons; nor do I advise you, Araspes, to let your eyes dwell long on beauties, for as fire burns those that touch it, beauties catch hold of those that look at them, though at a distance, and set them on fire with love."

"Be easy," said he, "Cyrus; though I look at her without ceasing, I will not be so conquered as to do any thing that I ought not." "You speak," said he, "very handsomely; guard her, therefore," said he, "as I bid you, and be careful of her; for perhaps this woman may be of service to us on some occasion or other." And having discoursed thus they parted.

The young man, partly by seeing the woman to be extremely beautiful, and being apprized of her worth and goodness, partly by waiting on her, and serving her, with intention to please her, and partly by his finding her not to be ungrateful in return, but that she took care by her servants that all things convenient should be provided for him when he came in, and that he should want nothing when he was ill; by all these means he was made her captive in love: and perhaps what happened to him in this case was what need not be wondered at.

Thus were these things transacted.

But Cyrus, designing that both the Medes and allies should stay with him of their own accord, summoned together all the proper persons, and when they were met, spoke to this effect; "Medes, and all you that are here present, I know very well that you came with me, not out of any desire of getting money, nor with the thought of serving Cyaxares by it, but you were willing to oblige me by it, and, in honour to me, you resolved to undertake a march by night, and to embark yourselves in dangers and hazards with me; and if I am not very unjust, I must acknowledge myself indebted to you for these things. But I do not think I am yet able to make you a due return for them: this I am not ashamed to say. But that I will make you just returns if you stay with me; this, be it known to you, I should be ashamed to tell you; for I should think that it would look as if I said this only to make you the more willing to stay with me. Instead of that, therefore, I say this; if you now go away in obedience to Cyaxares, yet will I endeavour, if I act with success, to deal by you in such a manner as shall make you applaud me. For my own part, I will not go; and the Hyrcanians, to whom I have given my oath and my right hand, I will stand by; I will not be caught betraying them. And for Gobryas, who delivers us up his fortress, his territory, and his whole force, I will endeavour to bring it about that he shall not repent of his journey to me; and, what is above all, when the gods so evidently deliver all these advantages into our hands, I ought to reverence them, and be ashamed to make a rash retreat and abandon all. Thus, therefore," said he, "will I act; do you as you judge proper, and tell me what your mind is." Thus he spoke.

And he who before had said that he was related to Cyrus replied: "As for me," said he, "O king! for you I take to be as much, by birth and nature, my king, as the particular bee in a hive is born the leader of the bees; for that one they willingly obey; where that remains, not one from thence departs; that remove, not one of them is left behind, so strong is the affection they are inspired with to be governed by it: and men seem to me to be almost exactly thus disposed towards you; for when you left us, and went into Persia, what Mede, either young or old, stayed behind, and did not follow you, till Astyages made us turn back? When you set out from Persia to our assistance, we again saw almost all your friends voluntarily following you; and when you were desirous to undertake the expedition hither, all the Medes willingly attended you; and we now stand so disposed, as that, with you, though we are in an enemy's country, we have courage, and without you we are afraid even to go home. Let the rest therefore speak for themselves, and declare what they will do. I, Cyrus, and they that are under my command, will remain with you, and, comforted with the sight of you, and supplied by your bounty, we will undergo any thing, and bear it with bravery."

On this Tigranes spoke thus: "Do not at all wonder," said he, "Cyrus, if I am silent; for my soul," said he, "is not prepared for advising you, but for executing what you command."

Then the Hyrcanian said: "For my part, O Medes! if you now go away, I should say it were the pleasure of some deity not to suffer you to be highly fortunate and happy; for what human creature can determine for turning back when the enemies are flying? or when they deliver their arms, would refuse to accept them? or when they deliver up themselves, and all that belongs to them, would refuse to receive them; especially when we have such a leader as, in my opinion, and I swear it to you by all the gods, is more pleased with doing us good than with enriching himself?" On this the Medes all said thus: "You, O Cyrus! have led us out, and do you, when you think it proper to retire, lead us back again with you."

Cyrus, having heard these things, made this prayer: "But do thou, greatest Jove! I beg thee, grant me to exceed in good offices those that pay me such honour!"

On this he ordered the rest to place their guards, and attend to the care of themselves. But the Persians he ordered to take possession of their tents; the horsemen such as were proper for them, and the foot such as were sufficient for the foot; and he ordered things to be so regulated, that they who were in the tents despatching the business there, should bring all necessaries to the Persians in their ranks, and see that the horses were taken care of, that the Persians might have no other work to do but the business of war. This day they thus passed.

II. And the next morning when they rose they marched to join Gobryas. Cyrus marched on horseback, as did also the Persian horsemen, who were about two thousand. They who held the shields and the swords of these men followed after them, being equal to them in number; and the rest of the army marched in order of battle. He ordered every one to tell their new servants, that whoever of them should be seen either behind the rear-guard or before the front, or should be caught on the outside of those that were in their ranks on either wing, should be punished. On the second day, towards the evening, they reached the habitation of Gobryas. They saw it to be an exceeding strong fortress, and that all things were provided upon the walls proper for a vigorous defence; and they saw abundance of oxen and sheep brought under the fortifications. Gobryas then, sending to Cyrus, bade him ride round, and see where the access was most easy, and send in to him some of those that he confided in, who, having seen how things stood within, might give him an account of them. So Cyrus, desiring in reality to see if the fortress might be taken on any side, or whether Gobryas might be discovered to be false, rode round on every side, but saw every part too strong to be approached. They that Cyrus sent in to Gobryas brought him an account, that there was such plenty of all good things within as could not, as they thought, even in the age of a man, come to fail the people that were there. Cyrus was under concern about what all this might mean. But Gobryas himself came out to him, and brought out all his men; some carrying wine, some meal, and others driving oxen, sheep, hogs, and goats, and of every thing that was eatable; they brought sufficient to furnish a handsome supper for the whole army that was with Cyrus. They that were appointed to this service made distribution of all these things, and they all supped. But Gobryas, when all his men were come out, bade Cyrus enter in the manner that he thought the most safe. Cyrus therefore, sending in before certain people to view and search into things, and a force with them, then entered himself; and when he was got in, keeping the gates open, he summoned all his friends and the commanders that had attended him: and when they were come in, Gobryas, producing cups of gold, and vessels of various kinds, all manner of furniture and apparel, daricks without number, and magnificent things of all kinds; and at last bringing out his daughter (who was astonishingly beautiful and tall, but in affliction on the death of her brother), spoke thus:

" Cyrus, all these treasures I give you, and this daughter of mine I intrust you with to dispose of as you think fit: but we are both of us your supplicants: I, before, that you would be the revenger of my son; and she, now, that you would be the revenger of her brother."

Cyrus to this said: " I promised you, then, that, if you were not false to us, I would revenge you to the utmost of my power; and now that I find you true to us, I am under the obligation of that promise. And I now promise her, with the help of the gods, to perform it. These treasures," said he, " I accept, but give them to this your daughter, and to the man that shall marry her. But I 'go off with one present from you, that I could not go off with more pleasure with the treasures of Babylon, where there are abundance; nor even with those of the whole world, were they to be exchanged for this that you have now presented me with."

Gobryas, wondering what it should be, and suspecting that he meant his daughter, asked him thus: " O Cyrus!" said he, " what is it?"

Then Cyrus replied: " Gobryas," said he, " it is this. I believe there may be abundance of men that would not be guilty either of impiety, injustice, or falsehood; and yet, because nobody will throw either treasures, or power, or strong fortresses, or lovely children in their way, die before it comes to appear what they were. But you, by having now put into my hands both strong fortresses, and riches of all kinds, your whole force, and your daughter, who is so valuable a possession, have made me clearly appear to all men to be one that would neither be guilty of impiety towards friends that receive and entertain me, nor of injustice for the sake of treasure, nor willingly false to faith in compacts. This therefore, be you assured, I will not forget, while I am a just man, and while as such I receive the applause of men, but I will endeavour to make you returns of honour in all things great and noble: and do not be afraid of wanting a husband for your daughter, and such a one as shall be worthy of her; for I have many excellent friends, and, amongst them, whoever it is that marries her, whether he will have either as much treasure as you have given, or a great deal more, I am not able to say; but be assured that there are some of them who, for all the treasures you have bestowed, do not on that account esteem you one jot the more. But they are at this time my rivals; they supplicate all the gods that they may have an opportunity of showing themselves that they are not less faithful to their friends than I am: that, while alive, they will never yield to their enemies, unless some god should blast their endeavours; and that for virtue and good reputation, they would not accept of all the treasures of the Syrians and Assyrians added to yours. Such men, be you assured, are sitting here."

Gobryas, smiling at this—" By the gods!" said he, " Cyrus, pray show me where these men are, that I may beg one of them of you to be my son." " Do not trouble yourself," said he· " it will not be at all necessary for you to inquire that of me. If you will but attend us, you yourself will be able to show them every one to any body else."

And having said this, he took Gobryas by the right hand, rose, went out, and brought out all that were with him; and though Gobryas repeatedly desired him to take his supper within, yet he would not do it, but supped in the camp, and took Gobryas to sup with him. After he had laid himself down on a mattress, he asked him thus: " Tell me," said he, " Gobryas, whether do you think that you, or we here, have the greatest plenty of furniture for couches?" He replied: " By Jove! I know very well that you have the furniture of this kind in greatest abundance, and couches too in greater number: and then your habitations are much larger than mine; for you have heaven and earth for a habitation, and couches you have as many as there are places on the earth to lie on: and for their furniture, you do not only think that you have as much of it as there grows of wool on the backs of sheep, but as much as there is of stubble and brushwood that the mountains and plains produce."

But Gobryas then supping with him for the first time, and observing the coarseness of the meats that were set before them, thought that they themselves lived in a much nobler manner than these people. But he afterwards considered their great temperance; for no disciplined Persian ever appeared struck with any sort of meats or drink, either by eagerness in his eyes, or by greediness, or by any such intenseness of mind, as not to give the same attention to things as if he were not taken up in eating; but as good horsemen, by keeping themselves easy and undisturbed on horseback, are able at the same time to see, to hear, and to speak what is proper; so they think, that while they are at their food, they ought to appear discreet and temperate; and to be much moved with any sort of meat or drink, they take to be selfish and brutal. He considered likewise their manner of converse, in asking each other such questions as were more agreeable to be asked than not; in jesting with each other in such a manner as was more pleasing than if let alone; and of their sporting with each other, but so as to keep at the greatest distance from being abusive, or from doing any thing indecent and ugly, and from giving one another offence. But what seemed to him to be above all was, that men engaged in military service should think that none of those engaged in the same dangers should be served with greater plenty than others; but they reckoned it their noblest feast to provide in the best manner for those that were to be their fellow-combatants. And when Gobryas rose up to go to his house, he is reported to have said:

" It is no longer a wonder to me, Cyrus, that we possess these fine vessels, gold, and rich habits, in greater abundance than you do, and that we are much less deserving than you are; for we do our endeavours to obtain as many of these things as we can, and your endeavours are to make yourselves the most excellent men." Thus he spoke; and Cyrus said: " Take care, Gobryas, to attend in the morning with your horse, ready in arms, that we may see your force, and at the same time, that you may conduct us through your territory, that we may know what we are to reckon belonging to our friends, and what to our enemies."

And having thus discoursed, they parted, each retiring to his proper business.

When day came, Gobryas attended with his horse, and led them the way. But Cyrus, as became a commander, was not only attentive to his present march, but as he advanced, considered whether it was in his power, by any means, to distress and weaken the enemy, and to strengthen themselves. Calling, therefore, the Hyrcanian and Gobryas to him, for he judged that these understood best the things that he thought it necessary for him to be informed of —" My friends," said he, " I do not think that I am in the wrong, when I consult with you on the subject of this war, as with men that are faithful and true; for I find that it is more your business than mine to take care that the Assyrian do not get the better of us: I, perhaps, though I fail in my undertaking here, may yet have a farther resource; but if he get the better, I see that all is lost for you. He is, indeed, my enemy, but not out of any hatred he bears me, but because he thinks it a damage to himself that we should be considerable, and this was the reason he made war on us. But you he hates, and by you he thinks himself unjustly dealt with." To this they both answered: " That he should proceed as he intended, and as concluding that they were convinced of what he said, and under the greatest care and concern for the turn that the present state of their affairs might take." Here then he thus began: " Tell me," said he, does the Assyrian think that you are the only people at enmity with him? or do you know any body else that is his enemy?" "Yes, by Jove!" said the Hyrcanian, "the Cadusians are his enemies in the highest degree, and are a strong and numerous people: the Sacians too, that are our borderers, and who have undergone a great many hardships under the Assyrian, for he endeavoured to subdue them as he did us.' "Do not you think, therefore," said he, "that they would both, with pleasure, fall on the Assyrian, in conjunction with us?" "With a great deal of pleasure," said they, "if they could join us." What is there then between," said he, "to hinder our joining?" "The Assyrians," said they; "the very nation that you are now marching through."

After Cyrus had heard this—" Well, Gobryas," said he, "do you not charge this young man that is now established as king with great pride and insolence of temper?" "Yes," said Gobryas, "for I have suffered by him accordingly." "And has he then," said Cyrus, "been so only to you? or has he been so to others besides?" "By Jove!" said Gobryas, "to many others. But what need I mention the wrongs he has done to the inconsiderable? There is one man abundantly more powerful than myself, on whose son, being his companion, as mine was, and drinking with him at his own house, he inflicted a most serious injury; because, as some say, his courtesan had commended him as a handsome man, and pronounced that woman happy who was to be his wife. But, as he himself now says, it was because he had made advances to his courtesan. This man, however, since the death of his father, holds that government." "Do you not think, therefore," said he, "that this man would see us with pleasure if he thought we would support him?" "I know it very well," said Gobryas: "but to come at the sight of him, Cyrus, is a difficult matter." "How so?" said Cyrus. "Because if any one has a mind to join him, one must pass by Babylon itself." "And what difficulty then is there in this?" "The difficulty, by Jove!" said Gobryas, "is, that the forces that belong to that place alone, I know to be much greater than those you have at present with you; and be assured that the Assyrians are now less forward than before to bring you arms and horses; for this reason, that your force appears to be but little to those that have had a view of it; and the discourse

of this has been already much spread abroad among them. So it seems to me," said he, "to be best for us to be on our guard, and cautious to our march."

Cyrus hearing this from Gobryas, spoke to him in this manner:

"In my opinion, Gobryas, you say very well when you bid us take the safest course we can with respect to our march: and therefore, on consideration, I am not able to find that any other march is safer for us than that to Babylon itself, if the principal strength of the enemy lies there; for you say they are very numerous; and, if they are in spirit, then I say they will be terrible to us. By not seeing us therefore, and by imagining that it is our fear of them that keeps us from appearing; be assured," said he, "that they will be released from the fear that has been on them; courage will spring up in its stead, and a courage that will be so much the greater, as they are the longer without seeing us. If we march instantly up to them, we shall find many of them lamenting for those that we have killed, many still bound up by reason of the wounds they received from our people, and all of them still well remembering the boldness of this army as well as their own misfortune and flight. And be assured, Gobryas, of this besides, that a multitude, when they are in spirit by leading to the such a courage as nothing can withstand; but when they are in fear, they bring on themselves such a terror as is the greater, and strikes on them so much the more as they are the more in number: for it falls on them, increased by numerous stories of misfortune, and gathers to a head from many unhappy circumstances, and from multitudes of dejected and astonished looks. So that it grows to such a height, that it is no easy matter either to suppress it by any discourse, or to raise a spirit by leading to the enemy, or to nurse up a courage by retreating; but the more you exhort them to confidence, they imagine themselves to be in so much the more dangerous circumstances. And now let us examine strictly into this particular farther. And indeed if victories from henceforward are acts to be performed only by that party that can reckon the greatest numbers, you are in the right to fear for us, and we are in reality in dangerous circumstances. But if engagements, as heretofore they have been, are still decided by good combatants, you will not be at all in the wrong to be of good heart; for with the help of the gods, you will find more amongst us that are forward to engage than amongst them. And that you may be still more in spirit, consider this: that the enemies are at this time much weaker than they were before they were beaten by us, and still weaker than when they fled from us; but we are more in vigour since we have been victorious, and stronger since you have joined us: for do not still think contemptuously of your people, now that they are with us; for be assured, Gobryas, that they that attend the victorious, follow with confidence: nor let this escape your notice," said he, "that the enemy is now at full liberty to see us; but we cannot, by any means, make our appearance with greater terror to them than by our marching up to them. As this therefore is my fixed opinion, do you lead us directly the way to Babylon."

III. So marching on, they reached the boundaries of Gobryas' territory on the fourth day. When he had got into the enemy's country, he took the foot to himself, and as many of the horse as he thought proper, and formed them. The rest of the horse he sent out on excursions: he ordered them to kill those that were in arms, but to bring the rest to him, together with whatever sheep or cattle they should take. He ordered out the Persians likewise on this service with the others; and many of them returned, after having got falls from their horses; but many of them brought off considerable booty. When the booty arrived, and that he had called together the commanders of the Medes and Hyrcanians, together with the alike-honoured, he spoke thus:

"Gobryas, my friends, has entertained us all with good things in great abundance: therefore," said he, "after having taken out what is due to the gods, and what will be sufficient for the army, if we should give the remainder of the booty to him, we should do a handsome thing, by making it immediately appear that we endeavour in benefits to exceed our benefactors."

When they had heard this they all commended and applauded it; and one of them spoke thus: "This we will do, Cyrus," said he, "by all means; for I believe that Gobryas took us for beggarly people, because we came not with daricks in abundance, and do not drink out of golden cups; but if we do this that you propose, he may then understand that it is possible to be generous, even without gold. Go,

then," said he, "and having delivered to the magi what is due to the gods, and taken what is sufficient for the army, call Gobryas, and give him the remainder."

So these men, having taken as much as was proper, gave the rest to Gobryas. On this he marched on to Babylon itself, making the same disposition as when he fought: and the Assyrians declining to come out against him, Cyrus commanded Gobryas to ride on before, and to declare that if the king were willing to come out and fight for his territory, he would fight him; but if he would not defend his territory, that then of necessity he was to submit to his conquerors. Gobryas, riding on as far as it was safe, notified these things. And the other sent out one to return him an answer in this manner:

"Gobryas, your sovereign says to you thus: that I have killed your son, I do not repent; but I repent that I have not killed you likewise! If you would fight, come hither on the thirtieth day from hence: we are at this time not at leisure, for we are yet employed in our preparations."

Then Gobryas said: "May that repentance never quit you! for it is plain I am a torment to you, from the moment that this repentance takes place."

Gobryas brought back the message from the Assyrian; and Cyrus having heard it, drew off the army; and calling Gobryas to him—"Tell me," said he, "did you not say that you thought a certain person who had been seriously injured by the Assyrian would take part with us?" "I think I know it very well," said he; "for he and I have often conferred together with great freedom." "When you think it proper therefore do you go to him; and, in the first place, you must manage so as to know what he says on the subject; and when you have conferred with him, if you find him inclined to be our friend, you must then contrive that his friendship for us may be kept concealed; for no one can by any other means do greater service to his friends in war, than by appearing to be their enemy; nor can he by any other means do greater mischief to his enemy than by appearing to be their friend." "I know indeed," said Gobryas, "that Gadatas would pay any price to do some considerable mischief to the Assyrian king: but then we must consider what it is that he can do." "Tell me, then," said Cyrus, "that fortress that lies on the frontiers of this country, and that you say was built as a barrier and defence to it, in war against the Hyrcanians and Sacians; do you think," said he, "that the commander of it would admit Gadatas into it if he came thither with his forces?" "Certainly," said Gobryas, "if he came unsuspected as he now is." "Therefore," said he, "he would stand the clearest from all suspicion, if I should fall on the places that are in his possession, as intending to make myself master of them, and he should act with his forces against me; if I should take something of his, and he on the other side should take either some others of our people, or some of those messengers that I send to such people as you say are enemies to the Assyrian; and if the people so taken declare that they were going to get forces, and to fetch ladders for the attack of the fortress; and if Gadatas then pretend, that on hearing these things, he attended him with intention to give him an account of them——"

Then Gobryas said, "If these things are thus transacted, I know very well that he would admit him, and would beg him to stay till you were gone." "And then," said Cyrus, "if he were once got in, could he not give up the fortress into our hands?" "Very probably," said Gobryas, "if he prepared matters within, and you brought a considerable strength on them from without." "Go, then," said he, "and after you have given him your instructions and accomplished these matters, endeavour to be here with us again: but as for his securities of our keeping faith with him, I desire you would neither mention nor intimate to him any greater than those that you yourself received from us."

On this Gobryas went his way. Gadatas seeing him, with great pleasure consented in every thing, and settled with him the things that were proper to be done.

And when Gobryas brought back an account that the whole business of his errand was firmly settled and agreed with Gadatas, then the next day Cyrus fell on him. He defended himself against the attack: the place that Cyrus took was that that Gadatas had appointed: of the messengers that Cyrus sent, directing them beforehand which way they should go, some Gadatas suffered to escape, that they might bring forces and fetch ladders; but those that he took he put to the torture before a great many people; and when he had heard what they declared to be the business they went about, he immediately prepared all things, and marched in the night, as intending to go and give an account of it: to conclude, he was trusted, and he entered the fortress as an assistant in defence of it: for a while he concurred with the governor in all preparations as far as he was able; but when Cyrus came up he seized the fortress, making the prisoners he had taken from Cyrus his assistants in the work.

When this was accomplished, Gadatas, having settled matters within, came out immediately to Cyrus, and having paid him his adoration in the accustomed manner, he said: "Happiness, O Cyrus, and joy to you!" "I have it," said he, "already; for, with the help of the gods, you not only bespeak joy to me, but you oblige me to rejoice: for be assured," said he, "I take it to be a thing of great importance to leave this place to my friends and allies in these parts. Your having of children, Gadatas, is what the Assyrian, it seems, has rendered hopeless; but the power of acquiring friends he has not deprived you of; and be assured that, by this action, you have made friends of us, who will endeavour, if we are able, to be as good supporters to you as if you had sons or posterity." Thus he spoke.

On this the Hyrcanian, who had just got notice of what had happened, ran to Cyrus, and taking him by the right hand, said: "O how great a blessing, Cyrus, are you to your friends! what a debt of gratitude and thanks do you bring me under to the gods, for having united me to you!" "Go then, presently," said Cyrus, "and take possession of the place you are so pleased with me for, and dispose of it in such a manner as it may be of most advantage to your own nation and to our other allies; but chiefly," said he, "to Gadatas, here, who has taken it, and delivered it up to us." "Therefore," said the Hyrcanian, "when the Cadusians, the Sacians, and my countrymen are come, shall we call in this man too, that all we who are concerned may consult in common how we may make use of this fortress to the best advantage?" Cyrus applauded the proposal; and when all that were concerned in the affair of this fortress were met, they jointly determined that it should be kept by those who had an advantage by its being in their interest, that it might be a bulwark and defence to them, and their rampart against the Assyrians. When this was done the Cadusians engaged with much more readiness and zeal in the service, as did likewise the Sacians and Hyrcanians; and from that time there was formed an army of Cadusians, consisting of twenty thousand shield-men, and four thousand horse; of Sacians, an army consisting of ten thousand bowmen on foot, and two thousand on horseback. The Hyrcanians sent out all the foot that they were able, and filled up their horse to the number of two thousand; for most of their horse were at first left behind, because the Cadusians and Sacians were enemies to the Assyrians. And all the time that Cyrus lay employed about the regulating this fortress, many of the Assyrians in those parts brought horses, and many brought arms, being afraid of all their neighbours.

On this Gadatas comes to Cyrus, and tells him that there were messengers arrived, who told him that the Assyrian, when he was informed of what had passed in the affair of the fortress, was extremely incensed, and made preparations to fall on his territory. "Therefore, Cyrus, if you would dismiss me, I would endeavour to save my places of strength: of the rest I make less account." Then Cyrus said: "If you set out now, when shall you be at home?" And Gadatas said: "I shall sup in my own territory the third day." "And do you think," said he, "that you will find the Assyrian already there?" "I know very well," said he, "that I shall; for he will make so much the more haste, as he thinks you to be at the greater distance." "And in how many days," said Cyrus, "might I get thither with the army?" To this Gadatas said: "O my sovereign! you have a very great army, and you would not be able to reach my habitation in less than six or seven days." "Do you then," said Cyrus, "go your way as soon as you can, and I will march with all possible despatch."

Gadatas then went his way, and Cyrus called together all the commanders of his allies; and he seemed now to have a great many, and full of courage; and in their presence he spoke to this effect: "Friends and allies! Gadatas has performed such things as we all judge to be of very great value to us, and this before he has received the least advantage whatever at our hands. It is reported that the Assyrian is now fallen on his territory with design, it is evident, both to be revenged of him, because he thinks himself to have been highly injured by him, and perhaps he considers withal that if they that revolt to us receive no hurt or damage from him, and if they that take part with him are destroyed by us, he must probably very soon have nobody that will stand by him; therefore, friends, we shall do in my opinion a very handsome thing if we yield our assistance with readiness and zeal to Gadatas, a man who has been our benefactor; we should besides do an act of justice, by discharging a debt of gratitude; and in my opinion we should at the same time do what would be of advantage to ourselves: for if we make it appear that we endeavour to outdo in injuries those that are injurious and hurtful to us, and to exceed our benefactors in good services, it is probable that by means of such conduct many will be willing to be friends to us, and nobody will desire to be our enemy; but if we appear neglectful of Gadatas, in the name of all the gods, with what arguments can we persuade others to do us any kindnesses? how can we dare to commend ourselves? and how can any of us possibly look Gadatas in the face, if we are outdone by him in good offices?—we, who are so many, by him who is a single man, and a man in such circumstances?"

Thus he spoke, and they all highly approved it. "Come on, then," said he, "since you agree with me in opinion. Let every man of us leave, with the carriages and with the beasts of burden, those that are the most proper to march with them, and let Gobryas command and conduct them; for he is skilled in the roads, and able in every other respect. Let us march with the best of our men and horse, taking necessaries with us for three days; and the lighter and more frugal provision we make, the pleasanter shall we dine and sup, and the pleasanter shall we sleep on the days that follow after. Now let our march be in this manner: let Chrysantas, in the first place, lead those that wear corslets, with all the centurions in front, since the way is level and open; and let each century march one by one in a line; for, by keeping in close order, we shall march with the more despatch and the more safety. And it is for this reason that I order those that have corslets to lead, because they make the heaviest part of the army; and when the heaviest lead the way, of necessity all the lighter follow with ease; but when the lighter and nimbler part leads in the night, it is not at all to be wondered at that the forces disperse; for the body that is at the head runs off from the rest. After these," said he, "let Artabazus lead the Persian shield-men and archers : after these, let Andranicas the Mede lead the Median foot: after these, Embas the Armenian foot: after these, Artuchas the Hyrcanians : after these, Thambradas the Sacian foot : after these, Damatas the Cadusians. Let all these lead with their centurions in front, and with their shield-men on the right, and their archers on the left of their own oblong bodies ; for by marching in this manner they are the more ready for service. After these," said he, "let the baggage servants of the whole army follow. Let their commanders take care of them all, that they have all things ready put up before they sleep, that they attend early in the morning in their appointed posts, and follow in an orderly manner. After the baggage servants," said he, "let Madatas the Persian lead the Persian horse, and let him likewise have the centurions of horse in front ; and let the centurion lead his century in a line one after another, in the same manner as the officers of foot. After these, let Rambacas the Mede lead his horse in the same manner. After these, do you, Tigranes, lead your own horse ; and so the rest of the commanders of horse, the horse that each of them joined us with. After these, let the Sacians march ; and the Cadusians, as they came in to us the last, so let them bring up the rear of the whole army. And do you, Alceuna, that command them, take care to be in the rear of all, and do not suffer any to be behind your horse. And do you, commanders, and all you that are wise, take care to march silently ; for it is by means of the ears, rather than the eyes, that all things must of necessity be discovered and transacted in the night. And to be put into disorder is a thing of worse consequence than in the day, and more difficult to be recovered. For this reason silence must be kept and order preserved. And when you are to settle the night-watches, you ought always to make them as short and as many as is possible, that much watching on the night-guard may not exhaust and disable any one for the march ; and when the time comes for marching, the signal must be given by the sound of the horn. And do you all attend ready on the road to Babylon, each of you with all things proper. And let him that advances before always exhort the man behind him to follow."

On this they went to their tents, and in going discoursed among themselves how great a memory Cyrus had, and how he gave his orders, naming all the persons that he gave directions to. This Cyrus did out of his great care and exactness ; for he thought it very strange that mean artificers should each of them know the names of the tools belonging to their art ; and that a physician should know the names of all the medicines and instruments that he uses ; but that a general should be such a fool as not to know the names of the commanders that are under him, and that he must necessarily use as his instruments. And whenever he had a mind to possess himself of any thing, or to preserve it, when he had a mind to raise courage or to strike terror, or when he had a mind to do honour to any one, he thought it became him to call the men by their names. And he was of opinion, that they who thought themselves known to their commander would be the more desirous to be seen performing some noble action, and more zealous to abstain from doing any thing that was base. He thought it very foolish, when one had a mind that any thing should be done, to give orders as some masters in their private families give theirs—" Let somebody go for water—let somebody cleave the wood ;" for when such orders were given, he thought that all looked one on another, and that nobody despatched the thing that was ordered ; and that all were in fault, yet nobody was ashamed or afraid, because the blame was shared amongst several. For these reasons he named all the persons when he gave his orders. This was Cyrus' judgment in this matter.

The soldiers having taking their suppers, settled their watches, and put up all things that were proper, went to rest. When it was midnight the signal was given by the sound of the horn ; and Cyrus having told Chrysantas that he would wait in the road on the front of the army, went off, taking his servants with him. In a short time after Chrysantas came up at the head of those that wore corslets. Cyrus therefore giving him guides, ordered him to march gently on till a messenger came to him, for they were not yet all on the march. He, standing in the same place, dismissed away in order those that came up, and sent off to call forward those that were dilatory. When they were all on the march, he sent certain horsemen to Chrysantas, to tell him that all were now on the march:—" Lead on therefore with more despatch!"—He himself on horseback, putting forward towards the van, observed at leisure the several bodies, and those that he saw marching orderly and silently, he rode up to, and inquired who they were; and when he was informed, he commended them: but if he perceived any of them to be tumultuous, he inquired into the cause of it, and endeavoured to allay the disturbance.

There is only one part of his care in the night that has been omitted; which is, that at the head of the whole army he sent out certain light and expeditious foot, not many in number, that Chrysantas was to keep within the reach of his eye, and who were to keep Chrysantas within the reach of theirs; who getting notices of things by the ear, or if by any other means able to receive any intelligence, were to signify to Chrysantas what the occasion seemed to require. There was one commander over them, who kept them in order, and notified what was worthy of notice, and what was not so, he gave no disturbance by the telling. And thus he marched in the night.

But when it was day, he left the Cadusian horse with the Cadusian foot, because they marched the last, and that they might not march unprovided with horse. But the rest of the horse he ordered to push forward to the front, because the enemy were before them; and that in case any opposed him, he might meet and engage them with his forces in order under him; and that if any were seen flying, he might be in the greatest readiness for the pursuit. And he had always ready in order, both those that were to pursue, if pursuit were proper, as well as those that were to remain by him; but the general order of the whole he never suffered to be broken. Thus Cyrus led he army. He himself was not always in the same station, but riding about here and there, kept viewing, and where any thing was deficient, took care of it. Thus did Cyrus' men march.

IV. But a certain person, one of authority and consideration, belonging to Gadatas' body of horse, as soon as he saw that he had revolted from the Assyrian, concluded that if any misfortune happened to Gadatas, he himself might obtain from the Assyrian all that belonged to Gadatas. So he sent one of the most trusty of his people to the Assyrian; and he ordered the man that went, if he found the As-

syrian army already in Gadatas' territory, to tell the Assyrian, that if he would form an ambuscade, he might take Gadatas and all that were with him. He ordered the man to tell what force Gadatas had, and that Cyrus did not go with him; and he told him the road that he intended to take. Besides, that he might be the more readily trusted, he sent orders to his servants to deliver up to the Assyrian the fort that he had the possession of, in the territory of Gadatas, and all that was in it. He said that he would come himself, and if he was able, it should be after he had killed Gadatas; but if he could not do that, it should be to attend on the Assyrian for the future. When the person appointed for this service, having rode with all possible speed, was come to the Assyrian, and had declared the purpose of his coming, the Assyrian having heard it, immediately seized the fort; and having a great force, both of horse and chariots, he lay in ambuscade in certain villages that stood very close together. Gadatas, as soon as he approached these villages, sent some people to examine and make discovery. The Assyrian, when he found these scouts approaching, ordered two or three chariots and a few horse to quit their post, and betake themselves to flight, as being terrified, and but few in number. The scouts themselves, as soon as they saw this pursued, and made signs to Gadatas. He being thus deceived, pursued with all his might. The Assyrians, when they thought Gadatas within reach of being taken, broke out from their ambuscade. They that were with Gadatas, seeing this, fled, as was natural for them to do; the others likewise, as was natural, pursued. On this the contriver of this affair against Gadatas struck at him, but missed the mortal blow, hit him on the shoulder, and wounded him; and having done this, he made off to join the pursuers. When it was known who he was, he, pressing his horse on with a great deal of zeal, in company with the Assyrians, attended the pursuit with the king. It is plain that on this occasion they that had the slowest horses were taken by those that had the fleetest. And all Gadatas' horse, having before been harassed by their march, were quite spent. When they saw Cyrus advancing with his army, one must needs think they made up to them with as much joy and pleasure as if they were entering a harbour after a storm.

Cyrus was at first astonished; but when he

understood what the matter was, he led the army forward, in order, during the whole time that all these men that faced him were riding up towards him. But when the enemy, understanding how things were, turned and fled, then Cyrus commanded those that were appointed to that purpose to pursue. He himself followed with the rest, in the manner that he thought proper. On this occasion several chariots were taken, some by means of the drivers falling off, and this partly by being overturned, partly by other means, and some were taken by being intercepted by the horse; and they killed a great many, and amongst them the man that struck Gadatas. Of the Assyrian foot that were besieging the fortress of Gadatas, some fled to the fort that had revolted from Gadatas, and some escaped to a considerable city that belonged to the Assyrian, and whither the Assyrian himself, with his chariots and horses, fled.

Cyrus having done this, retired into the territory of Gadatas, and having given his orders to the proper persons on the subject of the prisoners, he presently went to see how Gadatas was of his wound; and as he was going Gadatas met him with his wound already bound up. Cyrus was pleased at the sight of him, and said, " I was going to see how you did." " And I, by the gods !" said Gadatas, "was going again to view the outward form of the man who has such a soul ! you who are not, that I know, in any manner of need of me; who never promised to do these things for me; who, as to your own particular, never received any benefit whatever from me: and only because I was thought to have done a service to your friends, have so affectionately assisted me. So that, as far as I was concerned myself, I had now perished, but am by your means saved. By the gods, Cyrus! if I had children, I do not think that I could ever have a son so affectionate to me. For I know this present king of the Assyrians particularly to have been the cause of more affliction to his father than he can be now to you, and many other sons the same."

To this Cyrus said: " Now, Gadatas, do you admire me, and pass by a much greater wonder?" " And what is that ?" said Gadatas. " That so many Persians," said he, "have been so diligent in your service, so many Medes, so many Hyrcanians, as well as all these Armenians, Sacians, and Cadusians, here present."

Then Gadatas made this prayer: " O Jove! may the gods bestow many blessings on them, but most on him who is the cause of their being such men! And that we may handsomely entertain these men that you commend, Cyrus, accept these presents of friendship, which are such as I am able to tender you." At the same time he brought him great abundance and variety of things, that he might make a sacrifice, if he pleased, or entertain the whole army suitably to things so nobly performed, and so happily succeeding.

Meanwhile the Cadusian still made the rear-guard, and had no share in the pursuit; but being desirous to perform something himself that was conspicuous, he made an excursion into the territory of Babylon, without communicating it, or saying any thing of it to Cyrus. But the Assyrian, from that city of his, whither he had fled, and with his army entirely together, and in order, coming up with the horse of the Cadusian that were dispersed, as soon as he knew them to be the Cadusians alone, attacks them, kills their commander and a great many others, takes a great many horses, and takes from them the booty that they were carrying off. The Assyrian then, after having pursued as far as he thought it safe, turned back, and the Cadusians made their escape to the camp, where the first of them arrived towards the evening.

Cyrus, as soon as he perceived what had happened, went and met the Cadusians, and of all that he saw wounded, some he took and sent to Gadatas, that they might be taken care of, and others he lodged together in tents, and took care that they had all things necessary, taking some of the Persian alike-honoured to be his assistants ; for on such occasions men of worth are willing to bestow their joint pains : he evidently appeared to be extremely afflicted; so that while others were taking their suppers, when the time for it was come, Cyrus, attended by servants and physicians, willingly left no one neglected, but either saw with his own eyes, or if he could not despatch all himself, he was observed to send others to take that care of them. Thus then they went to rest.

As soon as it was day, having made proclamation that the commanders of the other nations, and all the Cadusians in general, should assemble, he spoke to this effect: " Friends and allies ! the misfortune that has happened to us is what human nature is liable to; for, in my opinion, it is not to be wondered at, that being men, we should be guilty of error. However, we are not unworthy of reaping some advantage by this accident; and that is to learn never to separate from the whole a smaller force than that of the enemy. Yet I do not say," said he, "that we are never to march where it is proper, with a part, even yet less than the Cadusian marched with on this occasion. But if a man march after having concerted matters with another, who is able to support him, he may indeed be deceived; but he that remains behind, by deceiving the enemy, may turn them to another part, and out of the way of those that have marched off; it is possible for him to procure safety to his friends, by giving other employment to his enemies; and thus, he that separates does not become entirely disjoined, but remains annexed to the main strength of the whole. He on the other hand, that marches off without giving any information whither it is that he is going, is in the same case as if he made war alone. But," said he, "if it please the gods, it shall not be long before we have our revenge of the enemy, in return for this. And as soon as ever you have dined I will lead you out to the place where this affair was transacted; we will bury our dead at the same time, if it please the gods; we will let the enemy see men superior to themselves, on the very place where they think they have been victorious, that they may not look with pleasure on that spot of ground where they butchered our fellow-combatants. If they will not come out to us, we will burn their villages and destroy their country, that they may not be delighted, on viewing what they themselves have done, but be afflicted at the sight of their own misfortunes. Let the rest then," said he, "go and take their dinners; and do you, Cadusians, first go your ways, and choose you a commander according to your usage, who, with the help of the gods, and together with us, shall take care of you in whatever may be wanting to you; and when you have made your choice and taken your dinners, then send the person you have chosen to me."

These men did accordingly. And Cyrus, when he had led out the army, and placed the person who was chosen by the Cadusians in his station, ordered him to lead his body of men near to himself, "That if we are able," said he, "we may recover the courage of the men."

So they marched, and coming up to the place, they buried the Cadusians, and laid the country waste. And having done this, and supplied themselves with necessaries out of the enemy's country, they again retreated into the territory of Gadatas.

But then, considering that they who had revolted to him, being in the neighbourhood of Babylon, would suffer severely, unless he himself was always at hand, he therefore commanded all those of the enemy that he dismissed to tell the Assyrian, that he himself sent a herald to declare to him that he was ready to let the labourers that were employed in the culture of the lands alone, and not to do them any injury; if he, on the other side, would allow such labourers as belonged to those that had revolted to himself to go on with their work; and indeed," said he, "if you are able to hinder them, you will hinder but a few, for the land that belongs to those that have revolted to me is but little; and on the other hand, I should allow a great quantity of land to be cultivated for you. Then at the time of gathering the crop, if the war continues, he that is superior in arms, in my opinion, must gather it. If there be peace, it is plain," said he, "that it must be you; but if any of my people use arms against you, or any of yours against me, on these we will both of us return mutual hostilities, if we can." Having given the herald these orders, he sent him away.

And when the Assyrians had heard these things, they did all that they were able to persuade the king to yield to them, and to leave as little of the war remaining as was possible. The Assyrian, either at the persuasion of those of his nation, or inclined to it himself, consented: and agreements were made, that there should be peace to those that were employed in labour, and war to those that bore arms. These things did Cyrus effect with respect to the labouring people. But the pastures of their cattle he ordered his own friends to settle, if they thought fit, within the extent of their own power, and to make prey on the enemy wherever they were able, that the service might be more agreeable to his allies; for the dangers were the same, even without their seizing necessaries for their subsistence; and the maintaining themselves on the enemy seemed to make the service the lighter.

But when Cyrus was now preparing to be gone, Gadatas came to him, having collected presents of all kinds, and in great abundance, as arising from a very great estate, and having taken a great many horses from his own horse-men that he mistrusted, on account of the late contrivance against him ; and when he accosted him, he spoke thus : " I bring you these things, Cyrus, at this time, that you may make pre-sent use of them in case you want them. And count on it," said he, " that all things else that belong to me are yours ; for I am not likely to have one descended from myself to leave my estate to ; but my race and name," said he, " will be extinguished with myself when I die. And this I suffer, Cyrus," said he, " (I swear it to you, by the gods, who see all things, and hear all things,) without having been guilty of any thing unjust or base, either in word or deed." At the same time that he said this, he burst out into tears at his unhappy fate, and it was not in his power to say more.

Cyrus having heard this, pitied him for his misfortune, and spoke thus : " The horses," said he, " I accept ; for I shall do you service by giving them to men better affected to you, it seems, than they who had them before ; and shall fill up the Persian body of horse to ten thousand men, a thing that I have long desired ; the rest of your valuable effects do you take away, and keep till such time as you see me in a condition not to be outdone by you in pre-sents ; for if you part with me, and your pre-sents amount to more than you receive at my hands, I know not how it is possible for me not to be quite ashamed."

To this Gadatas said : " But I trust them to you, for I see your temper. As to the keep-ing of them myself, pray see whether I am fit for it ; for, while we were friends with the Assyrian, my father's estate seemed to be the noblest that could be ; for, being near to our capital city, Babylon, we enjoyed all the ad-vantages that we could possibly be supplied with from that great city ; and as often as we were disturbed with the crowd and hurry, by retiring hither to our home, we got out of the way of it. But now that we are become ene-mies, it is plain that when you are gone, both we ourselves, and our whole family and estate, shall have contrivances formed against us. We shall, in my opinion, live very miserably, both by having our enemies just by us, and by seeing them superior to ourselves. Perhaps you will presently therefore say, and why did I not consider this before I revolted ? Why,

because, Cyrus, by means of the injuries I had received, and the anger I was in, my soul never dwelt on the consideration of what was safest for me ; but was always big with the thought, whether it would be ever in my power to take my revenge on this enemy both to the gods and men, who passes his days in hatred, and that not to the man that may have done him any in-jury, but to any one that he suspects to be a better man than himself. And this wicked wretch therefore, in my opinion, will make use of such assistants as are all more wicked than himself ; or if there be any that may appear to be better than he, take courage, Cyrus," said he, " you will not be under any necessity to engage against any such men of worth ; but he himself will be sufficient to carry on this work till he has taken off every better man than him-self ; and yet, distressing me, I am of opinion that with his villains he will easily get the better."

In all this Cyrus, who heard it, was of opin-ion that the man said what was worthy of his attention and care ; and he presently said : " And have not you therefore strengthened your fortress with a garrison, that you may make use of it with safety when you get thither ? And as to yourself, you accompany us in the service, that if the gods please to be with us, as now they are, he may be in fear of you, and not you of him. Take of what belongs to you, whatever you like to see about you ; and of your people, take whoever you like to converse with, and march with me. You will be, in my opinion, extremely useful to me, and I will en-deavour to be as useful to you as I can."

Gadatas hearing this, recovered himself, and said : " Shall I be able," said he, " to put up all, and be ready before you march away ? for," said he, " I would willingly carry my mother with me." " Yes, by Jove !" said he, " you will be ready time enough ; for I will wait till you say that all is well." So Gadatas, going his way, settled, in concert with Cyrus, garri-sons in the several fortresses he had made : he packed up all kinds of things, enough to fur-nish a very great house, in a handsome manner. He took with him from amongst those he con-fided in such whose company he was pleased with ; and many of those too that he distrusted, obliging some of them to take their wives, and some their sisters with them, that by their means he might keep them as it were in fetters.

Cyrus himself marched, and amongst the

rest of those that were about him, he kept Gadatas to inform him about the ways and the waters, about forage and provisions, that he might carry on the service with the greatest plenty of all things. But when, in the course of his march, he got sight of the city of Babylon, and fancied that the way he was going led him just under the walls of the place, he called Gobryas and Gadatas, and asked if there was any other way, that he might not lead the army near to the wall.

Then Gobryas spoke: " My sovereign, there are many ways; but I thought," said he, " that you desired to lead on as near to the city as possible, that you might show them the army, and let them see that you have now a great and a noble one; because, when you had a less you marched up to the walls, and they saw us when we were not very numerous. And now, though the Assyrian be prepared, as he told you he would be prepared to give you battle, I know that when he sees your strength, his preparations will not appear to him to be sufficient."

Cyrus to this said : " You seem to me, Gobryas, to wonder that when I came with a less army I led up to the very walls ; but that now, with a greater, I have no mind to march the army under them : but make no wonder of this," said he, " for to lead up to a place, and to march by it is not the same thing. All men lead up in such an order as they think is best for them to engage in. And people that are wise retreat so as to go off in the safest manner, and not in the quickest. But it is necessary to march by with the carriages extended in length, and with the beasts of burden, and those that are concerned in the baggage, all in loose order; all this must be covered by the soldiers that bear arms ; and the baggage-train must in no part appear to the enemy naked of arms : and, marching in this manner, the strength of the army must of necessity be extended into a thin and weak order. If then they have a mind from within the walls to make an attack, in a close, firm body, wherever they close in, they do it with a strength much superior to those that are on the march ; and to men that are marching in a train at length, the proper helps are at a great distance ; but to those that march out from within their walls, the distance is little that they have either to march up to the enemy that is at hand, or to retreat back again ; but if we pass by at no less a distance than so as that they may just see us,

and if we march extended, as we now are, they will see the multitude that we are ; and every multitude, by means of arms interwoven amongst them, appears terrible. If they really do march up to us in any part, by our seeing them at a considerable distance, we shall not be taken unprepared : and then, my friends," said he, " they will the rather avoid attacking us, when they are obliged to march a great distance from their walls, unless they think themselves, in the whole, superior to us, for they will have cause to be in fear for their retreat."

When he had said this, the persons present were of opinion that he said right, and Gobryas led the way as he had directed him. And while the army was moving on by the city, that part of it that was left behind he always made the strongest, and in that manner retreated.

When marching thus the following days, he reached the borders of the Assyrians and Medes, from whence he came before, and where there were three forts belonging to the Assyrians ; the weakest of these he attacked and took by force, and two of them, Cyrus by terror, and Gadatas by persuasion, prevailed with the garrisons to give up.

V. When he had done this he sent to Cyaxares, and by message desired him to come to the army, that they might consult what use to make of the forts they had taken ; and, after having taken a view of the army, he might, in the whole of their affairs, advise what he thought proper to be done for the future. " And if he orders it," said he, " tell him that I will come and encamp with him." The messenger in order to deliver this message went his way ; and on this Cyrus ordered Gadatas to furnish out the Assyrian's tent that the Medes had chosen for Cyaxares, and this in the handsomest manner ; and not only with all the other furniture that it was provided with, but he ordered him to introduce the two women into that apartment of the tent that belonged to the women, and together with them the women musicians that had been chosen out for Cyaxares. These men did as they were ordered. But when he that was sent to Cyaxares had delivered his message, Cyaxares, having heard him, determined it to be best that the army should remain on the borders ; for the Persians that Cyrus had sent for were come, and they were forty-thousand archers and shieldmen. Therefore, when he saw that these men did prejudice in many ways to the Median territory, he thought it better to get rid of these, rather than admit another multitude. And that Persian who commanded the army, having inquired from Cyaxares, according to the orders of Cyrus, whether he had any service for the army, when he told him that he had none, and when he heard that Cyrus was at hand, on that very day marched, and conducted the army to him. The next day Cyaxares marched with the Median horse that remained with him ; and as soon as Cyrus perceived him approaching, then taking the Persian horse, who were now very numerous, all the Medes, Armenians, and Hyrcanians, and of all the other allies, such as were best horsed and armed, he met him, and showed Cyaxares his force.

Cyaxares, when he saw a great many brave men attending Cyrus, and but a small company attending on himself, and those but of little value, thought it mean and dishonourable to him, and was seized with a violent concern. But when Cyrus, alighting from his horse, came up to him, as intending to embrace him in the customary manner, Cyaxares likewise alighted, but turned from him, refused to embrace him, and burst openly into tears. On this Cyrus ordered all the rest that were there to retire and wait. He himself, taking Cyaxares by the right hand, and conducting him out of the road under certain palm-trees, ordered some Median quilts to be laid for him, and making him sit down, he sat himself down by him, and asked him thus :

" O uncle !" said he, " tell me, I beg you by all the gods, what are you angry with me for ? And what bad thing have you discovered that you take thus amiss ?" Then Cyaxares answered in this manner : " It is, Cyrus," said he, " that I, who, as far as the memory of man can reach, am reckoned to be sprung from a long train of ancestors, and from a father who was a king, and who am myself accounted a king, should see myself marching thus meanly and contemptibly, and see you with my attendance, and with other forces, appear here great and conspicuous. I should think it hard to suffer this treatment at the hands of enemies, and much harder, O Jove ! to suffer it at the hands of those that I ought least to have it from ; for I think I could sink down under the earth ten times over with more satisfaction, than be seen in this mean condition, and see my own people thus contemning and

laughing at me : for I am not ignorant, not only that you are more considerable than myself, but that my own slaves are above me in power, dare to oppose my pleasure, and are so set up as to be rather able to do me mischief, than liable to suffer it at my hands." And, in saying this, he was still more overwhelmed in tears, so that he drew down a flood of tears into the eyes of Cyrus.

But Cyrus, pausing a little, spoke to this effect : " In all this," said he, " Cyaxares, you neither say true nor judge right. If you think that the Medes by my presence are set on such a footing as to be able to do you mischief, I do not wonder that you are enraged and terrified. But, whether it be justly or unjustly that you are offended at them, this I shall pass by : for I know you must take it ill to hear me making their apology. But for a ruler to take offence at all his people at once, this I take to be an error ; for by striking terror into a multitude, of necessity that multitude must be made one's enemies, and by taking offence at them all together, they are inspired with unity of sentiments. On this account be it known to you, it was that I would not send these men away to you without me, being afraid lest something might happen by means of your anger that might have afflicted us all. By the assistance of the gods, therefore, while I am present, these things may be safely composed. But that you should think yourself injured by me, at this I am very much concerned, that while I have been doing all that is in my power to do all possible service to my friends, I am then thought to have done quite the contrary ; but do not let us thus charge one another at random, but if possible, let us consider clearly what the injury is that I have done. I will state then an agreement for us to come to, and such as is the justest that can be between friends. If I shall appear to have done you mischief, I will confess that I have wronged you ; but if I neither appear to have done you any harm, nor to have intended it, will not you then confess that you have not been wronged by me ?" " I must," said he, " of necessity." " If I plainly appear to have done you service, and to have been zealous to do you all the service that I was able, shall not I deserve your commendation, rather than your reproach ?" " It is but just," said he. " Come on, then," said Cyrus, " let us consider all the things that I have done, one by one, for by all this it will appear the most evidently which was good and which was bad. We will take it from the beginning of this affair, if this appear to you to be sufficient. When you perceived that the enemy were assembling their forces and were about making an attempt on you and on your country, you then sent immediately to the public council of Persia, begging assistance, and to me in particular, desiring me to endeavour, if any Persians came to you, to come as their commander. Was not I by you persuaded to this? Did I not come, and bring you as many and as brave men as I was able?" "You did come," said he. "First, therefore," said he, "in this particular, tell me whether you accounted it an injury or a benefit that I did you." "It is plain," said Cyaxares, "that in this you did what was a benefit to me." "Well then," said he, "when the enemies advanced, and we were to engage them, did you perceive that on this occasion I spared any pains, or that I shunned any danger." "No, by Jove!" said he, "not at all." "And then, when, with the assistance of the gods, we gained our victory and the enemy retreated, I exhorted you that we might jointly pursue them, take our joint vengeance on them, and if any thing good or ill should befall us, that we might jointly share it? And can you charge me with any thing of ambition, and desire of power, in any of these things?" To this Cyaxares was silent, and Cyrus again spoke in this manner: "Since it is your pleasure to be silent in this, rather than to give me a reply, tell me then," said he, "whether you think yourself injured, because that, when you were of opinion that it was not safe to pursue, I did not allow you to share in the danger, but only desired you to send some of your horse? For if I wronged you in asking this, especially after giving myself up to you as an assistant and ally, let this," said he, "be demonstrated by yourself." When Cyaxares kept himself silent to this too—"But," said he, "if you will give me no answer here neither, then tell me this: whether I did you any wrong when you gave me for answer that, on your observing the Medes to be indulging themselves in pleasure, you would not put a stop to it, and oblige them to march, and run themselves into danger? and whether you think that I put a hardship on you, when, avoiding all anger and resentment to you, I then again, on that, asked you a thing, than which I knew there

was nothing that you could more easily grant, and that nothing more easy could possibly be enjoined the Medes? for I asked you only to allow any of them that would to follow me: and when I had obtained this from you, there was nothing left but to persuade them. I went to them; I persuaded them, and those that I prevailed with I took, and marched with them at your allowance. If you reckon this to be deserving of blame, then to take from you what you yourself grant, is not, it seems, a thing void of blame. Thus then we set forward. When we had marched, what was there that we did that was not apparent? Was not the camp of the enemy taken? Were there not many of those that made war on you killed? and of those that remained alive, were there not a great many stripped of their arms, and a great many of their horses? The fortunes and effects of those that plundered and ravaged yours before, you see now taken and ravaged by your friends. Some of them belong to you, and others of them to those that are under your dominion. But what is the greatest and noblest thing, and above all, is, that you see your own territory enlarged, and that of your enemies diminished; and some forts that were possessed by the enemy, and some of your own that had been taken and annexed to the Assyrian dominion, now, on the contrary, you see yielded to you. Whether any of these things be good or ill, I cannot say that I desire to learn. But nothing hinders me from hearing what your opinion is concerning them, and do you tell it me."

Cyrus, having said this, was silent, and waited the reply.

And Cyaxares spoke thus in answer. "Indeed, Cyrus, I do not know how one can say those things you have performed are ill; but be it known to you," said he, "that these good things are of such a kind, as the more they appear to be in number, so much the more are they burdensome on me. I should rather choose to enlarge your territory by my forces, than see mine thus enlarged by yours. For these things, to you that do them, are glorious, but to me they are in some sort disgraceful. And I am of opinion that I should be better pleased to bestow of these rich effects on you, than to receive from you these things that you now present me with; for I perceive myself enriched by you with things that make me the poorer; and I believe I should be less grieved to see my

M

subjects in some degree injured by you, than I am now, to see them receiving great advantages at your hands. If I appear to you to think unreasonably in this, do not consider these things as in my case, but turn the tables, and make the case your own. And then," said he, "consider that in the case of dogs, that you maintained as a guard and protection to you and yours; supposing any other person should make his court to them, and should make them better acquainted with himself than with you, whether you should be pleased with this courtship and service. But if this appear to you to be but an inconsiderable matter, then consider this : you have servants that you have acquired as guards to you, and for service; if any one should manage these in such a manner, as that they should be more willing to serve him than to serve you, should you think yourself obliged to this man, in return of this benefit? Then in another concern, that men's affections are greatly engaged in, and that they cultivate in the most intimate manner : if any one should make such court to your wife, as to make her love him better than she loved you, should you be delighted with this benefit? I believe, far from it," said he; "nay, I know that in doing this, he would do you the greatest of injuries. But that I may mention what is most applicable to my concern : if any one should make such court to the Persians, that you have conducted hither, as should make it more agreeable to them to follow him than to follow you, should you think this man your friend? I believe you would not, but you would rather think him yet more your enemy than if he killed you a great many of them. Well, then, suppose any friend of yours, on your saying to him in a friendly way, Take as much of what belongs to me as you please, should, hearing this, go his way, take all that he was able, and enrich himself with what belonged to you, and that you, meanwhile, should not have wherewithal to supply your own uses in a very moderate way; could you possibly think such a one a blameless unexceptionable friend? Now, Cyrus, I take myself to have had from you, if not the same usage, yet such as is very like it. You say true, that when I bade you carry off those that were willing to go, you took my whole force, went off with them, and left me destitute; and now you bring me things that you have taken with my own force, and with my own force you enlarge my territory. But I, as not having

any hand in obtaining these advantages, look as if I gave up myself like a woman, to be served by others as well as by my own subjects; for you appear to be the man, and I to be unworthy of rule; and do you take these things, Cyrus to be benefits? Be it known to you, if you had any concern for me, there is nothing you would be so careful not to rob me of as my dignity and honour. What advantage is it to me to have my land extended and myself contemned? I have dominion over the Medes, not by being really the best of them all, but by means of their thinking us to be, in all respects superior to themselves."

Here Cyrus took up the discourse, while Cyaxares was yet speaking, and said : "I beg you, uncle," said he, "by all the gods, if I ever before did any thing that was agreeable to you, now gratify me now in the things that I shall ask of you. Give over blaming me at this time; and when you have had experience of us, how we are affected towards you, if the things that have been done appear done for your service, give me your embraces in return for the affection I have for you, and think that I have been of service to you. If things appear otherwise, then blame me."

"Perhaps, indeed," said Cyaxares," you say right." "Well, then," said Cyrus, "shall I kiss you?" "If you please," said he. "And will you not turn from me, as you did just now?" "I will not," said he. Then he kissed him.

As soon as this was seen by the Medes and Persians, and many others, for they were all under concern about the issue of this affair, they all presently became cheerful and pleased.

Then Cyaxares and Cyrus, mounting their horses, led the way : the Medes followed after Cyaxares; for Cyrus made a sign to them to do so; and the Persians followed Cyrus, and after these followed the rest. When they came to the camp, and had lodged Cyaxares in the tent that was furnished for him, they that were appointed to that service prepared all things fitting for him. And during the time that Cyaxares was at leisure, before supper, the Medes went to him, some of themselves, but most of them in consequence of directions from Cyrus, and they brought him presents; one a beautiful cup-bearer, another an excellent cook, another a baker, another a musician, one brought him cups, and another a fine habit. And almost every one presented him with something out of what they had taken; so that Cyaxares changed his opinion, and no longer thought either that Cyrus had alienated these men from him, or that the Medes were less observant of him than before.

When the time of supper came, Cyaxares invited Cyrus, and desired that, since he had not seen him for some time, he would sup with him; but Cyrus said: "I beg, Cyaxares, that you would not bid me do this. Do you not observe that all those that are here with us attend here at our instigation? It would not therefore be well in me to appear negligent of them, and mindful of my own pleasure. When soldiers think themselves neglected, the best of them become much more dejected, and the worst of them much more insolent. But do you, especially now after you have had a long journey, take your supper; and if people come to pay you respect, receive them kindly, and entertain them well, that they likewise may encourage you. I will go my ways, and apply myself to what I tell you. To-morrow," said he, " in the morning, all the proper persons shall attend here, at your doors, that we may consult together what we are to do henceforward. And you being yourself present, will propose to us, whether it be thought fit to go on with the war, or whether it be now the proper time to separate the army." On this Cyaxares went to supper.

And Cyrus, assembling such of his friends as were most able to judge what was fit to be done on any occasion, and to assist him in the execution of it, spoke to this effect: " The things that we at first wished for, my friends, we now, with the assistance of the gods, have obtained; for wherever we march, we are masters of the country: we see our enemies weakened, and ourselves increased in numbers and strength. And if they who are now our allies will still continue with us, we shall be much more able to succeed in our affairs, whether we have occasion to act by force, or whether it be proper to proceed by persuasion; therefore, that as many of our allies as is possible may be inclined to stay, is not more my business to effect than it is yours. But as, when fighting is necessary, he that subdues the greatest numbers will be accounted the most vigorous; so where counsel is necessary, he that makes the greatest numbers to be of his opinion ought justly to be esteemed the most eloquent and best skilled in affairs. However, do not be at pains, as if you were to show us what sort of discourse you made use of to every one, but that the people you prevail with may show it in their actions, let this be your business to effect. And that the soldiers, while they consult about the carrying on of the war, shall be supplied with all things necessary and fit, in as great plenty as I am able, this I will endeavour to take care of."

XENOPHON

ON THE

INSTITUTION OF CYRUS.

BOOK VI.

CONTENTS of BOOK VI.

INSTITUTION OF CYRUS.

BOOK VI.

I. HAVING passed the day in this manner, and having taken their suppers, they went to rest. The next day, in the morning, all the allies came to the doors of Cyaxares; and while Cyaxares (who had heard that there was a great multitude of people at his doors) was setting himself out, Cyrus' friends presented to him several people, who begged him to stay; some presented the Cadusians, some the Hyrcanians; one presented Gobryas, and another the Sacian; and Hystaspes presented Gadatas, who begged Cyrus to stay. Here Cyrus, who knew before that Gadatas had been almost killed with fear lest the army should be separated, laughed, and spoke thus: "O Gadatas!" said he, "it is plain that you have been persuaded by Hystaspes here to be of the opinion you express." Then Gadatas, lifting up his hands to heaven, swore, that "indeed he was not persuaded by Hystaspes to be of this opinion; but I know," said he, "that if you depart, my affairs fall entirely to ruin. On this account," said he, "I came myself to this man, and asked him whether he knew what your opinion was concerning the separation of the army." Then Cyrus said: "It seems then that I accuse Hystaspes unjustly?" Then Hystaspes spoke: "By Jove, Cyrus!" said he, "unjustly indeed; because I gave Gadatas for answer, that it was impossible for you to stay, and told him that your father had sent for you." "What?" said Cyrus, "durst you assert this, whether I would or no?" "Yes, indeed," said he; "for I see you are exceedingly desirous to be making a progress about among the Persians, to be seen and to show your father how you performed every thing." Then Cyrus said, "And are you not desirous to go home?" "No, by Jove!" said Hystaspes, "nor will I go, but stay and discharge my duty as a commander till I

make Gadatas here master of the Assyrian." Thus did these men with a mixture of seriousness, jest with each other.

Then Cyaxares, dressed in a magnificent manner, came out, and sat himself on a Median throne; and when all the proper persons were met, and silence made, Cyaxares spoke thus: "Friends and allies! since I am here present, and am an older man than Cyrus, it is proper for me perhaps to begin the discourse. It appears therefore to me, that now is the time to debate whether it be thought proper to go on with the war, or to separate the army. Therefore," said he, "let somebody speak what his opinion is concerning this affair." On this the Hyrcanian first spoke: "Friends and allies! I do not at all know whether words be necessary where facts themselves declare what is best to be done; for we all know that by keeping together we do more mischief to our enemies than we suffer from them; and, when we are asunder, they deal by us as is most agreeable to them, and most grievous to us." After him spoke the Cadusian: "What can we say," said he, "concerning a general departure and separation, when it is not for our interest to separate, even while we are engaged in the service? accordingly, we not long ago undertook a piece of service separate from the rest of our body, and paid for it as you all know."

After him Artabazus, he who had said that he was related to Cyrus, spoke thus: "Cyaxares," said he, "thus much I differ in my opinion from those who spoke before. They say that we ought to proceed in the war, remaining here together; and I say that we were in war when we were at home, for I was frequently forced to run to the relief of our own country when the enemies were plundering what belonged to us: frequently I had business on my hands, with respect to our fortresses, that the enemies were said to have formed designs on, and I was continually in fear, and kept myself on my guard. All this I did, and was all this while on expense out of my own stock; but now I am in possession of the fortresses of the enemy, I am not in fear of them: I feast on what belongs to them, and I drink at the enemy's expense; therefore, as being in one case at war, and in the other case as at a festival, I am not of opinion to dissolve this public assembly." After him spoke Gobryas: "Friends and allies! thus far I applaud the faith of Cyrus, for he has been false in nothing that he has promised. But, if he quit the country, it is plain that the Assyrian will be at rest, and escape the punishment due to him for the injuries that he endeavoured to do you, and that he has in fact done me; and I, on my side, shall again suffer punishment at his hands, and now it will be for having been a friend to you."

After all these Cyrus spoke. "Nor am I ignorant, friends, that if we separate the army our own affairs will sink, and the affairs of the enemy will rise again; for as many of them as have had their arms taken from them will make others out of hand; they that have lost their horses will immediately get others; in the room of those men that are killed others will grow up and succeed them; so that it will not be to be wondered at if they become able to give us disturbance again very soon. Why then did I desire Cyaxares to propose the debate on the separation of the army? Be it known to you," said he, "it was because I was in fear for the future; for I perceive certain adversaries advancing on us, that, if we go on with the war on the footing we now stand, we shall not be able to struggle with: for the winter is coming on; and if we have roofs to cover our own heads, we have them not, by Jove! for our horses, nor for our servants, nor for the common soldiers; and without these we cannot proceed in the service. The provisions, wherever we have come, have been consumed by ourselves, and where we have not been, there, for fear of us, they have been carried off and secured in fortresses; so that the enemies have them, and we are not able to procure them. And who is there that has bravery and vigour enough to go on with the service, and struggle at the same time with hunger and cold? Therefore, if we are to continue the war

on these terms, I say that we ought rather to separate the army of our own accord than be driven away against our wills by distress, and by not knowing what to do. But, if we have a mind to go on still with the war, I say we ought to do this: we should endeavour, as soon as possible, to take from the enemy as many of their strong places as we are able, and to erect as many places of strength as we can for ourselves. For if this be done, then they will have provisions in the greatest plenty who can take and secure the most of them, and they that are inferior in strength will be besieged. But now we are just in the same case with those that are on a voyage at sea; for the part that they have sailed over they do not leave so as to make it safer for them than the other part that they have not sailed; but if we have fortresses, these will alienate the territory from the enemy, and all things will be with us serene and quiet. As for what some of you may be apprehensive of, in case you are obliged to keep garrison at a distance from your own territory, do not let this be any concern to you; for we will take on us to guard those parts that are the nearest to the enemy, since we are at a great distance from home. And do you take possession of the borders between you and the Assyrian territory, and cultivate them. And if we are able to guard and preserve those parts that are in the enemy's neighbourhood, you who keep those other parts that are at a greater distance from them will certainly live in great peace and quiet; for I do not believe that they can think of forming designs on you that are at a distance, and neglect dangers that are at hand."

After this had been said, all the rest of them rising up, declared that they would join heartily in putting these things in execution. And Cyaxares, Gadatas, and Gobryas said, that if the allies would give them leave they would each of them build a fort, that the allies might have those places in their interest. Cyrus therefore, when he saw them all so zealous in the execution of the things he had mentioned, concluded thus: "If we intend therefore to effect what we agree ought to be done, we ought, as soon as possible, to be supplied with engines to demolish the forts of the enemy, and with builders to erect bulwarks of our own." On this Cyaxares promised to make and supply them with one engine; Gadatas and Gobryas promised another; Tigranes another and another Cyrus said that he would endeavour to make. When they were determined on these things, they procured artificers for the making of these engines, and every one provided the materials necessary for their fabric; and they established, as presidents and overseers of the works, certain persons that seemed the most proper for the employment.

Cyrus, when he found that there would be some time taken up in these affairs, encamped the army in a situation that he judged to be the most healthy and most easily accessible, with respect to all things that were necessary to be brought thither. And he did whatever was necessary to the making it strong, that they who always remained there might be in safety, though the main strength of the army should, at any time, march at a distance from the camp. And, besides, he inquired of those he thought knew the country best, from what parts of it the army might be supplied with all things that were of use to them in the greatest plenty. He led them always abroad to get provision and forage, both that he might procure the greatest plenty of necessaries for the army, that his men, inured to labour by these marches, might gain health and vigour; and that in marching they might preserve in their memories the order they were to keep.

Cyrus was employed in these affairs when deserters from Babylon, and prisoners taken, gave an account that the Assyrian was gone to Lydia, carrying with him many talents of gold and silver, and other treasures, and rich ornaments of all kinds. The body of the soldiery supposed that he was already putting his treasures out of the way for fear; but Cyrus, judging that he went in order to collect a force against him, if he were able to effect it, prepared himself, on the other hand, with a great deal of vigour, as thinking that he should be again forced to come to an engagement. Accordingly he completed the Persian body of horse; some horses he got from the prisoners, and some from his friends; for these things he accepted from all, rejected nothing, neither a fine weapon nor a horse, if any one presented him with it. Chariots, likewise, he fitted up, both out of those that were taken, and from whencesoever else he was able to get supplied with what was necessary towards it.

The Trojan method of using chariots, that was practised of old, and that way of managing them that is yet in use amongst the Cyreneans,

he abolished. For formerly the Medes, Syrians, and Arabians, and all the people of Asia, used the same method, with respect to their chariots, that the Cyreneans do at this time; and he was of opinion, that the very best of the men being mounted on chariots, they that probably constituted the chief strength of the army had the part only of skirmishers at a distance, and had no great share in the gaining of a victory. For three hundred chariots afford three hundred combatants, and these take up twelve hundred horses; then their drivers probably are such as these men, that are the best of the army, chiefly confide in; and here again are three hundred others, and they such as do the enemy no manner of mischief. Therefore this sort of management, with respect to their chariots, he abolished; and instead of this, he provided a sort of warlike chariots, with wheels of great strength, so as not to be easily broken, and with axletrees that were long, because things that carry breadth are less liable to be overturned. The box for the drivers he made like a turret, and with strong pieces of timber; and the highest of these boxes reached up to the elbows of the drivers, that reaching over these boxes they might drive the horses. The drivers he covered, all but their eyes, with armour. To the axletrees, on each side of the wheels, he added steel scythes of about two cubits in length; and below, under the axletree, he fixed others pointing to the ground, as intending with these chariots to break in on the enemy. As Cyrus at that time contrived these chariots, so, to this day, they use them in the king's territory. He had likewise camels in great number, such as were collected from amongst his friends, and those that were taken from the enemy, being all brought together.

Thus were these things performed. But he, being desirous to send some spy into Lydia, and to learn what the Assyrian did, was of opinion that Araspes, the guardian of the beautiful woman, was a proper person to go on that errand; for with Araspes things had fallen out in this manner:

Having fallen in love with the woman, he was forced to make proposals to her. But she denied him, and was faithful to her husband, though he was absent; for she loved him very much. Yet she did not accuse Araspes to Cyrus, being unwilling to make a quarrel between men that were friends. Then Araspes,

N

thinking to forward the success of his inclinations, threatened the woman that if she would not yield to his wishes, she should be forced to submit against her will. On this the woman, being in fear, concealed the matter no longer, but sent a messenger to Cyrus with orders to tell him the whole affair. He, when he heard it, laughed at this man, that had said he was above the power of love. He sent Artabazus with the messenger, and commanded him to tell Araspes that he should respect the conduct of such a woman. But Artabazus, coming to Araspes, reproached him, calling the woman a deposit that had been trusted in his hands; and telling him of his passion, so that Araspes shed many tears for grief, was overwhelmed with shame, and almost dead with fear, lest he should suffer some severity at the hands of Cyrus. Cyrus, being informed of this, sent for him, and spoke to him by himself alone.

" I see, Araspes," said he, " that you are very much in fear of me, and very much ashamed. But give them both over, for I have heard that gods have been conquered by love; I know how much men that have been accounted very wise have suffered by love; and I pronounced on myself, that if I conversed with beautiful people, I was not enough master of myself to disregard them. And I am the cause that this has befallen you, for I shut you up with this irresistible creature." Araspes then said in reply : " You are in this too, Cyrus, as you are in other things, mild, and disposed to forgive the errors of men; but other men," said he, " overwhelm me with grief and concern; for the rumour of my misfortune is got abroad, my enemies are pleased with it, and my friends come to me and advise me to get out of the way, lest I suffer some severity at your hands, as having been guilty of a very great injustice."

Then Cyrus said : " Be it known to you therefore, Araspes, that, by means of this very opinion that people have taken up, it is in your power to gratify me in a very high degree, and to do very great service to our allies." " I wish," said Araspes, " that I had an opportunity of being again of use to you." " Therefore," said he, " if you would make as if you fled from me, and would go over to the enemy, I believe that the enemy would trust you." " And I know, by Jove !" said Araspes, " that I should give occasion to have it said by my friends that I fled from you." " Then you

might return to us," said he, " apprised of all the enemy's affairs. I believe that on their giving credit to you, they would make you a sharer in their debates and counsels, so that nothing would be concealed from you that I desire you should know." " I will go then," said he, " now, out of hand; for be assured that my being thought to have made my escape as one that was just about to receive punishment at your hands, will be one of the things that will give me credit."

" And can you," said he, " leave the beautiful Panthea?" " Yes, Cyrus; for I have plainly two souls. I have now philosophized this point out by the help of that wicked sophister Love : for a single soul cannot be a good one and a bad one at the same time, nor can it, at the same time, affect both noble actions and vile ones. It cannot incline and be averse to the same things at the same time; but it is plain there are two souls, and when the good one prevails, it does noble things; when the bad one prevails, it attempts vile things. But now that it has got you for a support, the good one prevails, and that very much." " If you think it proper therefore to be gone," said Cyrus, " thus you must do in order to gain the greater credit with them. Relate to them the state of our affairs, and relate it so as that what you say may be as great a hinderance as possible to what they intend to do : and it would be some hinderance to them, if you should say that we are preparing to make an incursion into some part of their territory; for when they hear this, they will be less able to assemble their whole force together, every one being in fear for something at home. Then stay with them," said he, " as long as you can; for what they do when they are the nearest us, will be the most for our purpose to know. Advise them likewise to form themselves into such an order as may be thought the strongest; for when you come away, and are supposed to be apprised of their order, they will be under a necessity to keep to it, for they will be afraid of making a change in it; and if they do make a change, by their being so near at hand, it will create confusion amongst them."

Araspes, setting out in this manner, and taking with him such of his servants as he chiefly confided in, and telling some certain persons such things as he thought might be of service to his undertaking, went his way.

Panthea, as soon as she perceived that Araspes was gone, sending to Cyrus, told him thus: "Do not be afflicted, Cyrus, that Araspes is gone off to the enemy; for if you will allow me to send to my husband, I engage that there will come to you one who will be a much more faithful friend to you than Araspes. I know that he will attend you with all the force that he is able; for the father of the prince that now reigns was his friend, but he who at present reigns, attempted once to part us from each other; and reckoning him therefore an unjust man, I know that he would joyfully revolt from him to such a man as you are."

Cyrus, hearing this, ordered her to send to her husband. She sent; and when Abradatas discovered the signs from his wife, and perceived how matters stood as to the other particulars, he marched joyfully away to Cyrus, having about two thousand horse with him. When he came up with the Persian scouts, he sent to Cyrus, to tell him who he was: Cyrus immediately ordered them to conduct him to his wife.

When Abradatas and his wife saw each other they mutually embraced, as was natural to do, on an occasion so unexpected. On this Panthea told him of the sanctity and virtue of Cyrus, and of his pity and compassion towards her. Abradatas having heard of it, said: "What can I do, Panthea, to pay my gratitude to Cyrus for you and for myself?" "What else," said Panthea, "but endeavour to behave towards him as he has done towards you?" On this Abradatas came to Cyrus, and as soon as he saw him, taking him by the right hand, he said: "In return for the benefits you have bestowed on us, Cyrus, I have nothing of more consequence to say, than that I give myself to you as a friend, a servant, and an ally; and whatever designs I observe you to be engaged in, I will endeavour to be the best assistant to you in them that I am able." Then Cyrus said: "I accept your offer, and dismiss you at this time, to take your supper with your wife; but, at some other time, you must take a meal with me in my tent, together with your friends and mine."

After this Abradatas, observing Cyrus to be employed about the chariots armed with scythes, and about those horses and horsemen that were clothed in armour, endeavoured, out of his own body of horse, to fit him up a hundred such chariots as his were; and he prepared himself, as being to lead them, mounted on a chariot himself. His own chariot he framed with four perches, and for eight horses. His wife Panthea, out of her own treasures, made him a corslet of gold, and a golden head-piece, and armpieces of the same; and the horses of his chariot she provided with brass defences. These things Abradatas performed. And Cyrus, observing his chariot with four perches, considered that it might be possible to make one with eight, so as to draw the lower frame of this machine with eight yoke of oxen. This engine, together with its wheels, was upwards of fifteen feet from the ground. And he believed that turrets of this kind, following in the line, might be of great help to his own phalanx, and do great injury to the line of the enemy. On these frames he made open places to move about in, and strong defences, and on each of these turrets he mounted twenty men. When all things with respect to these turrets were completed to his hand, he made an experiment of their draught, and eight yoke of oxen drew a turret, and the men on it, with more ease than each yoke drew the common baggage weight; for the weight of baggage was about five-and-twenty talents to each yoke; but the draught of a turret, whose wooden frame was as broad as a tragic stage, together with twenty men and their arms, amounted but to fifteen talents to each yoke. When he found that the draught was easy, he prepared for the marching these turrets with the army, reckoning that to take all advantages was both safe and just, and of happy consequence in war.

II. At this time there came from the Indian certain persons, who brought treasure, and gave him an account that the Indian sent him word thus: "I am pleased, Cyrus, that you gave me an account of what you wanted; I have a mind to engage in friendship with you, and I send you treasure; if you want any thing else send me word. They that come from me have it in charge to do whatever you order them."

Cyrus hearing this, said: "I order then, that some of you remaining here, where you have pitched your tents, may guard the treasure, and live as is most agreeable to you. But let three of you go on to the enemy, as coming from the Indian, to treat of an alliance, and getting yourselves informed of what is said and done there give me and the Indian an account of it as soon as possible. And, if you serve me well in this, I shall be yet more obliged to you, than for your coming hither, and bringing me treasure; for such spies, as appear men of servile condition, are not able to know or give an account of any thing more than what all people know. But such men as you are often led into the knowledge of designs and counsels." The Indians, hearing this with pleasure, and being on that occasion entertained by Cyrus, made all things ready: and the next day went away, promising faithfully to get informed of as many of the enemy's concerns as they were able, and to come away as soon as possible.

Cyrus made all other preparations for the war, in the most magnificent manner, as being a man who projected to perform no inconsiderable things, and withal, did not only take care of such things as he thought proper for his allies, but raised amongst his friends an emulation to appear armed in the handsomest manner, to appear the most skilled in horsemanship, at throwing the javelin, and in the use of the bow, and the most ready to undergo any fatigue. This he effected by leading them out to hunt, and rewarding those that were the ablest in the several performances. And those commanders that he observed to be most careful to make their soldiers excel, those he animated by praising them, and by gratifying them in all that he was able. If at any time he made a sacrifice, or solemnized a festival, he appointed games on the occasion, in all the several things that men practise on account of war, and gave magnificent rewards to the conquerors; and there was a mighty cheerfulness in the army.

All things that Cyrus had a mind to have with him for the service were now almost completed to his hands, except the engines; for the Persian horsemen were filled up to ten thousand. The chariots, armed with scythes that he himself provided, were now a hundred complete. Those that Abradatas the Susian undertook to provide, like those of Cyrus, were likewise a hundred complete. And the Median chariots, that Cyrus had persuaded Cyaxares to change from the Trojan and Libyan form and method, were likewise made up to another hundred. The camels were mounted by two archers on each; and most of the army stood so disposed, as if they had already conquered, and the affairs of the enemy were reduced to nothing.

While they were in this disposition the Indians that Cyrus had sent to get intelligence came back from the enemy, and said that Crœ-

sus was chosen general and leader of all the enemy's forces: that all the princes in their alliance had determined to attend each with his whole force, to contribute mighty sums of money, and to lay them out in stipends to all those that they could hire, and in presents, where it was proper: that they had already hired a great number of Thracians, armed with large swords: that the Egyptians were under sail to come to them, and the number of these they said amounted to a hundred and twenty thousand, armed with large shields that reached down to their feet, with mighty spears, such as they use at this day, and with swords. They said that a body of Cyprians was under sail to join them, and that all the Cilicians, the men of both the Phrygias, the Lycaonians, Paphlagonians, Cappadocians, Arabians, Phœnicians, and Assyrians, with the prince of Babylon, were already joined: that the Ionians, the Æolians, and all the Greek colonies in Asia, were obliged to attend Crœsus: and that Crœsus had sent to Lacedæmon, to treat of an alliance with them: that this army assembled about the river Pactolus, and was about to advance to Thybarra, where all the barbarians of the Lower Syria, that are subject to the king, assemble at this day: that orders were given out to all, to convey provisions and all things thither, as to the general market. The prisoners likewise related almost the same things; for Cyrus took care that prisoners should be taken, in order to get information; and he sent out spies, that seemed to be of servile condition, as deserters.

When the army of Cyrus came to hear all this, every body was under concern, as it was natural for them to be. They went up and down in a sedater way than they used to do, and the multitude did not appear cheerful. But they got together in circles; and all places were full of people, asking each other questions concerning these matters, and discoursing together. When Cyrus perceived that terror was spreading apace through the army he called together the commanders of the several bodies, together with all such whose dejection might prove to be any wise prejudicial, or their alacrity of use; and told his servants beforehand, that if any other of the soldiers attended to hear his discourse, they should not hinder them. When they were assembled he said:

" Friends and allies! I have called you

together, because I observed that since these accounts are come from the enemy, some of you appear like men that are terrified: for to me it appears strange that any of you should be really terrified at the enemies' being said to assemble their forces, because we are at this time met in much greater numbers than we were when we beat them; and, with the help of the gods, are now better prepared than before: and when you see this, does it not give you courage? In the name of the gods!" said he, "if you are afraid now, what had you done if people had given you an account that the enemies were advancing on you with all the advantages on their side which we have on ours? and, in the first place," said he, "had you heard that they who had beaten us before were coming on us again, with minds full of the victory they had obtained? That they, who at that time slighted the distant discharge of arrows and javelins, were now coming with multitudes more armed like themselves? And then, that as these heavy-armed men at that time conquered our foot; so now, their horsemen, provided in the same manner, advanced against our horse? And that, rejecting bows and javelins, each of them, armed with one strong lance, had it in their intention to push up to us and engage hand to hand? That there are chariots coming, that are not to be planted as heretofore, and turned away as for flight, but that the horses of these chariots are covered with armour, the drivers stand in wooden turrets, and all upwards are covered with their corslets and helms, and steel scythes are fixed to the axle-trees; and that these are ready to drive in immediately on the ranks of those that stand in opposition to them? Besides, that they have camels on which they ride up to us, and one of which a hundred horses will not bear the sight of? And yet, farther, that they advance with certain towers, from whence they can support their own people; and, by discharging their weapons on you, hinder you from fighting on even ground with them?—Had any one told you that the enemies were possessed of all these things, if you are afraid now, what had you done then? But when you have an account that Croesus is chosen the enemies' general, he who behaved himself so much worse than the Syrians; that the Syrians were beaten before they fled, but Croesus, when he saw them beaten, instead of supporting his allies, fled and made his escape!

And, when it is told you that the same enemies are not thought sufficient to engage us, but that they hire others that they think will fight their battles for them better than they do for themselves!—If these are such things as appear terrible to any, and that the state of our own affairs appears mean and contemptible to them, —these men, my friends, I say ought to go their ways to the enemy; for by being there they will do us more service than they will by being amongst us."

When Cyrus had said this, Chrysantus the Persian spoke thus: "O Cyrus! do not wonder that some people carry sad countenances on having heard these accounts; for it is not fear that affects them thus, but it is grief. For," said he, "if people that had a mind to get their dinners, and were just in expectation of it, were told of some work that was necessary to be done before they dined, nobody, I believe, would be pleased with hearing it. Just so therefore, while we are in present expectation of enriching ourselves, and then hear that there is still some work left that of necessity must be done, we look sad, not out of fear but because we want to have that work already over. But since we are not only contending for Syria, where there is corn in abundance, flocks, and fruitful palms; but for Lydia too, where wine, and figs, and oil abound, and a land whose shores the sea washes; by which means such numbers of valuable things are brought thither as no one ever saw. Considering these things, we are no longer dejected, but have full confidence that we shall soon enjoy these valuable productions of Lydia." Thus he spoke; and all the allies were pleased with his discourse, and applauded it.

"And, indeed, my friends," said Cyrus, "my opinion is, to march up to them as soon as possible, that if we can we may prevent them, and first reach those places where all their conveniences are got together for them; and then, the sooner we march to them, the fewer things we shall find them provided with, and the more things we shall find them in want of. This I give as my opinion; if any one think any other course safer and easier to us, let him inform us."

After a great many had expressed their concurrence in its being proper to march as soon as possible to the enemy, and that nobody said to the contrary; on this Cyrus began a discourse to this effect:

" Friends and allies! our minds, our bodies, and the arms that we are to use, have been, with the help of the gods, long since provided to our hands: it is now our business to provide necessaries on our march for not less than twenty days, both for ourselves and as many beasts as we make use of: for on calculation I find that the way we are to go will take us up more than fifteen days, and on the road we shall find no sort of necessaries; for every thing that was possible has been taken and carried off, partly by ourselves, and partly by the enemy. We must therefore put up a sufficient quantity of food, for without this, we can neither fight nor can we live; but of wine as much as is enough to accustom us to drink water; for great part of the way that we are to take is entirely unprovided with wine, and were we to put up a very great quantity of it, it would not suffice us. Therefore, that we may not fall into distempers by being deprived of wine all on a sudden, we must do thus; we must begin now immediately to drink water with our food; for by doing thus now we shall make no very great change: for whoever feeds on things made of flour, eats the mass mixed up with water; and he that feeds on bread, eats the loaf that is first moistened and worked up with water; and all boiled meats are made ready with a great quantity of water. But if after our meal we drink a little wine on it, our stomach, not having less than usual, rests satisfied. Then, afterwards, we must cut off even this allowance after supper, till at last we become insensibly water-drinkers: for an alteration, little by little, brings any nature to bear a total change. The gods themselves teach us this, by bringing us, little by little, from the midst of winter, to bear very great heat; and from the heat, to bear very great cold; and we, in imitation of them, ought by custom and practice to reach the end we should attain to. Spare the weight of fine quilts and carpets, and make it up in necessaries; for a superfluity of things necessary will not be useless. But if you happen to be without these carpets, you need not be afraid that you shall not lie and sleep with pleasure. If it prove otherwise than I say, then blame me; but to have plenty of clothes with a man is a great help to one both in health and sickness. And of meats we ought to put up those that are a good deal sharp, acid, and salt; for they create appetite, and are a lasting nourishment. And when we come into those parts of the country that are untouched, where probably we shall find corn, we ought to be provided with hand-mills, by taking them with us from hence, that we may use them in making our bread; for of all the instruments that are used in making bread these are the lightest. We ought likewise to put up quantities of such things as are wanted by sick people; for their bulk is but very little, and if such a chance befall us, we shall want them very much. We must likewise have store of straps; for most things, both about men and horses, are fastened by straps, and when they wear out or break there is a necessity of standing still, unless one can get supplied with them. Whoever has learned the skill of polishing a lance, it will be well for him not to forget a polisher, and he will do well to carry a file: for he that sharpens his spear sharpens his soul at the same time; for there is a sort of shame in it, that one who sharpens his lance should himself be cowardly and dull. We ought likewise to have plenty of timber with us for the chariots and carriages; for, in many affairs, many things will of necessity be defective. And we ought to be provided with the tools and instruments that are the most necessary for all these things, for artificers are not every where to be met with, nor will a few of them be sufficient for our daily work. To every carriage we should have a cutting-hook and a spade; and to each beast of burden a pick-axe and a scythe; for these things are useful to every one in particular, and are often serviceable to the public. Therefore, with respect to the things that are necessary for food, do you, that are the commanders of the soldiery, examine those that are under you; for in whatever of these things any one is defective, it must not be passed by; for we shall be in want of these. And as to those things that I order to be carried by the beasts of burden, do you that are commanders of those that belong to the baggage-train examine into them, and the man that has them not do you oblige to provide them. And do you that are the commanders of those that clear the ways take down, in a list from me, such as are turned out from among the throwers of the javelin, the archers, and the slingers. And those that are taken from amongst the throwers of the javelin you must oblige to serve with an axe for cutting wood; those that are taken from the archers with a spade; and those from the lingers with a cutting-hook. These must march in troops before the carriages, that in case the way wants to be mended, you may presently set to work, and that, if I want any thing to be done, I may know from whence to take them for my use. And I will take with me smiths, carpenters, and leather-cutters, with all their proper tools, and who shall be men of an age fit to attend the service, that nothing of what is necessary to be done in the army, in the way of those arts, may be wanting. And these shall all be exempt and disengaged from the military ranks, but shall be placed in their proper order, ready to do service for any one that will hire them, in the ways that they are severally skilled in. And if any tradesman has a mind to attend with intention to sell any thing, he must have necessaries for the days before mentioned; and if he be found to sell any thing during those days, all that he has shall be taken from him; but when these days are past, he may sell as he pleases. And whoever of these traders shall be found to furnish the greatest plenty of the things that he deals in, he shall meet with reward and honour from our allies and from me. If any one thinks that he wants money to purchase things, let him bring people that know him, and will be responsible for him, that he will certainly attend the army, and then let him take of what belongs to us.

"These are the things that I order. If any one knows of any other thing that is proper, let him signify it to me. Do you go your ways, and put up every thing. I intend to make a sacrifice on our setting forward; and when our divine affairs stand right we will give the signal. All must attend with the things before ordered, in their proper posts, under their several commanders. And do you, commanders, each of you, putting his division into good order, all come and confer with me, that you may learn your several posts." They, bearing this, made their preparations, and he made a sacrifice.

III. When the sacred rites were performed in a happy manner, Cyrus set forward with the army, and the first day encamped at as small a distance as he could, that in case any one had forgot any thing, he might fetch it; and that if any one found himself in want of any thing, he might provide it. Cyaxares, therefore, with the third part of the Medes, stayed behind, that affairs at home might not be left destitute.

And Cyrus marched with the utmost despatch, having the horse at the head of the whole, but always making the discoverers and scouts mount up before, to such places as were most proper to take their views from. After the horse he led the baggage-train, and where the country was open and plain, he marched the carriages and beasts of burden in several lines. The phalanx marched after; and if any of the baggage-train was left behind, those of the commanders that were at hand took care of it, that they might not be hindered in their march. But where the road was more contracted, he ranged the train in the middle, and the soldiers marched on each side, and if they met with a hindrance, those of the soldiers that were at hand took care about it. The several regiments marched for the most part with their own baggage near them, for it was given in charge to those of the train, to march each part of them by the regiment they belonged to, unless some necessity kept them from doing it; and every officer of the train led on with the colonel's ensign, or mark that was known to the men of their several regiments; so that they marched in close order, and every one took very great care of their own, that it might not be left behind; and by doing thus, they were in no need of seeking for each other, all things were at hand and in more safety, and the soldiers were the more readily supplied with what they wanted.

But as soon as the advanced scouts thought that they saw men in the plain getting forage and wood, and saw beasts of burden laden with such kind of things, and feeding, and then again taking a view at a greater distance, they thought that they observed smoke or dust rising up into the air. From all these things they concluded that the enemy's army was somewhere near at-hand. The commander of the scouts therefore immediately sent one to Cyrus to tell him these things.

He having heard these things, commanded them to remain in the same viewing places, and whatever new thing they saw, to give him an account of it. He sent a regiment of horse forward, and commanded them to endeavour to take some of the men that were in the plain, that they might get a clearer insight into the matter. They that were thus ordered did accordingly. He made a disposition of the rest of his army in such a manner, that they might be provided with whatever he thought fitting before they came up close to the enemy ; and first, he made it be proclaimed, that they should take their dinners, and then wait in their ranks, attentive to their farther orders. When they had dined he called together the several commanders of the horse, foot, and chariots of the engines, baggage-train, and carriages, and they met accordingly. They that made an excursion into the plain, taking certain people prisoners, brought them off.

These that were taken, being asked by Cyrus, told him, that they came off from their army, and passing their advanced guard, came out, some for forage and some for wood ; for by means of the multitude that their army consisted of, all things were very scarce. Cyrus, hearing this, said : " And how far is the army from hence ?" They told him about two parasangs. On this Cyrus asked, " And is there any discourse amongst them concerning us ?" " Yes, by Jove !" said they, " a great deal, particularly that you are already near at hand advancing on them." " Well, then," said Cyrus, " did they rejoice at the hearing it ?" And this he asked for the sake of those that were by. " No, by Jove !" said they, " they did not rejoice, but were very much concerned." " And at this time," said Cyrus, " what are they doing ?" " They are forming into order," said they, " and both yesterday and the day before they were employed in the same work." " And he that makes their disposition," said Cyrus, " who is he ?" " Crœsus himself," said they, " and with him a certain Greek, and another besides, who is a Mede ; and this man was said to be a deserter from you." Then Cyrus said : " O greatest Jove, may I be able to take this man as I desire."

On this he ordered them to carry off the prisoners, and turned to the people that were present, as if he were going to say something. At that instant there came another man from the commander of the scouts, who told him that there appeared a great body of horse in the plain : " And we guess," said he, " that they are marching with intention to take a view of the army ; for before this body there is another party of about thirty horse, that march with great diligence, and directly against us, perhaps with intention to seize our station for viewing, if they can, and we are but a single decade on that station." Then Cyrus ordered a party of those horse that always attended him to march and put themselves in a place under the viewing station, and keeping themselves concealed from the enemy, to be quiet. " And when our decade," said he, " quits the station, then do you rush out and attack those that mount it ; and that the enemy's greater body may not do you mischief, do you, Hystaspes," said he, " march with a thousand horse, and appear in opposition to the enemy's body ; and do not pursue up to any undiscovered place ; but when you have taken care to maintain the possession of your viewing stations, then come back to me. And if any men ride up to you with their right hands extended, receive them as friends." Hystaspes went away and armed himself. Those that attended Cyrus marched immediately, and on this side the viewing places Araspes, with his servants, met them ; he that had been some time since sent away as a spy, and was the guardian of the Susian woman.

Cyrus, therefore, as soon as he saw him, leaped from his seat, met him, and received him with his right hand. The rest, as was natural, knowing nothing of the matter, were struck with the thing, till Cyrus said : " My friends, here comes to us a brave man ; for now it is fit, that all men should know what he has done. This man went away, not for any base thing that he was loaded with, or for any fear of me, but he was sent by me, that learning the state of the enemy's affairs for us, he might make us a clear report of them. What I promised you therefore, Araspes, I remember, and, with the assistance of all these that are here, I will perform it. And it is just that all you, my friends, should pay him honour as a brave man ; for, to do us service, he has thrown himself into dangers, and has borne that load of reproach that fell so heavy on him." On this they all embraced Araspes, and gave him their right hands.

Then Cyrus, telling them that there was enough of this said : " Give us an account, Araspes, of these things, and do not abate any thing of the truth, with respect to the enemy's affairs ; for it is better that we should think them greater, and see them less, than hear them to be less, and find them greater." " I acted," said Araspes, " in such a manner as to get the clearest insight into them ; for I assisted in person at their making their disposition." " You therefore," said Cyrus, " know not only their numbers, but their order too." " Yes, by Jove !" said Araspes, " and I know the manner that they intend to engage in." " But, in the first place, tell

, however," said Cyrus, "in general, what their numbers are?" " Well, then," said he, "they are all ranged thirty in depth, both foot and horse, except the Egyptians, and they extended front forty stadia, for I took very great care know what ground they took up." "And then, as to the Egyptians," said Cyrus, "tell how they are ranged; for you said—except the Egyptians." " The commanders of ten thousand formed each of their bodies into a hundred every way; for this they say is their order, according to their custom at home; but Craesus allowed them to form in this manner very much against his will, for he was desirous over-front your army as much as possible." And why," said Cyrus, "does he desire his?" " Why, by Jove!" said he, "in order to encompass you with that part that exceeds on in front." Then Cyrus said: " But let him look to it, that the encompassers be not themselves encompassed. But we have heard what is proper for us to be informed of by you, and you, my friends, must act in this manner:

" As soon as you go from hence, examine the arms that belong both to the horses and to ourselves; for, frequently, by the want of a little thing, both man, and horse, and chariot become useless. To-morrow, in the morning, whilst I sacrifice you must first get your dinners, both men and horse, that whatever opportunity of action offers itself we may not balk it. Then do you, Araspes, keep the right wing as you do now, and let the other commanders of ten thousand keep the stations they now are in; for when a race is just ready to be entered on, there is no longer opportunity for any chariot to shift horses. Give orders to the several colonels and captains to form into a phalanx, with each company drawn up two in front." And each company consisted of four-and-twenty men. Then one of the commanders of ten thousand said: " And do we think, Cyrus," said he, " that when we are ranged but so many deep we shall be strong enough against phalanxes of that great depth?" And Cyrus replied: " Phalanxes that are deeper than to be able to reach the enemy with their weapons, what injury," said he, " do you think they will do to the enemy; or what service to their fellow-combatants? For my part," said he, "those soldiers that are ranged a hundred in depth, I would rather choose to have ranged ten thousand in depth, for by that means we should have the fewer to engage;

but by the number of men that form our phalanx in depth, I reckon to make the whole act and support itself. The throwers of the javelin I will range behind the corslet-men, and behind the throwers of the javelin the archers: for who would place those in front who, themselves, can confess that they cannot bear any engagement hand to hand? But when the corslet-men are interposed before them, then they stand. And the one casting their javelins, and the other discharging their arrows over the heads of those that are ranged before them, do execution on the enemy. And as much mischief as any one does the enemy, it is plain that so far he gives relief to his fellow-combatants. Last of all, I will place those that are called the rear; for as a house without a strong stone-work, and without men that have the skill to form the roof, is of no value, so neither is a phalanx of any value without such as are serviceable both in front and rear. Do you, then," said he, " form as I order you. And do you, commanders of the javelin-men, form your several companies in the same manner behind these. Do you, commanders of the archers, form in the same manner behind the javelin-men; and you, who command the rear, with your men placed last, give orders to those under you, each of them to keep his eye to those before him, to encourage those that do their duty, to threaten severely such as behave cowardly; and, if any one turn away with intention to desert his station, to punish him with death: for it is the business of those that are placed before, both by words and actions, to encourage those that follow; and you that are placed in the rear of all must inspire the cowardly with greater terror than the enemies themselves give them. These things do you do; and do you, Abradatas, who command those that belong to the engines, take care that the oxen that draw the turrets and men belonging to them follow up as close to the phalanx as possible. And do you, Daouchas, who command the baggage-train, lead up all that kind of people behind the turrets and engines, and let your attendants severely punish those that are either more advanced or more behind than they ought to be. And do you, Cardouchus, who command the waggons that carry the women, place these last behind the baggage-train; for all these following each other will make the appearance of a great multitude, and will give us an opportunity of forming an ambuscade; and, in case the enemy have a mind to encompass us, will oblige them to a greater circuit; and the more ground they encompass, so much the weaker must they of necessity be. And thus do you. But you, Artabazus and Artagersas, each of you, with the thousand foot that attend you, keep behind these. And you, Pharnouchus and Asiadatas, each with your thousand horse, do not you form in the phalanx, but arm by yourselves, behind the waggons, and then come to us, together with the rest of the commanders; but you ought to prepare yourselves, as being the first to engage. And do you, who are the commanders of the men mounted on the camels, form behind the waggons, and act as Artagersas shall order you. And of you, leaders of the chariots, let that man range his hundred chariots in front, before the phalanx, who obtains that station by lot, and let the other hundreds attend the phalanx ranged on the wings, one on the right side and the other on the left."

Thus Cyrus ordered. But Abradatas, king of the Susians, said: "I take it voluntarily on myself, Cyrus, to hold that station in front against the opposite phalanx, unless you think otherwise." Then Cyrus, being struck with admiration of the man, and taking him by the right hand, asked the Persians that belonged to others of the chariots. "Do you," said he, "yield to this?" When they replied, that it would not be handsome in them to give it up, he brought them all to the lot; and by the lot Abradatas obtained what he had taken on himself, and he stood opposite to the Egyptians. Then going their way, and taking care of the things that were before mentioned, they took their suppers, and, having placed their guards, they went to rest.

IV. The next day, in the morning, Cyaxares sacrificed: but the rest of the army, after having taken their dinners and made their libations, equipped themselves with fine coats, in great number, and with many fine corslets and helmets. The horses, likewise, they armed with forehead-pieces and breast-plates, the single horses with thigh-pieces, and those in the chariots with plates on their sides; so that the whole army glittered with the brass, and appeared beautifully decked with scarlet habits.

The chariot of Abradatas, that had four perches and eight horses, was completely adorned for him; and, when he was going to put on his linen corslet, which was a sort of armour used by those of his country, Panthea brought him a golden helmet, and arm-pieces, broad bracelets for his wrists, a purple habit, that reached down to his feet, and hung in folds at the bottom, and a crest dyed of a violet colour. These things she had made unknown to her husband, and by taking the measure of his armour. He wondered when he saw them, and inquired thus of Panthea: "And have you made me these arms, woman, by destroying your own ornaments?" "No, by Jove!" said Panthea, "not what is the most valuable of them; for it is you, if you appear to others to be what I think you, that will be my greatest ornament." And saying this she put on him the armour; and, though she endeavoured to conceal it, the tears poured down her cheeks. When Abradatas, who was before a man of fine appearance, was set out in these arms, he appeared the most beautiful and noble of all, especially being likewise so by nature. Then taking the reins from the driver, he was just preparing to mount the chariot; on this Panthea, after she had desired all that were there present to retire, said:

"O Abradatas! if ever there was another woman who had greater regard to her husband than to her own soul, I believe you know that I am such a one; what need I therefore speak of things in particular? for I reckon that my actions have convinced you more than any words I can now use. And yet though I stand thus affected towards you, as you know I do, I swear by this friendship of mine and yours, that I certainly would rather choose to be put under ground jointly with you, approving yourself a brave man, than to live with you in disgrace and shame; so much do I think you and myself worthy of the noblest things. Then I reckon we both lie under a great obligation to Cyrus, that when I was a captive, and chosen out for himself, he thought fit to take me neither as a slave, nor, indeed, as a free-woman of mean account; but he took and kept me for you, as if I were his brother's wife. Besides, when Araspes, who was my guard, went away from him, I promised him, that if he would allow me to send for you, you would come to him, and approve yourself a much better and more faithful friend than Araspes."

Thus she spoke; and Abradatas, being struck with admiration at her discourse, laying his hand gently on her head, and lifting up his eyes to heaven, made this prayer: "Do thou, O greatest Jove! grant me to appear a husband worthy of Panthea, and a friend worthy of Cyrus, who has done us so much honour!"

Having said this, he mounted the chariot by the door of the driver's seat; and after he got up, when the driver shut the door of the seat, Panthea, who had now no other way to salute him, kissed the seat of the chariot. The chariot then moved on, and she, unknown to him, followed, till Abradatas turning about, and seeing her, said: "Take courage, Panthea! Fare you happily and well; and now go your ways." On this her women and servants took and conducted her to her conveyance, and laying her down, concealed her by throwing the covering of a tent over her. The people, though Abradatas and his chariot made a noble spectacle, were not able to look at him till Panthea was gone.

But when Cyrus had happily sacrificed, the army was formed for him according to his orders, and taking possession of the viewing stations, one before another, he called the leaders together and spoke thus:

"Friends and fellow-soldiers! the gods, in our sacred rites, have exposed to us the same happy signs they did before, when they gave us victory; and I am desirous to put you in mind of some such things as, by your recollecting them, will, in my opinion, make you march with more courage to the enemy: for you are better practised in the affairs of war than our enemies are, and you have been bred up together in this, and formed to it a much longer time than our enemies have been. You have been fellow-conquerors together, whereas many of our enemies have been fellow-sharers in a defeat: and of those on both sides that have not yet been engaged in action, they that are of our enemy's side know that they have for their supports men that have been deserters of their station and runaways; but you that are with us know that you act with men zealous to assist their friends. It is probable then that they who have confidence in each other will unanimously stand and fight; but they who distrust each other will necessarily be every one contriving how they shall the soonest get out of the way. Let us march then, my friends, to the enemy with our armed chariots against those of the enemy unarmed; with our cavalry in like manner, both men and horses armed, against those of the enemy unarmed, in order to a close engagement. The rest of the foot are such as you have engaged already. But as for the Egyptians, they are both armed and formed in the same manner, both equally bad; for they have shields larger than they can act or see with, and being formed a hundred in depth, it is evident they will hinder one another from fighting, except only a very few. If they think by their might in rushing on, to make us give way, they must first sustain our horse, and such weapons as are driven on them by the force of horses; and if any of them make shift to stand this, how will they be able to engage our horse, our phalanx, and our turrets at the same time? For those mounted on the turrets will come up to our assistance, and by doing execution on the enemy, will make them, instead of fighting, be confounded, and not know what to do. If you think that you are still in want of any thing, tell it me; for, with the help of the gods, we will be in want of nothing. And if any one have a mind to say any thing, let him speak; if not, go your ways to sacred affairs; and having made your prayers to the gods, to whom we have sacrificed, then go to your ranks; and let every one of you remind those that belong to him of the things which I have put you in mind of. And let every one make it appear to those whom he commands that he is worthy of command, by showing himself fearless in his manner, his countenance, and his words!"

XENOPHON

ON THE

INSTITUTION OF CYRUS.

———

BOOK VII.

CONTENTS of BOOK VII.

INSTITUTION OF CYRUS.

BOOK VII.

I. THESE men, having made their prayers to the gods, went away to their ranks. And the servants brought meat and drink to Cyrus, and to those that were with him, while they were yet taken up in their holy rites. Cyrus, standing as he was, and beginning with an offering to the gods, took his dinner, and distributed around always to the man that most wanted. Then, having made his libations, and prayed, he drank, and the rest that were with him did the same. After this was done, and he had made supplication to Jove Paternal, to be their leader and support, he mounted his horse, and ordered those about him to do the same. All they that were with Cyrus were armed with the same arms that he was; in scarlet habits, brass corslets, brass helmets, white crests, swords, and every one with a single spear, made of the cornel-tree. Their horses were armed with forehead-pieces, breast-plates, and side-pieces, and these served as thigh-pieces to the rider. Thus much only did the arms of Cyrus differ from the others, that these were done over with a gold colour, but those of Cyrus cast a brightness like a mirror. When he was mounted, and stood looking which way he was to go, it thundered to the right: he then said: "We will follow thee, O greatest Jove!" And he set forward with Chrysantas, a commander of horse, and his body of horse on his right hand, and Arasambas, with his body of foot on his left. He gave orders that all should have their eyes to his ensign, and follow on in an even pace. His ensign was a golden eagle held up on the top of a long lance. And this remains the ensign of the Persian king to this day. Before they got sight of the enemy he made the army halt three times. When they had marched on about twenty stadia, they began then to observe the enemies' army advancing; and when they were all in view of each other, and the enemies found that they exceeded very much in front on both sides, then making their own phalanx halt, for otherwise there was no fetching a compass to inclose the opposite army, they bent themselves in order to take that compass, that by having disposed themselves into the form of the letter Γ, on each side, they might engage on every side at once.

Cyrus seeing this, did not slacken his pace for it, but led on just as before: and taking notice at how great a distance on each side they took their compass, and extended their wings around—"Do you observe," said he, "Chrysantas, where they take their compass?" "Yes," said Chrysantas, "and I wonder at it, for to me they seem to draw off their wings very far from their own phalanx." "Yes, by Jove!" said Cyrus, "and from ours too; and what is the meaning of this?—It is plainly," said he, "because they are afraid, in case their wings get near to us, while their phalanx is yet at a distance, that we shall charge them." Then said Chrysantas, "How will they be able to be serviceable to one another, when they are at such a distance from each other?" "It is plain," said Cyrus, "that when their wings have gained so much ground as to be over against the sides of our army, then turning themselves, and forming in front, they will march on us on every side, that they may engage on every side at once." "And do you not think then," said Chrysantas, "that they contrive well?" "Yes, with respect to what they see; but with respect to what they do not see, they contrive worse than if they advanced on us with their wings. But do you, Arasambas, lead on quietly with your foot, as you observe that I do. And do you, Chrysantas, follow on with your horse in the same even pace. I will march away to the place where I think it proper to begin the engagement, and as I pass on I will view how we stand disposed in every part. After I get to the place, and when we are marching up against each other, I will begin the hymn, and do you follow me. When we are engaged with the enemy, you will perceive it, for I reckon there will be no small noise and rout. Then will Abradatas set forward to charge the enemy with his chariots, for so it shall be told him to do. You must follow up immediately after the chariots, for by this means we shall fall on the enemy while they are the most in disorder. I will be myself at hand, as soon as I can, to pursue them, if the gods so please."

Having said this, and transmitted the word, which was this, " Jove our Saviour and Leader!" he then marched : and taking his way between the chariots and corslet-men, and looking on some of the men that were in their ranks, he then said : " My friends, how pleasing it is to see your countenances !" Then to others he said : " Consider, my friends, that our present contest is not only for victory to-day, but to maintain the victory we gained before, and for all manner of happy success hereafter." Then coming up with others, he said : " From henceforward, my friends, we shall have no cause to blame the gods, for they have put it in our power to acquire many great advantages to ourselves. But then, my friends, let us be brave." To others he spoke thus : " My friends, to what nobler society of friendship can we ever invite one another than to the present ? for it is now in our power, by being brave men, to confer on each other benefits in great number." And to others again thus : " I believe you know, my friends, that the prizes now lie before you. And to the victors they are these : to pursue, to deal their blows, to kill, to reap great advantage, to gain praise, to be free, and to rule. But the reverse of these, it is plain, will be the lot of the cowardly. Whoever therefore has a kindness for himself, let him fight after my example, for I will not willingly admit of any thing mean or base in my behaviour." When he came up with others that had been in the engagement with him before, he said : " And to you, my friends, what should I say? for you know how those that are brave in action, pass the day, and how those do it that are cowardly."

When he had got over against Abradatas, as he passed along he stopped. And Abradatas

delivering the reins to the driver, came to him, and several others that were posted near, and belonged both to the foot and to the chariots, ran to him; and when they were come, he spoke to them in this manner : " As you desired, Abradatas, the gods have vouchsafed to grant the principal rank amongst all us allies to those that are with you. And when it comes to be your part to engage, remember that the Persians are to see you, and to follow you, and not suffer you to engage alone." Then Abradatas said : " Affairs here with us, Cyrus, seem to stand on a good footing, but our flanks disturb me ; for along our flanks I observe are extended the enemies' wings that are very strong, and consist of chariots and all other military strength : but of ours there is nothing opposed to them but chariots ; so that," said he, " had I not obtained this post by the lot, I should be ashamed to be here ; so much do I think myself in the safest station." Then Cyrus said : " If things are on a good footing with you, be at ease as to them ; for, with the help of the gods, I will show you our flanks entirely clear of the enemy. And do not you attack the enemy, I charge you, before you see those people flying that you are now afraid of. (Thus presumptuously did he talk of the approaching engagement, though at other times he was not presumptuous in his discourse.) But when you see these men flying, then count on it that I am at hand, and begin your attack, for you will then deal with the enemy while they are in the greatest consternation, and your own men in the most heart. But, while you have leisure, Abradatas, drive along by your own chariots, and exhort your people to the attack. Give them courage by your countenance, raise them with hopes, and inspire them with emulation to appear the bravest amongst all that belong to the chariots : for be assured that if things fall out thus, they will all say, for the future, that nothing is more profitable than virtue and bravery." Abradatas, mounting his chariot, drove along, and put these things in execution.

But Cyrus, moving on again, when he came to the left, where Hystaspes was with half the Persian horse, calling him by his name, said : " Hystaspes, you now see a work for your quickness in the execution of business ; for, if we are beforehand with the enemy in charging and doing execution on them, we shall not lose a man." Hystaspes, laughing at this, said :

" We will take care of those that are over against us; do you give some others the charge of those that are on our flanks, that they likewise may not be idle." Then Cyrus said : " I am going to those myself. But remember this, Hystaspes, whichever of us it is that the gods favour with victory, if the enemy make a stand any where, let us always join in with our forces, and charge where the fight continues." Having said this he moved on, and, when in his passage he got to the flank, and to the commander of the chariots that were there posted, he said to him : " I am come to your assistance : but when you perceive us to have made our attack at the extremities, then do you endeavour, at the same time, to make your way through the enemy, for you will be much safer when you are at large than while you are inclosed within them." Then passing on, when he got behind the waggons he ordered Artagersas and Pharnouchus, each with his thousand men, one of foot, and the other of horse, there to remain. " And when you perceive," said he, " that I have made my attack on those that are posted over against our right wing, then do you charge those that are over against you. You will engage them by their wing and in flank, where an army is the weakest, and with your own men formed into a phalanx, that you yourselves may be in that form and disposition which is the strongest. Then the enemy's horse, as you see, are the hindmost. By all means therefore advance the body of camels on them, and be assured that before you come to engage you will see the enemy in a ridiculous condition." Cyrus, having finished these affairs, went on to the right wing.

And Crœsus, judging that his phalanx that he marched with was now nearer to the enemy than his extended wings, gave the signal to the wings to march no farther on, but to turn about in the station they were in. And as they all stood facing the army of Cyrus, he gave them the signal to march to the enemy. And thus three phalanxes advanced on the army of Cyrus; one in front, and, of the other two, one on the right side and the other on the left; so that a very great terror seized the whole army of Cyrus. For, just like a little brick placed within a large one, so was the army of Cyrus surrounded by the enemy, with their horse, their heavy-armed men, their shield-men, archers, and chariots, on every side, except on

the rear. However, when Cyrus gave the signal they all turned and faced the enemy; and there was a deep silence on every side, in expectation and concern for the event. As soon as Cyrus thought it the proper time he began the hymn, and the whole army sung it with him. After this they all of them together made a shout to the god of battle.

Then Cyrus broke out, and instantly with his horse, taking the enemy in flank, fell on them as soon as possible. The foot that were with him, in order of battle, followed immediately, and they inclosed the enemy on each side; so that they had very much the advantage : for with a phalanx of their own they charged the enemy on their wing, so that the enemy presently fled with the utmost speed. As soon as Artagersas perceived that Cyrus was engaged, he attacked on the left, making the camels advance as Cyrus had ordered; and the enemy's horses, even at a great distance, were not able to stand them, but some of them run madly away, some started from their ranks, and others fell foul of one another, for thus are horses always served by camels. Artagersas, with his men formed, charged in good order the enemy that were in confusion. And the chariots, both to the right and left, fell on at the same time. Many of the enemy that fled from the chariots were killed by those who pursued the wing, and many of them in their flight from these, were met by the chariots.

Abradatas then delayed no longer, but crying out with vehemence, " Follow me, my friends !" rushed on, without sparing his horses in any sort, but with the spur fetched a great deal of blood from them. His other charioteers broke out with him. The chariots of the enemy immediately fled before them, some of them taking up their men that mounted them, and some leaving them behind. Then Abradatas, making his way directly through these, fell on the Egyptian phalanx, and they that were placed in order near him fell on with him. On many other occasions it has been made evident, that no phalanx can be of greater strength than when it is made up of joint combatants that are friends : and it was made evident on this; for the companions and table acquaintance of Abradatas attacked jointly with him; but the other drivers, when they saw the Egyptians in a compact body stand their ground, turned off to the chariots that were flying and pursued them; the Egyptians

P

not being able to make way, because they who were on every side of them stood their ground. They that were with Abradatas therefore in that part where they fell on, running on those that stood against them, overturned them by the rapid course of the horses; and those that fell they tore to pieces, both men and arms, horses and wheels, and whatever the scythes caught hold of they cut their way through by force, whether arms or bodies of men. In this inexpressible confusion, the wheels making their way by jolts over heaps of all kinds, Abradatas fell, as did likewise the rest that broke in with him. And here were these brave men cut down and killed.

The Persians who followed up after them, falling on those that were in disorder, where Abradatas and his men had broken in, did execution on them. But, where the Egyptians were undisturbed, (and of these there were great numbers,) they marched up against the Persians. Here began a terrible combat of lances, javelins, and swords; and the Egyptians had the advantage, both by their multitude and by their arms, for their lances were very strong and of great length, (such as they yet use at this day,) and their large shields were a better defence to them than corslets and the smaller sort of shield; and being fastened to their shoulders, were of service to them to make the strongest push. Therefore, closing their large shields together, they moved and pushed on. The Persians holding their smaller sort of shields in their hands at arm's length, were not able to sustain them, but retreated gradually, dealing and receiving blows, till they came to the engines. When they got thither, the Egyptians were again galled from the turrets. And they that were in the rear of all would not suffer either the archers or javelin-men to fly; but, holding their swords at them, forced them to shoot and to throw. And great havoc and destruction there was of men, great clashing of arms and weapons of all kinds, and great noise of people, some calling to each other, some making exhortations, and some calling on the gods.

On this Cyrus, pursuing those that were opposite to him, came up; and when he saw the Persians forced from their station, he was grieved, and knowing that he could by no other means sooner stop the progress of the enemy forward, than by riding round, and getting to their rear, he commanded those that were with

him to follow. He rode round, and came up with their rear, where his men, charging them, fell on them as their backs were turned, and killed a great many. The Egyptians, as soon as they perceived this, cried out that the enemy was behind them, and, in this distress, faced about. Here foot and horse fought promiscuously, and a man falling under Cyrus' horse, and being trampled on, struck his sword into the horse's belly: the horse, thus wounded, tossed and staggered, and threw Cyrus off. On this occasion, one might see of what advantage it was for a ruler to have the love of those that are under his command; for all immediately cried out, fell on, and fought; they pushed, and were themselves pushed in their turn; they gave blows, and received them; and one of the attendants of Cyrus, leaping from his horse, mounted Cyrus on him. When Cyrus was mounted he perceived that the Egyptians were now hard pressed on every side, for Hystaspes was come up with the Persian horse, and Chrysantas in like manner. But he would not now suffer them to fall on the Egyptian phalanx, but to gall them with arrows and javelins at a distance; this he gave them orders to do. Then, in riding round, as he came up to the engines, he thought it proper to mount a turret to view whether any body of the enemy made a stand and fought. When he had got up he saw the whole plain full of horses, men, and chariots, some flying, some pursuing, some victorious, some defeated, the enemy flying, and his own men conquering. But he was no longer able to discover, in any part, any that stood but the Egyptians; and these, when they were at a loss what to do, forming themselves into a circle, with their arms turned to the view of their enemy, sat quietly under the shelter of their shields, no longer acted, but suffered in a cruel manner.

Cyrus being struck with admiration of these men, and touched with pity that such brave men should perish, made all those retreat that engaged against them, and suffered none to continue fighting. He then sent to them a herald to ask, "whether they intended to be all destroyed for men that had deserted and betrayed them, or whether they chose to be saved with the reputation of being brave men?" Their reply was this: "How can we obtain safety and be reputed brave?" Then Cyrus again said: "Because we see that you are the only men that stand your ground and dare fight!"

"But then," said the Egyptians, "what is that we can handsomely do and obtain safety?" Cyrus to this said: "If you can obtain it without betraying any of your allies and friends; if you deliver up your arms to us, and become friends to those who choose to save you, when it is in their power to destroy you." Having heard this, they asked this question: "If we become your friends, Cyrus, how will you think fit to deal with us?" Cyrus replied: "Both to do you good offices, and to receive them from you." Then the Egyptians again asked: "What good offices?" And to this Cyrus said: "As long as the war continues I will give you larger pay than you now receive; when we have peace, to every one of you that will stay with me I will give lands, cities, women, and servants." The Egyptians hearing this, "begged that they might be exempted from engaging in the war with him against Crœsus; for he was the only one," they said, "that they forgave." But, consenting to all the rest, they on both sides pledged their faith reciprocally. The Egyptians that then remained continue still to this day faithful to the king. And Cyrus gave them the cities Larissa and Cyllene, that are called the cities of the Egyptians, and lie up in the country in the neighbourhood of Cuma, near the sea; and their posterity have them at this day in their possession.

Cyrus having performed all these things, and it now growing dark, retreated, and he encamped at Thybarra. In this battle the Egyptians only, of all the enemy's people, gained reputation; and of those that were with Cyrus, the Persian cavalry were thought to have been the best; so that the same sort of arms that Cyrus at that time equipped his horsemen with continue yet in use. The chariots that carried scythes gained likewise great fame; so that this remains yet the chariots for war in use with the prince still reigning on in succession. The camels did no more than frighten the horses; they that mounted them did no execution on the horsemen; nor were they any of them themselves killed by the horsemen, for no horse would come near them. This was then reckoned of use; but no brave man will breed a camel for his own mounting, nor exercise and manage them, as intending to serve in war on them; so that, taking up their old form again, they keep in the baggage-train. Cyrus' men having taken their suppers, and placed their guards, as was proper, went to rest.

II. But Crœsus immediately fled with his army to Sardis. The other nations retreated as far as they could in the night, taking their several ways home. As soon as it was day Cyrus led the army to Sardis; and when he got up to the walls of the place he raised engines, as intending to form an attack on the walls, and provided ladders. Whilst he was doing these things, the next night, he made the Chaldeans and Persians mount that part of the Sardinian fortifications that was thought the most inaccessible; and a certain Persian led them the way, who had been a slave to one of the garrisons in the citadel, and had learnt the descent down to the river and the ascent from it. As soon as it was known that the heights above were taken, all the Lydians fled from the walls, all shifting for themselves as they were able. Cyrus, as soon as it was day, entered the city, and gave out orders that no one should stir from his rank. Crœsus, shut up in his palace, called out on Cyrus; but Cyrus, leaving a guard on Crœsus, turned off, and mounted up to the castle that was taken.

And when he saw the Persians keeping guard there, as became them, and the arms of the Chaldeans left alone, (for they themselves were run down to plunder the houses,) he presently summoned their commanders, and bade them quit the army immediately; "for I cannot bear," said he, "to see disorderly men get the advantage of others. And be it known to you," said he, "I was providing to manage so, as to make all the Chaldeans pronounce those fortunate and happy that engaged with me in the war; but now," said he, "do not wonder if somebody superior to you in strength happen to meet with you as you go off." The Chaldeans hearing this, were in great terror, begged him to allay his anger, and said, "That they would restore him all the rich effects they had taken." He told them, "That he was not in any want of them; but," said he, "if you would ease me of my trouble and concern, give up all that you have got to those that keep guard in the castle; for when the rest of the soldiers find that the orderly are the better for their being so, all will be well with me." The Chaldeans did as Cyrus had commanded them, and they that had been obedient to their orders got a great many rich effects of all kinds. Then Cyrus, having encamped his men towards that part of the city that he thought the most convenient, gave them all orders to stand to their arms and take their dinners; and, having done this, he ordered Crœsus to be brought to him.

Crœsus, as soon as·he saw Cyrus, said; " Joy and happiness to you, my soverign lord! for, from henceforward, fortune has ordered you to receive that name, and me to give it you." " The same I wish to you, Crœsus," said he, " since we are men both of us. But Crœsus," said he, " would you give me a little advice?" " I wish, Cyrus," said he, " that I were able to find any good for you, for I believe it might be of advantage to myself." " Here then, Crœsus," said he; " observing that the soldiers, after having undergone many fatigues, and run many dangers, reckon themselves now in possession of the richest city in Asia, next to Babylon, I think it fit that they should receive some profit in return: for I make account," said he, " that, unless they receive some fruit of their labours, I shall not have them long obedient to my orders; but I am not willing to give them up the city to plunder; for I believe that the city would be destroyed by it; and, in a plunder, I know very well that the worst of our men would have the advantage of the best." Crœsus, hearing this, said; " Allow me," said he, " to speak to such of the Lydians as I think fit, and to tell them that I have prevailed with you not to plunder, nor to suffer our wives and children to be taken from us; but have promised you, that in lieu of these you shall certainly have from the Lydians, of their own accord, whatever there is of worth and value in Sardis. For when they hear this, I know they will bring out whatever there is here of value in the possession either of man or woman. And yet by the time the year is completed, the city will be again in like manner full of things of value in great abundance: but if you plunder it, you will have all manner of arts, that are called the springs of riches, and of all things valuable, destroyed. And then you are at still liberty, after you have seen this, to come and consult whether you shall plunder the city or no. Send," said he, " in the first place, to my treasurers, and let your guards take them from those that have the keeping them for me."

Cyrus agreed to act in all things as Crœsus said: " But by all means," said he, " tell me how things have fallen out, in consequence of the answers you receive on your application to the Delphian oracle; for you are said to have paid the utmost devotion to Apollo, and to have done every thing at his persuasion." " Indeed, Cyrus," said he, " I could wish that things stood thus with me; but now have I gone on immediately from the beginning doing things in direct opposition to Apollo." " How so?" said Cyrus; " pray inform me; for you tell me things that are unaccountable." " Because," said he, " in the first place, neglecting to consult the god in what I wanted, I made trial of him whether he was able to tell the truth. Now, not only a god, but even men that are of worth, when they find themselves distrusted, have no kindness for those that distrust them. And after he had found me doing things that were absurd, and knew that I was at a great distance from Delphi, then I sent to consult concerning my having sons. He at first made me no answer; but by my sending him many presents of gold, and many of silver, and by making multitudes of sacrifices, I had rendered him propitious to me, as I thought; and he then, on my consulting him what I should do that I might have sons, answered, " that I should have them." And I had them; for neither in this did he deal falsely with me. But when I had them, they were of no advantage to me, for one of them continues dumb, and he that was the best of them perished in the flower of his age. Being afflicted with the misfortune of my sons, I sent again, and inquired of the god what to do, that I might pass the remainder of my live in the happiest manner? and he made answer, ' O Crœsus! by the knowledge of thyself, thou wilt pass thy days in happiness!' When I heard this oracle, I was pleased with it: for I thought he had granted me happiness, by commanding me to do the easiest thing that could be; for of the rest of men, some I thought it was possible for one to know, and some not, but that every man knew what he was himself. After this, during the whole time that I continued in peace, and after the death of my son, I accused my fortune in nothing. But when I was persuaded by the Assyrian to make war on you, I fell into all manner of dangers, but came off safe without getting any harm. Now, neither in this can I lay any thing to the god's charge; for after I knew myself not to be sufficient to make war with you with the help of the god, I came off with safety, both myself and those that attended me. But then again, being as it were dissolved by the riches I was possessed of, by those that begged me to be their chief, by the presents they made me, and by men that in flattery told me, that if I would take on me the command, all men would obey me, and I should be the greatest of men ; and being puffed up by discourses of this kind, as all the kings around chose me their chief in the war, I accepted the command, as if I were sufficient to be the first of men, ignorant of myself, in imagining that I was able to make war with you ; you who, in the first place, are descended from the gods, are born of a race of kings, and have been, from a boy, exercised to virtue. But of my own ancestors, the first that reigned, I have heard, became a king and a freeman at the same time. Having been therefore," said he, " thus ignorant, I am justly punished for it : but now," said he, " Cyrus, I know myself. And can you yet think that the words of Apollo are true, that, by knowing myself, I shall be happy? Of you I make the inquiry, for this reason, because you seem to me to be the best able to guess at it at this time, for you can make it good."

Then Cyrus said : " Do you give me your opinion, Crœsus, on this ; for, taking into consideration your former happiness, I have compassion for you, and now give up into your possession the wife that you have, together with your daughters, (for daughters I hear you have,) your friends, servants, and table that you used to keep, but combats and wars I cut you off from." " By Jove ! then," said Crœsus, "consult no farther to make me an answer concerning my happiness ; for I tell you already, if you do these things for me that you say you will, that then I am already in possession of that course of life that others have, by my confession, thought the happiest, and I shall continue on in it." Then Cyrus said : " Who is he that is in possession of that happy course of life ?" " My own wife, Cyrus," said he ; " for she shared equally with me in all tender, good, pleasing, and agreeable things ; but in the cares about the success of these things in wars and battles, she shared not at all. So that, in my opinion, you provide for me in the manner that I did for the person that, of all mankind, I loved the most ; so that I think myself indebted to Apollo in some farther presents of gratitude and thanks." Cyrus, hearing this discourse, admired his good humour : and he carried him about with him wherever he went, either thinking that he was of use, or reckoning it the safest way to do so. Thus then they went to rest.

III. The next day Cyrus, calling together his friends and the commanders of the army, ordered some of them to receive the treasures, and some to take from amongst all the riches that Crœsus should deliver up, first, for the gods, such of them as the magi should direct ; then to receive the rest, put it into chests, and pack it up in the waggons, putting the waggons to the lot, and so to convey it wherever they went, that, when opportunity served, they might every one receive their deserved share. These men did so accordingly.

And Cyrus, calling to some of his servants that were there attending him, " Tell me," said he, " has any of you seen Abradatas? for I admire that he, who was so frequently in our company before, now does not appear." One of the servants therefore replied : " My sovereign, it is because he is not living, but died in the battle as he broke in with his chariot on the Egyptians. All the rest of them, except his particular companions, they say, turned off when they saw the Egyptian's compact body. His wife is now said to have taken up his dead body, to have placed it in the carriage that she herself was conveyed in, and to have brought it hither, to some place on the river Pactolus, and her servants they say are digging a grave for the deceased on a certain elevation. They say that his wife, after having set him out with all the ornaments she has, is sitting on the ground with his head on her knees." Cyrus hearing this, gave himself a blow on the thigh, mounted his horse presently, at a leap, and taking with him a thousand horse, rode away to this scene of affliction ; but gave orders to Gadatas and Gobryas to take with them all the rich ornaments proper for a friend and an excellent man deceased, and to follow after him ; and whoever had herds of cattle with him, he ordered them to take both oxen, and horses, and sheep, in good number, and to bring them away to the place where, by inquiry, they should find him to be, that he might sacrifice there to Abradatas.

As soon as he saw the woman sitting on the ground, and the dead body there lying, he shed tears at the afflicting sight, and said : " Alas! thou brave and faithful soul ! hast thou left us ?— and art thou gone?" At the same time he took him by the right hand, and the hand of the deceased came away, for it had been cut off with a sword by the Egyptians. He, at the sight of this, became yet much more concerned than before. The woman shrieked out in a lamentable manner, and, taking the hand from Cyrus, kissed it, fitted it to its proper place again as well as she could, and said : " The rest, Cyrus, is in the same condition; but what need you see it ?—And I know that I was not one of the least concerned in these his sufferings; and, perhaps, you were not less so; for I, fool that I was ! frequently exhorted him to behave in such a manner as to appear a friend to you worthy of notice; and I know he never thought of what he himself should suffer, but of what he should do to please you. He is dead, therefore," said she, " without reproach, and I, who urged him on, sit here alive !" Cyrus, shedding tears for some time in silence, then spoke; " He has died, woman, the noblest death; for he has died victorious ! do you adorn him with these things that I furnish you with." (And Gobryas and Gadatas were then come up and had brought rich ornaments in great abundance with them.) " Then," said he, " be assured he shall not want respect and honour in all other things : but, over and above, multitudes shall concur in raising him a monument that shall be worthy of us; and all the sacrifices shall be made him that are proper to be made in honour of a brave man. You," said he, " shall not be left destitute; but, for the sake of your modesty and every other virtue, I will pay you all other honours, as well as place those about you who shall convey you wherever you please. Do you but make it known to me who it is that you desire to be conveyed to." And Panthea replied : " Be confident, Cyrus," said she, " I will not conceal from you who it is that I desire to go to."

He, having said this, went away with great pity for the woman, that she should have lost such a husband, and for the man that he should have left such a wife behind him, never to see her more. The woman gave orders to her servants to retire, " Till such time," said she, " as I have lamented my husband as I please." Her nurse she bid to stay, and gave her orders that, when she was dead, she should wrap her and her husband up in one mantle together. The nurse, after having repeatedly begged her not to do thus, and meeting with no success, but observing her to grow angry, sat herself down, breaking out into tears. She, being beforehand provided with a sword, killed herself, and laying her head down on her husband's breast, she died. The nurse set up a

lamentable cry, and covered them both as Panthea had directed.

Cyrus, as soon as he was informed of what the woman had done, being struck with it, went to help her if he could. The servants, being three in number, seeing what had been done, drew their swords and killed themselves, as they stood at the place where she had ordered them. And the monument is now said to have been raised by continuing the mount on to the servants; and on a pillar above they say, the names of the man and woman were written in Syriac letters. Below, they say, there were three pillars, and that they were inscribed thus : " Of the servants." Cyrus, when he came to this melancholy scene, was struck with admiration of the woman, and having lamented over her, went away. He took care of them, as was proper, that all the funeral rites should be paid them in the noblest manner; and the monument, they say, was raised up to a very great size.

IV. After this the Carians, falling into factions, and the parties making war on each other, and having their habitations in places of strength, both called in Cyrus. Cyrus, remaining at Sardis, made engines and battering-rams to demolish the walls of those that should refuse to submit; and sent Adusius, a Persian, one who was not unable, in other respects, nor unskilled in war, and a very agreeable man, into Caria, and gave him an army. The Cilicians and Cyprians very readily engaged with him in that service; for which reason he never sent a Persian as governor over the Cilicians or Cyprians, but contented himself with their national kings, only receiving a tribute from them, and appointing them their quotas for military service whenever he should want them. Adusius, at the head of his army, came into Caria ; and, from both parties of the Carians, there were people that came to him, and were ready to admit him into their places of strength, to the prejudice of their opposite faction.

Adusius behaved to both in this manner : whichever of the parties he conferred with, he told them that what they had said was just; he said that they must needs keep it concealed from their antagonists that he and they were friends, that by this means he might fall on their antagonists whilst they were unprepared. As testimonials of their faith, he required that the Carians should swear, without fraud, to admit him and his people into their places of strength, for the service of Cyrus and of the Persians ; and he would himself make oath to enter their place of strength for the service of those that admitted him. Having done this, then privately and unknown to each other, he appointed them both the same night ; and that night he got within their walls, and seized the fortifications of both. As soon as day came he sat himself between them with his army about him, and summoned the proper persons on both sides to attend. These men when they saw each other, were astonished, and thought themselves both deceived. And Adusius spoke to this effect : " I swore to you, men of Caria, that I would without fraud enter your fortifications, to the advantage of those that admitted me ; therefore, if I destroy either of you, I reckon that I have made this entry to the damage of the Carians ; but if I procure you peace, and liberty to you both to cultivate your lands with security, I then reckon I am come for your advantage. From this day therefore, it is your part to join in correspondence with each other in a friendly manner, to cultivate your lands ; to give and receive each other's children mutually in marriage ; and if any one attempt to deal unjustly in any of these matters, to all such Cyrus and we will be enemies." After this the gates of the fortresses were thrown open, the ways were full of people passing from one to another, the lands were full of labourers, they celebrated festivals in common, and all was full of peace and satisfaction.

Meanwhile there came people from Cyrus to inquire whether he wanted either a reinforcement or engines. Adusius returned answer : " That, for the present, he might turn his forces another way." And at the same time that he made this answer he led the army away, leaving garrisons in the castles. The Carians prayed him to stay ; and on his refusal, they sent to Cyrus, begging him to send Adusius to them as their governor. Cyrus, meanwhile, had sent Hystaspes away with an army to Phrygia, on the Hellespont ; and when Adusius arrived, he ordered him to lead his army on in the way that Hystaspes was gone before, that those people might the more readily submit to Hystaspes, when they heard that there was another army advancing. The Greeks that inhabited on the seaside prevailed, by many presents, not to admit the barbarians within their walls ; but they engaged to pay a tribute, and serve in war where Cyrus

should command them. The king of Phrygia prepared himself, as intending to keep possession of his places of strength, and not to submit, and he sent word accordingly. But when the commanders under him revolted from him, he became destitute, and at last fell into the hands of Hystaspes, to receive the punishment that Cyrus should think fit to inflict on him. Hystaspes then, leaving strong Persian garrisons in the castles, went away, and, together with his own men, carried off considerable numbers of the Phrygians, both horse and shield-men. Cyrus sent orders to Adusius to join Hystaspes, and to take such of the Phrygians as took part with them, and bring them away with their arms ; but such as had shown an inclination to make war on them, to take both their horses and arms from them, and command them all to attend them with slings. These men did accordingly.

Cyrus then set forward from Sardis, leaving there a numerous Persian garrison, and taking Cræsus with him, and a great many waggons loaded with abundance of rich effects of all kinds. And Cræsus came to him with an exact account in writing of what was in each waggon, and delivering the writings to Cyrus, said : " By these, Cyrus," said he, " you will know who it is that justly delivers the things that he takes with him into his charge, and who it is that does not." Then Cyrus said : " You do extremely well, Cræsus, in being thus provident and careful ; but they that have the charge of these things for me, are such as deserve to have them, so that if they steal any of them, they steal what belongs to themselves." At the same time he delivered the writings to his friends and chief officers, that they might know which of those that were intrusted with these things delivered them up to them safe, and which of them did not. Such of the Lydians as he saw setting themselves out handsomely in their arms, horses, and chariots, and using all their endeavours to do what they thought would please him, these he took with him in arms. But from those that he saw attended with dissatisfaction he took their horses, and gave them to the Persians that first engaged in the service with him ; he burnt their arms, and obliged them to follow with slings. And all those that he disarmed, of the several nations that he subjected, he obliged them to practise the sling, reckoning it a servile sort of arms : for there are occasions when slingers, accompanied with other forces, are of very great use; but when a force consists all of slingers, they are not able of themselves to stand against a very few men, that march up close on them with arms proper for close engagement.

In his march to Babylon he overthrew the Phrygians of the Greater Phrygia. He overthrew the Cappadocians, and he subjected the Arabians. And out of all these he armed no less than forty thousand Persian horsemen. Abundance of the horses that belonged to prisoners taken, he distributed amongst all his allies. He came at last to Babylon, bringing with him a mighty multitude of horse, a mighty multitude of archers and javelin-men, but slingers innumerable.

V. When Cyrus got to Babylon he posted his whole army round the city, then rode round the city himself, together with his friends, and with such of his allies as he thought proper. When he had taken a view of the walls he prepared for drawing off the army from before the city; and a certain deserter coming off, told him that they intended to fall on him when he drew off the army. "For, as they took their view from the walls;" said he, "your phalanx appeared to them to be but weak." And no wonder that it really was so; for his men encompassing a great extent of wall, the phalanx was, of necessity, to be drawn out into but little depth. Cyrus having heard this, and standing in the centre of his army with those that were about him, gave orders that the heavy-armed men, from both the extremities, closing up the phalanx, should move away, along by that part of the army that stood still, till each extremity came up and joined in the centre. On their doing this, therefore, it gave the greater courage to those that stood, because they were now of double the depth they were of before; and it gave courage in like manner to those that moved away, for they that stood their ground were immediately on the enemy. When both the extremities marched and joined up to each other, they stood still, being now much the stronger; they that moved off, by means of those that were before them, and they that were in front, by means of those that were now behind them. The phalanx being thus closed up, the best men came of necessity to be ranged first and last, and the worst in the middle. And a disposition of this kind seemed to be the best adapted both for fighting and to prevent flight.

Then the horse and light-armed men on the wings came up nearer always to the commander-in-chief, as the phalanx became less extended by being thus doubled in depth. When they were thus collected together they retreated, by falling back till they got perfectly out of weapon's cast from the walls: when they were got out of weapon's cast they turned, and moving forward a few steps, they turned again to their shields about, and stood facing the walls; and the greater distance they were off, so much the seldomer they faced about; and when they thought themselves safe, they made off in a continued march till they reached their tents.

When they were encamped Cyrus summoned to him the proper persons, and said: "Friends and allies! we have taken a view of the city round, and I do not find that I can discover it is possible for one, by any attack, to make oneself master of walls that are so strong and so high. But the greater the numbers of men in the city are, since they venture not out to fight, so much the sooner, in my opinion, they may be taken by famine. Therefore, unless you have some other method to propose, I say that these men must be besieged and taken in that manner." Then Chrysantas said: "Does not this river, that is above two stadia over, run through the midst of the city?" "Yes, by Jove!" said Gobryas, "and it is of so great a depth, that two men, one standing on the other, would not reach above the water; so that the city is yet stronger by the river than by its walls." Then Cyrus said: "Chrysantas, let us lay aside these things that are above our force: it is our business, as soon as possible, to dig as broad and as deep a ditch as we can, each part of us measuring out his proportion, that by this means we may want the fewer men to keep watch."

So measuring out the ground around the wall, and from the side of the river, leaving a space sufficient for large turrets, he dug round the wall on every side a very great ditch; and they threw up the earth towards themselves. In the first place, he built the turrets on the river, laying their foundation on palm-trees, that were not less than a hundred feet in length: for there are those of them that grow even to a yet greater length than that; and palm-trees, that are pressed, bend up under the weight as asses do that are used to the pack-saddle. He placed the turrets on these;

for this reason, that it might carry the stronger appearance of his preparing to block up the city, and as if he intended that if the river made its way into the ditch it might not carry off the turrets. He raised likewise a great many other turrets on the rampart of earth, that he might have as many places as were proper for his watches. These people were thus employed. But they that were within the walls laughed at this blockade, as being themselves provided with necessaries for above twenty years. Cyrus hearing this, divided his army into twelve parts, as if he intended that each part should serve on the watch one month in the year. And when the Babylonians heard this they laughed yet more than before; thinking with themselves that they were to be watched by the Phrygians, Lydians, Arabians, and Cappadocians, men that were better affected to them than they were to the Persians. The ditches were now finished.

And Cyrus, when he heard that they were celebrating a festival in Babylon, in which all the Babylonians drank and revelled the whole night; on that occasion, as soon as it grew dark, took a number of men with him, and opened the ditches into the river. When this was done the water ran off in the night by the ditches, and the passage of the river through the city became passable. When the affair of the river was thus managed, Cyrus gave orders to the Persian commanders of thousands, both foot and horse, to attend him, each with his thousand drawn up two in front, and the rest of the allies to follow in the rear, ranged as they used to be before. They came accordingly. Then he making those that attended his person, both foot and horse, to go down into the dry part of the river, ordered them to try whether the channel of the river was passable. And when they brought him word that it was passable, he then called together the commanders both of foot and horse, and spoke to them in this manner:

" The river, my friends, has yielded us a passage into the city: let us boldly enter, and not fear any thing within, considering that these people that we are now to march against are the same that we defeated while they had their allies attending them, while they were awake, sober, armed, and in order. But now we march to them at a time that many of them are asleep, many drunk, and all of them in confusion; and when they discover that we are got in, they

will then, by means of their consternation, be yet more unfit for service than they are now. But in case any one apprehend, (what is said to be terrible to those that enter a city,) lest, mounting to the tops of their houses, they discharge down on us on every side:—as to this, be still more at ease; for if they mount to the tops of their houses, we have then the god Vulcan for our fellow-combatant; their porches are easily set fire to; their doors are made of the palm-tree, and anointed over with bituminous matter, which will nourish the flame. We have torches in abundance, that will presently take fire; we have plenty of pitch and tow, that will immediately raise a mighty flame; so that they must of necessity fly from off their houses immediately, or immediately be burnt. Come on then; take to your arms, and, with the help of the gods, I will lead you on. Do you," said he, " Gobryas and Gadatas, show us the ways; for you are acquainted with them, and when we are got in, lead us the readiest way to the palace." " It may be no wonder, perhaps," said they that were with Gobryas, "if the doors of the palace are open, for the city seems to-night to be in a general revel, but we shall meet with a guard at the gates, for there is always one set there." " We must not then be remiss," said Cyrus, " but march, that we take them as much unprepared as is possible."

When this was said they marched; and, of those that they met with, some they fell on and killed, some fled, and some set up a clamour. They that were with Gobryas joined in the clamour with them, as if they were revellers themselves, and marching on the shortest way that they could, they got round about the palace. Then they that attended Gadatas and Gobryas in military order found the doors of the palace shut; and they that were posted opposite to the guards fell on them, as they were drinking, with a great deal of light around them, and used them immediately in a hostile manner. As soon as the noise and clamour began, they that were within perceiving the disturbance, and the king commanding them to examine what the matter was, ran out, throwing open the gates. They that were with Gadatas, as soon as they saw the gates loose, broke in, pressing forward on the runaways, and dealing their blows amongst them, they came up to the king, and found him now in a standing posture, with his sword

Q

drawn. They that were with Gadatas and Gobryas, being many in number, mastered him; they likewise that were with him were killed; one holding up something before him, another flying, and another defending himself with any thing that he could meet with. Cyrus sent a body of horse up and down through the streets, bidding them kill those that they found abroad, and ordering some who understood the Syrian language to proclaim it to those that were in the houses to remain within, and that if any were found abroad they should be killed. These men did accordingly. Gadatas and Gobryas then came up, and having first paid their adoration to the gods for the revenge they had had on their impious king, they then kissed the hands and feet of Cyrus, shedding many tears in the midst of their joy and satisfaction.

When day came, and they that guarded the castles perceived that the city was taken and the king dead, they gave up the castles. Cyrus immediately took possession of the castles, and sent commanders with garrisons into them. He gave up the dead to be buried by their relations, and ordered heralds to make proclamation that the Babylonians should bring out their arms, and made it be declared that in whatever house any arms should be found, all the people in it should suffer death. They accordingly brought out their arms, and Cyrus had them deposited in the castles, that they might be ready in case he should want them on any future occasion.

When these things had been done, then, first summoning the magi, he commanded them to choose out for the gods the first-fruits of certain portions of ground for sacred use, as out of a city taken by the sword. After this he distributed houses and palaces to those that he reckoned had been sharers with him in all the actions that had been performed. He made the distributions in the manner that had been determined, the best things to the best deserving; and if any one thought himself wronged he ordered him to come and acquaint him with it. He gave out orders to the Babylonians to cultivate their land, to pay their taxes, and to serve those that they were severally given to. The Persians, and such as were his fellow-sharers, and those of his allies that chose to remain with him, he ordered to talk as masters of those they had received.

After this, Cyrus, desiring now to set himself on such a footing as he thought becoming a king, that he might appear but seldom, and in an awful manner, with the least envy that was possible, was of opinion to effect it with the consent of his friends, he contrived in this manner: as soon as it was day, taking a station in some place where he thought it proper, he admitted any one that had a mind to speak with him, and, after having given him his answer, dismissed him. The people, as soon as they knew he gave admittance, resorted to the place in disorderly and unmanageable multitudes; and, by their pressing round about the entrance, there was a mighty struggle and contention; and the servants that attended, distinguishing as well as they could, let them in. When any of his friends, by pressing their way through the crowd, appeared before him, Cyrus, holding out his hand, drew them to him, and spoke to them thus: "Wait here, my friends, till we have despatched the crowd, and then we will confer at leisure." His friends waited, and the crowd flocked in more and more till the evening came on them, before he could be at leisure to confer with his friends. So Cyrus then spoke: "Now, good people," said he, "it is time to separate; come again to-morrow morning, for I have a mind to have some discourse with you." His friends hearing this ran off, and went their way with great satisfaction, having done penance in the want of all kind of necessaries. Thus they went to rest. The next day Cyrus attended at the same place; and a much greater multitude of people that were desirous to be admitted to him, stood round about, attending much sooner than his friends. Cyrus, therefore, forming a large circle of Persian lance-men, bade them let none pass but his friends, and the Persian commanders of his allies. When these men were met he spoke to them to this effect:

"Friends and allies! we have nothing that we can lay to the charge of the gods, as not having hitherto effected whatever we have wished for: but if this be the consequence of performing great things, that one cannot obtain a little leisure for oneself, nor enjoy any satisfaction with one's friends, I bid farewell to such happiness. You observed," said he, "yesterday, that beginning in the morning to give audience to those that came, we did not make an end before the evening; and now you see that these, and many more than those that attended yesterday, are hereabout, intending to give us trouble. If one submit oneself therefore to this, I reckon that but a very little part of me will fall to your share, and but a little of you to mine; and in myself, I know very well I shall have no share at all. Besides," said he, "there is another ridiculous thing that I take notice of: I stand affected to you, as it is natural for me to do; but of those that stand here around, I may know here and there one, or perhaps none at all; and these men stand so disposed as to think, that if they can get the better of you in crowding, they shall effect what they desire at my hands sooner than you shall. Yet I should think it proper, that if any of them want me, they should make their court to you that are my friends, and beg to be introduced. But somebody then perhaps may say: ' Why did I not set myself on this footing from the beginning? and why did I give myself up so in common?' Why, because I knew that the affairs of war were of such a nature that the commander ought not to be behindhand either in knowing what was fit to be known, or in executing what the occasion required. And such commanders as were seldom to be seen, I thought, let slip many things that were proper to be done: but since war, that requires the utmost labour and diligence, is now ceased, my own mind seems to me to require some rest: as I am therefore at a loss what to do, that our own affairs and those of others that it is our part to take care of may be established on the best footing, let some one or other give us such advice as he thinks the most advantageous." Thus Cyrus spoke.

Then Artabazus, he who had said heretofore that he was his relation, rose up after him and spoke: "You have done very well, Cyrus," said he, "in beginning this discourse; for while you were yet very young I set out with a desire to be your friend; but observing that you were not at all in want of me, I neglected coming to you. When you came afterwards to want me, as a zealous deliverer of Cyaxares' orders to the Medes, I counted on it, that if I undertook this for you with zeal, I should become your intimate friend, and converse with you as long as I pleased. These things were so effectually done, that I had your commendation. After this the Hyrcanians first became our friends, and this while we were in great distress for assistants; so that, in the transport, we almost carried them about with us

in our arms. After this, when the enemy's camp was taken, I did not think that you were at leisure for me, and I excused you: after this Gobryas became your friend, and I was rejoiced at it: then Gadatas too, and it became a downright labour to share of you. When the Sacians and Cadusians became your allies and friends, it was probably very fit for them to cultivate and serve them, for they had served you. When we came back again to the place from whence we set out, then seeing you taken up with your horse, your chariots, and your engines, I thought that when you were at leisure from all this, then you would have leisure for me: but when the terrible message came, that all mankind were assembling against us, I determined with myself that this was the decisive affair; and, if things succeeded well here, I thought myself sure that we should then plentifully enjoy each other's company and converse. Now we have fought the decisive battle and conquered; we have Sardis and Croesus in our hands; Babylon we have taken; and we have borne down all before us; and yet, by the god Mithras! yesterday, had not I made my way with my fist through the multitude, I had not been able to get to you. And when you had taken me by the hand and bade me stay by you, then there I stood to be gazed at, for passing the whole day with you without either meat or drink. Now therefore if any means can be found, that they who have been the most deserving shall have the greatest share of you, it is well; if not, then would I again give out orders from you that all should depart excepting us that have been your friends from the beginning."

At this Cyrus and many others laughed. Then Chrysantas the Persian rose, and spoke thus: "Heretofore probably, Cyrus, you kept yourself open to the eyes of all, for the reasons you have yourself expressed, and because we were not the people that you were chiefly to cultivate, for we attended for our own sakes; but your business was, by all methods, to gain the multitude, that they might, with all possible satisfaction, be ready to undergo labours and run dangers with us: but since you are not only in circumstances to do this, but are able to acquire others that you may have occasion for, it is now very fit that you have a house yourself. Or what enjoyment can you have of your command, if you are the only one that does not share a home? than which there is no place that to men is more sacred, none more agreeable to them, and none nearer to them in their affections. And then," said he, "do you not think that we must be ashamed to see you abroad, faring hard, when we ourselves are in houses, and seem to have so much the advantage of you?" When Chrysantas had said this many more concurred with him in it.

After this he entered the royal palace, and they that conveyed the treasures from Sardis delivered them up here. When Cyrus entered, he first sacrificed to the goddess Vesta, and then to Regal Jove, and to whatever other deity the magi thought proper. Having done this, he now began to regulate other affairs; and considering what his business was, and that he was taking on him the government of great multitudes of men, he prepared to take up his habitation in the greatest city of all that were of note in the world, and this city had as great enmity to him as any city could have to a man.

Taking these things into his consideration, he thought himself in want of a guard about his person; and well knowing that men are at no time so much exposed as while they are eating, or drinking, or bathing, or on their bed, or asleep, he examined with himself what sort of people he might have about him that might be best trusted on these occasions; and he was of opinion that no man could ever be trusted who should love another more than the person who wanted his guard. Those men therefore that had sons or wives that were agreeable to them, or youths that they were fond of, he judged to be under a natural necessity of loving them best; and therefore thought that those who were emasculated would have the greatest affection for such as were able to enrich them the most, to redress them in case of any wrong done them, and to bestow honours on them: and, in his bounty to these people, he thought that no one could exceed himself. Besides all this, they being the object of other men's contempt, are, for this reason, in want of a master to countenance and support them; for there is no man that does not think it his due to assume the upper hand of them in every thing, unless some superior power control him in it; but nothing hinders such a servant from having the upper hand of all in his fidelity to his master. That they were destitute of all vigour, which is what most people think, did not appear to him to be so; and he grounded his

argument on the example of other animals; for vicious horses are thus made to give over biting, and indeed being vicious, but are not at all the less fit for service in war: and bulls, in like manner, throw of their insolence and untractableness, but they are not deprived of their strength and fitness for labour. Dogs also give over the trick of leaving their masters; but, for their watching, and their use in hunting, they are not at all the worse. Men, in the same manner, become the more gentle; but they are not the less careful of things that are given them in charge, nor are they worse horsemen, nor less able at throwing the javelin, nor less desirous of honour. And they have made it evident, that both in war and in hunting they still preserve emulation in their minds. And, with respect to their fidelity on occasion of their masters' being destroyed, they have stood the greatest trials; and no men have ever shown greater instances of fidelity in the misfortunes of their masters than such men have done. But, if they may be thought to have lost something of the strength of their bodies, arms perhaps may make it up, and put the weak and the strong on the same level in war.

Judging things to be thus, he began from his door-keepers, and selected from such persons all those that officiated about his person. But then being of opinion that this was not a sufficient guard against the great multitude of people that were disaffected towards him, he considered whom he should take from amongst all the rest, as the most faithful for his guard round the palace. Observing therefore that the Persians, while at home, were those that fared the hardest on account of their poverty, and lived in the most laborious manner, because their country was rocky and barren, and they themselves forced to work with their own hands, he thought these would be the most pleased with that sort of life that they lived with him. Out of these therefore he took ten thousand lance-men, who kept guard both night and day round about the palace, whilst he kept quiet at home; and when he went abroad they marched with him, ranged in order on every side of him. Then thinking it necessary that there should be a guard sufficient for the whole city, whether he were there present himself, or absent abroad, he established a sufficient garrison in Babylon, and appointed the Babylonians to supply these men likewise with their pay, intending to distress them as much as he could, that they might be reduced to the lowest condition, and be the most easily managed. This guard, that was then established about his own person and in Babylon, continues on the same footing at this day.

Then taking into his consideration how his whole dominion might be maintained, and more might be acquired, he was of opinion that these mercenaries were not so much better than the people subjected, as they were fewer in number. He determined therefore that he ought to retain those brave men, who had, with the assistance of the gods, helped him to his conquest, and to take care that they should not grow remiss in the practice of virtue. And that he might not seem to order and direct them, but that, as judging of themselves what was best, they might persevere in virtue, and cultivate it, he called together the alike-honoured, and all such as were proper, as well as those whom he thought worthy to share with him, both in his labours and advantages, and when they were met he spoke to this effect:

" My friends and allies! we owe the greatest thanks to the gods for having granted us the things of which we thought ourselves worthy; for we are now possessed of a very large and noble country, and of people who, by their labour in the culture of it, will maintain us. We have houses and furniture in them; and let none of you imagine that by this possession he holds things that are foreign and not belonging to him; for it is a perpetual law amongst all men, that when a city is taken from an enemy, both the persons and treasures of the inhabitants belong to the captors. Whatever it is therefore that you possess, you do not possess it unjustly; but whatever you suffer them to keep, it is in benignity and love to mankind that you do not take it away. As to the time to come, my judgment is this: if we turn ourselves to a negligent and abandoned course of life, and to the luxury and pleasure of vicious men, who think labour to be the greatest misery, and a life of ease to be a pleasure, then, I say, we shall presently become of less value in ourselves, and shall presently lose all our advantages. For to have been once brave men is not sufficient in order to continue brave men, unless one continue careful of oneself to the end. But as all other arts when neglected sink in their worth; and as in the case of our bodies, when in good condition, if we abandon them to a course of laziness and inactivity, they become again faulty and deficient; so a discreet temper of mind, temperance, and the command of our passions, and courage, when a man remits the practice of them, from thenceforward turn again into vice. We ought not therefore to be remiss, nor throw ourselves immediately on every present pleasure; for I think it a great thing to acquire a dominion, and yet a greater to preserve it when acquired. For to acquire often befalls a man who contributes nothing towards it but boldness in the attempt; but to preserve an acquisition that one has made, this cannot be done without discretion, nor without the command of one's passions, nor without much care: and knowing things to be thus, we ought to be much more careful in the practice of virtue now, than before we made these valuable acquisitions; well knowing that when a man has most in his possession, he then most abounds in those that envy him, that form designs against him, and that are his enemies: especially if he hold the possessions and service of men, as we do, against their wills. The gods, we ought to believe, will be with us; for we are not got into an unjust possession of these things by designs and contrivances of our own to get them, but on designs that have been formed against us, we have revenged ourselves in the punishment of the contrivers. The next best thing after this is what we must take care to provide ourselves with; and that is, to be better than the people that are subjected, and to deserve a rule. In heat, therefore, and in cold, in meat and drink, in labours and in rest, we must of necessity allow our servants a share. But while we share with them in these things, we should endeavour to appear superior to them in all of them: but in the knowledge and practice of military affairs, we are not to allow any share at all to such as we intend to have as labourers and tributaries to us, but in all exercises of this kind, we must preserve the ascendant; determining within ourselves that the gods have set these things before men, as the instruments and means of liberty and happiness. And as we have taken arms away from them, so ought we never to be without them ourselves: well knowing that they who have always their arms the nearest at hand, have what they desire the most at their command. If any one suggest to himself such things as these; as, what advantage is it to us to effect what we desire, if we must still bear hunger and thirst, labour and application? This man ought to learn that good things give so much the more delight, as one takes the more pains beforehand to attain them. Labour and pains are what give a relish to all good things. Without being in want of a thing, there is nothing that can be acquired, though ever so noble, that can be pleasant. If some divinity have afforded us the things that men most desire; in order to have them appear the pleasantest, every one will make them so to himself. And such a man will have as much the advantage of those that live more necessitous, as he will get the pleasantest food when he is hungry, enjoy the pleasantest drink when he is thirsty, and when he wants rest can take it in the pleasantest manner. On all these accounts, I say, we must charge ourselves with the part of brave and excellent men, that we may enjoy our advantages in the best manner, and with the most pleasure, and that we may never come to experience the greatest hardship in the world; for it is not so hard a matter to gain advantages, as it is afflicting to be deprived of them after one has obtained them. Consider then what pretence we can have to choose to be worse than before. It is because we have obtained dominion! But it does not become a prince to be more vicious than those that are under his command. But perhaps it may be because we seem to be more prosperous and happy than before. Will any man say then that vice is to be indulged to pros-

perity? But perhaps, since we have acquired slaves, if they are vicious, we will punish them; and how does it become one that is vicious himself to punish others for vice and sloth? Consider this farther, that we are preparing to maintain abundance of men as guards to our houses and persons, and how can it be otherwise than base in us, to think it fit to have others as guards of our own safety, and not to be guards to ourselves? And you ought to be well assured that there is no other guard so secure as to be oneself an excellent and worthy man. This must keep you company; for with one that is destitute of virtue, nothing else ought to go well. What then do I say you should do? where practice virtue? where apply to the exercise of it? Nothing new, my friends, will I tell you; but as the alike-honoured among Persians pass their time about the courts; so I say, it is our parts being all alike honoured here, to practise the same things that are practised there. It is your part to attend here, keeping your eyes on me, to observe if I continue careful of the things that I ought to be careful of. I will keep my eyes intent on you, and such as I see practising things good and excellent I will reward. The sons that we have we shall here instruct; we shall be ourselves the better by being desirous to show ourselves the best examples to them that we can; and the boys will not easily become vicious, not even though they incline to it, when they neither see nor hear any thing that is mean or base, and pass their whole time under excellent institutions."

XENOPHON

INSTITUTION OF CYRUS.

BOOK VIII.

CONTENTS of BOOK VIII.

INSTITUTION OF CYRUS.

BOOK VIII.

I. THUS then Cyrus spoke; after him Chrysantas rose and spoke in this manner: " I have frequently, at other times, observed, my friends, that a good prince is not at all different from a good father: for fathers are careful to provide that their children may never come to fail of what is for their advantage; and Cyrus seems now to me to advise us to such things as will make us pass our days in the most fortunate and happy manner. But what I think he has been defective in laying open, this I will endeavour to explain to those that are not apprised of it; for have you considered what city belonging to an enemy can possibly be taken by men that are not obedient to command? And what city that belongs to those that are friends can be preserved by men that are not obedient? And what army consisting of men disobedient and refractory can be victorious? How can men sooner be defeated in battle than when every one begins separately to consult his own particular safety? or what other valuable thing can be performed by such as do not submit to the direction of their betters? What cities are they that are justly and wisely regulated? What are those families that preserve themselves in safety? And how come ships to arrive whither they are bound? By what other means have we obtained the advantages we have, more than by obedience to our commander? By this we have been presently ready at our proper posts; and by following our commander in compact order, we have been irresistible; and of things that have been given us in charge, we have left none executed by halves. Therefore, if obedience to command be of the greatest advantage, with respect to the making acquisitions, be you assured that it is, in the same manner, of the greatest advantage with respect to the preserving what is fit for us to preserve. Heretofore we were subject to the commands of many, and commanded none ourselves; but now you are all on a footing of bearing rule, some over more, and some over less. Therefore as you desire to rule those that are under you, so let us all submit to those that it becomes us to submit to. We ought to distinguish ourselves so far from slaves, as that slaves do service to their masters against their wills; and if we desire to be free, we ought willingly to perform what appears to be most excellent and worthy. You will find," said he, "that where a people are under a government that is not monarchical, and are most ready to pay obedience to their rulers, they are always least liable to the necessity of submitting to their enemies. Let us therefore attend about the palace as Cyrus orders; let us practise those things that will best enable us to hold what we ought; and let us yield ourselves to Cyrus, to make use of us in what is proper; for you ought to be well assured that it is not possible for Cyrus to find any thing that he can make an advantage of to himself, and that is not so to us, since the same things are alike serviceable to us both, and we have both the same enemies."

When Chrysantas had said this, many more, both Persians and allies, rose up, and spoke to the same effect; and it was determined that the men of note and quality should always attend at Cyrus' doors, and yield themselves to his service in whatever he thought fit, till he himself dismissed them. And according as it was then determined, so do those in Asia, that are under the king, do yet at this day: and they attend at the doors of their princes. And as in this discourse it is shown how Cyrus established things, in order to secure the dominion to himself and to the Persians; so do the kings, his successors, continue to put the same things in practice as laws to this day. But it

R

is in this, as in other things, when there is a better director, the established rules are executed more strictly; and when tnere is a worse, more negligently. The men of note therefore frequented the gates of Cyrus with their horses and lances; this being the joint determination of all the best of those that concurred with him in the overthrow of this empire.

Cyrus then constituted different officers to take care of different affairs. He had his receivers of the revenues, his paymasters, overseers of his works, keepers of his treasures, and officers to provide things that were proper for his table. He appointed as masters of his horse and of his dogs such as he thought would provide him with the best of these kinds of creatures for his use. But as to those whom he thought fit to have as joint guardians of his power and grandeur, he himself took care to have them the best; he did not give this in charge to others, but thought it his own business. He knew that in·case he were at any time obliged to come to a battle, they that were to stand by him on each side, and to support him in the rear, were to be taken from amongst these; with these he was to engage in the greatest dangers: out of these he knew he was to constitute the commanders of his several bodies of foot and horse; and if he were in want of generals, to serve any where in his own absence, out of these he knew they were to be sent. Some of these he knew he was to use as guardians and satraps of cities and whole nations; and some of them were to be sent out as ambassadors; and this he thought a thing of the greatest consequence with respect to the obtaining what he desired without a war. If they therefore that were to be intrusted with the management of most affairs, and of affairs of the greatest consequence, were not such as they should be, he thought matters would go very ill with him; but if they were such as they should be, he reckoned that affairs would go very well.

This being his judgment, he therefore took this care on him, and he reckoned that he himself was to engage in the same exercise of virtue; for he thought it not possible for one who was not himself such as he should be, to incite others to great and noble actions. On these considerations, he thought leisure, in the first place, necessary, if he intended to have it in his power to take care of the principal affairs. He reckoned it therefore impossible for him to be negligent of his revenues; foreseeing that, in a great dominion, he must of necessity be at a great expense. But then, on the other side, his possessions being very great to be himself always taken up about them, he thought would leave him no leisure to take care of the safety of the whole.

So taking into his consideration how his economy might be settled on a good footing, and he at the same time might have leisure, he observed the order of an army: for as the commanders of tens take care of their several decades; the captains, of the commanders of tens; the commanders of thousands, of the captains; the commanders of ten thousand, of the commanders of thousands; by which means, no one is left without care, though an army consists of many times ten thousand men; and when a general has any service for the army to do, it is enough for him to give his orders to the commanders of ten thousand; in like manner as these affairs were regulated, Cyrus accordingly ranged the affairs of his household under certain heads: and thus Cyrus, by discoursing with a few people, was enabled to have the affairs of his economy taken care of; and after this, he had yet more leisure than another man, who had but a single house or a single ship in charge. Having thus settled his own affairs, he taught others to use the same method, and so procured leisure both for himself and for those about him.

He then began to take on him the business of making his companions in power such as they should be. And in the first place, as many as were able to subsist by the labour of others, and were not attending at his doors, these he inquired into; reckoning that they who did attend would not be guilty of any base and vile action, both by reason of their being near their prince, and that in whatever they did, they would be observed by the most excellent men. They that did not attend he reckoned absented themselves, either out of their indulgence to some vicious passion, or on account of some unjust practice, or out of negligence. Being first therefore convinced of this in his judgment, he brought all such men under a necessity of attending: for he ordered some one of those about him, that were his chief friends, to seize what belonged to the person that did not attend, and to declare that it belonged to himself. When this was done, they that were dispossessed immediately came and complained, as persons that had been wronged. Cyrus, for a great while, was not at leisure to give such men a hearing; and when he had heard them, he deferred the decision of the matter a long while. By acting thus, he thought he accustomed them to make their court, and with less ill-will to him than if he himself had forced them to attend, by inflicting punishments on them. This was one method of instruction that he used, in order to make men attend on him. Another was, to command those that attended on such services as were most easy to execute and most profitable. Another was, never to allow the absent a share in any advantage. But the chief method of all that he used to necessitate men to attend was this, that in case a man did not yield obedience to these other methods, he then took what he had from him, and gave it to another man that he thought would be able to attend on the proper occasions. And thus he gained a useful friend, instead of a useless one; and the present king still makes inquiry whether any one of those be absent whose part it is to attend.

In this manner did he carry himself to those that did not attend on him: but those that afforded him their attendance and service, he thought he should best excite to great and noble actions, if he, being their prince, should endeavour to show himself to those whom he governed the most accomplished of all in virtue; for he thought he observed that men were the better for written laws; but a good prince, he reckoned, was to men a seeing law, because he was able both to give directions, to see the man that acted irregularly, and to punish him.

This being his judgment, he showed himself, in the first place, the more industrious to discharge himself in all dues to the gods at that time when he was in the most fortunate circumstances: and then were first appointed certain magi to sing a hymn to the gods, always as soon as it was day, and every day to sacrifice to such deities as the magi should direct. And the establishments that were thus made at that time continue in use with the king that still succeeds in the government, on to this day. The rest of the Persians therefore were the first that followed his example in these things; reckoning that they should be the more fortunate, if they served the gods as he did, who was the most fortunate of all, and their prince. And they thought by doing thus

they should please Cyrus. But Cyrus accounted the piety of those about him an advantage to himself; reckoning, as they do, who choose to undertake a voyage in company with men of piety, rather than with such as appear to have been guilty of any thing impious. And besides this, he reckoned that, if all his associates were religious, they would be the less apt to be guilty of any thing impious towards each other, or towards him, who thought himself their benefactor. Then by showing himself to be under great concern and fear of doing injury to any friend or ally, and keeping steadily to the rule of justice, he thought that others would abstain the more from base gains, and would take care that their revenue should arise to them by just methods. And he was of opinion that he should the better inspire other men with respect and awe, if he himself appeared to pay so great a respect to all, as never to say or do any thing shameful and vile: and that it would fall out thus, he grounded his argument on this; that not only in the case of a prince, but even of such as men had no fear of, they paid more respect to those that behaved respectfully than they did to the impudent. And such women as they observed to be modest and respectful they were the more ready to pay respect to. And he thought that a temper of obedience would be the more firmly established in those about him, if he appeared to bestow greater rewards on the obedient, than on those that seemed possessed of the greatest and most elaborate virtues. In this opinion, and in this practice, he always continued: and then, by showing his own goodness and modesty of temper, he made all others the more ready to practise it; for when men see one, that has it most in his power to behave with haughtiness and insolence, behave with this modesty and goodness of temper, then even those of the lowest degree are the more willing to be seen acting without any manner of insolence. He distinguished that respect and awe from this goodness of temper in this manner; that they who were possessed with this awe avoided things that were shameful and vile, while they were exposed to the eyes of others; but that the modest and good-tempered did it even in the dark. He thought likewise to make men practise a command of their passions best, by showing that he himself was not drawn away by present pleasures from the pursuit of good and excellent things; and that he preferred

toil and labour in the pursuit of a noble end
before all delights. Being therefore such a
man himself, he established an excellent order
at his doors; the meaner sort submitting to the
better, and all behaving with great awe and
decency one towards another. You would not
see any one there in anger, breaking out into
noise and clamour, nor expressing an insulting
pleasure in insolent laughter. But to see them,
you would think that they really lived in
the most comely and noble manner. In the
practice of such things as these, and with
such things always before their eyes, they
passed their days at the doors of Cyrus.

But then, in order to inure them to the practice of military affairs, he led out all those to
hunt that he thought proper to exercise in that
manner; reckoning this the best method of
practising all such things as relate to war, as
well as the truest exercise of the art of riding;
for this helps them the most of any thing, to
sit firm on horseback, in all sorts of ground,
by means of their pursuing the wild beasts in
their flight; and this, the most of any thing,
makes them capable of acting on horseback, by
means of their love of praise and desire of
taking their game. And by this he chiefly
accustomed his associates to gain a command
over their passions, and to be able to bear toil,
to bear cold and heat, hunger and thirst. And
the king that now reigns, together with those
that are about him, continue still the same
practice.

It is evident, therefore, by what has been
before said, that he thought dominion became
no one that was not himself better than those
whom he governed; and that by thus exercising these about him, he inured himself, the
most of all, to a command of his passions, and
to all military arts and exercises. For he led
out others abroad to hunt, when there was no
necessity that obliged him to stay at home;
and when there was any such necessity, he then
hunted the beasts that were maintained in his
parks. He never took his supper before he
gave himself a sweat; nor did he ever throw
food to his horses before they were exercised:
and he invited his servants abroad with him to
this hunting. He himself, therefore, greatly excelled in all noble performances; and they that
were about him likewise did so, by means of their
continual exercise. In this manner he made
himself an example to others. And, besides

this, whoever he saw the most zealous in the
pursuit of generous actions, such he rewarded
with presents, with commands, with placing
them in the principal seats, and with all other
honours. So that he raised a mighty emulation amongst all, to try by what means every
one might appear to Cyrus the most deserving.

And I think I have likewise heard, concerning Cyrus, that he was of opinion that
princes ought to excel those that are under
their dominion, not only in being better than
they, but that they ought likewise to play the
impostors with them. He chose therefore to
wear the Median robe, and persuaded his associates to put it on; for in case a man had any
thing defective in his person, he thought that
this concealed it, and made those that wore it
appear the handsomest and the tallest. And
they have a sort of shoe, where they may fit in
something under their feet, without its being
seen, so as to make themselves appear taller
than they really are. He allowed them also
to colour their eyes, that they might seem to
have finer eyes than they really had, and to
paint themselves, that they might appear to be
of better complexions than they naturally were
of. He took care, likewise, to use them not
to be seen to spit, or blow the nose, or to turn
aside to gaze at any spectacle, as if they were
men that admired nothing. And all these
things, he thought, contributed something to
their appearing the more awful to the people
that were subject to his dominion.

Those that he thought the proper persons to
share, by his own means, in the dominion with
him, he disciplined in this manner, and by
acting himself, at the head of them, in the
same venerable and majestic way. But those
that he trained for servitude, he never encouraged to the practice of ingenious labours, nor
allowed them the possession of arms, but took
care that they should never go without their
meat and drink for the sake of these liberal
exercises; for when with their horse they
drove out the wild beasts into the plains, he
allowed meat and drink to be carried for the
use of these people during the hunt, but not
for any of the ingenious. And when he was
on a march he led them to water as he did the
beasts of burden; and when the time for dinner came, he waited till they had eaten something, that they might not be distressed with
hunger. So that these people, as the better

sort likewise did, called him their father, for taking care that, beyond all doubt, they should always continue slaves.

Thus he provided for the security of the whole Persian dominion: but he was very confident that he himself was in no danger of meeting with any mischief from the people that were conquered, for he reckoned them weak and dispirited, and he observed them destitute of all order; and besides, none of them ever came near him by night or day. But such as he reckoned the better sort, that he saw armed and in compact order; some of them commanders of horse, and some of foot, and many of them that he perceived with spirits equal to rule, that were next to his own guards, and many of whom were frequently in company with himself, (for there was a necessity that it should be so, because he was to make use of them,) from these there was the most danger of his receiving mischief many ways. Therefore, taking into his consideration how matters might be made safe for him in this respect, to take away their arms from them and render them unfit for war, he did not approve, both accounting it unjust, and believing it to be a dissolution of his empire. And then again not to admit them to his presence, and openly to distrust them, he reckoned the beginning and foundation of a war. Instead of all these things, there was one that he determined to be the best for his security, and the handsomest of all, which was to try if possibly he could make the better sort of men more friends to himself than to one another. By what means therefore it was that in my opinion he came to be beloved, I will endeavour to relate.

II. For, first, he constantly at all times displayed, as much as he could, his own good-nature and love to mankind; reckoning that as it is no easy matter for men to love those who seem to hate them, or to bear good-will to those that have ill intentions towards them; so it was not possible for those that were known to love and bear good-will, to be hated by such as thought themselves beloved. Therefore, whilst he had it not so much in his power to bestow rich benefits on them, he endeavoured to captivate their affections by anticipating his companions in care and in pains, by appearing pleased with their advantages, and afflicted at their misfortunes; but when he had wherewithal to be bountiful to them, he seems to me to have known, in the first place, that there is no benefaction amongst men that is of equal expense, and is so grateful as that of sharing meat and drink with them.

And being of this opinion, he first regulated his table so as to have placed before him as many of the same things that he ate of himself as were sufficient for great numbers of people. And all that was set before him, except what was used by himself and his guests, he distributed to such of his friends as he intended to show that he remembered or had a kindness for. He sent likewise about to such as he happened to be pleased with, whether they were employed on the guard any where, or attended to pay their court to him, or were concerned in any other affairs. And this he did in order to signify that they who were desirous to do what was pleasing to him were not to be concealed from him. He paid the same honour from his table to his own domestics when he had a mind to give any of them his commendation. And all the meat that belonged to his domestics he placed on his own table, thinking that, as in the case of children, so this would gain him some good-will from them. And if he had a mind that any of his friends should have great numbers of people attend and pay their court to them, he sent them presents from his table: for even yet, at this day, all people make the greater court to such as they observe to have things sent them from off the king's table; because they reckon them men in great honour and esteem, and that in case they want any thing to be done, they are able to effect it for them. And besides, it is not only on these accounts that have been mentioned that the things sent from the king are pleasing, but things that come from the king's table do really very much excel in point of pleasure. And that it should be so is not at all to be wondered at; for, as other arts are wrought up in great cities to a greater degree of perfection, in the same manner are the meats that come from the king dressed in greater perfection: for, in little cities, the same people make both the frame of a couch, a door, a plough, and a table; and frequently the same person is a builder too, and very well satisfied he is if he meet with customers enough to maintain him. It is impossible therefore for a man that makes a great many different things to do them all well. But in great cities, because there are multitudes that want every particular thing, one art alone is sufficient for the maintenance of every one: and frequently not an entire one neither, but one man makes shoes for men, another for women. Sometimes it happens that one gets a maintenance by sewing shoes together, another by cutting them out; one by cutting out clothes only, and another without doing any of these things, is maintained by fitting together the pieces so cut out. He therefore that deals in a business that lies within a little compass, must of necessity do it the best. The case is the same with respect to the business of a table; for he that has the same man to cover and adorn the frame of a couch, to set out the table, to knead the dough, to dress the several different meats, must necessarily, in my opinion, fare in each particular as it happens. But where it is business enough for one man to boil meat, for another to roast it; for one to boil fish, and for another to broil it; where it is business enough for one man to make bread, and that not of every sort neither, but that it is enough for him to furnish one sort good, each man, in my opinion, must of necessity work up the things that are thus made to a very great perfection. He therefore by this kind of management greatly exceeded all other people in this sort of courtship, by presents of meat.

And how he came likewise to be greatly superior in all other ways of gaining on men, I will now relate; for he that so much exceeded other men in the multitude of his revenues, exceeded them yet more in the multitude of his presents. Cyrus therefore began it; and this custom of making abundance of presents continues to this day practised by the kings his successors. Who is there that is known to have richer friends than the Persian king has? who is known to set out the people about him in finer habits than this king does? whose presents are known to be such as some of those which this king makes? as bracelets and collars, and horses with bridles of gold? for it is not allowed there that any one should have these things but he that the king gives them to. What other man is there that can be said to make himself be preferred before brothers, fathers, or children, by his great presents? what other man has power to chastise his enemies that are many months' journey distant from him, as the Persian king has? what other man but Cyrus, after having overturned an empire, ever died and had the title of

father given him by the people he subjected? for it is plain that this is the name of one that bestows rather than one that takes away.

We have been likewise informed that he gained those men that are called the eyes and the ears of the king, by no other means than by making them presents, and by bestowing honours and rewards on them; for by being very bountiful to those that gave him an account of what was proper for him to be informed of, he set abundance of people on the search both with ears and eyes, to find what information they should give the king that might be useful to him. On this the eyes of the king were reckoned to be very numerous, and his ears so too. But if any one think it proper for a king to choose but one person as his eye, he judges not right; for one man would see but few things, and one man would hear but few things; and if this were given in charge to one only, it would be as if the rest were ordered to neglect it. Besides, whoever was known to be this eye, people would know that they were to be on their guard against him. This then is not the course that is taken; but the king hears every one that says he has heard or seen any thing worthy his attending to. By this means the ears and eyes of the king are reckoned to be in great number; and people are every where afraid of saying any thing to the king's prejudice, as if he himself heard them; and of doing any thing to his prejudice, as if he himself were present. So that no one durst mention any thing scandalous concerning Cyrus to any body: but every one stood so disposed, as if they were always amidst the eyes and ears of the king, whatever company they were in.

I know not what cause any one can better assign for such disposition in men towards him than that he thought fit to bestow great benefits in return for little ones. And it is not to be wondered at, that he who was the richest of all, exceeded others in the greatness of his presents; but that one possessed of the royal dignity should exceed others in the culture and care of his friends, this is a thing more worthy of notice. He is said never to have appeared so much ashamed of being outdone in any thing as in the culture of his friends: and a saying of his is recorded, expressing, "That the business of a good herdsman and of a good king were very near alike; for a herdsman," he said, "ought to provide for the welfare and happiness of the herd, and make use of them consistently with the happiness of those creatures ; and that a king ought, in the same manner, to make men and cities happy, and in the same manner to make use of them." It is no wonder therefore, if this were his sentiment, that he had an ambition to outdo all in the culture of men.

And Cyrus is said to have given this noble instance to Crœsus, on a certain time, when Crœsus suggested to him that, by the multitude of presents that he made, he would be a beggar, when it was in his power to lay up at home mighty treasures of gold for the use of one. It is said that Cyrus then asked him thus : " What sums do you think I should now have in possession, if I had been hoarding up gold, as you bid me, ever since I have been in power ?" And that Crœsus, in reply, named some mighty sum ; and that Cyrus to this said . " Well. Crœsus, do you send with Hystaspes here some person that you have most confidence in ; and do you, Hystaspes," said he, " go about to my friends, tell them that I am in want of money for a certain affair (and in reality I am in want of it), and bid them furnish me with as much as they are each of them able to do ; and that, writing it down and signing it, they deliver the letter to Crœsus' officer to bring me." Then writing down what he had said, and signing it, he gave it to Hystaspes to carry it to his friends : but added in the letter to them all, " That they should receive Hystaspes as his friend." After they had gone round, and Crœsus' officer brought the letters, Hystaspes said : " O Cyrus! my king, you must now make use of me as a rich man, for here do I attend you abounding in presents that have been made me on account of your letter." Cyrus on this said : " This then is one treasure to me, Crœsus ; but look over the others, and reckon up what riches there are there ready for me, in case I want for my own use. Crœsus on calculation is said to have found many times the sum that he told Cyrus he might now have had in his treasury, if he had hoarded. When it appeared to be thus, Cyrus is reported to have said :

" You see, Crœsus, that I have my treasures too ; but you bid me hoard them up, to be envied and hated for them : you bid me place hired guards on them, and in those to put my trust. But I make my friends rich, and reckon them to be treasures to me, and guards both to myself and to all things of value that belong to us, and such as are more to be trusted than if I set up a guard of hirelings. Besides, there is another thing that I will tell you : what the gods have wrought into the souls of men, and by it have made them all equally indigent, this, Crœsus, I am not able to get the better of ; for I am, as others are, insatiably greedy of riches : but I reckon I differ from most others in this ; that when they have acquired more than is sufficient for them, some of those treasures they bury under ground, and some they let decay and spoil, and others they give themselves a great deal of trouble about, in telling, in measuring, in weighing, airing, and watching them ; and though they have all these things at home, they neither eat more than they are able to bear, for they would burst, nor do they put on more clothes than they can bear, for they would suffocate, but all their superfluous treasures they have only for business and trouble. Whereas I serve the gods, and am ever desirous of more.; and when I have acquired it, out of what I find to be more than suffices me, I satisfy the wants of my friends ; and by enriching men with it, and by doing them kindnesses, I gain their goodwill and their friendship, and obtain security and glory, things that do not corrupt and spoil, and do not distress one by over-abounding ; but glory, the more there is of it, the greater and more noble it is, and the lighter to bear, and those that bear it, it often makes the lighter and easier. And that you may be sensible of this, Crœsus," said he, " they that possess the most, and have most in their custody, I do not reckon the happiest men ; for then would guards on the walls be the happiest of all men, for they have the custody of all that there is in whole cities ; but the person that can acquire the most with justice, and use the most with honour, him do I reckon the happiest man ; and this I reckon to be riches."

And as he expressed these things, so he apparently practised them. But, besides all this, having observed that most men, if they enjoy health, take care to provide themselves with all things fitting, and lay up all things that are of use with respect to a healthy course of life ; but how to be supplied with things that are of service, in case they are sick, of this he observed they were not very careful. He therefore thought proper to be at pains to provide himself with these things. He got together the best physicians about him, by his being willing to be at the expense of it; and whatever instruments, medicines, meats, or drinks, any one told him to be of use, there was nothing of all these that he did not provide himself with, and treasure up.   And when any of those whom it was proper for him to take care of fell ill, he went himself to see them, and furnished them with whatever they wanted; and was thankful to the physicians whenever they cured any one, and took the things which they used from out of what he had in store.   These and many such things did he contrive, in order to gain the principal place in the affections of those by whom he desired to be beloved.

Then all those affairs, wherein he appointed games, and established prizes, with intention to raise an emulation in men, to perform great and noble things, those gained Cyrus the applause of taking care that virtue should be kept in practice.   But these very games created strife and emulation amongst the better sort of men. And, besides, Cyrus established as a law, that whatever required a determination, whether it were a matter of right, or a dispute relating to games, the parties requiring such determination should have joint recourse to certain judges. It is plain therefore that both the parties at variance aimed at pitching on such judges as were the best and the most their friends; and he that lost his cause envied him that carried it, and hated those that did not give the cause for himself; he that carried his cause attributed the success to the justice of it, so reckoned he owed nobody thanks.   They that aimed at being chief in the friendship and esteem of Cyrus, like others in certain cities, bore envy to each other, so that most of them rather wished each other out of the way, than ever acted in concert together for their mutual advantage. These things make it evident by what means he made all the considerable men more affectionate to himself than they were one to another.

III. But now we will relate how Cyrus, for the first time, marched in procession out of the palace; for the majesty of this procession seems to me to have been one of those arts that made his government not liable to contempt.   First, therefore, before he made this procession he called in to him all those, both Persians and others, that were possessed of commands, and distributed to them Median

robes: and it was then that the Persians first put on the Median robe.   Having distributed these, he told them that he intended to march in procession to those portions of ground that had been chosen and set apart for the gods, and to make a sacrifice, accompanied by them.   "Attend, therefore," said he, "at the gates before the rising of the sun, adorned with these robes, and form yourselves as Pheraulas the Persian shall give you orders from me; and when I lead the way, do you follow on in the station assigned you.   But, if any of you think that our procession will be handsomer in any other manner, than as we march at this time, when we return again let him inform me; for every thing ought to be so disposed as shall appear to you to be most beautiful and noble."   When he had distributed the finest robes to the greatest men, he then produced other robes of the Median sort; for he had provided them in great numbers, and was not sparing either in the purple habits, or those of a dark colour, or in the scarlet, or the murrey.   And having distributed a certain portion of these to each of the commanders, he bade them adorn and set out their friends with them, "as I," said he, "adorn you." And one of those that were present then asked him, "But when will you, Cyrus," said he, "be adorned yourself?"   To this he replied: "And do you not think," said he, "that I am already adorned in adorning all you? No matter," said he, "if I am but able to serve my friends, whatever robe I wear, I shall appear fine in it."   So these men going their ways, and sending for their friends, adorned them with these robes.

Cyrus, taking Pheraulas, one of the inferior degree of people, to be a man of good understanding, a lover of what was beautiful and orderly, and careful to please him—the same that heretofore spoke for every one's being rewarded according to his desert; and calling this man to him, he advised with him how he might make this procession in a manner that might appear the most beautiful to his friends, and most terrible to those that were disaffected.   And when, on joint consideration, they both agreed in the same things, he ordered Pheraulas to take care that the procession should be made the next morning, in the manner that they had thought proper.   "I have ordered," said he, "all to obey you in the disposition and order of this procession.   And that they may attend to your orders with the more satisfaction, take these coats," said he, "and carry them to the commanders of the guards; give these habits for horsemen to the commanders of the horse; and these other coats to the commanders of the chariots." On this he took them and carried them off. When the commanding officers saw him, they said to him: "You are a great man, Pheraulas, now that you are to order us what we are to do." "No, not only so, by Jove!" said Pheraulas, "but it seems I am to be a baggage bearer too: therefore I now bring you these two habits, one of them is for yourself, the other for somebody else; but do you take which of them you please." He that received the habit, on this forgot his envy, and presently advised with him which he should take; then giving his opinion which was the best, he said, "If ever you charge me with having given you the choice when I officiate, another time you shall have me officiate for you in a different manner." Pheraulas, having made this distribution thus, as he was ordered, immediately applied himself to the affairs of the procession, that every thing might be settled in the handsomest manner. On the following day all things were in order before day-break.

There were ranks of people standing on each side of the way, as they yet stand at this day, wherever the king is to march; and within these ranks none but men of great dignity are allowed to come. There were men posted with scourges in their hands, who scourged any that made disturbance. There stood first before the gates four thousand of the guards drawn up, four in front: two thousand on each side of the gates. All the horsemen that were there attending alighted from their horses, and with their hands passed through their robes, as they still pass them at this day when the king takes a view of them. The Persians stood on the right hand, and the allies on the left hand of the way. The chariots, in the same manner, stood half of them on each side. When the gates of the palace were thrown open, first there were led certain bulls, very beautiful beasts, four abreast, devoted to Jove, and to such other of the gods as the magi directed; for the Persians are of opinion that artists ought to be made use of in divine affairs much more than in others. Next to the bulls there were horses led for a sacrifice to the Sun. After these proceeded a white chariot, with

its perch of gold, adorned with a crown, or wreath, around it, and sacred to Jove. After this a white chariot, sacred to the Sun, and adorned with a crown, as that before. After this proceeded a third chariot, with its horses adorned with scarlet coverings; and behind it followed men that bore fire on a large altar. After these Cyrus himself appeared without the gates with a turban on, that was raised high above his head, with a vest of a purple colour, half mixed with white; and this mixture of white none else is allowed to wear: about his legs he had a sort of stockings of a yellow colour, a robe wholly purple, and about his turban a diadem or wreath. (His relations had likewise this mark of distinction, and they have it still to this day.) And his hands he kept out of their coverings. By him rode his driver, a tall man, but less than himself: whether it really was so, or whether by some means or other it so fell out, Cyrus appeared much the taller. All the people at the sight of him paid their adoration, either because some people were before appointed to begin it, or because they were struck with the pomp and solemnity, and thought that Cyrus appeared exceedingly tall and beautiful; but no Persian ever paid Cyrus adoration before. When the chariot of Cyrus advanced, four thousand of the guards led the way before, two thousand of them attended on each side of it. And the staff-officers about his person being on horseback, finely clothed, with javelins in their hands, to the number of about three hundred, followed after. Then were led the horses that were maintained for Cyrus himself, with their bridles of gold; and thrown over with coverings wrought with a raised work in stripes; and these were about two hundred. After these marched two thousand spear men. After these the first formed body of horse, ten thousand in number, ranged a hundred every way, led by Chrysantas. After these another body of ten thousand Persian horse ranged in the same manner, led by Hystaspes. After these another body of ten thousand, in the same manner, led by Datarnas. After these another led by Gadatas. After these marched the Median horse; after these the Armenian horse; then the Hyrcanian; then the Cadusian; then the Sacian. And after the horse went the chariots, ranged four abreast, and led by the Persian Artabates.

As he marched along abundance of people

without the ranks followed by the side, petitioning Cyrus, one about one affair and another
about another. Sending therefore to them
some of the staff-officers who attended his
chariot, three on each side, for this very purpose of delivering messages, he bid them tell
them, "That if any of them wanted him on
any business, they should acquaint some of the
chief officers under him with what they wanted,
and they," he said, "would tell him." These
people, going their ways, immediately went to
the horsemen, and consulted who they should
each of them apply to. But those of his friends
that Cyrus had a mind to have the greatest
court and application made to, these he sent
somebody to, and called them severally to him,
and spoke to them in this manner : "If any of
these men that follow by my side acquaint
you with any thing, do not give attention to
any one that you think says nothing to the purpose ; but whoever desires what is just, give
me an account of it, that we may consult together, and effect their business for them."
Others, when they were called on, riding up
with the utmost despatch, obeyed, contributing
to the support of Cyrus' empire, and showing
their own readiness to obey. But there was
one Daipharnes, a man of absurd and uncouth
manners, who thought that by not paying
obedience with such despatch he should appear
a man of more dignity and freedom. As soon
therefore as Cyrus perceived this, before the
man came up so near as that he might speak to
him, he sent one of his staff-officers, and bade
him tell him that he had now no longer any
need of him ; and he never sent for him afterwards. But there was one who was sent
later, who rode up to him sooner than he ;
and to this man Cyrus gave one of the horses
that followed in his train, and ordered one of
the staff-officers to conduct the horse for him
wherever he should order. This appeared to
those that saw it to be a very great honour ;
and after this many more people made their
court to this man.

When they came to the sacred inclosures
they sacrificed to Jove, and burnt the bulls entirely. Then they sacrificed to the Sun, and
burnt the horses entirely : then killing certain
victims to the Earth, they did as the magi
directed. Then they sacrificed to the Heroes,
guardians of Syria.

After this, the country thereabouts being
very fine, he appointed a certain limited piece of
ground, of about five stadia, and bade them, nation by nation, put their horses to their speed.
He himself rode the race with the Persians, and
gained the victory, for he was extremely
well practised in horsemanship. Amongst the
Medes, Artabates got the victory, for Cyrus
had given him a horse. Amongst the Syrians,
their chief got the victory. Amongst the Armenians, Tigranes. Amongst the Hyrcanians,
the son of the commander of their horse. And
amongst the Sacians, a private man, with his
horse, left the other behind by almost half
the course.

And on this occasion Cyrus is said to have
asked the young man if he would accept of a
kingdom in exchange for his horse? and the
young man is said to have replied thus : "A
kingdom I would not accept for him, but I
would consent to oblige a worthy man with
him." Then Cyrus said : "Come, I will
show you where you may throw blindfold, and
not miss a worthy man." "By all means,
then," said the Sacian, taking up a clod,
"show me where I may throw this clod."
Then Cyrus showed him a place where a great
many of his friends were ; and the man, shutting his eyes, threw his clod and hit Pheraulas
as he was riding by ; for Pheraulas happened
to be carrying some orders from Cyrus, and
when he was struck he did not turn aside, but
went on the business that was ordered him.
The Sacian then looking up, asked, "Whom
he had hit ?"—None, by Jove !" said he, "of
those that are present." "But, surely," said
the young man, "it was none of those that are
absent." "Yes, by Jove !" said Cyrus, "you
hit that man that rides hastily on there by the
chariots." "And how came he not to turn
back ?" said he. Then Cyrus said : "Why,
in probability, it is some madman." The
young man hearing this went to see who it
was, and found Pheraulas with his chin all
over dirt and blood, for the blood gushed from
his nose on the stroke that he received.
When he came up with him, he asked him,
"Whether he had received a blow ?" He answered : "Yes, as you see." "Then," said
he, "I make you a present of this horse."
He then asked, "For what ?" and on this the
Sacian gave him a relation of the things ;
and, in conclusion said : "And I believe I
have not missed of a worthy man." Pheraulas
then said : "But if you had been wise, you
had given it to a richer man than I ; but I now

accept it, and beseech the gods, who have made me the receiver of this blow from you, to grant that I may behave so as to make you not repent your present to me." "Now," said he, "do you mount my horse, and ride off on him, and I will be with you presently." Thus they parted.

Amongst the Cadusians, Rathonices gained the victory. He likewise put their chariots severally to the trial of their speed: and to the victors he gave oxen, that they might sacrifice and feast, and he gave them cups. He himself took the ox that was his prize, but his share of the cups he gave to Pheraulas, because he thought that he had directed the procession from the palace in a very handsome manner.

This method of procession, then settled by Cyrus, continues still in use with the king to this day, excepting only that the victims make no part of it when he does not sacrifice. When all was at an end they returned again to the city, and they that had houses given them quartered in their houses, and they that had not, in their ranks

But Pheraulas, inviting the Sacian that presented him with the horse, gave him an entertainment; he furnished him with all other things in abundance. And after they had supped, he filled him the cups that he had received from Cyrus, drank to him, and made him a present of them. But the Sacian observing a great many fine carpets and coverlets, a great deal of fine furniture, and abundance of domestics: "Tell me." said he, "Pheraulas, were you one of the rich when you were at home?" "How rich do you mean?" said Pheraulas: "I was one of those that lived directly by the work of their own hands; for my father, maintaining himself very poorly by his own labour, bred me up under the discipline of the boys; but when I became a youth, not being able to maintain me idle, he took me into the country and ordered me to work. Here did I maintain him whilst he lived, digging and planting with my own hands a little piece of land, that was not ungrateful, but the justest in the world; for the seed that it received it returned me justly and handsomely again, with an overplus that indeed was not very abundant; but sometimes, out of its generosity, returned me double of what it received. Thus then I lived at home: but now all these things that you see Cyrus has given me." Then the Sacian said: "Oh!

happy are you in other respects as well as in this; that, from being poor before, you are now become rich! For I am of opinion that you grow rich with the more pleasure as you come to be possessed of riches, after having thirsted for them before." Pheraulas then said; "And do you think, Sacian, that I live with the more pleasure the more I possess? Do you not know," said he, "that I neither eat, nor drink, nor sleep with one jot more pleasure now than when I was poor? But, by all this abundance, thus much I gain: that I am to guard more, to distribute more to others, and to have the trouble of taking care of more: for a great many domestics now demand their food of me, their drink, and their clothes; some are in want of physicians; one comes and brings me sheep, that have been torn to pieces by wolves, or oxen killed by falling from a precipice, or tells me of a distemper got amongst the cattle; so that I think," said Pheraulas, "by possessing abundance, I have now more afflictions than I had before by having but little." "But, by Jove!" said the Sacian, "when all is well, and you are able to cast your eyes around on numerous possessions, you are certainly much better pleased than I am." Pheraulas then said: "Sacian, it is not so pleasant to possess riches as it is afflicting to lose them; and you will find that what I say is true; for there are none of those that possess riches that are forced from the enjoyment of rest by the pleasure which they afford; but of those that lose them, you will see none that are able to sleep because of the concern it gives them." "By Jove!" said the Sacian, "nor will you see any of those fall asleep that at first obtain them, because of the pleasure it gives them." "You say true," said he; "for if the possessing them was as pleasant as the obtaining them the rich would very much exceed the poor in happiness. But then, Sacian," said he, "he that possesses abundance must, of necessity, expend abundance, both on the gods, on his friends, and on strangers. Whoever therefore is greatly pleased with the possession of riches be assured will be greatly afflicted at the expense of them." "By Jove!" said the Sacian, "I am not one of those; but I take it to be a happiness for a man to have abundance, and to expend abundance." "Why then," said Pheraulas, "in the name of all the gods, are not you this instant that happy man, to make me so at the same time? for do you take possession of all these things, and use them as you please; maintain me only as a stranger; or yet more sparingly than a stranger; for it shall be enough for me to share with you in what you have." "You jest," said the Sacian. Pheraulas then asserted with an oath that he spoke in earnest. "And I will gain you, Sacian, something farther from Cyrus; and that is, that you shall not be obliged to attend at his doors, nor to engage in military service? but you shall stay at home, abounding in riches. And those other affairs I will perform for you and for myself; and, if I get any thing valuable by my attendance on Cyrus, or by any military expedition, I will bring it to you that you may still have the command of more; do you," said he, "but free me from this care; for if I can be at leisure from these affairs, I think that you will be of very great use both to me, and to Cyrus."

Having thus discoursed they settled these affairs and put them in practice. The one thought himself made a happy man, by having the command of great riches, and the other reckoned himself the most fortunate man in the world, in having a steward, who afforded him leisure to do what was agreeable to him. Pheraulas was in his temper extremely kind and friendly to his acquaintance; and no care or culture bestowed on any thing appeared so pleasing to him, or so profitable, as that bestowed on men; for man, he thought, was, of all other creatures, the best and the most grateful: because he observed of men, that when they were commended by any one, they were zealous in their returns of praise; that they used their endeavours to do kindnesses to those that had done kindnesses to them; that they were kindly affected to those whom they knew to be kindly affected to them; and those who they knew had a love for them, they could not possibly hate; and that, of all other creatures, they were the most inclined to make their parents all returns of respect and service, both while living and when dead. And all other animals he reckoned more ungrateful and more ill-natured than man. This Pheraulas was much delighted, that, by being freed from the care of other possessions, he should be at leisure to mind his friends. And the Sacian was delighted, because he was to have the possession of abundance, and was to spend abundance. The Sacian loved Pheraulas, because he was always bringing him something; and Pheraulas loved the Sacian, because he was willing to take all; and though he charged himself with the care of still more and more, yet he gave him no more trouble. Thus did these men live.

IV. Cyrus having sacrificed, and making an entertainment with the prize of his victory, invited those of his friends that appeared the most desirous to increase his power, and that paid him honour in the most affectionate manner: and with them he invited Artabazus the Mede, Tigranes the Armenian, the Hyrcanian commander of horse, and Gobryas. Gadatas was the commander of his eunuchs; and all the management within doors was settled as he thought fit to regulate it. When there were any that supped with him, Gadatas did not sit down, but minded the business; but when there was no company, he then supped with him; for he was pleased with his conversation; and, in return, he was presented with many great and noble things, both by Cyrus himself, and by many others on Cyrus' account.

As the persons who were invited to supper came, he did not place every one as it happened by chance to fall out; but the man that he most esteemed he placed on his left hand, as if this side were more exposed to dangerous designs than the right. The next in his esteem he placed on his right hand; the third again on his left, and the fourth on his right; and if there were more, he went on with them in the same manner. He thought it of service to make it evident how far he esteemed every one; because where men think that he who excels others is not to have his praises published, nor to receive his rewards, there it is plain they have no emulation to each other; but where he be that excels has the advantage, there they appear to struggle with the utmost zeal. Thus Cyrus made those known that were chief in his esteem; beginning first with their place, as they sat, and as they stood by him. Yet this privilege of place, in sitting, he did not make perpetual, but made it a rule, that a man might advance, by noble actions, to the more honourable seat; and if he grew negligent and remiss, might sink down to the less honourable. And if he that was possessed of the principal seat did not appear to have received the greatest number of valuable things at his hands, he was ashamed. And these things that were practised in the time of Cyrus I perceive continue still thus to this day.

When they had supped, it did not appear at all wonderful to Gobryas that a man who had the command of many should have every thing in great abundance; but that Cyrus, who had performed such great things, if he thought that he had got any thing that was delicate, should never spend it himself alone, but give himself trouble in desiring his friends that were present to share it; this he thought wonderful, and frequently he saw him send to some of his absent friends things that he happened to be pleased with himself. So that when they had supped, and Cyrus, by presents to several, had cleared his table of all that plenty that was on it, then Gobryas said: "Before, Cyrus, I thought that you most excelled the rest of men in being the most able in the command of an army; but now, I swear by the gods, that you excel more in benignity and love to mankind, than in military conduct!" "And, by Jove!" said Cyrus, "it is much more agreeable to show acts of love to men than acts of skill in the conduct of an army." "How so?" said Gobryas. "Because these," said he, "must be shown by doing mischief to men, and those by doing them good."

After this, when they had drunk a little, Hystaspes put this question to Cyrus: "Would you be offended, Cyrus," said he, "if I should ask you something that I am desirous to know from you?" "By the gods!" said he, "quite the contrary; I should be offended if I perceived that you retained what you had a mind to ask me." "Tell me then," said he, "when you have called me, did I ever refuse to come?" "Pray, be quiet," said Cyrus. "Or did I ever obey your summons slowly?" "No, nor this neither." "Have I ever neglected to do what you have ordered me?" "I do not lay it to your charge," said he. "And in what I have done, can you accuse me of not having done it with alacrity and pleasure?" "This," said Cyrus, "the least of all." "In the name of all the gods, then, Cyrus!" said he, "by what means is it that Chrysantas has prevailed on you so as to be placed before me in the more honourable seat?" "Shall I tell you?" said Cyrus. "By all means," said he. "And will you not be offended with me when you hear the truth?" "No, I shall be pleased," said he, "if I find that I am not wronged." "Then," said he, "Chrysantas here, in the first place, never waited my call, but before he was called, was ready at hand for our service:

and then, not only what he was ordered, but whatever he himself thought best for us to be done, that he did. When it was necessary to say any thing to our allies, he advised me what he thought was becoming and proper for me to say; and what he perceived I was desirous that our allies should know, but was ashamed to say of myself, this he spoke as if he were declaring his own opinion. So that, in these matters, what hinders him from being reckoned of more use to me even than myself? As to himself, he always says that the things that he has are sufficient for him; but it appears evidently that he is always looking out for what it may be of service for me to have: and with the advantages that befall me he is more delighted and pleased than myself." To this Hystaspes said: "By Here, Cyrus, I am pleased that I have asked you these things!" "And why?" said he. "Because I will endeavour too to practise them. One thing only there is," said he, "that I do not know; and that is, how to make it evident that I rejoice at your advantages, whether I must clap my hands, or laugh, or what I must do?" Artabazus to this said: "You must dance the Persian dance." And at this they laughed.

As the entertainment went on Cyrus put this question to Gobryas: "Tell me," said he, "Gobryas, do you think that you should give your daughter to one of these that are here with more satisfaction now than when at first you became acquainted with us?" "And must I tell the truth then?" said Gobryas. "Yes, by Jove!" said Cyrus, "since no question requires falsehood in answer to it." "Be assured then," said he, "that I should do it with much more satisfaction now." "And can you give," said Cyrus, "a reason why?" "I can." "Give it me then." "Because, at that time, I saw these men bear toils and dangers with alacrity; but now I see them bear prosperity with discretion and good temper. And to me, Cyrus, it appears more difficult to find a man that bears prosperity well, than one that bears adversity well; for prosperity inspires most men with pride and insolence, but adversity, gives discretion and modesty of temper to all." Then Cyrus said: "Do you hear, Hystaspes, this saying of Gobryas?" "Yes, by Jove!" said he, "I do; and if he pronounce many such, he shall much sooner have me for a suitor to his daughter, than if he showed me abundance of cups of great value." "Truly," said Gobryas, "I have a great many such written down; and I will not grudge them to you, if you have my daughter for a wife: but my cups," said he, "since you seem to dislike them, I do not know but I will give to Chrysantas here, especially since he has run away with your seat."

"Well," said Cyrus, "if you, Hystaspes, and the rest that are here present will acquaint me when any of you are endeavouring after a wife, you will then know how good an assistant I shall be to you." Gobryas then said: "But if one has a mind to dispose of a daughter, who must one tell it to?" "This," said Cyrus, "must be told to me too; for I am a notable man in this art." "What art?" said Chrysantas. "Why, in knowing what match will best suit each particular man." Then Chrysantas said: "In the name of all the gods, then, tell me what wife you think will best suit me!" "First," said he, "she must be little, for you are little yourself; and if you marry a tall wife, and would kiss her as she stands, you must leap up like a little dog." "You are much in the right," said he, "to provide against this, for I am by no means a good caperer." "And then," said he, "she must have a nose that sinks in the middle." "And what is this for?" "Because," said he, "you have a crooked nose, and a rising hook would best suit a sinking in." "Do you say then that a fasting wife would best suit one that had feasted plentifully as I have done now?" "Yes, by Jove!" said Cyrus "for the bellies of those that are full rise, and the bellies of those that are fasting sink in." "But, in the name of all the gods!" said Chrysantas, "can you tell what wife will be best for a frigid king?" Here Cyrus fell a-laughing, and so did the others. And as they were laughing Hystaspes said: "In the whole compass of your royal dignity, Cyrus, I envy you the most for this." "For what?" said Cyrus. "Why, that, as frigid as you are, you can make people laugh." "And would not you give a great deal," said Cyrus, "then, that these things had been said by you, and that she, that you desire should think well of you, should be informed that you are a polite agreeable man?" Thus they jested one with another.

After this he produced a woman's attire for Tigranes, and bade him give it his wife, because she bravely attended her husband in the service. To Artabazus he gave a golden cup; to the Hyrcanian, a horse. And many other noble presents he made. "But, Gobryas," said he, "I will give you a husband for your daughter." "And shall not I," said Hystaspes, "be the man that you will give, that I may get those writings?" "Have you substance enough," said Cyrus, "to deserve the girl?" "Yes, by Jove! I have much more than enough." "And where," said he, "is this substance of yours?" "Here," said he, "where you, my friend, sit." "That is enough for me," said Gobryas; and holding out his right hand—"Give him me, Cyrus," said he, "for I accept him." Then Cyrus, taking Hystaspes' right hand, presented it to Gobryas and he received it. After this he made a great many noble presents to Hystaspes, that he might send them to the maid; and pulling Chrysantas to him, he kissed him. On this Artabazus said. "By Jove! Cyrus, you have not given me my cup of the same gold with this present that you have made Chrysantas." "But I will give you the same," said he. He asked him—"When?" "Thirty years hence," said he. "Well, prepare yourself for me," said he, "as one that intends to wait, and not to die before the time." Thus then ended this conversation: and when they rose, Cyrus rose with them, and conducted them to his doors.

The next day all those of his allies that had voluntarily attended him he dismissed to their homes, excepting such as chose to live near him. To these he gave lands and houses, which the descendants of those who then staid possess still to this day: and they were, for the most part, Medes and Hyrcanians. To those that went off he gave many presents, and dismissed them, both commanders and soldiers, without leaving them the least cause to complain. After this he divided the treasure that he gained at Sardis among the soldiers that were about him. And to the commanders of ten thousand, and to the officers that were about him, he gave the choice things, according to the merit of every one. The rest he parcelled out, and giving a share to each of the commanders of ten thousand, he left it to them to distribute it in the same manner as he had distributed to them. And these other treasures each commander distributed to the commanders under him, giving judgment on the merit of every one. And the commanders of six, giving judgment on the private men that were under them, distributed the last remaining treasures severally to them, according to their desert. So they all received their just share.

When they had received what was then given them, some of them spoke of Cyrus in this manner: "Surely he must have abundance, when he gives so much to every one of us." But others of them said: "What is the abundance that he has? Cyrus is not of a temper to mind wholly the heaping up of treasure; but he is more pleased with bestowing than with having it." Cyrus, perceiving these discourses, and the opinions that men had of him, assembled his friends and all the other proper persons together, and spoke to this effect: "My friends, I have seen men that were willing to be thought possessed of more than they really had, and who thought by that means to appear the more generous and noble. But these men, in my opinion, are drawn into the very reverse of what they intend; for he that seems to have abundance, and does not appear to do that service to his friends that is suitable to his substance, gains, in my opinion, the character of being mean and sordid. There are those," said he, "on the other side, who desire that what they have may be concealed. And these too, in my opinion, are faulty to their friends: for frequently friends that are in want avoid telling it to their companions, because they are ignorant of what they have, and so are deceived. But the plainest, simplest part, in my opinion, is to make the whole strength of one's fortune appear, and with it to try to get the better of others in generosity. I intend, therefore," said he, "to show you every thing that is possible for you to see of what I have; and, of what you cannot see, to give you an account." Having said this he showed them abundance of rich and valuable things; and those that lay so as not easily to be seen he gave them an account of; and, in conclusion, said thus: "All these things, my friends," said he, "you ought to reckon not more mine than yours; for I have collected them in together, not that I may spend them myself, nor that I may myself wear them out, for I should not be able to do it; but that I may always have wherewithal to present any of you, on your performance of any thing great and noble; and that in case any of you think you are in want of any thing, you may come to me and take what you happen to be in want of." Thus were these things said.

V. But when he thought that affairs were now so well settled in Babylon that he might venture to travel abroad, he himself prepared for a journey into Persia, and gave out orders on it to others. And when he judged that he was sufficiently provided with the things he thought he should want, he departed. Now, we will give an account how so great an equipage was, in the most orderly manner, set out, and then again put up together, in the same manner, and disposed into the place where it ought to be; for, wherever the king encamps, they that are about his person attend the service with tents, both winter and summer.

Cyrus then immediately thought fit to place his own tent fronting to the east: then he first directed at what distance from the royal tent the guards should pitch theirs; he then appointed the bakers, and those that were concerned in making the bread, their station on the right; the cooks theirs on the left. To the horses he appointed their station on the right; and to the other beasts of burden, theirs on the left. And all the rest was so disposed, that every one knew his own station, both as to measure and place. When they are to put all up, every one packs up such baggage as it was appointed him to use, and there are others that place it on the beasts of burden; so that all the baggage carriers come up at the same time to the things that are severally appointed them to carry; and they all, at the same time, place them on the beasts that severally belong to them; so that the same time that suffices for the striking of one tent suffices for all. The case is the same in the displaying and setting out of all. And with respect to the doing all things that are necessary in proper time, every one is, in the same manner, appointed what he is to do; and by this means the same time suffices for the doing things in one part and in all. And as the servants that despatched all the necessary business had all severally their proper stations, so they that bore arms had their stations in their encampment suitable to the sort of arms they severally had: they knew what their station was, and all disposed themselves in it without any hesitation: for Cyrus thought the proper placing of things a noble rule in a house; because, if one happen to want any thing, it is known whither one must go to take it. But the proper placing of the several different sorts of military men he reckoned a much nobler thing; as the occasions of putting all to their use, in the affairs of war, are more sudden, and the faults arising from those that are dilatory in them are of worse consequence; and the most valuable advantages in war, he observed, arose from having all things ready for the occasion. On these accounts therefore he took the greatest care of this propriety of place.

First, then, he placed himself in the midst of the camp, as being the strongest and securest station. Then those whom he chiefly confided in he had, according to custom, about himself. Next to these, in a circle round, he had the horsemen and charioteers; for he was of opinion that a secure station was necessary for these people, because they encamp without having at hand any of those arms that they engage with, and require a considerable time to arm themselves, if they are to advance so as to do any service. To the right and left of himself, and of the horsemen, was the station of the shield-men. The station of the archers was before and behind himself and the horsemen. The heavy-armed men, and such as had large shields, he had in a circle round all, as a rampart, that in case there was any occasion for the horsemen to make ready, they that were the fittest to make a stand being placed before them might give them time to arm securely. And as the heavy-armed men slept there, in order round him, so did the shield-men and archers. So that even in the night-time, if the occasion required, as heavy-armed men were ready prepared to come to blows with such as came up close with them, so the archers and javelin-men, if any people approached them, were ready to discharge their javelins and arrows over the heads of the heavy-armed. And all the commanders had ensigns on their tents. And as in cities discreet and good servants know the habitations of most people, but chiefly of those that it is proper for them to know, so did the servants of Cyrus know the stations that the chief leaders had in the encampments, and knew the ensigns that belonged to each of them; so that whatever Cyrus might want, they were not to seek for them, but ran the shortest way directly to each of them. And by means of the several sets of people being distinct, it was much the more readily observed when any one was disorderly, and when any one did not perform what he was commanded. And things standing thus, he

was of opinion, that if any body attacked him, either by night or day, such aggressor would fall into his camp, as into an ambuscade.

And he did not only think it a part of the tactic art for a man to be able to draw up a phalanx easily and cleverly, or to increase it in depth, or to form a phalanx on the wing, or on the enemy's appearing to the right, the left, or the rear, to wheel properly, but to separate men when it was proper, he took to be a part of this art: to post each part where they might be most serviceable, and to make despatch where it might be fit to prevent the enemy. All these things, and such like, he took to be the business of a man skilled in tactics. He took care of all these things alike; and in his marches he moved always in a disposition suitable to what occurred: but in his encampments he placed his people, for the most part, as has been said.

When, in the course of their march, they arrived in the Median territory, Cyrus turned off to visit Cyaxares; and after they had embraced each other, Cyrus first told Cyaxares that there were domestics and palaces set apart for him in Babylon, that when he came thither he might have what was his own to come to. And he then made him a great many other noble presents. Cyaxares received them, and sent his daughter to him with a crown of gold, and with bracelets, with a collar and Median robe, that was as fine as was possible; and the maid put the crown on Cyrus' head. Cyaxares then said: " I give you the maid too, Cyrus, for your wife. She is my own daughter. Your father married my father's daughter, and from her you are descended. This is she that, when you were a boy and amongst us, you used to fondle; and when any one asked her, "Who she would marry?" she said, " Cyrus." And with her I give all Media as her dowry, for I have no legitimate male issue." Thus he spoke, and Cyrus replied: " O Cyaxares! I applaud the race, the maid, and the presents that attend her: and, with the consent," said he, " of my father and mother, I am ready to agree with you." Thus Cyrus spoke; but yet he presented the maid with all that he thought would be pleasing to Cyaxares; and having done this he continued his march to Persia.

And when, in the course of his march, he arrived at the borders of Persia, there he left the rest of the army; but he himself, together with his friends, proceeded on to the city, carrying with him such numbers of victims as were sufficient for all the Persians to sacrifice and feast on. He brought with him such presents as were proper for his father and mother and his other friends, and such as were proper for the elders and magistrates, and for all the alike-honoured. He gave likewise to all the Persians, both men and women, such presents as the king still makes at this day, when he comes into Persia. After this Cambyses assembled the Persian elders and magistrates who had the direction of the greatest affairs: he summoned likewise Cyrus, and spoke to this effect:

" Men of Persia, and you, O Cyrus! I have justly an affection for you both; for over you I am king, and you, Cyrus, are my son. It is just therefore that I should lay before you whatever I judge to be of advantage to you both. With respect to the time past, you have advanced Cyrus in his fortune by granting an army, and by constituting him the commander of it. Cyrus, in the conduct of his army, has, with the help of the gods, gained you, O Persians! glory amongst all men, and honour throughout all Asia. Of those that served with him the better sort he has enriched, and the multitude he has provided with their pay and with their maintenance: and, by constituting a Persian cavalry, he has given the Persians a share in the command of the plains. If you continue therefore for the future in the same sentiments, you will be the authors of many advantages to each other. But if either you, Cyrus, elevated with your present happy circumstances, attempt to rule the Persians as you do the others, with regard only to your own interest; or if you, citizens, envying him his power, endeavour to wrest the empire from him, be assured that you will hinder each other from obtaining many advantages. Therefore, that things may not fall out thus, but rather happily for you, my opinion is," said he, " that we make a sacrifice in common; and, calling the gods to witness, stipulate that you, Cyrus, in case any one make war on the Persian territory, or attempt to destroy the Persian laws, shall assist in their defence with your whole force: and that you, Persians, in case any one attempt to put an end to Cyrus' empire, or to excite any of his subjects to revolt, shall yield such assistance in defence of yourselves and of Cyrus as he shall order. Whilst I live, the royal dignity amongst the Persians is mine;

when I am dead, it then plainly belongs to Cyrus, if he lives. And when he comes into Persia, it may be perhaps of religious concern to you that he should make these sacrifices for you that I now make: but, when he is abroad, I think it will be proper that that person of our race that appears to you to be the most worthy should perform the sacred rites."

On Cambyses' saying this, Cyrus and the Persian magistrates joined in opinion with him. And having at that time agreed on these things, (calling on the gods as witnesses,) the Persians and the king continue still to this day to put them in practice one towards another.

When these things were performed Cyrus went away; and when he came into Media, in his journey back, on its being agreed to by his father and mother, he married the daughter of Cyaxares, who at this day has still the fame of having been extremely beautiful. There are some authors who say that he married his mother's sister; but she must have been a woman in years, much more probably than one so young. When he had married her he presently departed, and took her with him.

VI. When he was at Babylon he thought it now proper for him to constitute governors, or satraps, over the conquered nations. But the commanders of the garrisons in castles, and the commanders of thousands that were appointed for the guard of the country, he would not allow to obey the orders of any but himself. He used this foresight on consideration, that if any of the satraps, by means of their riches and the numbers of their people, should grow insolent, and attempt to withdraw their obedience from him, they might immediately meet with opposers on the place. Desiring therefore to bring this about, he determined first to call together all the proper persons, and to declare it to them, that they who went on these employments might know on what footing they went; for by this means he thought they would the more easily bear it. But if any one was first constituted a commander and then made the discovery, he was of opinion that men would bear this with difficulty, imagining that it was done out of distrust of them.

So, assembling them together, he spoke to this effect: " My friends, in the cities that have been conquered, there are garrisons and commanders over them that I left there at the time; and when I went away I gave them orders not to take on themselves any other

T

business than to preserve the fortresses : therefore I will not deprive these men of their power since they have discharged themselves handsomely in the guarding of what they had in charge. But I think it proper for me to send other governors, who shall take on them the rule of the inhabitants ; and who, receiving the revenues, shall give the garrisons their pay, and discharge whatever else is necessary. And to those of you here that I shall give employment, and send to perform any business in the several nations, I think it proper to distribute lands and houses there, that the tribute may be there paid them, and that they may bring it to this place, and when they go thither, that they may have what is their own to go to." Thus he said. And to many of his friends he gave houses and dependents throughout all the conquered cities. And these precincts remain still at this day in the possession of the descendants of those who then received them, some in one country and some in another, and they themselves reside with the king. "And we ought," said he, "to look out for such satraps to go into these precincts as will remember to send hither whatever there is that is excellent and valuable in every country, that we who are here may share of all that is excellent in every part ; for if any misfortune befall them, it will lie on us to defend them from it."

Having said this, he ended his discourse. And then from amongst his friends, that he knew were desirous to go on the terms expressed, choosing out such as he thought the most proper, he sent them as satraps. To Arabia he sent Megabyzus ; to Cappadocia, Artabatas ; to the Greater Phrygia, Artacamas ; to Lydia and Ionia, Chrysantas ; to Caria, Cadusius, as that people themselves had desired ; to Phrygia on the Hellespont and Æolia, Pharnuchus. To Cilicia, to Cyprus, and to the Paphlagonians, he sent no Persian satraps, because they seemed to have joined of their own accord with him in his expedition against Babylon. But he appointed these likewise a tribute that they were to pay, according to Cyrus' establishment at that time ; so that there are still at this day garrisons belonging to the king in the fortresses, and commanders of thousands appointed by the king to command those forces, and set down in a list belonging to the king.

The satraps that were thus sent out he beforehand directed to imitate, as near as was possible, whatever they saw him practise.

And in the first place, that each satrap, out of such of the Persians and of the confederates as attended him, should establish a number of horsemen and charioteers ; and then should oblige such as had lands and palaces to pay their attendance at his doors, and, practising discreet and modest manners, to yield themselves to the service of the satrap, if any occasion should so require ; and that he should discipline at his doors the boys that these men had, as was practised by himself ; and that the satrap should take those that attended at his doors out with him to hunt, and exercise himself and those about him in military affairs. "And the man," said he, "that, in proportion to his ability, produces the most chariots, and the most and best horsemen, him will I reward, as an excellent fellow-soldier, and as an excellent fellow-guardian and preserver of the empire to the Persians and myself. Let the best men with you be honoured with the principal seats, as they are with me ; and let your table, as mine does, maintain in the first place your domestics, and then let it be sufficiently furnished to afford your friends to partake of it, and allow you every day to reward any one that may have done a handsome action. Get yourselves parks, and maintain wild beasts. And neither set meat at any time before yourselves without having taking pains, nor throw food to your horses unexercised ; for it is impossible for me, who am but one, with all the virtue that belongs to human nature, to preserve all you in safety and prosperity ; but it is my part, making myself a worthy man, together with other worthy men about me, to be an assistant to you. And it is, in like manner, your part, making yourselves worthy men, together with other men of worth about you, to be friends and supports to me. And I desire likewise that you would observe that of all these orders that I now give you, I give none to those that are of servile condition ; and that the things which I say you ought to do, these I endeavour myself to practise. And as I exhort you to imitate me, so do you instruct those that are in command under you to imitate you."

Cyrus having thus regulated these affairs at that time, all the garrisons under the king are still at this day kept likewise in the same method. The doors of all the commanders are frequented in the like manner. All families, both great and little, are in the like manner regulated. The most deserving men, in all companies, are honoured with the principal seats. All marches are ordered in the same method; and the great multitude of affairs is parcelled out into distinct heads, under a few principal directors.

Having told them in what manner they were each of them to manage in these affairs, and having given to each of them a force, he sent them away, and told them all beforehand, that in the following year an expedition would be undertaken, and a review taken both of men and arms, horses and chariots.

There is another thing that we have observed, which, they say, was begun by Cyrus, and continues to this day; that there is a certain person, who, at the head of an army, takes a progress every year; and who, in case any of the satraps want assistance, affords it them, and if any of them grow insolent, reduces them to temper. And if any neglect the payment of his tribute, or the protection of the inhabitants, or the care of having the land cultivated, or leaves any other of his orders unexecuted, he puts all these things to rights; or if he is not able to do it himself, he makes a report to the king; and when the king has had an account of it, he takes advice how to deal with the transgressing person. And commonly he who takes this progress is the king's son, or the king's brother, or one of those they call the king's eye. And sometimes they do not appear, for they each of them return on the first orders from the king.

We have likewise been informed of another contrivance of his, with regard to the extent of his empire, by means of which he had immediate intelligence of what passed in the most remote parts of his government: for observing how far a horse was able to travel in a day, he built stables at that distance, and supplied them with horses, and persons to have the care of them. And he appointed a certain person at each of these stages to receive the letters and to deliver them out, and to receive those horses that had completed their stage, and to furnish fresh ones. And it is said that the night did not give any interruption to these stages; for as soon as he arrived who had been on his progress all day, another continued it during the night. And in this manner they are said to fly swifter than cranes; but though that be false, yet it is manifest that this is the quickest way of travelling for men. Besides, it is of use to have early intelligence of every thing, that immediate provision may be made.

At the conclusion of the year Cyrus assembled his army together at Babylon, which is said to have consisted of one hundred and twenty thousand horse, two thousand chariots armed with scythes, and sixty thousand foot; and having prepared them for it, he undertook that expedition, in which he is reported to have subdued all those nations which lie from the entrance into Syria as far as the Red Sea. His next expedition is said to have been against Egypt, which he also subdued. Then Cyrus' empire was bounded to the east by the Red Sea, to the north by the Euxine Sea, to the west by Cyprus and Egypt, to the south by Ethiopia; the extremities of which countries are difficult to inhabit, some of them from excess of heat, some of them from excess of cold, some from too great abundance of water, others from a scarcity of water.

Cyrus, residing in the centre of these countries, spent the seven winter months at Babylon, because that climate is warm, the three spring months at Susa, and the two summer months at Ecbatana: by which means he is said to have enjoyed a perpetual spring with respect to heat and cold. And men stood so affected towards him, that every nation thought they did themselves an injury if they did not send Cyrus the most valuable productions o their country, whether they were the fruits of the earth, or creatures bred there, or manufactures of their own; and every city did the same. And every private man thought himself rich if he could oblige Cyrus; for as Cyrus accepted from each of what they possessed in abundance, so in return he distributed to them what he observed they were in want of.

VII. After he had thus spent some considerable time, Cyrus, now in a very advanced age, takes a journey into Persia, which was the seventh from the acquisition of his empire, when his father and mother had probably been for some time dead. Cyrus made the usual sacrifices, and danced the Persian dance, according to the custom of his country, and distributed to every one presents, as usual. Then, being asleep in the royal palace, he had the following dream. There seemed to advance towards him a person with a more than human majesty in his air and countenance, and to say to him; "Cyrus, prepare yourself, for you are now going to the gods!" After this appearance in his dream he awaked, and seemed assured that his end drew near. Therefore, taking along with him the victims, he sacrificed on the summit of a mountain (as is the custom in Persia) to Jove Paternal, the Sun, and the rest of the gods, accompanying the sacrifices with this prayer:

"O Jove Paternal, Sun, and all ye gods! receive these sacrifices as the completion of many worthy and handsome actions; and as grateful acknowledgments for having signified to me, both by the victims, by celestial signs, by birds, and by omens, what became me to do, and not to do. And I abundantly return you thanks, that I have been sensible of your care and protection; and that, in the course of my prosperity, I never was exalted above what became a man. I implore you now to bestow all happiness on my children, my wife, my friends, and my country; and for myself, that I may die as I have always lived."

When he had finished his sacrifices and prayer he returned home, and finding himself disposed to be quiet, he lay down. At a certain hour proper persons attended, and offered him to wash. He told them that he had rested very well. Then, at another hour, proper officers brought him his supper; but Cyrus had no appetite to eat, but seemed thirsty, and drank with pleasure. And continuing thus the second and third days, he sent for his sons, who, as it happened, had attended their father, and were then in Persia. He summoned likewise his friends, and the magistrates of Persia. When they were all met, he began in this manner:

"Children, and all you, my friends, here present! the conclusion of my life is now at hand, which I certainly know from many symptoms. You ought, when I am dead, to act and speak of me in every thing as a happy man: for, when I was a child, I seemed to have received advantage from what is esteemed worthy and handsome in children; so likewise, when I was a youth, from what is esteemed so in young men; so, when I came to be a man, from what is esteemed worthy and handsome in men. And I have always seemed to observe myself increase with time in strength and vigour, so that I have not found myself weaker or more infirm in my old age than in my youth. Neither do I know that I have desired or undertaken any thing in which I have not succeeded. By my means my friends have been made happy, and my enemies enslaved; and my country, at first inconsiderable in Asia, I

leave in great reputation and honour. Neither do I know that I have not preserved whatever I acquired. And though, in time past, all things have succeeded according to my wishes, yet an apprehension lest, in process of time, I should see, hear, or suffer some difficulty, has not suffered me to be too much elated, or too extravagantly delighted. Now if I die, I leave you, children, behind me, (whom the gods have given me,) and I leave my country and my friends happy. Ought not I therefore, in justice, to be always remembered, and mentioned as fortunate and happy? I must likewise declare to whom I leave my kingdom, lest that, being doubtful, should hereafter raise dissensions among you. Now, children, I bear an equal affection to you both; but I direct that the elder should have the advising and conducting of affairs, as his age requires it, and it is probable he has more experience. And as I have been instructed by my country and yours to give place to those elder than myself, not only brothers, but fellow-citizens, both in walking, sitting, and speaking; so have I instructed you, from your youth, to show a regard to your elders, and to receive the like from such as were inferior to you in age; receive then this disposition as ancient, customary, and legal. Do you therefore, Cambyses, hold the kingdom as allotted you by the gods and by me, so far as it is in my power. To you, Tanoaxares, I bequeath the satrapy of the Medes, Armenians, and Cadusians; which when I allot you, I think I leave your elder brother a larger empire, and the title of a kingdom, but to you a happiness freer from care and vexation: for I do not see what human satisfaction you can need; but you will enjoy whatever appears agreeable and pleasing to men. An affection for such things as are difficult to execute, a multitude of pains, and an impossibility of being quiet, anxiety from an emulation of my actions, forming designs yourself, and having designs formed against you: these are things which must more necessarily attend a king than one in your station; and be assured these give many interruptions to pleasure and satisfaction. Know, therefore, Cambyses, that is not the golden sceptre which can preserve your kingdom; but faithful friends are a prince's truest and securest sceptre. But do not imagine that men are naturally faithful (for then they would appear so to all, as other natural endowments do); but every one must render others faithful to himself: and they are not to be procured by violence, but rather by kindness and beneficence. If therefore you would constitute other joint guardians with you of your kingdom, whom can you better begin with than him who is of the same blood with yourself? and fellow-citizens are nearer to us than strangers, and those who live and eat with us, than those that do not. And those who have the same original, who have been nourished by the same mother, and grown up in the same house, and beloved by the same parents, and who call on the same father and mother, are not they, of all others, the nearest to us? Do not you therefore render those advantages fruitless, by which the gods unite brothers in affinity and relation; but to those advantages add other friendly offices, and by that means your friendship will be reciprocally solid and lasting. The taking care of a brother is providing for oneself. To whom can the advancement of a brother be equally honourable, as to a brother? Who can show a regard to a great and powerful man equal to his brother? Who will fear to injure another, so much as him whose brother is in an exalted station? Be therefore second to none in submission and good-will to your brother, since no one can be so particularly serviceable or injurious to you. And I would have you consider how you can hope for greater advantages by obliging any one so much as him? Or whom can you assist that will be so powerful an ally in war? Or what is more infamous than want of friendship between brothers? Who, of all men, can we so handsomely pay regard to as to a brother? In a word, Cambyses, your brother is the only one you can advance next to your person without the envy of others. Therefore, in the name of the gods, children, have regard for one another, if you are careful to do what is acceptable to me. For you ought not to imagine, you certainly know, that after I have closed this period of human life I shall no longer exist: for neither do you now see my soul, but you conclude, from its operations, that it does exist. And have you not observed what terrors and apprehensions murderers are inspired with by those who have suffered violence from them? What racks and torture do they convey to the guilty? Or how do you think honours should have continued to be paid to the deceased, if their souls were destitute of all power and virtue? No, children, I can never

be persuaded that the soul lives no longer than it dwells in this mortal body, and that it dies on its separation; for I see that the soul communicates vigour and motion to mortal bodies during its continuance in them. Neither can I be persuaded that the soul is divested of intelligence, on its separation from this gross, senseless body; but it is probable, that when the soul is separated, it becomes pure and entire, and is then more intelligent. It is evident that, on man's dissolution, every part of him returns to what is of the same nature with itself, except the soul; that alone is invisible, both during its presence here, and at its departure. And you may have observed that nothing resembles death so much as sleep; but then it is that the human soul appears most divine, and has a prospect of futurity; for then it is probable the soul is most free and independent. If therefore things are as I think, and that the soul leaves the body, having regard to my soul, comply with my request. But if it be otherwise, and that the soul continuing in the body perishes with it, let nothing appear in your thoughts or actions criminal or impious, for fear of the gods, who are eternal, whose power and inspection extend over all things, and who preserve the harmony and order of the universe free from decay or defect, whose greatness and beauty is inexplicable! Next to the gods, have regard to the whole race of mankind, in perpetual succession: for the gods have not concealed you in obscurity; but there is a necessity that your actions should be conspicuous to the world. If they are virtuous, and free from injustice, they will give you power and interest in all men; but if you project what is unjust against each other, no man will trust you; for no one can place a confidence in you, though his inclination to it be ever so great, when he sees you unjust, where it most becomes you to be a friend. If therefore I have not rightly instructed you what you ought to be to one another, learn it from those who lived before our time, for that will be the best lesson. For there are many who have lived affectionate parents to their children, and friends to their brothers; and some there are who have acted the opposite part towards each other. Whichsoever of these you shall observe to have been most advantageous, you will do well in giving it the preference in your choice. But perhaps this is sufficient as to these matters. When I am dead, children, do not enshrine my body in gold, nor in silver, nor any thing else; but lay it in the earth as soon as possible; for what can be more happy than to mix with the earth, which gives birth and nourishment to all things excellent and good? And as I have always hitherto borne an affection to men, so it is now most pleasing to me to incorporate with that which is beneficial to men. Now," said he, "it seems to me that my soul is beginning to leave me, in the same manner as it is probable it begins its departure with others. If therefore any of you are desirous of touching my right hand, or willing to see my face while it has life, come near to me: for, when I shall have covered it, I request of you, children, that neither yourselves, nor any others would look on my body. Summon all the Persians and their allies before my tomb, to rejoice for me; that I shall be then out of danger of suffering any evil, whether I shall be with the gods, or shall be reduced to nothing. As many as come, do you dismiss with all those favours that are thought proper for a happy man. And," said he, "remember this as my last and dying words. If you do kindnesses to your friends, you will be able to injure your enemies. Farewell, dear children, and tell this to your mother as from me. And all you, my friends, both such of you as are here present, and the rest who are absent—farewell!" Having said this, and taken every one by the right hand, he covered himself, and thus expired.

VIII. That Cyrus' empire was the noblest and most extensive in Asia, is even confirmed by itself. It was terminated to the east by the Red Sea, to the north by the Euxine Sea, to the west by Cyprus and Egypt, to the south by Ethiopia; and though of such an extent, was governed by the single will of Cyrus. And to those who were subject to him he showed all kindness and regard, as to children; and they paid Cyrus duty and respect, as to a father. Immediately on Cyrus' death his sons fell into dissension; cities and nations revolted; every thing tended to ruin. To show that what I assert is truth, I will begin by things divine.

I know that in the early times of their institution, the king, and those that were subject to him, were religious observers of their oaths, and steady to their promises, even to the most criminal. If they had not been so, and that opinion of them had prevailed, no one would have trusted them; as at this time no one will, since their impiety is notorious: neither had the commanders of the army, in the expedition with Cyrus, put the confidence in them they did; but, relying on the ancient opinion of their faith, they delivered themselves into their hands, and being brought to the king, had their heads cut off. And many barbarians in that expedition perished, in different ways, by their treachery and deceit.

With respect likewise to these things, they are now degenerated from what they were: for, in their primitive institution, if any one hazarded himself for his king, or subdued any city or nation, or performed any great or excellent action, he had honours conferred on him. Now, if any one, as Mithridates did Ariobarzanes, betrays his father, and as Leomithres his wife and children, and his friend's children, left as hostages in Egypt, in violation of the most solemn oaths and engagements, he is esteemed to have done what is profitable to his prince, and is loaded with the highest honours. The Asiatics, being spectators of these things, are themselves sunk into impiety and injustice: for governments always resemble their governors, and the prosperity or declension, the vigour or decay of all states is derived from the virtues and vices, the abilities or weakness of their rulers. For this reason, they are more unjust now than they were formerly. They are likewise more corrupt with respect to riches; for they do not only imprison such as are highly criminal, but the innocent; and, contrary to justice, enforce the payment of their arbitrary impositions. So that they who have great estates are under the same apprehensions as those that are involved in great crimes: for this reason, they will not associate with the better sort, nor dare they enlist themselves in the king's army. Therefore those that are at war with them may securely ravage the country, without any opposition, if they are disposed to do it; which is owing to the impiety of the Persians towards the gods, and their iniquity towards men. Thus are their minds and dispositions debauched to what they had been in their first institution.

How defective they are in the care of their bodies I will, in the next place, relate. It was part of their institution not to spit, or blow the nose; but it is manifest this was not intended to spare the discharges of the body, but they intended to disperse those humours by exercise, and by that means to fortify their bodies. And the custom of not spitting or blowing the nose yet continues, though that of exercising is not practised. They likewise originally used to make only one meal a day, that the rest of the day might be employed in action and the despatch of business : and that custom yet continues. But, beginning their meal very early, they continue eating and drinking till the latest sitters up go to bed.

It was likewise an institution among them not to bring large bottles to their banquets; evidently thinking that, by not drinking to excess, they should neither weaken their bodies nor impair their understandings. And that custom too continues, of not bringing such bottles; but they drink to such excess, that instead of bringing in, they are carried out themselves, not being able to walk without help. It was also a custom of their countries, when they were on a journey, neither to eat nor drink, nor to do publicly what is the necessary consequence of both. Abstinence from these things yet continues; but their journeys are so short, that their abstaining from these necessities is nothing wonderful or extraordinary.

Formerly they went a-hunting so often, that those chases were sufficient exercises for themselves and their horses; but, since king Artaxerxes and his companions have debauched themselves with wine, they do not so frequently go out themselves, nor lead others to those chases. Wherefore, if some, from a fondness for exercise, have gone out a-hunting, they have manifestly incurred envy and hatred from those who thought it a mark of superiority, and of being better than themselves.

The custom yet likewise continues of a public education of the children; but the practice of horsemanship is neglected, because there are no public assemblies where they can gain applause by those exercises. And this institution is, in every circumstance, altered. That the boys, hearing the just and equitable determinations of private causes, were instructed in justice and equity; for now they see those certainly prevail who give the most exorbitant bribes. Formerly, likewise, boys were taught the virtues of the several productions of the earth, by which means they made use of such as were good, and abstained from those that were noxious. At this time they seem to be only instructed how to do the most hurt; therefore deaths and poisonings are nowhere so frequent as amongst them. And they are now much more luxurious than in Cyrus' time; for then they practised the Persian institutions and temperance, and conformed to the dress and elegance of the Medes; but now they have suffered the severity of the Persians to be quite extinguished, and retain the effeminacy of the Medes, which effeminacy and delicacy of theirs I have a mind to explain.

In the first place, it is not sufficient for them to have soft couches, but they must have carpets for their feet, that the floors may not, by resistance, make a noise, but that the carpets may break the sound. There is no diminution of what victuals used formerly to supply their tables, but new continually invented. And the like in sauces; for they are provided with cooks, who supply them with variety in both kinds. In winter it is not sufficient for them to cover their heads, their bodies, and their feet, but they have hair-gloves for their hands. In summer, the shade of trees and of rocks does not satisfy them; but under these, men stand near them with artificial shades contrived on purpose. If they possess a great number of cups, they are puffed up with it as a piece of magnificence; and, if these be unjustly acquired, they do not consider it as infamous; for injustice, and a sordid love of gain, is mightily increased among them. Formerly, it was a custom of their country never to be seen on foot on their journeys, for no other reason but in order to become more skilful horsemen; now, they have more coverings on their horses than on their couches; for they are not so careful of what concerns their horses, as to sit soft and at their ease.

With respect to the affairs of war, it is probable they should not be very much inferior to what they were at first? It was customary, in the beginning that those who possessed lands should furnish horsemen for their army, and pay those that were in garrisons, if they fought in defence of the country : now, porters, cooks, drawers, bed-makers, dressers, waiters at the baths, servants at table, and perfumers, are enlisted in their horse by the great men, that they themselves may make an advantage of their pay. These make an appearance in number, but are of no use in war; which is manifest in experience, for their enemies have a freer passage through their country than their friends. When Cyrus had broken them of the

custom of engaging at a distance, he armed
with breast-plates both them and their horses,
and gave every one a javelin in his hand, which
they might use in a close battle; but now, they
neither engage at a distance nor at hand. The
foot have yet shields and small swords, or cutlasses, as in Cyrus' time, but they will not venture to come to an engagement. Neither are
the chariots of that use Cyrus designed them:
for he had made brave and skilful drivers, by
bestowing rewards and honours on them who
would fall on the heavy-armed part of an army.
The Persians now, scarcely knowing who are
in the chariots, imagine that such as are unexercised in driving understand it as well as
those that have practised it: they do indeed
make an attack; but before they can break in-
into the enemy's ranks some of their own
accord fall off, others jump down and get
away; so that the chariots, being without
any guides, frequently do more injury to
their friends than to their enemies. Since
they themselves have been sensible how much
they are defective in martial affairs, they yield
to others, and none of them engage in a war
without the help of the Greeks, whether it be
a domestic quarrel or with the Greeks themselves; for they cannot engage in a war with
the Greeks without the assistance of Greeks.

Now I think I have executed what I undertook; for I say it is evident that the Persians
and their allies have less piety towards the gods,
less duty and regard to their relations, are less
just and equitable in their dealings with
others, more effeminate, and less fitted for
war than they were in their first institution.
If any one thinks differently, let him consider
their actions, and he will find them confirm
what I say.

XENOPHON

ON THE

EXPEDITION OF CYRUS.

TRANSLATED

By EDWARD SPELMAN, Esq.

PREFACE.

THERE is not, possibly, a more difficult, a more discouraging, or a more useful task than that of a translator; when I say this, I mean one who writes a translation, not a paraphrase, under which name most modern performances of this kind ought to be comprehended. It was very judiciously observed by Mr Pope, in the preface to his incomparable translation of the Iliad, that there have not been more men misled in former times by a servile dull adherence to the letter, than have been deluded in ours by a chimerical insolent hope of raising and improving their author. If these liberties are not to be allowed in translating poets, much less ought they to be indulged in translating historians. These paraphrasts, it seems, are men of too exalted a genius to stoop to a literal translation; they must improve their author, by adding something which he ignorantly omitted, or by omitting something which he thought material; by this means, the readers, who cannot compare the translation with the original (for whose use chiefly translations are intended) have either some wretched modern interpolation imposed on them for the thoughts of an ancient, or lose some of the author's thoughts, which the title of a translation gave them a right to. But these gentlemen have another reason for paraphrasing, instead of translating, if they will own it; they find less difficulty in clothing modern thoughts in a modern dress, than in making those of an ancient appear gracefully in a language so very different from that in which they were conceived: for it is a work of greater difficulty, than those, who have not experienced it, can possibly imagine, to give an appearance of novelty to antiquity, to give light to those things, which the ignorance of ancient customs and manners has rendered obscure, to give beauty to those that are obsolete, to give credibility to those that are doubtful, and above all, to give to a copy the air of an original. Yet all these, however difficult, belong to the province of a translator; these are embellishments, which he is to acquire, if he can; but his first duty is fidelity to his author: without that, his performance is not what it professes to be, and, in that case, these embellishments, like royal robes upon the back of an impostor, are rather a mockery than an ornament. If to the most exact fidelity a translator joins beauty of language, strength of expression, and, above all, perspicuity; and if, with these, he has genius enough to animate his translation with the spirit of his original, he then performs every duty belonging to his profession. I am far from thinking that my translation of Xenophon has all these perfections; on the contrary, I am sensible that it is in this, as in most other things, much easier to point out a duty, than to fulfil it. But I should be very much wanting in that respect which every author owes to the public, if I did not assure them, that no endeavours, no application, no labour, has been spared to render this translation fit to be laid before them. If the difficulties a translator meets with are considerable, the discouragements he labours under are no less so. The great number of anonymous translations, the great number of translations of translations, for which we in England are famous; but, above all, some very unfortunate versions of lives from the Greek into our language, to which the names of authors justly admired for every other kind of writing are prefixed, show the small account the world has reason to make of translations, as well as the difficulty of succeeding in them. These considerations, I say, are powerful discouragements to the undertaking any thing of this kind; but, if these are not sufficient to deter, let it be considered how unjust a way of thinking prevails with most readers; if there is any merit in the performance, it is placed to the account of the author; and if any fault, to that of the translator. Yet it should seem that translations might deserve more indulgence, when it is considered how many persons of great parts, who happen to be unacquainted with the learned languages, particularly with Greek, would, without that assistance, be deprived of the satisfaction and improvement of reading ancient histories written by ancient authors; for, I dare say, those, who are conversant with both, will allow that those histories are generally so much disfigured and distorted by modern relators, as scarce to be known: an instance of this we see in our countryman Sir Walter Raleigh, who has, in my opinion, treated ancient history with more strength and dignity than any modern writer of any other nation, and yet, let his account of the battle of Cannæ, though a military subject, and therefore particularly within his province; let his account, I say, of that battle be compared with the relation given of it by Polybius, from whom he took it, and what I have advanced will plainly appear. When I say this, I do not mean to insinuate that Sir Walter Raleigh was inferior, either as a soldier or a scholar, to Polybius; for I am thoroughly convinced of his great abilities, his fate alone is a proof of them: the only disadvantage he lay under, was in being less acquainted with the manners, customs, and discipline of the two contending nations at Cannæ; so that I am confident, whoever reads the two relations of that battle, will agree with me that a close translation of the account given of it by Polybius, would have been much more satisfactory and instructive, to those who cannot read the original.

The reader will observe that I have, in the course of my notes, principally taken notice of three translations, that of Leunclavius, of Hutchinson, and of D'Ablancourt; there is, besides, an Italian translation of the Expedition of Cyrus by Gandini, which I have occasionally consulted; but, as in cases of difficulty I found no assistance from thence, and, as I thought a criticism upon a translation in a third language would encumber the Notes, I have chosen to take no notice of it. I am also sensible there is a Latin translation of this history by Stephens, which I have mentioned as occasion required. But I cannot part with this subject without taking particular notice of Mr Hutchinson's edition of the Expedition of Cyrus, which I look upon to be the best edited book in the world, except the Cyropædia published by the same author: if I have sometimes differed from him, I hope it will be thought I have supported my opinion in such a manner that he will have no just reason to find fault with me. I have observed the same conduct with regard to D'Ablancourt, the looseness of whose translation I have been frequently obliged to condemn; on the other side, it will be allowed that I have often commended him; though I cannot carry my commendations of him so far as his countryman Menage, who says that D'Ablancourt has surpassed even Xenophon himself in the elegance of his style. Another celebrated Frénch critic, Balzac, says, that D'Ablancourt's translation of Xenophon would be incomparable, if he had placed nothing before it, but that his preface is so fine, that it obscures the finest things that can be compared to it; he adds that, if it were possible for D'Ablancourt to have lived in the time of Cyrus the Younger, and for Xenophon to be now alive, the prefaces of D'Ablancourt would deserve to be translated by Xenophon. The reader will observe, that this forced style was in fashion among the French in Balzac's time, that is, in the infancy of their taste: the writers of that age seem to have imposed an obligation upon themselves of being for ever witty; they were often so, but that was not enough; this eternal straining after wit obliged them many times to have recourse to forced turns of thought, and, sometimes, to what their language calls Phœbús, that is, shining expressions that seem to signify something. After the reader has compared the passages I have taken the liberty to censure in D'Ablancourt with the original, he will be able to judge how far he has surpassed Xenophon in the elegance of his style, and how far, according to the supposition of Balzac, his works might deserve to be translated by Xenophon. But there is an old English translation of the Expedition of Cyrus by John Bingham, printed in 1623, and dedicated to the Right Worshipful the Artillery Company. The first notice I had of this translation was by a note of Hutchinson about the middle of the last book; he also mentions it towards the end of the same book, where Xenophon says Gongylus marched out to the assistance of the Greeks βίᾳ τῆς Μητρὸς, upon which occasion, Hutchinson says, *vis phraseos omnino latuit versionis Anglicanæ authorem;* and, indeed, he had great reason to say so; for, upon looking into Bingham's translation, I find he has rendered that passage, "by compulsion of his mother," whereas he should have said, "against his mother's will," in which sense all the other translators have rendered it. I do not remember that Hutchinson has taken any notice of this translation but upon these two occasions. Finding, therefore, by Hutchinson's note before-mentioned, when I had not more than half the last book remaining to complete my translation, that there was an old English version of the Expedition, I employed several of the most eminent booksellers in town to get it for me, but all in vain; for none of them could find it, neither would they be persuaded there was any such book extant, till I referred them to that note of Hutchinson: however, at last I got a sight of it from a public library. Upon comparing it with the original, I found the author was a man of some learning, from whence I conclude that he must have made use of some very faulty edition, otherwise, it is not possible that a man of learning (for such he really seems to have been) should ever have been guilty of so many mistakes, as are to be met with through the whole course of his translation: as to his style, it seems to be, at least, a century older than that in which he writ. There is, in the fourth book, a conversation between Xenophon and Cheirisophus, in which they rally one another upon the art of stealing, so much practised by their respective countries; the foundation of which raillery is the advice given by Xenophon to steal a march to some part of a mountain they were to pass. As the spirit of raillery is, of all others, the most likely to be lost in a translation, for that reason, raillery itself is the last thing one would choose to translate, if it did not necessarily come in one's way; upon this occasion, therefore, I was in hopes of receiving some assistance from the old English translation, which I should both have made use of, and acknowledged very readily; but, upon examination, I found this passage translated in the following manner, "it seemeth to me not impossible to steal some part or other of the hill." After this, I dare say, it will easily be concluded that I could entertain no great hopes of any assistance from that quarter. Many ancient authors, both Greek and Latin, and particularly those who were themselves fine writers, as well as judicious critics, such as Dionysius of Halicarnassus, and Tully, have celebrated the beauty of our author's style, his perspicuity and peculiar sweetness in his composition, which made his writings be called the language of the muses: the latter goes so far as to say that Lucullus, being sent to make war upon Mithridates, which was no easy province, and being unacquainted with the duty of a general, acquired, by reading the Expedition of Cyrus, so great a knowledge in the art of war, as to owe his victories against that prince to the information he received from it. However this may be, we find, by the Commentaries of Cæsar, that he often made use of the same dispositions against the Gauls, which Xenophon had employed, with so great success, against the Persians: but, what is much more for the credit of our author, it is obvious that the Expedition of Cyrus was the model of these Commentaries; the same elegance, the same clearness of expression, the same unaffected grace, are the distinguishing characters of both; and, possibly, the Greek and Latin languages have nothing in their kind more perfect than these two admirable performances. I am sensible that all commendations bestowed upon the original, tend to expose the translation to censure, which I ought not, in prudence, wantonly to solicit: but I was willing, if I could not do justice to Xenophon by translating him, to endeavour to do it, at least, by commending him: this may be thought a small amends for the former: however, the determination of this question must be left to the voice of the people, who are still sovereigns in this; and who, as they were formerly remarkable for their justice in deciding the fate of mankind, are still not less so in determining that of their productions; so that, to use the words of my ancestor,* in the preface to his Glossary, I submit my labours and errors to the public.

* Sir Harry Spelman, who was great great-grandfather to the author.

AN ACCOUNT

OF

XENOPHON.

———

XENOPHON was an Athenian; his father's name was Gryllus. All that we know of him till he attended Cyrus in his expedition, is, that he was a disciple of Socrates. If, to have been a disciple of that great man was an instance of his good fortune, the improvement he made of that education is an instance of his merit; and, indeed, nothing less than the happiest disposition, the best education, and the greatest improvement of both, could render Xenophon that universal man we find him in his writings; his Cyropædia shows him to have possessed, in a sovereign degree, the art of government; his Expedition of Cyrus shows him a complete general; his History, an entertaining, an instructive, and a faithful historian; his Panegyric of Agesilaus, an orator; and his Treatise of Hunting, a sportsman; his Apology for Socrates, and the account he gives of his manner of conversing, show that he was both a friend, and a philosopher; and all of them, that he was a good man. This appears remarkably in his preserving Byzantium from being plundered by his soldiers, who having gained no other reward of the dangerous expedition they had been engaged in, but their preservation, were not only strongly tempted to plunder that town by the hope of making their fortunes, but justly provoked to it by the disingenuous behaviour of the Lacedæmonian governor; yet these two lawless passions, avarice and revenge, the authority and eloquence of Xenophon quite subdued.

As Cyrus had assisted the Lacedæmonians in their war against the Athenians, the latter looked upon Xenophon's attachment to that prince as criminal, and banished him for engaging in his service. After this, Xenophon attended Agesilaus, when he was sent for by the Lacedæmonians with his army from Asia; where the success of his arms gave something more than uneasiness to Artaxerxes, who, not without cause, began to fear the same fate from Agesilaus, which his successor, Darius, afterwards found from Alexander; but the former, by corrupting the Greek cities, and, by that means, engaging them to make war upon the Lacedæmonians, suspended the fate of Persia for a time: but, in all evils, relief, obtained by corruption, is only a respite, not a cure; for, when Alexander invaded Persia, the same low arts were again practised by Darius to recall him from Asia by a diversion in Greece; but these proving ineffectual, the Persians, by trusting more to the vices of their enemies, than to their own virtue, became an easy conquest. Agesilaus soon after he returned, fought the battle of Coronea, where, though wounded, he defeated the Thebans and their allies: at this battle Xenophon was present. After that, he retired to Scilus, where he passed his time in reading, the conversation of his friends, sporting, and writing history. But this place being over-run by the Eleans, in whose neighbourhood it was, Xenophon went to Corinth, where he lived till the first year of the hundred and fifth Olympiad, when he died in the ninety-first year of his age: so that, he must have been about fifty years of age at the time of the expedition of Cyrus, which was the fourth year of the ninety-fourth Olympiad, just forty years before. I am sensible some learned men are of opinion that he was not so old at the time of the expedition, though I see no reason to disbelieve Lucian in this particular, who says that Xenophon was above ninety years of age when he died. However, this is beyond all dispute, that he lived till after the battle of Mantinea, which, according to Diodorus Siculus, was in the second year of the hundred and fourth Olympiad, because he closes his History of the Affairs of Greece with the account of that battle: in which account it is very extraordinary that he should say nothing more of the most remarkable incident in it, I mean the death of Epaminondas, than *that he fell* in the action; but this may be accounted for by that modesty, which was the distinguishing character of our author, because it is well known that Epaminondas fell by the hand of Gryllus, the son of Xenophon, who was sent by his father to the assistance of the Athenians. It will easily be imagined that a general, at the head of a victorious army, then pursuing his victory, could not be attacked, much less slain, without manifest danger to the daring enemy, who should attempt it. This Gryllus found, for he had no sooner lanced the fatal dart, which deprived Thebes of the greatest general of that age, but he was cut to pieces by the friends of Epaminondas. When the news of his death was brought to Xenophon, he said no more than that *he knew he was mortal.*

INTRODUCTION.

Nothing seems to contribute more to the forming a clear idea of any transaction in history than a previous knowledge both of the persons and things that gave birth to it; for when the reader is once acquainted with the characters and views of the principal actors, and with what has been done in consequence of both, the scene unfolds in so natural a manner, that the most extraordinary events in history are looked upon in the same light as the most surprising phenomena in philosophy; that is, like these, they are found to be the necessary result of such principles as the all-wise Creator has thought fit to establish; and, like these, are as little to be wondered at, and as easy to be accounted for. In order, therefore, to enable the reader to view the consequences in their principles, and contemplate the embryo plant in its seed, I shall lay before him a short account of the most remarkable transactions that seem to have had an immediate influence upon that which Xenophon has chosen for the subject of his history. The affairs of the Athenians and Lacedæmonians had been, for some time before the expedition of Cyrus, so much interwoven with those of Persia, that all three seemed to have had a share in every remarkable event that happened to each of them. Thus the supplies of money with which Lysander, the Lacedæmonian general, was furnished by Cyrus, enabled him to carry on the war against the Athenians with advantage, and, at last, to give them a decisive blow at Ægos Potamos, which ended in the taking of Athens; and, on the other side, the assistance which Cyrus received from the Lacedæmonians, both by sea and land, in return, encouraged him to an attempt of no less moment than the dethroning his brother Artaxerxes. The several steps which led to this enterprise equally great, unfortunate, and unwarrantable, shall be taken notice of in the order of time in which they happened. In his short survey, I shall avoid entering into any chronological discussions, which often puzzle, seldom inform, and never entertain, but confine myself almost entirely to Diodorus Siculus, who, besides the character he has deservedly obtained for fidelity and exactness, had the advantage of living many centuries nearer the transactions he recounts, than those who differ from him in chronology, as well as that of consulting many authors, whose works are unfortunately lost to modern ages. Neither shall I go further back than the taking of Athens by the Lacedæmonians, which happened in the fourth year of the ninety-third Olympiad, and put an end to the Peloponnesian war, after it had lasted twenty-seven years. The same year died Darius Ochus, king of Persia, after a reign of nineteen years, and left his kingdom to his eldest son Artaxerxes, who was born before he was king. Parysatis, his queen, the most artful of all women, and mother both to Artaxerxes and Cyrus, tried the power of every practice to engage Darius to imitate his predecessor, Darius Hystaspes, who preferred his son Xerxes, born after his accession, to Artobazanes, who was born before it; but all her efforts proved ineffectual, and Artaxerxes succeeded his father without opposition. If the arts of Parysatis could not prevail with Darius to set his eldest son aside, her fondness for Cyrus not only encouraged him to form a design against his brother's life, but rescued him, if not from disgrace, at least, from punishment, when it was discovered. The next year, which was the first of the ninety-fourth Olympiad, there happened an eclipse of the sun, which is only taken notice of, as it is no small satisfaction to find history, upon this occasion, supported by astronomy, by which it appears that the eclipse of the sun, mentioned by Xenophon in his Greek History, to have happened this year, fell out on the third day of September upon a Friday, at twelve minutes after nine o'clock. The same year Cyrus returned to his government in Asia Minor, with a mind more exasperated at his disgrace, than terrified with his danger, and immediately resolved to repair the disappointment of private treason by open hostility; to this purpose, he addresses himself to the Lacedæmonians who cheerfully espouse his quarrel. This intercourse between Cyrus, and the Lacedæmonians, could not be carried on so privately, as to escape the notice of Alcibiades, who being banished from his country, was now retired to Grynium, a strong place in Phrygia, appointed by Pharnabazus for his residence, to whom he immediately communicates his intelligence, desiring him, at the same time, to appoint proper persons to conduct him to court, that he might give Artaxerxes an account of the whole: but Pharnabazus, being willing to have the merit of a discovery of so great importance, sent persons of trust to Artaxerxes to lay the information before him. Alcibiades, suspecting his design, left Pharnabazus, with an intention to apply himself to the satrap of Paphlagonia, to the end that, through him, he might be recommended to Artaxerxes; but Pharnabazus, fearing the king should, by this means, be informed of the truth, prevented his design, by ordering him to be put to death.

The next year, that is, the second of the ninety-fourth Olympiad, brings Clearchus upon the stage; he makes so considerable a figure in the ensuing history, both by his conduct and his fate, that the incident we are going to speak of, which happened just before he engaged himself in the service of Cyrus, and which seems to have driven him into it, must not be omitted. It seems, the inhabitants of Byzantium being engaged in factions, the Lacedæmonians sent Clearchus to compose their differences, who uniting them in nothing but their complaints against himself, the ephori recalled him: but he refusing to obey their orders, they sent Panthœdas with some troops, to force him to a submission. With these he defeated Clearchus, and obliged him to fly to Ionia; here he was received with open arms by Cyrus, to whom his experience in military affairs, his enterprising genius, and, possibly, even his rebellion, were, at this juncture, no small recommendation; since, he could not but look upon a man, who had dared to fly in the face of his country, as a proper person to bear command in an army, which he was raising to invade his own. It was upon this occasion that Cyrus gave him the ten thousand daricks mentioned by Xenophon, with which he levied a considerable number of forces, and engaged them in his service.

The next year Diodorus Siculus passes over without taking notice of any thing relating to this expedition, so we may conclude that Cyrus employed it in continuing his preparations under various pretences, particularly since we find him in the field early the year after. Sardes, the capital of Lydia, and formerly the residence of its kings, was the place of general rendezvous; from hence Cyrus marched at the head of about 12,800 Greeks, and 100,000 Barbarians, to dispute the crown of Persia with his brother Artaxerxes; and, from hence, Xenophon, who came to him to Sardes, begins his history of this Expedition.

he year, which decided this great contest, was the 783d year from the taking of
y, the 351st of Rome, Publius Cornelius, Cæsar Fabius, Spurius Nautius, Caius Va-
s, Marcus Sergius, and Junius Lucullus, being military tribunes; and the fourth year
he ninety-fourth Olympiad, Exænetus being archon at Athens. This expedition has,
ed, been thought of consequence enough to be taken notice of in the Arundel Mar-
; the 60th era of which has these words: "From the time those, who ascended
th Cyrus, returned, and Socrates, the philosopher, died, being seventy years of age,
e hundred and thirty-seven years, Laches being archon at Athens."[a]

The year the Greeks returned was the year after they marched from Sardes, since
Xenophon says they were fifteen months in their expedition, and consequently that year
ra the first of the ninety-fifth Olympiad; the authority of the Arundel Marble is supported by Diodorus Siculus, who says that Laches was archon that year at Athens, and
that Socrates was put to death the same year.

[a] The words of the Arundel Marble are these.

Αφ ου ανηλθον οι μετ A KYPOY ANABANTEΣ KAI ΣωKPATHΣ ΦIAOΣOΦος ἐτελεύτησε βιος ΕΤΗ
ΗΔΔΔ ΕΤΗ ΗΔΔΔΙΙΙΙ APXONTOΣ AΘHNHΣI ΔΑΧΗτος.

XENOPHON

ON THE

EXPEDITION OF CYRUS.

BOOK I.

CONTENTS of BOOK I.

THE

EXPEDITION[1] OF CYRUS.[2]

BOOK I.

1 CYRUS was the youngest son of Darius,[3] by Parysatis, and brother to Artaxerxes. Darius being sick, and apprehensive of his approaching end, desired both his sons might attend him. Artaxerxes the eldest being then present, he sent for Cyrus from his government with which he[4] had invested him, as a[5] satrap, having also appointed him general of all the people, who assemble in the plain of Castolus. Hereupon, Cyrus came to court, accompanied by Tissaphernes as his friend, and attended by three hundred [6] heavy-armed Greeks, under the command of Xenias of Parrhasie.

---

1 D'Ablancourt has thought fit to change the title given by Xenophon to his history, and, instead of *The Expedition of Cyrus*, to call it, *La Retraite des dix mille*: the reason he gives for it is this, he says, Things ought to derive their name from that which is most remarkable in them, and that the Expedition is nothing in comparison to the Retreat. I own this reason does not persuade me; whatever weight it ought to have had with the author, I think it should have none with a translator.

2 Ἀναβάσεως. Every one who is conversant with the Greek authors knows, that whenever they speak not only of military expeditions, but even of journeys undertaken by private persons from the Lesser Asia to Babylon or Susa, the residence of the Persian kings, they use the words ἀναβαίνειν: the same words came afterwards to be applied to the city of Rome, though more rarely. Arrian, who, in his Expedition of Alexander, has followed our author, not only in the distribution of his work into seven books, but in his style as far as he was able, has also copied him in his title, calling his history also, ἀνάβασις Ἀλεξάνδρου. Hutchinson thinks that the river of that part of Asia in question falling into the Ægean and Mediterranean seas, gave occasion to these terms ἀναβαίνειν and καταβαίνειν; but it is certain that almost all the great rivers of that part of Asia run either to the north or south, as the Halys, the Iris, the Thermodon, the Tigris, and the Euphrates.

3 Δαρείου καὶ Παρυσάτιδος, &c. This first period is much celebrated by Demetrius Phalareus, as full of dignity and historical simplicity.

4 Καὶ στρατηγὸν δὲ αὐτὸν ἀπέδειξε. D'Ablancourt has visibly mistaken this passage; he makes Darius consti-

tute Cyrus general at his arrival at court, *a sa venue*; whereas it not only appears from this passage, but from history also, that he was actually invested with that employment when he was sent for: I wish the old Latin translation, which says, *prætorem designat*, did not lead him into this error: Hutchinson has translated it properly *præfectum designaverat*. I said that this also appeared from history. Our author, in his account of the affairs of Greece, mentions a letter to have been written by Darius to the people of Lesser Asia, six years before this Expedition of Cyrus: in this letter, Darius gives them notice of his having appointed Cyrus commander-in-chief of those people, who assemble in the plain of Castolus. The words of the letter are these : κατασταμένου Κύρου κάρανον τῶν εἰς Καστωλὸν ἀθροιζομένων. τὸ δὲ κάρανόν ἐστι κύριον.

5 Σατράπης, though used both by Latin and Greek authors, is a Persian word, and signifies a commander, a general ; Σατράπαι, Ἀρχηγοί, στρατηλάται, Πέρσαι δὲ ἡ λέξις. Hesychius. Herodotus says, Darius Hystaspes appointed twenty of these governments, ἀρχὰς κατεστήσατο εἴκοσι τὰς αὐτοὶ καλίουσι σατραπηίας.

6 Ὁπλίτας. D'Ablancourt excuses himself for not distinguishing these heavy-armed men in his translation ; but I do not only think it necessary to distinguish them from the light-armed, but to give some account of their distinction. There are three different kinds of foot-soldiers chiefly mentioned by our author in the course of this history, the ὁπλῖται, the ψιλοί, and the πελτασταί ; of whom, and of their respective armour, Arrian gives the following account in his Tactics : τὸ ὁπλιτικὸν, says he, ἔχω θώρακας, καὶ ἀσπίδας παραμήκεις, καὶ μαχαίρας, καὶ δόρατα, ὡς Ἕλληνες, καὶ σαρίσας, ὡς Μακεδόνες. The heavy-armed men have corslets, long shields, and

After the death of Darius, and the accession of Artaxerxes,[1] Tissaphernes accuses Cyrus to his brother of treason. Artaxerxes gives credit to the accusation, and orders Cyrus to be apprehended, with a design to put him to death ; but his mother having saved him by her intercession, sends him back to his government. Cyrus, as soon as he left the court after this danger and disgrace,[2] deliberates by what means he may no longer be subject to his brother, but if possible reign in his palace. In this he was[3] supported by his mother Parysatis, who had a greater love for Cyrus than for the king Artaxerxes ; and when any persons belonging to the court resorted to him, he sent them back more disposed to favour him than the king. Besides, he took so great care of the Barbarians who were with him, as to render them both good soldiers, and affectionate to his service : he also levied an army of Greeks with all possible secrecy, that might find the king in no degree prepared to resist him. And whenever he recruited the garrisons that were dispersed in the several cities under his command, he ordered each of their officers to enlist as many Peloponnesians as possible, and of those the best men they could get, under pretence that Tissaphernes had a design upon those cities. For the cities of Ionia formerly belonged to Tissaphernes, having been given to him by the king, but at that time they had all revolted from him to Cyrus, except[4] Miletus ; the inhabitants of which being engaged in the same design, and Tissaphernes having early notice of their intentions, put some of them to death, and banished others ; these Cyrus received, and raising an army besieged Miletus both by sea and land, endeavouring to restore the banished citizens : thus he made another pretence for raising an army ; and sending to the king, he desired, that, as he was his brother, he might have the command of these cities rather than Tissaphernes. In this also he was assisted by his mother ; so that the king was not sensible of the design that was formed against him, but looking upon these preparations as directed against Tissaphernes, was under no concern at their making war upon one another ; for

---

swords, and pikes like the Greeks, and spears, like the Macedonians, τὸ δὲ ψιλὸν ἐναντιώτατον ἔχει τῷ ὁπλιτικῷ πᾶς, ὅτι σὺν ἄνω δόρασιν, καὶ ἀσπίδες, καὶ κνημίδες, καὶ πρόλοφοι, ἐκυζόλως τοῖς ὁπλοῖς διαχράμενοι, ταξεύμασιν, ἢ ἀκοντίοις, ἢ σφενδόναις, ἢ λίθοις ἐκ χειρός. The light-armed men are armed in a quite different manner from the heavy armed ; they have no corslets, or shields, greaves, or helmets, but altogether make use of missive weapons, such as arrows, darts, and stones thrown by slings, and out of the hand. τὸ δὲ πελταστικὸν δὲ ναυφότερον μὲν τυγχάνει ἐν τοῦ ὁπλιτικοῦ· ἡ γὰρ πέλτη, σμικρότερον τῆς ἀσπίδος δὲ ἐλαφρότερον, καὶ τὰ ἀκόντια τῶν δοράτων δὲ σαφεστῶν λυσόμενα, βαρύτερον δὲ τοῦ ψιλοῦ· The targeteers are armed in a lighter manner than the heavy armed men, for their bucklers are smaller and lighter than the shields of the latter, and their darts shorter than their pikes and spears ; but their armour is heavier than that of the light-armed. These three kinds of foot-soldiers are so often mentioned by Xenophon to have been employed by the Greek generals, and particularly by himself upon different occasions, according to the difference of their armour and manner of fighting, that I thought it necessary at first to give the reader a clear idea of that difference.

1 Τισσαφέρνη. This is the same Tissaphernes, over whom Alcibiades gained so great an ascendant, that he governed him not only in his politics, but in his pleasures. We shall find him in the course of this history at the head of the Persian army, that endeavoured in vain to cut off the retreat of the Greeks. But the treachery he was guilty of in relation to the Greek generals, after they had incautiously put themselves in his hands, must render his name so odious, that it may not be unacceptable to the reader to be informed of his fate after this history leaves him. Agesilaus being sent by the Lacedæmonians at the head of an army into Asia, and having gained many advantages over the Persians, Artaxerxes looked upon Tissaphernes as the cause of the ill success of his arms ; and being incensed against him by Parysatis, in revenge for his behaviour to Cyrus, he appointed Tithraustes to succeed him in his government, with orders to cut off his head : this happened in the first year of the ninety-sixth Olympiad, that is, about five years after the expedition of Cyrus.

2 Βουλεύεται ὡς μήποτε ἔτι ἔσται ἐπὶ τῷ ἀδελφῷ. This is rendered by D'Ablancourt il songea aux moyens de se venger de cet affront, which may be a translation of any other passage, as well as of this.

3 Παρύσατις μὲν δὴ μήτηρ ὑπῆρχε τῷ Κύρῳ, &c. Leunclavius has translated this passage as if ὑπῆρχε signified here εἰμί in the same sense as Plutarch uses the word, speaking of this very thing, ἡ δὲ μήτηρ ὑπῆρχε μᾶλλον τὸν Κῦρον φιλοῦσα ; but every body knows that ὑπάρχω with a dative case, signifies to favour : Hutchinson has said very properly mater a Cyri partibus stetit. D'Ablancourt has thought fit to leave out this period entirely.

4 Μιλήτου. A considerable city of Ionia, not far from the mouth of the Mæander : at the time of the Trojan war it was inhabited, according to Homer, by the Carians, whom he mentions among the allies of Troy.

Νάστης αὖ Καρῶν ἡγήσατο βαρβαροφώνων
Οἳ Μίλητον ἔχον.

This town, having revolted from the Persians, at the instigation of Aristagoras, was retaken by them six years after that revolt. About sixty-seven years after the time our author speaks of, Alexander took Miletus, after a brave resistance from the garrison, consisting of three hundred Greeks, then in the service of the king of Persia.

Cyrus sent the king all the taxes that were raised in those cities, which had been under the government of Tissaphernes.

He had also another army raised for him in the Chersonesus, over against Abydus, in this manner. There was a banished Lacedæmonian, his name Clearchus; Cyrus, becoming acquainted with him, [5] admired the man, and made him a present of ten thousand [6] daricks; with which money Clearchus raised an army, and marching out of the Chersonesus, made war upon the Thracians, who inhabit above the Hellespont, which, being a great advantage to the Greeks, induced the cities upon the Hellespont to subsist his forces with greater cheerfulness. Thus was this army also secretly maintained for his service. Aristippus of Thessaly, between whom and Cyrus there was an intercourse of [7] hospitality, being oppressed by a contrary faction at home, came to him, demanding two thousand mercenaries, and their pay for three months, in hope, by their assistance, to subdue his adversaries. Cyrus granted him four thousand men, and six months' pay, desiring him to come to no terms with his adversaries without [8] consulting him. In this manner the army in Thessaly was also privately maintained for his use. At the same time he ordered Proxenus, the Bœotian, a friend of his, to attend with all the men he could raise, giving it out that he designed to make war upon the [9] Pisidians, who, it was said, infested

---

5 Ἠγάσθη τε αὐτόν. Ἄγαμαι θαυμάζω. Phavorinus. In this sense I have translated it, though I must own I am pleased with what D'Ablancourt says, *Cyrus le voulut*. As Clearchus makes a considerable figure in this expedition, our author has given his character at the end of the second book; but there being some particulars relating to him mentioned in Diodorus Siculus, which are not there taken notice of, I thought the reader might not be displeased to be informed of them, for which reason I have mentioned them in the introduction.

6 Δαρικούς. The darick was a Persian gold coin. Suidas, Harpocration, and the Scholiast of Aristophanes, say it was of equal value with the Attick χρυσοῦς, or with twenty silver drachms, that is, the 5th part of a river mine, sixty of which made a talent, which last amounted to £193 : 15 : 0 sterling; so that 10,000 daricks will make 33 talents and 1-3d, or £6458 : 6 : 8 of our money. On the reverse of this coin was an archer, which gave occasion to Agesilaus to say, that he was driven out of Asia by thirty thousand archers, meaning so many daricks distributed among the Greek cities by the king of Persia. The authors before mentioned inform us that this coin did not derive its name from Darius, the father to Xerxes, but from another more ancient king: who that should be, is not so well understood, since Darius Hystaspes, the father to Xerxes, and one of the seven Persian noblemen, who put the Magi to death, was the first Persian king of that name. I am sensible Prideaux is of opinion, that Cyaxares, brother to Mandane, and uncle to the first Cyrus, is Darius the Mede mentioned by Daniel, from whom, he says, this coin took its name, and who caused it to be struck at Babylon during the two years he reigned there; but Xenophon, in his Cyropædia, mentions some of this coin to have been found, among other riches, by Cyrus, in a castle belonging to Gobryas, even before the taking of Babylon by the Medes and Persians. Sir Isaac Newton thinks that Darius the Mede, when he and Cyrus took Sardes, melted down all the Lydian money he found there, and re-coined it with his own effigies. But Xenophon speaks of daricks upon the occasion already mentioned even before the taking of Sardes, which preceded that of Babylon. It is not possible this could have escaped a man, to whom nothing either in history or nature was unknown; it is much more probable that he looked upon it as an anticipation in Xenophon, which opinion, I find, prevails with some learned men. There is however a passage in Herodotus in Melpomene, which almost inclines one to think, that Darius Hystaspes was the author of this coin, notwithstanding what Suidas, Harpocration, and the Scholiast of Aristophanes say to the contrary; he says there, that Darius Hystaspes refined gold to all the pureness that was possible, and coined it into money, Δαρεῖος μὲν χρυσίον καθαρώτατον ἀπεψήσας εἰς τὸ δυνατώτατον, νόμισμα ἐκόψατο.

Now it is certain that all authors celebrate the daricks for the fineness of the gold; and, a few lines before, the same author says, Darius did this with a view of leaving behind him such a monument as no other king had done, μνημόσυνον ἑαυτῷ λιπέσθαι τοῦτο τὸ μὴ ἄλλῳ εἴη βασιλεῖ κατεργασμένον.

7 Ξίνος. Ξίνος καλεῖται ὁ ὑποδεχόμενος, καὶ ὁ ὑποδεχθείς. Phavorinus. In the same manner ἄοσπος, every one knows, has both an active and passive signification. These rights of hospitality were of ancient date, and of so sacred a nature, that Jupiter himself was thought to preside over them, and to punish the violations committed against them, for which reason he was called Ξίνιος; with whom Ulysses in Homer endeavours, to very little purpose, to threaten Polypheme.

Ζεὺς δ' ἐπιτιμήτωρ ἱκετάων τε ξείνων τε
Ξείνιος, ὃς ξείνοισιν ἅμ' αἰδοίοισιν ὀπηδεῖ.

This tradition Virgil has, among many others, transplanted into his Æneid; where the unhappy Dido, when she first entertained her Trojan guest, implores the favour of Jupiter:

Jupiter, hospitibus nam te dare jura loquuntur.

Pliny has translated ξίνος, *hospitalis*, in the account he gives of a statue of Jupiter under that denomination; this statue was the work of Pamphilus a disciple of Praxiteles, and to be seen in the collection of Asinius Pollio. The same word signifies mercenaries a little lower, whence comes ἐπιτύεσθαι, μισθοφορεῖν, ξίνοι δὶ οἱ μισθοφόροι. Harpocration.

8 Συμβουλεύσηται. The difference between συμβουλεύεσθαι, and συμβουλεύειν, appears very particularly from a passage in Herodotus in Polyhymnia, συμβουλευομένων τε ἂν συμβουλεύουσι τὰ ἄριστα; where the former signifies to ask advice, and the latter to give it.

9 Πισίδας. The Pisidians inhabited the mountainous part of Asia Minor, which lies between the Phrygians, Lydians, and Carians, to whom they were very troublesome neighbours.

his country. He then ordered Sophænetus the Stymphalian, and Socrates the Achaian, with whom also he had an intercourse of hospitality, to come to him with as many men as they could raise, pretending to make war upon Tissaphernes, in conjunction with the banished Milesians. These too obeyed his commands.

Having now determined to march into the Upper Asia, he pretended his design was to drive the Pisidians entirely out of the country: and, as against them, he assembles there both his Barbarian and Greek forces ; commanding at the same time Clearchus with all his troops to attend him, and Aristippus to come to an agreement with his fellow-citizens, and send his army to him. He also appointed Xenias the Arcadian who had command of the mercenaries in the several cities, to come to him with all his men, leaving only sufficient garrisons in the citadels. He next ordered all the troops that were employed in the siege of Miletus, together with the banished citizens, to join him,[1] engaging to the last, if his expedition was attended with success not to lay down his arms, till he had restored them. These cheerfully obeyed him (for they gave credit to what he said), and, taking their arms with them, came to Sardes. Xenias also came thither with the garrisons he had drawn out of the cities, consisting of four thousand heavy-armed men. Proxenus brought with him fifteen hundred heavy-armed and five hundred [2]light-armed men. Sophænetus, the Stymphalian, a thousand heavy-armed ; Socrates, the Achaian, about five hundred heavy-armed ; Pasion, the Magarean, seven hundred men. Both he and Socrates were among those who were employed in the siege of Miletus. These came to him to [3]Sardes, Tissaphernes observing all this, and looking upon these preparations as greater than were necessary against the Pisidians, went [4] to

the king with all the haste he could, taking with him about five hundred horse ; and the king being informed by Tissaphernes of the intended [5]expedition of Cyrus, prepared himself to oppose him.

Cyrus, with the forces I have mentioned, marched from Sardes ; and advancing through Lydia in [6]three days, made twenty-two [7]parasangs, as far as the river Mæander.   This

---

[1] 'Υποσχόμενος αὐτοῖς, ἢ καλῶς κατωρθάξειν ἐφ' ἃ ἐστρατεύετο, μὴ πρόσθεν παύσασθαι, πρὶν, &c.   This sentence is thus translated by D'Ablancourt, avec assurance de ne plus faire d'entreprise avant leur retablissement, which is so apparently foreign from the author's sense, that it is unnecessary to make any observations upon it.

[2] Γυμνήτας.   These are the same with ψιλοὶ, mentioned above.

[3] Σάρδις.   Sardes was the capital of Lydia, and the seat of its kings : the first Cyrus took it after a siege of fourteen days, and in it Crœsus, after he had reigned as many years.   It was afterwards set on fire by the Ionians, and with the temple of the goddess Cybele ; which was the pretence afterwards made use of by Xerxes for burning the temples of the Greeks.

[4] 'Ως βασιλέα.   ὡς is frequently used by the Attic

writers for πρὸς, which possibly may be understood.   In this sense it is employed in the first of those two verses which Pompey repeated, when he put himself in the hands of Ptolemy, king of Egypt.

Ὅστις γὰρ ὡς τύραννον ἐμπορεύεται
Κείνου ἐστὶ δοῦλος κἂν ἐλεύθερος μόλῃ.

[5] Τὸν Κύρου στόλον.   Στόλος καὶ τὸ στζͅνὰ στρατεύματα.   Suidas.   καὶ ἡ διὰ γῆς πορεία.   Phavorinus.   The author first mentioned quotes a passage out of Arrian, in which στόλος is taken in the same sense our author uses it in this place.   Στεράμις μαθὼν τὸν στόλον βασιλέως ἐπὶ τὴν αὑτοῦ ἐπικρατέιαν γινόμενον, ἔφυγε.

[6] Σταθμοὺς τρεῖς.   I have said three days' march, in the same manner as the Roman authors say, tertiis castris, without any regard to the particular distance from one place to another, but only to the motion of the army.   In this I am confirmed by Diodorus Siculus, who speaking of the march of the Greek army in their retreat through the country of the Mosynœcians, explains ἱνℓὰ σταθμοὺς, mentioned by our author upon that occasion, by ἐν ἡμέραις ἑπτά.

[7] Παρασάγγας.   Παρασάγγης, μέτρον ἰδοὺ τριάκοντα σταδίους ἔχων.   Hesychius.   Herodotus says the same thing.   On the other hand, Strabo says, some make it sixty, others thirty or forty stadia ; but this may in some degree be reconciled by the Etymological Lexicon, which explains it thus, παρασάγγαι, τριάκοντα στάδιοι παρὰ Πέρσαις, παρ' Αἰγυπτίοις δ' ἑξήκοντα ; so that the parasang was thirty stadia among the Persians, and sixty among the Egyptians ; but as the march of the Greek army, described by our author, lay through Persia, there can be no doubt but he followed their account.   It may not be improper to observe, that a stadium contains one hundred ἀργυιαὶ or fathoms, στάδιον ἀργυιαὶ ἑκατόν.   Phavorinus, that is, 600 feet, ἀργυιὰ being, according to the same author, ἡ ἔκτασις τῶν χειρῶν σὺν τῷ πλάτει στήθους, that is, a fathom.   I know very well, that the Greek foot contained .0875 decimals more than an English foot, so that whoever has a mind to be exact, must compute according to that fraction. As the parasang, stadium, and plethrum are frequently mentioned in the course of this history, I thought it proper to explain them at first, that we may have done with them : the plethrum has not yet been taken notice of : Suidas, says it contains one hundred feet, ἔχει δὲ τὸ πλέθρον πόδας ρ΄ : or, as both he and Phavorinus affirm, together with the Greek scholiast upon this passage of Homer, where he speaks of Tityus

————'Ὁ δ' ἐπ' ἐννία πᾶσι πίλεθρα,

τὸ τοῦ σταδίου ἕκτον μέρος ; the sixth part of a stadium, that is, one hundred feet.   As the Latin tongue has no word to express πλέθρον in this sense, with accuracy, jugerum, signifying a square measure, (though I am sensible the poets use it also for πλέθρον) the Latin translators have thought themselves under a necessity of using the word plethrum : I hope I shall also be allowed to use the words parasang, stadium, and plethrum, after having explained them.

iver is two plethra in breadth; and having a ridge over it, supported by seven boats, he passed over, and advanced through Phrygia, making in one day's march eight parasangs, to Colosæ, a large city, rich and well inhabited, there he staid seven days, when Menon the Thessalian, came to him, with a thousand heavy-armed men, and five hundred targeteers, consisting of Dolopians, Ænians, and Olynthians. From thence he made, in three days' march, twenty parasangs to Celænæ, a city of Phrygia, large, rich, and well inhabited. Here the palace of Cyrus stood, with a large [8] park full of wild beasts, which Cyrus hunted on horse-back, when he had a mind to exercise himself and his horses. Through the middle of this park runs the river Mæander, but the head of it rises in the palace; it runs also through the city of Celænæ. There is besides a fortified palace belonging to the [9] great king in Celænæ, at the head of the river Marsyas, under the citadel. This river likewise runs through the city, and falls into the Mæander. The Marsyas is twenty-five feet broad: here Apollo is said to have slain Marsyas, whom contending with him [10] in music, he had overcome, and to have hung up his skin in the cave, from whence the springs flow: for this reason the river is called Marsyas. Here Xerxes, when he fled from Greece after his defeat, is said to have built both this palace and the citadel of Celænæ. Here Cyrus staid thirty days, and hither Clearchus the banished Lacedæmonian came with a thousand heavy-armed men, five hundred Thracian [11] targeteers, and two hundred Cretan

archers. At the same time Sosias the Syracusan came with a thousand heavy-armed men, and Sophænetus the Arcadian with a thousand more. Here Cyrus reviewed the Greeks in the park, and took an account of their numbers; they amounted in the whole to eleven thousand heavy-armed men, and about two thousand targeteers.

From hence Cyrus made in two days' march ten parasangs, and arrived at Peltæ, a city well inhabited: there he staid three days, during which Xenias the Arcadian solemnized the [12] Lupercalian sacrifice, and celebrated a game; the prizes were golden [13] scrapers; at this game Cyrus was present. From thence he made in two marches twelve parasangs, and came to the market of the Cramians, a city well inhabited, the last of the country of Mysia. From thence he made in three days' march thirty parasangs, and arrived at a well peopled city, called [14] the Plain of Caystrus, where he staid five days. There was now due to the soldiers above three months' pay, which they, coming often to [15] his door, demanded. He continued to give them hopes, and was visibly concerned; for he was not of a temper to deny money, when he had it. Hither Epyaxa, the wife to Syennesis king of the Cilicians, came to Cyrus;

8 Παράδεισος. This word is, no doubt, of Persian original, and like many other Persian words, as Julius Pollux says, commonly used by the Greeks. These parks, planted with stately forest and fruit-trees of every kind, well watered, and stocked with plenty of wild beasts, were very deservedly in great request among the Persians. Plutarch tells us, that Tissaphernes, to shew his opinion of the elegance of Alcibiades's taste, gave this name to that which belonged to him. The ecclesiastical writers after St Jerome have thought fit to translate the garden of Eden in Moses, *Paradisus volup. tatis*; and the Septuagint ἐν τῷ παραδείσῳ τρυφῆς, making Eden an appellative, though they oftener make it a proper name. The English translation says the garden of Eden, which agrees with the Hebrew.

9 Μεγάλου βασιλέως. This is the title given by all the Greek authors to the king of Persia, which is preserved to the successors of Mahomet in that of the Grand Seignior.

10 Περὶ σοφίας. Hutchinson has proved from several authorities that σοφία in this place signifies skill in music, rather than wisdom.

11 Πελτασταί. Here πελτασται seems to be taken in a

comprehensive sense, and to include all those who were not heavy-armed men.

12 Τὰ Λύκαια. This was an Arcadian sacrifice, instituted in honour of Pan, and brought by Evander into Italy, when he, with his followers, settled upon the Palatine Hill. Dionysius of Halicarnassus, from whom I have this, adds, that after the sacrifice was over, the priests ran through the streets naked all but their middle, which was covered with the skins of the victims newly sacrificed; this sacrifice, he says, continued to his time, which is confirmed by Dion Cassius and Plutarch. Virgil has taken notice of this circumstance of the Lupercalian priests running naked, among the other points of history, with which the shield of Æneas is embellished:

Hic exultantes Salios, andosque Lupercos,
Lanigerosque apices, et lapsa ancilia cælo
Extuderat.

13 Στλεγγίδες. In Latin, *strigiles*. They were instruments used in bathing, both by the Greeks and Romans; with these they scraped their bodies. D'Ablancourt has rendered it, *des etrilles d'or*; for which he makes an excuse: the best I can make for the word I have made use of is, that I know no other.

14 Καύστρου πεδίον. D'Ablancourt suspects this passage to be corrupted: but Hutchinson says, this plain may very probably have given name to the city.

15 Ἰόντες ἐπὶ τὰς θύρας. The custom of attending at the door of the kings of Persia, was introduced by the first Cyrus, as we find in the Cyropædia, οὕτω καὶ νῦν ἔτι παιδεύειν οἱ παντὰ τὴν Ἀσίαν ὑπὸ βασιλεῖ ὄντες θεραπεύουσι τὰς τῶν ἀρχόντων θύρας. It was in use in the time of Herodotus and Xenophon, and continued as long as the Persian empire. This compliment was paid to the satraps

it was said she made him a present of great sums of money. Cyrus therefore gave the army four months' pay at that time. The Cilician queen had a guard of Cilicians and Aspendians; and Cyrus was reported to have an amour with her.

From thence he made, in two days' march, ten parasangs, and came to the city of [1] Thymbrium, a town well inhabited. Here was a fountain near the road, called the fountain of Midas, king of Phrygia, where Midas is said to have [2] caught the satyr, by mixing the fountain with wine. From thence he made, in two days' march, ten parasangs, and arrived at Tyriæum, a populous town, where he staid three days. And here, it is said, the Cilician queen desired Cyrus to show her his army; in compliance therefore with her request, Cyrus reviewed in the plain, both his Greek and Barbarian forces; ordering the Greeks to dispose themselves, according to their custom, and stand in order of battle, and that each of the commanders should draw up his own men; so they were drawn up [3] four deep. Menon had the right with his people, and Clearchus the left with his men; the rest of the generals being in the centre. First therefore Cyrus viewed the Barbarians, (they marched by him drawn up in troops [4] and companies,) then the Greeks, Cyrus driving by them on a car, and the Cilician queen in a chariot. [5] They had all brazen helmets, scarlet vests, greaves, and burnished shields. After he had [6] passed by them he stopped his car in the centre of the fro and sending Pigres his interpreter to Greek generals, he ordered the whole lin to present their pikes, and advance in order battle : these conveyed his orders to the se diers; who, when the trumpets sounded, pr sented their pikes and advanced; then, marc ing [8] faster than ordinary, with shouts, ran their own accord to the tents. Upon thi many of the Barbarians were seized with fea the Cilician queen quitted her chariot, ar fled; and the sutlers leaving their commod ties, ran away: the Greeks, not withou laughter, repaired to their tents. The Cili cian queen, seeing the lustre and order of thei army, was in admiration, and Cyrus pleased t see the terror with which the Greeks ha struck the Barbarians.

Thence, in three days' march, he made twen ty parasangs, and came to Iconium, the last city of Phrygia, where he staid three days. Thence he made in five days' march, thirty parasangs through Lycaonia; which, being an enemy's country, he gave the Greeks leave to plunder it. From hence he sent the Cilician queen into Cilicia the shortest way, and appointed Menon the Thessalian, himself, with his soldiers, to escort her. Cyrus, with the rest of the army, moved on through Cappadocia, and in four days' march, made five and twenty parasangs to Dana, a large and rich city, well inhabited. Here he staid three days, during which he put to death Megaphernes, a Persian, one of his courtiers, [9] with another

---

as well as to the kings. It is possible the name of the Port given to the court of the Grand Seignior was derived from hence, rather than from the great gate leading to the seraglio, as is generally thought.

1 Θύμβριον. A town of Phrygia.

2 Θηρῶσαι. I have translated this in the same manner as if our author had said λαζῶν, which is the word made use of by Maximus Tyrius, speaking of this adventure; λαμζάνει τὸν Σάτυρον κεράσας οἴνῳ κρήνην. For this reason I am of opinion, that satyrum venatus is not so proper in Leunclavius and Hutchinson.

3 Ἐπὶ τεττάρων. This is what Arrian in his Tactics calls τὴν τάξιν ἱστάναι ἐπὶ τέσσαρας. Leunclavius and Hutchinson have said, in quaternis dispositi, which, I think, signifies rather that they were drawn up in platoons of four men each. D'Ablancourt is much clearer, à quatre de hauteur.

4 Κατ' ἴλας, καὶ κατὰ τάξις. Ἴλη in Greek, and turma in Latin, are proper to the horse, as τάξις and σῖδστε are to the foot; though I know there are some examples where the two last are applied to the horse also; however in this place there can be no doubt but τάξις signifies companies of foot.

5 Ἀρμαμάξαν. Plutarch employs this word for a close carriage used by women. D'Ablancourt has not distinguished it in his translation from ἄμαξα.

6 Ἐπεὶ πάντας παρέλασε. This is rendered by D'Ablancourt, après les avoir contemplé.

7 Προβαλέσθαι τὰ ὅπλα. There is a passage quoted by Suidas out of Demosthenes in his first Philippic, in which προβάλλεσθαι is used in the same sense our author uses it here, προβάλλεσθαι δὲ τὰς χεῖρας καὶ βλέπειν ἐναντίον οὔτε εἴδον, οὔτε ἐθέλω, where Suidas explains προβάλλεσθαι τὰς χεῖρας by προτείνειν τὰς χεῖρας ὡς εἰς μάχην : so that προβάλλειν τὰ ὅπλα will be the same with καθὶς τὰ δόρατα, a word of command mentioned by Arrian in his Tactics. D'Ablancourt has, I think, said very properly qu'ils fussent baisser les piques.

8 Θᾶττον. I am sensible that θᾶττον is not always used in a comparative sense; it sometimes, though rarely, signifies no more than εὐθὺς, ταχέως, as Hesychius explains it; however, it is generally used in the sense I have given it by the Attic writers, Θᾶττον Ἀττικοὶ τάχιον, Ἕλληνες. Phavorinus.

9 Φοινικιστὴν βασιλέως. I have never met with the word φοινικιστὴς in any author but Xenophon, or in any Lexicon ancient or modern, but Hesychius, who quotes this passage without explaining it; so that the readers

...men who had a principal command, accus-
...them of treachery. Thence they prepared
penetrate into Cilicia; the entrance[10] was
...broad enough for a chariot to pass, very
...ep, and inaccessible to an army, if there had
...any opposition; and Syennesis was said
...have possessed himself of the eminences,
...order to guard the pass; for which reason,
...was staid one day in the plain. The day
...after, news was brought by a messenger that
Syennesis had quitted the eminences, upon
...information that both Menon's army were in
Cilicia, within the mountains, and also that
Tamos was[11] sailing round from Ionia to
Cilicia with the galleys that belonged to the
Lacedæmonians, and to Cyrus, who immediately marched up the mountains without opposition, and[12] made himself master of the
tents, in which the Cilicians lay to oppose his
passage. From thence he descended into
a large and beautiful plain, well watered, and
full of all sorts of trees and vines; abounding
in[13] sesame, panic, millet, wheat, and barley;
and is surrounded with a strong and high ridge
of hills from sea to sea.

After he had left the mountains, he advanced
through the plain, and having made five and
twenty parasangs in four days' march, arrived
at[14] Tarsus, a large and rich city of Cilicia,
where stood the palace of Syennesis king of
Cilicia; having the river[15] Cydnus running
through the middle of it, and is two hundred
feet in breadth. This city was[16] abandoned by
the inhabitants, who, with Syennesis, fled to a
fastness upon the mountains, those only excepted who kept the public houses: but the inhabitants of[17] Soli and Issi, who lived near the sea,
did not quit their habitations. Epyaxa, the

---

and translators are left to shift for themselves as well as
they can. Leunclavius and Hutchinson have said,
regium purpuræ tinctorem, which I can by no means
approve of, since the king's purple dyer does neither
seem to be a proper person to attend Cyrus in a military expedition, neither does he appear a proper ac-
complice in a design of this nature, with so considerable
a person as the other is represented. D'Ablancourt
has said *maitre de sa garderobe*; this indeed answers
the two objections I made to the other interpretation,
but I am apt to believe, if Xenophon had designed to
denote any particular notice, he would have made use
of the article, and have said τὸν φοινικιστὴν βασιλέως.
H. Stephens has employed a very classical word, *purpu-
ratus*, which answers properly to φοῖνιξ, whence φοι-
νικωτὴς is derived; this is the sense I have given to the
word, though I am very far from being fond of it.

10 Ἡ δὲ εἰσβολή. This is the pass which Arrian calls
τὰς πύλας τῆς Κιλικίας, which Alexander possessed
himself of, as he marched into Cilicia to engage Darius.
The day before, he encamped in the place, where we
now find Cyrus, ἀφικόμενος, says Arrian, ἐπὶ τὸ Κύρου
τοῦ ξὺν Παρσοφέρνει στρατόπεδον, where he left Parmenion,
when he went himself to attack the pass.

11 Περιπλεούσας. Hutchinson very justly observes,
that περιπλέων is properly used by Xenophon to describe
the course a ship must take from the coast of Ionia to
that of Cilicia: but this has not been preserved either in
his or Leunclavius's translation, any more than in that
of D'Ablancourt.

12 Εἶλε. I have followed the conjecture of Muretus,
who reads εἷλε instead of εἶδε, in which I am supported
by Hutchinson.

13 Σήσαμον. This plant is common in the Levant,
and is called by Tournefort, *digitalis orientalis*; of the
seed of which they make an oil, that is good to eat, and

for several other uses. Panic and millet are so like one
another, that they are scarce to be distinguished but by
the manner in which they bring forth their grain, the
former bearing it in ears, and the latter in bunches;
they both make very bad bread, and are chiefly used to
fat fowls. D'Ablancourt has thought fit to render this
period by *remplie de toutes sortes de fruits et de grains*;
but his reason for it is still more curious than his translation. I was so much entertained with the vivacity of
it, that I cannot help transcribing his words: *Je l'ai
tranché*, says he, *en deux mots, pour ne pas venir à
un detail ennuyeux*.

14 Ταρσούς. Tarsus, a considerable city of Cilicia, was
built by Sardanapalus, who built both that and Anchia-
lus, another city not far from it, in one day; which,
though incredible to those who do not consider how
many millions of men the Assyrian kings had at their
command, is however attested by an Assyrian inscription, which Arrian has translated. This inscription was,
it seems, engraved on the monument of this prince, upon
which stood his statue, in the attitude of a person who
expresses a contempt, with his hands clapped together,
or, as Strabo says, I think more probably, by seeming to
snap his fingers. The sense of this inscription is so very
philosophical, that I cannot omit it, though at the same
time, the phrase is so very libertine, that I shall not
translate it. Σαρδανάπαλος ὁ Ἀνακυνδαράξεω παῖς, Ἀγ-
χίαλον καὶ Ταρσὸν ἐν ἡμέρᾳ μιᾷ ἐδείματο. σὺ δὲ, ὦ ξένε,
ἔσθιε, καὶ πίνε, καὶ παῖζε, ὡς τ' ἄλλα τὰ ἀνθρώπινα οὐκ
ὄντα τούτου ἄξια: instead of παῖζε, others read ὄχευε,
which Arrian says is the sense of the Assyrian word:
and which Plutarch, speaking of this inscription, has
rendered by ἀφροδισίαζε.

15 Κύδνος.—This river rises out of Mount Taurus and
running through a clean country, is remarkable for the
coldness and clearness of its stream; this tempted Alexander after a long and sultry march to bathe in it, which
had like to have put an end both to his life and his victories: but the care of his physician, or the strength of
his constitution, soon recovered him, and once more let
him loose upon mankind.

16 Ἐξέλιπεν, &c. I agree entirely with Hutchinson
against Leunclavius and Stephens that there is no necessity of having recourse to φυγόντες or of any thing of that
kind to perfect this sentence. These aposiopeses are
frequent in the Attic writers.

17 Σόλοι. This city was afterwards called Pompeio-
polis. It was formerly a colony of the Athenians, who
forgetting by length of time their mother-tongue, or at
least the grammar of it, spoke a barbarous language,
from whom the word *solecism*, so dreadful in the ears
of school-boys, took its name.

wife of Syennesis came to Tarsus five days before Cyrus. In the passage over the mountains into the plain, two companies of Menon's army were missing. It was said by some, that, while they were intent on plunder, they were cut off by the Cilicians, and by others, that being left behind, and unable to find the rest of the army, or gain the road, they wandered about the country, and were destroyed : [1] The number of these amounted to one hundred heavy-armed men. The rest, as soon as they arrived, resenting the loss of their companions, plundered both the city of Tarsus, and the palace that stood there. Cyrus, as soon as he entered the city, sent for Syennesis ; but he alleging that he had never yet put himself in the hands of any person of superior power, declined coming, till his wife prevailed upon him, and received assurance from Cyrus. After that, when they met, Syennesis gave Cyrus great sums of money to pay his army, and Cyrus made him such presents as are of great value among kings ; these were a horse with a golden bit, a chain, bracelets, and a scimitar, of gold, with a Persian robe, besides [2] the exemption of his country from further plunder ; to this he added the restitution of the prisoners they had taken, wherever they were found.

Here Cyrus and the army staid twenty days, the soldiers declaring they would go no further ; for they suspected he was leading them against the king, and said they were not raised for that service. Clearchus was the first who endeavoured to force his men to go on ; but as soon as he began to march, they threw stones at him and at his sumpter horses, so that he narrowly escaped being then stoned to death. Afterwards, when he saw it was not in his power to prevail by force, he called his men together, and first stood still a considerable time, shedding many tears, while the soldiers beheld him in amaze and silence : then spoke to them in the following manner :

" Fellow-soldiers ; wonder not that I am concerned at the present posture of affairs : for I am engaged to Cyrus by the rights of hospitality, and when I was banished, among other marks of distinction with which he honoured me, he gave me ten thousand daricks. After I had received this money, I did not treasure it up for my own use, or [3] lavish it in pleasures, but laid it out upon you. And first, I made war upon the Thracians, and with your assistance revenged the injuries they had done to Greece, by driving them out of the Chersonesus, where they were endeavouring to dispossess the Greek inhabitants of their lands. After that, when I was summoned by Cyrus, I carried you to him with this view, that, if there were occasion, I might in return for his favours be of service to him ; but, since you refuse to go on with me, and I am under a necessity either, by betraying you, to rely on the friendship of Cyrus ; or, by being false to him, to adhere to you, though I am in doubt whether I shall do right or not. However, I have determined to give you the [4] preference, and with you to suffer every thing that may happen. Neither shall any one say, that, having led the Greeks among Barbarians, I betrayed the Greeks, and preferred the friendship of the Barbarians ; but, since you refuse to obey me, and to follow me, I will follow you, and share in all your sufferings ; for I look upon you as my country, my friends, and fellow-soldiers, and that with you I shall live in honour wherever I am ; but without you, that I shall neither be useful to my friends, nor formidable to my enemies. Be assured, therefore, that whithersoever you go, I resolve to go with you." Thus spoke Clearchus. The soldiers, both those who belonged to him and the rest of the army, hearing this, commended him for declaring he would not march against the king : and above two thousand left Xenias and Pasion, and taking their arms and [d] baggage with them, came and encamped with Clearchus.

---

1 Ἧσαν δὲ οὗτοι ἱκανὸν ὁπλῖται. By this passage it seems that their companies consisted of fifty men each.

2 Καὶ τὴν χώραν μηκέτι, &c. This period is celebrated by Demetrius Phalareus for the proper placing of this uncommon gift, which, he says, if it had been placed either in the beginning, or in the middle, would have been disagreeable, but is graceful at the close of it.

3 Οὐδὲ καθηδονὰς ἔτρεψα. Que je n'ai pas emploié à mes plaisirs, in D'Ablancourt, does not, I think, come up to the strength of the Greek word : nec per voluptatem et luxum abrumpsi, in Hutchinson, is far better. Sure this word, which has great energy, was never more properly employed than by Plutarch to Mark Antony's lavishing the most precious thing he could throw away, his time, in the arms of Cleopatra, καθηδονὰς ἔτι τὸ πολυτελέστατον ἀνάλωμα, τὸν χρόνον, where by the way Plutarch has taken that fine application of πολυτελὲς ἀνάλωμα to time, from Theophrastus.

4 Ὑμᾶς ἐγὼ αὐτὸν. Leunclavius and Hutchinson have said, ut ei commodarem, which is not only the sense, but elegantly expresses ut ei commodo essem ; Tully uses the word in the same sense in his Epistles. D'Ablancourt has said, pour payer ses faveurs de quelque service, which I think, at least, equal to the other.

5 Αἱρήσομαι δ' οὖν ὑμᾶς. αἱρήσομαι, προαιρήσω. Phavorinus.

6 Ξκευοφόρα. The passage quoted by Hutchinson out

These things gave Cyrus great perplexity and uneasiness: so he sent for Clearchus, who refused to go, but despatched a messenger to him, unknown to the soldiers, with encouragement that this affair would take a favourable turn. He advised Cyrus to send for him, but at the same time let him know that he did not design to go to him. After this, assembling his own soldiers, with those who were lately come to him, and as many of the rest as desired to be present, he spoke to them as follows:

"Fellow-soldiers! it is certain the affairs of Cyrus are in the same situation in respect to us, with ours in regard to him; for neither are we any longer his soldiers, since we refuse to follow him, neither does he any longer give us pay. I know he thinks himself unjustly treated by us; so that, when he sends for me, I refuse to go to him, chiefly through shame, because I am conscious to myself of having deceived him in every thing; in the next place, through fear, lest he should cause me to be apprehended and punished for the wrongs he thinks I have done him. I am therefore of opinion, that this is no time for us to sleep, or to neglect the care of ourselves, but to consult what is to be done. If we stay, we are to consider by what means we may stay with the greatest security; and if we resolve to go away, how we may go with the greatest safety, and supply ourselves with provisions; for without these, neither a commander, or a private man, can be of any use. Cyrus is a very valuable friend, where he is a friend; but the severest enemy, where he is an enemy. He is also master of that strength in foot, horse, and at sea, which we all both see and are acquainted with, for truly we do not seem to be encamped at a great distance from him; so that this is the time for every one to advise what he judges best." Here he stopped.

Upon this some rose up of their own accord to give their opinions; others, by his direction, to show the difficulties either of straying, or going without the approbation of Cyrus. One, pretending to be in haste by returning to Greece, said, that if Clearchus refused to conduct them thither, they ought immediately to choose other generals, to buy provisions

(there being a market in the Barbarians' camp) and pack up their baggage; then go to Cyrus and demand ships of him to transport them; which if he refused, to desire a commander to conduct them, as through a friend's country; and, if this also be refused, continued he, we ought forthwith to draw up a declaration of battle, and send a detachment to secure the eminences, that neither Cyrus, nor the Cilicians (many of whom we have taken prisoners, and whose' effects we have plundered, and still possess) may prevent us. After him Clearchus spoke to this effect:

"Let none of you propose me to be general in this expedition, (for I see many things that forbid it,) but consider me as one resolved to obey, as far as possible, the person you shall choose, that you may be convinced I also know, as well as any other, how to submit to command." After him another got up, showing the folly of the man who advised to demand the ships, as if Cyrus would not resume his expedition. He showed also how weak a thing it was to apply for a guide to that person whose undertaking we had defeated. "If," says he, "we can place any confidence in a guide appointed by him, what hinders us from desiring Cyrus himself to secure those eminences for us? I own I should be unwilling to go on board the transports he may give us, lest he should sink the 'ships. I should also be afraid to follow the guide he may appoint, lest he should lead us into some place, out

---

7 Χρήματα. This word in this and in many other places in Xenophon, as well as in other good authors, signifies effects rather than money: in this sense it is explained by Hesychius, χρήματα, οἷς τις δύναται χρᾶσθαι, κτήματα, βοσκήματα. This explains a passage in Homer, where Eurymachus, one of the suitors, tells Halitherses, that, if Penelope continues to amuse them,

Χρήματα δ' αὖτε κακῶς βεβρώσεται.

Hutchinson has rendered χρήματα here bona, and Leunclavius, opes, the latter not so properly. D'Ablancourt has said ceux du pais qu'on avoit pillé, which, in my opinion, is too general, because it is applicable both to their money and effects: on the other side it is not applicable to the seizing their persons; for I dare say those who are critics in the French language will own, that piller quelqu'un does not signify to seize a man's person.

8 Ἀπείη ταῖς τριήρεσι καταδύσοι. This ellipsis is very frequent in Thucydides and Homer; the latter speaking of the waste made by the wild boar on the lands of Œneus, says, in the same figure,

Πολλὰ δ' ὅγε προθέλυμνα χαμαὶ βάλε δένδρεα μακρὰ
Αὐτῆσιν ῥίζῃσι, καὶ αὐτοῖς ἄνθεσι μήλων.

---

of Herodian, which is also quoted by Constantine in his Lexicon, plainly shows, that σκευοφόρα signifies both the carriages and the beasts of burden.

of which we could not disengage ourselves; and since it is proposed we should go away without the consent of Cyrus, I wish we could also go without his knowledge, which is impossible. These then are vain thoughts; I am therefore of opinion that proper persons, together with Clearchus, should go to Cyrus, and ask him in what service he proposes to employ us; and to acquaint him, that, if the present undertaking be of the same nature with that in which he before made use of foreign troops, we will follow him, and behave our_ selves with equal bravery to those who [1] at tended him upon that occasion; but if this enterprise appears to be of greater moment than the former, and to be attended with greater labour [2] and danger, that we desire he will either prevail on us by persuasion to fol low him, or suffer himself to be prevailed upon to allow us to return home. By this means, if we follow him, we shall follow him as friends, with cheerfulness; and if we return, we shall return with safety. And let them report to us what he says, which we may then consider of." This was resolved.

Having chosen the persons therefore, they sent them with Clearchus, who asked Cyrus the questions appointed by the army; to which he made this answer: "I am informed, that Abrocomas, my enemy, lies near the Euphrates, at the distance of twelve days' march: therefore, my intention is, if I find him there, to punish, by leading my army against him; but if he flies from the place, I will there consider what we are to do." This coming to the ears of those who were ap pointed to attend Cyrus, made their report to the soldiers, who suspected his design was to lead them against the king; yet they resolved to follow him; and when they demanded an increase of pay, he promised to give them half as much more as they had already; that is, instead of one darick, a darick and a half every month to each man. But it was not even then known that he intended to lead them against the king, at least, it was not public.

IV. Hence he made in two days' march ten

parasangs, to the river Pharus, which was three hundred feet broad; from thence to the river Pyramus, which is one stadium in breadth, making in one march five parasangs from which place he made, in two days' march fifteen parasangs, and arrived at Issus, [3] the last town of Cilicia, situated near the sea; a large city, rich, and well inhabited; where he staid three days, during which time, five-and-thirty ships, with Pythagoras, a Lacedæmo nian, (the admiral) at the head, sailed from Peloponnesus, and came to Cyrus, being con ducted from Ephesus by Tamos, an Egyp tian, who carried with him five-and-twenty other ships belonging to Cyrus, with which he had besieged Miletus, because that city was in friendship with Tissaphernes, against whom Tamos made war in conjunction with Cyrus. With these ships also came Cheirisophus, the Lacedæmonian, whom Cyrus had sent for, with seven hundred heavy-armed men, which he commanded under Cyrus, before whose tent the ships lay [4] at anchor. Hither also four hundred heavy-armed Greeks came to Cyrus, (leaving Abrocomas, in whose service they were,) and marched with him against the king.

Hence Cyrus made in one march five para sangs to the [5] gates of Cilicia and Syria.

1 Συναναβάντων. This relates to the three hundred Greeks, who, as our author tells us, attended Cyrus to court under the command of Εἶνας of Parrhasie.

2 'Επιπονωτέρα καὶ ἐπικινδυνοτέρα. These are the proper characters that distinguish this expedition from the former: however, D'Ablancourt has not taken the east notice of it in his translation.

3 'Ισσούς. Hard by stands a town now called Scan deroon, a place very well known to our Turkey mer chants, built by Alexander in memory of the great vic tory he obtained there over Darius, whose mother, wife, and children were taken prisoners in the action. The bay called by Strabo κόλπος 'Ισσικὸς, took its name from this town, and is now called the Bay of Scanderoon.

4 Αἱ δὲ νῆες ὥρμουν, &c. I will not say that ὁρμεῖ is never used to signify a ship that comes to land, but I am sure it is generally applied to a ship that lies at an chor, and that ὁρμίζω is almost universally the word made use of to express the former: the difference be tween the two words is particularly set forth by Pha vorinus, ὁρμέω, says he, ἐν τῷ λιμένι ἵσταμαι, ὁρμίζω δὲ τὸ εἰς τὸν λιμένα ὑπάγομαι. I will not therefore absolute ly say that the French and Latin translators have mis taken this passage, but wish the former, instead of say ing, elles vinrent mouiller l'ancre, had said, elles etoient a l'ancre pres de la tente de Cyrus; and that the lat ter, instead of saying naves propter Cyri tentorium ad pullerant, had said, in anchoris stabant.

5 'Επὶ πύλας τῆς Κιλικίας καὶ τῆς Συρίας. There are two passes upon the mountains that divide Cilicia from Syria, as we find in Pliny and Tully's Epistles, where the latter gives the reasons why he led the army, which he commanded as proconsul, into Cappadocia rather than into Cilicia: duo enim sunt aditus in Ciliciam ex Syria; one of these is called πύλαι 'Αμανικαὶ, by Pliny porta Amani montis, and the other simply πύλαι, or, as

These were two fortresses, of which the inner next Cilicia was possessed by Syennesis with a guard of Cilicians, and the outer next to Syria, was said to be defended by the king's troops. Between these two fortresses runs a river called Kersus, one hundred feet in breadth. The interval between them was three stadia in the whole, through which it was not possible to force a way; the pass being narrow, the fortresses reaching down to the sea, and above were inaccessible [6] rocks. In both these fortresses stood the gates. In order to gain this pass, Cyrus sent for his ships, that, by landing his heavy-armed men both within and without the gates, they might force their passage through the Syrian gates, if defended by the enemy; which he expected Abrocomas, who was at the head of a great army, would attempt: however, Abrocomas did not do this, but as soon as he heard Cyrus was in Cilicia, he suddenly left Phœnicia, and went back to the king, with an army consisting, as it was said, of three hundred thousand men.

Hereupon Cyrus proceeded through Syria, and, in one march, made five parasangs to Myriandros, a city near the sea, inhabited by the Phœnecians, [7] which being a mart-town, where many merchant ships lay at anchor, they continued seven days; during which Xenias the Arcadian general, and Pasion the Megarean, took ship, and putting their most valuable effects on board, sailed away. It was the general opinion, that this was owing to their resentment against Clearchus, whom Cyrus had suffered to retain the troops that left them, and put themselves under his command with a view of returning to Greece, and not of marching against the king. As soon therefore as they disappeared, a rumour was spread that Cyrus would follow them with his galleys. Some wished that, having acted perfidiously, they [8] might be taken, others [9] pitied them, if they should fall into his hands.

Cyrus immediately assembled together the general officers, and spoke thus to them: "Xenias and Pasion have left us, but let them be assured that they are not [10] gone away so as to be concealed (for I know whither they are

---

the last mentioned author calls them, *portæ Ciliciæ*; the former are to the eastward of the latter, which, as we find in this account of Xenophon, lie close to the sea. There is a doubt which of these is meant by our author; but this will be clearly rectified, if we look into Arrian, where we shall find Alexander to have taken the same route with Cyrus for a great way, and to have often encamped in the same places. After that prince had passed these πύλαι, mentioned by Xenophon, and while he lay with his army at Myriandros, the same place where Cyrus encamped after he had passed them, he received advice that Darius had left his camp at Sochi, within two days' march of the Πύλαι; and having passed the mountains at the Πύλαι Ἀμανικαί, or the eastern pass, was got behind him, and marching to Issus. Alexander was pleased to find his enemy had abandoned the advantage of a campaign country, and shut up his numerous army, the chief strength of which consisted in horse, between the mountains and the sea; and, marching back, possessed himself again of the πύλαι that night; the next day he engaged Darius, and the ground beneath this pass and Issus was the scene of that memorable victory. This happened in the 4th year of the 111th Olympiad, 68 years after Cyrus marched through Cilicia.

6 Πέτραι ἠλίβατοι. This expression is very poetical, and often made use of by Homer, whose scholiast explains it in this manner, ἣ ὁ ἥλιος μόνος ἐπιβαίνει, a rock inaccessible to every thing but to the rays of the sun. When Patroclus reproaches Achilles with his cruelty for suffering the Greeks to be slain in such numbers for want of his assistance, he tells him,
—οὐκ ἄρα σοί γε πατὴρ ἦν ἱππότα Πηλεὺς,
Οὐδὲ Θέτις μήτηρ· γλαυκὴ δὲ σε τίκτε θάλασσα
Πέτραι τ' ἠλίβατοι, ὅτι τοι νόος ἐστὶν ἀπηνής.

7 Ἐμπόριον δ' ἦν τὸ χωρίον, καὶ ὥρμουν αὐτόθι ὁλκάδες πολλαί. Here Hutchinson has translated ὥρμουν in the manner I have contended for in note, page 176. Leunclavius has still adhered to *adpulerant*. D'Ablancourt has left out the whole period in his translation. ὁλκὰς, παρὰ Θουκυδίδη, ἡ ἐμπορικὴ ναῦς. Suidas.

8 Οἱ δ' ηὔχοντο εἰ ἁλώσοιντο. I own I cannot, with the Latin translators, see the necessity of supplying this sentence with any word in order to complete it: I think the expression elegant, the sense plain, and the eventual commiseration fully pointed out by the conditional particle εἰ.

9 Ἀπωδύροντο. Ammonius and Phavorinus are quoted upon this occasion by Hutchinson, to show the difference between ἀποδύρεται and ἀπορύγνυ; the first, say they, signifies τὸ ἀσχημόνεσταντά τινα εὔδηλον εἶναι ἕνεκα ἐστι, the other τὸ μὴ δύνασθαι ἐπιληφθῆναι; and, to support this, the passage now before us in Xenophon is cited by Ammonius. Now I own, that, notwithstanding the very great deference which I have, and which every one ought to have, for those two grammarians, and the person who quotes them, yet I cannot help thinking that the very passage they quote destroys the difference they have established; for, if ἀποδύραι signifies, as they say, to retire in such a manner that the place of retreat is known, ἀποδιδράσκει here must signify the reverse; for Cyrus tells the Greeks that they have *not* retired to a place unknown to him, οὐδὶ ἀποδιδράκασι, because he says he knows whither they are going. Hutchinson himself confirms what I say by this translation, even against his own quotation; for he says, *nec clam se aufugisse*; whereas, if the observation of the authors he quotes is just, and that ἀποδύραι signifies ἀσχημονήσαντά τινα εὔδηλον εἶναι, he should have translated it, *nec palam se aufugisse*. I wish, I do not say for the advantage of the sense, but for the ease of the translator, that Xenophon had said ἀποδιδράκασι μὲν, οὐκ ἀποτορίψαει δὲ; I should then have translated it, they are fled, but not escaped.

10 Μὰ τοὺς Θεούς. Μὰ is a negative asseveration, and ναὶ an affirmative one.

Z

going, neither are they escaped (for my galleys can come up with their ship.) But I ¹ call the gods to witness that I do not intend to pursue them, neither shall any one say, that while people are with me, I use their service; but that, when they desire to leave me, I seize them, treat them ill, and rob them of their fortunes. Let them go therefore, and remember they have behaved themselves worse to me than I to them. Their wives and children are under a guard at Tralles; however, not even these shall they be deprived of, but shall receive them in return for the gallant behaviour they have formerly shown to my service." The Greeks, if any before showed a backwardness to the enterprise, seeing this instance of Cyrus's virtue, followed him with greater pleasure and cheerfulness.

After this, Cyrus, in four days' march, made twenty parasangs, and came to the river Chalus, which is one hundred feet broad, and full ² of large tame fish, which the Syrians look upon as gods, and do not suffer them to be hurt any more than pigeons. The villages in which they encamped belonged to Parysatis, and were given to her for her table. ³ Thirty parasangs more, in five days' march, brought him to the source of the river Daradax, the breadth of which was one hundred feet, having near it the palace of Beleais, who was formerly governor of Syria, with a very large and beautiful park, producing every thing proper to the season. Cyrus laid waste the park, and burned the palace. From thence, in three days' march, he made fifteen

---

1 Ἰόντων. The use of the genitive case plural of the participle is very common with the Attic writers, instead of the third person plural of the imperative mood in the same tense, unless ἔντωσαν, according to the opinion of some critics, is upon those occasions to be understood. Diogenes Laertius gives a remarkable instance of something like this: it relates to the trial of Socrates, where Plato offering to speak to the judges in defence of his master, began his speech in this manner: Νεώτατος ὢν, ὦ ἄνδρες Ἀθηναῖοι, τῶν ἐπὶ τὸ βῆμα ἀναβάντων, upon which the judges interrupted him by calling out καταβάντων for καταβηθι, and made him come down. But the Attic authors are not singular in the use of this phrase: Homer says ·

   —πάρυκες μὲν Ἀχαιῶν χαλκοχιτώνων
   Λαὸν ἀκήσοντες ἀγειρόντων κατὰ νῆας,

for ἀγειρόντων. This atticism is often made use of by the best authors.

2 Πλήρη δ' ἰχθύων μεγάλων, &c. Lucian, in his treatise of the Syrian goddess, has a passage that will explain this of Xenophon; he says, the Syrians looked upon fish as a sacred thing, and never touched them; and that they ate all birds but pigeons, which they esteemed holy: he adds, these superstitions were owing to their respect for Derceto and Semiramis, the first of whom had the shape of a fish, and the other was changed into a pigeon. That author has affected to write this treatise in the Ionic style, his words are these: ἰχθύας, χρῆμα ἱρὸν νομίζουσι καὶ οὔκοτι ἰχθύων ψαύουσι· καὶ ὄρνιθας τοὺς μὲν ἄλλους σιτέονται, περιστερὴν δὲ μούνην οὐ σιτέονται, ἀλλά σφίσι ἥδε ἱρή. Τὰ δὲ γιγνόμενα δοκεῖ αὐτοῖς ποιέεσθαι Δερκετοῦς, καὶ Σεμιράμιος οὕνεκα τὸ μὲν, ὅτι Δερκετὼ μορφὴν ἰχθύος ἔχει· τὸ δὲ, ὅτι τὸ Σεμιράμιος τέλος ἐς περιστερὴν ἀπίκετο. This tradition is somewhat varied by Diodorus Siculus; who says, that Derceto being brought to bed of Semiramis, threw herself into a lake, and was changed into a fish; for which reason, he says, the Syrians worship fish as gods. The same author

adds, that Semiramis, when a child, was fed by pigeons, till a person who had the superintendency over the king's herds, took her home to his own house, and called her Semiramis, a name derived, as he says, from pigeons, in the Syrian language; and that this was the occasion of the worship the Syrians paid to pigeons. It may not be improper to acquaint the reader, that the goddess called Derceto by the Greeks, and Atargatis by the Syrians, was looked upon by the last as the mother of Semiramis, and worshipped as a goddess in Bambyce, by them called Magog. Lucian says she was represented in Phœnicia as a woman to the waist, and from thence as a fish; which made Selden of opinion, that Derceto and Dagon who was also represented in the same manner, were the same divinity, though it is certain that Dagon was looked upon as a god, and Derceto as a goddess. Had D'Ablancourt considered these matters, he would not have been so hasty in condemning Xenophon of too great credulity; neither would he have thought himself under any obligation of softening, as he calls it, these facts, for fear of corrupting the truth of history: particularly since Diodorus Siculus also says, the fabulous tradition of Derceto being changed into a fish, prevailed so far, that the Syrians, even in his time, abstained from fish, and honoured them as gods.

3 Εἰς ζωὴν διδόμεναι, &c. Hutchinson has departed from the text, and without the authority of any manuscript, has followed Muretus and Jungermannus in reading ζώνην instead of ζωὴν. Indeed the passages he has supported this correction with, out of Tully, Plato, and Herodotus, show plainly that the kings of Persia used to give some particular cities to their queens to find them in girdles, others to find them in necklaces, and others in shoes: so that it cannot be denied but εἰς ζώνην is here very proper: but it is as certain from those authors he has quoted, and indeed from every author who has treated of the affairs of Persia, that the Persian kings also assigned particular cities to those whom they had a mind to honour, to find them in bread, others to find them in wine, and others in meat, or, as some will have it, in fish. In this manner Artaxerxes Mnemon distinguished Themistocles, εἰς ἄρτον καὶ οἶνον καὶ ὄψον, as Plutarch and Thucydides say; so that it is not at all improbable the villages our author here speaks of, might be assigned to Parysatis to supply her table: but if the reader prefers ζώνην it must then be translated, that these villages were given to Parysatis to find her in girdles.

parasangs, and came to the river Euphrates, which is four stadia in breadth; where, being the large and flourishing city of [4] Thapsacus, they remained five days; during which, Cyrus, sending for the generals of the Greeks, told them that he proposed marching to Babylon against the great king, and ordered them to acquaint the soldiers with it, and to persuade them to follow him. Hereupon, they called them together, and informed them of it; but the soldiers were angry with their generals, saying, they knew this before, but concealed it from them; therefore refused to march unless they had money given them, as the other soldiers had, who before attended Cyrus to his father, and that not to fight, but only to wait upon him when his father sent for him. The generals immediately gave an account of this to Cyrus, who promised to give every man five [5] mines of silver as soon as they came to Babylon, and their full pay, till he brought them back to Ionia; by which means great part of the Greeks were prevailed upon: but Menon, before it appeared whether the rest of the soldiers would follow Cyrus or not, called his own men together apart, and spoke thus to them:

"Fellow-soldiers! if you will follow my advice, you shall, without either danger or labour, be in greater esteem with Cyrus, than the rest of the army. What then do I advise? Cyrus is this minute entreating the Greeks to follow him against the king, I say, therefore, we ought to pass the Euphrates, before it appears what answer the rest of the Greeks will make to him; for if they determine to follow him, you will be looked upon as the cause of it by first passing the river, and Cyrus will not only think himself under an obligation to you, as to those who are the most zealous for his service, but will return it (which no man better understands;) but if the rest determine otherwise, we will [6] then all return. As you only are obedient to his orders, he will look upon you as persons of the greatest fidelity,

and as such employ you in the command both of garrisons and of companies; and I am confident you will find Cyrus your friend' in whatever else you desire of him." The soldiers, hearing this, followed his advice, and passed the Euphrates, before the rest had returned an answer. When Cyrus heard they had passed the river, he was pleased, and sending Glus to them, ordered him to say to them, in his name, "Soldiers! I praise you for what you have done, and will take care that you also shall have reason to praise me; if I do not, think me no longer Cyrus." Hereupon, the soldiers conceiving great hopes, prayed for his success; after which, having, as it was reported, sent magnificent presents to Menon, he, at the head of his army, passed the river, the water not reaching above their breasts, notwithstanding the inhabitants of Thapsacus declared, that the river was never fordable before, or passable but in boats, which Abrocomas had burned, as he marched before them, to prevent Cyrus from passing over; it seemed therefore providential,[8] and that the river visibly submitted to Cyrus, as to its future king.

V. From thence he advanced through [9] Syria, and, having in nine days' march made fifty parasangs, came to the river [10] Araxes; where, being many villages full of corn and

---

4 Θά-ψαχος. Here Darius passed the Euphrates with the broken remains of his army, after his defeat at Issus.

5 Πέντε ἀργυρίου μνᾶς. See note, page 169.

6 ᾿Αν-μεν. Hutchinson has observed from Stephens that ἵμεν is remarkable among those verbs which the Attic writers use in the present tense instead of the future.

7 ῾Ως φίλον. I agree with Hutchinson that this is an ellipsis, and that ὄντα, or something like it, is to be understood; without condemning ὄντα, I should like παρὰ full as well: thus Telemachus tells Menelaus in the same phrase,

παρὰ σὼ τυχὼν φιλότητος ἁπάσης

"Ἔρχομαι.

8 Ἐδόκει δὲ θεῶν ὕται. I make no doubt but what Xenophon says concerning this submission of the Euphrates was the style of Cyrus's court upon this occasion. It seems that the Euphrates was not endued with the same spirit of prophecy that Horace gives to Nereus; otherwise, like him, he would have cried out mali ducis avi; and not have suffered his army to have forded him so easily, a favour he afterwards denied to Alexander, whose success might have given him a better title to it, and who was obliged to pass this river at the same place over two bridges.

9 Διὰ τῆς Συρίας. Let not the reader be surprised to find Xenophon mention Syria in Mesopotamia, through which he is now conducting Cyrus; forit appears both by Pliny and Strabo, that the country lying between Thapsacus and the Scenite Arabians, of whom he will speak presently, was part of Syria.

10 ᾿Αράξην. I never yet could find this river in any other author but Xenophon; I mean a river called

wine, they staid three days, made their provisions, and then proceeded through [1] Arabia, keeping the river Euphrates on his right hand, and in five days' march through a desert, made thirty-five parasangs. The country was a plain throughout, as even as the sea, and full of wormwood; if any other kinds of shrubs or reeds grew there, they had all an aromatic smell; but no trees appeared. Of wild creatures, the most numerous were wild asses,[2] and not a few ostriches,[3] besides [4] bustards and roe-deer[5] which our horsemen sometime chased. The asses, when they were pursue having gained ground of the horses, stood sti (for they exceeded them much in speed,) an when these came up with them, they did th same thing again; so that our horsemen coul take them by no other means but by dividin themselves into relays, and succeeding on another in the chase. The flesh of those tha were taken was like that of red deer, but mor tender. None could take an ostrich; th horsemen, who pursued them, soon giving i over; for they flew far away, as they fled making use both of their feet to run, and o their wings, when expanded, as a sail to waf them along. As for the bustards, they may be

---

Araxes, that runs through this part of Syria: for every body knows there are rivers of this name in other parts of Asia, so I must submit it to the learned, whether this river is the Aboras of Marcellinus, which Strabo calls Ἀβύβρας, and Ptolemy Χαβώρας, and the Arabians Al Chabur.

1 Διὰ τῆς Ἀραβίας. The inhabitants of this part of Arabia are called by Strabo Σκηνίτας Ἀραβις; they were a vagabond people, and, like most of their countrymen, great robbers. Nomades, infestioresque Chaldæorum, Scenitæ, says Pliny, a tabernaculis cognominati: they were afterwards called Saracens, which name Scaliger derives from Saric, which, in Arabic, signifies a robber. Those who have travelled through Asia will not think this etymology forced.

2 Ἀγρίοι ὄνοι. All authors, both ancient and modern, agree, that wild asses are exceeding swift. Appian, in his Treatise of Hunting, calls the wild ass ἀελλόποδα, swift as the wind, an epithet given by Homer to the horses which Jupiter bestowed on the father of Ganymede, to make him some amends for the loss of his son. The wild ass is very different, both in its shape and colour, from the common ass. There is a skin of this animal at the college of Physicians in London; another I have seen among many other curiosities, natural and artificial, ancient and modern, belonging to my neighbour Sir Andrew Fontaine. The first of these is stuffed, and by that the creature appears to have been between twelve and thirteen hands high; the colour of every part about him is composed of white and chesnut stripes, his ears, mane, and tail, like those of a common ass; his forehead is long and thin, his shoulders fine, his back straight, his body full, his hoofs a little bound, his legs perfectly fine; seems a little goose-rumped; his quarters are thin, and lying under him, and his hams bent inward; to these three last shapes he very probably owes his speed. This doctrine I know all sportsmen will not allow; but many observations in sporting have convinced me of its truth. Wild asses were sometimes made use of by the ancients to cover mares, in order to breed mules: but all their authors agree, that the best stallion for that purpose was an ass bred between a wild male ass, and a female of the common kind. Pliny tells us also, that the foals of wild asses were called lalisiones, and were delicate meat. Wild asses are common in the deserts of Numidia and Libya, and particularly in Arabia; they are sold at an excessive price when reclaimed, and it is said the kings of Persia have always stables of them. When they are young, their flesh is like that of a hare, and when old, like red venison.

3 Στρουθοὶ αἱ μεγάλαι. Ostriches are animals very well known; they are common in Africa, South America, and many parts of the Levant, as Arabia and Mesopotamia, &c. I remember to have seen two that were shown at London; we were informed they came from Buenos Ayres; they answered the description given of them in books. Their feathers, in so great request for several kinds of ornaments, particularly upon the stage, and anciently in war, conos galeasque adornantes penna, says Pliny; these, I say, come from their tail and wing, and are generally white. The feather of an ostrich was among the Egyptians the emblem of justice. All authors agree, that in running they assist themselves with their wings, in the manner described by Xenophon. Some have thought that this compound motion, which contains both of flying and running, gave occasion to the fiction of the poetical horse, Pegasus. It is said they eat iron, which is so far true, that in those dissected in the Academy of Sciences at Paris, they found several pieces of iron-money in them more than half diminished; but this was occasioned by the mutual attrition of those pieces, and not by digestion, for they swallow iron to grind their meat, as other birds swallow pebbles for the same purpose.

4 Ὠτίδες. Bustards are very well known to sportsmen; we have great numbers of them in Norfolk; they are remarkable for having no more than three claws, like the dotterel, and some few other birds: they are scarce to be approached by any contrivance, as I have been taught by many disappointments: possibly this may be owing to their exquisite sense of hearing; no bird having, in proportion to its size, so large an aperture to convey it. What Xenophon says concerning their short flights, can only be understood of them before they are full grown; for, when they are so, they make flights of five or six miles with great ease. Pliny and Xenophon, like many other people, differ in their taste with relation to bustards; the first calls them damnatus in cibis, the last, we find, commends them.

5 Δορκάδις. We have no roe-deer in the south of England. They are common in France, des chevreuils: I have often seen them hunted there; they run the foil more than a hare, and hunt shorter; they have great speed, but, as they do not run within themselves, but often lapse, and consequently give frequent views, they seldom stand long even before their hounds. They are vastly less than our fallow deer, and are very good meat, when fat, which seldom happens.

aken, if one springs them hastily, they making
short flights, like partridges, and are soon tired.
Their flesh was very delicious.

In marching through the country they came
to the river Masca, a hundred feet in breadth,
surrounding a large city uninhabited, called
Corsote; whence, after continuing three days,
making their provisions, he made ninety parasangs in thirteen days' march, through a desert, still keeping the Euphrates on his right,
and came to Pylæ; during which marches,
many sumpter horses died of hunger, there
being no grass, nor any other plant, but the
whole country entirely barren; the inhabitants
being employed near the river with digging
[*] mill-stones, which they afterwards fashioned
and conveyed to Babylon for sale, to buy provisions for their support. By this time the
army wanted corn, and there was none to be
bought, but in the Lydian market, which was
in the camp of the Barbarians, belonging to
Cyrus, where a [7] capithe of [8] wheat or barley-
meal was sold for four [9] Sigli. The Siglus is
worth seven Attic oboli [10] and a half; and the
capithe holds two Attic [11] chœnixes; so that
the soldiers lived upon flesh. Some of these
marches were very long, when Cyrus had a
mind his army should go on till they came to
water or forage. And once where the road
was narrow and so deep, that the carriages
could not pass without difficulty, Cyrus stopped
with those about him of the greatest authority
and fortune, and ordered Glus and Pigres to
take some of the Barbarians belonging to his
army, and help the carriages through; but,
thinking they went slowly about it, he commanded, as in anger, the most considerable
Persians, who were with him, to assist in hastening on the carriages, which afforded an instance of their ready obedience; for, throwing
off their purple [12] robes, where each of them
happened to stand, they ran, as if it had been
for a prize, even down a very steep hill, in their
costly vests, and embroidered [13] drawers, some
even with chains about their necks, and bracelets round their wrists; and, leaping into the
dirt with these, they lifted up the carriages,
and brought them out sooner than can be
imagined. Upon the whole, Cyrus appeared
throughout to hasten their march, stopping no
where unless to get provisions, or for other
things that were very necessary; he judging
the quicker he marched, the more unprepared
the king would be to encounter him, and the
slower, the more numerous would be the king's
army; for it was obvious to any person of attention, that the Persian empire, though strong
with regard to the [14] extent of country, and
numbers of men, was however weak by reason
of the great distance of places, and the division
of its forces, when surprised by a sudden
invasion.

In their march through the desert, they discovered a large and populous city situated on
the other side of the Euphrates, called Car-

---

6 Ὅπως ἁλέσας. Ὅπος ὁ ἀνώτερος λίθος τοῦ μύλου.
Phavorinus. So that ἵνα ἁλέται signify properly the
upper mill-stones.

7 Καπίθη. From this passage it appears that the
καπίθη held two Attic chœnixes.

8 Ἀλεύρων. Hutchinson has, with great judgment,
supported the Greek text against Muretus, who wanted
to strike out ἀλεύρων, as signifying the same thing with
ἀλφίτων; whereas Phavorinus, from the scholiast of
Æschylus, plainly distinguishes ἄλευρα from ἄλφιτα,
showing that the first signifies the flour of wheat, and
the other that of barley. Ἄλευρα πυρίου τὸ ἐκ σίτου,
ἄλφιτα τὸ ἐκ κριθῶν ἄλευρα. Phavorinus.

9 Σίγλος. This was a Persian coin. Hesychius and
Phavorinus make it worth eight ὀβολοί, but this passage
shows it was worth but seven and a half.

10 Ὀβολῶν. The ὀβολός was the sixth part of a
drachm; it was called so from its resemblance to a spit.
See in a preceding note concerning the Greek coins.

11 Χοῖνιξ. A dry measure containing three κοτύλαι,
which were equal to one and a half of the ξέστης; the
χοῖνιξ contained 49,737 solid inches.

12 Κάνδυς. Κάνδυς, χιτὼν Περσικός. A Persian robe.
13 Ἀναξυρίδας. Ἀναξυρίδες were also part of the
dress of the old Gauls, according to Diodorus Siculus,
who says, they called them Βράκαι, which Braccæ, it is
certain, gave name to a very considerable part of France,
called from thence, Gallia Braccata, the same with
Gallia Narbonensis. The French language has retained
this word, Bragues, which is softened into a more
modern one, Brayes. I leave it to some profound anti-
quary, who may be disposed to employ his idle labour in
this inquiry, to consider how far this dress, from which
Persius calls the Medes, Medos Braccatos, and which
Ovid calls Persica Bracca; how far, I say, this dress,
which we find to have been common both to the Persians and Gauls of old, may be a proof of their being
descended originally from the same people, that is, the
Scythians, who, after they had conquered the Medes,
continued masters of that part of Asia for eight and
twenty years: particularly since we find in Herodotus,
that among the Persians there was a people called
Γερμάνιοι, Germans.

14 Πλῆθος. This word signifies quantity in this place,
when applied to the country; and number, when applied to the men; it is frequently used, by the best
authors, in the first sense as well as the last.

mande, where the soldiers bought [1] provisions, having passed over to it upon [2] rafts, by filling the [3] skins, which they made use of for tents, with dry hay, and sewed them together so close, that the water could not get therein : these provisions were such as wine made of the [4] fruit of the palm-trees and panic, there being great plenty of this in the country. It was here that a dispute arose between Menon's soldiers, and those of Clearchus ; the latter, thinking one of Menon's men in the wrong, struck him ; the

soldier thereupon informed his companions of it, who not only resented it, but were violently incensed against Clearchus,[5] who, the same day, after he had been at the place where the men passed the river, and inspected the provisions, rode back to his own tent with a few attendants through Menon's army ; and before the arrival of Cyrus, who was on his way thither, it happened that one of Menon's soldiers, as he was riving wood, saw Clearchus riding through the camp, and threw his axe at him, but missed him ; then another, and another threw stones at him, upon which, a great outcry ensuing, many did the same. However, Clearchus escaped to his own quarter, and immediately ordered his men to their arms ; commanding the heavy-armed soldiers to stand still, resting their shields against their knees, and taking with him the Thracians, and the horse, of whom he had above forty in his army, the greatest part Thracians, he rode up to Menon's men, who thereupon were in great consternation, as well as Menon himself, and ran to their arms, while others stood amazed, not knowing what to do ; Proxenus, for he happened to be coming after them at the head of his heavy-armed men, advanced between them both, and [6] making his soldiers

---

1 Ἠγέραζον. Somebody has violently provoked Hutchinson, by finding fault with the Scripture writers, for making use of this word in the sense Xenophon uses it upon this occasion. There can be no doubt but ἀγοράζων is to be found in the best authors in this sense. I remember a passage in Isocrates to Nicocles, which will not only support what I have said, but may well deserve translating : δσφιὰς ὑμᾶς πολὺ πλείονς ἀγοράζετι παρὰ τῶν διδόντων ἢ παρὰ τῶν πωλούντων. You (men of fortune) purchase presents much dearer from those who give, than from those who sell.

2 Σχιδίαις. Whenever Homer speaks of the boat which Ulysses built with his own hands, in four days, in Ogygia, Calypso's island, he calls it σχιδίη, which is thus explained by the scholiast, ὑπαίου καταπκευασθεῖσα ναῦς, a boat built on a sudden ; it signifies also an extemporary bridge ; in which sense Herodotus applies it to the two bridges of boats, over which Xerxes passed the Hellespont. Here Xenophon uses it for a raft (if I may be allowed to make use of that word upon this occasion) made of skins stuffed with hay.

3 Διφθέρας. This method of passing rivers was formerly much in use ; as the soldiers' tents were generally made of skins, instead of canvas, they had always great numbers of them at hand : the tents of the Romans were also made of skins, whence come these phrases, sub pellibus durare, and sub pellibus contineri, which we find in Livy and Cæsar. Alexander, in his victorious march through Asia, passed several rivers in this manner, particularly the Oxus, the passage of which is described by Arrian, in such a manner, that it is obvious to any one he had this description of Xenophon in his eye, which, I think, he explains much better than I can. His words are these : ξυναγαγὼν οὖν τὰς διφθέρας ὑφ' αἷς ἐσκήνουν οἱ στρατιῶται. φορυτοῦ ἐμπλήσας ἐπέκλωσεν ὡς ξηροτάτου, καὶ καταδήσαί τι καὶ ξυββάψαι ἀκριβῶς τοῦ μὴ ἐνδύεσθαι ἐς αὐτὰς τοῦ ὕδατος.

4 Τῆς βαλάνου. The fruit of the palm tree is properly called dates, of which there is an infinite variety. Of these they make in Persia a wine, which is very agreeable, but does not keep well. Of this wine Cambyses, when he was in Egypt, sent a hogshead to the king of the Ethiopians, as a present ; with this wine, the Egyptians washed their dead bodies before they embalmed them. By the way, I have always thought, that the fruit of a certain palm-tree, described by Pliny, who calls the trees syagri, answers exactly to the cocoa nut. This palm-tree, he says, grew in that part of the Lower Egypt which he calls Chora Alexandriæ ; the description he gives of its fruit is as follows : Ipsum pomum grande, durum, horridum et a cæteris generibus distans

sapore ferino, quem ferme in apris novimus, evidentissimeque causæ est nominis.

5 Κλίαρχος ἰλθὼν ἐπὶ τὴν διάβασιν τοῦ ποταμοῦ, καὶ ἐπὶ κατασκεψάμενος τὴν ἀγοράν. D'Ablancourt has left out all this in his translation, as he has this parenthesis also, Κῦρος δ' οὔπω ἥκει, ἀλλ' ἔτι προσήλαυνι.

6 Ἔθετο τὰ ὅπλα. Hutchinson, with great reason, finds fault with Leunclavius for translating this arma deponebat ; it really signifying the reverse, as he has very properly rendered it armis rite disponitis, and as Harpocration explains this phrase, θέμενος τὰ ὅπλα πηξάμενος, ὁπλισάμενος ; and as Shakspeare has said, according to his custom, more beautifully than any other author, "the powers above put on their instruments." Not that I imagine Proxenus, when he advanced between Menon and Clearchus, had his armour to put on, but that he ordered his men to stand to their arms, that he might be prepared to prevent their engaging by force, if he could not prevail by fair means. Upon the whole, I look upon it, that Proxenus put his men in the same posture, into which Eurypylus, in Homer, threw the Greeks, in order to secure the retreat of Ajax, when he was pushed by the Trojans,

οἱ δὲ παρ' αὐτὸν
Πλησίοι ἕστασαν σάκι ὤμοισι κλίναντις
Δούρατ' ἀνασχόμενοι.

D'Ablancourt foresaw the difficulty of this passage, and prudently avoided it by leaving it quite out ; a conduct he observed about three lines above, where he also omitted to translate οἱ δὲ καὶ ἕστασαν ἀποροῦντες τῷ πράγματι.

stand to their arms, begged of Clearchus to desist. But he took it very ill, that, having narrowly escaped being stoned to death, the other should speak tamely of his grievance; and therefore desired he would withdraw from beween them. In the meantime Cyrus came up, and being informed of what had happened, immediately took his arms, and with the Persians who were present, rode between them, and spoke to them in the following manner: " Clearchus! and Proxenus! and you Greeks who are present! you are not sensible of what you are doing; for, if you fight with one another, be assured, that I shall this day be destroyed, and you not long after; for, if our affairs decline, all these Barbarians, whom you see before you, will be greater enemies to you than those belonging to the king." Clearchus, hearing this, came to himself, and both sides resigning their anger, laid up their arms' where they were before.

VI. While they were marching forward, there appeared the footing and dung of horses, which, by the * print of their feet, were judged to be about two thousand, marching before, burning all the forage, and every thing else that could be of any use. There was a Persian, by name Orontas, a prince of the blood, and of reputation in military affairs, equal to the most considerable among the Persians; having formed a design to betray Cyrus, with whom he had before been at war; but, being now reconciled, told Cyrus, that, if he would give him a thousand horse, he would place himself in ambuscade, and either destroy those horse that burned all before him, or take many of them prisoners, which would prevent them both from burning the country, and from being able to inform the king that they had seen his army. Cyrus thinking this proposal for his service, ordered him to take a detachment out of every troop belonging to the several commanders.

Orontas, presuming the horse were ready, wrote a letter to the king, acquainting him, that he should come to him with as many horse as he could get, and desiring him to give orders at the same time, to his own horse, that they * should receive him as a friend; reminding him also of his former friendship and fidelity. This letter he gave to a trusty person, as he thought, who, as soon as he had received it, delivered it to Cyrus: who immediately commanded Orontas to be apprehended, and caused [10] seven of the most considerable Persians about him to assemble in his tent; and, at the same time, upon giving orders to the Greek generals for bringing their heavy-armed men, and place them round his tent, with their arms in their hands, they obeyed his commands, and brought with them about three thousand heavy-armed men. He also called Clearchus to the council, as a man, whom both he and the rest looked upon to be of the greatest dignity among the Greeks. When he came out, he gave his friends an ac-

---

7 Κατὰ χώραν. I own I cannot agree with Hutchinson, that κατὰ χώραν, in this place, signifies suo ordine et loco, ubi arma iter facientium disponi par est: I think that is rather the signification of ἐν χώρᾳ, than of κατὰ χώραν, the last implying no more than that a thing remained in the same place it was in before. In this sense Aristophanes says, ἀλλ' οὐδὲ τὸ βλίμμ' αὐτὸ κατὰ χώραν ἔχει, his look even is not the same. So that a thing may be κατὰ χώραν, and not ἐν χώρᾳ, in the place it was, and not in the place it ought to be.

8 'Ο στίβος. I make no doubt but στίβος signifies, as Hutchinson has translated it, ℬος: but I hope it will be allowed that it signifies also the print of feet: there being a passage in Homer, in his Hymn to Mercury, which plainly proves that στίβος has both these significations, for which reason I shall transcribe it.

"Ορρα μὲν οὖν ἰδίωκι διὰ ψαμαθώδια χῶρον,
'Ρῖα μάλ' ἴχνια πάντα διέφαινε ἐν κονίησιν·
Αὐτὰρ ἐπὶ ψαμάθοιο μέγαν στίβον ἐξεπέρησεν,
"Αφραστος γένετ' ὄκα βοῶν στίβος, ἠδὲ καὶ αὐτοῦ
Χῶρον ἀνὰ κρατερόν.

I hazard an observation, to show, that our author uses the word here to signify the print of the horses' feet: it is this: the article ἡ before στίβος, seems to me to refer to ἴχνη ἴππων, mentioned in the foregoing line.

9 'Αλλά. 'Αλλὰ is here, as Hutchinson has observed, παρακελευστικὸν, an exhortative particle; in which sense it is frequently used by Xenophon, and indeed by all authors, particularly by Homer. There is a necessity of so frequent a repetition in this place, that it unavoidably renders the translation disagreeable; the difference in the termination of ἱππέας and ἱππεῦσι, and in the Latin of equites and equitibus, makes the reader insensible of this repetition; this is one disadvantage, among many others, to which a literal translation, in a modern language, is subject. D'Ablancourt always avoids these repetitions, and every thing else that lays him under any restraint, whatever violence he may do to the author's sense; it must be owned, his method gives a translation the air of an original, but then it often makes it one.

10 Τοὺς ἀρίστους τῶν περὶ αὐτὸν ἑπτά. We often find a council of seven mentioned by the writers, who treat of the affairs of Persia; which council seems to have been instituted in memory of the seven Persian noblemen, who put the Magi to death: of whom Darius Hystaspes, afterwards king of Persia, was one.

count of the [1] trial of Orontas, (for secrecy was not enjoined,) and of the speech which Cyrus made, as follows:

"Friends! I have called you hither to the end that I may consider with you of what is most just both in the sight of gods and men, and accordingly proceed against this criminal Orontas. In the first place, my father appointed [2] this man to be my subject; afterwards, by the command, as he says, of my brother, he made war upon me, being then in possession of the citadel of Sardes; this war I prosecuted in such a manner, as to dispose him to desire an end of it, and I received his [4] hand, and gave him mine; since that time, say, Orontas, have I done you any injury?" To which he answered, "None." Cyrus again asked him, "Did not you afterwards, without any provocation from me, as you yourself own, revolt to the Mysians, and lay waste my country to the utmost of your power?" Orontas owned it. "After that," continued Cyrus, "when you again became sensible of your want of power, did not you fly to the [5] altar of Diana, profess repentance, and having prevailed with me, give me again your faith, and received mine?" This also Orontas confessed. "What injury, then," says Cyrus, "have I done you, that you should now, for the

third time, be found endeavouring to betray me?" Orontas saying that he was not provoked to it by any injury, Cyrus continued, "You own then you have wronged me?" "I am under a necessity of owning it," replied Orontas: upon which Cyrus asked him again, "Can you yet be an enemy to my brother, and a friend to me?" "Though I should," says Orontas, "O Cyrus! you will never think me so."

Hereupon, Cyrus said to those who were present, "Such are the actions of this man, and such his words:" at the same time, desiring the opinion of Clearchus, who delivered it as follows: "My advice is, that this man be forthwith put to death, to the end that we may no longer be under a necessity of guarding against his practices, but have leisure, being freed [6] from him, to do good to those who desire to be our friends:" after which, upon declaring the rest were unanimous in this advice, they all rose up, and, together with his relations, by order of Cyrus, laid hold on [7] Orontas's girdle, as a token of his being con-

---

1 Τὴν κρίσιν τοῦ Ὀρόντου. Sure, comme le proces d' Oronte avoit ete juge, would have been as proper a translation of these words, as comme le chose s'etoit passee, in D'Ablancourt.

2 Τοῦτο γὰρ. Γὰρ in this place is not designed to introduce a reason for what precedes, but to enforce what follows, as in Homer,

Ἀντήσω γὰρ ἐγὼ τοῦ δ' ἀνέρος, ὄφρα δαείω,
Ὅστις δὲ κιατίν.

D'Ablancourt has rendered ὑπήκοον ἐμοὶ ὕναι in the same sentence, pour m'accompagner.

3 Ἐπὶ δέ. I have translated this as if Xenophon had said ἔπειτα δὲ, in which sense ἐπὶ δὲ seems to answer better to πρῶτον μέν. Hutchinson has said posteaquam, which has no relation to primum. I think deinde would have been better.

4 Δεξιὰ ἔλαβον. Hutchinson, in his annotations upon the Institution of Cyrus, has brought several authorities to prove, that the kings of Persia used to pledge their faith by giving their right hands, which to be sure is true; but the custom was also observed by all nations, and by the Greeks, so early as in Homer's days, as we learn from Nestor's speech to the Greek commanders,

Σπονδαί τ' ἄκρητοι, καὶ δεξιαὶ, ᾗς ἐπέπιθμεν:

Which I need not translate, because Ovid has almost done it for me:

Jura, Fides ubi nunc, commissaque dextera dextra?

5 Ἐπὶ τὸν τῆς Ἀρτέμιδος βωμόν. Hutchinson is of opin-

ion, that this must be the altar of Diana at Ephesus: which to me seems very probable, for this reason, because that altar was a very ancient sanctuary: so ancient that Eustathius, in his annotations on Dionysius περιηγητῶν, says, the Amazons being pursued by Hercules, and flying to this altar, were protected by the religion of it. As the Persians worshipped the sun and moon, it is no wonder they had a respect for the altar of Diana, which may be the reason why they spared Delus and Ephesus, when they burned all the other Greek temples. It is equally certain this could not be a Persian altar, if what Herodotus says be true, that the Persians erected none to their gods. Though it is certain there was a temple in Ecbatana dedicated to Diana, under the name of Anitis; since Plutarch tells us, that Artaxerxes made Aspasia a priestess of that goddess, to disappoint Darius, τῆς Ἀρτέμιδος τῆς ἐν Ἐκβατάνοις, ἣν Ἀνῖτιν καλοῦσι, ἱερὰν ἀνέδειξεν αὐτήν. (τὴν Ἀσπασίαν.) But, as Ecbatana was far distant from the government of Cyrus, it is not at all probable that Orontas fled to that temple for protection. However, the Persians had a particular respect for Diana of Ephesus, an instance of which may be seen in Thucydides, where we find Tissaphernes offering sacrifice to that goddess.

6 Τὸ κατὰ τούτου ὕναι. This addition of ὕναι is very common in all the Attic writers. Herodotus has also admitted it into his Ionic style: thus he makes Damaratus say to Xerxes, Ἐκὼν γε ὕναι οὐδ' ἂν μοισμαχέσιμι: D'Ablancourt, I imagine, found some difficulty in this passage, for he has left it out.

7 Ἐλάβοντο τῆς ζώνης. Hutchinson has showed from a passage in Diodorus Siculus, in the affair of Charidemus, who was ordered to be put to death by Darius, that it was a custom among the Persians to lay hold on a criminal's girdle when they condemned him to die.

demaned; and instantly led out by the proper officers; when, although in that dishonourable situation, those who used to prostrate themselves before him, even then paid him the same [8] veneration, though they knew he was leading to death. He was carried into the tent of Artapates, who was in the greatest trust with Cyrus of any of his sceptre-bearers; [9] from which time, no one ever saw Orontas either [10] alive or dead, nor could any one certainly relate how he was put to death, though various conjectures were made about it; neither was it ever known that any monument was erected to his memory.

VII. Cyrus next proceeded through the country of Babylon, and after completing twelve parasangs in three days' march, reviewed his forces, both Greeks and Barbarians, in a plain, about midnight, (expecting the king would appear the next morning, at the head of his army, ready to give him battle,) giving the command of the right wing to Clearchus, and that of the left to Menon the Thessalian, while he himself drew up his own men. After the review, and as soon as the day appeared, there came deserters from the great king, bringing an account of his army to Cyrus, who thereupon called together the generals and captains of the Greeks, and advised with them concerning the order of battle; at the same time encouraging them by the following persuasions; " O Greeks! it is not from any want of Barbarians, that I make use of you as my auxiliaries, but, because I look upon you as superior to great numbers of them; for that reason I have taken you also into my service: show [11] yourselves therefore worthy of that liberty you enjoy, in the possession of which I think you extremely happy; for be [12] assured that I would prefer liberty before all things I possess, with the addition of many others. But, that you may understand what

8 Προσεκύνησας. Hence it appears, that this custom of adoration was not only used by subjects to the kings of Persia, but by subjects of an inferior degree to those of a superior. We have the whole ceremonial in Herodotus; if two Persians of equal degree met, says he, they kissed one another's mouths; if one of them is something inferior to the other, he kisses his cheek; if much inferior, he falls down and adores him. When Alexander, intoxicated with success, endeavoured to prevail with the Macedonians to imitate the conquered Persians in their servility, Calisthenes opposed him to his face, with a spirit becoming both a Greek and a philosopher; by what he says to Alexander upon that occasion, we find that Cyrus, the founder of the Persian empire, was the first of all mankind, to whom adoration was paid, which from thence was looked upon as a duty from the Medes and Persians to his successors. To this day the Greeks call the compliments they send one to another προσκυνήματα, adorations.

9 Σκηπτούχων. Sceptres, both in the ancient and modern world, are ensigns of great dignity. All authors agree, that they were borne by the kings of Persia; upon which occasion, I cannot help translating a fine sentiment made use of by the first Cyrus, (or rather by our author) in the speech he makes to his children; " You are sensible," says he, " O Cambyses! that this golden sceptre is not the support of the empire, but that faithful friends are the truest and securest sceptre of kings," οἶσθα μὲν οὖν καὶ σὺ, ὦ Καμβύση, ὅτι οὐ τόδε τὸ χρυσοῦν σκῆπτρον τὸ τὴν βασιλείαν διασώζόν ἐστιν, ἀλλ' οἱ πιστοὶ φίλοι σκῆπτρον βασιλεῦσιν ἀληθέστατον καὶ ἀσφαλέστατον. This thought Sallust has paraphrased in the speech of Micipsa. Non exercitus, neque thesauri, præsidia regni sunt, verum amici. Homer gives all his Greek commanders sceptres; with him a king is σκηπτοῦχος βασιλεὺς, which Milton has rendered, " sceptred kings." By this passage in Xenophon, we find that Persian noblemen were also distinguished by this mark of dignity. However, I look upon the σκηπτοῦχος, or sceptre-bearers, to have been a kind of guard attending upon the persons of the Persian kings, since we find in Xenophon, that three hundred of them, richly dressed, attended the first Cyrus upon a very solemn occasion, ἐφείποντο οἱ περὶ αὐτὸν σκηπτοῦχοι κεκοσμημένοι—ἀμφὶ τοὺς τριακοσίους. D'Ablancourt has strangely mistaken this passage. He supposes Artapates to have been one of those whose duty it was to carry the sceptre of Cyrus; but I do not think it fair to censure him, without quoting his words, " l'un des plus fideles serviteurs de Cyrus, d'entre ceux qui portoient son sceptre."

10 Μετὰ ταῦτα οὔτε ζῶντα Ὀρόντην, οὔτε τεθνεῶτα οὐδεὶς πώποτε ἴδεν. Hutchinson has left out this line in his translation. When I say this, I desire not to be mistaken; I am convinced that his leaving it out was owing to some accident; for he is certainly not, like some others, a shy translator, where he meets with a difficulty.

11 Ὅπως οὖν ἔσεσθε ἄνδρες ἄξιοι τῆς ἐλευθερίας, &c. These ellipses, as well in prohibitions as in exhortations, are often to be met with in the best authors, particularly the Attic writers: in the former φυλάττου, or something like it, is to be understood, and in the latter τυρᾶ, or something equivalent to it; and as ὅπως leads to the ellipsis in exhortations, so μήπως leads to it in prohibitions; a remarkable instance of which we find in Homer, where Sarpedon says to Hector,

Μήπως ὡς ἀψῖσι λίνου ἁλόντε πανάγρου,
Ἀνδράσι δυσμενέεσσιν ἕλωρ καὶ κύρμα γένησθε,

where, by the way, the dual number is used for the plural, which is not uncommon.

12 Εὖ γὰρ ἴστε ὅτι τὴν ἐλευθερίαν ἑλοίμην ἂν ἀντὶ ὧν ἔχω πάντων καὶ ἄλλων πολλαπλασίων. Cyrus with great judgment expresses himself with so much warmth upon the subject of liberty, which he knew to be the reigning passion of the people to whom he addresses his discourse. Whether D'Ablancourt found any difficulty in this sentence, or whether he was afraid of offending the tender ears of his monarch with the harshness of it, I know not; but so it is, that he has left out every syllable of this period.

2 A

kind of combat you are going to engage in, I shall explain it to you. Their numbers are great, and they come on with mighty shouts, which if you can withstand, for the rest, I am almost ashamed to think what kind of men you will find our country produces. But you are [1] soldiers; behave yourselves with bravery, and, if any one of you desire to return home, I will take care to send him back the envy of his country; but I am confident that my behaviour will engage many of you rather to follow my fortunes than return home."

Gaulites, a banished Samian, a man of fidelity to Cyrus, being present, spoke thus: " It is said by some, O Cyrus! that you promise many things now, because you are in such imminent danger, which, upon any success, you will not remember; and by others, that, though you should remember your promises, and desire to perform them, it will not be in your power." Cyrus then replied; " Gentlemen! my [2] paternal kingdom to the south, reaches as far as those climates that are uninhabitable through heat, and the north, as far as those that are so through cold: every thing between is under the government of my brother's friends; and if we conquer, it becomes me to put you, who are my friends, in possession of it: so that I am under no apprehension, if we succeed, lest I should not have enough to bestow on each of my friends: I only fear, lest I should not have friends enough, on whom to bestow it; but to each of you Greeks, besides what I have mentioned, I promise a crown of gold." Hereupon, the officers espoused his cause with greater alacrity, and made their report to the rest; after which, the Greek generals, and some of the private men, came to him to know what they had to expect, if they were victorious; all whom he sent away big with hopes, and all who were admitted, advised him not to engage personally, but to stand in the rear. Clearchus himself put this question to him: " Are you of opinion, O Cyrus! that your brother will hazard a battle?" " Certainly," answered Cyrus: " if he is the son of Darius and Parysatis, and my brother, I shall never obtain all this without a stroke."

While the soldiers were accomplishing themselves for the action, the number of the Greeks was found to amount to ten thousand four hundred [3] heavy-armed men, and two thousand four hundred targeteers; and that of the Barbarians in the service of Cyrus, to one hundred thousand men, with about [4] twenty chariots armed with scythes. The enemy's army was said to consist of twelve hundred thousand men, and two hundred chariots armed with scythes, besides six thousand horse, under the command of Artagerses, all which were drawn up before the king, whose army was commanded by four generals, commanders and leaders, Abrocomas, Tissaphernes, Gobryas, and Arbaces, who had each the command of three hundred thousand men; but of this number, nine hundred thousand only were present

1 'Ανθρώπους' ὑμῶν δὶ ἀνδρῶν ὄντων. This opposition between ἀνθρώπων and ἀνδρῶν is finely supported in Herodotus, where he says that Leonidas and his four thousand Greeks, having repulsed the Persians in several attacks at Thermopylæ, made it plain to all the world that they were many men but few soldiers, δῆλον ἐποίουν—ὅτι πολλοὶ μὲν ἄνθρωποι ὦσιν, ὀλίγοι δὲ ἄνδρες: I am apt to think our author had that passage of Herodotus in his eye upon this occasion. This opposition is preserved in Latin by homines et viri, of which Hutchinson and Leunclavius have very properly taken advantage in rendering this passage. I imagine D'Ablancourt thought his language would not support this distinction, having left out the whole passage: but I do not see why the opposition which his language allows between des hommes and des soldats, might not have encouraged him to attempt it. There is a fine instance of that opposition in a very beautiful, though a very partial writer of his nation, Father D'Orleans, where, speaking of the French army at the ever memorable battle of Crecy, he says, les Francois avoient beaucoup de troupes et point d'armes, grand multitude d'hommes et peu de soldats, des rois a leur tete, et point de chefs.

2 'Η ἀρχὴ ἡ πατρώα. Plutarch has given us the substance of a most magnificent letter, written by Cyrus to the Lacedæmonians, desiring their assistance against his brother; he there tells them, that " if the men they send him are foot he will give them horses; if horsemen, chariots; if they have country houses, he will give them villages; if villages, cities; and that they shall receive their pay by measure, and not by tale." Οἷς ἔφη δώσειν ἰὰν μὲν πεζοὶ παρῶσιν, ἵππους· ἰὰν δὲ ἱππεῖς, συνωρίδας· ἰὰν δὲ ἀγροὺς ἔχωσι, κώμας· ἰὰν δὲ κώμας πόλεις· μισθὸν δὲ τοῖς στρατευομένοις οὐκ ἀριθμὸν, ἀλλὰ μέτρον ἔσεσθαι. This letter seems to be full of the same eastern Fast with the speech Cyrus makes to the Greeks upon this occasion.

3 'Ασπὶς. 'Ασπὶς is taken here in the same sense Suidas gives it, ἡ τάξις, that is ἀσπιστῶν, which is very properly explained by the scholiast upon these words of Homer,
———κρατεραὶ στίχες ἀσπιστάων
λαῶν,
by στίζων, ὁπλιτῶν, heavy-armed men.

4 Ἅρματα δρεπανηφόρα. Xenophon, in his Cyropædia, ascribes the invention of these chariots armed with scythes to the first Cyrus; though Diodorus Siculus, from Ctesias, says Ninus had greater numbers of them in his expedition against the Bactrians: it is certain they were not in use in the Trojan war, for which reason Arrian in his Tactics, opposes ἅρματα Τρωϊκὰ to Περσικὰ, as he does ψιλὰ to δρεπανηφόρα.

at the battle, together with one hundred and fifty chariots armed with scythes; for Abrocomas, coming out of Phœnicia, arrived five days after the action. This was the account the deserters gave to Cyrus before the battle, which was afterwards confirmed by the prisoners. From thence Cyrus, in one day's march, made three parasangs, all his forces, both Greeks and Barbarians, marching in order of battle : because he expected the king would fight that day; for, in the middle of their march, there was a trench cut five fathom broad, and three deep, extending twelve parasangs upwards, traversing the plain as far as the wall of Media. In this plain are four [5] canals derived from the river Tigris; being each one hundred feet in breadth, and deep enough for barges laden with corn to sail therein : they fall into the Euphrates, and are distant from one another one parasang, having bridges over them.

The great king hearing Cyrus was marching against him, immediately caused a trench to be made (by way of fortification) near the Euphrates ; close to which, also, there was a narrow pass, through which Cyrus and his army marched, and came within the trench ; when, finding the king did not engage that day, by the many tracks that appeared both of horses and men which were retreated, he sent for Silanus, the soothsayer of Ambracia, and, agreeable to his promise, gave him three thousand daricks, because the eleventh day before that, when he was offering sacrifice, he told Cyrus, the king would not fight within ten days ; upon which, Cyrus said, " If he does not fight within that time, he will not fight at all ; and, if what you say proves true, I will give you [6] ten talents." Since, therefore, the king had suffered the army of Cyrus to march through this pass un-

molested, both Cyrus and the rest concluded that he had given over all thoughts of fighting : so that the next day Cyrus marched with less circumspection ; and the third day rode on his car, very few marching before him in their ranks ; great part of the soldiers observed no order, many of their arms being carried in waggons, and upon sumpter horses.

VIII. It was now about the time of day, when the market is usually crowded, the army being near the place where they proposed to encamp, when Patagyas, a Persian, one of those whom Cyrus most confided in, was seen riding towards them full speed, his horse all in a sweat, and he calling to every one he met, both in his own language and in Greek, that the king was at hand with a vast army, marching in order of battle ; which occasioned a general confusion among the Greeks, all expecting he would charge them, before they had put themselves in order : but Cyrus leaping from his car, put on his corslet, then mounting his horse, took his javelins in his hand, ordered all the rest to arm, and every man to take his post: by virtue of which command they quickly formed themselves, Clearchus on the right wing close to the Euphrates, next to him Proxenus, and after him the rest : Menon and his men were posted on the left of the Greek army. Of the Barbarians, a thousand Paphlagonian horse, with the Greek targeteers, stood next to Clearchus on the right : upon the left Ariæus, Cyrus's lieutenant-general, was placed with the rest of the Barbarians : they had large corslets, and cuirasses, and all of them helmets but Cyrus, who placed himself in the centre with six hundred horse, and stood ready for the charge, with his head unarmed : [8] in which

---

5 Αἱ διώρυχις ἀπὸ τοῦ Τίγρητος ποταμοῦ ῥέουσι. Arrian differs very much from our author, in relation to these canals ; he says, that the level of the Tigris is much lower than that of the Euphrates, and consequently all the canals that run from the one to the other, are derived from the Euphrates, and fall into the Tigris. In this he is supported by Strabo and Pliny, who say that in the spring, when the snow melts upon the hills of Armenia, the Euphrates would overflow the adjacent country, if the inhabitants did not cut great numbers of canals to receive and circulate this increase of water in the same manner as the Egyptians distribute that of the Nile.

6 Δέκα τάλαντα. By this it appears, as Hutchinson has observed, that three thousand daricks, and ten talents, were of equal value. See note 4, page 160.

7 Ἀμφὶ ἀγορὰν πληθοῦσαν. It is very common with the Greek authors to denote the time of the day by the employment of it ; thus περὶ λύχνων ἀφὰς is often used by Dionysius Halicarnassensis to signify the evening, and ἀμφὶ πληθοῦσαν ἀγοράν, as Kuster has proved in his notes upon Suidas, what they called the third hour, that is, nine o'clock with us. Possibly πληθοῦσαν ἀγορὰν may not improperly be rendered in English Full Change. There is a very particular description of the evening in the Odyssey, where Ulysses says he hung upon the wild fig-tree, till Charybdis had cast up his raft, which appeared at the time when the judge left the bench to go to supper,

———Ἦμος δ' ἐπὶ δόρπον ἀνὴρ ἀγορῆθεν ἀνέστη,
Κρίνων νείκεα πολλὰ δικαζομένων αἰζηῶν,
Τῆμος δὴ τάγε δοῦρα Χαρύβδιος ἐξεφαάνθη.

8 Λέγεται δὲ καὶ τοὺς ἄλλους Πέρσας ψιλαῖς ταῖς κεφαλαῖς ἐν τῷ πολέμῳ διακινδυνεύειν.—D'Ablancourt has left

manner, they say, it is also customary for the rest of the Persians to expose themselves in a day of action : all the horses in Cyrus's army had both frontlets and breast-plates, and the horsemen Greek swords.

It was now in the middle of the day, and no enemy was yet to be seen ; but [1] in the afternoon there appeared a dust like a white cloud, which not long after spread itself like a darkness over the plain ! when they drew nearer, the brazen armour flashed, and their spears and ranks appeared, having on their left a body of horse armed in white corslets, (said to be commanded by Tissaphernes,) and followed by those with [2] Persian bucklers, besides heavy-armed men with wooden shields, reaching down to their feet, (said to be Egyptians) and other horse, and archers, all which marched [3] according to their respective countries, each nation being drawn up in a [4] solid oblong square ; and before them were disposed, at a considerable distance from one another, chariots armed with scythes fixed aslant at the axle-trees, with others under the [5] body of the chariot, pointing downwards, that so they might cut asunder every thing they encountered, by driving them among the ranks of the Greeks to break them : but it now appeared that Cyrus was greatly mistaken when he exhorted the Greeks to withstand the shouts of the Barbarians ; for they did not come on with shouts, but as silently and quietly as possibly, and in an equal and slow march. Here Cyrus riding along the ranks with Pigres the interpreter, and three or four others, commanded Clearchus to bring his men opposite to the centre of the enemy, (because the king was there,) saying, " If we break that our work is done :" but Clearchus observing their centre, and understanding from Cyrus that the king was beyond the left wing of the Greek army, (for the king was so much superior in number, that, when he stood in the centre of his own army he was beyond the left wing to that of Cyrus,) Clearchus, I say, would not, however, be prevailed on to withdraw his right from the river, fearing to be surrounded on both sides ; but answered Cyrus, he would take care all should go well.

Now the Barbarians came regularly on ; and the Greek army standing on the same ground, the ranks were formed as the men came up ; in the meantime, Cyrus riding at a small distance before the ranks, surveying both the enemy's army and his own, was observed by Xenophon, an Athenian, who rode up to him, and asked whether he had any thing to command ; Cyrus, stopping his horse, ordered him

---

out all this, unless he designed that *selon la costume des Perses* should be taken for a translation of it. I have said that Cyrus *stood ready for the charge with his head unarmed*, and *not bare*, in which I have differed from all the translators, but am supported by Brissenius, who in his third book *de Regno Persarum*, from whom Hutchinson has taken his whole annotation upon this passage, is of opinion, which he proves from Herodotus, that both Cyrus and the rest of the Persians, though they had no helmets in a day of battle, wore however tiaras upon their heads. This is confirmed by Plutarch, who says, that in this battle *the tiara of Cyrus fell from his head*. Besides, ψιλὸς, which is the word our author uses upon this occasion, has a visible relation to what goes before ; after he has said, therefore, that the six hundred horse had all helmets but Cyrus, when he adds that he had ψιλὴν τὴν κεφαλὴν, he does not mean that he stood with his head bare, but that he had no helmet ; in the same manner when Arrian calls the light-armed men ψιλὸς, he does not mean they were naked, but that they had neither corslets, shields, greaves, or helmets, which the reader will see in his own words in note 6, page 187.

1 Ἡνίκα δὲ δείλη ἐγένετο. Hutchinson quotes upon this occasion a passage out of Dio Chrysostomus, in which he divides the day into five parts ; 1. πρωΐ. 2. πλήθουσαι ἀγορᾶν. 3. τὰς μεσημβρίας. 4. δείλην. 5. ἑσπέρας : this division of the day perfectly agrees with that of Xenophon ; and, as πλήθουσα ἀγορὰ is the middle hour between the morning and noon, so δείλη will be the middle hour between that and the evening, that is, three o'clock.

2 Γέῤῥοφόρω. Πέρσικὰ μὲν τινα ὅπλα τὰ γέῤῥα ἐστί. Harpocration. This kind of buckler is also mentioned by Homer in the following verse,

Τῇ δ' ἑτέρῃ σάκος εὐρὺ, γέρον πεπαλαγμένον ἄζη,

where Eustathius explains γέῤῥα by ἀσπίδες Περσικαὶ in λόγον, Persian bucklers made of wickers.

3 Κατὰ ἴδνη. This seems to have been customary among the Persians : for we find in Herodotus, that in the prodigious army with which Xerxes invaded Greece, each nation was drawn up by itself, κατὰ ἴδνεα διατάσσοντα.

4 Ἐν πλαισίῳ. As πλαίσιον and πλινθίον are disposi tions often mentioned by Xenophon and other Greek authors, it may not be amiss to show the difference between them. They are thus defined by Arrian in his Tactics, πλαίσιον ὀνομάζεται, ὁπόταν πρὸς πάσας τὰς πλευρὰς παρατάξηται τις ἐν ἑτερομήκει σχήματι· πλινθίον δὲ, ὅταν ἐν τετραγώνῳ σχήματι αὐτὸ τοῦτο πράξῃ, (rather πράχθῇ ;) so that πλαίσιον is an oblong square, and πλινθίον an equilateral square. Had D'Ablancourt attended to this, he would not have translated ἐν πλαισίῳ, avec autant de front que de hauteur.

5 Ὑπὸ ταῖς δίφραις. The grammarians derive δίφρος from δίφορος ; because both the ἡνίοχος, the charioteer, and the παραβάτης, the soldiers, sat in the body of the chariot. This hint may be of use to historical painters, who oftentimes place the charioteer upon a seat by himself in the modern way.

to let them all know, that the[6] sacrifices and victims promise success.

While he was saying this, upon hearing a noise running through the ranks, he asked him what meant it? Xenophon answered, that the word was now giving for the second time; Cyrus, wondering who should give it, asked him what the word was: the other replied, "[7] Jupiter the preserver, and victory:" Cyrus relied, " I accept it, let that be the word;" after which, he immediately returned to his post, and the two armies being now within three or four stadia of each other,[8] the Greeks sung the pæan, and began to advance against the enemy; but the motion occasioning a small[9] fluctuation in the line of battle, those who were left behind, hastened their march, and at once gave a general[10] shout, as their custom is when they invoke the god of war, and all ran forward, striking their shields with their pikes (as some say) to frighten the enemy's horses; so that, before the Barbarians came within reach of their darts, they turned their horses and fled, but the Greeks pursued them as fast as they could, calling out to one another not to run, but to follow in their ranks: some of the chariots were borne through their own people without their charioteers, others through the Greeks, some of whom, seeing them coming, [11]divided; while others, being

amazed, like spectators in the [12] Hippodrome, were taken unawares; but even these were reported to have received no harm, neither was there any other Greek hurt in the action, except one upon the left wing, who was said to have been wounded by an arrow.

Cyrus seeing the Greeks victorious on their side, rejoiced in pursuit of the enemy, and was already worshipped as king by those about him; however, he was not so far transported as to leave his post, and join in the pursuit: but, keeping his six hundred horse in a body, observed the king's motions, well knowing that he was in the centre of the Persian army; [13] for in all Barbarian armies, the generals ever place themselves in the centre, looking upon that post as the safest, on each side of which

---

6 Τὰ ἱερὰ καὶ τὰ σφάγια. The last of these properly signifies victims, though I am sensible the first is sometimes taken also for ἱερὰ; but in this place I should rather think it means some religious rites, upon which conjectures were formed of future events.

7 Ζεὺς Σωτὴρ καὶ Νίκη. Dion Cassius tells us, that at the battle of Phillippi, Brutus's word was ἐλευθερία, libertas; at the battle of Pharsalia, Cæsar's word was Ἀφροδίτη νικηφόρος, Venus victrix; and that of Pompey, Ἡρακλῆς ἀνίκητος, Hercules invictus.

8 Ἐπαιάνιζον οἱ Ἕλληνες. Achilles, after he has slain Hector, says thus to his men, in Homer,

Νῦν δ' ἄγ', ἀείδοντες παιήονα, κοῦραι Ἀχαιῶν,
Νηῶσιν ἴσι γλαφυρῇσι νιώμεθα ——

whence the Greek Scholiast observes, that the ancients sung two pæans; the first before the battle, to Mars; and the second after it to Apollo.

9 Ἐξεκύμανέ τι τῆς φάλαγγος. This expression is celebrated by Demetrius Phalereus, as an instance of the beauty which metaphors give, when they descend from greater things to smaller.

10 Ἐλελίζουσι. Ἐλελῦ, ἐπιφώνημα πολεμικόν. Hesychius. From thence comes ἐλελίζω. I am at a loss to guess what D'Ablancourt means by translating this, comme on fait dans les solemnites de Mars.

11 Οἱ δὲ, ἐπὶ σφείδους, ἵεναντο. Hutchinson has employed his whole annotation upon this passage, in show-

---

ing that οἱ δὲ in this place signifies τινὲς, which to be sure is so ; but he has said nothing of a much greater difficulty that occurs in it. If we are to read ἵεναντο in this place, as all the translators have rendered it, the sense will be, that when the Greeks saw the chariots coming towards them, they stood still, which surely was not the way to avoid them. I find in Leunclavius's edition the word διίεναντο in the margin, and also in the Eton manuscript, quoted by Hutchinson in his addenda, though neither of them have followed it in their translations, or said any thing to support it; however, I make no doubt but this is the proper reading, and then the sense will be very plain: the Greeks avoided the chariots, by dividing. This is confirmed by a passage in Arrian which fully explains that before us. At the battle of Arbela, or, as he will have it, of Gaugamela, Darius had placed before his left wing one hundred of these chariots armed with scythes, which proved of no greater effect than those of Artaxerxes; for Alexander, who was upon the right of his own army, and consequently opposite to the chariots, had ordered his men to divide, when they saw them coming, which they did accordingly, and by that means rendered them ineffectual. But the words of Arrian are the best comment upon this passage, which it is probable he had in view, ἔστι δὲ ἃ καὶ διεξίεσαν διὰ τῶν τάξεων· διίσχον γὰρ, ὥσπερ παρήγγελτο αὐτοῖς, ἵνα προσπίπτοντι τὰ ἅρματα.

12 Ἐν ἱπποδρόμῳ. This word is used also by Homer, to signify the place where the chariots ran the lists :

—— λίοι δ' ἱπποδρομος ἀμφίς.

At the battle of Thurium, where Sylla defeated Archelaus, one of the generals of Mithridates, the Roman soldiers treated these chariots, armed with scythes, with so great contempt, that after the first which were sent against them had proved ineffectual, as if they had been spectators of a chariot race, they called out for more, ἄλλα ἤτουν, as Plutarch says, ὥσπερ εἰώθασιν ἐν ταῖς διατριχαῖς ἱπποδρομίαις.

13 Καὶ πάντες δὲ οἱ τῶν Βαρβάρων ἄρχοντες μέσον ἔχοντες τὸ αὑτῶν ἡγοῦντα. Thus Arrian tells us that Darius placed himself in the centre of his army at the battle of Issus, according to the custom of the kings of Persia : the reason of which custom, he says, Xenophon assigns in the passage now before us.

their strength is equally divided; and, if they have occasion to give out any orders, they are received in half the time by the army. The king, therefore, being at that time in the centre of his own battle, was, however, beyond the left wing of Cyrus; and, when he saw none opposed him in front, nor any motion made to charge the troops that were drawn up before him, he wheeled to the left in order to surround their army; whereupon Cyrus, fearing he should get behind him, and cut off the Greeks, advanced against the king, and charging with his six hundred horse, broke those who were drawn up before him, put the six thousand men to flight, and, as they say, killed Artagerses, their commander, with his own hand.

These being broken, and the six hundred belonging to Cyrus dispersed in the pursuit, very few were left about him, and those almost all persons who used to eat at his table: however, upon [1] discovering the king properly attended, and unable to contain himself, immediately cried out, " I see the man !" then ran furiously at him, and striking him on the breast, wounded him through his corslet (as Ctesias the physician says, who affirms that he cured the wound,) having, while he was giving the blow, received a wound under the eye, from somebody, who threw a javelin at him with great force; at the same time, the king and Cyrus engaged hand to hand, and those about them, in defence of each. In this action Ctesias (who was with the king,) informs us how many fell on his side; on the other, Cyrus himself was killed, and eight of his most considerable friends [2] lay dead upon him. When Artapates,

who was in the greatest trust with Cyrus of any of his sceptred ministers, saw him fall, they say, he leaped from his horse, and threw himself about him; when (as some say) the king ordered him to be slain upon the body of Cyrus; though others assert, that, drawing his scimitar, he slew himself; for he wore a golden scimitar, a chain, bracelets, and other ornaments which are worn by the most considerable Persians; and was held in great esteem by Cyrus, both for his affection and fidelity.

IX. Thus died Cyrus ! a man universally acknowledged by those who were well acquainted with him, to have been, of all the Persians since the ancient Cyrus, endued with the most princely qualities, and the most worthy of empire. First, while he was yet a child, and educated with his brother, and other children, he was looked upon as superior to them all in all things. For all the children of the great men in Persia are brought up [3] at court, where they have an opportunity of learning great modesty, and where nothing immodest is ever heard or seen. There the children have constantly before their eyes those who are honoured and disgraced by the king, and hear the reasons of both; so that, while they are children, they presently learn to command as well as to obey. Cyrus was observed to have more docility than any of his years, and to show more submission to those of an advanced age than any other children, though of a condition inferior to his own. He was also observed to excel not only in his love of horses, but in his management of them; and in those exercises that relate to war, such as archery and lancing of darts, they found him the most desirous to learn, and the most indefatigable. When in the flower of his age, he was, of all others, the fondest of hunting, and in hunting, of danger: and once, when a bear rushed upon him, he did not decline the encounter, but closed with her, and was torn from his horse, when he received those wounds,

1 I cannot help translating a very fine passage in Plutarch, in his Life of Artaxerxes, where he excuses himself for not entering into the detail of this battle, because Xenophon had already described it in so masterly a style, that he thinks it folly to attempt it after him ; he says, that " many authors have given an account of this memorable action, but that Xenophon almost shows it, and, by the clearness of his expression, makes his reader assist with emotion at every incident, and partake of every danger, as if the action was not past but present." However, that I may neither rob Xenophon of the praise Plutarch gives him, or Plutarch of his manner of giving it, I shall transcribe the whole passage : τὴν δὲ μάχην ἐκείνην, says Plutarch, πολλῶν μὲν ἀπαγγελλόντων, Εἰνοφῶντος δὲ μονονουχὶ δεικνύοντος ὄψει, καὶ τοῖς πράγμασιν, ὡς οὐ γεγενημένοις, ἀλλὰ γινομένοις, ἐφιστάντος τὸν ἀκροατὴν ἐν πάθει, καὶ συγκινδυνεύοντα, διὰ τὴν ἐνάργειαν, οὐκ ἔστι νοῦν ἔχοντος ἐπεξηγεῖσθαι, πλὴν ὅσα τῶν ἀξίων λόγου. The same author calls the place where this battle was fought Cunaxa.

2 Ἔκειντο ἐπ' αὐτῷ. I am so much pleased with the

reason D'Ablancourt gives for not translating these words, that I must mention it ; he says, le Grec dit, qui se firent tous tuer sur lui, mais cela est repeté ensuite dans son eloge, et j'avois besoin de cette expression la dix lignes aprez. There is a frankness in this acknowledgment that has more merit in it than the best translation.

3 'Εν ταῖς βασιλέως θύραις παιδεύονται. Literally at the door of the king, concerning which, see note 9, page 172.

of which he ever wore the scars : at last he killed the bear, and the person that ran to his assistance, he made a happy man in the eyes of all that knew him.

When he was sent by his father governor of Lydia, the greater Phrygia, and Cappadocia, and was declared general of all those who are obliged to assemble in the plain of Castolus, the first thing he did was to show, that, if he entered into a league, engaged in a contract, or made a promise, his greatest care was never to deceive ; for which reason, both the cities that belonged to his government, and private men, placed a confidence in him. And if any one had been his enemy, and Cyrus had made peace with him, he was under no apprehension of suffering by a violation of it. So that when he made war against Tissaphernes, all the cities, besides Miletus, willingly declared for him ; and these were afraid of him, because he would not desert their banished citizens ; for he showed by his actions, as well as his words, that after he had once given them assurance of his friendship, he would never abandon them, though their number should yet diminish, and their condition be yet impaired. It was evident that he made it his endeavour to out-do his friends in good and his enemies in ill offices ; and it was reported, that he wished to live so long, as to be able to overcome them both, in ⁴ returning both. There was no one man, therefore, of our time, to whom such numbers of people were ambitious of delivering up their fortunes, their cities, and their persons.

Neither can it be said that he suffered malefactors and robbers to triumph ; for to these he was of all men the most inexorable. It was no uncommon thing to see such men in the great roads deprived of their feet, their hands, and their eyes ; so that any person, whether Greek or Barbarian, might travel whithersoever he pleased, and with whatsoever he pleased, through the country under his command, and provided he did no in-

jury, be sure of receiving none. It is universally acknowledged that he honoured, in a particular manner, those who distinguished themselves in arms. His first expedition was against the Pisidians and Mysians, which he commanded in person ; and those whom he observed forward to expose themselves, he appointed governors over the conquered countries, and distinguished them by other presents ; so that ⁵ brave men were looked upon as most fortunate, and cowards as deserving to be their slaves ; for which reason, great numbers presented themselves to danger, where they expected Cyrus would take notice of them.

As for justice, if any person was remarkable for a particular regard to it, his chief care was, that such a one should enjoy a greater affluence than those who aimed at raising their fortunes by unjust means. Among many other instances, therefore, of the justice of his administration, this was one, that he had an army which truly deserved that name, for the officers did not come to him from countries on the other side of the sea, for gain, but because they were sensible that a ready obedience to Cyrus's commands was of greater advantage to them than their monthly pay ; and, indeed, if any one was punctual in execution of his orders, he never suffered his diligence to go unrewarded ; for which reason, it is said, that Cyrus was the best served of any prince in all his enterprises. If he observed any governor of a province joining the most exact economy with justice, improving his country, and increasing his revenue, he never took any share of these advantages to himself, but added more to them : so that they laboured with cheerfulness, enriched themselves with confidence, and never concealed their possessions from Cyrus, who was never known to envy those who owned themselves to be rich ; but endeavoured to make use of the riches of all who concealed them. It is universally acknowledged, that he possessed, in an eminent degree, the art of cultivating those of his friends, whose good-will to him he was assured of, and whom he looked upon as proper instruments to assist him in accomplishing any thing he pro-

---

4 Ἀλεξόμενος. It is to be observed that ἀλέξασθαι, in this place, signifies to reward and to revenge, both which significations this word admits of. Ἀλέξεσις, βοήθεια καὶ ἀντίτισις. Hesychius ἀμύνεσθαι is used in the same manner by Thucydides, where Hermocrates of Syracuse tells the inhabitants of Sicily, τὸν εὖ καὶ κακῶς δρῶντα ἐξ ἴσου ἀρετῇ ἀμυνούμεθα, where ἀμυνούμεθα is thus explained by the Greek Scholiast, ἐνταῦθα ἐπὶ τῶν δύο σημασιῶν ἱλαβὼν αὐτὸ καὶ ἐπὶ καλοῦ, καὶ ἐπὶ κακοῦ.

5 Ὥστε φαίνεσθαι τοὺς μὲν ἀγαθοὺς, εὐδαιμονεστάτους, τοὺς δὲ κακοὺς, δούλους τούτων ἀξιοῦσθαι. D'Ablancourt has not taken the least notice of these lines in his translation ; if the reader will give himself the trouble of comparing his version with the original in this character of Cyrus, he will find many omissions, as well as strange liberties.

posed; as an acknowledgment for which, he endeavoured to show himself a most powerful assistant to them in every thing he found they desired.

As, upon many accounts, he received, in my opinion, more presents than any one man; so, of all men living, he distributed them to his friends with the greatest generosity, and in this distribution consulted both the taste and the wants of every one. And as for those ornaments of his person that were presented to him, either as of use in war, or embellishments to dress, he is said to have expressed his sense of them, that it was not possible for him to wear them all, but that he looked upon a prince's friends, when richly dressed, as his greatest ornament. However, it is not so much to be wondered at, that, being of greater ability than his friends, he should out-do them in the magnificence of his favours; but that he should surpass them in his care and his earnestness to oblige, is, in my opinion, more worthy of admiration. He frequently sent his friends small [1] vessels, half-full of wine, when he received any that was remarkably good, letting them know, that he had not for a long time tasted any that was more delicious; besides which, he also frequently sent them half-geese, and half-loaves, &c. ordering the person who carried them to say, Cyrus liked these things, for which reason he desires you also to taste of them. Where forage was very scarce, and he, by the number and care of his servants, had an opportunity of being supplied with it, he sent to his friends, desiring they would give the horses that were for their own riding their share of it, to the end they might not be oppressed with hunger, when they carried his friends. When he appeared in public upon any occasion, where he knew many people would have their eyes upon him, he used to call his friends to him, and affected to discourse [2] earnestly

with them, that he might show whom he honoured. So that, by all I have heard, no man, either of the Greeks or Barbarians, ever deserved more esteem from his subjects. This, among others, is a remarkable instance : no one ever deserted from Cyrus, though a subject, to the king: Orontas alone attempted it,[3] yet he soon found, that the person on whose fidelity he depended, was more a friend to Cyrus than to him. Many who had been most in favour with Cyrus, came over to him from the king, after the war broke out between them, with this expectation, that in the service of Cyrus their merit would be more worthily rewarded than in that of the king. What happened also to him at his death, made it evident, that he was not only himself a good man, but that he knew how to make choice of those who were faithful, affectionate, and constant; even when he was killed, all his friends and his [4] favourites died fighting for him, except Ariæus, who, being appointed to the command of the horse on the left wing, as soon as he heard that Cyrus was killed, fled with all that body which was under his command.

X. When Cyrus was dead, his head and right hand were cut off upon the spot, and the king, with his men, in the pursuit, broke into his camp; while those with Ariæus no longer made a stand, but fled through their own camp to their former post, which was said to be four parasangs from the field of battle. The king, with his forces, among many other things, took Cyrus's mistress, a [5] Phocæan, who

---

1 Βἰνος. Βἰνος, στάμνος ἔτα ἴχων. Hesychius. It was a wine vessel.

2 Ἐσπουδαιολογεῖτε. Hutchinson has rendered this *gravibus de rebus sermonem habebat*, which is, no doubt, the general sense of the Greek word, but does not, in my opinion, explain that which our author has given it in this place. The subject of the discourse between Cyrus and his friends was of little consequence; to let the spectators know how much he honoured them, his manner of conversing with them could only do it; and, as σπουδὴ signifies earnestness in the manner of speaking, as well as the seriousness of the subject, I thought

proper to give it that sense in the translation. This puts me in mind of a practice of some persons of quality in Scotland, when King Charles the First made a progress thither : my Lord Clarendon says, that in order to render themselves considerable in the eyes of their countrymen, they used to whisper the king when he appeared in public, though the subject of those whispers was often of very little consequence. I have known some men of gallantry so happy in this practice, that, upon no other foundation than the art of whispering trifles, they have been thought to be well with women of distinction, which possibly was all they aimed at.

3 Οὗτος δὲ, &c. The Latin translators have rendered this parenthesis, as if οὗτος related to the king, for which, I think, there is no foundation. I have understood it of Orontas, who intrusted a person, in whom he thought he might confide, with his letter to the king; but soon found, to his cost, that he was more attached to Cyrus than to him.

4 Συντράπεζοι. Properly those who eat at his table.

5 Τὴν Φωκαῖδα. As this favourite mistress of Cyrus was afterwards very near being the cause of a revolution in the Persian empire, it may not be amiss to give

was said to be a woman of great sense and beauty. The other, a Milesian, who was the younger of the two, was also taken by the king's troops, but escaped naked to the quarter of the Greeks, who were left to guard the baggage. These, forming themselves, killed many of those who were plundering the camp, and lost some of their own men; however, they did not fly, but saved the Milesian, with the men and effects, and, in general, every thing else that was in their quarter. The king and the Greeks were now at the distance of about thirty stadia from one another, pursuing the enemy that were opposite to them, as if they had gained a complete victory; and the king's troops plundering the camp of the Greeks, as if they also had been every where victorious. But, when the Greeks were informed that the king, with his men, were among their baggage, and the king, on his side, heard from Tissaphernes, that the Greeks had put those before them to flight, and were gone forward in the

pursuit, he then rallied his forces, and put them in order. On the other side, Clearchus consulted with Proxenus, who was nearest to him, whether they should send a detachment, or should all march to relieve the camp.

In the meantime, the king was observed to move forward again, and seemed resolved to fall upon their rear: upon which, the Greeks [6] faced about, and put themselves in a posture to march that way, and receive him. However, the king did not advance that way; but, as before, passed [7] beyond their left wing, led his men back the same way, taking along with him those who had deserted to the Greeks during the action, and also Tissaphernes with his forces; for Tissaphernes did not fly at the first onset, but penetrated with his horse, where the Greek targeteers were posted, quite as far as the river. However, in breaking through, he killed none of their men, but the

---

some account of her. She was of Phocæa in Ionia (the mother-city of Marseilles,) and the daughter of Hermotymus, her name Milto; she was mistress of so much wit and beauty, that Cyrus, who was very fond of her, called her Aspasia, from Aspasia, the mistress of the great Pericles, who was so much celebrated for those accomplishments. After the death of Cyrus, she was in the same degree of favour with his brother Artaxerxes, whose eldest son Darius had so unfortunate a passion for her, that, upon his being declared by his father successor to the crown, when, it seems, it was customary for the successor to ask some favour of the king, which was never refused, if possible to be granted, he demanded Aspasia. The king, though besides his wife Atossa, he had three hundred and sixty ladies in his seraglio, one for every night, according to the old Babylonian year, yet was unwilling to part with Aspasia, though she was now far from being young; so told his son that she was mistress of herself, and, if she consented to be his, he should not oppose it, but forbid him to use violence. It seems this caution was unnecessary, for Aspasia declared in favour of the son, which so displeased Artaxerxes, that, though he was under a necessity of yielding her to Darius, yet he shortly after took her from him, and made her a priestess of Diana. This exasperated Darius to that degree, that he conspired with Teribazus to put his father to death: but his design being discovered, ended in his own destruction. After this short account of Aspasia's adventures, I believe the reader will smile to find her called la belle and la sage by D'Ablancourt. She was the occasion of so much mischief, that I am persuaded even the Persian ladies could not refuse her the first of these qualities; but there is little room to call her chaste, for that is the sense of the word sage in his language when applied to a woman. Had Xenophon designed to give her that character, he would have called her σώφρονα, instead of σοφὴν: the last of which, I should think, might be more properly translated in French by sensee than sage.

6 Συντραφέντες. I am sorry to find myself obliged to differ from Hutchinson in translating this. I agree with him that conglobati, the sense he has given of it, is the general sense of the word, as he has proved from Hesychius and Phavorinus; as for those synonymous words he has quoted from Julius Pollox, I do not look upon them to concern the present case, since they relate only to the contraction of the human body, as the title of that chapter plainly shows, Περὶ τοῦ συστρέψαι τὸ σῶμα, καὶ ἁπλῶσαι. But, in order to form a right judgment of the sense of this word in this place, we are to consider the situation of the two armies; the Greeks, after they had broken that part of the enemy's army that stood opposite to them, were engaged in pursuing them; and the king, having plundered Cyrus's camp, followed the Greeks, in order to fall upon their rear, προσιὼν ὄπισθεν; but the latter seeing this motion of the king, faced about to meet him. Now I believe it will be allowed, that it was not enough for the Greeks (though they had been dispersed, which we do not find) to get together in a body, in order to meet the king, who was following them; I say, I believe it will be thought that it was also necessary for them to face about, in order to put themselves in a proper posture to receive him. This motion of facing about to receive the enemy, is often described by this verse in Homer,

Οἱ δ' ἐλελίχθησαν καὶ ἐναντίοι ἔσταν Ἀχαιῶν.

Which the Greek Scholiast explains by the very word made use of by our author in this place, συνεστράφησαν, μεταβαλλόμενοι ἐλήθησαν. It is with pleasure I lay hold on this opportunity of doing justice to D'Ablancourt, who had said, I think, in a very proper and military manner, " les Grecs firent la conversion pour l'aller recevoir; cela s'appelle parler guerre." Leunclavius has also given it the same sense.

7 Ἡ δὲ παρήλθετο ἴξω τοῦ εὐωνύμου κέρατος. Xenophon considers the Greek army as it stood when the battle began, otherwise after they had faced about, their left wing was become their right. This D'Ablancourt has observed, but Leunclavius and Hutchinson take no notice of it.

2 B

Greeks [1] dividing, wounding his people both with their swords and darts. Episthenes of Amphipolis commanded the targeteers, and is reported to have shown great conduct upon this occasion. Tissaphernes, therefore, as sensible of his disadvantage, departed, when coming to the camp of the Greeks, found the king there, and reuniting their forces, they advanced and presently came opposite to the left of the Greeks, who being afraid they should attack their wing, by wheeling to the right and left, and annoy them on both sides, they resolved to open that wing, and cover the rear with the river. While they were consulting upon this, the king [2] marched by them, and drew up his army opposite to theirs in the same order in which he first engaged : whereupon, the Greeks, seeing they drew near in order of battle, again sung the pæan, and went on with much more alacrity than before ; but the Barbarians did not stay to receive them, having fled sooner than the first time to a village, where they were pursued by the Greeks, who halted there : for there was an eminence above the village, upon which, the king's forces faced about. He had no foot with him, but the hill was covered with horse, in such a manner that it was not possible for the Greeks to see what was doing. However, they said they saw the royal ensign there, which was a [3] golden eagle with its wings extended, resting upon a spear. When the Greeks advanced towards them, the horse quitted the hill, not in a body, but some running one way, and some another. However, the hill was cleared of them by degrees, and at last they all left it. Clearchus did not march up the hill with his men, but, halting at the foot of it, sent Lycius the Syracusan, and another, with orders to reconnoitre the place, and make their report : Lycius rode up the hill, and, having viewed it, brought word that the enemy fled in all haste. Hereupon the Greeks halted, (it being near sunset) and lying under their arms, rested themselves : in the meantime wondering that neither Cyrus appeared, nor any one from him, not knowing he was dead, but imagined that he was either led away by the pursuit, or had rode forward to possess himself of some post : however, they consulted among themselves

1 Διαστάντις. This is the word contended for in note 11, p. 189. The motion made by the Greeks to let Tissaphernes and his men pass through their body, upon this occasion, is the same they then made to let the chariots pass through them.

2 Παραμαιψάμενος, ὡς τὸ αὐτὸ σχῆμα κατέστησεν ἐναντίαν τὴν φάλαγγα, ὅντες, &c. I have translated this passage, as if there was a comma after παραμαιψάμενος, which I have rendered "marching by them," a signification very common to the word ; for Xenophon does not say that the Greeks did actually open their wing ; but that, while they were consulting about doing so, the king drew up his army against theirs, upon which the Greeks advanced to attack him : this I do not understand how they could well do, while the enemy was upon their flank ; but, if we suppose the king marched by them, and drew up upon the same ground, and in the same disposition in which he first came on, we may easily understand how the Greeks, by facing about again, might put themselves again in a posture to attack him. And this seems to agree very well with their pursuing the king's troops to a village, which pursuit led them to some distance from their camp, since they made it a matter of consultation, whether they should send for their baggage, or return thither.

3 Ἀετόν τινα χρυσοῦν ἐπὶ ξυστοῦ ἀνατεταμίνον. I think, Hutchinson has been very happy in substituting ξυστοῦ for ξύλου, but then I do not see what ἐπὶ σίλτω has to do here, unless it is supposed to signify a shield upon which the eagle rested ; however, I cannot think Xenophon said ἀετὸ ἐπὶ σίλτος, ἐπὶ ξυστοῦ ἀνατεταμίνον, and, if ἐπὶ σίλτω is to be changed into ἐπὶ παλτοῦ as Leunclavius will have it, it will be visibly a marginal explanation of ἐπὶ ξυστοῦ. Xenophon, in his Institution of Cyrus, tells us, that the ensign of the first Cyrus was a golden eagle upon a spear, with its wings extended, which, he says, still continues to be the ensign of the Persian kings, and which we find by Curtius continued to be so, as long as the Persian empire subsisted. The description Xenophon gives us of this eagle, comes so very near to that given by Dion Cassius of the Roman eagle, and also to the representation of it upon Trajan's pillar, that one may reasonably conclude the Romans received theirs from the eastern part of the world. I own it is very probable that the Romans had an eagle for their ensign before the battle in which the first Cyrus defeated Crœsus, and in which Xenophon says he had an eagle for his ensign ; for this battle was fought in the first year of the 58th Olympiad, that is, about the 205th year of Rome. Indeed the earliest mention I can find of the Roman eagle, is in the year of Rome 299, and the third of the eighty-first Olympiad, T. Romilius and C. Veturius being consuls ; where Siccius Dentatus tells the people, that, in an action he there mentions, he recovered the eagle from the enemy ; but it must be owned also, that it is there spoken of as a thing already established. I say this to show the mistake of some learned men, who have maintained that Marius was the first who introduced the use of this ensign. I will hazard a conjecture : it is this—If the account given by Dionysius Halicarnassensis be true, which he supports by so many probable circumstances, that Æneas, after the destruction of Troy, came into Italy, and built Lavinium, whose inhabitants built Alba, of which the city of Rome was a colony ; if, I say, this account be as true as it is probable, why may not Æneas have brought this ensign with him from the East ? where possibly it might have been in use long before the conquest of Cyrus.

whether they should stay where they were, and send for their baggage, or return to their camp. To the latter they resolved upon, and arriving at their tents about supper-time, found the greatest part of their baggage plundered, with all the provisions, besides the carriages, which, as it was said, amounted to four hundred, full of flour and wine, which Cyrus had prepared, in order to distribute them among the Greeks, lest at any time his army should labour under the want of necessaries; but they were all so rifled by the king's troops that the greatest part of the Greeks had no supper, neither had they eaten any dinner; for, before the army could halt in order to dine, the king appeared. And in this manner they passed the night.

XENOPHON

ON THE

EXPEDITION OF CYRUS.

BOOK II.

CONTENTS OF BOOK II.

EXPEDITION OF CYRUS.

BOOK II.

I. In the foregoing book we have shown, by what means Cyrus raised an army of the Greeks, when he marched against his brother Artaxerxes; what was performed during his march, and in what manner the battle was fought; how Cyrus was killed; and the Greeks, thinking they had gained a complete victory, and that Cyrus was alive, returned to their camp, and betook themselves to rest. As soon as the day approached, the generals, being assembled, wondered that Cyrus neither sent them any orders, nor appeared himself; resolved therefore to collect what was left of their baggage, and armed themselves to move forward in order to join Cyrus; but just as they were on the point of marching, and as soon as the sun was risen, [1] Procles, who was governor of Teuthrania, a descendant from Damaratus the Lacedæmonian, and Glus, the son of [2] Tamos, came to them, and declared that Cyrus was dead, and that Arisæus had left the field, and was retired, with the rest of the Barbarians, to the camp they had left the day before; where [3] he said he would stay for them that day, if they thought fit to come; but that the next, he should return to Ionia, whence he came. The generals, and the rest of the Greeks, hearing this, were greatly afflicted: and Clearchus with astonishment said, "'Would to God Cyrus was alive! but since he is dead, let Arisæus know, that we have overcome the king, and, as you see, meet with no further resistance, and that, if you had not come, we had marched against the king; at the same time, assure Arisæus from us, that, if he will come hither, we will place him on the throne; for those who gain the victory, gain with it a right to command." After he had said this, he directly sent back the messengers, together with Cheirisophus the Lacedæmonian, and Menon the Thessalian; for Menon himself desired it, he being a friend to Arisæus, and engaged to him by an intercourse of hospitality. Clearchus staid till they returned, making provisions as well as he could, by killing the oxen and asses that belonged to the baggage; and instead of other wood, made use of the arrows, which they found in great quantities in the field of battle, not far from the place where their army lay, (and which the Greeks obliged the deserters to pull out of the ground,) and also of the Persian bucklers, and the Egyptian shields, that were made of wood, besides a great many targets, and empty waggons;

---

[1] Προκλῆς. Teuthrania was a city of Mysia in Asia Minor, of which Procles was governor; he was descended from Damaratus, one of the kings of Sparta, who was deprived of his kingdom by his colleague Cleomenes; upon which he fled to Darius Hystaspes, who entertained him with great magnificence: he afterwards attended Xerxes in his expedition to Greece.

[2] Ταμώ. He was of Memphis, and admiral to Cyrus; after his death, he sailed with his fleet to Egypt, and, having formerly conferred some obligations on Psammitichus, who was then king of that country, he made no doubt of his protection; but Psammitichus, forgetting all obligations, as well as the laws of hospitality, put him to death, and seized his fleet.

[3] Καὶ λέγει ὅτι ταύτῃ μὲν τὴν ἡμέραν περιμένειν ἂν αὐτούς, εἰ μέλλοιεν ἥκειν τῇ δὲ ἄλλῃ ἀπιέναι φαίη ἐπ᾿ Ἰωνίας, ἐλεύσεσθαι ἔλεγε. All this is left out by D'Ablancourt.

[4] Ὄφελι μὲν Κύρος ζῆν. Ὄφελον is here joined with an infinitive mood, though in an optative sense. In all these phrases ὄφελον, or the Ionic ὤφελον, is not an adverb, whatever the grammarians say, ὡς or εἴθε being always understood, which construction of the phrase is so true, that one of them is frequently expressed. Thus Helen, reproaching Paris for his inglorious behaviour in the duel between him and Menelaus, tells him,

Ἤλυθες ἐκ πολέμου ὡς ὤφελες αὐτόθ᾿ ὀλέσθαι,
Ἀνδρὶ δαμεὶς κρατερῷ, ὃς ἐμὸς πρότερος πόσις ἦεν.

Many other examples may be given from the same author, where αἴθι or εἴθι is expressed.

with all which they dressed their victuals, and in this manner supported themselves that day.

It was now [1] about the time the market is generally full, when the heralds arrived with the message from the king and Tissaphernes, all of whom were Barbarians, (except Phalinus, who was a Greek, and happened then to be with Tissaphernes, by whom he was much esteemed; for he pretended to understand tactics and the [2] exercise of arms) who, after assembling together the Greek commanders, said, that the king, since he had gained the victory, and killed Cyrus, ordered the Greeks to deliver up their arms, and, repairing to [3] court, endeavour to obtain some favourable terms from the king. The Greeks received this with much indignation; however, Clearchus said no more to them than that, "It was not the part of conquerors to deliver up their arms: but," addressing himself to the generals, "do you make the best and most becoming answer you can, and I will return immediately;" he being called out by one of his servants to inspect the entrails of the victim, which he was then offering up in sacrifice. Whereupon, Cleanor the Arcadian, the oldest person present, made answer, "They would sooner die than deliver up their arms." Then Proxenus the Theban, said, "I wonder, O Phalinus! whether the king demands our arms

as a conqueror, or as a friend desires them by way of present? If, as a conqueror, what occasion has he to demand them? [4] Why does he not rather come and take them? If he would persuade us to deliver them, say, what are the soldiers to expect in return for so great an obligation?" Phalinus answered, "The king looks upon himself as conqueror, since he has killed Cyrus; for who is now his rival in the empire? He looks upon you, also, as his property, since he has you in the middle of his country, surrounded by impassable rivers; and can bring such numbers of men against you, that, though he delivered them up to you, your strength would fail you before you could put them all to death."

After him, Xenophon, an Athenian, said, "You see, O Phalinus! that we have nothing now to depend upon, [5] but our arms, and our courage; and, while we are masters of our arms, we think we can make use of our courage also; but that, when we deliver up these, we deliver up our persons too; do not therefore expect we shall deliver up the only advantages we possess; on the contrary, be assured, that with these we are resolved to fight with you, even for those you are in possession of." Phalinus, hearing this, smiled, and said, [6] "Young man! indeed you seem to be a philosopher,

---

1 Περὶ πληθαουσαν ἀγοραν. See note 7, page 197.

2 Ὁπλομαχίας. Leunclavius has translated this gladiatoriæ peritiam, which I cannot think so proper as artem armis depugnandi, in Hutchinson: D'Ablancourt has artfully evaded this difficulty, by comprehending both τῶν περὶ τὰς τάξις τι καὶ ὁπλομαχίας in these general words, l'art militaire. It is very certain the Romans took many things, both in civil and military affairs, from the Greeks, but I believe the gladiatorian spectacles were in use in Rome, before they were heard of in Greece; the origin of which seems to have been the early custom in use among most nations, of sacrificing captives to the manes of great generals, who were slain in war. Thus Achilles sacrifices twelve Trojans to the manes of Patroclus; and Æneas sends captives to Evander, to be sacrificed at the funeral of his son Pallas. Valerius Maximus says, that M. and D. Brutus in the consulship of App. Claudius and M. Fulvius, honoured the funeral of their father with a gladiatorian spectacle, which from that time became frequent upon those occasions; but this was many years after the time our author speaks of, when I am convinced the Greeks had never heard of these spectacles: my reason is, that whenever any Greek author of, or near the age, Xenophon lived in, speaks of ὁπλόμαχον, I dare say they always understand masters appointed to teach military exercises.

3 Ἐπὶ τὰς βασιλέως θύρας. See note 9, page 171.

4 Τί δὴ αὐτὸν αἰτῶν, ἀλλ' οὐ λαβὼν ἐλθόντα; Thus, when Xerxes sent to Leonidas at Thermopylæ to deliver up his arms, the latter bid him come and take them; λαβὶ μολὼν, says he, according to the concise style of this country.

5 Εἰ μὴ ὅπλα καὶ ἀρετή. Ἀρετὴ is here taken for courage, in which sense it is frequently used by the best authors; in this sense Idomeneus says an ambuscade is the trial of a soldier's courage,

　—λόχον ἔνθα μάλιστ' ἀρετὴ διαείδεται ἀνδρῶν,
　"Ἔνθ' ὅτε δειλὸς ἀνὴρ, ὅς τ' ἄλκιμος, ἐξεφαάνθη.

In this sense also Virgil says,

　—Dolus, an virtus quis in hoste requirit?

After this, I believe, it will be allowed, that D'Ablancourt does not give the author's sense, when he says, il ne nous est reste autre chose, que les armes et la liberte; to justify this, he says the Greek word signifies la vertu, though ἀρετὴ in this place signifies neither liberty nor virtue.

6 Ὦ νεανίσκε. I find all the translators have rendered this in the same manner I have done; though, if Lucian's account of our author be true, that is, that he was above ninety years old when he died; and if, according to Laertius, he died in the first year of the hundred and fifth Olympiad, he must have been fifty, at least, at the time of this expedition; which I mention for the sake of some worthy gentlemen of my acquaintance, who will not be sorry to find a man of fifty treated as a young man.

EXPEDITION OF CYRUS.

BOOK III.

. In the foregoing discourse, we have related the actions of the Greeks, during the expedition of Cyrus, to the battle; and what happened after his death, when the Greeks marched away with Tissaphernes upon the peace. After the generals were apprehended, and the captains and soldiers who accompanied them put to death, the Greeks were in great distress; knowing they were not far from the king's palace, surrounded on all sides with many nations and many cities, all their enemies; that no one would any longer supply them with provisions: that they were distant from Greece above ten thousand stadia, without a guide to conduct them, and their road thither intercepted by impassable rivers; that even those Barbarians, who had served under Cyrus, had betrayed them, and that they were now left alone, without any horse to assist them. By which it was evident, that if they overcame the enemy, they could not destroy a man of them in the pursuit, and if they themselves were overcome, not one of them could escape. These reflections so disheartened them, that few ate any thing that evening, few made fires, and many that night never came to their ¹ quarter, ² but laid themselves down, every man in the place where he happened to be, unable to sleep through sorrow, and a longing for their country, their parents, their wives and children, whom they never expected to see again. In this disposition of mind they all lie down to rest.

There was in the army an Athenian, by name Xenophon, who, without being a general, a captain, or a soldier, served as a volunteer; for, having been long attached to Proxenus by the rights of hospitality, the latter sent for him from home, with a promise, if he came, to recommend him to Cyrus; from whom, he said, he expected greater advantages than from his own country. Xenophon, having read the letter, consulted Socrates the Athenian concerning the voyage, who ³ fearing lest his country might look upon his attachment to Cyrus as criminal, because that prince was thought to have espoused the interest of the Lacedæmonians against the Athenians with great warmth, advised Xenophon to go to Delphos, and consult the god of the place concerning the matter. Xenophon went thither accordingly, and asked Apollo to which of the gods he should offer sacrifice, and address his prayers, to the end that he might perform the voyage he proposed in the best and most reputable manner, and, after a happy issue of it, return with safety. Apollo answered, that he should sacrifice to the proper gods. At his return, he acquainted Socrates with this answer; who blamed him, because he had not asked Apollo in the first place, whether it were better for him to undertake this voyage, than to stay at home: but, having himself first determined to undertake it,

---

1 'Επὶ τὰ ὅπλα. See note 6, page 203. Here it plainly signifies that part of the camp which was appointed for the quarters of the several companies, particularly of the heavy-armed men. D'Ablancourt has left it out, as he generally does this expression where he meets with it.

2 'Ανταξίως δὲ ὅπου ἐτύγχανεν ἕκαστος, οὐ δυνάμενοι καθεύδειν ὑπὸ λύπης καὶ πόθου πατρίδων, γονέων, γυναικῶν, παίδων, οὓς οὐ ποτε ἐνόμιζον ἔτι ὄψεσθαι. This period, so beautifully melancholy, is cruelly mangled by D'Ablancourt, whose translation I shall also transcribe, that the reader may compare it with the original. "Ils etoient si abbatus qu'ils ne pouvoient reposer, comme ne devant plus revoir ni femme, ni enfans, ni patrie."

he had consulted him concerning the most proper means of performing it with success; but since, says he, you have asked this, you ought to do what the god has commanded. Xenophon, therefore, having offered sacrifice to the gods, according to the direction of the oracle, set sail, and found Proxenus and Cyrus at Sardes ready to march towards the Upper Asia. Here he was presented to Cyrus, and Proxenus pressing him to stay, Cyrus was no less earnest in persuading him, and assured him that, as soon as the expedition was at an end, he would dismiss him; this he pretended was designed against the Pisidians.

Xenophon, therefore, thus imposed on, engaged in the enterprise, though Proxenus had no share in the imposition, for none of the Greeks, besides Clearchus, knew it was intended against the king: but, when they arrived in Cilicia, every one saw [1] the expedition was designed against him. Then, though they were terrified at the length of the way, and unwilling to go on, yet the greatest part of them, out of [2] a regard both to one another, and to Cyrus, followed him: and Xenophon was of this number. When the Greeks were in this distress, he had his share in the general sorrow, and was unable to rest. However, getting a little sleep, he dreamed he thought it thundered, and that a flash of lightning fell upon his paternal house, which upon that was all in a blaze. Immediately he awoke in a fright, and looked upon his dream as happy in this respect, because, while he was engaged in difficulties and dangers, he saw a great light proceeding from Jupiter. On the other side, he was full of fear, when he considered that the fire, by blazing all around him, might portend that he should not be able to get out of the king's territories, but should be surrounded on all sides with difficulties.

However, the events, which were consequent to this dream, sufficiently explain the nature of it; for presently these things happened. As soon as he awoke, the first thought that occurred to him was this, Why do I lie here? the night wears away, and as soon as the day appears, it is probable the enemy will come and attack us: and if we fall under the power of the king, [3] what can preserve us from being spectators of the most tragical sights, from suffering the most cruel torments, and from dying with the greatest ignominy. Yet no one makes preparation for defence, or takes any care about it: but here we lie, as if we were allowed to live in quiet. From what city, therefore, do I expect a general to perform these things? what age do I wait for? But, if I abandon myself to the enemy this day, I shall never live to see another. Upon this, he rose, and first assembled the captains who had served under Proxenus; and when they were together, he said to them, "Gentlemen! I can neither sleep (which I suppose is your case also) nor lie any longer, when I consider the condition to which we are reduced. For it is plain the enemy would not have declared war against us, had they not first made the necessary preparations, while, on our side, none takes any care how we may resist them in the best manner possible. If we are remiss, and fall under the power of the king, what have we to expect from him, who cut off the head and hand of his brother, even after he was dead, and fixed them upon a stake? How then will he treat us, who have no support, and have made war against him, with a design to reduce him from the condition of a king to that of a subject; and, if it lay in your power, to put him to death? Will he not try the power of every extremity, to the end, that, by torturing us in the most ignominious manner, he may deter all men from ever making war against him? We ought, therefore, to do every thing, rather than fall into his hands. While the peace lasted, I own I never ceased to consider ourselves as extremely miserable, and the king, with those who belonged to him, equally happy. When I cast my eyes around, and beheld how

---

[1] 'O στόλος. See note 5, page 170.

[2] Δι' αἰσχύνην δὲ ἀλλήλων. Where any number of men are embarked in the same design, they generally meet with success, but always deserve it, if they are once brought to be ambitious of one another's praises, and to stand in awe of one another's reproaches. Homer, who knew every spring of the human soul, was sensible how powerful a motive this mutual respect is to a proper behaviour in a day of battle, when he makes Agamemnon say to his men,

'Αλλήλους τ' αἰδῶσθε κατὰ κρατερὰς ὑσμίνας·
Αἰδομένων ἀνδρῶν πλέονες σόοι, ἠὲ πέφανται.

By the way, it is from this sense of the word αἰδὼς, that the Latin authors have used verecundia to signify respect.

[3] Τί ἐμποδὼν μὴ οὐχὶ πάντα μὲν τὰ χαλεπώτατα ἰσιδόντας, πάντα δὲ τὰ δεινότατα παθόντας, ὑβριζομένους ἀποθανεῖν; thus translated by D'Ablancourt, "quelle espérance nous reste il que d'une mort cruelle?" So pathetic a description of the miseries, which our author had then in view, deserved, methinks, that he should have been more particular in his translation.

spacious and beautiful a country they were masters of, how they abounded in provisions, slaves, cattle, gold, and rich apparel; and, on the other hand, reflected on the situation of our men, who had no share of all these advantages, without paying for them, which I knew very few were any longer able to do, and that our oaths forbade us to provide ourselves by any other means; when I reflected, I say, on these things, I was more afraid of peace than now I am of war. But since they have put an end to the peace, there seems to be an end also both of their insolence and our jealousy. And these advantages lie now as a prize between us, to be given to the bravest. In this [4] combat the gods are the umpires, who will, with justice, declare in our favour; for our enemies have provoked them by perjury, which we, surrounded with every thing to tempt us, have, with constancy, abstained from all, that we might preserve our oaths inviolate. So that, in my opinion, we have reason to engage in this combat with greater confidence than they. Besides, our bodies are more patient of cold, of heat, and of labour than theirs, and our minds, with the divine assistance, more resolved. And if, as before, the gods vouchsafe to grant us the victory, their men will be more obnoxious to wounds and death. But possibly others may also entertain these thoughts. For heaven's sake, then, let us not stay till others come to encourage us to glorious actions, but let us present them, and excite even them to virtue. Show yourselves the bravest of all the captains, and the most worthy to command of all the generals. As for me, [5] if you desire to lead the way in this, I will follow you with cheerfulness, and if you appoint me to be your leader, I [6] shall not excuse myself by reason of my age, but think myself even in the vigour of it to repel an injury."

The captains, hearing this, all desired he would take upon him the command, except a certain person, by name Apollonides, who affected to speak in the Bœotian dialect. This man said, that whoever proposed any other means of returning to Greece, than by endeavouring to persuade the king to consent to it, talked impertinently; and, at the same time, began to recount the difficulties they were engaged in. But Xenophon, interrupting him, said, " Thou most admirable man! who art both insensible of what you see, and forgetful of what you hear. You were present when the king, after the death of Cyrus, exulting in his victory, sent to us to deliver up our arms; and when, instead of delivering them up, we marched out ready to give him battle, and encamped near him, what did he leave undone, by sending ambassadors, begging peace, and supplying us with provisions, till he had obtained it? And afterwards, when our generals and captains went to confer with them, as you advise us to do, without their arms, relying on the peace, what has been their treatment? Are not these unfortunate men daily scourged, [7] tortured, and insulted, and forbid even to die, though I dare say they earnestly desire it? When you know all this, can you say that those who exhort us to defend ourselves, talk impertinently, and dare you advise us to sue again to the king for favour? For my part, gentlemen! I think we ought not to admit this man any longer into our company, but use him as he deserves, by removing him from our command, and employing him in carrying our baggage; for, by being a Greek with such a mind, he is a shame to his country, and dishonours all Greece."

Then Agasias of Stymphalus said, " This man has no relation to Bœotia, or to any other part of Greece; for, to my knowledge, both his ears are bored, like a Lydian." Which was found to be true: so they expelled him their company. The rest went to all the quarters of the army, and where any generals were left, they called them up; where they were wanting, their lieutenants; and where there were any

---

4 'Αγωνοθέται δ' οἱ θεοί εἰσι. This alludes to the umpires who were chosen to preside at the Olympic and her games. This allusion, which gives great beauty the whole passage, is entirely left out by D'Ablancourt.

5 Εἰ μὲν ἐθέλετε ἐξεμεῖτ' ἐπὶ ταῦτα. The reader will observe, that ἐξεμεῖν is here used neutrally, it was used tively a few lines above.

6 Οὐδὲν προφασίζομαι τὴν ἡλικίαν. See note 5, page 0, and particularly the life of Xenophon.

7 Κιττούμενα. I have ventured to depart from the Latin translators in rendering this word. Leunclavius has said vulneribus affecti, and Hutchinson vulnera passi; D'Ablancourt has left it out: I have translated it tortured; in the same sense Xenophon, a little above, speaking of the usage the Greeks were to expect, if they fell into the king's hands, says ἡμᾶς τὰ αἴσχιστα αἰκισάμενος, and a little before that, πάντα τὰ δυνατώτατα παθόντας. It is from this sense of the word κιττάω, that Suidas tells us a thief is called κίντρος, because, as he says, κίντρα were part of their torture. Κίντρῳ ὁ κλίστης· διὰ τὸ βασανιζομένους τοῖς κλίσταις καὶ κίντρῳ προσφέρεσθαι.

captains left, they called up them. When they were all assembled, they placed themselves [1] before the quarter where the heavy-armed men lay encamped; the number of the generals and captains amounting to about a hundred. While this was doing, it was near midnight. Then Hieronymus of Elis, the oldest of all the captains, who had served under Proxenus, began thus: "Gentlemen! we have thought proper, in the present juncture, both to assemble ourselves, and call you together, to the end we may, if possible, consider of something to our advantage. Do you, O Xenophon! represent to them what you have laid before us." Upon this Xenophon said,

"We are all sensible that the king and Tissaphernes have caused as many of us as they could to be apprehended, and it is plain they design, by the same treacherous means, if they can, to destroy the rest. We ought, therefore, in my opinion, to attempt every thing not only to prevent our falling under their power, but, if possible, to subject them to ours. Know then, that, being assembled in so great numbers, you have the fairest of all opportunities; for all the soldiers fix their eyes on you: if they see you disheartened, their courage will forsake them; but, if you appear resolute yourselves, and exhort them to do their duty, be assured, they will follow you, and endeavour to imitate your example. It seems also reasonable that you should excel them in some degree, for you are their generals, their leaders, and their captains; and as in time of peace you have the advantage of them both in riches and honours,[2] so now in time of war, you ought to challenge the pre-eminence in courage, in counsel, and, if

necessary, in labour. In the first place then, it is my opinion, that you will do great service to the army, if you take care that generals and captains are immediately chosen in the room of those who are slain: since, without chiefs, nothing either great or profitable can indeed be achieved upon any occasion, but least of all in war; for as discipline preserves armies, so the want of it has already been fatal to many. After you have appointed as many commanders as are necessary, I should think it highly seasonable for you to assemble and encourage the rest of the soldiers; for no doubt you must have observed, as well as I, how dejectedly they came to their quarters, and how heavily they went upon guard: so that, while they are in this disposition, I do not know what service can either by night or day be expected from them. They have at present nothing before their eyes but sufferings: if any one can turn their thoughts to action, it would greatly encourage them; for you know, that neither numbers nor strength give the victory: but that side which, with the assistance of the gods, attacks with the greatest resolution, is generally irresistible. I have taken notice also, that those men who in war seek to preserve their lives at any rate commonly die with shame and ignominy; while those who look upon death as common to all, and unavoidable, and are only solicitous to die with honour, oftener arrive at old age, and while they live, live happier. As therefore we are sensible of these things, it behoves us, at this critical juncture, both to act with courage ourselves, and to exhort the rest to do the same."

After him Cheirisophus said: "Before this time, O Xenophon! I knew no more of you than that you were an Athenian; but now I commend both your words and actions, and wish we had many in the army like you; for it would be a general good. And now, gentlemen! let us lose no time: those of you who want commanders depart immediately and choose them: and when that is done, come into the middle of the camp, and bring them with you: after that, we will call the rest of the soldiers hither: and let Tolmides the crier attend." Saying this, he rose up, that what was necessary might be transacted without delay. After this, Timasion, a Dardanian, was chosen general in the room of Clearchus; Xanthicles, an Achaian, in the room of Socrates; Cleanor, an Orchomenian, in the room of

---

1 Εἰς τὸ πρόσθεν τῶν ὅπλων. See note 6, page 203.

2 Καὶ νῦν τοίνυν, ἐπεὶ πόλεμός ἐστιν, ἀξιοῦν δὲ ὑμᾶς αὐτοὺς ἀμείνους τὶ τοῦ πλήθους εἶναι, καὶ προβουλεύειν τούτων, καὶ προπονεῖν, ἣν τοῦ δίῃ.—D'Ablancourt has left out every title of this fine period; the reason he gives for it in his own words is; parce qu'elle est deja exprimee: I am afraid the reader will not think that reason to have much weight. The Attic writers, when they speak of their affairs, always use the word προβούλευμα, for an act passed by the senate before it was sent down to the people; for the same reason the Greek writers of the Roman History call a senatus consultum προβούλευμα, and this sense seems to agree better with διαφέρειν and ἐπλεονεκτεῖς, which our author applies to the generals a few lines above, and which seem very naturally to introduce ἀμείνους εἶναι, προβουλεύειν, and προπονεῖν. The Latin translators have given it another sense; Leunclavius has said horum causa consilia suscipienda, and Hutchinson pro iis consilia capere: the decision therefore is left to the reader.

Agias, an Arcadian; Philysius, an Achaian, in the room of Menon; and Xenophon, an Athenian, in that of Proxenus.

II. As soon as the election was over, it being now near break of day, the officers advanced to the middle of the camp, and resolved first to appoint outguards, and then to call the soldiers together. When they were all assembled, Cheirisophus, the Lacedæmonian, first got up, and spoke as follows: " Soldiers! we are at present under great difficulties, being deprived of such generals, captains, and soldiers. Besides, the forces of Arizus, who were before our auxiliaries, have betrayed us. However, we ought to emerge out of our present circumstances like brave men, and not be cast down, but endeavour to redeem ourselves by a glorious victory. If that is impossible, let us die with honour, and never fall alive under the power of the enemy: for in that case, we should suffer such things, as I hope the gods keep in store for them."

After him Cleanor, of Orchomenus, rose up and said : " You see, O soldiers ! the perjury and impiety of the king, as well as the perfidy of Tissaphernes, who amused us by saying that he lived in the neighbourhood of Greece, and should of all things be most desirous to carry us in safety thither. It was he that gave us his oath to perform this; he that pledged his faith ; he that betrayed us, and caused our generals to be apprehended : and this he did in defiance even of [3] Jupiter, the avenger of violated hospitality ; for having entertained Clearchus at his table, by these arts he first deceived, and then destroyed our generals. Arizus also, whom we offered to place upon the throne, with whom we were engaged by a mutual exchange of faith not to betray one another ; this man, I say, without either fear of the gods, or respect for the memory of Cyrus, though of all others the most esteemed by him when alive, now revolts to his greatest enemies, and endeavours to distress us who were his friends. But of these may the gods take vengeance ! It behoves us, who have these things before our eyes, not only to take care that these men do not again betray us, but also to fight with all possible bravery, and submit to what the gods shall determine."

Then Xenophon rose up, dressed for the war in the most gorgeous armour he could pro-

vide; for he thought, if the gods granted him victory, these ornaments would become a conqueror, and, if he were to die, they would decorate his fall. He began in the following manner : " Cleanor has laid before you the perjury and treachery of the barbarians : which, to be sure, you yourselves are no strangers to. If, therefore, we have any thoughts of trying their friendship again, we must be under great concern, when we consider what our generals have suffered, who, by trusting to their faith, put themselves in their power. But, if we propose to take revenge of them with our swords for what they have done, and persecute them for the future with war in every shape ; we have, with the assistance of the gods, many fair prospects of safety." While he was speaking one of the company sneezed : upon this, the soldiers all at once adored the god. Then Xenophon said, " Since, O soldiers ! while we were speaking of safety, Jupiter the preserver sent us an [4] omen, I think we ought to make a vow to offer sacrifice to this god, in thanksgiving for our preservation, in that place where we first reached the territories of our friends ; and also to the rest of the gods, in the best manner we are able. Whoever, then, is of this opinion, let him hold up his hand " And they all held up their hands ; and then made their vows, and sung the Pæan. After they had performed their duty to the gods, he went on thus :

" I was saying that we had many fair prospects of safety. In the first place, we have observed the oaths, to which we called the gods to witness, while our enemies have been guilty of perjury, and have violated both their oaths and the peace. This being so, we have reason to expect the gods will declare against them, and combat on our side : and they have it in their power, when they think fit, soon to humble the high, and, with ease, to exalt the low, though in distress. Upon this occasion, I shall put you in mind of the dangers our ancestors were involved in, in order to convince you that it behoves you to be brave, and that those who

---

3 Διὰ ξένιον. See note 7, page 169.

4 Οἰωνὸς τοῦ Διὸς τοῦ Σωτῆρος. Οἰωνὸς is here taken for the omen itself; in which sense we find it in that noble sentiment of Hector to Polydamas,

Εἰς οἰωνὸς ἄριστος ἀμύνεσθαι περὶ πάτρης.

This superstition of looking upon sneezing as ominous, is very ancient, and to be met with in many Greek authors : possibly it may have given rise to the modern custom of saying, God bless you ! upon that occasion.

are so, are preserved by the gods amidst the greatest calamities: [1]for when the Persians, and their allies, came with a vast army to destroy Athens, the Athenians, by daring to oppose them, overcame them; and having made a vow to Diana to sacrifice as many goats to her as they killed of the enemy, when they could not find enough, they resolved to sacrifice five hundred every year: and even to this day they offer sacrifice in thanksgiving for that victory. [2]Afterwards when Xerxes invaded Greece, with an innumerable army, then it was that our ancestors overcame the ancestors of these very men, both by sea and land;

of which the trophies that were erected upon that occasion, are lasting monuments still to be seen. But of all monuments, the most considerable is the liberty of those cities, in which you have received your birth and education: for you pay adoration to no other master but the gods. From such ancestors are you descended: neither can I say that you are a dishonour to them, since, within these few days, you [3]engaged the descendants of those men, many times superior to you in number, and, with the assistance of the gods, defeated them. Then you fought to place Cyrus on the throne, and in his cause fought bravely: now your own safety is at stake, you ought certainly to show more courage and alacrity. You have also reason now to entertain a greater confidence in your own strength than before; for though you were then unacquainted with the enemy, and saw them before you in vast numbers, however you dared to attack them with the spirit of your ancestors: whereas now you have had experience of them, and are sensible that, though they exceed you many times in number, they dare not stand before you, why should you any longer fear them? Neither ought you to look upon it as a disadvantage, that the Barbarians belonging to Cyrus, who before fought on your side, have now forsaken you; for they are yet worse soldiers than those we have already overcome.

"They have left us, therefore, and are fled to them: and it is our advantage that those who are the first to fly, should be found in the enemy's army rather than in our own. If any of you are disheartened, because we have no horse, in which the enemy abound, let them consider that ten thousand horse are no more than ten thousand men; for no one was ever killed in an action by the bite or kick of a horse. The men do every thing that is done in battle. But further we are steadier upon the ground than they on horseback: for they, hanging upon their horses, are not only afraid of us, but also of falling; while we, standing firmly upon the ground, strike those who

---

1 Ἐλθόντων μὲν γὰρ Περσῶν. This was the first expedition of the Persians against the Greeks, when, under the command of Datis and Artaphernes, they invaded their country, and were defeated by Miltiades at the battle of Marathon. This invasion seems to have been occasioned by the twenty ships which the Athenians sent to Miletus, under the command of Melanthius, at the instigation of Aristagoras, to assist the Ionians against the Persians; this, and their peremptory refusal to receive Hippias their tyrant, who had fled to Persia for refuge, provoked Darius Hystaspes to send a powerful fleet to invade Athens, the success of which has been mentioned. In this defeat the Persians lost six thousand four hundred men, and the Athenians, with their allies, the Platæans, only one hundred and ninety-two: but on the Persian side fell Hippias, and lost that life in the field, which had been long due to the sword of justice. This battle was fought on the sixth day of the Attic month Boedromion, (with us, September,) the third month from the summer solstice, and the third year of the seventy-second Olympiad, Phenippus being archon, and four years before the death of Darius.

2 Ἔπειτα ὅτι Ξέρξης. This is the second expedition of the Persians against the Greeks, in which Xerxes himself commanded. The year in which this was undertaken, was the tenth from that in which the battle of Marathon was fought. Xenophon had reason to call this army innumerable, since Herodotus makes it amount to about three millions; which number is expressed in the epitaph that was inscribed on the monument erected at Thermopylæ, in honour of those Greeks who died there in the service of their country. This inscription says, that in that place four thousand Peloponnesians engaged three millions of the enemy. The words are these:

Μυριάσι ποτὲ τῇδε τριηκοσίαις ἐμάχοντο
Ἐκ Πελοποννάσου χιλιάδες τέτορες.

This seems very authentic, though I am sensible that Diodorus Siculus has διηκοσίαις instead of τριηκοσίαις; however, an army of two millions of men, will, I am afraid, scarce gain that general credit which possibly it may deserve. The victories here hinted at by Xenophon, which the Athenians, with their allies, gained over the Persians, by sea and land, were Artemisium and Salamine, Platæ and Mycale; the two last being gained the same day, that is, the third of the Attic month Boedromion, September, a day, it seems, auspicious to the cause of liberty, the first in Bœotia, and the last at Mycale, a promontory of Ionia.

---

3 Ἀντιταξάμενοι τούτοις τοῖς Ἰασόνων ἐγγόνοις—ἱππεῖς. This is ridiculously translated by D'Ablancourt, "vous avez vaincu les descendans de Xerxes en bataille rangee." Xerxes must indeed have a numerous posterity, if the whole army of Artaxerxes were his descendants; but οἱ Ἰασόνων ἐγγονοι visibly signifies the descendants of those Persians who were defeated under Xerxes.

approach us with greater force, and a surer
aim. The horse have but one advantage over
us, they can fly with greater security. But if
you are confident of your strength in battle, yet
look upon it as a grievance that Tissaphernes
will no longer conduct us, or the king supply
us with a market; consider which is the most
advantageous, to have Tissaphernes for our
conductor, who, it is plain, has betrayed us, or
such guides as we shall make choice of who
will be sensible that, if they mislead us, they
must answer it with their lives. Consider
also whether it is better for us to purchase, in
the markets they provide, small measures for
great sums of money, which we are no longer
able to furnish, or, if we conquer, to make use
of no other measure but our will. If you are
convinced that these things are best in the way
they are in, but think the rivers are not to be
repassed, and that you have been greatly deluded
in passing them, consider with yourselves
whether the Barbarians have not taken very
wrong measures even in this; for all rivers,
though, at a distance from their springs, they
may be impassable, yet if you go to their
sources, you will find them so easily fordable,
as not even to wet your knees. But if the
rivers refuse us passage, and no guide appears
to conduct us, even in that case we ought not
to be disheartened; for we know that the
Mysians, who are certainly not braver men
than ourselves, inhabit many large and rich
cities in the king's territories against his will.
The Pisidians, we also know, do the same.
We have ourselves seen the Lycaonians, who,
after they had made themselves masters of the
strong places that command the plains, enjoy
the product of the country. And I should
think we ought not yet to betray a desire of
returning home; but prepare every thing as if
we proposed to settle here: for I am well assured that the king would grant many guides
to the Mysians, and give them many hostages,
as a security, to conduct them out of his territories without fraud; he would even level
roads for them, if they insisted upon being
sent away in chariots. And I am convinced he would, with great alacrity, do the
same for us, if he saw us disposed to stay
here: but I am afraid, if once we learn to
live in idleness and plenty, and converse with
the fair and stately wives and daughters
of the Medes and Persians, we shall, like

the ⁴ Lotophagi, forget to return home. It
seems, therefore, to me both just and reasonable that we first endeavour to return to Greece,

---

4 Ὥστε οἱ λωτοφάγοι. This tradition seems derived
from Homer, who says that those who eat of the lotus
never think of returning home,

Τῶν δ' ὅστις λωτοῖο φάγοι μελιηδέα καρπόν,
Οὐκ ἔτ' ἀπαγγεῖλαι πάλιν ἤθελεν, οὐδὲ νέεσθαι.

Eustathius, in his explication of this passage, quotes
many authors, but, I think, none whose account of the
lotus seems so satisfactory as that of Herodotus, who
says that when the Nile overflows the country, there
grow in the water great quantities of lilies, which the
Egyptians call lotuses; these, he says, they dry in the
sun, and of the heads of them, which are like the heads
of poppies, they make bread; the root of it, he says, is
also eatable and sweet; he adds, that it is round, and
about the size of an apple. But there is another kind of
lotus, described by Theophrastus, and after him by Pliny.
This is a tree of the size of a pear-tree, or something
less, εὐμέγεθες, ἡλίκον ἄπιος, ἢ μικρὸν ἐλάττον, magnitudo
quæ piro, says Pliny: the leaves are jagged like those of
the ilex, φύλλον δὲ ἐντομὰς ἔχον, καὶ πρινῶδες, thus translated by Pliny, incisuræ folio crebriores quæ ilicis videntur. Theophrastus and his translator Pliny thus
pursue the description; the wood is black, τὸ μὲν ξύλον,
μέλαν, ligno color niger. There are different kinds of
this plant distinguished by the difference of their fruit,
διΐη δὲ αὐτοῦ πλείω διαφορὰς ἔχοντα τοῖς καρποῖς, differen-
tiæ plures eæque maxime fructibus fiunt. The fruit is
like a bean, and changes its colour, as it ripens, like
grapes. The fruit of this lotus grows opposite to one
another, like myrtle-berries, and thick upon the boughs;
ὁ δὲ καρπὸς ἡλίκον κύαμος· συναίνεται δὲ, ὥσπερ οἱ βότρυες,
μεταβάλλων τὰς χροιάς. φύεται δὲ καθάπερ τὰ μύρτα πα-
ράλληλα· πύκνος ἐστι τῶν βλαστῶν. Magnitudo huic
fabæ, color ante maturitatem alius atque alius, sicut in
uvis; nascitur densus in ramis myrti modo: Theophrastus adds that the fruit is sweet, pleasant to the taste,
and without any ill quality; on the contrary, that it
helps digestion; the most delicious are those that have
no stone, which one of the kinds has not; he says the
inhabitants also make wine of them, γλυκὺς· ἡδύς· καὶ
ἀσινής· καὶ ἔτι πρὸς τὴν κοιλίαν ἀγαθόν· ἥδιον· δὲ ὁ ἀπύρη-
νος· ἔστι γὰρ καὶ τοιοῦτον γένος· ποιοῦσι δὲ καὶ οἶνον ἐξ
αὐτοῦ. Tam dulci ibi cibo, ut nomen etiam genti ter-
ræque dederit, nimis hospitali advenarum oblivione
patriæ. Ferunt ventris non sentire morbum, qui eum
mandant. Melior sine interiore nucleo, qui in altero
genere osseus videtur; vinum quoque exprimitur illi. I
have been so particular in translating the description of
this plant, because I have never yet met with an account
of it in any modern writer that agreed with this given
by Theophrastus; and, what is more extraordinary,
Monsieur Maillet, who was many years consul at Cairo,
says he never saw any plant in that country that had
any resemblance to the lotus of the ancients. I have
read the description of the lotus given by the polite and
learned author of the Spectacle de la Nature, which
agrees no doubt very well with the Nelumbo of the East
Indies; but, I believe, he will own that it does not, in
all respects, answer this description of Theophrastus.
But there seems to be a third kind of lotus, upon which
the horses belonging to the companions of Achilles fed
during his inaction,

and to our families, and let our countrymen see that they live in voluntary poverty, since it is in their power to bring their poor hither and enrich them; for all these advantages, gentlemen! are the rewards of victory. The next thing I shall mention to you is, in what manner we may march with the greatest security, and, if necessary, fight with the greatest advantage. In the first place," continued he, "I think we ought to burn all the carriages, that the care of them may not influence our march, but that we may be directed in it by the advantage of the army. After that, we ought to burn our tents also; for they are troublesome to carry, and of no use either in fighting or in supplying ourselves with provisions. Let us also rid ourselves of all superfluous baggage, and reserve only those things that are of use in war, or for our meat and drink; to the end as many of us as possible may march in their ranks, and as few be employed in carrying the baggage; for the conquered, you know, have nothing they can call their own; and, if we conquer, we ought to look upon the enemy as servants to be employed in carrying our baggage. It now remains that I speak to that which is, in my opinion, of the greatest consequence. You see that even the enemy did not dare to declare war against us, till they had seized our generals; for they were sensible that, while we had commanders, and yielded obedience to them, we were able to conquer them: but, having seized our commanders, they concluded that we should, from a want of command and discipline, be destroyed. It is necessary, therefore, that our present generals should be more careful than the former, and the soldiers more observant, and more obedient to them than to their predecessors; and, if you make an order, that whoever of you happens to be present, shall assist the commander in chastising those who are guilty of disobedience, it will be the most effectual means to frustrate the designs of the enemy; for, from this day, instead of one

Clearchus, they will find [1] a thousand, who will suffer no man to neglect his duty. But it is now time to make an end, for it is probable the enemy will presently appear; and, if you approve of any thing I have said, ratify it immediately, that you may put it in execution. But if any other person thinks of any thing more proper, though a private man, let him propose it; for our preservation is a general concern."

After that, Cheirisophus said, "If it is necessary to add any thing to what Xenophon has laid before us, it may be done by and by: at present I think we ought to ratify what he has proposed, and whoever is of that opinion, let him hold up his hand:" and they all held up their hands. Then Xenophon, rising up again, said, "Hear then, O soldiers! what, in my opinion, we are to expect. It is evident that we must go to some place where we may get provisions. I am informed there are many fair villages, not above twenty stadia from hence; I should not therefore be surprised if the enemy, like cowardly dogs that follow, and, if they can, bite those who pass by, but fly from those who pursue them, should also follow us when we begin to move. Possibly therefore we shall march with greater safety, if we dispose the heavy-armed men in a hollow square, to the end the baggage, and the great number of those who belong to it, may be in greater security. If then we now appoint the proper persons to command the front, each of the flanks, and the rear, we shall not have to consider of this, when the enemy appears; but shall presently be ready to execute what we have resolved. If any other person has any thing better to propose, let it be otherwise; if not, let Cheirisophus command the front, [2] since he is a Lacedæmonian; let two of the oldest generals command the flanks; and Timasion and myself, who are the youngest, will, for the present, take charge of the rear. Afterwards, when we have had experience of this disposi-

---

————Ἴστω δὲ παρ᾽ ἅρμασιν οἷσιν ἕκαστος
Λωτὸν ἐρεπτόμενοι, ἐλεόθρεπτόν τε σέλινον·
Ἕκτασαν.
This is thought to be a kind of trefoil, and this, I imagine, was the lotus that, together with saffron and hyacinth, formed the couch of Jupiter and Juno upon a very amiable occasion,

Τοῖσι δ᾽ ὑπὸ χθὼν δῖα φύεν νεοθηλέα ποίην,
Λωτόν θ᾽ ἑρσήεντα, ἰδὲ κρόκον, ἠδ᾽ ὑάκινθον
Πυκνὸν καὶ μαλακόν.

1 Μυρίους ὁρῶντας. Μυρία πολλὰ, καὶ ἀναρίθμητα·
μύρια δὲ, ὁ ἀριθμός. Suidas. Sexcenti is used in the
same manner in Latin to signify an indefinite number:
I have translated μυρίους a thousand, because I think our
language makes use of this number in that sense: in
French cent has the same effect, for which reason I was
surprised D'Ablancourt did not say, ils en verront re-
naître cent, rather than dix mille.
2 Ἐπειδὴ καὶ Λακεδαιμόνιός ἐστι. The reason why
Xenophon does this honour to the Lacedæmonians, will
appear in the Introduction.

tion, we may consider what is best to be done, as occasion offers. If any one thinks of any thing better, let him mention it." But nobody opposing what he offered, he said, " Let those who are of this opinion hold up their hands :" so this was resolved. " Now," says he, " you are to depart, and execute what is determined: and whoever among you desires to return to his family, let him remember to fight bravely, for this is the only means to effect it : whoever has a mind to live, let him endeavour to conquer ; for the part of the conqueror is to inflict death, that of the conquered to receive it. And if any among you covet riches, let him endeavour to overcome : for the victorious not only preserve their own possessions, but acquire those of the enemy."

III. After he had said this, they all rose up, and, departing, burnt their carriages and tents ; as for the superfluous part of their baggage, they gave that to one another where it was wanted, and cast the rest into the fire, and then went to dinner. While they were at dinner, Mithridates advanced with about thirty horse, and, desiring the generals might come within hearing, he said, " O Greeks! I was faithful to Cyrus, as you yourselves know, and now wish well to you : and do assure you, that while I remain here, I am under great apprehensions. So that, if I saw you taking salutary resolutions, I would come over to you, and bring all my people with me. Inform me therefore of what you resolve, for I am your friend and well-wisher, and desire to join you in ²your march." After the generals had consulted together, they thought proper to return this answer, Cheirisophus speaking in the name of the rest. " We resolve," says he, " if we are suffered to return home, to march through the country with as little damage to it as possible ; but, if any one oppose our march, to fight our way through it in the best manner we are able." Mithridates, upon this, endeavoured to show how impossible it was for them to return in safety, without the king's consent. This rendered him suspected : besides, one belonging to Tissaphernes was in his company as a spy upon him. From this time forward, the generals determined that they would admit of no other treaty, while they continued in

the enemy's country : for, by coming in this manner, they not only debauched the soldiers, but Nicarchus, an Arcadian, one of the captains, deserted to them that night, with about twenty men.

As soon as the soldiers had dined, the army passed the river Zabatus, and marched in order of battle, with the baggage, and those who attended it, in the middle. They had not gone far before Mithridates appeared again with about two hundred horse, and four hundred archers and slingers, very light and fit for expedition. He advanced as a friend ; but when he came near, immediately both horse and foot discharged their arrows ; the slingers also made use of their slings, and wounded some of our men, so that the rear of the Greeks received great damage, without being able to return it ; for the bows of the Cretans did not carry so far as those of the Persians. The former also, being lightly armed, had sheltered themselves in the centre of the heavy-armed men, neither could our darters reach their slingers. Xenophon, seeing this, resolved to pursue the enemy ; and the heavy-armed men and targeteers, who were with him in the rear, followed the pursuit. But they could come up with none of them ; for the Greeks had no horse, and their foot could not in so short a space, overtake those of the enemy who had so much the start of them. Neither durst they in the pursuit separate themselves too far from the rest of the army: for the Barbarian horse wounded them as they fled, shooting backward from their horses ; and as far as the Greeks were advanced in the pursuit, so far they were obliged to retreat fighting ; insomuch that they could not march above five and twenty stadia all that day ; however, in the evening they arrived in the villages. Here the troops were again disheartened, and Cheirisophus, with the oldest generals, blamed Xenophon for leaving the main body to pursue the enemy, and exposing himself without ⁴any possibility of hurting them.

Xenophon hearing this, said they had reason to blame him, and that they were justified by the event. " But," says he, " I was under a necessity of pursuing the enemy, since I saw our men suffer great damage by standing still, without being able to return it ; but when we were engaged in the pursuit," continued he, " we found what you say to be true ; for we were not more able to annoy the enemy than before, and retreated with great difficulty. We have reason, therefore, to thank the gods that they came upon us only with a small force and a few troops, so that, instead of doing us great damage, they have taught us our wants. For now the enemy's archers and slingers wound our men at a greater distance than either the Cretans or the darters can reach them; and when we pursue them, we must not separate ourselves far from the main body; and in a short space our foot, though ever so swift, cannot come up with theirs, so as to reach them with their arrows. If we mean, therefore, to hinder them from disturbing us in our march, we must immediately provide ourselves with slingers and horse. I hear there are Rhodians in our army, the greatest part of whom, they say, understand the use of the sling, and that their slings carry twice as far as those of the Persians, who, throwing large [1] stones, cannot offend their enemy at a great distance: whereas the Rhodians, besides stones, make use of leaden balls. If, therefore, we inquire who have slings, and pay them for them, and also give money to those who are willing to make others, granting at the same time some other immunity to those who voluntarily list among the slingers, possibly some will offer themselves who may be fit for that service. I see also horses in the army, some belonging to me, and some left by Clearchus; besides many others that we have taken from the enemy, which are employed in carrying the baggage. If, therefore, we choose out all the best of these, and accoutre them for the horse, giving to the owners [2] sumpter horses in exchange, possibly these also may annoy the enemy in their flight." These things were resolved upon, and the same night two hundred slingers listed themselves. The next day proper horses and horsemen were appointed to the number of fifty, and [3] buff coats and corslets were provided for them, and the command of them was given to Lycius, the son of Polystratus an Athenian.

IV. That day the army staid in the same place, and the next day they began their march earlier than usual, for they had a valley [4] formed by a torrent to pass, and were afraid the enemy should attack them in their passage. As soon as they had passed it, Mithridates appeared again with a thousand horse, and four thousand archers and slingers; for so many Tissaphernes had granted him at his desire, and upon his undertaking with that number to deliver the Greeks into his power: for having, in the last action, with a small force, done them (as he imagined) great damage, without receiving any, he had a contempt for them. When the Greeks were advanced about eight stadia beyond the valley, Mithridates also passed it with the forces under his command. The Greek generals had given orders to a certain number, both of the targeteers and heavy-armed men to follow the chase, and also to the horse to pursue them boldly, with assurance that a sufficient force should follow to sustain them. When, therefore, Mithridates overtook them, and was now within reach of their slings and arrows, the trumpet sounded, and those of the Greeks, who had orders, immediately attacked the enemy, the horse charging at the same time. However, the Persians did not stand to receive them, but fled to the valley. In this pursuit, the Barbarians lost many of their foot, and about eighteen of their horse were taken prisoners in the valley. The Greeks of their own accord mangled the bodies of those that were slain, to create the greater horror in the enemy.

After this defeat the Persians retired, and the Greeks, marching the rest of the day without disturbance, came to the river Tigris, where stood a large uninhabited city, called [5] Laris-

---

1 Χαρσαλήθσοι τοῖς λίθαις. Literally, stones so large, that every one of them is a handful.

2 Σευσφόρα. See note 6, in page 174.

3 Σπολάδις. Hutchinson inclines to read σπολάδις, which has the sense I have here given to σπολάδας, though Suidas acknowledges σπολάδας in the sense our author takes it.

4 Χαράδραν. In this sense χαράδραι is taken by Homer in that sublime description of an inundation, in which the Bishop of Thessalonica thinks he had the universal deluge in his eye—

Τῶν δέ τε πάντες μὲν ποταμοὶ πλήθουσι ῥέοντες,
Πολλὰς δὲ κλιτῦς τότ' ἀποτμήγουσι χαράδραι,

where χαράδραι is thus explained by the Greek Scholiast, Οἱ ἀπὸ τῶν χυμαῤῥων ἱερφπτόμενοι αὐλῶνες· παρὰ τὸ χαράσσειν, καὶ τρηχύνειν τὴν γῆν· οἱ πάλαι ῥέοντα καὶ χείμαῤῥοι, so that χαράδρα is a valley formed by a torrent.

5 Λάρισσα. It is very judiciously remarked by the great Bochart that it is improbable there should be any such name of a town in this part of the world as Larissa, because it is a Greek name; and though there were several cities so called, they were all Greek: and as no Greeks settled in these parts till the time of Alexander's conquests, which did not happen till many years after Xenophon's death, so he concludes they could meet

sa, anciently inhabited by the Medes, the walls of which were five and twenty feet in breadth, one hundred in height, and two parasangs in circuit; all built with bricks, except the plinth, which was of stone, and twenty feet high. This city, when besieged by the king of Persia, at the time the Persians were wresting the empire from the Medes, he could not make himself master of by any means; when it happened that [5] the sun, obscured by a cloud, disappeared, and the darkness continued till the inhabitants being seized with consternation, the town was taken. Close to the city stood a [7] pyramid of stone, one hundred feet square, and two hundred high, in which a great number of Barbarians, who fled from the neighbouring villages, had conveyed themselves.

Thence they made, in one day's march, six parasangs, to a large uninhabited castle, standing near a town, called Mespila, formerly inhabited also by the Medes. The plinth of the wall was built with polished stone full of shells, being fifty feet in breadth, and as many in height. Upon this stood a brick wall fifty feet also in breadth, one hundred in height, and six parasangs in circuit. Here Media, the king's consort, is said to have taken refuge, when the Medes were deprived of the empire by the Persians. When the Persian king besieged this city, he could not make himself master of it either by length of time or force, but Jupiter [8] having struck the inhabitants with a panic fear, it was taken.

From this place they made, in one day's march, four parasangs. During their march Tissaphernes appeared with his own horse, and the forces of Orontas, who had married the king's daughter, together with those Barbarians who had served under Cyrus in his expedition; to these was added the army which the king's brother had brought to his assistance, and the troops the king had given him. All these together made a vast army. When he approached, he placed some of his forces against our rear, and others against each of our

---

with no such name so far from Greece as beyond the river Tigris. He therefore conjectures that this city is the Resen, mentioned by Moses, Gen. x. 12. where he says, " Ashur built Resen between Nineveh and Calah: the same is a great city."[1] This agrees exactly with what Xenophon says of it, who calls it πόλις μεγάλη, and affirms the walls of it to be in circumference two parasangs. Bochart, therefore, supposes, that when the Greeks asked the people of the country, what city are these the ruins of? they answered לרסן Larseen, that is, of Resen. It is easy to imagine how this word might be softened by a Greek termination, and made Larissa.

6 Ἥλιον δὲ νεφέλη προκαλύψασα, etc. This passage, I find, admits of different readings; however, I prefer that of Hutchinson, which is supported by Stephens and Muretus, but differ both from him and Leunclavius, and also from D'Ablancourt, in translating it. They all make ἡράνισε to relate to the town, which, I think, is neither so agreeable to the sense, nor to the genius of the Greek language, since ἥλιον being the accusative case, governed by προκαλύψασα, I think ἡράνισε ought to relate to the same, which every body knows is very common in Greek, and not to another thing, which has not been mentioned in this sentence.

7 Πυραμὶς λιθίνη, τὸ μὲν εὖρος ἑνὸς πλέθρου, τὸ δὲ ὕψος δύο πλέθρων. These are very extraordinary dimensions for a pyramid, and very different from those of the Egyptian pyramids; so that we find the Egyptian and Asiatic taste disagreed very much in this respect. For, though there is some diversity in the accounts given by the ancient authors of the dimensions of the Egyptian pyramids, yet they all make them very different in their proportions from this described by Xenophon. Herodotus makes the great pyramid at Memphis eight hundred Greek feet square, and as many in height, τῆς ἐστὶ πανταχῆ μέτωπον ἕκαστον ὀκτὼ πλέθρα, ἐούσης τετραγώνου, καὶ ὕψος ἴσον. If the reader pleases to turn to page 170, note 7, of the first book, he will find that the Greek foot exceeded ours by .0875 decimals of an inch. Diodorus Siculus says the great pyramid was four square, and that each side of the base was seven hundred feet, and the height above six hundred. Μέγιστον, τετράπλευρος οὖσα τῷ σχήματι, τὴν ἐπὶ τῆς βάσεως πλευρὰν ἑκάστην ἔχει πλέθρων ἑπτὰ, τὸ δ' ὕψος ἔχει πλέον τῶν ἓξ πλέθρων. There is another account given of its dimensions by a modern author, Thevenot, who says the great pyramid is five hundred and twenty feet high and six hundred and eighty-two square. Of these three

accounts, that of Diodorus Siculus seems to give the most rational proportion of a pyramid, which, if supposed to be an equilateral triangle, and the base to contain seven hundred feet, as he says, will, in that case, have six hundred and six feet, and a fraction of two thousand one hundred and seventy-seven for its perpendicular height; for if an equilateral pyramid, of which the base contains seven hundred feet, be divided into two equal parts by a perpendicular let down from the top, it will make two right angled triangles, of which the hypothenuse will contain seven hundred feet, the square of which will consequently be equal to the square of the two other sides. If, therefore, from four hundred and ninety thousand, the square of seven hundred, you deduct one hundred and twenty two thousand five hundred, the square of three hundred and fifty, of which the base consists, there will remain three hundred and sixty-seven thousand five hundred for the square of the perpendicular, the square root of which will be six hundred and six, with a fraction of two thousand one hundred and seventy-seven; so that the perpendicular height of an equilateral pyramid, the base of which is seven hundred feet, will be six hundred and six feet with that fraction.

8 Ἐμβροντήτους. Ἐμβρόντητος· καρδιόπληκτος· μαινόμενος· ἔμφρων. Suidas.

flanks, but durst not attack us, being unwilling to hazard a battle: however, he ordered his men to use their slings and bows. But when the Rhodians, who were disposed in platoons, began to make use of their slings, and the Cretan bowmen, in imitation of the Scythians, discharged their arrows, none of them missing the enemy (which they could not easily have done, though they had endeavoured it) both Tissaphernes himself quickly got out of their reach, and the other divisions retired. The remaining part of the day the Greeks continued their march, and the others followed without harassing them any more with skirmishes: for the slings of the Rhodians not only carried further than those of the Persians, but even than most of the archers could throw their arrows. The Persian bows are long, so that their arrows, when gathered up, were of service to the Cretans, who continued to make use of them, and accustomed themselves to take a great elevation, in order to shoot them to a greater distance. Besides, there were found a considerable quantity of bow-strings in the villages, and some lead, both which were employed for the slings.

This day, after the Greeks were encamped in the villages, the Barbarians, having suffered in the skirmish, retired: the next the Greeks staid where they were, and made their provisions; for there was plenty of corn in the villages. The day after, they marched over the open country, and Tissaphernes followed, harassing them at a distance. Upon this occasion the Greeks observed that an equilateral square was not a proper disposition for an army when pursued by the enemy: for whenever the square has a narrow road, a defile between hills, or a bridge to pass, the wings must close, and consequently the heavy-armed men be forced out of their ranks, and march uneasily, being both pressed together and disordered; so that of necessity they become useless for want of order. On the other side, when the wings come to be again extended, the men who before were forced out of their ranks must divide, and consequently leave an opening in the centre, which very much disheartens those who are thus exposed, when the enemy is at their heels. Besides, when they have a bridge or any other defile to pass, every man is in a hurry, wanting to be first, upon which occasion the enemy has a fair opportunity of attacking them. After the generals had discovered this, they formed

six companies of one hundred men each, whom they subdivided into others of fifty, and these again into others of twenty-five, and appointed officers to all of them. The captains of these companies upon a march, when the wings closed, staid behind, so as not to disorder the rear, they at that time marching clear of the wings. And when the sides of the square came to be again extended, [1] they then filled up the centre,

1 Τὸ μέσον ἀναξιοπίμπλασαν, εἰ μὲν στενότερον ἴη τὸ διάχον, κατὰ τοὺς λόχους· εἰ δὲ πλατύτερον, κατὰ πεντηκοστῦς, εἰ δὲ πάνυ πλατύ, κατ' ἐνωμοτίας· ὥστε αἰεὶ ἔκπλεων εἶναι τὸ μέσον. Here a great difficulty presents itself, which the translators have either not seen, or if they have seen it, they have not thought fit to take notice of it. But let us follow Xenophon in stating the inconveniences to which the equilateral square was subject, with the remedies proposed by the generals to cure them. The inconveniences, it seems, were two; the first, that in passing through defiles, the wings closed, which put the men in disorder; the second, that, after they had passed the defiles, and the wings were again extended, the men were forced to run to the wings, in order to recover their ranks, by which means there was a void in the middle. In order, therefore, to remedy these inconveniences, the generals formed six companies or bodies of one hundred men each, which they subdivided into others of fifty, and these again into others of twenty-five, and appointed officers to each of these bodies. The captains of these companies, when the wings closed, marched clear of them, so as not to put them into any disorder: by this means the first inconvenience was cured, but how was the second to be remedied? If you believe the text as it now stands, by filling up the void, if it was narrow, with the companies of one hundred men each, if larger, with those of fifty, and if very large, with those of twenty-five; so that the narrower the interval, the greater was the number of men to be made use of in filling it up, and the larger, the fewer were to be employed for that purpose. But this is obviously contrary to common sense. If, therefore, the text be so far altered as to transpose κατὰ τοὺς λόχους and κατ' ἐνωμοτίας, every thing will be natural. This correction, however, I have not followed in the translation, because it is very possible to explain the text as it now stands, and if so, no alteration ought to be made in it. It is possible, I say, very possible, that the meaning of Xenophon may be this. Let it be supposed that the square has passed some defile, and that the men running to each of the wings in order to recover their ranks, there remains a void in the centre; in that case, I say, possibly the captains of these six companies, marching in the rear, filled up the void, if it was narrow, with their six companies of one hundred men each, drawn up, for example, twenty-five in front, and twenty-four in depth; if the void was larger, with those of fifty men each, drawn up fifty in front, and twelve in depth; and if very large, with the companies of twenty-five men each, drawn up one hundred in front, and six in depth; and by this means, as our author says, the centre was always full. This passage seems very well to have deserved the attention of the translators, for if I am not mistaken, this is a very fine disposition, and very well calculated to cure the two inconveniences to which a square was subject when an enemy followed. But the merit of this,

if the opening was narrow, with the companies of one hundred men each; if larger, with those of fifty; and if very large, with those of five and twenty; so that the centre was always full. If, therefore, the army were to pass any defile or bridge, there was no confusion, the captains of these several companies bringing up the rear; and if a detachment were wanted upon any occasion, these were always at hand. In this disposition they made four marches.

While they were upon their march the fifth day, they saw a palace and many villages lying round it. The road which led to this palace lay over high hills that reached down from the mountain, under which there stood a village. The Greeks were rejoiced to see these hills, and with great reason, the enemy's forces consisting in horse. But after they had left the plain, and ascended the first hill, while they were descending thence in order to climb the next, the Barbarians appeared, and from the eminence showered down upon them, under [1] the scourge, darts, stones, and arrows. They wounded many, and had the advantage over the Greek light-armed men, forcing them to retire within the body of the heavy-armed; so that the slingers and archers were that day entirely useless, being mixed with those who had charge of the baggage. And when the Greeks, being thus pressed, endeavoured to pursue the enemy, as they were heavy-armed men, they moved slowly to the top of the mountain, while the enemy retreated; and when the Greeks retired

to their [3] main body, the same thing happened to them again. They found the same difficulty in passing the second hill; so that they determined not to order out the heavy-armed men from the third hill; but instead of that, brought up the targeteers to the top of the mountain from the right of the square. When these were got above the enemy, they no longer molested our men in their descent, fearing to be cut off from their own body, and that we should attack them on both sides. In this manner we marched the rest of the day, some in the road upon the hills, and others abreast of them upon the mountain, till they came to the villages; when they appointed eight [4] surgeons, for there were many wounded.

Here they staid three days, both on account of the wounded, and because they found plenty of provisions, as wheat-meal, wine, and a great quantity of barley for horses; all which was laid up for the satrap of the country. The fourth day they descended into the plain, where, when Tissaphernes had overtaken them with the army under his command, he taught them how necessary it was to encamp in the first village they came to, and to march no longer fighting; for some being wounded, some employed in carrying those that were so, and others in carrying the arms of the latter, great numbers were not in a condition to fight. But when they were encamped, and the Barbarians, coming up to the village, offered to skirmish, the Greeks had greatly the advantage of them; for they found a great difference between sally-

---

and of all other dispositions practised by our author in this memorable retreat, must be submitted to the military men, who alone are the proper judges in these cases. As to the signification of στρατευτικὴ and ἐνωμοτία, they were both military terms among the Lacedæmonians; the first explains itself, and the second is thus explained by Suidas. 'Ενωμοτία· τάξις τις στρατιωτικὴ ἀνδρῶν ι' καὶ κ', παρὰ Λακεδαιμονίοις, ὥρισται δὲ ἐκ τοῦ ὁμότας αὐτοὺς μὴ λείψιν τὴν τάξιν, a body of soldiers among the Lacedæmonians, consisting of twenty-five men. It must be observed, that in the first book, where Xenophon mentions two of Menon's λόχοι or companies to have been cut off, he says they amounted to one hundred men, whereas these companies consisted of one hundred men each, but these seem to have been formed for this particular purpose.

[1] Τὴν μαστίγων. It was part of the Persian discipline to make their soldiers do their duty, as Xenophon says, ὑπὸ μαστίγων, under the scourge. So Xerxes, after he had landed in Europe, saw his army passing the Hellespont under the scourge, ἰθύνε τὴν στρατὸν ὑπὸ μαστίγων διαβαίνοντα;—D'Ablancourt has left it quite out, choosing rather to leave his readers uninformed of this custom, than to clog his translation with so uncommon a circumstance.

[3] Πρὸς τὸ ἄλλο στράτευμα. Schil. Barbarorum, says Hutchinson in his notes: Leunclavius has also translated it in the same sense. I am sorry to find myself obliged to differ from them both; but I think it plain that τὸ ἄλλο στράτευμα here signifies the main body of the Greeks, from which these heavy-armed men were detached to drive the enemy from the eminence, which after they had effected, the enemy attacked them in their retreat to their main body. Our author used the same expression in the same sense some pages before, καλὰ γὰρ οὐχ εἶοντι ἦν ἀπὸ τοῦ ἄλλου στρατεύματος διώκειν, where all the translators have translated τὸ ἄλλο στράτευμα, in the same manner I have rendered it here: besides, the word ἀπίασι shows clearly that the thing here spoken of is their return.

[4] Ἰατροὺς. I have said surgeons instead of physicians, because both professions being anciently exercised by the same persons, they were chiefly employed as surgeons upon this occasion. There are two verses in Homer, upon Machaon's being wounded by Paris, which show both the great regard that was paid to the profession, and that surgery, as I said, was a branch of it.

Ἰητρὸς γὰρ ἀνὴρ πολλῶν ἀντάξιος ἄλλων
Ἰοὺς τ' ἐκτάμνειν, ἐπί τ' ἤπια φάρμακα πάσσειν.

ing from their camp to repulse the enemy, and being obliged to march fighting, whenever they were attacked. When the evening approached, it was time for the Barbarians to retire; because they never encamped at a less distance from the Greeks than sixty stadia, for fear these should fall upon them in the night. A Persian army being then subject to great inconveniences, for their horses are tied, and generally shackled, to prevent them from running away; and if an alarm happens, a Persian has the [1] housing to fix, his horse to bridle, and his corslet to put on, before he can mount. All these things cannot be done in the night without great difficulty, particularly if there is an alarm. For this reason they always encamped at a distance from the Greeks. When these perceived they designed to retire, and that the word was given, they in the enemy's hearing received orders to make ready to march; whereupon the Barbarians made a halt; but when it grew late they departed; for they did not hold it expedient to march and arrive at their camp in the night.

When the Greeks plainly saw they were retired, they also decamped, and marching away, advanced about sixty stadia. The two armies were now at so great a distance from one another, that the enemy did not appear either the next day or the day after. But on the fóurth, the Barbarians having got before the Greeks in the night, possessed themselves of an eminence that commanded the road through which the Greeks were to pass. It was the brow of a hill, under which lay the descent into the plain. As soon as Cheirisophus saw this eminence possessed by the enemy, he sent for Xenophon from the rear, and desired him to bring up the targeteers to the front. Xenophon did not take these with him, (for he saw Tissaphernes advancing with his whole army) but riding up to him himself, said, " Why do you send for me?" Cheirisophus answered, " You see the enemy

have possessed themselves of the hill that commands the descent, and unless we dislodge them it is not possible for us to pass: but," adds he, "why did you not bring the targeteers with you?" Xenophon replied, because he did not think proper to leave the rear naked, when the enemy was in sight: " but," says he, " it is high time to consider how we shall dislodge those men." Here Xenophon observing the top of the mountain that was above their own army, found there was a passage from that to the hill where the enemy was posted. Upon this he said, " O Cheirisophus! I think the best thing we can do is to gain the top of this mountain as soon as possible; for if we are once masters of that, the enemy cannot maintain themselves upon the hill. Do you stay with the army; if you think fit, I will go up to the hill; or do you go, if you desire it, and I will stay here." Cheirisophus answered, I give you your choice; to this Xenophon replied, that as he was the younger man, he chose to go: but desired he would send with him some troops from the front, since it would take a great deal of time to bring up a detachment from the rear. So Cheirisophus sent the targeteers that were in the front: Xenophon also took those that were in the middle of the square. Besides these, Cheirisophus ordered the three hundred chosen men, who attended on himself in the front of the square, to follow him.

After that they marched with all possible expedition. The enemy, who were upon the hill, the moment they saw them climb the mountain, advanced at the same time, striving to get there before them. Upon this occasion there was a vast shout raised both by the Greek army, and that of Tissaphernes, each encouraging their own men. And Xenophon, riding by the side of his troops, called out to them, " Soldiers! think you are this minute contending to return to Greece, this minute to see your wives and children: after this momentary labour we shall go on without any further opposition." To whom Soteridas, the Sicyonian, said, " We are not upon equal terms, O Xenophon! for you are on horseback, while I am greatly fatigued with carrying my shield." Xenophon, hearing this, leaped from his horse, and thrust him out of his rank; then, taking his shield, marched on as fast as he could. He happened to have a horseman's corslet on at that time which was very troublesome. How-

---

1 Ἐπισάξαι τὸν ἵππον. I was surprised to find this translated by D'Ablancourt, selle son cheval, which I had rather attribute to his inadvertence than to his ignorance, since he could not but know that the ancients, instead of saddles, used a kind of housing or horse-cloth, which the Greeks called σάγη, and the Latins sagum. This housing is to be seen upon the horses represented on Trajan's pillar, and in many other monuments of antiquity. The Romans called these housings also strata, the invention of which, together with that of bridles, Pliny ascribes to Pelethronius, frænos et strata equorum Pelethronium.

ever, he called to those who were before to mend their pace, and to those behind, who followed with great difficulty, to come up. The rest of the soldiers beat and abused Soteridas, and threw stones at him, till they obliged him to take his shield, and go on. Then Xenophon remounted, and led them on horseback, as far as the way would allow; and, when it became impassable for his horse, he hastened forward on foot. At last they gained the top of the mountain, and prevented the enemy.

V. Hereupon the Barbarians turned their backs, and fled every one as he could, and the Greeks remained masters of the eminence. Tissaphernes and Ariæus with their men, turning out of the road, went another way, while Cheirisophus with his forces came down into the plain, and encamped in a village abounding in every thing. There were also many other villages in this plain, near the Tigris, full of all sorts of provisions. In the evening the enemy appeared on a sudden in the plain, and cut off some of the Greeks who were dispersed in plundering; for many herds of cattle were taken, as the people of the country were endeavouring to make them pass the river. Here Tissaphernes and his army attempted to set fire to the villages; whereby some of the Greeks were disheartened, from the apprehension of wanting provisions if he burned them. About this time Cheirisophus and his men came back from relieving their companions, and Xenophon being come down into the plain, and riding through the ranks, after the Greeks were returned, said, " You see, O Greeks! the enemy already acknowledge the country to be ours; for when they made peace with us, they stipulated that we should not burn the country belonging to the king, and now they set fire to it themselves, as if they looked upon it no longer as their own. But wherever they leave any provisions for themselves, thither also they shall see us direct our march. But, O Cheirisophus! I think we ought to attack these burners, as in defence of our country." Cheirisophus answered, " I am not of that opinion. On the contrary, let us also set fire to it ourselves, and by that means they will give over the sooner."

When they came to their tents, the soldiers employed themselves in getting provisions, and the generals and captains assembled, and were in great perplexity; for on one side of them were exceeding high mountains, and on the other a river so deep, that when they sounded it with their pikes, the ends of them did not even appear above the water. While they were in this perplexity, a certain Rhodian came to them, and said, " Gentlemen, I will undertake to carry over ² four thousand heavy-armed men at a time, if you will supply me with what I want, and give me a ³talent for my pains." Being asked what he wanted, " I shall want," says he, " two thousand leather bags. I see here great numbers of sheep, goats, oxen, and asses: if these are flayed, and their skins blown, we may easily pass the river with them. I shall also want the girths belonging to the sumpter-horses: with these," adds he, " I will fasten the bags to one another, and hanging stones to them, let them down into the water instead of anchors, then tie up the bags at both ends, and when they are upon the water, lay fascines upon them, and cover them with earth. I will make you presently sensible," continues he, " that you cannot sink, for every bag will bear up two men, and the fascines and the earth will prevent them from slipping."

The generals, hearing this, thought the invention ingenious, but impossible to be put in practice; there being great numbers of horse on the other side of the river to oppose their passage, and these would at once break all their measures. The next day the army turned back again, taking a different road from that which leads to Babylon, and marched to the villages that were not burned, setting fire to those they abandoned, insomuch that the enemy did not ride up to them, but looked on, wondering which way the Greeks meant to take, and what their intention was. Here, while the soldiers were employed in getting provisions, the generals and captains re-assembled, and ordering the prisoners to be brought in, inquired concerning ⁴ every country that lay round them. The prisoners informed them that there was to the south a road that led to Babylon and Media, through which they came: another to the east, leading to Susa and Ecbatana, where the king is said to pass the summer and the spring; a third to the west over the Tigris, to Lydia and Ionia; and that the road, which lay over the mountains to the

§ Κατὰ τετραχισχιλίους. This is the known force of the preposition κατὰ, as might be shown by many examples taken from the best authors.

3 Τάλαντον. See note 6, page 169.

4 ʽΗλύγχον. Ἐλίγξι· βασανίσω. Hesychius.

north, led to [1] the Carduchians. This people, they said, inhabited those mountains, and that they were a warlike nation, and not subject to the king; and that once the king's army, consisting of one and twenty thousand men, penetrated into their country, whence not one of them returned, the roads being hardly passable.

---

1 Καρδούχους. This people came afterwards to be better known under the name of Parthians. I should not have advanced this upon an authority of less weight than that of Strabo; Πρὸς δὶ τῷ Τίγρι, says he, τὰ τῶν Παρθυαίων χωρία ὥς οἱ πάλαι Καρδούχους ἔλεγον. It was the posterity of this very people with whom we shall find the Greeks engaged in the next book, who, under the conduct of their king Arsaces, freed their country from the dominion of the Seleucides, and afterwards became a terror even to the Romans, who were so to the rest of mankind. They are still called Curdes, and their country Curdistan. Plutarch informs us that Artaxerxes (the same against whom this expedition was formed) afterwards marched into the country of the Carduchians, at the head of three hundred thousand foot and ten thousand horse, and that his army had in all probability been destroyed by famine, had not Taribazus, by infusing into the minds of the two kings of the Carduchians a mutual distrust, induced them to make peace with the Persians.

But that whenever there was a peace subsisting between them and the governor residing in the plain, there was an intercourse between the two nations.

The generals, hearing this, kept those prisoners by themselves from whom they received the intelligence of each country, without discovering what route they designed to take. However, they found there was a necessity to pass the mountains, and penetrate into the country of the Carduchians: for the prisoners informed them, that, as soon as they had passed through it, they should arrive in Armenia, which was a spacious and plentiful country, and of which Orontas was governor: whence they might, without difficulty, march which way soever they pleased. Upon this they offered sacrifice to the end that when they found it convenient they might depart, (for they were afraid the pass over the mountains might be possessed by the enemy,) and commanded the soldiers, as soon as they had supped, to get their baggage ready, then all to go to rest, and march upon the first order.

XENOPHON

ON THE

EXPEDITION OF CYRUS.

BOOK IV.

.

CONTENTS of BOOK IV.

EXPEDITION OF CYRUS.

BOOK IV.

I. WE have hitherto given an account of what happened in the expedition of Cyrus to the time of the battle; of what happened after the battle, during the truce concluded between the king and the Greeks who had served under Cyrus; and in what manner, after the king and Tissaphernes had broken the truce, the Greeks were harassed, while they were followed by the Persian army.

When the Greeks came to the place, where the river Tigris is, both from its depth and breadth, absolutely impassable, and no road appeared, the craggy mountains of the Carduchians hanging over the river, the generals resolved to march over those mountains: for they were informed by the prisoners, that, after they had passed them, they would have it in their power to cross the head of the Tigris, in Armenia, if they thought proper; if not, to go round it. [1] The source of the Euphrates

also was said not to be far distant from that of the Tigris: and, indeed, the distance between these two rivers is in some places but small. To the end, therefore, that the enemy might not be acquainted with their design of penetrating into the country of the Carduchians, and defeat it, by possessing themselves of the eminences, they executed it in the following manner: when it was [2] about the last watch, and so much of the night was left, as to allow them to traverse the plain while it was yet dark, they encamped; and, marching when the order was given, came to the mountains by break of day. Cheirisophus commanded the vanguard with his own people, and all the light-armed men; and Xenophon brought up the rear with the heavy-armed, having none of the light-armed, because there seemed no danger of the enemy's attacking their rear,

---

1 Καὶ τοῦ Εὐφράτου τι τὰς πηγὰς ἐλέγετο οὐ πρόσω τοῦ Τίγρητος εἶναι. Strabo informs us that the Euphrates and Tigris both rise out of mount Taurus, the former on the north of it, and the latter on the south, and that the sources of these rivers are distant from one another about two thousand five hundred stadia, διέχουσι δὲ ἀλλήλων αἱ πηγαὶ τοῦ τε Εὐφράτου καὶ τοῦ Τίγρητος περὶ δισχιλίους καὶ πεντακοσίους σταδίους. I cannot omit, upon this occasion, an observation of the learned bishop of Avranches, who says that the name of mount Taurus comes from the general word טור *toru*, which in the Chaldaic language signifies a *mountain*, and is applicable to every mountain in the world: this he confirms by the testimony of Diodorus Siculus, who speaking of the building of Taurominium in Sicily, calls the mountain Taurus upon which it stood λόφος, *a hill*. But it must be observed, that the mountain from whence the Euphrates rises, is more properly a branch of mount Taurus, which Strabo in the same book calls Abos. Tournefort, who was upon the place, says, that the Euphrates has two sources rising out of that mountain, which sources form two beautiful rivulets, both called

by the name of *Frat;* and that these rivulets make a kind of peninsula of the plain, in which Erzeron, the capital of Armenia, stands, and afterwards unite their streams at a village called Mommacotum, which, he says, is about three days' journey from Erzeron. I shall only add that Moses, in his description of paradise, calls this river פרת *Phrath*, which the Septuagint has translated Εὐφράτης: though by the way it is pretty plain these letters were not those made use of by Moses; since the Jews used the Samaritan letters till their captivity at Babylon, and adopted the Syriac or Chaldaic at their return.

2 Τελευταίαν φυλακήν. The author of the Etymologicum thinks that φυλακή comes from φυλή; the reason he gives for it is, because the watches were kept by the tribes, λέγουσι γὰρ ὅτι τὰς φυλακὰς αἱ φυλαὶ ὦχον· ὅθεν λέγεται καὶ πρώτη φυλακὴ τῆς νυκτὸς, καὶ δευτέρα, καὶ τρίτη· κατὰ γὰρ τρεῖς ὥρας ἐφύλαττεν μία φυλή. From thence, says he, they say the first, second, and third watch, because one tribe watched three hours. The invention of these watches, together with that of many other military institutions, Pliny ascribes to Palemedes, "Ordinem exercitus, signi dationem, tesseras, vigilias invenit Palemedes Trojano bello."

while they were marching up the mountain. Cheirisophus gained the top before he was perceived by the enemy: then led forward; and the rest of the army, as fast as they passed the summit, followed him into the villages, that lay dispersed in the valleys and recesses of the mountains.

Upon this, the Carduchians left their houses, and, with their wives and children, fled to the hills, where they had an opportunity of supplying themselves with provisions in abundance. The houses were well furnished with all sorts of brass utensils, which the Greeks forbore to plunder: neither did they pursue the inhabitants, in hope, by sparing them, to prevail upon the Carduchians, since they were enemies to the king, to conduct them through their country in a friendly manner: but they took all the provisions they met with, for they were compelled to it by necessity. However, the Carduchians paid no regard to their invitations, nor showed any other symptoms of a friendly disposition; and when the rear of the Greek army was descending from the top of the mountains into the villages, it being now dark, (for as the way was narrow, they spent the whole day in the ascent of the mountains, and the descent from thence into the villages,) some of the Carduchians, gathering together, attacked the hindmost, and killed and wounded some of them with stones and arrows. They were but few in number, for the Greek army came upon them unawares. Had the enemy been more numerous at that time, great part of the army had been in danger. In this manner they passed the night in the villages: the Carduchians made fires all round them upon the mountains, and both had their eyes upon one another.

As soon as it was day, the generals and the captains of the Greeks assembled, and resolved to reserve only those sumpter-horses upon their march that were necessary and most able, and to leave the rest, and dismiss all the slaves they had newly taken: for the great number of sumpter-horses and slaves retarded their march; and many of their men, by having charge of these, were unfit for action. Besides, there being so many mouths, they were under a necessity of providing and carrying double the quantity of provisions. This being resolved, they gave orders to have it put in execution.

While, therefore, they were upon their march after dinner, the generals placed themselves in a narrow pass, and, whatever they found reserved by the soldiers, contrary to order, they took it away; and the men submitted, unless any of them happened privately to have retained some boy or beautiful woman he was fond of. In this manner they marched that day, sometimes fighting, and sometimes resting themselves. The next day there was a great storm: however, they were obliged to go on; for their provisions failed them. Cheirisophus led the van, Xenophon brought up the rear. Here, the ways being narrow, the enemy made a brisk attack upon them, and, coming up close, discharged their arrows, and made use of their slings: so that the Greeks, sometimes pursuing, and sometimes retreating, were obliged to march slowly: and Xenophon often ordered the army to halt, when the enemy pressed hard upon them. Upon one of these orders, Cheirisophus, who used to stand still on the like occasions, did not stop, but marched faster than usual, and ordered the men to follow. By this it appeared there was something extraordinary, but they were not at leisure to send to him to inquire the cause of this haste; so that the march of those in the rear had the resemblance more of a flight than a retreat. Here fell a brave man, Cleonymus, a Lacedæmonian, who was wounded in the side by an arrow, that made its way both through his shield and his buff coat. Here also fell Basias, an Arcadian, whose head was pierced quite through with an arrow. When they arrived at the place, where they designed to encamp, Xenophon immediately went as he was to Cheirisophus, and blamed him for not stopping, but obliging the rear to fly and fight at the same time. "Here we have lost two brave and worthy men," says he, "without being able either to bring them off, or to bury them." To this Cheirisophus answered, "Cast your eyes upon those mountains, and observe how impassable they all are. You see there is but one road, and that a steep one. It is, you may observe, possessed too by a great multitude of men, who stand ready to defend it. For this reason, I marched hastily, without staying for you, that, if possible, I might prevent the enemy, and make myself master of the pass; for our guides assure us there is no other road." Xenophon replied, "I have two prisoners; for, when the enemy molested us in our march, we placed some men in ambush, which gave us time to breathe, and, having killed some of them, we were also desirous of taking some alive, with this view, that we might have guides who were acquainted with the country."

The prisoners, therefore, being brought before them, they [1] questioned them separately, whether they knew of any other road than that which lay before them. One of them said he knew no other, though he was threatened with divers kinds of torture. As he said nothing to the purpose, he was put to death in the presence of the other. The survivor said, this man pretended he did not know the other road, because he had a daughter married to a man who lived there; but that he himself would undertake to conduct us through a road that was passable even for the sumpter-horses. Being asked whether there was any difficult pass in that road, he said there was a summit, which, if not secured in time, would render the passage impracticable. Upon this it was thought proper to assemble the captains, the targeteers, and some of the heavy-armed men; and, having informed them how matters stood, to ask them whether any of them would show their gallantry, and voluntarily undertake this service. Two of the heavy-armed men offered themselves: Aristonymus of Methydria, and Agasias of Stymphalus, both Arcadians. But Callimachus of Parrhasie, an Arcadian, and Agasias, had a contest who should undertake it. The latter said that he would go, and take with him volunteers out of the whole army. "For I am well assured," says he, "if I have the command, many of the youth will follow me." After that they asked if any of the light-armed men, or of their officers, would also be of the party. Upon which Aristeas of Chios, presented himself. He had, upon many occasions of this nature, done great service to the army.

II. The [2] day was now far advanced; so the generals ordered these to eat something, and set out, and delivered the guide to them bound. It was agreed that if they made themselves masters of the summit, they should make it good that night, and as soon as it was day, give them notice of it by sounding a trumpet; and that those above should charge that body of the enemy that was posted in the passage that lay before them, while those below marched up to their assistance with all the expedition they were able. When things were thus ordered,

they set forward, being about two thousand in number. And, notwithstanding it rained most violently, Xenophon marched at the head of the rear-guard towards the passage before them, [3] in order to draw the attention of the enemy that way, and conceal as much as possible the march of the detachment. When Xenophon, with the rear-guard, came to [3] a valley which they were to pass, in order to climb the ascent, the Barbarians rolled down [4] vast round stones, each a ton in weight, with others both larger and smaller. These being dashed against the rocks in their fall, the splinters [5] were hurled every way, which made it absolutely impossible to approach the road. Some of the captains despairing to gain this passage, endeavoured to find out another, and employed themselves in this manner till it was dark. When they imagined they could retire without being seen, they went away to get their supper; for the rear-guard had not dined that day. However, the enemy continued to roll down stones all night, as was perceived by the noise they made in their fall. In the meantime, those who marched round with the guide, surprised the enemy's guard as they were sitting round a fire; and having killed some of them, and forced others

---

1 Ἤλεγχον. See note 4, page 231.

2 Καὶ ἦν μὲν δείλη. That is, the middle of the afternoon. See note 5, page 202.

3 Χαράδραν. See note 4, page 226.

4 Ὁλοτρόχους ἀμαξιαίους. Ὁλότροχος is here a substantive, like ὀλοίτροχος in Homer, and used in the same sense with that in the following verse,

———ὀλοίτροχος ὣς ἀπὸ πέτρης

Ὅντε κατὰ στεφάνης ποταμὸς χειμάρροος ὤσῃ,

Ῥήξας ἀσπέτῳ ὄμβρῳ ἀναιδέος ἔχματα πέτρης,

Ὕψι τ' ἀναθρῴσκων πέτεται———

where ὀλοίτροχος is thus explained by the Greek scholiast, λίθος στρόγγυλος, στρογγύλος. Ἀμαξιαίοι literally signifies stones so large, that each of them was a cart load, or what we call a ton weight.

5 Διεσφενδονῶντο. This word happily expresses the impetuous dispersion of the splinters, when the stones were shattered by falling against the rocks. There is a passage in Euripides where this word without the preposition is very beautifully, or rather dreadfully, made use of, to express the scattering of the limbs of Capaneus, when he was dashed to pieces by a thunderbolt just as he was scaling the battlements of Thebes.

Ἤδη δ' ὑπερβαίνοντα γεῖσα τειχέων

Βάλλει κεραυνῷ Ζεύς νιν· ἐκτύπησε δὲ

Χθὼν ὥστε δεῖσαι πάντας· ἐκ δὲ κλιμάκων

Ἐσφενδονᾶτο χωρὶς ἀλλήλων μέλη.

Κόμαι μὲν εἰς Ὄλυμπον· αἷμα δ' εἰς χθόνα

Χεῖρες δὲ καὶ κῶλ' ὡς κύκλωμ' Ἰξίονος

Ἐλίσσετ'· εἰς γῆν δ' ἔμπυρος πίπτει νεκρός.

" While o'er the battlements Capaneus sprung,
Jove struck him with his thunder, and the earth
Resounded with the crack; mean while mankind
Stood all aghast; from off the ladder's height
His limbs were far asunder hurl'd, his hair
Flew towards Olympus, to the ground his blood,
His hands and feet whirl'd like Ixion's wheel,
And to the earth his flaming body fell."

down the precipice, they staid there, thinking they had made themselves masters of the summit. But in this they were mistaken, for there was still an eminence above them, near which lay the narrow way, where the guard sat. There was indeed a passage from the post they had taken, to that the enemy were possessed of, in the open road. Here they remained that night.

As soon as it was day, they put themselves in order, and marched in silence against the enemy; and, there being a mist, came close to them before they were perceived. When they saw one another, the trumpet sounded, and the Greeks, shouting, made their attack. However, the Barbarians did not stand to receive them, but quitted the road, very few of them being killed in the flight: for they were prepared for expedition. Cheirisophus and his men bearing the trumpet, immediately marched up the passage which lay before them. The rest of the generals took bye-paths, each of them where he happened to be, and, climbing as well as they could, [1] drew up one another with their pikes; and these were the first who joined the detachment that had gained the post. Xenophon, with one half of the rear guard, marched up the same way those who had the guide went, this road being the most convenient for the sumpter-horses; the other half he ordered to come up behind the baggage. In their march they came to a hill that commanded the road, and was possessed by the enemy, whom they were either to dislodge, or to be severed from the rest of the Greeks. The men, indeed, might have gone the same way the rest took, but the sumpter-horses could go no other. Encouraging, therefore, one another, they made their attack upon the hill [2] in columns, not surrounding it, but

leaving the enemy room to run away, if they were so disposed. Accordingly, the Barbarians, seeing our men marching up the hill, every one where he could, without discharging either their arrows or their darts upon those who approached the road, fled, and quitted the place. The Greeks, having marched by this hill, saw another before them also possessed by the enemy. This they resolved to attack likewise; but Xenophon, considering that if he left the hill they had already taken without a guard, the enemy might repossess it, and from thence annoy the sumpter-horses as they passed by them; (for the way being narrow, there was a long file of them.) He therefore left upon this hill, Cephisodorus, the son of Cephisiphon, an Athenian, and Archagoras, a banished Argive, both captains; while he with the rest marched to the second hill, and took that also in the same manner. There yet remained a third, by much the steepest. This was the eminence that commanded the post where the guard was surprised at the fire, the night before, by the detachment. When the Greeks approached the hill, the Barbarians quitted it without striking a stroke: so that every body was surprised and suspected they left the place, fearing to be surrounded and besieged in it. But the truth was, that seeing from the eminence what passed behind, they all made haste away with a design to fall upon the rear.

Xenophon, with the youngest of his men, ascended to the top of this hill, and ordered the rest to march slowly after, that the two captains, who were left behind, might join them: and that when they were all together, they should choose some even place in the road, and there stand to their arms. He had no sooner given his orders than Archagoras, the Argive, came flying from the enemy, and brought an account, that they were driven from the first hill, and that Cephisodorus and Amphicrates, and all the rest who had not leaped from the rock and joined the rear, were slain. The Barbarians, after this advantage, came to the hill opposite to that where Xenophon stood; and Xenophon treated with them, by an interpreter, concerning a truce, and demanded the dead. They consented to deliver them, provided he agreed not to burn their villages. Xenophon came into this. While the other part of the army approached, and these were employed in treating, all the men

---

1 Ἀτίμων, from ἱμάς; but ἀπιμάς in the best authors signifies to draw up any thing generally. So Dion. Cassius uses the word, when he says Mark Antony begged of those who were about him to carry him to Cleopatra's sepulchre, and draw him up to the top of it by the ropes that hung down to draw up the stones employed in the structure of it: ἱκέτευε τοὺς παρόντας, ὅπως πρός τι τὸ μνῆμα αὐτὸν κομίσωσι, καὶ διὰ τῶν σχοινίων τῶν πρὸς τὴν ἀναλκὴν τῶν λίθων κρεμαμένων ἀνιμήσωσι.

2 Ὀρθίαις τοῖς λόχοις. What λόχος ὀρθιος, or φάλαγξ ὀρθία, is, we may learn from Arrian in his Tactics: ὀρθία (φάλαγξ) says he, ὅταν ἐπὶ κέρας, (or κέρως) παρίηνται· οὕτω, δὲ αὖ τὸ βάθος τοῦ μήκους πολλαπλάσιον παρέχεται· ὅλως τι παρέμηκες μὲν τάγμα ὀνομάζεται, ὅτι πᾶς ἂν τὸ μῆκος ἔχῃ ἐσπλώιον τοῦ βάθους· ὀρθιον δὲ, ὅτι πᾶς ἂν τὸ βάθος τοῦ μήκους. So that ὀρθία φάλαγξ is properly an army, and λόχοι ὀρθιοι are companies drawn up in columns, where, as Arrian says, there are many more men in depth than in front.

moved from the post they were in towards the same place. Upon this the enemy made a stand, and when the Greeks began to descend from the top of the hill to join those who were drawn up in order of battle, they advanced in great numbers, and with tumult; and, after they had gained the top of the hill, which Xenophon had quitted, they rolled down stones, and broke the leg of one of our men. Here Xenophon's armour-bearer deserted him, taking away his shield: but Eurylochus of Lusia, an Arcadian, and one of the heavy-armed men, ran to his relief, and covered both himself and Xenophon with his shield, while the rest joined those who stood ready drawn up.

And now the Greeks were altogether, and quartered there, in many fine houses, where they found provisions in abundance: for there was so great a plenty of wine, that they kept it in plastered cisterns. Here Xenophon and Cheirisophus prevailed upon the Barbarians to deliver up their dead in exchange for the guide. These, as far as they were able, they buried with all the honours that are due to the memory of brave men. The next day they marched without a guide, and the enemy, both by fighting with them, and seizing all the passes, endeavoured to hinder them from advancing. Whenever, therefore, they opposed the vanguard, Xenophon, ascending the mountains from behind, endeavoured to gain some post that commanded the enemy, and by this means opened a passage for those who were in the van: and, when they attacked the rear, Cheirisophus ascended the hills, and endeavouring also to get above the enemy, removed the obstruction they gave to the march of the rear. Thus they were very attentive to relieve one another. Sometimes also the Barbarians, after the Greeks had ascended the eminences, gave them great disturbance in their descent, for they were very nimble; and, though they came near to our men, yet still they got off, having no other arms but bows and slings. They were very skilful archers; their bows were near three cubits in length, and their arrows above two. When they discharged their arrows, [a] they drew the string by pressing upon

the lower part of the bow with their left foot. ' These arrows pierced through the shields and corslets of our men, who, taking them up, made use of them instead of darts, by fixing thongs to them. In these places the Cretans were of great service. They were commanded by Stratocles, a Cretan.

III. This day they staid in the villages situate above the plain that extends to the river Centrites, which is two hundred feet broad, and the boundary between Armenia and the country of the Carduchians. Here the Greeks rested themselves. This river is about six or seven stadia from the Carduchian mountains. Here, therefore, they staid with great satisfaction, having plenty of provisions, and

---

[a] Εἶλκον δὲ τὰς νευρὰς, ἐνότε τοξεύοιεν, πρὸς τὸ κάτω τοῦ τόξου τῷ ἀριστερῷ ποδὶ προβαίνοντες. This passage has, I find, very much puzzled the translators. Both Leunclavius and Hutchinson have attempted to mend it: but without entering into the merits of those amendments, I shall produce a passage out of Arrian, which will, I be-

lieve, not only explain this, but also show that no amendment at all is necessary. The passage I mean, is, where he is speaking of the Indian archers, who, like these Carduchians in Xenophon, assisted themselves with their left foot in drawing their strong bows. It is this, οἱ μὲν πεζοὶ αὐτοῖσι (τοῖσιν Ἰνδοῖσι) τόξον τι ἔχουσιν ἰσόμηκες τῷ φέροντι· τὸ τόξον· καὶ τοῦτο κάτω ἐπὶ τὴν γῆν θέντες, καὶ τῷ ποδὶ τῷ ἀριστερῷ ἀντιβάντες· οὕτως ἐκτοξεύουσι, τὴν νευρὴν ἐπὶ μέγα ὀπίσω ἀπαγαγόντες. Where Xenophon says προβαίνοντες, which all translators have been desirous to alter, Arrian says ἀντιβάντες, which, I think, sufficiently explains it. The only thing that remains is to take away the comma after τόξου, that πρὸς τὸ κάτω τοῦ τόξου may belong to τῷ ἀριστερῷ ποδὶ προβαίνοντες, and not to ἶλκον τὰς νευρὰς, as both Leunclavius and Hutchinson have translated it; the first having said, nervos, emissuri sagittas, versus imam partem arcus tendebant; and Hutchinson nervos, cum sagittas missuri essent, ad imam arcus partem adducebant: neither of which has any meaning, for I appeal to all my brother archers, (having the honour to be of that number,) or indeed to any other person, whether they understand what is meant by drawing the string to the lower part of the bow. After all this, I desire I may not be thought to claim any advantage over those two learned gentlemen by this discovery, since I am entirely persuaded, that had they chanced to cast their eyes upon Arrian, while the difficulties of this passage were fresh in their memories, which happened to be my case, they would have made the same or a better use of it. D'Ablancourt has left out that part of the passage that occasions the difficulty.

' Τὰ δὲ τοξεύματα ἰσχύφει διὰ τῶν ἀσπίδων καὶ διὰ τῶν θωράκων. We find the posterity of these Carduchians using the same weapons with the same success against the Romans in the expedition of Marcus Crassus, the death of whose son, who was pierced by these irresistible arrows is so pathetically described by Plutarch. Mark Antony, and his men, in their unfortunate retreat, felt the violent effect of them, which drew from him this exclamation, Ὦ μύριοι! Happy the ten thousand Greeks, who, being pursued by the same enemies, retreated with so much better success! but, alas! his thoughts and heart were in Egypt, whither he was hastening, for which reason all the disadvantages his army suffered from the Parthians were grievous to him, rather as they were delays than defeats.

often calling to mind the difficulties they had undergone; for, during the seven days they had marched through the country of the Carduchians, they were continually fighting, and suffered more than from all the attempts of the king and Tissaphernes. Looking upon themselves, therefore, as freed from these hardships, they rested with pleasure. But, as soon as it was day, they saw a body of horse on the other side of the river, completely armed, and ready to oppose their passage; and, above the horse, another of foot drawn up upon an eminence, to hinder them from penetrating into Armenia. These were Armenians, Mygdonians, and Chaldæans, all mercenary troops, belonging to Orontas and Artuchus. The Chaldæans were said to be a free people, and warlike; their arms were long shields and spears. The eminence upon which they were drawn up, was about three or four hundred feet from the river. The only road the Greeks could discover, led upwards, and seemed to have been made by art. Over against this road the Greeks endeavoured to pass the river: but, upon trial, they found the water came up above their breasts; that the river was rendered uneven by large slippery stones; and that it was not possible for them to hold their arms in the water; which, if they attempted, they were borne away by the stream, and, if they carried them upon their heads, they were exposed to the arrows, and the other missive weapons of the enemy. They retired, therefore, and encamped on the banks of the river.

From hence they discovered a great number of armed Carduchians, who were got together upon the mountain, in the very place where they had encamped the night before. Here the Greeks were very much disheartened, seeing on one side of them a river hardly passable, and the banks of it covered with troops to obstruct their passage, and, on the other, the Carduchians ready to fall upon their rear, if they attempted it. This day, therefore, and the following night, they remained in the same place under great perplexity. Here Xenophon had a dream: he thought he was in chains, and that his chains breaking asunder of their own accord, he found himself at liberty, and went whithersoever he pleased. As soon as the first dawn of day appeared, he went to Cheirisophus, and told him he was in hopes every thing would be well, and acquainted him with his dream. Cheirisophus was pleased to hear it:

and, while the morn advanced, all the generals who were present offered sacrifice, and the very first victims were favourable. As soon therefore as the sacrifice was over, the generals and captains departing ordered the soldiers to [1] get their breakfast. While Xenophon was at breakfast, two young men came to him, for it was well known that all persons might have free access to him at his meals; and, that, were he even asleep, they might wake him, if they had any thing to communicate concerning the operations of the war. These youth informed him, that while they were getting brush-wood for the fire, they saw on the other side of the river, among the rocks that reached down to it, an old man, and a woman with some maid-servants, hiding something, that looked like bags full of clothes, in the hollow of a rock. That, seeing this, they thought they might securely pass the river, because the place was inaccessible to the enemy's horse. So they undressed themselves, and taking their naked daggers in their hands, proposed to swim over; but the river being fordable, they found themselves on the other side before the river came up to their middle, and having taken the clothes, repassed it.

Xenophon hearing this made a libation himself, and ordered wine to be given to the youths to do the same, and that they should address their prayers to the gods, who had sent the dream, and discovered the passage to complete their happiness. After the libation, he immediately carried the two youths to Cheirisophus, to whom they gave the same account. Cheirisophus, hearing this, made libations also. After that, they gave orders to the soldiers to get their baggage ready. Then, assembling the generals, they consulted with them in what manner they should pass the river with most advantage, and both overcome those who opposed them in front, and secure themselves against the others, who threatened their rear. And it was resolved that Cheirisophus should lead the van, and pass over with one half of the army, while the other staid with Xenophon: and that the sumpter-horses, with all those that attended the army, should pass in

---

1 'Αριστοποιεῖσθαι. I have translated this in the same sense Homer says of Ulysses and Eumæus,

Τὸ δ' αὖτ' ἐν κλισίης 'Οδυσσεὺς καὶ δῖος Τφορβὸς
'Εντύοντ' ἄριστον ἅμ' ἠοῖ.——
where ἄριστον is thus explained by the Greek Scholiast, τὴν ἑωθινὴν τροφήν.

the middle. After this disposition was made, they began their march. The two youths led the way, keeping the river on their left. They had about four stadia to go before they came to the ford.

As they marched on one side of the river, several bodies of horse advanced on the other opposite to them. When they came to the ford, and to the bank of the river, the men stood to their arms, and first Cheirisophus, with a garland upon his head, pulled off his clothes, and, taking his arms, commanded all the rest to do the same : he then ordered the captains to draw up their companies in [2] columns, and march some on his left hand, and some on his right. In the meantime the priests offered sacrifice, and poured the blood of the victims into the river; and the enemy, from their bows and slings, discharged a volley of arrows and stones, but none of them reached our men. After the victims appeared favourable, all the soldiers sung the pæan and [3] shouted, all the women answered them; for the men had many mistresses in the army.

Immediately Cheirisophus, with his men, went into the river; and Xenophon, taking those of the rear-guard, who were most prepared for expedition, marched back in all haste to the passage opposite to the road that led to the Armenian mountains, making a feint as if his design was to pass the river in that place, and intercept the horse that were marching along the bank of it. The enemy, seeing Cheirisophus with his men passing the river with great ease, and Xenophon with his forces marching back in all haste, were afraid of being intercepted, and fled with precipitation to the road that led from the river up into the country. Having gained that road, they continued their march up the mountains. As soon as Lycius, who had the command of the horse, and Æschines, who commanded the targeteers belonging to Cheirisophus, saw the enemy flying with so much haste, they pursued them, the rest of the soldiers crying out

to them that they would not be left behind, but would march up the mountain in a body. When Cheirisophus had passed the river with his forces, he did not pursue the horse, but marched along the bank against the other body of the enemy that was posted upon the upper ground. These, finding themselves abandoned by their horse, and seeing our heavy-armed men coming up to attack them, quitted the eminence that commanded the river.

Xenophon therefore perceiving every thing went well on the other side, returned in all haste to the army that was passing over; for, by this time the Carduchians were seen descending into the plain, as if they designed to fall upon the rear. Cheirisophus had now possessed himself of the eminence, and Lycius, while he was pursuing the enemy, with a few of his men, took part of their baggage that was left behind, and in it rich apparel, and drinking cups. The baggage of the Greeks, with those who had charge of it, was yet passing; when Xenophon, facing about, [4] drew up his men against the Carduchians. He ordered all the captains to divide their several [5] companies into [6] two distinct bodies of twenty-five men each, and to extend their [7] front to the [8] left, and that the captains with the leaders of these distinct bodies should march against the Carduchians, while the [9] hindmost men of every file posted themselves upon the bank of the river.

Now the Carduchians, when they saw the rear reduced to a few by the departure of those who had the charge of the baggage, advanced the faster, singing as they came on. Upon this, Cheirisophus, seeing all on his side was secure, sent the targeteers, the slingers, and archers to Xenophon, with directions to do whatever he commanded : but he, as soon as he saw them

2 Λόχους καθίστη. See note 1, page 238.
3 Οἱ στρατιῶται ἀνηλάλαξον, συνωλόλυζον δὲ αἱ γυναῖκες. The first is known to be a military shout, the other is properly a supplicatory acclamation of women : so Homer says of the Trojan women addressing their prayers to Minerva,
Αἱ δ᾽ ὀλολυγῇ πᾶσαι 'Αθήνη χεῖρας ἀνέσχον.
Upon which the Greek Scholiast observes, φωνὴ δὲ αὕτη γυναικῶν εὐχομένων θεοῖς.

4 'Αντία τὰ ὅπλα ἔθετο. See note 2, page 188.
5 Λόχον. See note 1, page 174.
6 Κατ᾽ ἐνωμοτίας. See note 1, page 228.
7 'Επὶ φάλαγγος. This is the reverse of ἐπὶ κέρως, which was explained in note 1, page 238. As therefore ἐπὶ κέρως is a disposition, in which the depth very much exceeds the front, so ἐπὶ φάλαγγος is another, in which the front very much exceeds the depth.
8 Παρ᾽ ἀσπίδα. All the ancient masters of tactics inform us that ἐπὶ δόρυ κλῖνον, ἐπ᾽ ἀσπίδα κλῖνον, were words of command among Greeks for the foot; the first signifying to the pike, that is to the right, and the second to the shield, that is to the left : and that the words of command for the horse were the same as to the first, but that instead of the second they said ἐφ᾽ ἡνίαν κλῖνον, to the bridle.
9 Οὐραγούς. These in Arrian are what we call the bringers-up, that is, the hindmost men of every file.

coming down the hill, sent a messenger to them with orders to halt, as soon as they came to the river; and that, when they saw him begin to pass it with his men, they should come forward in the water on each side opposite to him, [1] the darters with their fingers in the [2] slings of their darts, and the archers with their arrows on the string, as if they designed to pass over, but not advance far into the river. At the same time he ordered his own men, when they came near enough to the enemy to reach them with their slings, and the heavy-armed men [3] struck their shields with their pikes, to [4] sing the pæan, and rush at once upon the enemy: and, when they were put to flight, and the trumpet from the river [5] sounded a charge, to face about to the right, [6] and that the hindmost men of every file should lead the way, and all make what haste they could to the river, which they were to pass in their ranks, that they might not hinder one another; telling them that he should look upon him as the bravest man, who first reached the opposite side.

The Carduchians, seeing those who remained, but few in number, (for many even of those who had orders to stay, were gone, some to take care of the sumpter-horses, some of their baggage, and others of [7] other things) came up boldly towards them, and began to use their slings and bows. But, when the Greeks, singing the pæan, ran forward to attack them, they did not stand to receive them, (for though they were well enough armed for a sudden onset, and retreat upon the mountains they inhabited, yet they were not all so to fight hand to hand.) In the meantime the trumpet sounded, upon which the enemy fled much faster than before; and the Greeks, facing about, passed the river in all haste. Some of the enemy seeing this, ran back to the river, and wounded a few of our men with their arrows; but many of them, even when the Greeks were on the other side, were observed to continue their flight. In the mean time those who had met them in the river, carried on by their courage, advanced unseasonably, and repassed it after Xenophon and his men were on the other side; by this means some of them also were wounded.

IV. The army having passed the river about noon, drew up in their ranks, and, in this manner, marched at once over the plain of Armenia, intermixed with hills of an easy ascent, making no less than five parasangs: for there were no villages near the river, by reason of the continual wars with the Carduchians. However at last they came to a large village, that had a palace in it belonging to the [8] satrap, and upon most of the houses there were turrets: here they found provisions in abundance. From this place they made, in two days' march, ten parasangs, till they were advanced above the head of the Tigris. From thence they made fifteen parasangs in three days' march, and came to the river Teleboas. The [9] river, though not large, was beautiful, and had many fine villages on its banks: this country was called the western part of Armenia. The governor of it was Teribazus, who had behaved

---

1 'Ακοντιστάς. The ἀκόντιον, or dart, was properly part of the arms both of the targeteers and light-armed men, as the reader will see, if he pleases to cast his eye upon note 6, page 167, where he will also find that these were different corps, and differently armed; so that D'Ablancourt should not have comprehended under the general name of *gens de trait*, the targeteers, slingers, and archers, whom Cheirisophus sent to the relief of Xenophon.

2 Διαγκυλισμένους, etc. Διαγκυλῶσθαι τὸ ἐνιέναι τοὺς δακτύλους τῇ ἀγγύλῃ τοῦ ἀκοντίου. Hesychius. 'Αγγύλη is what the Romans called *amentum*, the thong or sling, with which they lanced their darts.

3 'Ασπὶς ψοφῇ. I have said " when the heavy-armed men struck their shields with their pikes," because the ἀσπὶς, or shield, properly belonged to the heavy-armed men, as may be seen in note 6, page 167. The light-armed men being ἄνευ ἀσπίδος, as Arrian says there, without a shield, and the targeteers having πέλτην, their pikes upon an attack, continued among the Greeks in Alexander's time, as may be seen in Arrian.

4 Παιανίσαντες. See note 8, page 180.

5 'Ο σαλπιγκτὴς σημήνῃ τὸ πολεμικόν. This seems to have deserved the attention of the commentators; τὸ πολεμικὸν σημαίνειν, every body knows, signifies to sound a charge, as τὸ ἀνακλητικὸν σημαίνειν, to sound a retreat: why therefore should Xenophon order a charge to be sounded, when his men were to retreat? I imagine his intention was to make the enemy fly the faster, that so they might be at a greater distance from them, when they were engaged in passing the river; and this seems to have been the effect of it, for Xenophon will tell us presently, that when the trumpet sounded, the enemy fled much faster than before.

6 'Επὶ δόρου. See note 8, page 241.

7 'Ετέρων. I have followed the Eton manuscript in translating this word. Hutchinson says it should be ἑταίρων, because Xenophon has very lately told us, that the soldiers had a great many mistresses with them; but in that case it should have been ἑταιρῶν, not ἑταίρων.

8 Τῷ σατράπῃ. See note 5, page 167.

9 Οὗτος δ' ἦν μέγας μὲν οὔ, καλὸς δέ. Demetrius Phalereus gives great commendations to this period. He says, that by the conciseness of it, and its termination in δέ, the author almost lays before our eyes the smallness of the river.

himself with great fidelity to the king, and, when he was present, no other, [10] lifted the king on horseback. This person rode up towards the Greeks with a body of horse, and, sending his interpreter, acquainted them that he desired to speak with their commanders. Upon this the generals thought proper to hear what he had to say, and, advancing within hearing, asked him what he wanted. He answered that he was willing to enter into a league with them upon these terms : that he should not do any injury to the Greeks, or they burn the houses, but have liberty to take what provisions they wanted. The generals agreed to this : so they concluded a league upon these conditions.

From thence they advanced through a plain, and in three days' march made fifteen parasangs, Teribazus following them with his forces at the distance of about ten stadia, when they came to a palace, surrounded with many villages, abounding in all sorts of provisions. While they lay encamped in this place, there fell so great a [11] snow in the night, that it was

resolved the next morning the soldiers, with their generals, should remove into the villages, and quarter there, for no enemy appeared; and the great quantity of snow seemed a security to them. Here they found all sorts of good provisions, such as cattle, corn, old wines exceeding fragrant, raisins, and legumens of all kinds. In the meantime, some of the men, who had straggled from the camp, brought word that they had seen an army, and that in the night many fires appeared. For this reason the generals thought it not safe for the troops to quarter in the villages at a distance from one another : so resolved to bring the army together. Upon this they re-assembled, and it was determined to encamp abroad. While they passed the night in this camp, there fell so great a quantity of snow, that it covered both the arms and the men as they lay upon the ground; the sumpter-horses also were so benumbed with the snow, that it was with difficulty they were made to rise. It was a miserable sight to see the men lie upon the ground still covered with snow. But, when Xenophon was so hardy as to rise naked, and rive wood, immediately another got up, and taking the wood from him, cleft it himself. Upon this they all rose up, and, making fires, anointed themselves ; for they found there many sorts of ointments, which served them instead of oil, as hog's-grease, oil of sesame, of bitter almonds, and of turpentine. There was also found a precious ointment made of all these.

After this they determined to disperse themselves again in the villages, and quarter under cover. Upon which the soldiers ran with great shouts and pleasure to the houses and provisions ; but those who had set fire to the houses, when they left them before, were justly punished by encamping abroad, exposed to the inclemency of the weather. From hence they sent that night a detachment to the mountains, where the stragglers said they had seen the fires, under the command of Democrates of Temenus, because he was ever thought to give a true account of things of this nature, reporting matters as they really were. At his return he said he had seen no fires, but, having taken

---

10 Οὐδεὶς ἄλλος βασιλέα ἐπὶ τὸν ἴππον ἀνέβαλλον. I was desirous to excuse D'Ablancourt, when in the third book, he made the Persians saddle their horses ; but do not know what to allege in his defence upon this occasion, where he has given them stirrups as well as saddles. I shall say no more than that " il lui tenoit l'etrier lorsqu'il montoit a cheval," is an unfortunate translation of βασιλέα ἐπὶ τὸν ἴππον ἀνέβαλλεν. It is very well known that the ancients, having no stirrups, had a person whom the Greeks called ἀναβαλὼν, and the Latins strator, to lift them on horseback.

11 Ἐπιπίπτει χιὼν ἄπλητος. Lest the veracity of our author should be suspected, when he speaks of deep snows and excessive frosts in Armenia, a country lying between the fortieth and forty-third degrees of latitude, I desire it may be considered that all authors, both ancient and modern, agree that the hills of this country are covered with snow ten months in the year. Tournefort, who was an eye-witness of it, thinks that the earth, upon these hills, being impregnated with sal ammoniac, the cold occasioned by it, may hinder the snow from melting : to support this, he says, that this salt being dissolved into any liquor, renders it excessive cold. This puts me in mind of an experiment mentioned by Boerhaave, as having been made by himself : he says, that four ounces of this salt being infused in twelve of water generated twenty-eight degrees of cold ; though I rather believe that the reason why the tops of mountains in the warmest climates are generally covered with snow, while the plains below are often parched with heat, is, because the atmosphere is vastly less compressed upon the top than at the foot of those mountains. Whatever may be the cause, the fact is certain. When Lucullus, in his expedition against Mithridates, marched through Armenia, his army suffered as much by the frost and snow, as the Greeks under Xenophon. And when Alexander Severus returned through this country, many of his men lost their hands and feet

through excessive cold. Tournefort also complains, that, at Erzeron, though situated in a plain, his fingers were so benumbed with cold, he could not write till an hour after sun-rise.

a prisoner, he brought him with him. This man had a [1] Persian bow and quiver, and [2] an Amazonian battle-axe; and, being asked of what country he was, he said he was a Persian, and that he went from the army of Teribazus to get provisions. Upon this they asked him of what numbers that army consisted, and with what intention it was assembled. He answered, that Teribazus, besides his own army, had mercenary troops of Chalabians and Taochians; and, that his design was to attack the Greeks in their passage over the mountains, as they marched through the defile, which was their only road.

The generals, hearing this, resolved to assemble the army, and, leaving a guard in the camp under the command of Sophænetus of Stymphalus, they immediately set forward, taking the prisoner with them for their guide. After they had passed the mountains, the targeteers, who marched before the rest, as soon as they discovered the enemy's camp, ran to it with shouts, without staying for the heavy-armed men. The Barbarians, hearing the tumult, did not stand their ground, but fled. However some of them were killed, and about twenty horses taken, as was also the tent of Teribazus, in which they found beds with silver feet, and drinking cups, with some prisoners, who said they were his bakers and cup-bearers. When the commanders of the heavy-armed were informed of all that passed, they determined to return in all haste to their own camp, lest any attempt should be made upon those they had left there; and immediately ordering a retreat to be sounded, they returned, and arrived there the same day.

V. The next day they resolved to march away with all the haste they could, before the enemy should rally their forces, and possess themselves of the pass. Their baggage therefore being presently ready, they set forward through a deep snow with many guides; and having the same day passed the eminence upon which Teribazus designed to attack them, they encamped. From thence they made three marches through a desert, and came to the Euphrates, which they passed, the water coming up to their navel. It was said the sources of this

river were not far off. From thence they made, in three days' march, fifteen parasangs, over a plain covered with deep snow. The last day's march was very grievous, for the north wind, blowing full in their faces, quite parched and benumbed the men. Upon this one of the priests advised to sacrifice to the wind, which was complied with, and the vehemence of it visibly abated. The snow was a fathom in depth, insomuch that many of the slaves and sumpter-horses died, and about thirty soldiers. They made fires all night, for they found plenty of wood in the place where they encamped; and those who came late, having no wood, the others who were before arrived, and had made fires, would not allow them to warm themselves till they had given them a share of the wheat, or of the other provisions they had brought with them. By this exchange they relieved one another's wants. In the places where the fires were made, the snow being melted, there were large pits which reached down to the ground; this afforded an opportunity of measuring the depth of the snow.

From thence they marched all the next day through the snow, when many of them contracted the [3] bulimy. Xenophon, who commanded the rear, seeing them lie upon the ground, knew not what their distemper was: but being informed by those who were acquainted with it, that it was plainly the bulimy, and that, if they ate any thing, they would rise again, he went to the baggage, and, whatever refreshments he found there, he gave some to those who were afflicted with this distemper, and sent persons able to go about, to divide the rest among others, who were in the same condition: and as soon as they had eaten something, they rose up, and continued their march. During which, Cheirisophus came to a village, just as it was dark, and, at a fountain, without

---

1 Τόξον Περσικόν. See page 226, where Tissaphernes attacks the Greeks.

2 Σάγαρις. Σάγαρις· πελέκυς' ἢ πόλεμος. Suidas. Where he quotes this passage.

3 Ἐξεβουλιμίασαν. The bulimy is a distemper creating excessive hunger. It is thus described with all its symptoms by Galen : Βούλιμός ἐστι διάθεσις, καθ᾽ ἣν ἐπιζήτησις ἐκ μικρῶν διαλειμμάτων γίνεται τροφῆς. Ἐκλύονται δὲ καὶ καταπίπτουσι, καὶ ἀχρόουσι, καὶ καταψύχονται τὰ ἄκρα, θλίβονταί τι τὸν στόμαχον, καὶ ὁ σφυγμὸς ἐκ αὐτῶν ἀμυδρὸς γίνεται. "The bulimy is a disorder in which the patient frequently craves for victuals, loses the use of his limbs, falls down, and turns pale; his extremities become cold, his stomach oppressed, and his pulse scarcely sensible." The French Philosophical Transactions speak of a countryman who was violently afflicted with this distemper, but was cured by voiding several worms of the length and bigness of a tobacco pipe.

the walls, he found some women and girls, who belonged to it, carrying water. These inquired who they were? The interpreter answered, in Persian, that they were going to the satrap from the king. The women replied, that he was not there, but at a place distant about a parasang from thence. As it was late, they entered the walls together with the women, and went to the bailiff of the town. Here Cheirisophus encamped with all that could come up. The rest, who were unable to continue their march, passed the night without victuals or fire, by which means some of them perished: and a party of the enemy following our march, took some of the sumpter-horses that could not keep pace with the rest, and fought with one another about them. Some of the men also, who had lost their sight by the snow, or whose toes were rotted off by the intenseness of the cold, were left behind. The eyes were relieved against the snow by wearing something black before them, and the feet against the cold, by continual motion, and by pulling off their shoes in the night. If any slept with their shoes on, the latchets pierced their flesh, and their shoes stuck to their feet: for when their old shoes were worn out, they wore 'carbatines made of raw hides. These grievances therefore occasioned some of the soldiers to be left behind; who, seeing a piece of ground that appeared black, because there was no snow upon it, concluded it was melted; and melted it was by a vapour that was continually exhaling from a fountain in a valley near the place. Thither they betook themselves, and, sitting down, refused to march any further. Xenophon, who had charge of the rear, as soon as he was informed of this, tried all means to prevail upon them not to be left behind, telling them that the enemy were gotten together in great numbers, and followed them close. At last he grew angry. They bid him kill them, if he would, for they were not able to go on. Upon this, he thought the best thing he could do, was, if possible to strike a terror into the enemy that followed, lest they should fall upon the men that were tired. It

was now dark, and the enemy came on with great tumult, quarrelling with one another about their booty. Upon this, such of the rear-guard as were well, rising up, rushed upon them; while those who were tired, shouted out as loud as they could, and struck their shields with their pikes. The enemy, alarmed at this, threw themselves into the valley through the snow, and were no more heard of.

Then Xenophon, with the rest of the forces, went away, assuring the sick men, that, the next day, some people should be sent to them; but before they had gone four stadia, they found others taking their rest in the snow, and covered with it, no guard being appointed. These they obliged to rise, who acquainted him, that those at the head of the army did not move forward. Xenophon, hearing this, went on, and sending the ablest of the targeteers before, ordered them to see what was the occasion of the stop. They brought word that the whole army took their rest in that manner. So that Xenophon and his men, after they had appointed such guards as they were able, passed the night there also without either fire or victuals. When it was near day, he sent the youngest of his men to oblige the sick to get up and come away. In the meantime Cheirisophus sent some from the village to inquire into what condition the rear was. These were rejoiced to see them, and having delivered their sick to them to be conducted to the camp, they marched forward; and, before they had gone twenty stadia, they found themselves in the village where Cheirisophus was quartered. When they came together, they were of opinion that the army might quarter in the villages with safety. So Cheirisophus staid in the place he was in, and the rest went to the several villages that were allotted to them.

Here Polycrates, an Athenian, one of the captains, desired he might have leave to absent himself; and, taking with him those who were most prepared for expedition, he made such haste to the village that had fallen to Xenophon's lot, that he surprised all the inhabitants together, with their bailiff, in their houses. He found here seventeen colts, that were bred as a tribute for the king; and also the bailiff's daughter, who had not been married above nine days. However, her husband being gone to hunt the hare, was not taken in any of the villages. Their houses were under

---

4 Καρβατίναι. Καρβατίνη μὲν, ἀγροίκων ὑπόδημα, αἰχθὲν ὑπὸ Καρῶν. Julius Pollux. I hope I shall be excused for calling these ὑποδήματα, shoes. All the monuments of antiquity show the ancients wore a kind of sandal instead of shoes, but, as this is not generally understood, I have chosen the latter.

ground; the mouth resembling that of a well, but spacious below; there was an entrance dug for the cattle, but the inhabitants descended by ladders. In these houses were goats, sheep, cows, and fowls, with their young. All the cattle were maintained within doors with fodder. There was also wheat, barley, and legumens, and [1] beer in jars, in which the malt itself floated even with the brims of the vessels, and with it reeds, some large and others small, without joints. These, when any one was dry, he was to take into his mouth and suck. The liquor was very strong, when unmixed with water, and exceeding pleasant to those who were used to it.

Xenophon invited the bailiff of this village to sup with him, and encouraged him with this assurance, that his children should not be taken from him, and that, when they went away, they would leave his house full of provisions in return for those they took, provided he performed some signal service to the army, by conducting them, till they came to another nation. The bailiff promised to perform this, and, as an instance of his good-will, informed them where there was wine buried. The soldiers rested that night in their several quarters in the midst of plenty, keeping a guard upon the bailiff, and having an eye at the same time upon his children. The next day Xenophon, taking the bailiff along with him, went to Cheirisophus, and, in every village through which he passed, made a visit to those who were quartered there; and found them every-where feasting and rejoicing. They all would force him to sit down to dinner with them, and he every where found the tables covered with lamb, kid, pork, veal, and fowls; with plenty of bread, some made of wheat, and some of barley. When any one had a mind to drink to his friend, he took him to the jar, where he was obliged to stoop, and, sucking, drink like an ox. The soldiers gave the bailiff leave to take whatever he desired; but he took nothing; only wherever he met with any of his relations, he carried them along with him.

When they came to Cheirisophus, they found them also [2] feasting, and crowned with garlands made of hay, and Armenian boys, in Barbarian dresses, waiting on them. To these they signified by signs what they would have them do, as if they had been deaf. As soon as Cheirisophus and Xenophon had embraced one another, they asked the bailiff, by their interpreter who spoke the Persian language, what country it was. He answered, Armenia. After that they asked him for whom the horses were bred. He said for the king, as a tribute. He added that the neighbouring country was inhabited by the Chalybians, and informed them of the road that led to it. After that Xenophon went away, carrying back the bailiff to his family, and gave him the horse he had taken some time before, which was an old one, with a charge that he should recover him for a sacrifice (for he had heard he was consecrated to the sun), being afraid that, as he was very much fatigued with the journey, he should die. At the same time he took one of the young horses for himself, and gave one of them to each of the generals and captains. The horses of this country are less than those of Persia, but have a great deal more spirit. Upon this occasion the bailiff taught us to tie bags to the feet of the horses and beasts of burden, when they travelled through the snow, for, without them, they sunk up to their bellies.

VI. After they had staid here eight days, Xenophon delivered the bailiff to Cheirisophus,

---

1 Οἶνος κρίθινος. Literally, barley wine. Diodorus Siculus tells us, that Osiris, that is, the Egyptian Bacchus, was the inventor of malt liquor, as a relief to those countries where vines did not succeed, which is the reason assigned by Herodotus for the Egyptians using it. This was also the liquor used in France, till the time of the emperor Probus, when vines were first planted there. Pliny says they called it cerevisia, a word probably derived from cervoise, which, among the ancient Gauls, signified beer. Julian, who was governor of France, before he was emperor, vents his spleen against malt liquor, which necessity, or rather ignorance in his time, had made the drink of that country. As there is a great deal of poetry in the invention both of the person of this unknown Bacchus, and of his qualities, the reader may not be displeased to find the epigram here:

Τίς; πόθεν δ' Διόνυσε; μὰ γὰρ τὸν ἀληθέα Βάκχον
Οὔ σ' ἐπιγιγνώσκω· τὸν Διὸς οἶδα μόνον.
Κεῖνος νέκταρ. ἔδωδε σὺ δὲ τράγον· ἦ ῥά σε Κελτοὶ,
Τῇ πενίῃ βοτρύων, τεῦξαν ἀπ' ἀσταχύων.
Τῷ σε χρὴ καλέειν Δημήτριον οὐ Διόνυσον.
Πυρογενὴ μᾶλλον, καὶ Βρόμον, οὐ Βρόμιον.

2 Σκηνοῦντας. Xenophon uses σκηνή in the same sense in his Cyropædia, where he says τὴν σκηνὴν εἰς κοίτην διέλυον, they dissolved the feast to retire to rest. Hutchinson has supported this sense of the word from other passages out of our author. Had Leunclavius attended to them, he would not have rendered this passage illos etiam milites et ab tectis reperiunt. D'Ablancourt has said much better, ils trouverent tout le monde a table.

to serve him as a guide, and left him all his family, except his son, a youth just in the flower of his age. This youth he committed to the charge of Episthenis of Amphipolis, with a design to send him back with his father, if he conducted them in a proper manner. At the same time they carried as many things as they could into his house, and, decamping, marched away. The bailiff conducted them through the snow unbound. They had now marched three days, when Cheirisophus grew angry with him for not carrying them to some villages. The bailiff said there were none in that part of the country. Upon this Cheirisophus struck him, but did not order him to be bound: so that he made his escape in the night, leaving his son behind him. This ill treatment and neglect of the bailiff was the cause of the only difference that happened between Cheirisophus and Xenophon during their whole march. Episthenis took an affection to the youth, and, carrying him into Greece, found great fidelity in him.

After this they made seven marches at the rate of five parasangs each day, and arrived at the river [3] Phasis, which is about one hundred feet in breadth. From thence they made, in two marches, ten parasangs; when they found the Chalybians, Taochians, and Phasians posted upon the passage that led over the mountains to the plain. As soon as Cheirisophus saw the enemy in possession of that post, he halted at the distance of about thirty stadia, that he might not approach them while the army marched in a column; for which reason he [4] ordered the captains to bring up their companies in the front, that the army might be drawn up in a line.

When the rear-guard came up, he called the

generals and captains together, and spoke to them in this manner. " The enemy, you see, are masters of the pass over the mountains. We are therefore now to consider in what manner we may charge them with the greatest advantage. It is my opinion, that while the soldiers get their dinner, we should consult among ourselves, whether it will be most proper to attempt the passage to-day, or stay till to-morrow." " My advice is," says Cleanor, " that, as soon as we have dined, we should take our arms, and attack the enemy; for, if we defer it till to-morrow, this delay will inspire those who observe us with confidence, and their confidence will, in all probability, draw others to their assistance."

After him Xenophon said, " This is my sense of the matter. If we are obliged to fight, we ought to prepare ourselves to fight with all possible bravery; but if we propose to pass the mountain in the easiest manner, we are to consider by what means we may receive the fewest wounds, and lose the fewest men. The mountain that lies before us, reaches above sixty stadia in length, and, in all this extent, no guard appears to be posted any where, but only in this part. For which reason I should think it more for our advantage to endeavour to surprise some unguarded place upon the mountain, and, if possible, prevent their seizing it, than to attack a post already fortified, and men prepared to resist; for it is easier to climb a steep ascent, without fighting, than to march upon plain ground, when the enemy are posted on both sides of us. We can also better see what lies before us in the night, when we are not obliged to fight, than in the day time, when we are; and the roughest way is easier to those who march without fighting, than an even way to those whose heads are exposed to the darts of an enemy. Neither do I think it impossible for us to steal such a march, since we may have the advantage of the night to conceal us, and may take so great a circuit as not to be discovered. I am also of opinion, that, if we make a false attack upon the post which is possessed by the enemy, we shall, by that means, find the rest of the mountain more unguarded; for this will oblige them to keep all their forces in a body. But why do I mention stealing? [5] Since

3 Παρὰ τὸν Φάσιν ποταμόν. It must be observed that this is not the river Phasis which falls into the Euxine sea, and to which sportsmen are obliged for the breed of pheasants. Delisle is of opinion, that the Phasis here mentioned is the Araxes, which falls into the Caspian sea, the same whose impetuous course is so boldly described by Virgil,

———Pontem indignatus Araxes.

4 Παρήγγειλε δὲ τοῖς ἄλλοις παράγειν τοὺς λόχους, ὅπως ἐπὶ φάλαγγος γίνοιτο τὸ στράτευμα. The translators do not seem to have attended to the force of the word παράγειν in this place; it is a military term, and signifies to bring up the files in front, and march in a line, in which disposition Cheirisophus proposed to attack upon this occasion: this is called παραγωγὴ by Arrian, the reverse of which is ἐπαγωγὴ as ἐπιστάτης is of παραστάτης.

5 Ὑμᾶς γὰρ ἔγωγε, ὦ Χειρίσοφε, ἀκούω τοὺς Λακεδαιμονίους, ὅσοι ἐστὲ τῶν ὁμοίων, εὐθὺς ἐκ παίδων κλέπτειν μελετᾷν.

I am informed, O Cheirisophus! that among you Lacedæmonians, those of the first rank, practise it from their childhood, and that, instead of being a dishonour, it is your duty to steal those things which the law has not forbidden: and to the end you may learn to steal with the greatest dexterity and secrecy imaginable, your laws have provided that those who are taken in a theft, shall be whipped. This is the time, therefore, for you to show how far your education has improved you, and to take care that, in stealing this march, we are not discovered, lest we smart severely for it."

Cheirisophus answered, " I am also informed, that you Athenians are very expert in stealing the public money, notwithstanding the great danger you are exposed to, and that your best men are the most expert at it, that is, if you choose your best men for your magistrates. So this is a proper time for you also to show the effects of your education." " I am ready," replies Xenophon, " to march with the rear-guard, as soon as we have supped, in order to possess myself of the mountain. I have guides with me: for our light-armed men have, in an ambuscade, taken some of the marauders, that follow the army. By these I am informed that the mountain is not inaccessible, but that goats and oxen graze upon it, so that, if we are once masters of any part of it, it will be accessible also to our sumpter-horses. Neither do I believe the enemy will keep their post, when they see we are masters of the summit, and upon an equality with themselves; because they are now unwilling to come down to us upon equal ground." But Cheirisophus said, " Why should you go, and leave the charge of the rear? Rather send others, unless any offer themselves to this service." Upon this Aristonymus of Methydria presented himself with his heavy-armed men; and Aristeus of Chius, and Nicomachus of Oete, both with their light-armed. And it was agreed that, when they had possessed themselves of the summit, they should light several fires. When these things were settled, they went to dinner. After which Cheirisophus led the whole army within ten

stadia of the enemy, as if he had absolutely resolved to march that way.

Supper being ended, and night coming on those who had orders marched away, and made themselves masters of the top of the mountain. The others went to rest where they were. The enemy finding our men were possessed of that post, remained under arms, and made many fires all night. As soon as it was day, Cheirisophus, after he had offered sacrifice, led his forces up the road, while those who had gained the summit attacked the enemy: great part of whom staid to defend the pass, and the rest advanced against those who were masters of the eminence. But before Cheirisophus could come up to the enemy, those upon the summit were engaged; where our men had the advantage, and drove the enemy before them In the meantime, the Greek targeteers ran on from the plain to attack those who were ready drawn up to receive them, and Cheirisophus at the head of the heavy-armed men, followed as fast as was consistent with a regular march. However, the enemy that were posted in the pass, when they saw those above give way, fled also; when great numbers of them were slain, and many of their bucklers taken, which the Greeks, by cutting them to pieces, rendered useless. As soon as they had gained the ascent, they offered sacrifice, and having erected a trophy, marched down into the plain, where they found villages well stored with all sorts of provisions.

VII. From hence they came to the country of the Taochians, making, in five marches, thirty parasangs: and here their provisions began to fail them; for the Taochians inhabited fastnesses, into which they had conveyed all their provisions. At last the army arrived at a strong place, which had neither city nor houses upon it, but where great numbers of men and women, with their cattle, were assembled. This place Cheirisophus ordered to be attacked the moment he came before it, and when the first company suffered, another went up, and then another; for the place being surrounded with precipices, they could not attack it on all sides at once. When Xenophon came up with the rear guard, the targeteers and heavy-armed men, Cheirisophus said to him, " You come very seasonably, for this place must be taken, otherwise the army will be starved."

Upon this they called a council of war, and

Those who among the Lacedæmonians were called ὁμοῖοι, and among the Persians ὁμότιμοι, by the Greeks, under which name Xenophon often speaks of them in his Institution of Cyrus, agree very well with what the Gothic government calls peers, with us, and with the French, pairs, persons of equal dignity.

Xenophon demanding what could hinder them from carrying the place, Cheirisophus answered, " There is no other access to it but this, and when any of our men attempt to gain it, they roll down stones from the impending rock, and those they light upon are treated as you see ;" pointing, at the same time, to some of the men whose legs and ribs were broken. " But," says Xenophon, " when they have consumed all the stones they have, what can hinder us then from going up? for I can see nothing to oppose us, but a few men, and of these not above two or three that are armed. The space, you see, through which we must pass, exposed to these stones, is about one hundred and fifty feet in length, of which that of one hundred feet is covered[1] with large pines, growing in groups, against which, if our men place themselves, what can they suffer, either from the stones that are thrown, or rolled down by the enemy? The remaining part of this space is not above fifty feet, which, when the stones cease, we must despatch with all possible expedition." " But," says Cheirisophus, "the moment we offer to go to the place that is covered with the trees, they will shower down stones upon us." " That," replies Xenophon, " is the very thing we want, for by this means they will be consumed the sooner. However," continues he, " let us, if we can, advance to that place from whence we may have but a little way to run, and from whence we may also, if we see convenient, retreat with ease."

Upon this, Cheirisophus and Xenophon, with Callimachus of Parrhasie, one of the captains, advanced, (for the last had the command that day of the officers in the rear;) all the rest of the officers standing out of danger. Then about seventy of the men advanced under the trees, not in a body, but one by one, each sheltering himself as well as he could ; while Agasius the Stymphalian, and Aristonymus of Methydria, who were also captains belonging

to the rear, with some others, stood behind, without the trees, for it was not safe for more than one company to be there. Upon this occasion, Callimachus made use of the following stratagem. He advanced two or three paces from the tree under which he stood ; but as soon as the stones began to fly, he quickly retired, and, upon every excursion, more than ten cart-loads of stones were consumed. When Agasius saw what Callimachus was doing, and that the eyes of the whole army were upon him, fearing lest he should be the first man who entered the place, he, without giving any notice to Aristonymus, who stood next to him, or to Eurylochus of Lusia, both of whom were his friends, or to any other person, advanced alone, with a design to get before the rest. When Callimachus saw him passing by, he laid hold on the [2] border of his shield. In the meantime, Aristonymus, and after him Eurylochus, ran by them both : for all these were rivals in glory, and in a constant emulation of each other. And, by contending thus, they took the place ; for the moment one of them had gained the ascent, there were no more stones thrown from above.

And here followed a dreadful spectacle indeed ; for the women first threw their children down the precipice, and then themselves. The men did the same. And here Æneas the Stymphalian, a captain, seeing one of the Bar-

<hr />

[1] Δασὺ πίτυσι διαλείπουσαις μεγάλαις. The explication of διαλείπουσα, brought by Hutchinson out of Suidas and Phavorinus, ἀλλήλων ἀπέχουσαι, does not, in my opinion, give the author's sense of it in this place : nobody doubts but these pines grew at some distance from one another : but Xenophon means that they grew in groups, and then διαλείπουσαι will have the same sense with κατασχθέντα in the second book, where he speaks of the Rhodians being disposed in platoons, for groups in planting and painting are the same thing with platoons in tactics. D'Ablancourt has artfully avoided the difficulty by saying generally, semez de grands pins.

[2] Ἐπιλαμβάνεται αὐτοῦ τῆς ἴτυος. I am surprised to find ἴτυς, rendered both by Leunclavius and Hutchinson, umbo, when Suidas has explained it so particularly by περιφέρεια ὅπλου, and to support that explanation, has quoted this very passage of Xenophon now before us ; and for fear this authority should not be thought sufficient to establish this sense of the word, the same author quotes part of an inscription on the shield of Alexander of Phyllos, where ἴτυς is very particularly distinguished from ὀμφαλός, which is properly umbo.

Τρεχαλία μὲν ἴτυν σαλίμων ὑπὸ, γυραλία δὲ
Ὀμφαλόν.

D'Ablancourt has evaded this difficulty also, by translating it generally, " le prit en passant par son bouclier ;" ἴτυς therefore is what Homer calls ἄντυξ συμάτη, where the ocean flowed in the divine shield which Vulcan made for Achilles.

Ἐν δ' ἰτίθι ποταμοῖο μέγα σθένος Ὠκεανοῖο
Ἄντυγα πὰρ πυμάτην σάκεος πύκα ποιητοῖο.

Which Mr Pope has translated with his usual elegance and exactness :

" In living silver seem'd the waves to roll,
And beat the buckler's verge, and bound the whole."

The Latin translators, therefore, ought to have rendered it ora, as Virgil has in that verse, where he speaks of the javelin thrown by Pallas at Turnus,

———Viam clypei molita per ora.

Tandem etiam magno strinxit de corpore Turni.

barians, who was richly dressed, running with a design to throw himself down, caught hold of him; and the other drawing him after, they both fell down the precipice together, and were dashed to pieces. Thus we made very few prisoners, but took a very considerable quantity of oxen, asses, and sheep.

From thence the Greeks advanced through the country of the [1] Chalybians, and, in seven marches, made fifty parasangs. These being the most valiant people they met with in all their march, they came to a close engagement with the Greeks. They had linen corslets that reached below [2] their navel, and, [3] instead of tassels, thick cords twisted. They had also greaves and helmets, and at their girdle [4] a short falchion, like those of the Lacedæmonians, with which they cut the throats of those they overpowered, and afterwards, cutting off their heads, carried them away in triumph. It was their custom to sing and dance, whenever they thought the enemy saw them. They had pikes fifteen cubits in length, [5] with only one point. They staid in their cities till the Greeks marched past them, and then followed, harassing them perpetually. After that they retired to their strongholds, into which they had conveyed their provisions: so that the Greeks could supply themselves with nothing out of their country, but lived upon the cattle they had taken from the Taochians.

They now came to the river Harpasus, which was four hundred feet broad; and from thence advanced through the country of the Scythians, and, in four days' march, made twenty parasangs, passing through a plain into some villages; in which they stood three days, and made their provisions. From this place they made, in four days' march, twenty parasangs, to a large and rich city well inhabited: it was called Gymnias. The governor of this country sent a person to the Greeks, to conduct them through the territories of his enemies. This guide, coming to the army, said he would undertake, [6] in five days, to carry them to a place from whence they should see the sea. If not, he consented to be put to death. And when he had conducted them into the territories belonging to his enemies, he desired them to lay waste the country with fire and sword: by which it was evident that he came with this view, and not from any good-will he bore to the Greeks. The fifth day, they arrived at the holy mountain called Theches. As soon as the men who were in the van-guard ascended the mountain, and saw the sea, they gave a great shout; which, when Xenophon and those in the rear heard, they concluded that some other enemies attacked them in front; for the people belonging to the country they had burned, followed their rear, some of whom those who had charge of it had killed, and taken others prisoners in an ambuscade. They had also taken twenty bucklers made of raw ox-hides, with the hair on.

The noise still increasing as they came nearer, and the men, as fast as they came up, running to those who still continued shouting, their cries swelled with their numbers, so that Xenophon, thinking something more than

---

1 Διὰ Χαλύβων. It is difficult to say what nation these were; I am sensible Diodorus Siculus calls them Chalcideans; but we are much in the dark as to them. The reader will, however, observe, that these Chalybians were a different people from those he will find mentioned by our author in the next book.

2 Μέχρι τοῦ ἥτρου. Τὸ μένται ὑπὸ τὸν ὀμφαλὸν πᾶς, ἄχρι τῶν ὑπὲρ αἰδοῖα τειχόειαν, ἥμερι τι καὶ ὑπογάστειον. Julius Pollux.

3 Ἀντὶ τῶν πτερυγίων. These tassels with which the skirts of the ancients' armour were adorned, are, by our author, in his treatise of horsemanship, called πτέρυγα, which he says should be so large and in so great quantity, as to hide the lower part of the belly and thighs of the horseman, πτέρι δὲ τὸ ἥτρον καὶ τὰ αἰδοῖα καὶ τὰ μῆλα αἱ πτέρυγες τοιαῦται καὶ τοσαῦται ἱστάσαι, ὥστε στέγειν τὰ μῆλα.

4 Κνήλην. Κνήλη· ξιφίδιον, ὃ τινες δρέπανον λίγουσι. Hesychius.

5 Μίαν λόγχην ἔχον. This seems to have deserved some attention from the translators. What Xenophon calls λόγχη here, Julius Pollux, speaking of the different parts of a spear, calls αἰχμή. The sharp iron at the other end, with which they fixed their pikes in the ground, the same author calls σαυρωτήρ, after Homer, who describes the pikes of Diomede and his companions in that posture,

———ἔγχεα δέ σφιν
Ὄρθ' ἐνὶ σαυρωτῆρι ἐλήλατο.———

I imagine the pikes of the Chalybians had not this lower iron.

6 Ὅθεν πέντε ἡμερῶν ὄψονται θάλατταν. I do not know whether the Latin translators have rendered this passage with perspicuity enough; they have said, "a quo et unde dierum quinque spatio mare conspecturi essent." Of which this seems to be the sense, that the guide said he would carry them to a place, from whence they should see the sea in five days after they arrived there; but this is not the sense of our author; for it is obvious from what follows, that the five days were to be counted from the time he began to conduct them, not from the time they arrived at the place to which he was to conduct them. Accordingly we find, that in five days he led them to the mountain, from which they saw the sea. D'Ablancourt has said much better, "il promit de montrer la mer aux soldats dans cinq jours."

ordinary had happened, mounted on horseback, and, taking with him Lysius and his horse, rode up to their assistance; and presently they heard the soldiers calling out, 'SEA! SEA!' and cheering one another. At this they all set a running, the rear-guard as well as the rest, and the beasts of burden, and horses were driven forward. When they were all come up to the top of the mountain, they embraced one another, and also their generals and captains, with tears in their eyes; and immediately the men, by whose order it is not known, bringing together a great many stones, made a large mount, upon which they placed a great quantity of shields made of raw ox-hides, staves, and bucklers taken from the enemy. The guide himself cut the bucklers in pieces, and exhorted the rest to do the same. After this, the Greeks sent back their guide, giving him presents out of the public stock: these were a horse, a silver cup, a Persian dress, and ' ten daricks. But, above all things, the guide desired the soldiers to give him some of their rings, many of which they gave him. Having therefore shown them a village, where they were to quarter, and the road that led to the Macronians, when the evening came on, he departed, setting out on his return that night. From thence the Greeks, in three days' march, made ten parasangs, through the country of the Macronians.

VIII. During their first day's march, they came to a river, which divided the territories of the Macronians from those of the Scythians. The Greeks had on their right an eminence of very difficult access, and on their left another river, into which the river that served for a boundary between the two nations, and which the Greeks were to pass, emptied itself. The banks of this river were covered with trees, which were not large, but grew close to one another. These the Greeks immediately cut down, being in haste to get out of the place. The Macronians were drawn up on the opposite side, to obstruct their passage. They were armed with bucklers and spears, and wore vests made of hair. They animated one another, and threw stones into the river; but as they did not reach our men, they could do us no damage.

Upon this one of the targeteers coming to

Xenophon, said, he had formerly been a slave at Athens, that he understood the language of these people: " and," says he, " if I am not mistaken, this is my own country, and, if there is no objection, I will speak to the people." Xenophon answered, " There is none, so speak to them," says he, " and first inquire what people they are." He did so, and they answered, they were Macronians. " Ask them, therefore," says Xenophon, " why they are drawn up against us, and seek to be our enemies?" To which they answered, " Because you invade our country." The generals then ordered him to let them know, it was not with a view of doing them any injury; " but that, having made war against the king, we were returning to Greece, and desirous to arrive at the sea." The Macronians asked, " whether they were willing to give assurance of this." The Greeks answered, that they were willing both to give and take it. Upon this the Macronians gave the Greeks a Barbarian spear, and the Greeks gave them one of theirs; for this, they said, was their method of pledging their faith; and both parties called upon the gods to be witnesses to their treaty.

When this ceremony was over, the Macronians came in a friendly manner among the Greeks, and assisted them in cutting down the trees, in order to prepare the way for their passage. They also supplied them with a market, in the best manner they were able, and conducted them through their country during three days, till they brought them to the mountains of the * Colchians. One of these was

---

7 Δαρμκὸς δίσα. See note 6, page 169.

8 Τῶν Κάλχων. We have been a long time following Xenophon through countries, the greatest part of whose inhabitants are scarcely known but by his history. We are now beginning to tread upon classical ground, where almost every mountain, every river, and every city, is rendered famous by the actions of the Greeks and Romans, but more so by their writings. The Colchians are immortalized by the Argonautic expedition, but their origin is not so generally known. Dionysius Periegetes, after Herodotus, makes them a colony of the Egyptians.

Πὰς δὲ μαχὸν Πάντας, μετὰ χθόνα Τυνδαριδάων
Κόλχοι ναιετάωσι, μετέλυδες Αἰγύπτοιο,
Καινάσιω ἐγγὺς ἰόντε——

Herodotus says they were either settled there by Sesostris, or, being unwilling to follow him any further, remained there. This he supports by several arguments as that they were blacks, and had curled hair, but chiefly because the Colchians, the Egyptians, and,

very large, but not inaccessible. And upon this the Colchians stood in order of battle. The Greeks, at first, drew up their army in a line, with a design to march up the mountain in this disposition; afterwards, the generals, being assembled, thought proper to deliberate in what manner they should engage the enemy with most advantage; when Xenophon said it was his opinion they ought to change the disposition, and dividing the heavy-armed men into companies of a hundred men each, to throw every company into a separate column; " for," says he, " the mountain being in some places inaccessible, and in others of easy ascent, [1] the line will presently be broken, and this will at once dishearten the men; besides, if we advance with many men in file, the enemy's line will outreach ours, and they may apply that part of it which outreaches us, to what service they think proper; and if with few we ought not to wonder, if they break through our line wherever their numbers and weapons unite to make an impression; and if this happens in any part, the whole line must suffer. To avoid, therefore, these inconveniences, I think the several companies being thus drawn up in separate columns, ought to march at so great a distance from one another, that the last on each side may reach beyond the enemy's wings: by this means, not only our last companies will outreach their line, but, as we make our attack in columns, the bravest of our men will charge first; and let every company ascend the mountain in that part where it is of easy access: neither will it be an easy matter for the enemy to fall into the intervals, when the companies are placed on each side, or to break through them, when they advance in columns; and if any of the companies suffer, the next will relieve them, and if any one of them can by any means gain the summit, the enemy will no longer stand their ground." This was resolved on, so they divided the heavy-armed men into companies, and threw every company into a separate column; then Xenophon, going from the right of the army to the left, spoke thus to the soldiers: " Gentlemen! the enemy you see before you, are now the sole remaining obstacle that hinders us from being already in the place whither we are long since hastening. These, if we can, we ought even to eat alive."

When every man stood in his place, and all the companies were drawn up in columns, they amounted to about eighty companies of heavy-armed, each of which consisted of near a hundred men; the targeteers and archers they divided into three bodies of near six hundred men each, one of which they placed beyond the left wing, another beyond the right, and the third in the centre. Then the generals ordered the soldiers to make their vows to the gods, and after they had made them, and sung the pæan, they marched. Cheirisophus and Xenophon advanced at the head of those targeteers, who were beyond the enemy's line; these, seeing them coming up, moved forward to receive them, and some filed off to the right, and others to the left, leaving a great void in the centre. When the Arcadian targeteers who were commanded by Æschines, the Arcadian, saw them divide, they ran forward in all haste, thinking they fled, and these were the first who gained the summit. They were followed by the Arcadian heavy-armed men, commanded by Cleanor the Orchomenian. The enemy, when once they began to give ground, never stood after, but fled some one way, and some another. After the Greeks had gained the ascent, they encamped in many villages full of all sorts of provisions. Here they found nothing else worthy of their admiration; but their being

---

Ethiopians, were the only people in the world that originally used circumcision; the Phœnicians and Syrians in Palestine themselves acknowledging that they learned it from the Egyptians: Herodotus adds, that the Egyptians and Colchians agreed also in their way of living, and spoke the same language. If by the Syrians in Palestine, he means the Jews, as it is very probable, his opinion opens so large a field for argument, that, to treat it cursorily would not be doing justice to a subject of so much consequence, and to go the whole length of it, would be not only invading the province of gentlemen much more capable of discussing it than myself, but would also swell this annotation much beyond its due length.

[1] 'H μὲν γὰρ φάλαγξ διασπασθήσεται εὐθὺς. The reasons given here by Xenophon for attacking this mountain in columns, rather than in a line, being the same with those alleged by Polybius, in his dissertation upon the Macedonian phalanx, for the advantages which the Roman legions had over it, I thought the English reader would not be displeased with a translation of this Dissertation, wherein we find a much more particular description of the Macedonian phalanx, and of all its operations, than is to be met with in any other author, particularly, since the seventeenth book of Polybius, in which this Dissertation is, not being entire, has not, that I know of, been translated into our language. From the reasoning both of Xenophon and Polybius, it may be gathered that Philip, the son of Amyntas, and father to Alexander the Great, who we find, by Diodorus Siculus, instituted the Macedonian phalanx, did not improve the Greek discipline by that institution.

great quantities of [2] bee-hives in those villages, all the soldiers who ate of the honeycombs lost their senses, and were seized with a vomiting and purging, none of them being able to stand upon their legs. Those who ate but little, [3] were like men very drunk, and those who ate much, like madmen, and some like dying persons. In this condition great numbers lay upon the ground, as if there had been a defeat, and the sorrow was general. The next day, none of them died, but recovered their senses about the same hour they were seized; and the third and fourth day, they got up as if they had taken physic.

From thence they made, in two days' march, seven parasangs, and arrived at the sea, and [4] at Trebisond, a Greek city, well inhabited, and situated upon the Euxine sea; it is a colony of the Sinopians, but lies in the country of the Colchians. Here they staid about thirty days, encamping in the villages of the Colchians, and from thence made excursions into their country, and plundered it. The inhabitants of Trebisond supplied them with a market in their camp, and received the Greeks with great hospitality, making them presents of oxen, barley-meal, and wine; they also concluded a treaty with them in favour of the neighbouring Colchians, the greatest part of whom inhabit the plain, and from these also the Greeks received more oxen, as a mark of their hospitality. After this, they prepared the sacrifice they had vowed. They had received oxen enough to offer to Jupiter the preserver, and to Hercules, in return for their having conducted them with safety, and also to the other gods what they had vowed. They also celebrated a Gymnic game upon the mountain where they encamped, and chose Dracontius of Sparta (who having involuntarily killed a boy with his falchion, fled from his country, when he was a child) to take care of the course, and preside at the game.

When the sacrifice was over, they delivered the hides of the victims to Dracontius, and desired he would lead them to the place, where he had prepared the course. This hill, says he, pointing to the place where they stood, is the properest place for running, let them take which way they will. But, said they, how is it possible for them to wrestle in so uneven and so bushy a place? He that is thrown, replied he, will feel the greater anguish. [5] The course was run by boys, the greatest part of whom were prisoners, and the long course by above sixty Cretans: others contended in wrestling, boxing, and the pancratium. All which made a fine sight: [6] for many entered the lists, and, as their friends were spectators, there was great emulation. Horses also ran;

---

2 Τὰ δὲ σμήνη. The accident, here mentioned by Xenophon, is accounted for by Pliny, and further explained by Tournefort. The first says there is a kind of honey found in this country, called, from its effect, *maemomenon*; that is, that those who eat of it are seized with madness. He adds, that the common opinion is, that this honey is gathered from the flowers of a plant, called *rhododendros*, which is very common in those parts. Tournefort, when he was in that country, saw there two plants, which he calls *chamaerhododendros*, the first with leaves like the medlar, and yellow flowers; and the other with leaves like the *laurocerasus*, and purple flowers; this, he says, is probably the rhododendros of Pliny, because the people of the country look upon the honey that is gathered from its flowers to produce the effects described by Xenophon.

3 Σφόδρα μεθύουσιν ἐῴκεσαν. Ressembloient a des *yvrognes*, says D'Ablancourt. Methinks he should have rather said, a des gens yvres, for I believe it will be allowed, that in his language, un yvrogne signifies an habitual drinker, and un homme yvre, a man who is actually drunk.

4 Εἰς Τραπεζοῦντα. As this was a Greek city, the Greeks found themselves here in safety, after their long and glorious march. The port, which is on the east of the town, was built by the emperor Adrian, as we find by Arrian, who, in his Periplus of the Euxine Sea, which he dedicates to that emperor, says, "that he was making a port there, for, before, there was no more than a station, where ships could only ride at anchor, with safety, in the summer-time." ἐνταῦθα σὺ σαυῖς λιμένα· πάλαι γὰρ ὅσον ἀποσαλεύειν ὥρα ἔτους, ὁρμος ἦν. Tournefort says this part is now called Platana, and is much neglected by the Turks.

5 Στάδιον, δόλιχος, πάλη, πύγμη, παγκράτιον. The five games, so much celebrated in Greece, are contained in the following pentameter verse,

Ἅλμα, ποδωκίην, δίσκον, ἄκοντα, πάλην.

Leaping, running, throwing of the disk, and of darts, and wrestling. The first is not here taken notice of; under the second is comprehended στάδιον and δόλιχος, the former being a course of six hundred feet, τὸ στάδιον ἔχει πόδας χ'. Suidas, and the latter containing twenty-four stadia, ἔστι δὲ ὁ δόλιχος κδ'. στάδια. id. It is possible that πάλη may, in that verse, be taken for ἀναπαλαιοπάλη, that is, that both boxing and wrestling might be comprehended under the word πάλη, which in that case will be the same with παγκράτιον, since this consisted both of boxing and wrestling, παγκρατιασταῖς· ἀθληταῖς πύκταις, οἳ ταῖς χερσὶ καὶ τοῖς ποσὶ πυκτυμαχοῦσι. Suidas. However, we find them distinguished by Xenophon upon this occasion.

6 Πολλοὶ γὰρ κατέβησαν. In this sense Horace uses the word *descendo*.
———— hic generosior
Descendat in campum petitor.

they were obliged to run down to the sea, and turning there, to come up again to the [1] altar. In the descent, many rolled down the hill, but, when they came to climb it, the [2] ascent was so very steep the horses could scarcely come in at a foot pace. Upon this the spectators shouted, and laughed, and animated their friends.

---

[1] Πρὸς τὸν βωμόν. It is very probable, as Hutchinson has observed, that this altar might be one of those taken notice of by Arrian, in his Periplus, which, he says, were standing in his time, and built of rough stone.

[2] Ἄνω δὲ πρὸς τὸ ἰσχυρῶς ὄρθιον μόλις βάδην ἐπορεύοντο οἱ ἵπποι. Not only the sense of the words, but their order admirably represents the labour of the horses, in climbing the steep ascent. Homer has led the way in this, as in all other beauties both of thought and style. With what difficulty does Sisyphus crowd up the stone to the top of the hill !

Λᾶαν ἄνω ὤθεσκε ποτὶ λόφον—

And then, with what celerity does it come bounding down !

—ἔπειτα πέδονδε κυλίνδετο λᾶας ἀναιδής.

DISSERTATION OF POLYBIUS

MACEDONIAN PHALANX.

Having promised, in the [1] fourth Book, to compare, upon a proper occasion, the arms of the Romans and Macedonians, and the different dispositions of their respective armies, as also to consider the advantages and disadvantages of both; I shall take the opportunity of their being engaged together, to endeavour to perform my promise. For since the Macedonian disposition, recommending itself by success, formerly prevailed over that of the Asiatics and Greeks; and on the other side, the Roman disposition has been victorious over that of the Africans, and of all the inhabitants of the western part of Europe; and since, in our time, there has been not only one, but many trials of the dispositions and soldiers of both nations; it will be a useful and a creditable undertaking to inquire into the difference of their discipline, and consider the cause of the victories of the Romans, and of their excelling all other nations in military achievements, to the end we may not, by attributing their success to fortune, like weak men, compliment the victorious without foundation; but, by being acquainted with the true reasons of it, celebrate and admire the conquerors with justice.

As to what relates to the battles, in which the Romans were engaged with Hannibal, and the defeats they received from him, it is unnecessary to enlarge upon them, since they were not owing either to their arms, or their disposition, but to a superiority of genius, and conduct in Hannibal. This we have made appear in the relation of those battles: and this is farther confirmed by the event of the war, (for as soon as the Romans were commanded by a general equal to Hannibal, they presently became victorious,) and also by the conduct of Hannibal himself, who, disliking the arms his men had till then made use of, upon the first victory he gained over the Romans, immediately armed his forces with the arms of the latter, and continued to use them ever after. It is also certain, that Pyrrhus not only made use of Italian arms, but also of Italian forces, in his engagements with the Romans, placing a body of Italians, and of his own men, drawn up in a phalanx, alternately: however, not even by this means, was he able to beat the Romans, but the event of all their battles proved doubtful. It was necessary to premise these things, to the end that nothing may seem to contradict our assertions. I now return to the proposed comparison. Many arguments may convince us that nothing can resist the phalanx in front, or withstand its onset, when possessed of all the advantages that are peculiar to it: for each man, with his arms, when drawn up in order of battle, takes up three feet in depth; and their pikes, though originally sixteen cubits in length, are, however, in reality, fourteen; of these, four are taken up by the distance between his hands, and so much of the hinder part of the pike, as is necessary to balance the fore part, when presented to the enemy. This being so,

---

it is plain that the pike, when grasped with both hands and presented, must project ten cubits before each man. Hence it happens, that the pikes of the fifth rank will project two cubits, and those of the second, third, and fourth, will project more than two before the file leaders, and when the intervals between the ranks and files of the phalanx are properly observed, as Homer has shown in these verses,

" An iron scene gleams dreadful o'er the fields,
Armour in armour lock'd, and shields in shields,
Spears lean on spears, on targets targets throng,
Helms stuck to helms, and man drove man along."
Pope.

This being truly and beautifully expressed, it follows, that five pikes, differing two cubits from one another, in length, must project before each of the file-leaders; so that it is an easy matter to represent to one's self, the appearance, and strength of the whole phalanx, when being, as usual, drawn up sixteen deep, presenting its pikes, it makes an attack. Of these sixteen ranks, those that exceed the fifth cannot contribute, with their pikes, to annoy the enemy; for which reason they do not present them, but each rank inclines them over the shoulders of that before it, in order to secure them from above; the pikes, by their closeness defending them from the missive weapons, which might otherwise, by flying over the foremost ranks, fall upon those who stand behind them. Besides, each of these ranks, pressing in file, with the whole weight of their body, the rank which immediately precedes, they not only strengthen the attack, but make it impossible for the foremost ranks to retreat. This being the disposition of the phalanx in the whole, and in part, we are now to give an account of the properties and difference of the Roman arms and disposition, by comparing them together. The Romans likewise, with their arms, take up three feet in depth: but, as they cover their bodies with their shields, changing their guard at every stroke, and make use of their swords both to cut, and thrust, it happens that their line of battle is in a perpetual fluctuation; this makes it necessary for each man to have room, and an interval of, at least, three feet, both in rank and in file, if it is expected he should do his duty; from whence it follows, that one Roman will stand opposite to two file-leaders of the phalanx, and consequently be exposed to, and engaged with ten spears which it is not possible

for one man, when once the armies close, to cut to pieces, before he is annoyed by them, or easy to break through, since the hindmost ranks can contribute nothing either to the force of the file-leaders, or to the efficacy of their swords. From what has been said it may be easily concluded that, as I before observed, nothing can withstand the onset of the phalanx in front, while it preserves all the advantages that are peculiar to it. What, therefore, is the cause that gives the victory to the Romans, and defeats those who make use of the phalanx? It is this: military operations are uncertain both in time and place; whereas the phalanx has but one time, one place, and one disposition, in which it can perform the service that is expected from it. If, therefore, there was a necessity for the enemy to engage the phalanx at its own time and place, in every decisive action, it is reasonable to conclude, from what has been said, that the latter would always prove victorious. But, if this is possible, and easy to be avoided, why should that disposition be any longer looked upon as formidable? And, indeed, it is allowed that the phalanx stands in need of an even and open ground, where there is no impediment, such as ditches, chasms, valleys, eminences, and rivers: for all these are capable of confounding, and breaking its ranks. It must also be allowed, that it is almost impossible, at least, very rare, to find places of twenty or more stadia, in which there is nothing of this nature; however, admit there are such places; if the enemy does not think fit to engage the phalanx there, but, instead of that, marches round, and lays waste the towns and country of their friends, what will be the service of such a disposition? Since, while the phalanx remains in the places that are proper for it, so far is it from being able to relieve its friends, that it is incapable even of preserving itself; for the enemy will easily cut off their provisions, the moment they have, without opposition, made themselves absolute masters of the country: and, if the phalanx quits the places that are proper for it, to engage in any enterprise, it will become an easy conquest. But if the enemy, resolving to engage the phalanx in an even place, should, instead of exposing his whole army at once to the onset of the phalanx, retreat a little the instant it charges, the event may be easily foreseen from what the Romans now practise. For I desire no judgment to be formed of my assertions from what say, but from what has already happened: once the Romans do not engage the phalanx with all their legions drawn up in a line parallel to the former; but some divisions of them lie behind in reserve, while others are engaged; so that, whether the phalanx forces those who are opposite to it to give way, or is itself forced by them to give way, the property of it is destroyed: or, in order to pursue those who fly, or to fly from those who pursue, some parts of the line must leave the rest; which no sooner happens, than an opening is given for the reserve to take the ground they left, and, instead of attacking those who remain in front, to break in upon their flanks, or their rear. Since, therefore, it is an easy matter to avoid the opportunities and advantages of the phalanx, but impossible for the latter to avoid those the Romans have over it, how is it possible there should not in reality be a great difference between them? Besides, it is sometimes necessary for the phalanx to march through, and encamp in all sorts of places; at others, to prevent the enemy by seizing some advantageous post; sometimes to besiege, at others, to be besieged, and to meet with unexpected occurrences; for all these things are incident to war, and either decide the victory, or greatly contribute to it: and, in all these, the disposition of the Macedonians is of little or no use; it being impossible for the men, either in companies, or singly, to perform any service: whereas that of the Romans is properly adapted to all; for every Roman, when once armed for action, is equally fit for all places, for all times, and all occurrences; he is also ready and equally disposed either for a general, or a particular action, to charge with his company, or engage in a single combat. As, therefore, the disposition of the Romans is vastly superior to that of the Macedonians in the use of all its parts, so the enterprises of the former are vastly more successful than those of the latter.

The following Geographical Dissertation is a work of so much learning, that I am con-
fident it will be thought not only to explain, but even to adorn the Expedition of Cy-
rus: and though at first, I believe, only designed as a compliment to my book-
seller, is received with as great acknowledgment by the author, as it will be with ap-
probation by the public. There are, I observe, some points, in which this learned
gentleman differs from me in Chronology, and the computation of the Greek mea-
sures, or rather from Diodorus Siculus, and Arbuthnot, whom I have followed; but
I could never answer it either to the public, or myself, if any difference of opinion in
those points could create in me a wish to deprive them of so great an improvement, or
my work of so great an ornament.

GEOGRAPHICAL DISSERTATION.

It is observed by a late ingenious author, that a prince so entirely bent upon the enlarging of his territories, as Lewis XIV. was, could not be very well pleased with the mathematicians who measured his kingdom; for that, by fixing the true boundaries of his dominions, they robbed him of more land, than he could have any hopes of regaining by four or five of his most successful campaigns. The Mahommedan princes have still a stronger tie (if stronger can be than ambition) in this respect: their religion obliges them, both to extend their borders, and to be in a peculiar manner tenacious of what they already possess. How therefore the Grand Seignior may relish the measures of our modern geographers, I cannot take upon me to say; but certain it is, that they have deprived him of so much land (which before he had an uncontested title to), that had the Grand Monarque suffered in such a degree, the world would never afterwards have had any reason to fear the Gallic power.

The Arabians, who are the geographers the Turks are most conversant with, lay down Byzantium, and the northern parts of Asia Minor, in about 45 degrees of north latitude; Ptolemy in [1] about 43; and the southern parts of Cilicia, Pamphilia, &c. in [2] 36° 30'; where-

as in fact the former lie in about 41°, and the latter in 37°. So that the Arabians make this part of the Grand Seignior's dominions four degrees and a half; Ptolemy, and by far the greatest part of the geographers ever since, two degrees and a half broader than in reality it is; which, considering the length of the Euxine sea, namely, more than a thousand miles, is so considerable a portion of country, as a superstitious Mahommedan could not be easily brought to part with.

I think I may venture to say, that the Arabians are not to be complimented with having made any great improvements in geography. It is probable, the first of them made use of a faulty copy of Ptolemy in laying down the places above mentioned, or, it may be, instead of 43° 5', he mistook the letters, and made it 45°, and the rest followed him without every inquiring into the truth. But for Ptolemy, who will, I believe, be allowed to be the greatest geographer the world ever produced, to fall into such a mistake, is very surprising; when we consider, that [3] Herodotus positively affirms, that a man, prepared for expedition, could go on foot from the Cilician sea to the Euxine in five days. Indeed Ptolemy makes a degree of the great circle to consist of but five hundred stadia, and consequently the breadth of Asia Minor (as it is commonly called) will not be increased in proportion to the number of degrees, it being, according to this computation, about four hundred miles English: but this is a great deal too much, especially as the country is very mountainous, for a footman to despatch in so short a time as five days.

Strabo, from Eratosthenes, [4] places the

---

1 He places Byzantium in 43° 5'. Bithyniæ Promontorium in 43° 20'. Heraclea, Ponti 43° 10'. Parthenii Ostia 43° 10'. Sinope 44°. Halys Ostia 43° 10'. Amisus 43° 6', and Trapezus 43° 5'. So that M. Greaves (Philosoph. Transact. No. 178.) had no occasion to have recourse to Ptolemy's Almagest. Magn. to prove there is no error crept into the text, with regard to the latitude of Byzantium, since all these places correspond with it, and particularly Chalcedon, which stood over against it, he puts exactly in the same latitude, viz. 43° 5'.

2 I say in 36° 30', though I might have said less: for he places the middle of Rhodes in 35°. Xanthi Fluv. Ostia in 36° 0'. Phaselis 36° 25'. and Issus 36° 25'.

---

3. In Clio, cap. 72.   4. Book ii. in the beginning.

Sinus Issicus in the same parallel with the Fretum Gaditanum; which is pretty near the truth: but then he says again from Hipparchus, [1] that Narbon, Massalia, and Byzantium lie under one parallel. This it is probable [2] led Ptolemy into the mistake above-mentioned. The latitude of Massalia had been determined to be about 43°, by the observations of Pytheas. He therefore placed Byzantium and the shore of the Euxine in the same latitude, and of consequence made all this country almost double what it is in reality. Indeed Strabo proves afterwards, by an [2] odd sort of reasoning, that

the parallel of Byzantium is much more northward than that of Massalia: because from Byzantium to Rhodes, (which lies in the same parallel with the Fretum Gaditanum) he says, is allowed by all, to be four thousand nine hundred stadia: but that from Massalia to the aforesaid parallel is not quite two thousand five hundred. We may presume that Strabo, though a very cautious and very modest writer, did not attend to the words of Herodotus: for, if he had, he must have concluded, that upon the supposition of Hipparchus and Eratosthenes, a footman could travel in five days the whole breadth of Spain, that is, from the Fretum Gaditanum (the straits of Gibraltar) to the Mare Cantabrium, (the bay of Biscay) and upon his own supposition in much less; either of which a man of his intelligence must know to be quite impracticable.

All that can be said in this case is, that the greatest part of the ancients looked upon Herodotus, as an author that indulged himself too much in the privilege of travellers; and therefore in general seem to give very little credit to what he advances: though time and experience have at last convinced the world, that he had a genius superior to the rest of mankind: that his diligence and veracity were equal to his genius; and that he, like our countryman R. Bacon, discovered truths too sublime for the contemplation of the age he lived in.

This I thought proper to premise, because several modern map-makers, and [4] some late authors, still adhere to Ptolemy, in placing Byzantium and the Euxine two degrees too far to the northward. I shall for the future confine myself to the proper subject of this dissertation, namely, to the route which the Greek army took,

---

1 Book ii. page 212, and in other places.

2 There might another reason be assigned for Ptolemy's placing Byzantium so far to the northward, and that is his making a degree of the great circle to consist of but five hundred stadia, whereas in reality it contains very near six hundred and five: so that the greater the distance, the more in proportion are the number of degrees increased; six of Ptolemy's not being quite equal to five of the great circle. And thus we find that the distance between Alexandria, in Egypt, the place of Ptolemy's residence, and Byzantium, is in reality about ten degrees, the former being near thirty-one, the latter in forty-one; whereas Ptolemy increasing one degree in five, has placed Byzantium in forty-three. However, as Hipparchus in Strabo does affirm, that Byzantium is by observation exactly in the same latitude with Massalia, Φησὶ γὰρ ἐν Βυζαντίῳ τὸν αὐτὸν εἶναι λόγον τοῦ γνώμονος πρὸς τὴν σκιὰν, ὃν ἔστιν ὁ Πυθέας ἐν Μασσαλίᾳ; and as Ptolemy makes them exactly the same, viz. μγ. ιϛ. 43, 5, I think it is most probable he was misled by those authorities. We may from this be convinced how little stress ought to be laid upon the observations of the ancients, and how far their authority is to be relied on, with regard to the motion of the poles of the earth. Mr Cassini, in the Mem. of the Acad. Royale, has treated this subject in a very curious and ample manner; after which I am surprised how M. Voltaire (Philosophie de Nucton, cap. 25) could espouse this opinion of the poles shifting after the rate of one minute in 100 years, and affirm that the Egyptian astronomers had made regular observations of the heavens for two whole revolutions of the poles: which makes the Egyptians a very ancient nation indeed; for two revolutions amount to no less than 4,320,000 years. This he gathers from Herodotus, who says that the Egyptian annals mention the sun's rising twice in the west. A consequence this, which nothing but an exalted genius could have drawn! But we must remember this gentleman is a poet as well as a philosopher.

2 He says, "It is allowed by most people, that the line which is drawn from the straits of Gibraltar through the fare of Messina, Athens, and Rhodes, makes all these places lie under the same parallel. It is also allowed that this line (from the Straits to the fare) passes somewhere very near the middle of the sea. Now we are assured by navigators, that the greatest distance from France (from the gulf of Lyons to Africa is no more than 5000 stadia: and consequently that this is the breadth of the Mediterranean in the

broadest place. So that from the aforesaid line to the farthest corner of the gulf of Lyons, must be 2500 stadia, and to Massalia somewhat less, because it stands more southward than the bight of the Bay. But from Rhodes to Byzantium is 4900 stadia: so that the parallel of Byzantium must be a great deal more northward (πολὺ ἀρκτικώτερον) than that of Massalia." page 115. The fallacy of this argument is quickly perceived, by only casting an eye upon any common map where we shall find the difference of latitude between Rhodes and Constantinople is not four degrees, that is, not 2500 stadia; and that the parallel of the Straits runs into the coast of Africa.

4 Some of these Mr Spelman has followed in note 11, book iv. page 243, where he says that Armenia lies between the 40th and 43rd degrees of latitude; whereas Trebisond lies in 4° 4′, so that Armenia cannot reach at most to above forty and a half.

in their expedition to Babylon, and in their return back again.

Xenophon begins his account of their march from Sardes, the capital of Lydia, because he there joined the army, but afterwards constantly computes from Ephesus the sea-port, from whence he began his journey. They directed their[a] march through the middle of the country; through Lydia, Phrygia, Lycaonia, Cappadocia, and [b] Cilicia, to the gates of Syria, near the upper end of Sinus Issicus.

From thence they proceeded to Myriandrus, a sea-port town, of which no footsteps that I can hear of at present remain. Ptolemy[7] places it twenty minutes south of Alexandria penes Issum (Scanderun,) upon the same meridian; but whoever casts his eye upon the chart of the bay of Scanderun, will soon perceive this to be impossible; because the bay lies near the north-east and south-west, and both these towns stood upon the shore. All that we can gather from it is, that they were distant from each other twenty of Ptolemy's minutes, i. e. nineteen English miles; and that therefore Myriandrus is to be placed at the entrance into the bay, just within the Scopulus Rhossicus, now called, Ras al Khanzir.

From hence, the army, in four days' march, made twenty parasangs, (in our language leagues) and came to the river Chalus, very justly, by the great Delisle, supposed to be the Chalib, or Alep, the river of Aleppo; because the name is not only the same, allowing for the different genius of languages; but the distance shows it can be no other. For as Aleppo is about twenty small hours' journey from Scanderun, so it must be something more from Myriandrus, which lay near south-west from the latter of those places; and as there lies a great bog in the direct road, which was made

passable but of late years, and which Cyrus's army was to go almost round; we may conclude, that all these put together, must make the distance from Myriandrus to the Chalus, twenty parasangs, or Persian leagues. In mentioning the Chalus, I cannot but make one remark, and that is, that it is, in one respect, very different from what it was formerly. Xenophon says, it was full of fish in his time; and give a very good[8] reason for it. Rauwolf says, there is great scarcity of fish at Aleppo, though the inhabitants do not esteem them; but the reason he gives for their indifference to this sort of victuals, seems to me a little extraordinary; he says, " It is because most of them drink water instead of wine."

From the Chalus, in five days' march, they made thirty parasangs, and came to the sources of the river Daradax, which Xenophon affirms to be one hundred feet broad; by which we must naturally conclude, that the army marched along the bank of it a considerable way; because we cannot suppose any river in this country, the edge of the desert of Arabia, to be one hundred feet in breadth at the source. What river this was, or what is the present name of it, is difficult, perhaps impossible, to determine. The plethrum, or measure of one hundred feet, is but a lax way of reckoning, and might, perhaps, be applied to rivers a [10]great deal less than one hundred feet in breadth: as our [11]measures, in modern times, are often applied to rivers in a very random manner. However, as modern travellers take no notice of any such river, we must let it rest as it is, till more satisfactory discoveries are made in these parts. What surprises me most in this very particular account of their march is, that our author takes no notice of the river, now called [12]Ephrin, about half way between the bay

<hr>

5 I shall speak more particularly of this march, when I come to take notice of M. Delisle's computations.

6 I would recommend the following passage in Diodorus Siculus to the consideration of the next editor of that author; 'Ο δὲ Κῦρος, ἐπειδὴ διῆλθε τὴν Κιλικίαν, καὶ παρεγενήθη πρὸς πόλιν Ἰσσόν, ἐπὶ θαλάττη μὲν κειμένην, ἐσχάτην δ' οὖσαν τῆς Κιλικίας, κατασλεύσας εἰς αὐτήν. Booth translates it, " Having marched almost through all Cilicia, he took shipping, and arrived at last by sea at Issus, the utmost city of that country, near the seaside." Which is indeed a verbal translation of the Latin version; but how to reconcile it with the original, or with Xenophon's account of this march, I confess, I cannot tell.

7 Alexandria penes Issum long. 69° 10', lat. 30° 10' Myriandus 69° 10', lat. 35° 50'. Mr Delisle has placed this town fifteen minutes to the north of Alexandrete.

8 Because the inhabitants of that country worshipped them as gods. See Book I. page 172.

9 Travels published by J. Ray, part, i. c. 2.

10 Thus we find Xenophon applies the measure of one hundred feet to some of the rivers of Cilicia, which other authors call no more than brooks falling from Mount Taurus cross a small plain into the sea.

11 In this manner Rauwolf says the Euphrates is half a league broad at Babylon; whereas Sir Thomas Herbert says it is only almost double the breadth of the Thames at London. At Bir, Rauwolf says, it is a mile broad; Maundrel, that it is as broad as the Thames at London.

12 Tavernier mentions two rivers between Alexandretta and Aleppo; over the first he says is a bridge very long and strongly built, Book ii. cap. 1. But in this he is mistaken, the bridge and causeway being laid

of Scanderun and Aleppo; and which the army must of necessity pass in their march to the East; for it rises in the mountains above Korus, and falls into the lake of Antioch. This river is at least as considerable as the Chalus, and much more so, I dare venture to say, than any river between Aleppo and the Euphrates. This, among a great many others, some of which I shall have occasion to mention in the sequel of this discourse, does almost prevail upon me to think, that Xenophon kept no journal, at least no regular one, of this expedition; but that he drew it up a great many years afterwards, at his leisure, in his [1] exile, from the several particulars, which must have made a very strong impression upon his memory. This will not seem so strange, when we consider that, in Xenophon's days, writing was not what it is in our's; the materials were not easy to be had, nor were they easy to be carried in such marches as they performed.

From the source of the Daradax, they marched, in three days, fifteen parasangs, to Thapsacus, upon the Euphrates. This city, though nothing at present remains of it but the name, was formerly a place of great note: it was the frontier town of the kingdom of Israel, in the days of David and Solomon: for it is said, 1 Kings iv. 24, that Solomon רשלמה היה רדה בכל עבר הנהר מתפסח ועד עזה בכל מלכי עבר הנהר that is, He had dominion over all on this side the river, from Thapsakh even to Ngaza over all the kings on this side the river, viz. the Euphrates. Our translators have rendered them Tiphsah and Azzah, which puts such a disguise upon these two noted cities, that I dare to say, very few people, upon seeing these names in the Bible, have been able to know them. Such confusion has the pointing of the Hebrew brought into that primitive and sacred language! Thapsakh, in the original, signifies a pass, or passing over, or perhaps, in this place, more properly a ford; for as in our nation, there are at present bridges over most of the rivers at such places as end in

ford, such as Oxford, Wallingford, Hertford, and the like, yet it is certain that these names were given them from fording the rivers at those places before the bridges were built. In like manner, it is more than probable, that Thapsakh was so called, from the Euphrates being fordable at that place; because it was a town of note in David's time, and consequently must have had its name long before, in those times of simple nature, when ferry-boats, and bridges of boats, were not invented. Ptolemy makes the Euphrates fordable here; and Rauwolf, about the same place, found the river so full of shoals, that though their boats could draw but little water, the navigation was extremely dangerous. And, indeed, Menon, who was a man of great cunning, must have drawn this secret from somebody, else it can scarcely be supposed, he would attempt to pass a river near half an English mile in breadth, that is broader than the Thames at Woolwich. This I have been the more particular in, with a design to show what a notable compliment the inhabitants of Thapsacus paid Cyrus, when they told him that the gods had wrought a miracle in his favour, by making the river, the great river, to submit to his authority; inasmuch as it was never known to be fordable before this time.

I cannot here pass without taking notice of a great error crept into the copies of Strabo; where speaking of Alexander's design of subduing the Arabs, he tells us, " That great conqueror, seeing the impossibility of attacking them by land, proposed to build a great quantity of boats, in Phœnicia and Cyprus, and [2] transporting them seven stadia, to Thapsacus, to convey them, by means of the river, to Babylon." Which makes it not a mile from the coast of the Mediterranean to Thapsacus, whereas, it must be at least one hundred and fifty. I cannot find that any of the learned

---

over the b'g above mentioned: the other he calls Afrora, and says that upon rains it is not fordable. This is the Ephrin, the fording of which does frequently so much damage to the bales of goods, that our Turkey merchants, some years ago, proposed to build a bridge over it at their own expense; but the Turks would not consent, and so the design was dropped.

[1] I shall speak of this more particularly towards the end of this Dissertation.

2 Book xvi. page 741. "Α πεμισθέντα δὶς Θάψακον, σταδίους ίπτὰ ὕπα τῷ ποταμῷ καταπομισθῆραι μέχρι Βαβυλῶνος. It is certain that Strabo, in composing such a work as his Geography is, must consult a very great variety of authors; and though he himself always makes use of the stadium in computing of distances, yet in transcribing other writings, he might sometimes be forced to adopt other terms: for instance, in this place, he might meet with σταθμοὶς ίπτὰ, and put it down so, as not being able to determine the exact quantity: which some ignorant scribe, seeing σταδίους in all other places made use of, might change, and think he had done his author great service.

men, who have made their observations upon this author, have taken any notice, much less made any attempt towards the clearing up of this passage.

Pliny, Stephanus of Byzantium, and Lucan, affirm, that Alexander passed the Euphrates at Zeugma, (a place near two hundred and thirty miles higher up the river than Thapsacus,) contrary to the authority of all other historians, and the nature of the thing itself; for as Alexander was at Tyre, in his return from Egypt, and was to direct his march towards Arbela, it would have been near four hundred miles out of his way to have gone to Zeugma. What might probably lead Pliny and the rest into this mistake, was the name of the place: for [2] Zeugma was so called, because a bridge was laid over the Euphrates there; and as there was also a bridge over the Euphrates at Thapsacus, it might easily lead authors, at so great a distance, into such a mistake. The reason Mr Hutchinson gives, namely that [4] these authors must speak of different expeditions, sounds somewhat strange to me: because it is certain, that Alexander made but one expedition against the Persians; at least, (which is most to our purpose) that he never passed the Euphrates but once in these parts.

As to Ptolemy's placing Thapsacus in Arabia Deserta, whereas all other authors place it in Syria, it is but very little material; because though it is really within the limits of Syria, yet it stands [5] in the desert which adjoins to Arabia. This great geographer places Thapsacus in thirty-five degrees of latitude; but as he puts all the sea-coast half a degree too far towards the south, so I have ventured to place this in 35° 30'.

---

3 What Pliny says, Book v. cap. 26. *Scinditur Euphrates a Zeugmate octoginta tribus millibus passuum; et parte læva in Mesopotamiam, vadit per ipsam Seleuciam, circa eam præfluenti infusus Tigri,* is sufficient to persuade us, that either there is some error in the text, or that Zeugma was a lax term applied to several places; for Zeugma, properly so called, stood somewhere near the place where Bir now stands, from whence, to the end of the mountains of Mesopotamia, is near three hundred miles; and from thence to the plain country of Babylonia, where this division most assuredly was, must be above four hundred miles; so that instead of eighty, perhaps it should be eight hundred.

4 *De diversis nimirum expeditionibus intelligenda videntur discrebantes auctorum narrationes.* Dissert. page 8.

5 The desert begins two or three leagues from Aleppo. Tavernier, Book ii. cap. 3.

The army having passed the Euphrates, marched upon the banks of it, for the most part: I say, for the most part, because they did not do it constantly; since Xenophon tells us, pag. 26. b. i. that some of their marches were very long, when Cyrus had a mind the army should go on, till they came to water or forage. Now they cannot be supposed to quicken their marches for want of water, while they travelled on the bank of so fine a river. We are but little acquainted with the course of the Euphrates, though several travellers have sailed down it. It is probable, that the river makes some great windings towards the south, where no man that is acquainted with the country, would keep to the bank of it; one of these Rauwolf mentions, [6] which took them up more than half a day to pass.

Strabo makes the distance between Thapsacus and Babylon, following the course of the Euphrates, (that is, the route this army took,) [7] to be four thousand eight hundred stadia, and, as it is repeated very often, we depend upon it, there is no error crept into the text: and as the Greeks in Alexander's time, and for several years afterwards, travelled this way, the distance must be very well known. However, Xenophon, in his account of this march, makes it a great deal more, as we shall see by laying the several numbers together: namely,

	Parasangs.
From Thapsacus, through Syria, to the river [8] Araxes, in 9 days,	50
To the river Masca, unknown to modern writers, in 5 days,	35
To Pylæ, in 13 days, ...	90
In Babylonia, 3 days, ...	12
March in order of battle, p. 187, 1 day,	3
March with less circumspection, 1 day, suppose,	3

---

6 He says, that " on the ninth of October they came to a point called Eusy, which took them up more than half a day to pass." So that if they were above half a day in reaching the point, it is probable that the bent of the river was more than double, and must take them more than a day to get round, which could not be an inconsiderable distance, as the stream was in their favour.

7 Book ii. page 82, &c.

8 This river Rauwolf calls Chabu, (not observing the r in the termination) and says there is a castle named Sere at the mouth of it, p. ii. cap. 5. There was a castle in this place in the days of Julian the Apostate, which Zosimus calls Circesium, Book iii.

It is plain from what is said con- ⎫
cerning the retreat of Arimus, |
after the battle, p. 192, that up- ⎬   4
on the day of battle, they had |
marched,   ⎭

—————
197

Which amounts to no less than five thousand nine hundred and ten stadia: now if we consider that they were yet a considerable distance [1] on this side Babylon, (Plutarch says five hundred stadia) we must perceive this account swelled prodigiously above the truth. All the solution that I can pretend to give to this difficulty is, that the Persians, who were the guides of this expedition, must mark out the distances according to their fancies: that excessive heat and hunger are companions, that make a journey seem tedious and long; and consequently, when their Persian friends told them they had marched so many parasangs, the Greeks made no hesitation to believe them, in order to rest themselves. And, indeed, if we attentively consider the marches, as set down in Xenophon, we shall find most of them too long for so great an army to perform, especially as they must have a prodigious quantity of carriages along with them, not only to convey their provisions, but also the accoutrements of the heavy-armed men. For instance, from the Araxes to the Masca, they marched in five days thirty-five parasangs, which is very near twenty-four miles a day. From Masca to Pylæ, they despatched in thirteen days ninety parasangs, which is very near twenty-four miles one day with another; too much to be performed by an army of near one hundred and twenty thousand men, in the middle of summer, in the latitude of thirty-four, and with such great numbers of attendants as they must of necessity have along with them.

In marching through the country of Babylon, they came to the canals which were cut between the Tigris and Euphrates, in order, as most authors agree, to circulate the waters of the latter, which would otherwise drown all the adjacent country, when the snows melt upon the Armenian mountains. Xenophon says, these canals fall out of the Tigris into the Euphrates; whereas [2] Strabo and Pliny

say the contrary, and Arrian goes so far as to affirm, that the level of the Tigris is much lower than that of the Euphrates; so that the water must necessarily run always one way. Our modern travellers inform us, that the country between these two rivers is, in these parts, rich low land, something like the province of Holland: so that it is more than probable, that these canals were cut to circulate the waters of the one river as much as the other; and that as the Tigris is by much the most rapid of the two, the water must come down with greater fury, and stand in more need of being diverted when it arrived in the level country. It is worth our observation, that these two great rivers could never swell at the same season; because as the mountains out of which the Tigris rises, lie in the south of Armenia, and those in which the Euphrates has its source in the north, it is certain that the snows upon the former must melt sooner than those upon the latter. Accordingly, we find the author of Ecclesiasticus mentions the overflowing of the Tigris [3] in the latter end of March, and beginning of April. And Pliny assures us, that the Euphrates overflows in [4] July and August. It might so happen that the Greek or Roman travellers, from whom these authors could have had their intelligence (all travellers generally choose the spring to perform long journeys in) might not arrive at Babylon early enough in the season, to see any thing of the rise of the Tigris. But having spent March, April, May, and perhaps June, in their journey, they must find the channel of the Euphrates quite full, and discharging the superfluous waters with great rapidity, into the Tigris; sufficient to persuade any common observer, that the level of the former must be above that of the latter. However, had it been so in reality, the Euphrates must quickly have forsook his old course, and in a few years have joined the Tigris, by one or more of these

———

1 Xenophon says no less than three thousand and sixty stadia, but this I shall speak more particularly to by and by.

2 See Mr Spelman's note 5, page 187.

3 Chap. xxiv. 25. Pliny also says, that the Tigris overflows in such a manner, as to run into a river which falls into the Euphrates, B. vi. cap. 27. Now, if it does this in the upper parts, where its current is so very swift, as to merit the appellation of arrow, what can we expect in the lower country, where the land is flat, and its stream more gentle?

4 *Increscit (nempe Euphrates) statis diebus, Mesopotamiam inundans, sole obtinente vicesimam partem Cancri : minui incipit in Virgine, Leone transgresso. In totum vero remeat in vicesima nona parte Virginis,* B. v. 26.

canals; for Strabo, and modern observers have assured us, that the land between these rivers is fat and very rotten, and, consequently must soon have been worn deep and broad enough to convey any quantity of water, which, for a constancy, could run through it. When our author was in this country, I find, by computation, was towards the latter end of September, a time when both the Euphrates and Tigris must be very low; and, therefore, some art must be used in order to make these canals so full of water. Clearchus, we see, suspected it to be the case, and no doubt but he had good reason for these suspicions. The Tigris was much the smaller river of the two, and consequently the more manageable. It is therefore probable, that they had some works in it, in order to raise the water to a proper height; and that when Cyrus approached with his army, it is likely the king ordered the country to be laid under water, as far as they were able to do it, with a design to retard and harass them as much as possible. This would turn the water through the canals into the Euphrates, and may be the reason why Xenophon differs from other authors in this particular.

Speaking of the magnitude of the Euphrates, puts me in mind of what Strabo says of it, where he informs us that it runs through the middle of ancient Babylon, and was a stadium in breadth, [5] Ὁ γὰρ ποταμὸς διὰ μέσον ἦν τῆς πόλεως σταδιαῖος τὸ πλάτος: which Calmet, with the generosity of [6] modern writers, takes for granted, without examining what difficulties such an assertion is loaded with. Xenophon, who forded it himself, affirms, that this river is four stadia broad at Thapsacus, above five hundred miles higher than Babylon: and all the world is sensible, that rivers do not grow narrower the further they proceed in their course. What surprises me most is, that

Calmet should fall into this mistake, when he had Rauwolf before him, and quotes him in this very article, as an author of considerable credit. This writer travelled through these parts two hundred years ago, and speaking of the bridge of Babylon (some of the piers of which at this day remain), says thus: " The arches of it are built of burnt brick, and so strong that it is admirable: and that so much the more, because all along the river, as we came from Bir, where the river is a great deal smaller, we saw never a bridge: wherefore, I say, it is admirable which way they could build a bridge here, where the river is at least [7] half a league broad, and very deep besides." p. ii. c. 7. Sir Thomas Herbert, who had been in these parts, and it is probable had taken a view of the river hereabouts, who, though he falls into a great many [8] mistakes in matters of learning, yet he must be allowed to be a competent judge in those things that are the objects of sense, assures us, that the Euphrates at ancient Babylon was well nigh double the breadth of the Thames at London. That Xenophon was not mistaken in the breadth of the river at Thapsacus, and that there is no error crept into the text, we may be convinced from what our ingenious countryman Maundrel says on the same subject, where he assures us, [9]

---

5 Book xvi. p. 738.

6 Dean Prideaux, Connec. Part I. Book ii. adheres to this sense of Strabo, though he quotes Diodorus Siculus, who tells us, Book ii. that the bridge of Babylon was five stadia long. Now instead of correcting Strabo by such an authority, he gives it this unnatural turn, viz. that the bridge must be a great deal longer than the river was broad: though he himself has but just before told us, that the person who built this bridge had banked up the river on each side with brick, in such a manner as the river could never overflow; so that to make the bridge five times as long as the distance between these two banks, must be a needless, not to say a ridiculous piece of work.

7 It must here be observed, that when travellers mention the breadth of rivers, we must not take what they say to be strictly true: they have no instruments with them to determine distances; and had they instruments, the generalty would not know how to make use of them. What Rauwolf says in this place, must be understood as spoken very much at large, half a league being thirteen stadia. Diodorus Siculus, we have seen, makes the bridge over it five stadia. Now as a bridge is by much more easily measured than a river, and as Xenophon makes it four stadia at Thapsacus, we may suppose that five stadia, a little more than half an English mile, was the breadth of the Euphrates at Babylon.

8 For instance, he tells us that Ninus enlarged Nineveh the Great upon Tigris, formerly called Nysib and Rauhaboth, and since Mosul, being indeed rather the ruins of Seleucia. Page 226. He also informs us from Xenophon, that Cyrus had one hundred and twenty-five millions of pounds when he marched against his brother Artaxerxes. Page 249.

9 Journey from Aleppo to Beer, April 20, where he tells us, that the river is as broad as the Thames at London, and that a long bullet-gun could not shoot a ball over it, but it dropped into the water. By this it appears that it is a great deal broader than the Thames at London, for a common fowling-piece will carry a ball, without any elevation, more than twice the breadth of the Thames at Blackwall. At London bridge the Thames is nine hundred feet over: now supposing it one hundred feet more at Blackwall, will make it one thousand, that

that a long bullet-gun could not shoot a ball over the Euphrates at Jerabolus. This I take to be the [1] ancient Zeugma, above two thousand stadia, or two hundred and thirty miles, higher up the river than Thapsacus. So that if it is so broad at Jerabolus, we cannot think four stadia (not quite half a mile) any thing extraordinary for its breadth at Thapsacus.

As to the situation of Babylon, I confess, I can find nothing to determine it with any exactness. Though astronomical observations were made there constantly for several centuries, yet less remains (if less can remain) of these, than of that once so famous city. Mr Bedford [2] has reckoned up a great variety of opinions concerning the situation of this place, and at last himself adheres to one of the worst. He quotes three of the principal Arabians, who, it is highly probable, had every one of them been upon the spot, and made some sort of observation to determine the latitude. For as they differ among themselves, they could not copy from any that went before, nor from one another; and as the difference is but very small, it might be owing to the inaccuracy of their instruments. But he chooses to forsake these, and follow Bochart, who places it [3] almost a whole degree further to the north. As to the longitude, he, again from Bochart, makes it 77° 46′, which is a great deal too much: for as the longitude of Scanderun has been determined [4] to be 55° 25′, so upon the foregoing

supposition, the meridian distance between Babylon and Scanderun must be 22° 21′, which, upon a little examination, will be found very much to exceed the truth. For instance, from Scanderun to Aleppo, is not sixty miles; which, considering the winding of roads and the difference of latitude, cannot exceed one degree. From Aleppo to Thapsacus, Xenophon makes forty-five parasangs, which upon this parallel, the difference of latitude above one degree, cannot make above two and a half degrees. From Thapsacus to Babylon was four thousand eight hundred stadia, following the course of the Euphrates. Now, allowing for the difference of latitude, and bending of the river, we will suppose [5] Babylon more to the east by three hundred geographical miles, (and this I am persuaded will be thought too much) which being reduced, will be found to be six degrees. So that the meridian distance between Scanderun and Babylon, cannot upon any reasonable calculation be supposed more than [6] nine and a half degrees, which added to the longitude of Scanderun, makes 64° 55′, the longitude of Babylon. Bochart therefore has placed this city no less than thirteen degrees too far to the east. As for the Arabians, Eachard, &c. they followed Ptolemy ; and as he had, for the most part, nothing but imagination to determine the longitude of places by, it is not to be wondered at, if he generally does it in a manner very wide from the truth.

---

doubled is two thousand, almost three stadia and one half : so that we may conclude this at least to be the breadth of the Euphrates at Jerabolus. Pliny says, Book v. cap. 24. "Arabiam inde læva, Oroen dictam regionem, trischœna mensura, dextraque Commagenem, disterminat (nempe Euphrates)." P. Hardouin observes upon the place, "Amnem ibi latum esse ait schœnis tribus." Now Pliny assures us, Book xii. cap. 14. the schœnus consists of forty stadia, or five Roman miles ; so that according to Hardouin, the Euphrates must be fourteen English miles broad at Bir. However, as the sentence will admit another construction, we have no occasion to father such an absurdity upon Pliny. I do not know whether it is worth while to take notice of a small mistake or two in Delisle's maps. He makes the Euphrates five hundred feet broad, and the pyramid near Larissa upon the Tigris two hundred paces high, and one hundred paces square. Whereas Xenophon makes the river four stadia broad, i. e. five hundred paces, or two thousand five hundred feet ; and the pyramid one hundred feet square, and two hundred high.

1 I conclude so from the many beautiful ruins found there, and especially from the remains of a bridge said to be thereabouts. Vide Maundrel *ubi supra.*

2 Scripture Chronology, Book i. cap. 1.

3 The Arabians place it in 33° 20′. Bochart in 34° 15′.

4 The French place Paris in 20° long. and therefore Mr Delisle makes the longitude of Alexandretta to be but 54° 15′. However, as we reckon London 19° east from Ferro, and Paris 2° 25′ from London, and as Mr Chaselles found the meridian distance between Paris and Scanderun to be 2° 16′, i. e. 34° , so the true longitude of Scanderun is 55° 15′.

5 This way of reckoning is in some measure confirmed by Josephus, Antiq. viii. c. 6. where he says that Thadomira (that is Palmyra) was one day's journey from the Euphrates, and six from Great Babylon. Here by day's journey, is meant the horseman's journey, or sixty miles ; so that from the Euphrates over-against Palmyra to Babylon is three hundred miles. But Thapsacus stands somewhat more to the west than this part of the Euphrates ; that is, the course of the river is S. and by E. and S. S. E. so that three hundred geographical miles must be pretty near the true meridian distance between Thapsacus and Babylon. Pliny indeed affirms, Book v. cap. 25. that from Palmyra to Seleucia upon the Tigris is three hundred and thirty-seven miles ; but as other copies say five hundred and thirty-seven, I must leave it to the decision of the critics.

6 Mr Delisle makes the distance between Babylon and Scanderun to be pretty nearly equal to that between Babylon and Smyrna. Now the meridian distance of

After the[7] battle, and the death of Cyrus, the Greeks, though victorious, had no hope left, but that of getting back again to their own country. But to effect this was a matter of considerable difficulty. To return by the same way they came, was impossible, because all their provisions were spent, and they were to march through the deserts of Arabia: and they wanted guides to show them another road. At last they entered into a truce with the king, one of the conditions of which was, that he should conduct them safe to their own country. The officers sent by the king to perform this, led them through the middle of Babylonia, a country intersected with canals and ditches kept full of water, in order to convince the Greeks that all endeavours to arrive at Babylon must be in vain, if the people of the country were their enemies. I am far from being of Mr Spelman's opinion, where he supposes the distance mentioned by Xenophon between the field of battle and Babylon, three thousand and sixty stadia, to be a mistake of the transcriber. The Persians, without doubt, persuaded them the distance was so great, and led them through the country with a design to convince them, that whoever should attempt to march thither, must be entirely discouraged and baffled by the many difficulties he would meet with. They were no strangers, it is likely, to Daniel's prophecies, which were wrote in their capital, and in their language: and which plainly foretold that their empire should be overturned by the Greeks.

This they might endeavour to avert by such arts as I have mentioned; with a design that if any of these soldiers should get back again to Greece, (which however they did all in their power to obstruct) they should spread such an account among their countrymen of the difficulties they had met with, as should for the future put a stop to all undertakings of this kind. There can no other reason, I believe, be assigned for conducting them to Sitace: for it was entirely out of their way, and they must pass[8] by Babylon to arrive at it. This town stood near the Tigris, and part of the province of Babylon was from it called Sitacene. Strabo says, the road from Babylon to Susa lay through it. Now, as Susa was near S. E. from Babylon, Sitace must lie beyond Babylon from hence, at the distance of five hundred stadia, as the same author informs us. Xenophon confirms this, by making it twenty parasangs, or six hundred stadia, from Sitace to Opis, a large trading town upon the Tigris, about the place where Bagdat now stands.

From Opis the army marched up the Tigris, till they arrived at the mountains of the Carduchians, at present called the Curdes, the same untractable people, and show the same regard to travellers they did to these Greek wanderers. They stroll about upon the mountains from hence as far as the springs of the Euphrates, and plunder every one they meet with, that is weaker than themselves. They will be under no sort of government, and pay as little respect to the Turk, who pretends to be their master, as their forefathers did to the kings of Persia. In all this tract, I can find very little for a geographer to exercise himself upon. If Rauwolf had Xenophon's Anabasis along with him, or the contents of it fresh in his memory, he might have made several remarks, which would have given great light into our author; for he travelled over the same ground from Bagdat to these mountains.

It took up the army seven days to cross this inhospitable country, wherein they suffered more than from all the great armies of the Persians. At last they came to the Centrites, a river which, in those days, served as a boundary between the Curdes and Armenia. Mons. Delisle has made this river run eastward, and

---

the two latter of these places is by observation found to be nine degrees; so, as the difference of longitude between Scanderun and Babylon is nine degrees.

7 Plutarch (in Artax.) speaking of the loss of this battle, lays all the blame upon Clearchus, for not according to Cyrus's order, bringing his Greeks to front the king's centre; but I think the conduct of Clearchus may be easily vindicated. This general very well knew, from the mock-encounter at Tyriæum, what was to be expected from the rest of Cyrus's forces, viz. that they would run away at the first onset, and himself with his handful of Greeks be left alone to encounter with the king's army. A handful they might be called with the greatest propriety, being thirteen thousand against one million two hundred thousand, (for so many the king's army was supposed to consist of) Clearchus therefore kept close to the river, with a design not be surrounded by such prodigious numbers; which had it happened at the beginning of the battle, before the Greeks had tried the Persian metal, might have disheartened his men, and lost the day. Had Cyrus relied upon Clearchus's promise, (viz. that all should go well) and waited patiently for the event, all had gone well, he had won the day, and been king of Persia.

8 I suppose here that they were conducted to the left towards the Tigris, and not suffered to pass within sight of Babylon.

fall into the [1] lake of Van. I have ventured to turn its course westward; because I take it to be a branch of the Lycus, which, when it falls into the Tigris, is so very considerable a river, that Rauwolf [2] says, is at least a long mile broad, and must come out of this country from the east; for had it come from the north, the Persians, after the rout at [3] Arbela, would have been under no necessity of running such risks in attempting to pass it. Besides, we ought to reflect, that in these seven days the Greeks could not have travelled more than seventy miles, considering the many obstructions they met with in the country of the Carduchians; and that as the course of the Tigris is in these parts from the N. W. and the course of the army to the north, they could not be fifty miles from the Tigris at the place where they crossed the Centrites. This river was not a very small one; Xenophon makes it two hundred feet broad, and consequently, if it runs towards the east, must rise at least thirty miles towards the west; and then what room can we find for the rise and progress of so large a river as the Lycus, which must drain the East for a considerable distance?

From hence the army marched over the plains of Armenia to the river Teleboas, which Mons. Delisle in his [4] dissertation and map, in the Memoirs of the Royal Academy of Sciences, entirely overlooks, and passes from the [5] head of the Tigris to the Euphrates, without taking any notice of, or laying down any river between them; however, in his large map published in the year 1723, entitled,

Retraites des Dix Mille, he has rectified mistake, and laid down the Teleboas as arm of the most easterly branch of the I phrates, which M. Delisle has discovered fr Ptolemy, to rise fifty leagues to the south-e of the springs above Ertzrum : and which makes the Greeks pass just at the fount: So that their passing of this branch of the I phrates must be more to the eastward by least two degrees than the meridian of Er rum : but how little this squares with the si ation of these countries, a small degree of fsection will convince us. We have seen abo that, upon the most favourable calculation, t longitude of Babylon cannot be more th 64° 55'. After the battle, the Greeks trave led upon the banks of the Tigris, till th came to the Carduchian mountains : now, the course of this river is from the N. W. an W. N. W. so they must diminish the longitud considerably by this long march. Delisle map makes it three degrees; so that they en tered the Carduchians' country in longitud 51° 55'. But the Royal Academy of Sciences of which M. Delisle was geographer, place Ertzrum [6] in 68° 45', so that the sources of th Euphrates, which M. Delisle, from Ptolemy places fifty leagues S. E. of the Ertzrum, mus be at least in 70° 45' longitude. Upon this supposition, therefore, the Greeks, in travelling three degrees of latitude, for so much M. Delisle makes it from their entering the Carduchians' country to their fording the Euphrates, must deviate to the east no less than nine degrees; which is quite incredible, especially as Xenophon himself tells us, and M. Delisle repeats his words, that their course was north. Again, let us view this affair in another light : Tournefort informs us, (vol. ii.

1 He does not indeed give it any name in his maps of this expedition, but in his other maps he makes it the lake of Van.

2 Part ii. cap. ix. This must be understood with some allowance : Rauwolf assures us he was in very great fear while he forded this river, and therefore might think it four or five times bigger than in reality it is.

3 This place is still known by the name of Harpel. Rauwolf, ubi sup.

4 Entitled, "Determination Geographique de la Situation et de l'Etendue de Pays Traversee," &c. in the Memoirs of the Acad. Royale, An. 1725, p. 55.

5 M. Delisle brings Herodotus to prove, that there were in these parts three rivers of the name of Tigris. This he does in order to show that the Greeks did not approach near the head of the Tigris properly so called, viz. that which flows by Diarbekir; but supposes it the most easterly branch. However, he might have saved himself a good deal of trouble, had he attended to Xenophon's words, who does not say they passed the head of the Tigris, or were near it, but only, that they were now advanced above it. Vol. i. page 268.

6 This places Ertzrum farther to the east, than any geographer I can meet with will allow. I am surprised that neither Mr D'Anville, nor the English editor of Du Halde's China, in folio, takes any notice at all of this circumstance, in determining the situation of the Caspian sea. The greatest longitude they are willing to allow to Astrakhan, is but 68° 55', very little more than this of Ertzrum; whereas there must be at least four degrees of difference between them. Observations are material evidences in geography. The Acad. Royal, An. 1699, assures us these situations were grounded upon observations. How therefore this article could slip the notice of persons so much interested in the discovery of it, is to me very surprising. Not but that I have reasons (to myself very strong ones) to think that those places are not situated so far to the east; however, as there is no reasoning against facts, I desist.

let. 6.) that from Ertzrum to Aleppo is thirty-five days' journey; and Tavernier (book ii. c. 4.), that from Bir to Mousul is but fifteen days' journey. Now, as Bir is in the road from Aleppo to Ertzrum, or very near it, and [7] four days' journey from Aleppo, so it will be thirty-one days' journey from Bir to Ertzrum. Bir is in lat. 37° 10'; Ertzrum in 39° 56' 35'', and Mousul is about 35° 30'. So that Ertzrum is more to the northward with respect to Bir, than Mousul is the southward by 1° 6' 35'', for which we must allow five days' journey; therefore Ertzrum is more to the east than Mousul by eleven days' journey. But M. Delisle makes the Greeks enter the Carduchian mountains a little [8] to the west of Mousul; and consequently as they travelled north, must pass the Euphrates a great deal to the west of Ertzrum; whereas he has laid down their route above two hundred miles to the east of Ertzrum. M. Delisle tells us of one M. Duval, formerly geographer to the king of France, who drew a map of this expedition, and laid down the countries as best suited his own notions, without any regard to their true dimensions; by which he doubled the Persian dominions, and made Asia Minor to contain one thousand five hundred square leagues, instead of six hundred. How much M. Delisle has succeeded better, we have in some measure seen above. He quotes P. Beze's authority for the latitude of Trebisond, but says not one word about the longitude: the reason of this seems to me to be, that, if he had, it would have overset his whole scheme. He places Babylon in 62° long. the Royal Academy places Trebisond in 65° long., so that had the places been laid thus down, and the route of the army made somewhere towards the north, they must have arrived [9] at the Euxine a good deal to the west of Trebisond. In order to

remedy this, he has laid down Trebisond in 57 and a half, and Ertzrum in 58; has made the ten thousand, from the Carduchian mountains, steer a N. N. E. course: so that when they came into Georgia, they turned to their left, and, travelling afterwards near three hundred miles due west, arrived at Trebisond. Whereas had the Black Sea been [10] extended to its due length, the Greeks must have arrived at the shore of it where he places Taochir, the place where he makes them turn to the left.

I think I may venture to say, that M. Delisle is equally unhappy in his guesses, with respect to the ancient measures of the Greeks. He compares the distances of places, mentioned by Xenophon, with their true distance determined by astronomical observations. Xenophon makes the distance between Ephesus and the gates of Syria nearly equal to that between the gates of Syria and Babylon. Modern observers have discovered, that from Smyrna (near Ephesus) to Scanderun (near the gates of Syria) is pretty near equal to the distance of Scanderun from Bagdat (near ancient Babylon.) [11] The same, he tells us, may be said of their return from Babylon to Trapezus: but that comparing these distances together, he concludes, that the measures of the ancient Greeks were much smaller than we suppose them; that a stadium in Xenophon's days was but about half so much as it was in the times of the Romans. He supposes, that in ancient times they made use of a common pace in the mensuration of land, which is no more than [12] two feet and a half; whereas, afterwards the pace was double, i. e. five feet. He says, what confirms him in this opinion is, the quantity of a degree determined by Aristotle, who says, in his book De Cœlo, that the circumference of the earth is four hundred thousand stadia, which being reduced, gives one thousand one

---

7 Tavernier says it is four days' journey for the horse caravan: but then I imagine he must reckon the passing of the river into the time. Book ii. cap. iv.

8 This cannot be, because had they advanced up the Tigris as far as Mousul, they must have passed the Lycus, which, as it is larger than any river they passed after the Tigris, Xenophon must have taken notice of it.

9 Especially if we allow, as above, three degrees for their westing on the banks of the Tigris. There is in Xenophon one material article not taken notice of by Mr Delisle, and that is, that where they crossed the river Telebous, the country was called the Western Armenia; which name would but ill suit with the country two hundred miles east of Ertzrum.

10 Arrian, who measured the Euxine, makes it from the mouth of the Thracian Bosphorus to Trebisond seven thousand and thirty-five stadia, that is, about eight hundred and five miles English. Tournefort does not always mention the distances; but, by what he says, we may gather he made it about eight hundred miles, whereas Tavernier makes it nine hundred and seventy miles, and Gimelli nine hundred.

11 His meaning is, that upon his supposition it agrees pretty well with modern observations, i. e. from Babylon to Trebisond is about half as much as Xenophon makes it.

12 One step or common stride in walking; whereas the pace was the return of the same foot, or two strides.

hundred and eleven and one-third to each degree. However, upon examination, we cannot find that Aristotle ever determined the quantity of a degree, or that it was at all determined in his days. He is in this book speaking of the smallness of the body of the earth, plainly discoverable from the different elevations of the stars at different places, not far distant from each other; where he says, " [1] That all the mathematicians who have attempted by reasoning to discover the earth's circumference, affirm that it is four hundred thousand-stadia." All we can gather from hence is, that, comparing the different elevations at several places together, they made a guess at the earth's periphery. Strabo seems to intimate, that Eratosthenes was the first who applied celestial observations to determine the magnitude of the earth; and [2] M. Cassini is positive in this opinion. However, we will suppose that Aristotle did determine the quantity of a degree to be one thousand one hundred and eleven and one-third of the stadia of his time, and that Eratosthenes discovered it to contain seven hundred of his time, it will then of consequence follow, that between the days of Aristotle and Eratosthenes, the Greek measures were changed in the same proportion as one thousand one hundred and eleven and one-third bears to seven hundred, which is a supposition that will hardly be allowed, when we consider, that from the death of the one to the birth of the other was little more than [3] forty-years. Besides, if this method of arguing is to take place, there would be no end of altering the measures of antiquity. Xenophon makes it from Thapsacus to the place of battle five thousand nine hundred and ten stadia, which, with the five hundred mentioned by Plutarch, makes the distance from Thapsacus to Babylon six thousand four hundred and ten stadia. But in Aristotle's time, i. e. at Alexander's expedition, about seventy years after Xenophon was in this country,. it was found to be four thousand eight hundred; so that the stadium must be increased near one-fourth in this space of time.

It is very unlucky for M. Delisle's hypothesis, that the ancient Greeks never made use of such a measure as the pace, or had any such term, that I can find: all their measures were by the foot, and by such compositions of it, as are very well known, such were the fathom, six feet; plethrum, one hundred; and stadium, six hundred. This last was the longest measure, and therefore they always compute large distances by it. When the Greek foot was first fixed, is, like the beginning of most other things, I believe, quite unknown; but to be sure, a great many centuries before the times we are treating of. And when the standard-measure of any nation is once fixed, and becomes current, it is not only needless, but extremely difficult, afterwards to alter it. Perhaps nothing less than the total destruction of a people, or a universal change of customs can effect this. But suppose, for argument's sake, we allow that the Greeks had such a measure as the pace, and that originally this pace contained two feet and a half, but afterwards was disused, and the geometrical pace, that of five feet, took place: yet how could this affect the stadium, which contained six hundred of such feet as the pace was composed of? As the foot was the foundation of both, so they could have no influence the one upon the other. Indeed, had the stadium been composed of a determinate number of paces, as the Roman mile was, M. Delisle's argument would have had some show of reason in it, some probability to support it: but to apply two sorts of paces, which consisted of different numbers of feet, to the stadium which consisted of a determinate number of feet of the same length, is such an impropriety, as I am surprised so sagacious a person as M. Delisle most assuredly was, should fall into.

But it may be answered, that the difficulty still remains. If Xenophon's measures are applied to the true distances, determined by astronomy, they will be found double : for from Ephesus to the gates of Syria, is made to be about eight thousand stadia; whereas its real distance is not five thousand. To this it may be replied, that great armies, with such numbers of carriages as they must always have with

---

1 Καὶ τῶν μαθηματικῶν ὅσοι τὸ μέγεθος ἀναλογίζεσθαι συρῶνται τῆς περιφερείας, εἰς τετταράκοντα λέγουσιν εἶναι μυριάδας σταδίων.—Which cannot be understood that any one had actually measured the contents of a degree; but only that they had guessed at the whole by a computation or reckoning.

2 Acad. Royale, anno 1694. Pliny calls this undertaking of Eratosthenes, Improbum annum; but adds, Verumita subtili argumentatione comprehensum, ut pudeat non credere. Book ii. cap. 108.

3 Aristotle died in the hundred and fourteenth Olympiad, and Eratosthenes was born in the hundred and twenty-sixth.

em, cannot go the nearest way; they must serve the disposition of mountains and rivers, and call at towns a good distance from the direct road, upon the account of provisions. This was undoubtedly the case of the army before us, which, if joined to what I said above about their Persian guides, may give a tolerable account why the distances are so magnified in their march from Ephesus to Babylon. But their return the case is very different: at this time they reckoned for themselves, and if we take the distance from Opis (near which Bagdat now stands) to their passing the Euphrates below Ertzrum, we shall find, allowing for their course westward along the bank of the Tigris, I say we shall find it correspond pretty near with the astronomical observations.

Whereabouts they passed the Euphrates, I cannot take upon me to say; but we have seen above, that it must be considerably to the west of Ertzrum, below the junction of its [4] two branches; for had they passed two rivers by the name of Euphrates, Xenophon would certainly have taken notice of it. Indeed he says the springs of this river were not far off; but he speaks not of his own knowledge, and οὐ πρόσω is an indeterminate expression, which does not at all fix the distance; besides, the river was so deep, that it reached up to their middle, which is very considerable, as it was in the depth of winter, the snow lay upon the ground, and consequently could be supplied with no water but from the springs.

---

[4] I cannot pass without taking notice of a mistake in Tournefort, who says, vol. ii. let. 6. that one of these ranches runs a days' journey to the south of Ertzrum, he other a day and a half, or two days' journey to the orth of it; whereas, he has told us but just before, that he bridge of Elijah is but about six miles from Ertzrum. t is well known that, in the East great distances are measured by days' journeys, small ones by hours: it is therefore probable, that in discoursing about the country, he was told it was so many hour's journey, which he put down journee, without distinguishing it from a day's journey. Calmet says, that Strabo and Pliny differ from each other almost in every thing concerning the Euphrates. For that Pliny represents it first running in the south, and then to the west: whereas Strabo affirms that it first runs west, and then south. However, upon examination, I believe they will be found to agree exactly; and that Calmet has mistaken Pliny's meaning. This great naturalist, B. v. cap. 24. compares Mount Taurus and the Euphrates to two great champions contending with each other; that the mountain, though twelve miles broad, is not able to stop the river; but, however, prevails so far, as not to suffer it to have its way, but diverts it to the south, whereas before its course was westward.

From the Euphrates they proceeded still north for three days. We are certain that their course was north, because our author informs us, that ἄνεμος Βορρᾶς ἐναντίος ἔπνει· viz. that the north wind blew full in their faces, in so fierce a manner as to scorch and benumb the men. Now had they not thought themselves under a necessity of travelling north, they would never have chose to face so terrible a wind as this. They still proceeded one day farther; we must naturally conclude towards the same point of the compass: and then put themselves under the conduct of the bailiff of the village.

And here we meet with the greatest difficulty in the whole book. [5] Ertzrum is but five days' journey from the Euxine: and the Greeks, where they passed the Euphrates, could not be much farther from it. We have seen they marched to the northward three days fifteen parasangs; and another day, the distance not mentioned, (suppose five parasangs) which amount to above sixty miles; so that they must be at this time half way to the coast of the Black Sea. Insomuch that, had they kept still on in the same course, they must in three or four days more have arrived at Cerazunt, Trebisond, or somewhere thereabouts. But, instead of this, we find they made it no less than forty-five days' march, and several of these very long ones, before they came to Trebisond. This is very surprising, and the more so, when we consider, that from the sources of the Euphrates to the banks of the Caspian, is not more than thirteen days' journey. So that these wanderers were enclosed between the Euxine, the Caspian, the Euphrates, and Mount Caucasus: and how they could make such marches for forty-five days together, in this space, is, I confess, entirely beyond my comprehension.

We find after the battle, when the Greeks were without guides, that they directed themselves [6] by the sun; and Xenophon in his speech to the army, in the fifth book plainly shows, that they understood their compass well enough to know the four principal points. How therefore they could be so prodigiously misled, is very strange. However, we must remember, that in after-times, when these parts were better known, Artavasdes, the king

---

[5] Tournefort, vol. ii. let. 6.
[6] Page 203.

of the country, abused Anthony [1] by mislead-
ing him. We must consider also, that when
the Greeks were in this country it was in the
middle of winter; my account makes it January; and that these countries are at this time
of the year extremely subject to fogs; so that
they might not see the sun for several days together: and consequently the old bailiff, like a
true subject of the king of Persia, might take
such an opportunity to mislead them, in order
to distress and destroy them. It is highly probable it was this that made him run away, and
leave his son behind him: [2] for had he done
his duty, it is not at all likely that he would
have left his son in such circumstances. He
might have some ambition in him, though his
estate was low; though he was but the superior of a [3] Troglodyte village, yet he might
hope that the sacrificing of a son might raise
him to the government of a province; as we see
great numbers of garreteers among us, who
think themselves qualified to be at least ministers of state.

After the Greeks had lost their guide, they
marched seven days thirty-five parasangs, and
arrived at the Phasis. This M. Delisle strives
[4] to prove is the Araxes. But by what is

said above, it is quite improbable they c
deviate so far to the east. And to sup
they came to the Araxes, after they had
ed the Euphrates, is still more unlikely;
cause these two rivers rise out of the
mountain, about [5] six miles distant from
other; the Euphrates runs west, and the Ar
east, and then south-east. Now, as the Gr
had passed the Euphrates, and travelled nc
ward four days, they must have left the Ar
so far behind them, that it is very unlikely
could ever come back again to it. I would
ther for the present, till this country is be
discovered, suppose it to be the noted Colc
Phasis. Strabo affirms, that this river has
source in Armenia, [6] Φάσις μέγας ποταμὸς ἐξ
μανίας τὰς ἀρχὰς ἔχων. Dionysius the geograp
says,

———————Φάσις

'Αρξάμενος τὸ πρῶτον ἀπ' οὔρεος 'Αρμενίοιο.

So that the ancients, who knew these countr
much better than we do, gave the Phasis a v
different rise to what is assigned to it by
moderns, placing its source in the mountains
Armenia, probably, by what they say of
long course, not at a great distance from
fountains of the Euphrates and Araxes, espe
ally as Dionysius calls it, the Armenian mou
tain, out of which the Euphrates rises.

This will appear still the more probable,
we seriously attend to what Moses says in I
description of Paradise, Gen. ii. v. 10, 8
where he informs us, that a river proceeded o
of Ngeden to water the garden; and there שׁ
in that place, i. e. in the garden, it was divid
and became into four heads ראשׁים Capita,
the Latin accurately expresses it. The nan
of the first Phisun, which encompasses th
whole country of [7] Khoilh, for so it is written
the original, or perhaps Kloilkh,) where there

---

1 B. xi. p. 524. Where he says he led him round
about more than double the direct way, ἐσούρτε πλίω ἢ
διπλασίαν τῆς εὐθείας, διὰ ἐρῶν, καὶ ἀνοδιῶν, καὶ κυκλευο-
μένος.

2 That is, had he conducted them to towns where they
could get provisions. But instead of this, he carried
them into desolate countries, where he concluded they
must of course be starved; where the first people they
could meet with were the Taochians and Chalybians,
who kept all their provisions in such fastnesses, as the
bailiff might imagine it was impossible for them to force.
And indeed he was not much mistaken in his aim; for
had they not with great courage, and no small address,
stormed the Taochian mountain, it is more than probable
they had every one perished with hunger.

3 The villages of this country do retain the same form
to this day. Gimelli, P. i. b. 3. c. 3. tells us, " He was
in dispute with himself, whether to call the houses caves
or stables, for they are dug out of the earth; that the
roofs are upon a level with the surface of the earth, and
that the men and beasts lodge together in them."

4 The main of his argument consists in this, that Constantine Porphyrogenetes says, that the Phasis runs near
Theodosiopolis, that it parted his empire from Iberia, and
was likewise called Erax. Now Theodosiopolis stood
near the place where Ertzrum now stands; and therefore if the Colchian Phasis rises somewhere in this country, and flows north, it would run as near that city as
the Araxes could do, and would naturally serve as a
boundary between Iberia and the Greek empire. As to
the name, it proves very little; for as araxes signifies a rapid stream, the Persians applied it to a great many rivers.

5 Pliny, Book vi. cap. 9. says, "Araxes eodem mon
oritur, quo Euphrates vi. mill. passuum intervallo
which is confirmed in some measure by Tournefort, w
tells us, vol. ii. l. 7. that the Araxes runs by Ertzrum
which is but six hours from Ertzrum.

6 B. x. p. 498. and again B. xi. p. 529. he say
Ποταμοὶ δὲ πλείους μὲν εἰσιν ἐν τῇ χώρᾳ· γνωριμότατοι
Φάσις μὲν καὶ Λύκος.

7 I can find nothing to convince me that the Hebrew
ever used the ו as a consonant. The ב pronounced sof
as some European nations do at present, supplied th
place of v. Thus קין תובל Thubal Cain, is Vulcan
שׁבע shebang, is seven, and the like. The ו is, I in

gold, and the gold of that country is good; there is also the בדלח and the stone שהם. All which particulars, viz. the name of the river, for Phisun and Phasis are very near the same, the name of the country, and the products of it, do plainly point out the Colchian Phasis, we are now treating of. The ancients are so full of the Colchian gold, that it would be endless to quote all they say upon this subject. The bare mentioning the Argonautic expedition (whether real or fictitious) will be sufficient to persuade any one that Colchis was formerly noted for the best gold. What Pliny [8] says of it may convince us, that the character Moses gives of it is just, where he tells us that the gold of that country is good. As to the בדלח it is supposed by the most learned writers, both Jews and Christians, to signify Crystal, and שהם Emeralds; both which the ancients make Scythia, the country about Phasis, famous for. Solinus [9] informs us, that though crystal was the produce of several parts of Europe, and some places in Asia, yet that of Scythia was the most valuable. And Pliny mentions the emeralds of Scythia in such strong terms, that I must beg leave to transcribe his words, it not being an easy matter to translate them, [10] " Nobilissimi Scythici, ab ea gente, in qua reperiuntur, appellati : nullis major austeritas, nec minus vitii : et quantum Smaragdi a ceteris gemmis distant, tantum Scythici e ceteris Smaragdis."

It may be objected against what I have here said, that it is entirely improbable four rivers should have the same source, and that accordingly these four, which I suppose the rivers of Paradise, namely the Phasis, the Aras, the Tigris, and the Phrat, have their sources at a considerable distance from one another. To this I answer, that the time Moses speaks of was before the flood, when the surface of the earth was very different from what it is at present : For that the universal deluge wrought prodigious changes in the outward parts of this globe, I think, is manifest from the very ruinous appearance of mountains, the unequal dis-

position of their parts, (I mean the heaviest bodies mixed with and often placed above the lightest) and sea-shells found in great quantities, and surprising varieties upon some of the highest of them. Should I attempt to explain the cause and manner of these alterations, or to write a geographical dissertation upon the antediluvian earth, what fate could I expect, when so many great men have handled this subject with so little success.

I am sensible the current of learned men is against me, who almost all agree that Paradise was situated about the place where Babylon afterwards stood ; that the Tigris and Euphrates meet near that place, and afterwards part again : and, therefore, that the heads mentioned by Moses, are those two partings, making four divisions; the two upper being Hiddekil and Phrat, the two lower Phison and Gihon. But with due submission to those great names, who have espoused this opinion, I believe it is founded upon a [11] mistake : for that the Euphrates and Tigris do not meet together till a

---

[11] The original of this mistake seems to have come from Pliny, who says that the Euphrates is divided : (vide p. 20.) that one branch falls into the Tigris at Seleucia, the other runs through Babylon, and is lost in the bogs. However, in another place he informs us, that this part of the river which runs through Seleucia was an artificial canal. Book vi. cap. 28. he calls it Fosa, and tells us who it was that made it. This was known afterwards by the name of Nahar Malcha, the King's River. Strabo tells us the land was so rotten, that the canals which circulated the water were very subject to fill up, so that Alexander caused new ones to be made. At the junction of one of these with the Tigris, Seleucia was built. Trajan and Severus afterwards cleansed this canal for the passage of their fleets to the Tigris Ammianus Marcellinus, lib. xxiv. cap. 6. says, id. (viz. " Fumen Regium, (which he also calls fossile flumen,) antehac Trajanus, postesque Severus, egesto solo, fodiri in modum canalis amplissimi studio curaverat summo, ut aquis illuc ab Euphrate transfusis, naves ad Tigridem commigrarent." Notwithstanding which, when Julian the Apostate came hither, he was forced to cleanse it Zosimus indeed says (B. iii.) the King's River had water in it, but not enough to carry the emperor's fleet without being cleansed : whereas Amm. Marcell. positively affirms that it was quite dry ; all which plainly proves that this was not the natural course of the river. Rauwolf and Herbert both affirm that these two rivers meet a little below Babylon; but as they took it upon trust we must believe Tavernier, who was an eye-witness. Besides, did the rivers join so near Bagdat, why do they complain of selling their boats for a trifle at Elago ? They might carry them to Bagdat, and have as good a market for them as any in the East. But the truth is, the canals are choked up, and there is no getting thither in a boat, but by going above eight hundred miles round about.

---

arine, the הוה, the o or u of the East, and is always u-ed as a vowel.

[8] B. xxxiii. c. 3.

[9] C. xv. speaking of Scythia, " Istic et crystallus, quem licet pars major Europæ et particula Asiæ subministret, pretiosissimam tamen Scythia edit."

[10] B. xxxvii. c. 5.

great many hundred miles below Babylon; nay, it is positively affirmed by the ancients, that originally they did not meet at all, but had their channels distinct quite to the sea; and that the [1] inhabitants of the country by stopping up the Euphrates, in order to water their lands, diverted its course, and turned it into the Tigris. In this manner were the Rhine and the Maese joined together by an earthquake in latter times; Tavernier, who himself sailed down the Tigris, makes the present [2] junction of these two rivers, to be at Gorno, at the distance of one hundred and forty-five leagues, or four hundred and thirty-five miles from Bagdat, only fifteen leagues from Balsora. Indeed, Della Valle, and the East India Pilot, make the river to part again, and fall into the Persian Gulf, by two mouths; but then whoever considers the situation of the country, that it is near the sea, and marshy, that the river is three or four miles broad, and that it overflows the adjacent country every year, will think it a very improper place to make a garden of, for the entertainment and delight of man in his state of innocence. Moses, indeed, says, that this garden was in the east from the place he wrote in, that is, from Arabia Petræa; but this will prove nothing at all, because the Hebrews took no notice of the intermediate points; so that when a place lay any where towards the east, they said it was situated מקדם in the east; in the same manner as we say, that Riga, Revel, and Petersburg, are in the east country. Job says, that "Gold cometh out of the north;" meaning, without doubt, the gold of the Phasis; but then we must consider, that Job lived a great deal further east, than where Moses wrote, bordering upon the Sabeans and Chaldeans, and consequently would have the Colchians near full north.

But to return from this long, and, I am afraid, tedious digression: The Greeks, after they had passed the Phasis, wandered into countries, of which there are but few marks at present to know them by. There is, indeed, a province of Georgia, called Taochir, which, as it has a plain resemblance to the Taochians,

and as the Greeks must be in these parts, it may be presumed to have been formerly inhabited by this people. Who the Chalybians were, or where they lived, I can find nothing remaining. What Mr Hutchinson [3] quotes from Strabo, that Χαλδαίοι Χάλυβις τὸ παλαιὸν ὠνομάζοντο, is plainly meant of the Chalybians, in the next book, who, as Mr Hutchinson himself allows, were very distant both in country and manners, from the people the Greeks had to deal with in this place.

After this they came to the river Harpassus. I do allow with Delisle, that there is a river of this name in this country, which Tournefort calls [4] Arpagi, and makes to fall into the Araxes; but how to bring the Greeks hither, and where to assign them the long marches they had before performed, is, I confess, quite above my sphere. To do any thing tolerable in this particular, we must wait till this country is perfectly discovered; and whenever there shall be a complete map of it exhibited to the world, we may venture to affirm, that then the learned will be able to lay down the march of this army with some accuracy. The next people the Greeks met with in their progress, were the Scythians; probably the same with those Scythians, [5] whom Diodorus places in this country. From hence they came to a city called Gymnias; of which I can meet with nothing, but that the same is called Gymnasia by Diodorus. At this place they were furnished with a guide, who was more just to them than the bailiff had been: for in five days [6] he conducted them to the top of a mountain, from whence they could plainly discern the sea. A sight they had long desired! In a short time after this, they arrived at [7] Trebisond, a Greek city; and keeping near the sea-shore, marched, all that were able, to Cotyora.

And here Xenophon puts an end to his journey; making this the conclusion of the Κατά-

---

1 Pliny, B. vi. c. 27. "Inter duorum amnium ostia xxv. mill. passuum fuere, aut (ut alii tradunt vii.) mill. utroque navigabili: sed longo tempore Euphratem præclusere Orcheni et accolæ agros rigantes: nec nisi Pasitigri defertur in mare."

2 Book ii. c. 8.

3 Dissert. p. xiv.

4 So that Mr Hutchinson had no occasion to correct Diodorus.

5 B. ii. c. 43. Τὸ μὲν οὖν πρῶτον (sc. Σκύθαι) παρὰ τὸν Ἀράξην ποταμὸν ὀλίγοι κατώκουν παντελῶς καὶ διὰ τὴν ἀδοξίαν καταφρονούμενοι.

6 Diodorus Siculus says fifteen days: but in this, and several other particulars, he differs so much from Xenophon, that I suspect, in drawing up the account of this expedition, he made use of some other author.

7 I take no notice of the places they touched at, because Mr Spelman's notes are as full as can be desired.

λευς (Retreat,) as the place of battle was of he 'Ανάβασις (Expedition). The reason of this s, because they afterwards sailed much the greatest part of their way to Greece.

Xenophon himself says that from the field of battle, in Babylonia, to Cotyora, they made eight months; and in the conclusion he informs us, that the whole expedition and retreat took up fifteen months. Now whoever will be at the pains to compute the marches and halts from Sardis to the battle, will find them to amount to exactly six months; but as Xenophon begins the expedition from Ephesus, we should reckon the time from the same place. Therefore, allowing something for their march to, and stay at Sardis; their [8] consulting, and passing the Cilician mountains; their [9] stay and quarrel at Carmande; and the [10] affair of Orontas, (where the soothsayer's ten days plainly show the time not accounted for:) I say, allowing for these, as Xenophon has said nothing about their continuance, we cannot think a month too long a time for them all: which will make just fifteen months from their departure from Ephesus to their arrival at [1] Cotyora. Our author placing this account at the end of his book, has induced all the learned men, I can meet with, to suppose, that the whole of their transactions, from their first setting out, to their joining of Thimbron, took up no more than fifteen months. This has introduced still a worse mistake, by misplacing the year of the expedition in all the chronological tables. Diodorus Siculus places the expedition in the last of the ninety-fourth Olympiad; and Thimbron's passing over into Asia, to make war upon Tissaphernes, in the first of the ninety-fifth Olympiad, and all have followed him, as far as I can perceive, without examining into the affair. However it is most certain, that from their departure under Cyrus, to their junction with Thimbron, was very

near if not quite two full years; and consequently that the year of the expedition ought to be fixed in the third of the ninety-fourth Olympiad, and this will account for the chasm or non-action which Mr Spelman has [15] discovered in Diodorus, that year. In order to make out what I advance, I reckon up the time thus: namely,

	Months.
From Ephesus to the battle,	7
From the battle to Cotyora,	8
From their arrival at Cotyora, to their joining Seuthes, (upon a moderate computation,)	6
Serve under Seuthes,	2
From their leaving Seuthes, to their joining Thimbron, must be near	2
	25

The two months they served under Seuthes, were in the middle of winter (suppose December and January), which is the only mention of the season of the year in the whole book. From thence we gather, that the battle was fought about the latter end of September; that they were in the snows of Armenia about the beginning of January, came to Trebisond towards the end of February, and arrived at Cotyora about the beginning of June. They set out from hence towards the latter end of July, joined Seuthes at the end of November, and were incorporated with the troops under Thimbron, the March following, two full years from their first departure from Ephesus, to serve under Cyrus. The Greeks, it is well known, began their year from the [12] summer solstice. Therefore, as this army returned when Thimbron passed over into Asia, (as is plain from Xenophon) that is, in the spring of the first of the ninety-fifth Olympaid; so it is apparent, that Cyrus mustered his forces, and departed from Sardes in the spring of the third of the ninety-fourth Olympiad; which was two years before their junction with the Lacedæmonian general. Archbishop Usher plainly saw some difficulty in this particular; for, in repeating Xenophon's words, where he tells us, they were eight months from the battle to Cotyora, this learned prelate says, [14] "It ought to be five,

<hr>

8 Page 173.
9 Page 182.
10 Page 184.
11 What puts this beyond all dispute, are the distances, which are only computed to Cotyora: for from Ephesus to the battle are one million six thousand and fifty, and from the battle to Cotyora one million eight thousand six hundred stadia, in all three million four thousand six hundred and fifty, the whole sum mentioned by Xenophon at the end of the book, without taking any notice of their tavels after they left Cotyora.

12 Introduction, p. viii.
13 That is, the first month after the summer solstice.
14 "Cotyora venerant octo (vel quinque potius ut Series Historiæ postulare videtur) post pugnam mensibus."

as the course of the history afterwards requires;" meaning, without doubt, that out of the fifteen months mentioned by Xenophon, at the end of the book, some time ought to be allowed for their joining the Lacedæmonians. But, with all due respect be it spoken, three months is not sufficient for this by a great deal; for instance, they staid at Cotyora forty-five days, and served under Seuthes two months, besides a very considerable train of actions both before and after; all of which together could not, according to my computation, take up much less than ten months. But further, if we collect the days from the field of battle, to their arrival at Cotyora, as they lie scattered in Xenophon, we shall find more than seven months accounted for, besides two or three places where time is not strictly mentioned; which plainly shows that no error can be crept into the text; but that eight months was the time they spent in this march.

It is true, indeed, that the battle was fought in the fourth of the ninety-fourth Olympiad; but then it was in the beginning of it; whereas, Diodorus affirms, that Cyrus[1] hired his mercenaries, sent to the Lacedæmonians for assistance, mustered his army at Sardes, and began his march this same year; ([2]supposing, without doubt, that they spent but fifteen months in the whole of their travels) all which, as I think, I have proved beyond all contradiction, ought to be placed in the third of the ninety-fourth Olympiad, Micion being archon of Athens.

At Cotyora they took shipping, and sailed to Harmene, a port near Sinope; and from thence to Heraclea. In this second trip, Xenophon informs us, that they saw the mouths of several rivers; first, that of the Thermodon, then of the Halys, and, after this, that of the Parthenius; whereas it is most certain, that the Thermodon and Halys are a great way on the other side of Sinope, and consequently, Xenophon must have seen the mouths of them

in the former run, that is, from Cotyora to Harmene. This will render what I hinted at above very probable, viz. that our author kept no regular journal of this expedition; for, if he had, where could he have more leisure to write than on board, where he could have nothing else to do, there being pilots to steer the course, and sailors to manage the ships?

It is evident, from the digression in the fifth book[3] about Diana's offering, that our author did not write 'this history in its present form, till several years after his return from the Expedition: for he there makes mention of his sons going a-hunting; whereas it is pretty plain, that at the time we are speaking of, [4]he had no children. He staid in Asia with the troops, till Agesilaus was recalled, and after the battle of Chæronea he retired to Scilus. This battle was fought in the second of the ninety-fourth Olympiad, near five years after his return from the expedition. In this interval he married, and had two sons; and when these were grown up, which we must suppose would take up about twenty years, [6]he wrote

---

[1] Usher copies Diodorus in all these particulars, and yet afterwards says, "commissa pugna est sub initium Anni 4 Olympiadis xciv."

[2] He supposes that Cyrus, having spent the summer and winter in preparing for the expedition, set out in the spring of the fourth of the ninety-fourth Olympiad, and that the Greeks returned late in the spring following.

[3] Page 287.

[4] This work came out under the name of Themistogenes of Syracuse; and Xenophon himself refers to it under this title in the second book of his history. But the world was soon convinced who was the true author; for there are not only several passages in it which Xenophon himself alone could know, but it is likewise penned with so much harmony and sweetness, as could flow from no other than the Attic Bee. Indeed it is the opinion of some learned men, that Themistogenes did write an account of the expedition, which Xenophon refers to, as above; but that he afterwards wrote one himself, which is the work we have now extant. However we shall find this very unlikely, when we reflect that our Ἀνάβασις was wrote while Xenophon lived in ease and peace at Scilus, and his sons were alive; whereas his Greek history was not drawn up till after the battle of Mantinea; when Scilus was destroyed, Xenophon removed to Corinth, and one of his sons slain; so that Scilus was destroyed some time before this battle, and the expedition must be written before the Greek History.

[5] See Book vii.

[6] It is probable he wrote this history to vindicate his honour, and published it under another name to avoid the imputation of vanity. There were other accounts, it is likely, of this expedition, which either blamed his conduct, or were silent as to its merit. What confirms me in this opinion, is the relation which Diodorus Siculus gives of the same transactions, which not only varies from Xenophon in abundance of particulars, but never mentions his name where he most deserves it, viz. in conducting the most memorable retreat that ever was performed in any period of time. This he attributes to Cheirisophus, by saying that he was chosen general,

this account of the transactions of the Greeks, in Upper Asia. So that if some trivial matters have slipped his memory, it is not at all to be wondered at, since it was penned so many years after the affairs it mentions were transacted.

And here I cannot forbear to express some doubt, concerning our author's age at the time we are treating of. Diogenes Laertius affirms that he died in the first of the one hundred and fifth Olympiad; and Lucian, that he lived to be upwards of ninety years of age. So, when he accompanied Cyrus into Asia, he must be at least fifty-one: which to me seems quite irreconcilable with the account he gives us of himself. When their commanders were all destroyed, the Greeks were under great anxiety, as being in the heart of the Persian empire, in the neighbourhood of a great army, and all their best officers murdered. The army was so dispirited, that no one seemed to take any care for its preservation. Xenophon, revolving these things in his mind, says to himself, [7] "Do I stay for the arrival of a general from Greece to take the command upon him? Or do I wait for years to accomplish myself? But I shall in vain hope to grow older, if I this day surrender myself up to the enemy." He therefore immediately calls up the captains who had served under his friend Proxenus, and proposes the election of officers in the room of those who were put to death; and concludes his speech with saying, that if they should choose him for their commander, he would not excuse himself by reason of his age. These two passages, compared with Phalinus calling him boy [8] in the second book, and his taking notice of himself frequently as the youngest officer, do almost prevail upon me to think, that he was no more than twenty-three or twenty-four years of age; his beard not fully grown, and therefore he might with some propriety be called boy. Proxenus was but thirty when put to death, and consequently we must suppose Xenophon to be less, when he talks

of excusing his age to the officers who served under Proxenus; else what he said must have been looked upon as a banter upon the years of his friend, and upon the men who served under such a boy. It may be answered, that as the Athenians never pressed men into their armies, who were above the age of forty, so Xenophon might say he would not refuse the command by pleading this custom: but this will be found to square but very indifferently with all the other particulars; for had he been upwards of fifty, he had been older than Clearchus, [9] whom all the rest submitted to of course, and consequently can never be supposed to be the youngest commander, when new ones were chosen. Besides, it is not credible, that a man would go volunteer in such an expedition as this, that is, to march one thousand two hundred miles into an enemy's country, and then, when a command was offered him, talk of refusing it upon the account of his advanced age. And though the Athenians did exempt men from forced service at the age of forty, yet this was only with respect to the common soldiers; their generals were not thought the worse for being above that age. I think I may leave it to all the world to judge, whether it would not be ridiculous in any general to talk of resigning upon account of his age at fifty-one, especially when he was affirming upon every occasion, that he was one of the youngest officers in the army.

I cannot take my leave without pointing out a very considerable error in Arbuthnot's tables, which has misled Mr Spelman in reducing the Greek to the English measures at the end of the book; for who could have any suspicion of the correctness of a work, which, it is supposed, was overlooked by some of the greatest geniuses in Europe? These tables make the Greek foot somewhat larger than the English foot: the pace to contain five feet English, and yet the stadium to contain about one hundred paces, four feet four and a half inches; so that six hundred Greek feet are not equal to five hundred and five English feet: and so the μίλιον, which contains four thousand eight hundred Greek feet, is made equal to eight hundred and five paces five feet, that is four thou-

---

B. xiv. c. 5. The only time I can find he mentions Xenophon's name, is his warring against the Thracians. B. xiv. c. 6.

7 Ἐγὼ οὖν τὴν ἐκ ποίας πόλεως στρατηγὸν προσδοκῶ ταῦτα πράξειν; ποίαν δ᾽ ἡλικίαν ἐμαυτῷ ἐλθὼν ἀναμένω; οὐ γὰρ ἔγωγ᾽ ἔτι πρεσβύτερος ἔσομαι, ἐὰν τήμερον προδῶ ἐμαυτὸν τοῖς πολεμίοις, where it is plain by πρεσβύτερος, that he looked upon himself as too young to command.

8 Page 201.

9 Page 203. As the oldest officer, the rest being without experience. If we may guess at the rest by the ages of those mentioned, they must all be young men. Proxenus was but thirty, Agias and Socrates about forty, when put to death.

sand and thirty English feet. This error arises from computing by the fathom, instead of the pace; and if this mistake be rectified in the next edition, the tables will be correct for any thing I know at present to the contrary. The surest way of reducing the ancient measures to those of the moderns, is to keep in mind the true proportion of their respective feet. Thus nine hundred and sixty Greek feet are equal to nine hundred and sixty-seven English, and therefore the thirty-four thousand six hundred and fifty stadia, contained in the whole expedition and return of this army, will, when reduced to our measures, amount to three thousand nine hundred and sixty-six miles. The Greek mile, or μίλιον is less than an English mile by four hundred and forty-five English feet. An English mile contains five thousand two hundred and forty-one Greek feet.

R. FORSTER.

XENOPHON

ON THE

EXPEDITION OF CYRUS.

BOOK V.

in order to be safe, and not wander about the country without them, and that the care of providing them be left to us." This being resolved, he went on. " Hear also what I have farther to say. Some of you will, no doubt, desire to go out for plunder. Let all such therefore acquaint us with their intentions, and to what part of the country they propose to go ; that we may know the number both of those who go, and of those that stay, and assist the former in any thing they want ; and if it shall be found necessary to send out succours, that we may know whither to send them : and that, if any person of less experience undertakes any thing, by endeavouring to know the strength of the enemy, we may be able to advise him." This also was resolved. " In the next place, consider this," says he : " The enemy having leisure to make reprisals, may, with justice, lay snares for us, for we have possessed ourselves of what belongs to them, and they have the advantage of us by being posted upon eminences that command our camp. For which reason I think we ought to place out-guards round the camp ; and if, by turns, we mount the guard, and watch the motions of the enemy, we shall be the less exposed to a surprise. Take this also into your consideration. If we were as-

sured that Cheirisophus would return with a sufficient number of ships to transport us, what I am going to say would be unnecessary : but, as that is uncertain, I think we ought, at the same time, to endeavour to provide ourselves with ships from hence : for, if we are already supplied, when he arrives we shall have a greater number of ships to transport us ; and, if he brings none, we shall make use of these we have provided. I observe many ships sailing along this coast ; these, if we desire the inhabitants of Trebisond to supply us with ships of strength, we may bring to the shore, and, taking off their rudders, place a guard upon them, till we have enough to transport us in such a manner as we propose." This also was resolved. " The next thing I would recommend to your consideration," says he, "is, whether it may not be reasonable to subsist those belonging to the ships, as long as they stay in our service, out of the public stock, and pay them their freight, that they may find their account in serving us." This was also resolved. " I think," added Xenophon, " that if by this means we should be disappointed of a sufficient number of ships, we ought to order the towns, that border on the sea, to repair the roads, which, as we are informed, are hardly passable : for they will obey our orders, both through fear, and a desire to be rid of us."

Upon this they all cried out, that there was no necessity to repair the roads. Xenophon, therefore, seeing their folly, declined putting

---

dulged before ; it is this, I would read *σὺν ἡγεμόσι* instead of *σὺν σεσσαμαῖς* ; but, in order to support this alteration, I find myself obliged to put the reader in mind of what our author says immediately before ; he tells the men they will expose themselves, *ἢν ἁμιλῶς τι καὶ ἀφυλάκτως σεεύωνται ἐπὶ τὰ ἐπιτήδεια* : the first of these I think he guards against, by advising them to go out for provisions *σὺν ἡγεμόσι*. This reading seems to lead naturally to what he adds, *ἄλλως δὲ μὴ πλανᾶσθαι*, and further to *ἡμᾶς τούτων ἐπιμελησθῆναι*. Those who are acquainted with the ancient writers, must be sensible that there is so much method in them, and so close a connection between their general assertions and the detail of them, the latter perpetually growing out of the former, that I hope this alteration will not seem too violent, particularly where some was necessary. But there was another danger against which he was to warn them, and that related to private plunder, for that is the sense of *ἐπὶ λείαν σεεύεσθαι*, as it is particularly distinguished from public expeditions in the sixth book, where Xenophon tells us the soldiers made an order that when the army staid in the camp, *ἐξὸν ἐπὶ λείαν ἰέναι*, the men were then allowed to go out for private plunder ; and presently he will give us an account of the misfortune of Cleænetus, when the Greeks went out upon that account, *ἐπὶ λείαν ἐξῆσαν οἱ Ἕλληνες* : but when he comes to the public expeditions of the army to get provisions, which he calls *ἐπὶ τὰ ἐπιτήδεια σεεύεσθαι*, and which were made in consequence of their resolution upon what he proposed, he there tells us that he himself took the guides appointed by the Trapezuntians, and led out one half of the army, leaving the other to guard the camp.

1 *Ἐσυψήφιζε μὲν οὐδέν*. Leunclavius mistook this passage when he said *nihil sanxit*, which Hutchinson has properly explained by *nihil eos sententias rogavit*. Thus in *ἐπεψήφιζε* made use of more than once by Thucydides, and in this sense he makes use of Nicias use it upon a very important occasion : the Athenians, at the instigation of Alcibiades, resolved to send a fleet of sixty ships under his command, and that of Nicias and Lamachus, to assist the Egestæans against the Selinuntians, or rather to conquer Sicily. Five days after this resolution, there was another assembly of the people, where every thing that was necessary towards equipping and manning the fleet was to be provided. Here Nicias did all that was in his power to divert them from the expedition, and after many very solid arguments to that purpose, he proposes to them to revoke their former votes, and leave the Sicilians to enjoy what they possessed, and compose those differences without their interposition; after proposing this, he calls upon the president of the assembly, (if he thought it his duty to take care of the commonwealth, and desired to show himself a good citizen) to put the question, and again to take the opinion of the Athenians ; *καὶ οὐ ξ κρύναι; ταῦτα (ὥστε ἤγῇ τοι σεορτάκυι κινδυνεύσαι τι τῆς πόλεως, καὶ βούλει γενέσθαι πολίτης ἀγαθὸς) ἐπιψήφιζε, καὶ γνώμας σεροτίθει αὖθις Ἀθηναίοις*. D'Ablancourt has said very carelessly, *ne laissa pas d'y donner ordre*.

any question relating to that, but prevailed on the towns near the sea to mend their roads, of their own accord; telling them, that if the roads were good, the Greeks would the sooner leave their country. The inhabitants of Trebisond let them have a galley with fifty oars, of which they gave the command to [2] Dexippus, who lived in the neighbourhood of Sparta : but he, neglecting to take any transport ships, went away with the galley, and sailed out of the Euxine sea. However, he afterwards received condign punishment; for, being in Thrace in the service of Seuthes, and carrying on some intrigues there, he was slain by Nicander the Lacedæmonian. The inhabitants of Trebisond also supplied them with a galley of thirty oars, of which Polycrates an Athenian, had the command, who brought all the transport ships he seized to the shore before the camp, and the Greeks, taking out their cargoes, appointed guards to take charge of them, and retained the ships for their passage. In the meantime, the soldiers went out to get plunder, some succeeding, and others not. But Cleænetus, in attacking a strong place with his own, and another company, was slain together with many others.

II. When the provisions in the neighbourhood were so far consumed, that the parties could not return the same day, Xenophon, taking some of the inhabitants of Trebisond for his guides, led out one half of the army against the Drillians, leaving the other to guard the camp : because the Colchians, being driven out of their houses, were got together in great numbers, and encamped upon the eminences. These guides did not lead them to those places where provisions were easy to be had, because the inhabitants were their friends; but conducted them with great chearfulness into the territories of the Drillians, by whom they had been ill treated. This is a mountainous country, and of difficult access, and the people the most warlike of all those who live near the Euxine sea.

As soon as the Greeks entered their country, the Drillians set fire to all the places they thought easy to be taken, and then went away. So that the Greeks found nothing but swine and oxen, and some other cattle that escaped the fire. There was one place called their metropolis, whither they had all betaken themselves. This place was surrounded by a [3] valley, exceeding deep, and the access to it was difficult. However, the targeteers, advancing five or six stadia before the heavy-armed men, passed the valley, and seeing there a great many cattle with other things, attacked the place. They were followed by many pikemen, who had left the camp to get provisions : so that the number of those who passed the valley, amounted to above two thousand men. These finding themselves unable to take the place by storm (for it was surrounded with a large ditch and a rampart, upon which there were palisades, and many wooden towers) endeavoured to retreat; but the enemy attacked the rear, so that, not being able to make their retreat (for the pass, which led from the place to the valley, was so narrow they could only go one by one) they sent to Xenophon, who was at the head of the heavy-armed men. The messenger acquainted him that the place was furnished with great quantities of effects; "But," says he, "it is so strong, we cannot make ourselves masters of it : neither is it easy for us to retreat; for the enemy sallying from the place, attacks our rear, and the recess is difficult."

Xenophon, hearing this, advanced to the brink of the valley, and ordered the heavy-armed men to stand to their arms; then passing over with the captains, he considered whether it were better to bring off those who had already passed, or to send for the heavy-armed men to come over also, in expectation of taking the place. He found the first could not be brought off without considerable loss, and the captains were also of opinion that the place might be taken. So Xenophon consented,

2 Δεξίππον Λακωνικὸν τιχίωκον. Hutchinson has rendered this Dexippum Laconem istius loci accolam, and D'Ablancourt, in the same sense, qui demeuroit en ces quartiers là. This I do not take to be the sense of τιχίωκος, in this place, which I think Leunclavius has rendered very properly Dexippum Laconem e Spartæ vicinia. The ancient authors in treating of the affairs of the Lacedæmonians, almost always distinguish between the inhabitants of Sparta and those of Lacedæmon, that is of the country adjoining to it, the former of whom at the time of the invasion of Xerxes, consisted but of eight thousand men, and were looked upon as better soldiers than the latter; for we find Demaratus, in Herodotus, saying to Xerxes at the affair of Thermopylæ ἐστι ἐν τῇ Λακεδαίμονι Σπάρτα, πόλις ἀνδρῶν ὀκτακισχιλίων μάλιστα· καὶ οὗτοι πάντες ὅμοιοί εἰσι τοῖς ἐνθάδε μαχισαμένοις· οἱ γε μὴν ἄλλοι Λακεδαιμόνιοι, τούτοισι μὲν οὐχ ὅμοιοι, ἀγαθοὶ δέ. These inhabitants of the country of Lacedæmon are particularly called τιχίωκοι by Strabo: who, he tells us, were freed by the Romans, when those of Sparta were under the oppression of their tyrants.

3 Χαράδρα. See note 4, page 221.

relying upon the victims; for the priests
had foretold there would be an action, and
that their ¹ excursion would be attended with
success.   He sent therefore the captains
to bring over the heavy-armed men, and himself staid there, and drew off the targeteers
without suffering any of them to skirmish.
As soon as the heavy-armed men came up, he
ordered each of the captains to draw up their
several companies in such a manner as they
thought most advantageous.   He did this, because those captains, who were in a perpetual
emulation of gallantry, stood near to one another.   While these orders were putting in execution, he commanded all the targeteers to
advance with their fingers ² in the slings of
their darts, which, when the signal was given,
they were to lance, and the archers with their
arrows on the string, which, upon a signal also,
they were to discharge; at the same time he
ordered the light-armed men to have their
pouches full of stones; and appointed proper
persons to see these orders executed.   When
every thing was ready, and the captains and
lieutenants, and the men, who valued themselves no less than their leaders, stood all in
their ranks, and viewed one another, (for by
reason of the ground the army made a fine appearance) they sung the pæan, and the trumpet
sounded; then the army shouted, the heavy-
armed men ran on, and javelins, arrows, leaden
balls, and stones thrown by hand, flew among
the enemy; some of the men even throwing
fire at them.   The great quantity of these missive weapons forced them both from the palisades and the towers; so that Agasias of
Stymphalus, and Philozenus of Pelena, laying
down their arms, mounted the rampart in their
vests only; when some, being drawn up by
their companions, and others getting up by
themselves, the place was taken, as they imagined.   Upon this, the targeteers and light-armed
men, rushing in, plundered every thing they
could find, while Xenophon, standing at the
gates, kept as many of the heavy-armed men
as he could, without: because other bodies of
the enemy appeared upon some eminences,

strongly fortified.   Not long after, there was a
cry heard within, and the men came flying,
some with what they had got, and others, possibly, wounded.   Upon this, there was great
crowding about the gates.   Those who got
through, being asked what the matter was, said
there was a fort within, from which the enemy
sallied, and wounded our men who were in the
place.

Xenophon, hearing this, ordered Tolmides
the crier to publish, that all who desired to
partake of the plunder should go in; many,
therefore, prepared themselves to enter, and,
rushing in, drove back those who were endeavouring to get out, and shut up the enemy
again within the fort.   The Greeks plundered
and carried off every thing they found without
it; while the heavy-armed men stood to their
arms, some round the palisades, and others
upon the road that led to the fort.   Then Xenophon and the captains considered whether it
were possible to take it, for in that case, they
secured their retreat, which, otherwise, would
be exceeding difficult: but, upon consideration,
the fort was found to be altogether impregna-
ble.   Upon this they prepared for their retreat,
and each of the men pulled up the palisades
that were next to him; then the useless people, together with the greatest part of the
heavy-armed men, were sent out to get plunder; but the captains retained those, in whom
each of them confided.

As soon as they began their retreat, the enemy sallied upon them, in great numbers, armed
with bucklers, spears, greaves, and Paphlagonian helmets; while others got upon the houses
on each side of the street that led to the fort,
so that it was not safe to pursue them to the
gates of it, for they threw great pieces of timber from above, which made it dangerous both
to stay, and to retire; and the night coming on,
increased the terror.   While they were engaged
with the enemy under this perplexity, some god
administered to them a means of safety; for
one of the houses on the right hand took fire
on a sudden: who set fire to it is not known;
but, as soon as the house fell in, the enemy
quitted all those on the right, and Xenophon
being taught this expedient by fortune, ordered
all the houses on the left to be set on fire.
These being built of wood were soon in a
flame, upon which the enemy quitted them also.
There only now remained those in the front
to disturb them, it being evident they designed

1 Τίλος τῆς ἐξόδου. Hutchinson understands ἐξόδος
in this place to relate to the retreat of the Greeks from
the place, where they seem to have engaged themselves
rashly; I have rather chosen to explain it of their excursion in quest of provisions, which sense I find Leunclavius has followed.

2 Διαγκυλισμένοι ἵεναι. See note, 2, page 242.

to attack them in their retreat and descent
from the fort. Upon this, Xenophon ordered
all who were out of the reach of the missive
weapons, to bring wood, and lay it in the midway between them and the enemy. When
they had brought enough, they set fire to it;
setting fire at the same time to the houses that
were next the rampart, in order to employ the
enemy. Thus, by interposing fire between
themselves and the Barbarians, they, with difficulty, made good their retreat; the city, with
all the houses, towers, palisades, and every
thing else but the fort, was reduced to ashes.

The next day the Greeks marched away with
the provisions they had taken; but, apprehend-
ing some danger in the descent to Trebisond
(for it was a steep and narrow defile) they
placed a false ambuscade. A certain Mysian
by birth as well as name, taking four or five
Cretans with him, stopped in a thicket, affecting an endeavour to conceal himself from the
enemy, while the flashing of their brazen buck-
ers discovered them here and there. The enemy, therefore, seeing this, were afraid of it, as
if a real ambuscade; in the meantime the army descended. As soon as the Mysian judged
they were advanced far enough, he gave the
signal to his companions to fly in all haste; and
he himself, leaving the thicket, fled, and they
with him. The Cretans (expecting to be overtaken) left the road, and rolling down into the
valleys, got safe to a wood; but the Mysian, keeping the road, called out for help, when some ran
to his assistance, and brought him off wounded.
These, after they had rescued him, retreated
slowly, though exposed to the enemy's missive
weapons, while some of the Cretans discharged
their arrows in return. Thus they all arrived
at the camp in safety.

III. When neither Cheirisophus returned,
nor the ships they had provided were sufficient
to transport them, and no more provisions were
to be had, they determined to leave the country. To this end they put on board all their
sick, and those above forty years of age, together with the women and children, and all their
baggage, that was not absolutely necessary, and
appointed Philesius and Sophænetus, the oldest of the generals, to go on board, and take
care of them. The rest travelled by land, the
roads being mended; and the third day they
arrived at Cerasunt; [3] a Greek city, situated

in the country of the Colchians near the sea,
and a colony of the Sinopians. Here they
staid ten days, during which the soldiers were
reviewed in their arms, and an account taken
of their number, which amounted to eight
thousand six hundred. These were all that
were saved out of about ten thousand; the res
were destroyed by the enemy and by the snow,
and some by sickness. Here each man received his share of the money that had been raised
by the sale of the captives, the tenth part ot
which they consecrated to Apollo, and to Diana of Ephesus. Of this each of the generals
received a part, to be appropriated by them to
that service. Neon the Asinian received that
which was designed for Cheirisophus.

Xenophon, therefore, having caused an offering to be made for Apollo, consecrated it in
the treasury of the Athenians at Delphos, in-
scribing it with his own name and that of
Proxenus, who was slain with Clearchus, there
having been an intercourse of hospitality between them. As to that part of the money
which was appropriated to Diana of Ephesus,
he left it with Megabysus, the sacristan of
that goddess; [4] when he departed out of Asia
in company with Agesilaus, with a design to
go to Bœotia, conceiving it might be exposed
to some danger with him at Chæronea. He
enjoined Megabysus, if he escaped, to restore
the money to him, otherwise to make such an
offering with it, as he thought would be most
acceptable to the goddess, and dedicate it to
her. Afterwards, when Xenophon was banished from Athens, and lived at Scilus, a town
built by the Lacedæmonians near Olympia,
Megabysus came to Olympia to see the games,
and restored the deposit. With this money,
Xenophon purchased some lands in honour of
the goddess, in the place directed by the oracle, through which the river Sellenus happens
to run; a river of the same name running also
hard by the temple of the Ephesian Diana,

Lucullus, in his return from his expedition against Mithridates, brought cherry-trees into Italy, in the year of
Rome 680; one hundred and twenty years after that
they were carried into Britain: they seem to have had
their name from this city, or the city from them. Tournefort tells us, that he found all the hills, in the neighbourhood of it, covered with those trees. Cerasunt was
afterwards called Pharnaccia, though Ptolemy, Strabo,
and Pliny make them different towns.

4 Ὅτι ἀσφι τῷ Ἀγησιλάῳ. See the Life of Xenophon
prefixed to this translation, where this and many other
subsequent passages are explained.

and in both there are shell-fish, [1] as well as other fish; besides, there are in this place, near Scilus, wild beasts of all kinds that are proper for the chase. Xenophon also built a [2] temple and an altar with this consecrated money; and from that time, offered to the goddess an annual sacrifice of the tenth of the product of every season; and all the inhabitants, with the men and women in the neighbourhood, partook of the feast; and all who were present at it have barley meal, bread, wine, and sweetmeats in honour of the goddess, and also their share of the victims that are killed from the consecrated lands, and of the game that is taken. For the sons of Xenophon, and those of the rest of the inhabitants, always make a general hunting against the feast, when all who desired it hunted along with them; and wild boars, with [2] roe and red deer, were taken both upon the consecrated lands, and upon a mountain called Pholoe. The place lies near the road that leads from Lacedæmon to Olympia, about twenty stadia from the temple of Jupiter, that stands in the last of these cities. There are groves belonging to it, and hills covered with trees, very proper to feed swine, goats, sheep, and horses; so that those belonging to the persons who come to the feast, find plenty of pasture.

The temple itself stands in a grove of fruit trees, that yield all sorts of fruit proper to the season.[4] It resembles, in little, the temple of Ephesus, and the statue of the goddess is as like that of Ephesus, as a statue of cypress can be to one of gold. Near to the temple stands a pillar with this inscription: " These lands are consecrated to Diana. Let the possessor offer up the tenth part of the annual product in sacrifice, and out of the surplus, keep the temple in repair. If he fails, the goddess will punish his neglect."

---

1 Κύγχαι. Under the title of Κύγχαι in Greek, and conchæ in Latin, are comprehended the infinite variety of shell fish described by Pliny; most of which, I dare say, I have seen in Sir Hans Sloane's magnificent and curious collection of the product of all the four parts of the earth; which collection I look upon as a much better comment upon that author, than all that has been written to explain him.

2 Ἐσσήσει δὲ καὶ ναὸν, etc. Pausanias tells us that near to this temple stood a monument, said to be erected for Xenophon, with his statue in Pentelesian marble. The quarry of this marble, so much celebrated among the statuaries, was upon a mountain of that name near Athens; whatever merit this marble might have, we find in Pliny that the first statuaries made use of no other than that of Paros, though, since that time, he says, many whiter kinds of marble have been discovered, and, not long before he wrote, in the quarries of Luna, a sea-port town of Tuscany. I have lately seen, in the hands of a very curious person, a piece of marble just brought from the island of Paros; it is exceedingly white, and sparkles like the fragments of the most ancient statues, which, by these circumstances, as well as by the authority of the best authors, plainly appears to have been of that marble.

3 Δερκάδες. See note 5, page 180, upon the first book. The mountain Pholoe in Arcadia was famous for all sorts of game.

4 Ὁ δὲ ναὸς, ὡς μικρὸς μεγάλῳ τῷ ἐν Ἐφέσῳ εἴκασται καὶ τὸ ξόανον ἔοικεν, ὡς κυπαρίσσινον χρυσῷ ὄντι τῷ ἐν Ἐφέσῳ. Hutchinson has, upon this occasion, quoted a passage out of Pliny, wherein that author gives the dimensions of the temple of Ephesus; but it must be observed, that the temple there described by Pliny, was not in being at the time of our author; since it was only begun after the first was burned down by Herostratus, which happened the same night Alexander the Great was born, that is, in the Attic month Boedromion (September), in the first year of the hundred and sixth O'lympiad: which gave occasion to Timæus, the historian, to say, that it was no wonder Diana's temple was burned, since the goddess was from home attending Olympias in her labour. The temple, therefore, which was burned down by Herostratus, not that described by Pliny, (which was not begun till some years after Xenophon's death, and was two hundred and twenty years in building) must have been the model of the temple built by Xenophon at Scilus. The last temple of Ephesus, Alexander, it seems, was so desirous to have inscribed with his name, that he offered the Ephesians to bear all the expense they had been, and should be at, in building it, provided they would consent to the inscription. This they refused with as great vanity as he desired it; but, being sensible that a flat denial might be attended with dangerous consequences, they clothed theirs with a piece of flattery, and told Alexander that it was not decent for one god to dedicate temples to another. The same judgment is to be made of the quotation brought by Hutchinson out of Pliny, in relation to the wood of which the statue of the Ephesian Diana was made, since we find, by this passage of Xenophon, that the statue in the first temple was of gold. I am apt to believe also that the representations of the Ephesian Diana, which are to be met with in several monuments of antiquity, are all taken from the statue in the last temple. The great numbers of breasts, with which the body of this statue is surrounded, (from which she was called multimammia, πολύμαστος) confirm the opinion of some learned men, that the Egyptian Isis, and the Greek Diana, were the same divinity with Rhœa from the Hebrew word רעה, Rahah, to feed. The Diana of Ephesus also, like Rhœa or Cybele, was crowned with turrets, which symbol of Rhœa, together with her fecundity, are both set forth in those beautiful verses, where Virgil compares Rome to this goddess:

" En hujus, Nate, Auspiciis illa inclyta Roma
Imperium Terris, animos æquabit Olympo;
Septemque una sibi Muro circumdabit Arces,
Felix Prole virum; qualis Berecynthia mater
Invehitur curru Phrygias turrita per urbes,
Læta Deum partu, centum complexa Nepotes,
Omnes Cœlicolas, omnes supera alta tenentes."

I am surprised that Montfaucon, in his account of the

CONTENTS of BOOK V.

EXPEDITION OF CYRUS.

BOOK V.

I. WE have hitherto related the actions of the Greeks in their expedition with Cyrus, and in the march to the Euxine sea; how they arrived at Trebisond, a Greek city, and offered the sacrifices they had vowed to the gods, in return for their safety, in the place where they first came into the territories of their friends.

After that they had assembled to consider of the remainder of their march, and Antileon of Thuria first rose up, and spoke in the following manner. " For my part, gentlemen! I am already tired with preparing my baggage, with walking and running, carrying my arms, and marching in my rank, and with mounting the guard and fighting; and therefore now desire, since we are arrived at the sea, to [1] sail from hence forward, freed from these labours, and stretched out, [2] like Ulysses, sleeping to arrive

in Greece." The soldiers, hearing this, applauded him, and first another, and then all present expressed the same desire. Upon this Cheirisophus rose up and said, " Gentlemen ! Anaxibius is my friend, and, at present, admiral; if, therefore, you think proper to send me to him, I make no doubt of returning with galleys and ships to transport you; and since you are disposed to go by sea, stay here till I return, which will be very suddenly." The soldiers, hearing this, were very well satisfied, and decreed that he should set sail immediately.

After him, Xenophon got up and spoke to this effect. " Cheirisophus is gone to provide ships for us; in the meantime, we propose to stay here. I shall therefore acquaint you with what I think proper for us to do during our stay. In the first place, we must supply ourselves with provisions out of the enemy's country, for the market here is not sufficient to supply us: besides, few of us are furnished with money to provide ourselves with what we want, and the country is inhabited by the enemy. We shall therefore expose ourselves to lose many of our men, if, when we go in search of provisions, we are careless and unguarded: so that I am of opinion, when you go out upon these expeditions, you ought to take [3] guides,

---

1 Πλῖν τὰ λοιπὰ. Xenophon, as we shall see afterwards, perpetually uses πεζῇ πορεύεσθαι, to travel by land, in opposition to πλῖν, to travel by sea. There is a very remarkable passage in the Institution of Cyrus, where our author, speaking of the posts instituted by the first Cyrus, says that these posts, performed by horses, were the most expeditious method of travelling by land, τῶν ἀνθρωπίνων πεζῇ πορειῶν αὕτη ταχίστη. But our author is not singular in this use of the word; Diodorus Siculus, speaking of the expedition of Artaxerxes against Evagoras, king of Cyprus, calls his land-army, though it consisted of horse, as well as foot, πεζὸν στράτευμα: his words are these; τὸ μὲν γὰρ πεζὸν στράτευμα μυριάδων ἦν τριάκοντα σὺν ἱππεῦσι. I imagine this sense of the word in Greek may have given occasion to the phrase pedibus ire in the Latin authors, and to Cæsar, in particular, to say, Lucius Cæsar pedibus Adrametum profugerat.

2 Ὥσπερ Ὀδυσσεὺς. This relates to Ulysses arriving asleep in Ithaca, where the Phæacian sailors left him in that condition.
Κὰδδ' ἄρ' ἐπὶ ψαμάθῳ ἔθεσαν, δεδμημένον ὕπνῳ.
I mention this verse to show that D'Ablancourt had no reason to excuse his leaving out dormant, by saying that it is only an ornament, and not a point of history.

3 Σὺν προνομαῖς. I suspect there is here some corruption in the text; I do not know what to make of σὺν προνομαῖς; Muretus has a mind it should be σὺν προδόχοις, but that does not satisfy: both the Latin translators have said per excursiones; but how could they get provisions otherwise than by excursions? D'Ablancourt has made very good sense of it by saying, gu'on n'y aille point sans escorte; but I do not think it can be shown that προνομὴ signifies the escort that attends on foragers. I shall therefore venture to make a small variation in the text, a liberty I believe I have not above twice in-

IV. From Cerasunt those who went on board before continued their voyage by sea, and the rest proceeded by land. When they came to the confines of the [5] Mosynoecians, they sent Timesitheus of Trebisond to them, (between whom and them there was an intercourse of hospitality) to ask them, in their name, whether they desired the Greeks should march through their country as friends or as enemies? The Mosynoecians answered it was equal to them; for they trusted to their places of strength. Upon this, Timesitheus informed the Greeks, that the Mosynoecians, who inhabited the country beyond these, were at enmity with them: so they resolved to send to this people to know whether they were disposed to enter into an alliance; and Timesitheus being sent upon this occasion, returned with their magistrates. When they were arrived, they had a conference with the generals of the Greeks,

and Xenophon spoke to them in this manner, Timesitheus being the interpreter:

"O Mosynoecians! we propose to go to Greece by land, for we have no ships: but these people, who, as we understand, are your enemies, oppose our passage. You have it in your power, therefore, if you think proper, by entering into an alliance with us, both to take revenge of them for any injuries they may have formerly done you, and to keep them in subjection for the future. Consider then, whether, if you neglect this opportunity, you are ever like to be supported with so powerful an alliance." To this the chief magistrate of the Mosynoecians made answer, that he approved of this, and accepted our alliance. "Let us know then," said Xenophon, "what use you propose to make of us, if we become your allies? And of what service you can be to us in our passage?" They answered, "We have it in our power to make an irruption, on the other side, into the country of those who are enemies to us both, and to send hither ships with men, who will be both auxiliaries, and your guides."

Upon these terms they gave their faith and received ours, and then returned. The next day they came back with three hundred canoes, three men being in each, two of whom disembarking, stood to their arms in order of battle, and the third remained on board. These went away in their canoes, and the rest disposed themselves in the following manner. They drew up in several lines, each consisting of about one hundred men, which, like rows of dancers, faced one another; they had all bucklers, made of the hides of white oxen with the hair on, and shaped like an ivy-leaf; and in their right hands a spear, six cubits in length, with a point on the upper part, and on the lower a ball of the same wood. They wore vests, which did not reach to their knees, of the thickness of the linen bags [6] in which carpets are usually packed up: and on their heads helmets made of leather, like those of the Paphlagonians, from the middle of which there rose a tuft of hair [7] braided to a point, resem-

---

Diana of Ephesus, and of the various representations of that goddess, does not distinguish between the two temples and the two statues, but contents himself with quoting the same passage out of Pliny, to show the different opinions of people concerning the wood of which the statue was made. But to return to the Greek Diana, the Phrygian Rhœa, or the Egyptian Isis, all emblems of fecundity, it is very observable that almost all the statues of the Ephesian Diana have a crab upon the breast: of which Montfaucon, after he has given the opinions of the antiquaries, says the signification is uncertain. However uncertain it may be, I beg I may be allowed to offer a conjecture about it. Every one agrees that the representation of the Ephesian Diana was taken from the Egyptian Isis, and all authors, both ancient and modern, affirm that the overflowing of the Nile becomes remarkable generally at the summer solstice; how then could the Egyptians represent fertility better than by placing on the breast of their goddess Isis, or universal nature, that sign in the zodiac, which denotes the summer solstice, when the fertile water of the Nile begins to diffuse plenty over the face of their country? This hieroglyphical manner of representing fertility is agreeable to the genius of the Egyptians, who seem to have pursued it in the composition of their fictitious animal, the sphinx, a figure composed of the body of a lion, and the head of a virgin, with the same view of denoting plenty spread over Egypt by the overflowing of the Nile, during the time the sun passes through the signs of the lion and virgin, which immediately follow the summer solstice, שוב, Sphang, in Hebrew, from whence the word sphinx is visibly derived, signifying overflowing.

5 Μοσυνοίκων. The Mosynoecians are thus paraphrased by Dionysius Periegetes,

· ————οἱ μόσσυνας ἴχωσι

Δουρατίους.————

Upon which Eustathius observes λέγει μόσσυνας ἴχειν δουρατίους ἤγουν ξυλίνους. It seems the Greeks gave them the name of Mosynoecians, from the wooden towers they inhabited, μόσυν signifying in Greek a wooden tower.

6 Linen bag.—Στρωματόδεσμον. It was in one of these sacks that Cleopatra conveyed herself in order to deceive Cæsar's guards, and solicit him against her brother—Δυτέρω δὲ, says Plutarch, τοῦ λαθεῖν ὄντος ἄλλου, ἡ μὲν εἰς στρωματόδεσμον ἐνδῦσα, προτείνει μακρὰν ἑαυτήν· ὁ δὲ Ἀπολλόδωρος ἱμάντι συνδήσας τὸν στρωματόδεσμον εἰσκομίζει πρὸς τὸν Καίσαρα.

7 Tuft of hair.—Κρώβυλον. I shall quote a passage of

bling a tiara. They had also battle-axes made of iron. Then one of them led the way, and all the rest followed, singing also, and marching in time; when, passing through the ranks of the Greeks, as they stood to their arms, they advanced immediately against the enemy, to a fort that seemed in no degree capable of making resistance. This fort stood before the city, which they called the metropolis, that contained within it the most considerable citadel of the Mosynœcians. This citadel was the subject of the present war between them; for those who were in possession of it were always looked upon to have the command of all the rest of the Mosynœcians: they told us, that the others had seized this place contrary to all justice, it belonging to both nations in common, and by seizing it had gained the ascendant over them.

Some of the Greeks followed these men, not by the orders of their generals, but for the sake of plunder. The enemy, upon their approach, kept themselves quiet for a time; but, when they came near the fort, they sallied out, and, putting them to flight, killed many of the Barbarians, together with some of the Greeks who were of the party, and pursued them till they saw the Greek army coming up to their assistance. Upon which they turned and fled:

and, cutting off the heads of the slain, they showed them both to the Greeks and to the Mosynœcians, their enemies; dancing at the same time, and singing a particular tune.[1] This accident gave the Greeks great uneasiness, both because it encouraged the enemy, and because their own men, who were of the party, in great numbers ran away; which had never happened before during the whole expedition. Upon this Xenophon, calling the soldiers together, spoke to them in this manner. "Gentlemen! do not suffer yourselves to be cast down by what has happened; for the good that attends it is not less than the evil. In the first place, this has convinced you, that our guides are in reality enemies to those to whom we are so through necessity. Secondly, those Greeks who despised our discipline, and thought themselves able to perform as great things, in conjunction with the Barbarians, as with us, are justly punished; so that, for the future, they will be less desirous of leaving our army. Prepare yourselves, therefore, to let those Barbarians, who are your friends, see that you are superior to them in courage, and to show those who are your enemies, that they will not find you the same men now, as when they engaged you, while you were in disorder."

Thus they passed this day. The next, as soon as they had offered sacrifice, and found the victims favourable, they took their repast. After that, the army being drawn up in columns, and the Barbarians placed on their left in the same disposition, they went on, the archers marching in the intervals, a little within the foremost ranks of the heavy-armed men; for the enemy's forlorn consisting of light-armed, advanced before the rest, and discharged a volley of stones among the Greeks. These were repulsed by the archers and targeteers. The rest marched slowly on, and first went against the fort, before which the Barbarians and the Greeks, who were with them, had been put to flight the day before: for here the enemy was drawn up. The Barbarians received the targeteers, and fought with them: but, when the heavy-armed men came up, they fled; and the targeteers immediately followed,

Thucydides, upon this occasion, not only to explain the signification of this word, but also because the passage itself contains an account of a very odd dress in use among the Athenians of old, with the observation of the Greek Scholiast upon it. Thucydides tells us, that not long before his time, the old men at Athens, of the richer sort wore linen vests, and the braids of their hair interwoven with golden grasshoppers: καὶ οἱ πρεσβύτεροι αὐτοῖς τῶν εὐδαιμόνων, διὰ τὸ ἀξροδίαιτον, οὐ πολὺς χρόνος ἐπειδὴ χιτῶνάς τε λινοῦς ἐπαύσαντο φορῦντες καὶ χρυσῶν τεττίγων ἐνέρσει κρώβυλον ἀναδούμενοι τῶν ἐν τῇ κεφαλῇ τριχῶν. The Greek Scholiast, in his observation upon this passage, fully explains the word κρώβυλος, made use of by Xenophon in that now before us: κρώβυλος, says he, ἐστὶν εἶδος πλέγματος τῶν τριχῶν, ἀπὸ ἑκατέρων εἰς ἓν ἀπολῆγον· ἐκαλῦτο δὲ τῶν μὲν ἀνδρῶν, κρώβυλος· τῶν δὲ γυναικῶν, κόρυμβος· τῶν δὲ παίδων σκορπίος— ἱέρρων δὲ τέττιγας, διὰ τὸ μουσικὸν, ἢ διὰ τὸ αὐτόχθονας εἶναι, καὶ γὰρ τὸ ζῶον γηγινές. And this is the sense I have given to the word κρώβυλος, in my translation of this passage. The last reason given by the Greek Scholiast for the Athenians wearing grasshoppers in their hair seems the best founded, that is, that they did it to show they were the original inhabitants of the country; for every body knows this was their pretension. I am at a loss to know what induced D'Ablancourt to translate κρώβυλος, un cercle de fer. He has been equally unfortunate in rendering the following passage—χιτωνίσκους δὲ ἐνδεδύκεσαν ὑπὲρ γονάτων, "ils avolent des cottes d'armes, qui leur passoient lex genoux."

[1] Singing a particular tune.—Νόμῳ τινὶ ᾄδοντες. Νόμος is used in the same sense by Herodotus, where speaking of the adventure of Arion, he says, τὸν δὲ ('Αρίονα) ἰνδύντα τε πάντα τὴν σκευὴν, καὶ λαβόντα τὴν κιθάραν, στάντα ἐν τοῖσι ἐδωλίοισι διεξελθεῖν νόμον τὸν ὄρθιον.

ursuing them up the hill to the metropolis, while the heavy-armed men marched on in their ranks. As soon as the Greeks had gained the top of the hill, and came to the houses of the metropolis, the enemy being now got together in a body, engaged them, and lanced their javelins ; and with other spears, which were of that length and thickness that a man could scarce wield one of them, they endeavoured to defend themselves hand to hand.

However, the Greeks pressing hard upon them, and engaging them in a close fight, they fled, and presently all the Barbarians quitted the town. But their king, who resided in a wooden tower situated upon an eminence, (whom, while he resides there, and guards the place, they maintain at the public expense,) refused to leave it, as did also those who were in the place that was first taken ; so they were burned there, together with their towers. The Greeks, in sacking the town, found in the houses great heaps of bread, made according to the custom of the country, the year before ; as the Mosynoecians assured us ; and the new corn laid up in the straw ; [2] it was most of it spelt. They found also dolphins cut to pieces, lying in pickle in jars ; and in other vessels the fat of the same fish, which the Mosynoecians used as the Greeks do oil. In their garrets were great quantities of [3] chestnuts. These they boil, and generally use instead of bread. There was found wine also, which when unmixed was so rough that it appeared sour, but being mixed with water became both fragrant and sweet.

The Greeks, having dined there, went forward, delivering up the place to those Mosynoecians who had assisted them in taking it. As for the rest of the towns they arrived at, which belonged to the enemy, the easiest of access were either abandoned or surrendered ; the greatest part of which are of this nature. They are distant from one another eighty stadia, some more and some less ; and yet, when the inhabitants call out to one another, they can be heard from one town to another ; so mountainous and so hollow is the country. The Greeks proceeding still forwards, arrived among their allies, who showed them boys belonging to the rich men, fatted with boiled chestnuts : their skin was delicate and exceeding white, and they were very near as thick as they were long. Their backs were painted with various colours, and all their fore parts [4] impressed with flowers. They wanted publicly to make use of the women the Greeks brought with them. It seems this is their custom. The people of this country, both men and women, are very fair. All the

---

[2] *Zuaì·* Ζύα, or ζία in Greek, is what the Romans called *far*, as we find very particularly in Dionysius Halicarnassensis, where speaking of the matrimonial ceremony, by them called, "confarreatio," he says it had its name ἀπὸ τῆς κοινωνίας τοῦ φαρῥὸς, ὁ καλοῦμεν ἡμεῖς ζίαν ; I am apt to believe it was what we call spelt. Pliny says the epithet of ζείδωρος, which Homer gives so often to ἄρουρα, is derived from ζία, not from ζῆν, according to the general opinion.

[3] Κάρυα τὰ πλατία οὐκ ἔχοντα διαφυὴς οὐδεμίας. Literally "flat nuts without any cleft ;" κάρυα signifies *nuts* in general ; by these additions they are distinguished both from common nuts and walnuts.

[4] 'Εστιγμένοι ἀνθέμων. I am not at all surprised that the translators are puzzled at the word ἀνθέμων in this place, for I believe it is no easy matter to find it used in this sense by any other author. Hutchinson has said, after Leunclavius, "pictura florida distinctis," which though I am far from condemning, yet I think ἀνθέμων is the word used by all authors in that sense. This is the epithet Homer gives to the basin or charger, which Achilles proposes as one of the prizes to the victor in throwing the dart.

Καλλὶ λίζητ' ἄπυρον βοὸς ἄξιον ἀνθεμόεντα
Θῆκ' ἐς ἀγῶνα φέρων.———

Which Mr Pope has translated, as he ever does, with great propriety,

" An ample charger of unsullied frame,
With flowers high wrought."

The lexicons are as silent, in relation to this sense of the word ἀνθέμων, as the authors. Hesychius says it signifies a winding line in pillars, γραμμή τις ἑλικοειδὴς ἐν τοῖς κίοσι, I suppose he means twisted pillars ; it is therefore submitted to the reader whether Xenophon may not say that the fore-parts of this people were impressed with this kind of flourishes. D'Ablancourt has said, with great art and little fidelity, " ils avoient le dos et l'estomac peints de diverses couleurs," by this means he has left out ἀνθεμίων. The custom, mentioned by Xenophon, to have been in practice among the Mosynoecians, of painting their bodies, was also used by our ancestors, as we find in Cæsar, who says that all the Britons painted themselves with woad, which makes a blue dye. " Omnes se Britanni vitro inficiunt, quod cœruleam efficit colorem." This word vitrum has, I find, puzzled the commentators : but it signifies here the plant which the Greeks call ἰσάτις, in English, woad, a plant well known to the dyers, who use great quantities of it to make their blue dye. " Herba," says Marcellus Empiricus, " quam nos vitrum, Græci Isatida vocant." The French called this herb, in Pliny's time, glastum, and, to this day, they call it *guesde*, as well as *pastel*. I am, informed that the Welch, as well as the inhabitants of lower Brittany in France, still call it glass, so that it is probable the equivocal application of vitrum may have given occasion to the equivocal sense of the word glass.

army agreed that these were the most barbarous people they had met with in all their expedition, and the most distant from the manners of the Greeks.   For [1] they do those things
in public which others do in private, otherwise
they dare not do them at all: and in private,
they behave themselves as if they were in public.   They talk to themselves, they laugh by
themselves, and dance, wherever they happen
to be, as if they were showing their skill to
others.   The Greeks were eight days in passing through the enemy's country, and that
which belonged to the Mosynœcians their
allies.

V. After · that they arrived among the
[2] Chalybians.   These are few in number, and
subject to the Mosynœcians; and the greatest
part of them subsist by the manufacture of
iron.   From thence they came to the [3] Tibarenians.   This is a much more campaign country, and their towns near the sea are not so
strong.   These the generals were disposed to
attack, that the army might have the advantage
of some plunder.   For this reason they declined receiving the presents which the Tibarenians
sent them, as a token of hospitality : but, having ordered those who brought them, to wait
till they had conferred together, they offered
sacrifice ; and, after many victims were slain,
all the priests agreed that the gods by no means
allowed them to make war upon this people.
Hereupon they accepted their presents, and
marching as through a country belonging to
their friends, they came to [4] Cotyora, a Greek

city, and a colony of the Sinopians, situa[te]
the territory of the Tibarenians.

Thus far the army travelled by land, h[a]
in their retreat from the field of battle
Babylon to Cotyora, made, in one hundre[d]
twenty-two marches, six hundred and t[ ]
ty parasangs, that is, eighteen thousan[d]
hundred stadia, in which they spent [ ]
months.   Here they staid forty-five d[ ]
during which they first offered sacrifice t[o]
gods; [5] then, dividing themselves accordin[g]
their several nations, made processions,
celebrated gymnic games.   After that [ ]
went out to get provisions, taking some ou[ ]
Paphlagonia, and the rest out of the cou[ ]
of the Cotyorians : for they refused to sup[ ]
them with a market, or to admit their sick
to the city.

In the meantime ambassadors arrived fr[ ]
Sinope ; these were in pain both for the c[ ]
of the Cotyorians, which belonged to them, a[ ]
paid them tribute, and for the country, whi[ ]
they heard was plundered.   When they ca[ ]
to the camp of the Greeks, they spoke th[ ]
Hecatonymus, who was esteemed a man [ ]
great eloquence, speaking for the rest : " Ge[ ]
tlemen ! the city of Sinope hath sent us hith[e]
first to commend you, for that, being Greek
you have overcome the Barbarians ; next, [ ]
congratulate you upon your safe arrival, throug[ ]
many, and, as we are informed, grievous har[d]
ships.   But we have reason to expect that, [ ]
we are Greeks also, we shall rather receiv[e]
favours, than injuries from Greeks : parti[ ]
cularly, since we have never provoked you b[ ]
any ill treatment.   I must acquaint you the[n]
that Cotyora is our colony, and that havin[g]
conquered this country from the Barbarians, w[e]
have given it to them.   For which reason,
they pay us the tribute at which they are taxed,
in the same manner with the inhabitants of
Cerazunt and Trebisond ; so that whatever injury you do them, the city of Sinope will look
upon it as done themselves.   Now, we are informed that you have entered their town by

---

1 Ἔστι γὰρ ὄχλῳ ὄντες.   This account of the very
odd manners of this people is transcribed almost word
for word by Eustathius, in his notes upon Dionysius
Periegetes.   Upon this occasion, I cannot help mentioning what Strabo says of the Irish, φανερῶς μίσγε-
σθαι ταῖς τε ἄλλαις γυναιξί, καὶ μητράσι καὶ ἀδελφαῖς ;
but, lest we should think ourselves less barbarous than
our neighbours, Cæsar says the same thing of the
Britons.

2 Εἰς Χάλυβας.   Strabo is of opinion that these were
the same with the Alizonians mentioned by Homer,

   Αὐτὰρ Ἀλιζώνων Ὀδίος δὲ Ἐπίστροφος ἦρχεν
   Τολόθεν ἐξ Ἀλύβης ὅθεν ἀργύρου ἐστι γενέθλη.

And that either the poet wrote ἐκ Χαλύβης, or that the
inhabitants were originally called Alybiana.   By this
passage of Homer it seems they were, at that time, as
famous for their mines of silver as they were afterwards
for those of iron.

3 Τιβαρηνούς.   These were called by Dionysius Periegetes, πολύρρηνες Τιβαρηνοί, which epithet agrees very
well with the account our author gives of their country.

4 Κοτύωρα.   This town was no more than a village
in Arrian's time, and, as he says, a small one.

---

5 Κατ' ἔθνος.   Leunclavius has translated this, I think
properly, " Græcis per singulas nationes distinctis," and
Hutchinson, who takes notice of this translation of
Leunclavius in his notes without any mark of disappro-
bation, has, however chosen to render it " quisque pro
more gentis ;" I own I doubt whether κατὰ ἴδιε signifies " pro more gentis."   By the little acquaintance I
have had with the Greek authors, I observe that κατὰ
τὰ σύντεια is almost always the expression they make
use of upon that occasion.

force; that some of you are quartered in their houses, and that you take what you want, out of the country, without their consent. These things we cannot approve of; and, if you continue this behaviour, we shall be obliged to enter into an alliance with Corylas, and the Paphlagonians, and with any other nation we can prevail upon to assist us."

Then Xenophon rose up, and spoke thus in behalf of the soldiers. "We come hither, O men of Sinope! well satisfied with having preserved our persons, and our arms; for, to bring our booty along with us, and at the same time to fight with our enemies, was impossible. And now, since we arrived among the Greek cities, at Trebisond, for example, we paid for all the provisions we had, because they supplied us with a market; and, in return for the honours they did us, and the presents they gave to the army, we paid them all respect, abstaining from those Barbarians who were their friends, and doing all the mischief we are able to their enemies, against whom they led us. Inquire of them what usage they have received from us: for the guides, whom that city has sent along with us through friendship, are here present. But wherever we find no market provided for us, whether among the Barbarians or Greeks, we supply ourselves with provisions, not through insolence, but necessity. Thus we made the Carduchians, the Chaldæans, and the Taochians, (though no subjects of the king, yet very warlike nations,) our enemies, by being obliged to take what we wanted, because they refused to supply us with a market; while we treated the Macronians, though Barbarians, as friends, and took nothing from them by force, because they supplied us with the best market they were able. And if we have taken any thing from the Cotyorians, who, you say, are your subjects, they are themselves the cause of it: for they have not behaved themselves to us as friends; but, shutting their gates, would neither suffer us to come within their walls, nor supply us with a market without: and of this they lay the fault upon the person you have sent hither as their governor. As to what you say concerning our quartering in their houses by force, we desired them to receive our sick under their roofs: they refusing to open the gates, we passed through them into the city, without committing any other act of violence, and our sick lodged

now in their houses, without putting them to any expense. We have, it is true, placed a guard at the gates, that our people may not be under the power of your governor, but that we may be at liberty to carry them away whenever we may think proper. The rest of us, as you see, encamp, in order, in the open air, prepared, if any one does us a favour, to return it, if an injury, to resent it. You threaten to enter into an alliance with Corylas and the Paphlagonians, if you see convenient, against us. Know then, that if you force us to it, we will encounter you both (for we have already engaged much more numerous enemies;) besides, we have it also in our power, if we think fit, to enter into an alliance with the Paphlagonian; for we are informed that he wants to make himself master both of your city and of the maritime towns. We shall therefore endeavour, by assisting him in attaining what he desires, to gain his friendship."

Upon this, the rest of the ambassadors showed a visible dislike of what Hecatonymus had said; and another of them advancing, said they were not come to declare war, but to express their friendship. "And if," says he, "you think fit to come to Sinope, we will receive you in a hospitable manner, and, for the present, directions shall be given to the inhabitants of this place to supply you with every thing; for we are sensible you advance nothing but what is true." After this, the Cotyorians sent presents to the army, and the generals of the Greeks also treated the ambassadors with all hospitality. They all conferred together a considerable time in a very friendly manner; and, among other things, the generals inquired concerning the remainder of the way, and both of every thing that related to their respective concerns. And thus ended that day.

VI. The next day the generals thought proper to call the soldiers together, and to consider of the rest of their march, in the presence of the Sinopians; for, if they determined to travel by land, they thought these might be of service to conduct them, for they were well acquainted with Paphlagonia; and, if by sea, they imagined they should also want the assistance of the Sinopians, for they alone seemed capable of providing a sufficient number of ships to transport them. Calling therefore the ambassadors, they consulted together: and the generals desired that, as they themselves were Greeks, they would first show their hospitality by their benevolence to Greeks, and by giving them the best advice they were able.

Then Hecatonymus rose up, and first made an apology, for having said that they would enter into an alliance with the Paphlagonian, alleging, that he did not say this with a view of making war upon the Greeks, but to let them see, that, having it in their power to make an alliance with the Barbarians, they preferred that of the Greeks. Being called upon to give his advice, he first invoked the gods: then said thus: " If the advice I am going to give you, appears to me the best, may I be prosperous; otherwise, miserable; for the present counsel seems to be of the nature of those, which are termed ¹ holy. If, therefore, I am found to advise you well, I shall have many to applaud me, and, if ill, many to curse me. I am sensible, then, that we shall have much more trouble, if you return by sea; for in that case we shall be obliged to supply you with ships : whereas if you go by land, it will be incumbent on you to fight your way through. However, I must speak what I think; for I am well acquainted both with the country of the Paphlagonians, and with their strength. Their country contains many very fair plains, and mountains of a prodigious height. And first of all, I know the place where you must, of necessity, enter it; for there is but one pass, and that lies between two points of a rock exceeding high. These a very few men, posted there, may defend; and, if the enemy are once masters of this pass, all the men in the world cannot force their way. This I can make appear to any one you think proper to send along with me. On the other side of this pass, I am well assured, you will find plains, and upon them a body of horse, which the Barbarians themselves think exceeds all the cavalry the king is master of. These, though lately summoned, did not attend him, their commander

being too haughty to obey. But, admit you could even seize the pass between these mountains unobserved, and prevent the enemy, and, afterwards, in the plain, defeat their horse and foot, whose numbers amount to above one hundred and twenty thousand men, you will still find several rivers in your way. First, the ² Thermodon, which is three hundred feet over; the passage of which seems to me very difficult, particularly, when you have a numerous army in front, and another in your rear. Secondly, the ³ Iris; this is also three hundred feet broad. The third river you will meet with, is the ⁴ Halys, not less than two stadia in breadth. This you cannot pass without boats; and who is there to supply you with them? The ⁵ Parthenius is, in like manner, impassable. This river you would arrive at, if you could pass the Halys. So that I do not look upon this road as only difficult but absolutely impassable. Whereas if you go by sea, you may sail from hence to Sinope, and from Sinope to Heracles ; and, from Heracles, there will be no difficulty, either in going by land, or by sea : for there you will find great numbers of ships."

When he had done speaking, some suspected he said this out of friendship to Corylas, for there was an intercourse of hospitality between them; others, that he expected to be rewarded for his advice; and some, that he said it, fearing lest, if they went by land, they should do some damage to the country of the Sinopians. However, the Greeks voted to go by sea. After that Xenophon said, " O men of Sinope! the soldiers have determined to go in a manner you advise. But thus the case stands. We are contented to go by sea, provided we are furnished with such a number of ships, that not a man of us shall be left behind. But if it is proposed, that some of us should be left, and some set sail, we are resolved not to go on board at all : because we are sensible, that wherever we are the strongest, we shall not only be safe, but get provisions also ; and that, if we are any where found weaker than our enemies, we expect no better

---

1 Ἱερὰ συμβουλή· We find by this passage of Xenophon, and by another in Plato, that it was a common saying among the Greeks, that counsel was a divine thing. " If," says the latter to Demodocus, "counsel is called a divine thing, none can be more so than that which relates to the present question;" this was education, ἀλλὰ μὲν δὴ ὦ Δημόδοκε, καὶ λέγεταί γε συμβουλὴ ἱερὸν χρῆμα εἶναι. Εἴπερ οὖν καὶ ἄλλη ἡτισοῦν ἐστιν ἱερὰ καὶ αὕτη ἂν εἴη, περὶ ἧς σὺ νῦν συμβουλεύῃ. D'Ablancourt was sensible this parenthesis could have no grace in a modern language; but I doubt whether that reason will be thought to justify his leaving it out.

2 Τὸν Θερμώδοντα. See note upon the sixth book.

3 Ἴριν. This river rises out of the kingdom of Pontus, and, having received the Lycus, runs through the plain of Themiscyra, and, from thence, falls into the Euxine sea.

4 Ἅλυν. See note upon the sixth book.

5 Παρθένιος. See note upon the sixth book.

age than to be made slaves." The Sino-ians, hearing this, desired the Greeks to send nbassadors to them, and accordingly they int Callimachus an Arcadian, Ariston an thenian, and Samylas an Achaian; who set ut immediately.

In the meantime Xenophon, considering the reat number of Greek heavy-armed men, of rgeteers, archers, slingers, and horse, who, by ong experience, were now become good troops, oked upon it as an enterprise of great repu-ation to add to the acquisitions of Greece, hat of a country, with the power annexed to t, by building a city upon the Euxine sea, rhere so great an army could not be got toge-ber without a vast expense. He had reason o think this city would grow considerable, oth from the number of his own men, and of he neighbouring inhabitants. Calling, there-ore, Silanus of Ambracia, to him, the same rho had been soothsayer to Cyrus, he offered acrifice upon this occasion, before he commu-icated his thoughts to any of the soldiers. But Silanus, fearing this should take effect, nd that the army would settle in some place, cquainted the soldiers that Xenophon pro-osed to detain them there, and, by building a ity, to acquire reputation and power to him-elf. The design of Silanus in this was to get o Greece as soon as possible, having saved he three thousand [6] daricks which he received rom Cyrus, when sacrificing by his order, he old him the truth concerning the ten days. As soon as the soldiers were informed of this, ome thought it was best for them to stay here; but the greatest part disapproved f it; and Timasion the Dardanian, and Thorax the Bœotian, told some merchants of Heraclea and Sinope, who were present, that, f they did not supply the men with money ufficient to buy provisions when they set sail, hey were in danger of having so great an army ettle in their neighbourhood. "For," said hey, "Xenophon is the author of this resolu-ion, and advises us, as soon as the ships arrive, mmediately to speak to the army in these erms: Gentlemen! we observe you are at a oss both how to get provisions for your voy-ge, and enrich your families in some measure rhen you come home; but if you have a

mind to make choice of some part of the inha-bited country that lies round the Euxine sea, and possess yourselves of it, and that those who are desirous to return home, may go away, while the rest stay here, we are now furnished with ships for that purpose; so that you have it in your power to make an unexpected descent upon any part of the country you think fit."

The merchants, hearing this, informed their cities of it; and Timasion of Dardanus sent Eurymachus, also of Dardanus, and Thorax of Bœotia with them, to confirm it. As soon as the inhabitants of Sinope and Heraclea were acquainted with this, they sent to Timasion, to engage him, in consideration of a sum of money, to persuade the army to sail out of the Euxine sea. He was pleased with the offer, and spoke thus to the assembly of the soldiers : "Gentle-men! we ought not to think of staying here, or to prefer any other country to Greece. I hear some people are offering sacrifice upon this occasion, without even acquainting you with their purpose; but I promise you, if you sail from hence, the first [7] day of the month, to

7 Ἀπὸ νουμηνίας. We find by several passages in Xenophon and other authors, that the soldiers among the Greeks received their pay monthly. The interest of money was also payable monthly among the Greeks, as it was among the Romans. As the payment both of the principal and interest, and the rigorous methods al-lowed by law to compel it often occasioned great con-vulsions among the latter, it may not be amiss to make some cur ory observations upon this subject, particular-ly since Dacier, in his notes upon Horace, and many other modern authors, have very much misrepresented it. It is certain, then, that this monthly interest was one per cent. by the law of the twelve tables, that is, twelve per cent. per annum; this they called "unciarium fœnus:" and, what is very extraordinary, Livy says, that by the establishment of this interest, usury was made easy, "unciario fœnore facto levata usura erat;" an evident sign of the scarcity of money; but then it must be considered that the year to which this reflection of Livy relates, was so early as the three hundred and ninety-ninth of Rome. Afterwards, that is, in the four hundred and eighty year of Rome, T. Manlius Torqua-tus and C. Plautius being consuls, this monthly interest was reduced to half per cent. that is, to six per cent. per annum, "semunciarum ex unciario fœnus factum." But to return to the νουμηνία, the year of the Greeks was luni-solar, that is, formed of twelve synodical months, making in all but three hundred and fifty-four days, with an intercalation of seven months in nineteen years, invented by Meton, (from whom it was called Μέτωνος ἐνιαυτός) to answer the annual difference of eleven days between the lunar and solar year; this was their civil year; and as their new year began at the first new moon of the summer solstice (the Romans begin-ning theirs at the first after the winter solstice) it neces-

6 Δαρικούς. See note 6. page 160.

give each of you a ¹ Cyzicene, for your monthly pay. My design is to lead you into Troas, from whence I am banished; where my fellow-citizens will assist you, for I know they will receive me with pleasure. Thence I propose to carry you to those parts, where you shall enrich yourselves; for I am acquainted with Æolia, Phrygia, and Troas, and with all the country belonging to the government of Pharnabazus; with one of them by being born there, and with the other, by having served there under Clearchus and Dercellidas."

Immediately Thorax the Bœotian, who had a perpetual contest with Xenophon for the command, rose up, and said, if they sailed out of the Euxine sea, they might settle in the Chersonesus, a country of great beauty and fertility; where those who were willing, might inhabit, and from whence those, who were not so, might return home. He added, that it was ridiculous to hunt after lands, among the Bar-

barians, when others, of a great extent, offered themselves in Greece. "And, till you arrive there," says he, "I, as well as Timasion, promise you pay." This he said from being acquainted with what the inhabitants of Heraclea and Sinope had promised to Timasion, upon condition the army set sail. All this time Xenophon was silent. Then Philesius and Lycon, both Achaians, said, it was not to be suffered, that Xenophon should persuade the soldiers in private to stay, and offer sacrifice upon this occasion, without letting the army partake of the sacrifice, yet say nothing of all this in public. So that he was under a necessity of rising up, and of speaking as follows:

"Gentlemen! I offer sacrifice, as you are sensible, to the utmost of my abilities, both for you and myself, to the end that my words, my thoughts, and actions may be employed in those things that are most for the credit and advantage of us all. And even now I was consulting the gods by sacrifice, whether it would be more expedient to mention this and treat with you about it, or not to concern myself at all in the matter. Here Silanus, the soothsayer, assured me, that the victims, which is of the greatest moment, were favourable, (for he knew that I, by being constantly present at the sacrifices, was not unacquainted with these things) but informed me, at the same time, that, according to them, some fraud and treachery seemed to threaten me: and in this, indeed, he was in the right, since he himself designed treacherously to accuse me before you: for he has spread a report that I had already purposed to effect this without your approbation. But the truth is, when I saw you in want, I considered by what means you might possess yourselves of some town, to the end that those among you who are willing, might set sail immediately, and that those who were not so, might stay till they had acquired something to carry home to their families. But now I find both the inhabitants of Heraclea and Sinope are sending us ships, and that these men promise you your pay from the beginning of the month, I look upon it as an advantageous circumstance for us to be conducted with safety to the place we desire, and to be ² paid for be-

---

sarily happened that the first day of the year of both began about sun-set, for at that time only the new moon became visible. It is very possible that the crescent with which Diana is represented, is owing to the custom of proclaiming the new moon, particularly if, as I observed upon another occasion, Diana and the Egyptian Isis, who is often represented with a crescent upon her head, were the same divinity. This ceremony of proclaiming the new moon still continues in the Levant, where the Turks, whose year is lunar, publish, with great solemnity, the first appearance of the new moon of their month of Ramazan, which is their Lent.

1 Κυζικηνόν. Hesychius and Phavorinus inform us, that the Cyzicene was a coin famous for being well struck; and that it had a woman's head on one side; to which Suidas adds, that, on the other, was the head of a lion. Demosthenes tells us they were worth twenty-eight Attic drachms, that is 18s. and 1d. sterling. The woman's head is possibly Cybele, who was supposed to be drawn by lions, and who was worshipped in a particular manner at Pessinus in Phrygia, not far from Cyzicus, whose tutelar god, however, was, I imagine, Hercules, whom they looked upon as the founder of their city, as may be seen by a medal of Domitian, on the reverse of which is a Hercules, with this inscription: ΤΟΝ ΚΤΙΣΤΗΝ ΚΥΖΙΚΗΝΩΝ. But we have great reason to conclude that the woman's head is designed for Cybele, from what we find in Strabo, who says, that near to Cyzicus stood a temple of Cybele built by the Argonauts, upon the mountain Dindymon, from which Cybele was called Dindymene. This being so, the globe and the fish, and particularly the ears of corn and bunches of grapes with which she is crowned, will be very proper symbols of universal nature which, as I endeavoured to show upon another occasion, was represented by Cybele. D'Ablancourt is of opinion that the Turkish sequin is derived from Cyziquin; but Menage says that it comes from the Italian zecchino, a Venetian ducat, which takes its name from Zecca, the place where it is coined.

2 Μισθὸν τῆς σωτηρίας. This appears to me far preferable to μισθὸν τῆς σωτίας; it not only makes the sense stronger, but seems to be the natural result of σωζομένους, which immediately precedes it. I am sorry to dif-

ng preserved. For this reason, I not only give over all thoughts of that kind myself, but desire those who came to me to declare themselves in favour of that measure, to desist also. For this is my sense of the matter; while you continue together as you are now, in great numbers, you will be sure to find esteem, and never to want provisions, for victory carries with it a right to whatever belongs to the conquered. But, if you suffer yourselves to be divided, and the army to be broken into small bodies, you will neither be able to find subsistence, nor have reason to be pleased with your treatment. My opinion, therefore, is the same with yours, that we ought to go on to Greece: and further, if any one stays behind, or is taken endeavouring to desert his companions before the whole army arrives in a place of safety, that he be punished as an offender. And whoever is of this opinion, let him hold up his hand." And they all held up their hands.

However Silanus cried out, and endeavoured to show that every one ought to be at liberty to go away. This the soldiers would not bear, but threatened him, if they took him endeavouring to make his escape, to inflict the punishment on him. After this, when the inhabitants of Heraclea were informed that the Greeks had resolved to sail out of the Euxine sea, and that Xenophon himself had [2] put the question, they sent the ships, but disappointed Timasion and Thorax of the money they had promised them to pay the soldiers. Hereupon those who undertook for it were confounded, and afraid of the army; and taking with them the rest of the generals, who were privy to their former designs, (these were all, except Neon the Asinian, who commanded under Cheirisophus, then absent) they came to Xenophon, and told him they were sorry for what had passed, and thought the best thing they could do, since they had ships, was to sail to the river Phasis, and possess themselves of the country belonging to the Phasians; of whom the son of Ætas was at that time king. Xenophon made answer, that he would mention nothing of this kind to the army; "But,"

says he, "do you assemble them, and if you think fit, propose it." Upon this, Timasion the Dardanian gave his opinion that they ought not to call the soldiers together; but that each of the generals should first endeavour to persuade his own captains to come into it. So they departed to put this in execution.

VII. In the meantime the soldiers were informed of what was in agitation; and Neon told them that Xenophon having prevailed upon the rest of the generals, designed to deceive the army, and carry them back to the Phasis. The soldiers hearing this, resented it, and holding assemblies and private meetings among themselves, gave great reason to apprehend they would break out into the same violences they had committed upon the persons of the heralds of the Colchians, and the commissaries of provisions, all of whom they had stoned to death, except those who escaped to the sea. As soon as Xenophon perceived this, he resolved immediately to call the army together, and not to suffer them to meet of their own accord: so he ordered the crier to assemble them. They readily obeyed the summons. Then Xenophon, without accusing the other generals of coming to him privately, spoke to them in the following manner:

"I am informed, gentlemen! that some people accuse me of a design to deceive you, and carry you to the Phasis. Hear me, therefore, for heaven's sake, and, if I appear guilty, I do not desire to depart hence, before I receive the punishment that is due to my crime: but if they find they accuse me wrongfully, I hope you will treat them as they deserve. I make no doubt but you all know in what quarter the sun rises, and where it sets; and that the way to Greece lies westward, that to the Barbarians, eastward. Is there any one therefore who can make you believe that the sun rises where it sets, and sets where it rises? You are also sensible that the north wind carries you out of the Euxine sea to Greece, and the south to the Phasis; and when the wind is in the north, you always say it is fair for Greece. Can any one therefore so far impose upon you, as to persuade you to go on board when the wind is in the south? But suppose I embark you in a calm: I shall however sail but in one ship, while you sail, at least, in a hundred. How therefore can I

<hr>

ter both from Leunclavius and Hutchinson upon this occasion. D'Ablancourt has said *de recevoir recompense pour retourner en votre pais*, which gives the sense, but not the beauty of the Greek expression.

3 'Εστιψηφισάς. See note 1, page 297.

either compel you to keep me company against your consent, or deceive you with regard to the place to which I carry you? But let us further suppose that I do deceive you, and, by some magic art, carry you to the Phasis, and also that we land there; you will soon be sensible that you are not in Greece; and I who have deceived you shall be but one man, while you who have been deceived by me, will be near ten thousand with your arms in your hands. By what means therefore can one man court punishment more effectually, than by forming designs so prejudicial both to himself and you? But these rumours are spread by weak men, who envy me because I am honoured by you; though without reason: for which of them do I hinder from proposing any thing for your advantage, if he can, from fighting both for you and himself, if he is willing, or from watching for your safety, if he is disposed to undertake that care. Why should I hinder them? When you choose your commanders, do I oppose the pretensions of any person? I [1] resign; let him take the command; only let him make it appear he can do something for your advantage: but I have said enough of this. If any of you thinks himself in danger of being deceived, or that any other person has deceived him in this, let him declare it; but since you have heard enough of this subject, I desire you would not depart until I have acquainted you with a thing, that I find begins to show itself in the army; which, if it makes any progress, and becomes what it threatens to be, it is high time for us to take proper measures, that we may not appear both to gods and men, to friends and enemies, the most abandoned, and most infamous of all men, and consequently incur a general contempt." The soldiers hearing this, wondered what it might be, and desired him to go on; so he resumed his discourse. " You know there were some towns upon the mountains belonging to those Barbarians who were in alliance with the inhabitants of Cerazunt; from whence some of the people came down to us, and sold us cattle and other things. Some of you, I believe, went into the nearest of these towns,

and after you had bought provisions there, returned to the camp. Clearatus, one of the captains, finding this place both small and unguarded, because the inhabitants looked upon themselves to be in friendship with us, marched against them in the night, with a design to plunder it, without acquainting any of us with his purpose. For he determined, if he had made himself master of the place, to have returned no more to the army, but to have gone on board the ship in which his companions were sailing by the coast, and, with his booty, to have escaped out of the Euxine sea. And all this was concerted between him and his companions, who were on board, as I am now informed. Calling, therefore, together as many as he could prevail upon to follow him, he led them against the town. But the day surprising them in their march, the inhabitants got together, and defended themselves from their strong places so well, both with missive weapons, and their swords, that Clearatus himself, and several others, were slain; part of them, however, escaped to Cerazunt. This happened the same day we left Cerazunt to march hither. Some of those also who were to sail along the coast, were still in that city, having not as yet weighed anchor. After this, as the inhabitants of Cerazunt inform us, three of the elders came from the town, desiring to be introduced to the assembly of the Greeks; but not finding us, they told the citizens of Cerazunt, they wondered what we meant by attacking them. These assured them, that the attempt was not countenanced by public authority; with which they were very well satisfied, and resolved to sail hither, in order to give us an account of what had passed, and to let us know that they gave leave to those who were willing to carry off the dead, and bury them. It happened that some of the Greeks, who had fled to Cerazunt, were still there. These, perceiving whither the Barbarians purposed to go, had the confidence to throw stones at them themselves, and to encourage others to do the same. By this means these ambassadors, being three in number, were stoned to death. After the fact was committed, some of the inhabitants of Cerazunt came to the generals, and informed us of what had happened. These proceedings gave us great concern, and we consulted together with them, in what manner the

---

1 Παρίημι. Nicias, at the close of one of his speeches to the Athenians, uses this word in the same sense, with the addition of ἀρχὴν· εἰ δὲ τῷ ἄλλως δοκεῖ, παρίημι αὐτῷ τὴν ἀρχήν.

reeks who were slain might be buried. While e were sitting in consultation without the master of the heavy-armed men, on a sudden a heard a great uproar, and people crying out, Knock [2] them down, knock them down, stone them, stone them ;' and immediately we saw reat numbers running to those who cried out, some with stones in their hands, others taking them up. Upon this the inhabitants of Cerazunt, [3] having been witnesses of what had happened in their own town, were frightened, and as to their ships : some of us also, I do assure you, were not without fear. For my part, I went directly up to them, and asked them what the matter was ? Some of those I inquired of knew nothing about it ; yet had stones in their hands. At last, meeting with one who did know, he told me that the commissaries of provisions oppressed the army in a most grievous manner. While he was saying this, one of the soldiers perceived the commissary Zelarchus, retiring towards the sea, and cried out ; the rest, hearing this, as if a wild boar or a stag had been roused, ran at him. The citizens of Cerazunt, seeing the soldiers making towards them, and thinking themselves aimed at, fled in all haste, and ran into the sea. Some of our men ran in after them, and those who could not swim were drowned. What do you think these men were afraid of? They had committed no crime ; they must imagine that some madness like that of dogs had seized our men. If these things continue, consider what will be the condition of the army. You will not have

it in your power, by a general consent, to make either war or peace, as you see convenient ; but every private man may lead the army upon whatever enterprise he pleases. And if, at any time, ambassadors come to you to sue for peace, or for any thing else, any one may put them to death, and thereby prevent your being informed of their demands. The consequence of which will be, that those, whom you, by a general voice, appoint to command you, will be no longer regarded ; but whoever erects himself to be your general, and pleases to cry ' Stone them, stone them,' may, if he finds the same obedience that was lately given, put to death not only your commander, but any private man, untried. Consider what services these self-elected generals have done for us. If Zelarchus, the commissary, is guilty, he has, by sailing away, escaped punishment ; if he is innocent, he has left the army, from the fear of being unjustly put to death without trial. Those who have stoned the ambassadors, have done you this piece of service—they have made it unsafe for you alone, of all the Greeks, to go to Cerazunt, without a force sufficient to protect you : and not less so even with [4] a herald to bring off your dead, whom, before this, the same persons who killed them, gave you leave to bury : for who that had a hand in killing heralds, will serve in that capacity ? However, we have desired the citizens of Cerazunt to bury them. If these things are right, give them a public sanction, that, as attempts of this kind are to be expected, every man may be upon his guard, and endeavour to pitch his tent upon places of advantage and strength. But, if you look upon them rather as the actions of wild beasts, than of men, consider how to put a stop to them : otherwise, how, in the name of the gods, shall we offer sacrifice with cheerfulness, if we are guilty of impiety ? Or how shall we fight with our enemies, if we kill one another ? What city will receive us

---

2 Παῖς, ταῖς, βάλλε, βάλλι. Literally, attack them both sword in hand, and with missive weapons, cominus eminusque incesso, which I should think might do as well as cædo, cædo, feri, feri, in the Latin translators. I have considered the Greeks here as a mob, which they were upon this occasion, and have consequently made use of terms very familiar to an English mob in tumults. For the same reason I think D'Ablancourt has said very properly tue, tue, though I am very sensible that the French troops use this word when they pursue the enemy, as they call it, l'epee dans les reins.

3 'Ὃς ἂν ἰωρακότες τὸ σαφ' ἱαυτοῖς σεῆγμα. If the Latin translators, by rendering this, ut qui facinus apud se designatum etiam vidissent, mean perpetratum, I think that signification of the word designo, is too uncommon for a translation ; but, if they mean it in the ordinary acceptation of the word, the fact was not only designatum but commissum ; for what is said of the fear of the inhabitants of Cerazunt, visibly relates to the outrage committed by the Greeks upon the persons of the three ambassadors, who were stoned to death in their town. D'Ablancourt has I think said much better, instruits parce qui s'etoit passe dans leur ville.

4 Σὺν κηρυκίῳ. Κηρύκιον or κηρύκιον, for it is written both ways, was the caduceus which heralds carried in their hands, when they were sent upon public occasions from one army to another. It is particularly described by the Greek Scholiast upon Thucydides ; but so many bas-reliefs, and other monuments of antiquity represent Mercury with his caduceus in his hand, that I think it needless to translate what he says of it. It is reported to have been a present from Apollo to Mercury, in exchange for the harp, which tradition I find, by Diodorus Siculus, was derived from the Egyptians.

as friends, when they see us guilty of such enormities? Who will bring provisions to us, with any confidence, if we are found to offend in things of so great moment? As to the applause which we promised ourselves with so much confidence, who will speak well of us if we dishonour ourselves by such actions? For I am well assured, that we should condemn others, were they guilty of them."

Upon this, they all rose up, and said the authors of these disorders should be punished; that it should be unlawful to begin such enormities for the future, and that those who were guilty of it, should be put to death. They then ordered that the generals should bring them all to their trial; where it should be inquired whether any person had received any other injury since the death of Cyrus; and appointed the captains to be the judges. At the same time, upon Xenophon's ¹ motion, and the concurrence of the priests, it was resolved to purify the army. And the army was purified accordingly.

VIII. They further decreed that the generals themselves should be called to an account for their past conduct; and, upon their trial, Philesius and Xanthicles were condemned in a fine of twenty mines, to the amount of which sum they had embezzled ² the effects that had

been taken out of the ships, and committed to their charge. Sophænetus was fined ten mines, for that, being chosen a commander, he had neglected his duty. Some accused Xenophon, complaining they had been beaten by him, and brought their accusation against him for abusing them. Upon this, Xenophon rising up, desired the first person who appeared against him, to acquaint the judges where he had been beaten. He answered, "Where we were dying with cold, and there was abundance of snow." Xenophon replied: "If, during the storm you speak of, when we had no victuals, nor so much wine as would serve us to smell to; when many of us were spent with labour, and the enemy at our heels, if, in that season I was abusive, I own myself more ³ vicious than asses, which, through viciousness, are said to be insensible to fatigue. However, say for what reason you were beaten. Did I demand any thing of you, and beat you because you refused it? Did I insist upon your restoring any thing? Was it in struggling to subdue you to my passion, or when I was drunk, that I abused you?" And upon his saying that it was nothing of all this, Xenophon asked him "whether he belonged to the heavy-armed men?" He answered, "No." "If to the targeteers?" "Neither," says he: "but I was driving a mule at the desire of my comrades, being a free man." Upon this Xenophon called him to mind, and asked him, "Are you not the man who carried a sick person?" "The

---

1 Παραινοῦντος δὲ Ξενοφῶντος——ἐδοξε καὶ καθαίρειν τὸ στράτευμα. Xenophon seems to imitate Agamemnon upon this occasion, who, as Homer tells us, having at last sent Chryseïs back to her father with a hecatomb, to appease the anger of Apollo, orders the Greek army to be purified, and it was purified accordingly:

Λαοὺς δ' Ἀτρείδης ἀπολυμαίνεσθαι ἄνωγεν,
Οἱ δ' ἀπελυμαίναντο, καὶ εἰς ἄλα λύματ' ἔβαλλον.

Thus translated by Mr Pope,

The host to expiate, next the king prepares,
With pure lustrations, and with solemn prayers,
Wash'd by the briny wave, the pious train
Are cleansed; and cast th' ablutions on the main.

There can be no doubt, as Mr Pope has very properly observed from Eustathius, that λύματα is derived from λούω, which justifies him in the use of the word ablutions, a word much more decent than those made use of upon this occasion by all former translators. It was a prevailing opinion, it seems, among the ancients, that the water of the sea had a sovereign virtue in explations: it was from this opinion that Iphigenia says in Euripides,

Θάλασσα κλύζει πάντα τ' ἀνθρώπων κακά.

2 Τῶν γαυλιτικῶν χρημάτων. The ancient Lexicons say that γαῦλος signifies a certain kind of ship used by the Phœnicians, but I find γαῦλος in Herodotus for a Phœnician ship, where he says that Dionysius of Phocæa

sailed to Phœnicia, and having sunk the merchant ships, and taken a great booty, sailed to Sicily, Διονύσιος δὲ ὁ Φωκαεὺς——ἔπλεε εἰς Φοινίκην· γαυλοὺς δὲ ἐνθαῦτα καταδύσας, καὶ χρήματα λαβὼν πολλὰ, ἔπλεε εἰς Σικελίω; so that γαυλικὰ χρήματα may, no doubt, signify the freight of those ships; but in this place I imagine it means the cargoes of those ships the Greeks had taken, which cargoes our author in the beginning of this book calls ἀγώγιμα; he also says in the same place that the Greeks having taken out the cargoes of these ships, appointed guards to take care of them. It is very probable that Philesius and Xanthicles might have the command of these guards, and consequently the charge of these effects, and that they might have embezzled as much of them as amounted to twenty mines; if the reader will cast his eye on note 7, page 175, he will find that χρήματα is often made use of by the best authors to signify effects. There seems to be so great a relation between this passage, and that in the beginning of this book, that I cannot approve of pecuniam de navigiis coactam in Leunclavius and Hutchinson, and much less of du prix des navires in D'Ablancourt.

3 Τῶν ὄνων ὑβριστικώτεροι εἶναι. Every body knows that asses, and mules, their offspring, have such an inbred viciousness, that no fatigue can subdue it.

ame," says he; " for you forced me to it, and threw about the baggage that belonged to my comrades." " But," says Xenophon, " in this manner I threw about their baggage ; I distributed it to others to carry, with orders to return it to me ; and having received every thing safe, I restored them to you, after you had shown me the man I gave you in charge." " But I desire," says he, " you will hear how this matter was, for it is well worth while."

" One of the men being unable to continue his march, was left behind. This man I knew no otherwise than that he belonged to the army ; however, I obliged you to carry him, that he might not perish: for, as I remember, the enemy were at our heels." This the other confessed. " Then," says Xenophon, " after I had ordered you to go before, I quickly overtook you again, as I came up with the rear guard, and found you digging a pit, with a design to bury the man ; and stopping, I commended you: but the man drawing in his leg while we stood by, all who were present cried out, that he was alive ; and you said whatever you thought fit, as, ' I will not carry him.' Upon which I struck you, you say, and you say true: for you seemed to me to be sensible that the man was alive." " But," says the other, " did he die the less after I showed him to you ?" " We must all die," replies Xenophon, " but are we for that reason to be buried alive ?" At this they all cried out, that he had not beaten him so much as he deserved. Then Xenophon desired the rest to inform the judges for what reason each of them had been beaten ; but they not rising up, he spoke thus :

" I own, gentlemen, that I have struck a great many of the men, for not keeping their ranks. These ought to have been contented with being preserved by your means, while you marched in order, and fought where it was necessary ; but instead of that, they wanted to leave their ranks, and run before you for plunder, that they might have the advantage over you. Had we all done the same, we had all been destroyed. I own also, that finding some overcome with sloth, unwilling to rise, and ready to abandon themselves to the enemy, I struck them, and forced them to march. For being myself once obliged, when it was excessive cold, to stay for some of the men who were getting their baggage ready, and sitting for a considerable time, I found myself scarcely able to rise and stretch out my legs. Having, therefore, had the experience of this in myself, afterwards, when I saw any one sitting down, and indulging his sloth, I drove him before me ; for motion and vigorous efforts created warmth and * suppleness, while sitting down and rest, I observed, made the blood to congeal, and the toes to rot off ; which you are sensible was the case of a great many. Others, who suffered themselves to be left behind through laziness, and by that means hindered you, who were in the van, and us, who were in the rear, from advancing, I might possibly strike with my fist, that they might not be struck by the spear of the enemy. These, therefore, who have been thus preserved, may, if they have suffered any unjust treatment from me, now be relieved: whereas, had they fallen under the power of the enemy, what relief could they have had though their treatment had been ever so grievous ? I speak to you in all simplicity. If I have punished any one for his own good, I am willing to submit to the same chastisement that parents receive from their children, and masters from their scholars. Physicians, also, use incisions and caustics for the good of their patients. If you imagine I did these things through insolence, consider with yourselves, that now, with the assistance of the gods, I entertain greater hopes and confidence than at that time, and drink more wine, yet strike no man ; for I see you are now in a calm. But when a storm arises, and the sea runs high, do not you find that the * pilot, for a nod only, quarrels with those who are at the head of the ship, and the steersman with those at the stern ? because, upon those occasions, the least fault is enough to ruin every thing. You yourselves then determined that their chastise-

---

5 'Τγρότητα. 'Τγρότης, in this place, is used by Xenophon in the same sense in which the Greeks say ύγρού άγκάλαι, which Horace has finely translated in that ode, where he represents the false Neæra holding him in her arms, while she swears fidelity to him.

Arctius atque hedera procera astringitur ilex,
Lentis adhærens brachiis.

And when our author, in his Art of Horsemanship, recommends a colt that moves his knees with freedom, he says τάγε μὴν γόνατα ἣν βαδίζων ὁ πῶλος ὑγρῶς κάμπτη.

6 Πρωρεύς. Πρωρεὺς in Greek, and proreta in Latin, signify an officer, whose business it was to keep a look out, as the sailors call it, at the head of the ship. I am informed that we have no term in our naval institution, that properly explains it ; that of pilot, the gentlemen of the navy tell me, comes the nearest to it.

ment was just; for you were present with arms in your hands, to assist them if you had thought proper, not [1] with billets to give your votes in their behalf. However, in reality, you neither assisted them in escaping the punishment due to their irregularity, nor me in inflicting it. Thus by suffering their insolence, you have given a sanction to their remissness: for I am of opinion, if you observe, you will find that those who were then most remarkable for their neglect of duty, are now so for their insolence. An instance of this you see in Boiscus, the Thessalian boxer: he then contended, under pretence of sickness, not to carry his shield, and now, I am informed, he has stripped several of the inhabitants of Cotyora. If you are wise, therefore, your treatment of this man will be the reverse of that bestowed on dogs; for these, when they are cursed, are tied up in the day-time, and let loose in the night; whereas, if you do well, you will tie him up in the night, and let him loose in the day. I own I am surprised to find, that if I have given offence to any of you, you call it to mind, and publish it; but if I have defended any from the cold, or from the enemy, or relieved them when they were sick, or in want, these things are remembered by none of you: if I have commended any for a proper behaviour, or honoured brave men to the utmost of my power, these things also are not remembered. Yet it is certain, there is more honesty, justice, piety, and pleasure in remembering good than ill offices."

Upon this the assembly rose, and called to mind what was passed: so Xenophon was [2] acquitted, and all was well.

---

1 Ψῆφος. Ψῆφος signifies literally a pebble; and as the Greeks give their votes with these, their votes came to be called ψῆφοι: this literally translated would not be intelligible to an English reader, so that it seems necessary to render it in such a manner as may relate to our customs; and as every person who votes by ballot puts a billet into the ballot box, signifying his sense of the question, I thought ψῆφοι could not upon this occasion be properly translated by any other word than billets. D'Ablancourt seems to have been sensible of the difficulty of translating ψῆφοι with propriety, by his leaving it out.

2 Περιγίνετο. Both the Latin translators have said hic exitus erat: I have rather chosen to render it in the same sense in which Thucydides uses the word in the speech of the Corinthians to the Lacedæmonians, where they tell them that in the war between them and the Athenians they often owed the advantages they gained to the oversights of the enemy, rather than to the assistance they received from the Lacedæmonians: καὶ πρὸς αὐτοὺς τοὺς Ἀθηναίους πολλὰ ἡμᾶς ἤδη τοῖς ἁμαρτήμασιν αὐτῶν μᾶλλον ἢ τῇ ἀφ' ὑμῶν τιμωρίᾳ περιγεγενημένους. So that I imagine Xenophon means that at his trial he had the advantage over his enemies, that is, he was acquitted.

XENOPHON

ON THE

EXPEDITION OF CYRUS.

BOOK VI.

CONTENTS of BOOK VI.

EXPEDITION OF CYRUS.

BOOK VI.

I. FROM this time, some of the Greeks, while they staid here, subsisted themselves by the provisions they bought in the market, and others, by those they got in plundering the country of Paphlagonia. On the other side, the Paphlagonians lost no opportunity of robbing the stragglers, and, in the night-time, endeavoured to annoy those who were encamped in places more advanced than the rest. These proceedings increased the ill blood that was between them. Upon this, Corylas, who was at that time governor of Paphlagonia, sent ambassadors to the Greeks in costly robes, and well mounted, with instructions to acquaint them that Corylas desired neither to do an injury to the Greeks, nor receive any from them. To this the generals answered, that they would consider of it with the army. In the meantime, they entertained them with all hospitality, and invited such of the army as they judged most proper: then having killed some of the oxen they had taken, and other cattle, they gave them a handsome entertainment, the company lying [1] on beds made of brushwood, covered with grass and leaves, and drinking out of horn cups which they found in the country.

As soon as the libations were over, and they had sung the pæan, two Thracians first rose up, and danced with their arms to the sound of a flute : they capered very high, and with great agility ; then made use of their swords. At last one of them struck the other in such a manner, that every one thought he had killed him, (but the stroke was given with art,)

upon which the Paphlagonians cried out ; and the other, having despoiled him of his arms, went out [2] singing a song of triumph in honour of Sitalces : then other Thracians carried off the man as if he had been dead, though indeed he was not hurt. After this, some [3] Ænians and Magnesians rose up, and danced [4] in their arms, what they call the Carpæan

---

2 Ἀλῶν Σιτάλκαν. Herodotus, Thucydides, and Diodorus Siculus speak much in commendation of Sitalces, king of Thracia, in whose honour, no doubt, this song of victory was composed by the Thracians : Thucydides tells us that he was slain in a battle against the Tribalians, and that his nephew Seuthes succeeded him. As this happened the first year of the eighty-ninth Olympiad, that is, the eighth of the Peloponnesian war, and only twenty years before the time of this expedition, it is possible this Seuthes may be the prince in whose service the Greeks engaged, as we shall find in the seventh book ; though I am sensible that Thucydides makes him the son of Sparadocus, and Xenophon of Mæsades.

3 Αἰνιᾶνες καὶ Μάγνητες. Possibly the first might belong to Ænea, a town said by Dionysius of Halicarnassus to have been built by Æneas, after the taking of Troy.

4 Οἱ ἀρχοῦντο τὴν καρπαίαν καλουμένην ἐν τοῖς ὅπλοις. The pantomime representation of the ancients is so often confounded in translations of their works into modern languages with what is now called dancing, that I think myself obliged to explain my sense of this passage, in order to prevent my translation of it from being thought to fall under the general mistake. It is certain that the Greeks and Romans had, besides their tragedies and comedies, a mute pantomime representation, which was called by the former ὄρχησις, and by the latter saltatio. This is that representation, in praise of which Lucian has written a particular treatise ; what he designed for praise, we may make use of for information. After having run through a detail of the vast knowledge an ὀρχηστής or pantomime ought to be master of, he says, that as his profession consists in imitation, and as he undertakes to represent, by his gestures, what the chorus sings or recites, his chief business is perspicuity, to the end that none of his actions may stand in need of an explanation, but that the spectators may, like the Pythian

dance; the manner of which is as follows. One of them having laid down his arms, sows, and drives a yoke of oxen, looking often behind him, as if he were afraid; then a robber approaches, whom the other perceiving, he catches up his arms, and advancing, fights with him [1] in defence of his oxen (and all this these men performed in time to the flute). At last, the robber binds the ploughman, and carries him off with the oxen. Sometimes the ploughman overcomes the robber, and, fastening him to the oxen, ties his hands behind him, and so drives him away.

After this, Mysus entered with a buckler in each hand, and danced sometimes, as if he had been engaged with two adversaries; then used his bucklers, as if engaged with only one;

sometimes he [2] whirled round; then threw himself head foremost and fell upon his feet, without parting with the bucklers: this made a fine sight. Last of all he danced the Persian dance, striking his bucklers against each other, and in dancing, fell upon his knees, then sprung up again, and in all this he kept time to the flute. He was succeeded by some Mantineans and other Arcadians, who, being dressed in the handsomest armour they could provide, rose up, and advanced in time to a flute that played a point of war. They sung the pæan, and danced in the same manner that is practised in solemn processions. The Paphlagonians were amazed to see all these dances performed by men in arms. Upon this, Mysus, perceiving their astonishment, prevailed upon one of the Arcadians, who had a woman dancer, to let him bring her in; which he did accordingly, after he had dressed her in the handsomest manner he was able, and given her a light buckler. She danced the Pyrrhic [3] dance with great agility: upon which there was great clapping; and the Paphlagonians asked whether the women also charged with their troops. The others answered, that it was they who drove the king out of their camp. This was the end of that night's entertainment.

The next day the generals brought the ambassadors to the army: when the soldiers came to a resolution neither to do any injury to the Paphlagonians, nor suffer any from them. After that, the ambassadors departed; and the Greeks, finding they had as many ships as they wanted, embarked and sailed with a fair wind all that day and the next night, keeping Paphlagonia on their left hand; and the day after they arrived at Sinope, and anchored in [4] Harmene,

---

oracle, understand the pantomime though mute, and hear him though he does not speak. By the way, the Greek verse attributed to the Pythian oracle, to which Lucian alludes, is preserved by Plutarch,

Καὶ κωφοῦ συνίημι καὶ οὐ λαλέοντος ἀκούω.

Upon this occasion Lucian tells a story of a famous pantomime in Nero's time, who, to show the excellence of his art to Demetrius the Cynic, commanded the music and even the chorus to be silent, while he represented by himself (ἐφ' ἑαυτοῦ ὀρχήσατο) the amour of Venus and Mars, the Sun giving information, and Vulcan catching them both in a net, the gods standing by, Venus blushing and Mars trembling and asking forgiveness: Lucian adds, that Demetrius was so well pleased with the performance, that he cried out, I not only see but hear what you represent, for you seem even to speak with your hands. The reader will pardon this short dissertation upon an art, which is so far lost, that it is thought by many never to have existed. Lucian applies the word ἐχόμενος with great humour to the unfortunate companion of his captivity and his labour, as he calls him, τὸν ἀθλιον κοινωνὸν καὶ τῆς αἰχμαλωσίας, καὶ τῆς ἀχθοφορίας, I mean the poor ass that was thrown down the precipice, upon which he says, ὁ δὲ, ἀσφὶ κάτω, τὸν θάνατον ἐχόμενος, which I do not translate, because I cannot. The dance here mentioned by Xenophon is, by Hesychius, called a Macedonian dance; it is so particularly described by Xenophon, that I think I may venture to call it after him, the Carpæan dance, without translating the word.

[1] Μάχεται πρὸ τοῦ ζεύγους. Both the Latin translators have said ante jugum dimicat, which D'Ablancourt has followed; but as πρὸ is very frequently used in the sense I have given it upon this occasion, that is for ὑπὲρ, I thought it more natural to say that the husbandman fought with the robber in defence of his oxen, than before them, particularly as the oxen seem to be the prize contended for: since, when the robber gets the better, he drives away the oxen; but, if there can be any doubt whether πρὸ is used in this sense, the following passage in Euripides will clear it up; it is in Alcestis, where Admetus says to Pheres,

Οὐκ ἠθέλησας οὐδ' ἐτόλμησας θανεῖν
Τοῦ σοῦ πρὸ παιδός. . . . .

[2] Τοτὲ δὲ ἰδινοῦτο καὶ ἐξεκυβίστα. Homer tells us that Vulcan represented two dancers performing a dance of this kind upon Achilles's shield,

——δοιὼ δὲ κυβιστῆτε κατ' αὐτοὺς
Μολπῆς ἐξάρχοντες ἐδίνευον κατὰ μέσσους.

And Tournefort says that the Turkish dervises preserve this kind of dancing, which they make a religious ceremony; and that upon a signal from their superior, they turn round with an amazing velocity.

[3] Πυῤῥίχην. This dance is called by Dionysius of Halicarnassus and Hesychius ἐνόπλιος ὄρχησις, the first leaving it in doubt whether Minerva or the Curetes were the authors of it; and the second whether one Pyrrhichus a Cretan, or Pyrrhus, the son of Achilles, was the inventor of it.

[4] Ἁρμήνην. Both Strabo and Arrian make mention of Armene or Harmene as a sea-port belonging to Sinope, from which the former says it was distant fifty stadia.

one of its ports. Sinope is situated in Paphlagonia; it is a colony of the Milesians. The inhabitants sent the Greeks, as a mark of hospitality, three thousand medimni [4] of flour, and fifteen hundred [5] ceramia of wine. Hither Cheirisophus came with some galleys. The soldiers expected he would bring them something: however he brought nothing, but gave them an account that both Anaxibius the ad-

miral, and the rest of the Lacedæmonians, celebrated their praise, and that the former promised them, if they would come out of the Euxine sea, they would have pay.

The soldiers staid five days at Harmene: and looking upon themselves to be in the neighbourhood of Greece, they were more desirous than before to carry some booty home with them. [7] They thought, if they made choice of one general, that single person would find a readier obedience from the army both by night and day, than if the command were vested in many: where it was necessary for him to conceal his designs, he would conceal them better, and where to prevent the enemy, he would use greater expedition, for there would then be no need of conferences, but whatever that single person resolved upon, would be put in execution: for hitherto in all operations the generals were governed by the majority. While they had these things under consideration, they cast their eyes on Xenophon; and the captains came to him and acquainted him with the resolution of the army: and each of them, expressing his affection to him, endeavoured to prevail upon him to undertake the command. Xenophon was not averse to it, when he considered that he should, by this means, increase both his credit with his friends, and his reputation in his country, and that possibly also, he might be the cause of some advantage to the army.

These considerations led him to desire to be commander-in-chief. On the other side, when he reflected that future events being concealed from all mankind, he might, for that reason, run a hazard of losing the glory he had already gained, he was in suspense. While he was in this doubt, he thought the best thing he could do was to consult the gods: in the presence therefore of two priests, he offered sacrifice to [8] Jupiter the king, to whom he was directed by

---

and the latter forty. Herodotus says that the Cimmerians flying from the Scythians into Asia, built a town upon the peninsula, where Sinope, a Greek city, now stands. But we find by Strabo that the inhabitants of Sinope looked upon Autolycus, one of the Argonauts, to be their founder, whose statue, made by Sthenis, Lucullus carried away when he took the town. The same author tells us, that the Milesians, observing the advantageous situation of the place, and the weakness of the inhabitants, sent a colony thither. And by the account that author gives of Sinope, no city could be more advantageously situated; for he says it stood upon the isthmus that joined the peninsula to the main land, having on each side a sea-port, where great quantities of the tunny fish were taken as they swam along the Asiatic coast, from the Palus Mæotis, where they are bred, to the Bosphorus. He adds, that the peninsula was surrounded with sharp rocks which made the access to it very difficult, that the land above the town was very fertile, and disposed into gardens, and that the city was well built and adorned with a place of exercise, a market, and magnificent porticoes. This account both of the situation of Sinope, and of the country round it, is confirmed by Tournefort, who was there himself; and, in the relation he gives of it, is grievously out of humour with the modern geographers for taking no notice either of the peninsula, or of the sea-ports lying on each side of it. Sinope is famous for having given birth to two considerable men of very different characters, Diogenes, the Cynic philosopher, and the great Mithridates. Strabo says it was in his time (that is, in the reign of Augustus) a Roman colony. I cannot part with this subject without taking notice that Sinope furnished the ancient painters with a red earth, which is one of the four colours with which alone, Pliny tells us, Apelles, Echion, Melanthius, Nicomachus painted those immortal works; "quatuor coloribus solis immortalia illa opera fecere; ex albis Melino, ex silaciis Attico, ex rubris Sinopide Pontica, ex nigris Atramento, Apelles, Echion, Melanthius, Nicomachus."

5 Μέδιμνοι. Μέδιμνος—μέτρον ἐστὶ ξηρῶν, οἷον συρῶν ἢ πριθῶν· ἔχει δὲ χοίνικας ὀκτὼ καὶ τεσσαράκοντα. Harpocration. So that the medimnus was a dry measure containing forty-eight chœnixes, each of which Arbuthnot makes equal to an English pint; but then he says a medimnus contains four pecks and six pints, which is a mistake; for if, as he says, sixteen pints make a peck, it is plain that forty-eight pints will make but three pecks: so that, in reality, a medimnus is equal to three English pecks.

6 Κεράμια. Κεράμιον, τὸ τοῦ οἴνου ἢ ὕδατος σταμνίον. Hesychius. And in another place κάδος, κεράμιον. Now the cadus Arbuthnot makes equal to the metretes, which he says contains ten gallons, two pints, so that κεράμιον, upon these authorities, will be a liquid measure containing ten gallons, two pints.

7 Ἡγήσαντο οὖν, εἰ ἕνα ἕλοιντο ἄρχοντα, μᾶλλον ἂν, ἢ πολυαρχίας οὔσης, δύνασθαι τὸν ἕνα χρῆσθαι τῷ στρατεύματι καὶ νυκτὸς καὶ ἡμέρας· καὶ εἴ τι δέοι λανθάνειν, μᾶλλον ἂν καὶ κρύπτεσθαι, καὶ εἴ τι αὖ δέοι φθάνειν, ἧττον ἂν ὑστερίζειν· οὐ γὰρ ἂν λόγων δεῖν πρὸς ἀλλήλους, ἀλλὰ τὸ δόξαν τῷ ἑνὶ περαίνεσθαι ἄν. I have transcribed this whole passage, that the reader may see how dreadfully D'Ablancourt has mangled it; these are his words, "Les soldats donc, pour mieux couvrir leur enterprise, et l'exécuter plus promptement resolurent d'élire un général."

8 Διὶ τῷ βασιλεῖ. Harpocration mentions two porti-

the oracle of Delphos to address himself; and whom he looked upon to be the author of the dream he had, when, together with the other generals, he was first appointed to take charge of the army. He called to mind also, that, when he left Ephesus in order to be presented to Cyrus, ¹ an eagle cried on his right, sitting however on the ground, which the priest, who accompanied him, said was an omen, that por-

---

coes dedicated at Athens to Jupiter under two different appellations; the first to Jupiter ἱλαςθέριος, because the people of Athens, as Dydimus says, were freed from the Persians by his assistance; the other to Jupiter βασιλιύς. This passage explains what our author mentions in the third book, where he says the oracle of Delphos directed him to sacrifice to the proper gods, by which, we find here, he means Jupiter the king.

1 Ἀετὸν ἀνιμμμνήσκετο ἱαυτῷ δεξιὸν. It was an old superstition among the Greeks to look upon all appearances, and particularly that of an eagle on the right hand, as an omen of success. When Telemachus takes his leave of Menelaus, Homer makes an eagle appear on his right, with a goose in his talons,

Ὣς ἄρα οἱ εἰπόντι ἱπίπτατο ἱαυτῷ δεξιὸς ἐρνις
Αἰετός, ἀργὴν χῆνα φέρων ὀνύχεσσι πέλωρον,
Ἥμερον ἐξ αὐλῆς.

This omen Helen, who was present, takes upon herself to interpret, and says it signifies that Ulysses shall return and punish the suitors, who, it seems, were represented by the white goose. By the way, Homer makes Helen rather than Menelaus interpret this omen, possibly to avoid making the good man indirectly reproach his wife by this interpretation; for Menelaus seems to have forgotten or forgiven all that was past, and they then lived very well together. It may be asked why the Greeks looked upon the omens that appeared on their right to be prosperous, and the Romans on those that appeared on their left to be so? This question, though, at first sight, it may appear frivolous, is of so great consequence to the understanding many passages both in the Greek and Roman authors, that I really think it very well deserves to be discussed. The first thing to be considered is, that the Greeks and Romans did not turn their faces towards the same quarter of the heavens when they took their stand in their augural ceremonies, the former turning theirs to the north, and the latter theirs to the south. But this deserves something more than a bare assertion. Homer, who is always a religious observer of the ceremonies of his country, makes Hector reprimand Polydamas for advising him to attend to the flight of birds, and says he cares not whether they fly to the right, that is, to the east, or to the left, that is, to the west,

—τῶν οὔτι μεταστρέφομα', οὐδ' ἀλεγίζω,
Εἴτ' ἐπὶ δεξὶ ἴωσι πρὸς ἠῶ τ' ἠέλιον τι,
Εἴτ' ἐπ' ἀριστερὰ τοίγε, ποτὶ ζόφον ἠερόεντα.

It may not possibly be so easily allowed that the Romans, upon these occasions, turned their faces towards the east: I say this because I remember to have seen the contrary asserted by a very learned man, I mean Dacier, in his Notes upon Horace; he there says, "ceux qui prenoient les auspices, tournoient toujours le visage vers le midi;" and a little after he adds, "cela a toujours ete observe de meme par les Romains, sans qui'l y ait jamais eu aucun changement; et c'est une verite si constante, que l'on ne scauroit expliquer ni consilier autrement tous les passages des anciens, ou il est parle de ces matieres." Errors in authors of little merit are of little consequence; but when ushered into the world under the sanction of a name deservedly famous for critical learning, they are either taken for truths, or at best pass uncontradicted. That this is an error will appear to a demonstration, from the two following passages of those two oracles of the Roman history, Livy and Dionysius of Halicarnassus. The first, speaking of the inauguration of Numa Pompilius, says, "Augur ad laevam ejus, capite velato sedem coepit dextra manu baculum sine nodo aduncum tenens, quem lituum appellaverunt. Inde, ubi, prospectu in urbem agrumque capto, Deos precatus, regionem ab oriente ad occasum determinavit; dextras ad meridiem partes, laevas ad septentrionem esse dixit." In this division then we find the south was on his right hand, and the north on his left, consequently his face was turned to the east. Dionysius of Halicarnassus not only confirms this, but gives several reasons why the augurs, upon these occasions, turned their faces to the east. The first is this, ὅτι καθῆδρα μέν ἐστι καὶ στάσις ἀρίστη τῶν οἰωνοῖς μαντευομένοις ἡ βλέπουσα πρὸς ἀνατολὰς, ὅθεν ἥλιον τε ἀναφοραὶ γίνονται καὶ σελῆναι, καὶ ἀστέρων πλανητῶν τε καὶ ἀπλανῶν ἥσι τοῦ κόσμου περιφοραὶ, δι' ἣν ποτὲ μὲν ὑπὲρ γῆς ἅπαντα τὰ ἐν αὐτῷ γίνεται, ποτὲ δ' ὑπὸ γῆς, ἰωσθεν ἀρξαμένη τὴν ἐγκύκλιον ἀποδίδωσι κίνησιν. This reason, according to the system of astronomy then in vogue, was a very plausible one, that is, because the heavenly bodies began their motion from the east. To this I shall add the reason given by the same author, why the Romans looked upon the lightning that appeared on the left hand, as a happy omen. I mention this not only to confirm what has been said, but also to show that a passage in Virgil, which, like many others, is looked upon as poetical, is, like them, merely historical. Dionysius says that Ascanius, the son of Æneas, being besieged by the Tuscans, under Mezentius, and upon the point of making a sally, prayed to Jupiter, and to the rest of the gods, to send him a happy omen; upon which, they say, the sky being clear, it lightened on his left. Now let us see what use Virgil has made of this tradition. Ascanius is besieged by the Rutulans and Tuscans, commanded by Turnus and Mezentius; he is insulted by Remulus, but, before he takes revenge of him, he prays to Jupiter to favour his coup d'essai; Upon this a clap of thunder was heard on the left, where the sky was clear,

" Audiit, et cœli genitor de parte serena
Intonuit laevum."

This is told almost in the same words by the Greek historian, φασὶν αἰθρίας οὔσης ἐκ τῶν ἀριστερῶν ἀστράψαι τὸν οὐρανόν.

However, I desire I may not be understood as if I meant by this that Virgil took this passage from Dionysius. I am very sensible that the Greek historian speaks of the seven hundredth and forty-fifth year, as of the year then present, in the preface to his history, Claudius Nero for the second time, and Calpurnius Piso being consuls; and that Donatus tells us, in his life of Virgil, that, designing to return to Rome with Augustus, whom he met at Athens, as the latter was coming out of the east, he died at Brundusium, Cn. Plautius and Qu. Lucretius, being consuls. Now Dion Cassius says, that Augustus went into the east in the spring of the year, in which M. Apuleius and P. Silius were contended something great, and above a private station, something illustrious, though toilsome; for other birds attack the eagle chiefly when she is sitting upon the ground. He added that the omen foretold nothing lucrative, because, when the eagle preys, she is generally upon the wing. While therefore he was offering sacrifice upon this occasion, the god plainly signified to him, that he ought neither to seek the command, nor, if they chose him, to accept it : and this was the issue of the affair. However the army assembled, and they all agreed to choose a single person to command them : this therefore being determined, they proposed him : when it was manifest they would choose him, if any one put the question, he rose up, and spoke as follows :

" Gentlemen ! as I am a man, I take a pleasure in the honour you design me, and return you thanks for it ; I also beseech the gods to give me an opportunity of being the occasion of some advantage to you : but I cannot think it will be any either to you or myself to give me the preference, when a Lacedæmonian is present : on the contrary, if you should want their assistance in any thing, you will, by this means, be the less entitled to it. Neither do I look upon this as a thing altogether safe for me to engage in ; for I am sensible they never ceased making war upon my country, till they made the whole city acknowledge, that the Lacedæmonians were the masters of Athens, as well as of the rest of Greece : however, upon this acknowledgment, they desisted, and immediately raised the siege of that city. If, therefore, I, who am sensible of this, should seem, where I have it in my power, to invalidate their authority, I have reason to fear that I should very soon be taught my duty. As to your opinion, that the command of a single person will leave less room for contest, than that of many, be assured that, if you choose another, you shall find I will not oppose him : for I look upon it, that, in war, whoever opposes his commander, opposes his own safety : whereas, if you choose me, I shall not be

surprised, if you find others, who will be offended both at you and me."

After he had said this, much greater numbers than before rose up, and said, he ought to take upon him the command. And Agasias the Stymphalian alleged it would be ridiculous to suppose what was mentioned to be true ; because, at any rate, the Lacedæmonians might as well be angry, if, when they met to sup together, they did not choose a Lacedæmonian for their president ; for, says he, if that is the case, neither ought we, it seems, to be captains, because we are Arcadians. Upon this the assembly showed by their murmur that they approved of what they said.

Xenophon seeing it was necessary to enforce what he had alleged, advanced and went on. " But, gentlemen ! that you may know all the circumstances of this affair, I swear by all the gods and goddesses, that, after I was acquainted with your resolutions, I sought by sacrifice to know whether it were for your advantage to confer this command upon me, and for mine to accept it : and the gods signified to me, by the victims, in so clear a manner that the most ignorant man could not mistake it, that I ought to decline the command." Upon this they chose Cheirisophus, who, after he was chosen, came forward and said, " Be assured, gentlemen ! I should have given you no opposition, if your choice had fallen upon another. But," says he, " you have done a service to Xenophon by not choosing him, since Dixippus has lately accused him to Anaxibus, in the strongest manner he was able, though I endeavoured all I could to silence him." Cheirisophus added that he thought Anaxibus would rather desire Timasion of Dardanus, who had served under Clearchus, for his colleague, than himself, though he was a Lacedæmonian. " But," says he, " since you have made choice of me I shall endeavour, on my part, to do you all the service in my power. In the meantime, be ready to sail to-morrow, if the weather is favourable. Heraclea is the port we must all endeavour to arrive at. When we are there we will consider of what we have farther to do."

II. The next day they weighed anchor with a fair wind, and sailed two days along the coast : and, in their passage, saw the Jasonian shore, where the ship Argo is said to have come to land ; and the mouths of several rivers:

---

suls, which, in the *fasti consulares*, is the 733d of Rome, and that he returned to Rome the next year. All that I mean by what I have said, is that both the poet and the historian took the passage from the history of Rome.

² Ἃς δ' ἐμὶ ἴληφθι, οὐκ ἂν θαυμάσαιμι εἰ τινα εὕροιτι καὶ ὑμῖν καὶ ἐμοὶ ἀχθόμενον. D'Ablancourt has left out all this sentence.

first that of the [1] Thermoden ; then of the [2] Halys, and, afterwards that of the [3] Parthenius : and having sailed by the last, they arrived at [4] Heraclea, a Greek city, and a colony of the Megarians, situated in the country of the Maryandenians. They came to anchor near to the peninsula of Acherusias, where Hercules is said to have descended to bring up Cerberus, and where they show, at this day, a chasm, two stadia in depth, as a monument of his descent. The inhabitants of Heraclea sent the Greeks three thousand medimni of barley meal, and two thousand ceramia of wine, as hospitable presents, with twenty oxen, and one hundred sheep. Here the river Lycus, about two hundred feet broad, runs through the plain.

The soldiers being assembled, deliberated whether they should proceed the rest of the way till they were out of the Euxine, by land or by sea ; when Lycon of Achaia rising up,

said, " I [5] wonder, gentlemen ! at our generals, for not endeavouring to find money for us to buy provisions ; for the presents we have received will not subsist the army three days ; neither is there any place," says he, "from whence we can supply ourselves. My advice therefore is, that we demand of the inhabitants of Heraclea no less than three thousand [6] cyzicenes." Another said a month's pay, no less than ten thousand : and that " we ought to choose ambassadors, and send them immediately to the town while we were assembled, to the end ' we might know what answer they thought proper to return, and thereupon consider what measures to take." Upon this they proposed sending, as ambassadors, first Cheirisophus, because they had chosen him for their general ; and some named Xenophon. But both these declined it absolutely ; for they concurred in opinion, that they ought not to constrain a Greek city, in friendship with them, to supply them with any thing against their will. When they found these were unwilling to go, they sent Lycon of Achaia, Callimachus of Parrhasie, and Agasias of Stymphalus. These, going to the town, informed the inhabitants of the resolutions of the army : it was said Lycon even added threats, if they did not comply with all their demands. The inhabitants hearing this, said they would consider of it, and immediately removed all their [7] effects out of the country, and carried all their provisions into the town : at the same time the gates were shut, and men in arms appeared upon the walls.

Hereupon, the authors of these disturbances accused the generals of having defeated the design ; and the Arcadians and Achaians assembled together ; (they were chiefly headed by Callimachus the Parrhasian, and Lycon the Achaian. They said it was a shame that one Athenian, who brought no forces to the army, should have the command both of the Peloponnesians and Lacedæmonians. They said they had the labour, and others the profit,—which was the less to be suffered, because the preservation of the army was owing to them ; for they said the Arcadians and Achaians had

---

[1] Τοῦ Θερμώδοντος. This river, after it has received many others, runs through a plain called Themiscyra formerly inhabited by the Amazons, and then falls into the Euxine sea.

[2] Τοῦ Ἅλυος. This river, Strabo says, took its name from the beds of salt, through which it runs, ἀπὸ τῶν ἁλῶν ἃς παταρρεῖ. He adds, that its source is in the Greater Cappadocia : and, upon this occasion, Arrian blames Herodotus for saying it flows from the south, whereas it comes, as he says, from the east. This river formerly parted the Persian and Lydian empires. Tournefort says this country is so full of fossil salt, that it is to be found in the high roads, and ploughed lands.

[3] Τοῦ Παρθενίου. The Parthenius rises, according to Strabo, in Paphlagonia, and derives its name from the cheerful meadows through which it runs.

4 Εἰς Ἡράκλειαν. Heraclea was anciently a city of great consideration, and in alliance with Rome, till Mithridates made himself master of it by corrupting Lamachus, one of their magistrates, which furnished Cotta, who served under Lucullus, with a pretence both of plundering it, and reducing it to ashes, for which he was deservedly censured at his return to Rome. I find Strabo makes Heraclea to have been a colony of the Milesians, but Xenophon seems to deserve most credit, since he is supported by Diodorus Siculus, Pausanias, and many other authors of the best note. Heraclea was afterwards called by the modern Greeks, to whom it belonged, Penderachi, and by the Turks, in whose possession it now is, Eregri. There are many medals to be seen at this day, formerly struck by this city in honour of the Roman emperors, with a Hercules on the reverse, by which it appears that he was the patron of it : and when Cotta took it, there was a statue of Hercules in the market place, with all his attributes of gold. But it must be observed, that this was the Grecian, not the Egyptian Hercules, from whom Diodorus Siculus observes the Greeks borrowed most of the great actions which they ascribed to their Hercules.

5 Θαυμάζω μὲν, ὦ ἄνδρες, τῶν στρατηγῶν. Θαυμάζω, ὅτι πρὸς γυναῖκα συντάσσομαι, τὸ καταγελάσεαι συμαίνω πρὸς δὲ αἰτιατικὴν, τὸ ἱκανῶ. Suidas.

6 Κυζικηνούς. See note 1, p. 296, upon the fifth book.

7 Χρήματα. See note 7, page 175, upon the first book.

preserved it, and that the rest of the army was nothing; (and it was true the Arcadians and Achaians made above half the army) if, therefore, they were wise, they ought to assemble, and having chosen their own generals, to march by themselves, and endeavour to get some booty. This was resolved: and those Arcadians and Achaians, who served under Cheirisophus, leaving him and Xenophon, joined to the rest, and chose their own generals, to the number of ten. These they voted to execute whatever should be approved of by the majority. Here, therefore, ended the generalship of Cheirisophus, the sixth or seventh day after he was chosen.

Xenophon was inclined to march in their company, looking upon that as safer than for every one to travel by himself; but Neon, who had been informed by Cheirisophus, that Cleander, the Lacedæmonian [8] governor of Byzantium, said he would come to the port of Calpe, with some galleys, persuaded him to go by himself. He gave him this advice to the end that none should partake of this opportunity, but only they, with their own soldiers, should go on board the galleys; and Cheirisophus, partly discouraged at what had happened, and partly through the hatred he, from that time, conceived against the army, permitted Xenophon to do as he thought fit. The latter had some thoughts also of leaving that part of the army that remained with him, and of sailing away; but while he was offering sacrifice to Hercules the Conductor, and consulting that god, whether it were better for him to march on with the rest of the soldiers, or to leave them, the god signified, by the victims, that he should go on with them. By this means the army was divided into three bodies: the first consisted of Arcadians and Achaians, being above four thousand five hundred in number, all heavy-armed men; the second, of fourteen hundred heavy-armed men, and seven hundred targeteers, belonging to Cheirisophus, the last being Thracians, who had served under Clearchus; and the third of seventeen hundred heavy-armed men, and three hundred targeteers, who followed Xenophon; the horse, which amounted to about forty, were solely commanded by him.

The Arcadians, having furnished themselves with ships from the inhabitants of Heraclea, first set sail, that, by falling upon the Bithynians unawares, they might get the greater booty. With this view they landed in the port of Calpe, situated about the middle of [9] Thrace. Cheirisophus, leaving Heraclea, travelled through the country; but when he arrived in Thrace, he kept near the sea, because he was in an ill state of health; and Xenophon, having provided himself with ships, landed upon the confines of Thrace, and of the territory of Heraclea, and from thence, marched through the middle of the country.

III. In what manner, therefore, the generalship of Cheirisophus was abrogated, and the Greek army divided, has been already related. The actions of each of them were as follows: the Arcadians, landing by night at the port of Calpe, marched to the next villages, at the distance of about fifty stadia from the sea. When it was light, each of their generals led his own division to a village, and, where any of the villages seemed larger than the rest, they marched in a body formed of two divisions: at the same time they fixed upon a hill where they were all to re-assemble; and, as their irruption was unexpected, they [10] took many slaves, besides great numbers of cattle.

The Thracians who escaped, got together: for, being targeteers, many of them made their escape from the Greeks, who were heavy-armed men. Being now assembled in a body, they first attacked the division commanded by Smicres, one of the Arcadian generals, while he was upon his march to the place of rendezvous with a considerable booty. For some time, the Greeks fought as they marched; but, while they were passing a valley, the Thracians put them to flight, and killed Smicres with all his men. They also defeated another division commanded by Hegesander, one of the ten generals, eight only escaping; and with them Hegesander himself. The rest of the generals came to the place of rendezvous, some

---

8 Ἀςμωστήκ. Ἀςμωσταὶ, οἱ ὑπὸ Λακεδαιμονίων εἰς τὰς ὑπεκόους πόλεις ἄρχοντες ἐκπεμπόμενοι. Harpocration.

9 Τῆς Θράκης. These are the Thracians, who, as Herodotus says, having settled in Asia, were called Bithynians. He adds, that they were driven out of Thrace by the Teucrians and Mysians.

10 Περιβάλοντο. Περιβαλλόμενος· προστορισάμενος. Suidas. Phavorinus. So that I cannot think the word collego, made use of by both the Latin translators, so proper upon this occasion.

with difficulty, and others without any at all. The Thracians, after this advantage, gave notice to one another, and assembled, with great resolution, in the night: and as soon as it was day, great numbers of horse and targeteers were drawn up round the hill, upon which the Greeks were encamped; and their numbers continually increasing, they attacked the heavy-armed men, with great security; for the Greeks had neither archers, darters, or horse; while the others, advancing with their light-armed men, and horse, lanced their darts, and when the Greeks offered to attack them, retreated with ease; and assailing them in different places, gave several wounds, without receiving any; so that the Greeks could not stir from the place, and were at last debarred from water by the Thracians. Being reduced to great extremity, terms of accommodation were proposed, and other things were agreed upon; but the Thracians refused to give hostages, which the Greeks insisted on. This put a stop to the treaty; and this was the situation of the Arcadians.

In the meantime, Cheirisophus, marching with safety along the coast, arrived at the port of Calpe. While Xenophon was upon his march through the middle of the country, his horse, who were upon the scout, met with some ambassadors, who were travelling the road. When they were brought to Xenophon, he asked them, whether they had any where heard of another Greek army. These men informed him of every thing that had passed; that the Greeks were actually besieged upon a hill, and that the whole army of the Thracians had surrounded them on all sides. Upon this he ordered the men to be strictly guarded, that he might use them as guides, where it was necessary; and having placed his scouts, he assembled the soldiers, and spoke to them as follows:

"Gentlemen! part of the Arcadians are slain, and the rest besieged upon a hill. It is my opinion, that if these are destroyed, all hopes of our own safety are desperate, the enemy being so numerous, and so much emboldened by their success. The best thing therefore, we can do, is immediately to march to their relief: that if they are still alive, we may have their assistance in battle, rather than, by being left alone, be alone exposed to the danger of it. Let us, therefore, for the present, march on till supper-time, and then

encamp; and while we are upon our march, let Timasion, with the horse, advance before, keeping us still in sight, and reconnoitre the country, to prevent surprise." At the same time, he sent those of the light-armed men, who were most prepared for expedition, to the sides and tops of the hills, with orders if they saw any thing to give notice. He ordered them also to set fire to every combustible thing they met with. "For," says he, "we have no place to fly to: it is a great way back to Heraclea; a great way through the country to Chrysopolis, and the enemy is near at hand. Indeed, it is not far from the port of Calpe, where we conclude Cheirisophus is arrived, if he has met with no accident; but, when we are there, we shall find neither ships to transport us, nor provisions to subsist us even for one day. However, if those who are besieged should perish, it will be more disadvantageous for us to hazard a battle in conjunction with the troops belonging to Cheirisophus only, than, if they are preserved, to join all our forces, and make our preservation a common concern. But let us go with this resolution, either to die with honour, upon this occasion, or perform the greatest of all actions in preserving so many Greeks. Possibly, God has ordained this with a design of humbling those who magnified their prudence, as superior to ours, and of rendering us, who derive all our hopes from the gods, more renowned than they. Follow then your leaders, and be attentive to the orders you receive, that you may obey them."

When he had said this, he put himself at their head. The horse, spreading themselves over the country, as far as was proper, set fire to every thing where they passed, and the targeteers, marching abreast upon the eminences, set fire also to every thing they found combustible, as did the army also to what the others happened to leave; so that the whole country seemed in a blaze, and the army appeared very numerous. When it was time, they encamped on a hill, and discovered the enemy's fires, from whom they were distant about forty stadia; upon this they made as many fires as they could. But when they had supped, orders were given that all the fires should immediately be put out: and having placed guards they went to sleep. The next morning, by break of day, after they had invoked the gods, they put themselves in order of battle, and marched with all the haste they could. Timasion and the horse, with the guides, advancing before the army, found themselves, before they were aware, upon the hill where the Greeks had been besieged. Here they saw neither friends nor enemies, (of which they gave notice to Xenophon and the army) but only some old men and women, with a few sheep and oxen that were left behind. At first, they wondered what the matter was, but, afterwards, they understood by the people who were left, that the Thracians went away, as soon as the evening came on; and the Greeks the next morning; but whither, they said, they could not tell.

Xenophon and his men, hearing this, after they had eat their breakfast, got their baggage ready, and marched on, desiring, as soon as possible, to join the rest of the Greeks at the port of Calpe. In their march, they saw the footing of the Arcadians and Achaians in the road leading to Calpe; and, when they overtook them, they were pleased to see one another, and embraced like brothers. The Arcadians asked Xenophon's men, why they had put out their fires? "For," said they, "we thought at first, when we saw no more fires, that you designed to attack the enemy in the night; (and they, as we imagined, were apprehensive of this, and for that reason went away, for they retired about that time,) but you not coming, and the time wherein we expected you being expired, we concluded, that, being informed of our situation, you were terrified, and had retired to the sea-side. Whereupon, we resolved not to be far behind you: and this was the reason of our marching hither also."

IV. That day they encamped upon the shore near the port. This place, which is called the port of Calpe, is situated in the Asiatic Thrace. This Thrace begins at the mouth of the Euxine Sea, and extends on the right hand, as far as Heraclea. To which place, from Byzantium, [1] it is as far as a trireme galley can row in the longest day. Between these two cities there is no town belonging either to the Greeks, or their allies; but all the coast is inhabited by Thracians or Bithynians; and whatever Greeks are thrown upon their coast by shipwreck, or

by any other accident fall into their hands, they are said to abuse them in the most savage manner. The port of Calpe lies in the midway between Heraclea and Byzantium. A promontory runs out into the sea, of which that part which lies contiguous to it, is a craggy rock, in height, where it is lowest, not less than twenty fathom. The neck of land, by which this promontory is joined to the continent, is about four hundred feet in breadth; and the space within this neck is ample enough to afford habitation for ten thousand men. The port lies under the rock upon the western shore; and, close to the sea, flows a spring plentifully supplied with fresh water; this spring is commanded by the rock. This place affords great plenty of timber, particularly that which is proper for building ships, in great quantities, and in great perfection close to the sea. The mountain that lies next the port, reaches about twenty stadia into the midland. The soil is a mould free from stones; but that part of it which lies next the sea, and extends above twenty stadia, is covered with great numbers of stately trees of every kind. The rest of the country is pleasant and spacious, abounding with villages well inhabited; for it produces barley, wheat, and all sorts of legumens, panic, sesame, a sufficient quantity of figs, vines in abundance, yielding a sweet wine, and every thing else but olive-trees. This is the nature of the country.

The soldiers encamped along the shore: had they entered into any of the villages, they would not have quartered there; because they suspected they were drawn thither by the artifice of some people, who were desirous to build a city there. For the greatest part of them had not engaged in this service through want, but induced by the reputation of Cyrus, some even bringing soldiers with them, who had spent their fortunes, some having left their fathers and mothers, and others their children, with a design to return, when they had acquired enough to enrich them; for they heard that the other Greeks, who before served under Cyrus, had made their fortunes. This being their situation, they were desirous to return in safety to Greece.

The morning after the junction of their forces Xenophon offered sacrifice concerning their going out of the camp; (for there was a necessity to lead them out in order to get provisions) he also proposed to bury the dead.

---

1 Ἡμέρας μάλα μακρᾶς πλοῦς. Xenophon has great reason to say that it is a long day's work for a galley to go from Byzantium to Heraclea, since Arrian, in his Periplus, makes it 1670 stadia, 870 of which he reckons from Byzantium to the port of Calpe, which agrees very well with Xenophon's account.

The victims being favourable, the Arcadians also followed him, and they buried the greatest part of the dead, where each of them lay, (for their bodies having lain five days, there was no possibility of bringing them away) some of them they removed out of the roads, and, laying them in a heap, buried them with all the decency that their present circumstances would admit of. As for those whose bodies could not be found, they erected a large [1] cenotaph, with a great funeral pile, which they crowned with garlands. Having performed these things they returned to their camp: and after they had supped, went to rest. The next day there was a general meeting of the soldiers, (they were chiefly assembled by Agasias of Stymphalus, one of the captains, and Hieronymius of Elis, a captain also, and by the oldest Arcadian officers) in which they came to this resolution, that, for the future, whoever proposed dividing the army should be punished with death; that the army should march in the same disposition it was in before, and that the same generals should command. Cheirisophus having lost his life by a medicine he took in a fever, Neon the Asinæan succeeded him.

After this Xenophon rising up, said, "Gentlemen! it seems we are under a necessity both of travelling by land, for we have no ships, and of marching away immediately; for, if we stay, we shall want provisions. We, therefore, shall offer sacrifice; in the mean time, if, upon any other occasion, you were prepared to fight, prepare yourselves for it now, for the enemy have resumed their courage." After this, the generals offered sacrifice in the presence of Arexion of Arcadia, the priest: for Silanus of Ambracia had hired a ship, and made his escape from Heraclea. But the victims they sacrificed concerning their departure were not favourable; so they staid there that day: and some had the confidence to report, that Xeno-

phon, being desirous to build a city there, had prevailed upon the priest to declare that the victims were not favourable to their departure. Upon this, Xenophon ordered a herald to publish that any one, who was willing, might be present at the sacrifice the next day, and that, if there was any priest among them, he should also attend, and assist in inspecting the victims; he offered sacrifice accordingly in the presence of great numbers; and, though victims were three times sacrificed concerning their departure, still they were not favourable. This gave the soldiers great concern; for the provisions they had brought with them were all consumed, and there was no market near.

Hereupon they re-assembled, and Xenophon said, "Gentlemen! the victims you see, are not yet favourable to our departure; at the same time, I see you are in want of provisions; it is necessary, therefore, in my opinion, to offer sacrifice concerning this." Upon which one of the men, rising up, said, "It is with reason the victims do not favour our departure: for a ship coming in yesterday by accident, I was informed that Cleander, the Lacedæmonian governor of Byzantium, designed to come hither from thence with transports and gallies." Upon this they all concluded to stay for him. However they could not avoid going out to get provisions concerning which he again offered sacrifice three times, and still the victims were not favourable; the soldiers now came to Xenophon's tent, complaining they had no provisions: but he told them he would not lead them out, while the victims forbade it.

The next day he sacrificed again, and, it being a general concern, almost all the army crowded round the sacrifice: but the victims fell short. Still the generals did not think fit to lead out the army, however they called them together; and Xenophon said, "Possibly the enemy may be assembled in a body, and, then we shall be under a necessity of fighting: if, therefore, we leave our baggage in the place of strength, and march out prepared to fight, it is possible the victims may be more favourable." The soldiers, hearing this, cried out it was to no purpose to lead them to the place he mentioned, but that they ought immediately to offer sacrifice. They had no victims left: so they bought some oxen out of a cart, and sacrificed them; and Xenophon begged of Cleanor the Arcadian, to show an earnestness, if this sac-

---

1 Κενοτάφιον. In the same manner we find in Thucydides, that the Athenians, in the funeral of the first of their countrymen, who were killed in the Peloponnesian war, besides a coffin for every tribe, carried also an empty one in honour to the memory of those whose bodies could not be found. Virgil has translated the Greek word by *tumulus inanis* in the third Book, where he says Andromache had raised an empty monument to the manes of Hector,

"Manesque vocabat
Hectoreum ad tumulum; viridi quem cespite inanem,
Et geminas, causam lachrimis, sacraverat aras."

rifice promised any thing. Notwithstanding this the victims were not favourable.

Here Neon, who had succeeded Cheirisophus, seeing the men oppressed with want, was desirous to gratify them, and, having found out a man belonging to Heraclea, who said he was acquainted with some villages in the neighbourhood, where they might get provisions, ordered proclamation to be made, that whoever was willing might go out to supply themselves, there being a guide ready to conduct them. Upon this two thousand men went out of the camp with javelins, leather bags, sacks, and other vessels. While they were in the villages dispersed in plunder, some horse, belonging to Pharnabazus, first fell upon them : these were come to the assistance of the Bithynians, designing, jointly with them, to hinder, if possible, the Greeks from penetrating into Phrygia. This body of horse killed no less than five hundred of the Greeks : the rest fled to a mountain.

The news of this defeat was brought to the camp by one of those who escaped. Xenophon, since the victims were not favourable that day, taking an ox out of one of the carts (for there were no other victims) sacrificed it, and then went out to their relief with all the men who were not above forty years of age ; and, having brought off the rest, they returned to the camp. It was now near sunset, and the Greeks ate their supper in great consternation ; when, on a sudden, some Bithynians, coming up through the thickets, surprised the advanced guard, and, killing some of them, pursued the rest to the camp ; and, the alarm being given, all the Greeks ran to their arms. But it was not thought advisable to pursue the enemy, or leave their camp in the night ; for the country was full of thickets ; so they lay that night upon their arms, taking care effectually to reinforce their out-guards.

V. In this manner they passed the night. The next day, as soon as it was light, the generals led them to the place of strength, and the army followed, with their arms and baggage, and before noon they had dug a trench quite across the neck of land that leads to the promontory, and fortified the whole length of it with palisades, leaving three gates. In the meantime a ship arrived from Heraclea, laden with barley-meal, cattle, and wine. Xenophon rising early offered sacrifice concerning an ex-

pedition against the enemy, and the first victim was favourable. When the sacrifice was near an end, Arexion of Parrhasie, the priest, saw an eagle on the favourable side, and called out to Xenophon to lead on. After the men had passed the trench, they stood to their arms, and the generals ordered proclamation to be made, that the soldiers, as soon as they had dined, should march with their arms, leaving those who had care of the baggage, and the slaves behind. All the rest went out except Neon ; for it was thought most advisable to leave him to command those who remained in the camp ; but, when the captains and soldiers were about to leave them, they were ashamed to stay behind, while the rest marched out ; so they left only those who were above five and forty years of age. These, therefore, staid in the camp, and the rest marched forward. Before they had gone fifteen stadia, they came to the dead bodies, and, [2] extending one of their wings upon a single line, where the first of them lay, they buried all those that fell within the line. After they had buried these as they marched along, they formed a line of the other wing, where the first of the bodies lay unburied, and in the same manner buried those that fell in their way : and when they came to the road that led from the villages, where the dead bodies lay in heaps, they brought them all together, and buried them.

It being now past noon, they marched clear of the villages, and, while the men were employed in taking whatever provisions they met with within reach of the line, on a sudden they discovered the enemy marching over some hills opposite to them. Their army was disposed in a line, and very numerous both in horse and foot ; for Spithridates and Rathines were there with the forces they had received from Pharnabazus. As soon as the enemy saw the Greeks, they halted at the distance of about fifteen stadia. Upon this, Arexion the Greek priest, immediately offered sacrifice, and the

2 Τὴν οὐρὰν τοῦ κέρατος συσπειράσαι, κατὰ τοὺς πρώτους φωνίτεας νεκρούς, ἰδαντες σάντας ὑπτίους ἐσυλλόμβασι τὸ κέρας. 1 very much suspect that οὐρὰν τοῦ κέρατος συσπειρᾶσθαι signifies to extend one of the wings of an army upon a line ; but, as I do not find this sense of the expression supported by the authority of any author, or lexicon, though I have consulted many, I only offer it as a conjecture, and leave it to the consideration of the learned.

very first victim was favourable. Then Xenophon said to the generals, " Gentlemen ! it is my opinion that we ought to place some bodies of reserve behind the line of battle, to sustain it, if necessary, and that the enemy when disordered may be received by these bodies of reserve, that will be fresh and in order." All this met with general approbation. " Do you therefore," continues he, " advance against the enemy, that now we have seen them, and been seen by them, we may not stand still ; and I will form the bodies of reserve in the rear, in the manner you approve of, and follow you."

Upon this the generals advanced in silence ; and Xenophon having separated from the main body, the three hindmost ranks, consisting of about two hundred men each, placed one, commanded by Samolas of Achaia, behind the right wing, another of which Pyrias of Arcadia had the command, behind the centre ; and the third, commanded by Phrasias, an Athenian, behind the left wing ; these had orders to follow the line of battle at the distance of about one hundred feet. As they marched on, those in the front (. . . . . was large and difficult to . . . . wing whether it was . . . . der was given for all . . . . s to come up to the . . . . dered what should stop their march ; but, as soon as he heard the order, he rode up in all haste. As soon as the officers were got together, Sophænetus, the oldest of the generals, said it [2] was not advisable to pass a valley of such difficulty ; but Xenophon, answering with some earnestness, said,

" You know, gentlemen ! that I never willingly sought dangers for you ; because I am sensible you want safety, more than glory ; but this is our present situation. It is not possible for us to go hence without fighting ; for, if we do not engage the enemy, as soon as we offer to depart, they will pursue us, and fall upon us in our retreat. Consider therefore with yourselves, whether it is better for us to attack them with our arms to cover us, or to see them pursuing us, when we are defenceless. You know also that there is no honour to be got by flying from an enemy, while even cowards gain courage by pursuing ; for which reason I had rather pursue with half the number of forces, than retreat with twice as many. Besides, I am confident that you yourselves do not [3] expect the enemy will stand, if we attack them ; but we are all sensible, that if we retire, they will have courage enough to follow us. However, to be on the other side, with a difficult valley in our rear when we engage, is not that an advantage worth contending for ? May the enemy [4] find every passage open to their flight ! whereas the situation of the place ought to instruct us that we can have no hope of safety, but in victory. I wonder any one should think this valley more dreadful than so many other places we have passed through. Shall we not find this very place, where we now are, difficult to march over, if we do not overcome the horse ? Will not the mountains we have traversed be difficult to repass with such numbers of targeteers at our heels ? But admit even that we arrive at the sea-coast in

---

1 'Επὶ πάσι μεγάλῳ. I cannot approve of the word saltus, which both Leunclavius and Hutchinson have made use of, upon this occasion, for πάσος ; I am very sensible that πάσος signifies saltus, but I do not look upon that to be the signification of the word in this place, because he tells us afterwards, that there was a bridge over this πάσος, which I am sure is, in no degree, applicable to saltus, particularly, since he calls it πάσος μέγα, which addition puts it out of all doubt that bocage epais, in D'Ablancourt, is improper, since bocage is a diminutive. I have called it a valley, in which I am supported by Phavorinus, who explains the word in that sense ; πάσος, ὁ κοιλότης τοῦ ὄρους.

2 "Οτι οὐκ ἄξιον εἴη διαβαίνειν. I agree with Hutchinson, that Stephanus and Muretus had no reason to find fault with this reading. I go further ; he calls it satis sana scriptura, but I think the phrase perfectly elegant, and of the same turn with a passage in Demosthenes, quoted by Suidas—διὰ γὰρ τοῦτο μάλιστα ἄξιόν ἐστι σιωπᾶν, ἵν' οὐκ ἐστὶν ὁ κατακλήσειαι, οὐδ' ὁ κολάσων ὑμᾶς. Upon which occasion Suidas explains the word in this manner, ἄξιον· οἱ ῥήτορες ἐπὶ τοῦ εὐλόγου καὶ δικαίου ἐλαμβάνουσι.

3 'Ελπίζειν. In this sense Thucydides uses the word in the beginning of his history, where he says, that he chose the Peloponnesian war for his subject, because he expected it would be of more importance than any before it, ἐλπίσας μέγαν τε ἔσεσθαι, καὶ ἀξιολογώτατον τῶν προγεγενημένων. Upon which the Greek Scholiast observes, τὸ ἐλπίσας, οὐ μόνον ἐπὶ ἀγαθῷ, ἀλλ' ἁπλῶς ἐπὶ τῇ τοῦ μέλλοντος λαμβάνει λέγεται. After the example of the Greeks, the Latins also gave this sense to the word spero, as we find in Virgil, where Dido, in the agony of her mind, tells her sister,

" Hunc ego si potui tantum sperare dolorem,
Et perferre, soror, potero."

4 Τοῖς μὲν γὰρ πολεμίοις ἔγωγε βουλοίμην ἂν εὔπορα πάντα φαίνεσθαι, ὥστε ἀποχωρεῖν. This soldierly wish of Xenophon, that the enemy might have hopes of safety in a retreat, while his own men had none but in victory, is thus disfigured by D'Ablancourt : " Je voudrois que nous fussions si bien remparés de toutes parts, qu'ils ne soussent pas par ou nous attaquer, afin qu'ils se retirassent plutot."

safety, how [5] large a valley is the Euxine sea? Where we shall neither find ships to transport us, or if we stay there, provisions to subsist us. And, if we make haste thither, we must haste abroad again to get provisions. We had better therefore fight, now we have eaten something, than to-morrow, when we are fasting. Gentlemen! the sacrifices are favourable, the omens happy, and the victims assure us of success. Let us go on. Since the enemy have seen us all, they ought not to eat their supper with satisfaction, or encamp where they please."

Upon this the captains bid him lead on, and no one contradicted it: he therefore put himself at their head, and ordered every man to pass the valley in his rank, for he thought it would be more expeditious for the army to pass over in a body, than if they filed off over the bridge, that lay across the valley. After they had passed it, Xenophon, coming up to the foremost ranks, said, " Remember, gentlemen! how many battles, with the assistance of the gods, you have gained, and what those are to expect who turn their backs upon the enemy. Consider also that we are at the gates of Greece. Follow Hercules your conductor, and exhort one another by name. There is a pleasure in reflecting that whoever, upon this occasion, says or does any thing brave and glorious, will be remembered by those whose applause he is ambitious of."

This he said as he rode along the ranks: then put himself at the head of the line of battle, and, having placed the targeteers upon the wings, he marched against the enemy. He had also ordered the heavy-armed men to carry their pikes on their right shoulders, till the trumpet sounded; then to present them, and move slowly on : and that none should run, when they pursued. Upon this the word was given, " Jupiter the preserver, and Hercules the conductor." The enemy encouraged by the advantage of their post, stood their ground; and, when our men

drew near, the Greek targeteers shouted, and ran on before they were ordered. The enemy's horse, with the body of Bithynians, advanced against them, and both together put the targeteers to flight: but, when the line of battle, consisting of the heavy-armed men, marched briskly up to meet them, and, at the same time, the trumpet sounded, and the men sung [*] the pæan, then shouted and presented their pikes, they no longer stood their ground, but fled. Timasion pursued them with the horse; and his men, being but few in number, killed as many of them as they could. The enemy's left wing, which was opposite to the Greek horse, was presently dispersed; but the right, not being closely pursued, rallied upon a hill. As soon as the Greeks saw them make a stand, they thought the easiest and safest thing they could do, was to charge them immediately. Accordingly, they sung the pæan, and advanced directly; but the enemy did not stand: the targeteers pursued them till their right wing was also dispersed. However, few of them were killed, for the enemy's horse being very numerous, kept the Greeks in awe. When our men saw the body of horse belonging to Pharnabazus still unbroken, and the Bithynian horse flocking to them, and observing, from a hill, what was doing, though they were spent with labour, yet they resolved to charge them also, as well as they could, that they might give them no time to recover their spirit and breath. So they formed themselves, and marched against them. Upon this, the enemy's horse fled down the hill with as much precipitation, as if they had been pursued by horse : for there was a . valley to receive them, which the Greeks knew nothing of, because, as it was late, they had given over the pursuit, before they came to it. Then returning to the place, where the first action happened, they erected a trophy, and came back to the sea about sunset. For they had near sixty stadia to their camp.

VI. After this, the enemy employed themselves in their own concerns, removing their families and [7] effects to the greatest distance they could. In the meantime, the Greeks waited for the arrival of Cleander, with the gallies and transports ; and going out every day with their sumpter-horses and slaves, they fur-

---

5 Πλέον τι τάσσε ὁ πόντος· Methinks this expression should have convinced the Latin translators that τάσσε was not, upon this occasion, to be translated by saltus. However, they have, I find, still adhered to it. Hutchinson has said, "quantus tandem saltus ipse pontus est ?" And Leunclavius, " quantus quæso saltus ipsum pelagus Ponticum erit ?" I expected D'Ablancourt would also have pursued this translation, and have said, " quel bocage sera le Pont Euxin ?" But he has prudently avoided this absurdity, by leaving out the whole sentence

6 Καὶ ἐπιμάνζον. See note 8, page 189, upon the first book.

7 Τὰ χρήματα. See note 1, page 175, upon the first book.

nished themselves in all security, with wheat, barley, wine, legumens, panic, and figs; for the country produced every thing but oil. While the army lay in their camp to refresh themselves, the men had liberty to go out for plunder; and upon those occasions, the booty was their own: but when the whole army went out, if any one straggled from the rest, and got any thing, they determined it should belong to the public. The camp now abounded in all things, for provisions came from every side out of the Greek cities; and people, who sailed along the coast, being informed that a city was going to be built with a haven, willingly put in there: and those of the enemy, who lived in the neighbourhood, sent to Xenophon, hearing he had the conduct of the intended settlement, to know what they should do to deserve his friendship; and he showed them to the soldiers. In the meantime, Cleander arrived with two galleys, but no transports. It happened, that when he came, the army was gone out to get provisions, and a party of stragglers, going up the mountain in search of plunder, took a great number of sheep; but being afraid they would be taken from them, they informed Dexippus of it, the same who ran away with the fifty-oar galley from Trebisond, and desired him to secure the sheep, agreeing that he should retain some of them for his pains, and restore the rest. Immediately Dexippus drove away the soldiers who stood round them, and told them the sheep belonged to the public; then went to Cleander, and informed him that they endeavoured to take them away by force. Cleander ordered him to bring the man who attempted it before him. Upon that, Dexippus seized one of the men, and was carrying him away, when Agasias, meeting him, rescued the man; for he belonged to his company: and the rest of the soldiers who were present, threw stones at Dexippus, calling him traitor. This put not only him, but many of the men also, who belonged to the galleys, in fear, and made them fly to the sea; and Cleander himself was among those who fled. Hereupon, Xenophon and the rest of the generals endeavoured to suppress the tumult, and told Cleander, that there was no danger, and that all this was occasioned by the standing order of the army, But Cleander, being inflamed by Dexippus, and himself nettled for having discovered so much fear, said he would sail away, and cause

them to be proclaimed enemies, and that as such, none of the Greek cities should receive them: for the [1] Lacedæmonians were, at that time, the masters of all Greece.

The Greeks looked upon this as an affair of bad consequence, and begged of him not to do it; but he said it could not be otherwise, unless they delivered up the man who began throwing stones, together with the person who rescued him. This was Agasias the constant friend of Xenophon; for which reason Dexippus had accused him. In this perplexity, the commanders called the army together, and some of them treated Cleander as a man of no importance; but Xenophon thought the affair of no small consequence, and, rising up, said:

"Gentlemen! I look upon it as a matter of great moment, if Cleander goes away, as he threatens, in this disposition: for we are now in the neighbourhood of the Greek cities, and as the Lacedæmonians preside over Greece, every single Lacedæmonian can effect whatever he pleases in these cities. If, therefore, this man first shuts us out of Byzantium himself, then gives notice to the rest of the Lacedæmonian governors, not to receive us into their cities, as men refusing obedience to the Lacedæmonians, and absolutely ungovernable; this character of us will at last reach the ears of Anaxibius, the admiral, and then it will be difficult for us either to stay where we are, or to sail away; for, at this time, the Lacedæmonians command both at sea and land. We ought not, therefore, for the sake of one or two men, to exclude ourselves from Greece, but to obey them in every thing; for the cities to which we belong, obey them. As to my own particular (for I hear Dexippus tells Cleander, that Agasias had never done this, if I had not given him orders,) for my part, I say, I am ready to clear both you and Agasias of this accusation, if he will say that I was the author of any of these things, and to condemn myself, if I began throwing stones, or any other violence, to the last of punishments, and will submit to it. My advice also is, that if Cleander should accuse any other person, he ought to surrender himself to him to be tried; by this means you will be free from censure. As things now stand, it will be hard if we, who expect to meet with applause and honour in Greece,

1 Ἦρχον δὲ τότε πάντων τῶν Ἑλλήνων οἱ Λακεδαιμόνιοι. See the Introduction, p. 161.

should, instead of that, not even be in the same condition with the rest of our countrymen, but be excluded from the Greek cities."

After this, Agasias rose up, and said, " Gentlemen! I call the gods and goddesses to witness, that neither Xenophon, nor any other person among you, ordered me to rescue the man ; but seeing Dexippus (who you know has betrayed you) carrying away a brave man belonging to my company, I thought it was not to be borne, and own I rescued him. Think not of delivering me up, for I will surrender myself to Cleander, as Xenophon advises, to be tried by him, and used as he thinks fit. Let this be no cause of war between you and the Lacedæmonians ; but let every man return with safety to whatever part of Greece he pleases. I only desire you will choose some of your own number, and send them with me, to Cleander, that if I omit any thing, they may both speak and act in my behalf." Upon this, the army gave him leave to choose such persons as he thought proper -to accompany him ; and he chose the generals. Agasias and the generals accordingly went to Cleander, together with the man who had been rescued by Agasias ; and the generals spoke to Cleander in the following manner :

" The army has sent us to you, O Cleander, and desires, if you accuse them all, that you will yourself pass sentence upon them all, and treat them as you think fit : if one, or two, or more of them, they have thought proper they should surrender themselves to you, and submit to your judgment. If, therefore, you accuse any of us, here we are before you : if any other, let us know it ; for no man shall refuse to submit to your judgment, who will submit to our command." After this, Agasias, advancing, said, " I am the person, O Cleander, that rescued the man whom Dexippus was carrying away, and that gave orders to our men to strike Dexippus ; for I knew the soldier to be a good man, and that Dexippus, who had been chosen by the army to command the galley we begged of the inhabitants of Trebisond, in order to get ships together to transport us, had run away with the galley, and betrayed the soldiers, to whom he owed his preservation. Thus he is the cause not only of our having deprived the inhabitants of Trebisond of their galley, but of our being looked upon as ill men, and, as far as it lay in his power, of our ruin ; for he had heard, as well as we, that if we went by land, it was impossible for us to pass the

rivers that lay in our way and return to Greece. Such is the character of the person from whom I rescued the man. If either you, or any one belonging to you, had been carrying him away, and not one of our own deserters, be assured that I should have attempted no such thing. Know, then, that if you put me to death, you will destroy a brave man, for the sake of a coward and a villain."

Cleander, hearing this, said he could not approve of the conduct of Dexippus, if he had been guilty of these things ; " But," adds he, " in my opinion, though Dexippus were the worst of men, no violence should be offered to him, but that he ought to be tried, (in the manner you yourselves propose,) and punished, if guilty. As for you, leave Agasias with me, and depart : and when I give you notice, be present at his trial. I neither accuse the army, nor any other person, since Agasias himself owns he rescued the man." Upon this, the soldier who had been rescued said, " Though you seem to think, O Cleander, that I was apprehended as an offender, yet know, that I neither struck any one, or threw stones at any ; I only said the sheep belonged to the public : for the soldiers had made an order, that when the whole army went out, whatever booty was taken by any particular person, should belong to the public. This was all I said, and for this, Dexippus seized me with a design to carry me away, that every man's mouth being stopped, he might have his share of the booty, and secure the rest for his accomplices, contrary to ª the standing order of the army." To this Cleander answered, " Since you are that kind of man, stay here, that we may consider what to do with you also."

After this Cleander and his company went to dinner ; and Xenophon assembling the army, advised them to send some persons to Cleander to intercede for the men. Hereupon they resolved to send the generals and captains, together with Dracontius the Spartan, and other proper persons, to entreat Cleander, by

2 Παρὰ τὴν ῥήτραν. I have taken ῥήτρα here in the same sense that Plutarch says Lycurgus used it when he called his decrees by that name. I am sensible that the word also signifies an agreement, but as our author calls the same thing τῶν στρατιωτῶν δόγμα a few lines before, I have chosen to give it that sense here also. Leunclavius has said very properly contra edictum, and Hutchinson, I think, not so well, contra pactum. D'Ablancourt has, according to his custom where he meets with a difficulty, left it out.

all means to release them. As soon as Xenophon came to him, he said, " The men you demanded, O Cleander! are in your hands, and the army makes you not only master of their fate, but of its own. However, they now conjure you to give up these two men to them, and not to put them to death; because, upon all occasions, both of them have taken great pains to do service to the army. If they can prevail upon you in this, they promise you, in return, if you think fit to be their general, and the gods are propitious, to let you see both how observant they are, and how incapable, while they obey their commander, and heaven assists them, of fearing an enemy. They also beg of you, that, when you are with them, and have taken upon you the command, you will make trial of Dexippus, and of themselves and others, and then reward each, according to his merit." Cleander, hearing this, said, " By [1] Castor and Pollux, I will return you an answer immediately. I not only give you up the men, but will come to you myself; and, if the gods are in any degree favourable, I will conduct you into Greece. Your discourse is very different from the reports I have heard of some of you, as if you were endeavouring to render the army disaffected to the Lacedæmonians."

After this those who were sent by the army, applauded him, and returned with the two men. Cleander offered sacrifice concerning the journey, and conversed in a friendly manner with Xenophon, and they two contracted an [2] intercourse of hospitality; and when he saw the obedience, and exact discipline of the army, he was still more desirous of commanding them : but after he had offered sacrifice for three days, and the victims were not favourable, he called the generals together, and said, " The victims will not allow me to conduct the army, but let not that discourage you, for it looks as if this was reserved for you. Go on, therefore;

and, when you are arrived at Byzantium, we will receive you in the best manner we are able."

Upon this, the soldiers thought proper to make him a present of the sheep that belonged to the public; these he accepted, and gave them to the army again, and then sailed away. The soldiers having [3] sold the corn they had brought with them, and the rest of the booty they had taken, marched on through Bithynia; and meeting nothing in the direct road to carry with them into the territories of their friends, they resolved to march back one day and a night : and, having done so, they took great numbers both of slaves and cattle ; and after six days' march, arrived at [4] Chrysopolis, a town

<hr>

[1] Nai μὰ τὼ Σιώ. This was an oath much used by the Lacedæmonians : by τὼ Σιώ are meant the two brother gods, Castor and Pollux, as we find by what the Greek scholiast observes upon the following passage of Aristophanes, where Mercury says to Trygæus, in the Lacedæmonian style.

Nai τὰ Σιώ, τὸν ᾽Αττικὸν δόντα δίκην.

Upon this the scholiast says οὕτω τοὺς Διοσκόρους οἱ Λακιδαιμόνιοι Σιὼς ἔλεγον· ὡς ᾽Αθηναίοι Θεοὺς, Δήμητρα καὶ Περσεφόνην.

[2] Μίντας. See note 7, page 169, upon the first book.

[3] Διαθέμενοι τὸν εἶτον. I have been obliged to differ from all the translators, both Latin and French, in the sense I have given to the word διαθέμενοι: the former have rendered it " diviso, distributo frumento," and D'Ablancourt " les soldats le partagerent," which signification I will not say absolutely the word will not bear, though I believe it very uncommon : but I really think the sense will not really bear it here, for our author says they marched back, that they might carry something with them into the territories of their friends, which they might have done without marching back, had they before divided among themselves the booty they had taken. I have therefore said, after they had sold the corn, and the rest of their booty, which is a very common acceptation of the word διατίθεσθαι, and the very sense in which our author uses it in his Cyropædia, where he makes Cyrus tell his officers, and those of the Hyrcanians, that they should divide the money in such a proportion among the horse and foot, ὑμεῖς δὲ λαβόντες διαδίδοτε, ἱππεῖ μὲν, τὸ διπλοῦν, πιζῷ δὲ, τὸ ἁπλοῦν, and a little after that they should publish an order for the sutlers and merchants to sell their commodities, and when they had sold them to bring others, πωλεῖν δὲ τοὺς καπήλους καὶ ἱππέρους ὃ, τι ἔχῃ ἕκαστος πράσιμον· καὶ ταῦτα διαθέμενος, ἄλλα ἄγειν. Upon this occasion I desire the reader will take notice, first that διαδίδοτε, not διατίθεσθε, is the word made use of there, by our author, for "dividite, distribuite ;" secondly, that he there uses διατίθεμαι in the same sense I have translated it upon this occasion ; in which sense also both Leunclavius and Hutchinson have rendered the word, in translating that passage of the Cyropædia.

[4] Εἰς Χρυσόπολιν. Chrysopolis was no more than a village in Strabo's time, that is, in the time of Augustus, καὶ κώμη Χρυσόπολις; it is now called Scutari, and though separated from Constantinople by the Bosphorus is looked upon by the Turks as one of the suburbs of their capital. Polybius informs us that the Athenians, being in possession of Chrysopolis, endeavoured, by the advice of Alcibiades, to oblige those who sailed through the Bosphorus into the Euxine sea, to pay toll. This was many ages after put in practice with greater effect by Mahomet the Second, by means of a castle which he built upon a cape, on the side of Europe, where the temple of Mercury, called by Polybius Ἑρμαῖον, formerly

... days,

... the sacred hill, ... Acropolis, called by the ... This castle Mazeppa the ... fortified ... two castles, Babylon

... says, is the narrowest of the whole Bosphorus, it being but about five stadia (near half an English mile) over. The same author adds that this was the spot over which Darius Hystaspes caused Mandrocles of Samos, as he is called by Herodotus, an eminent architect, to lay a bridge, over which he passed his army, consisting of seven hundred thousand men, to make war upon the Scythians.

A

DISSERTATION

UPON THE

ARGONAUTIC EXPEDITION.

I SHALL take this opportunity to consider what the learned and polite author of the History of Heaven has advanced upon the subject of the Argonautic Expedition; he contends, it seems, that it is all a fiction; his reasons are these: he begins by proving, from Herodotus and Strabo, that the Colchians, who are supposed to have been the possessors of the Golden Fleece, were a colony of the Egyptians, and that, like them, they were famous for their linen manufacture, which drew the Greeks to Colchis, in order to traffic with them: upon this foundation that gentleman builds the following system; he supposes that when the Colchians were to be summoned to leave their fishing for gold, with fleeces, in the river Phasis, in order to apply themselves to their linen manufacture, they put a shuttle into the hands of Isis, and because ארגואטון Argonatoun signifies, in Hebrew, the manufacture of linen, he concludes that the Greek merchants, who were at Colchis, called this shuttle, from the resemblance which it has to a ship, Argonaus. He goes on, and says that ישון jashon, signifies, in Hebrew, to sleep, and מדיה mideh, a measure; and that, when the Colchians were summoned to leave fishing for gold, with their fleeces, and apply themselves to their linen manufacture, they were obliged to watch great part of the night, and, consequently, their sleep was regulated: from whence he infers, that the Greeks hearing the words jashon and mideh often pronounced by the Colchians, framed the fable of the ship Argo, Jason, Medea, and the Golden Fleece. This is the system of that learned gentleman, which, I am apt to believe, will hardly find so great success in the world as all the rest of that author's writings have deservedly met with. I am very willing to allow that the Colchians were a colony of the Egyptians, and that, according to the testimony of Herodotus, they spoke the same language, and had the same religion, the same laws, the same customs, and the same manufactures, particularly that of linen. But is an affinity between some Hebrew words, and the names of Argonaut, Jason, and Medea a sufficient authority to overthrow an expedition supported by the concurrent testimony of all ancient authors, both Greeks and Romans, poets and historians? But this affinity will still have less weight, when it is considered that the language the Colchians spoke being, with great reason, supposed, by this gentleman, to be the Egyptian, an affinity between the Hebrew words, and those names, will be no proof of what is contended for, unless an affinity between the Egyptian and Hebrew languages be first established: but that is a task not easy to be performed, since the Egyptian language is so far lost, that not one letter of it has escaped: there are, indeed, some few Egyptian words to be met with in the Greek and Latin authors, but then they are written in the characters of the language those authors write in; but even these few words contradict the supposition of that affinity between the Egyptian and Hebrew languages; as for example, Pliny tells us that Obeliscus signifies, in Egyptian, a ray of the sun, which is very probable, because their obelisks were dedicated to the sun, whereas, in Hebrew, קרן kran, signifies a ray of the sun. But the author, of all others, who will furnish us with most materials for this purpose, is Diodorus Siculus, from whom I shall take some passages, which will evidently show that the supposition of an affinity between the Egyptian and Hebrew languages, which is the point laboured throughout by the author of the History of Heaven, is without foundation. Diodorus tells us that the two foremost of the long catalogue of divinities, adored by the Egyptians, were the sun and moon, worshipped by them under the well-known names of Osiris and Isis, and that the first is an Egyptian word, which being translated into the Greek language, signifies πολυόφθαλμος, many-eyed: this word is not, I believe, to be met with in the sacred writings, but רב rab, in Hebrew signifies many, and עין ngin an eye, neither of which has the least affinity to the Egyptian word Osiris: the same author tells us that Isis is an Egyptian word also, which, being translated into Greek, signifies παλαιὰ old, this, in Hebrew, is זקן zeken: here again there is not the least shadow of an affinity. The same author says that Athena, the Egyptian Pallas, is also an Egyptian word, signifying in Greek, ἀὴρ the air, the sky, or visible heaven, so that he very justly gathers that the epithet γλαυκῶπις blue-eyed, was much more applicable to Pallas from that sense of the word, than because she was supposed by the Greeks to have blue eyes. In Hebrew, the sky is שמים shamaim. Here again there is no pretence to any affinity between the two languages. Towards the end of the first book, the same author observes that Charon, in Egyptian, signifies πορθμὸς in Greek, a pilot, from whence he says the Greeks took the name of their imaginary ferry-man, as they took the fable of his carrying over the souls of the departed, and of their trials before the three infernal judges, from the real trial which all the deceased, among the Egyptians, underwent, before they were suffered to be honoured with funeral rites. Upon this occasion, Diodorus Siculus, with great reason, complains that the Greeks, by turning this practice of the Egyptians into a fable, have defeated the end of its institution; for, he says, the fictions propagated by their poets, of the rewards of the virtuous, and of the pun-ishments of the wicked, instead of promoting a reformation of manners, are laughed at by ill men, and received with general contempt; whereas, among the Egyptians, the punishments of the wicked, and the rewards of the virtuous, being not fictitious, but visible to all the world, and the daily subject of honour or infamy to the families of both, are, of all others, the greatest incitement to virtue. Now the Hebrew word for a pilot is חבל Hhoble, which is far enough from Charon. The last Egyptian word I shall make use of, shall be from Herodotus, who says that, in the Egyptian language, crocodiles are called champsæ, καλίονται δὲ, οὐ κροκόδειλοι· ἀλλὰ χαμψαί. I am sensible there is some diversity of opinions concerning the sea monster, called in the book of Job, לויתן Leviathan; however, there is little room to doubt of its being a crocodile, which opinion is supported by Bochart, who proves it by a passage of the Thalmud, where it is said that the כלבית Calbith, or the Ichneumon, as he calls it, is the terror of the Leviathan. But the description of it, in the book of Job, will, I believe, be found to be applicable to no other animal. "Canst thou fill his skin with barbed irons? or his head with fish-spears? Behold the hope of catching him is vain: Shall not a man be cast down even at the sight of him? None is so fierce that dare stir him up.—Who can open the doors of his face? His teeth are terrible round about. His scales are his pride, shut up together as with a close seal; one so near to another that no air can come between them: they are joined one to another, they stick together, that they cannot be sundered. When he sneezes, the light flashes, and his eyes are like the eye-lids of the morning.—When he raiseth up himself, the mighty are afraid.—The sword of him that layeth at him cannot hold; the spear, the dart, or the breast-plate. He esteemeth iron as straw, and brass as rotten wood." After this description of the fierceness of the Leviathan, and of his offensive and defensive weapons, I am surprised that it should ever have been taken for the whale, which is a creature terrible in nothing but his bulk, and of a sluggish, rather than a fierce disposition. Now, it is certain that no two words can be, in all respects, more distant from one another, than Leviathan and Chamsæ: and, indeed, how should the Egyptian language have any resemblance to any other, when, if the account given by Herodotus is to be depended on, the Ionians and Carians, who assisted Psammitichus in destroying his brother kings, being eleven in number, were the first persons, speaking a different language, who ever settled in Egypt, πρῶτοι γὰρ οὗτοι ('Ιωνές τε καὶ οἱ Κᾶρες) ἐν Αἰγύπτῳ ἀλλόγλωσσοι κατωκίσθησαν. From this settlement of the Ionians and Carians in Egypt, Herodotus dates the beginning of the intercourse between the Egyptians and the Greeks, and, very probably, their intercourse with the Phœnicians began soon after, from whom possibly they may have taken some terms relating to commerce, and to some other things they might have learned from them, which, from the affinity between the Phœnician and Hebrew languages, may have some distant resemblance to a few terms of the latter. There are a few more Egyptian words to be met with in Herodotus and Diodorus Siculus, which have no more affinity with the Hebrew, than those I have mentioned; it is possible the Chinese language may, for some reasons that do not belong to this subject, be found to have more affinity with that of the Egyptians. But, if the concurrent testimony of so many authors is not thought sufficient to establish the reality of the Argonautic Expedition, we must call in the assistance of the stars to support it; half the sphere is peopled with Argonauts, or furnished with something relating to them: no wonder when either Chiron, the master of Jason, or Musæus, one of the Argonauts, was the first inventor of it, and adorned it with asterisms. There is the golden ram, the ensign of the vessel in which Phryxus fled to Colchis; the bull with brazen hoofs tamed by Jason; and the twins, Castor and Pollux, two of the Argonauts, with the swan of Leda, their mother. There is the ship Argo, and Hydrus the watchful dragon, with Medea's cup, and a raven upon its carcase, the symbol of death. There is Chiron the master of Jason with his altar and sacrifice. There is the Argonaut Hercules with his dart and the vulture falling down; and the dragon, crab, and lion, which he slew; and the harp of the Argonaut Orpheus. But, it may be said that the Argonautic Expedition is as fictitious as the asterisms by which it is delineated. However, the position of the equinoxes, and solstices, in relation to those asterisms, at the time of that expedition, is not fictitious; and we know that those four cardinal points then answered in the middle, that is the fifteenth degrees, of Aries, Cancer, Chelæ, and Capricorn; this position, I say, is not fictitious, any more than the retrogradation of the equinoxes and solstices, not after the rate of one hundred years to a degree, as Hipparchus and the Greek astronomers thought, but after the rate of seventy-two only, as the modern philosophers have discovered; the cause of which retrogradation, or, to speak in the language of the astronomers, of which precession of the equinoxes, was unknown to all of them, till Sir Isaac Newton, by that amazing sagacity, which was peculiar to him, and which gave him so visible a superiority over all other philosophers of all nations and all ages, not only discovered, but clearly demonstrated, that it is owing to the broad spheroidical figure of the earth, and that this figure arises from the rotation of the earth round its axis. It will, I believe, be thought strange that such a cloud of authorities should be dispelled by the single breath of one man, supported by no other arguments than a strained analogy between three or four Hebrew words, and the names of Argonaut, Jason, and Medea. I shall end this long, and I fear, tedious note with declaring, that, though I have the misfortune of differing in opinion with the author of the History of Heaven upon this occasion, yet I have all the deference in the world both for his learning and his polite manner of communicating it to the public; and all possible gratitude for the pleasure and instruction I have had in reading his works.

XENOPHON

ON THE

EXPEDITION OF CYRUS.

BOOK VII.

CONTENTS of BOOK VII.

EXPEDITION OF CYRUS.

BOOK VII.

. THE preceding discourse contains a relation of the actions the Greeks performed, during their Expedition with Cyrus to the battle, of those they achieved after his death, during their retreat, till they came to the Euxine sea, and of those they performed, after their departure thence, both by sea and land, till they arrived at Chrysopolis, a city of Asia, situated without the mouth of that sea.

After this, Pharnabazus, fearing lest the Greeks should make an irruption into the country under his command, sent to Anaxibius, the admiral, (who happened to be then at Byzantium,) to desire he would transport the army out of Asia, with assurance, that in return, he would do every thing that could reasonably be expected. Hereupon, Anaxibius sent for the generals and captains to Byzantium; and promised, if the army came over, they should have pay. The rest of the officers told him they would consider of it, and let him know their resolution; but Xenophon said he proposed to leave the army, and wanted to sail away. However, Anaxibius desired he would come over with the army, before he left it, which the other consented to.

In the meantime, Seuthes the Thracian, sent Medosades to Xenophon, to desire he would let him have his assistance in prevailing upon the army to pass into Europe, assuring him he should have no reason to repent it. Xenophon said, "The army will certainly pass over: let him not, therefore, give any thing either to me, or to any other person, upon that account. As soon as it is transported, I shall depart; let him, therefore, apply to those who stay, and may be of service to him, in such a manner as he thinks fit."

After this, the whole army passed over to Byzantium; but Anaxibius gave them no pay; however, he published an order, that the soldiers should go out of the town, with their arms and baggage, as if he designed to dismiss them, and to take an account of their numbers at the same time. The soldiers were uneasy at this, because they had no money to furnish themselves with provisions for their march, and packed up their baggage with reluctance.

Xenophon, having before contracted an intercourse of hospitality with Cleander, the Lacedæmonian governor, went to take his leave of him, designing to set sail immediately. But, he said to him, "I desire you will not do it; if you do, you will be blamed; for you are already accused by some people as the cause of the army's creeping so slowly out of the town." Xenophon answered, "I am not the cause of this; but the soldiers, being in want of money to buy provisions, are for that reason, of themselves, unwilling to leave the town." "However," says Cleander, "I advise you to go out with them, as if designing to proceed; and, when the army is out of the town, to depart." "Let us go then," says Xenophon, "to Anaxibius, and settle it in this manner:" and coming to him, they informed him of what they had determined. He advised them to pursue it, and that the army should immediately go out with their baggage: at the same time he desired they would also give notice, that whoever absented himself from the review and muster, should incur their censure. Upon this the generals first, and after them, the rest of the army went out of the town. They were now all out, except a few, and Eteonicus stood already at the gates to shut and bolt them, as soon as they were all gone.

Anaxibius, therefore, calling together the

generals and captains, said, " You may supply yourselves with provisions out of the Thracian villages, where there is great plenty of barley and wheat, and of all things necessary : as soon as you have furnished yourselves, go on to the [1] Chersonesus, where Cyniscus will give you pay." Some of the soldiers overheard this, or, possibly, one of the captains informed the army of it. In the meantime, the generals inquired concerning Seuthes, whether he were a friend, or an enemy ; and whether they were to march over the holy mountain, or round through the middle of Thrace.

While they were engaged in this discourse, the soldiers snatched up their arms, and ran hastily to the gates, with a design to force their way back into the town. But Eteonicus, with those about him, when they saw the heavy-armed men running to the gates, immediately shut and bolted them. Upon this, the soldiers [2] knocked at the gates, and complained they were treated with great injustice, in being shut out of town, as a prey to the enemy ; threatening to cut the gates asunder, if they would not open them. Some ran to the sea, and got over the [3] mole into the town ; and others, who happened to be within, observing what was doing at the gates, cleft the bars with hatchets, and set them open : upon this they all rushed in.

Xenophon, seeing what passed, and being afraid the army should fall to plundering, and, by that means, an irreparable mischief should be done, not only to the town, but to himself, and the soldiers, ran in all haste, and got within the gates, together with the crowd. As soon

as the inhabitants saw the army break in, they fled out of the market, some hurrying to the ships, others to their houses, and those, who were within doors, ran out : some hauled down the galleys into the sea, in hopes of saving themselves in them : and all thought themselves undone, the town being taken. Upon this, Eteonicus fled to the citadel ; and Anaxibius running down to the sea, sailed round to the same place, in a fisher-boat, and immediately sent for the garrison from Chalcedon ; for he did not think that in the citadel sufficient for its defence.

As soon as the soldiers saw Xenophon, they crowded about him, and said, " You have now an opportunity, O Xenophon ! of making yourself a man. You are master of a town, of galleys, of money, and of so many people : you have now the power, if you think fit, of making us rich, and we that of making you considerable." " You say well," says Xenophon ; " and I will follow your advice ; if, therefore, this is your desire, place yourselves in your ranks immediately, and handle your arms." He gave these orders with a design to quiet them, and, for the same reason, directed the rest of the officers to give orders that their men also should stand to their arms. The soldiers drew up of their own accord, the heavy-armed men presently forming themselves into a body of fifty deep, and the targeteers repairing to each of the wings. The place where they stood was called the Thracian square, and being free from houses, and even, was very proper for a parade. When they all stood armed in their ranks, and their minds were appeased, Xenophon addressed himself to the assembly, in the following manner.

" Gentlemen ! I am not at all surprised at your resentment, and that you look upon yourselves as very ill used, by being imposed on. But, if we indulge our anger, and not only take revenge of the Lacedæmonians, who are present, for this imposition, but plunder the city, that is in no degree guilty, consider what will be the consequence : we shall, from that moment, be the declared enemies both of the Lacedæmonians, and of their allies ; and of what nature this war will be, may be easily guessed, by those who have seen, and call to mind what has happened of late years. For, when [4] we Athenians entered upon the war with the Lacedæmonians, and their allies, we had a fleet of

---

1 Εἰς τὴν Χερρόνησον. The Thracian Chersonesus was separated from the rest of Thrace by a wall, reaching from the Propontis, to the sea called Sinus Melas, in the Ægean Sea. This wall was built by Dercyllidas, the Lacedæmonian general, the second year of the ninety-fifth Olympiad, that is the year after Xenophon brought back the remains of the soldiers, who had served under Cyrus. This wall was begun in the spring, and ended before the autumn of the same year ; it reached from sea to sea, quite across the Isthmus, and was in length thirty-seven stadia, that is, about three English miles and three quarters : this Chersonesus contained in it eleven towns, many sea-ports, and a large extent of arable land, woods, and rich pastures. It afterwards belonged to Agrippa, son-in-law to Augustus, and one of the greatest men of that or of any other age. At his death it came to Augustus. It is a great pity that part of the seventh book of Strabo is lost, where he treats of this Chersonesus.

2 Ἔκοπτον τὰς πύλας. Lucian for ever uses this word in the sense I have given it here.

3 Παρὰ τὴν χηλὴν. Χηλαί· αἱ ἐμφερεῖσι τοῦ πρὸς θάλασσαν τείχους προβεβλημέναι λίθοι, διὰ τὴν τῶν κυμάτων βίαν, μὴ τὸ τεῖχος βλάπτοιτο· παρὰ τὸ ἐοικέναι χηλῇ βοός. Suidas.

4 Ἡμεῖς γὰρ οἱ Ἀθηναῖοι. See the Introduction.

no less than four hundred galleys, some of which were at sea, and others in [5] the docks : we had a great sum of money in the treasury, and an annual revenue payable both by the citizens, and foreigners, of no less than [6] one thousand talents : we had the command of all the islands; we were possessed of many cities both in Asia and Europe, and even of Byzantium, where we now are: yet, with all these advantages, we were overcome by them, as you all know. What then have we now to expect, when the Lacedæmonians and the Achæans are united, and the Athenians, with those who were then in alliance with them, are all become an accession to their power? When [7] Tissaphernes, and all the rest of the Barbarians, who inhabit the sea-coast, are our enemies, and the king of Persia himself the most inveterate of all, against whom we have made war with a design to deprive him of his kingdom, and, if possible, of his life too? When all these join their forces is there any one so void of sense, as to flatter himself that we shall prove superior to them? For heaven's sake, gentlemen! let us not go mad, and perish with dishonour, by becoming the proclaimed enemies to our fathers, our friends, and our relations? ' For these all live in the cities that will make war upon us : and not without reason ; if, having declined to possess ourselves of any town belonging to the Barbarians, whom we vanquished, we should plunder the first Greek city we arrive at. For my part, I wish, before I see you guilty of such things, I may be buried ten thousand fathom deep : and would advise you, as you are Greeks, to endeavour, by your obedience to the masters of Greece, to obtain justice. But, if your endeavours should prove ineffectual, we ought not, however, though wronged, to deprive ourselves of all possibility of returning home. My opinion therefore now is, that we should send some persons to Anaxibius, to acquaint him, that we did not come into the town with a design to commit violence, but if possible, to obtain favour ; and, if we fail in this, to let

him see that we are ready to leave it again, not because we are imposed upon, but because we are willing to obey."

This was resolved upon : so they sent Hieronymus of Elis, Eurylochus of Arcadia, and Philesius of Achaia to him with these instructions. While the soldiers were yet assembled, Cyratades, a Theban, came to them. This man was not banished from Greece, but wandered about, from an ambition to command armies, offering himself to any city or nation that had occasion for a general. He told them he was ready to conduct them to that part of Thrace, called the [8] Delta, where they should make their fortunes, and that till they arrived there, he would supply them with meat and drink in plenty. While he was saying this, the soldiers received an answer from Anaxibius, who assured them they should have no cause to repent of obeying him ; that he would give an account of this to the magistrates of Sparta, and would, himself, consider in what he could be of most service to them. Upon this, they accepted Cyratades for their general, and went out of the town. And Cyratades appointed to come the next day to the army, with victims, and a priest, and also meat and drink for the men. As soon as they were out of the town, Anaxibius caused the gates to be shut, and public notice to be given, that if any of the soldiers were found within the walls, they should be sold for slaves. The next day, Cyratades came to the army with the victims, and the priest : he was followed by twenty men, loaded with barley-meal, and as many with wine ; three more brought as many olives, another, as much garlic, and a third, as many onions as he could carry ; and having ordered these things to be set down, as if he intended to [9] divide them among the troops, he offered sacrifice.

Here Xenophon sent for Cleander, and desired him to procure liberty for him to go into the town, and embark at Byzantium. When Cleander came, he said, " It is with great difficulty that I have prevailed ; for Anaxibius says

5 'Εν τοῖς νεωρίοις. Νεώριον λέγεται ὁ τόπος ἅπας, ὡς ὃν ἀνέλκονται αἱ τριήρεις, καὶ πάλιν ἐξ αὐτοῦ καθέλκονται. Harpocration. For which he cites Lycurgus and Andocides.

6 Χιλίων ταλάντων. See note 6, page 169, upon the first book.

7 Τισσαφέρνους. See note 1, page 168, upon the first book.

8 Τὸ Δέλτα καλούμενον τῆς Θράκης. Besides the Egyptian Delta, other places were, from their triangular figure, called by that name by the ancients ; for Strabo mentions an island, called Pattalene, lying at the mouth of the Indus, which he says, Onesicritus, calls by the name of Delta.

9 'Ως ἐπὶ δάσμωσιν. Δάσμωσις διαίρεσις. Hesychius.

it is not proper that the soldiers should be near the town, and Xenophon within; the inhabitants being engaged in factions and animosities: however, he says, you may come in if you propose to sail with him." Upon which, Xenophon took leave of the soldiers, and went into the town with Cleander.

The victims not being favourable to Cyratades, the first day he distributed nothing to the soldiers. The next, both the victims and Cyratades, with a garland upon his head, preparing to offer sacrifice, stood before the altar, when Timasion the Dardanian, Neon the Asinian, and Cleanor the Orchomenian, came to Cyratades, and forbade him to offer sacrifice, adding, that unless he gave provisions to the army, he should not command it. Upon this, he ordered them to be distributed; but the provisions falling short of one day's subsistence for every man, he renounced the generalship, and, taking the victims, departed.

II. Hereupon Neon the Asinian, Phryniscus of Achaia, and Timasion of Dardanus, who staid with the army, led them into some villages of the Thracians, that lay near Byzantium, where they encamped. Here the generals disagreed, Cleanor and Phryniscus being desirous to carry the army to Seuthes (for he gained them by making a present of a horse to one, and of a woman to the other), and Neon, to the Chersonesus, upon this presumption, that, if they came into the dominions of the Lacedæmonians, he should have the sole command. Timasion wanted to go back into Asia, expecting, by this means, to return home. The soldiers were for this: but, much time being spent in this contest, many of the soldiers sold their arms in the country, and sailed away as they could; others gave them to the country-people, and settled in the cities, mingling with the inhabitants. Anaxibius was pleased to hear the army was disbanding, for he concluded this would be most acceptable to Pharnabazus.

While [1] Anaxibius was upon his voyage from Byzantium, Aristarchus met him at Cyzicus. He was sent to succeed Cleander, as governor of Byzantium. He informed Anaxibius, that Polus was upon the point of coming into the Hellespont, to succeed him in the command of the fleet; and Anaxibius ordered Aristarchus to sell all the soldiers of Cyrus, whom he found in Byzantium. As for Cleander, he had sold none of them, but, out of compassion, took care of those who were sick, and obliged the inhabitants to receive them into their houses; but Aristarchus, as soon as he arrived, sold no less than four hundred of them. When Anaxibius came to [2] Parium, he sent to Pharnabazus in pursuance of their agreement; but he finding that Aristarchus was going to Byzantium, in quality of governor, and that Anaxibius was no longer admiral, neglected him, and made the same terms with Aristarchus, concerning the army of Cyrus, that he had before made with Anaxibius.

Upon this, Anaxibius, calling Xenophon to him, desired, by all means, that he would set sail for the army immediately, and both keep them in a body, and draw together as many as he could of those who were dispersed, then leading them to [3] Perinthus, transport them forthwith into Asia. He ordered at the same time, a thirty-oar galley to attend him, and not only gave him a letter, but sent an express with him, to let the Perinthians know that they were immediately to furnish Xenophon with horses to carry him to the army. Xenophon crossed the Propontis, and arrived at the army. He was received by the soldiers with great joy, who followed him cheerfully, in hopes of passing over from Thrace into Asia.

[4] Seuthes, hearing that Xenophon was returned, sent Medosades to him by sea, to

1 Ἀποπλέοντι δὲ Ἀναξιβίῳ ἐκ Βυζαντίου συναντᾷ Ἀριστάρχῳ ἐν Κυζίκῳ. I was surprised to find Hutchinson translate this passage, " At Anaxibio, e Byzantio solventi obviam venit apud Cyzicum Aristarchus;" and Leunclavius, " Quum autem Byzantio solveret, obviam ei venit apud Cyzicum Aristarchus." How could Aristarchus meet Anaxibius at Cyzicus, as the latter was weighing anchor from Byzantium? They have translated it as if our author had said, ἀπαντομένῳ δὲ Ἀναξιβίῳ. It is very plain the sense is, that Aristarchus, who was

2 Παραπλεύσας εἰς Πάριον. Parium was a town upon the Propontis situated between Cyzicus and the Hellespont: it was built, according to Strabo, by the inhabitants of the island of Paros ; the same author adds, that in Parium there was an altar, the sides of which were six hundred feet in length.

3 Εἰς Πέρινθον. Perinthus was a city of Thrace, in the neighbourhood of Byzantium: it was otherwise called Heraclea. Harduin says it is now called Pantiro.

4 Σεύθης. See note 2, page 305, upon the sixth book.

sent to succeed Cleander, met Anaxibius at Cyzicus, which every body knows is a city upon the Propontis, not far from the Hellespont, through which Anaxibius was to sail on his return home. It is with pleasure I do justice to D'Ablancourt, upon this occasion: he has said very properly, " Comme il fut parti de Byzance, et arrive a Cyzique, il rencontra Aristarque.

desire he would bring the army to him, promising whatever he thought most effectual to persuade him. Xenophon answered, "that it was not possible for any thing of this kind to be done:" whereupon the other went away. When the Greeks came to Perinthus, Neon drew off his forces, and encamped apart with about eight hundred men; the rest remained together under the walls of the town.

After this, Xenophon was employed in getting ships to transport the troops into Asia; when Aristarchus the governor, arriving from Byzantium with two galleys, at the desire of Pharnabazus, forbade the masters of the ships to transport them; and, going to the army, commanded the soldiers not to go over into Asia. Xenophon told them that "Anaxibius had ordered it, and," says he, "he sent me hither for that purpose." Upon which Aristarchus replied, "Anaxibius is not admiral, and I am governor here; and if I take any of you attempting to go over, I will throw them into the sea." Having said this, he went into the town. The next day he sent for the generals and captains; and when they came near the walls, Xenophon had notice given him, that if he went into the town, he should be apprehended, and either suffer some punishment there, or be delivered over to Pharnabazus. When he heard this, he sent them on before him, saying, "he had a mind to offer sacrifice;" and returning, he sacrificed, in order to know whether the gods would allow him to endeavour to carry the army to Seuthes: for he saw that it was neither safe to pass over into Asia, since the person who would oppose it had galleys at his command; neither was he willing to shut himself up in the Chersonesus, and expose the army to a general scarcity, where, besides the want of provisions, they would be under a necessity of obeying the governor of the place.

While Xenophon was thus employed, the generals and captains came from Aristarchus, and brought word that he had sent them away, for the present, but had ordered them to come back to him in the evening. This made the treachery still more manifest: Xenophon therefore, finding the sacrifice promised security both to himself and the army, in going to Seuthes, took with him Polycrates the Athenian, one of the captains, and from each of the generals, except Neon, a person in whom they confided; and went that night to the army of Seuthes, which lay at the distance of sixty stadia. When they drew near to it, he found several fires, but nobody near them, which made him at first conclude that Seuthes had decamped; but hearing a noise, and the men calling out to one another, he understood that Seuthes had, for this reason, ordered fires to be made before his night-guards, that they, being in the dark, might not be seen, neither might it be known where they were; while those who approached the camp could not be concealed, but were discovered by the light. Observing this, he sent the interpreter, whom he happened to have with him, and ordered him to acquaint Seuthes that Xenophon was there, and desired a conference with him. They asked whether it was Xenophon the Athenian, one of the army; and upon his saying it was he, they returned with great alacrity, and presently after, about two hundred targeteers appeared, who conducted Xenophon and his company to Seuthes. They found him in a [5] castle very much upon his guard, and round the castle stood horses ready bridled: for, living in continual fear, he fed his horses in the day-time, and stood upon his guard all night. It was reported that formerly, [6] Teres, the ancestor of this man, having entered this country with a considerable army, lost great numbers of his men, and was stripped of his baggage by the inhabitants: they are called Thynians, and, of all people, are said to be the most dangerous enemies in the night.

When they were near the castle, Seuthes ordered Xenophon to come in with any two of his company: as soon as they were entered, they first saluted each other, and, according to the Thracian custom, drank to one another in horns full of wine, (Medosades being present, who was the ambassador of Seuthes upon all occasions,) then Xenophon began to speak: "You sent Medosades to me, O Seuthes! first to Chalcedon, to desire I would co-operate with you in getting the army transported out of Asia; and promised, if I effected it, to return the obligation, as Medosades informed me." Having said this, he asked Medosades if it was true, who owned it. Then Xenophon

---

5 'Εν τύρση. Τύρσιν· πύργος. Hesychius.
6 Τήρης ὁ τούτου πρόγονος. This Teres was the father of Sitalces, who was uncle to Seuthes; see note 2, page 305, upon the sixth book.

went on, "after I arrived at the army from Parium, Medosades came to me again, and assured me, if I brought the army to you, that you would not only treat me as a friend, and a brother, in other respects, but that you would deliver up to me those maritime towns, of which you are in possession." After this, he again asked Medosades if he said so, who owned that also. "Then," said Xenophon, "let Seuthes know the answer I made to you at Chalcedon." "You answered first that the army had resolved to go over to Byzantium, and, therefore, there was no reason to give any thing, either to you, or to any other person, upon that account: you added that, as soon as you had crossed the sea, you designed to leave the army, which happened accordingly." "What," says Xenophon, "did I say when you came to ¹ Selymbria?" "You said that what I proposed was impracticable, because the army had determined to go to Perinthus, in order to pass over to Asia." "Here I am then," said Xenophon, "with Phryniscus, one of the generals, and Polycrates, one of the captains; and, without, are those who are most confided in by each of the generals, except Neon, the Lacedæmonian: and, if you desire that our stipulation should receive a greater sanction, let them also be called in. Do you, therefore, Polycrates! go to them, and tell them, from me, that I desire they would leave their arms without, and do you leave your sword there also, and come in."

Seuthes, hearing this, said, he should distrust no Athenian; for he knew them to be ² related to him, and looked upon them as his

affectionate friends. When all proper persons were come in, first Xenophon asked Seuthes what use he proposed to make of the army? To this he answered: "Mæsades was my father, under whose government were the Mælandeptans, the Thynians, and the Thranipsans. My father, being driven out of this country, when the affairs of the Odrysians declined, died of sickness, and I, being then an orphan, was brought up at the court of Medocus, the present king. When I grew up, I could not bear to subsist upon another man's liberality. As I was sitting therefore, by him, I begged of him to give me as many troops as he could spare, that, if possible, I might take revenge on those who had expelled our family, and be no longer, like a dog, supported at his table. Upon this, he gave me those forces, both of horse, and of foot, which you shall see, as soon as it is day; and I now subsist by plundering my paternal country with these troops : to which if you join your forces, I have reason to believe, that, with the assistance of the gods, I shall easily recover my kingdom. This is what I desire at your hands."

"Let us know then," says Xenophon, "what you have in your power to give to the army, the captains, and the generals, if we come; to the end that these may make their report." He promised to every common soldier a cyzicene, two to the captains, and four to the generals ; with as much land as they desired, besides yokes of oxen, and a walled town near the sea. "If," says Xenophon, "I endeavour to effect what you desire, but am prevented by the fear that may be entertained of the Lacedæmonians, will you receive into your country any who shall be desirous to come to you?" He answered, "Not only that, but I will treat them like brothers, give them a place at my table, and make them partakers of every thing we shall conquer : to you, Xenophon! I will give my daughter, and if you have one, I will buy her, according to the Thracian custom, and give you Bisanthe for your habitation, which is the handsomest town belonging to me near the sea."

III. After they heard this, they exchanged hands, and went away; and arriving at the camp before day, each of them made his report to those who sent them. As soon as it was

<hr>

1 Ἐν Σηλυμβρίᾳ. Selymbria was a town of Thrace upon the Propontis, near Perinthus. Strabo says that βρία in the Thracian language, signifies a town. Leunclavius says it is now called both by the Turks and Greeks, Silyurian.

2 Καὶ γὰρ ὅτι συγγενεῖς ἦσαν αὐτῶν. Hutchinson, upon this occasion, quotes a passage out of the second book of Thucydides, where that author says that Perdiccas gave his sister Stratonice in marriage to Seuthes. I own I do not understand how Seuthes could be said to be related to the Athenians by marrying a daughter of a king of Macedon. We find in another part of the second book of Thucydides, that the Athenians entered into an alliance with Sitalces, and made his son Sadocus a citizen of Athens; but this, I own, does not seem to support what Seuthes says of their relation : it is certain that Tereus, the father to Sitalces, was not the person who married Procne, the daughter of Pandion, the son of Erectheus, king of Athens, since Thucydides expressly tells us that the name of the latter was Tereus, and that they were not of the same part of Thrace ; so that Seuthes could not ground his relation to the Athenians upon the marriage of Tereus with Procne.

ght, Aristarchus sent again for the generals
d captains to come to him, but they declined
, and determined, instead of going to Aristar-
hus, to call the army together: and all the
ldiers assembled, besides those belonging to
eon; who encamped at the distance of about
n stadia from the rest. When they were
assembled, Xenophon rose up, and spoke as
ollows:

"Gentlemen! Aristarchus, with his galleys,
inders us from sailing to the place we pro-
osed; so that it is not safe for us to embark.
Ie would have us force our way, over the holy
ountain, into the Chersonesus. If we gain
at pass, and arrive there, he says he will nei-
er sell any more of you, as he did in Byzan-
um, nor deceive you any longer; but that you
rill then be the better entitled to receive pay.
Ie promises also that he will no longer suffer
s, as he does now, to want provisions. Thus
Aristarchus says. On the other side, Seuthes
ngages that, if you go to him, you shall find
our account in it. Consider, therefore, whe-
her you will deliberate upon this matter, while
ou stay here, or after you are returned to the
lace, where you may supply yourselves with
rovisions. My opinion is, since we have nei-
her money to purchase what we want, nor are
uffered to supply ourselves without it, that we
return to the villages, where the inhabitants,
being weaker than we are, do not oppose it;
and where, after we are supplied with what is
necessary, and have heard in what service each
of them propose to employ us, we may choose
that measure which shall appear most to our
advantage. Whoever, therefore, is of this
opinion, let him hold up his hand." And they
all held up their hands. "Go then," continued
he, "and get your baggage ready, and, when
the order is given, follow your leader."

After this, Xenophon put himself at their
head, and they followed him. But Neon, together with some other persons sent by Aristarchus, would have persuaded them to turn
back: however, they regarded them not. When
they had marched about thirty stadia, Seuthes
met them. As soon as Xenophon saw him,
he desired he would draw near, that as many of
the army as possible might bear what he had
to propose for their advantage. When he came
up, Xenophon said, "We are marching to
some place, where the army may find provisions, and where, after we have heard what you

and the Lacedæmonians have to propose to us,
we shall be determined by that which appears
most to our advantage. If, therefore, you will
conduct us to some place, where there is great
abundance, we shall look upon ourselves under
the same obligation to you as if you entertained
us yourself." Seuthes answered, "I know
where there are many villages that lie together,
and are well supplied with all sorts of provisions;
they are so near that you may march thither,
with ease, before dinner." "Lead the way,
therefore," said Xenophon. The army being
arrived in the villages in the [3] afternoon, the
soldiers assembled, and Seuthes spoke to them
in the following manner: "Gentlemen! I desire you will assist me with your arms; and I
promise to each of you a [4] cizycene for your
monthly pay, and to the captains and generals,
what is customary. Besides this, I will do
honour to every man, who shall deserve it. As
to meat and drink, you shall supply yourselves
with both, as you do now, out of the country.
But, I must insist upon retaining the booty,
that by selling it, I may provide for your pay.
We ourselves shall be sufficient to pursue and
discover those of the enemy who fly, and seek
to conceal themselves, and, with your assistance, we will endeavour to overcome those who
resist." Xenophon then asked him, "how far
from the sea he proposed the army should follow him?" He answered, "never more than
seven days' march, and often less."

After that, every man who desired to offer
any thing, had liberty to speak, and several of
them agreed that the proposals of Seuthes were
very advantageous: for, it being now winter,
it was neither possible for those who desired
it, to sail home, nor for the army to subsist in
the territories of their friends, if they were to
pay for every thing they had. They considered also that it would be safer for them to remain, and find subsistence in an enemy's country, jointly with Seuthes, than by themselves;
and that, if, while they were in possession of
so many advantages, they also received pay, it
would be a piece of good fortune they had no
reason to expect. Then Xenophon said, "If
any one has any thing to say against this, let
him speak, if not, [5] let him give his vote for

3 Ἐπὶ δὲ ἀρίαστε τὶς αὐτὰς τῆς δείλης. See note 1,
page 198, upon the first book.
4 Κυζικηνόν. See note 1, page 296, upon the fifth book.
5 Ἐπιψηφίσεσθω ταῦτα. I have followed the manu-

it ;" and, there being no opposition, they gave their votes for it, and it was resolved accordingly; and Xenophon immediately told Seuthes, "they would enter into his service."

After that, the soldiers encamped in their ranks; while the generals and captains were invited by Seuthes to sup with him at his quarters in a neighbouring village. When they came to the door, one Heraclides of Maronea addressed himself to those he thought in a capacity of making presents to Seuthes, and first to some Parian deputies, who were there, being sent to establish a friendship with Medocus, king of the Odrysians, and had brought presents both for him and his queen: to these he said, "that Medocus lived up in the country, twelve days' journey from the sea; and that Seuthes, now he had taken this army into his service, would be master of the sea-coast: being therefore your neighbour," says he, "it will be very much in his power to do you both good and harm: so that, if you are wise, you will make a present to him of what you have brought, which will be laid out much more to your advantage, than if you give it to Medocus, who lives at so great a distance from you:" by this means, he prevailed upon them. Afterwards he came to Timasion of Dardanus, hearing he had cups, and [1] Persian carpets, and told him it was the custom of those who were invited to supper by Seuthes, to make him presents; adding, that, "if he becomes considerable in this country, he will be able both to restore you to yours, and to enrich you when you are there." In this manner, he [2] procured for Seuthes, addressing himself to each of them. When he came to Xenophon, he said, "You are not only of the most considerable city, but are yourself in the greatest reputation with Seuthes, and may possibly desire to be master of some place of strength with lands, in these

parts, as others of your countrymen are: it is therefore worth your while to honour Seuthes in the most magnificent manner. I give you this advice, because I wish you well; for I am satisfied the more your presents exceed those of your companions, the more the advantages you will receive from Seuthes will exceed theirs." When Xenophon heard this, he was in great perplexity; for he had brought with him, from Parium, only one servant, and just money enough for his journey.

Then the most considerable of the Thracians, who were present, together with the Greek generals and captains, and all the deputies of towns who were there, went in to supper; at which they placed themselves in a ring. After that, every one of the guests had a tripod brought him: these were about twenty in number, full of meat cut in pieces, and large leavened loaves were skewered to the meat. The [3] dishes were always placed before the strangers preferably to the rest of the company; for that was their custom. Seuthes then set the example of what follows; he took the loaves that lay before him, and breaking them into small pieces, threw them about to those he thought proper; he did the same by the meat, leaving no more for himself than what served for a taste. The rest, before whom the meat was served, did the same thing. There was an Arcadian in company, whose name was Aristus, a great eater: this man, instead of employing his time in throwing about the victuals, took a loaf of three [4] choenixes in his hand, and, laying some meat upon his knees, ate his supper. In the meantime, they carried about horns of wine, and every body took one. When the cup-bearer brought the horn to Aristus, he, seeing Xenophon had done supper, said, "Go, give it to him, he is at leisure; I am not so yet." When Seuthes heard him speak, he asked the cup-bearer what he said,

---

script quoted by Hutchinson, rather than his conjecture, though I think ἐπιψηφίζωθι, in him, is much better than ἐπιψηφίζοιτ in Leunclavius; but ἐπιψηφίσθω seems to me to answer better to λίγεται, that immediately precedes it.

1 Τάπιδας βαρβαρικάς. Persian carpets have always been famous for their beauty, for which reason, and because these carpets were part of the spoils taken by the Greeks from the Persians, I have ventured to call them Persian carpets, rather than Barbaric after Milton:

> Where the gorgeous East, with richest hand,
> Showers on her king barbaric pearl and gold.

2 Ταῦτα προυμήτα. Προμιόμενοι, προμνηστευόμενοι. Hesychius. D'Ablancourt has left it out.

3 Μάλιστα δὲ αἱ τράπεζαι κατὰ τοὺς ξίνους ἀεὶ ἐτίθεντο. Leunclavius and Hutchinson have very properly, I think, rendered τράπεζαι in this place, Fercula; to support which, they quote a passage out of Julius Pollux, where he says that τράπεζαι were also called the victuals that were placed upon the tables. There is a passage in Athenæus, by which it appears that the word was understood in that sense by every body, πάντων τραπέζας καλούντων τὰς παραθέσεις ταύτας. From hence I imagine the Latins took their "secunda mensa, et altera mensam," for their second course.

4 Τριχοίνικτι ἄρτον. See note 11, page 181, upon the first book.

ho told him; for he could speak Greek; on this, there was great laughing.

The * cup going round, a Thracian entered, ading in a white horse, and taking a horn full f wine, " Seuthes !" says he, " I drink to you, ad make you a present of this horse, with hich you may take any one you pursue, and, a retreat, you will have no reason to fear the nemy." Another brought a boy, which he, in he same manner, presented drinking to him: nd another, clothes, for his wife. Timasion, inking to him, made him a present of a silver up, and a carpet worth ten * mines. Then ae Gnesippus, an Athenian, rose up, and aid, " There was a very good old custom, hich ordains that those who have any thing, hall make presents to the king, to show their espect; but the king shall make presents to hose who have nothing. Let this custom be beerved," says he, " that I also may have omething to present you with, and show my espect." Xenophon was at a loss what to do; or he had the honour done him to be placed ext to Seuthes; and Heraclides had ordered he cup-bearer to give him the horn. However he stood up boldly, (for by this time he ad drunk ' more than usual) and taking the orn, said, " O Seuthes! I present you both vith myself, and with these my companions, as our faithful friends : I am confident none of hem will refuse the condition, but all contend vith me in their zeal for your service. Here hey now are, with a view of asking no other avour * of you, but to undertake labours and angers for your sake. By whose assistance, f the gods are favourable, you may become naster of a large tract of country, by recovering that part of it which belonged to your aternal kingdom, and conquering the rest: by heir assistance, also, you will make yourself naster of many horses and of many men, and easutiful women, whom you need not take way by force; on the contrary, they will come nd offer themselves to you, with presents in heir hands." Upon this Seuthes got up, and ledged Xenophon, pouring * what remained

in the horn upon the person who sat next to him. After this, some Cerasuntæans came in; these sounded a charge with pipes, and trumpets made of raw hides, keeping time, as if they played upon the [10] magade. Upon this, Seuthes himself got up, and shouted in a warlike manner, then, with great agility, sprung out of the place where he stood, imitating a man who avoids a dart. There came in also buffoons.

When it was about sunset, the Greeks rose up, and said it was time to place the guards for the night, and give the word. At the same time, they desired Seuthes to give orders that none of the Thracians might come into the Greek camp in the night; " for," said they, " some of that nation are our enemies, though you are our friends. As they went out, Seuthes got up, showing no signs of being drunk, and going out also, he called the generals to him, and said, " Gentlemen! the enemy as yet knows nothing of our alliance; if, therefore, we fall upon them, before they are either upon their guard against a surprise, or prepared for their defence, it will be the most effectual means of gaining great booty, and taking many prisoners." The generals were of the same opinion, and desired him to lead them. Then Seuthes said, " Do you make yourselves ready, and stay for me; when it is time, I will come back to you; and taking the targeteers and you with me, with the assistance of the gods, I will lead you against the enemy." Upon this Xenophon said, " Consider, then, since we are to march by night, whether the Greek custom is not preferable. In the day-time either the heavy-armed men or the horse march in the van, according to the nature of the ground; but in the night it is always the custom among the Greeks for the slowest corps to lead the way. By this means the army is less subject to be separated, and the men have fewer opportunities of straggling without being taken notice of; it often happening in the

---

5 Ἐπὶ δὲ περιχάρει ὁ οἶνος. Περὶς μὲν τὸ εὐνόμενον, οἶνος δ τὸ συμπόσιον. Suidas.

6 Ἀξίας δίκα μνῶν. See note 6, page 169, upon the first ook.

7 Τεωτωκόος. Ἀντὶ τοῦ μεθίσκεσθαι. Suidas.

8 Προσέμενον. Προσίεται, ἀρέσκεται, ἀρεσθίχεται, ἰδίως αιοδόνοι. Hesychius.

9 Ἐγκατασπίλατι. Suidas, upon the word κατασπι-

λάζων, says, it was a custom among Thracians, when they had drunk as much wine as they could, to pour the rest upon the clothes of the company, for which he quotes Plato : this, he says, they called κατασπιλάζων. It was necessary just to take notice of this ridiculous custom, in order to explain this passage of Xenophon.

10 Οἷον μαγάδι. This musical instrument is said to have been a kind of flute. Strabo reckons it among those whose names were taken from the Barbarians. It was probably an instrument of war.

night, that the troops, when separated, fall up-on one another, and not being able to distin-guish friends from enemies, both do and suffer great damage." Seuthes answered, "You say well, and I will conform to your custom; and will take care you shall have guides, such as, among the oldest of my people, are best ac-quainted with the country; while I bring up the rear with the horse; and if there is occa-sion, I can soon come up to the front." The Athenians gave the word by reason of their al-liance to Seuthes. After this, they went to rest.

When it was about midnight, Seuthes came to them with the horse clad in their coats of mail, and the targeteers with their arms. Af-ter he had delivered the guides to them, the heavy-armed men marched in the van, the tar-geteers followed, and the horse brought up the rear. As soon as it was day, Seuthes, riding up to the front, extolled the Greek custom: "For it has often happened to me," said he, "when I have been upon a march in the night, though with a few troops, to have my horse separated from the foot; where-as now, at break of day, we appear, as we ought, all together. But do you halt here, and repose yourselves, and when I have ta-ken a view of the country, I will come back to you." Having said this, he met with a path, which led him to the top of a mountain, where, coming to a great deal of snow, he examined the road, to see whether there were any foot-steps of men pointing either forward or back-ward: and finding the way untrodden, he returned presently, and said, "Gentlemen! our design will succeed, God willing: we shall surprise the people: but I will lead the way with the horse, that if we discover any one, he may not escape, and give notice to the enemy: do you come after; and, if you are left behind, follow the track of the horse. After we have passed these mountains, we shall come to a great many rich villages."

When it was noon, Seuthes, having reached the summit of the mountains, and taken a view of the villages, rode back to the heavy-armed men, and said, "I now propose to send the horse to scour the plain, and the targeteers to attack the villages; do you follow as fast as you can, that, if they find any resistance, you may support them." When Xenophon heard this, he alighted from his horse: upon which

Seuthes said, "Why do you alight, when ex-pedition is required?" The other answered, "I know that, by myself, I can be of no ser-vice; besides, the heavy-armed men will   with greater speed and alacrity, if I lead on foot."

After this Seuthes, and, with him, Tima-sion, with about forty of the Greek horse, went away. Then Xenophon ordered those of each company, who were under thirty years of age, and prepared for expedition, to advance; and, with these, he ran forward; while Cleanor brought up the rest of the Greeks. When they were in the villages, Seuthes riding up to Xenophon with about fifty horse, said, "What you foretold has happened: the men are taken; but our horse have left me, and are gone away without a commander, some following the pur-suit one way, some another; and I am afraid lest the enemy should rally, and do us some mischief: some of us must also remain in the villages, for they are full of men." Xenophon answered, "With the troops I have, I will pos-sess myself of the eminences. Do you order Cleanor to extend his line in the plain, against the villages." After they had put these things in execution, they got together about one thou-sand slaves, two thousand oxen, and ten thou-sand head of other cattle: and there they quar-tered that night.

IV. The next day, after Seuthes had burned all the villages, without leaving a single house, (in order to terrify the rest by letting them see what they were to expect, if they refused to submit,) he returned; and sent the booty to Perintheus to be sold by Heraclides, that he might, by that means, raise money to pay the soldiers. In the meantime, Seuthes and the Greeks encamped in the plain of the Thyniaus: but the inhabitants left their houses and fled to the mountains.

Here fell a great snow, and the cold was so severe, that the water the servants brought in for supper, and the wine in the vessels, were frozen, and the noses and ears of many of the Greeks were parched with the cold. This explained to us the reason that induces the Thracians to wear [1] foxes skins over their

---

1 Τὰς ἀλωπεκίδας ἐς τ... ἀσφαλαῖς φοςοῦσι καὶ τοῖς ἀσι. After Xerxes had passed t... Hellespont with his pro-digious army, he reviewed the... in the plain of Doriscus; among his troops were Thracia... who, according to Herodotus, wore foxes skins up... their heads, and

heads and ears, and vests, that not only cover their breasts, but their thighs also, with cassocks reaching down to their feet, when they go instead of cloaks. Seuthes sent some of the prisoners to the mountains, to acquaint the inhabitants that, if they did not come down, and, returning to their habitations, submit to him, he would burn their villages also, together with their corn, and then they must perish with hunger. Upon this, the women and children, with the old men, came down, but the younger sort encamped in the villages under the mountain: which when Seuthes observed, he desired Xenophon to take with him the youngest of the heavy-armed men, and follow him; and, leaving their camp in the night, they arrived by break of day at the villages: but the greatest part of the inhabitants quitted them: for the mountain was near. However, Seuthes ordered all they took to be pierced with darts.

There was present an Olynthian, his name Episthenes, who was a lover of boys: this man, seeing a handsome boy, just in his bloom, with a buckler in his hand, going to be put to death, ran to Xenophon, and begged of him to intercede for so beautiful a youth. Upon this, Xenophon went to Seuthes, and desired he

would not put the boy to death, acquainting him at the same time, with the character of Episthenes, and that he once raised a company, in which he considered nothing but the beauty of his men; at the head of whom he always behaved himself with bravery. Hereupon, Seuthes said, " O Episthenes! are you willing to die for this boy?" The other, stretching out his neck, answered, " Strike, if the boy commands, and will think himself obliged to me." Seuthes then asked the boy whether he should strike Episthenes, instead of him. This the boy would not suffer, but begged he would kill neither. Upon this, Episthenes, embracing the boy, said, " Now Seuthes! you must contend with me for him; for I will not part with the boy." This made Seuthes laugh; who, leaving this subject, thought proper they should encamp where they were, to the end the people who had fled to the mountains, might not be subsisted out of these villages. So he, descending a little way into the plain, encamped there; and Xenophon, with the chosen men, quartered in the village that lay nearest the foot of the hill, and the rest of the Greeks, not far from him, among those they call the mountain Thracians.

A few days after, the Thracians, coming down from the mountains to Seuthes, treated concerning hostages and a peace. Hereupon, Xenophon went to him, and let him know that the post they were in was very disadvantageous, that the enemy was not far off, and that he had rather encamp abroad in any other place, than in a strait, where they were in danger of being destroyed: but Seuthes bid him fear nothing, and showed him their hostages, then in his custody. Some of the Thracians, coming down from the mountain, besought Xenophon also to assist them in obtaining a peace. He promised his assistance, and encouraged them with this assurance, that, if they submitted to Seuthes, they had nothing to fear. But they, it seems, were spies sent to amuse them with these proposals.

This passed in the day time: the following night, the Thynians came down from the mountain, and attacked them; their leaders were the masters of every house, it being difficult for any other to find the houses in the dark; because they were surrounded with great palisades to secure the cattle. When they came to the door of each habitation, some threw in

---

whose dress he describes not unlike that of the Thracians, with whom Xenophon was acquainted. Whether these Thracians wore foxes skins upon their heads to preserve them from the cold, as our author seems to think, or whether they wore them by way of armour, and as a distinction in war, I shall not determine; but we find that many nations, inhabiting the warmest climates, wore the skins of several beasts upon their heads, when they went to war: upon those occasions, the upper jaw, or forehead of the animal, was fixed to the top of their heads, I suppose to give them a fierce look. Herodotus tells us, that, in the same army, the Indians, whom he calls the Asiatic Ethiopians, οἳ ἐκ τῆς Ἀσίης Αἰθίοπες, wore upon their heads the skins of horses' heads, with the mane flowing, and the ears erect. I cannot help mentioning, upon this occasion, a passage of Diodorus Siculus, because it shows the origin of a very great folly committed by a very wise people, I mean the worship of Anubis by the Egyptians; he tells us that Anubis and Marcedon, two sons of Osiris, attended him in his expedition to the Indies, and that their armour was taken from animals, that bore some resemblance to their fortitude, Anubis wearing the skin of a dog, and Macedon that of a wolf; for which reason, he says, these animals were worshipped by the Egyptians. The Roman Signiferi, upon Trajan's pillar, have most of them their heads and shoulders covered with the skins of lions, something like Aventinus in Virgil:

" Ipse pedes tegmen torquens immane leonis
Terribili impexum seta cum dentibus albis
Indus capiti ———."

2 U

darts, others clubs, which they carried, with a design as they said, of breaking off the points of the pikes; and some were employed in setting fire to the houses: these called out to Xenophon by name, to come out, and meet his fate, threatening, if he refused, to burn him in the house.

By this time the fire came through the roof, and Xenophon and his men were within, with their corslets on, their shields and swords in their hands, and their helmets upon their heads; when Silanus Macestius, a youth of eighteen years of age, gave the signal by sounding a trumpet; upon which, the rest also, at once, rushed out of the other houses with their swords drawn. Whereupon the Thracians fled, covering their backs with their bucklers, according to their custom: and some of them, endeavouring to leap over the palisades, were taken hanging on them, their bucklers being set fast; others, missing the way out, were killed, and the Greeks pursued them out of the village. However, a party of the Thynians, coming back in the dark, threw darts at some of the Greeks, as they ran by a house that was on fire, taking their aim from an obscure place at those who were in the light, and wounded Hieronymus, Enodius, and Theagenes, a Locrian, all captains; but nobody was killed, though some had their clothes and baggage burned. Seuthes came to their relief with seven horse, the first he met, bringing with him a Thracian trumpeter, who, from the time the other found they were attacked, and set out to relieve them, continued sounding till the action was over; which did not a little contribute to terrify the enemy: when he came, he embraced the Greeks, saying he expected to find a great number of them slain.

After this, Xenophon desired Seuthes to deliver to him the hostages, and march up to the mountain with him, if he thought proper: if not, that he would leave it to his conduct. The next day, therefore, Seuthes delivered to him the hostages, who were elderly men, the most considerable, as they said, of the mountain Thracians, and he himself set out with his own forces. By this time, the army of Seuthes was increased to three times the number it before consisted of; for many of the Odrysians, being informed of what Seuthes was doing, came down to his assistance. When

the Thynians saw, from the mountain, great numbers of heavy-armed men, of targeteers, and of horse, they came down and sued for peace, promising to do every thing that was required of them, and desired Seuthes would take pledges for their fidelity. He, calling Xenophon to him, informed him of what they said, letting him know at the same time, that he would not make peace, if he desired to take revenge of them for attacking him. Xenophon answered, that he was sufficiently revenged, if these people were, instead of free men, to become slaves: but withal, advised him, for the future, to take for hostages those who had most power to do him harm, and to let the old men stay at home. All the Thracians, therefore, in this part of the country submitted to Seuthes.

V. They next marched into the country called the Delta, belonging to the Thracians, which lies above Byzantium. This country did not belong to the kingdom of Mæsides, but to that of Teres the Odrysian, one of their ancient kings; here they found Heraclides, with the money he had raised by the sale of the booty. And here Seuthes, having ordered three yokes of mules (for there were no more) and several of oxen to be brought out, sent for Xenophon, and desired he would accept the first, and distribute the rest among the generals and captains; but Xenophon said, " I shall be satisfied, if I, receiving your favours another time, give these to the generals and the captains, who, with me, have attended you in this expedition." Upon which, Timasion the Dardanian, received one yoke of mules, Cleanor the Orchomenian, another, and Phryniscus the Achaian, the third. The yokes of oxen he distributed among the captains; but gave the army no more than twenty days' pay, though the month was expired; for Heraclides said he could not sell the booty for more. Xenophon was concerned at this, and said, " O Heraclides ! you do not seem to have so great a regard for Seuthes, as you ought to have : if you had, you would have brought the army their full pay: though you had taken up at interest, and even sold your own clothes to raise as much as would have completed it, if you could not get the money by any other means."

This reproach gave Heraclides great uneasiness, and made him apprehend he should lose the favour of Seuthes; and from that day, he laboured all he could, to give Seuthes ill impressions of Xenophon; on whom not only the soldiers laid the blame of their not receiving their pay, but Seuthes also resented his earnestness in demanding it. And whereas, before, he was for ever telling him that, when he arrived at the sea, he would put him in possession of [1] Bisanthe, Ganus, and Neon Teichus; from this time he never mentioned any thing of that kind; for Heraclides, upon this occasion, had also recourse to calumny, suggesting that it was not safe to intrust places of strength with a person who was at the head of an army.

Upon this, Xenophon considered with himself what was to be done[2] about pursuing their expedition against the upper Thracians; when Heraclides, carrying the rest of the generals to Seuthes, desired them to assure him that they could lead the army as well as Xenophon, and promised that, in a few days, he would give them their pay complete for two months, advising them at the same time to continue in the service of Seuthes. Upon which Timasion said, " If you would give me five months' pay, I would not serve without Xenophon;" and Phryniscus and Cleanor said the same thing.

This made Seuthes chide Heraclides for not calling in Xenophon; so they sent for him alone; but he, being sensible this was an artifice in Heraclides, contrived to create a jealousy in the rest of the generals, took not only all the generals, but likewise all the captains along with him: and, all of them approving of what Seuthes proposed, they pursued their expedition, and marching through the country of the Thracians, called the Melinophagi, with the Euxine sea on their right hand, they arrived at [3] Salmydessus. Here many ships upon their arrival in the Euxine sea

strike, and are driven ashore, the coast being full of shoals, that run a considerable way into the sea. The Thracians, who inhabit this coast, raise pillars, in the nature of boundstones; and every man plunders the wreck that is cast upon his own coast. It is said, that before they erected these pillars, many of them lost their lives by quarrelling with one another about the plunder. In this place are found many beds, boxes, books, and several other things which sailors usually carry in their chests. The army, after they had subdued this people, marched back: that of Seuthes was now grown superior in number to the Greeks; for many more of the Odrysians were come down to him, and the Thracians, as fast as they submitted, joined the army. They now lay encamped in a plain about Selymbria, about fifty stadia from the sea: as yet no pay appeared, and not only the soldiers were displeased at Xenophon, but Seuthes himself was no longer disposed in his favour: and whenever he desired to be admitted to him, business of many kinds was pretended.

VI. Two months were very near elapsed, when Charminus the Lacedæmonian, and Polynicus, arrived from Thimbron. They gave an account that the Lacedæmonians had resolved to make war upon Tissaphernes, and that Thimbron had sailed from Greece with that design. They added that he had occasion for this army, and that every common soldier should have a [4] darick a month, the captains two, and the generals four. Upon arrival of the Lacedæmonians, Heraclides, hearing they were come for the army, immediately told Seuthes it was a happy incident; " For," says he, " the Lacedæmonians are in want of the army, and you are not so. In resigning it, you will confer an obligation on them, and the soldiers will no longer ask you for their pay; but will leave the country."

Seuthes, hearing this, ordered the Lacedæmonians to be brought in: and upon their saying they came for the army, he told them he was willing to resign it, and desired they would account him their friend and ally: he also invited them to his table pursuant to the laws of hospitality, and gave them a magnificent entertainment. But he did not invite Xenophon,

---

1 Βισάνθην, καὶ Γάνον καὶ Νέον Τεῖχος. Towns of Thrace near the sea: if the reader pleases to turn to the first note upon this book, he will find that the last has nothing to do with the wall built by Dercyllidas, for that was not built till the year after Xenophon engaged the Greeks in the service of Seuthes.

2 Περὶ τοῦ ἔτι ἄνω στρατεύεσθαι. D'Ablancourt understands this concerning his going over into Asia, but I have chosen rather to make it relate to the expedition of Seuthes, and the Greeks against those Thracians who inhabited above Byzantium, in which I am supported by Leunclavius and Hutchinson.

3 Σαλμυδησσόν. Salmydessus was a sea-port lying upon the Euxine sea; it is mentioned by Arrian in his

Periplus: the river, the town, and the bay had all the same name.

4 Δαρεικός. See note 6, page 169.

or any one of the other generals. The Lacedæmonians inquiring what kind of man Xenophon was, he answered that he was in other respects, no ill man, but a friend to the soldiers; which hurts him. "But," said they, "is he a popular man with them?" "Altogether so," says Heraclides. "Then," answered the Lacedæmonians, "will not he oppose our carrying away the army?" "If you call the soldiers together," says Heraclides, "and promise them pay, they will have no regard for him, but will quickly follow you." "How," replied they, "shall they be assembled for that purpose?" "Early to-morrow morning," says Heraclides, "we will bring you to them and I am confident, added he, that as soon as they see you, they will cheerfully assemble." This was the result of that day's business.

The next, Seuthes, and Heraclides brought the Lacedæmonians to the army, which assembled for that purpose. These informed them, that the Lacedæmonians had resolved to make war upon Tissaphernes, "who," said they, "has injured you. If, therefore, you engage with us, you will both revenge yourselves of an enemy, and receive each of you a darick a month, the captains two, and the generals four." This was well received by the soldiers: and presently one of the Arcadians rose up to accuse Xenophon. Seuthes was also present, being desirous to know the result, and, for that purpose, had placed himself within hearing with his interpreter; though he himself understood most things that were spoken in Greek. The Arcadian said: "Know then, O Lacedæmonians, that we should long since have engaged ourselves in your service, if Xenophon had not prevailed upon us to come hither; where, though we have been upon duty both night and day, during this severe winter, we have [1] acquired nothing, while he enjoys the reward of our labour, and Seuthes enriches him personally, and deprives us of our pay: so

that," continued he, "if I could see this man stoned to death, and punished for leading us about, I should think I had received my pay, and no longer regret my labour." After him, another got up, and then another: upon which Xenophon spoke as follows:

"There is nothing a man ought not to expect, since I find myself accused by you for that, in which my conscience tells me I have had all the zeal in the world for your service. I was already set out in order to go home, when I turned back, be assured, not because I heard you were in prosperity, but rather because I was informed you were in difficulties, with this intent, that I might serve you, if it was in my power. When I came to the army, though Seuthes sent several messengers to me with many promises, in case I prevailed upon you to go to him, yet I never endeavoured it, as you yourselves know; but led you to that place, from whence I thought you would have the quickest passage into Asia. This I looked upon as a measure the most agreeable both to your interest and inclination. But when Aristarchus arrived with the galleys, and prevented your passage, I then (as it became me) called you together, that we might consider what was to be done. Upon that occasion you heard, on one side, Aristarchus ordering you to go to the Chersonesus, and, on the other, Seuthes proposing terms to engage you in his service, when all of you declared you would go with Seuthes, and all gave your votes for it. Say, then, if I committed any crime in carrying you whither you all resolved to go. If, when Seuthes began to break his promise concerning your pay, I then commended him, you would have reason both to accuse and hate me; but if I, who was before his greatest friend, am now his greatest enemy, how can you any longer with justice blame me, who have given you the preference to Seuthes, for those very things about which I quarrel with him? Possibly, you may say that I have received your pay of Seuthes, and that all I say is artifice; but, is it not plain, that if Seuthes paid me any thing, it was not with a view of being deprived of that part of your pay which he gave me, and of paying you the rest? On the contrary, if he had given me any thing, I dare say, his design would have been to excuse himself from paying you a large sum, by giving me a small one. If, therefore, you are of opinion, that this is the case, it is in your power presently

---

1 Οὐδὲν σταάμεθα. Πισᾶσθαι κιστῆσθαι. Hesychius. Both which, in my opinion, signify much oftener to acquire than to possess. I look upon the word to have the same sense also in that very moral and sensible epigram of Solon, the Athenian legislator, as quoted by Plutarch, in his life of him,

Χρήματα δ' ἱμείρω μὲν ἔχειν, ἀδίκως δὲ σταάσθαι
Οὐκ ἰθίλω, πάντως ὕστερον ἦλθε δίκη.

But as σταάσθαι signifies also to possess, I will not blame Hutchinson for translating it upon this occasion nihil possidemus, though I have translated it otherwise myself; a little farther in signifies, beyond all doubt, to possess.

to render this [2] collusion useless to both of us, by [3] insisting upon your pay: for it is evident that Seuthes, if I have received a bribe from him, will, with justice, redemand it, when I fail in performing the contract, in consideration of which I was bribed. But my conscience tells me that I am far from having received any thing that belongs to you: for I swear by all the gods and goddesses, that I have not even received from Seuthes what he promised me in particular. He is present himself, and, as he hears me, he knows whether I am guilty of perjury or not; and that you may still have more reason to wonder, I also swear, that I have not only received less than the rest of the generals, but even than some of the captains. For what reason then did I do this? I flattered myself, gentlemen, that the greater share I had of this man's poverty, the greater I should have of his friendship, when it was in his power to show it; but I see him now in prosperity, and, at the same time, discover his temper. Possibly, some may say, are you not then ashamed to be thus stupidly deceived? I should, indeed, be ashamed to be thus deceived by an enemy; but, in my opinion, there is a greater shame in deceiving a friend, than in being deceived by him. If it is allowed to be upon one's guard against a friend, I know you have all been very careful not to give this man a just pretence to refuse the payment of what he promised? for we have neither done him any injury, neither have we hurt his affairs through negligence, or through fear declined any enterprise he proposed to us. But, you will say, we ought then to have taken some assurance, that although he had been desirous to deceive us, he might not even have had it in his power. Hear then what I should never have mentioned before him, unless you had shown yourselves either entirely inconsiderate, or very ungrateful to me. You remember under what difficulties you laboured, from which I extricated you by carrying you to Seuthes. When you offered to go into Perinthus, did not Aristarchus the Lacedæmonian, shut the gates against you? Did not you, upon that, encamp in the open field? Was not this in the middle of winter? Was there not a scarcity of provisions in the market, and a

scarcity of the means to purchase them? In the meantime, you were under a necessity of staying in Thrace, (for the galleys lay at anchor [4] to observe your motions, and hinder your passage,) and while you staid, you staid in an enemy's country, where great numbers both of horse and targeteers were ready to oppose you. It is true, we had heavy-armed men, who, by going into the village in a body, might possibly provide themselves with a small quantity of corn; but we were not prepared to pursue the enemy, or supply ourselves with slaves and cattle; for, at my return, I found neither the horse nor targeteers any longer in a body. While, therefore, you were in so great necessity, if, without even insisting upon any pay, I had procured Seuthes to become your ally, who had both horse and targeteers, which you were in want of, do you think I should have made ill terms for you? It was owing to their assistance, that you not only found greater quantities of corn in the villages, the Thracians being thereby obliged to precipitate their flight, but had also your share both of cattle and slaves. From the time also we had the assistance of these horse we saw no enemy, though before they boldly harassed us both with their horse, and targeteers, and by hindering us from going in small parties, prevented our supplying ourselves with provisions in any quantity. But if the person whose assistance procured you this security, has not also paid you very considerably for being secure, can you look upon this as a moving calamity? And, for this, do you think yourselves obliged, by no means, to suffer me to live? But in what circumstances are you, now you are leaving this country? After you have passed the winter in plenty, have you not as an occasion to this advantage, the money you have received from Seuthes? For you have lived at the expense of the enemy; and while you have been thus employed, none of you have either been killed or taken prisoners. If you have gained some reputation against the Barbarians in Asia, is not that entire, and have you not added a new glory to it by the conquest of the European Thracians? I own I think you ought to return thanks to the gods for those very things, as for so many blessings, for which you are displeased with me. This is the situation of your af-

---

2 Πρᾶξις. Προδοσία. Suidas.
3 Πράττητι αὐτὸν τὰ χρήματα. Πράττεσθαι· ἀπαιτεῖσθαι Phavorinus.

4 Τριήρεις ἐφορμοῦσαι. Ἐφορμεῖν· Ἐνεδρεύειν ἐν πλοίοις. Suidas.

fairs: consider now, I beg of you, that of mine. When I first set sail in order to return home, I went away attended with great praise from you, and, through you, with reputation from the rest of Greece: I had also the confidence of the Lacedæmonians: (otherwise they would not have sent me back to you;) now, I go away suspected by the Lacedæmonians, through your means, and hated by Seuthes, upon your account, whom I proposed, by uniting my services to yours, to have made an honourable refuge both to myself and my children, if I should have any; while you, for whose sake chiefly I have made myself odious, and that to persons far more powerful than myself; while you, I say, for whom I cease not, even now, to procure all the advantages I am able, entertain such thoughts of me. You have me in your power, I neither fled from you, nor endeavoured it; and if you do what you say, know that you will put to death a man who has often watched for your safety; who has undergone many labours and dangers with you, while he not only did his own duty, but that of others; who, by the favour of the gods, has with you raised many trophies of the Barbarians' defeats, and who laboured to the utmost of his power to engage you to make none of the Greeks your enemies. For you are now at liberty to go whithersoever you please, either by sea or land, without control. This then is the season, when there is so great an appearance of prosperity; now you are going to sail for a country, where you have long since desired to be; when those, who are most powerful, want your assistance; when pay is offered, and the Lacedæmonians, who are allowed to be the best generals, are come to command you; this, I say, you think the proper season to put me to death. You did not think fit to do it when we were in difficulties; O men of admirable memories! then you called me father, and promised ever to remember me as your benefactor. However, those who are now come to command you are not void of sense; so that I believe your behaviour to me will not recommend you to them." Xenophon said no more.

Then Charminus the Lacedæmonian rose up and spoke in the following manner: Gentlemen! you seem to have no just cause of displeasure against this man; since I myself can give testimony in his favour: for Seuthes, when Polynicus and I inquired what kind of man Xenophon was, had nothing else to lay to his

charge, but that he was a great friend to the soldiers, which, says he, hurts him both with regard to the Lacedæmonians and to myself." After him Eurylochus of Lusi, an Arcadian, got up, and said: "My opinion is, O Lacedæmonians, that the first act of generalship you exercise, should be to obtain our pay of Seuthes, either with or without his consent; and that till then you ought not to carry us away." Polycrates the Athenian next rose up, and spoke in favour of Xenophon. "Gentlemen!" says he, "I see Heraclides also present in the assembly, who, having received the booty we acquired by our labour, and sold it, has neither paid the [1] money to Seuthes, nor to us; but, having robbed both, still keeps possession of it. If, therefore, we are wise, let us apprehend him; for this man is no Thracian, but, being himself a Greek, does an injury to Greeks."

Heraclides, hearing this, was thunder-struck, and coming to Seuthes, said, "If we are wise, we shall withdraw ourselves out of the power of these people." So they mounted on horseback, and rode off to their own camp; from whence Seuthes sent Eboselmius his interpreter to Xenophon, to desire him to remain in his service, with a thousand of the heavy-armed men, assuring him, at the same time, that he would give him the places of strength near the sea, and every thing else he had promised him. To this he added, as a secret, that he was informed by Polynicus, that if he put himself in the power of the Lacedæmonians, he would certainly be put to death by Thimbron. Many other persons, also, between whom and Xenophon there was an intercourse of hospitality, gave him notice, that he lay under a suspicion, and ought to be upon his guard. Xenophon, hearing this, offered two victims to

---

1 Τὰ γινόμενα. I cannot agree with Hutchinson that this word is taken by Thucydides, in the passage quoted by him, nearly in the same sense our author takes it here. In the passage quoted by him out of Thucydides, that author says the Athenian tyrants, Hippias and Hipparchus, adorned the city, carried on the wars, and performed the sacrifices by exacting only the twentieth part of the product of the country from the Athenians, 'Αθηναίους εἰκοστὴν μόνον πραττόμενοι τῶν γιγνομένων, which signification of the word is put out of all dispute by what Meursius says of the tax of the tenth part of the product of the country imposed upon the Athenians by Pisistratus, which he calls δεκάτην τῶν ἐν τῇ χώρᾳ γινομένων. In the passage, therefore, of Thucydides, τὰ γιγνόμενα signifies the product of the country; but here it signifies, as Hutchinson himself, and all the other translators have rendered it, the money raised by the sale of the booty.

Jupiter the king, and consulted him whether it were better and more advantageous for him to stay with Seuthes upon the terms he proposed, or to depart with the army; and Jupiter signified to him that he ought to depart.

VII. After that, Seuthes encamped at a greater distance, and the Greeks quartered in the villages, from whence they might get most provisions, before they returned to the sea. These villages Seuthes had given to Medosades, who, seeing every thing in them consumed by the Greeks, resented it; and taking with him an Odrysian, a man of the greatest power of all those who had come from the Upper Thracia, to join Seuthes, and about fifty horse, came to the Greek army, and called Xenophon to come to him, who, taking some of the captains and other proper persons, went to him. Then Medosades said: "You do us an injury, O Xenophon, in laying waste our villages. Wherefore we give you notice, I in the name of Seuthes, and this man from Medocus, king of the Upper Thrace, to leave the country; otherwise we shall not allow you to remain here; and if you continue to infest our territories, we shall treat you as enemies."

When Xenophon heard this, he said: "What you say is of such a nature, that it is even a pain to me to give an answer to it: however, I shall return one for the information of this youth, that he may be acquainted both with your behaviour, and with ours. Before we entered into an alliance with you, we marched through this country at our pleasure, and laid waste and burned any part of it we thought proper; and you yourself, when you came to us in the quality of an ambassador, staid with us, without the apprehension of an enemy. Whereas you, who are subjects of Seuthes, either never came into this country at all, or, if you came hither, you kept your horses ready bridled while you staid, as in a country belonging to those who were more powerful than yourselves. But now, since, by becoming our allies, you have got possession of it, you would drive us out of this country, though you received it from us as a conquest we were willing to resign, for you yourself are sensible the enemy was not strong enough to dispossess us; and not only want to send us away [2] without any acknow-

ledgment for the benefits you have received, but also to hinder us, as far as you are able, from encamping in the country, as we pass through it; and this you urge, without reverence either to the gods, or to this man, who sees you now abounding in riches; you, who before you entered into an alliance with us, lived by plunder, as you yourself have owned. But why do you say this to me?" continues he, "for I have no longer the command; but the Lacedæmonians, to whom you resigned the army, that they might carry it away, which you did without consulting me, most admirable men! and without giving me an opportunity of obliging them by delivering the army to them, as I had disobliged them by carrying it to you."

As soon as the Odrysian heard what Xenophon said; "O Medosades!" says he, "I am ready to sink into the earth with shame, when I hear this. Had I known it before, I should not have accompanied you, and shall now depart; for Medocus, my sovereign, will not approve of my conduct, if I should drive our benefactors out of the country." Having said this, he mounted on horseback, and rode away with all the rest of the horse, except four or five. Upon which, Medosades (for he was uneasy to see the country laid waste) desired Xenophon to call the two Lacedæmonians. He, taking some proper persons along with him, went to Charminus and Polynicus, and told them Medosades desired they would come to him, designing to order them, as he had him, to leave the country. "It is my opinion, therefore," says he, "that you will receive the pay due to the army, if you let him know that the soldiers have desired you to assist them in obtaining it, either with or without the consent of Seuthes; and that they engage to follow you with cheerfulness if they succeed in their demands. Tell him, at the same time, that you find their claim is founded in justice, and that you have promised them not to depart till they succeed in it." The Lacedæmoni-

---

2 Τῷ Διὶ τῷ Βασιλεῖ. See note 1, page 306, upon the sixth book.

3 Οὐχ ὅπως ἀδικα δούς. Οὐχ ὅπως signifies here not only not in the same manner as Dion Cassius uses it, where he says that Gabinius, being asked by Clodius what he thought of the law he had brought in against Cicero, not only did not commend Tully, but accused the Roman knights to the senate. Οὐχ ὅπως ἐκείνου ἐσήγητο, ἀλλὰ τῶν ἱππέων τῆς βουλῆς κρεσκατηγόρησεν. I make no doubt but this Grecism induced the Latins to give the same force to "non modo;" the following passage of Tully is a remarkable instance of it. "Regnum non modo Romano homini, sed ne Persæ quidem cuiquam tolerabile."

ans, hearing this, said they would acquaint him with it, and with whatever else would prove most effectual: and immediately set out with proper persons to attend them. When they arrived, Charminus said, "O Medosades! if you have any thing to say to us, speak; if not, we have something to say to you." Medosades, with great submission, answered, "Seuthes and I have this to say: we desire that those who are become our friends, may suffer no ill treatment from you; for whatever injury you do to them, you will now do to us, since they are our subjects." The Lacedæmonians replied, "We are ready to depart, as soon as those who have forced them to submit to you have received their pay: otherwise, we are come to assist them, and take revenge of those men, who, in violation of their oaths, have wronged them. If you are of that number, we shall begin by doing them justice against you."

Then Xenophon said: "Are you willing, O Medosades! to leave it to the people, in whose country we are, (since you say they are your friends) to determine whether you or we shall leave it?" This he refused, but desired, by all means, the two Lacedæmonians would go to Seuthes about the pay, and said it was his opinion Seuthes would hearken to them: but if they did not approve of that, he desired they would send Xenophon with him, assuring them of his assistance in obtaining it. In the meantime, he begged they would not burn the villages. Upon this, they sent Xenophon with such persons as were thought most proper to attend him. When he came to Seuthes, he said, "I am not come, O Seuthes! to ask any thing of you, but to demonstrate to you as well as I am able, that you had no just cause to be displeased with me for demanding of you, on the behalf of the soldiers, the pay which you cheerfully promised them; since I was convinced that it was not less your interest to give it, than theirs to receive it: for I know, in the first place, that next to the gods, they have rendered you conspicuous, by making you king over a large extent of country, and great numbers of people: so that your actions, whether commendable or infamous, cannot possibly be concealed from public notice. In this situation, I look upon it as a matter of great moment to you not to have it thought that you send away your benefactors without rewarding their services; and not less so, to have your praise celebrated by six thousand men. But, above all, that it concerns you, in no degree, to derogate from the credit of what you say; for I observe the discourse of men without credit to be vain and ineffectual, and to wander disregarded; while that of persons who are known to practise truth, is not less effectual to obtain what they desire than the power of others; I know, also, that if they propose to reform any one, their threats are not less powerful to that end, than the immediate punishment inflicted by others; and if such men promise any thing, they succeed no less by promising than others by giving presently. Recollect with yourself what you paid us, before you received our assistance. I know you paid us nothing. But the confidence you created in us of your performance of what you promised, induced such numbers of men to join their arms to yours, and conquer a kingdom for you, not only worth fifty talents, (the sum these men now look upon to be due to them,) but many times that sum. In the first place, therefore, for this sum you sell your credit, to which you owe your kingdom. After that, call to mind of what consequence you thought it to you to obtain what you now have conquered and possess. I know you wished to obtain it rather than to gain many times that sum. Now I look upon it to be a greater injury, as well as disgrace, to lose the possession of this conquest, than never to have gained it; as it is more grievous to a rich man to become poor than never to have been rich, and more afflicting to a king to become a private man than never to have been a king. You are sensible that these people, who are now become your subjects, were not prevailed upon to submit to you by their affection for you, but by necessity: and that they would endeavour to recover their liberty, if they were not restrained by fear. Whether, therefore, do you think they will be more afraid and more devoted to your interest, if they see not only these soldiers disposed to stay, if you desire it, and presently to return, if necessary, but others, from the advantageous character these give of you, ready to come to your assistance in any thing you require of them; or, if they are possessed with an opinion that hereafter none will ever engage in your service from a distrust created by your present behaviour; and that these have a greater affection for them than for you? Besides, these people

id not submit to you because they were infe-
or to us in numbers ; but because they wanted
'aders. This danger, therefore, you are also
xposed to : they may choose for their leaders
)me of our men, who think themselves wrong-
d by you, or those who have still more power,
)e Lacedæmonians : especially, on one side
he soldiers show greater alacrity to engage in
heir service, upon condition that they force
ou to give them their pay ; and, on the other,
he Lacedæmonians, from the want they have
f the army, consent to the condition. It is
lso no secret that the Thracians, who are now
ecome your subjects, had rather march against
ou than with you : for, if you conquer, they
re slaves ; and, if you are conquered, free.
3ut if you think it incumbent on you to have
ny regard to the country, now it is your own,
'hether do you think it will receive less dam-
ge if these soldiers, having received what they
insist upon, leave it in peace, or if they stay in
, as in an enemy's country ; while you endea-
our to raise more numerous forces, which
nust also be supplied with provisions, and
rith these make head against them ? And
'hether do you think the expense will be
reater, if the money due to these is paid, or
: this is still suffered to remain due, and it be-
omes necessary for you to take other forces
ito your pay [1] powerful enough to subdue the
ormer? But Heraclides, I find, by what he
eclared to me, thinks this sum very consider-
ble. It is certainly much less considerable to
ou now both to raise and pay than the tenth
art of it was before we came to you : for the
uantity of money is not the measure of the
reatness or smallness of the sum, but the
bility of the person who is either to pay or to
eceive it : and your annual income now ex-
eeds the whole of what before you were
rorth. In what I have said, O Seuthes! I
ave had all the consideration for you that is

due to a friend, to the end that both you may
appear worthy of the favours the gods have bestowed on you, and I not lose my credit with the
army. For be assured that if I desired to punish an enemy, it is not in my power to effect it
with this army, or to assist you, if I were again
inclined to attempt it : such is their disposition
with regard to me. And now I call both upon
you, and the gods, who know the truth of what
I say, to witness that I never had any thing
from you in return for the services you have
received from the army, or ever demanded of
you, for my own use, any thing that was due to
them, or claimed what you promised me. I
also swear that though you had been willing to
perform your promise to me, yet I would not
have accepted any thing, unless the soldiers, at
the same time, had received what was due to
them : for it would have been a shame for me
to succeed in my own pretensions, and to suffer theirs to remain without effect ; particularly, since they had done me the honour to
choose me for one of their generals. Heraclides, I know, looks upon all things as trifles
when compared to possession of riches, by
what means soever acquired : but I, O Seuthes! am of opinion, that no possession does
more become and adorn a man, particularly a
prince, than that of virtue, justice, and generosity ; for whoever enjoys these, is not only rich
in the numerous friends he has, but in those
who desire to become so : if he is in prosperity,
he has many ready to rejoice with him ; and, if
in adversity, to relieve him. But if neither
my actions nor my words are able to convince
you that I am your sincere friend, consider
what the soldiers said ; for you were present
and heard the speeches of those who were desirous to asperse me. They accused me to the
Lacedæmonians, that I was more devoted to
your interest than to that of the latter ; and,
at the same time, objected to me that I studied
your advantage more than theirs : they also
said that I had received presents [2] from you.

---

[1] *Ἄλλους τι περίττους τούτων μισθωσαι.* Hutchinson
as great reason to find fault with Leunclavius and
Amasæus for translating *περίττους* here, *majores copiæ,
major exercitus.* It most certainly signifies, as he has
rendered it, *armis potentiores.* D'Ablancourt's translation is still more loose than that of the two first, he has
said *faire de nouvelles levees pour nous faire tete.* I
shall add to what Hutchinson has said a passage in Thucydides, where he not only uses *περίττους* in the same
sense, but explains it himself by *δυνατώτεροι;* he is giving an account of the state of Greece before the Trojan
war, and says, *ἐσόμεναι γὰρ τῶν κερδῶν, οἴτε ἥσσους ὑπέμενον
ἣν τῶν κρεισσόνων δουλείαν, οἴτε δυνατώτεροι, περιουσίας
ἔχοντες, προσεποιοῦντο ὑπηκόους τὰς ἐλάσσους πόλεις.*

[2] *Ἔφασαν δέ με καὶ δῶρα ἔχειν παρά σου.* I have rendered *δῶρα* here presents, not bribes, which would have
been inconsistent with what he says afterwards, though
I doubt not but every English reader will have the same
satisfaction I have in observing that neither *δῶρον* in
Greek, *donum* in Latin, or *un present* in French, have
the force of our word bribe. A foreigner, who does not
know us, may say that our manners have coined the
word, but we, who know ourselves, know how much
we are above such an imputation.

2 X

Now, do you think they accused me of receiving these presents, because they discovered in me any indisposition to your service, or because they observed in me the greatest zeal to promote it? I am indeed of opinion that all men ought to show an affection to those from whom they have received presents. Before I did you any service, you gave me a favourable reception by your looks, your words, and your hospitality, and never could satisfy yourself with making promises. Now, you have accomplished what you desired, and are become as considerable as I could make you, finding me thus fallen into disgrace with the soldiers, you dare neglect me. But I am confident, time will inform you that you ought to pay them what you promised, and also that you yourself will not suffer those who have been your benefactors to load you with reproaches. I have, therefore, only this favour to ask of you, that when you pay it, you will study to leave me in the same credit with the army in which you found me."

When Seuthes heard this, he cursed the man who had been the cause of their not having been paid long since (every one concluding he meant Heraclides). "For my part," says he, "I never designed to deprive them of it, and will pay them what is due." Then Xenophon said again, "Since you are resolved to pay the money, I desire it may pass through my hands, and that you will not suffer me to be in a different situation with the army now, from what I was in when we came to you." Seuthes answered, "You shall not suffer in the opinion of the soldiers by my means; and if you will stay with only one thousand heavy-armed men, I will give you not only the places of strength, but every thing else I promised." The other made answer, "That is not possible, so dismiss us." "I know," replies Seuthes, "you will find it safer for you to stay with me, than to depart." Xenophon answered, "I commend your care of me: however I cannot possibly stay, but wheresoever I am in credit, be assured that you shall also find your advantage in it." Upon this Seuthes said, "I have very little money; no more than one [1] talent, which I give you; but I have six hundred oxen, four thousand sheep, and one hundred and twenty slaves; take these with you, together with the hostages of those who wronged you." Xenophon replied smiling, "But if

these are not sufficient to raise the money that is due, whose talent shall I say I have? Is it not more advisable for me, since my return is attended with danger, to take care I am not stoned? You heard their threats." The remainder of the day they staid there.

The next he delivered to them what he had promised; and sent persons with them to drive the cattle. In the meantime, the soldiers said that Xenophon was gone to Seuthes with a design to live with him, and to receive what the other had promised him: but, when they saw him returned, they were rejoiced, and ran to him. As soon as Xenophon saw Charminus and Polynicus, he said, "The army is obliged to you for these things. I deliver them to you; do [2] you sell them, and distribute the money among the soldiers." They, having received the things, and appointed persons to dispose of them, sold them accordingly, and incurred great censure. Xenophon had no share in the management, but openly prepared to return home; for he was [3] not yet banished from Athens. But his [4] friends in the army came to him, and begged he would not leave them until he had carried away the army, and delivered it to Thimbron.

VIII. After this they crossed the sea to [5] Lampsacus, where Euclides the Phliasian priest, the son of [6] Cleagoras, who painted

---

1 Τάλαντον. See note 1, page 168, upon the first book.

2 Διατίθημαι. Διάδοτε. See note 3, page 320, upon the sixth book.

3 Οὐ γάρεσι ψῆφος αὐτῷ ἰσίωτε Ἀθήνησι περὶ τῆς φυγῆς. See the author's life at the beginning of this translation.

4 Ἐπιτήδειοι. Ἐπιτήδειος· φίλος· εὔνους· ἀρμόδιος. Suidas. I have chosen the first of these with D'Ablancourt. The two Latin translators have preferred the last.

5 Εἰς Λάμψακον. Lampsacus was a sea-port town in Asia upon the Hellespont, over against Ægos Potamos; that strait is there about fifteen stadia over, that is, about an English mile and a half. Lysander, the Lacedæmonian general, took Lampsacus just before he defeated the Athenians at the last mentioned place. See the Introduction.

6 Κλεαγόρου υἱὸς τοῦ τὰ ἐνύπνια ἐν Λυκείῳ γεγραφότος. Dr Potter, the late worthy primate of England, in his Archæologia Græca, that treasure of Greek learning, says Lyceum was situated upon the banks of the Ilissus, and received its name from Apollo Λυκεακτῶνος or Λύκιος, to whom it was dedicated. The Greek scholiast upon Aristophanes and Suidas says it was a place designed for military exercises. I am sorry I cannot get any light concerning the painter and picture mentioned by Xenophon, but nothing is to be found in Pliny or Pausanias concerning either, though several considerable painters, who flourished before this time, are mentioned by the former, as Polygnotus and Micon, who painted a portico at Athens called the Pœcile; and particularly Panænus, brother to Phidias the famous

be dreams in the Lyceum, met Xenophon, and after congratulating him upon his safe return, asked him how much gold he had. The other swore to him that he had not money enough to carry him home, unless he sold his horse and his equipage. However Euclides gave no credit to him; but after the inhabitants of Lampsacus had sent him presents in token of their hospitality, and Xenophon was offering sacrifice to Apollo in his presence, Euclides, upon viewing the entrails of the victims, said, he was now convinced he had no money: "But," added he, "I find if there should ever be a prospect of any, that there will be some obstacle, and, if no other, that you will be an obstacle to yourself." Xenophon owned this; upon which Euclides said, " The [7] Meilichian Jupiter is an obstacle to

you ;" and asked him whether he had, at any time, offered sacrifice in the same manner, "as I," says he, "used to sacrifice for you at Athens, and offer a holocaust." Xenophon answered that since he had been from home, he had not sacrificed to that god; the other advised him to offer sacrifice to that divinity, assuring him that it would be for his advantage. The next day, Xenophon going to [8] Ophrynion offered sacrifice, and burned hogs whole, according to the custom of his country; and the entrails were favourable. The same day, Biton and Euclides arrived with money for the army. These contracted an intercourse of hospitality with Xenophon, and hearing he had sold his horse at Lampsacus for fifty daricks, and suspecting he had sold him through want, because they were informed he was fond of him, they redeemed the horse, and restored him to Xenophon, refusing to accept the price they had paid for him.

From thence they marched through Troas, and passing over Mount Ida, came first to [9] Antandrus: then continued their march along

---

statuary, who painted the battle of Marathon, where the generals, both Greeks and Persians, were represented as big as the life, which I take to be the signification of *iconici duces*, the words made use of by Pliny upon that occasion, since Athenæus calls statues as big as the life *εἰκονικὰ ἀγάλματα*, and Plato says *εἰκόνα ἰσομέγεθες* in the same sense.

7 'Ο Ζεὺς ὁ Μειλίχιος. There is a passage in Thucydides, where, speaking of Cylon's seizing the citadel of Athens, he mentions the Athenian festival celebrated without the walls of the city in honour of the Meilichian Jupiter, which he calls Διάσια, *Diasia*, at which, he says, all the people attended, and sacrificed not victims, but cakes made in the shape of animals, "according to the custom of the country," οὐχ ἱερεῖα ἀλλ' θύματα ἐπιχώρια; for so the Greek scholiast explains the word θύματα. The reason of my being so particular is, that Xenophon says he offered sacrifice to the same Jupiter, and burned hogs whole to him, according to the custom of his country, Εὐσφῶν ἰδίατι, καὶ ὁλοκαύτει χοίρους τῷ πατρίῳ νόμῳ. Are we then to imagine, that either Thucydides or Xenophon were uninformed of the custom of their country upon so great a solemnity? I should almost be tempted to think the hogs, Xenophon says he burned whole, were also cakes made in the shape of hogs. There is a passage in Herodotus, that in some degree favours this conjecture; he says, the Egyptians, notwithstanding their known aversion to hogs, sacrificed them one day in the year to the Moon and Bacchus, when they eat their flesh, which they tasted upon no other day, and that the poorer sort made cakes resembling hogs, and, roasting them, offered them in sacrifice: οἱ δὲ πένητες αὐτῶν ὑπ' ἀσθενίης βίου, σταιτίνας πλάσαντες ὖς, καὶ ὀπτήσαντες, ταύτας θύουσι.—But what affinity is there between the religious customs of the Egyptians and the Athenians? So great an affinity that we find in Diodorus Siculus, the Egyptians pretended that the Athenians were one of their colonies, and had received the Eleusinian mysteries from them, which they said Erichtheus, an Egyptian, and afterwards king of Athens, carried from Egypt, and instituted among the Athenians in honour of Ceres. I cannot say that I ever met with an account, in any Greek author, of cakes offered by the Greeks in the resemblance of hogs; but, besides the authority of the Greek scholiast upon the passage already mentioned in Thucydides, where he explains θύματα,

τινὰ πέμματα εἰς ζῶα μορφὰς τετυπωμένα, cakes made in the shape of animals generally; I say, besides that passage, we find in Julius Pollux that the Greeks offered cakes to all the gods, which cakes had their names from their different shapes, as an ox, which was a cake with horns, and was offered to Apollo, and Diana, and Hecate, and the Moon. τέλασοι δὲ καιναὶ πᾶσι θεοῖς, πλησμέναι δὲ ἀπὸ τοῦ σχήματος, ὥσπερ ὁ βοῦς· πέμμα γάρ ἐστι, κέρατα ἔχον εἰσηγμένα προσφερόμενον 'Απόλλωνι, καὶ 'Αρτέμιδι, καὶ 'Εκάτη, καὶ Σελήνη. I shall conclude this note with observing that Apollo, when taken for the sun, was the same, among the Egyptians, and, afterwards, among the Greeks, with Dionysius, or Bacchus, as Diodorus Siculus proves from this verse of Eumolpus,

'Αστερφαῆ Διόνυσον ἐν ἀκτίνεσσι πυρωπόν,

And from another in Orpheus. Now, every body knows that these were the same with Osiris, as Diana, Hecate, and the Moon were the same divinity with Isis; so that the custom mentioned by Julius Pollux, of offering cakes in the shape of animals, to have been in practice among the Greeks, seems to be derived from that mentioned by Herodotus to have been in use among the Egyptians; especially, since we find they were offered to the same divinities. D'Ablancourt seems to have forgot that Jupiter was worshipped at Athens under the title of Meilichius; for he takes the name to be allegorical to the mildness of Xenophon's character, who did not make his fortune "pour avoir trop de pudeur," as he says, because he was too bashful.

8 'Οφρύνιον. A town of Dardania, near which stood the grove of Hector upon a conspicuous place.

9 Διὰ τῆς Τρῳάς, καὶ ὑπερβάντες τὴν Ἴδην, εἰς 'Αντάνδρον ἀφικνοῦνται. The misfortunes of Troy, or rather the fine relations of them, have rendered all these parts famous, so that there is no necessity of saying any thing either of Troas or mount Ida: Antandrus was the seaport where Æneas built his fleet to preserve the remains

the coast of the Lydian sea, to the plain of Thebes. From thence through [1] Atramyttium, and Certonicum, by Aterne to the plain of Caicus, and reached Pergamus, a city of Mysia. Here Xenophon was entertained by Hellas, the wife of Gongylus the Eretrian, and the mother of Gorgion and Gongylus. She informed him that Asidates, a Persian, lay encamped in the plain, adding, that with three hundred men, he might surprise him in the night, and take him with his wife and children and all his riches, which were very considerable. At the same time, she sent a person who was her cousin-german, together with Daphnagoras, for whom she had a particular value, to conduct them in the enterprise. Xenophon, therefore, while these were with him, offered sacrifice: and Agasias the Helean priest, being present, said the victims were very favourable, and that the Persian might be taken prisoner. Accordingly, after supper, he set out, taking with him those captains who were most his friends, and had ever been faithful to him, that he might procure them some advantage. Others, to the number of six hundred, accompanied him whether he would or no; but the captains rode on before them, lest they should be obliged to give them a share of the booty, which they looked upon as their own.

They arrived about midnight, when they suffered the slaves that lay round the castle, together with a considerable quantity of effects, to escape, to the end they might take Asidates himself with his riches; but not being able to take the place by assault, (for it was both high and large, well fortified with battlements, and defended by a good number of brave men,)

they endeavoured to make a breach in the wall, which was eight bricks thick. However, by break of day the breach was made; which was no sooner effected, than one of those who were within, ran the foremost man through the thigh with a [2] large spit. After that, they sent such a shower of arrows, that it was no longer safe to approach the wall. In the meantime, their cries, and the signals they made by lighting fires, drew Itabelius, with his forces, to their assistance. There came also from Comania, the garrison, consisting of heavy-armed men, together with some Hyrcanian horse, who were in the king's pay, being about eighty in number, and eight hundred targeteers; besides others from Parthenium, Apollonia, and the neighbouring places, and also horse.

It was now time for the Greeks to consider how to make their retreat. To effect this, they took all the oxen and sheep that were there, and then forming themselves into a hollow square, and placing them with the slaves in the middle, they marched away. They were now no longer solicitous for their booty, but only lest, by leaving it behind, their retreat might seem a flight, which would have increased both the confidence of the enemy, and the dejection of their own men. Whereas, while they made their retreat in this disposition, they seemed resolved to defend their booty. In the meantime Gongylus, seeing the number of the Greeks was small, and that of the enemy, who hung upon their rear, very considerable, came out himself against his mother's will, at the head of his own forces, being desirous to have a share in the action. [3] Procles, also, who was descended from Damaratus, came to their assistance from Elisarne, [4] and Teuthrania. Now as Xenophon's men suffered very much from the enemy's arrows and slings, while they marched in a ring, in order to cover themselves from the arrows with their shields, it was with great difficulty they passed the river Caicus, near half their number being wounded. Here Agasias of Stymphalus, one of the captains, was wounded, having the whole time

---

of his country: but one thing must not be forgot; above Antandrus was a mountain, called Alexandria, from Paris, where they say he passed judgment upon the three contending goddesses. The town that gave name to the plain of Thebe, was called by the same name, and belonged to Eetion, the father to Andromache.

'Ωχόμεθ' ἐς Θήβην ἱεζὴν πόλιν 'Ηετίωνος.

In the taking of this town Chryseis was taken prisoner, and given to Agamemnon; the restoring of whom, with the difficulties that attended it, and the consequences that flowed from it, are the subject of the Iliad.

1 Δι' 'Ατραμυττείου καὶ Κερτονίου παρ' 'Αταρνία εἰς Καΐκου πεδίον ἐλθόντες, Πέργαμον καταλαμβάνουσι τῆς Μυσίας. The first of these is a sea-port that gives its name to the bay, the other two are towns in, or near the road from the first to the plain that is watered by the river Caicus. Pergamus was the residence of the Attalic kings, the last of whom left it with his kingdom by will to the Roman people.

2 Βουτόρῳ ὀβελίσκῳ. Βουτόρους ὀβελοὺς, μεγάλους ὀβελίσκους. Phavorinus. In this sense Euripides takes it in his Cyclops, where Ulysses tells him,

Οὐκ ἀμφὶ βουτόροισι πυχθέντας μέλη

'Οβελοῖσι, τηδὲ καὶ γνάθον πλῆσαι σίθω.

3 Προκλῆς――――ὁ ἀπὸ Δαμαράτου. See note 1, page 199, upon the second book.

4 Παρθένιον―'Απολλώνια―'Ελισάρνη―Τευθρανία. These four towns are also placed by Pliny in Mysia.

fought with great bravery. At last they arrived[?] with about two hundred slaves, and cattle enough for sacrifice.

The next day Xenophon offered sacrifice, and in the night led out the whole army with a design to march as far as possible into Lydia, to the intent that the Persian seeing him no longer in his neighbourhood, might be free from fear and unguarded. But Asidates bearing that Xenophon had again offered sacrifice concerning a second expedition against him, and that he would return with the whole army, quitted the castle, and encamped in some villages reaching to the walls of Parthenium. Here Xenophon's men met with him, and took him with his wife and children, his horses, and all his riches; and this was the success promised in the former * sacrifice. After that they returned to Pergamus. Here Xenophon had no reason to complain of Jupiter Meilichius; for the Lacedæmonians, the captains, the rest of the generals, and the soldiers, all conspired to * select for him not only horses, but yokes of oxen, and other things: so that he had it now in his own power even to oblige a friend.

After this, Thimbron arrived, and taking the command of the army, joined it to the rest of the Greek forces, and made war upon Tissaphernes and Pharnabazus.

The following persons were the king's governors of the countries, through which we marched; of Lydia, Artimas; of Phrygia, Artacamas; of Lycaonia and Cappadocia, Mithridates; of Cilicia, Syennesis; of Phoenicia and Arabia, Dernis; of Syria and Assyria, Belesis; of Babylon, Roparas; of Media, Arbacas; of the Phasians and Hesperitans, Teribazus; (the Carduchians, the Chalybians, the Chaldæans, the Macrones, the Colchians, the Mosynœcians, the Coetans, and the Tibarenians being free nations) of Paphlagonia, Corylus; of the Bithynians, Pharnabazus; and of the European Thracians, Seuthes.

The whole of the way, both of the Expedition and Retreat, consisted of two hundred and fifteen days' march, of * eleven hundred fifty-five parasangs, and of thirty-four thousand six hundred and fifty stadia; and the time employed, in both, of a year and three months.

---

2 Τὰ σφάγια ἱερά. I imagine with Hutchinson, that Xenophon means the sacrifice he says he offered in the presence of Agasias of Elis, to distinguish it from that which he offered the day after their unsuccessful expedition.

6 Ὅσσα ἐξαίρετα λαμβάνειν. It was an early custom among the ancients to select the most valuable part of the booty for their generals, which makes the following reproach from Thersites to Agamemnon very impertinent, and consequently very agreeable to the character of the men who makes it:

'Αντρὸς, τὶς δ' αὖτ' ἐπιμέμφεαι, ἠδὲ χατίζεις;
Πλεῖαί τοι χαλκοῦ κλισίαι, πολλαὶ δὲ γυναῖκες
Εἰσὶν ἱνὶ κλισίης ἐξαίρετοι, ἅς τοι 'Αχαιοὶ
Πρωτίστῳ δίδομεν, εὖτ' ἂν πτολίεθρον ἕλωμεν.

Where ἐξαίρετοι is thus very properly explained by the Greek scholiast, αἱ κατὰ τιμὴν ληθεῖσαι ἀπὸ τῶν αἰχμαλώτων. Virgil has preserved this custom, and translated ἐξαιρῶ in the ninth book, where he makes Ascanius promise Nisus the war-horse, the shield, and helmet of Turnus, at his return from the enterprise he and Euryalus had undertaken,

" Vidisti quo Turnus equo, quibus ibat in armis
Aureus? ipsum illum, clypeum cristasque rubentes
Excipiam sorti, jam nunc tua præmia Nise."

In the eighth book, Virgil calls the horse, which was reserved for Æneas's own riding, when he went to the Tuscans to implore their assistance, exsortem, which is a literal translation of ἐξαίρετον.

7 Παρασάγγας χίλια ἱκατὸν πεντήκοντα πέντε, στάδια τετρακόσια τετρακισχίλια, δισμύρια εὑρίσκεται εἴντι. I have followed Hutchinson's correction, who, very properly, I think, instead of δισμύρια, reads ἑξμύρια, and takes away the word εὑρίσκεται. Concerning these measures of length, see note 7, page 170, upon the first book. To which I shall only add, that these parasangs or stadia being reduced to English miles, amount to no more than 3305 miles and a half, and not to 4331, as Hutchinson has computed it, who, I find, reckons eight stadia to an English mile: eight stadia, indeed, make a milliare or Greek mile, but do not, by a great deal, amount to an English mile: since an English mile, according to Arbuthnot, contains 1056 geometrical paces, and a Greek mile only 806: so that an English mile is to a Greek mile as 1056 to 806. 4331 Greek miles being, therefore, contained in 34,650 stadia, if we say 1056 : 806 : : 4331 : the proportional number will be 3305, with a fraction of 668, so that 3305, and one half will be, to a trifle, the number of English miles contained in the 34,650 stadia mentioned by Xenophon to have been the amount both of the expedition and retreat.

XENOPHON'S HISTORY

THE AFFAIRS OF GREECE

WILLIAM SMITH

XENOPHON'S HISTORY

OF

THE AFFAIRS OF GREECE.

TRANSLATED BY

WILLIAM SMITH, A. M.

ΕΚ ΤΗΣ ΘΑΛΑΤΤΗΣ ΑΠΑΣΑ ΥΜΙΝ ΗΡΤΗΤΑΙ ΣΩΤΗΡΙΑ.

PREFACE.

THE Translator of this valuable piece of Xenophon looks upon himself as now discharging a debt to the public. The favourable reception of his translation of Thucydides was urged, and, with gratitude be it spoken, was urged by the late Earl Granville, as an obligation upon him to copy in the English language what Xenophon had written orginally in Greek in regard to the Peloponnesian war; namely, the continuation of it till the naval power of the Athenians was demolished, and the city of Athens surrendered to her foes. This is properly the end of the Peloponnesian war. But, as the state of Lacedæmon, elated with the consequential enlargement of her power, exerted it in too haughty and imperious a manner, the resentment of other states was raised, and a war ensued, in which Sparta was well nigh ruined, and the sovereignty of Greece transferred to Thebes. The battle of Mantinea, in which the Thebans by losing Epaminondas lost their all, closed this eager struggle for supremacy in Greece, and left its several states a commodious prey to Philip of Macedon, who soon after began to act. In this piece of Xenophon, the history of Greece is continued from the time Thucydides breaks off, down to that famous battle, including the space of near fifty years.

Never had historian who left his work imperfect so illustrious a continuator as Thucydides found in Xenophon. They were both of them men of excellent sense. They both lived in the times, and had competent knowledge of the facts, they describe. They were both Athenians, had been generals, and were both in exile when they wrote their histories. But a man more accomplished in all respects than Xenophon will not easily be found. He was the greatest hero, and at the same time the genteelest writer of his age. Instructed and formed by Socrates, he exemplified his useful philosophy in the whole conduct of his life. And it will be hard to decide, which are most excellent in their kind, his historical or his philosophical writings. The style of both hath that sweetness, that ease, that perspicuity, and that simplicity, which remain envied and unequalled, and must give all his translators no small anxiety about their own success. He especially has abundant reason to be alarmed, who after being so long employed in copying a different style in Thucydides, has attempted the manner of Xenophon. He is sensible of the daringness of such an attempt, has no small terrors about its success, and puts his whole confidence in the judgment of the late Earl Granville, who had perused some parts of it in manuscript, and honoured the Translator with his commands to complete and publish the work.

As the Greek text is sometimes faulty, the translator hath made no scruple to adopt the marginal reading of the best editions, if it fixed or cleared the sense to an English reader. He hath also ventured to translate some passages according to the conjectural but sagacious emendations of the late Rev. Dr Taylor, residentiary of St Paul's.

The translator, in the life of Thucydides, hath said, " There is a chasm between the time the history of Thucydides breaketh off, and the Grecian history of Xenophon beginneth."—He said it upon the authority of Archbishop Usher, but hath seen abundant reason since to be diffident of the fact. The *Annales Xenophontei* of the learned Dodwell seem to prove from variety of arguments a close connexion between them.

THE

AFFAIRS OF GREECE.

BOOK I.

CONTENTS of BOOK I.

AFFAIRS OF GREECE.

BOOK I.

I. Not many days after this, Thymochares arrived from Athens with a few ships; and immediately the Lacedæmonians and Athenians had another engagement at sea; but the Lacedæmonians, commanded by Hegesandridas, got the victory.

Soon after, in the beginning of winter, Dorieus the son of Diagoras stands into the Hellespont, at daylight, with fourteen ships from Rhodes. The sentinel of the Athenians, having a sight of him, made proper signals to the commanders. They put out against him with twenty ships; and Dorieus, flying before them, ran his ships on shore, as he was clearing it, on the cape of Rhæteum. But, the enemy coming up close to them, they defended themselves both from their ships and the shore, till at length the Athenians stood away to their naval station at Madytus, after a fruitless attack. Mindarus, who saw this attack, as he was then at Ilium sacrificing to Minerva, hastened down to the sea to help his friends; and, after laying his vessels afloat, he sailed up [1] to fetch off the ships under Dorieus. Upon this the Athenians, putting out again, engaged him on the coast near Abydus, and fought from morning till night. One while they had the better of it, another while they had the worse, till Alcibiades joins them with eighteen sail. Then began the flight of the Peloponnesians to Abydus. But Pharnabazus marched down to their relief; and, advancing on horseback into the sea as far as possibly he could, he exerted himself in their defence, and encouraged his troops both horse and foot to do their best. The Peloponnesians, closing their ships firm together with their heads towards the enemy, continued the fight on the very beach. At length the Athenians, carrying off with them thirty empty ships of the enemy and all their own that were disabled, sailed away to Sestus. From thence, all their ships excepting forty, went out of the Hellespont on different cruises to fetch in contributions. And Thrasylus, one of the commanders, set sail for Athens, to notify the late success, and to beg a reinforcement of men and ships.

After these transactions, Tissaphernes came to the Hellespont, where he arrested Alcibiades, who came in a single ship to visit him, and to offer him the presents of hospitality and friendship. He then sent him prisoner to Sardis; alleging express orders from the king to make war upon the Athenians. Yet, thirty days after, Alcibiades, and Mantitheus too, who had been taken prisoners in Caria, having provided themselves with horses, escaped by night from Sardis to Clazomenæ. In the meantime, the Athenians at Sestus, having received intelligence that Mindarus was coming against them with sixty ships, fled away by night to Cardia. And here Alcibiades joined them with five ships and a row-boat from Clazomenæ. But receiving advice that the fleet of the Peloponnesians was sailed from Abydus to Cyzicus, he went himself to Sestus by land, and ordered the ships round to the same place. When the ships were arrived at Sestus, and he was fully bent on going out to sea and engaging, Theramenes joins him with twenty ships from Macedonia, and Thrasybulus at the same time with twenty more from

---

1 The Greek text is ἀπικλυ, but the word required by the sense is ἐπικλυ. Dr Taylor.

Thasus, having both of them collected contributions. Alcibiades, leaving orders with them to follow, after they had taken out the great masts of their vessels, sailed himself to Parium. And when the whole fleet was assembled at Parium, to the number of eighty-six ships, the night following they went to sea, and next day about the hour of repast they reach Proconnesus. Hear they were informed that " Mindarus is at Cyzicus, and Pharnabazus too with the land force." This day therefore they continued at Proconnesus. But the day following Alcibiades called an assembly, and expatiated on the necessity they were under of engaging the enemy at sea, and engaging them too at land, and also of attacking their towns : " For we," says he, " are in want of money, whilst our enemies are plentifully supplied by the king." But the day before, when they came to this station, he had drawn round about his own vessel the whole force, both the great and the smaller ships, that no one might be able to inform the enemy exactly of their number ; and made public proclamation, that " whoever should be caught attempting to cross over the sea should be punished with death." And now, after holding the assembly, and making all needful preparations for an engagement, he set sail for Cyzicus in a heavy rain. And when he was near it, the weather clearing up and the sun breaking out, he had a view of the ships of Mindarus, to the amount of sixty, exercising themselves at a distance from the harbour, and fairly intercepted by him. On the other hand, the Peloponnesians, seeing the ships of Alcibiades to be much more numerous than usual, and close in with the harbour, fled away to the shore ; and there, having ranged into regular order, they received the enemy's attack. But Alcibiades, after stretching to a distance with twenty of the ships, landed with his men. Mindarus seeing this, landed also, and engaging was killed on shore ; but all his men were at once in flight. The Athenians returned to Proconnesus, carrying away with them all the ships of the enemy excepting three of the Syracusans, for these were burnt by the Syracusans themselves. Next day the Athenians returned from thence to Cyzicus. And the inbabitants of Cyzicus, as the Peloponnesians and Pharnabazus had abandoned the place, received the Athenians. But Alcibiades, after continuing with them twenty days, and exacting a large

sum of money from the Cyzicenes, though doing no other harm in any shape to the city, sailed back to Proconnesus. From thence he sailed to Perinthus and Selymbria ; and the Perinthians received his forces into their city ; whereas the Selymbrians received them not, but gave him a sum of money. Going from thence to Chrysopolis of Chalcedonia, they fortified the place, and appointed it to be the station for collecting tenths : and here a tenth was levied on all vessels from Pontus. Leaving therefore thirty ships for the guard of Chrysopolis, and two of the commanders, Theramenes and Eubulus, to take care of its preservation, to oblige the ships to pay the duty, and to lay hold of every opportunity to annoy the enemy, the rest of the commanders departed to the Hellespont.

The letter sent to Lacedæmon from Hippocrates, lieutenant to Mindarus, was intercepted and carried to Athens. The contents were these—" Success is at an end. Mindarus is killed. The men are starving. We know not what to do."

But Pharnabazus was animating all the Peloponnesians and Syracusans ; exhorting them, " not to despond, so long as themselves were safe, for the loss of a parcel of timber, since enough might again be had in the dominions of his master ;" and then he gave to every man a suit of apparel and two months' pay. He also distributed proper arms to the mariners, and stationed them as guards of his own maritime provinces. He then summoned the generals of the different states and the captains of ships to assemble, whom he ordered to rebuild at Antandros as many vessels as they had severally lost, furnishing them with money, and directing them to fetch the necessary timber from Mount Ida. Yet, amidst the hurry of rebuilding the fleet, the Syracusans assisted the Antandrians in finishing a part of their walls, and of all the people now within that garrison, were the most obliging to them. Upon this account the Syracusans are honoured with the solemn acknowledgment of being benefactors to Antandros, and with the freedom of the city. But Pharnabazus, after putting affairs in this new train, departed in all haste to the relief of Chalcedon.

Just at this time it was notified to the generals of the Syracusans, that " they are sentenced to exile by the people of Syracuse." Calling therefore all their men together, Hermocrates speaking in the name of the rest, they deplored their " wretched fortune in being thus iniquitously doomed to exile in their absence, ¹ quite contrary to the laws." They advised the men "to adhere to the same spirited behaviour they had hitherto shown, and with fidelity and bravery to execute all the orders of their country." And then they ordered them " to go and elect a set of generals, till the persons appointed to take the command should arrive from Syracuse." The whole assembly called aloud upon them to continue in the command; and the captains of ships, the land-soldiers, and the pilots, were loudest in their shouts. They replied, that "generals ought not to mutiny against the orders of their country. But, in case any criminal accusations were laid to their charge, it was but justice to expect a true account from them, who would be still keeping in remembrance—how many victories at sea you have gained under our direction without the concurrence of others; how many ships you have taken; and how often with the rest of the confederates you have been saved from defeats; distinguished above all by having the post of honour both at land and sea, whilst we prudently issue and you gallantly executed our orders." Not one amongst them having any thing to object, and all persisting in the former demand, they continued with them till their successors arrived from Syracuse, Demarchus the son of Pidocus, and Myscon the son of Menecrates, and Potamis the son of Gnosias. Most of the captains of ships promised them with an oath, that on their return to Syracuse they would endeavour their restoration; and then dismissed them to go where themselves thought proper; loading them all with abundant commendations; but such as were intimately acquainted with Hermocrates most highly regretted the loss of so vigilant, so humane, and so affable a commander: for it had been his daily custom to invite, both morning and evening, to his own tent, such of the captains of ships and pilots and land-soldiers as he knew to be men of merit, and to communicate to them whatever he intended either to say or to do, begging them to favour him with their sentiments of things, sometimes without premeditation, and sometimes with a more deliberate answer. By this means Hermocrates was heard with the highest deference in all councils of war: his expression and his matter were ever judged the best. But having afterwards preferred at Lacedæmon an accusation against Tissaphernes, which was supported by the evidence of Astyochus, and had a great air of truth, he went to Pharnabazus, and before he could ask it received a subsidy from him, which enabled him to provide himself both with men and ships for his return to Syracuse. But now the successors of the Syracusan commanders were arrived at Miletus, and received the ships and troops.

About the same time a sedition broke out in Thassus, which ended in the ejection of the party attached to the Lacedæmonians, and of Eteonicus the Lacedæmonian commandant. Pasippidas the Lacedæmonian, who was accused, in concert with Tissaphernes, of being the author of such miscarriages, was declared an exile from Sparta; and Cratesippidas was despatched to take the command of the fleet, which the other had assembled from the confederates; and he received it at Chios.

About this time also, while Thrasylus was at Athens, Agis, making a grand forage from Decelea, marched up to the very walls of Athens. But Thrasylus, putting himself at the head of the Athenians and of all persons then residing in the city, drew up in order of battle near the Lyceum, determined to fight in case the enemy approached. Agis perceiving this, immediately retired, with the loss of a few men in the extremity of his rear, who were killed by the light-armed Athenians. For this piece of conduct the Athenians became more and more disposed to grant to Thrasylus the reinforcements he came for; and decreed him in form a thousand heavy-armed from the public roll, a hundred horsemen, and fifty ships. But Agis, seeing from Decelea that numerous vessels laden with corn were running into the Piræus, declared it "to be of no avail for his army to block up the Athenians so long by land, unless some stop could be put to the importation of corn by sea; and that it was most advisable to send Clearchus the son of Ramphias, who was public host of the Byzantines, to Chalcedon and Byzantium." This being approved, and fifteen ships, though transports rather than ships of war, being manned out by the Megareans and the rest of the confederates, Clearchus departed. Three indeed of these his ships are destroyed in the Hellespont by nine ships of the Athenians, stationed there to awe the enemy's navigation: the rest of them fled to Sestus: and from thence got safe to Byzantium.

And now the year ended, in which the Carthaginians commanded by Hannibal, having invaded Sicily with an army of a hundred thousand men, take in three months' time two Grecian cities, Selinus and Himera.

II. The year after (when the ninety-third Olympiad was solemnized, in which Evagoras the Elean conquered in the chariot-race, and Eubotas the Cyrenian in the foot-race, Euarchippides presiding in the college of Ephori at Sparta, and Euctemon being Archon at Athens) the Athenians fortified Thoricus. Now Thrasylus taking the command of the ships decreed him, and having provided five thousand seamen with proper arms to act as targeteers, in the beginning of summer sailed out to Samos. Having staid there three days, he stood over to Pygela, where he laid the adjacent country waste, and made an assault on the city. But a body of troops, marching out of Miletus to aid the Pygeleana, put to flight the light-armed Athenians who were dispersed about the country. Yet the targeteers and two companies of heavy-armed, coming up to the relief of the light-armed, put almost the whole body from Miletus to the sword. They also took about two hundred shields, and erected a trophy. Next day they sailed to Notism; and, after making all needful preparations, marched from the ? to Colophon. ? Colophonians readily ? the night after they ? Lydia as the harvest w. ? ? many villages, and took ? money and slaves and other ? es the Persian, who was now in this province, when the Athenians were straggled from their camp to pick up private plunder, fell in amongst them with a party of horse. He took but one Athenian prisoner, though he killed seven. After this, Thrasylus led off his army to the sea-coast, as resolved to sail to Ephesus. But Tissaphernes, perceiving his intent, collected together a numerous army, and sent his horsemen round the country to summon every body into Ephesus to the aid of Diana. It was the seventeenth day after his incursion into Lydia that Thrasylus arrived before Ephesus. He disembarked his heavy-armed at Coressus; but his horse and targeteers and land-soldiers, and all the rest of his

force, at the marsh on the other side of the city; and thus at break of day he approached with two different bodies. The whole force of Ephesus marched out in its defence; the confederates too, whom Tissaphernes had brought up; the Syracusans also, as well from the former ships as from the five others, which happened to be just arrived, under the command of Eucles the son of Hippo, and Heraclides the son of Aristogenes, and were accompanied by two ships from Selinus. All these advanced first against the heavy-armed from Coressus; and, after giving them an utter defeat, taking about a hundred of them prisoners, and pursuing them down to the sea, they turned to meet the body from the marsh. Here also the Athenians were put to flight, and about three hundred of them were slain. The Ephesians erected a trophy on the marsh, and another at Coressus. But on many of the Syracusans and Selinuntians, who had distinguished their bravery on the late occasions, they conferred the highest marks both of public and private gratitude; a liberty of residing amongst them at pleasure, with exemption from taxes, was granted to them all in general; and to the Selinuntians in particular, since their own city was destroyed, a complete naturalization. The Athenians, after fetching off their dead under truce, sailed away to Notium; and from thence, after interring their dead, they sailed for Lesbos and the Hellespont. But, as they were lying at anchor at Methymne of Lesbos, they had a view of five-and-twenty sail of Syracusans on their course from Ephesus. They immediately gave chase, and took four of them with all their crews, and pursued the rest into Ephesus. All the prisoners taken on this occasion Thrasylus sent away to Athens, except Alcibiades an Athenian, a cousin of and involved in the same sentence of exile with Alcibiades, whom he stoned to death. From thence he made the best of his way to Sestus to join the rest of the fleet.

From Sestus the whole united force crossed over to Lampsacus. And the winter now came on, in which the Syracusan prisoners confined in the quarries of the Piraeus, having dug themselves a passage through the rock, made their escape by night to Decelea, and some of them to Megara. But at Lampsacus, where Alcibiades was bringing the whole force into regular order, the former soldiers refused to rank with those who came with Thrasylus, because themselves had continued hitherto without a defeat, whereas the latter came to them defeated. Here however they all of them wintered, and fortified Lampsacus. They also made an expedition against Abydus ; and Pharnabazus came to its aid with a numerous body of horse : but, being defeated in battle, he fled. Alcibiades, accompanied with some horse and a hundred and twenty heavy-armed belonging to Menander, went in pursuit of him till the darkness of the night insured his safety. But this action reconciled the whole soldiery to one another, and those that came with Thrasylus were heartily caressed. In the progress of the winter they made some other incursions on the continent of Asia, and laid waste the dominions of the king.

About the same time, the Lacedæmonians, by granting a truce, fetched off such of their Helots as had deserted from Malea to Coryphasium.

About the same time also, when all parties were drawn up in order of battle against their enemies the Oeteans, the Achæans betrayed all those who belonged to the new colony of Heraclea in Trachinia, so that seven hundred of them, with Labotas the Lacedæmonian commandant, were put to the sword.

And thus the year ended, in which the Medes, who had revolted from Darius king of Persia, returned to their obedience.

III. In the succeeding summer the temple of Minerva in Phocea was set on fire by lightning, and entirely consumed.

But when the winter was over (Pantacles presiding amongst the Ephori, and Antigenes being Archon,[1] five and twenty years of the war being now completed) the Athenians with their collected force sailed in the beginning of spring to Proconnesus : and, proceeding from thence against Chalcedon and Byzantium, they encamped themselves near to Chalcedon. But the Chalcedonians, who had notice of the approach of the Athenians, had deposited all their effects with their near neighbours the Bithynian-Thracians. Alcibiades, taking with him a few of the heavy-armed and the horse, and having ordered the ships to coast it, marched up to the Bithynians, and demanded the effects belonging to the Chalcedonians ; in case of a refusal, he declared, he would make war upon them ; upon which they delivered them up. And now

returning to the camp, possessed of his booty and secure of no future disturbance from the Bithynians, he employed the whole of his troops in throwing up a work of circumvallation round Chalcedon from sea to sea, and secured as much of the river as he possibly could by a wooden rampart. Upon this, Hippocrates the Lacedæmonian commandant led his troops out of the city, as determined to engage. The Athenians formed immediately for battle. And Pharnabazus with his army and a numerous cavalry came up to the outside of the works of circumvallation, to be ready with his aid. Hippocrates therefore and Thrasylus, each with their heavy-armed, had a long engagement, till Alcibiades marched in with some more heavy-armed and the horse. Now Hippocrates was slain, and his troops fled back into the city. And at the same time Pharnabazus, who was prevented from joining Hippocrates by the narrowness of the passage between the river and the wall of circumvallation, retreated to his camp at the temple of Hercules in the district of Chalcedon. After this, Alcibiades went off to Hellespont and the Chersonesus to fetch in contributions ; but the rest of the generals made an agreement with Pharnabazus in relation to Chalcedon,—that " Pharnabazus should pay down twenty talents, to the Athenians ' and should convey an Athenian embassy to the king." They swore to Pharnabazus and took an oath from him, that " the Chalcedonians should punctually pay their former tribute to the Athenians with the full arrears, and the Athenians should suspend all hostilities against the Chalcedonians, till their ambassadors were again returned from the king." Alcibiades was not present when these conditions were sworn, for he was then before Selymbria. But taking that place, he went afterwards against Byzantium, having under him the whole military force of the Chersonesus, and the soldiers from Thrace, and more than three hundred horse. Pharnabazus, insisting that Alcibiades also should swear to the articles, waited at Chalcedon till he returned from Byzantium. But, when returned, he would not swear, unless Pharnabazus would swear again to him. In consequence of this, he gave his oath at Chrysopolis to Metrobates and Arnapes, whom Pharnabazus sent thither to receive it ; and Pharnabazus swore again at Chalcedon to Euryptolemus and Diotimus

---

and beside the public oath, they mutually exchanged the solemn pledges of private regard
and friendship.   Pharnabazus therefore immediately departed, and ordered that the ambassadors who were to go to the king should meet
him at Cyzicus.   Those sent by the Athenians were Dorotheus, Philodices, Theogenes,
Euryptolemus, Mantitheus ; they were accompanied by Cleostratus and Pyrrholochus from
Argos.   An embassy also went from Lacedæmon, Pasippidas and his colleagues, and were
accompanied by Hermocrates, now an exile from
Syracuse, and his brother Proxenus.   And
Pharnabazus began conducting them to the
king.

The Athenians were busy in the siege of
Byzantium.   They had raised a circumvallation round it, and carried their skirmishes and
attacks quite up to the wall.   Clearchus was
the Lacedæmonian commandant in Byzantium.
He had with him some persons of the neighbourhood of Sparta, a few of the Spartans
newly enfranchised, some Megareans commanded by Helixus, general from Megara, and
Bœotians commanded by their general Cæratadas.   But the Athenians, when they were
not able to prevail by force, persuaded some of
the Byzantines to betray the city.   Clearchus
the commandant, never suspecting that any of
them could be guilty of such treachery, had
made the best dispositions that occurred to his
own judgment : and, leaving the care of the
place to Cæratadas and Helixus, crossed over
the sea to Pharnabazus.   He went to receive
from him the pay for his troops ; and he designed to collect together all the ships, both
such as were left in the Hellespont for guard-
ships by Pasippidas, and such as were stationed
at Antandrus, and those under the command
of Hegesandridas, who [1] had been posted by
Mindarus on the coast of Thrace ; to procure
farther the building of more : and to draw them
all into one grand fleet, in order to annoy the
confederates of the Athenians, and oblige them
to quit the siege of Byzantium.   So soon as
Clearchus was sailed, the Byzantines joined in
the plot to betray the city—These were Cydon,
and Aristo, and Anaxicrates, and Lycurgus,
and Anaxilaus ; the latter of whom, when tried
for his life at Lacedæmon for betraying this
place, pleaded successfully in his own defence,
that " so far from betraying, he had only pre-

served it.   He who was a Byzantine and not a Lacedæmonian, saw their children and their wives
perishing with famine" (for Clearchus had distributed all the provisions in the town to the
soldiers of the Lacedæmonians).   " For this
reason therefore, he declared, he had given
admission to the enemy, and not for the sake
of money, or to gratify any rancour against the
Lacedæmonians."—The Byzantines therefore
in the plot, when they had made all necessary
preparations, opened in the night the Thracian
gates, as they are called, and let in the troops
and Alcibiades.   Helixus and Cæratadas, who
were quite ignorant of the plot, hastened with
all their men to the market-place to make head
against them.   But, as the enemy were masters
of the avenues, and resistance was unavailing,
they surrendered themselves, and were sent
prisoners to Athens.   Yet, as they were landing in the Piræus, Cæratadas slipped into the
crowd of people there ; and lurking for a time,
at length escaped safe to Decelea.

IV. The account of what had been lately
done at Byzantium reached Pharnabazus and
the ambassadors at Gordium in Phrygia, where
they spent the winter.   But as they were continuing their journey to the king early in the
spring, they were met by the Lacedæmonian
ambassadors, Bœotius and his colleagues, and
by other envoys who were on their return.   By
these they were assured, that the Lacedæmonian had been gratified by the king in all their
demands, and that Cyrus was appointed governor of all the maritime provinces, and was to
co-operate with the Lacedæmonians in the
war ; he also carried with him a letter to all
the people of those provinces, sealed with the
royal signet, and in these words—" I send down
Cyrus to be Caranus of all the troops assembled
at Castolus."   The word Caranus signifies
commander-in-chief.   When the Athenian
ambassadors heard all this, and afterwards saw
Cyrus himself, they were desirous more than
ever to go up to the king ; if that was denied
them, to have a safe-conduct back.   But Cyrus,
who would fain have the people of Athens
kept in ignorance of what had been done, advised Pharnabazus, either to deliver up these
ambassadors to him, or by no means to give
them their dismission.   Pharnabazus therefore
for the present detained the ambassadors ; one
while pretending, that he would conduct them
forwards to the king ; another while that he
would convey them back : managing so well

---

1 Ἐπιστάτω, the marginal reading, Ed. Par. 1625.

that no one could blame him. But when three years were thus elapsed, he begged leave from Cyrus to dismiss them: alleging the oath he had sworn, to re-conduct them to the sea, since he could not carry them to the king. Upon this they are sent to Ariobarzanes with an order to him to carry them back. He conducted them to Chium in Mysia, and from thence they went by sea to the other station of the Athenians.

Alcibiades, who now had a great desire with a military force to return to Athens, set sail immediately for Samos. Taking twenty ships from that station, he stood over into the Ceramic bay of Caria; and, after collecting there a hundred talents,[2] he returned to Samos. Thrasybulus with thirty ships was gone to Thrace, where he reduced the other cities that had revolted to the Lacedæmonians and Thasus too, miserably distressed by war, by seditions, and by famine: and Thrasylus with another part of the fleet was sailed for Athens. Yet before his arrival the Athenians had chosen for generals, Alcibiades though yet in exile, and Thrasybulus who was absent, and, thirdly, Conon who was now at Athens. But Alcibiades, taking the money from Samos, sailed with twenty ships to Paros. From thence he stood over to Gytheum, to discover in what progress the thirty vessels were that he heard the Lacedæmonians were fitting out there, and what was the disposition of the Athenians in regard to his returning home. And so soon as he perceived they were in the right disposition, nay, had even chosen him general, and his friends privately invited him to make his appearance, he sailed into the Piræus the very day that the city was celebrating the Plynteria, when the image of Minerva's temple was covered with a veil; which some interpreted to be a very bad omen both to himself and the state, because on this day no Athenian whatever dares to intermeddle in any serious affair. But on his entering the harbour the whole people, both from the Piræus and the city, came flocking down to his ships, all full of wonder, and full of desire too to see Alcibiades. Some of them were maintaining, "he was the most excellent citizen that Athens ever bred: the only one who beyond all dispute had been banished un-

justly; since he had been merely circumvented by the cabals of men of much less weight than himself, of snarling malicious haranguers, who had no other principle than that of plundering the state. He, on the contrary, had always been promoting the public welfare, so far as his own and the efforts of true patriots could promote it. And when the accusation was preferred against him for irreligious behaviour in regard to the mysteries, he had declared his readiness to submit to an immediate trial; whereas his enemies, who had overruled so equitable a demand, had during his absence deprived him of his country. In the meantime, his very necessities had reduced him to a state of servility; he had been forced to caress even the bitterest of foes, and not a day past but his life was in danger. He could henceforth perform no services to such of his fellow-citizens as were most endeared to him, none to his relations, none even to the state, though he saw how sadly it was conducted, since he was cramped by the restrictions of his exile. Such a man, they affirmed, could not be suspected of designing innovations in the state or a revolution of government. He could ever have obtained, from the favour of the people, precedency over those of his own age, and equality with his seniors. Nay, his very enemies knew him, even when they banished him, to be the same true patriot he had always been: and yet they, by forcing themselves into power, had destroyed the best citizens of Athens; and then, being left alone in the administration of affairs, had been countenanced by their fellow-citizens for no other reason than because they had no better men to countenance." In the meantime others were averring, that "he was the sole author of all the miseries they had lately experienced; and was still the man, that would precipitate his country into all the distresses by which at present it was threatened."

Alcibiades was now at the shore. He did not however quit his ship, since he was afraid of his enemies; but standing upon the deck, he cast his view around to see whether his friends were at hand; and spying at length his cousin Euryptolemus the son of Peisinax and his other relations accompanied by their friends, he then stepped ashore, and marcheth along with them up into the city, having parties placed near him ready to guard him against any violence. He then spoke in his own justification both in the senate and the assembly of the peo-

---

1 The learned Usher in his Annals doubts, and with reason, whether it should not be months.
2 19,375l.

ple, maintaining he had never been guilty of impiety, but had himself been sadly injured." Much was said to this purpose, and nobody presumed to say a word against him, because the people would never have suffered it. Being afterwards declared a general-plenipotentiary, as if he was able to raise the state to its former power, he first of all placed himself at the head of. the whole military strength of Athens, to guard by land the procession of the mysteries, which during the war had gone by sea. After this, he picked out a levy from the public roll, fifteen hundred heavy-armed, a hundred and fifty horsemen, and a hundred ships. And in the third month after his return to Athens, he set sail on an expedition against Andros, which had revolted from the Athenians. Aristocrates and Adimantus the son of Leucorophidas, who were chosen to command the land-forces, were sent along with him.

Alcibiades landed his troops at Gaurium on the coast of Andros, who repulsed the Andrians that sallied out to stop them, and shut them up within the city. Some few of them, though not many, and what Lacedæmonians were with them, they killed in the engagement. Alcibiades upon this erected a trophy; and, after continuing there a few days, sailed away to Samos; and having fixed his station there, carried on the war against the enemy.

. V. It was no long time before these last transactions, that the Lacedæmonians, as the time of the command of Cratesippidas was elapsed, had sent away Lysander to command the fleet. Lysander, after arriving at Rhodes, and taking upon him the command, stood away to Cos and Miletus. He proceeded from thence to Ephesus at the head of seventy sail, where he continued till he was sure that Cyrus was arrived at Sardis. But so soon as Cyrus was there, he went up to him along with the embassy from Lacedæmon. Here they made remonstrances against the past behaviour of Tissaphernes, and begged of Cyrus that with his utmost alacrity he would attend to the war. Cyrus answered " his father had expressly enjoined him to do so ; and for his own part, it was a point he had entirely at heart : he had brought down with him five hundred talents [1] in specie ; and, if that was insufficient, he would spend his own private money, which his father had given him ; and, if that should fail, he would

turn into coin the very throne on which he was sitting," which was all silver and gold. This they received with high applause ; but begged him " to raise the pay of their seamen to an Attic drachma;" [2] insisting upon it, that " if the pay was thus advanced, the seamen of the Athenians would desert their ships, and himself on the whole would be a considerable saver." He replied, that " they talked in a rational manner ; but, for his own part, it was not in his power to act otherwise than his father had enjoined him : besides it was expressly stipulated by treaty, that he was to pay only thirteen minæ [3] a month to each ship, the number employed to be wholly at the option of the Lacedæmonians." Lysander said no more at present : but after supper, when Cyrus drank to him, and desired to know " in what instance he could oblige him most ?" he replied, " if you give each seaman an obole a-day over and above their present pay." From this time their pay was advanced from three to four oboles a-day. [4] Cyrus also paid off the arrears, and advanced a month's pay beforehand, which gave fresh alacrity and spirit to all the men. But the Athenians, when they had news of this, were sadly dejected ; however, they despatched ambassadors to Cyrus under the safe conduct of Tissaphernes. He indeed refused to grant them audience, though Tissaphernes earnestly entreated for them, representing that " all he had hitherto done was in pure compliance with the advice of Alcibiades, studying only that no party of the Grecians should grow too strong, but that all might be kept in weakness through their own embroilments."

So soon as all the naval points were settled, Lysander laid all the ships to the number of ninety on the ground at Ephesus, and minded no other business than cleaning and refitting them for service. But Alcibiades had received intelligence, that Thrasybulus was come from the Hellespont to fortify Phocæa. He therefore crossed over to him, leaving Antiochus his own pilot in the command of the fleet, with an order not to put to sea against the ships of Lysander. And yet Antiochus with his own ship and one more from Notium ventured even to enter the harbour of Ephesus, and to sail under the very heads of the ships of Lysander. Lysander got a few of his vessels immediately

---

1 £6,875l.

2 7½d.   3 96l. 17s. 6d.
4 See Smith's Thucydides, book V.

on float, and gave him chase. But as the Athenians came out with a greater number of ships to the aid of Antiochus, he then collected all his own, and bore down upon the enemy. And then the Athenians, getting into the water all their ships at Notium, went out to meet him, each ship as fast as she could clear. An engagement immediately ensued; the enemy fought in the regular line; the Athenians with their ships irregularly dispersed, till at length they fled with the loss of fifteen ships. The greatest part of the men escaped, but some of them were taken prisoners. Lysander, after carrying off the ships in tow, and erecting a trophy at Notium, sailed back to Ephesus; and the Athenians to Samos.

But after this Alcibiades, being returned to Samos, stood over with the whole fleet to the harbour of Ephesus, and formed into line of battle before the mouth of the harbour, to defy the enemy. Yet, when Lysander would not come out against him, because inferior in number by many ships, he stood back to Samos. And a little while after the Lacedæmonians take Delphinium and Eion.

· When the news of the late engagement at sea was brought to Athens, the Athenians conceived high indignation against Alcibiades, ascribing the loss of their ships entirely to his negligent and wild behaviour. They nominated ten others to be generals, Conon, Diomedon, Leon, Pericles, Herasinides, Aristocrates, Archestratus, Protomachus, Thrasylus, Aristogenes. Alcibiades therefore, whose credit also was low in the fleet, taking a single vessel, sailed away to the Chersonesus, to a fortress of his own.

· And now Conon, pursuant to the decrees of the state, sailed away from Andros with the twenty ships he had there, in order to take the command at Samos. But to replace Conon at Andros, they sent away Phanosthenes with four ships from Athens. In his passage he fell in with two ships belonging to Thurium, and took both of them with their crews. The Athenians put all these prisoners into close confinement, but were moved with compassion for Dorieus the commander of them, who in reality was a Rhodian, but had long since been exiled both from Athens and Rhodes, and for fear of the Athenians, who had sentenced both himself and all his kindred to death, had got himself naturalised amongst the Thurians; they therefore gave him his liberty without a ransom.

When Conon was arrived at Samos, and had received the command of the fleet which was sadly dispirited, instead of the former number of ships which amounted to a hundred, he completely manned out seventy; and with these putting out to sea, accompanied by the other commanders, he landed at many different places on the enemy's coast, and plundered the country. And the year ended, in which the Carthaginians, having invaded Sicily with a hundred and twenty ships and a land-force of a hundred and twenty thousand men, reduced Agrigentum by famine, after being defeated in battle, and bestowing seven months on the siege.

VI. But in the following year, in which the moon was eclipsed in the evening, and the old temple of Minerva was burnt down at Athens (Pitys presiding among the Ephori, and Callias being Archon at Athens), when the time of Lysander's command and six [b] and twenty years of the war were elapsed, the Lacedæmonians sent Callicratidas to command the fleet. When Lysander delivered him the ships, he told Callicratidas, that "master of the sea and conqueror of a naval engagement, he resigned them to him." Upon this the latter advised him "to set sail from Ephesus, and keeping Samos on the left where the Athenian fleet was lying, afterwards to deliver up the ships at Miletus, and then he would own him to be master of the sea." But Lysander replying that "he ought not to interfere in another person's command," Callicratidas, besides the ships he received from Lysander, manned out fifty more from Chios and Rhodes and other places in the confederacy. And having collected them all together to the number of a hundred and forty, he made the needful preparations for meeting the enemy. But finding that all his measures were seditiously opposed by the friends of Lysander, who not only obeyed his orders with an open reluctance, but were clamouring also in all the cities against the most impolitic conduct of the Lacedæmonians, in perpetually changing their admirals, sending out persons not qualified for the office, or who had a very slender notion of naval affairs, and knew not how to manage the tempers of mankind; intimating farther the great danger they run of suffering severely for giving the command to men unexperienced at sea, and unknown to their friends

---

b Marginal reading, Paris Ed. 1625. Leunclav.

in these parts—for these reasons, Callicratidas, having called together the Lacedæmonians now on board the fleet, expressed himself thus:

"I should have been well contented to have staid at Sparta; nor, if Lysander or any other person hath a mind to be thought a better seaman than myself, have I any thing to object. But since I am commissioned by the state to command the fleet, I am bound in duty to execute their orders to the utmost of my power. You therefore I adjure, as I would always behave with honour, and as the state expects us to do our duty (and you know your duty as well as I can tell it you), to give me your opinions without any reserve, whether it be more expedient I should continue here, or return immediately to Sparta to report [1] there the posture of your affairs."

No person presumed to give his opinion otherwise, than that "he ought to obey the state, and execute their orders:" He therefore made a journey to Cyrus, and demanded pay for the seamen. Cyrus ordered him to wait two days. [2] But Callicratidas, chagrined at this delay, and vexed at frequently attending at his door, could not forbear deploring the lamentable lot of the Grecians in being obliged to cajole Barbarians for money; affirming, that "if ever he returned to Sparta, he would exert his endeavours to bring about a reconciliation between the Athenians and Lacedæmonians;"—and then he departed to Miletus. From thence he sent away some ships to Sparta for a supply of money; and, having called an assembly of the Milesians, he addressed them thus:

"It is my indispensible duty, Milesians, to obey the orders of my country. And you I expect to signalize yourselves in a cheerful prosecution of the war, as you live in the very midst of the Barbarians, and have already suffered greatly by them. It is therefore incumbent upon you to set an example to the rest of the confederates, in devising the most expedi-

tious and most effectual means to hurt the enemy, till the persons return from Sparta whom I have sent thither to fetch us money. For Lysander, at his departure, sent back all the money in his hands to Cyrus, as if it was a useless article to us: and Cyrus, when I addressed myself to him, was for ever studying excuses to avoid a conference; and for my part, I could not prevail with myself to dance attendance at his doors. But I pledge my faith to you, that I will make it my study to be grateful to you for all the good services you may do us, during this interval of our waiting for a supply from Sparta. And if it please the gods, we will convince these Barbarians, that without fawning upon them, we are able to chastise our enemies."

When Callicratidas had ended, many persons rose up, and most remarkably those who were accused of crossing his measures. They were frightened, and therefore told him the means of raising a supply, and promised to contribute from their own private purses. When he had thus got money, and had also levied five drachmas for each of his seamen at Chios, he sailed against Methymne in Lesbos, which belonged to the enemy. But the Methymnæans refusing to come over, as the Athenians had a garrison in the place, and the Atticizing party had all the power in their hands, he assaults and takes the city by storm. The soldiers instantly made booty of all the money in the place, but Callicratidas gathered all the slaves together in the market-place. The confederates called upon him to put even the citizens of Methymne up to sale: but he answered, that "whilst he was in command, he would exert his utmost endeavours that no Grecian whatever should be made a slave." The day after he set all the freemen and the [3] Athenian garrison at liberty, but the slaves were sold at public sale. He also sent word to Conon, that "he would stop him from whoring the sea."

But early one morning, perceiving Conon out at sea, he immediately gave chase, to intercept his passage to Samos, that he might not escape thither. Conon, however, made the best of his way with ships that went at a great rate, because he had picked the best rowers out of many crews to make up a few, and flies to Mitylene of Lesbos, accompanied by two of

---

[1] *Εφαντα, marg. read. Paris Edit. 1625. Leunclav.

[2] The first time he went, he desired that Cyrus might be informed that "admiral Callicratidas was there, and desired to speak with him." But the person waiting at the door answering, "Cyrus is not at leisure at present, for he is drinking;" Callicratidas with the greatest simplicity replied—"That signifies nothing at all; I can easily stand and wait here till he has finished his draught." Upon which the Barbarians, who thought him quite a rustic, laughing heartily at him, he went away. Plutarch's Life of Lysander.

[3] Τους τι, margin. reading, Ed. Par. 1625. Leunclav.

the ten commanders, Leon and Herasinides. Callicratidas pursuing with a hundred and seventy ships, stood into the harbour along with him. And Conon, now shut up by the enemy who were got quite round him, was obliged to engage in the harbour, and lost thirty ships, but their crews escaped to land, and the forty remaining ships of his fleet he drew ashore under the walls of Mitylene. But Callicratidas, having moored his ships in the harbour, besieged the place. He was entirely master of the road; and, having sent a summons to the Methymneans to march up with their whole military force, he also fetched over the troops from Chios. Now too he received the money from Cyrus.

But Conon, now that Mitylene was invested both by land and sea, and all importation of provisions was effectually cut off, and great numbers of people were crowded into the city, and the Athenians sent him no aid, because utterly ignorant of his situation, drew two of his best sailers into the water before it was day, and completely manned them with the best rowers he could pick out from the fleet. He then made the soldiers go down below decks, and stowed the materials of defence. During the whole day they were at work on board: and in the evening, so soon as it was dark, he made them all go again on shore, that the enemy might gain no suspicion of his design. But on the fifth day, having got a moderate stock of provision on board, exactly at noon, when the enemy who blocked him up were drowsy with heat, and some were taking their repose, they expeditiously stood out of the harbour, One of the ships made the best of its way to Hellespont, but the other stretched out to sea. The enemy, who blocked him up, made haste to prevent their escape, each ship as fast as they could clear, by cutting away the cables and anchors, alarming the crews, calling the men on board who had been taking their repasts on shore, and were now flocking down to the ships in a violent hurry. At length, having got on board their vessels, they gave chase to the ship that stretched out to sea, and at sunset came up with her. And after a struggle making themselves masters of her, they took her in tow, and brought her back with all her crew on board to the naval station. But the ship, that took her course towards the Hellespont, completed her escape, and carried the news of the siege to Athens.

Diomedon, who went to the aid of Conon thus besieged, came to an anchor with twelve ships in the road of Mitylene. But Callicratidas, having suddenly borne down upon him, seized ten of his ships at once, whilst Diomedon fled away with his own and with another vessel.

The Athenians, having received advice of all that happened, and of the siege, immediately decreed an aid to consist of a hundred and ten ships, compelling all of an age to bear arms to go on board, as well slaves as freemen. And, having manned out the hundred and ten ships in the space of thirty days, they put to sea: nay, even many of those persons who belonged to the cavalry of the state went on board this fleet. They first touched at Samos, and from thence took ten sail of Samians. They collected also above thirty ships more from the rest of the confederates, obliging men of all conditions to go on board. All vessels too they met at sea were embargoed, so that they amounted at last to more than a hundred and fifty sail. Callicratidas, having received intelligence that this aid was come to Samos, left fifty ships under the command of Eteonicus to continue the siege: but, putting to sea himself with a hundred and twenty, he took his evening-repast at Cape Malea in Lesbos over-against Mitylene. This very evening the Athenians were taking their repast at Arginusæ, which is over-against the isle of Lesbos. But in the night-time perceiving fires, and some persons bringing him intelligence that "they are the Athenians," he set sail at dead of night, with a design to fall suddenly amongst them. The great quantity of rain that fell in the night, accompanied with thunder, prevented him from going across. But at break of day, when the tempest was ceased, he sailed over to Arginusæ, where upon the left the Athenians were drawn out at sea in line of battle in the following disposition:

Aristocrates with fifteen ships was posted on the left; next him was Diomedon with fifteen more. Pericles was posted behind Aristocrates, and Herasinides behind Diomedon. Next to Diomedon were the Samians with ten ships drawn up in line a-head; a Samian by name Hippeus had the command of the Samians. Next them were ten ships of private captains, these also in the line a-head; and after them, three ships of the commanders-in-chief and the rest of the confederates. Protomachus with fifteen ships commanded the right; next him was Thrasylus with fifteen more. Lysias with an equal number of ships was posted behind Protomachus; and Aristogenes behind Thrasylus. They had made this disposition to prevent the enemy from breaking through their line; for their ships sailed worse than those of the enemy.

But all the ships of the Lacedæmonians were drawn up in a single line, with a view of being ready, as they were better sailers, to break through and tack about again upon the enemy; and Callicratidas commanded in their right wing. Yet Hermon the Megarean, who was steersman to Callicratidas, told him now it was most advisable for him to sheer off in time, since the ships of the Athenians were far superior in number to his own." Callicratidas made him this reply—" Sparta will not be worse inhabited when I am dead, but it would be infamous in me to flee."

And now the fleets engaged in a fight of long continuance. At first, all the ships kept close together, yet afterwards were separately engaged. But so soon as Callicratidas was tumbled into the sea by the shock of his ship when she struck on an enemy, and was never seen any more, and Protomachus with those posted with him on the right had defeated the enemy's left; then began the flight of the Peloponnesians to Chios, though most of them fled to Phocea: and the Athenians sailed back again to Arginusæ. Five and twenty ships of the Athenians were lost in this action with their crews, some few men excepted, who swam ashore. But on the Peloponnesian side nine ships belonging to Lacedæmon were lost, though the whole number of them was but ten, and upwards of sixty more belonging to the rest of the confederates.

It was now judged expedient by the Athenian commanders to order Theramenes and Thrasybulus, who commanded ships, and some other officers, with seven and forty of the ships, to sail round to the wrecks and fetch off the men; and to proceed with the rest to Mitylene against the fleet commanded by Eteonicus. But in these designs they were prevented by a gale of wind which grew to be a violent tempest. Upon which they erected a trophy, and passed the night at Arginusæ.

In the meantime, a fly-boat had carried Eteonicus the news of the late battle at sea. But he sent the boat out again with an order to those on board, to move silently off without saying a syllable to any person whatever, and soon after to return again to the naval station crowned with garlands, and shouting aloud, that " Callicratidas had gained a victory at sea," and that " the whole Athenian fleet was destroyed." They punctually observed his instructions. And when they returned again, Eteonicus offered up a sacrifice for the good tidings they brought. He then issued an order to the soldiers to take their evening repast, and to the sutlers quietly to carry all their effects on board, and sail away in the ships with all expedition to Chios, for the wind favoured the passage; whilst he himself, after setting his camp on fire, drew off the land-army to Methymne. And now Conon, having got his ships afloat, as the enemy was gone and the wind considerably abated, went out to sea, and met the Athenians who were under sail from Arginusæ. He told them what Eteonicus had done, upon which the Athenians put into Mitylene. From thence they proceeded to Chios; but being unable to do any thing there against the enemy, they stood away for Samos.

VII. But at Athens the people turned out all the commanders excepting Conon, to whom they assigned for his colleagues Adimantus and Philocles. However, of those who commanded in the late engagement, Protomachus and Aristogenes returned not to Athens, but six of them came home, namely Pericles and Diomedon, and Lysias and Aristocrates, and Thrasylus and Herasinides. Archedemus, who at this time was the greatest demagogue in Athens, and had the management of all affairs relating to Decelea, laying a fine [1] upon Herasinides, preferred an accusation against him in public court, importing, that " he had embezzled some money from Hellespont belonging to the state," and charged him farther with misdemeanors during his command. It was adjudged by the court that " Herasinides be committed to prison." After this, the commanders made their report in full senate about the late engagement at sea, and the violence of the storm. But Timocrates having moved, that " the rest of the commanders as well as Herasinides should be imprisoned in order to be tried by the people of Athens," the senate ordered their com-

---

1 I read ἐπιβαλὼν for ἐπιβουλὴν, on the authority of Dr Taylor.

mitment. In the next place a general assembly of the people was holden, in which several persons preferred accusations against the commanders, though Theramenes distinguished himself most on this occasion. He affirmed "they ought to be brought to a trial for not fetching off the men from the wrecks." He produced their own letter sent by them to the senate and people as full evidence that "no necessary avocation had prevented their doing it, since they alleged no other excuse but the storm." Each of the commanders was then permitted to make a short apology for himself; the course of law did not yet allow them to make a formal defence. They made a bare recital of facts, that "they had stood out to sea in quest of the enemy: had given an order to proper officers amongst the captains of the ships, nay, to such as had formerly commanded fleets, to Theramenes, and Thrasybulus, and some others of equal rank, to fetch off the men from the wrecks. If any therefore were accountable for nonperformance of this point, it certainly ought to be charged upon them alone who received the order to perform it: and yet (they continued) the accusation preferred against ourselves shall not make us deviate from truth, by assigning any other reason for their not having done it than the violence of the storm." They then called upon the pilots and many other persons who were on board the ships, to give their evidence in confirmation of the truth. By such pleas they mollified the people, many of whom immediately rose up, and offered to be security for their future appearance. It was resolved however, "to adjourn the affair to another assembly;" (for it was now so late in the evening that they could not distinguish the majority of hands) "the senate in the meantime to draw up a resolution to be reported to the people in what manner they should be tried."

The Apaturian festival now came on, in which it is the custom for fathers of families and near relations to entertain one another. Theramenes therefore and his party employed the festival in dressing up a number of persons in mourning garments, having first shaven them clean to the skin, who were to present themselves to the assembly of the people for the relations of such as had perished on the wrecks. They also prevailed upon Callixenus to accuse the commanders in form before the senate, The general assembly was afterwards holden,

when the senate reported their resolution by the mouth of Callixenus, and in the very words in which he had moved to have it drawn up:

" Whereas in the last assembly of the people, not only the accusers of the commanders, but also the commanders themselves, were heard in their own justification: let the people of Athens proceed to give their votes by tribes. Let two urns be placed for every tribe. In each tribe let the herald proclaim—' As many as are of opinion that the commanders have misbehaved in not fetching off from the wrecks the men who had earned them a victory, let such cast their ballots into this urn; as many as are of the contrary opinion, into that. And if a majority declare them guilty, let them be sentenced to death, let them be delivered over to the public executioners, let their estates be confiscated, reserving a tenth part for the goddess.' "

And now a person stood forth in the assembly who affirmed, that "he had swam ashore upon a barrel of flour: that the poor wretches who were lost had solemnly conjured him, if he escaped with life, to tell the people of Athens, that their commanders would not save the lives of those very men who had fought with the utmost bravery for their country." A clamour was already begun against Callixenus, for proposing a method of procedure that was manifestly against due course of law. Euryptolemus the son of Peisionax, and some other leading men amongst the people, declared themselves of this opinion. But the multitude roared aloud, that "Athens was undone, if the people were restrained from proceeding at their own discretion." Upon this a motion was made by Lyciscus, that whoever interrupted the free votes of the assembly of the people, should be involved in the same sentence that was given against the commanders." This motion was approved by a loud tumultuous shout from the multitude, and the others are forced to withdraw their opposition; but now again, the presidents refusing to put a question which was contrary to law, Callixenus stood up again, and accused them for their refusal. The people demanded aloud, that "such of them as refused should be called to account." This terrified the presidents, who immediately declared they were ready to comply, all but Socrates the son of Sophroniscus, who still insisted that "he would not do an act which was not according to law." But after this Euryptolemus rose up, and spoke thus in favour of the commanders :

" I rise up, my fellow-citizens of Athens, partly with a design to blame my near and dear relation Pericles, and my friend Diomedon ; and partly to offer some plea in their behalf ; and farther to give you such advice, as in my opinion will best promote the welfare of the Athenian state. I therefore blame my relation and my friend for persuading their colleagues in the command to insert in the letter they were desirous to send to the senate and you, that they had issued an order to Theramenes and Thrasybulus to repair with forty-seven ships to the wrecks, and fetch off the men, which order was never put in execution. In consequence of this, they are now involved in the guilt of a crime which others separately incurred : and, in requital for all their humanity, are now, by the treachery of those very persons and a party here, brought into imminent danger of their lives. No danger neither, if you will but comply with my advice, and obey the dictates of piety and justice. And by this means you will best be enabled to discover all the truth, and preserve yourselves from a subsequent fit of remorse, when in process of time, convinced that you have enormously offended both against heaven and your ownselves.

" Let me therefore recommend such a conduct to you, as will guard you from all deception either by myself or by any other person, as will clearly discover the guilty, how far they all and in what degree each person amongst them is guilty, and will enable you to assign the proper measure of punishment to each. Indulge them therefore with only one day, if more time must not be granted, to make their defence ; and pay a higher deference to your own than to the judgment of other men. And all of you know, my fellow-citizens of Athens, that the law of Canonus is still in force, which enacts, that " if any person hath aggrieved the people of Athens, he shall be imprisoned and brought to a trial before the people : and, in case he be convicted, shall be put to death and thrown into the pit, his goods and chattels to be forfeited to the state, reserving the tenth part for the goddess." By this law I exhort you to try the commanders ; and by heaven to begin, if you think proper, with Pericles my own relation. It would be baseness indeed in myself to place a higher value upon him than upon my country.

" But if you rather choose it, try them by the other law against persons accused of sacrilege and treason, which enacts that—" if any man betrays the city or robs the temples, he shall be tried in the courts of judicature ; and, if adjudged to die, shall not be buried in Attica, his goods and chattels to be forfeited to the state."

" Make use of either of these laws, my fellow-citizens. Let a separate day be assigned for the trial of each : that day to be divided into [1] three parts ; in the first of which you ought to assemble and give your ballots whether or no they ought to be put upon their trial ; in the second, the accusation should be opened against them ; in the third, they should be heard in their own defence. And if this method be observed, the guilty will receive the severest punishment, and the innocent be saved by you, Athenians, and not be put to death by an iniquitous condemnation. You then, without offending heaven, without violating your oaths, will judge them according to law, and will not make war in combination with the Lacedæmonians by putting to death without a trial, in express violation of the laws, the very men who have taken seventy of their ships, and gained a notable victory over them.

" But of what are you afraid, that you are in such vehement haste to pass a sentence ? Are you afraid of losing your right to put to death or to save whom you please, in case you try men in a regular conformity with and not in open violation of the law ? Yes ; such was the motive of Callixenus, when he persuaded the senate to subject them all to one summary vote from the people. Yet this way perhaps you may put an innocent man to death ; and then, in a subsequent fit of remorse, you may bitterly reflect what a dreadful and unjustifiable act you have committed ; and more bitterly still, if you iniquitously put to death a number of them. Horrible indeed would the procedure be, if you, the very persons that indulged Aristarchus, who formerly overturned the popular government, and afterwards betrayed Oenoe to our enemies the Thebans, with a day of his own appointment to make his defence, and observed every form of law in regard to him, should deny every indulgence and every right to commanders who in all respects have

---

1 Διηγημένων τῆς ἡμέρας τριῶν μέρων, Leunclavius. Paris Ed. marg. reading, p. 450, and the Appendix.

answered your expectations, and have gained a victory over your enemies! Forbid it heaven, that Athenians should behave in such a manner. Keep your attention fixed on the laws, on laws which are entirely your own, on laws by whose immediate influence you have been so highly exalted; and, let it never enter your hearts to deviate from them. Bring back your thoughts to the sole consideration of the matters of fact, in which your commanders seem to have incurred your displeasure.

" For, after they had obtained the victory at sea and were returned to their station, it was Diomedon's advice, that the whole fleet should proceed in regular line to fetch off the disabled ships and the crews on board them. Herasinides was for repairing immediately with the whole fleet against the enemy at Mitylene. Thrasylus declared for the execution of both these points, by leaving part of the fleet behind, and going with the rest against the enemy. His advice received the general approbation. Each commander was to leave three ships of his own division; the number of the commanders was eight; besides the ten ships belonging to private captains, and the ten belonging to the Samians, and the three ships belonging to the commander-in-chief. All these together are forty-seven, four for the care of every disabled vessel, which were twelve in all. The officers left behind to command them were Thrasybulus and Theramenes, that very Theramenes, who in the last assembly accused these commanders; and then, with the rest of the fleet, they went out to sea against the enemy.

" In what article therefore hath their conduct been defective or inglorious? If the behaviour hath been faulty in regard to the enemy, those who went out against the enemy ought by all the rules of justice to be accountable for it. But such only as were assigned to fetch off the men, and yet did not execute the order of their superiors, should be put on their trial for not fetching them off. Thus much indeed I can safely allege in vindication of Thrasybulus and Theramenes too, that the storm prevented them from executing that order. The persons who by good fortune were preserved, are evidence that this is true; in

which number is one of your own commanders, who escaped with life from one of the wrecks; and whom, though then he stood in need of all their assistance, they now will have involved in the same sentence with those who were to bring it, and yet brought it not.

" Take care, therefore, my fellow-citizens of Athens, that successful as you are, you act not the part of men who are on the brink of despair and ruin; that, instead of submission to the gods in points that are subject to their will alone, you condemn not men for treachery when they were incapable of acting at all, since the violence of the storm entirely prevented the execution of orders. You would behave much more agreeably to justice if you honoured your victorious commanders with crowns, rather than, in compliance with the instigations of wicked men, to punish them with death."

Euryptolemus, after this address, proceeded to move, that " the accused should be separately put on their trials according to the law of Canonus." The proposal of the senate was, that " one summary vote should be passed upon them all." Upon holding up of hands, a majority appeared for the motion of Euryptolemus. But as Menecles entered a protest against the regularity of it, and of course the question was put again, it was carried for the proposal of the senate. And after this they condemned to death the eight commanders in the sea-fight of Arginusæ. Six of them, who were now at Athens, were actually put to death. Yet no long time after the Athenians repented of what they had done, and passed a decree, that " the persons who had beguiled the people in this matter should be impeached for the crime, and procure bail till they should be brought to a trial, Callixenus in particular to be one of the number." Four other persons were also impeached, and were kept in safe custody by their own bail. But the sedition breaking out afterwards in the city, in which Cleophon was killed, they all made their escape before they could be brought to a trial. Callixenus, however, who afterwards returned to Athens with those who came up from the Piræus into the city, was so universally detested, that he starved himself to death.

THE

AFFAIRS OF GREECE.

BOOK II.

CONTENTS of BOOK II.

AFFAIRS OF GREECE.

BOOK II.

I. THE soldiers that were at Chios with Eteonicus subsisted during summer on the fruits of the season, and the money they earned by working in the fields. But when winter came on, and they had no subsistence, and were both naked and barefoot, they ran into cabals, and formed a conspiracy to make seizure of Chios. It was agreed amongst them, that all such as approved of the scheme should carry a reed in their hands, in order to discover to each other a just account of their numbers. Eteonicus, who had gained intelligence of the plot, was highly perplexed in what manner to disconcert it, because of the great number of those who carried reeds. He judged it too hazardous to attack them openly, lest they should run to arms; and then, seizing the city and turning enemies, might ruin all affairs at Chios in case they prevailed. On the other side he thought it would be dreadful to destroy so many persons who were old confederates, which might open the mouths of the rest of Greece against them, and give the soldiery an aversion to the service. Taking therefore along with him fifteen persons armed with daggers, he walked about the city; and lighting on a fellow who had a disorder in his eyes, and was just come from the surgeon's, with a reed in his hand, he killed him on the spot. Hereupon a tumult beginning to rise, and some demanding " for what reason that man was killed?" Eteonicus orders them to be answered aloud, "because he carried a reed.' This answer was no sooner given, than all such as carried reeds threw them instantly away; every one within hearing was afraid lest he should have been seen with one of them in his hand. Eteonicus, after this, having assembled the Chians, issued out an order to them to advance a proper sum of money, that the seamen might receive their pay, and all kinds of mutiny be prevented. The Chians advanced the money, and then Eteonicus ordered all the men on board. Repairing afterwards on board every vessel in its turn, he encouraged and he advised them much, as if he was entirely ignorant of the late conspiracy, and then distributed a month's pay to each.

The Chians and the rest of the confederates, assembling afterwards at Ephesus, determined to send ambassadors to Lacedæmon concerning the present state of their affairs, who were to make their report, and then desire, that " Lysander might be sent to command the fleet," who had highly recommended himself to the alliance during his former command, and by gaining the sea-fight at Notium. The ambassadors were accordingly despatched away, and with them some envoys for Cyrus, who were to second them. But the Lacedæmonians complied only so far as to send Lysander to be the lieutenant, for they appointed Aracus to be admiral-in-chief: for their law doth not permit the same person to be twice in the chief command. The fleet therefore was resigned to Lysander, when twenty-seven years of the war were now completed.

In this year Cyrus put to death Autobœsaces and Mitræus, the sons of a sister of Darius and daughter of Artaxerxes, who was father of Darius, because at meeting him they had not drawn their hands within the sleeve, a compliment paid to the king alone. The sleeve reacheth down below the hand, and the person who draws his hand within it is incapable of doing any act at all. Hieramenes and his wife represented to Darius, that he could not in justice connive at such outrageous behaviour. Darius therefore, pretending himself much out of order, sends couriers to Cyrus to summon him to court.

In the following summer (when Archytas presided in the college of ephori, and Alexius was archon at Athens) Lysander, now arrived at Ephesus, sends for Eteonicus with the ships from Chios, and collected all the rest from their several stations into one grand fleet. He refitted them all for service, and was building others at Antandros. He also made Cyrus a visit, and asked for money. Cyrus told him, that " all his father's money and a great deal more besides had already been expended," reciting particularly, what each admiral in chief had received: however, he gave him a supply. Lysander, thus furnished with money, assigned proper commanders to the ships, and paid the seamen their arrears. In the meantime the Athenian commanders were making preparations at Samos to go out to sea with the fleet.

At this juncture Cyrus sent again for Lysander, when the messenger was come to him from his father with the news, that " he was much out of order and wanted to see him," being now at Thamneria in Media near the Cadusians, against whom he had marched because they had revolted. When Lysander was come, he expressly forbade him " to engage the Athenians at sea, unless he had by far the larger number of ships, since both the king and himself were masters of abundance of wealth, and the fleet might be properly enlarged to secure the point." He then showed him an account of all the tributes from the cities which were his own appointments, and gave him what money he could spare. And then, having put him in mind " of the great friendship he bore to the Lacedæmonian state, and particularly to Lysander," he set out on a journey to his father.

Lysander, when Cyrus had thus intrusted him with all his concerns, and was departed in obedience to the summons to visit his sick father, after distributing pay to his fleet, sailed into the Ceramic bay of Caria; where, assaulting a city called Cedrea, that was confederate with the Athenians, he took it the second day by storm, and sold the inhabitants for slaves; these inhabitants were half-barbarians; and from thence he sailed away to Rhodes. The Athenians, having stood out from Samos, were infesting the coasts belonging to the king; they even sailed up to Chios and Ephesus, and were prepared for battle. They associated also in the command of the fleet, Menander, Tydeus, and Cephisodotus. Lysander was now coasting along Ionia, from Rhodes towards the Hellespont, and the track of vessels out of it, and against the cities that had revolted. The Athenians were also at sea, being bound to Chios; for Asia was entirely against them. Lysander from Abydus sailed up to Lampsacus, which was confederate with the Athenians. The Abydenians and others marched their troops thither by land. They were commanded by Thorax the Lacedæmonian; and assaulting Lampsacus they take it by storm. The soldiers plundered this city, a rich one, and plentifully stocked with wine and other needful stores: but Lysander dismissed all persons that were free without a ransom. The Athenians, who closely chased him, were now arrived at Eleus in the Chersonese, with a hundred and eighty ships. Here they had no sooner taken their repast, than news is brought them of what had been done at Lampsacus, when immediately they proceed to Sestos: from whence, after victualling with the utmost despatch, they sailed into Ægos-potamos, over-against Lampsacus. The distance between them across the Hellespont is about [1] fifteen stadia : and here they took their evening repast. Night came on; but so soon as it was break of day, Lysander made a signal for his men to eat their meal and repair on board their ships. Having now got things in readiness for an engagement, and made all fast on board for defence, he issued out orders, that no ship should stir out of the line or go out to sea. The Athenians, when the sun was up, appeared before the harbour in a line abreast, as ready to engage. But when Lysander would not come out against them, and it grew late in the day, they sailed back again into Ægos-potamos.

Lysander now ordered the nimblest vessels to follow the Athenians. They were to take a view in what manner they behaved so soon as they quitted their ships, and then to return and bring him a report. Nor did he suffer any of his own men to quit their vessels before these ships returned. He did the same thing for four days successively; and the Athenians

---

1 One mile and a half.

overcame, the same number of days, against him.

Alcibiades from his own fortress had a view of the Athenians in their present station, on the open beach, near no city, and obliged to go [2] fifteen stadia from their ships to fetch provisions from Sestos; whilst the enemy lay in a harbour, and were supplied with every thing from the adjacent city. He told them therefore " they had chosen an improper station ;" he advised them to remove to Sestos, to a harbour and to a city; " Only station yourselves there," said he, " and you will be able to fight the enemy at your own discretion." But the commanders, and especially Tydeus and Menander, ordered him to be gone—since they, and not he, were at present in the command of the fleet. Accordingly he went his way.[3]

But Lysander, on the fifth day the Athenians thus came over to offer him battle, ordered those who followed them in their retreat, that, " so soon as they saw them landed again, and straggled about the Chersonese," which they continued to do more and more every succeeding day, to buy provisions at a great distance, heartily despising Lysander for not coming out against them, " they should immediately return, and when they were got out half way, should hoist a shield up in the air." They punctually obeyed his orders; and Lysander immediately made the signal for standing out to sea with all expedition. Thorax, also, with the land-forces under his command, was taken on board to go along with them. Conon no sooner had a view of the enemy, than he made a signal to the ships to be ready for defence with all their might. But as the seamen were dispersed about, some ships had but two benches of rowers aboard, some only one, and some none at all. Conon's own ship, with about seven more and the Paralus, had their crews on board, and immediately put out to sea; but all the rest Lysander took close to the shore. They had indeed drawn together most of their men on the land, but they fled away to places of safety. Conon flying with nine ships, as he found all was over with the Athenians, sailed up to Cape Abarnis near Lampsacus, and carried from thence the great masts belonging to

the ships of Lysander. And then with eight ships he sailed away for Cyprus to Evagoras, whilst the Paralus went for Athens to notify what had happened. But Lysander brought over the ships, and the prisoners, and every thing else to Lampsacus. And, besides others of the commanders, he had got for his prisoners Philocles and Adimantus. But the very day he performed these exploits, he sent away Theopompus the Milesian partizan to Lacedæmon, to notify what had been done, who performed the journey in three days, and published the victory.

Lysander afterwards called the confederates together, and desired their advice about the prisoners. On this occasion many bitter charges were exhibited against the Athenians : —" what sad transgressors they had formerly been !—what horrid designs they would have put in execution had they obtained the victory, even to cut off the right hands of all the prisoners they should take ! They had thrown overboard and drowned all the men belonging to two ships they had taken, one a Corinthian, and the other an Andrian : and Philocles was the very Athenian commander who had thus destroyed them." Much more was said at this meeting, and a resolution was taken " to put all the Athenians who were prisoners to death except Adimantus," who in the council of war had singly opposed the proposal to cut off hands ; however, he was charged by some persons with betraying the fleet to the enemy. Lysander therefore, having first put the question to Philocles, who had thrown the Corinthians and Andrians overboard—" What he deserved to suffer, who had set the example of such outrageous behaviour in Greece ?" put him instantly to death.

II. And, so soon as he had settled affairs at Lampsacus, he sailed to Byzantium and Chalcedon. They gave him a reception, having first sent away under truce the Athenian garrisons. The persons indeed, who had betrayed Byzantium to Alcibiades, fled away to Pontus and afterwards to Athens, where they were naturalized.

But Lysander sent home all the garrisons belonging to that state, and all Athenians whatever that fell into his hands, to Athens ; thither he permitted them to sail without any molestation, but no where else. He knew, that the greater the numbers that were collected together in the city and the Piræus, the

---

2 One mile and a half.

3 This is the last time any mention is made of Alcibiades, who soon after, through the instigations of Critias and Lysander, was treacherously put to death by Pharnabazus.

sooner they must want the necessaries of life. And now, leaving Sthenelaus the Lacedæmonian, to be commandant of Byzantium and Chalcedon, he himself returned to Lampsacus and refitted the fleet.

At Athens, where the Paralus arrived in the night, the calamity was told, and a scream of lamentation ran up from the Piræus through the long walls into the city, one person repeating the news to another; insomuch that no single soul that night could take any rest, not merely for lamenting those who were lost, but much more for reflecting what themselves in all probability were soon to suffer—the like no doubt as themselves had inflicted upon the Melians, when they had reduced by siege that colony of the Lacedæmonians, on the Istians also, and Scioneans, and Toroneans, and Æginetæ, and many other people in Greece. The next day they summoned a general assembly, in which " it was resolved to barricade all their harbours excepting one, to repair their walls, to fix proper watches, and prepare the city in all respects for a siege." All hands accordingly were immediately at work.

Lysander, who now from the Hellespont was come to Lesbos with two hundred sail, took in and re-settled the cities in that island, and especially Mitylene. He also sent away to the towns of Thrace ten ships commanded by Eteonicus, who reduced every thing there into subjection to the Lacedæmonians. But immediately after the fight at Ægos-potamus all Greece revolted from the Athenians, excepting Samos. At Samos the people, having massacred the [1] nobility, held the city for the Athenians.

In the next place, Lysander sent notice to Agis at Decelea, and to Lacedæmon, that " he is sailing up with two hundred ships. The Lacedæmonians immediately took the field with their own force, as did the rest of the Peloponnesians, except the Argives, upon receiving the order circulated by Pausanias the other king of Lacedæmon. When they were all assembled, he marched away at their head, and encamped them under the walls of Athens, in the place of exercise called the Academy. But Lysander, when come up to Ægina, collected together all the Æginetæ he could possibly find, and replaced them in their city. He did the same to the Melians, and to the other

people who formerly had been dispossessed. In the next place, having laid Salamis waste, he stationed himself before the Piræus with a hundred and fifty ships, and prevented all kind of embarkations from entering that harbour.

The Athenians, thus besieged both by land and sea, and destitute of ships, of allies, and of provisions, were miserably perplexed how to act. They judged they had nothing to expect but suffering what without provocation themselves had made others suffer, when they wantonly tyrannized over petty states, and for no other reason in the world than because they were confederate with the state of Lacedæmon. From these considerations, after restoring to their full rights and privileges such as were under the sentence of infamy, they persevered in holding out; and, though numbers began to die for want of meat, they would not bear any motion of treating. But when their corn began totally to fail, they sent ambassadors to Agis, offering " to become confederates with the Lacedæmonians, reserving to themselves the long walls and the Piræus," and on these terms would accept an accommodation. Yet Agis ordered them " to repair to Lacedæmon, since he himself had no power to treat." When the ambassadors had reported this answer to the Athenians, they ordered them to go to Lacedæmon. But when they were arrived at Sellasia on the frontier of Laconia, and the ephori were informed " they were to offer no other proposals than had been made by Agis," they sent them an order " to return to Athens, and when they heartily desired peace, to come again with more favourable instructions." When therefore the ambassadors returned to Athens, and had reported these things to the state, a universal despondency ensued : " slavery," they judged, " must unavoidably be their portion ; and whilst they were sending another embassy numbers would die of famine." No one durst yet presume to advise the demolition of the walls; since Archestratus, who had only hinted in the senate that " it would be best for them to make peace on such terms as the Lacedæmonians proposed," had immediately been thrown into prison. But the Lacedæmonians proposed, that " each of the long walls should be demolished to the length of [2] ten stadia ;" and a decree had been passed that " such a proposal should never be debated."

---

1 Γνωριμων.

2 About a mile.

In this sad situation, Theramenes offered to the general assembly, that "if they would let him go to Lysander, he could inform them at his return, whether the Lacedæmonians insisted on the demolition of the walls with a view entirely to enslave them, or by way of security only for their future behaviour." He was ordered to go; and he staid more than three months with Lysander, waiting till a total want of provisions should necessitate the Athenians to agree to any proposal whatever. But on his return in the fourth month, he reported to the general assembly, that "Lysander had detained him all this time, and now orders him to go to Lacedæmon, since he had no power to settle the points of accommodation, which could only be done by the ephori." Upon this he was chosen with nine others, to go ambassador-plenipotentiary to Lacedæmon. Lysander sent Aristotle, an Athenian, but under sentence of exile, in company with other Lacedæmonians, to the ephori, to assure them that "he had referred Theramenes to them, who alone were empowered to make peace and war." When therefore Theramenes and the other ambassadors were arrived at Sallasia, and were asked—"What instructions they had?"—their answer was,—"They had full powers to make a peace." Upon this the ephori called them to an audience: and on their arrival at Sparta they summoned an assembly, in which the Corinthians and Thebans distinguished themselves above all others, though several joined in their sentiments. They averred that "the Athenians ought to have no peace at all, but should be utterly destroyed." The Lacedæmonians declared, "they would never enslave a Grecian city that had done such positive service to Greece in the most perilous times." Accordingly they granted a peace, on condition "they should demolish the long walls and the Piræus, should deliver up all their ships except twelve, should recall their exiles, should have the same friends and the same foes with the Lacedæmonians, and follow them at command either by land or sea." Theramenes and his colleagues returned to Athens with these conditions of peace. At their entering the city a crowd of people flocked about them, fearing they had been dismissed without any thing done: for their present situation would admit of no delay at all, such numbers were perishing by famine. On the day following, the ambassadors reported the terms on which the Lacedæmonians peace. Theramenes was their mouth on this occasion, and assured them "they had no resource left, but to obey the Lacedæmonians and demolish the walls." Some persons spoke against, but a large majority declaring for it, it was resolved—"to accept the peace."

In pursuance of this, Lysander stood into the Piræus, and the exiles returned into the city. They demolished the walls with much alacrity, music playing all the time, since they judged this to be the first day that Greece was free.

Thus ended the year, in the middle of which Dionysius, the son of Hermocrates, made himself tyrant of Syracuse, after the Carthaginians had been defeated in battle by the Syracusans, though the former had first made themselves masters of Agrigentum, which the Sicilians too evacuated for want of provision.

III. [In the year following were celebrated the Olympic games, in which Crocinas the Thessalian gained the prize in the stadium or foot-race, Eudius presiding amongst the ephori at Sparta, and Pythodorus being archon at Athens, whom the Athenians, because he was appointed during the oligarchy, never name in their list of archons, but style that year the Anarchy.]

The oligarchy was thus set up:—It was decreed by the people, that "thirty persons should be chosen to draw up a body of laws for the future government of the state." The persons chosen were these—Polyarches, Critias, Melobius, Hippolochus, Euclides, Hiero, Mnesilochus, Chremon, Theramenes, Aresias, Diocles, Phædrias, Chærelaus, Anetius, Piso, Sophocles, Eratosthenes, Charicles, Onomacles, Theognis, Æschines, Theogenes, Cleomedes, Erasistratus, Phido, Dracontides, Eumathes, Aristotle, Hippomachus, Mnesithides. When these things were done, Lysander sailed away for Samos: and Agis, marching away the land army from Decelea, disbanded them to their several cities.

About the same time, and when the sun was eclipsed, Lycophron the Pheræan, who was scheming to be king over all Thessaly, defeated in battle the Larisseans and other people of Thessaly who had made head against him, and slew many of them. At the same time also, Dionysius, tyrant of Syracuse, being defeated in battle by the Carthaginians, lost Gela and Camarina; and a little time after, the Leontines who lived at Syracuse revolted from Dionysius and the Syracusans, and withdrew to their own city, upon which the cavalry of Syracuse were immediately sent by Dionysius to Catana.

The Samians, invested on all sides by Lysander, treated for the first time about a surrender when he was just proceeding to a general assault. The capitulation was, that "all the freemen should depart with only the clothes on their backs, and should deliver up every thing beside;" accordingly they departed. Lysander, having delivered over the city and all within it to its ancient inhabitants, and appointed ten commanders for the preservation of the place, sent home all the quotas of shipping belonging to the confederates; and with those belonging to that state he sailed away to Lacedæmon, bringing with him all the ornaments of the ships he had taken from the enemy, and the ships out of the Piræus, twelve excepted, and the crowns that had been presented personally to himself from the states of Greece, and four hundred and seventy talents [1] of silver, being the surplus of the tributes which Cyrus assigned him for the war, and whatever else he had got in the course of his command. All these articles he delivered in to the Lacedæmonians in the close of this summer, at which time twenty-eight years and a half [2] put an end to this war, during which the ephori of Sparta are reckoned up in the following order: first Æneslas, in whose time the war began, in the fifteenth year of the truce made for thirty years after the conquest of Eubœa. After him are these—Brasidas, Isanor, Sostratidas, Hexarchus, Agesistratus, Angenidas, Onomacles, Zeuxippus, Pityas, Pleistolas, Clinomachus, Hilarchus, Leon, Chæridas, Patesidas, Cleosthenes, Lycarius, Aperatus, Onomantius, Alexippidas, Misgolaidas, Hysias, Aracus, Avarchippus, Pantacles, Pityas, Archytas, and Audieus, in whose time Lysander, having finished the war as is above related, returned with the fleet to Sparta.

The Thirty were put into commission at

Athens, so soon as ever the long walls and those of the Piræus were demolished. They were appointed to draw up a body of laws for the future government of the state, and yet were continually delaying to draw up such laws, and make them public: but then they filled up the senate and other offices of state by nominations of their own. In the next place, it was their principal care to apprehend and subject to capital punishment all such as, during the democracy, had subsisted by the trade of informers, and had been a nuisance to honest and good men. Such persons the senate readily condemned to death; and the whole body of Athenians who were conscious to themselves that they had never been guilty of such practices, were not at all dissatisfied. But when they began to cabal together how to erect themselves into an arbitrary council of state, their first step was to send Æschines and Aristotle to Lacedæmon, to persuade Lysander to send them a guard, that they might effectually rid themselves of a malignant party, in order to settle their future polity; and they promised to take the expense upon themselves. Lysander was persuaded, and procured a body of guards to be sent them under the command of Callibius. But when they had got this guard, they paid all possible court to Callibius, that his commendation might be given to all their measures. By this sending them parties to execute their orders, they now apprehended whatever persons they pleased, no longer bad men and scoundrels, but such as they imagined would never acquiesce in their violent proceedings, would attempt resistance, and had influence enough to raise a large party against them.

Critias and Theramenes at first had acted with great unanimity and friendship. But when the former, who had been exiled by the people, was impetuous for putting numbers to death, Theramenes began to clash. He maintained it "to be quite iniquitous to put men to death only because they were honoured by the people, and had never done any harm to the worthy and good. For," he added, "even I myself, and you too, Critias, have advised and executed many public measures merely for the sake of obliging the people." But Critias (for he was still well with Theramenes) replied—"It was an inconsistency for men, who had schemed to get the power into their own hands, not to rid themselves of

1 91062l. 10s.

2 That is, if reckoned by the complete years of the ephori at Sparta. But as the war began in the year of Æneslas, the first year of it ended in the year of Brasidas. Count Brasidas therefore first, and the duration of the war will appear to be twenty-seven years and a half, since it ends in the year of Eudicus. This perfectly reconciles Thucydides and Xenophon.

such as were best able to disappoint their scheme. You judge very simply indeed, if, because we are thirty in number, you think we ought to be less vigilant in establishing our power, than a single person would be for his own personal tyranny." Yet, when numbers had unjustly been put to death, and it was visible, that the Athenians began to form associations, and to be alarmed for their future safety, Theramenes again declared, that " unless they strengthened themselves by taking in a number of able assistants, it was impossible the oligarchy could be of long continuance." Here Critias and the rest of the thirty beginning to be alarmed, and not least of all about Theramenes lest the Athenians should put themselves under his protection, draw up a list of three thousand persons, who were to be associated with them in the administration. But Theramenes again declared his sentiments, that " it seemed an absurdity to him, for men, who had at first proposed to form a union only of the best men in the community, to draw up a list amounting to three thousand, as if that number necessarily implied that all of them were men of honour and virtue; as if it was impossible for any one not in the list to be a man of worth, or any one in it to be a villain. But in short," said he, " I plainly see that you are intent on two schemes utterly inconsistent with one another, a government to be supported by violence, and the agents in it much less considerable in point of power than those who are to be governed." In this manner Theramenes talked.

They now summoned the whole city to a review; the three thousand to assemble in the forum, but all the rest who were not in the list at a distant place. The former they ordered to arms; and, whilst the rest were remotely engaged, they despatched the guards and such of the citizens as were in combination with them, to seize the arms of all the Athenians excepting the three thousand. And, having carried them into the citadel, they laid them up safe within the temple.

These things being done, as if now with security they might act all their pleasure, they put many to death from personal enmity, and many because they were rich.[3] And to enable

them to pay the Lacedæmonian guards, they also made a decree, that " each person of the thirty might apprehend one of the sojourners

philosopher, as if he had given him improper lessons. Xenophon had justified Socrates from these reproaches in a neat and most convincing manner. He also relates a severe censure that Socrates passed upon the impurity of his manners; and how, when Critias became one of the thirty tyrants, and had put many worthy men to death, Socrates made in public the following observation : " It would be strange (said he) if a person, who was appointed to take care of a herd of cattle, should lessen their number, and reduce the remainder to a state of weakness, and yet not confess that he was a bad keeper of cattle : but then it is much stranger that a person, who governing in a community of men, lessens the number of the people under him, and reduces the rest to a state of desolation, can avoid taking shame to himself, and not confess that he is a wretched governor indeed." This (says Xenophon) was carried to the tyrants ; upon which Critias and Charicles sent for Socrates, and, showing him the law they had made, by which he was forbidden to teach the art of reasoning, they strictly enjoined him to hold no discourse at all with young men of Athens. Socrates begged leave to propose some questions, that he might be sure of the meaning of this prohibition. They told him he might. " I declare myself (he then went on) always ready to obey the laws. But lest I should transgress through ignorance, I would know explicitly from you, whether you forbid me to teach the art of reasoning, because you judge it to consist in saying what is right, or saying what is wrong. For if it consists in saying what is right, you clearly forbid me to say what is right ; if it consists in saying what is wrong, it is certain indeed I ought always to endeavour to say what is right." Charicles upon this grew angry, and replied : Since you are so ignorant, Socrates, we word the prohibition in such a manner that you cannot mistake ; you are to hold no discourse at all with the young men of Athens. " But still (said he) to prevent mistakes, and to guard me from the least breach of your commands, declare to me, till what age you deem men young?" Till the age prescribed for their entrance into the senate (said Charicles), till then they are not to be deemed at years of discretion. Hold therefore no discourse at all with persons under thirty years of age. " Suppose I want something of a tradesman who is under thirty, must I not ask him the price of what I want ?" Ay, ay, certainly you may, said Charicles. But it is your way, Socrates, to ask questions about points in which you want to inform and not to be informed. You are to ask no such questions as those. " Suppose then a person may ask me, where Charicles lives, or where Critias may be found, am I forbidden to give him any answer ?" Here Critias put in : You are to hold no discourse at all about shoemakers, and carpenters, and brasiers ; though I fancy you have already vexed them with fetching them in for comparisons in your daily loquacity. " Why then (said Socrates) I must refrain too from the consequences I draw from such comparisons, and say nothing about justice, and piety, and things that are right and proper ?" Ay, by Jove, you must, and from ever mentioning again your keepers of cattle ; if not, you may depend upon it, you shall suffer for it in your own goods and chattels too. From hence it is plain, it had been told them what Socrates had said about a keeper of cattle, which had made them exceeding angry with him.—Xenophon's Memorable Things of Socrates, Book I.

---

3 Critias had been in the earlier part of his life a disciple of Socrates, and his bad conduct afterwards occasioned several reproaches to be thrown upon this divine

residing in the city, might put him to death, and appropriate his wealth." They then encouraged Theramenes to apprehend what sojourner he pleased. But the answer of Theramenes was, " To me it appears base indeed, that men, who pique themselves on being the best men in Athens, should give in to such outrages as the vile tribe of informers could not commit. The latter only extorted their money, but deprived not men of their lives. But as for us, if we shall murder persons who have done us no wrong, merely to get their money, will not our behaviour be in every respect more outrageous than theirs ?" ¹ Judging from hence that Theramenes would obstruct them in all their designs, they combine against him, and calumniate him privately to every member of the senate apart, as a determined opposer of their new polity. And then, having issued out orders to a party of young men, such as they judged would act most daringly, to repair to the senate-house with daggers under their skirts, they convened the senate. No sooner was Theramenes come in, than Critias rose up, and spoke as follows :

" If there be a man in this house, who imagines that more persons suffer death than the public welfare requireth, let him only reflect, that in all revolutions of government such everywhere is the case. And when revolutions end here in an oligarchy, the greatest number of adversaries must necessarily start up, because Athens is the most populous community in Greece, and because for the longest series of time the people here have been pampered in liberty. For our parts, gentlemen of the senate, who know what an oppressive yoke the democracy hath ever proved to men of such qualifications as we are and as you are ; who know besides, that the people can never be well affected to the Lacedæmonians, to whom we owe our preservation, whereas the most worthy men amongst us may ever be their hearty friends ; on these considerations, and by advice of the Lacedæmonians, we are now modelling our constitution ; and, whomsoever we perceive to be an enemy to the oligarchy, we rid ourselves of him to the utmost of our power. But then, if any one of our own body gives a dangerous opposition to our own fa-

vourite scheme, nothing on our principles can be so equitable as to make him suffer for it. And yet we are well assured, that this Theramenes, who sits here amongst us, is labouring his utmost to destroy both us and you. I speak nothing but the truth. You will be convinced of it yourselves if you only reflect, that nobody is so lavish of his censure on the present measures as this very Theramenes, nobody so ready to oppose when we are willing to put one of the demagogues out of our way. If indeed his principles had originally been the same, though this would prove him our enemy, it would not justly expose him to the title of villain. But now, this very man, the author of our confidence in and our friendship towards the Lacedæmonians, the author of the late demolition of the power of the people, and who was most active at exciting us to inflict due punishment on our first set of enemies,—now, I say, when you, gentlemen, have shown yourselves to be utter enemies to the people, this very man takes upon him to be displeased with your conduct, in order to secure his own personal safety, and leave us to be punished for all that hath been done.—Here, beyond all doubt, we are obliged to take vengeance upon him, not only as an enemy but also as a traitor. And treachery of a truth is a much more heinous crime than open enmity, by how much more difficult it is to guard against what is not seen than against what is. Nay, it carries a more implacable enmity with it, since men at open variance with one another become reconciled, and renew a mutual confidence ; but with a man, who is a traitor convict, no one ever yet was, and no one can ever again be reconciled. But, to give you complete conviction that Theramenes is not merely a changeling, but by nature a traitor, I will remind you of his former behaviour.

" This man, who in the early part of his days was in the highest credit with the people, as his father Agnon had been before him, showed himself the most impetuous zealot in shifting the power of the people into the hands of the four hundred, and accordingly became the leading man amongst them. And yet, he no sooner perceived that a sufficient party was formed against the four hundred, then he set himself again at the head of the people against his own accomplices. And this in truth is the reason why he is styled the Buskin. The buskin you know seems to fit both of the feet, and is a

---

1 I am for making one sentence of two by a small but necessary correction : viz. 'Ημᾶς δὲ εἰ ἀπαντίσομεν . . . λαμβάνομεν, πῶς οὐ.—This is more in the manner of Xenophon. The future verb ἀπαντίσομεν calls for this alteration. Dr Taylor.

buskin for either of them. But let me tell you, Theramenes, a man, who deserves to live at all, ought not to signalize himself by leading his fellow-citizens into dangerous schemes, and when things go wrong to make a sudden turn and desert them. Embarked as it were in the same ship with them, he ought to share their toil, till they meet with more favourable gales. For in case he refuseth this, how shall they ever reach their harbour in safety, when at every adverse blast they must immediately invert their course?

" It must be owned, that revolutions in political bodies carry death and destruction with them. But you, sir, most dexterous in making your turns, were the cause, that an unusual number was put to death by the people when the oligarchy was demolished, and an unusual number put to death by the few when the democracy was again suspended. And this again is that very Theramenes, who, after the seafight on the coast of Lesbos, being ordered by the commanders to fetch off their countrymen from the wrecks, never executed that order, and yet accused those very commanders, and got them to be put to death, though merely to save himself. And what mercy ought ever to be shown to that man, who hath made it the business of his life to convince the world of his own selfishness of heart, and of his total disregard of his duty and his friends? And how cautiously ought we to behave, who are conscious of his unsteady shifting temper, that he may never be able to turn the tables upon us?

" We therefore charge him before you as a dangerous and subtle plotter, as a traitor to us and to you. That we act on just and cogent reasons, you will be convinced from hence—The polity of the Lacedæmonians is allowed by you all to be the finest in the world. Yet if any one of the ephori at Sparta, instead of conforming to the determinations of the body, should asperse their conduct and oppose their measures, can you think he would not be judged worthy of the severest punishment by all the rest of the ephori, and by the whole community? You therefore, gentlemen, if you are wise indeed, will have no mercy on him, but will have mercy on yourselves. For if Theramenes escapes with life, he will give fresh and higher spirits to many who are already your determined foes; but at once put to death, he will totally confound the hopes of all the factious either within the city or without."

Critias having spoke thus sat down. And Theramenes rising up made this defence :

" I shall, gentlemen, first reply to the finishing article of his charge against me. He says, it was I who accused and got the commanders to be put to death; but I did not begin the prosecution against them. It was pleaded by themselves in their own justification, that I was ordered to do it, and did not save the lives of our unhappy countrymen in the sea-fight near Lesbos. I was heard in my own defence; and, insisting on the impossibility of putting to sea, or fetching off the men because of the storm, was judged by all Athens to have spoken nothing but the truth. And so the charge of the commanders against me turned wholly upon themselves : for though, by their own confession, it was possible to save them, yet they sailed away with the fleet, and left them all to perish.

" I am not however surprised, that Critias hath violated the laws of equity. He was not at Arginusæ; he saw no part of the transactions there; but was at that time in Thessaly, assisting Prometheus to set up a democracy, and arming[1] vassals against their lawful superiors. His exploits in Thessaly were fine ones indeed! and grant Heaven we may never see the like in Athens!

" And yet in one point I entirely agree with him, that if any man endeavours to put an end to your administration, and to strengthen the hands of your determined enemies, he ought in all justice to suffer the severest punishment. And in my judgment, you yourselves, if you will only fix your recollection on what hath already been done, and what each of us are now doing, will be able most clearly to find out the man, on whom the guilt of such practices ought entirely to be fastened.

" So long therefore as the points in agitation were only these—to establish you, gentlemen, in the possession of the senate-house, to appoint proper magistrates for the state, and to rid the community of a notorious set of informers, we all of us proceeded in perfect unanimity. But when Critias and his faction began to apprehend the worthy and the good, I too began that moment to differ in sentiments with them. I was well convinced, when Leon of Salamis, who was reputed to be, and in reality was, a worthy

---

1 Τας Πανσας.

man, without being guilty of the least misdemeanor, was put to death, that all such persons as he would with reason be alarmed for themselves, and thus alarmed for themselves, must needs turn out enemies to the new administration. I was well assured, when Niceratus the son of Nicias was apprehended, a man of so large a fortune, and who had never dabbled in popular intrigues, nor his father before him, that all such men as Niceratus must needs conceive an aversion towards you. And again, when Antipho was put to death by you, Antipho, who during the war fitted out two ships that were excellent sailers at his own expense, I was firmly persuaded, that all men, who from pure generosity were desirous to serve their country must entertain suspicions of you. I also opposed, when they urged the necessity for each person to seize one of the sojourners residing in the city. For it was plain to me, that by putting these men to death, the whole body of sojourners must be made enemies to such an administration. I also declared my opposition to taking away their arms from the body of the citizens, judging, that we ought not in this manner to weaken our own community. I knew the Lacedæmonians could never intend, when they determined to save us, that we should be reduced so low as never again to be able to do them service. For had this been their scheme, it was once in their power to have left not one single Athenian alive, since famine in a little time would have done it for them. And I never could give my consent to take into pay these foreign guards, when we might have been supported by a competent number of honest Athenians, till by gentle methods we had brought those who were to be governed into quiet submission to us who were to govern. And when I perceived that numbers of men in Athens were actually become enemies to the new administration, and numbers of our countrymen were driven into exile, I could never approve that either Thrasybulus or Anytus or Alcibiades should be sent into exile after the rest. For I plainly saw that an accession of strength accrued to our enemies, when able heads were driven out to command the multitude, and numbers showed themselves ready to follow such as were willing to command them.

" Ought therefore the man who openly remonstrates aloud against such violent measures, to be esteemed an honest man or a traitor? You are mistaken, Critias. The persons who restrain you from increasing the number of your foes, who persuade you to enlarge to the utmost the number of your friends, can in no light be regarded as agents for your foes. By every rule of judging, that character belongs to others, to such as make plunder of the property of their neighbours, to such as unjustly put the innocent to death. Such men, beyond all contradiction, enlarge the number of our enemies; such men are traitors not only to their friends but even to their ownselves, for the sake of filthy lucre.

" But if you are not yet convinced that I speak the truth, consider it in another light. What set of measures, whether those which I recommend or those to which Critias and his faction adhere, do you think are most pleasing to Thrasybulus and Anytus and the rest of the exiles? For my own part, I am thoroughly persuaded, that this very moment they are confident that all the world is on their side. But were only the best families of Athens well affected to us, they would judge it difficult indeed to get the least footing anywhere within our borders.

" And now examine attentively with me the remaining part of his charge, that I have been for ever turning about.—It was the people of Athens, and they alone, who placed the government in the hands of the Four-hundred. They were convinced that the Lacedæmonians would trust to any form of government whatever sooner than the democracy. But, when after all they would not relax in their demands, and a factious parcel of our own commanders, such as Aristotle, Melanthius, and Aristarchus, were raising a work at the end of the pier, and with a manifest design to let the enemy in amongst us, and subject the state to themselves and others; —if I detected and put a stop to their scheme, am I therefore a traitor to my friends? He styles me indeed the Buskin, as if I endeavoured to fit both parties. And how then, good Heaven! must we style that man, who could never yet ingratiate himself with any party at all? When the democracy was in being, you, Critias, were judged the bitterest enemy the people ever had; and, during the aristocracy, you signalized your abhorrence of all good men. But I, good Sir! have ever been waging war against those who formerly thought a democracy never to be safe, till every slave and every scoundrel, who, to gain a drachma, would have sold the community, should have a share in the government for the price of a drachma;

and have as constantly signalized myself in opposition to those who think an oligarchy can never be safe, till they have enslaved the whole community to a small parcel of tyrants. Athens was then best constituted, when a competent number of citizens were ready to defend her with their horses and their shields. I thought so formerly: and this very moment I think the same. If you have any objections, Critias, tell these gentlemen on what occasion I ever attempted, in conjunction either with a factious populace or a small parcel of tyrants, to deprive any good and worthy Athenian of the right and privileges to which he had just pretensions. For in case I am convicted of doing so now, or ever to have done so in the former part of my life, I frankly own that death in its severity ought in all justice to be my doom."

Here Theramenes ended his defence: and a murmur, intimating their good-will to him, ran round the senate. Critias was convinced by this, that, should he suffer the senate to proceed to a vote, Theramenes would escape him. But, regarding this as worse than death to himself, after drawing near and conferring a while with the Thirty, he went out, and ordered those who had daggers about them, to go into the house and take their stand at the bar. And then, coming in again, he spoke as follows :

"Gentlemen of the senate, I reckon it the duty of a good magistrate, not to stand by quietly and suffer gross impositions to pass upon his friends: and it shall be my care at present to discharge that duty. For even those gentlemen, who now stand round the bar, declare they will never suffer us to let a man escape with impunity, who openly avows himself an enemy to the oligarchy. It is indeed enacted in the new body of laws, that no person in the list of the Three-thousand shall be put to death unless by a vote of the senate, but that the Thirty be empowered to put any to death who are not in that list. I therefore (he went on), with your entire approbation, strike the name of this Theramenes here out of the list; and we (he added) order him to be put to death."

Theramenes, hearing this, leaped upon the altar, and cried out :—

"I make to you, gentlemen of the senate, the most righteous request that ever can be made, by no means to suffer Critias to strike out my name or any of your names, at pleasure, but to adhere to the law which these very persons have enacted concerning those in the list,

that both I and yourselves may be judged according to the law. Of this, by Heaven! I am well persuaded, that even this altar will avail me nothing. But I would willingly convince you all, that these men are not only most unjust in regard to their fellow-creatures, but most irreligious too towards the gods. And yet I am surprised at you, men as you are of honour and worth, that you will not succour your ownselves, though so well aware that my name is not easier to be struck out of the list, than the name of any one amongst you."

But here the crier belonging to the Thirty ordered the Eleven [1] to go and seize Theramenes. Accordingly they came in, attended by their own servants, with Satyrus, the most reprobate and audacious fellow alive, at their head. Critias thus addressed himself to them— "We deliver over to you that Theramenes yonder, who by law is condemned to die. Seize him you whose office it is ; and then, convey him hence to the proper place, and do your duty. So soon as Critias had spoken, Satyrus was pulling him from off the altar, the servants too were helping to pull him down. Theramenes, as was likely he should, called aloud upon gods and men to take notice of what was doing. The senate continued quietly in their seats, seeing the bar surrounded by fellows like Satyrus, and the area before the senate-house quite filled with the foreign guards, not ignorant besides that those within had daggers about them. They hurried Theramenes away across the forum, in very loud lamentations deploring his fate. One thing he said is still talked of, and it is this—When Satyrus told him—" If he did not hold his tongue, he would make his heart ache,"—he replied—"But will not my heart ache, though I should hold my tongue ?" And at the time of his execution, when he had drank off the poison, they say he dashed the little that was left in the cup upon the ground, and said—" May the brave Critias pledge me !" I am not ignorant indeed, that such sententious escapes are not worth relating ; but this I think worthy of admiration in the man, that, in the very hour of death, neither his good sense nor his pleasantry forsook him. And in this manner Theramenes died.[2]

IV. The Thirty, as if they were now at li-

---

1 Public executioners of justice.

2 And soon after Alcibiades was murdered by Pharnabazus at the request of Lysander, owing entirely to the instigations of Critias.

berty to tyrannize without restraint, issued out an order to all whose names were not in the list, not to come into the city. They drove them also out of the country, that themselves and their friends might get into possession of their estates. It was to the Piræus that they went chiefly for refuge : but numbers of them, driven out also from thence, filled both Megara and Thebes with Athenian exiles.

Immediately after this it was that Thrasybulus, setting out from Thebes with about seventy persons in company, possesseth himself of the strong fort of Phyle. The Thirty marched immediately out of Athens to recover the place, attended by the Three-thousand and the horsemen of the state ; and the weather was very calm and fine. On their approach to Phyle, some of the younger sort, who piqued themselves on their bravery, immediately attacked the fort with no manner of success, since they were obliged to retire with plenty of wounds. But, the Thirty having formed a design to throw up a work, in order, by cutting off the conveyance of all necessaries, the more easily to reduce them, there fell in the night an exceeding deep snow. Next morning, having been well drenched by the snow, they marched back to Athens, after losing many of their baggage-men in the retreat by a party that pursued them from Phyle. Apprehensive too, that they would plunder the adjacent country, if a guard was not properly posted, they despatch almost all the Lacedæmonian guards and two troops of horse to the extremity of their frontier, about [1] fifteen stadia from Phyle : these, having encamped themselves on a rough spot of ground, set themselves on the watch.

But Thrasybulus, as now seven hundred persons were got together at [2] Phyle, put himself at their head, and marched out by night. Having ordered them to ground their arms [3] at

the distance of three or four stadia from the guard, he halted for a time. But at the approach of day, and the enemy beginning to get up and straggle on their necessary business from the camp, and the noise being heard which the grooms made in currying their horses, at this juncture the party under Thrasybulus recovered their arms, and came running in amongst them. They made some of them prisoners ; and put all the rest to flight, pursuing them to the distance of six or seven stadia. They slew more than one hundred and twenty of the heavy-armed, and Nicostratus (who was called the handsome) of the horsemen : two other horsemen they had seized in their beds. After quitting the pursuit and erecting a trophy, they packed up all the arms and baggage they had taken from the enemy, and marched back to Phyle. The horsemen who marched out of Athens to succour their brethren, were too late to gain the sight even of a single foe. They continued however in the field, till their relations had carried off the dead, and then withdrew into the city.

The Thirty, who now apprehended that their power began to totter, bethought themselves of securing Eleusis, that, when things were at the worst, they might be sure of a place of shelter. Having therefore issued out orders to the Athenian horse to attend, Critias and the rest of the Thirty repaired to Eleusis ; where, having ordered out to a review the horsemen of Eleusis, pretending they must know exactly how many they were

---

1 One mile and a half.

2 Marginal reading of the Paris edition, 1625.

3 This passage, with two others cited below, justifies the English translation *ground their arms*. I am persuaded it ought always to be so translated, when the Greek phrase Θέμενος τὰ ὅπλα stands simply and absolutely by itself ; for ἐπὶ τὴν γῆν or something like it is in this case understood. The addition indeed of another or of more words may vary the meaning. But in these passages the context determines the meaning beyond a doubt. Need it be mentioned, that when soldiers halt or are upon a guard, it easeth them much to ground their arms, the men sometimes standing, sometimes lying down in their ranks, nay sometimes walking about, yet, if discipline be alive, to no greater distance than to be able, on the most sudden alarm, to fall

again into their ranks, and recover their arms. But to the point in hand :

Thrasybulus under favour of the dark is got undiscovered within three or four stadia of the enemy. The better to direct his attack he waits for daylight ; and in the meantime to ease his men and preserve their vigour for action, Θέμενος τὰ ὅπλα ἡσυχίαν εἶχεν—but at daylight ἀναλαβόντες τὰ ὅπλα—προσήκιντον.

See farther p. 387, where the action is rather more distinct, for the men only ground their shields and not their spears or javelins, τοὺς μετ' αὐτοῦ Θέσθαι κέλευσας τὰς ἀσπίδας, καὶ αὐτὸς Θέμενος, τἆδ' ἄλλα ὅπλα ἔχων—ἔλεξεν. And when the speech is ended, the corresponding phrase soon occurs, ἀνέλαβε or ἀνέλαβον τὰ ὅπλα.

See also book vii. near the end, where Epaminondas is preparing for the battle of Mantinea—ἔθετο τὰ ὅπλα, ὥστε οἴεσθαι στρατοπεδευομένῳ. This could never be standing to their arms, which could not have imposed upon the enemy. But he ordered the arms to be grounded, as if he was going not to fight but to encamp. The enemy observed the action and was deceived, for Epaminondas soon saw his opportunity—τότε δὴ ἀναλαβὼν παραγγείλας τὰ ὅπλα—and began the attack.

and how many more were wanting to garrison the place, they commanded them all to give in their names; and each person, so soon as his name was taken down, was ordered to go through the wicket to the sea. They had posted their own horse on either side of the wicket upon the beach; and the servants seized and bound every Eleusinian as he came out of the wicket. And, when all of them were bound in this manner, they ordered Lysimachus, who commanded the horse, to deliver them into the custody of the Eleven. Next day they assembled in the Odeum the heavy-armed in the list and the rest of the horsemen, where Critias rose up, and addressed them thus: "We, gentlemen, are settling a new form of government for your benefit as much as for our own. You therefore are obliged, as you will share the honours, to take an equal share in all the dangers. You must therefore sentence to death the Eleusinians whom we have secured, that both in your hopes and in your fears you may be united with us."—Then, having pointed out a certain spot, he ordered them to give their ballots in the presence of all the assembly. But the Lacedæmonian guards were this moment drawn up under arms so as to fill half the Odeum. Yet even this behaviour was not displeasing to some citizens of Athens, to such as had no regard for any thing but their own-selves.

The number of those who had gathered together at Phyle was now increased to a thousand: and Thrasybulus, putting himself at their head, marcheth by night into the Piræus. No sooner had the Thirty intelligence of it than in person they sallied out against them with the Lacedæmonian guards, the horsemen, and the heavy-armed. They took their march along the cart-way that goes down to the Piræus. Those from Phyle for some time attempted to stop their approach. But as so large a compass of ground was judged to require a very large number of men to guard it, and themselves were few indeed, they wheeled off by regular bodies into Munychia. Those from the city immediately repaired into the forum of Hippodameia, where having formed into regular order, they afterwards filled up the way that leads to the temple of Diana in Minuchia and to the Bendideum. They were in depth not less than fifty shields; and, thus drawn up, they were mounting the ascent. But those from Phyle likewise filled up the road, though

they were not more than ten heavy-armed in depth. The targeteers and light-armed darters were posted behind them, and behind these were the slingers. The latter were numerous indeed, since now they were in a way of continual increase. But during the enemy's approach, Thrasybulus ordered his men to ground their shields: and, having laid down his own, though keeping the rest of his arms, he placed himself in the midst of them, and harangued them thus:

"I am desirous, my fellow-citizens, to inform some of you, and put the rest in mind, that of yonder body now approaching to fight us, those posted on the right are the very people whom you beat and pursued but five days ago. But those in the extremity of the left are the Thirty, who have deprived us, though guilty of no offence at all, of our rights and liberties, have driven us from our houses, and by an illegal sentence stripped our dearest friends of all their property. But now we have them fast, where they expected never to have been found, and we have continually been praying to find them. With arms in our power we are now drawn up and face them. All the heavenly powers know we have been seized upon during the hours of repast, and the hours of repose, and our peaceable walks upon the forum: and that some of us, so far from having offended at all, and not even residing in the city, have been doomed to exile; and all these heavenly powers at present declare themselves on our side. For instance, in the finest weather they raise a storm, when it serves our cause; and, when we give the assault to a more numerous body of our foes, they have enabled us, though but a handful of men, to erect our trophies. And now they have led us to a spot of ground, in which the enemy cannot throw their darts or javelins over the heads of the heavy-armed in their own front, because they are mounting an ascent; whilst ourselves, who are to throw our javelins and darts and stones down-hill, shall reach them at every throw, and shall wound numbers. It was but reasonable to judge we should have been obliged to engage the heavy-armed in their van on level ground; but now, if you will only throw your weapons in the proper and judicious manner, the way is so crowded with them that every weapon must do execution, and they have no defence left but to be skulking perpetually under their shields. Disabled thus from seeing their assailants, we shall have opportunities to strike at our own discretion, and of driving each fighting man from his rank.

"But you, my fellow-citizens, should act with the full conviction, that each man amongst you must personally earn the victory at present: for that victory, if heaven awards it us, will instantly restore us our country and our habitations, and our liberty and our honours, and to some amongst us our children and our wives. Happy men indeed will such of us be, as, after the victory, shall see the sweetest day that men can live. And blessed will he be too who dies in the struggle: for all the wealth in the world cannot purchase so noble a monument as will be that man's portion. I myself, at the proper time, shall begin the pæan; and when we have invoked the god of battle, then with one heart and all our hands united, let us revenge ourselves on yonder men for all the wrongs they have made us suffer."

After this harangue, he returned again to his post, and stood quietly facing the enemy; for the soothsayer had strictly enjoined him, " in no wise to begin the attack before one of their own people was either killed or wounded.—So soon as ever that happens, we ourselves (said he) shall lead you forwards. The consequence to you will be victory, and death to me, if I prophesy right." He was no false prophet: for, the moment they recovered their arms, he jumped out of the rank, like a man hurried by divine impulse; and, rushing among the enemy, dies in a moment, and was buried at the ford of the Cephissus. His friends obtained a victory, and carried their pursuit down into the plain.

Critias and Hippomachus of the Thirty, and Charmidas the son of Glauco, one of the ten governors of the Piræus, and others to the number of seventy, lost their lives in the engagement. The conquerors plundered them of their arms, but stripped off the garment from none of their fellow-citizens. And when all was over, and they had granted a truce for fetching off the dead, they began to approach and confer with one another, till at length Cleocritus, herald of the Mystæ, remarkable for the loudness of his voice, proclaimed silence, and spoke as follows:

" What is the reason, my fellow-citizens, that you drive us from Athens? What is the reason you are so intent on destroying us? On no occasion whatever have we done you any wrong, but have ever shared along with you the most solemn temples, the most pompous sacrifices and feasts. We have assisted in the same choruses, we have walked in the same processions, we have served in the same armies, and have partaken the same dangers with you both by sea and land, in defence of the common safety and liberty of us all. I conjure you, therefore, by our parental gods, by the ties of affinity, consanguinity, and friendship, (for in all these respects we are many of us connected together)—I conjure you to show some reverence both to gods and men, by ceasing to sin against your country, and by no longer obeying these execrable tyrants, who for their own private gain have nearly slain as many citizens of Athens in the space of eight months, as all the Peloponnesians slew in ten years' war. We might have lived together in an orderly and peaceable manner; but these tyrants oblige us to make war upon one another—a war, the basest, the most grievous, most impious, and most abominated by gods and men, that human creatures were ever engaged in. But know, for most true it is, that some of those persons who died by our hands in the late engagement, have cost abundance of tears to ourselves as well as to you."

In this manner Cleocritus spoke; but the commanders on the other side, and the sooner too for having heard such a speech, marched away their people into the city.

The day following, the Thirty, solitary and quite dejected, took their seats in council : but the Three-thousand, wheresoever posted, were at variance one with another. So many of them as had committed any acts of violence, and were now alarmed for their own safety, declared in a vehement tone against submission in any shape to those in the Piræus. But as many as were conscious they had done no harm, immediately saw matters in a true light, and were persuading the rest, that " the present evil situation was not in the least conducive to their welfare." They insisted "it was no longer their duty to obey the Thirty, nor suffer them to destroy their country." And at last they passed a decree to put an end to the Thirty, and elect others. Accordingly they chose Ten, one out of every tribe. The Thirty went off immediately to Eleusis : but the Ten, as the city was full of confusion and mutual diffidence, applied themselves to preserve the peace, with the aid of the generals of the horse. The horsemen, with both horses and shields, passed the night in the Odeum. Distrustful as they were, they patroled from the beginning of night towards the walls with their shields, and when it was near day on horseback, being under continual apprehensions, lest a body of men from the Piræus might break in amongst them. The latter, as they were now become exceeding numerous, and a collection of all sorts of persons, were busy in making themselves shields of wood or the twigs of osier, and these were afterwards whitened. Yet before ten days were passed, proper security being given that "whoever would join them in arms, even though they were not natives of Athens, should be admitted to an equal share of right and privilege," many of the heavy-armed, and many of the light-armed too, went off to the Piræus. Their horsemen also were now increased to the number of seventy. In the day-time they went out to forage, and having fetched in wood and the fruits of the season, reposed themselves by night in the Piræus. Not one of the heavy-armed in the city sallied out against them; but the horse came once to a skirmish with the plundering parties from the Piræus, and threw the body that covered them into disorder. Another time they fell in with some [1] persons of the borough of Æxone, going to their own lands to fetch provisions, and took them prisoners; and these Lysimachus, one of the generals of horse, immediately butchered, though they begged hard for their lives, and many of the horsemen expressed an abhorrence at putting them to death. And those in the Piræus retaliated upon them, by butchering in like manner Callistratus of the horse of the Leontine tribe, whom they took prisoner in the country. For now their spirits were raised so high that they even gave an assault to the walls of the city. And here it may be excusable to mention a mechanic of the city, who, becoming well assured that the enemy would place their battering machines in the course that goes out of the Lyceum, ordered all the carts to load with single stones, and throw them down at their own discretion in the course. For when this was performed, the removal of each of these stones gave the enemy a deal of trouble.

Ambassadors were now sent away to Lacedæmon, not only by the Thirty from Eleusis,

but by those in the list from Athens, who entreated their speedy aid, since the people had revolted from the Lacedæmonians. Lysander, reasoning with himself that "a siege both by land and sea must quickly reduce the enemy in the Piræus, if they were deprived of all future supplies," exerted himself so effectually, that a hundred talents [2] were advanced by way of loan for this service, and himself was ordered to go and command by land, and his brother Libys by sea. He himself went off immediately to Eleusis, where he collected into a body the heavy-armed from Peloponnesus. Libys in the meantime kept so strict a watch at sea, that not one boat with provisions could get into the Piræus. By this means those in the Piræus were soon distressed by famine, whilst those in the city were greatly animated by the coming of Lysander.

When affairs were in this situation, Pausanias, king of Sparta, envious of Lysander, since, if he succeeded now, his glory would be greater than ever, and Athens would become entirely his own, obtained the consent of three of the ephori, and proclaims a foreign expedition. All the confederates put themselves under his command, except the Bœotians and Corinthians, who alleged that "they could not, in any consistence with their oaths, make war against the Athenians, who had broken no one article of the peace." The true motive of their refusal was their own persuasion, that the Lacedæmonians designed to get possession of all Attica, and to make it a province of their own. Pausanias, however, encamped the army near the Piræus at Halipedum. He himself commanded in the right, and Lysander with the mercenary troops had the left. He sent ambassadors to those in the Piræus, commanding them "to separate and be gone." But as they refused compliance, he proceeded to an assault, to the noise of one at least, that he might conceal his real design to save them: and, when no advantage could be gained by such an assault, he again retired.

The day following, putting himself at the head of two Lacedæmonian brigades and three troops of the Athenian horse, he marched down to the Still Harbour, examining in what manner a circumvallation might be thrown up quite round the Piræus. But, in his return to the camp, as some of the enemy sallied out upon

---

[1] Τῶν ἐξ τῶν in the Greek; but I translate it Αἰξωνέων, according to the reading of Palmerius.

[2] 20,050l.

him and retarded his march, he grew angry, and ordered the horse to ride out upon them, and the first class of Spartans to advance with the horse, whilst himself followed with the rest of his force. They slew about thirty of the light-armed, and pursued the rest to the theatre in the Piræus. All the targeteers happened to be drawn up there in arms, and the heavy-armed too of the Piræus. The light-armed sallied out in a moment against the enemy; they were poising, were throwing, were shooting, were slinging. The Lacedæmonians, as numbers of them were wounded, unable to withstand the attack, gave ground. Their enemies, perceiving this, plied upon them more briskly than ever. Here Chæron and Thibracus, both of them general officers, are slain; Lacrates also, an Olympic victor, and other Lacedæmonians, who are buried in the Ceramicus near the gates. Thrasybulus saw what was doing, and with the rest of the heavy-armed marched to the aid of his own people: and they were soon formed eight deep before the light-armed. But Pausanias, who was greatly .distressed, and had already retreated four or five stadia to some rising ground, sent orders to the Lacedæmonians and the rest of the confederates to march up to him: and then, having drawn his whole army into a very deep and compact body, he led them against the Athenians. The latter stood the shock; but some of them were soon driven into the mud at Alæ, and some took to flight. About a hundred and fifty of them were slain: and Pausanias, after erecting a trophy, marched away to his camp.

He was not after all this exasperated against them: but, secretly sending his emissaries amongst them, instructs those in the Piræus "to address themselves by an embassy to himself and the ephori with him, with such and such proposals." They followed his instructions. He raiseth farther a division in the city, and orders as large a number of them as could be got together to repair to his camp with a remonstrance, that "they saw no reason at all to continue the war against those in the Piræus, but they ought to be reconciled, and all parties unite in being friends to the Lacedæmonians." Nauclides, one of the ephori, heard this remonstrance with pleasure; for, since by the laws of Sparta two ephori must accompany the king in the field, and he himself and another person were now attending in that capacity, both of them were more in the sentiments of Pausanias than in those of Lysander. For this reason, therefore, they readily despatched away to Lacedæmon the ambassadors from those in the Piræus, (who carried with them the articles agreed upon in relation to the Lacedæmonians,) and some persons without a public character from those in the city, besides Cephisophon and Melitus. After these were set out for Lacedæmon, those who had now authority in the city sent a deputation after them, declaring that "they actually surrender the walls that are yet in their power, and their own persons, to the Lacedæmonians at discretion; but they think it reasonable that they in the Piræus, if they pretend to be friends to the Lacedæmonians, should also surrender to them the Piræus and Munychia." The ephori and council of state, having heard all sides, despatched fifteen persons to Athens, and ordered them, in concurrence with Pausanias, to complete the reconciliation on the most honourable terms that could be made. They completed it on these; that "they should be at peace with one another: should on each side repair to their own habitations, except the Thirty and the Eleven, and the Ten who had commanded in the Piræus:—but in case any of those in the city were afraid to continue there, they might withdraw to Eleusis."

All points being now adjusted, Pausanias disbanded his army; and they of the Piræus, marching up under arms into the citadel, sacrificed to Minerva. But when the commanders were come down again from the citadel, Thrasybulus spoke as follows:

"To you, Athenians, who have been of the party in the city, I give this advice, that you would know your ownselves. This knowledge you will readily gain, if you will reflect, for what reason you took so highly upon you as to attempt to make us your slaves. Are you men of more integrity than we? Why, the body of the people, poor indeed as they are in comparison with you, have never for money done you any injury: but you, who have more wealth than all the people put together, from the mere motives of avarice, have done many scandalous injuries to them. Since therefore the plea of integrity cannot avail you, consider another. Have you taken so highly upon you, because you are men of greater bravery? Why, what clearer decision can be made of this point, than the manner we have warred upon

ıe another? But it is wisdom, you may say,
which you excel. You had fortifications,
ju had arms, you had wealth, you had besides
ıe Peloponnesians for your confederates, and
:t have been overpowered by men, who had
one at all of these advantages. Yet perhaps
ju took so highly upon you, because the La-
:dæmonians were your friends?—But how?
Vhy, as men fasten ª biting curs by a collar,
ıd give them up to those they have bitten,
ıst so the Lacedæmonians, after giving up you
ɔ an injured people, have rid themselves of you
nd are gone. Far be it however from me,
Athenians, to excite any of you to a violation
ı any degree of the oaths you have sworn. I
ınly exhort you to show all mankind, that, be-

ª "Ωσπερ οἱ τοὺς δάκνοντας κύνας κλοίω, marg. reading,
Paris Ed. 1625.

sides all your other glories, you can keep your
oaths, and be religiously good."

Having spoken thus, and said a great deal
more, about refraining from giving any farther
disturbance to one another, and adhering firmly
to their ancient laws, he dismissed the assembly. Having next appointed a new set of
magistrates, the government went regularly
forwards. But hearing some time after, that
those at Eleusis were taking foreigners into
pay, they marched against them with the whole
force of the city, and slew the commanders when
they came out to parley. They sent their
friends and relations amongst the rest to persuade them to a reconciliation. At length,
having sworn to one another that "they would
never remember grievances," they do to this
day live quietly together, and the people stand
firm to their oaths.

THE
AFFAIRS OF GREECE.

BOOK III.

.

3 D

CONTENTS of BOOK III.

AFFAIRS OF GREECE.

BOOK III.

I. THE sedition at Athens was in this manner brought to an end.

After this, Cyrus sent envoys to Lacedæmon, and demanded that "as he had behaved towards the Lacedæmonians in the war against the Athenians, so now the Lacedæmonians should behave towards him." The ephori, acknowledging the equity of his demand, sent orders to Samius, who was at this time admiral of their fleet, "to do all the service in his power to Cyrus." Samius accordingly performed with cheerfulness whatever Cyrus desired of him. For, having joined his own fleet with that of Cyrus, he sailed round to Cilicia, and disabled Syennesis, governor of Cilicia, from giving any molestation by land to Cyrus in his march against the king. Yet in what manner Cyrus drew an army together, and conducted the expedition against his brother, and how the battle was fought, and how Cyrus lost his life, and how afterwards the Greeks retreated safe to the sea, hath been written by Themistogenes the Syracusan.[1]

But now when Tissaphernes, who was judged to have done the king excellent service in the war against his brother, was sent down again to be governor of the provinces he himself had governed before, and of those also which had belonged to Cyrus, he immediately insisted that all the cities of Ionia should acknowledge him for their master; but these, from a desire to be free, added to their dread

of Tissaphernes, with whom they had never acted, but had always joined Cyrus so long as he was living, refused to receive him within their walls. On the contrary, they despatched away ambassadors to Lacedæmon, representing there, that "as the Lacedæmonians are the ruling state in Greece, they were bound to take under their protection the Greeks in Asia, that their lands might not be ravaged and they might still be free." The Lacedæmonians therefore sent Thimbro to take upon him the command, having assigned him a thousand soldiers of those who were newly enfranchised and four thousand other Peloponnesians. Thimbro desired farther to have three hundred horse from the Athenians, promising that he himself would take care to pay them. They sent him that number, composed of such persons as had served in the cavalry under the Thirty, judging it clear gain to the people, if these were sent into a foreign country and perished there.

When these were arrived in Asia, Thimbro further drew the troops together that belonged to the Greek cities on that continent. For all those cities readily obeyed, as a Lacedæmonian was now in the command. And yet with all this army, Thimbro would not march down into the plains: he was awed by the enemy's horse, and contented himself to preserve the country where he was from devastation. But when those who had been in the expedition with Cyrus were safely returned, [2] and had joined his army, he ever after that drew up boldly in the plains against Tissaphernes. He became master

---

[1] There is no such history now to be met with. So fine a subject no doubt excited others to write as well as Themistogenes. But Xenophon only was equal to the task of penning his own achievements. It seems probable from hence that he had not yet written or at least not finished his own history of the Anabasis.

[2] Under the command of Xenophon himself.

of some cities; of Pergamus, by voluntary surrender; of Teuthrania also and Alisarnia, which belonged to Eurysthenes and Procles, the descendants of Demaratus the Lacedæmonian; for this country had been given to Demaratus by the king in requital for his serving with him in the invasion of Greece. Gorgio also and Gongylus came over to him. They were brothers; and one of them was master of Gambrium and Palægambrium, the other of Myrine and Grynium. These cities also were a present from the king to Gongylus, the only person who had been exiled from Eretria for his attachment to the Medes. There were cities too, which because of their weakness Thimbro reduced by storm. Yet he was obliged to encamp before Larissa, which is styled the Ægyptian, and besiege it in form, because it would not hearken to any capitulation. And when he could not reduce it by other methods, he sunk a deep pit, from whence he continued a subterraneous trench, with a design to draw off their water. But as the besieged by frequent sallies from the walls filled up the pit with pieces of timber and stones, he built a wooden penthouse and placed it over the pit. And yet the Larisseans, who made a sudden sally in the night, set fire to this penthouse and burnt it to ashes. As he was now judged to be doing nothing, the ephori sent him an order to raise the siege and march into Caria. But, when he was got to Ephesus in order to begin that expedition, Dercyllidas came with orders to supersede him in the command; a man in high reputation for the subtlety of his genius, and for that reason known by the name of Sisyphus. Thimbro therefore departed for Sparta, where he was fined and sent into exile, since the confederates preferred an accusation against him, for permitting his soldiers to plunder their friends.

Dercyllidas was no sooner in the command, than knowing that Tissaphernes and Pharnabazus were suspicious of each other, he had an interview and made a private bargain with the former, and then led off his army into the country of Pharnabazus, choosing rather to make war against one of them singly than against both of them at once. Besides this, Dercyllidas had been of long time an enemy to Pharnabazus. For having been commandant at Abydus whilst Lysander was admiral of the fleet, a complaint had been made against him by Pharnabazus, for which he was obliged to stand holding his shield. By all Lacedæmonians of spirit this is reckoned high disgrace, as it is the punishment for breach of discipline. And for this reason he marched with more pleasure to himself against Pharnabazus. He soon convinced the world, that he was a much better man for command than Thimbro; for, as he marched his army through a friendly country all the way to Æolia that belonged to Pharnabazus, he did no damage at all to the confederates.

Æolia indeed belonged to Pharnabazus; but one Zenis, a Dardan, so long as he lived, had been governor of the province under him. But when Zenis was carried off by sickness, and Pharnabazus was preparing to dispose of the government to another person, Mania the wife of Zenis, who also herself was a Dardan, having got her equipage in order, and taken money with her to make presents to Pharnabazus, and to gratify his mistresses and favourites, performed her journey, and being admitted to an audience, addressed him thus:

" My husband, Pharnabazus, was in other respects your hearty friend, and was punctual in the payment of his tributes. For this you gave him praise, and you gave him honour too. If therefore I myself can serve you in no worse a manner than he did, why should you appoint any other person to command the province? If indeed I should not answer your expectations, it will be always in your power to remove me, and to bestow the government upon another."

Pharnabazus, having heard her, determined that the lady should be governante of the province. And when she was settled in it, she paid the tributes with as much punctuality as her husband had paid them; and besides that, whenever she waited upon Pharnabazus, she constantly brought him presents. Nay, whenever he came into her province, she entertained him in a more generous and elegant manner than any of his sub-governors. All the cities that originally belonged to her district she kept firm in their obedience, and enlarged the number by the acquisition of some on the sea-coast; for instance, of Larissa, Hamaxitus, and Colonæ. She assaulted these high places with troops she had hired from Greece. Seated in a high chariot she viewed every attack, and was remarkably liberal in her gratuities to those whom she had a mind to distinguish for their good behaviour; and by this means was become mistress of a most splendid body of mercenaries. She even took the field in com-many with Pharnabazus, whenever he invaded the Mysians or Pisidians, for committing hostilities on the dominions of the king. Pharnabazus in return loaded her with honours, and on some occasions gave her even a seat in his council. She was now above forty years of age, when Midias, her daughter's husband, buoyed up by some of his flatterers, who represented " how base it was that a woman should rule and himself be only a private person," whilst she was on her guard against all the world beside, as people in such invidious stations must necessarily be, but had an entire confidence in, and even a fondness for him, as much as a mother-in-law can have for her daughter's husband,—this Midias, I say, is reported to have stolen into her chamber and strangled her. He also put her son to death, who was a most beautiful youth, and not above seventeen years of age. And after these murders he took possession of Scepsis and Gergis, two fortified cities, in which Mania had reposited the greatest part of her treasures. The other cities would not submit to him, but the garrisons within preserved them for Pharnabazus. Midias after this sent presents to Pharnabazus, and solicited the government of the province which had belonged to Mania. He was ordered to keep his presents, " till Pharnabazus came in person to take into his custody both the presents and the sender." For he declared " he would either lose his life, or be revenged for Mania."

At this very time Dercyllidas arrives; and immediately, in one and the same day, was master, by their voluntary surrender, of the cities on the coast, Larissa, Hamaxitus, and Colonæ. He also sent round to the Æolian cities, insisting upon it, that they should assert their freedom, should receive him within their walls, and become confederates. Accordingly, the Neandrians and Ilians and Cocylitans obeyed the summons; for, as these cities were garrisoned by Grecians, they had not been well dealt with since the death of Mania. But the commandant of Cebren, who found himself at the head of a garrison in a well fortified town, had judged that, in case he preserved the town for Pharnabazus, he should be nobly recompensed for it, and therefore refused to receive Dercyllidas. Exasperated at this refusal, Dercyllidas prepared for an assault. But when on the first day's sacrifice the victims were not favourable, he sacrificed again the day after.

And when nothing appeared favourable at this second sacrifice, on the third day he sacrificed again. Nay he continued to do so four days together, though inwardly very much dissatisfied. He was eager to compass the reduction of all Ætolia, before Pharnabazus could come up to its succour.

One Athenadas of Sicyon, who commanded a company of heavy-armed, took it into his head, that Dercyllidas trifled sadly on this occasion, and that he himself could cut off the water of the Cebrenians. Running up therefore with his own company, he endeavoured to fill up their fountain. But the inhabitants, sallying out against him, wounded Athenadas, killed two of his men, and sometimes fighting close and sometimes at a distance, entirely repulsed them. Whilst Dercyllidas was fretting at this incident, and judged it might slacken the ardour of the assault, the heralds of the Greeks came out from the wall, and assured him " they did not concur in the behaviour of their commander, but chose rather to be along with their countrymen than along with a Barbarian." Whilst they were yet speaking, a messenger came also from the commandant, declaring that " what the heralds said was his own sense of things." Dercyllidas therefore the next day, for he had now sacrificed with favourable signs, ordered his soldiers to their arms, and led them towards the gates. They threw open the gates, and gave them admittance. Having therefore fixed a garrison here, he marched immediately against Scepsis and Gergis.

But Midias, who expected Pharnabazus, and was even afraid of the inhabitants, sent a message to Dercyllidas, and assured him, that " if he would give him hostages, he would come out to a conference." He immediately sent him one from each of the confederate cities, and bade him take which of them and as many of them as he pleased. Midias took ten of them, and came out. And now advancing to Dercyllidas he asked him, " on what conditions he might be a confederate?" He answered, " by leaving the inhabitants of the cities in a state of freedom and independence;"—and saying these words he moved forwards to Scepsis. Midias, sensible that if the inhabitants were willing to admit him he could not prevent it, suffered him to enter the city. Dercyllidas, after sacrificing to Minerva in the citadel of the Scepsians, made the garrison of Midias withdraw; and having delivered the city to the inhabitants, and exhorted them to behave for the future as Grecians and as freemen ought, he left it and marched towards Gergis. But many of the Scepsians, as they honoured the man and were highly pleased with his behaviour, accompanied his march. Midias further, who was still in company, begged him to leave in his custody the city of the Gergithians; to which Dercyllidas replied, that "he should have justice done him in every respect." And saying these words, he went up to the gates with Midias; and his army followed him by two and two in a most peaceful manner. The people on the turrets, which were exceeding lofty, as they saw Midias with him, threw not so much as a single dart. But when Dercyllidas said to him, "order the gates to be opened, Midias, that you may show me the way, and I go with you to the temple, and sacrifice to Minerva," here Midias boggled about opening the gates. Afraid however that he should instantly be put under arrest, he ordered them to be opened. Dercyllidas was no sooner in the town, than, with Midias still at his side, he went to the citadel. He ordered his soldiers to ground their arms round the walls, but with his own attendants he sacrificed to Minerva. When he had finished the sacrifice, he ordered the guards of Midias to go and ground their arms in the front of his own troops, as now taken into his pay, since Midias had no longer any thing to fear. Midias, however, who began to be in great anxiety, said to him, "I must leave you for the present, to go and get ready for you the hospitable feast."—"That is what I shall never permit," replied Dercyllidas, "since it would be base in me, who have offered the sacrifice, to accept of an entertainment from the man whom I ought to feast. Stay therefore here with us; and, whilst supper is preparing, let you and me confer together about what ought to be done, and then we will do it."

When the company was seated, Dercyllidas began with this question, "Tell me, Midias, did your father leave you in possession of all his substance?" "He did," said Midias. "And how many houses have you in all? how many fields have you? how many pastures?" Whilst he was reciting the particulars, some of the Scepsians who were present cried out, "He tells lies, Dercyllidas." "You need not insist," replied Dercyllidas, "on his being quite exact." When he had recited all his inheritance, "But

tell me," Dercyllidas went on, "whom did Mania belong to?" The whole company answered, "To Pharnabazus." "Then all she had belonged also to Pharnabazus?" "It did," was the general answer. "Therefore it now belongs to us," said Dercyllidas, "by right of conquest, for Pharnabazus is an enemy to us. And let somebody show me where the effects of Mania and Pharnabazus are lodged." Some persons led him directly to the house of Mania, which Midias had appropriated to his own use, and Midias himself followed. So soon as he entered the house, Dercyllidas called for the upper servants, and, having ordered his own people to take them into custody, he threatened them, that "if they were caught secreting any thing that belonged to Mania, they should be instantly put to death:" but they made a clear discovery. When he had surveyed the whole, he made all fast, clapped on his own seal, and appointed a guard. As he was coming out of the house, he saw many of his officers at the door, and said to them, "We have here a fine supply for the army; near a year's pay for eight thousand men; and if we can earn any more in good time, it will be so much the better." This he said purposely, concluding that all who heard him would observe discipline better, and would study more to oblige him. But Midias asking him now, "And where am I to live, Dercyllidas?" "Just where you ought," he replied, "in Scepsis, where you were born, and in the house you inherit from your father."

II. Dercyllidas, having so far acted with success, and taken nine cities in eight days, consulted with himself how he might avoid taking up his winter-quarters in a friendly country, lest he might be burdensome to the confederates, as Thimbro had been, and yet so that Pharnabazus might be sufficiently awed from harassing the Greek cities with his horse. He sends therefore to the latter, and asks him, whether he chose to have war or peace? Pharnabazus, reflecting that Æolia was now become a continued fortification against Phrygia, in which he himself resided, declared for a truce. And when the point was settled, Dercyllidas, marching into Bithynian-Thrace, passed the winter there; at which Pharnabazus was very little, if at all concerned, for these Bithynians were often making war upon him. In this country Dercyllidas spent his time, sending out parties who harassed all Bithynia, and furnished his quarters with necessaries in the most plentiful manner. And when about two hundred Odrysian horse, and about three hundred targeteers were crossed over from Seuthes to join him, they formed a separate camp, which they fortified with a circular work, at the distance of [1] twenty stadia from the camp of the Grecians: and having begged Dercyllidas to send them some of his heavy-armed to guard their camp, they went out for plunder, and took many slaves and valuable effects. When their camp was at length quite crowded with prisoners, the Bithynians, who had gained intelligence how many went out to plunder, and how many Grecians were left behind to guard their camp, having drawn together a vast body of targeteers and horsemen, about break of day rush upon the heavy-armed, who were about two hundred. At the first approach, some were throwing in their darts, others were tossing in their javelins amongst them. The defendants, who though amidst wounds and death could yet do nothing for their own preservation, shut up as they were within a work as high as their own heads, tore down an opening in it, and sallied out against them. But their enemies retreated before them at every sally, and being but targeteers, slipped with ease out of the way of men in heavy armour. But they still were galling them on their flanks with javelins, and struck many of them to the ground at every sally. In short, pent up as it were in a fold, they were slain by darts and javelins. Not but that about fifteen of this number escaped in safety to the camp of the Grecians: but these had wheeled off in time, when they first perceived the enemy's design, and, as in the hurry of engaging, the Bithynians had not attended to their motions, effected their escape. The Bithynians, after so much success and putting all the tent-keepers of the Odrysian-Thracians to the sword, marched quickly away, and carried off with them all the prisoners; so that the Grecians, who marched thither, so soon as they had notice of the affair, found nothing at all in the camp but naked dead. The Odrysians at their return, after interring their own dead, swallowing a great quantity of wine on the occasion, and solemnizing a horse-race, encamped themselves for the future along with the Grecians, and continued to lay Bythynia waste with fire and sword.

So soon as it was spring, Dercyllidas left Bithynia, and arrived at Lampsacus. Whilst he was there, Aracus, and Navates, and Antisthenes arrive from the magistracy of Sparta. They were commissioned to inspect the state of affairs in Asia, and notify to Dercyllidas that he must continue in the command another year. They had further been particularly enjoined by the ephori, to assemble all the soldiers, and tell them in their name, that " they had justly been displeased at their behaviour in former years; but as lately they had been guilty of no misbehaviour, they commended them for it: and, in regard to the time to come, to assure them, that "if they behaved amiss, they should find no connivance in them; but in case they behaved justly towards the confederates, they will give them all due commendation." When therefore they called an assembly of the soldiers and delivered their instructions,[2] the commander of those who had served under Cyrus made the following answer:

" We, for our parts, Lacedæmonians, are the very same persons now that we were the preceding year; but the commander-in-chief is quite another person now than he who commanded then. You are capable yourselves to discern the reasons, why we committed so many irregularities then, and commit none at all at present."

At an entertainment that Dercyllidas gave in his own quarters to the commissioners from Sparta, some persons, who belonged to the retinue of Aracus, let fall the mention of an embassy now at Sparta from the Chersonesus. It was said, they were representing at Sparta, that " they were not able to till the lands in the Chersonesus, where every thing was continually ravaged and plundered by the Thracians; but in case a fortification was raised from sea to sea, they should possess in security a great quantity of good land, enough for themselves and for all Lacedæmonians that would settle upon it." It was added, " they should not be surprised, if some Lacedæmonian was sent out by the state with a body of men to carry this work into execution." Dercyllidas, who listened to this discourse, discovered nothing at all of his present sentiments to the company, but sent away the commissioners through the Grecian cities to Ephesus.[1] He was delighted with the thought, that they would see those cities living happily in peace. The commissioners accordingly proceeded on their journey.

Dercyllidas, as he knew he was to continue another year in the command, sent once more to Pharnabazus and demanded—"whether he was for a truce, as during the last winter, or for war?" And Pharnabazus preferring at this time too a continuation of the truce, Dercyllidas, leaving all the confederate cities that were near to Pharnabazus in peace, passeth over the Hellespont into Europe with his army. And then, marching through the part of Thrace in friendship with him, where he was hospitably entertained by Seuthes, he arrives at the Chersonesus. Finding now that it contained eleven or twelve cities, was the best and most fruitful country in the world, though sadly ravaged, as was said before, by the Thracians, he measured the isthmus, and found it to be [2] thirty-seven stadia over. He lost no time, but after a sacrifice began to raise a fortification. He divided out the ground to the different parties of his army. He promised rewards to such as soonest completed the parts assigned them, and to all in proportion to their diligence. He began it in the spring, and before autumn he had completely finished the work. He inclosed within it eleven cities, many harbours, a large quantity of excellent ground for tillage, a large quantity too of plantations, and a vast number of the finest pastures for all sorts of cattle. And now he again repassed into Asia.

Taking here a survey of the cities, he found all well in every respect, except that the exiles from Chios had possessed themselves of Atarna, a strong town, and by incursions from thence were extending their ravages all over Ionia, and subsisting themselves by this practice. But learning that they had a great store of corn, he invested the place, and besieged it in form. And having in eight months reduced it to a surrender, and appointed Draco of Pellene to take care of the place, and filled the magazines in it with all kinds of stores, that it might supply him with every thing he wanted, whenever he came to Atarna, he marched for Ephesus, which is three days' journey from Sardis.

Till this time there had been peace between Tissaphernes and Dercyllidas, and also between the Grecians of those parts and the Barbarians. But when ambassadors from the Grecian cities had been at Lacedæmon, and had represented to the state, "that Tissaphernes, if he had a mind, might leave all the cities quite free and independent;" adding, that "in case a war was carried vigorously into Caria, where Tissaphernes resided, they judged he might soon be prevailed upon to leave them all in perfect liberty;" the ephori, after listening to these representations, sent over to Dercyllidas, and ordered him to march with his army into Caria, and Pharax, who commanded at sea, to attend the expedition with the fleet. They accordingly obeyed their orders.

But just at this time Pharnabazus was arrived on a visit to Tissaphernes, as well to compliment him on his being declared governor in chief over all, as to testify for himself that he was ready to concur in a general war, to join his troops with Tissaphernes, and drive the Greeks out of their master's dominions. But at the bottom he was sadly mortified at the pre-eminence given to Tissaphernes, and was also grieved at the loss of Æolia. Tissaphernes, after giving him the hearing, answered—" In the first place, therefore, come along with me into Caria, and there we will afterwards consult together about these other points." And when they were in Caria, they thought proper to place sufficient garrisons in all the fortified places, and then to proceed against Ionia.

When Dercyllidas had received intelligence that they had again passed the Mæander, he made known his fears to Pharax, lest Tissaphernes and Pharnabazus, finding no resistance in the country, might extend their devastations at pleasure; and then he immediately repassed the Mæander. His troops were advancing forward without any regular order, as judging the enemy to be got already on the lands of the Ephesians;[3] when on a sudden they discover from the opposite shore some of their scouts[4] mounted on the tombs. Upon which, climbing up themselves on the tombs and some turrets that were near, they had a view of their army drawn up in order of battle on the very ground they were to march over. It consisted of the

---

1 The text is ἀπ' Ἐφέσου, but I translate it according to Dr Taylor's reading ἐν Ἐφέσω.
2 Near four miles.
3 The marginal reading, πολεμίων εἰς τὴν Ἐφεσίαν.
4 For σκοπῶ read σκοποὺς.

Carians, distinguished by the name of Leucaspidæ, of all the Persian troops they had been able to draw together, of the Grecian troops in the pay of both these chiefs, and a very numerous cavalry, those belonging to Tissaphernes being posted in the right wing, those belonging to Pharnabazus in the left. When Dercyllidas saw this, he issued out his orders to the officers of the heavy-armed to draw them up eight in depth, and to post the targeteers, and the horse, as many and such as he had, upon the flanks; and then he offered sacrifice. All the troops from Peloponnesus observed on this occasion a deep silence, and prepared for battle. But of the men from Priene, and Achilleum, and the islands and the cities of Ionia, some ran instantly away, throwing their arms into the corn (for in the plains of Mæander the corn was very high), and such as were left showed plainly they would not stand. It was reported that Pharnabazus declared strongly for fighting. Tissaphernes, however, who recalled to his remembrance in what manner the Greeks under Cyrus had fought against them, and judged that all Greeks were men of the same spirit and resolution, would not be persuaded to fight. But sending to Dercyllidas he notified to him, that "he desired to meet and have a conference with him." Dercyllidas, taking with him such persons both of the horse and foot as made the finest appearance, advanced towards the messengers, and said—"I was ready here prepared for battle, as yourselves perceive: but since your master is desirous of a conference, I have nothing to object. Yet before the conference begins, we must receive and exchange securities and hostages." This point being agreed to and executed, the armies drew off; the Barbarian army to Tralles of Phrygia, and the Grecian to Leucophrys, where was a temple of Diana, held in high veneration, and a lake more than a stadium in length, of a sandy bottom, kept full by perpetual springs, its water fine for drinking and warm. And these were the incidents of the present day.

On the following day they met at the place of conference; and it was agreed on each side to propose the terms on which a peace should be made. Dercyllidas said, "it should be on condition the king would leave the Grecian cities entirely free." Tissaphernes and Pharnabazus answered, "on condition the Grecian army evacuates the dominions of the king, and the commandants from Lacedæmon do the same by the cities." On these conditions they made a truce, till the treaty could be reported for ratification, by Dercyllidas at Lacedæmon, and by Tissaphernes to the king.

Whilst Dercyllidas was thus employed in Asia, the Lacedæmonians, who had long been exasperated against the Eleans; [5] because they had entered into an offensive and defensive league with the Athenians, and Argives, and Mantineans; and because, on the pretext that themselves had not paid a fine set upon them, they had refused them a share in the equestrian and gymnic games; and not satisfied with this refusal, when Lichias had entered his chariot in the name of the Thebans, and they accordingly were proclaimed victors, because Lichias came forwards and crowned the charioteer, they scourged that venerable man, and expelled him the assembly; and later in time, when Agis had been sent in pursuance of an oracle to sacrifice to Jupiter, the Eleans would not suffer him to pray for a successful war, pretending it was an old established rule, that Grecians should not consult an oracle in relation to a war against their countrymen, on which account he was obliged to depart without sacrificing at all;—upon all these provocations, it was decreed by the ephori and the council of state, to "reduce them to a more submissive temper." They despatched therefore an embassy to Elis with the notification that "the regency of Lacedæmon had judged it equitable that the Eleans should leave all the cities adjacent to Elis in perfect liberty." The Eleans answering, "they would not do it, since they were masters of those cities by right of war," the ephori proclaimed an expedition against them.

Agis, who commanded the army, marched through Achaia, and entered Elea not far from Larissa. But the army being now in the enemy's country, and extending their devastations, an earthquake is felt. Agis, reckoning this an inhibition from heaven, retreated out of the country, and disbanded his army. After this the Eleans were in higher spirits than ever, and sent embassies round to every state whom they knew to be disaffected to the Lacedæmonians.

But the year after, the ephori again proclaim an expedition against Elis; and, excepting the Bœotians and Corinthians, all the con-

5 See Thucydides, Book V.

federates, nay, even the *Athenians*, attended with their troops in this army under *Agis*. As Agis entered now by the way of *Aulon*, the Lepreate revolted from the *Eleans* and immediately joined him. The Macystians soon did the same, and immediately after them the Epitalians. And, when he had passed the river, the Leprinians, and Amphidolians, and Marganians came over to him. After this, he went to Olympia, and sacrificed to Olympian Jove, no creature any longer endeavouring to stop him. After the sacrifice, he advanced towards Elis, putting all the country to fire and sword; nay, a vast number of cattle and a vast number of slaves were taken on this occasion. Very many of the Arcadians and Achæans, who had heard what was doing, flocked down to the army as volunteers, and got a share of the plunder. And this expedition was as it were a general forage for the benefit of Peloponnesus. But when Agis had reached the city, he destroyed the suburbs and the gymnasiums which were very splendid; yet as to the city itself (which was not fortified) the world judged it was not in his choice, rather than not in his power, to take it.

The country being thus destroyed, and the army being now in the neighbourhood of Cyllene, one Xenias and his accomplices, who, according to the proverb, were measuring their wealth before they had it, being desirous of securing Elis for the Lacedæmonians, rushed out from his house by night with daggers, and began a massacre. Amidst the number of those they put to death, they had killed a person very much resembling Thrasydæus, who was head of the popular party, and were persuaded they had killed Thrasydæus himself, insomuch that the people were quite dispirited, and made no resistance at all. The assassins now judged that all was secure; and their whole party were coming out in arms to join them in the market-place. In the meantime Thrasydæus was still sleeping in the house where he had been spending the evening. So soon therefore as the people knew he was not dead, they came flocking in crowds about the house, like a swarm of bees about their monarch. And when Thrasydæus had put himself at their head, and marched them up, a battle ensued, in which the people were victorious. But those who had been concerned in the assassinations made their escape to the Lacedæmonians. When Agis in his retreat had repassed the Alpheus, he left a garrison to be commanded by Lysippus, and the fugitives from Elis in Epitalium near the Alpheus; after which he disbanded the army, and returned to Sparta. But during the rest of the summer and the ensuing winter, the territory of the Eleans was exposed to the continuing ravage of Lysippus and his soldiers.

The summer after, Thrasydæus sent his agents to Lacedæmon, declaring his assent to a demolition of the fortifications, and to setting at perfect liberty Cyllene and the cities of Triphylia, Phrixa, and Epitalium, and Ladrin, the Amphidolians too, and the Marganians; adding to these the Acronians also and Lasium that was claimed by the Arcadians. The Eleans however insisted on still keeping Epeum, which is situated between the city of Heræa and Macisthus. They said, " they had purchased the whole district at the price of thirty talents[1] from the persons who at the time of the sale were possessed of the city, and had actually paid the money. But the Lacedæmonians, who knew the injustice was the same between forcing people to sell, or forcing them to quit their property, obliged them also to set Epeum at liberty. However they would not strip them of the privilege to be guardians of the temple of Olympian Jove, though it did not originally belong to the Eleans. They judged the people[2] who claimed it to be only a company of peasants, and not at all qualified for so important a trust. These points being settled, a peace and a confederacy ensued between the Eleans and the Lacedæmonians. And thus the war between the Lacedæmonians and the Eleans was brought to an end.

III. Agis after this repaired to Delphi, and offered up the tenth of the spoil. But in his return, since he was far advanced in years, he fell sick at Heræa, and being with some difficulty brought home alive, died soon after at Sparta, and was buried in too pompous a manner for mortal man. When the usual time of mourning was expired, and his successor to be declared, two competitors appeared—Leotychides, who called himself the son, and Agesilaus, who was the brother of Agis. Leotychides said,[3] The law, Age-

---

1 5812l. 10s.   2 The Pisans.

3 The text of Xenophon is, in the following dispute about the succession, very perplexed and certainly corrupt. In the translation I have made use of three various readings in the margin of the Paris edition by Leunclavius, 1625. But there is no marginal reading to help

silaus, expressly enjoins, that not the brother but the son of the king shall reign." "Yet, if there be no son," Agesilaus replied, "the brother reigns: the right therefore is in me." "What! is there no son, and I alive?" "None; because he whom you call your father never owned you for his son."[4] "But my mother, who knows the truth much better than he, protests that I am." "Yes, but then Neptune hath clearly proved that it is all a fiction, who by an earthquake drove your father abroad from cohabiting with her; and time itself, which is said to be the surest witness, joins evidence with Neptune, since you were born the tenth month after he separated from and had no cohabitation with her." In this manner they disputed. But Diopithes, who was a great dealer in oracles, supported the claim of Leotychides, and affirmed there was an oracle of Apollo, "which bade them be on their guard against a halting reign." Lysander, who favoured Agesilaus, replied, "That he did not imagine it was the sense of the oracle to put them on their guard against a king who was lame of a foot; but rather, that no person should reign who was not of the royal blood. For the kingdom would halt to all intents and purposes, when men ruled the state who were not of the race of Hercules." The Spartans, having thus heard the plea of both parties, chose Agesilaus for their king.

Agesilaus had not reigned a year, when, during his performance of a solemn sacrifice for the public welfare, the soothsayer told him, that "the gods showed him a conspiracy of the most dangerous kind." Upon his repeating the sacrifice, he affirmed that "the victims showed worse than before." But when he sacrificed a third time, he said, "It is plainly signified to me, that we are, Agesilaus, in the midst of enemies." They sacrificed afterwards to the gods who avert calamities or were guardians of the state; and the victims after several repetitions at length appearing favourable, they ceased. Within five days after the sacrifices, somebody gives the ephori information of a conspiracy, and that "Cinadon was the chief director of it." This Cinadon was a very handsome young man, of great solidity of mind, but not in the first class of Spartans. The ephori questioned the informer "on what grounds the plot was to be carried on?" He answered, that "Cinadon, drawing him aside in the farthest part of the forum, bade him count the number of Spartans who were then walking upon it. And I (said he) having counted the king, and the ephori, and the seniors, and about forty others, demanded, But why, Cinadon, did you bid me count them? Reckon these (he replied) to be enemies, but all others now upon the forum, who amount at least to four thousand, to be assuredly friends." He added, that "as they went along the streets, Cinadon pointed sometimes at one, and sometimes at a couple of enemies, but all others were firm accomplices; and on all the estates in the country belonging to Spartans, the master singly was an enemy, whilst all the people were their own.' The ephori then demanded, "what number of persons he told him were in the secret of the plot?" He answered, that "Cinadon told him, the number yet let into the design by the principal agents was not large, but were men on whom they could depend. Yet all agreed that the Helots, the new-enfranchised, those incapacitated by law from being magistrates, and the people in the neighbourhood of Sparta, were all ripe for a rebellion; since, whenever any discourse arose about the Spartans, not a soul amongst them could conceal the longing he had to eat them up alive." They asked him next, "By what methods they were to procure arms?" He answered, that "such as were already in the secret had told him—We ourselves are already

---

us out in the close, where this knotty expression occurs μὴ προσταίσας τὶς χωλύση.... The learned Dr Taylor hath favoured me with his sentiments upon it, to which I have paid a due regard in the translation. "The words, (he says) may possibly be mended by the help of Plutarch, who, in the Life of Lysander, reciting this story, has μὴ προσταίσας τὶς ἄρχη, and in that of Agesilaus μὴ προσταίσας τὶς βασιλύση; one of which words must be given here to Xenophon. For as the text stands, it is just as if he had said μὴ χωλύων τὶς χωλύση. Possibly χωλὸς may be added in the margin to explain προσταίσας (as being a more unusual word), and so was reduced to χωλύσης and jostled out the true word βασιλύση or ἄρχη. Or it may be thus; There wants no verb at all in this place. See how it runs, φυλάξασθαι μὴ προσταίσας τὶς, ἀλλὰ μᾶλλον μὴ οὐκ ὂν τοῦ γίνους, βασιλύση. Let us apply the words of Plutarch to the whole passage; Οὐ γὰρ ἢ προσταίσας τὶς τὸν πόδα βασιλύση τῷ Διῒ διαφέρον· ἀλλ' εἰ μὴ γνήσιος ὂν, μάδι Ἡρακλύδας, τοῦτο τὴς χωλὴν ἴσαι βασιλύαν. Plutarch in Agesil.

4 He is said to have been the son of Alcibiades, who during his residence at Sparta had an intrigue with Timæa. She was excessively fond of this gallant Athenian, and within doors always called this son Alcibiades. But Alcibiades was used to profess, that he carried on the intrigue with Timæa, not from any lewd or wanton motive, but only that his own posterity might reign at Sparta. Plutarch's Life of Alcibiades.

provided;—and in regard to the multitude, Cinadon had led him to the shops of the mechanics, and showed him many swords, many daggers, many spits, many hatchets and axes, and many scythes; adding farther on this occasion, that all the utensils which men employ in agriculture and the working of timber and stone were so many weapons, and even the tools used in most trades would serve the purpose, especially against enemies who had no arms at all." Being interrogated again, "in what time they were to put the plot in execution?" he said, "he had already received an order to keep in the way."

The ephori, having finished the examination, were persuaded he had discovered a deep-laid plot, and were terribly alarmed. Yet they summoned no meeting on this occasion even of the lesser council; but assembling some of the senior Spartans just as they could pick them up, they determined to send Cinadon to Aulon, accompanied by a party of the younger Spartans, to arrest and bring away some inhabitants of that city and some Helots, whose names he would find in his scytale. They also ordered him to bring away with him a woman, who was reported to be the greatest beauty in the place, but was thought to debauch all the Lacedæmonians, as well old as young, who frequented Aulon. Cinadon had executed some such orders of the ephori on former occasions, and readily took the scytale they gave him now, in which were the names of the persons he was to apprehend. But when he asked, "what youths he was to take with him?" "Go," they said, "and order the senior of the prefects of youth to send six or seven of his band along with you, of such as happen to be rt hand." They had taken care beforehand, that this prefect should know whom he was to send, and that the persons sent should know they were to secure Cinadon. They told Cinadon further, "they would send three carriages, that they might not bring away their prisoners on foot;" concealing from him as much as possible, that they only aimed at his single person. They would not venture to apprehend him in the city, as they did not know how far the plot might have spread, and were desirous to learn first from Cinadon himself who were his accomplices, before they would discover that any information was given against them, in order to prevent their flight. The party along with him were first to secure

him, and then getting out from him the names of his accomplices, to send them in writing in all haste to the ephori. Nay, so intent were the ephori on securing the point, that they also ordered a troop of horse to march with this party to Aulon.

But as soon as Cinadon was secured, and a horseman returned with the names that Cinadon had discovered, they instantly apprehended Tisamenus the soothsayer, and the most dangerous persons amongst the conspirators. And when Cinadon was brought to Sparta and examined, he confessed the particulars of the plot, and named all the persons concerned in it. At last they asked him, "With what view he had engaged in such a project?" His reply was, "That I might be inferior to no man in Sparta." Immediately after this he was tied neck and arms in the wooden collar, [1] and along with his accomplices was led round the city, being all the way scourged with rods and pricked with javelins. And thus they received the punishment inflicted by the laws. [2]

IV. After these transactions, one Herod a Syracusan, who was along with the master of a vessel in Phœnicia, and saw several Phœnician vessels arriving from other places, and more of them already manned where he was, and more still fitting out, and heard farther that they were to be completed to the number of three hundred;—this Herod took his passage on board the first vessel that sailed for Greece, and gave intelligence to the Lacedæmonians, that "the king and Tissaphernes were fitting out so great a fleet, but whither designed, he said, he had not discovered.' The Lacedæmonians were all in a flutter, and summoned a meeting of the confederates to consult what was to be done. Lysander, who reckoned that the Grecians would be far superior at sea, and remembered the fine retreat of his countrymen who had served in the expedition under Cyrus, persuades Agesilaus to engage, if they would assign him thirty noble Spartans, two thousand of such as were newly enfranchised, and a body of six thousand confederates, to carry the war into Asia. He had it farther in his intention to accompany Agesilaus in this expedition, that under his protection he might re-establish the forms of government consisting of ten persons, which himself

1 Κλοιῳ.
2 Leunclavius's marginal reading, μὸ δὲ τὰς ὕλαυς. . .

had set up in the cities, and the ephori had since abolished, who ordered them to return to their primitive models. Agesilaus having therefore offered to undertake the expedition, the Lacedæmonians, beside all the rest of his demands, granted him a six months' supply of corn. When he had performed his sacrifices, particularly the solemn ones usual before foreign expeditions, he set forwards. He had already by messengers circulated his orders to the confederate states, to what place they were to send their quotas, and in what number they were to be ready for him. For his own part, he intended to go and sacrifice at Aulis, as Agamemnon had done when he set out against Troy. When arrived at Aulis, the rulers of Bœotia, who heard he was sacrificing, sent thither a party of horse, who forbade his sacrificing any more, and threw off from the altar the victims he was offering at the time of their approach. Making loud appeals to heaven, and full of indignation, he went on board his ship, and put to sea. And after reaching Gerastus, and collecting together as large a number as he could of the troops assigned him, he crossed the sea at the head of the armament to Ephesus.

On his arrival at Ephesus, he was accosted by messengers from Tissaphernes, who demanded, "what was his business in Asia?" He replied, "To set the Greek cities in Asia in as perfect liberty as our own cities enjoy in Greece." The answer of Tissaphernes to this was—"If therefore you will come into a truce, whilst I send up to the king, I think I shall get that point settled so that you may go home again at pleasure." "I would agree to a truce," said Agesilaus, "was I not afraid that you will deceive me. But you shall have," he added, "what security you please from us, that if you solicit the point without fraud, we will refrain during the truce from doing any damage to the country under your government." This point being agreed to, Tissaphernes swore to Herippidas, Dercyllidas, and Megialius, who were sent to him for this purpose, that "without fraud he would procure a peace:" and they in return swore to Tissaphernes, in the name of Agesilaus, that "whilst Tissaphernes was employed in this negotiation, he would faithfully observe the truce." Tissaphernes swore, indeed, but immediately broke his oath. For instead of soliciting a peace, he sent to the king for a number of troops to reinforce the army he already had. But Agesilaus, though sensible of such behaviour, most steadily observed the truce.

Whilst Agesilaus was thus passing his time in a quiet and leisurely manner at Ephesus, there was high confusion in all the Greek cities of Asia, as the democracy, which had prevailed when they were under the Athenians, no longer existed, nor the administration of ten persons, which had been the establishment of Lysander. But, as every body there was acquainted with Lysander, they applied themselves to him, requesting his interest with Agesilaus to get their favourite forms established. And hence it was, that a prodigious crowd of people was constantly attending upon and paying court to Lysander, so that in short Agesilaus seemed only a private person, and Lysander looked like a king. What followed showed indeed that these things chagrined Agesilaus. The rest of the thirty Spartans were so filled with envy, that they could not refrain from giving it vent. They told Agesilaus, that "Lysander's behaviour was quite unjustifiable, since he assumed a pomp even too high for a king." But as soon as Lysander began to introduce them to Agesilaus, he dismissed with a flat refusal of their petitions all such as he knew were strenuously supported by Lysander. And as things were now taking a quite different turn to what Lysander expected, he soon discovered the cause. And then he no longer suffered such a crowd of people to pay attendance upon himself, and ingenuously owned to such as begged his support, that they would succeed the worse if he appeared in their favour. He took his disgrace to heart, and going to Agesilaus expostulated thus—"Are you then, Agesilaus, become an artist at lessening your friends?" "Upon honour, I am," he replied, "when they betray a design of appearing greater than myself. But I should blush indeed, if I was not as great a proficient in the art of honouring those who endeavour to promote my honour." "Why then I am convinced," said Lysander, "that your conduct is much easier to be justified than my own. But for the future, that I may avoid the disgrace of having no interest at all in you, and may be no obstacle to your personal glory, send me to some remote employ. For wherever I go, I will spare no pains to serve you." He made this proposal which Agesilaus approved, and sends him to Hellespont. When there, Lysander having made a discovery, that Spithridates the Persian had suffered some oppressions from Pharnabazus, gets a conference with him, and persuades him to revolt with his children, with his wealth, and about two hundred horse. He placed the rest of his people and his effects in Cyzicus, but set out himself on the journey, and conducted Spithridates and his son to Agesilaus. Agesilaus, when he knew the whole affair, was highly pleased, and immediately began his inquiries about the country and government that belonged to Pharnabazus.

But when Tissaphernes, highly animated by the army that came down to his assistance from the king, declared war against him, unless he evacuated Asia, the rest of the confederates and even the Lacedæmonians who were there, betrayed great signs of dejection, as they judged the force at present with Agesilaus was by no means a match for that of the king. Agesilaus however, with a countenance exceeding cheerful ordered the ambassadors to acquaint Tissaphernes, that "he had high obligations to him, since by perjuring himself he had got the gods for his enemies, and had made them friends to the Greeks." Immediately after this he issued out orders to his soldiers to get all things in readiness to take the field. He gave notice also to the cities, by which he must of necessity pass in the route towards Caria, to prepare their markets. He sent farther to the Ionians, and Æolians, and Hellespontines to march up their quotas that were to serve under him to Ephesus. Tissaphernes, therefore, because Agesilaus had no horse, and Caria was not a country proper for them, and because he judged him exasperated personally against himself for having deceived him, actually concluded that he would march into Caria to ruin the place of his residence. He therefore sent away all his infantry into Caria, but led his horse round into the plains of Mæander, accounting himself able with his horse alone to trample the Grecians under foot before they could reach that part of the country in which cavalry could not act. But Agesilaus, instead of taking the route of Caria, took instantly one quite contrary, and marched for Phrygia. He reduced the cities on his march, and by an incursion so entirely unexpected, he took an infinite quantity of most valuable spoil.

Hitherto he had seen no enemy at all. But when he drew near Dascylum, the horse in his van rode up to an eminence, that they might take a view of the country before them. It so happened that the horse of Pharnabazus, commanded by Rathines and Bancæus his bastard-brother, in number about equal to the Grecians, had been detached by Pharnabazus, and were riding up the same eminence that very moment. Thus getting a view of and not distant from one another above four plethra,[1] each side at first made a halt. The Grecian horse was drawn up four deep, like a body of foot; but the Barbarians had formed their ranks to no more than twelve men in front, but of a very great depth. After this halt, the Barbarians advanced first to give the charge. When the engagement was begun, whatever Grecian struck an enemy, his spear broke off short with the blow: but the Persians, whose weapons were made of less brittle materials,[2] had soon slain twelve men and two horses; and soon after the Grecians were put to flight. Yet, as Agesilaus was advancing with the heavy-armed to their relief, the Barbarians retreated in their turn, and one of the noble Persians is slain.

After this engagement between the horse, when Agesilaus sacrificed next day for proceeding forwards, the victims were inauspicious. This plainly appearing, he turned off and marched down to the sea-coast. Being now convinced, that, unless he could procure a sufficient body of horse, he should never be able to march down into the plains, he resolved to procure them, that he might not be obliged to make war like a fugitive. He therefore drew up a list of the persons in all the adjacent cities who could best afford to keep horses. And having promised, that whoever contributed towards the cavalry either arms or an approved horseman should be excused from personal service, he made them exert themselves with as much activity as if each was seeking out a man to die in his own stead.

But afterwards, so soon as it was spring, he drew them all in a body to Ephesus. And here resolving to exercise his troops, he proposed rewards to the companies of heavy-armed which ever appeared in the finest condition, and to the squadrons of horse which should perform their duty best. He also proposed rewards to the targeteers and archers, to such as should best behave in their respective duties. In

<hr/>

1 Four hundred feet.
2 Κρειττω παλτα εχοντες.

consequence of this one might have seen all the places of exercise crowded with persons at their exercise, and the riding-schools with horsemen practising the manage, the darters also and archers exercising their parts; in short, he made the whole city of Ephesus a fine spectacle indeed; for the market-place was filled with arms of all sorts and horses for sale. The braziers, carpenters, smiths, curriers, and furbishers were all busy in preparing the instruments of battle, insomuch that you would actually have judged that city to be the workhouse of war. And it inspirited every spectator to see, beside all this, Agesilaus marching first, his soldiers following with garlands on their heads, when they came from their exercise and went to offer up their garlands to Diana. For wherever men worship the gods, perfect themselves in martial exercise, and carefully practise obedience to their superiors, now is it possible that all things there should not be full of the warmest hope? But thinking further, that a contempt of the enemy might invigorate his men the more for battle, he ordered the criers to sell such barbarians quite naked as were taken by their plundering parties. The soldiers therefore seeing them with skins exceeding white, because they never had used themselves to strip, delicate also and plump in body, because they always travelled upon wheels, imagined there was no difference between fighting against such men and fighting against women.

A whole year was now completely come round since Agesilaus sailed from Greece, so that the thirty Spartans in commission with Lysander departed for Sparta, and their successors with Herippidas were ready to succeed them. To Xenocles, one of the number, and to another person Agesilaus gave the command of the horse; to Scythes that of the heavy-armed who were newly enfranchised; to Herippidas the command of those who had served under Cyrus; and to Migdon the command of the troops belonging to the cities. And now he gave out, that he would immediately march them by the shortest route into the strongest parts of the country, that from this consideration, they might best prepare their bodies and resolution too for action. Tissaphernes judged indeed, that he gave this out merely from a desire to deceive him again, but now undoubtedly he would break into Caria. His infantry therefore, as before, he sent away into Caria, and posted his horse in the plain of Mæander.

Agesilaus told no falsehood at all; but, exactly as he had given out, immediately marched for the province of Sardis; and for three days passing through a country quite clear of enemies, he got subsistence in abundance for all his troops. But on the fourth day the enemy's horse came in sight, and [3] their commander ordered the officer who took care of the baggage to pass the river Pactolus and encamp. And then, beholding the followers of the Greeks to be straggling about for plunder, they slew many of them. Agesilaus, perceiving this, ordered the horse to advance to their relief. On the other side, the Persians, when they saw the horse advancing, gathered close together, and drew up their whole numerous cavalry in order of battle. And here Agesilaus, knowing that the enemy had no foot at hand, whereas none of his own forces were absent, thought it a proper opportunity to engage if possible. Having sacrificed therefore, he immediately led the main body towards the horse who were drawn up to face him; but he ordered some [4] heavy-armed Spartans of the first military class to march up with the main body; and bade the targeteers advance at the same time running; and then he sent orders to the horse to charge the enemy, since himself and all the army were ready to support them. The Persians stood indeed the charge of his horse. But when at once every thing terrible was upon them they were forced to give way; and some of them were immediately pushed into the river, whilst the rest fled outright. The Grecians pursue, and are masters of their camp. And now the targeteers, as it is likely they should, were gone off to plunder. But Agesilaus, inclosing friend and foe, encamped round about them in a circle. A vast quantity of booty was taken by him on this occasion, which he found to be in value above seventy talents.[5] The camels also were taken at this time, which Agesilaus brought afterwards into Greece.

At the time this battle was fought, Tissaphernes happened to be at Sardis: for which reason he was accused by the Persians, as one who had betrayed them all to the enemy. But the king of Persia, conscious himself that the bad state of his affairs was owing entirely to

---

3 The marginal reading of the Paris edition by Leunclavius.
4 Marginal reading of Leunclavius.
5 13,562l. 10s.

Tissaphernes, sent Tithraustes down, and cuts off his head.

When Tithraustes had executed this order, he sends ambassadors to Agesilaus, who said —" The author, Agesilaus, of the present war between you and us, hath received his punishment. But the king now insists that you return back to Greece, and that the cities in Asia, continuing to govern themselves by their own laws, shall pay to him the tribute they formerly paid." Agesilaus replied, that " he would settle nothing without instructions from the magistrates of Sparta." Tithraustes rejoined, " But till you can know their pleasure, quit these parts and make war upon Pharnabazus, since I myself have amply avenged you on your enemy here." Agesilaus answered, " As I shall be some time on my march thither, you must pay for the supply of my army." Accordingly Tithraustes gives him thirty talents,[1] on receipt of which he proceeded towards Phrygia, in quest of Pharnabazus.

Being now on his march and in the plain beyond Cyme, an express from the magistrates of Sparta comes to him with an order, " to take the fleet under his own command, and to appoint whom he pleased to be admiral of it." The Lacedæmonians acted thus from these considerations, that if he was commander of both, the land-army would act more firmly because of their union with the fleet, and the fleet would act more firmly by the sight of the land-army ready to support them whenever it was needful. When Agesilaus had received this authority, he immediately circulated orders to the cities in the islands and on the sea-coast to build triremes, the number to be left to the discretion of each city. Accordingly, about one hundred and twenty new ones were built, partly at the public determination of those cities, and partly by the zeal of private persons who studied to oblige him. He then appointed Pisander, his wife's brother, to be admiral, a man desirous to signalize himself, and of great natural abilities, but of small experience in naval matters. Pisander accordingly departed to take care of the fleet, whilst Agesilaus, continuing his first design, proceeded in his march against Phrygia.

V. In the meantime Tithraustes, who judged it plain that Agesilaus had a real contempt for the power of his master, and had no manner of intention to go out of Asia, but on the contrary entertained high hopes of demolishing the king ;—Tithraustes, I say, after balancing about the measures he should take, sends into Greece Timocrates the Rhodian. He furnished him with gold to the value of fifty talents,[2] and instructed him to distribute the money amongst the leading men in the several states, after procuring from them the strongest engagements that they would make war upon the Lacedæmonians. Timocrates, when arrived, distributes his gold, at Thebes to Androclides and Ismenias and Galaxidorus, at Corinth to Timolaus and Polyanthes, at Argos to Cyclon and his faction. The Athenians, even without getting any share of the money, were ready for a war, and judged they ought to be principals in it. The persons who had received their shares, began the outcry against the Lacedæmonians in their own several communities. When they had once raised in these a hatred against the Lacedæmonians, they next drew the principal states of Greece into their scheme. But the leading men at Thebes, being well assured that unless somebody began the rupture the Lacedæmonians would never break the peace with their allies, persuade the Locrians of Opus to levy contributions on a certain district, about which there was a controversy between them and the Phocians, judging that upon this provocation the Phocians would break into Locris. They were not deceived ; for the Phocians breaking immediately into Locris, carried off a booty of many times the value. Androclides therefore and his party soon persuaded the Thebans to assist the Locrians, since the Phocians had actually levied war, not upon a district that was in dispute, but on Locris itself, that was confessedly in friendship and alliance with them. And when the Thebans, by way of retaliation, had broke into Phocis and laid the country waste, the Phocians send ambassadors in all haste to Lacedæmon, and demanded assistance, representing that " they had not begun the war, but had acted against the Locrians in self-defence." The Lacedæmonians caught with pleasure at this pretext to make war upon the Thebans, having long been irritated against them for their detention at Decelea of the tenth due to Apollo, and for their refusal to march with them against the Piræus. They accused them farther of

---

[1] 5,812l. 10s.

[2] 9,685l. 10s.

persuading the Corinthians too, not to accompany them on that occasion. They also recalled to remembrance, how they would not permit Agesilaus to sacrifice at Aulis, and threw the victims actually sacrificed from off the altar, and that none of them were serving at this time under Agesilaüs in Asia. They judged the present, therefore, a fine opportunity to march an army against them, and put a stop to their insolent behaviour; for matters went well in Asia under the command of Agesilaus, and they had no war at present upon their hands in Greece. These being the general sentiments of the Lacedæmonians, the ephori proclaimed a foreign expedition. But first they sent Lysander to the Phocians, and ordered him to conduct the Phocians with all their strength, and the Oeteans and the Heracleots and the Meliensians and Ænianians to Haliartus. Pausanias, who was to command the army, agreed to be there on a certain day with the Lacedæmonians, and the rest of the Peloponnesian confederates. Lysander truly obeyed all his orders, and, what is more, procured the revolt of the Orchomenians from the Thebans. But Pausanias, after completing the solemn sacrifices, lingered for a time at Tegea, sending out the persons who were to command the confederate quotas, and waiting the coming up of the troops from the neighbouring cities.

When now it was clear to the Thebans that the Lacedæmonians would soon march into their country, they sent ambassadors to Athens, who spoke as follows:

" You have, Athenians, complaints against us, as men who made proposals to ruin you, in the close of the late war: but ye have no manner of reason for such complaints. These proposals were not issued by the people of Thebes; they were merely the declaration of one single Theban, who assisted then at the consultations of the confederates. But when the Lacedæmonians solicited us to march with them against the Piræus, the whole state unanimously joined in a refusal. It is principally therefore on your account that the Lacedæmonians now are exasperated against us; and it is natural for us to esteem it incumbent upon you to assist our state against them.

" Nay, we have much stronger reasons for insisting, that so many of you as were of the party in the city should march cheerfully now against the Lacedæmonians. For, after setting up an oligarchy here, and throwing you into enmity with the people, hither they marched with a numerous force, pretending themselves your confederates, and then delivered you up to the people. So far as Lacedæmonians could do it, you were utterly undone : it was your own people here assembled that saved you.

" We know, moreover, Athenians, we know it well, how desirous you are again to recover that empire, of which you were formerly possessed. And what more probable method to accomplish this desire, than in person to succour those whom your enemies oppress ? Those enemies, it is true, give law to numerous states. But suffer not yourselves to be awed by this consideration, which rather abounds in motives to courage and resolution. Your own recollection will inform you, that the number of your enemies was always the greatest when your rule was most enlarged. So long indeed as no favourable opportunities offered for revolt, people concealed the enmity they bore you; but no sooner had the Lacedæmonians set up for leaders, than they openly showed what they thought of you : and at present would but we Thebans and you Athenians appear together in arms against the Lacedæmonians, be assured that many who hate them will openly declare it.

" Reflect within yourselves, and you will confess the truth of what we are alleging.— What people in Greece continues at present well affected to them ? Have not the Argives been from time immemorial their irreconcileable foes ? Even the Eleans, deprived by them as they now have been of a large territory and its cities, are added to the number of their enemies. And why should we mention the Corinthians and Arcadians and Achæans ? who, so long as the war was carrying on against you, were earnestly solicited by them, and were admitted to a share of every hardship, of every danger, and of every expense; and yet, when the Lacedæmonians had carried all their points, in what dominion, what honour, what wealth, were they suffered to partake ? Nay, so haughty are they grown, that they send out their very slaves to be governors over their friends; and, in the height of their good fortune, have declared themselves lords over their free confederates. Nay farther, it is manifest to all, how grossly they have deluded those very people whom they seduced to revolt from you,

3 F

since, instead of giving them liberty, they have doubled their portion of slavery upon them. For they are tyrannized over by the governors whom these Lacedæmonians send them, and by the committees of ten, which Lysander hath established in every city. Nay, even the monarch of Asia, who principally enabled them to get the better over you—what better treatment doth he now receive, than if he had joined with you to war them down?

" Is it not therefore quite reasonable to imagine, that would you but set yourselves at the head of those who were so manifestly aggrieved, you may again become a much greater people than ever you were in former times? For, during the former interval of your power, the sea was the only element in which you displayed it. But now you will be leaders of all, of us, of the Peloponnesians too, and of those who were subjected to you before, and of the king himself possessed of the amplest share of power. In regard to us, you yourselves well know, how very valuable confederates we proved to them. But now, we want no motive to join you with higher alacrity and more effectual strength than we then joined the Lacedæmonians. For we shall unite our aid on this occasion, not in behalf of the inhabitants of the isles or the inhabitants of Syracuse, not in behalf of remote people as we did at that time, but in behalf of our ownselves, so grievously injured as we have been.

" There is one truth more, of which you ought to rest well assured, that the ravenous appetite after power in the Lacedæmonians may much easier be demolished than the power you once enjoyed. You then were a maritime power, and could awe the most reluctant states. The Lacedæmonians, though a mere handful of men, are greedily assuming power over people many times more numerous than, and in arms not one jot inferior to themselves.

" These considerations therefore we lay before you; and rest perfectly convinced, Athenians, that it is our firm persuasion we are inviting you now to do greater services to Athens than to Thebes."

With these words the Theban ambassador put an end to his discourse.

A very large number of Athenians spoke afterwards in their favour, and it was unanimously decreed to aid the Thebans. Thrasybulus presented the decree by way of answer, in which it was expressly recited, that " though

the Piræus was not yet restored to a state of defence, they would however run all hazards to return greater services than they had themselves received.—You Thebans," he then added, " did not join your arms against us, but we Athenians will fight along with you against the Lacedæmonians, in case they invade you." The Thebans therefore departing got ready all the means of their defence, and the Athenians were making preparations for their succour.

The Lacedæmonians lost no more time, for Pausanias their king marched into Bœotia at the head of the troops of Sparta and the troops of Peloponnesus; the Corinthians were the only people who did not attend. Lysander, however, at the head of the troops from Phocis and Orchomenus and the adjacent cities had arrived at Haliartus before Pausanias. And when arrived, he could not bear to wait inactively till the Lacedæmonian army came up, but with the force he already had he marched up to the walls of the Haliartians. At first he persuaded them to revolt from the Thebans, and declare themselves free and independent: but when some of the Thebans, who were within the walls, hindered them from making any such declaration, he made an assault upon the wall. The Thebans hearing this set forward, heavy-armed and horse, with all speed to its succour. How the fact really was, whether they suddenly fell upon Lysander, or whether, aware of their approach, he slighted them from a confidence of victory, is still uncertain. Thus much only is clear, that a battle was fought under the walls, and a trophy was erected at the gate of Haliartus. And no sooner was Lysander slain, than his troops fled away to the mountain, and the Thebans followed resolutely in pursuit. The pursuers were now on the ascent of the mountain, and had pushed forwards into the strait and narrow pass, when the heavy-armed faced suddenly about, and poured their javelins with good effect upon them. When two or three of the foremost were dropped, they rolled down great stones along the declivity upon the rest, and kept plying at them with great alacrity, so that the Thebans are driven quite down the hill, and more than two hundred of them perish. This day therefore the Thebans were dispirited, reckoning they had suffered as much as they had made the enemy suffer before. However, on the morrow, when they heard the Phocians had marched off in the night and the rest of the confederates were departed to their several homes, they conceived a much higher opinion of their late success. But when again Pausanias appeared in sight at the head of the Lacedæmonian army, they thought themselves once more in very imminent danger, and it was said there was a deep silence and much dejection among the troops. Yet when, upon the arrival of the Athenians the day after, and their junction with them, Pausanias came no nearer and no battle ensued, the Thebans began to be much higher in spirit than ever. Pausanias, it is true, had called a council of his general officers and captains, and demanded their opinions, "whether he should give the enemy battle, or fetch off Lysander and those who were killed with him under truce." For Pausanias and the other Lacedæmonians who were in authority reasoned with themselves that Lysander was actually slain, that the army under his command was defeated and dispersed, that the Corinthians had flatly refused to join them, and the troops now in the army served plainly against their inclinations: the cavalry also were taken into their account; that of the enemy was numerous: their own was very small: the dead moreover were lying under the walls of Haliartus: so that, should they get a victory, they could not easily fetch them off because of the defendants upon the turrets. Upon all these considerations, they judged it most advisable to demand a truce for fetching off their dead. The Thebans answered, that "they would not restore the dead, unless the enemy evacuated the country." They received this condition with pleasure, and fetching off their dead marched out of Bœotia. But after such things had passed, the Lacedæmonians march away with minds sadly dejected, and the Thebans with all the marks of insolence. If any one of the enemy straggled the least into the inclosures, they drove them out again with blows into the high road.

In this manner the expedition of the Lacedæmonians was brought to a conclusion. Pausanias however, upon his return to Sparta, was summoned to a trial for his life. He was accused in form, for not marching up to Haliartus so soon as Lysander, though they had jointly agreed on a day for their junction, for demanding a truce to fetch off their dead when he ought to have endeavoured to recover them by a battle, and for letting the people of Athens escape him formerly when he had got them fast in the Piræus. Upon the whole, as he did not appear at his trial, he was condemned to die. He fled indeed to Tegea, and died there of sickness. These things were done in Greece.

THE

AFFAIRS OF GREECE.

BOOK IV.

CONTENTS OF BOOK IV.

AFFAIRS OF GREECE.

BOOK IV.

I. Agesilaus, who about autumn reached the Phrygia of Pharnabazus, put the country to fire and sword, and possessed himself of the cities either by siege or voluntary surrender. But Spithridates telling him that "if he would go along with him into Paphlagonia, he would persuade the king of the Paphlagonians to a conference with him, and make him his confederate," he readily went with him, having long been desirous to procure the revolt of this nation from the king. And when he was arrived in Paphlagonia, Cotys came to him and agreed to a confederacy; for he had already refused to obey a summons sent him by the king. And, at the persuasion of Spithridates, he left with Agesilaus a thousand horse and two thousand targeteers.

Agesilaus, esteeming himself highly obliged to Spithridates for this good service, said to him, "tell me, Spithridates, would not you give your daughter to Cotys?" "With much more pleasure," he replied, "than Cotys would receive her from me, an exile as I am, whilst he is a mighty king and of large dominions." This was all that was said at that time about the match. But when Cotys was about departing, he waited upon Agesilaus to take his leave. The thirty Spartans were present; Spithridates had purposely been sent out of the way; when Agesilaus began thus to open the affair: "Tell me, Cotys, (said he) is Spithridates a man of noble birth?" He replied, "No Persian is more nobly born." "You have seen his son, (said he) who is a very handsome youth?" "Beyond all doubt he is; I supped last night in his company." "They tell me he hath a daughter, who is much handsomer." "Oh heavens! (replied Cotys) she is a beauty indeed." "Cotys, (said

he) you are now my friend; I regard you as such, and must advise you to marry this lady. She is exceedingly beautiful, than which, what can be sweeter to a man? She is the daughter of a man of the highest nobility, and so extensive a power, that in return to the wrongs Pharnabazus hath done him, he hath taken such ample revenge, as to force him to be a fugitive from all his dominions, as yourself can witness. And rest convinced, that as he knows how to avenge himself upon an enemy, so he knows as well how to serve his friend. And be farther assured, that if this match be completed, you not only gain a relation in Spithridates, but in me also, and all the Lacedæmonians, and consequently, (as we are the head of Greece,) in all Greece itself. Nay, in case you comply, what man can ever marry with so much pomp as yourself? What bride can ever be conducted home with so many horsemen, so many targeteers, and so many heavy-armed, as shall conduct yours home to you?" Here Cotys demanded, whether he made this proposal with the privity of Spithridates? "I call the gods to witness (said he) that he gave me no orders to mention it to you. But I can say for myself, that though I rejoice above measure when I punish an enemy, yet methinks I receive much more abundant pleasure when I find out any good for my friends." "Why therefore (replied Cotys) did you not ask him whether he approves the match?" "Go you there, Herippidas, (said Agesilaus) and persuade him to give us his consent." Herippidas and his colleagues rose up and went on their commission. But as their stay was long, "Are you willing, Cotys, (said Agesilaus) that we send for him ourselves?" He replied, "with all my heart; for I am convinced, you have more influence over him than all the rest of mankind." And upon this Agesilaus sent for Spithridates and the others.   On their approach, Herippidas said, "what need Agesilaus to repeat to you all that hath passed between us ?   For in short Spithridates says he will consent with pleasure to whatever you please to propose." "It is therefore my pleasure," said Agesilaus, "that you Spithridates give your daughter to Cotys, and that you Cotys accept her, and heaven bless the match !   We cannot indeed before spring bring the lady home by land." Cotys cried out, "But, by heaven, Agesilaus, if you are willing, she may be sent immediately by sea."   And now having given their hands to one another to ratify the contract, they dismissed Cotys.   Agesilaus, as he knew his eagerness, without loss of time commanded a trireme to be manned, and ordered Callias the Lacedæmonian to carry the lady to him.

In the meantime he marched himself to Dascylium, where was the palace of Pharnabazus, surrounded with a number of villages, all of them large and abundantly stored with the necessaries of life.   There was excellent hunting, both in the parks that were paled about and in the open fields.   A river, full of all sorts of fish, flowed round the whole spot of ground; and birds were everywhere to be found for those who could fowl.   It was here that Agesilaus passed the winter, having supplies at hand for his army, or fetching them in by his foraging parties.   But as once the soldiers were fetching in necessaries in a very careless and unguarded manner, since hitherto they had met with no interruption, Pharnabazus, who had with him two chariots armed with scythes, and about four hundred horse, fell suddenly amongst them as they were dispersed about the plains.   The Grecians, when they saw him riding up, ran together in a body to the number of seven hundred.   He lost no time, but setting his chariots in the front, and posting himself behind with his horse, ordered them to drive full upon the enemy.   No sooner was that body broken by the fury of the chariots than his horsemen instantly demolished the rest of the Greeks.   The rest fled away to Agesilaus, for he was near at hand with the heavy-armed.

The third or fourth day after this, Spithridates discovers that Pharnabazus was encamped at Caue, a large village about a [1] hundred and sixty stadia off, and sends this intelligence immediately to Herippidas.   Herippidas, always eager to distinguish himself by some grand exploit, requests of Agesilaus two thousand horse, an equal number of targeteers, the horsemen farther belonging to Spithridates and the Paphlagonians, and so many of the Greeks as he could persuade to go with him.   Agesilaus having complied with his request, he began his sacrifices; and the victims appearing favourable in the evening, he sacrificed no more.   He then issued his orders for the troops to be ready after supper in the front of the camp.   It was now dark, and half the number were not come out; but reflecting, that if he gave up the affair, the rest of the Thirty would sadly ridicule him, he marched away with what force he got : and, falling in by break of day upon the camp of Pharnabazus, many of the Mysians, who were then upon the guard, were slain; the enemy took to their heels, the camp is taken, with a great quantity of plate and the whole field-equipage of Pharnabazus, with the addition of all the baggage and the carriages, with the beasts that drew them.   For as Pharnabazus was in constant fear of staying too long in a place, lest he should be surrounded and blocked up, Scythian-like, he was for ever changing his ground, and most cautiously concealing his encampments.   But when the Paphlagonians and Spithridates brought in the booty they had taken, Herippidas, who had posted his officers for the purpose, took every thing away from Spithridates and the Paphlagonians, in order to enlarge the booty he himself should deliver in to the commissioners of sale.   Treated in this manner, they could not brook it; but as men who had been injured and disgraced, they packed up their baggage and went off by night to Sardis, to offer their service to Ariæus, confident of a good reception from him, as he too had revolted from and was making war upon the king.   Agesilaus took nothing to heart during this expedition so much as this desertion of Spithridates, and Megabyzus, and the Paphlagonians.

But there was one Apollophanes of Cyzicus, who had an hospitable connexion of long standing with Pharnabazus, and at this time had the same connexion with Agesilaus.

---

[1] About sixteen miles.

This man therefore told Agesilaus, that he thought he could bring Pharnabazus to a conference with him about a peace. And when Agesilaus, listening to him, pledged his right hand and granted a truce, he soon brought Pharnabazus to the place agreed on. Agesilaus truly and his thirty Spartans were lying down upon the grass, and waiting for him. At length Pharnabazus appeared, dressed up in a most sumptuous attire. His servants spread the carpets, on which the Persians seat themselves softly down before Pharnabazus, who seeing the mean figure that Agesilaus made, became ashamed to indulge himself in his usual manner; in his finery therefore he threw himself down on the bare ground. In the first place, they gave one another a short verbal greeting. Pharnabazus then offering his right hand, Agesilaus in return held out his own. This done, Pharnabazus thus began the conference, for he was the elder man.

" To you, Agesilaus, and to all you Lacedæmonians here present, I address myself. I was a firm friend and confederate to you, when you warred with the Athenians. I furnished you with money, and at sea I strengthened your fleet. But by land I fought on horseback in company with you, and drove your enemies into the sea. And no one person amongst you can upbraid me with ever acting a double part with you, as Tissaphernes did, either in word or deed. Such I have been towards you, and such treatment in return I have received from you, that in all my dominions at present I cannot get one meal's meat, unless like a dog I pick up the scraps you have left behind you. As to all the fine houses, and the parks well stocked with cattle and with timber, that my father left me, and which formerly rejoiced my heart, I see them all destroyed by fire and sword. I cannot think these proceedings to be either just or pious; but I beg to learn from you whether such should be the actions of men who know how to be grateful?"

In this manner Pharnabazus spoke. The Thirty Spartans to a man were quite out of countenance, and kept a dead silence. But after some pause Agesilaus replied as follows :

" I imagine, Pharnabazus, you cannot be ignorant, that in the cities of Greece it is usual for men to connect themselves together by the ties of hospitality. But yet those very persons, when the states of which they are members are at war, adhere to their own country,

and make war on their hospitable friends; nay, sometimes it happens, that in the field they kill one another. In like manner we are now at war with your king, and are obliged to execute all hostilities against whatever belongs to him. In regard to yourself, there is nothing we so much desire as to have you for our friend ; but even I myself would scorn to advise you to make a bare exchange, and merely to take us for your masters instead of the king. But you have it in your power, by joining with us, to live henceforth in ample enjoyment of all that belongs to you, without adoring a fellow-creature, or acknowledging any master at all. For my own part, I reckon freedom to be of greater value than all the riches in the world. And yet I am far from inviting you to be free and at the same time poor ; but, by accepting our service as confederates, to enlarge for the future not the dominions of the king but your own, and oblige those who are now your fellow-slaves to be subjects to yourself. And if at one and the same time you become both free and rich, what more will you need to make you completely happy ?"

" I shall therefore tell you frankly," said Pharnabazus, " what it is I intend to do."

" Spoken like a man of honour."

" It is my full resolution," Pharnabazus went on, " in case the king sends another person to take my place and lord it over me, to be a friend and ally to you. But then, in case he continues me in the command, I shall by the laws of honour be bound, and am determined, I declare it before you all, to make war upon you to the utmost of my power."

Agesilaus, hearing this, caught him by the hand, and said,

" I wish, most generous of men, that you were a friend to us. But of one thing you may rest assured, I will march out of your country as fast as I can ; and for the time to come, so long as the war continues, whilst we have another person to attack, we will give no molestation to thee or thine."

These words being spoken, they ended the conference ; and Pharnabazus, mounting on horseback, rode away. But his son by Parapite, a handsome youth, lingered behind, and running up to him, cried out—" O Agesilaus ! I take thee for my hospitable friend." " I accept you as such," he replied. " Remember me, therefore," said the youth, and immediately gave the javelin in his hand, a very fine one it was, to Agesilaus. He received it, and taking off the trappings from the horse of Idæus the painter, he gave them in return. The youth, now leaping upon his horse, rode after his father. And afterwards, when, during the absence of Pharnabazus, another brother took away his provinces from this son by Parapite, and drove him into exile, Agesilaus showed him all possible kindness; and particularly, exerted himself so much in the favour of an Athenian, the son of Evalces, who was loved by this youth, that he got him admittance into the Stadium at Olympia, though he was too tall for the rest of the lads.

Agesilaus, however, pursuant to his promise, marched immediately out of the territory of Pharnabazus, and the spring by this time was drawing on. But when he was arrived in the plains of Thebe, he encamped near the temple of Astyrinian Diana, and there collected from all quarters a very large reinforcement to his army. He was preparing now to penetrate as far as possible into the country, judging, that whatever nations he should leave behind him, would all, without exception, revolt from the king. Such at this time were the employments of Agesilaus.

But the Lacedæmonians, when once convinced that money was come over into Greece, and that the greatest states were caballing together for war, thought themselves in imminent danger, and judged it necessary to take the field. Accordingly they set about their preparations, and without loss of time despatch Epicydides to Agesilaus. He, on his arrival, reported to him the present situation of Greece, and that "the state commands him with his utmost speed to succour his country." Agesilaus, when he heard this, was sadly chagrined, recollecting of what honours and hopes he was going to be deprived![1] Calling however the confederates together, he communicated to them the orders he had received from

Sparta, and told them, "he was indispensably obliged to succour his country. If affairs turn out well at home, you may depend upon it, my friends and confederates, I will not forget you, but will be here again amongst you, to accomplish all your wishes." At hearing him talk thus many tears were shed; and it was unanimously resolved to accompany Agesilaus to the aid of Sparta, and if affairs turned out well in Greece, to reconduct him back into Asia. And in fact they were getting all things in readiness to bear him company.

Agesilaus left Euxenus behind to command in Asia, and assigned him no less than four thousand men for garrisons, that he might be enabled to keep the cities fast in their obedience. But observing that the soldiers were much more inclined to stay where they were than to march against Grecians, and yet willing to take as many as possible and the best of them too along with him, he proposed to give prizes to the city which sent in the choicest body of men, to the commanders of hired troops who attended the expedition with their party most completely armed, and the same in regard to the heavy-armed and the archers and the targeteers. He also declared to the commanders of horse, that he would give prizes to such of them as brought in their squadron best mounted and best accoutred. He said the decision should be made in the Chersonesus, so soon as they had passed over from Asia into Europe, that all of them might be well convinced, that they who served in this expedition must needs undergo a very accurate review. The prizes were chiefly arms of the most beautiful make, as well for heavy-armed as horsemen. There were also crowns of gold. The value of them upon the whole amounted to not less than four talents.[2] By submitting in truth to such an expense, arms of the greatest value were provided for this expedition: and so soon as he had crossed the Hellespont, the judges were appointed; of the Lacedæmonians, Menascus and Herippidas and Orsippus; of the confederates, one of every city: and Agesilaus, after he had finished the distribution of the prizes, began his march, and took the same road as Xerxes took formerly when he invaded Greece.

In the meantime the ephori proclaimed a foreign expedition; and, as Agesipolis was yet a

---

1 According to Plutarch, he immediately wrote to the ephori as followeth: " Agesilaus to the ephori, greeting. We have subdued a large part of Asia, have driven the Barbarians before us, and have taken a great quantity of arms in Ionia. But since you order my return by a day prefixed, I follow this letter, and shall almost arrive before it. For I am in this command not for myself but for my country and allies: and then a commander commandeth in the rightful manner, when he is submissive to the laws and the ephori, or whatever magistrates are supreme in his country." Plu. *Laconic Apophthegms.*.

2 775*l.*

minor, the state ordered Aristodemus, who was a relation and guardian to the young king, to command the army. When the Lacedæmonians had taken the field, the enemy, who were now gathered in a body, assembled together in consultation how, with the best advantage, to bring on a battle. Timolaus of Corinth on this occasion said thus:

" It is my opinion, confederates, that the course of the Lacedæmonian affairs very much resembles the course of rivers: for rivers near their sources are never large, and are easy to be passed. But then the farther they run, other rivers, by having emptied themselves into them, increase the depth and impetuosity of the current. It is just so with the Lacedæmonians. When they first come out into the field, they are alone; but taking in on their route the other states, their numbers are enlarged, and they are harder to be resisted. I see again, that such as have a mind to destroy wasps, in case they attempt to hurt them when they are come out of their nest, are grievously stung for their pains; but if they fire them when they are all within their nest, they suffer no harm, and demolish the wasps. It is therefore my judgment, that we should reflect on these points, and fight the Lacedæmonians in Sparta itself, which would indeed be best; but if that cannot be, as near to Sparta as possible."

As Timolaus was judged to advise them well, they unanimously resolved to follow his advice. But whilst they were settling the points of command, and agreeing together in what depth to draw up the whole of their army, lest if the several states drew up their files too deep, the enemy might have it in their power to surround them—whilst, I say, they were settling these points, the Lacedæmonians, who had been joined by the Tegeans and Mantineans, were advancing along the coast. The enemy marching about the same time, the Corinthians and all on their side were now at Nemea, and the Lacedæmonians and confederates at Sicyon. As the latter had forced their way by the pass of Epiœcœa, the light-armed of the enemy had at first terribly annoyed them, by darting and shooting at them from the eminences; but when they came down again to the sea, they continued their march along the plains, putting the country to fire and sword. The enemy at length drew near and encamped, having a rivulet in their front.

The Lacedæmonians still advancing were now but ² ten stadia distant from the enemy; halting therefore, and encamping, they remained quiet: and I will now reckon up the numbers on either side.

There were now assembled, of the Lacedæmonians, to the amount of six thousand heavy-armed: of the Eleans and Triphyllians and Acrorians and Lasionians, nearly three thousand; fifteen hundred of the Sicyonians; and the number of Epidaurians, Trazenians, Hermionians, and Haliensians was not less than three thousand. Beside these, there were about six hundred horse belonging to the Lacedæmonians, accompanied by about three hundred Cretan archers. The slingers of the Marganeans and Ledrinians and Amphidolians were not fewer than four hundred. The Phliasians indeed had not joined them; for they excused themselves by alleging a truce. This was the force on the side of the Lacedæmonians. On the side of the enemy were now assembled, of the Athenians, six thousand heavy-armed; the Argives were said to amount to seven thousand; the Bœotians, since the Orchomenians were not come up, were about five thousand: the Corinthians were three thousand: and from the whole isle of Eubœa there were not fewer than three thousand. Such was the amount of their heavy-armed. The horse of the Bœotians, as the Orchomenians were not come up, were eight hundred; of the Athenians, six hundred: of the Chalcideans of Eubœa, one hundred; of the Locrians of Opus, fifty. The light-armed, added to those belonging to the Corinthians, were very numerous indeed, for the Locrians of Ozolæ and the Meliensians and the Arcanians were with them. Such was the force on either side.

The Bœotians, so long as they were on the left wing, were in no hurry at all for a battle. But so soon as the Athenians were posted over-against the Lacedæmonians, and they themselves took post on the right where they faced the Achæans, they immediately declared that the victims were auspicious, and proclaimed that all should be ready for a battle. But neglecting, in the first place, the rule of drawing up by sixteens, they formed their battalion exceeding deep; and farther, still kept creeping

---

² About a mile.

forwards to the right, in order to overstretch the enemy's wing. The Athenians, that they might not be separated from the rest of the army, followed their motion, though sensible at the same time how great a risk they ran of being quite surrounded.

So far the Lacedæmonians had no perception at all of the enemy's approach, for the ground was covered over with shrubs. But when the pæan began, they knew what was doing. They instantly issued out orders for the whole army to prepare for battle. So soon as they were formed, the commanders of the auxiliary bodies enjoined them to follow their leaders in the order they had now placed them. The Lacedæmonians kept inclining towards the right, and thus they far overstretched the enemy's wing, so that only six regiments of Athenians faced the Lacedæmonians, whilst four of them were over-against the Tegeans. When they were not above a stadium asunder, the Lacedæmonians, after sacrificing in obedience to their laws a she-goat to the goddess of the chase, led on towards the enemy bending circularly the part of their line that overstretched to surround the enemy. But when the battle was joined, all the confederates on the Lacedæmonian side were defeated by their antagonists, though the Pellenians, who faced the Thespians, maintained the fight some time, and some of both sides perished on the spot. The Lacedæmonians themselves beat all the Athenians whom they charged, and, surrounding them with the part of their line that overstretched, slew numbers of them, and still, as they suffered nothing from the enemy, kept pushing forwards in their regular array. It was thus that they clearly passed the four Athenian regiments till they returned from the pursuit; by which means those Athenians saved their lives, excepting some few who in the charge were slain by the Tegeans. The Lacedæmonians, farther, met the Argives full in their retreat; and the first general officer was going to fall in full upon their front; when somebody is said to have roared out aloud "to let the first of them pass by." This was permitted; and then, running upon their flank and wounding them on their unarmed sides, they slew many of them. They also fell in with and attacked the Corinthians in their retreat. The Lacedæmonians farther fall in with some of the Thebans retreating from their pursuit,

and slew a great number of them. These things being done, the vanquished fled at first to the walls; but afterwards, the Corinthians setting the example, they posted themselves again in their former camp. The Lacedæmonians, on the other side, repairing to the spot of ground where they first charged the enemy, erected the trophy. And this is an exact account of the battle.

III. Agesilaus from Asia was marching forwards with all expedition. He was now at Amphipolis, when Dercyllidas meets him with the news, that "the Lacedæmonians have gained a victory, with the loss of only eight of their own citizens, but a vast slaughter of the enemy;" he added at the same time that "no small number of the confederates were slain." Agesilaus put this question to him, "Would it not be proper, think you, Dercyllidas, to communicate the news of this victory without loss of time to the cities which have sent their troops hither under my orders?" Dercyllidas answered, that "the hearing of it must in all probability raise their spirits." You then can best report it, because you yourself was present at the action." He was highly delighted at hearing this. All his life long he had been very fond of going abroad. He said therefore, "Do you order me to go?" "I do," said he, "and enjoin you to tell them farther, that if affairs turn out well in Greece, we will be with them again according to promise." Dercyllidas immediately continued his journey for the Hellespont, whilst Agesilaus, having passed through Macedonia, arrived in Thessaly.

But now the Larisseans, Cranonians, Scotusians, and Pharsalians confederate with the Bœotians and all the Thessalians, such excepted as were then under sentence of exile, pursued and gave him molestation. At that juncture he was leading his army in the long march, with half his cavalry in the van and the other half in the rear. But because the Thessalians by harassing those in the rear retarded the march, he sends off the cavalry in the van, except his own body-guard, to strengthen the rear. When both sides were now drawn up to face one another, the Thessalians, thinking it by no means advisable to fight on horseback against heavy-armed, wheeled about and retreated in a leisurely manner, and the heavy-armed too eagerly and rashly pursued them. Agesilaus perceiving bad conduct on both sides, sends off the finest body of horse that was his own guard, with orders for the others to pursue, and themselves to do the same with their utmost speed, and not give the enemy time to face about. The Thessalians no sooner saw them riding down upon them beyond their expectation, than some of them fled outright, some faced about, and some in the very endeavour to face, as they had the enemy on their flanks, were taken prisoners. Polycharmus the Pharsalian indeed, a commander in the horse, faced about, and fighting at the head of his own troop is slain. But so soon as he had dropped, a most dreadful flight ensued amongst the Thessalians, in which numbers were slain, numbers were taken alive, and none stopped their flight till they were got on the mountain Narthacium. And then Agesilaus set up a trophy between Pras and Narthacium. There too he halted highly delighted with this day's work, in which with cavalry of his own creation he had vanquished those who reckoned themselves the best horsemen in the world. The next day, having crossed the Achaic mountains of Phthia, he marched through a friendly country till he reached the frontiers of Bœotia. But just as he was entering Bœotia, the sun appeared in the form of the crescent of the moon, and news was received, that the Lacedæmonians were beaten at sea, and their admiral Pisander killed. It was also told him, in what manner the battle had been fought.

That near Cnidus the fleets had borne down upon one another: that Pharnabazus, who was admiral on the side of the enemy, was in the Phœnician fleet, and Conon, who commanded the Grecian squadron, had drawn up his ships in the van: but when Pisander had formed his line of battle, his ships appeared much inferior in number to the Greeks under Conon; upon which the confederates in the left wing immediately took to flight, whilst Pisander, rushing in amongst the enemy with his own vessel, well-armed with beaks, was driven on shore: that the other persons of the fleet who were driven on shore, abandoned their ships and fled safely off to Cnidus, but Pisander, continuing to fight from his decks, was killed.

Agesilaus at first was exceedingly mortified at this piece of news; but he soon recollected, that the disposition of the bulk of his army was such, that they would readily take a share in all joyful occurrences, and there was no necessity to communicate to them such things as were opposite to their wishes. Hereupon he assumed another countenance, and gave out that "Pisander indeed had lost his life, but however had gained a victory at sea." He had no sooner published this than he sacrificed oxen for the good tidings received, and sent round to several persons a share of the victims. A skirmish immediately ensued with the enemy, in which the soldiers of Agesilaus got the better, upon the strength of the report that the Lacedæmonians were victorious at sea.

There were now in the field against Agesilaus, the Bœotians, Athenians, Argives, Corinthians, Ænianians, Eubœans, and both the Locrians. He had with him one whole brigade of Lacedæmonians that joined him from Corinth, and the half of another brigade from Orchomenus. He had, farther, the newly enfranchised citizens of Sparta who had been with him in Asia; he had also the auxiliary body commanded by Herippidas. The rest were the quotas of aid from the Grecian cities in Asia, and from the Grecian cities in Europe which he had taken up on his march back. The heavy-armed from Orchomenus and Phocis were all the accession he had gained from the adjacent parts. The targeteers of Agesilaus were much superior in number; the number of the horse was nearly equal on both sides. Such was the force of either army. And I will now give an exact account of the battle, for such another hath not been fought in our days.

There were now facing one another in the plains of Coronea, the army under Agesilaus from the Cephissus, and the army along with the Thebans from Helicon. Agesilaus had the right of his own army, but the Orchomenians were posted in the extremity of his left. The Thebans, on the other side, stood on the right, but the Argives had the left. During the approach, there was a deep silence on both sides. When they were about the distance of a[2] stadium from one another, the Thebans having set up a shout, came running to the charge. But when there was no more than three [3]plethra of ground between them, the auxiliaries under the command of Herippidas started out before the main battle of Agesilaus to receive them, and were accompanied by the Ionians, Æolians

---

1 Xenophon himself was at this battle serving under Agesilaus. See the Anabasis, l. v.
2 About one tenth of a mile.   3 300 feet.

and Hellespontines. All these were now running together in one body to the charge, and coming to the point of the spear, broke the body of enemies they encountered. The Argives also were not able to stand before the body under Agesilaus, but fled towards Helicon. And here some of the auxiliaries were already putting the garland on the head of Agesilaus. But a message is brought him, that the Thebans, having cut to pieces the Orchomenians, were amongst the baggage; upon which he immediately put the main body in countermarch, and led them towards the Thebans. But the Thebans no sooner perceived that their confederates were fled to Helicon, than, designing to slip away and join them, they were briskly marching off in firm and close array. On this occasion it may be said beyond all dispute, that Agesilaus acted with the utmost bravery; he did not, however, prefer the securest method. For when it was in his power to let those who were sheering off pass by, and then by a close pursuit to defeat their rear, he did it not, but fell in their front he dashed against the Thebans. Here, thrusting shield against shield, they were pushing, were fighting, were slaying, were dying. At length some of the Thebans slip off to Helicon, and many of them retreating back, were slain. When thus the victory remained with Agesilaus, and he himself was brought back wounded to the main body, some horsemen riding up to him, acquaint him, that about eighty of the enemy with their arms are under the temple, and demanded how they must act. He, though sorely wounded in many parts of his body, forgot not, however, the duties of religion, but ordered that they might be permitted to depart where they pleased, and forbade all kind of insult. And then, for it was already evening, they took their supper and their repose. But early next morning he ordered Gylis, a general officer, to draw up the army and set up a trophy, all of them to be crowned with garlands in honour of the god, and all the music of the army to play. These things therefore they did.

The Thebans now sent heralds, desiring a truce to fetch off and inter their slain. A truce accordingly is granted; and Agesilaus repairing to Delphi, offered the tenth of his spoils to the god, in value not less than a hundred talents.[1] But Gylis, a general officer, taking

the command of the army, marched them off into Phocis, and from thence he made an incursion into Locris. All the next day the soldiers were carrying away the moveables and corn from the villages; but when evening was come, as the Lacedæmonians marched off in the rear, the Locrians were close at their heels, pouring in their javelins and darts upon them. Yet when the Lacedæmonians, by facing about and pursuing them, destroy some of the enemy, they gave over following them in the rear, but kept galling them from the eminences on the right. The Lacedæmonians then endeavoured to gain the ascent, but as it grew quite dark, they tumbled in their retreat because of the unevenness of the ground, some too, because they could see nothing before them, and some were struck down by the weapons of the enemy. Gylis the general officer, and most of the soldiers about him, in all eighteen Spartans, lose their lives on this occasion, some being killed with stones and some with other weapons. And had not those from the camp marched up after supper to their relief, the whole party was in great danger of perishing. After this the rest of the army was dismissed to their several cities, and Agesilaus went by sea to Sparta.

IV. The war, after this, was carried on by the Athenians, Bœotians, Argives and confederates, who took the field from Corinth, against the Lacedæmonians and their confederates from Sicyon. But the Corinthians, perceiving that the consequence of this was the entire devastation of their own lands, and a constant destruction of their people from the nearness of the enemy, whilst the rest of the confederates were enjoying peace at home and duly reaping the productions of their soil,— the greatest part of them and the best men amongst them grew desirous of peace, and laboured together to bring others into the same persuasion. But the Argives, Bœotians, and Athenians, and such of the Corinthians as had shared the king's money, and were principal authors of the war, saw plainly, that unless they could rid themselves of such as were bent on peace, the city of Corinth would fall under a Lacedæmonian influence, and therefore endeavoured to secure their point by a massacre. In the first place, they contrived the most impious scheme that ever men devised. For, though it is every where a rule not to put to death upon a festival even such as are legally

---

[1] 19,444l. 15s.

condemned to die, yet these men pitched upon the last day of the Euclean solemnity, as presuming they should then surprise the largest number upon the forum, to execute the massacre. When the marks of whom they were to despatch had been given to the persons employed, they drew their swords, and murdered one person standing in the circle, another sitting leisurely down, another in the theatre, and another on the very bench of justice. When once the alarm was spread, the very best men of Corinth betook themselves immediately, some to the statues of the gods in the forum, and some to the altars. But this most execrable band of assassins, entirely lost to all sense of duty, I mean equally those who contrived and those who executed the facts, murdered them even in the temples; insomuch that some, who received no harm, but retained a due sense of humanity, were most grievously afflicted at the sight of such impiety. In this manner most of the elderly Corinthians, as such generally frequented the forum, are put to death. The younger sort, as Pasimelus suspected what was in agitation, kept themselves quietly in Craneum. But when they heard the noise, and some came flying from the scene to take refuge amongst them, they at once ran up to the citadel of Corinth, and repulsed the Argives and others who were making an assault upon it. Whilst now they were consulting what was to be done, a capital falls off from a column, without either an earthquake or a blast of wind. They sacrificed, and the appearance of the victims was such that the soothsayers declared it was best for them to go down from thence. At first, therefore, like so many exiles, they withdrew out of the territory of Corinth. But their friends sending persuasions after them, nay, their mothers and their brethren coming to them with entreaties, and even some now invested with power, promising with an oath that no harm should be done them, they at length came back to their former habitations. Yet. now beholding the tyrants in authority, perceiving the actual ruin of the state, since the boundaries were demolished, and they were to style their country Argos instead of Corinth; necessitated, farther, to submit to the polity of Argos, so unsuited to their taste, and reduced within their own walls to a worse condition than that of mere sojourners;—some of them there were, who thought such a life not worth

the living, but well worth their while to try if they could not make Corinth, as it originally had been, their own country again, if they could not assert its freedom, clear it of those execrable assassins, and restore its excellent constitution : if indeed they could accomplish these points, they should become the preservers of their country; and in case they miscarried, they should manifest a desire of obtaining the most noble and most solid acquisitions, and should be sure to die a most glorious death.

In this disposition of mind, two of them, Pasimelus and Alcimenes, endeavoured by creeping in through the rivulet to confer with Praxitas, a general officer of the Lacedæmonians, who, with his own brigade, was now keeping guard in Sicyon, and told him, they could open him an entrance within the walls that reach down to Lecheum. Praxitas, who long since was well assured of their veracity, believed all they said ; and having obtained an order for his brigade, which was just going from Sicyon, to continue there, he settled with them the manner of this entrance. And when these two persons, either by regular rotation or purposed solicitation, were placed on the guard of the gates, Praxitas then approacheth that spot of ground where stood the trophy, with his Lacedæmonian brigade and the Sicyonians, and as many Corinthian exiles as were ready at hand. But when he was come up to the gates, and yet was afraid to enter, he desired he might first send in a person, in whom he confided, to take a view of what was within. The two projectors led him in, and with so much ingenuity showed him every thing, that the person introduced reported that all was safe exactly to their former description of things : now therefore Praxitas enters. The distance between the two walls was great; when therefore they were drawn up within, and their number was judged too small, they fortified themselves with a rampart and ditch, the best they could make, to secure the post till their confederates came up to their support. There was also, behind them in the harbour, a garrison of Bœotians.

This they entered by night, and passed the next day quietly without molestation. But the day after, came marching down against them the Argives with all their force, who finding the Lacedæmonians drawn up on the right, next to them the Sicyonians, and the exiles from Corinth, about a hundred and fifty in number, close to the eastern wall, they range themselves also in order of battle. Nearest to the western wall were the mercenaries under Philocrates, next to them the Argives, the Corinthians from the city had the left. Their own numbers made them despise the foe, and they immediately charged. They beat indeed the Sicyonians, and having opened a breach in the rampart, pursued them to the sea, and there slew many of them. But Pasimachus, who commanded the horse, though the number he had was very small, when he saw the Sicyonians defeated, ordered the horses to be fastened to the trees, and snatched away the shields from the fliers; and then, with such as were willing to follow him he marched up to the Argives. The Argives, who saw the letter S upon their shields, took them for Sicyonians, and were under no apprehensions at all. Pasimachus is now reported to have said, " By the twin gods, ye Argives, these SS will be your ruin;" and immediately charged them. Engaging in this manner with a handful of men against numbers, he is slain with those of his party.

In the meantime the Corinthian exiles, who had defeated their antagonists, were pushing upwards, and were now approaching the wall that encircled the city. But the Lacedæmonians, who perceived the defeat of the Sicyonians, marched downwards to their succour, keeping the rampart on their left. The Argives, hearing that the Lacedæmonians were in their rear, wheeled suddenly about and were throwing themselves over the rampart. The farthest of them in the right, being struck on the unarmed side by the Lacedæmonians, were dying apace. But those nearest the wall, close gathered in a body, were retreating in a great multitude towards the city. Yet no sooner did they fall in with the Corinthian exiles, and knew them to be enemies, than they again fled backwards. Here, indeed, some of them running up the stairs, jumped down from the wall, and were bruised to death; others, striving to get up, but beat off the stairs, were slain; and some trodden under foot by their companions, were trampled to death. The Lacedæmonians on this occasion had enow and enow again to kill. Full employ was here assigned them by God, beyond all they could have prayed for. For that a multitude of enemies, affrighted, astonished, exposing their unarmed sides, should thus be delivered up to slaughter, not a soul

amongst them endeavouring to resist, and all contributing in every respect to their own destruction—was not the hand of Heaven discernible here? Accordingly, in a small space of time, such numbers were slain, that men who had only been used to see heaps of corn, of wood, and of stones, saw at that time heaps of dead. The garrison of Bœotians also in the harbour, some of them having climbed upon the walls, and some of them upon the roof of the docks, were put to death.

When all was over, the Corinthians and Argives fetched off their dead under truce; and the confederates of the Lacedæmonians came up to join them. When they were thus assembled, the first resolution of Praxitas was, to lay open so much of the walls as would yield a sufficient passage to an army; and he then marched off, and led them towards Megara. He now, in the first place, takes Sidus by assault, and after that, Crommyon. Having fixed a garrison within the walls of these places he resumed his march. And having fortified Epiœcæa, that it might serve as a bulwark to cover the territories of the confederates, he then dismissed the army, and returned himself to Sparta.

Henceforth neither side took the field with their grand armies; they only marched garrisons into the cities, one side to Corinth and the other to Sicyon, to preserve these important places. Yet both sides being possessed of a body of mercenaries, were continually harassing and fighting one another. In this manner Iphicrates breaking into the territory of Phlius, placed an ambuscade, and then went about plundering the country with a handful of men, by which means he slew some of the Phliasians, who marched out of the city with too little circumspection to drive him off. For this reason the Phliasians, who before this accident would not receive the Lacedæmonians within their walls, lest they should restore those persons who said they had been exiled for their attachment to the Lacedæmonians, became so terrified at those who sallied out from Corinth, that they sent for the Lacedæmonians, and delivered up their city and citadel to their protection. The Lacedæmonians, however, though benevolently disposed towards these exiles, yet so long as they were masters of the city, never made the least mention of their recalment: and so soon as they saw the city had recovered its usual spirit, they evacuated the place, and restored them their town and their laws exactly as they received them.

But the party commanded by Iphicrates were making frequent incursions into Arcadia, in which they took much booty, and even attacked the fortified places: for the heavy-armed of the Arcadians durst never march into the field against them, so highly terrified they were at the targeteers: and yet these very targeteers were so afraid of the Lacedæmonians, that they durst never approach their heavy-armed within throw of javelin: nay, some of the younger Lacedæmonians had at times ventured to attack them even out of that distance, and had killed some of them. The Lacedæmonians, I say, had a contempt of these targeteers, but at the same time had a much greater contempt of their own confederates: for the Mantineans, when once they came out to join them, ran briskly towards the targeteers, but being galled with darts from the wall reaching down to Lecheum, they wheeled off, and some of them were killed in open flight; insomuch that the Lacedæmonians ventured to break a severe jest upon them, saying, " their confederates were as much afraid of the targeteers, as children are of bugbears." They marched however out of Lecheum, with a brigade of their own and the Corinthian exiles, and encamped themselves in a circle round the city of Corinth.

The Athenians now, who dreaded the Lacedæmonian strength, lest, as they had broken down a passage in the long walls of the Corinthians, they might march against them, thought it the most advisable expedient to rebuild the walls that were demolished by Praxitas. Thither accordingly they repaired with the whole force of Athens, attended by carpenters and masons, and in a few days' time completely rebuilt the part towards Sicyon and the west, and then proceeded in a more leisurely manner to repair the eastern wall.

But the Lacedæmonians, reflecting that the Argives, who are in a flourishing condition at home, were delighted at this war, march out to invade them. Agesilaus commanded in this expedition, and after laying waste all their territory, he departed thence by Tegea towards Corinth, and demolished the walls just rebuilt by the Athenians. His brother Teleutias also came up to him by sea with a squadron of about twelve triremes, so that their mother was now pronounced happy indeed, since in one and the same day one of her sons commanding by land demolished the walls of the enemy, and the other commanding at sea destroyed their ships and docks. Agesilaus, however, after these exploits, disbanded the confederates, and marched back the troops of that state to Sparta.

V. The Lacedæmonians after this received intelligence from the exiles, that the Corinthians of the city had lodged and secured all their cattle in Piræum, by which means they enjoyed a plentiful subsistence; upon which they march out afresh upon Corinth, Agesilaus commanding also on this occasion. In the first place he arrived at the Isthmus. It was now the month in which the Isthmian games are celebrated. The Argives were this moment there, presiding at the sacrifice to Neptune, as if Argos was Corinth. But they no sooner perceived the approach of Agesilaus, than, abandoning their sacrifices and their feasts in the highest consternation, they withdrew into the city of Corinth by the road of Cenchreæ. Agesilaus, however, would not pursue, though he saw their flight. But taking up his own quarters in the temple, he himself sacrificed to the god, and continued there till the Corinthian exiles had performed their sacrifices to Neptune, and the games. Yet, when Agesilaus was departed, the Argives did all over again. This year therefore it happened, that in some instances the same person was beaten twice over; and in others, that the very same persons were twice proclaimed to be victors.

It was on the fourth day that Agesilaus led his army towards Piræum: but finding it numerously guarded, after the time of repast he encamped before Corinth, as if he was sure of its surrender. The Corinthians therefore, being sadly alarmed lest the city might actually be betrayed to him, sent for Iphicrates with the greatest part of his targeteers. And Agesilaus, discovering that they had marched into Corinth by night, wheeled off so soon as it was day, and led directly towards Piræum. He himself advanced by the hot baths, and sent a brigade up to the highest part of the mountain. The night following he encamped near the baths, and the brigade spent the night on the summit of the mountain. And on this occasion Agesilaus gained high reputation by a small but seasonable piece of management: for though there were persons now employed in carrying up provisions to the brigade, yet nobody brought them any fire. They found it excessively cold, they were mounted quite aloft in the air, and hail and rain had fallen in the evening. Besides, they had got upon the mountain clad only in their thin summer garments. They were shivering, were quite in the dark, and had no appetite at all to their supper. Agesilaus sends them no less than ten persons with fire in chaffing-dishes. When these, getting up as they could by different paths, had reached the summit, many and large fires were soon kindled, since there was plenty of fuel at hand, and all the Lacedæmonians anointed themselves, and many of them made a hearty supper. This very night the temple of Neptune was seen all in flames; but by whom it was set on fire is still unknown. And now, when they in the Piræum perceived that the eminence was possessed by the enemy, they no longer thought of resisting: they betook themselves therefore for refuge into the temple of Juno, both men and women, slaves as well as freemen, with the greatest part of their cattle. Agesilaus marched at the head of the army along the sea-coast. But the brigade at the same time coming down from the eminence takes Oenoe, a fortress walled about, and made booty of every thing within it. That day every soldier in the army gained abundantly in plunder whatever he could stand in need of: for those who had refuged themselves in the temple of Juno came out, and left to the discretion of Agesilaus to determine what should be done with them. His sentence was, that "all such as had been concerned in the massacre should be delivered up to the exiles, and all their effects in general should be sold." In consequence of this all sorts of living creatures came out of the temple to surrender.

Many embassies from different states were attending here. Even the Bœotians were come with a demand —" What they must do to obtain a peace?" But Agesilaus with an air of high elevation would not condescend to look towards them, though Pharax the public host of the Bœotians stood at their head ready to introduce them to him. He was now sitting in the Rotundo at the harbour, and taking a view of the booty as they brought it out. A party of Lacedæmonians, belonging to the heavy-armed, with their spears alone, were guarding the prisoners along, and were gazed at with admiration by the standers-by: for the happy and the

victorious are generally regarded as fine spectacles indeed. Agesilaus still kept his seat, and seemed to be highly delighted with the scene before him, when a person on horseback came galloping that way with his horse in a foam. Many persons called upon him to tell his news, to whom he made no answer. But when he was come near to Agesilaus, throwing himself off, and running up to him with a very gloomy countenance, he told him the sad calamity of the brigade at Lecheum. Agesilaus no sooner heard it than he jumped from his seat, snatched his spear, and ordered the herald to call the general-officers, the captains of companies, and the commanders of the auxiliary troops. When these came running to him, he ordered the rest of them, for they had not yet dined, to take a little meat with their utmost despatch and follow him with all speed, whilst himself with Damasias and his company set out instantly though fasting. His guards too in their heavy armour set out eagerly with him: he went off at their head, they followed their leader. When he had passed by the hot baths and was got into the plain of Lecheum, three horsemen ride up and tell him, that "the dead bodies are recovered." When he heard this, he ordered his soldiers to ground their arms: and, after halting some time, he led them back again to the temple of Juno.

On the day following every thing they had taken was disposed of by sale. And the Bœotian ambassadors were then called for and asked the reason of their coming. But now, they made not the least mention of peace, saying only "they were desirous, if permission could be obtained, to go into the city to speak with their countrymen who were serving there." "I am well satisfied, Agesilaus replied with a smile; you have not so great a desire to see the soldiers, as to gain a view of the late success of your friends, and know how considerable it is. But have patience; I will conduct you thither myself. And if you go with me, you will be much more likely to come to an exact knowledge of the truth." He was as good as his word; for the next day, after a sacrifice, he led his army towards the city. He would not demolish the trophy; yet, if a single tree was left standing, felling it and breaking it in shatters, he convinced them that nobody durst come out into the field against him. After doing this, he encamped near Lecheum, and sent away the Theban ambassadors, not indeed to Corinth, but by the sea to Crusis. Yet such a calamity as the late one being an unusual thing to Lacedæmonians, a general dejection was visible throughout the camp, except in the persons, whose sons or fathers or brothers had died in their posts. These indeed, as if they had gained a victory, walked up and down with a cheerful countenance; exulting over their own private misfortunes. But the great calamity of that brigade fell out in the following manner.

The Lacedæmonians of Amyclæ, though they are in the field or abroad on any business whatever, always repair home at the Hyacinthan festival to join in the pæan. At this juncture therefore Agesilaus had picked the Amycleans out of all the troops, and left them at Lecheum. The officer who commanded that garrison ordered a body of the confederates to take care and guard the fortress, whilst himself with his brigade of heavy-armed and the horse conveyed the Amycleans in safety by the city of Corinth. When they were got to the distance of about twenty or thirty stadia [1] from Sicyon, the officer with his heavy-armed, who were about six hundred, was returning back again to Lecheum, but had left orders with the commander of the horse to proceed forwards with the Amycleans till they thought proper to dismiss him, and then likewise to return to Lecheum. They were not ignorant, it is true, that many both of the targeteers and heavy-armed were now in Corinth. They however entertained a contempt of them, as if nobody durst presume to attack Lacedæmonians, after their late successes. But they of Corinth, and Callias the son of Hipponicus, who commanded the heavy-armed Athenians, and Iphicrates who commanded the targeteers, seeing plainly that they were but few in number, and had neither targeteers nor horsemen with them, thought they might safely attack them with their own targeteers; for, should they proceed in their march, they could make havoc of them by throwing darts at their unarmed sides; and if they endeavoured to pursue, targeteers could easily avoid the nimblest men in heavy armour. Having thus considered the point, they lead out into the field. Callias, for his part, drew up his heavy-armed not far from the city, whilst Iphicrates with his targeteers began the attack upon the Lace-

dæmonian brigade. The Lacedæmonians being thus galled with darts, here one of them was receiving wounds, and there another was dropping, and such as stood next in the ranks were ordered to take them up and carry them to Lecheum: and those of the brigade who were thus employed, were the only persons in reality who escaped with life. In the meantime, the commanding officer ordered the Lacedæmonians of the first military class to pursue and drive away the enemy. They pursued, it is true, but not within javelin's throw of any of them, heavy-armed as they were in chace of targeteers. And he had farther enjoined them to retire from pursuit, before they came up to the heavy-armed of the enemy. When therefore they were retreating in a straggling manner, since they had pursued before with their utmost speed, the targeteers of Iphicrates faced about again, and kept pouring in their darts either directly upon them, or running up to their flanks on the unarmed sides. And immediately, in this first pursuit, they slew nine or ten of the Lacedæmonians. Being so far successful, they renewed their attacks with much greater spirit than before. The Lacedæmonians were grievously annoyed; and the commanding officer now ordered the two first military classes to pursue. They did so, but lost more persons in the retreat than they had done before. Their best men being thus destroyed, the horsemen are returned and join them; so now accompanied by the horse they renew the pursuit. But on this occasion, when the targeteers kept flying before them, the horse managed the pursuit in a very improper manner. They rode not after them so as to reach and slaughter the fliers, but keeping abreast with their own foot, either advanced or retreated with them. After repeating this method again and again, and suffering at every repetition, their numbers were continually lessening, their efforts were fainter and fainter, whilst the enemy attacked with redoubled spirit, and came thicker at them than before. Thus grievously distressed, they draw close together in a body on a little hillock about two stadia from the sea, and about sixteen or seventeen from Lecheum. Those at Lecheum, perceiving what was the matter, leap into their boats, rowed amain, and at length came to the hillock. But already grievously distressed, they were dying apace, they could do nothing at all in their own defence; and, what was

---

[1] Two or three miles.

worse, beholding the heavy-armed advancing to attack them,' they take to flight. Some of them now rush into the sea, and a small number get safe to Lechæum with the horse. But in all the skirmishes and the flight, no less than two hundred and fifty of them were destroyed. And in this manner was this affair conducted.

Agesilaus now marched off, taking with him the suffering brigade, and leaving a fresh one at Lechæum. Through the whole of his march to Sparta, he entered every city as late as possible in the evening, and resumed his march as early as possible every morning. Nay, he set out so early from Orchomenus, that he passed by Mantinéa before it was day-light. The soldiers could not bear to see the Mantineans with joy in their faces for the late calamity they had suffered.

After this, Iphicrates continued to act successfully in every thing he undertook. For as a garrison had been placed at Sidus and Crommyon by Praxitas when he took those places, and another at Oenoe by Agesilaus, when he took Piræum, Iphicrates reduced them all. The Lacedæmonians however and confederates still continued their guard at Lechæum; but the Corinthian exiles durst no longer march towards Corinth by land from Sicyon, being awed by the late calamity of the brigade; but going by water, and landing frequently near it, they carried on hostilities, vexatious indeed on both sides, with those in the city.

VI. After this, the Achæans, who were possessors of Calydon, anciently belonging to Ætolia, and had declared the Calydonians to be members of their own community, were obliged to keep a garrison in the place. For the Acarnanians made war upon it, assisted by some Athenians and Bœotians in pursuance of the confederacy between them. The Achæans therefore, being at this time distressed, send ambassadors to Lacedæmon. They arrived there, and said,—"they were treated wrongfully by the Lacedæmonians. For our own parts (said they) and you know it, Lacedæmonians, we readily take the field whenever you summon us, and march whithersoever you lead us. And now, that a city of ours is blocked up by the Acarnanians and their confederates the Athenians and Bœotians, you take no manner of care of us. Thus deserted as we are, we are no longer able to make head against them. But we must either entirely,

giving up the war in Peloponnesus, ¹ employ our whole force against the Acarnanians and their confederates, or submit to a peace the best we can get." Thus they spoke with a kind of threat to the Lacedæmonians to abandon their confederacy, unless they sent them succour in their turn. But after this representation, it was judged expedient by the ephori and council of state, to march with the Achæans against the Acarnanians. Accordingly they send out Agesilaus with two Lacedæmonian brigades and a body of confederates; and the Achæans joined in the expedition with the whole of their force. But when Agesilaus had made his passage, all the Acarnanians fled out of the country into the cities, and drove away their cattle to a very distant place, that they might not be taken by his army. Agesilaus, so soon as he arrived on the enemy's frontiers, sent to Stratus the capital of Acarnania, and declared, that "if they did not relinquish their confederacy with the Bœotians and Athenians and join the Lacedæmonians and their confederates, he would lay all their country waste, and not spare the least corner in it." And, as they gave no heed to this declaration, he kept his word. For without any intermission carrying on his devastations, he advanced in his marches not above ten or twelve stadia a day. The Acarnanians therefore, thinking they had little to apprehend from the slow marches of this army, fetched down their cattle from the mountains, and almost every where resumed their rural employments. When now they were judged by Agesilaus to have given up all fear, on the fifteenth or sixteenth day after he had entered the country, he sacrificed early in the morning, and before evening completed a march of ² one hundred and sixty stadia to the lake, about which were almost all the cattle of the Acarnanians, and took a vast many herds of oxen, and horses, and flocks of cattle of all other kinds, and many slaves. Having thus gained it, he halted there the next day, and sold all the booty; many targeteers however of the Acarnanians came up; and, as Agesilaus had encamped upon a mountain, were shooting and slinging without suffering any thing in return, and obliged the army to come down into the plain from the summit of the mountain, though they had just been preparing for sup-

---

1 Dr Taylor's reading, τάντε διατολιμέσμμε.
2 About sixteen miles.

per. The Acarnanians indeed drew off at night; and the army, having posted guards, took their repose in quiet: but the next day Agesilaus led them back. The issue from the meadow and plain round the lake was narrow, because the ground was on all sides surrounded by mountains. The Acarnanians had posted themselves upon them, and kept pouring down from above their darts and javelins. They even ventured down to the skirts of the mountains; they attacked and annoyed the army, so that they could no longer proceed in their march. The heavy-armed, it is true, from the main-body and the horse pursued them, but did no damage to such assailants: for the Acarnanians, whenever they thought proper to retire, were immediately in their strong-holds. Agesilaus, esteeming it a difficult piece of work for an army thus grievously annoyed to get clear through so narrow a pass, determined to pursue those who attacked on his left, as they were the most numerous body. The mountain also on this side was much easier of ascent for the heavy-armed and horse. Yet during the time that he sacrificed and consulted the victims, the Acarnanians still continued to pour down their darts and javelins, and approaching nearer and nearer wounded numbers. But at length, upon his giving the signal, the heavy-armed of the two first military classes started forwards, the horsemen were riding up, and Agesilaus followed with the rest. Such of the Acarnanians, therefore, as had ventured down the mountain and had been skirmishing with them, are soon forced to fly, and whilst scrambling up the ascent were put to death. The heavy-armed of the Acarnanians and many of their targeteers were drawn up on the summit of the mountain, where they stood their ground, and let fly their darts, and striking at them with their spears wounded the horsemen and slew some horses. But when they were very near falling into the hands of the Lacedæmonian heavy-armed, they took to flight, and this day about three hundred of them were slain.

After so much success, Agesilaus erected a trophy. And then marching round the country he laid it all waste with fire and sword. He even assaulted some of the towns, merely in compliance with the entreaties of the Achæans, but he took not one. And now, as autumn was coming on apace, he marched out of the country.

The Achæans, nevertheless, thought that he had done nothing at all, since he had not made himself master of a single town, either by force or voluntary surrender. They begged, therefore, that if nothing else could be done, he would only stay so long in the enemy's country as to hinder them from sowing their corn. His answer was, that "they are pleading against their own interest. I shall certainly march hither again next summer. The more seed they sow, the more desirous of course they will be of peace." Having said thus, he marched off his army through Ætolia, by such roads as neither a large nor small army could have passed without leave from the Ætolians. However they suffered him to proceed, for they hoped he would assist them to recover Naupactus. But when he came to the cape of Rhium, he crossed the sea and returned to Sparta. For the Athenians, who had stationed themselves with a squadron at Oeniadæ, stopped all passage to Peloponnesus from Calydon.

VII. When the winter was over, Agesilaus, in pursuance of his promise to the Achæans, declared an expedition in the very beginning of spring against the Acarnanians. The latter had notice of it, and reasoned right, that as their city lay in the heart of their country, they should suffer a siege as much from those who destroyed their corn, as if they were invested in form. They sent therefore ambassadors to Lacedæmon, and made a peace with the Achæans, and an offensive and defensive alliance with the Lacedæmonians. And thus ended the war of Acarnania.

Henceforth the Lacedæmonians judged it by no means safe to march their army against the Athenians or Bœotians, and leave the great and hostile state of Argos, lying on their own frontier, behind their backs: they proclaim therefore an expedition against Argos. Agesipolis, who knew that he was to command in this expedition, and found the victims favourable which he sacrificed for success, went to Olympia to consult the oracle. He demanded of the god, "Whether, in consistence with piety, he might reject the truce which the Argives would plead?" For the latter would begin to compute its expiration not from the day of the declaration, but from the time when the Lacedæmonians actually broke into their country. The god signified to him, that consistently with piety he might reject it so wrongfully.

pleaded. From thence, without loss of time, he repaired to Delphi, and there demanded of Apollo, " Whether he judged of the truce in the same manner with his father?" He answered positively to the same purpose. Accordingly Agesipolis put himself at the head of the army, and marched from Phlius, for there it had assembled whilst he was on his journey to the oracles, and broke in by the pass of Nemea. But the Argives, when they found themselves unable to make head against him, sent to him, as usual, two heralds with garlands on their heads, alleging that " the truce was not expired." Agesipolis having answered, that " the gods had decided against the justice of their plea," refused to observe it, and marched forwards into the country, and soon caused high perplexity and distress over all the country, and in Argos itself. But the first day they were in Argia, after Agesipolis had supped, and upon finishing supper they were making the libation, Neptune shook the earth. Upon this the Lacedæmonians, who were but just set out from home, joined in chorus and sung the pæan to the god ; but the rest of the troops concluded, that they ought to return home immediately, since Agis formerly upon the shock of an earthquake had marched them out of Elis. Agesipolis alleged, that " if the god had shaken the earth when he was only intending to break in, he should have construed it a prohibition ; but now that he actually had broken in, he judged it an exhortation ;" and so the next day, after sacrificing to Neptune, he advanced, though not far, into the country. As Agesilaus had lately commanded in an expedition against Argos, Agesipolis asked the soldiers, how near he had advanced to the walls of the city? how far he had extended his devastations ? and then, like the champion in public games, who struggles for every prize, he endeavoured to outdo him in every respect. He was once even within reach of darts from the turrets, but then he immediately repassed the trenches that surrounded the walls. And when most of the Argives were marched into Laconia, he approached so near to the very gates, that they shut them against some Bœotian horsemen who had just desired to be let in, afraid that the Lacedæmonians might rush in along with them ; insomuch that those horsemen were compelled to keep clinging under the battlements, like so many bats. And had not the Cretans at that time been absent on an ex-

cursion to Nauplia, many men and horses too must have been shot to death. But after this, when he lay encamped near Eircta a thunderbolt fell in the camp. Some were much affrighted, but some were actually killed by the lightning. And having afterwards a mind to fortify a castle at the entrance of the pass over the Colousa, he sacrificed, and the victims appeared without lobes. Determined by this, he led off the army and dismissed them, having done vast damage to the Argives by an invasion so little expected.

VIII. The war was on this manner carried on at land. And I shall now relate the concurrent transactions at sea and the cities on the sea-coast ; describing such of them only as are worthy of remembrance, and omitting such as deserve not a particular mention.

In the first place, therefore, Pharnabazus and Conon, after beating the Lacedæmonians at sea, sailing round to the isles and the maritime cities, drove out the Lacedæmonian commandants, and gained the hearty goodwill of the people, as they placed no garrisons in their citadels, but left them free and independent. Nay, such as only heard of this behaviour were delighted with and commended it much, and sent cheerfully their hospitable presents to Pharnabazus. For Conon had convinced him, that if he acted thus, " he would be sure of the friendship of all the cities : but in case he manifested any design to enslave them, then (he added) each single city is able to cut you out a deal of trouble, and the danger is, that all the Greeks, when they see into your schemes, will unite together against you." Pharnabazus therefore was persuaded by him : and, going on shore at Ephesus, he gave Conon forty ships ; and, having told him to meet him at Sestus, he went by land to his own dominions. Dercyllidas truly, an inveterate enemy to Pharnabazus, happened to be at Abydus at the time of the late battle at sea ; yet, instead of abandoning his town, as did the other commandants, he fast secured Abydus, and kept it firm to the Lacedæmonians. His first step had been to convene the Abydenians, and to harangue them thus :

" It is now, ye men of Abydus, in your power, as you long have been steady friends to the Lacedæmonian state, to prove yourselves their actual benefactors. To continue faithful during a course of prosperity hath nothing wonderful in it ; but, when any set of men continue steadily attached to friends in adversity, they ought on that account to be eternally remembered. Not that we are in so bad a situation as to be nothing at all, because we have been beaten at sea. For formerly, when the Athenians were the sovereigns of the sea, our state was very well able to do good to her friends and harm to her enemies. But by how much the larger is the number of the cities, which, veering about with fortune, at present desert us, by so much will your fidelity be actually the more conspicuous. Some persons it is true may apprehend that we are in danger here of being besieged both by land and sea: but let such reflect, that as yet, no Grecian fleet appears at sea, and that Greece will never suffer a fleet of Barbarians to ride masters of the sea. Greece undoubtedly will assist herself, and consequently will fight for you."

The Abydenians, having heard him, were readily without any reluctance persuaded. They received in a friendly manner the new governants, and invited to their posts such as had absented. But Dercyllidas, so soon as a large body of men well qualified for service were assembled in Abydus, passed over to Sestus, which is over-against Abydus, distant from it no more than eight stadia, and collected together all the persons who had been settled by the Lacedæmonians on the lands of the Chersonesus, and as many of the commandants as had been ejected out of the cities in Europe. He received them kindly, telling them, " they ought not to give way to dejection, but recall to mind, that even yet in Asia, which originally belongs to the king, there are Temnus, though not a large city, and the Ægians, and other places in which they might settle, and disdain submission to the king. Nay, where (he went on) can you find another place so strong as Sestus? what town more difficult to be reduced by siege? since it cannot possibly be blocked up without both a land and a naval force." And by talking to them in this manner, he preserved them from total dejection.

Pharnabazus, when he found that Dercyllidas had thus secured Abydus and Sestus, sent word to the inhabitants, that " if they did not send away the Lacedæmonians, he would make war upon them;" and, as they were not to be awed by this menace, he sent orders to Conon not to suffer them to stir by sea, and then he ravaged in person the territory of the Abydenians. But as nothing he did could induce them to surrender, he himself went home, and ordered Conon so to manage the cities in Hellespont, that as large a fleet as possible might be gathered together in the spring. Full of resentment against the Lacedæmonians for the harm they had done him, it was his high ambition to go even to Laconia, and revenge himself to the utmost of his power. They spent the winter therefore in making preparations ; and early in the spring, having manned out a numerous fleet, and hired a body of auxiliaries, Pharnabazus put to sea and Conon with him, and sailed through the islands to Melos, and from thence they proceeded towards Lacedæmon. In the first place, making a descent at Pheræ, he laid all the adjacent country waste ; and afterwards repeating his descents on the coast, he did them all possible damage. Yet, terrified at a coast where harbours were so scarce, and at the readiness of the people to resist him, added to the danger of wanting provisions, he soon turned back, and, standing off, cast anchor at Phænicus of Cythera. But when such of the Cytherians as guarded the city were afraid of being stormed and taken prisoners, they evacuated their works ; and these persons, according to terms granted them by Pharnabazus, were sent over by him into Laconia. He then repaired the fortifications of the Cytherians, and left a garrison there under the command of Nicophebus the Athenian. Having done this, he sailed up to the isthmus of Corinth ; and after encouraging the confederates to proceed briskly in the war, and to manifest their zeal for the king, he gave them all the money he had with him, and then departing sailed immediately home.

But Conon representing to him, that, "if he would put the fleet under his command, he would furnish it with all needful supplies from the islands, and then sailing back to Athens, would rebuild the long walls and the wall round the Piræus, than which (he assured him,) nothing would vex the Lacedæmonians more. Hereby too (he added) you yourself, Pharnabazus, will most highly oblige the Athenians, and take ample revenge on the Lacedæmonians, for you will undo at once what they have long been labouring with their highest application." Pharnabazus hearing this, readily sent him away to Athens, and furnished him with money to rebuild the walls. Accordingly on his arrival, he rebuilt great part of the wall, employing his own seamen in the work, advancing wages to carpenters and masons, and defraying every needful expense. The remaining part of it the Athenians themselves and the Bœotians, and other states, rebuilt voluntarily at the same time.

In the meanwhile the Corinthians, who by help of the money Pharnabazus left behind had manned out a fleet, and given the command of it to Agathinus, were quite masters by sea in the bay round Achaia and Lecheum. The Lacedæmonians indeed manned out a fleet against them, which was commanded by Polemarchus. But as an engagement came on, in which Polemarchus was killed, and Pollis his lieutenant was also carried ashore wounded, Herippidas takes upon him the command of the ships. However, Prœnus the Corinthian, who succeeded Agathinus in the command of the fleet, abandoned Rhium, and the Lacedæmonians took possession of it. Teleutias after this took the fleet from Herippidas, and now again he was master of the whole bay.

But the Lacedæmonians, having heard that Conon, at the king's expense, was rebuilding the walls of Athens, and by the same means subsisting his fleet, and settling the islands and maritime cities on the continent in a manner most agreeable to the Athenian interest, they imagined that could they give Teribazus, who was one of the king's generals, an information of these points, they should either bring him over to their own side, or at least put a stop to the subsistence of Conon's fleet. And thus resolved, they send Antalcidas to Teribazus, instructing him to inform Teribazus of all these points, and endeavour to make peace between the state of Lacedæmon and the king. The Athenians, aware of the design, send away an embassy along with Conon, consisting of Hermogenes, Dion, Callisthenes, and Callimedon. They also invited their confederates to despatch their embassies in company with them; accordingly they were sent by the Bœotians, and from Corinth, and from Argos. When all were arrived, Antalcidas told Teribazus that "he came to solicit a peace between his own constituents and the king, and such a peace as the king himself must be glad of. For the Lacedæmonians would have no dispute with the king about the Greek cities in Asia; they would rest contented if the islands and other cities were left free and independent. And why," says he, "when we are thus compliant, should either the Greeks or the king

carry on a war against us? or why should the king incur so vast an expense? For when we no longer lead, it will be impossible either for the Athenians to make war upon the king, or for us to do so ourselves, when the cities are free and independent." These words of Antalcidas were heard by Teribazus with high satisfaction; but to the opposite party they were to continue to be merely words; for the Athenians, in case it was agreed to leave the cities and islands free and independent, were afraid of losing Lemnos and Imbrus and Sciros; the Thebans were also afraid they should be obliged to set the cities of Bœotia at liberty; and the Argives were apprehensive of disappointment in their desire to keep as fast hold of Corinth as Argos, if such a treaty and such a peace was made. By this means no terms of peace could be agreed on, and every embassy again went home.

As to Teribazus, he thought it not consistent with his own personal security to make a separate peace with the Lacedæmonians without consulting the king. However, he gave Antalcidas a supply of money to enable the Lacedæmonians to keep a fleet at sea, in order to render a peace quite necessary to the Athenians and their confederates; and he shut up Conon in prison, as one who had injured the king, and was justly accused by the Lacedæmonians. After this, he made a journey to the king, to tell him what the Lacedæmonians had proposed, and that he had apprehended Conon for his ill behaviour, and to receive orders about his future conduct. The king, indeed, so soon as Teribazus arrives at court, sends Struthes down as governor of the maritime provinces on the coast. And Struthes exerted himself in warm attachment to the Athenians, remembering what damage the dominions of his master had suffered from Agesilaus.

The Lacedæmonians, when they saw that Struthes had turned out an enemy to them, but a friend to the Athenians, send Thimbro to make war against him: and Thimbro, when he had crossed the sea, and taken his march from Ephesus and the cities in the plains of Mæander, Priene, and Leucophrys, and Archilleum, put the dominions of the king to fire and sword. But in process of time, Struthes, having received intelligence that Thimbro ran over the country in that negligent manner which showed a contempt of his enemies, he sent his cavalry into the plains of Mæander, whom he ordered to ride quite round, and drive off every thing they could find. It happened that Thimbro was now passing the time after dinner in the tent of Thersander the musician: for Thersander was not only a good musician, but a good soldier too, since he had been trained at Sparta. Struthes, who perceived the enemy were marching about in a negligent manner, and to be few in number when he first discovered them, rushes at once upon them with a numerous and firmly compacted body of horse. Both Thimbro and Thersander were among the first whom they slew; and after killing them, they soon put the rest to flight, and pursuing, made a vast slaughter of them. There were some, indeed, who completed their escape to friendly cities; but there were more who saved themselves by being left behind, and not knowing in time of the engagement: for very often, and on this occasion too, Thimbro had advanced against the enemy, without giving any signal for the troops to follow. And these things were done in this manner.

But when those who had been exiled from Rhodes by the people, were arrived at Lacedæmon, they represented there how impolitic it would be to continue inactive, whilst the Athenians were reducing Rhodes, and gaining so great an accession of strength. The Lacedæmonians, therefore, well apprised that if the people were masters, all Rhodes would be in the power of the Athenians, but if the rich prevail it would be in their own, manned out eight ships for their assistance, and appointed Ecdicus to command them. On board these ships they also sent away Diphridas. The latter they ordered to go over into Asia, and there to secure the cities which had adhered to Thimbro, and to take upon him the command of the troops yet remaining, and, reinforcing them with all possible additions, to make war upon Struthes. Diphridas obeyed all his orders; and, amongst other parts of his successful conduct, takes prisoner Tigranes and his wife, who was the daughter of Struthes, as they were travelling to Sardis, and for a vast sum of money set them again at liberty. By this money he was immediately enabled to pay his troops: for Diphridas gave in every respect as great satisfaction as Thimbro had given; but, as a general, outdid him far in discipline and vigilant activity. No bodily indulgence ever gained the ascendant over him,

but on the contrary, he gave all his attention to the business in hand. But Ecdicus, after sailing to Cnidus, heard there that the people had the entire possession of Rhodes, and were masters both by land and sea. Nay, they were then out at sea with a number of triremes double to his own. He therefore continued quietly at Cnidus. But the Lacedæmonians, when they found his squadron was too small to give any effectual aid to their friends, ordered Teleutias, with the twelve ships he commanded in the bay along Achaia and Lecheum, to sail round to Ecdicus; and as to Ecdicus, to send him home, whilst himself took all the care he could of such as desired his protection, and did all possible damage to the enemy. Teleutias, when he arrived at Samos, enlarged his fleet with the ships from thence, and proceeded to Cnidus, but Ecdicus returned home.

Teleutias, having now twenty-seven ships, put to sea against Rhodes. But in his course he falls in with Philocrates the son of Ephialtus, who with thirteen ships was bound from Athens to Cyprus, to assist Evagoras; and he takes them all. Both parties on this occasion were acting in direct contrariety to their own interest. For the Athenians, who enjoyed the friendship of the king, were sending this aid to Evagoras, who was at war with the king; and Teleutias, whilst the Lacedæmonians were likewise at war with him, demolished those who were going to a war against him. But Teleutias, having steered back again to Cnidus, and disposed of his captures, proceeded afterwards to Rhodes to succour the friends of Sparta.

The Athenians, growing now apprehensive that the Lacedæmonians might re-establish their power at sea, send out for their annoyance Thrasybulus the Styrensian, with forty ships. He was now at sea, but pursued not the auxiliary squadron for Rhodes; judging, that he could not easily hurt the friends of the Lacedæmonians, who were possessed of a fortified place, and had Teleutias ready with his fleet to protect them; and that neither were the Athenians in danger of being reduced by their enemies, as they had possession of cities far superior in number, and had beat them in field of battle. He sailed therefore to the Hellespont, and no enemy appearing, he was intent on performing some notable service for the state. In the first place, therefore, having

3 I

received intelligence, that a rupture had happened between Amadocus, king of the Odrysians, and Seuthes who possessed the sea-coast of Thrace, he reconciled them to one another, and made both of them friends and confederates to the Athenians; concluding, that when these princes were in friendship, the Greek cities in Thrace would, even though against their inclinations, pay higher regard to the Athenians. All being now right in those cities, as well as in the cities of Asia, because the king was in friendship with the Athenians, he proceeded to Byzantium, and put to sale the tenths of the ships from Pontus. He also obliged the Byzantines to change their oligarchical government into a democracy, so that the people of Byzantium now beheld without chagrin the great number of Athenians at present in the city. Having done these things, and also made friends of the Chalcedonians, he sailed out of the Hellespont. But though he found in Lesbos that all the cities, except Mitylene, were in the Lacedæmonian interest, he let them alone till he had been at Mitylene, where he settled four hundred persons from on board his fleet, and all such exiles from the other cities as had taken refuge there. Then taking such of the Mitylenians as were best qualified for the service, and inspiring proper hopes into all, into the Mitylenians, that if he reduced the cities, they should be masters of the whole isle of Lesbos;—into the exiles, that if they would go with him to each city, they would all of them be of course enabled to recover their former state; and into those who went on board his fleet, that, would they make all Lesbos friends to Mitylene, they must necessarily acquire abundance of wealth. With these exhortations and their united strength he led them against Methymne. Therimachus, who commanded there for the Lacedæmonians, no sooner knew of the approach of Thrasybulus than he ordered all the mariners on shore, with whom and the Methymneans, and the exiles from Mitylene now at Methymne, he marched out and met him on the frontier. A battle ensued, in which Therimachus is slain: and the rest flying, a great slaughter is made of them. After this he brought over some of the cities, and he plundered the territories of such as did not come in, and supplied his soldiers with pay. He was now in a hurry to get to Rhodes; but in order to put the troops into higher spirits, he collect-

ed contributions from other cities; and proceeding to Aspendus, he anchored in the river Eurymedon. He had received their contribution from the Aspendians when his soldiers did some damage on their lands. The Aspendians growing angry at it, and falling upon him in the night, kill him in his tent. In this manner Thrasybulus, a man of so great accomplishments, ended his days. The Athenians, however, having chosen Argyrius for his successor, sent him to the fleet.

The Lacedæmonians hearing now, that the tenth of the ships from Pontus had been sold by the Athenians at Byzantium, that they are masters of Chalcedon, and that the other Hellespontine cities having the friendship of Pharnabazus were in a safe situation, saw plainly that all their care was needful. They had no reason however to blame Dercyllidas; and yet Anaxibius, who was favoured by the ephori, solicited successfully for himself, and was sent out to be the commandant of Abydus. Nay, would they give him money and shipping, he promised to carry on the war against the Athenians, and stop their career of prosperity in the Hellespont. Having assigned him therefore three triremes and pay for a thousand foreigners, they sent Anaxibius to sea. He was no sooner arrived, than he drew together by land his number of foreign troops; he forced over some cities from Pharnabazus; and as the latter with the aid of the other cities had invaded the territories of Abydus, he returned the invasion, marched against them, and laid waste their country. Then doubling the number of ships he brought by manning out three more at Abydus, he fetched into that harbour whatever vessel belonging to the Athenians or their confederates he could catch at sea.

The Athenians informed of this, and afraid lest all the fine dispositions Thrasybulus had made in Hellespont should be quite ruined, send out Iphicrates with eight ships and about twelve hundred targeteers. The greatest number of the latter were the same whom he commanded at Corinth: for when the Argives had made Corinth Argos, they said they had no farther need of them. Iphicrates, in fact, had killed some persons who had been in the Argive interest, and on that account withdrew to Athens, and lived retired. But when he was arrived at the Chersonesus, Iphicrates and Anaxibius at first carried on a piratical war against one another: but in process of time,

Iphicrates perceiving that Anaxibius was marched against Antandros with his foreign troops and what Lacedæmonians he had, and two hundred heavy-armed Abydenians; and hearing farther, that he had gained Antandros by composition, he suspected that after settling a garrison there, he would return the same way, and bring back the Abydenians to their own city. He therefore passed over by night into the least frequented part of the territory of Abydus, and marching up into the mountains he placed an ambuscade. He ordered the triremes that brought him over to keep cruising at day-light along the Chersonesus, that it might be judged he was then upon his usual employ of fetching in contributions. Having made these dispositions, every thing fell out just as he expected: for Anaxibius was now on his return, even though the victims at his morning sacrifice were inauspicious. But this he disregarded, since he was to march through a friendly country, and was going to a friendly city. And when he heard besides from persons he met that Iphicrates was sailed towards Proconnesus, he marched with more negligence than before. So long, however, as the troops of Anaxibius were upon the same level ground with himself, Iphicrates rose not from his ambuscade. But so soon as the Abydenians, who had the van, were got down into the plain near Cremastes, where are the mines of gold, and the rest of the troops were descending the mountain, and Anaxibius with his Lacedæmonians was just at the descent, that moment Iphicrates starts up from his place of ambush, and runs full speed towards him. Anaxibius, knowing there was no possibility of escape, as he saw his troops were in a narrow road, and extended in a long line forwards, as he judged that those who were gone on could not readily remount the ascent to his aid, and saw plainly that they were all in a panic on the appearance of the ambuscade, he said to those who were near him, " It is my duty, sirs, to die on this very spot; but do you make the best of your way to a place of safety, before the enemy can charge you." He said these words, and then snatching his shield from the person that carried it, he fights and is slain on the spot. A favourite boy stood by him to the last, and about twelve of the Lacedæmonian commandants of cities, who were in company fought and died with him. All the rest fled, and were slaughtered in their flight. They pursued them to Abydus. Of the other troops about two hundred were slain, and about fifty of the Abydenian heavy-armed. But after this exploit, Iphicrates returned again to the Chersonesus.

THE

AFFAIRS OF GREECE.

BOOK V.

CONTENTS of BOOK V.

AFFAIRS OF GREECE.

BOOK V.

THIS was the state of the war between the thenians and Lacedæmonians in the Helles-
nt.

The people of Ægina had for a long time
pt up intercourse with the Athenians. But
rw, as war was again openly renewed at sea,
teonicus, who was again in Ægina, empower-
l them, with the joint consent of the Ephori,
plunder Attica at pleasure. The Athenians,
ocked up by them, sent over a body of heavy-
med commanded by Pamphilus, into Ægina,
invest them with a work of circumvallation,
ocking them thus up at land, and with ten
iips at sea. Teleutias however, who hap-
med about this time to be going round the
lands to collect money, having received intelli-
rnce of the throwing up this circumvallation,
ime away to assist the Æginetæ. He indeed
rove off the ships, but Pamphilus kept fast
ossession of the work on shore.

But now Hierax arriveth from Lacedæmon
ɔ be admiral of the fleet, and accordingly re-
eiveth the command. Teleutias departed
'om Sparta, and in as happy a manner as his
ivn heart could wish: for when, upon the
oint of departure, he went down to the water
de, the whole soldiery crowded about him to
take him by the hand. One was crowning
im with a garland, another adorning him with
illets; and such as came too late, and found
im already under sail, threw their garlands
ito the sea after him, and prayed Heaven to
less him in all his undertakings. I am sensi-
le, indeed, that in relating such incidents, I
ive no shining proof of munificence, bravery,
r fine conduct. But by Heaven I think it
vorth any man's while to reflect, by what me-
bods Teleutias had thus gained the hearts of
hose whom he commanded: for such behavi-

our better deserveth our admiration that any
acquisition of wealth or conquest.

Hierax, with the rest of the fleet, sailed again
to Rhodes; but he left twelve ships at Ægina,
under the command of his lieutenant Gorgopas.
The consequence was, that the Athenian troops
were more closely blocked up in their own circumvallation than their countrymen were in A-
thens: insomuch that, five months after, the
Athenians, having by express decree manned out
a large number of ships, fetched off the people
on this service, and carried them back to Athens.
And yet after this they were sadly infested a
second time by the plunderers from Ægina and
by Gorgopas too. They therefore man out
against the latter thirteen ships, and elect Eunomus to take upon him the command of them.

Hierax being still at Rhodes, the Lacedæmonians send out Antalcidas to be admiral in
chief; judging that by giving this commission
to Antalcidas, they should most sensibly oblige
Teribazus. Antalcidas, when he came to
Ægina, took away with him the ships under
Gorgopas, and proceeded to Ephesus. But from
thence he sends back Gorgopas with the twelve
ships to his former station at Ægina, and gave
the command of the rest to his own lieutenant
Nicolochus. Nicolochus set sail from Ephesus
to go and assist the citizens of Abydus. But
in his passage landing upon Tenedos, he laid
the country waste, and, after getting a sum of
money, he stood away from thence to Abydus.
The Athenian commanders, collecting what
strength they could from Samothracia and
Thasus and the adjacent places, repaired to
the assistance of the Tenedians. But when
they found that Nicolochus was already gone
away to Abydus, they put to sea from the
Chersonesus, and with two and thirty sail of

their own blocked him up in Abydus, as he had but twenty-five. Gorgopas, in the meantime, repassing from Ephesus, falls in with Eunomus; and sheering off at first reached the island of Ægina a little before sun-set. He immediately landed his men, and ordered them to eat their suppers: but Eunomus, after a little stay, sheered off. It was now dark night; he therefore led the way with his own ship, which carried a light, as is the practice at sea, that the squadron might not disperse. But Gorgopas, having again got his men on board, followed after him by direction of the light, keeping at a proper distance, that he might not be perceived, and, to prevent all alarm, ordering the masters not to shout aloud, but to drop stones for their signals, and all oars to be gently moved: but so soon as the ships of Eunomus had made land near Zoster in Attica, he ordered the trumpets to sound, and to fall in amongst them. The crews belonging to the ships of Eunomus were some of them already on shore, some of them were this moment landing, and some were still drawing to land. A battle was fought by moonlight; and in it Gorgopas taketh four of the enemy's ships, which he fastened to his own, and returned with them in tow to Ægina; but the other Athenian ships of this squadron fled for shelter into the Piræus.

Chabrias after this was sailing out to Cyprus to the aid of Evagoras, having with him eight hundred targeteers and ten ships. But taking out at the same time from Athens other ships and some heavy-armed, he landed by night on the isle of Ægina, and with his targeteers sat down in ambuscade in a hollow, a good way beyond the temple of Hercules. So soon as it was day, as had been previously agreed, the heavy-armed from Athens came ashore under the command of Dimænetus, and marched likewise about sixteen stadia beyond the temple to the place called Tripyrgia. Gorgopas, having heard it, ran down with the Æginetæ, with the soldiers of his own squadron, and the eight Spartans who happened to be with him. He left orders for all persons belonging to the squadron who were free men to follow, so that numbers of them were approaching, each provided with such a weapon as he could get. When the first party had passed by the ambuscade, Chabrias starts up with his targeteers, who immediately attacked and galled them with javelins. The heavy-armed, who had

last landed, charged them at the same time. And thus this first party, as they were few in number, were immediately slain, amongst whom was Gorgopas and the Lacedæmonians. When these were killed, all the rest turned about and fled. Of the Æginetæ there perished about a hundred and fifty, and not less than two hundred of the strangers, and sojourners, and mariners, who had run together for aid.

The Athenians after this ranged the sea as quietly as in the midst of peace: for the seamen paid no regard to Eteonicus, though he would have compelled them to go on board, since he had no money to pay them. But now again the Lacedæmonians send Teleutias to command as admiral in chief. The soldiers, when they saw him arrive, were rejoiced above measure. He immediately called them together, and harangued them thus:

"Here I am again, my fellow-soldiers, but bring no money with me. And yet, with the blessing of heaven and your hearty concurrence, I will endeavour to provide abundantly every article that you can need. Be assured within yourselves, that so long as I am in command, I pray for your comfortable subsistence no less than for my own. And perhaps it may surprise you to hear me say, that I had rather want bread myself than see you want it. But by the gods I would rather choose to be without food two days together, than you should be without it one. My door in the former parts of my command was constantly open to any one that wanted me, and shall be open now. Insomuch that, when you are enjoying plenty and abundance, you shall then see my table too more plentifully provided. But again, when you behold me enduring cold and heat and want of sleep, remember that you are bound in duty to endure them with me. I would not subject you to any hardships of this nature merely to give you pain, but in order to put it in your power to reap a higher good. The community of which we are members, my fellow-soldiers, and a happy community it is, hath attained, you well know, the large share of happiness with which it is blessed, not by habitual sloth, but by an alacrity to endure every toil and every danger for the public welfare. You, I know it by long experience, were formerly good men: and now it behoves you to approve yourselves better men than ever, that we may unite with pleasure in every toil, and unite with pleasure too in the enjoyment of every success. What thing on earth can be so sweet, as to cajole no man, neither Greek nor Barbarian, for a precarious pay, but to be able to earn our own subsistence, and that too by the most glorious methods? For in time of war, affluence at the cost of our foes, be ye well assured, is the finest provision men can make for themselves, as it is the admiration of all mankind."

In this manner Teleutias spoke. The whole assembly shouted aloud upon him to issue his orders, since they were ready to obey. He next performed the solemn sacrifice, and then said to them—" Depart now, my honest souls, and eat your suppers as usual; then prepare for yourselves one day's provision. This done, repair hither immediately, that we may go whither heaven invites us, and arrive in time." When they were all returned, he ordered them on board, and set sail by night for the harbour of Athens. Sometimes he slackened his course, and ordered them to take a little rest, then he advanced farther by plying the oars. But in case any one blames him on this occasion, for going out imprudently with only twelve ships against a people possessed of such numerous shipping, let such a one reflect on the judicious motives on which he acted. He concluded, that as Gorgopas was killed, he should find the Athenians keeping little or no guard at all in the harbour; and though the ships of war should be lying there at anchor, he thought it safer to attack twenty of them in harbour than ten of them out at sea. When they were on a cruise, he knew that the seamen lay constantly on board the vessels; but at Athens, he was assured that the captains of the ships always went home to bed, and the seamen too had lodgings on shore. It was on these considerations that he engaged in this attempt.

When he was advanced within five or six stadia of the harbour, he made all stop quietly, and rest themselves for a time. But at break of day he led the way into the harbour, and the rest followed. He would not suffer any of his own ships to sink or to damage the trading vessels; but if they saw a ship of war any where at anchor, he ordered them to disable her for sea, and to fasten all the trading vessels and such as had cargoes on board, and tow them out to sea; to search also the larger ships, and make all persons prisoners whom they found on board. Nay, some of his people even leaped on shore on the quay, and laying hold on some merchants and masters of vessels, carried them on board their own ships.

In this manner Teleutias successfully conducted the business. Such of the Athenians as were within the houses ran out to learn the meaning of the noise; such of them as were out of doors ran home for their arms, whilst some were posting up to the city with the news. All Athenians, as well the heavy-armed as the horsemen, were now marching down in arms, as if the Piræus was taken. But Teleutias sent away his prizes to Ægina, and ordered three or four of his ships to accompany them thither. With the remainder he proceeded along the Attic coast, and in standing out of the harbour he took a great number of fishing-boats, and the ferries full of passengers coming in from the islands. When he was got up to the cape of Sunium, he also took some vessels laden with corn, and some with merchandise. After these captures he sailed back to Ægina; and disposing of his spoils by public sale, he advanced a month's subsistence to his men. Nay, he afterwards continued his cruises, and made prize of every thing he could. By acting in this manner he kept his ships full manned, and preserved the cheerful and prompt obedience of all his people.

It was at this time that Antalcidas in the company of Teribazus returned from the king. He had so conducted his negotiations, as to be assured of the king's future concurrence with the Lacedæmonians, if the Athenians and confederates did not acquiesce in the peace which he himself had proposed. But when he heard that Nicolochus with his squadron was blocked up in Abydus by Iphicrates and Diotimus, he went by land to Abydus. Resuming there the command of the fleet, he went out to sea by night, having scattered a report that he was sent for by the Chalcedonians. But he went only into the harbour of Percope, where quietly he stationed his ships. His departure was perceived by Dimænetus, Dionysius, Leontichus, and Phanias, who immediately went in pursuit after him towards Proconesus. And when they had clearly passed beyond him, Antalcidas returned and came again to Abydus. For he heard that Polyxenus was coming thither with twenty sail from Syracuse and Italy: and his design was now to join them to his own.

After this Thrasybulus of Colyttus set sail from Thrace with eight ships to join the rest of the Athenian fleet. But Antalcidas, when

3 K

the sentinel made a signal that eight ships were in sight, sending the seamen on board twelve of his prime sailers, and ordering their crews to be completed out of the rest of the ships, lay on the watch as much out of view as possible. When they had sailed by, he began a pursuit; they saw him and fled. He soon reached their slowest vessels with the swiftest of his own; but he had ordered such as came first up with them, not to meddle with the hindermost vessels of the enemy, but to pursue the foremost in flight. And so soon as he had taken these, the hindermost seeing their leaders taken, were so dispirited that they became easy captures to the slower vessels of the enemy, and every ship was taken.

Antalcidas, farther, when the twenty ships from Syracuse came up to him, and all the ships of which Teribazus was master had also joined him from Ionia;—the latter were manned out of the dominions of Ariobarzanes; for Teribazus, by the ties of hospitality, had long been connected with Ariobarzanes, and Pharnabazus was now by invitation gone up to the royal court, where he married the king's daughter;—Antalcidas, I say, by the junction of these ships, which were more than eighty in number, rode master of the sea; insomuch that he stopped the navigation of all vessels from Pontus to Athens, and carried them off to the confederates of the Lacedæmonians.

The Athenians now, who saw the enemy's ships so numerous, were highly alarmed, lest they should be warred down as they were before, now that the king was become a confederate with the Lacedæmonians, and they were blocked up at home by the plunderers from Ægina. For these reasons they were sincerely desirous of a peace.

On the other side the Lacedæmonians, who kept a brigade in garrison at Lecheum, and another brigade at Orchomenus; who besides were keeping a constant guard over the cities firmly attached to them lest they should be taken, and even such as they were diffident of lest they should revolt; who farther were harassed and harassing with successive hostilities about Corinth, were sadly tired of the war.

The Argives, farther, who found that an expedition was proclaimed against them, and were sensible that their insisting on the computation of the months would avail them nothing, began also heartily to wish for a peace.

Hence it was, that when Teribazus issued out the notification, that all states, who were desirous of a peace on the terms which the king prescribes, should assemble together, they were all soon assembled. And now in the presence of them all, Teribazus, having first showed the king's signet, read aloud to them the contents of his mandate, as followeth:

"Artaxerxes the king thinks it just, that the cities in Asia and the two isles of Clazomenæ and Cyprus should be his own; but, that all the rest of the Grecian cities, both small and great, should be left free and independent, except Lemnos, Imbros, and Sciros; these, as formerly, to continue in subjection to the Athenians. And whatever people refuseth this peace, I myself, with such as receive it, shall make war against that people, both by land and sea, both with ships and with money."

The ambassadors from the several states having heard this mandate, sent their report of it to their constituents. All the rest swore absolutely to the observance of it, but the Thebans insisted upon taking the oath in the name of all the Bœotians. Agesilaus positively refused to admit their oath, unless they swore according to the letter of the king's mandate, that "every city small and great shall be left free and independent." The Theban ambassadors urged in return, they were not empowered to do it. "Go then," said Agesilaus, "and consult your principals. But tell them at the same time from me, that if they do not comply they shall be excluded the peace." Accordingly the ambassadors departed.

Agesilaus, because of his long inveteracy against the Thebans, lost no time, but with the approbation of the ephori sacrificed immediately. And so soon as the victims had a favourable appearance, he passed the frontiers to Tegea. He sent his horsemen to summon in the neighbouring troops; he sent commanders round to the several states. But before he could march from Tegea the Thebans were with him, professing that they would leave the cities free and independent. And thus the Lacedæmonians returned home, and the Thebans were obliged to accept the peace and to leave the cities of Bœotia in freedom and independence.

On another side the Corinthians would not dismiss the garrison of Argives. But Agesilaus sent a notification to the Corinthians, "that if they did not send away the Argives," and to the Argives "that if they did not evacuate Corinth, he would make war upon them." This menace affrighted them both, and the Argives accordingly marched out, and Corinth became again the city of the Corinthians. The authors of the massacre, indeed, and their accomplices, of their own accord withdrew from the city: but the other citizens readily gave a re-establishment to the former exiles.

When these points were settled, and the states had sworn to the peace which the king prescribed, all the land armies were disbanded, and all the naval forces were disbanded too. And thus at length the first peace was ratified in form between the Lacedæmonians, Athenians, and confederates after the war between them subsequent to the demolition of the walls of Athens. But though through the whole course of the war the scale had generally turned in favour of the Lacedæmonians, yet they made a greater figure than ever through this peace, which took its name from Antalcidas. For now, assuming the execution of the peace prescribed by the king, and insisting that the cities should be free, they recovered the alliance of Corinth; they set the cities of Bœotia at liberty from the Thebans, a point which they had long desired; they had put an end to that appropriation which the Argives had made of Corinth, by declaring war against them unless they evacuated that city. All these points being accomplished to their wish, they now came to a determination to chastise such of their confederates as had been untractable during the war, and manifested any good-will to their enemies; and to order them so now, that they should not dare to be refractory in time to come.

II. In the first place, therefore, they sent to the Mantineans, commanding them "to demolish their walls;" affirming that "nothing less could convince them they would not take side with their enemies." They added, that "they well knew how they had supplied the Argives with corn during the late war; and sometimes, on pretext of truces, had refused to march with them against the enemy; and, even when they did march, were intent on doing them more hurt than good." They told them farther, "they were well convinced, how much they envied them upon every incident of success, and how heartily they rejoiced if any calamity befell them." A declaration was also made, that "the truce with the Mantineans for thirty

years, agreed upon after the battle of Mantinea, expired this present year." But as the Mantineans refused to demolish their walls, the Lacedæmonians proclaim an expedition against them.

Agesilaus on this occasion petitioned the state to excuse his commanding the army; alleging that "the Mantinean community had done many good services to his father in the war against Messene." Agesipolis therefore led out the army, notwithstanding that his father Pausanias too had always been in high friendship with the most popular men of Mantinea. So soon as he had entered the country, in the first place he laid it waste. But as even yet they refused to demolish their walls, he dug a trench in circle quite round the city, one moiety of the army sitting down before the city with the arms of those who were digging, whilst the other moiety carried on the work. When the trench was finished, he also erected without molestation a circular wall quite round the city. But finding there was abundance of corn within the place, as the last year had been a season of great plenty; and thinking it would be judged a hardship to harass both the Lacedæmonians and the confederate troops with a tedious siege, he dammed up the river, and a very large one it is, that runs through the city. The channel being thus dammed up, the water swelled above the foundations of the houses and the city walls. The lower brick-work was soon rotted by the wet, and shrunk under the upper buildings, by which means the city walls cracked, and afterwards were ready to tumble. For some time they under-propped them with timber, and made use of all their art to keep them from falling. But when they found they must be overpowered by the water, and were afraid lest a breach being made by the tumbling of any part of the wall, they should be taken sword in hand, they at length offered to demolish their walls. The Lacedæmonians refused to accept this condition now, unless they would also settle in villages. The Mantineans, judging there was no avoiding it, agreed to comply. But to such of them, as from their long connection with the Argives and their great influence over the people, feared they should be put to death, Agesipolis, at the earnest request of his father, granted their lives (and they were sixty in number), in case they withdrew themselves from Mantinea. On both sides of the road, beginning from the very gates of Mantinea, the Lacedæmonians ranged themselves with their spears in their hands, to take a view of such as were withdrawing; and, though they hated them, yet refrained themselves from any abuse much easier than did the oligarchical party at Mantinea. But be this only mentioned as a signal proof of their habitual obedience to their commanders.

After this the walls were demolished, and the Mantinean country was now settled in four villages, in the same manner as it had been formerly inhabited. At first, it is true, the Mantineans were highly dissatisfied, when thus obliged to pull down the houses they had built for their own convenience, and to erect new ones. But when the wealthier of them were settled on their estates which lay round the villages, when they were ruled by an aristocracy, and rid of their turbulent demagogues, they grew delighted with the change. And the Lacedæmonians sent them, not indeed one person to command the troops of the four, but a separate commander to every village. They afterwards marched upon summons from the villages with more cheerfulness than they had ever done when under a democratical government. And in this manner were things brought about in regard to Mantinea; mankind having learned one piece of wisdom by it, never to let a river run through their walls.

The exiles from Phlius, perceiving the Lacedæmonians were now examining into the behaviour of their several confederates during the war, thought it the proper season to apply for themselves. They went to Lacedæmon, and represented there, that so long as they were in Phlius, the citizens received the Lacedæmonians within their walls, and marched in their company wherever they led them. But no sooner had the people of Phlius ejected them, than they absolutely denied to march at the summons, and refused to the Lacedæmonians alone, of all men living, admittance into their city. When the ephori had heard this representation, they judged it deserving of their attention. They sent therefore to the state of Phlius, remonstrating that "the exiles were friends to the Lacedæmonian community, and for no offence at all had been exiled their country." They insisted upon it therefore "as a point of justice, that without compulsion and by mere voluntary act they should grant the restoration of these exiles." The Phliasians, having heard all this, conceived a suspicion, that some of their own citizens might open the gates, should the Lacedæmonians march against them. For many relations of these exiles were now in the city, who, besides their natural good-will toward them, were desirous (as is generally the case in most communities) to work some change in the society, and were very eager for the recall of the exiles. Moved therefore by such apprehensions, they passed a decree for the re-admission of the exiles—"all their real estates to be immediately restored, and the value of such as had been sold to be returned to the purchasers out of the public treasure; and, in case any dispute arose, the point to be determined by due course of law." These resolutions were carried at this time in favour of the exiles from Phlius.

Ambassadors were now arrived at Lacedæmon from Acanthus and Apollonia, which are the largest cities in the neighbourhood of Olynthus. The ephori, having been informed the reason of their coming, introduced them into a grand assembly of themselves and the confederates, where Cligenes the Acanthian spoke as followeth:

"Lacedæmonians and ye their confederates, an event of vast importance hath lately taken place in Greece, of which we suppose you are quite unapprized. There can, however, be very few amongst you, who know not that Olynthus is the greatest city on the coast of Thrace. These Olynthians therefore have prevailed with some other cities to unite with them in point of laws and political administration: and then they took into their union some larger cities. After this they endeavoured to free the cities of Macedonia from their subjection to Amyntas king of the Macedonians. Having succeeded with the nearest of these cities, they proceeded with rapidity to do the same by the more distant and the larger. And when we came away, they were masters of a great number of them, and even of Pella the capital of Macedonia. We have moreover intelligence, that Amyntas hath been forced successively to quit his cities, and is only not driven out from the whole of Macedonia.

"To us Acanthians also and to the Apollonians these Olynthians have likewise notified their pleasure, that unless we engage to act in confederacy with them, they will make war upon us. But for our parts, Lacedæmonians, we desire still to live under our own established laws, and to persevere as free as we have hitherto been. And yet, unless somebody condescends to assist us, we must of necessity submit to their will and pleasure. They are possessed at this very time of a body of heavy-armed not less than eight hundred, and of a body of targeteers in a much larger number; and their cavalry, if we should be obliged to join them, will amount to more than a thousand.

" We, farther, left behind us at Olynthus ambassadors from the Athenians and Bœotians: and we hear that the Olynthians are come to a resolution to send back with them ambassadors to these several states, to perfect an alliance offensive and defensive. If therefore so great an accession be made to the present strength of the Athenians and the Thebans, consider, Lacedæmonians, whether you will find them for the future so tractable as they ought to be.

" Since, farther, they are already masters of Potidæa on the isthmus of Pallene, you must take it for granted, that all the cities within that isthmus must of course submit to the Olynthians. But one particular and unquestionable proof may be given you, that these cities already are most grievously alarmed: for though they bear an irreconcileable hatred to the Olynthians, yet they durst not send ambassadors along with us to join in representing these things to you.

" Consider again of how much inconsistence you must be guilty, if you, whose chief study it is to prevent the union of Bœotia, should slight the conjunction of so great a power: a power that will show itself considerable indeed not only at land, but even at sea: for what can hinder the men from becoming so, who have timber of their own growth for the building of ships, who receive tribute from abundance of sea-ports and from abundance of trading towns, and who, from the fertility of their country, abound in people ? And more than this, the Thracians who have no king are their nearest neighbours, and have already begun to pay great court to these Olynthians: and should they submit to receive their law, the latter will acquire a vast accession of power by it. And by necessary consequence it must follow, that they then will seize for their own the gold mines in the mountains of Pangæus.

" We tell you nothing here but what hath been talked of a thousand times by the people of Olynthus. And what need is there to add how highly they are elevated upon it ? The author of our nature hath perhaps so framed mankind, that their ambition must keep increasing with their power.

" We are only, Lacedæmonians and confederates, to make you a just report of the present state of affairs. It behoveth you to consider whether or no they deserve your attention. We are bound, however, to assure you of one important truth, that the power of the Olynthians, be it actually as great as we have represented, is not yet too mighty for resistance: for even the cities, which, against their inclinations, are at present with them, will revolt the very moment an army taketh the field against them. But if they enter into closer connections with them by intermarriages and reciprocal acquisitions, which are at present the points in agitation ; and then grow convinced that it is most for their interest to adhere to the strongest party (as for instance the Arcadians, when they march with you, preserve what is their own, and plunder every body else,) then perhaps it may be impossible to reduce within due bounds this growing power."

These things being said, the Lacedæmonians referred the consideration of them to the confederates, and ordered them to consult and report what they thought most conducive to the interest of Peloponnesus and the whole confederacy. And now a majority of them voted for the march of an army, those especially who had a mind to ingratiate themselves with the Lacedæmonians. It was at length decreed " to demand their quotas from the several states to form a body of ten thousand men." Clauses were inserted in the decree, that, " instead of men, any state might be at liberty to advance a sum of money, three oboles [1] of Ægina instead of a man ; and if any furnished horse, the expense of every horseman should be deemed equivalent to the pay of four of the heavy-armed. But if any refused to concur in the service, the Lacedæmonians are empowered to lay a fine of a stater [2] a-day upon them for every man." After these points were decreed, the Acanthians rose up again and declared, that " these indeed were very fine decrees, but could not soon be carried into execution." They said, therefore, " it would be highly expedient, whilst this force was assembling, to send away immediately some proper person to command, at the head of what troops could march at once

1 About sixpence English. 2 £1 9d. sterling.

from Lacedæmon and any of the other states. For if this were done, the cities not yet gone over would stand their ground, and those already under compulsion would readily revolt." This proposal being also approved, the Lacedæmonians send away Eudamidas, and with him the Spartans newly enfranchised, the troops of the neighbourhood, and the Sciritæ, about two thousand in all. Eudamidas, however, at his departure begged of the ephori, that Phœbidas his brother might assemble the rest of the army destined for this service, and bring them up after him. As to himself, so soon as he arrived in Thrace, he sent garrisons round to such of the cities as petitioned for them, and by a voluntary surrender recovered Potidæa, which had been for a time confederate with the Olynthians. He afterwards marched from Potidæa to commence hostilities, which he conducted in the manner suitable to a commander who had the inferior force.

So soon as the troops destined to follow Eudamidas were assembled in a body, Phœbidas put himself at their head, and began the march. On their arrival at Thebes, they encamped without the city near the Gymnasium. The Thebans were now in sedition, and Ismenias and Leontiades were generals of the state. These two were enemies to one another, and each was at the head of his own faction. Ismenias, who hated the Lacedæmonians, never once came near Phœbidas. But Leontiades abundantly caressed him: and, when he had got his heart, addressed him thus:

"You have it, Phœbidas, this very day in your power to do the highest service to your country. If you will only follow me with your heavy-armed, I will introduce you into the citadel of Thebes: and the citadel once secured, assure yourself that Thebes will be entirely in the power of the Lacedæmonians and of us your friends. A proclamation is already gone out, you know it well, that no Theban shall march with you against the Olynthians. But do you only execute what I advise, and we will immediately send away with you a numerous body of heavy-armed, and a numerous body of cavalry too. And thus with a formidable army you will march up to reinforce your brother; and before he can reduce Olynthus, you yourself shall have reduced Thebes, a city of far more importance than Olynthus."

Phœbidas, having listened to him, was quite

in a rapture. He was fonder of distinguishing himself by some grand exploit than of life itself. But then he was not a man that could reason far, nor remarkable for any depth of thought. He soon assented to the proposal, and Leontiades bade him have his troops in motion, as if he had decamped and was for continuing his march. "I will be with you again," said Leontiades, "at the proper time, and will conduct you myself." Whilst therefore the senate was sitting in consultation in the portico of the forum, because the women were celebrating in the Cadmea the rites of Ceres, and scarce a creature could be seen in the streets; since it was about noon in the heat of summer, Leontiades returneth on horseback, makes Phœbidas file off secretly, and introduceth him into the citadel. Having thus put Phœbidas and his party in possession of the place, given him the key of the gates, and enjoined him to give no person admittance without a pass from him, he went his way directly to the senate. He entered it and said—

"The Lacedæmonians, gentlemen, are in possession of the citadel, but let not that alarm you. They profess themselves enemies to no man who is not fond of war. But as general of the state, and by virtue of the power lodged in me by the laws to apprehend all traitors, I now apprehend this Ismenias, as a public enemy. And you, who are officers in the army, and all of you whose duty it is, I order to secure him and convey him you know whither."

The conspirators were ready at hand, and obeyed it, and took Ismenias into their custody. But such as knew nothing of the plot, and were of the opposite party to Leontiades, fled some of them immediately out of the city, being afraid for their lives; whilst others withdrew at first to their own homes; but hearing afterwards that Ismenias was made prisoner in the Cadmea, all those who were of the same party with Androclides and Ismenias, to the number of four hundred persons, made the best of their way to Athens.

When these things were done, they chose another general in the room of Ismenias. But Leontiades set out immediately for Lacedæmon. He found there the ephori and every citizen of Sparta in high indignation against Phœbidas for having presumed to act in this manner without consulting the state. Agesilaus, it is true, represented that "if he had acted to the public detriment, he ought to be punished; but if he had served the public, it was an old established law, that his own good intentions sufficiently authorised him. We should therefore consider first," said he, "whether what hath been done hath been serviceable to the state or not." Leontiades, however, being introduced, on his arrival to the council of state, spoke thus :

" Your ownselves, Lacedæmonians, have for ever been declaring that the Thebans were your constant enemies, even before the last transactions. You have for ever seen them exerting their friendship towards your foes, and exerting their enmity against your friends. Did they not refuse to march with you against the Athenian people, your implacable enemy, when they had seized the Piræus? and did they not make war against the Phocians, merely because the latter were benevolently inclined to you? Nay, no sooner had they learned that you were going to make war upon the Olynthians, than they struck up a confederacy with them. Time was, you were attentive to all their motions, and alarmed at hearing they were extending their power in Bœotia. But all alarms are now at an end; you no longer have any reason to fear the Thebans. Henceforth a small scytale will suffice to keep every thing there in all regular and needful obedience to yourselves, provided you show the same zeal for us as we have manifested for you."

After hearing him, the Lacedæmonians decreed " to keep fast possession of the citadel, now that it was seized, and to proceed to the trial of Ismenias." Their next step was, to send judges to try him, three from Lacedæmon, and one from every state, as well small as great, in the Lacedæmonian league. When these judges were assembled, and had taken their seats in court, an accusation was preferred against Ismenias, that " he was in the interest of Barbarians, and had entered into the hospitable ties with the Persian with no good design in regard to Greece ; that he had received a share of the money from the king ; and that he and Androclides were principal authors of all the confusion in Greece." He made his defence against every part of the accusation, but could not convince his judges, that he had not been a very intriguing and mischievous man. He was accordingly condemned to die, and suffered death. The faction of Leontiades continued now to be masters of Thebes, and outstripped command in the officiousness of their zeal to serve the Lacedæmonians.

After these things were brought about, the Lacedæmonians, with much more alacrity than ever, sent away the army against Olynthus. They give the command of this army to Teleutias, and all the states furnished their quotas towards ten thousand men to march away with him, and scytales were circulated to the confederate cities, ordering them to obey Teleutias according to the decree of the confederates. Each separate people in the league with cheerfulness accompanied Teleutias. They were sure Teleutias would never be ungrateful to those who did him any service. And the Theban state, as he was the brother of Agesilaus, sent away with him heavy-armed and horsemen. Though in a hurry to reach his post, yet he marched but slowly, always careful not to hurt any friends in his march and to enlarge his numbers as much as possible. He sent messengers before him to Amyntas, and desired him to hire a body of mercenaries, and to lay out his money among the neighbouring kings to purchase their aid, if he really had a mind to recover his dominions. He sent also to Derdas, king of Elyma, admonishing him that the Olynthians had demolished the greater power of Macedonia, and will not refrain from doing the same by a lesser power, unless a stop be put to their insolence. Acting in this manner, he arrived at length with a very numerous army on the lands of the confederacy. And when he had made his entry into Potidæa, he there marshalled his troops, and then took the field. But, during his approach to Olynthus, he set nothing on fire, he committed no ravage; judging, that if he did such things, he should embarrass both his own approach and retreat. When he should be marching back, he judged it would be the proper time to cut down the trees and block up the roads against the enemy that might follow his rear. When he was advanced within [1] ten stadia of Olynthus, he made the army halt. He was himself on the left; and thus it happened that he appeared before the gates through which the enemy sallied. The rest of the confederate troops were drawn up on the right. He also posted on the right the Lacedæmonian and Theban horse, and what Macedonian cavalry was at hand. He kept Derdas and his four hundred horse on his own flank, because he admired this body of horse, and had a mind to compli-

---

[1] About a mile.

ment Derdas for joining him with so much alacrity. When the enemy was come out of Olynthus, and had formed into order of battle under the wall, their cavalry closed firm together, and rode down on the Lacedæmonian and Bœotian horse. They dismounted Polycharmus, the Lacedæmonian officer, gave him several wounds as he lay on the ground, and slew others; and at length compel the horse in the right wing to fly. The horse being thus first in flight, the foot also, drawn up nearest to them, began to give way. The whole army was now in great danger of defeat, had not Derdas, with his own cavalry, rode up directly to the gates of Olynthus; and Teleutias with the left wing marched after him in excellent order. The Olynthian horse had no sooner perceived these motions, than they were afraid of being shut out of the town. They wheeled about, therefore, with all speed, and came on a gallop towards the gates. And now Derdas slew a vast number of these horsemen as they were gallopping by him. The infantry of the Olynthians retired into the city; and very few of them were killed, since they were so near the walls. But after a trophy was erected, and the victory remained with Teleutias, he retreated and cut down the trees.

III. When the campaign was over for the summer, he dismissed the troops of Macedonia and those of Derdas. The Olynthians, however, were making frequent excursions against the cities confederate with the Lacedæmonians, carrying off much plunder and slaughtering the people. And very early in the succeeding spring, the Olynthian horse, to the number of six hundred, had made an excursion against Apollonia about noon, and were dispersed plundering about the country. That very morning Derdas, with his own horse, had marched into Apollonia, where he stopped to refresh himself and his men. When he beheld the enemy's incursion, he made no bustle at all. His horses were ready; the riders were armed and mounted: and so soon as the Olynthians, in a contemptuous manner, entered the suburb, and rode up to the very gates of the town, he then sallied out in excellent order. The Olynthians no sooner saw him than they fled. And Derdas, when once at their backs, continued the pursuit and slaughter of them for [1] ninety stadia, till he had chased them to the very walls of Olynthus.

Derdas was said this day to have slain eighty of their horsemen. From this time the enemy were obliged to keep more within their walls, and employ themselves entirely in cultivating the small tract of country that was yet in their power.

Some time after, when Teleutias was again in the field against the Olynthians, in order to demolish any tree yet standing, and to complete the ruin of their country, the Olynthian horse, who had sallied out and came marching quietly forwards, passed the river that runs near the city, and then again kept quietly advancing towards the enemy's army. When Teleutias saw them, he was vexed at their assurance, and ordered Tlemonides, who commanded the targeteers, to march full speed against them. But the Olynthians, when they saw the targeteers running forwards, wheeled about, retreated quietly, and repassed the river. The targeteers kept following in a very courageous manner, and, like men who were driving fugitives before them, passed the river too in pursuit. But here the Olynthian horse, who judged they had now got them fast, face about and attack them, and slew Tlemonides himself, and more than a hundred of his men. Teleutias no sooner saw this, than, quite mad with anger, he caught up his arms, and led the heavy-armed towards them, ordering the targeteers and horsemen to continue the pursuit and lose no ground. By this means many of the army, having unadvisedly continued the pursuit too near the walls, found a great difficulty in retreating again. They were galled with darts from the turrets; they were obliged to move off in the most disorderly manner, guarding themselves from the darts that came pouring upon them. And now the Olynthians ride down upon their horse, and their targeteers made what haste they could to assist them. At length the heavy-armed sallied out, and charge the main body of the enemy, who were all in confusion. And here Teleutias is killed fighting. He was no sooner dead, than all about him gave way. No man any longer stood his ground. The whole army fled: some towards Spartolus; some towards Acanthus; some to Apollonia; but most of them to Potidæa. As thus they were fleeing different ways, the pursuit by as many different ways was continued after them, in which a vast number of men, and indeed the very flower of this mighty army, perished. Such dreadful

---

1 About nine miles.

calamities as these should, in my judgment, be a lesson to mankind to guard against anger, nay, even when they are only to chastise their own domestics. For it frequently happens, that when masters are too angry, they do more hurt to themselves than to those they want to punish. But to attack an enemy in the heat of anger, and not with judgment, is the saddest fault of which we can be guilty: for anger foreseeth no consequences at all; whereas, judgment considereth as much its own preservation as doing harm to an enemy.

When the news of this defeat was brought to the Lacedæmonians, they determined, after mature consultation, to march up a considerable force, in order to damp the great exultation of the enemy, and lest all hitherto done should have been done in vain. Having thus determined, they send away Agesipolis the king, to take upon him the command, attended, as Agesilaus was in Asia, by thirty Spartans. Many of the bravest soldiers in the neighbourhood of Sparta went out with him volunteers, as did those strangers distinguished by the title of Trophimi, and the bastards of the Spartans. Volunteers farther from the confederates joined in the expedition, and the horsemen of Thessaly, who had a mind to recommend themselves to the notice of Agesipolis. Amyntas also and Derdas came in with more alacrity than ever: and Agesipolis, thus executing his commission, was marching against Olynthus.

The citizens of Phlius, who had been highly commended by Agesipolis for their handsome and prompt contribution towards his expedition, began now to imagine, that as Agesipolis was gone abroad, Agesilaus would not take the field against them, since it was not probable that both kings could, at the same time, be absent from Sparta; and therefore in a very haughty manner they refused justice to the exiles lately restored. In vain did these exiles insist that all disputes should be determined before impartial judges, for they compelled them to submit to the determinations of their own judges at Phlius. And when the returning exiles demanded, "what justice could be expected when the very persons who had injured them presided in the courts?" they gave not the least attention to them. The persons therefore thus aggrieved, go afterwards to Lacedæmon with accusations against the city of Phlius. Some other Phliasians also came with them, representing that many of the citizens

acknowledged the injustice of such behaviour. The Phliasians were nettled at these proceedings, and laid a fine upon all those who went to Lacedæmon without public authority. The persons on whom these fines were laid were afraid to return home. They continued at Sparta, representing that "the authors of all this violence were the same persons who had driven them from their homes, and excluded the Lacedæmonians too. The very same persons, who had bought their effects, and by violence refused to restore them, had now exerted their influence to have a fine laid upon them for repairing to Lacedæmon, that no one for the future might presume to go thither and report what was doing at Phlius." As this behaviour of the Phliasians was not to be justified, the ephori proclaim an expedition against them: and Agesilaus was not at all displeased with this resolution of the state, since Podanemus, who, with his family, had been the hospitable friend of his father Archidamus, was in the number of the exiles who had returned, and Procles the son of Hipponicus had likewise been his own. So soon therefore as the sacrifices were auspicious, he dallied not, but began his march. Many embassies met him, and offered him money to stop. His answer was, "he was now in the command, not to commit injustice himself, but to vindicate the oppressed." The last embassy of all declared "they would submit to any conditions, provided he would not enter their country." He replied, that "he could put no confidence in mere speeches; they had already broken their words: he could trust to nothing but a positive act." Being now asked what act he meant? he answered, "the very same you did once before, and received no damage at all from us by doing it." This was, to deliver up their citadel. But as they refused to comply, he marched into their territory, and throwing up a circumvallation, laid siege to their city.

It was now frequently said by the Lacedæmonians, that "for the sake of a few of his favourites, Agesilaus was going to ruin a city that contained more than five thousand men:" for to make them believe that this was so, the Phliasians were ever declaiming it to them from the walls. Agesilaus, however, contrived a scheme to convince them it was false: for whenever any of the Phliasians that were either friends or relations to the exiles, escaped out of the city to the camp, he ordered the Lacedæmonians to invite them to their tents, and to furnish such of them as had a mind to go through the exercises with them with all proper accommodations. He enjoined them farther to provide them with arms, and without hesitation to procure such arms upon credit. They did all this, and furnished out above a thousand Phliasians, whose bodies were in fine exercise, who were perfectly well disciplined, and most expert in the use of arms. At length the Lacedæmonians were obliged to confess, that "it was well worth their while to gain such brave fellow-soldiers as these." And Agesilaus was thus employed.

In the meantime Agesipolis, having with all expedition crossed Macedonia, showed himself in battle-array before the walls of Olynthus. And when nobody sallied out against him, he laid waste all that territory which had hitherto escaped devastation, and marching towards the cities confederate with Olynthus, destroyed their corn. He made also an assault upon Torone, and took it by storm. Thus busied as he was in the heat of summer, he is attacked by a burning fever. And as he had lately visited the temple of Bacchus at Aphyte, he conceived a violent longing after the shady bowers and the clear and cooling streams. He was therefore conveyed thither yet alive: but on the seventh day after he was seized, he expired without the verge of the temple. His body was preserved in honey and brought home to Sparta, where it was interred with regal pomp. Agesilaus, when he heard of his death, was not, as some would imagine, secretly glad at the death of a competitor, but he shed tears abundantly, and sadly regretted the loss of his companion. For, when they are at Sparta, both kings are lodged in the same apartment. And Agesipolis was qualified in all respects to entertain Agesilaus with his discourses about youthful exercises, about hunting and riding, or the more gay and lively topics. And what is more, when they were thus lodged together, he constantly paid high respect to Agesilaus, as his senior, in the manner that became him. The Lacedæmonians send away Polybiades to command in his stead against Olynthus.

Agesilaus had been a longer time before Phlius than it was said their provisions could have lasted. But of such excellent use it is to refrain from indulging the belly, that the Phliasians, who had made a decree that only half the usual allowance should be daily issued out, and had observed this decree, were enabled to hold out twice as long as had been expected. And a resolute spirit sometimes gains an entire ascendent over despondency, insomuch that one Delphio, a person who had made a great figure at Phlius, being supported by a party of three hundred Phliasians, was able at any time to stop the mouths of such as cried out for peace, was able farther to apprehend and secure in safe custody such as were not to be trusted. He could also force the multitude to mount regularly upon guard, and by constantly going the rounds kept them steady in their posts. Nay, he frequently sallied out with his select party, and drove such of the enemy as were guarding the circumvallation from their posts. But when at last this select party, after the strictest inquiry, found all the corn in the city to be spent, they then sent to Agesilaus desiring a truce for an embassy to go to Lacedæmon: adding, "they had come to a resolution to surrender the city on whatever conditions the magistrates at Lacedæmon should prescribe." Agesilaus was angry that they should slight him in this manner. He therefore sent to his friends at Lacedæmon, and by them solicited so effectually, that the terms of surrender for Phlius were left to his own determination; he, however, granted a truce for the embassy. He now kept a stricter guard than ever upon the besieged, that none of them might make their escape. But notwithstanding all his vigilance, Delphio, accompanied by a scoundrel fellow, a servant of his own, who had frequently plundered the besiegers of their arms, got away by night. When the messengers arrived from Lacedæmon, with a permission from the state to Agesilaus to settle the terms as he thought most advisable, he declared them thus; that "fifty persons of the late exiles, and fifty Phliasians who had not been exiled, should first agree upon a report, what persons deserved to be saved and what persons ought to be put to death; and then should draw up a body of laws for their future observation." And whilst these things were settling he left a garrison in Phlius, and had six months' pay secured to them. Having done this, he dismissed the confederates, and marched back himself with the domestic troops to Sparta. The whole time of these transactions about Phlius was one year and eight months.

Polybiades now compelled the Olynthians,

who were grievously afflicted with famine, since they could neither fetch in provisions by land nor import them by sea, to send an embassy to Lacedæmon to sue for peace. The ambassadors arrived there with full powers, and agreed " to have the same friend and the same foe with the Lacedæmonians, to follow them as their leaders, and be their confederates." And having sworn to observe these articles, they returned to Olynthus.

When every thing had thus succeeded with the Lacedæmonians, so that now the Thebans and the rest of the Bœotians were entirely submissive, the Corinthians adhered most faithfully to them, and the Argives were humbled, as their plea about computing the months could no longer avail them ; as the Athenians farther were left quite by themselves, and they had sufficiently chastised their own disaffected confederates, their empire over Greece seemed at present to be established with lustre and security.

IV. Many instances however might be brought from the histories both of Greeks and Barbarians, that the gods neglect not the punishment of men who behave irreligiously, or commit unrighteous acts : but at present I shall stick close to my subject. For even those Lacedæmonians, who had sworn to leave the cities in freedom and independence, and yet had seized the citadel of Thebes, were chastised for their crime by the very people they had injured, though hitherto superior to all their enemies. And as to those very Thebans, who had led them into the citadel and taken it into their heads to betray the city to the Lacedæmonians, that under their protection they might play the tyrant, no more persons than seven exiles were sufficient to wreak ample vengeance upon them. I shall relate in what manner it was done.

There was one Phyllidas, who served as secretary to the generals of the state, in the interest of Archias, and was highly esteemed for the faithful execution of his office. This man was by business carried to Athens, where Mello, one of the Thebans who had refuged himself at Athens, and was his old acquaintance, gets a conference with him. He asked him abundance of questions, how Archias executed his office? and Philip continued to play the tyrant? and discovering that Phyllidas abhorred all the management at Thebes even worse than himself, after proper pledges of fidelity to one another, they agreed about the exact method of executing the plot. In consequence of this, Mello, taking with him six [1] of the properest persons amongst the exiles, armed with daggers and no other weapon, goeth in the first place by night into the territory of Thebes. In the next place, having passed the day in some unfrequented spot, at evening they came to the gates, as if returning amongst the latest of those who had been working in the fields. When they had thus got into the city, they passed that night in the house of one Charon, with whom also they continued the following day. Phyllidas was now very busy in making preparations for his masters the generals of the state, that they might celebrate the feast of Venus at the expiration of their office. He had long before made them a promise to bring them some of the noblest and most beautiful ladies in the city, and fixed this night for the performance of it. The generals, libertines as they were, reckoned they should have a most joyous night. When supper was over, and they had drunk largely, for Phyllidas took care they should have plenty of wine, they called upon him again and again to fetch in the ladies. He went indeed, but fetched in Mello and his companions. He had finely dressed up three of them as women of quality, and the rest as their maids. He led them first into the pantry of the public mansion ; and then, going himself into the room where they were feasting, told them " the ladies positively refused to come in till all the servants were withdrawn." Upon this they immediately ordered all servants to leave the room. Phyllidas gave the servants wine, and sent them out to drink it in the house of one of the public officers. When this was done, he introduced the ladies, and seated them each to a man. The signal was, that so soon as they were seated, they should immediately discover themselves, and stab. It is thus that some say they were put to death. But others will have it, that Mello and his companions came as a party of masquers, and so killed the generals of the state.

Phyllidas, however, taking with him three of them, proceeded to the house of Leontiades ; and after knocking at the door, said he had some orders to deliver from the generals. Leontiades had just thrown himself upon a couch after supper, and his wife was sitting by him employed at her wheel. He looked upon Phyllidas as a trusty person, and therefore ordered him to come in. They were no sooner in the room, than after killing him [1] and sadly affrighting his wife, they enjoined her to be silent. And now departing, they left an order, " to keep the door fast. If they found it had been opened," they threatened " to put all the people in the house to death." Phyllidas, accompanied by two of the men, went away to the public prison, and told the keeper, " he had a prisoner to deliver from a general of the state, whom he must take care to secure." So soon as he opened the door, they immediately killed him, and set all the prisoners at liberty. They now ran and took arms out of the portico, with which they armed the prisoners; and then marching to the Amphieum, posted them there on guard. And no sooner was this done, than they proclaimed aloud, that " all the horsemen and heavy-armed of Thebes should come out since the tyrants were slain." The citizens, who in the night-time knew not what to believe, kept quiet in their houses. But so soon as it was day, and it was clearly seen what had been done, the heavy-armed and horsemen soon joined them in arms.[2] The exiles also, who had now returned to Thebes, despatch horsemen away to the rest of their associates, who were waiting on the frontiers of Athens, and two Athenian generals with them. These, knowing well why they were sent for, put themselves in march.

The Lacedæmonian, who commanded in the citadel, had no sooner heard of the proclamation that was made in the night, than he sent away to Platæa and Thespiæ for aid. But the Theban horsemen, who were aware of the approach of the Platæans, met them on the road, and slew more than twenty of them. Coming back into Thebes after this exploit, and the party from the frontier of Athens was now also arrived, they made an assault upon the citadel. When those within the citadel, whose number was but small, found what they were about, and saw with how much spirit each assailant behaved, and heard large rewards offered by proclamation to such as should first scale the wall, they were greatly intimidated, and offered to evacuate the place, " would they

give them leave to depart unmolested with their arms." They readily agreed to this demand; and then granting a truce and swearing to an observance of the articles, they ordered them to evacuate the citadel. However, as they were marching out, they seized and massacred all such amongst them as they knew were their enemies. And yet some persons there were, as were secreted by such of the Athenians who had marched up with the aid from the frontier, and conveyed safely off. But the Thebans apprehended and butchered even the children of those persons whom they had massacred on this occasion.

When the Lacedæmonians were informed of these affairs, they put to death their commandant, for evacuating the citadel and not remaining in it till aid came up. They also proclaim an expedition against Thebes. But Agesilaus alleged, that " he had been in constant service now forty years from his youth, and as the law exempted all persons of that standing from serving abroad in the army," he averred that " the king also was included in that exemption;" and having thus alleged a reasonable excuse, he did not command in this expedition. Yet this was a mere pretext to evade the service, as he well knew, in case he took the command himself, that his countrymen would murmur at him for giving them so much trouble that he might succour tyrants. He suffered them therefore to determine every point relating to it without interfering at all. The ephori at length, at the desire of those who had escaped from Thebes after the massacre, send out Cleombrotus for the first time to command the army, and in the very depth of winter. Chabrias, at the head of the Athenian targeteers, was guarding the pass of Eleutheræ; Cleombrotus therefore marched up by the road that leadeth to Platæa. His targeteers, who led the van, fell in upon the mountain with a guard of about one hundred and fifty persons, the very same men who had been set at liberty out of the prison. And all these, unless perhaps one or two who might escape, the targeteers immediately slew. He then marched down to Platæa, which was yet in friendship with them. But after he had been at Thespiæ, he marched from thence to Cynoscephale, which belonged to the Thebans, and encamped his army. He continued there about sixteen days, and then retired again to Thespiæ. He left Sphodrias to command in that place with a third part of

---

1 It was Pelopidas who killed him.
2 With Epaminondas at their head.

the confederate troops. He also gave him what money he had brought from Sparta, and ordered him to hire a body of auxiliaries. And Sphodrias set about obeying his orders.

Cleombrotus led the rest of the army back by the road of Crusis, his soldiers being yet very much in doubt, whether there was a war or not with the Thebans. He had entered with his army, it is true, upon the dominions of Thebes, but he was again withdrawing after doing them as little damage as possible. Yet during his retreat there happened a most violent tempest of wind, which some interpreted as an omen of what was soon to come to pass. Amongst other prodigious effects of this tempest, as Cleombrotus was crossing the mountain in the road from Crusis to the sea, it blew several asses loaded with baggage down the precipices, and carried abundance of weapons whirled out of the soldiers' hands into the sea. In short, many of them, unable to go on with their arms, left them behind here and there upon the top of the mountain, laying down their shields with the wrong side uppermost and filling them with stones. That night they refreshed themselves as well as they could at Ægosthenes in the district of Megara, but next day they returned and fetched off their arms. And from thence each party made the best of their way to their several homes, for Cleombrotus disbanded the army.

The Athenians, who now saw what the strength of the Lacedæmonians was, that there was war no longer at Corinth, and that the Lacedæmonians had even marched along by Attica against Thebes, were so highly intimidated, that they called down to a trial the two generals, who had been concerned in the conspiracy of Mello against the faction of Leontiades, and put one of them to death, and outlawed the other who fled before his trial.

The Thebans farther, who were under full and great apprehensions in case they should be compelled singly to war with the Lacedæmonians, have recourse to the following artifice.[3] They persuade Sphodrias, who was left commandant at Thespiæ, and it was supected by a handsome bribe, to make an incursion into Attica, in order to force the Athenians to a rupture with the Lacedæmonians. Sphodrias undertook the business, and pretended he would seize the Piræus, as it was not yet secured by gates. He put his troops on the march soon after supper, saying that before day he would be at the Piræus. But day-light overtook him at Thria, and he had not even the caution to conceal his design. For when he was forced to retreat, he drove off the cattle and gutted the houses. Some persons, too, who had fallen in with him on his march, flying with all speed into the city, alarmed the Athenians with the news that a very numerous army was approaching. Their horsemen and heavy-armed were soon accoutred, and posted themselves on the guard of the city. Etymocles, and Aristolochus, and Ocellus, the Lacedæmonian ambassadors, were now in residence at Athens, lodged with Callias the public host of their state: and no sooner was this news arrived, than the Athenians arrested and secured these ambassadors as privy to the scheme. They were strangely surprised at this incident, and pleaded in their own behalf that " they were not such fools as to have staid in the city in the power of the Athenians, had they known of any design to seize the Piræus, and least of all in their public lodgings, where they were sure to be met with." They said farther, " it should be cleared up to the satisfaction of the Athenians, that the state of Lacedæmon was not privy to the design ;" adding, " they were well assured of hearing soon that Sphodrias was put to death by his country for it." And thus, being clearly adjudged to have known nothing at all of the matter, they were set at liberty.

The ephori recalled Sphodrias, and preferred a capital indictment against him. He truly was affrighted, and would not undergo a trial. But after all, though he refused to stand his trial, he got himself acquitted. This was thought by many the most iniquitous sentence that ever was given by the Lacedæmonians. But the true history of it was this :

Sphodrias had a son, by name Cleonymus, of an age just beyond the class of boys, but the handsomest and most accomplished youth in Sparta ; and Archidamus the son of Agesilaus had a fondness for him. The friends therefore of Cleombrotus, who were great intimates with Sphodrias, were bent on getting him acquitted, but yet were afraid of Agesilaus and his friends, and indeed of all impartial persons, since beyond all doubt his offence was enormous. But Sphodrias at length spoke

3 According to Plutarch, Pelopidas was chief agent and promoter of this affair.

thus to Cleonymus: "It is in your power, my son, to save your father's life, would you prevail with Archidamus to get Agesilaus to favour me in court." After hearing this, he had the courage to go to Archidamus and beg him to save his father. Archidamus truly, seeing Cleonymus, in tears, stood all in suspense, and wept along with him.. And when he had heard his request, he answered thus: "But you must know, Cleonymus, that I never am able to look my father in the face; and whatever public point I want to carry, I solicit all the world much sooner than my father. However, since you request it, be assured I will do all in my power to serve you." And then, leaving the public room of entertainment where they were, he went home to bed. Next morning he was up betimes, and took care his father should not go out before he had seen him. But when he saw him appear, in the first place if any of the citizens came in, he let them talk over their business with him; and then if there came any stranger; and afterwards, he gave way to such of the domestics as had any thing to say. In short, when Agesilaus was returned home again from the Eurotas, he retired without daring to approach him. And the next day he behaved again exactly in the same manner. Agesilaus however suspected the true reason of his son's behaviour, but he asked no questions, and let him go on. Archidamus, as is now likely, was longing for a sight of Cleonymus, but durst not presume to face him, as he had not opened his lips to his father about his petition. And the friends of Sphodrias, finding that Archidamus, who used to be assiduous, came not near Cleonymus, were persuaded he had been chidden by his father. But, in short, Archidamus had at last the courage to go up to him and say, "I am, sir, desired by Cleonymus, to beg of you to save his father; I earnestly entreat you therefore to do it if you can." He answered, "I forgive you, my son, for asking it; but I do not see how I can be forgiven by my country, if I do not condemn the man, who hath taken a bribe to hurt my country." Archidamus had nothing to reply, but overpowered by a sense of justice went his way. Yet afterwards, whether of his own thought or the suggestion of somebody else, he came again and said, "But I am assured, my father, if Sphodrias had done no wrong, you would readily acquit him; and therefore, though he hath done wrong, forgive

him this once to gratify your son. Agesilaus replied, "Be it so, provided it can be done with honour." At this answer Archidamus went his way quite despairing of success.

One of the friends of Sphodrias being afterwards in discourse with Etymocles said to him, "All you, I suppose, who are the friends of Agesilaus, are for putting Sphodrias to death." "Far from it," replied Etymocles; should we not act in concert with him? And Agesilaus, I assure you, says to all with whom he talketh about him, that beyond all doubt Sphodrias hath been to blame; but then it would be a hardship indeed to put a man to death, who in every stage of life had behaved in the most honourable manner, for Sparta standeth in need of such gallant men." Hearing this, he went and told it to Cleonymus. Cleonymus, quite overjoyed, sought out Archidamus and said, "Now we are convinced you have a sincere regard for us; and rest assured, Archidamus, we shall always endeavour to show so high a regard for you, that you shall never blush you have been our friend." He made his words good, since quite through life he nobly discharged all the duties of a Spartan, and at Leuctra, fighting before the king in company with Dinon, a general-officer, he was the first of the Spartans who dropped and died in the midst of the enemy. His death gave the heartiest concern to Archidamus, though according to promise he never shamed, but on the contrary gloriously adorned his benefactor. And in this manner truly was Sphodrias acquitted.

At Athens, however, such persons as were in the Boeotian interest were representing to the people, that "the Lacedæmonians, far from punishing, had even commended Sphodrias for his treachery to them." The consequence was, that the Athenians made all fast about the Piræus, set ships on the stocks, and aided the Boeotians with high alacrity. On the other side, the Lacedæmonians declared an expedition against Thebes; and judging that Agesilaus would command the army with more prudence than Cleombrotus, they begged of him to undertake the service. He replied that "he could refuse no service for which the state judged him to be qualified," and began the preparations to take the field. But sensible that unless Cithæron was secured in time, it would not be easy to get into the territory of Thebes; and having learned that the Cletorians were at war with the Orchomenians, and subsisted a body of foreign troops, he treated with them for the aid of those troops in case he should want them. After the sacrifices for a successful campaign were over, before he had reached Tegea with his Lacedæmonians, he despatched a messenger to the commander of the troops in the service of the Cletorians, with a month's pay advance for those troops, and an order to possess themselves immediately of Cithæron. He sent also a notification to the Orchomenians "to suspend their war during his present expedition. But if any state, whilst he was in the field, presumed to make war upon any other state, he threatened to make war upon the state so offending, in pursuance of the standing decree of the confederates." And now, after passing Cithæron and arriving at Thespiæ, he resumed his march from thence, and entered the dominions of Thebes. But finding the plains and the richest parts of the country secured by ditches and ramparts, he shifted his encampments from one spot to another, and leading out his army in the afternoon laid all the country waste that he found not covered by ditches and ramparts. For the enemy, whenever Agesilaus appeared in sight, formed into order of battle behind their rampart as ready to defend it. And once, when he was returning to his camp, the Theban horse, who had kept themselves concealed, ride out suddenly through the sally-ports contrived on purpose in the rampart, and at the time the targeteers were dispersed to their supper, and were actually getting it ready, whilst the horsemen were either dismounting or mounting again upon their horses, gallop in amongst them. They made a slaughter of the targeeters, and of the horse slew Cleon and Epilytidas, both of Sparta, and Eudicus who belonged to a city in the neighbourhood of Sparta, and some exiles from Athens, who had not been able to remount their horses. But when Agesilaus had faced about with the heavy-armed, and was marching towards them, and the horse on each side began to ride at one another, and the first military class of Spartans ran out from the heavy-armed to support the horse, then indeed the horsemen of the Thebans resembled labourers exhausted by the noon-day heat. They kept their ground, it is true, against assailants, and threw their spears, but then they never threw them home. And at last, being obliged to wheel about, twelve of them were slain.

When Agesilaus was thus convinced that the enemy were always in motion after dinner, he sacrificed at early day; and then marching out his army with all expedition, he entered their lines by a quarter on which there was no guard at all. And after this he put every thing within their lines to fire and sword, quite up to the walls of Thebes. But having done this, and retreated again to Thespiæ, he fortified that city: and leaving Phœbidas behind to be commandant in Thespiæ, he repassed to Megara, dismissed the confederates, and led back the domestic troops to Sparta.

But after his departure, Phœbidas, by sending out his parties, was continually fetching in plunder from the Thebans, and by the incursions he made gave sad annoyance to the country. The Thebans on the other side, being eager for revenge, march with their whole united force into the territory of the Thespians. But though they had thus entered it, Phœbidas lay so close upon them with his targeteers, that none of the enemy durst on any occasion straggle from the main body. In short the Thebans were grievously disappointed in this fruitless incursion, and were retreating with much precipitation. And even their muleteers, throwing away what corn they had got, rode homewards as fast as possible: so great a panic had seized the army. But Phœbidas with high ardour kept plying in pursuit. He followed it close with the targeteers, having left orders for the heavy-armed to follow after in their regular order. He was full of hope to make it end in a general rout. He himself pressed with great bravery on their rear; he encouraged every person to keep up close at the enemy; and he ordered the heavy-armed of Thespiæ to follow him. But the Theban horse were now come in their retreat to a wood that was impassable, at which they first drew close together, and in the next place they faced about, since they were quite at a loss how to get any farther. The targeteers, and the number of them was but small, that first approached, were terrified and took to flight. When the horsemen saw this, the very fright of their own people instructed them to fall on; and here Phœbidas with two or three more were slain fighting. Perceiving Phœbidas was killed, all the mercenaries to a man took to flight. When in their flight they were come back to the heavy-armed of Thespiæ, these also, in spite of their former boasts that they would never give way before Thebans, fled too far for company. They saved themselves indeed from any warm pursuit, since it was now late in the day. Hence it was that few of these Thespians lost their lives. They fled, however, without once looking behind them, till they were got within their own walls.

The affairs of the Thebans took fresh life again after this success, and they marched against Thespiæ and the adjacent cities. The party, it is true, for the Thebans, in each of these cities had retired to Thebes, since their governments had been lodged in the hands of a few great men in the same manner as had been done in Thebans. The friends therefore of the Lacedæmonians in all these cities were petitioning for succour. And after the death of Phœbidas the Lacedæmonians sent by sea a general officer and one brigade to lie in garrison at Thespiæ.

But so soon as the spring came on, the Lacedæmonians again declared an expedition against Thebes, and begged Agesilaus, as the year before, to take upon him the command. He was still in the same sentiments about the manner of breaking into the country, so that before the solemn sacrifices were performed, he despatched away a messenger to the commanding officer at Thespiæ, with an order to him to possess himself immediately of the eminence that commands the pass of Cithæron, and maintain it till he came up with the army. When he himself had passed it and was got to Platæa, he again pretended to march to Thespiæ. He sent his couriers thither to order a market to be ready, and for all ambassadors to wait for him there, insomuch that the Thebans gathered all their strength together to stop his march to Thespiæ. But the day after, having sacrificed at early dawn, he began his march along the road of Erythra: and having made a double march that day, he passed the lines of the enemy at Scolus, before the Thebans could arrive from the place where he had passed last year, which they were intent on guarding. Having thus passed the lines, he laid all the country waste eastward of Thebes quite up to Tanagra (for Tanagra was still in the possession of Hypotadorus, who was a friend to the Lacedæmonians), and afterwards marched back again, keeping the walls of Thebes on his left. The Thebans took the field, and were posted in order of battle at Graos-stethos, having in their rear the ditch and rampart, and judging

themselves excellently well posted for hazarding a battle: for the ground here was sufficiently narrow and very rugged. But Agesilaus, seeing how they were posted, would not advance towards them; but making a sudden turn to the left, he marched directly for the city of Thebes. And now the Thebans, trembling for the city, empty as it was of all its people, started away from the post where they were formed in order of battle, and advanced full speed towards the city along the road of Potnia; for this was in reality the securest way. And yet it was undoubtedly a noble piece of conduct in Agesilaus, to retreat to a great distance from the enemy, and oblige them in the greatest hurry to quit their ground. Some however of the general officers with their own brigades ran at the Thebans, as they were rushing along full speed. But the Thebans poured their darts and javelins upon them from the eminences, and Halypetus, one of these officers, lost his life by a wound received from a javelin thrown at him. The Thebans, however, were obliged to dislodge from that eminence; and the Seiritæ and the horsemen rode up it, and kept striking at the rear of the enemy, whilst they were running towards the city. But so soon as they were got near the walls, the Thebans face about. The Sciritæ, seeing this, retreated back faster than a foot pace, and not one of them lost his life on this occasion. The Thebans however erected a trophy, since their assailants had thus retreated.

Agesilaus, as it was now high time, wheeled off, and encamped his army on the very ground where he had before seen the enemy posted in order of battle, and on the next day led them back to Thespiæ. The targeteers in the pay of Thebes kept following close in his rear, and were calling out on Chabrias for not keeping up with them, when the Olynthian horse (for now pursuant to oath they were in the army) wheeled about, forced them up an ascent by the closeness of their pursuit, and put very many of them to the sword: for foot-men, when labouring up a smooth ascent, are quickly overtaken by horse.

At his return to Thespiæ, Agesilaus found the citizens of that place embroiled in sedition; and, as the party attached to the Lacedæmonians were for putting their adversaries to death, amongst whom was Meno, he would not suffer it. On the contrary, he reconciled them; and having obliged them to swear not to hurt one another, he then repassed Cithæron and got back to Megara. At Megara he disbanded the confederates, and led away himself the domestic troops to Sparta.

The Thebans, who now were highly distressed by a scarcity of corn, since for the last two years they had not reaped the produce of their soil, send out proper persons on board two triremes to purchase corn at Pagasæ, giving them ten [1] talents for the purpose. But Alcetas the Lacedæmonian, who was now in garrison at Oreus, whilst they were purchasing and taking in their corn, manned out three triremes, taking all possible care they should have no intelligence of what he was about. And when the corn was carrying off, Alcetas seizeth it in all the triremes, and took prisoners all the persons on board, who were not fewer than three hundred. And these his prisoners he conveyed for security into the citadel where he was lodged himself. It was reported that a youth of Oreus, remarkably handsome, followed after the crowd on this occasion, and Alcetas walked down from the citadel to have some conversation with him. The prisoners therefore, observing this negligence of his, seize the citadel, and the town revolts; and now, without obstruction, the Thebans fetched away all the corn.

When the ensuing spring approached, Agesilaus was confined to his bed: for at Megara, when he led the army back from Thebes, as he was going up from the temple of Venus to the hall of the magistrates, he burst a vein somewhere in the inside of his body, and the blood flowed down from it into his sound leg. His ancle became excessively swelled, and the pain was not to be borne. A physician therefore from Syracuse lays open the vein upon the ancle-bone. The blood, having thus got a vent, continued to issue for a whole day and night, and in spite of all their arts, the flux could not be stopped till he fainted away; then indeed it ceased entirely. And being afterwards conveyed to Lacedæmon, he was very ill all the rest of that summer, and all the next winter too.

However, so soon as it was spring, the Lacedæmonians again declared an expedition against the Thebans, and ordered Cleombrotus to command the army. When in his march

he was near Cithæron, the targeteers advanced before him to secure the eminence above the pass. Some of the Thebans and Athenians had already possessed themselves of the summit of the mountain, and suffered them quietly to mount the ascent. But so soon as they were come within reach, they started up, pursued, and slew about forty of them. And after this repulse, Cleombrotus, judging it impossible to get over into the dominions of Thebes, led back and disbanded the army.

An assembly of the confederates was held afterwards at Lacedæmon, where they remonstrated at large, that " they should be ruined by such a sluggish conduct of the war. The Lacedæmonians, if they pleased, might man out a much larger number of ships than the Athenians, and might starve their city into a surrender. With the same ships they might also transport the land-army against Thebes: or, if they had rather, might march through Phocis ; or, if they chose it, by the pass of Crusis." In pursuance of these remonstrances, they manned out sixty triremes, and Pollis was appointed to be admiral. And indeed such as recommended this conduct were not disappointed, for by it the Athenians were blocked up at sea. Their corn ships were come up as far as Gerastus, but not a vessel durst stir from thence, as the fleet of the Lacedæmonians was on the stations of Ægina, and Ceos, and Andros. The Athenians, thus convinced they must run all hazards, went on board their ships; and, coming to an engagement with Pollis, they gain a victory at sea under the command of Chabrias : and then the corn was brought in safety to Athens.

The Lacedæmonians preparing now to transport the land-army against the Bœotians, the Thebans requested the Athenians to appear with their naval force on the coasts of Peloponnesus ; judging that, would the Athenians comply, it would be impossible for the Lacedæmonians at one and the same time to guard their own coast with all the confederate cities that lie round their dominions, and to send abroad an army large enough to make head against them. The Athenians, still full of resentment against the Lacedæmonians for the affair of Sphodrias, having manned out sixty ships, and chosen Timotheus for commander, despatched them with alacrity against Peloponnesus. And now, as their enemy had made no irruption into the territory of Thebes,

---

1 One thousand nine hundred and thirty-seven pounds ten shillings.

either during the command of Cleombrotus, or whilst Timotheus was hovering round their coasts, the Thebans boldly took the field against their neighbouring cities, and retook them all. Timotheus, also, after coasting round, reduced Corcyra without loss of time. However he reduced none to slavery, he drove none into exile, he made no change in their laws; and by such moderation he procured the good-will of all the neighbouring states. And now the Lacedæmonians manned out their ships to check Timotheus, and sent them to sea under the command of Nicolochus, a man of remarkable bravery. He was no sooner within sight of the ships of Timotheus, than, though six ships from Ambracia had not yet joined him, and he had under his command but fifty-five against sixty under Timotheus, he engaged without any hesitation. He was indeed defeated in the battle, and Timotheus erected a trophy at Ælyzia. But whilst the ships of Timotheus were drawn ashore in order to be repaired, and the six fresh ships from Ambracia had joined Nicolochus, he sailed up to Ælyzia where Timotheus was. But as the latter refused to come out and fight, Nicolochus also erected a trophy on the nearest island. Yet, when Timotheus had refitted his own ships, and manned out several more from Corcyra, his total number amounting now to more than seventy, he became far superior in strength at sea. He sent away to Athens for money; and much money he wanted, for he had many ships.

THE

AFFAIRS OF GREECE.

BOOK VI.

CONTENTS of BOOK VI.

THE

AFFAIRS OF GREECE.

BOOK VI.

I. THE Athenians and the Lacedæmonians were thus employed. But the Thebans, after they had reduced the cities of Bœotia, marched into Phocis. The Phocians sent away ambassadors to Lacedæmon, and represented there, that without a speedy aid they could not avoid submitting to the Thebans." The consequence was, that the Lacedæmonians transported by sea to aid them their king Cleombrotus, having under him four brigades and a part of their confederates.

About the same time Polydamas the Pharsalian also arriveth at Lacedæmon on business to the state. Polydamas was in high esteem all over Thessaly; and in his own city of Pharsalus was judged so honest and worthy a man, that his fellow-citizens, who had been embroiled in a sedition, had unanimously agreed as the safest expedient to entrust their citadel to his custody. They empowered him farther to receive all the public revenue, and make such disbursements for sacrifices and other points of the public administration as were according to law. Thus provided with money, he procured an effectual guard for the citadel, and at every year's end passed fair accounts of his administration. Nay, whenever the public money fell short, he advanced his own for the necessary payments, and reimbursed himself again when the public money came in. And more than all this, he lived in a course of great hospitality and magnificence too, according to the modes of Thessaly. When Polydamas therefore was arrived at Lacedæmon, he spoke as followeth:

"Not only my progenitors from time immemorial, but I myself too, Lacedæmonians, have been your public host and constant benefactor. I have therefore a right, when I want assistance, to apply to you for it, and to give you notice in time of any difficulty that starts up and may prove prejudicial to you in Thessaly.

"You are no strangers, I am well assured, to the name of Jason; for he is a man of great power, and in high reputation. This Jason, having demanded a truce, hath had a conference with me, in which he discoursed me thus:

"You may judge, Polydamas, from the reasons I am going to lay before you, whether I am not able to reduce Pharsalus your city to my obedience in spite of all opposition. I have (said he) now ready to act with me the largest number of the most powerful cities in Thessaly. I have reduced them into obedience to myself, though you united with them in carrying on a war against me. You know, further, that I have now a body of six thousand foreigners in my pay; and, in my judgment, no city in this part of the world can in battle be a match for them. I can bring (said he) full as many more into the field from other places in my own subjection. The troops that occasionally take the field from Thessalian cities, have several persons amongst them advanced in years, and several not yet of age for service; and small is the number of those belonging to any city whatever, who keep themselves in proper exercise for war. But not a man receiveth my pay, who is not able to undergo any toil as well as myself."

"And Jason himself (for I must not suppress the truth) is very strong by natural constitution, and is beside habitually hardy. And hence it is, that not a day passeth, in which he doth not put the hardiness of his men to trial. He is daily in armour, and daily at their head, either when they go out to exercise, or go out on actual service. Such of his mercenaries as he findeth unable to bear hardships, he throweth aside; but such as he findeth are eager to toil, and eager to face the dangers of war, he distinguisheth by an assignment of pay twice, thrice, nay four times as large as the common, besides the additional presents he maketh them, his great care to cure them when they are sick, and the handsome funerals he honoureth them with if they die. Thus it is, that all the foreigners in Jason's service are perfectly assured, that military valour affordeth all the honour and affluence of life.

" He then repeated to me what I well knew before, that the Maracians, Dolopians, and Alcetas, who govern in Epirus, were already subject to his orders.—What reason therefore (said he) have I to be frightened, or to think I am not able to reduce you Pharsalians too? Yet some that know me not may here demand, Why therefore do you dally? why do you not march at once against the Pharsalians? My answer is plain and honest truth, because I had rather gain you by a willing than a compelled submission. For should you act with me upon compulsion, you will for ever be contriving to do me mischief, and I shall for ever be contriving to weaken you as much as possibly I can. But if you join me upon the motives of persuasion, it is plain we shall be ready on both sides to do all the good we can for one another. I am very sensible, Polydamas, that Pharsalus, your own native city, placeth all confidence in you. If therefore you can bring it into friendship with me, I give you my honour (said he) I will make you next after myself the greatest man in Greece. And hear of how much good I offer you the second share; and believe nothing of what I am going to say, unless your own reason, upon reflection, convinceth you it is true. This therefore is certainly clear, that if Pharsalus and the cities that depend upon you, will act in union with me, I may easily get myself declared supreme governor of all the Thessalians. It is equally certain, that when Thessaly shall be united under one head, the number of horsemen riseth at once to six thousand, and the number of their heavy-armed to more than ten thousand men. And when I consider, how able-bodied and how brave they are by nature, I am persuaded that, when they are properly disciplined, there is not a nation to whom the Thessalians would not disdain the thoughts of submitting. And as Thessaly itself is a country of vast extent, no sooner are they united under

one head, than all the nations around must instantly submit. These people are expert in the use of missive weapons; and hence it may be judged, that our armies will exceed all others in the number of our targeteers. Besides this, the Bœotians, and all other people of Greece who are enemies to the Lacedæmonians, are confederates with me. They ever profess themselves ready to act under my guidance, provided I free them from the Lacedæmonians. The Athenians, farther, I am well persuaded, would do any thing in the world to be taken into our alliance. But I think it will not be my choice to be at friendship with them; since I judge it much easier at present to establish an empire by sea than by land. Whether I judge solidly or not, consider what I am going to add—When we are masters of Macedonia, from whence the Athenians fetch their timber, we shall be able to build a much larger number of ships than they. And shall we not be able to man these ships with much more expedition than the Athenians, as we have so many vassals amongst us capable of being made good seamen? And again, shall we not be better able to victual our fleets, we, who make large exportations of our corn from the great plenty we enjoy, than the Athenians can be, who have not enough for their home consumption without buying it at foreign markets? In money, too, we must certainly outdo them, since we are not to squeeze it from a parcel of paltry islands, but can collect it in most ample measure from whole nations on the continent; and all the circumjacent nations are subject to a tribute, when the government of Thessaly is lodged in the hands of a supreme governor. You yourself know, that the Persian monarch, who collects his tributes not from islands but the continent, is the richest man upon earth. And this very monarch, I think, I could reduce to my own subjection with more ease than even Greece. For I am sensible, that in all his dominions there is but one single person who takes not more pains to be a slave than to be free. And I am farther sensible, how that monarch was reduced to the last extremity by so small a force as marched up against him under Cyrus, and by that afterwards under Agesilaus.

" When Jason had run over all these points, my answer was—There is weight assuredly in all you have said. But for us, who are confederates with the Lacedæmonians and without having any thing to lay to their charge, to revolt to their enemies, seems to me (said I) a point that I shall not easily comply with. He praised my ingenuity, and said I was so honest a man that he would do all in his power to gain my friendship. He hath therefore given me leave to repair hither, and represent the truth to you, that unless we readily join him, he is fully determined to make war upon the Pharsalians. He enjoined me, farther, to demand assistance from you. If (said he) they grant you an aid, and such as you can judge sufficient to enable you to make head against me, bring them into the field (said he) and let us decide by battle what our future conduct must be: but, in case they give you not a sufficient aid, your country, which honoureth you, and which you nobly serve, may possibly have ample reason to censure your behaviour.

" It is for these reasons, that I am come now to Lacedæmon, and have given an exact recital of what I know myself, and what I have heard Jason say. And, in my own opinion, Lacedæmonians, the point rests here;—If actually you can send an army thither, in aid not only of me but of the rest of the Thessalians, sufficient to maintain a war against Jason, the cities will revolt from him. For they are all in great fear, how the mighty power of this man will end. But, if you judge that a body of new enfranchised citizens and a private Spartan to command will suffice, I then advise you not to meddle at all. For rest thoroughly convinced, it is a mighty strength you are to struggle against. That strength will be under the conduct of an able commander; who, when the point is either to conceal, or prevent, or to push, will be generally successful. He knoweth how to act as well by night as by day. On an emergency he will take either dinner or supper without abating his activity. He never thinketh it time to take his repose, till he is arrived at the place whither he resolved to go, or hath completed the point he was determined to complete. He hath made such practices habitual to all his troops. He is skilful at gratifying his soldiers, when by hardy perseverance they have accomplished any point of importance; so that all who serve under Jason have learned this lesson, that pleasure is the effect of toil; though as to sensual pleasures, I know no person in the world more temperate than Jason. They never break in upon his time; they always leave him leisure to do what must be done.

" Consider therefore these things; and tell me, in the manner that becometh you, what you shall be able to do, and what you will do in this affair."

Polydamas spoke thus, and the Lacedæmonians excused themselves from giving an immediate answer. Next day and the day after, they employed themselves in calculating how many brigades they had already abroad in different quarters, and how many ships they must keep at sea to make head against the fleet of Athens, and what was requisite for the war against their neighbouring enemies. And then they made this answer to Polydamas, that "at present they could not send him a competent aid; it was therefore their advice, that he should return, and accommodate both the public and his own private affairs with Jason in the best manner he was able." And Polydamas, after highly commending the ingenuity of the state, returned to Pharsalus.

He now made it his request to Jason, not to compel him to surrender the citadel of the Pharsalians, which he would fain preserve faithfully for those who had made him the depositary of it. But then he gave his own sons for hostages, promising he would persuade his fellow-citizens to act in hearty concert with him, and would himself co-operate to get him declared supreme governor of Thessaly. When therefore they had exchanged securities to one another, the Pharsalians had a peace immediately granted them, and Jason was soon without opposition appointed supreme governor of all Thessaly. When thus invested with authority, he fixed the number of horsemen and number of heavy-armed, that every city in proportion to their ability should be obliged to maintain. And the number of his horsemen now, including his confederates, was more than eight thousand, his heavy-armed were computed to be twenty thousand at least. His targeteers were numerous enough to fight all other targeteers in the world: it would be a toil to reckon up the names of the cities to which they belonged. He also ordered the people that lay round Thessaly to send in their tribute, in the same manner it was paid during the supremacy of Scopas. And in this manner were these things brought about. I now return again from whence I digressed to give this account of Jason.

II. The troops of the Lacedæmonians and confederates were now assembled in Phocis; but the Thebans, after withdrawing into their own territory, guarded all the passes. In the meantime the Athenians, seeing how much they had contributed towards the power of the Thebans, who notwithstanding paid nothing in return for the support of their fleet, and finding themselves exhausted by the vast taxes they paid and by the piratical cruizes from Ægina, and the guard of their lands, became highly desirous of bringing the war to an end. Accordingly they sent ambassadors to Lacedæmon, and made a peace. Two of these ambassadors set sail immediately from Lacedæmon in pursuance of an order from Athens, and commanded Timotheus to return home with the fleet, since now there was a peace. But in his homeward passage he landed all the exiles from Zacynthus on their own isle. But no sooner had the other Zacynthians sent notice to Lacedæmon of this action of Timotheus, than the Lacedæmonians resolved that " the Athenians had committed injustice," prepared again to send out a fleet, and ordered the equipment of sixty ships from Lacedæmon itself, Corinth, Leucas, Ambracia, Elis, Zacynthus, Achæa, Epidaurus, Trœzen, Hermione, and Haliæ. Having next declared Mnasippus admiral of this fleet, they ordered him to take due care of every thing within that sea, and to make an attempt upon Corcyra. They sent also to Dionysius, representing to him, that it was by no means for his interest, that Corcyra should remain in the power of the Athenians.

And now when the whole fleet was got together, Mnasippus sailed for Corcyra. He had with him, besides the troops from Lacedæmon, a body of mercenaries in number not less than fifteen hundred. When he had landed in Corcyra, he was master of all the country. He ruined their estates, so beautifully cultivated and so finely planted. He demolished the magnificent houses built upon them, in the cellars of which their wines were lodged. His soldiers are reported on this occasion to have grown so nice in palate, that they would not drink any wine that had not an odoriferous flavour. Slaves also and cattle in vast abundance were taken in the adjacent country. At length he had encamped with his land-forces on a hill, which had the country behind it, about [1] five stadia from the

city, in order to intercept any aid from the country that might endeavour to enter the city; and had further stationed his fleet on either side of the city, as he judged would best enable them to discover and stop in time whatever approached by sea; and, beside all this, he kept a guard at sea before the harbour, when the weather was not too tempestuous. In this manner he kept the city close blocked up.

And now the Corcyreans, who could receive none of the produce of their lands, since they were all in the enemy's possession, who could have nothing imported by sea, as their enemies were also masters there, were in great distress. They sent to the Athenians, and requested a speedy aid. They remonstrated to them, " How vastly they needs must suffer, if they were thus deprived of Corcyra, or resigned so great a strength to their enemies! No state in Greece, excepting Athens, had so much shipping, or so much wealth. The city of Corcyra was finely situated in respect to the bay of Corinth, and the cities which stood upon that bay; finely situated too for annoying the coast of Laconia; and most finely indeed in respect to the continent beyond it, and the passage from Sicily to Peloponnesus."

The Athenians, after listening to these remonstrances, agreed it was a point deserving all their care, and despatch away Stesicles with six hundred targeteers to take upon him the command, and begged Alcetas to transport and land them in Corcyra. Accordingly they were landed by night somewhere upon that island, and get into the city. They decreed farther, to man out sixty ships; and, by a majority of hands, elected Timotheus to command them. But, not being able to man them at home, Timotheus sailed to the islands, and endeavoured there to complete his crews; judging it no trifling matter to stand away hastily against a fleet so well prepared as was that of the enemy. But the Athenians, who now thought he was wasting the precious time, and ought at once to have made his passage, grew out of all patience with him, and suspending his command, choose Iphicrates in his room. Iphicrates, so soon as he was appointed to command, completed his crews with high expedition, obliging all captains of ships to exert themselves. He pressed into the service, by public permission, whatever ships were found upon the Attic coasts, nay even the Salaminian and the Paralus, saying " if things succeeded well at Corcyra, he

---

1 About half a mile

would send them back plenty of ships." And the number of his ships amounted at last to seventy.

In the meantime the Corcyreans were so sorely pressed with famine that vast numbers of them deserted to the enemy, insomuch that Mnasipnus at length made public proclamation, that "all deserters should be sold at public sale." But as this put no stop to their desertion, he at last scourged them, and then drove them back. Yet the besieged would not again receive any slaves into the town, so that many of them perished without the walls. Mnasippus, therefore, seeing these things, imagined he was already only not in possession of the city. He therefore made new regulations in regard to his mercenaries, and forced some of them to leave the service without their pay. And to those whom he still kept with him, he was already two months in arrear, though, as was said, he was in no want of money; for several of the cities sent money over to him instead of troops, as the expedition was across the sea. But now the besieged saw plainly from the turrets, that the guards did their duty with more negligence than before, and that the men straggled in a careless manner about the country. They therefore sallied out upon them suddenly, and took some prisoners, and some they slew. Mnasippus, perceiving this, caught up his arms in an instant, and marched with all the heavy-armed he had to their succour, and gave orders to the superior and inferior officers of the mercenaries to lead out their troops. But some of these inferior officers having answered, that "it would not be easy to bring soldiers out in proper discipline who could get no pay," he struck one of them with his staff and another with his spear. And thus at length they all come out into the field, though without any spirit at all, and with a hearty detestation of Mnasippus, the worst temper in the world for men going to fight. When he had drawn them up in order of battle, he put the enemy to flight that were drawn up between him and the gates, and followed briskly in pursuit. But the pursued, when they were near the wall, made a wheel, and kept galling him from the tombs with their darts and javelins. And another party, sallying out at another gate, pour down in great numbers on the extremity of his line. The men posted there, as they were drawn up but eight in file, judged the point of their line to be quite too weak, and endeavour

ed to make a wheel. But they had no sooner begun to fall back, than the enemy broke in upon them as if they were flying, and they made no attempt to recover their ranks. Such too as were posted nearest to them took instantly to flight. Mnasippus in the meantime was not able to assist the routed part of his line, as the enemy was lying hard upon him in front; he was every moment left with fewer and fewer men. And at last the enemy, gathering into a body, made a general attack upon those remaining with Mnasippus, who were very few. The heavy-armed of the enemy seeing how the case stood, now made a sally; and after killing Mnasippus, the whole force of the enemy continued the pursuit. The whole camp and the entrenchment were in great danger of being taken, had not the pursuers judged it advisable to retreat, when they saw the great crowd of people got together within the camp, whom, though servants and slaves, they judged might be serviceable in its defence. And then the Corcyreans erected a trophy, and restored the dead under truce.

The besieged, after this, were in the highest spirits, whilst the besiegers were in total dejection. For now it was reported, that Iphicrates was only not at hand, and the Corcyreans actually manned out their ships. But Hypermenes, who was at present in the command, since he had been lieutenant to Mnasippus, ordered every ship to be immediately manned, and standing round with them to the entrenchment of the camp, shipped all the slaves and treasure on board, and sent them off. He staid on shore, with the marines and such of the soldiers as yet remained, to guard the entrenchments. And at last even these, though with the utmost disorder, got on board the ships and put out to sea, leaving a great quantity of corn, and a great quantity of wine, and many slaves and sick persons behind them. They were in a terrible fright, lest they should be caught upon the island by the Athenians. And in fact they all got safe over to Leucas.

But Iphicrates, when once he had begun the passage, kept at the same time advancing in his course, and preparing his whole fleet for engagement. He had left behind him the great masts at setting out, as standing away for battle. He also made very little use of his sails even when the wind was favourable. He made the passage by the oar; and so kept the bodies of his men in excellent order, and his ships in an even motion.

3 N

Whenever the forces were to land for their dinner or supper, he led the fleet in a line a-head over-against the place; then making a tack, and bringing the heads of his vessels in a direct line with the shore, he gave a signal for all to make the best of their way to land. A great advantage thence accrued to such as could first take in their water or what else they wanted, and first finish their meal. A great punishment likewise fell upon such as were last on these occasions, because they got a less quantity of whatever they wanted, since they were obliged to put out to sea again when the signal was given. For it followed of course, that such as landed first had leisure enough for all their occasions, whilst the last were grievously hurried. And whenever he landed at meal-time on the shore of the enemy, he posted advanced guards, as was proper, at land: and raising the masts in his ships, placed sentinels on their tops. These latter therefore had generally a much more extensive view by being thus mounted aloft than men who stand upon level ground. And wherever he supped or refreshed his men, he suffered no fire to be kindled in the night-time within his encampment, but fixed his lights in the front of his station, that nobody might approach without being discovered. Oftentimes, too, when the weather was calm, he put out again to sea so soon as supper was over; and if a gale sprung up, the men took some repose whilst the vessels kept going before the wind. But if they were obliged to row, he made them take rest by turns. In the day-time, directing the course by signals, he one while advanced in the line a-head, and another while in the line a-breast. By this means, and during the passage, having acquired all needful skill for engaging, they arrived in the sea of which they imagined the enemy were masters. They frequently dined and supped upon the enemy's land; but as Iphicrates was solely intent upon doing what must needs be done, he prevented all attacks by the suddenness with which he again put to sea, and proceeded in his passage. About the time that Mnasippus was killed he was got to Sphagæ of Laconia. Advancing from thence to the coast of Elis, and passing by the mouth of the Alpheus, he came to an anchor near the place called Icthys. The next day he proceeded from thence to Cephallene, with his fleet so ranged and proceeding in their course, that every thing needful was ready for an en-

gagement, if it should be necessary to engage. He heard indeed of the death of Mnasippus, yet from none that could attest its truth; he suspected it was given out on purpose to deceive him, and kept upon his guard. However, when arrived at Cephallene, he was there convinced of the truth, and stopped to refresh his fleet.—I am sensible, indeed, that whenever men expect an engagement, exercise and discipline are constantly enforced. But I commend Iphicrates for this, that as he was to advance with the highest expedition to find his enemy and engage them, he contrived so well, that the expeditiousness of the voyage should not hinder his men from acquiring skill for battle, nor the methods of acquiring such skill should retard the expeditiousness of the voyage.

When therefore he had reduced the cities of Cephallene, he sailed to Corcyra. After his arrival there, the first thing he heard was, that ten ships were coming over from Dionysius as a succour to the Lacedæmonians. He went therefore himself in person to look for proper places on the coast, from whence the approach of these ships might be descried, and the signals made to notify it might be seen in the city; and there he posted sentinels, instructed by him in what manner to make their signals, when the enemy approached or came to anchor. He then ordered twenty captains of his own fleet to be ready to follow him at the call of the herald; and gave out that such as were not ready at the call must not complain at being punished for their neglect. So soon as the signal was made that these ships were approaching, and the herald had made the call, such diligence ensued as caused a fine spectacle indeed; for not a man of those who were to act upon this occasion, but ran full speed on board his ship. Having now stood away to the spot where the ships of the enemy were arrived, he findeth that from the rest of the squadron the men were already got on shore, whilst Melanippus the Rhodian was calling out upon them by no means to linger there, and himself with all his crew on board was getting out to sea. Melanippus by this means escaped, though he met with the ships of Iphicrates: but all the Syracusan ships were taken with their crews. And Iphicrates, after cutting off the beaks of these ships, brought them into the harbour of Corcyra. He then fixed a certain sum which each of the prisoners must pay for his ransom, except Anippus their commander. Him he confined under a close guard, as if he expected a vast sum for him, or otherwise would sell him. Anippus was so highly chagrined at this usage, that he chose to die by his own hand. And Iphicrates, taking security from the Corcyreans for the payment of their ransom, gave their liberty to the rest.

He after this subsisted his mariners by employing them in works of tillage for the Corcyreans, but with the targeteers and heavy-armed of the fleet he passed over himself to Acarnania. He there gave aid to all such of the cities in friendship as needed it, and made war upon the Thurians, a very warlike people, and possessed of a place strongly fortified. Then fetching away the fleet from Corcyra, now consisting of about ninety ships, he went first to Cephallene to raise contributions, and exacted them from all persons, whether willing or unwilling. He then prepared to lay waste the territory of the Lacedæmonians, and to reduce the other cities of the enemy in those parts, if they desired it, by an accommodation; but if they stood out, by war. For my own part, I have a deal of commendation to bestow on Iphicrates for his conduct during this command, but above all for getting Callistratus the popular haranguer, a man not easy to be managed, and Chabrias, who was reckoned an excellent general, associated with him in it. For if he judged them men of sense, and therefore desired to be assisted with their counsel, in my opinion he acted the prudent part: or, in case he regarded them as enemies, why then he showed his noble spirit, in being thus confident that they should discern no bad management and no negligence in him. And these were the acts of Iphicrates.

III. But the Athenians, who now saw their friends the Platæans driven out of Bœotia, and forced to take refuge at Athens, and the inhabitants of Thespiæ offering their petitions, that "they (the Athenians) would not stand quiet and let them be stripped of their city," could no longer approve the conduct of the Thebans. They were restrained by shame from an open rupture, and by the reflection too that it would be prejudicial to their own interest. Yet they positively refused to act any more in participation with them, when they saw them invade the Phocians who had long been in friendship with the state of Athens, and utterly destroying cities that had been faithful in the war with the Barbarians, and

steadily attached to themselves. The people of Athens were now persuaded to pass a decree for negotiating a peace, and accordingly sent in the first place ambassadors to Thebes, with an invitation to go with them to Lacedæmon, if it suited their own inclinations, about a peace. And then they despatched away their own ambassadors. The persons chosen for this employ were Callias the son of Hipponicus, Autocles the son of Strombichides, Demostratus the son of Aristophon, Aristocles, Cephisodotus, Melanopus, Lycanthus. When they were admitted to audience before the council of state at Lacedæmon and the confederates, Callistratus the popular haranguer was with them. He had promised Iphicrates, if he would give him his dismission, either to procure him money for his fleet, or to make a peace; he accordingly had been at Athens, and solicited a peace. But when they were introduced to the council of state at Lacedæmon and the confederates, Callias, whose office it was to bear the torch in the Eleusinian mysteries, was the first that spoke. He was a man that took as much delight in praising himself as in being praised by others. He began on this occasion, and spoke to this effect:

"I am not, Lacedæmonians, the only person of my family, who hath been the public host of your community. My father and his father too were so before me, and delivered the honour down to me as the privilege of my birth. I am desirous too to persuade you all, that Athens hath continually persisted in showing favour to us. For, whenever there is war, our Athens, our own community, chooseth us to command their armies; and when peace is again desired, sendeth us to negotiate a peace. Nay, twice already have I been at Lacedæmon to negotiate accommodations; both times so successfully, that I made peace between us and you. I am now a third time employed, and think I have more abundant reason than ever to depend on a mutual reconciliation. For now I see clearly, that you are not intent upon one system and we upon another; but both of us are united in indignation for the ruin of Platæa and Thespiæ. What therefore can hinder men, whose sentiments are exactly the same, from choosing to be friends rather than enemies to one another?

"It is indeed the part of wise men, not hastily to have recourse to arms, even though considerable dissentions arise. But when their sentiments of things exactly coincide, will it not be wonderful indeed, if such persons cannot agree about a peace? Common justice, it is true, hath always laid it as a duty upon us, never to make war upon one another. For it is acknowledged by all the world, that our progenitor Triptolemus communicated the ineffable mysteries of Ceres and Proserpine to Hercules your founder, and to the Dioscuri [1] your countrymen, the first time he did it to foreigners; and Peloponnesus was the first foreign land on which he generally bestowed the fruits of Ceres. How, therefore, could it be just, that you should ever in a hostile manner enter upon the lands and ravage the fruits of those from whom you first received your seed? or, that we ever should wish, that the very people on whom we bestowed it, should not enjoy in highest plenty the needful sustenance of life? But if the fates decree that war must take place amongst mankind, it is our part to begin it on all occasions with the utmost reluctance; and, when once begun, to bring it to an end with our utmost expedition."

After him Autocles, who was looked upon as an orator of great art and address, harangued them thus:

"I am going to say some things, Lacedæmonians, which I am very sensible you will not hear with pleasure. But I am well persuaded, that men who are desirous of peace, and to settle that peace in such a manner that it may be of lasting continuance, should not be shy in putting one another in remembrance of the reasons of the previous wars. You, Lacedæmonians, are ever giving out, that the cities of Greece ought to be free and independent; whilst after all, yourselves are the greatest hinderers of that freedom and independence. The very first condition you make with all the cities that enter into your confederacy is, that they shall march along with you wheresoever you lead them. And can this in any shape be consistent with freedom and independence? You declare enemies what people you please, without any previous consultation of your confederates; and then lead on the latter to make war upon them; insomuch that these free and independent people, as they are called, are often obliged to take the field against men to whom they bear the most benevolent affection.

"Again, and what of all things is most repugnant to a state of freedom and independence, you establish in some cities the government of ten, and in others of thirty persons. You take no care at all that these governors should rule according to laws, but merely that by oppressive methods they keep the cities in fast subjection to yourselves. In a word, you have convinced mankind, that not a polity but a tyranny is most agreeable to your own inclinations.

"When, farther, the Persian monarch signified his pleasure that the cities should be free and independent, you then made frank and open declarations that the Thebans could in no wise be judged to conform to the king's intention, unless they permitted each single city to be master of itself, and to make use of laws of their own proper choice. And yet, when you had seized the citadel of Thebes, you would not suffer even these Thebans to be free and independent.

"Men, let me add, who sincerely desire peace, ought not to expect from others a thorough compliance with their own demands, whilst they manifest an ambition to engross all power to themselves."

When Autocles had spoken thus, the consequence was, not only a general silence in the assembly, but an inward pleasure in the hearts of those who were displeased at the Lacedæmonian conduct.

But after him Callistratus spoke:

"Far be it from me, Lacedæmonians, to think that I could truly aver, that nothing wrong hath been done either by you or by us. And I am as far from thinking, on the other hand, that all intercourse must for ever be stopped with men who once do wrong; because I cannot see any mortal alive who goeth through life without committing some offence. It is rather my opinion, that sometimes men who have offended become afterwards more tractable and better tempered, especially if they have been chastised for those offences, as we Athenians have been. I see, Lacedæmonians, in your behaviour, too, some offences incurred for want of temper and reflection, for which you have since been abundantly crossed. But I shall produce no other instance of this at present than your seizure of the citadel of Thebes. And hence it is, since this flagrant injury you did the Thebans, that all the cities, in whose favour you once so earnestly exerted yourselves to restore them to freedom and independence, have united with the Thebans against you. I hope you are now convinced, how prejudicial it is to grasp at too much power, and are resolved for the future to use moderation, and to be steady in reciprocal friendship with others.

" There are people, I know, who, intending to dissuade you from a peace with us, mischievously insinuate, that we ask it not from sincerity of heart, but are brought hither by the fears we are under, lest Antalcidas may return with a fresh supply of money from the king of Persia. But consider, and be convinced, that such people are arrant triflers. The king, it is well known, hath told us in writing, that all the cities in Greece should be left free and independent. For our own parts, we conform both in word and deed to the intention of the king. What reason have we therefore to apprehend any thing from him? Is there a person so weak as to imagine, that the king had rather subject himself to a vast expense, and only to make other people great, than to accomplish what he thinketh is best for himself, without making any expense at all? Be it so. For what reason then are we come hither? Not because we are totally distressed; yourselves may perceive the contrary, if you will survey the present situation of our affairs at sea, and if you will survey the situation of them too at land. But what then is our meaning? It is plain to be discerned, since there are several of the confederates who behave in such a manner as can be pleasing neither to us nor to you. Perhaps, after all, our chief motive may be, to communicate our own sentiments of things to you, in requital for the kindness you did us in preserving Athens.

" But at present I shall only insist on the point of reciprocal interest. It is true of all the cities of Greece, that some by principle are more attached to us, and some to you: it is the case in every city, one party declares for the Lacedæmonian and another for the Athenian interest. If we therefore unite in friendship with one another, from what quarter can we with reason expect any effectual opposition? For who in good truth is the person who, when you are our friends, can presume at doing us Athenians any harm by land? And who will dare to annoy you Lacedæmonians by sea, when we are cheerful and warm in your service? Wars, it must be granted, are for

ever breaking out between us; and accommodations, as we well know, are soon again brought on. And, though it be not our case at present, yet the case will happen again and again, that we shall be desirous of a peace with you. But what reason can there be to put off our reconciliation to that distant day, when, through the weight of distress, we may be grown quite desperate, rather than to settle all things by an immediate peace, before any irremediable disaster hath taken place? For my part, I ingenuously own it, I never could commend those champions in the public games, who, after a series of victory, and a large acquisition of glory, are so litigiously ambitious of more, that they can never stop, till they are shamefully beaten, and compelled to forego the lists for ever after. Nor can I commend those gamesters who, after having gained the stake, will suffer it to be doubled, and throw again. Most of those who play with so much avidity, I have seen reduced to utter beggary. We ought therefore to catch instruction from such examples, and not reduce our contest to that state of desperation, that we must either win all or lose all. But whilst we yet are vigorous, whilst we yet are happy, let us become friends to one another: for then we through you, and you through us, may yet make a greater figure than hitherto we have ever made in Greece."

This speech met with general approbation, and the Lacedæmonians passed a decree to sign a peace on the following terms:—" To withdraw their commanders out of the cities; to disband all forces both by land and sea; and to leave the cities in a state of freedom and independence. And in case any of these commanders refuse to withdraw, any city that was willing might assist the injured cities; but such as were not willing might refuse to act in defence of the injured, without being guilty of a breach of faith." On these conditions the Lacedæmonians swore to a peace for themselves and their confederates; the Athenians and their confederates swore severally in the name of their principals. Even the Thebans were entered down by name in the list of the states that swore; but their ambassadors[2] made a fresh application the day after, and desired that " the name of Bœotians might be inserted instead of Thebans." Agesilaus answered,

---

2 Epaminondas was one of them, and spoke with so much spirit on this occasion, that he sadly nettled Agesilaus.

that " he would not alter a letter of what they had already sworn to, and to which they had set their name. If indeed they had no mind to be comprehended in the peace (he said) he would readily, at their own desire, expunge their name." And now, all others having signed the peace, and the Thebans being singly excluded, the Athenians were persuaded in their own minds that the Thebans could no longer save themselves, even, as is commonly said, by a decimation. The Thebans also, judging themselves in a desperate situation, went their way.

IV. After this the Athenians withdrew their garrisons out of the cities. They also recalled Iphicrates and the fleet, whom they obliged to restore all captures they had made since the peace was sworn to at Lacedæmon. In like manner, the Lacedæmonians brought away their commandants and garrisons from the cities within their own dependence. Cleombrotus was excepted, who being now at the head of the troops in Phocis, sent to the magistracy of Lacedæmon for orders how to act. Prothous had already declared that in his sentiments, " they ought according to oath to disband their troops, and circulate an order to the cities to make the present of a sum of money, but at their own discretion, to the temple of Apollo ; and then, if any restraint was laid on the freedom and independence of those cities, they ought to call their confederates together, so many as should be willing to assert this independence, and lead them out against the authors of such restraint. For by such behaviour (he said) it was his opinion the gods would become more propitious to them, and the cities have the least ground for discontent." But the whole council of Lacedæmon, hearing him talk in this manner, looked upon him as a very trifler, (for already it should seem as if the wrath of heaven was driving them on,) and despatched an order to Cleombrotus, not to disband his troops, but to march immediately against the Thebans, unless they set the cities at liberty. Cleombrotus, I say, so soon as he heard the peace was made, sent to the ephori for instructions how to act, who ordered him to march against the Thebans, unless they set the cities of Bœotia at liberty. When therefore he was become assured, that so far from setting those cities at liberty, they had not so much as disbanded their army, but kept them in readiness to make head against him, he

marcheth his army into Bœotia. He took not the route which the Bœotians imagined he would have taken out of Phocis, and had posted themselves in a narrow pass to stop him ; but on a sudden crossing the mountains by the pass of Thisbe he arriveth at Crusis, taketh the fortress there, and seizeth twelve triremes belonging to the Thebans. Having done this, and marched upwards from the sea, he encamped at Leuctra in the district of Thespiæ. The Thebans [1] encamped their own troops on an opposite hill at no great distance from the enemy, having none of their confederates with them but those of Bœotia.

The friends of Cleombrotus went to him here and discoursed him thus ;—" If, Cleombrotus, you now suffer these Thebans to depart without a battle, you will be in danger of the severest punishment from the state. They will then remember against you, how formerly when you reached Cynoscephale you committed no manner of devastation on the lands of the Thebans ; and that in the next campaign you were not able so much as to enter their country, though Agesilaus always broke in by the pass of Cithæron. If then you regard your own preservation, or have any value at all for your country, you must give the enemy battle." [a] His friends discoursed him thus. His enemies said—" Now will this man convince the world, whether or no he be a friend to the Thebans, as some report him." Cleombrotus of a truth, hearing these insinuations, was provoked to fight.

On the other side, the chief men amongst the Thebans were reckoning, " that if they did not fight, the circumjacent cities would revolt from them, and they must suffer a siege in Thebes ; and then, should the people of Thebes be distressed for want of necessaries, an insurrection might be the consequence." Many of them knew by experience what exile was ; they determined, therefore, " it was better to die in battle than to become exiles a second time." An oracle much talked of was also some encouragement to them. It imported that " the Lacedæmonians would be conquered on that spot of ground where stood the monument of the virgins," who are reported to have killed themselves, [b] because they had been violated

---

1 Epaminondas was their commander-in-chief.

2 Other writers differ in this circumstance. Plutarch relateth the whole story thus : " A poor man whose

by some Lacedæmonians. The Thebans therefore adorned this monument before the battle. Intelligence was also brought them from Thebes, that all the temples had opened of their own accord, and the priestesses declared that the gods awarded them a victory. All the arms in the temple of Hercules were also said to have disappeared, as if Hercules himself was sallied forth to battle. Some persons, after all, pretend that these things were only the artifices of the generals.

In regard to the battle, every thing turned out cross on the side of the Lacedæmonians, whilst fortune smoothed every difficulty on the side of the enemy. It was just after dinner that Cleombrotus held the last council about a battle. They had drunk briskly at noon, and it was said that the wine also was a provocative to fight. But when each side was armed, and it was plain a battle would be fought,—in the first place, the sellers of provisions and some of the baggage-men, all such as had no inclination to fight, were departing from the camp of the Bœotians. But the mercenaries with Hiero, the targeteers from Phocis, and the horsemen from Heraclea and Phlius, fetched a compass, and meeting them full in their departure, drove them back, and pursued them to the Bœotian camp. The consequence was, they made the Bœotian army stronger and more numerous than it was before. In the next place, as there was a plain between them, the Lacedæmonians drew up and posted their horse before their phalanx; the Thebans also did the same. But then the horse of the Thebans had been long in exercise because of the war against the Orchomenians and the war against the Thespians; whereas the Lacedæ-

---

name was Scedasus, dwelt at Leuctra, a village in the district of Thespiæ. He had two daughters; their names were Hippo and Militia, or (as some say) Theano and Euxippe. Now Scedasus was a good man, and though his substance was very small, exceedingly kind to strangers. He received with cheerful hospitality two young Spartans who came to his house; and they, though enamoured with the daughters, were so awed by Scedasus' goodness, that they durst make no attempt upon them. And next day they continued their journey to the Pythian oracle, whither they were going. But after consulting the god about the points in which they wanted his advice, they set out again for their own homes; and, after travelling through Bœotia, stopped again in their return at the house of Scedasus. It happened that Scedasus himself was absent at this time from Leuctra, but his daughters received the strangers and entertained them with the usual hospitality, who, finding them thus without protection or defence, commit a rape upon them. But perceiving them full of indignation for the violence they had suffered, they put them to death, and then throwing their bodies into a well, they went their way. Scedasus on his return could see his daughters no where, and yet found every thing in the house as safe as he had left it. He knew not what to think, till a bitch whining at him, then several times running up to him and away from him again to the well, he guessed how it was, and at length drew up by ropes the dead bodies of his daughters. Learning now upon inquiry from his neighbours, that they had seen the very Lacedæmonians who had formerly lodged with him go into his house again the day before, he concluded them to be the murderers, since on their first visit they had abundantly praised the young lasses, and affirmed that their husbands would be very happy. He now set out for Lacedæmon, to beg justice from the ephori. Night came upon him while he was in the territory of Argos, and he turned into an inn to lodge. There came into the same inn another traveller, an old man of Oreus a city of the Hestiæa. Scedasus hearing him often groan and curse the Lacedæmonians, asked him what hurt the Lacedæmonians had done him? The traveller told him a dreadful story about the murder of his son by a Lacedæmonian commandant, and though he had been with the ephori at Sparta, they would not at all listen to his complaints. Scedasus, having heard this story, was all despondency. He suspected, the magistrates of Sparta would listen as little to himself. Yet he related some part of his calamity to the stranger, who advised him not to have recourse to the ephori, but to return into Bœotia, and build a tomb for his daughters. Scedasus however would not comply with his advice; but going on to Sparta laid his complaint before the ephori. As they gave him no attention, he presenteth himself before the kings; and going from them to all the men in power, he let them know his deplorable case. But obtaining no justice from them, he ran through the midst of the city, now raising his hands towards the sun and now dashing them against the ground, invoking the furies to avenge him, and at length put an end to his own life. But in after times the Lacedæmonians paid dearly for it. For when they were masters over all the Greeks, and had put garrisons into their cities, Epaminondas the Theban, to set a pattern to others, put their garrison in Thebes to the sword. And the Lacedæmonians for this reason making war upon them, the Thebans met them in the field at Leuctra. The very ground was an omen to them of victory. On it formerly they had recovered their liberty, when Amphicton, driven into exile by Sthenelus, had refuged himself at Thebes, and finding the Thebans tributary to the Chalcideans, had put an end to the tribute by killing Chalcedon king of the Eubœans. And now on the same spot the Lacedæmonians were totally defeated at the very tomb of the daughters of Scedasus. It is said, that before the battle Pelopidas, one of the Theban generals, was highly alarmed at some incidents that he thought boded him ill success, till Scedasus appeared to him in a dream, and inspired him with new confidence, since the Lacedæmonians were now caught at Leuctra and must suffer vengeance for his daughters; and the day before the battle was fought, he ordered a white colt to be sacrificed at the tomb of the virgins; nay, that whilst the Lacedæmonians were encamped at Tegea, he sent persons to find out this tomb; and when he had learned from the people of the country where it stood, he marched his troops with high confidence to the spot, where he drew them up and gained a victory."—Plutarch's Love-stories.

monian cavalry had never been in a worse condition than at present. The horses were furnished by the wealthiest persons of the state; and, when a foreign expedition was declared, then came the appointed rider, who receiving such a horse and such arms as they pleased to give him went immediately on service. And thus, the weakest in body and the worst spirited part of the soldiery were generally mounted on horses. Such truly was the cavalry on both sides.—In the Lacedæmonian phalanx, it was said, that every platoon was drawn up three in front; consequently in depth they could not be more than twelve. But the Thebans were drawn up firm together not less than fifty shields in depth; reckoning, that could they break the body of the enemy posted around the king, all the rest of the army would be an easy conquest.

But so soon as Cleombrotus began to advance towards the enemy, and even before the bulk of the army knew that he was in motion, the horse had already engaged, and those of the Lacedæmonians were immediately defeated, and in their flight fell in amongst their own heavy-armed: and at that instant, the heavy-armed of the Thebans had made their attack. However, that the body posted round Cleombrotus had at first the better in the fight, any man may have clear and certain proof from hence; for they could not have taken him up and carried him off yet alive, unless those who fought before him had the better of it at that instant of time. But when Cleombrotus was dead, and Dinon a general-officer, and Sphodrias of the king's council of war, and his son Cleonymus were also slain, then the horse-guard, and the adjutants of the general-officer and the rest, being quite overpowered by the weight of the enemy, were forced to retire. The Lacedæmonians who composed the left, when they saw the right thus driven from their ground, quitted their own ground too. Yet, after a terrible slaughter and a total defeat, so soon as they had repassed the trench which was round their camp, they grounded their arms on the very spot from whence they had marched out to battle; for the ground of their camp was not quite on a level, it was rather an ascent. And now there were some of the Lacedæmonians, who, judging their defeat to be an insupportable disgrace, declared against suffering the enemy to erect a trophy, against fetching off their dead by truce, but ra-

ther to endeavour to recover them by another battle. But the general officers, who saw that in all near a thousand Lacedæmonians were slain; who saw that of seven hundred Spartans belonging to their army, about four hundred were killed; who perceived, besides, that all the confederates were averse to fighting again, and some of them too not even sorry for what had happened, calling a council of the most proper persons, demanded their advice of what ought to be done. And when it was unanimously agreed, that "they ought to fetch off the dead by truce," they sent a herald to beg the truce. And then truly the Thebans erected a trophy, and delivered up the dead.

These things being done, a messenger sent to Lacedæmon with the news of this calamity arriveth there on the last day of the naked games, and when the chorus of men had just made their entry. The ephori, when they heard of the calamity, were grievously concerned, and in my opinion could not possibly avoid it; but they ordered not the chorus to withdraw, letting them finish the games. And then they sent round the names of the dead to the relations of each, with an order to the women to make no noise, and to bear the calamity in silence. But the day after, such persons as were related to any of the slain appeared in public, and the signs of pleasure and joy were visible in their faces; whilst you could see but few of those whose relations were reported to be yet alive, and they too walked up and down discontented and dejected.

In the next place, the ephori ordered the two remaining brigades to march, not excepting such persons as had been forty years in the service. They ordered out also such of the same standing as belonged to the brigades already abroad. For such as had been thirty-five years in the service marched out before in the army that went against the Phocians. They even enjoined the very persons who were left at home to serve the offices of state to march out on this occasion. Agesilaus indeed was not yet recovered of his illness: the state therefore ordered his son Archidamus to take upon him the command. The Tegeatæ with great cheerfulness took the field along with Archidamus: for the party of Stasippus, ever strongly attached to the Lacedæmonians, were yet alive, and had a very great influence at Tegea. The Mantineans too with all their strength marched out of their villages and joined him, for they were under an aristocratical government. The Corinthians, Sicyonians, Phliasians, and Achæans very cheerfully followed him ; and other cities too sent out their troops. The Lacedæmonians immediately fitted out their own triremes ; the Corinthians did the same, and begged the Sicyonians to do so too, as the Lacedæmonians had thoughts of transporting the army by sea. And in the meantime Archidamus was offering sacrifices for a successful expedition.

The Thebans immediately after the battle despatched a herald to Athens with a garland on his head, whom they ordered at the same time to notify the greatness of the victory and to request their aid, saying that " now it was in their power to be revenged on the Lacedæmonians for all the evil they have ever done them." The senate of Athens happened to be sitting in the citadel. And when they heard the news, it was plain to all men that they were heartily mortified at it. For they neither invited the herald to take any refreshment, nor made any reply to the request of aid. And in this manner the herald returned from Athens.

The Thebans however sent in all haste to Jason their ally, pressing him to come and join them. Their thoughts were wholly intent on what might be the consequence of this battle. Jason at once manned out his triremes, as if he would repair by sea to their assistance ; but then, taking with him his body of mercenaries and his own horse, even though the Phocians were in implacable hostility with him, he marched by land into Bœotia ; making his entry into several cities, before any news could be brought that he was on the march. And before any strength could be collected to stop him, he was advanced quite beyond their reach ; exhibiting a certain proof, that expedition carrieth a point much better than strength. And when he was gotten into Bœotia, the Thebans declaring for an immediate attack on the Lacedæmonians, Jason to pour down from the hills with his mercenaries, whilst themselves charged them full in front, he dissuaded them from it, remonstrating to them that after so noble a victory, it was not worth their while to run the hazard of either gaining a greater or losing the fruits of the victory already gained. Are you not aware (said he) that you have just now conquered, because you were necessitated to fight ? You should remember therefore, that the Lacedæmonians, when necessitated too to fight for their very beings, will fight with the utmost desperation. And God, it must be owned, often taketh delight in making the little great and the great little." By such remonstrances he dissuaded the Thebans from running any fresh hazards. On the other side he was teaching the Lacedæmonians what a difference there was between a vanquished and a victorious army. " If therefore (said he) you are desirous to extinguish the memory of your late calamity, I advise you to breathe a while ; and when you are grown stronger, then to fight again against these unconquered Thebans. But at present (said he) you may rest assured, that there are some even of your own confederates, who are in treaty with your enemies. By all means endeavour to obtain a peace for yourselves. I will equally endeavour to procure one for you, as I desire nothing for your preservation, because of the friendship my father had for you, and because I myself by the laws of hospitality am connected with you." In this manner he talked ; and his motive possibly might be, that both these discordant parties might be reduced to a dependence upon himself. The Lacedæmonians, therefore, having hearkened to his advice, desired him to procure them a peace. But so soon as word was brought them that a peace was granted, the general officers issued out an order, for all the troops to be ready immediately after supper, since they should march off by night ; that next morning by day-break they might pass Mount Cithæron. When supper was over, before they could sleep, the order was issued for a march, and immediately after the close of evening their officers led them off by the road of Crusis, confiding more in the secrecy of their march than in the peace. And after a very difficult march indeed, since it was by night, in a very dejected mood, and through very bad roads, they reach Ægosthena in the territory of Megara. There they met with the army under the command of Archidamus. He halted there with them till all the confederates were come in, and then led them off in one body to Corinth. At Corinth he dismissed the confederates, and led home the domestic troops to Lacedæmon.

As to Jason, he returned back through Phocis, where he took the suburbs of Hyampolis, laid the adjacent country waste, and slew many persons ; and then continued his march forwards through the rest of Phocis in an orderly and quiet manner. But when he was come to Heraclea, he demolished the fortifications of that place. It is plain he was under no fear of opening a road to an enemy against himself by laying open this important pass. In fact, his true motive was, lest any should seize Heraclea that is situated so commodiously in the strait, and hinder him from marching into Greece at his own pleasure. On his return into Thessaly, he became great indeed, as well because by law he was supreme governor of the Thessalians, as because he kept constantly about him a large body of mercenary troops, both horse and foot, and these so finely disciplined as to excel all other troops in the world. He was greater still through the large number of confederates he already had, and the number of those who were desirous of his alliance. But he was greatest of all in his own personal character, since no man could despise him. The Pythian games were now approaching; he therefore circulated his orders to the cities to fatten oxen, sheep, goats, and swine, and prepare for the sacrifice. It was said, that though a moderate number was demanded from each separate city, yet the number of oxen amounted to not less than a thousand, and all other cattle together rose in number to above ten thousand. He also made public proclamation, that whatever city fed the finest ox to lead up the sacrifice to the god, should be rewarded with a prize of a golden crown. He also issued out his orders to the Thessalians to be ready to take the field at the time of the Pythian games. For he intended, as was said, to preside himself in the solemn assembly at the games in honour of the god. Whether indeed he had any intention to meddle with the sacred treasures remaineth yet uncertain. For it is reported, that when the Delphians asked " what must be done, in case Jason meddled with the treasures of the god?" the answer of the god was "he himself would take care of that." Yet after all, this extraordinary man, big with such great and splendid schemes, when after reviewing and scrutinizing the condition of the cavalry of Pheræ he had set himself down, and was giving answers to such as were offering petitions, is assassinated and murdered by seven young men, who came up to him with an air of having a dispute for him to settle. His guards indeed who were at hand bestirred themselves with spirit, and one of the assassins whilst striking at Jason was

killed by the thrust of a spear; another was stopped as he was getting on horseback, and put to death by a great number of wounds; but the rest mounted the horses, that were ready prepared for them, and made their escape; and in whatever cities of Greece they afterwards appeared, were generally received with honour. From whence it is plain, how much the Grecians dreaded Jason, lest he should turn out a tyrant.

After the murder of Jason, Polydorus his brother and Polyphron were appointed supreme leaders of Thessaly. But as they were going in company to Larissa, Polydorus dieth suddenly in his bed by night, and as was judged by the hands of his brother Polyphron. His death certainly was very sudden, and there was no other probable method of accounting for it. Polyphron held the supremacy for a year, and behaved in his office quite like a tyrant. For at Pharsalus he put to death Polydamas and eight more of the most illustrious Pharsalians, and from Larissa drove several persons into exile. For these outrageous acts he too is killed by Alexander, who pretended to be avenging the death of Polydorus and demolishing the tyranny. But when he had gotten the power in his own hands, he proved a terrible governor indeed to the Thessalians, terrible also to the Thebans, an enemy further to the Athenians, and an arrant robber both by land and sea. Such was his real character, and as such he is put to death by the hands of his wife's brothers, but entirely by her contrivance. For she told her brothers that Alexander had a design upon their lives; she concealed them therefore a whole day in the house. She received Alexander quite drunk into her chamber at night; and as soon as he was asleep she left the lamp still burning, but carried out his sword. And when she perceived that her brothers were afraid of going into the chamber to kill him, she told them if they boggled any longer, she would go and awake him. So soon as they were in it, she herself secured the door and held the bolt in her hand till her husband was despatched. The reason of her enmity to Alexander is supposed to be this, that Alexander had imprisoned his page, a beautiful youth, and when she begged hard for his liberty, he brought him out and put him to death. Others say, it was, because, having no children by her, he had sent to Thebes and entered into engagements to marry Jason's widow. The reasons of this plot against his life by the lady are given in this manner. But Tisiphonus, the eldest of the brothers who were agents in his murder, succeeded to his power, and hath continued in possession of it till the time this history is writing. And thus the affairs of Thessaly under the management of Jason, and down to the time of Tisiphonus, have now been opened. I return to the place from whence I digressed to give this recital.

V. When Archidamus, who had marched to the relief of those at Leuctra, had brought the army back, the Athenians began to reflect, that the Peloponnesians would still reckon it their duty to follow the Lacedæmonians, who were not yet reduced so low as they had reduced the Athenians. They summoned therefore the states, who were willing to be parties in the peace prescribed by the king of Persia. When all were assembled, they decreed, in conjunction with those who were willing to be parties, that the following oath should be taken,—" I will abide by the peace which the king hath sent, and the decrees of the Athenians and their confederates. And in case any enemy maketh war upon any state that hath taken this oath, I will assist that state with all my strength." All others present were satisfied with this oath; but the Eleans objected to it, "since they ought not thus to make the Marganians, and Scilluntians, and Triphyllians free and independent, all whose cities belonged to them." The Athenians however and the rest, having ratified the decree according to the king's mandate, that " the cities whether great or small should be left equally free and independent," sent out a deputation to administer the oath, and ordered that " the chief magistrates in every city should take it." And all took this oath except the Eleans.

The consequence was, that the Mantineans, who now looked upon themselves as sovereign masters of their own concerns, assembled together in a body, and resolved to settle again in the city of Mantinea, and fortify it as their own. But on the other hand, the Lacedæmonians judged, that if this was done without their consent, they should be much aggrieved. They send Agesilaus therefore ambassador to the Mantineans, because he was esteemed their hereditary friend. At his arrival, the men in power would not grant him an audience of the people, but ordered him to communicate his business to them alone. He then made them

a promise, that "if they would desist at present from fortifying Mantinea, he would engage that the state of Lacedæmon should soon consent to it, and ease them in the expense of doing it." But when they answered, that " it was impossible to desist, since their whole community had joined in the resolution for doing it," Agesilaus in great wrath departed. It was not however judged possible to stop them by force, since the grand article of peace was freedom and independence. And now some cities of Arcadia sent in their people to the Mantineans to assist them in carrying on the fortification: and the Eleans presented them with thirty talents[1] of silver towards defraying the expense of the work. And in this manner were the Mantineans very busy.

At Tegea, the party of Callibius and Proxenus were striving to get a general meeting of the whole body of Arcadians, in which whatever measures were voted by a majority should have the force of laws to all their cities. But the party of Stasippus was for leaving each city in its present separation, and in the enjoyment of their primitive constitutions. The party of Proxenus and Callibius, who were overpowered in all the sessions, imagining that in a general assembly of the people they should quite outvote their opponents, bring out their arms. The party of Stasippus, perceiving this, armed also to oppose them, and were not inferior to them in number. But when they came to an engagement, they killed Proxenus and a few more with him; and though they put the others to flight, went not after them in pursuit. For Stasippus was a man of that temper, that he would not put many of his fellow-citizens to death. But those with Callibius, having retreated to the part of the wall and the gates towards Mantinea, as their enemy gave them no farther annoyance, posted themselves there in a body. They had sent beforehand to the Mantineans to beg assistance, and the party of Stasippus now came to them with proposals of reconciliation. But the Mantineans no sooner appeared in sight, than some leaping upon the wall pressed them to advance with their utmost expedition, shouting aloud at them to make all possible haste, whilst others throw open the gates for their entrance. When the party of Stasippus found out what was done, they make their escape through the gates that lead to Palantium, and before their pursuers could overtake them, fly away in safety to the temple of Diana, where they shut themselves up and remained in quiet. But their enemies who came up in pursuit, after climbing the temple and stripping off the roof, pelted them with tiles. Conscious therefore of their own distressful situation they begged them to stop their hands and promised to come out. But their enemies, after thus getting them in their power, bound them fast, and putting them in a carriage drove them back to Tegea: and there, supported by the Mantineans, they formally put them to death. After this the Tegeatæ, who were of the party of Stasippus, to the number of about eight hundred, fled to Lacedæmon.

The Lacedæmonians now resolved it to be their duty to take the field with the utmost haste in the cause of the dead and the exiled Tegeatæ. Accordingly they make war upon the Mantineans, because contrary to their oaths they had marched in a hostile manner against the Tegeatæ. The ephori proclaimed a foreign expedition, and the state ordered Agesilaus to take upon him the command. The rest of the Arcadians were by this time assembled at Asea; but, as the Orchomenians had declared against all participation in the Arcadian league because of their enmity to the Mantineans, and had even received into their city a body of mercenaries commanded by Polytropus, which had been drawn together at Corinth, the Mantineans staid at home to look after their own concerns. But the Heræans and Lepreatæ joined with the Lacedæmonians in marching against the Mantineans. And Agesilaus, when the sacrifices for a successful expedition were finished, marched without loss of time into Arcadia.

He first took possession of Eutæa, a town on the frontier. He found in this place old men, women, and children, whilst all the fighting men were gone to join the Arcadic body. He did no harm at all to the city, but suffered these people still to continue in their houses, and his soldiers paid regularly for whatever they wanted. Or, if any thing had been taken by force when he entered the place, after a proper search he caused it to be restored. He also repaired such parts of the wall as needed it, whilst he halted there in expectation of the mercenaries under Polytropus.

In the meantime the Mantineans take the field against the Orchomenians. But after showing themselves before the walls, they found it a work of toil to make good their retreat, and some of them were slain on this occasion. But when they had secured their retreat as far as to Elymia, and the heavy-armed Orchomenians no longer pursued them, whilst the body under Polytropus kept plying on their rear with great impetuosity, the Mantineans were now convinced that, unless they could beat them back, a great part of their own people would perish by the missive weapons, upon which they suddenly faced about, and advancing close up to them, gave the charge. And there Polytropus died fighting. The rest taking to flight, many of them had been slain, had not the Phliasian horse come up that instant, and by riding round to the rear of the Mantineans obliged them to stop all pursuit. And after these transactions the Mantineans departed to their own home.

Agesilaus having heard these things, and judging now that the mercenaries from Orchomenus would not join him, set forwards from Eutæa. After the first day's march he supped his army in the district of Tegea; but in the second day's march, he passeth over into the dominions of Mantinea, and encamped under the mountains of Mantinea which lay to the west; and from thence he ravaged the country, and laid waste all the cultivated ground. The Arcadians however who had assembled at Asea marched by night into Tegea. The next day Agesilaus encamped his army at the distance of about [1]twenty stadia from Mantinea. The Arcadians from Tegea were now approaching with a very numerous body of heavy-armed, marching between the mountains of Mantinea and Tegea, and bent on completing their junction with the Mantineans. The Argives however had not yet joined them with all their force. Some persons therefore advised Agesilaus to attack them before the Argives came up. But apprehensive, that whilst he was advancing against them the Mantineans might sally out of their city, and then he might be attacked both in flank and rear; he judged it most prudent to let them complete their junction; and then, if they had a mind to fight, he could engage them upon fair and equal terms. But now

_____

[1] About two miles.

that the Arcadians had completed this junction, when the targeteers from Orchomenus, accompanied by the horsemen from Phlius, after marching by night under the walls of Mantinea, appear at break of day within the view of Agesilaus, who was sacrificing in the front of the camp, they made all others run to their posts, and Agesilaus retire to his heavy-armed. But when they were discovered to be friends, and Agesilaus had sacrificed with favourable omens, after dinner he led the army forwards; and at the approach of night he encamped, unobserved by the enemy, in a valley behind but very near Mantinea, and surrounded on all sides by mountains. The next day, so soon as it was light, he sacrificed in the front of his camp: and discovering that the Mantineans were come out of the city and gathering together on the mountains in the rear of his camp, he found the necessity of getting out of this valley without loss of time. But now in case he led the way in the van, he was apprehensive the enemy might attack his rear. He therefore stood to his post, and making the heavy-armed face towards the enemy, he ordered those in the rear to make a wheel to the right and march behind the phalanx on towards him. In this manner he got them out of this narrow ground, and was continually adding strength to the phalanx. And when once it was doubled, he advanced into the plain with his heavy-armed in this arrangement, and then opened the whole army again into files of nine or ten shields in depth. The Mantineans, however, gave him no opposition. For the Eleans, who now had joined them, persuaded them by no means to give him battle till the Thebans were come up. They said "they were well assured the Thebans would soon be with them, since themselves had lent them ten talents[1] to forward their march." And the Arcadians, hearing this account, rested quietly in Mantinea.

But Agesilaus, though vastly desirous to march the army off, for it was now the middle of winter, yet continued three days longer in his post, at no great distance from the city of Mantinea, that he might not seem to be too much in a hurry to be gone. Yet on the fourth day, after dinner, he led them off with a design to encamp on the ground he had encamped on before, after the first day's march

from Euteea. But as none of the Arcadians appeared in sight, he marched with all speed quite as far as Euteea, though it was exceedingly late before he reached it, desirous to carry off the heavy-armed before they could see the enemy's fires, that no one might say his departure was a flight. He judged that he had done enough to raise the spirits of his countrymen after the late dejection with which they had been oppressed, since he had broken into Arcadia, and no one durst give him battle whilst he was laying the country waste. And so soon as he was returned into Laconia, he sent the Spartans home, and dismissed the neighbouring people to their respective cities.

The Arcadians, now that Agesilaus was gone, and as they heard had disbanded the army, since they were all assembled in a body, march against the Heræans, because they would not be associated in the Arcadian league, and had joined the Lacedæmonians in the invasion of Arcadia. They broke into their country, where they set the houses on fire and cut down the trees. But as now they received intelligence that the Theban aid was come to Mantinea, they evacuate Heræa and join the Thebans. When they were thus all together, the Thebans thought they had done enough for their honour, since they had marched to the aid of their friends, and found the enemy had quite evacuated their country, and therefore they were preparing to return home. But the Arcadians, Argives, and Eleans persuaded them to march without loss of time into Laconia, expatiating much on their own numbers, and crying up to the skies this Theban army;[2] for, in fact, the Bœotians had kept to the constant exercise of arms ever since they had been elated with their victory at Leuctra. They were now attended by the Phocians, whom they had reduced to subjection; by the people of every city in Eubœa; by both the Locrians, Acarnanians, Heracleots, and the Maliensians. They had also with them some horsemen and targeteers from Thessaly. Delighted with so fine an army, and insisting on the desolate condition of Lacedæmon, they earnestly entreated them "not to go home again without making any irruption into the dominions of the Lacedæmonians." The Thebans, after giving them the hearing, alleged on the other side, that "to break into Laconia was a very difficult undertaking at

---

[1] 1,977l. 10s.

[2] Epaminondas and Pelopidas were chief commanders of it.

best, and they took it for granted that proper guards were posted at the places that were easiest of access." For in fact Ischolaus kept guard at Ium in the Skiritis with a party of four hundred men, consisting of Spartans newly enfranchised, and the most active exiles from Tegea. There was also another guard posted at Leuctra in the Maleatis. The Thebans reckoned besides, that the whole strength of the Lacedæmonians would soon be drawn together, and would never fight better than on their own ground. All these things occurred to their reflection, and they showed no eagerness to march against Lacedæmon. But when some persons came from Caryæ, who confirmed the account of their desolate state, and even undertook to be the guides of their march, with a frank desire " to be put to death if they deceived them in any point ;" and some people also of the neighbourhood of Sparta arrived with an invitation for them to come on, and a promise to revolt if they would only show themselves in the country; adding, that " some of those people distinguished by the title of their neighbours, would not give the Spartans the least assistance ;" hearing all this, and from all persons, too, the Thebans were at length persuaded. They broke in with their own army by way of Caryæ, and the Arcadians by the pass of the Skiritis. But if Ischolaus had posted himself on their route on the most difficult part of the ascent, they said not a single person could have entered by that pass. Yet, willing now to have the joint aid of the people of Ium, he had continued in that village. The Arcadians mounted the ascent in very numerous bodies. And here the soldiers under Ischolaus, so long as they had the enemy only in their front, had greatly the superiority over them, but when they were gotten in their rear and on their flanks, and climbing up to the tops of houses, were galling and pouring their javelins upon them, then Ischolaus himself and all his people were slain, except a person or two of no note who might possibly escape. And the Arcadians, having thus successfully carried their point, marched on and joined the Thebans at Caryæ.[1]

The Thebans, when they knew what had been done by the Arcadians, marched down into the country with much more spirit than before. They immediately put Sellasia to fire and sword; and, when they were gotten into the plains, encamped themselves within the verge of the temple of Apollo: but next day they continued their march. They made no attempt however to pass the bridge towards Sparta, for the heavy-armed were seen posted in the temple at Alea; but keeping the Eurotas on their right they continued their march, setting on fire and demolishing the houses, with all their grand and costly furniture. The women at Sparta had not spirits enough to look at the smoke, since never before had they seen an enemy. The citizens of Sparta, whose city had no wall round it, were stationed in different posts. Their number at each guard was thin in fact, and appeared so too. But the magistrates thought proper to acquaint the Helots by proclamation, that " if

less than seventy thousand men. It was seven hundred years since the Dorians had settled in Lacedæmon ; and during this long period of time no enemy had ever before been seen in Laconia, none had ever dared to invade the Spartans. Yet now an enemy was laying waste with fire and sword, and without any resistance too, a country that never before had suffered devastation. Agesilaus would not suffer the Lacedæmonians to expose themselves against so impetuous a flood and torrent of war ; but, having secured all the passes and eminences about Sparta with the heavy-armed, he heard with patience the threats and bravadoes of the enemy, who called out upon him by name, and bade him come out and fight for his country, since he was the author of all her distresses and had raised this war. Nor was his patience less severely tried by the tumultuous, clamorous, and disorderly behaviour of the elder Spartans who were all rage and vexation, whilst the women too could not contain, but were quite mad and frantic at the shouts and fires of the enemy. He was sadly alarmed about his own reputation, since, though Sparta had never been so great and powerful as when he succeeded to the government, he now saw her glory in grievous diminution, and his own big speeches proved insolent and vain ; for it had been his frequent boast, that " no woman at Sparta had ever seen an enemy's smoke." It is said too that Antalcidas, when once disputing with an Athenian about the bravery of their countrymen, and the latter saying, " We have often drove you from the Cephissus," replied briskly, " But we never drove you from the Eurotas." An answer of the spirited kind is also ascribed to a more obscure Spartan as made to an Argive : " Many of your countrymen," said the latter, " are interred in Argolica." " True," cried the Spartan, " but not one of yours in Laconia." And yet some affirm that Antalcidas, though at this very time one of the ephori, was under such a consternation, that he conveyed away his children to the island of Cythera.—Plutarch's life of Agesilaus.

---

1 The army now under Epaminondas consisted of not fewer than forty thousand heavy-armed. ¡The light-armed were also very numerous ; and numbers without any arms at all were following for plunder ; so that the number of enemies which now invaded Laconia was not

ny of them were willing to take up arms and o into the ranks, the public faith was pledged, hat all who assisted in this war should henceorth be free." It was said that more than six housand of them immediately gave in their ames ; so that, when formed into ranks, they truck a terror, and seemed to be quite too nany. But when the mercenaries from Orchonenus agreed to stay with them, and the Phlisians, Corinthians, Epidaurians, Pellenians, nd the troops of some other cities, were come ip to the aid of the Lacedæmonians, they be-;an to be less in fear about the number of Helots who gave in their names.

When the army of the enemy was advanced o Amyclæ, they there passed the Eurotas.* As for the Thebans, whenever they encamped, hey immediately cut down the trees, and piled ip as many of them as they could before their ines, and so kept upon their guard. But the Arcadians scorned all such precautions : they eft their arms, and minded nothing but break-ng and plundering of houses. The third or ourth day after, the horse advanced in regular irray to the Hippodrome and temple of Nep-une, all the horse of the Thebans and Eleans, ind so many of the Phocian and Thessalian horse as were at hand. The Lacedæmonian horse, whose numbers appeared very thin in-leed, were drawn up to oppose them. But as they had placed an ambuscade of about three hundred men of their younger heavy-armed near the temple of the Tyndaridæ, these started up against, and the horse at the same moment of time rode down on the enemy. The enemy stood not the charge, but turned their backs : and many of their infantry too seeing this took immediately to flight. However, as the pursuit was soon discontinued, and the Theban army stood firm to their ground, they all returned to their camp. But after this they thought it would be too desperate an undertaking to make any fresh attempts upon the city : the whole army therefore filed off towards Elis and Gytheum. They set all the unwalled cities in flames, and for three days successively made an assault on Gytheum, where were the docks of the Lacedæmonians. There were some too of the neighbouring peo-

ple, who acted against them, and joined the Thebans.

The Athenians, hearing this, were highly embarrassed about the conduct they ought to observe in regard to the Lacedæmonians, and pursuant to a decree of their senate held an assembly of the people. The ambassadors of the Lacedæmonians, and of the confederates who yet adhered to them, were introduced into this assembly. The Lacedæmonians, Aracus, Ocyllus, Pharax, Etymocles, and Olontheus, all spoke, and pretty much in the same strain, that, "from time immemorial the states of Athens and Lacedæmon had readily assisted one another in their most pressing necessities. Themselves," they said, "had co-operated to drive the tyrants out of Athens ; and the Athenians had marched to their assistance, when they were besieged by the Messenians." They proceeded to recite all the signal services they had done one another ; putting them in mind, " how they had fought in conjunction against the Barbarian ;" recalling to their remembrance, that " the Athenians were chosen by the body of Greece to command at sea, and to be treasurers of Greece, the Lacedæmonians advising it to be so ; and themselves were unanimously appointed by all the Grecians to be their leaders at land, the Athenians advising it might be so." One of them, however, made use of the following expression : " If you, Athenians, act unanimously with us, there will be hope again, according to the old saying, of decimating the Thebans."

The Athenians did not entirely relish what they said, since a murmur ran round the assembly, " This is their language at present ; yet, whilst they were in prosperity, they proved bitter enemies to us." But the argument of greatest weight alleged by the Lacedæmonians was this, that "when they had warred the Athenians down, and the Thebans insisted upon their utter ruin, the Lacedæmonians had refused to comply :" though the point chiefly insisted upon was this, that "in conformity to their oaths they ought to send them aid ; they (Lacedæmonians) had been guilty of no man-ner of injustice, when they were invaded by the Arcadians and their confederates ; they had only assisted the Tegeatæ, upon whom the Mantineans had made war in direct contrariety to their oaths." At these words a great clamour arose in the assembly : for some persons averred that " with justice the Mantineans

2 Epaminondas, as he was marching at the head of his troops, was pointed out to Agesilaus, who, looking steadfastly at him for a time, and sending his eyes after him as he passed on, dropped only these words :—" Oh ! that glorious man !"

had assisted the party of Proxenus, some of whom had been put to death by the party of Stasippus ;" whilst others maintained, that " they had unjustly made war upon the Tegeatæ." These points having raised a debate in the assembly, at last Cliteles the Corinthian rose up, and spoke as followeth :

" The point at present in debate, Athenians, is this, who were the first aggressors ? Yet in regard to us, after the peace was settled, who can accuse us of taking up arms against any state, or of taking any money from others, or of laying waste the lands of any people whatever ? But the Thebans it is certain have marched into our territories, have cut down our trees, have set our houses in flames, and made plunder of our effects and our cattle. How, therefore, unless you give assistance to us who have been beyond all denial most injuriously treated, how can you avoid a breach of oaths ? oaths, too, which you yourselves took the care of administering, that all of us might faithfully swear to all of you."

Here indeed the Athenians shouted aloud, that Cliteles spoke the words of truth and justice. And then Patrocles the Phliasian rose up, and made the following speech :

" When the Lacedæmonians are once out of their way, that you Athenians will be the first people the Thebans will attack, is a truth in which all the world will agree : since you they regard as the only people who will then be left to hinder them from obtaining the empire of Greece. And if this be so, I must give it as my opinion, that you are as strongly obliged to take up arms and assist the Lacedæmonians, as if the distress was your own. That Thebans, your inveterate enemies and your nearest neighbours too, should become the sovereigns of Greece, will, in my judgment, be a point of much harder digestion to you, than when you had your rivals for empire seated more remotely from you. And with a much finer prospect of success will you now aid the latter in your own behalf, whilst yet they have some confederates left, than if looking on till they are quite destroyed, you are then compelled to fight it out alone against the Thebans.

" But if any be apprehensive that if the Lacedæmonians are now rescued from destruction, they may hereafter prove very troublesome to you ; remember, Athenians, that none ought to be alarmed at the reviving power of men to whom you have done good, but of men

to whom you have done evil. You should farther recollect, that it ought to be the principal care both of individuals and public communities, when they are in their most flourishing state, to secure themselves a future support, that in case they are afterwards reduced, they may be sure of a ready redress in requital for former services. An opportunity is now offered to you by some one of the celestial powers, if you will hearken to their request and succour the Lacedæmonians, of gaining their eternal and sincerest friendship. You will do them a great kindness indeed, and numerous witnesses will be ever ready to attest it. For the powers above, who see all things both now and for ever, will know it ; your friends and your foes will be equally conscious of it ; to which must be added, all the Grecian, and all the Barbarian world. No act of yours on this occasion can be lost in oblivion ; insomuch that should they ever prove ungrateful to you, what state in the world will for the future manifest any regard for them ? But we are bound to hope, that gratitude and not ingratitude will always be the practice of the Lacedæmonians. For if ever people did, they may certainly be allowed to have persisted in the love of everything praiseworthy, and to have refrained from everything that is base.

" Let me suggest one point more to your reflection, that should Greece be ever again endangered by Barbarians, in whom could you confide more strongly than in Lacedæmonians ? whom could you see with so much delight in the same lines of battle with yourselves, as the men who once posted at Thermopylæ chose rather to fight and die to a man, than to save their lives and let the Barbarian into Greece ? With what justice therefore can you or can we refuse to show all alacrity in the behalf of men, who have acted such noble parts in company with yourselves, and who it is hoped would be ready to act them again ? But it is well worthy of you to show alacrity in their behalf, though merely because so many of your confederates are present to be eye-witnesses of it. For you may rest assured, that all such as remain faithful to the Lacedæmonians in their present distress, will hereafter scorn them should they prove ungrateful to you.

" If again we, who are ready to share the danger with you, should seem but petty inconsiderable states, reflect, Athenians, that when Athens hath put itself at our head, we shall march to the aid of the Lacedæmonians in numbers well worthy to be respected.

" I have long ago, Athenians, been stricken with admiration of this your community, when I heard that all men who suffered under injustice, or were afraid of suffering, betook themselves to you for redress, and always obtained it. But now I rely no longer on my ears; I am here present among you; and see with my own eyes the most famous Lacedæmonians, accompanied by their own most faithful friends, attending upon you and imploring your succour. I see even Thebans, too, who once in vain solicited the Lacedæmonians to enslave you all, now promoting the request, that you would not look quietly at the destruction of men who save been your preservers. It is handed down in honour of your progenitors, that they would not suffer the dead bodies of the Argives, who perished at the Cadmea, to remain uninterred. But it would be much more honourable for you, if you would not suffer such of the Lacedæmonians as are yet alive to be injuriously treated or utterly destroyed. There is too another glorious piece of behaviour, that when you had put a stop to the insolence of Eurystheus, you took all possible care to save the children of Hercules. But would it not be much more glorious, if you, who saved the founders, would proceed to save the whole community? And it would be most glorious of all, if, as once these Lacedæmonians saved you by a vote that cost them nothing, you would now with arms and through a series of dangers go to their relief. The case will then be, that whilst we are exulting for joy, we who have prevailed upon you by our exhortation to succour such worthy men, upon you, I say, who are able effectually to succour them, the credit of such high generosity will be all your own, who, after having been oftentimes friends and oftentimes enemies to the Lacedæmonians, forgot all the mischief, remembered only the good they had done you, and abundantly requited them, not merely in your own, but in behalf of Greece your common country, in whose cause they have ever bravely distinguished themselves."

After this the Athenians went to consultation, but would not hear with patience such as spoke against the aid. They passed a decree ' to march to their aid with the whole strength of Athens," and chose Iphicrates to command.

But when the sacrifices were auspicious, and he had issued out his orders, that " they should all take their suppers in the academy," it was said that numbers of them marched out of the city before Iphicrates. At length he put himself at their head; they followed their commander, imagining he was conducting them to some noble achievement. But when upon reaching Corinth he dallied away some days in that city, this gave them the first occasion to censure him for loss of time. Yet again, when he led them out of Corinth, they followed with alacrity wheresoever he led them, and with alacrity assaulted the fortress he pointed out to them. Of the enemies indeed at Lacedæmon, the Arcadians, and Argives, and Eleans were mostly departed, since they dwelt on the borders, driving before them and carrying off the booty they had taken. The Thebans and the rest had also a mind to be going, as from day to day they saw the army was lessening; partly, because provisions were grown more scarce, owing to the quantities that had been consumed, ravaged, wasted, or burnt. Beside this, it was winter, so that all persons were desirous to be at home. And when the enemy were thus retreated from Lacedæmon, Iphicrates too led the Athenians back out of Arcadia to Corinth.

In regard to any instances of fine conduct during his other commands, I have nothing to object against Iphicrates. But on the present occasion I find the whole of his conduct not only unavailing but even prejudicial. He endeavoured to post himself so at Oneum, that the Bœotians might not be able to go that way back, but he left the finest pass of all, that by Cenchrea, unguarded. Being farther desirous to know whether the Thebans took the route of Oneum, he sent out all the Athenian and Corinthian horse to observe their motions. A few horsemen might have performed this service full as well as larger numbers; and in case they were obliged to retire, a few with much more ease than a larger number might have found out a commodious road, and securely retreated. But to carry out large numbers, and after all inferior in number to the enemy, how can such a conduct escape the imputation of folly? For this body of horse, when drawn up in lines, were compelled by their very number to cover a large tract of ground; and, when obliged to retire, made their retreat through

3 P

several and all of them difficult roads ; insomuch that not fewer than twenty of them were
slain.   And then the Thebans had all the
roads open to march home as they pleased. [1]

---

[1] No sooner were they returned to Thebes, than,
through the envy and malevolence of some of their own
community, an attempt was made upon the lives of the
commanders.   A capital accusation was preferred
against them for having continued in the command four
months longer than their legal appointment.   Epaminondas persuaded his colleagues to exculpate themselves
by throwing all the blame upon him.   His own plea
was, that " if what he had done could not justify itself,
all that he could say would stand him in little stead.   He
should therefore trouble his judges on this occasion only
with this small request, that if he must suffer death, the
sentence to be inscribed on a pillar might be so drawn
up, that the Grecians might know that Epaminondas
had forced the Thebans against their will to lay Laconia
waste with fire and sword, which for five hundred years
had been free from any devastation ; that he had restored
the city of Messene two hundred and thirty years after
its demolition ; had united the Arcadians amongst themselves, and in firm friendship with the Thebans : and had
recovered the liberty and independence of Greece, since
all these things were done in his last expedition." His
judges immediately quitted the bench with a laugh, nor
would suffer any vote to be taken about him.—*Plutarch's
Apophthegms.*

AFFAIRS OF GREECE.

BOOK VII.

CONTENTS of BOOK VII.

THE

AFFAIRS OF GREECE.

BOOK VII.

I. Next year ambassadors from the Lacedæmonians and confederates arrived at Athens, fully empowered to settle the conditions of an alliance offensive and defensive between the Lacedæmonians and the Athenians. After many of the foreign ministers and many of the Athenians too had given their opinions that the alliance ought to be made upon fair and equal terms, Patrocles the Phliasian made the following speech:

"Since, Athenians, you are come to a resolution to make a league with the Lacedæmonians, it is my opinion that one point yet remaineth to be considered—by what method the friendship between you may be rendered as lasting as possible. If therefore we can settle the terms in such a manner as may be highly for the advantage of either party, then in all probability we may most firmly continue friends. Other points are already well nigh agreed on both sides; what at present remaineth to be considered is the point of command. It hath already been resolved by your senate, that it shall be yours at sea, and the Lacedæmonians shall have it by land. An adjustment this, which in my opinion is marked out for you by the constitution and determinaton both of earth and heaven. For, in the first place, your own situation is most finely adapted by nature to this very purpose. A very great number of states who want the sea for their support are seated round about your Athens, and all these states are weaker than your own. Besides this you have harbours, without which it is not possible to exert a naval power. You are moreover possessed of a great number of triremes, and the enlargement of your navy hath been from every generation your principal study. Nay, what is more, the arts needful for these purposes are all your own, and you far excel the rest of the world in naval skill: for most persons in your community earn their livelihood at sea; so that, whilst employed in your own personal concerns, you grow experienced in all the important points which are to be decided on the sea. Add to this, that such numerous fleets have never sailed out from any harbours as from your own; and hence accrues the strongest reason why you should have the command at sea. For all men flock with the most prompt alacrity to what hath been evermore invested with strength. And the gods, it must be added, have granted you a high measure of success in this respect. For in the very many and most important struggles you have undergone at sea, you have incurred the fewest losses, you have in general been remarkably successful. It standeth therefore to reason, that the confederates, with the most prompt alacrity, will take a share in all your dangers.

"But convince yourselves from what I am going to say, how indispensably needful to you it is to take all possible care of the sea. The Lacedæmonians made war upon you formerly for many years together, and though they became masters of your territory, yet were nothing nearer their grand scheme of demolishing your power. But no sooner had God given them a victory over you at sea, than instantly you became their vassals. Hence therefore it is clear beyond a scruple, that your own preservation is entirely connected with the sea. And if this is the true state of things, how can it be for your interest to suffer the Lacedæmonians to have the command at sea? In the first place, they own themselves that their skill on this element is inferior to yours. In the next place, you do not encounter dangers at sea upon equal terms; since they hazard only the men who serve on board their ships, but you your children, and your wives, and your whole community. This is the state of the point on your side, but it is very different on that of the Lacedæmonians. For, in the first place, they dwell within the land; insomuch that so long as they are masters at land, though they are hindered from putting out to sea, they can live in peace and affluence. Ever mindful therefore of this their situation, they train up their people from their infancy in that discipline of war which is suitable to the land; and especially, which is worth all the rest, in obedience to those who command them. They truly are strongest at land, and you are the strongest at sea. And in the next place, as you are soonest out at sea, so they draw out most expeditiously and in the greatest numbers at land: and likely it is, for this very reason, that the confederates with the greatest confidence will ever join them there. Nay, what is more, even God hath granted them very signal successes upon the land, in the same measure as he hath granted them to you at sea. For in the very many most important struggles they have undergone at land, they have received the fewest defeats, and have in general been remarkably successful. And hence, that to take care at land is no less necessary to them than to you at sea, you may readily learn from fact itself. For when for many years together you were at war with them, and oftentimes fought at sea successfully against them, yet you made no progress at all in warring them down. But no sooner were they once defeated at land, than the loss of their children, and their wives, and their whole community became instantly endangered. How therefore can it be but dreadful to them to suffer any other state to take command by land over them who have most bravely achieved the pre-eminence there!

" So much, in pursuance of the resolution of the senate, I have said on this occasion, and think I have advised the best for both. But may your determinations prove the best for all of us: and may success attend all your undertakings!"

In this manner Patrocles spoke; and the Athenians in general, and such Lacedæmonians as were present, heartily agreed in commending his advice. But Cephisodotus stood up and spoke as followeth:

" You perceive not, Athenians, how sadly you are going to be over-reached; but if you will give me attention, I will immediately show you. You yourselves, forsooth, are to command at sea. But it is clear, that if the Lacedæmonians act in confederacy with you, they will send you Lacedæmonian captains to command the vessels, and perhaps Lacedæmonian marines, but the seamen of a truth will be only Helots or hirelings; and then over such as these you will be invested with the command. But whenever the Lacedæmonians issue out their mandate for an expedition by land, you will for certain send to them your own cavalry and your heavy-armed. And thus beyond all dispute, they become the rulers of your very ownselves, whilst you can be such only over slaves and the very dregs of mankind. But (said he) answer me one question, you Timocrates of Lacedæmon: did you not say just now, that you come hither to make an alliance upon fair and equal terms?" I said so. " Can any thing therefore be more reasonable (said Cephisodotus) than that each should command alternately at sea, alternately too at land; and if there be any pre-eminent advantage at sea, that you should come in for your share of it; and we the same by land?"

The Athenians, upon hearing this, quite changed their sentiments, and drew up a decree, that, " each side should command alternately for the space of five days."

Both parties with their confederates now taking the field for Corinth, it was resolved to guard Oneum in conjunction. And when the Thebans and confederates [1] approached, the different parties of the enemy drew up on their several guards, the Lacedæmonians and Pellenians being posted in that quarter which was most likely to be attacked. But the Thebans and confederates, after advancing within [2] thirty stadia of the guard, encamped in the plain. Having then allowed a proper interval of time, which they thought they should spend in completely marching up, they advanced at twilight towards the guard of the Lacedæmonians. And they were not deceived in their allowance of time, but rush in upon the Lacedæmonians and Pellenians, when the nightly watch was already dismissed, and the others were rising up from the straw where they had taken their repose. At this very time the Thebans fall

---

1 Under the command of Epaminondas.
2 About three miles.

in amongst them, prepared for action against men unprepared, and in regular order against men in total disorder. But when such as could save themselves from the danger had fled to the nearest eminence, and the commander of the Lacedæmonians had it still in his power to take to his aid as many heavy-armed and as many targeteers from the confederates as he pleased, and keep possession of Oneum, (since all necessary provisions might have been safely brought them from Cenchrea,) he did it not; but on the contrary, when the Thebans were in great perplexity how to get down by the pass towards Sicyon, or about returning the same way they came, he clapped up a truce (as most people thought) more for the advantage of the Thebans than of his own party, and in pursuance of it retreated, and marched off his troops. In consequence of this, the Thebans having marched down in safety, and joined their own confederates the Arcadians, Argives, and Eleans, carried on their assaults without loss of time against Sicyon and Pellene. They marched also against Epidaurus, and laid waste all their territory. And retreating from thence in a manner that showed the utmost contempt of all their enemies, when they came near the city of Corinth, they ran full speed towards the gates that look towards Phlius, with a design if they were open to rush in at once. But a party of light-armed sallied out of the city, and met the chosen party of the Thebans at a distance not of four plethra from the wall. These mounted immediately on the monuments and eminences that were near, and pouring in their darts and javelins kill a great many of this foremost body, and having put them to flight pursued them three or four stadia. And when this was done, the Corinthians having dragged the bodies of the slain to the wall, and restored them afterwards by truce, erected a trophy. And by this turn of fortune the confederates of the Lacedæmonians were restored to better spirits.

These incidents had scarcely taken place, when the aid to the Lacedæmonians from Dionysius arrived, consisting of more than twenty triremes. They brought Celtæ and Iberians, and about fifty horsemen. But next day the Thebans and confederates having formed into order of battle, and filled all the plain quite down to the sea and quite up to the eminences which are near the city, de-

stroyed every thing in the plain that could be of use to the enemy. The horse of the Athenians and Corinthians never advanced within any nearness of the enemy, perceiving how very strong and numerous they were. But the horsemen of Dionysius, however inconsiderable in their number, straggled from one another and were scouring all over the plain; now riding up, they threw their javelins at the enemy; and so soon as the enemy rushed forwards they again rode off: and presently, wheeling about, they kept pouring in their javelins; and in the midst of these feats dismounted from their horses and rested. But in case any of the enemy rode at them whilst thus dismounted, they were again in their seats with great agility, and rode off safe. Nay, if pursued to any considerable distance from the army, no sooner were the pursuers on retreat, than close behind them and plying at them with their javelins, they made havoc, and merely of themselves obliged the whole army of the enemy alternately to advance and retire. And after this the Thebans making only a few day's stay went off for Thebes, and the rest of the confederates dispersed to their several homes.

But the aid from Dionysius march afterwards against Sicyon, and beat the Sicyonians in a battle on the plain, and slew about seventy of them. They also take by storm the fort of Dera. But after these exploits, this first aid from Dionysius sailed away for Syracuse.

Hitherto the Thebans, and all such as had revolted from the Lacedæmonians, had acted and taken the field together with perfect unanimity, the Thebans being in the command. But now one Lycomedes of Mantinea, a man in birth inferior to none, but superior in wealth and of extraordinary ambition, began to interfere. This man quite filled the Arcadians with notions of their own importance; telling them, " Peloponnesus was a country exclusively their own," (for they alone were the original inhabitants of it,) " the Arcadians were the most numerous people in all Greece, and had their persons most remarkably qualified for action." He then showed them to be the most valiant people in Greece: producing in proof, that " when other states had need of auxiliaries, they evermore gave preference to the Arcadians;" that, moreover, " without them the Lacedæmonians had never dared to invade the Athenians, and now without the Arcadians the Thebans durst not take the field against Lacedæmon. If therefore you can see your own interest, you will discontinue the custom of following whenever another state may call for your attendance; since formerly, by thus following the Lacedæmonians, you augmented their power; and now, if rashly you follow the Thebans, and do not insist upon your turn in the command, you may perhaps find them in a little time to be second Lacedæmonians."

The Arcadians by listening to these discourses were highly puffed up, quite doated on Lycomedes, and thought him the only man, insomuch that they chose such persons to be their magistrates, as he was pleased to point out to them. Many things had also coincided to give the Arcadians high notions of themselves. For when the Argives had invaded Epidaurus, and their retreat was cut off by the Athenians and Corinthians under Chabrias, they went to their aid when almost reduced to a surrender, and set the Argives at liberty, though they had not only the disadvantage of numbers, but even of situation to struggle against. Taking the field another time against Asine in Laconia, they beat the Lacedæmonian garrison, they slew Geranor the Spartan who commanded, and plundered the suburbs of Asine. Nay, whenever they resolved to act, neither night, nor winter, nor any length of march, nor mountains difficult of passage could stop them; insomuch that at the present juncture of time they esteemed themselves as the bravest of men. For these reasons truly the Thebans beheld them with envy, and could no longer manifest good-will to the Arcadians. The Eleans also, when on re-demanding from the Arcadians those cities which had been taken from them by the Lacedæmonians, they found that the Arcadians wholly slighted every thing they alleged, and even manifested high regard to the Tryphyllians and other people who had revolted from them, on the haughty pretext that they too were Arcadians,—for these reasons the Eleans were also bitterly incensed against them.

Whilst the states of the confederacy were thus severally setting up for themselves, Philiseus of Abydus arriveth from Ariobarzanes, furnished with a large sum of money. In the first place, therefore, he caused the Thebans and confederates, and the Lacedæmonians, to meet together at Delphi to treat about a peace. But when assembled there, they never re-

quested the advice of the god in relation to the peace, but made it a subject merely for their own consultations. And when the Thebans positively refused to leave Messene in the power of the Lacedæmonians, Philiscus drew together a large body of mercenaries to serve as aids on the side of the Lacedæmonians. And whilst these things were doing, the second aid arriveth from Dionysius. The Athenians allege "these ought to be sent into Thessaly to make head against the Thebans;" the Lacedæmonians are "for landing them in Laconia;" and the latter opinion carried it with the allies. When therefore the aid from Dionysius had sailed round to Lacedæmon, Archidamus taking them under his command marched out with the domestic troops of that state. He took Caryæ by storm, and put all the persons he found in it to the sword. From thence without loss of time he led them on against Parrhasia of Arcadia, and laid waste the country. But so soon as the Arcadians and Argives were come out into the field he retreated, and encamped on the high ground of Midea. Whilst he was in this post, Cassidas who commanded the aid from Dionysius notified to him, that "the time limited for his stay in Greece is expired;" and he had no sooner notified this, than he marched off for Sparta. But when the Messenians had stopped him on his route by besetting the narrow passes, he sent back to Archidamus and begged his assistance; and Archidamus immediately began his march. When they were got as far as the turning in the road that leadeth to Euctresii, the Arcadians and Argives were advancing into Laconia to stop his proceeding farther on the road to Sparta. Archidamus now turneth aside into the plain near the spot where the roads to Euctresii and Midea meet, and formeth into order of battle, as resolved on an engagement. It is said that he went up to the front of the army, and animated the men by the following exhortation:

" Countrymen and soldiers! let us now be brave, and look our enemies directly in the face. Let us bequeath our country to our posterity as we received it from our fathers. From this moment let us cease to make our children, our wives, our elders, and our foreign friends ashamed of the behaviour of men, who in former days were the admiration of Greece."

These words were no sooner uttered, than (according to report) though the sky was clear it lightened and thundered, being omens of success. There happened also to be on his right wing a grove and an image consecrated to Hercules, from whom Archidamus is said to be descended. The concurrence of such auspicious signs inspired, as they say, such vigour and spirit into his soldiers, that it was difficult for the commander to restrain them from rushing forwards towards the enemy. And indeed no sooner did Archidamus lead them to the charge, than those few of the enemy who had the courage to stand it were immediately slain; the rest were all in flight, and were slaughtered, many by the horse, and many by the Celtæ. When the battle was over and the trophy erected, Archidamus immediately despatched Demoteles the herald to Sparta, to notify there the greatness of the victory, since not one Lacedæmonian was slain, but a very great number indeed of the enemy. It is reported, that the news was no sooner heard at Sparta, than Agesilaus, the elders, and the ephori, began setting the example, and at length the whole community wept:[1] thus common are tears both to sorrow and joy. Not but that the Thebans and the Eleans were as much rejoiced as the Lacedæmonians themselves at this blow given to the Arcadians: so highly did they resent their late assuming behaviour.

As the point at which the Thebans were aiming was how to attain the sovereignty of Greece, they now thought, that should they send to the king of Persia, by his assistance they might accomplish their scheme. With this view they summoned their confederates to a meeting; and, on the pretext that Euthycles the Lacedæmonian was then with the king, Pelopidas is sent up by the Thebans: Antiochus the Pancratiast by the Arcadians; Archidamus by the Eleans; and an Argive ambassador went also in their company. The Athenians hearing this sent Timagoras and Leo to solicit against them. When they were all arrived, Pelopidas had soon gained the greatest interest in the Persian monarch. He could justly plead, that "of all the Grecians the Thebans alone had joined the royal army at Platæa, and ever since that time had never joined in any war against the king;" and that the Lacedæmonians had made war upon them for this reason only, because they had refused to act against him under the command of Agesilaus, nor would permit the latter to sacrifice at Aulis, where Agamemnon had formerly sacrificed, and thence beginning his expedition into Asia had taken Troy." Other circumstances also concurred to procure Pelopidas more honourable treatment, such as that the Thebans had been victorious in the battle of Leuctra; and farther, quite masters of the country, had laid waste the dominions of the Lacedæmonians. Pelopidas moreover insinuated, that "the Argives and Arcadians had been defeated in battle by the Lacedæmonians, merely because the Thebans were not there." Timagoras the Athenian bore witness to him, and vouched the truth of whatever Pelopidas said; he therefore was honoured by the king, in the next degree to Pelopidas. At length, Pelopidas was asked by the king, "what he would have him insist upon in his letter?" He answered, that "Messene should be left free and independent by the Lacedæmonians, and the Athenians should lay up their fleet. And in case they refused to comply, war should be declared against them. And if any state refused to join in the war, that state should be first invaded." These points being committed to writing, and then read aloud to the ambassadors, Leo cried out in the hearing of the king, "In good truth, Athenians, it is high time for you to look out another friend instead of the king." And when the secretary had interpreted what the Athenian said, the king ordered this qualifying article to be added; "But in case the Athenians are able to devise more

---

1 Plutarch in the life of Agesilaus gives a fuller account of the rejoicing at Sparta on this occasion, which he introduces with so pertinent but shrewd an observation, that the whole passage well deserves a notice :— "Nothing (says he) so much betrayed the weakness of the Spartan state as this victory. Ever before this time they had looked upon themselves as so entitled by prescription and by right to conquer in battle, that for the greatest victories they sacrificed nothing but a cock, the combatants never uttered any words of exultation, and the news of them inspired no hearer with any extraordinary joy. Even after the battle of Mantinea, which Thucydides hath described, the magistrates sent a piece of flesh from their own table as a reward to the person who brought them the news, and made him no other present. But after this victory was published, and Archidamus in his return drew near to Sparta, not a soul but was quite transported : his father Agesilaus cried for joy and went out to meet him, attended with the whole magistracy. The elders of the city and the women flocked down to the river Eurotas, lifting up their hands to heaven and giving thanks to the gods, as if Sparta now had cleared her reputation from all the late disgraces, and as bright a prospect as ever was opened before her."

effectual expedients, let them repair hither and communicate them to the king." No sooner were these ambassadors returned to their several homes than the Athenians put Timagoras to death; since Leo preferred an accusation against him, "for refusing to lodge in the same apartment with him, and for bearing a share in all the schemes of Pelopidas." As to the rest of the ambassadors, Archidamus the Elean highly applauded the king's declaration, because he had given the preference to the Eleans over the Arcadians. But Antiochus, because the Arcadic body was slighted by him, refused his presents, and told the magistrates of Arcadia at his return, that "the king, it is true, was master over an infinite number of bakers and cooks, butlers and door-keepers, but though he had looked about with his utmost diligence to discover the men, who were able to fight with Grecians, he had not been able to get the sight of any." He added, that "in his opinion his vast quantity of wealth was mere empty pageantry; since the very plane-tree of gold, so much celebrated by fame, was not large enough to afford shade to a grasshopper." But when the Thebans had summoned deputations from all the states to come and hear the king's epistle; and the Persian, who brought it, after showing the royal signet, had read aloud the contents, the Thebans commanded all "who were desirous of the king's friendship and of theirs, to swear observance;" but the deputies from the states replied, that "their commission was not to swear but to hear. And if oaths were necessary, they bade the Thebans send round to the several states." Lycomedes the Arcadian added farther, that "this congress ought not to have been holden in Thebes, but in the seat of the war." The Thebans however resenting this, and telling him "he was destroying the confederacy," Lycomedes would no longer assist at any consultation, but instantly quitted Thebes, and went home accompanied by all the deputies from Arcadia. Yet as those remaining at Thebes refused to take the oaths, the Thebans sent ambassadors round to the several states, commanding them "to swear to the observance of what had been written by the king;" concluding that each state, thus singly to be sworn, would be afraid of incurring the resentments of themselves and the king by a refusal. However, the first place to which they repaired was Corinth. And the Corinth-

ians standing out, and remonstrating that "they wanted no swearing to treaties with the king," many other states followed their example, and answered to the same effect. And thus the grand scheme of empire so long agitated by Pelopidas and the Thebans was totally disconcerted.

But now Epaminondas, being desirous to begin again with the reduction of the Achæans, in order to render the Arcadians and the rest of the confederates more attentive to the friendship of the Thebans, determined to make war upon Achaia. He therefore persuadeth Peisias the Argive, who commanded in Argos, immediately to seize Oneum. Peisias, accordingly, having made a discovery that the guard of Oneum was neglected by Naucles, who commanded the mercenary troops of the Lacedæmonians, and by Timomachus the Athenian, seizeth by night, with two thousand heavy-armed, the eminence above Cenchrea, having with him provisions for seven days. During this interval the Thebans begin their march, and complete the passage of Oneum; and then the confederates in one body invade Achaia, under the command of Epaminondas. And as such of the Achæans as were of the party of the few went over to him, Epaminondas exerteth his influence with so much weight, that afterwards none of that party were sentenced to exile, nor any change made in the polity of the state, but only security was given by the Achæans, that they would be firm allies, and follow the Thebans wheresoever they led them; and so the latter returned again to Thebes.

The Arcadians and all discontented parties now accusing Epaminondas for marching off so soon as he had put Achaia in a proper disposition to serve the Lacedæmonians, it was judged expedient by the Thebans, to send away governors into the cities of Achaia. The persons thus exiled, concurring together in the same measures, and being not few in number, returned to their several cities, and recovered the possession of them. And now, as they no longer observed any manage in their conduct, but with high alacrity supported the Lacedæmonian cause, the Arcadians were grievously harassed on one side by the Lacedæmonians, and on the other by the Achæans.

At Sicyon down to this time the administration had been carried on according to the laws of the Achæans. But Euphron, ambitious to play a leading part amongst the enemies of the

Lacedæmonians, though hitherto he had been regarded by the latter as their most steady friend, insinuateth to the Argives and Arcadians, that " were the most wealthy members of the community to be indisputable masters of Sicyon, then beyond all doubt on every occasion that city would act entirely in the Lacedæmonian interest ; whereas, if a democracy be set up in it, you may depend upon it (said he) that city will firmly adhere to you. If therefore you will give me your aid, I will engage to convene the people ; and at the same time I will give them this certain pledge of my own sincerity, and will keep the city firm in your alliance. My motives for acting, be you well assured, are the same with your own, since I have long suffered with regret the insolence of the Lacedæmonians, and would with the highest pleasure escape from their bondage." The Arcadians and Argives, therefore, who listened greedily to him, repaired to Sicyon to support him. On their arrival he immediately convened the people in the forum, and proposed a form of administration wherein each might have a fair and equal share. And in this very assembly he ordered them to choose what persons they pleased to be their commanders. The people accordingly choose Euphron himself and Hippodamus, Cleander, Acrisius, and Lysander. When these points were settled, he appointed his own son Adeas to command the mercenary troops, having discharged Lysimenes who commanded them before. Euphron by his generosity had soon attached many of the mercenaries firmly to his interest ; he quickly made many more of them his friends, sparing neither the public money nor the treasure in the temples in buying their service. And he employed to the same use the wealth of such persons as he drove into exile for being friends to the Lacedæmonians. Some also of his colleagues in command he slew by treachery, and some he banished ; insomuch that he grew to be absolute master of Sicyon, and past all doubt became a tyrant ; and he caused the confederates to connive at all his proceedings, sometimes by supplying them with money, and at other times by taking the field with his mercenaries whenever they summoned him to join them.

II. Affairs having so far succeeded, and the Argives having fortified Tricranum, situated above the temple of Juno in Phlius, and the Sicyonians at the same time fortifying Thyamia on the frontier of the Phliasians, the latter were grievously distressed, and reduced to the want of necessaries : yet notwithstanding this, they persevered in a most steadfast adherence to their allies. When any grand point is accomplished by powerful states, all historians are careful to propagate the remembrance of it. But in my opinion, if any petty state can accomplish a series of numerous and great achievements, such a state hath a much better title to have them honourably remembered.

The Phliasians, for instance, became friends to the Lacedæmonians, when the latter were possessed of the most ample power. And yet, after their overthrow at the battle of Leuctra, after the revolt of many neighbouring cities, and after the revolt of many of their Helots, and of their old allies, very few excepted, all Greece in a word being combined against them ; the Phliasians persevered in the most faithful attachment to them : nay, when even the Argives and Arcadians, the most powerful states in Peloponnesus were become their enemies, notwithstanding all this the Phliasians gave them aid, even though it fell to their lot to be the very last body of men of the whole confederacy, that could march up to Prasiæ to join them. The Corinthians, Epidaurians, Trœzenians, Hermionians, Haliensians, Sicyonians, and Pellenians, for these had not revolted, were at Prasiæ before them. Nay, when even the Spartan general, who was sent to command, would not wait for their arrival, but marched off with those who were already come up, the Phliasians notwithstanding scorned to turn back, but hiring a guide to Prasiæ, though the enemy was now at Amyclæ, came forwards as well as they could, and arrived at Sparta. The Lacedæmonians, it is true, gave them all possible marks of their gratitude, and by way of hospitality presented them with an ox.

When again, after the enemies' retreat from Lacedæmon, the Argives, exasperated against the Phliasians for their zealous attachment to the Lacedæmonians, invaded Phlius with their whole united force, and laid all that country waste, they would in no wise submit. And after the enemy had completed their ravage, and were again on their retreat, the horsemen of Phlius sallied out in good order, and pressed close on their rear ; and, though the whole Argive cavalry and some companies of heavy-armed composed this rear, though but sixty in number, they fell upon them, and put the whole rear to flight. They slew some of them, and even erected a trophy in the very sight of the enemy, nor could they have done more, though they had killed them to a man.

Again, when the Lacedæmonians and confederates were posted on the guard of Oneum, and the Thebans were approaching with a design to force the passage, the Eleans and Argives marching in the meantime by the road of Nemea in order to join the Thebans, some exiles from Phlius insinuated to the latter, that " if they would only show themselves before Phlius, they might take it." When they had resolved on a trial, these exiles with some auxiliaries, amounting in all to about six hundred, posted themselves by night under the wall of Phlius, having with them a number of ladders. When therefore the sentinels had given the signals that the enemy were marching down from Tricranum, and all the inhabitants of the city were thrown into alarm, that very instant the traitors gave the signal to those skulking under the wall to mount. Accordingly they mounted ; and first seizing at the stand the arms of the guard, they pursued the sentinels who were left to watch them, being ten in number : from every five one person was left to watch the arms. But one of these they murdered before he could wake out of sleep, and another as he was flying for shelter to the temple of Juno. As the sentinels had leaped from the walls down into the city to flee from the enemy, the latter were now masters of the citadel, and the former saw it plainly with their own eyes. But when they shouted for aid, and all the inhabitants came running to assist them, the enemy sallied immediately from the citadel, and engaged them before the gate that openeth into the city. Yet being afterwards surrounded by numbers of such as had flocked together to assist, they again retired into the citadel, and the heavy-armed rush in at the same time with them. The area of the citadel was immediately cleared of the enemy, who mounting the wall and the turrets, threw down darts and javelins upon the Phliasians below. They defended themselves, and fought their way to the stairs that lead up to the wall. And when the inhabitants had possessed themselves of the turrets on either side of the enemy, they then advanced with the utmost fury close up to them, who, unable to withstand such a bold and desperate attack, were all driven together on a heap. At this

very instant of time the Arcadians and Argives invested the city, and were directly opening a breach in the wall of the citadel. The Phliasians within it were levelling their blows fast ; some of them, at the enemy on the wall ; some, at the enemy on the ladders endeavouring to mount ; some also were fighting against those who had scaled and were got upon the turrets ; and, finding fire in the barracks, they set the turrets in a flame by the help of faggots, which had just happened to be cut down in the citadel itself. And now, such as were upon the turrets jumped off immediately for fear of the flames ; and such as were upon the walls were forced by the blows of their antagonists to leap over. And when once they began to give way, the whole citadel was soon cleared of the enemy, and the horsemen of Phlius rode out of the city. The enemy retreated at the sight of them, leaving behind their ladders and their dead, nay, the living too who had been lamed in the scuffle. The number of the slain, both of such as had fought within and such as had leaped down from the wall, was not less than eighty. And now you might have seen the men of Phlius shaking one another by the hand in mutual congratulation, the women bringing them refreshments of liquor, and at the same time weeping for joy. Nay, there was not a soul present on this occasion, whose countenance did not show the tearful smile.

Next year the Argives and Arcadians with their whole united force again invaded Phliasia. The reasons of this continued enmity against the Phliasians were, because they were very angry at them, and because they were situated between them, and they never ceased hoping that by reducing them to famine they might starve them into obedience. But in this invasion also the horsemen and chosen band of Phlisians, with the aid of Athenian horse, were at hand to attack the enemy as they are passing the river. Having the better in the action, they forced the enemy to retire for the rest of the day under the craggy parts of a mountain, since they avoided the plain, lest by trampling over it they might damage the corn of their friends.

Again, upon another occasion the commandant at Sicyon marched an army against Phlius. He had with him the Thebans and his own garrison, the Sicyonians, and the Pellenians (for these now had accustomed themselves to follow the orders of the Thebans.)

Euphron also accompanied this expedition, having with him about two thousand mercenaries. The rest of the army marched down by way of Tricranum to the temple of Juno, with a design to lay waste the plain. But the commandant left the Sicyonians and Pellenians behind, near the gates that open towards Corinth, that the Phliasians might not be able to fetch a compass round the eminence, and get above them whilst they were at the temple of Juno. When the Phliasians in the city were assured that the enemy were rushing down into the plain, their horsemen and their chosen band marched out in order of battle against them, and charged them, and effectually prevented their descent into the plain. Here they spent the greatest part of the day in throwing their darts and javelins at one another; the mercenaries of Euphron pursuing so far as the ground was not good for horse, and the Phliasians of the city driving them back to the temple of Juno. But when they judged it the proper time, the enemy retreated by the pass round about Tricranum, since the ditch before the wall hindered their marching the shortest road to the Pellenians. The Phliasians, after following close behind them till they came to the ascents, turned off and made full speed close under the wall towards the Pellenians and the troops with them. The enemy under the command of the Theban general, perceiving what a hurry the Phliasians were in, made all possible haste to reach the Pellenians with timely aid. But the horsemen of Phlius were too speedy for them, and had already attacked the Pellenians. The latter standing firm, the Phliasians again retreated backwards, till they had strengthened themselves by such of their foot as were now come up, and then renewed the attack, and closely engaged them. Now the enemy gave way, and some of the Sicyonians are slain, as also were very many, and those the flower too, of the Pellenians. These things being done, the Phliasians erected a splendid trophy and sung the pæan of victory, as they justly might; whilst their enemies under the Theban general and Euphron looked calmly at them, as if they came hither only to see a sight. And when the rejoicings were over, the latter marched off to Sicyon, and the Phliasians returned into their own city.

There is also another gallant action which the Phliasians performed. For, having taken a Pellenian prisoner who had formerly been their public host, they gave him his liberty without asking any ransom, though they were then in want of the necessaries of life.

To these, who did such things, what person can deny the praise of being generous and gallant men? It is plain to all the world, how steadily they persevered to the last in fidelity to their friends, though deprived of all the produce of their own lands, though subsisting merely on what they could plunder from the lands of their enemies or purchase from Corinth, when even to that market they could not go but through a series of dangers, with difficulty procuring money for the purpose, with difficulty finding any to advance it for them, and hardly able to find security for the loan of beasts to carry their provisions home. At length reduced to total distress, they prevailed upon Chares to undertake the guard of a convoy for them. And when this guard was arrived at Phlius, they persuaded Chares to take all their useless mouths along with him as far as Pellene, and there he left them. In the next place, having purchased their provisions, and laden as many beasts as they could possibly procure, they began their march by night, not ignorant that the enemy had laid an ambush on their road, but determined within themselves that it was more eligible to fight than to want necessary food. Accordingly, they set out on their return in company with Chares, and were no sooner got in with the enemy than they fell to work with them, and loudly exhorting one another fought with the utmost vigour, shouting aloud on Chares to give them aid. Victorious at length, and having cleared the road of their enemies, they returned safe with their whole convoy to Phlius. But as they had passed the night without a wink of sleep, they slept in the morning till the day was far advanced. And yet Chares was no sooner up than the horsemen and most active citizens of Phlius went to him, and accosted him thus:

" It is in your power, Chares, to perform this very day a most noble exploit. The Sicyonians are this moment busy in fortifying a post on our frontier. They have assembled a large number of mechanics for the purpose, and yet but a small number of heavy-armed. We ourselves with our horsemen and the most gallant men of our city will march out first; and if you at the head of your mercenaries will follow after us, perhaps you may find the business completed on your arrival; or perhaps, by barely showing yourself, you will put them all to flight as you did at Pellene. Yet in case you judge the proposal we make to be attended with difficulties, go and consult the gods by sacrifice. For we are fully persuaded, that the gods will, more forcibly than we can, exhort you to compliance. But, Chares, of this you ought to be assured, that if you succeed in this undertaking, you will have gained a high ascendent over the foe, you will have indisputably preserved a friendly city, you will become an Athenian of the highest esteem among your own countrymen, and a man of the highest reputation both with friends and foes."

Chares so far hearkened to what they said as to set about the sacrifice. But the Phliasian horsemen immediately put on their breastplates and bridled their horses; the heavy-armed too prepared to begin the march. And when taking up their arms they were repairing to the place of sacrifice, Chares and the soothsayer advanced to meet them, and declared that "the victims portended success. Halt a little," they added, "and we march out in company with you." Their herald called to arms without loss of time; and the mercenaries ran into their ranks with an alacrity that seemed inspired by heaven. Chares no sooner began his march, than the Phliasian horsemen and heavy-armed advanced and led the van. They moved off briskly at first, and then set up a trot; the horsemen were at length on the gallop; the heavy-armed ran after as fast as they could without breaking their ranks; and Chares followed the heavy-armed with all his speed. It was now near sunset. When arrived, therefore, at the fortification, they found the enemy, some of them employed in bathing, some dressing their meat, some kneading their bread, and some preparing their beds; who no sooner saw the impetuosity with which their enemy came on, than they took fright and fled, leaving all their victuals behind for the use of these gallant men. The latter accordingly made a hearty supper upon what was thus ready dressed, and what they had brought along with them from Phlius; and then, pouring forth a libation in acknowledgment of success, and singing their pæan of victory, and placing proper sentinels for the nightly guard, had a sound repose. A messenger arrived in the night, and told the Corinthians what had been done at Thyamia, who in a very hearty manner ordered the herald to call for all the carriages and beasts of draught in the city, which they loaded with provisions and drove away to Phlius. And afterwards, till the fortification was completely finished, they continued daily to send them in a convoy of provisions. All these incidents have been related, to show how faithful to their confederates the Phliasians were, with how much bravery they persisted in the war, and, though reduced to extreme distress, would still persevere in their alliance.

III. About the same space of time, Æneas the Stymphalian, who had been made general in chief of the Arcadians, judging what was doing at Sicyon to be past all sufferance, marched up with his forces into the citadel, whither he conveneth the best men of Sicyon resident in the city, and recalled such as had been driven into exile without a legal process. Euphron, alarmed at this, flies for refuge down to the harbour of Sicyon; and having sent for Pasimelus from Corinth, delivered up the harbour to him for the use of the Lacedæmonians; and thus he went over again into their alliance, averring that "whatever appearances were against him, he had been faithfully attached to the Lacedæmonians. For when it was publicly voted at Sicyon, whether or no they should revolt," he said, "he had given his own vote with the minority; and afterwards had set up the democracy only to execute his revenge upon such as had betrayed him. And, even now, all those who had betrayed the Lacedæmonians are driven into exile by me. If, therefore, I had been able to execute the whole of my design, I should have revolted to you with the whole city in my own disposal: but, as I was not able to accomplish this, I have now delivered up the harbour to you." These words were spoken by him in the hearing of many; but it did not appear that many believed him sincere. Yet since I have thus returned to the intrigues of Euphron, I will proceed and finish all that relateth to him.

A sedition happening afterwards between the parties of the nobility and the people at Sicyon, Euphron, at the head of some mercenaries picked up at Athens, returneth again into that city. Here, aided by the people, he became master of the whole place except the citadel, which remained in possession of the Theban commandant. But being clearly convinced that he could not stay long in the place, as the Thebans were masters of the citadel, he collected together every thing of value he possibly could, and went away for Thebes, intending to bribe the Thebans to eject the party of the few, and leave him master once more of the city of Sicyon. But the former exiles got notice of his journey and his whole scheme, and posted away after him to Thebes. And when they saw him conversing familiarly with the men in power at Thebes, and became apprehensive that he would succeed in the whole of his designs, some of them determine to run all risks, and stab him in the very citadel whilst the magistrates were sitting in council. The magistrates immediately ordered the assassins to be brought before the council, and then spoke as followeth:

" Citizens of Thebes! we accuse these persons here who have assassinated Euphron as guilty of a capital offence. We are convinced by experience, that men of honour and worth never commit such outrageous and impious acts; wicked men indeed commit them, and endeavour at the same time to remain undiscovered. But these wretches have far exceeded all mankind in a daring and abominable crime; for erecting themselves into judges and executioners too, they have murdered Euphron, almost in the presence of the magistrates of Thebes, and in the presence also of you, who are solely invested with the power of life and death. If these wretches therefore be suffered to escape the punishment of death, what stranger for the time forwards will dare to appear in this city? or, what will become of Thebes, if private persons may be permitted to murder a stranger, before he hath notified the reasons of his coming? We therefore accuse these men as impious and execrable wretches, and guilty of the highest contempt against the state. And, after hearing what they have to say, judge ye what punishment they best deserve, and sentence them accordingly."

In this manner the magistrates accused them; and each of the assassins pleaded in his own behalf, that he was not the person who gave the blow, till at length one of them boldly avowed it, and began his defence as followeth:

" No man, ye Thebans, can possibly entertain a contempt of you, who knoweth that you are sovereign arbiters of life and death within your own community. And you shall be clearly informed on what I place my confidence, when within your walls I gave Euphron the mortal blow.

" It was, in the first place, on my conviction that what I did was right; and, secondly, on my inward persuasion that you would judge righteously of the fact. I knew, that in the case of Archias and Hypates, whom you found guilty of practices like those of Euphron, you waited not for the legal decision, but wreaked your vengeance upon them the first opportunity that presented itself, convinced that the sentence of death is already passed by all mankind upon wretches openly abandoned, upon detected traitors, and ambitious tyrants. And Euphron in each of these characters deserved his fate. He had seized the temples of the gods, and stripped them of all their gold and silver oblations. And certainly no man was ever a more notorious traitor than Euphron, who being in the closest friendship with the Lacedæmonians, deserted them for you; and after the most solemn pledges of fidelity to you, again betrayed you, and delivered up the harbour of Sicyon to your enemies. And farther, how incontestably doth it appear to all the world that Euphron was a tyrant, who not only made freemen of slaves, but even raised them to all the privileges of citizens! He put to death, he drove into banishment, he deprived of their properties, not men who had acted unjustly, but whom he did not like; and these were the worthiest men of Sicyon. And, what is more, returning to that city by the aid of the Athenians your greatest enemies, he drew up his troops in opposition to your own commandant. But when he found himself unable to dislodge him from his post, he collected every thing of value he could, and even ventured hither. Now, had he been marching against you in a hostile manner, you would have bestowed your thanks upon me for taking his life. When therefore he had amassed all the wealth he could, and came hither to corrupt your members, and so persuade you to make him once more master of Sicyon; and at this very crisis I inflicted condign punishment upon him; with what justice can I be put to death by you? Men overpowered by arms are sufferers, it is true; yet are not thereby proved unjust; but men, who are corrupted to do iniquitous acts, are not only hurt but are disgraced for ever. Yet, supposing Euphron to have been only an enemy to me, but a friend to you, I then shall frankly confess, that I am not to be justified for having killed him. But who hath been a traitor to you, can that man be a greater enemy to me than he was to you? Good gods! it may be said, Euphron came hither on his own free accord. Granted. The person then who killed him out of your jurisdiction would have received your commendations for it. And shall any one deny that he was justly slain, because he was gotten within your walls to accumulate the mischiefs he hath done you? What proofs can such a one bring, that Grecians are bound to observe any terms with traitors, with habitual deserters, or with tyrants? And after all this remember, Thebans, that you yourselves have passed a decree which is yet in force, that exiles upon record may be fetched away from any of the confederate cities. Who therefore can deny the justice of putting that man to death, who, though exiled, presumed to return home without a previous decree from the confederate cities? I affirm, therefore, ye Thebans, that if you take my life, you are only going to revenge the man who was the bitterest enemy in the world to yourselves. But, should you declare that I have acted with justice, you will take revenge in behalf of yourselves and all your confederates."

The Thebans, after hearing this defence, declared that Euphron was justly killed. The Sicyonians however of his own faction carried him home as a man of bravery and worth, buried him in the forum, and honour him as guardian of their city. This, it seemeth, is the practice of the world, that men generally pronounce their own private benefactors to be persons of honour and worth. The account of Euphron is thus completed; I return to the place from whence I digressed to give it.

IV. Whilst the Phliasians were yet employed in fortifying Thyamia, and Chares continued with them, Oropus was seized by the exiles. The whole military force of Athens took the field on this occasion; and Chares being also sent for from Thyamia, the harbour of the Sicyonians is again taken by the inhabitants and the Arcadians. None of their confederates marched out to join the Athenians, who retreated, leaving Oropus in the hands of the Thebans, till the dispute should be judicially determined. But Lycomedes, perceiving the Athenians were displeased with their confederates, since, though involved in many troubles in their behalf, yet, in time of need not one would stir to their assistance, persuadeth the ten thousand to treat with them for an offensive and defensive alliance. Some of the Athenians were not at all satisfied with the proposal, that they, who were in friendship with the Lacedæmonians, should enter into such an alliance with the enemies of the latter. But when, after serious consideration, they found it might be as serviceable to the Lacedæmonians as to themselves, that the Arcadians should stand in no need of the Thebans, they at length accepted the alliance of the Arcadians. Lycomedes, who managed the negotiation, in his return from Athens, lost his life in a most wonderful manner. For, very many ships being on their departure, he pitched on a particular one from amongst the number, and having agreed with them to land him at whatever place be named, he chose to land in the very place where the exiles were at that moment assembled; and thus he loseth his life.

The alliance between Arcadians and Athenians was thus effectually settled. But Demotion saying in the assembly of the people at Athens, that "this alliance was in his judgment an honourable measure," he then added, that "it ought to be particularly recommended to the generals of the state, to take care that Corinth be kept firm in its duty to the people of Athens." This was reported to the Corinthians, who sending without loss of time detachments of their own people to all places garrisoned by the Athenians, ordered the latter to march out, as they had no longer any need of their service. Accordingly they evacuated the garrisons; and when they were all afterwards arrived at Corinth, the Corinthians made public proclamation, that "if any Athenian thought himself aggrieved, he should prefer his petition and have all equitable redress." But at this juncture Chares arrived at Cenchreæ with the fleet. And when he knew what had lately been done, he gave out that "having heard of a design against the city, he was come up with a timely aid." The Corinthians commended his alacrity in their service, but however would not permit him to enter the harbour, and ordered him to depart with the fleet: and then, after doing them all kind of justice, they sent away the heavy-armed. In this manner were the Athenians dismissed from Corinth. But in pursuance of the late alliance they were obliged to send their cavalry to the aid of the Arcadians, whenever any enemy invaded Arcadia; and yet, they never entered Laconia in a hostile manner. In the meantime the Corinthians were reflecting much with themselves, how difficult it would be to secure their own preservation, as they had already been quite overpowered at land, and the Athenians were now become intractable in regard to them. They determined, therefore, to take into their pay bodies both of foot and horse. And keeping these submissive to their own orders, they, at one and the same time kept guard at Corinth, and gave some annoyance to their enemies. They sent however to Thebes to demand of the Thebans, "whether, in case they requested it in form, a peace would be granted them ?" And when the Thebans encouraged them to come with their request, giving hopes of its success, the Corinthians offered a fresh petition, that "they would first permit them to go and consult their confederates, that they might associate such of them as were willing in this peace, and leave such as preferred war to the liberty of continuing it." The Thebans permitting them to take this step, the Corinthians repaired to Lacedæmon, and spoke as followeth :

"We Corinthians, your old and approved confederates, address ourselves to you, ye men of Lacedæmon. We solemnly conjure you, if you know any certain expedient of securing preservation for us in case we persevere along with you in this war, that you would explicitly inform us what it is. But if you are convinced in yourselves, that your affairs are irrecoverably distressed and no other resource remaineth, we then conjure you to make a peace in conjunction with us, since united with you, rather than with any other people in the world, we would gladly earn our preservation. But in case you judge it most advisable for yourselves to continue this war, we beg at least that you would give us permission to make a peace. Let us but save ourselves now, and the time again may come when we may do you some signal acts of friendship. But if now we must be ruined, it is plain we never any more can do you service."

The Lacedæmonians, after hearing this request, advised the Corinthians by all means to make their peace ; and gave permission to any other of their confederates, who were averse from a longer continuance of the war, to give it up. As to themselves, they said, "they would fight it out, and would submit to the will of God; but would never suffer themselves to be deprived of Messene, which they had received from their progenitors. The Corinthians hearing this, went away to Thebes to negotiate a peace. The Thebans insisted, that "they should swear to an alliance offensive and defensive." The Corinthians answered, that "such a settlement would be no peace, but a mere change of the war," adding that "the Thebans should candidly remember, that they came hither only to make an amicable peace." This struck the Thebans with high admiration of them, since in whatever distress involved, they would not be parties in a war against their old benefactors. They therefore granted a peace to them and to the Phliasians, and to others who now accompanied them at Thebes, on the sole condition that "each party should respectively keep their own ;" and oaths were sworn to the observance of it.

The Phliasians, when an accommodation was thus ratified, honestly and without hesitation departed from Thyamia. But the Argives, who had sworn to observe the peace on the very same condition with the Phliasians, when they could not prevail for the safe continuance of the Phliasian exiles at Tricranum, on pretence that the place was their own, seized it and kept a garrison in it ; averring the land on which it stood to be their own property, though a little while ago they had laid it waste in a hostile manner; and even refused to submit to a judicial determination, though the Phliasians summoned them to do it.

Almost at the same time Dionysius the elder being lately dead, his son sendeth over twelve ships under the command of Timocrates to the aid of the Lacedæmonians. Timocrates on his arrival acteth in conjunction with them at the siege and reduction of Sellasia, and after that sailed back again to Syracuse.

No long time after this the Eleans seize upon Lasion, a town formerly their own, but at present comprehended in the Arcadian league. The Arcadians would not calmly brook it, but immediately took the field and marched. Four hundred Eleans at first, who were soon after joined by three hundred more, made head against them. After facing one another a whole day in very low ground belonging to the Eleans, the Arcadians by night ascend the summit of the hill above their enemies, and early next morning rushed down upon them The Eleans now perceiving an enemy far more numerous than themselves pouring down upon them from higher ground, were a long time kept in their posts by mere vexation; nay, they even advanced to meet them, yet were no sooner charged than they broke and fled. They fled over rough and difficult ground, and lost many of their men and many of their arms. The Arcadians after so much success marched against all the towns in the upper country, and after taking all of them, except Thraustus, arrive at Olympia. Here they threw up an entrenchment round the temple of Saturn, where they posted themselves, and were masters of the mountain of Olympia. They farther took the city of the Marganians, which was betrayed to them by some of the inhabitants. Their enemies having had such a train of success, the Eleans began utterly to despond. And now the Arcadians march up to Elis, and into it as far as to the forum. But then the horsemen and some other of the inhabitants fall upon them, drive them out, and made some slaughter, and erected a trophy. There had been now a dissension of long standing in Elis. The faction of Charopus, Thrasonides, and Argeus, were striving to set up a democracy. The faction of Stalcas, Hippias, and Stratolus struggled for the oligarchy. And when the Arcadians with so much strength seemed to come opportunely thither as in aid of those who are inclined to a democracy, the faction of Charopus became more daring, and having bargained with the Arcadians for support, they seized the citadel of Elis. The horsemen and the three hundred, however, lost no time, but march thither immediately and drive them out, in consequence of which, Argeus and Charopus, with about four hundred Eleans more, were driven out into exile. And no long time after, these exiles, by the aid of a party of Arcadians, possess themselves of Pylus; whither many of the popular faction in Elis repaired afterwards to them, as the place was spacious and of great strength, and where they were certain of support from the Arcadians. The Arcadians also, at the instigation of these exiles, who assured them of the quick surrender of Elis, march soon after into the territory of the Eleans. But on this occasion the Achæans, who were in friendship with the Eleans, had securely garrisoned their city, so that the Arcadians, unable to do any thing more than lay waste the country, again retreated. But no sooner had they marched out of Elea, and discovered that the Pellenians were in Elis, than they made an exceeding long march in the night, and seized Olurus, belonging to the latter. The Pellenians had already returned into the alliance of the Lacedæmonians. And they no sooner heard of the seizure of Olurus than, marching a roundabout way, the better to conceal their motion, they entered their own city Pellene. And after this, they continued a war against the Arcadians in Olurus and all the people of Arcadia, notwithstanding their own great inferiority in number; nay, never slackened in their endeavours, till they had again recovered Olurus by a siege.

The Arcadians once more repeat their expedition against Elis. But, as they lay encamped between Cyllene and Elis, the Eleans make a sudden attack upon them; the Arcadians stood it out, and got the victory. And Andromachus the Elean commander, who was the principal adviser of this last attack, laid violent hands upon himself; the rest of the Eleans retired into their city. Soclidas, a Spartan who was present in this battle, lost his life in it, for the Lacedæmonians were once more allies to the Eleans. But the Eleans, now distressed about their own defence, despatched ambassadors, and begged the Lacedæmonians to make war upon the Arcadians; judging there was no other method to get clear of the Arcadians than to have them warred upon on both sides. In consequence of this, Archidamus taketh the field with the domestic force of Sparta, and seizeth Cromnus. Leaving three of the twelve battalions he had with them to garrison Cromnus, he again marched back to Sparta. The Arcadians, however, whose forces were all assembled for the expedition against Elis, hurried away to recover Cromnus, and invested it round with a double work of circumvallation; and having thus secured their own camp, continued in the siege of the place. The state of Lacedæmon, unable to brook this besieging of their own citizens, order their troops to march; and on this occasion also, Archidamus commanded. Entering their country, he laid waste as much of Arcadia and Skiritis as he possibly could, and did every thing that could be done to force them to raise the siege. Yet the Arcadians persisted steadfastly in it, and made no manner of account of all these devastations. Archidamus now took a view of an eminence, across which the Arcadians had carried their outward circumvallation. He thought he could secure it, and in case he did, that the enemy below it could not continue their siege. Whilst he was marching his troops a round-about way to seize this post, the targeteers of Archidamus advancing before the rest had a view of the chosen body of the enemy without the works, and rush suddenly upon them; and the horse at the same time endeavoured to charge. The enemy scorned to retreat, but drew up in regular order, and stood quiet. They then rushed a second time upon them; and when yet, so far from retiring, they actually advanced to meet them; every thing now being in hurry and confusion, Archidamus himself, who had made a turn into the cart-way that leadeth to Cromnus, appeared in sight, his men marching two by two in the order they had set out, and himself at their head. When they were thus come near the enemy, those under Archidamus, with their flanks exposed in consequence of the order of their march, but the Arcadians in regular array for battle and their shields closed firmly together, the Lacedæmonians were not able to stand their ground against this body of Arcadians, but on the contrary Archidamus had soon received a wound quite through his thigh, and the two Spartans who fought before him were actually slain. These were Poly-anidas and Chilon; the latter of whom had married the sister of Archidamus. Nay, the number of Spartans slain on this occasion was not less than thirty. Yet when, after falling back along the road, they were got into more open ground, the Lacedæmonians then formed again to receive the enemy. The Arcadians stood firm together in regular order, inferior it is true in numbers, but much higher in spirits, since they had fallen upon their enemy whilst retreating before them, and made some slaughter. The Lacedæmonians were sadly dejected; they saw that Archidamus was wounded; they heard the names of those who were slain, brave men, and almost the most illustrious of their body. And now, the enemy approaching nearer, one of the elder Spartans cried out aloud— "Why fight any longer, my countrymen? Why not rather demand a truce? He was heard with pleasure by all, and a truce was made. Accordingly, the Lacedæmonians took up their dead and marched away; and the Arcadians, returning to the spot from whence they first advanced, erected a trophy.

Whilst the Arcadians were thus employed in the siege of Cromnus, the Eleans marching out of their city, first against Pylus, fall in with the Pylians who were on their return after their repulse from Thalami. The Elean horsemen, who rode in the van, had no sooner a sight of them, than they seized the opportunity, and immediately fall in amongst them. Some of them they slaughter, whilst others of them flee for safety to an eminence that was near; but when the foot came up, they entirely defeated those upon the eminence; some of them they killed, and some they took prisoners, to the number of two hundred. So many of the latter as were strangers they sold for slaves; and so many as were exiles on record they put to the sword. And after this, as nobody came to the aid of the Pylians, they reduce them town and all, and recover the Marganians.

But the Lacedæmonians, some time after, marching by night towards Cromnus, force their way over the circumvallation, in the quarter of the Argives, and called out such of the Lacedæmonians as were besieged in the place. So many of them as happened to be near at hand and lost no time, completed their escape; but the rest, being prevented by the Arcadians who soon ran together in numbers to the place of escape, were again shut up within; and being afterwards taken prisoners were divided amongst the captors: the Argives had one part of them; the Thebans another; the Arcadians another; and the Messenians had a fourth. The whole number of Spartans and neighbours to Sparta taken prisoners on this occasion was more than a hundred.

The Arcadians, who had now cleared their hands of Cromnus, turned their attention again towards the Eleans, and not only strengthened their garrison at Olympia, but as it was the Olympic year made all needful preparation to celebrate the Olympic games in conjunction with the Pisans, who aver themselves to have been the original guardians of the temple. When, therefore the month was come in which the Olympic games are celebrated; nay, on the very days of the grand assembly, the Eleans, who had made open preparations for the purpose, and had sent for the Achæans to join them, came marching along the road to Olympia. The Arcadians had never imagined they would dare to give them any interruption, and jointly with the Pisans were conducting the order of the festival. They had already finished the race of chariots and the foot-race of the pentathlum, and the wrestlers had just entered the lists, not indeed on the course, since on this occasion they were to wrestle between the course and the altar; for the Eleans in military array were now come up to the sacred grove. The Arcadians however made no advance towards them, but stood drawn up by the river Cladaus, which running along the Altis dischargeth itself into the Alpheus. Their confederates were also at hand to the number of about two thousand heavy-armed Argives and about four hundred Athenian horse. The Eleans drew up in order on the other side of the river, and after a solemn sacrifice advanced to the charge. And thus a people, who in preceding times had been contemned by the Arcadians and Argives, contemned also by the Achæans and Athenians for the want of martial spirit, marched, however, that day at the head of their confederates in the most gallant manner. The Arcadians, for these were the first they charge, they instantly put to flight; they then stood the attack of the Argives who ran to aid the Arcadians, and gave them a defeat. And after they had pursued the fleets to the spot of ground that lieth between the council-house and the temple of Vesta and the adjacent theatre, they still fought on and drove them to the very altar. Here after being galled by darts and javelins from the porticoes and the council-house and the great temple, and fought with again on the level ground, a number of Eleans was slain, amongst whom was Stratolus the commander of the three hundred; after which they retreated to their own camp. The Arcadians however, and their associates were in so much dread of the ensuing day, that they busied themselves all that night in demolishing the fine pavilions they had erected for the festival, and throwing up a rampart for their better defence. And next day when the Eleans perceived that the work was strong, and that numbers had posted themselves upon the temples, they marched back to Elis, after showing themselves such gallant men, as God by particular inspiration can in one day enable men to be, though all human endeavours could not have made them such even in a long course of life.

The Arcadian commanders were now laying hands on the sacred treasures, and diverting them to the payment of their chosen bands, which the Mantineans first resented, and sent them an order "not thus to embezzle the sacred treasure." Nay, they even raised in their own city what pay was due to those chosen bands,

and sent it to the Arcadian commanders. The latter however alleged that "such behaviour was an infraction of the Arcadian league," and appealed against it to the council of ten thousand. But as the Mantineans slighted this appeal, the other proceeded to a judgment against them, and despatched the chosen bands to apprehend such persons as they had condemned by name. Upon this the Mantineans made fast their gates, and refused them admittance into their city. The consequence was, that even some of the other members of the council of ten thousand began also to affirm, that, " it was wrong to embezzle in this manner the sacred treasures, and to fix an eternal stain on their posterity by such sacrilege against the gods." At length it was voted in the council, that " these sacred treasures should not be embezzled," and then all such persons in the chosen bands as could not subsist without immediate pay slipped away from the service; and such as had a subsistence, after heartening up one another, entered themselves in these chosen bands, not indeed to be commanded, but to secure to themselves the command over them. Such also of the commanders as had dabbled most in the sacred treasure, being aware that their lives were in danger should they be called to a strict account, send messengers to Thebes, and give notice to the Thebans, that " unless they march up an army, the danger is great that the Arcadians will again go over to the Lacedæmonians." The Thebans accordingly were getting all things in readiness to take the field. Such persons, however, as were in their hearts true friends to Peloponnesus, persuaded the Arcadians state to despatch ambassadors to the Thebans with a notification to them " by no means to march with their forces into Arcadia, till they were formally invited." Nay, they not only notified this to the Thebans, but also came to a resolution amongst themselves, that " there was no need of war." They were now also convinced, that they had no manner of pretence to invade the presidency over the temple of Jove, but by restoring it to the Eleans should act with more piety and justice, and without doubt in a manner more acceptable to the god.

The Eleans were willing to accommodate affairs, and so both parties resolved upon a peace. A truce immediately ensued. And after the peace was sworn to, not only by all the other parties, but by the Tegeatæ also, and even by the Theban officer who was then in Tegea commanding four hundred heavy-armed Bœotians, such of the Arcadians as at that time were resident in Tegea feasted one another and were full of spirits, pouring forth their libations and singing their pæans as rejoicing for a peace. The Thebans, however, and such of the commanders as were apprehensive of being called to account for the sacred treasures, assisted by the Bœotians and their accomplices amongst the chosen bands, shut fast the gates of the wall round Tegea, and sending parties to their several lodgings, seized all the men of consequence who were not of their sentiments. As many people were here from every city in Arcadia, all of them highly delighted at the making of peace, the number seized in this manner must needs be very considerable. The public prison was soon filled with them; the town-house in like manner was filled as soon. After many persons were thus secured, and many had escaped by leaping over the wall, others there were who were let out through the gates, since no one acted with fury on this occasion that did not think his own life in danger. But, after all, the Theban officer and his accomplices were soon reduced to the greatest perplexity, when they found they had gotten into their hands but very few of those whom they chiefly desired to secure, and especially of the Mantineans, since almost all the Mantineans, had returned in good time to Mantinea, as it lay at so little distance from Tegea.

Upon the return of day, the Mantineans no sooner knew what had been doing, than they despatched their messengers round to the cities of Arcadia, with notice to them to take to their arms and stand on the defence of their cities. They themselves did so at Mantinea; and, sending at the same time to Tegea, demanded such of their citizens as were detained in that city; insisting withal that "no Arcadian whatsoever should be thrown into prison or put to death, before he had undergone a legal trial; and, in case any Mantineans were accused of a criminal behaviour, let their names be sent hither, and the state of Mantinea would pledge their faith to produce such persons in the public council of Arcadia, whenever they were called upon to do it." The Theban officer, hearing all this, was grievously perplexed in what manner to act, and in short delivereth up all the men. The day after, he had a meeting with as many of the Arcadians as were willing to meet him, and said in his justification, that "he had been sadly deluded." He affirmed "information had been given him that the Lacedæmonians were assembled in arms upon the frontier, and that some Arcadians had engaged to betray Tegea to them." They indeed gave him the hearing, and though assured that all he said was false, they let him depart. Yet they despatched ambassadors after him to Thebes, and preferred such a charge against him as might cost him his life. But they say that Epaminondas, who was then general of the state, made this declaration to them, that "the Theban officer did his duty better when he seized these persons than when he set them at liberty. For we Thebans, said he, went into a war purely on your account, whereas you have clapped up a peace without consulting us at all; may not any one therefore, consistently with justice, charge all the treachery in this affair upon you? But rest assured (he went on) that we shall soon march our forces into Arcadia, and will still continue the war with the assistance of such as remain in the same sentiments with ourselves."

V. No sooner was this declaration of Epaminondas reported to the general council of Arcadia and to the several cities, than it struck the reflection into the Mantineans, and such other Arcadians as were friends to the true welfare of Peloponnesus, as also into the Eleans and Achæans, "that it was plainly the design of the Thebans to reduce Peloponnesus to so low a condition, that they might easily enslave it. For what other view can they have in desiring us to continue the war, than to make us harass and distress one another, that both parties may be obliged to court them for assistance? For what other reason can they be preparing to march their army amongst us, when we tell them plainly we want them not at present? Is it not clear as the day that they are preparing to take the field with full purpose to do us mischief? They now sent away to Athens to beg an aid. They sent to Lacedæmon also an embassy consisting of persons enrolled in their chosen bands, with earnest entreaties to the Lacedæmonians, "readily to join their forces against such as are coming with a full design to enslave Peloponnesus." The point of command was also finally adjusted, that each people should command within their own territory.

Whilst these points were in agitation, Epaminondas took the field, at the head of all the Bœotians, and Eubœans, and numerous bodies of Thessalians, either by Alexander or such as were enemies to him. The Phocians, however, marched not with him, pretending "they were obliged by treaty only to give aid in case an enemy invaded Thebes; to act offensively with them against other states was no condition in the treaty." Epaminondas reckoned, that in Peloponnesus he should assuredly be joined by the Argives and Messenians, and such Arcadians as were in the interest of Thebes, for instance, the Tegeatæ and Megalapolitans, and Aseatæ and Palantians, and some other cities which, because they were surrounded by the greater states, would be compelled to join them. Epaminondas accordingly advanced towards Peloponnesus with the utmost expedition. But when he came up to Nemea he halted there, hoping he might intercept the Athenians in their march, and reckoning that such an incident would have a great effect in raising the spirits of his own confederates, and would strike despondency into his foes; at all events, that lessening the Athenians in any degree would be so much positive advantage to the Thebans. But during his halt at Nemea, all the states of Peloponnesus that acted with unanimity on this occasion assembled together at Mantinea. Epaminondas however had no sooner heard that the Athenians had given up their design of marching by land, and were preparing to pass over by sea, that they might go through Lacedæmon to the aid of the Arcadians, than he immediately decamped from Nemea, and advanceth to Tegea.

For my own part, I shall not take upon me to say that this expedition proved a happy one for him. But this I can affirm, that he was not deficient in exhibiting every proof that man can give of bravery and conduct. In the first place, I highly applaud him for encamping his troops within the walls of Tegea: for there he was posted in much greater security than he could have been on open ground, and all his motions were much better concealed from the enemy; since within a city he could much easier be supplied with any article he wanted: and as his enemies lay in open ground, he had a full view of what they were doing, and could see when they were right and when they blundered. And though he thought himself superior to the enemy, yet he never led out his troops against them, so long as he judged they had the advantage in ground. But finding at length that not one city came over to him, and that the time of his command was fast elapsing, he judged it necessary to strike a blow; since otherwise he foresaw the loss of his former glory. When therefore he was informed that the enemy kept close at Mantinea, and had sent for Agesilaus and all the Lacedæmonians; and was even assured that Agesilaus was marched out at their head, and was already advanced as far as Pellene; he ordered his army to take their repast, then gave the signal for a march, and led them on directly against Sparta. And had not a Cretan by an especial providence made away in all haste to Agesilaus, and told him of this march, he would have taken Sparta like a bird's nest quite destitute of all defence. But as timely notice of his march had been given to Agesilaus, he had returned in time to the aid of the city, and the Spartans, though exceeding few in number, had already posted themselves on its guard. The whole of their cavalry was absent in Arcadia, as were all their auxiliaries, and three out of their ten battalions of foot. When therefore Epaminondas was come up to Sparta, he made no attempt to enter the city, where the enemy could have charged him on level ground, or could annoy him with darts and javelins from the tops of houses, or where the ground might enable a few to be a match for far superior numbers. But having seized an eminence, which he judged would give him great advantage, he from thence marched down, instead of marching up into Sparta. The sequel was of so strange a nature, that we may either ascribe it to the special will of God, or confess that men reduced to a state of desperation are not to be resisted. For no sooner did Archidamus lead on against him, though attended by not one hundred persons; no sooner, I say, had Archidamus passed the river, which in all probability must have greatly delayed him, and advanced towards the enemy, than these Thebans, who breathed out fire and flame, who had gained such victories over the Lacedæmonians, who were now so far superior in numbers, and had all the advantage of higher ground, durst not even stand the charge of those under Archidamus, but wheel themselves off from before him; and the soldiers of Epaminondas, who formed the first ranks, are immediately slain. Exulting at so much success, the victors pursued them farther than was prudent, and are slaughtered in their turn. It looked as if heaven had beforehand settled the limits in which each party should be victorious. Archidamus, however, erected a trophy on the spot where he had gotten the better, and gave up under truce the bodies of the enemy who had fallen there.

Epaminondas now bethought himself, that, as the Arcadians would come with all speed to the aid of Sparta, it was not his business to fight with them and the whole Lacedæmonian strength in conjunction; especially as the enemy had hitherto been successful, and the contrary had happened to his own troops. He therefore marched off, and returned again with the utmost expedition to Tegea. He here ordered the heavy-armed to halt, but sent off the horse to Mantinea; begging them " to perform this service with their utmost perseverance ;" and telling them, " it was likely that all the cattle of the Mantineans were out abroad in the fields, and all the people too, especially in this season of fetching in their harvest." And accordingly they began the march.

The Athenian horsemen, who had set out from Eleusis, took their evening repast at the isthmus. From thence continuing their march through Cleone, they had just now reached Mantinea, and were quartering themselves in houses within the walls. So soon therefore as the enemy was seen riding up, the Mantineans besought these Athenian horse to give them all possible aid, "since all their flocks and herds were abroad in the fields, as were all their labourers and most of the youths and old men of the city." The Athenians complied and sally out immediately, though neither themselves nor their horses had yet tasted any food. Who on this occasion can help admiring the generosity of these men; who, with an enemy in sight much superior in number to their own, and with the late blow given at Corinth to their cavalry quite fresh in their remembrance, were not however disheartened, no not even at the thought that they were going to engage with Thebans and Thessalians, at that time reckoned the best horsemen in the world; but disdaining that their friends should suffer through the want of any assistance that themselves could give them, they were no sooner in sight of the enemy than they rode full speed upon them, desirous to preserve at all events

their hereditary glory? In this manner they engaged; and by engaging preserved every thing belonging to the Mantineans that was abroad in the fields. But several gallant men amongst them perished; and they killed as many gallant men on the side of the enemy. For not one person on either side had a weapon so short but it was long enough to reach his adversary. They took up the dead bodies of their friends, and restored some dead bodies of their enemies by truce.

Epaminondas was thus reflecting, that " he must needs be gone in a few days, since the time limited for this expedition was just expiring: and, in case he now abandoned his allies whom he came to save, they would be besieged and reduced by their adversaries, and he should entirely blemish all his former glory; defeated with his numerous heavy-armed as he had been at Lacedæmon by a handful of men; defeated also at Mantinea in the engagement of the horse; and the author, as he had really proved by this expedition into Peloponnesus, of a fresh coalition of Lacedæmonians, Arcadians, Achæans, Eleans, and Athenians." He therefore judged it impossible for him to quit the country without fighting a battle; concluding, "in case he was victorious, he should prevent all the great evils he foresaw; or, in case he fell in the attempt, his death would be honourable and glorious, since he was endeavouring to gain for his own country the sovereignty of Peloponnesus." It cannot appear in the least surprising to me, that Epaminondas should reason in such a manner. Men greedy of honour are aptest to encourage such thoughts as these. But what excites my surprise and admiration too is this; that he had so highly ingratiated himself with the troops he commanded that no toil whatever, either by day or by night, could at all fatigue them; no danger whatever could stop them; and though straitened for want of necessary provisions, that they should execute all his orders with prompt alacrity. For at last when he issued his final orders for all to get ready, since he was determined to fight, the horsemen at a word were cleaning up their helmets. The heavy-armed Arcadians, who carried clubs, were also enrolled and mustered as Thebans; and all they to a man were busied in sharpening their spears and their swords and brightening their shields.

But when they were all ready, and he was for leading them towards the enemy, it is worth while to observe the particulars of his conduct. In the first place, he made all the dispositions, as one would expect Epaminondas should make them ; and by his manner of doing it showed plainly to every body that he was preparing in earnest for a battle. And when his army was completely formed to his own liking, he then led on, not indeed directly towards the enemy, but declining towards the mountains on the west beyond the city of Tegea. By this he gave his enemies reason to imagine, that he had no design to fight that day. For when he came near the mountain, after he had formed his main army in a line of battle, he ordered them to ground their arms under the shelter of the eminence ; so that he yielded to his enemies the appearance of a general who was for encamping his army. But, by acting in this manner, he caused the bulk of his enemies to relax in the ardour they had conceived for engaging ; he caused them even to quit the ranks in which they were posted. Yet, no sooner had he made some bands of heavy-armed in the wings to march up and take post in the centre, by which he made the part of the army where he was posted himself as strong as the beak of a ship, than he gave the word for recovering their arms. He now again led on, and his army was in march. As for the enemy, who quite unexpectedly saw them thus advancing, they were at once all hurry and precipitation. Some were running to fall into their ranks, some were only forming ; the horsemen were bridling their horses and putting on their breast-plates ; and they all had the appearance of men, who were rather to suffer from than to hurt their foe.

Epaminondas was still advancing with his troops, which resembled a ship of war bearing down to the attack, assured that, on whatever part of the enemy's army he made his first effectual push, he must bear them down before him, and throw the whole into utter disorder. For his previous disposition was such, that he must begin the charge with the prime strength of his troops ; the weakest of them he had posted in the rear ; knowing that even the latter, if defeated, would strike terror into his own people, and give additional spirit to the enemy. The enemy on the other side had drawn up their horse like a battalion of heavy-armed, without giving them a proper depth or lining them with foot ; whereas Epami-

nondas had so formed his, that their attack must needs make the strongest impression ; and he had lined their ranks with parties of foot ; assured that, in whatever part they broke through the enemy, their whole body must at once be vanquished. For exceeding difficult it is to preserve a willingness in any part of a body to stand fast, when they see some of that body in actual flight. And to prevent the Athenians from stirring out of the left wing to aid such as were near them, he had posted over-against them on the higher ground a party of horse and heavy-armed ; intending to frighten them by this show of the danger they must run of being attacked in their rear, if they stirred to give aid to others.

In this manner he had made his dispositions for the attack : and he was not disappointed in the event he expected. For he made his first charge with so much force, that he compelled the whole body of the enemy to flee before him. But after Epaminondas dropped, there was no one left who could make a proper use of the victory. For though the whole of the enemy was in flight before them, his heavy-armed made no slaughter not even of a single foe, nor made any advance in the field of battle beyond the spot where they first attacked. And though the enemy's horse were also in open flight, his own horse slew neither horsemen nor heavy-armed in their pursuit ; but like men who had been vanquished, slipped tremblingly out of the way of their routed enemies. His foot indeed and targeteers, who had engaged along with the horse, advanced quite up to the left wing of the enemy, as masters of the field of battle ; and there most of them were put to the sword by the Athenians.

Such was this battle ; the event of which was quite contrary to what all the world expected it must be. For as almost all Greece was assembled together on this occasion to fight a decisive action against one another, there was no man but thought that, after such a battle, the conquerors would remain for ever masters, and the conquered must for ever be subject to them ; whereas God so ordered the event, that both parties erected trophies as claiming the victory, and neither side could hinder the erection of them. Both parties again, as conquerors, restored the dead under truce ; both parties too, as conquered, requested a truce for the delivery of them. Nay, though both parties gave out that the victory was their own, it was manifest that neither of them had gained any more ground, any other city, or any more dominion than they were masters of before the battle. On the con-trary, a greater confusion and a wilder hurry arose in Greece after this battle than had been known before it.

So far may suffice for me. Others perhaps will take care to relate what happened after-wards in Greece.

3 S

XENOPHON'S

MEMOIRS OF SOCRATES.

TRANSLATED BY

SARAH FIELDING.

PREFACE

TO

THE MEMOIRS OF SOCRATES.

———

ALTHOUGH the translator of the following Memoirs was fully persuaded, that the far greater number of those who favoured her with their names, and assisted her with their interest, were influenced by much nobler motives, than the expectation of receiving any thing very extraordinary from her hand; yet, so little did this appear to her any reason for relaxing her endeavours, that on the contrary, she considered it as laying her under an additional obligation to do all the justice she possibly could to her author. It was partly on that account; partly from sickness; and partly from some other accidents, not more within her power to regulate, than the state of her own health, that the publication of these Memoirs hath been deferred beyond the time first mentioned in the proposals: but if the task is, at last, discharged tolerably, the mind of the translator will be set much at ease; and the reader find somewhat to repay him for his waiting.

That the Memoirs of Socrates, with regard to the greatest part, are held in the highest estimation, is most certain; and if there are some passages which seem obscure; and of which the use doth not so plainly appear to us at this distance of time; and from the dissimilarity of our customs and manners; yet, perhaps, we might not do amiss, in taking Socrates himself for our example in this particular, as well as in many others; who being presented by Euripides with the writings of Heraclitus, and afterwards asked his opinion of their merit;—" What I understand," said he, " I find to be excellent; and therefore believe that to be of equal value, which I do not understand."—" And, certainly," continues the admired modern writer, from whom the quotation above was taken, " this candour is more particularly becoming us in the perusal of the works of ancient authors; of those works which have been preserved in the devastation of cities; and snatched up in the wreck of nations: which have been the delight of ages; and transmitted as the great inheritance of mankind, from one generation to another: and we ought to take it for granted, that there is a justness in the connexion, which we cannot trace; and a cogency in the reasoning, which we cannot understand." The translator of the following sheets would willingly bespeak the same candour, in reading the translations of the ancient writers, which hath above been thought so necessary for judging right of the originals. In the preface to the Life of Cicero, the celebrated writer of it thus expresses himself:—" Nor has that part of the task," said he, (speaking of the several passages he had translated from the writings of Cicero) " been the easiest to me; as those will readily believe who have ever attempted to translate the classical writings of Greece and Rome." It may, perhaps, be objected, " That candour alone is not sufficient for the present occasion:" to which it can only be answered, " That something was to be done: and, that no pains hath been spared, to do it as well as possible."

The translator is sorry to find, that the title affixed to this work hath not been approved of universally : and, in truth, that inundation of trifles, follies, and vices, lately introduced into the world, under the general appellation of Memoirs, hath occasioned such an unhappy association of ideas, as doth not well suit with a Xenophon's giving a relation of what a Socrates once said and did : but the translator takes shelter for her self, under the respectable names of Mr Johnson and Mrs Carter ; the one having, as she thinks, explained the word Memoir in a manner consistent with the present application of it ; and the other actually made choice of it for the very same purpose as is here done.

THE

DEFENCE OF SOCRATES

HIS JUDGES.

I HAVE always considered the manner in which Socrates behaved after he had been summoned to his trial, as most worthy of our remembrance; and that, not only with respect to the defence he made for himself, when standing before his judges; but the sentiments he expressed concerning his dissolution. For, although there be many who have written on this subject, and all concur in setting forth the wonderful courage and intrepidity wherewith he spake to the assembly—so that it remaineth incontestable that Socrates did thus speak—yet that it was his full persuasion, that death was more eligible for him than life at such a season, they have by no means so clearly manifested; whereby the loftiness of his style, and the boldness of his speech, may wear at least the appearance of being imprudent and unbecoming.

But Hermogenes, the son of Hipponicus, was his intimate friend; and from him it is we have heard those things of Socrates, as sufficiently prove the sublimity of his language was only conformable to the sentiments of his mind. For, having observed him, as he tells us, choosing rather to discourse on any other subject than the business of his trial; he asked him, "If it was not necessary to be preparing for his defence?" And "What!" said he, "my Hermogenes, suppose you I have not spent my whole life in preparing for this very thing?" Hermogenes desiring he would explain himself: "I have," said he, "steadily persisted, throughout life, in a diligent endeavour to do nothing which is unjust; and this

I take to be the best and most honourable preparation."

"But see you not," said Hermogenes, "that ofttimes here in Athens, the judges, influenced by the force of oratory, condemn those to death who no way deserve it; and, not less frequently, acquit the guilty, when softened into compassion by the moving complaints, or the insinuating eloquence of those who plead their cause before them?"

"I know it," replied Socrates; "and therefore, twice have I attempted to take the matter of my defence under consideration: but the Genius [1] always opposed me."

---

[1] Various have been the opinions concerning this Genius, or Demon of Socrates; and too many for the translator to enumerate. What seems the most probable and satisfactory is, that the Genius of Socrates, so differently spoken of, was nothing more than an uncommon strength of judgment and justness of thinking; which, measuring events by the rules of prudence, assisted by long experience and much observation, unclouded and unbiassed by any prejudices or passions, rendered Socrates capable of looking as it were into futurity, and foretelling what would be the success of those affairs about which he had been consulted by others, or was deliberating upon for himself. And, in support of this opinion, they urge his custom of sending his friends—Xenophon, for example—to consult the oracle when any thing too obscure for human reason to penetrate was proposed to him: to which might be added, as no mean testimony, his own practice on all such occasions. But from whence this notion arose, of his being thus uncommonly assisted, is not easy to determine. It might perhaps be from nothing more, as some have imagined, than from his having casually said on some occasion, "My Genius would not suffer me;" alluding to the notion which prevailed with many, that every one had a Genius to watch over and direct him.

Hermogenes having expressed some astonishment at these words, Socrates proceeded:

"Doth it then appear marvellous to you, my Hermogenes, that God should think this the very best time for me to die? Know you not, that hitherto I have yielded to no man that he hath lived more uprightly or even more pleasurably than myself; possessed, as I was, of that well-grounded self-approbation, arising from the consciousness of having done my duty both to the gods and men: my friends also bearing their testimony to the integrity of my conversation! But now,—if my life is prolonged, and I am spared even to old age,—what can hinder, my Hermogenes, the infirmities of old age from falling upon me? My sight will grow dim; my hearing, heavy; less capable of learning, as more liable to forget what I have already learned; and if, to all this, I become sensible of my decay, and bemoan myself on the account of it; how can I say that I still lived pleasantly? It may be t ," continued Socrates, "that God, through his goodness, hath appointed for me, not only that my life should terminate at a time which seems the most seasonable; but the manner in which it will be terminated shall also be the most eligible: for, if my death is now resolved upon, it must needs be, that they who take charge of this matter will permit me to choose the means supposed the most easy; free too from those lingering circumstances which keep our friends in anxious suspense for us, and fill the mind of the dying man with much pain and perturbation. And when nothing offensive, nothing unbecoming, is left on the memory of those who are present, but the man is dissolved while the body is yet sound, and the mind still capable of exerting itself benevolently, who can say, my Hermogenes, that so to die is not most desirable? And with good reason," continued Socrates, "did the gods oppose themselves at what time we took the affair of my escape under deliberation, and determined, that every means should be dil¹

gently sought after to effect it; since, if our designs had been carried into execution, instead of terminating my life in the manner I am now going, I had only gained the unhappy privilege of finding it put an end to by the torments of some disease, or the lingering decays incident to old age, when all things painful flow in upon us together, destitute of every joy which might serve to soften and allay them.

"Yet think not, my Hermogenes, the desire of death shall influence me beyond what is reasonable: I will not set out with asking it at their hands: but if, when I speak my opinion of myself, and declare what I think I have deserved both of gods and men, my judges are displeased, I will much sooner submit to it, than meanly entreat the continuance of my life, whereby I should only bring upon myself many and far greater evils, than any I had taken such unbecoming pains to deprecate."

In this manner Socrates replied to Hermogenes and others: and his enemies having accused him of "not believing in the gods whom the city held sacred; but as designing to introduce other and new deities; and, likewise, of his having corrupted the youth:" Hermogenes farther told me, that Socrates, advancing towards the tribunal, thus spake:

"What I chiefly marvel at, O ye judges! is this; whence Melitus inferreth that I esteem not those as gods whom the city hold sacred. For that I sacrifice at the appointed festivals, on our common altars, was evident to all others; and might have been to Melitus, had Melitus been so minded. Neither yet doth it seem to be asserted with greater reason, that my design was to introduce new deities among us, because I have often said, ' That it is the voice of God which giveth me significations of what is most expedient;' since they themselves, who observe the chirping of birds, or those ominous words spoken by men, ground their conclusions on no other than voices. For who among you doubteth whether thunder sendeth forth a voice? or whether it be not the very greatest of all auguries? The Pythian priestess herself; doth not she likewise, from the tripod, declare, by a voice, the divine oracles? And, truly, that God foreknoweth the future, and also showeth it to whomsoever he pleaseth, I am no way singular either in believing or asserting; since all mankind agree with me herein; this difference only excepted,

<hr>

And although nothing more was at the first either intended or understood by it, than when we say, "My good angel forbade me;" or, said so and so to me; yet, being verified by the event, it came at length to be considered, by a superstitious people, as something supernatural: and, as it added much weight to his counsel and instructions, neither Socrates nor his friends were in haste to discredit such an opinion; not looking upon themselves as obliged to it by any one duty whatsoever.

that whereas they say it is from auguries, omens, symbols, and diviners, whence they have their notices of the future; I, on the contrary, impute all those premonitions, wherewith I am favoured, to a genius; and I think, that, in so doing, I have spoken not only more truly, but more piously, than they who attribute to birds the divine privilege of declaring things to come: and that I lied not against God, I have this indisputable proof, that whereas I have often communicated to many of my friends the divine counsels, yet hath no man ever detected me of speaking falsely."

No sooner was this heard, but a murmuring arose among his judges; some disbelieving the truth of what he had said, while others envied him for being, as they thought, more highly favoured of the gods than they. But Socrates, still going on; "Mark!" said he, "I pray; and attend to what is yet more extraordinary, that such of you as are willing, may still the more disbelieve that I have been thus favoured of the deity: Chærephon, inquiring of the oracle at Delphos concerning me, was answered by Apollo himself, in the presence of many people, "That he knew no man more free, more just, or more wise than I."

On hearing this, the tumult among them visibly increased: but Socrates, still going on, —"And yet Lycurgus, the Lacedæmonian lawgiver, had still greater things declared of him: for, on his entering into the temple, the deity thus accosted him: "I am considering," said he, "whether I shall call thee a god, or a man!" Now Apollo compared me not to a god. This, indeed he said, "That I by far excelled man." Howbeit, credit not too hastily what ye have heard, though coming from an oracle; but let us thoroughly examine those things which the deity spake concerning me.

"Say, then, where have you ever known any one less enslaved to sensual appetite; whom more free than the man who submits not to receive gift, or reward, from the hands of any other? Whom can you deservedly esteem more just, than he who can so well accommodate himself to what he hath already in his own possession, as not even to desire what belongeth to another? Or how can he fail of being accounted wise, who, from the time he first began to comprehend what was spoken, never

1 See the learned Mr Harris's notes on these several particulars, infra, b. i. p. 16.

ceased to seek, and search out, to the very best of his power, whatever was virtuous and good for man? And, as a proof that in so doing I have not laboured in vain, ye yourselves know, that many of our citizens, yea, and many foreigners also, who made virtue their pursuit, always preferred, as their chief pleasure, the conversing with me. Whence was it, I pray you, that when every one knew my want of power to return any kind of pecuniary favour, so many should be ambitious to bestow them on me? Why doth no man call me his debtor, yet many acknowledge they owe me much? When the city is besieged, and every other person bemoaning his loss, why do I appear as in no respect the poorer than while it remained in its most prosperous state? And what is the cause, that when others are under a necessity to procure their delicacies from abroad, at an exorbitant rate, I can indulge in pleasures far more exquisite, by recurring to the reflections in my own mind? And now, O ye judges! if, in whatsoever I have declared of myself, no one is able to confute me as a false speaker, who will say I merit not approbation, and that not only from the gods, but men?

"Nevertheless, you, O Melitus, have asserted, that I,—diligently applying myself to the contemplation and practice of whatever is virtuous—corrupt the youth!—and, indeed, we well know what it is to corrupt them. But show us, if in your power, whom, of pious, I have made impious; of modest, shameless; of frugal, profuse? Who, from temperate is become drunken; from laborious, idle, or effeminate, by associating with me? Or, where is the man who hath been enslaved, by my means, to any vicious pleasure whatsoever?"

"Nay, verily!" said Melitus; "but I know of many whom thou hast persuaded to obey thee rather than their parents."

"And with good reason," replied Socrates, "when the point in question concerned education; since no man but knows that I made this my chief study: and which of you, if sick, prefers not the advice of the physician to his parents? Even the whole body of the Athenian people,—when collected in the public assembly,—do not they follow the opinion of him whom they think the most able, though he be not of their kindred? And in the choice of a general, do you not to your fathers, brothers, nay, even to yourselves, prefer the man whom ye think the best skilled in military discipline?"

"Certainly," returned Melitus; "neither can any one doubt of its being most expedient."

"How then could it escape being regarded even by you, Melitus, as a thing deserving the highest admiration, that while in every other instance the man who excels in any employment is supposed not only entitled to a common regard, but receives many, and those very distinguishing, marks of honour; I, on the contrary, am persecuted even to death, because I am thought by many to have excelled in that employment which is the most noble, and which hath for its aim the greatest good to mankind; by instructing our youth in the knowledge of their duty, and planting in the mind each virtuous principle!"

Now, doubtless, there were many other things spoken at the trial, not only by Socrates, but his friends, who were most zealous to support him; but I have not been careful to collect all that was spoken, yet think I have done enough to show, and that most plainly, that the design of Socrates in speaking at this time, was no other than to exculpate himself from any thing that might have the least appearance of impiety towards the gods, or of injustice towards men. For, with regard to death, he was no way solicitous to importune his judges, as the custom was with others: on the contrary, he thought it the best time for him to die. And, that he had thus determined with himself, was still the more evident after his condemnation: for, when he was ordered to fix his own penalty, [1] he refused to do it, neither would he suffer any other to do it for him; saying, that to fix a penalty implied a confession of guilt. And, afterwards, when his friends would have withdrawn him privately, he would not consent; but asked them with a smile, "If they knew of any place beyond the borders of Attica where death could not approach him?"

The trial being ended, Socrates, as it is related, spake to his judges in the following manner:

"It is necessary, O ye judges! that all they who instructed the witnesses to bear, by perjury, false testimony against me, as well as all those who too readily obeyed their instructions, should be conscious to themselves of much impiety and injustice: but that I, in any wise, should be more troubled and cast down than before my condemnation, I see not, since I stand here unconvicted of any of the crimes whereof I was accused: for no one hath proved against me that I sacrificed to any new deity; or by oath appealed to, or even made mention of the names of, any other than Jupiter, Juno, and the rest of the deities, which, together with these, our city holds sacred: neither have they once shown what were the means I made use of to corrupt the youth, at the very time that I was inuring them to a life of patience and frugality. As for those crimes to which our laws have annexed death as the only proper punishment,—sacrilege, man-stealing, [2] undermining of walls, or betraying of the city,—my enemies do not even say that any of these things were ever once practised by me. Wherefore I the rather marvel that ye have now judged me worthy to die.

"But it is not for me to be troubled on that account: for, if I die unjustly, the shame must be theirs who put me unjustly to death; since, if injustice is shameful, so likewise every act of it; but no disgrace can it bring on me, that others have not seen that I was innocent. Palamedes, likewise affords me this farther consolation: for being, like me, condemned undeservedly, he furnishes, to this very day, more noble subjects for praise, than the man who had iniquitously caused his destruction. [3]

1 In all cases where the laws had fixed the penalty, one single verdict was thought sufficient; but where the laws were silent, a second was necessary, to declare the punishment the offender had incurred. Before this second sentence was pronounced, the judges were ordered to value the crime, as Cicero calls it; and the offender himself was asked, What penalty he thought due to it? and the merits of the case being afterwards debated, the valuation was admitted, or rejected, as the judges saw reason: but Socrates incensed them so much with the answer he made them, that they proceeded, without any delay, to pass the second, or decretory sentence against him, and he was immediately condemned to suffer death.—Pott. Antiq.

2 It was the practice of many to steal slaves, or freemen's children in order to sell for slaves, which was made capital at Athens.—Potter.

3 When the Grecian kings were to go to the siege of Troy, Ulysses, to save himself from going, counterfeited madness; which Palamedes suspecting, ordered they should lay Ulysses's son in the furrow where the father was ploughing with an ox and an ass, and sowing salt. Ulysses immediately stayed the plough to save his child; by which being discovered, he was compelled to go to the wars. For this, and for other reasons, Ulysses hated Palamedes, and artfully contrived his death.—See infra, b. iv.

And I am persuaded that I also shall have the attestation of the time to come, as well as of that which is past already, that I never wronged any man, or made him more depraved; but, contrariwise, have steadily endeavoured, throughout life, to benefit those who conversed with me; teaching them, to the very utmost of my power, and that without reward, whatever could make them wise and happy."

Saying this, he departed; the cheerfulness of his countenance, his gesture, and whole deportment, bearing testimony to the truth of what he had just declared. And seeing some of those who accompanied him weeping, he asked what it meant. And why they were now afflicted. " For, knew ye not, " said he, " long ago, even by that whereof I was produced, that I was born mortal ? If, indeed, I had been taken away when the things which are most desirable flowed in upon me abundantly, with good reason it might have been lamented, and by myself, as well as others ; but if I am only to be removed when difficulties of every kind are ready to break in upon me, we ought rather to rejoice, as though my affairs went on the most prosperously."

Apollodorus being present,—one who loved Socrates extremely, though otherwise a weak man,—he said to him, " But it grieveth me, my Socrates ! to have you die so unjustly !" Socrates, with much tenderness, laying his hand upon his head, answered, smiling, " And what, my much-loved Apollodorus ! wouldst thou rather they had condemned me justly ?"

It is likewise related, that on seeing Anytus pass by, " There goes a man," said he, " not a little vain-glorious, on supposing he shall have achieved something great and noble, in putting me to death, because I once said, ' that since he himself had been dignified with some of the chief offices in the city, it was wrong in him to breed up his son to the trade of a tanner.' But he must be a fool," continued Socrates, " who seeth not that he who at all times performs things useful and excellent, is alone the hero. And, truly," added Socrates, " as Homer makes some, who were near the time of their dissolution, look forward into futurity ; I, likewise, have a mind to speak somewhat oraculously. Now it happened I was once, for a short time, with this same son of Anytus ; and plainly perceiving he neither wanted talents

nor activity, therefore I said, it was not fitting that the young man should continue in such a station : but continuing, as he still doth, destitute at the same time of any virtuous instructor, to guide and restrain him within the bounds of duty, he must soon fall a prey to some evil inclination, that will hurry him headlong into vice and ruin."

And, in thus speaking, Socrates prophesied not untruly ; for the young man delighted so much in wine, that he ceased not drinking, whether night or day ; whereby he became perfectly useless to his country, to his friends, and even to himself. The memory of Anytus was likewise held in the highest detestation ; [4] and that not only on the account of his other crimes, but for the scandalous manner in which he had educated his son.

Now, it cannot be doubted but Socrates, by speaking thus highly of himself, incurred the more envy, and made his judges still the more eager to condemn him ; yet I think, indeed, he only obtained that fate which the gods decree to those they most love ;—a discharge from life, when life is become a burthen ; and that by a means, of all others, the most easy. Yet here, as well as on every other occasion, Socrates demonstrated the firmness of his soul. For, although he was fully persuaded that to die would be the best for him, yet did he not discover any anxious solicitude, any womanish longings for the hour of his dissolution ; but waited its approach with the same steady tranquillity, and unaffected complacency, with which he afterwards went out of life. And, truly, when I consider the wisdom and greatness of soul, so essential to this man, I find it not more out of my power to forget him, than to remember and not praise him. And if, among those who are most studious to excel in virtue, there be any who hath found a person to converse with, more proper than Socrates for promoting his design,—verily, we may well pronounce him the most fortunate of all mankind.

[4] The Athenians soon became sensible of the mischief they had done in putting Socrates to death ; and so hated the authors of it, that they would not suffer any of them to light fire at their hearths : they would not answer them a question : they would not bathe with them : and if they were seen to touch ever so large a vessel of water, they threw it away as impure : till, at last, these men, unable to bear this usage any longer, hanged themselves.—*Plo.* in *Phæd.*

XENOPHON'S

MEMOIRS OF SOCRATES.

BOOK I.

CONTENTS OF BOOK I.

XENOPHON'S

MEMOIRS OF SOCRATES.

BOOK I.

I. I HAVE often wondered by what arguments the accusers of Socrates could persuade the Athenians that he had behaved in such a manner towards the republic as to deserve death; for the accusation proferred against him was to this effect:

"Socrates is criminal; inasmuch as he acknowledgeth not the gods whom the republic holds sacred, but introduceth other and new deities.—He is likewise criminal, because he corrupteth the youth."

Now, as to the first of these, that he acknowledged not the gods whom the republic held sacred,—what proof could they bring of this, since it was manifest that he often sacrificed both at home and on the common altars? Neither was it in secret that he made use of divination; it being a thing well known among the people, that Socrates should declare his genius gave him frequent intimations of the future; whence, principally, as it seems to me, his accusers imputed to him the crime of introducing new deities. But, surely, herein Socrates introduces nothing newer, or more strange,[1] than any other, who, placing confidence in divination, make use of auguries,[2] and omens,[3] and symbols,[4] and sacrifices.[5] For these men suppose not that the birds or persons they meet unexpectedly, know what is good for them: but that the gods by their means, give certain intimations of the future, to those who apply themselves to divination.

---

[1] The sense of this passage, together with the notes which here follow upon the several particulars contained in it, were obligingly given me by one not more known for his learning, than esteemed for his candour and benevolence,—Mr Harris of Salisbury.

[2] Auguries. In Greek Οἰωνοι, which originally signifying birds, was, by metaphor, taken to signify that discovery of futurity to which birds were supposed instrumental.

[3] Omens. In Greek Φήμαι, voices; either declarations of the gods, by express words of their own, heard in temples, groves, and other places; or incidental expressions dropt by human beings, who, without intending it themselves, were supposed to be made channels of divine communications. Thus, when Paulus Æmilius was just returned from the senate, when the conduct of the war with the Macedonian king Perses had been decreed to his care, he found his little daughter Tertia in tears. On his tenderly kissing her, and demanding the cause; "My dear father," says she, "poor Persia is dead." Persia (according to the Latin idiom for Perses) was the name of her lap-dog. The father, eagerly embracing her, cries out, "Accipio omen, mea filia."—My child, I seize the omen. Æmilius soon after went, and Perses was conquered. Cic. de Divinat. lib. i. cap. 46. According to this idea of the word omen, the old etymologists very properly inform us, that it was originally written "oremen quod fit ex ore," as being a method of divination which proceeds from the mouth.

[4] Symbols. In Greek Σύμβολα, or Σύμβολοι, signs, symbols, or external types, by which something else more latent was signified; on the explanation of which depended the skill of the diviner. Thus, from Cicero, in the same tract above quoted, we learn, that when king Midas was a child, the ants, as he was sleeping, filled his mouth with grains of corn; and that when Plato was sleeping in his cradle, the bees came and seated themselves on his lips. These symbols were explained to foretell the future riches of the first, and the future eloquence of the latter.—Cic. de Div. lib. i. cap. 36.

[5] Sacrifices. In Greek Θυσίας. The inspection of the entrails of victims, and the divination thence deduced, are too well known to need explanation.

And the same also was his opinion, only with this difference, that while the greatest part say they are persuaded, by the flights of birds, or some accidental occurrence, Socrates, on the contrary, so asserted concerning these matters, as he knew them from an internal consciousness; declaring it was his genius,from whom he received his information. And, in consequence of these significations, (communicated, as he said, by his genius,) Socrates would frequently forewarn his friends what might be well for them to do, and what to forbear; and such as were guided by his advice found their advantage in so doing, while those who neglected it had no small cause for repentence. [1]

Now, who is there that will not readily acknowledge, that Socrates could have no desire to appear to his friends either as an enthusiast or arrogant boaster? which, however, would have been unavoidable, had he openly asserted that notices of the future had been given him by the Deity; while a failure in the event made the falsehood of the assertion notorious to all. Wherefore, it is manifest Socrates foretold nothing but what he firmly believed would, hereafter, be fulfilled:—But where could he place this full confidence, exclusive of a deity; and how could one, who thus confided, be said to acknowledge no gods?

Farther:—although Socrates always advised his followers to perform the necessary affairs of life in the best manner they were able; yet, with regard to every thing, the event whereof was doubtful, he constantly sent them to consult the oracle, whether it ought or ought not to be undertaken. He likewise asserted, that the science of divination was necessary for all such as would govern successfully either cities or private families: for, although he thought every one might choose his own way of life, and afterwards, by his industry, excel therein;

whether architecture, mechanics, agriculture, superintending the labourer, managing the finances, or practising the art of war; yet even here, the gods, he would say, thought proper to reserve to themselves, in all these things, the knowledge of that part of them which was of the most importance; since he, who was the most careful to cultivate his field, could not know, of a certainty, who should reap the fruit of it. He who built his house the most elegantly, was not sure who should inhabit it. He who was the best skilled in the art of war, could not say, whether it would be for his interest to command the army: neither he who was the most able to direct in the administration, whether for his to preside over the city. The man who married a fair wife, in hopes of happiness, might procure for himself a source of much sorrow; and he who formed the most powerful alliances, might come in time, by their means, to be expelled his country. Socrates therefore, esteemed all those as no other than madmen, who, excluding the Deity, referred the success of their designs to nothing higher than human prudence. He likewise thought those not much better who had recourse to divination on every occasion, as if a man was to consult the oracle whether he should give the reins of his chariot into the hands of one ignorant or well versed in the art of driving; or place at the helm of his ship a skilful or unskilful pilot. He also thought it a kind of impiety to importune the gods with our inquiries concerning things of which we may gain the knowledge by number, weight, or measure; it being, as it seemed to him, incumbent on man to make himself acquainted with whatever the gods had placed within his power: as for such things as were beyond his comprehension, for these he ought always to apply to the oracle; the gods being ever ready to communicate knowledge to those whose care had been to render them propitious.

Socrates was almost continually in men's sight. The first hours of the morning were usually spent in the places set apart for walking, or the public exercises; and from thence he went to the forum, at the time when the people were accustomed to assemble. The remainder of the day was passed where might be seen the greatest concourse of the Athenians; and for the most part, he so discoursed, that all who were willing might hear whatsoever he said: yet no one ever observed Socra-

[1] As an instance of this, it is said, that after the defeat of the Athenians, at the battle of Delium, he told Alcibiades, and those who were with him, "that he had just received intimations from his genius, that they should not take the same road the greatest part of their broken forces had taken, but turn into some other." By which means those who paid regard to his admonitions escaped: while the rest, being overtaken by a party of the enemy's horse, were either killed on the spot or made prisoners. Neither doth this, or any of the like instances, oppose the opinion of those who say Socrates' genius was nothing more than sound judgment or reason, free from all the warpings and mists of passion; improved by experience and a careful observation of nature and things. Cornelius Nepos called prudence a kind of divination.

tes either speaking or practising any thing impious or profane; neither did he amuse himself, like others, with making curious researches into the works of Nature; and finding out how this, which sophists call the world, had its beginning, or what those powerful springs which influence celestial bodies. On the contrary, he demonstrated the folly of those who busied themselves much in such fruitless disquisitions; asking, whether they thought they were already sufficiently instructed in human affairs, that they undertook only to meditate on divine? Or, if passing over the first, and confining their inquiries altogether to the latter, they appeared, even to themselves, to act wisely, and as became men. He marvelled they should not perceive, it was not for man to investigate such matters; for those among them who arrogated the most to themselves, because they could with the greatest facility talk on these subjects, never agreed in the same opinion; but like madmen, some of whom tremble when no danger is near, while others fear no harm at the approach of things hurtful: so these philosophers; some of them asserting there was no shame in saying or doing any thing before the people; others sending their disciples into solitude, as if nothing innocent could be performed by us in public: some regarding neither temples nor altars, nor reverencing any thing whatsoever as divine; while others thought nothing could be found too vile for an object of their adoration. Even among those who laboriously employed themselves in studying the universe, and the nature of all things, some imagined the whole of being to be simply one only; others, that beings are in number infinite: some, that all things are eternally moving; others, that nothing can be moved at all: some, that all things are generated and destroyed; others, that there can never be any generation or destruction of any thing.[2]

He would ask, concerning these busy inquirers into the nature of such things as are only to be produced by a divine power, whether as those artists who have been instructed in some art, believe they are able to practise it at pleasure, so they, having found out the immediate cause, believe they shall be able, for their own benefit, or that of others, to produce winds and rain, the vicissitudes of time, or the change of seasons? Or if indeed altogether destitute of this hope, they could content themselves with such fruitless knowledge?

In this manner would he reason concerning those people who gave themselves up to such useless speculations. As for himself, man, and what related to man, were the only subjects on which he chose to employ himself. To this purpose, all his inquiries and conversation turned upon what was pious, what impious; what honourable, what base; what just, what unjust; what wisdom, what folly; what courage, what cowardice; what a state or political community, what the character of a statesman or politician; what a government of men,[3] what the character of one equal to such government. It was on these, and other matters of the same kind, that he used to dissert; in which subjects, those who were knowing he used to esteem men of honour and goodness; and those who were ignorant, to be no better than the basest of slaves.[4]

That the judges of Socrates should err concerning him, in points wherein his opinion might not be apparently manifest, I marvel not; but that such things as had been spoken plainly, and acted openly, should have no weight with them, is indeed wonderful; for, being of the senate, and having taken, as was customary, the senatorial oath, by which he bound himself to act in all things conformable to the laws, and arriving in his turn to be president of the assembly of the people,[5] he boldly refused to

---

2 This passage, with the following note upon it, together with note 3, were given to the translator by Mr Harris.

In this passage Socrates has reference to the speculations, partly physical, partly metaphysical, of the philosophers who lived before him, and whose writings now are either wholly lost, or only preserved in fragments by Aristotle, Cicero, Simplicius, &c. The names of these ancient sages were Melissus, Parmenides, Anaxagoras, Heraclitus, Democritus, &c. It would be superfluous in this place to say any thing concerning their opinions, the diversity among them is sufficiently set forth by our author, and it is on this diversity rests the force of his argument.

3 He speaks here of the government of men in contradistinction to that of brutes, as practised over sheep by shepherds, over cattle by herdsmen, over horses by horsemen. The brutes are all considered as irrational, but man as rational. See this matter finely illustrated by Xenophon, in the beginning of his Cyropædia.

4 Epictetus confines the study and inquiries of men to yet narrower bounds; for he says,—" As the subject-matter of a carpenter, is wood; of a statuary, brass; so of the art of living, the subject-matter is, each person's own life."—But the more enlarged scheme of Socrates seems more amiable, as more just.

5 Epistate.

3 U

give his suffrage to the iniquitous sentence which condemned the nine captains,[1] two of whom were Erasmides and Thrasellus, to an unjust death; being neither intimidated with the menaces of the great, nor the fury of the people, but steadily preferring the sanctity of an oath to the safety of his person; for he was persuaded the gods watched over the actions and the affairs of men in a way altogether different to what the vulgar imagined; for while these limited their knowledge to some particulars only, Socrates, on the contrary, extended it to all; firmly persuaded, that every word, every action, nay, even our most retired deliberations, were open to their view;[2] that they were every where present, and communicated to mankind all such knowledge as related to the conduct of human life: wherefore, I greatly wonder the Athenians could ever suffer themselves to be persuaded that Socrates retained sentiments injurious to the Deity! He in whom nothing was ever observed unbecoming that reverence so justly due to the gods; but, on the contrary, so behaved towards them, both in regard to his words and his actions, that whoever shall hereafter demean himself in such a manner, must be in fact, and ought also to be esteemed, a man of the truest and most exemplary piety.

II. But it is still matter of more wonder to me, that any one could be prevailed on to believe that Socrates was a corrupter of youth! Socrates, the most sober and the most chaste of all mankind! supporting with equal cheerfulness the extreme, whether of heat or cold![3] who shrunk at no hardships, declined no labour, and knew so perfectly how to moderate his desires, as to make the little he possessed altogether sufficient for him! Could such a one be an encourager of impiety, injustice, luxury, intemperance, effeminacy? But, so far from any such thing, that on the contrary he reclaimed many from these vices, by kindling in their minds a love of virtue; encouraging them to think, that by a steadfast perseverance they might make themselves esteemed by becoming virtuous men: and although he never undertook to be a teacher of others, yet, as he practised the virtues he sought to recommend, those who conversed with him were animated with the hopes of becoming one day wise, from the influence of his example. Not that Socrates ever omitted a due concern for his body; neither did he commend those who did: he would even frequently blame the people whose custom it was to eat to excess, and afterwards use immoderate exercise; saying, that men should only eat till nature was satisfied, and then apply themselves to some moderate exercise; which would not only keep the body in health, but set the mind at liberty for the more proper discharge of its peculiar duties.

In his apparel nothing was either delicate or ostentatious; and the same might be said with respect to his whole manner of living: yet no man ever became avaricious from having conversed with Socrates: on the contrary, many were reclaimed from this infamous vice by his example, as they had been already from many others; while they observed him not only to forbear the taking any reward of those who sought his conversation, but heard him earnestly contend it was necessary to do so, for any one who desired to avoid slavery: for such, he would say, as submit to receive a pecuniary return for the instructions they bestow, are no longer at liberty to give, or withhold them; but, like so many slaves, are at the will of those from whom they are content to receive wages: therefore he much admired, that the man who professed himself a teacher of virtue, should debase himself so far; unless he either understood not, that to gain a virtuous friend was the greatest of all acquisitions; or at least feared, that such as had been made wise and virtuous by his instructions, might yet be wanting in gratitude to their greatest benefactor.

But, far from any such absurdity, Socrates,

---

1 The crime alleged against these men was, their not having taken care to pay the last rites to the dead after a sea-fight with the Lacedæmonians, though they could plead in excuse for the not doing it, the being prevented by a violent storm. Socrates, notwithstanding Theramenes, one of his followers and friends, had preferred the accusation, opposed it strongly; and when called upon to put the judgment in writing, as his office required him, he told them at first he was unacquainted with the law-terms; and at last absolutely refused to do it.

2 "When you have shut your door," saith Epictetus, "and darkened your room, remember never to say you are alone: for God is within, and your genius is within, and what need they of light to see what you are doing?"—Carter's Epic.

3 It was his custom never to drink on his return from his exercises, till after having poured abroad the first bucket of water, though ready to die with thirst and heat; and this, as he said, to exercise his patience, and accustom his sensual appetites the better to obey his reason.

without setting himself up for an instructor, had full confidence, that all who attended to his discourses, and embraced his doctrines, would never fail in point of friendship, either to him or to each other:—How then could a man like this, be a corrupter of youth; unless, haply, the study of virtue should be the way to corrupt the morals, and incline mankind to become more dissolute?

But, say his accusers, "Socrates makes those who converse with him contemners of the laws; calling it madness to leave to chance the election of our magistrates; while no one would be willing to take a pilot, an architect, or even a teacher of music, on the same terms; though mistakes in such things would be far less fatal than errors in the administration." With these, and the like discourses, he brought (as was said) the youth by degrees to ridicule and contemn the established form of government; and made them thereby the more headstrong and audacious.

Now, it seemeth to me, that whoever applies himself to the study of wisdom, in hopes of becoming one day capable of directing his fellow-citizens, will not indulge, but rather take pains to subdue whatever he finds in his temper of turbulent and impetuous; knowing that enmity and danger are the attendants on force; while the path of persuasion is all security and good-will: for they who are compelled hate whoever compels them, supposing they have been injured; whereas we conciliate the affection of those we gain by persuasion; while they consider it as a kindness to be applied to in such a manner. Therefore it is only for those to employ force who possess strength without judgment; but the well-advised will have recourse to other means. Besides, he who pretends to carry his point by force, hath need of many associates; but the man who can persuade, knows that he is of himself sufficient for the purpose: neither can such a one be supposed forward to shed blood; for, who is there would choose to destroy a fellow-citizen, rather than make a friend of him, by mildness and persuasion?

"But," adds his accuser, "Critias and Alcibiades were two of his intimate friends; and these were not only the most profligate of mankind, but involved their country in the greatest misfortunes; for, as among the thirty none was ever found so cruel and rapacious as Critias; so, during the democracy, none was so audacious, so dissolute, or so insolent, as Alcibiades."

Now I shall not take upon me to exculpate either of these men; but shall only relate at what time, and, as I think, to what end, they became the followers of Socrates.

Critias and Alcibiades were, of all the Athenians, by nature the most ambitious; aiming, at what price soever, to set themselves at the head of the commonwealth, and thereby exalt their names beyond that of any other: they saw that Socrates lived well satisfied with his own scanty possessions; that he could restrain every passion within its proper bounds, and lead the minds of his hearers, by the power of his reasoning, to what purpose he most desired. Understanding this, and being such men as we have already described them, will any one say it was the temperance of Socrates, or his way of life, they were in love with; and not rather, that by hearing his discourses, and observing his actions, they might the better know how to manage their affairs, and harangue the people?

And, truly, I am thoroughly persuaded, that if the gods had given to these men the choice of passing their whole lives after the manner of Socrates, or dying the next moment, the last would have been preferred, as by much the most eligible. And their own behaviour bears sufficient testimony to the truth of this assertion; for, no sooner did they imagine they surpassed in knowledge the rest of their contemporaries, who, together with themselves, had attended on Socrates, but they left him, to plunge into business and the affairs of the administration; the only end they could propose in desiring to associate with him.

But, perhaps, it may be objected, that Socrates ought not to have discoursed with his followers on the affairs of government, till he had first instructed them how to behave with temperance and discretion. Far am I from saying otherwise, and shall only observe, that it is commonly the practice with those who are teachers of others, to perform in the presence of their pupils the things they would recommend; to the end, that while they enforced them on their minds, by the strength of their reasonings, they might set forth, by their example, the manner in which they are done.

Now, with respect to either of these methods of instruction, I know not of any who went beyond Socrates; his whole life serving as an example of the most unblemished integrity; at the same time that he ever reasoned with a peculiar force and energy, on virtue and those several duties which are becoming us as men. And it is certain, that even Critias and Alcibiades themselves behaved soberly and wisely all the time they conversed with him; not that they feared punishment; but as supposing a regular conduct would best serve the end they had in view.

Nevertheless, I know there are many who value themselves on the account of their philosophy; who allow not that a virtuous man can ever be any other than virtuous, but that he who is once temperate, modest, just, must always remain so; because the habits of these virtues being deeply imprinted, cannot afterwards be erased out of the minds of men. But I hold not this opinion; for, as the body from disuse may come in time to be deprived of all its powers, so the mental faculties may lose all their energy, through a neglect of their being exerted duly, and the man no longer able to act, or not act in the manner that best becomes him. Therefore fathers, although otherwise well assured of the good disposition of their children, forget not to warn them against the company of ill men; knowing, that as to converse with the good must exercise and improve every virtue, so to associate with the bad must prove no less pernicious and baneful. And to this purpose also the poet:[1]

" Although unconscious of the pleasing charm,
The mind still bends where friendship points the way;
Let virtue then thy partner's bosom warm,
Lest vice should lead thy soften'd soul astray."

And that other:

" In the same mind, now good, now bad, prevail."

And with these do I agree; for as we may observe people who have learnt verses soon forget them, if not frequently repeated, so will it prove with regard to the precepts of philosophy; they slip out of the memory, and along with them we lose the very ideas which kindled and nourished in our souls the love of virtue; which ideas once gone, no wonder if the practice of it ceases soon after. I have observed farther, that such men as are hurried

away with an inordinate love, whether of wine or women, become less capable of attending to what will be for their advantage, or refraining from what is to their harm; so that it hath often happened, that many, who before were remarkable for their economy, no sooner became slaves to one or other of these passions, but all things went to ruin; and having squandered away their substance, were compelled, through want, to submit to such offices as they themselves had once thought shameful. How then shall we say, that he who is once temperate cannot become intemperate? or that he who acts uprightly at one time, cannot at another act the very contrary? For myself, I am persuaded that no one virtue can subsist that is not diligently and duly exercised, and temperance more especially; because our sensual desires, being seated with our minds in the same body, are continually soliciting us to a compliance with those appetites nature hath implanted, though at the expense of virtue and all things virtuous; wherefore I can well imagine that even Alcibiades and Critias could restrain their vicious inclinations while they accompanied with Socrates and had the assistance of his example: but being at a distance from him, Critias retiring into Thessaly, there very soon completed his ruin, by choosing to associate with libertines rather than with such as were men of sobriety and integrity; while Alcibiades, seeing himself sought after by women of the highest rank, on account of his beauty; and at the same time much flattered by many who were then in power, because of the credit he had gained, not only in Athens, but with such as were in alliance with her; in a word, perceiving how much he was the favourite of the people, and placed, as it were, above the reach of a competitor, neglected that care of himself which alone could secure him; like the athletic, who will not be at the trouble to continue his exercises, on seeing no one near able to dispute the prize with him. Therefore, in such an extraordinary concurrence of circumstances as befell these men, puffed up with the nobility of their birth, elated with their riches, and inflamed with their power, if we consider the company they fell into, together with their many unhappy opportunities for riot and intemperance, can it seem wonderful, separated as they were from Socrates, and this for so long a time too, if at length they became altogether degenerate, and

1 Theognis.—The character of this poet is, " that he rescued poetry from trifling and useless subjects, to employ it in the service of virtue and goodness." He was born in the 39th Olympiad.

☞ This elegant translation was given me by a kind friend.

rose to that height of pride and insolence to which we have been witnesses?

But the crimes of these men are, it seems, in the opinion of his accuser, to be charged upon Socrates; yet allows he no praise for keeping them within the bounds of their duty in that part of life which is generally found the most intemperate and untractable; nevertheless, on all other occasions, men judge not in this manner. For what teacher of music, or any other art or science, was ever known to incur censure, because the scholar, whom he had well instructed, forgot all he had been taught, when placed under the care of some other master? Or what father would condemn those companions of his son with whom the first years of his life had been spent innocently, because afterwards he had been drawn aside into riot and debauchery by associating himself with very different people? Will he not rather bestow the greater praise on the one by how much more he sees his son hath been corrupted by the other? Even parents themselves are not blamed for the faults of their children, though educated under their own eye, provided they are careful not to set before them any ill example.

Here, then, is the test whereby to have tried Socrates: " Hath his life been wicked? let him be considered, and condemned, as a wicked man : but, if otherwise, if he hath steadily and invariably persevered in the paths of virtue, accuse him not of crimes which his soul never knew."

" Yet it may be he countenanced those vices in others which in his own person he chose not to commit."

But far from Socrates were all such compliances! On the contrary, when Critias was insnared with the love of Euthydemus, he earnestly endeavoured to cure him of so base a passion; showing how illiberal, how indecent, how unbecoming the man of honour, to fawn, and cringe, and meanly act the beggar; before him, too, whom of all others he the most earnestly strove to gain the esteem of, and, after all, for a favour which carried along with it the greatest infamy. And when he succeeded not in his private remonstrances, Critias still persisting in his unwarrantable designs, Socrates, it is said, reproached him in the presence of many, and even before the beloved Euthydemus; resembling him to a swine, the most filthy and disgusting of all animals. For this cause Critias hated him ever after; and when one of the Thirty, being advanced, together with Charicles, to preside in the city, he forgot not the affront; but, in order to revenge it, made a law, wherein it was forbidden that any should teach philosophy in Athens :[2] by which he meant, having nothing in particular against Socrates, to involve him in the reproach cast by this step on all the philosophers, and thereby render him, in common with the rest, odious to the people; for I never heard Socrates say that he taught philosophy; neither did I know any who ever did hear him; but Critias was stung, and he determined to show it.—Now, after the Thirty had put to death many of the citizens, and some of them of the best rank,[3] and had given up the reins to all manner of violence and rapine, Socrates had said somewhere " that it would astonish him much, if he who lost part of the herd every day, while the rest grew poorer and weaker under his management, should deny his being a bad herdsman; but it would astonish him still more, if he who had the charge of the city, and saw the number of his citizens decrease hourly, while the rest became more dissolute and depraved under his administration, should be shameless enough not to acknowledge himself an evil ruler." These words, therefore, of Socrates, being told to Critias and Charicles, they sent for him; and showing him the law, straitly forbade him to discourse any more with the young men. Socrates then asked, " if it was permitted him to propose some questions touching some parts of the said law, which he said he could not thoroughly understand;" and being answered it was permitted : " I am always," said he, " most ready to obey the laws; but, to the end I may not transgress unwittingly, inform me, I pray you, whether you take philosophy, as it stands here condemned by you, to consist in reasoning right, or reasoning wrong; since, if you intend it to imply the first, then must we henceforth beware how we reason right; but if the latter is meant, the consequence is plain, then must we endeavour to mend our reasoning."

---

2 This law was again abrogated upon the expulsion of the thirty tyrants.—See *Potter's Grecian Antiquities*, vol. i. chap. 25.

3 It is said, that the number of those put to death by these tyrants was fourteen hundred,—and this without the least form of law,—besides five thousand, who were driven into banishment.

At these words Charicles, being much enraged, said to him, " Since you are so ignorant, Socrates, and withal so dull of apprehension, we will express ourselves in terms somewhat more easy to be understood ; refrain altogether from talking with the young men."

" It is well," answered Socrates ; " but that nothing of ambiguity may remain in the present case, tell me, I pray you, how long are men called young ?"

" So long," replied Charicles, " as they are refused admittance into the senate, as supposed not yet arrived at maturity of judgment : or, in other words, till they are thirty."

" But suppose I should want to buy something of a merchant, must I not ask the price of it if the man is under thirty ?"

" Who says any such thing ?" returned Charicles. " But, Socrates," said he, " it is so much your custom to ask questions when you are not ignorant of the matter in hand, that I do not wonder at your doing so now. Let us, however, have done for the present with your trifling interrogatories."

" But what if some young man, as he passes along, should ask me in haste, ' Where lives Charicles ? where's Critias gone ?' Must I not answer him ?"

" It is hardly intended to prohibit such things," returned Charicles : when Critias interrupting them ; " And I, Socrates, I can inform thee of something more thou hast to refrain from : keep henceforth at a proper distance from the carpenters, smiths, and shoemakers ; and let us have no more of your examples from among them. And, besides, I fancy they are sufficiently tired with your bringing them in so often in your long discourses."

" Must I likewise give up the consequences," said Socrates, " deducible from these examples, and concern myself no longer with justice and piety, and the rules of right and wrong ?"

" Thou must, by Jupiter !" replied Charicles. " And, Socrates," said he, " to make all sure, trouble not thyself any more with the herdsmen, for fear thou shouldst occasion the loss of more cattle." [1]

Now, from this, it is evident, that what Socrates once said concerning the cattle, being told these men, had greatly inflamed their rage against him. Hence also may be seen how long Critias continued to associate with Socrates, and what the affection they had for each other. I might here likewise add, how seldom it is we make proficiency under people who are not pleasing to us ; and that the conversation of Socrates did not render him so either to Critias or Alcibiades, may well be supposed. Even at the very time they followed him, their chief delight was in conversing with such persons as they believed the most skilful in the affairs of state ; their only design being to govern the republic. And, agreeably to this, they tell us that Alcibiades, when under the age of twenty, coming to Pericles his tutor, and at that time sole director of the Athenian state, entered into the following conversation with him concerning the laws :

" My Pericles," said he, " can you explain to me what a law is ?" " Undoubtedly," returned the other. " Then, I conjure you by the immortal gods !" said Alcibiades, " instruct me in this point : for when I hear men praised for their strict observance of the laws, it seems to me evident, that he can no way pretend to that praise who is altogether ignorant what a law is."

" Your request," my Alcibiades, " is not difficult to be complied with : for that is a law, which the people agree upon in their public assemblies, and afterwards cause to be promulgated in a proper manner ; ordaining what ought or ought not to be done."

" And what do they ordain ; to do good, or to do evil ?"

" Not evil, most assuredly, my young man."

" But what do you call that," said Alcibiades, which in states where the people have no rule, is advised and ordained by the few who may be then in power ?"

" I call that likewise a law," replied Pericles ; " for the laws are nothing but the injunctions of such men as are in possession of the sovereign authority."

" But when a tyrant is possessed of this

---

1 Some understand this as referring to a certain coin in use among the Athenians, whereon was stamped the figure of an ox, as if Charicles had threatened Socrate... ...nt there are others, and seemingly ... think that Charicles aimed his ... than wealth of Socrates, when

he thus turns his own words upon him, and bids him take care " that he himself does not occasion the loss of more cattle." It seems a witticism, too, well suiting such a man.

sovereign authority, are the things he ordains to be received as laws?"

" As laws," returned Pericles.

" What then is violence and injustice?" said Alcibiades. " Is it not when the strong compel the more weak, not by mildness and persuasion, but force, to obey them?"

" I think it is."

" Will it not then follow, that what a tyrant decrees, and compels the observance of, not only without, but contrary to the will of the people; is not law, but the very reverse to it?"

" I believe it may," answered Pericles; "for I cannot admit that as a law, which a tyrant enacts, contrary to the will of the people."

" And when the few impose their decrees on the many, not by persuasion, but force, are we to call this also violence?"

" We are: and truly, I think," said Pericles, " that whatever is decreed and enforced without the consent of those who are hereafter to obey, is not law, but violence."

" Then ought that also, which is decreed by the people, contrary to the will of the nobles, to be deemed violence, rather than law?"

" No doubt of it," replied Pericles : " But, my Alcibiades," continued he, " at your age we were somewhat more acute in those subtilties, when we made it our business to consider them, as we now see you."

To which, it is said, Alcibiades returned answer: " Would to the gods then, my Pericles, I might have conversed with you at the time when you best understood these sorts of things!" In consequence, therefore, of this most ambitious disposition, no sooner did these men suppose they had acquired some advantages over the persons then employed in the administration, but they forbore to associate any longer with Socrates : for, besides that his company was no way pleasing to them, on other considerations, they could still less brook his frequent remonstrances for the many irregularities of their lives : therefore they plunged at once into business, and the affairs of the commonwealth ; the only end for which they had ever been among his followers.

But Crito, Chærephon, Chærecrates, Simmias, Cebes, Phædo, and many others, were continually with him ; not from the hope of becoming, by his means, better orators, whether at the bar, or before the people ; but better men : capable of discharging all those duties which they owed to themselves, to their country, to their families, their friends, their fellowcitizens. And, so far were these men from practising what was dishonest, that whether in youth or in age, not one of them ever incurred even the suspicion of any crime.

But, saith his accuser, " Socrates encourageth his followers to despise their parents ; inasmuch as he persuadeth them that he is able to make them wiser than they ; declaring still farther, that as it is lawful for a son to confine his father in chains when convicted of madness, so ought the ignorant also to be confined by him who is possessed of superior knowledge."

Now, whatever his accuser might endeavour to insinuate, it is certain Socrates was very far from being of such an opinion. On the contrary, it was common with him to say ; " that whoever pretended to confine another on the account of his ignorance, might himself be thus treated by those who were still more knowing.' And, to this purpose, he would often discourse on the essential difference between madness, and ignorance ; saying, on such occasions, plainly and clearly ; " that it was indeed necessary, and for the benefit of himself, as well as his friends, that the madman should be enchained ; but, that he who was ignorant in any thing useful, should only be instructed, by such persons as were qualified to give him proper instruction."

His accuser, however, went on to assert, " that Socrates not only taught the youth to have a contempt for their parents, but for the rest of their kindred ; since he would frequently declare, that when men were sick, or had a lawsuit upon their hands, they had not recourse to any of their kindred for relief ; but to the lawyer in one case, and the physician in the other. And, with regard to friendship, he would likewise say, " that a useless good-will, unaccompanied with the power of serving,,was little to be accounted of ; but the man to be esteemed and preferred, should be one who not only knows what is for our advantage, but can so explain it as to make us likewise know it ; thereby insinuating, as was pretended, into the minds of the youth, that he himself was the friend to be chosen before any other, as being the best able to direct in the way of wisdom : while the rest of mankind, in comparison with him, were of small estimation.

Now, that I myself have heard him talk after some such manner, concerning relations, fathers, and friends, is most certain. And I remember him saying, "that when the soul, in which thought and reason alone reside, retires from the body, although it may be the body of a father, or a friend, we remove it from our sight as speedily as well may be. And whereas no man can be doubted as to the love he beareth to his own body, yet who is there, would he ask, that scruples to take away from it the part that is superfluous? to cut the hair, or pair the nails; or remove the whole limb, when mortified? for which purpose the surgeon is called in, and the steel and the caustic not only readily submitted to, but the hand which applies them liberally rewarded. The spittle, he would say, men were glad to cast from them, because, remaining in the mouth, it was both useless and offensive. But, notwithstanding all this, Socrates never intended, though he talked in such a manner, that fathers were to be buried alive, or that he himself should have a limb taken off; but he intended to let us see, that whatever is useless can be of no estimation; in order to excite in his hearers a desire to improve, and make themselves, as far as may be, serviceable to others; to the end, that if they wished to be regarded by their parents, or respected and honoured by their brethren or kindred, they might urge their claim on the account of merit, and not owe the whole only to consanguinity." "But," says his accuser, "Socrates, the better to convey, and at the same time conceal the malignity of his intentions, hath chosen many passages from our most celebrated poets, whereby to convey his poison to the people, and dispose them the more readily to fraud and oppression;" for having often cited that line of Hesiod's,

"Employ thyself in any thing, rather than stand idle,"

it was pretended he meant to insinuate it as the poet's opinion, "that no employment whatever could be unjust or dishonourable from whence profit might arise:" whereas, in truth, nothing could be farther from the design of Socrates: for, although he constantly maintained that labour and employment were not only useful, but honourable, and idleness no less reproachful than pernicious to man; yet he never concluded without saying, "that he alone could be considered as not idle who was employed in procuring some good to mankind; but that the gamester, the debauchee, and every other whose end was only evil, were emphatically to be called so; and, in this sense, he

might, with good reason, adopt that line of Hesiod's,

"Employ thyself in any thing, rather than stand idle."

But it was still farther alleged, that Socrates frequently introduced these lines of Homer, where, speaking of Ulysses, he says,

"Each prince of name, or chief in arms approved,
He fired with praise, or with persuasion moved:
'Warriors like you, with strength and wisdom blest,
By brave examples should confirm the rest:'

"But if a clamorous vile plebeian rose,
Him with reproof he check'd, or tamed with blows:
'Be still, thou slave, and to thy betters yield;
Unknown alike in council and in field!'"   Pope.

These words, it was said, he would explain in such a manner, as if the poet hereby meant to recommend roughness, severity, and stripes, as the only proper arguments to be made use of against the vulgar and the indigent. But Socrates was not absurd enough to draw such conclusions; for how then could he have complained, if he himself had been rudely treated? But he asserted, and might strengthen his assertion with these lines from Homer, "that such as could neither counsel nor execute, equally unfit, whether for the city or the camp, these, and such as these, and more especially when insolent and unruly, ought to be reduced to reason, without any regard to the extent of their possessions."

And it is certain nothing more could be intended; for as to himself, Socrates loved the people: his benevolence even extended to all mankind; insomuch that, although he was sought after by foreigners as well as Athenians, he took no reward from any who applied to him, but freely imparted that wisdom he was endued with. Yet so did not others. On the contrary, many who were become rich by his liberality, sold at no mean price, but a small part of that which had cost them nothing: while, uninfluenced by his example, and bearing no resemblance to him in affection to the people, they refused to converse with any who were not able to pay, and that largely, for their instruction.

And, indeed, by this conduct Socrates had rendered the city of Athens renowned throughout all Greece; so that, if it was said of Lychas the Lacedæmonian, "that he was the glory of Sparta," because he entertained, at his own expense, the strangers who resorted thither at one of the feasts made in honour of Apollo, much rather might be said of Socrates, "that he was the glory of Athens," whose whole life was one continued largess; and who, dispensing with a liberal hand his inestimable treasure, sent no one ever away from him without making him, if willing, a wiser and a happier man. Wherefore, it should seem, that had Socrates been treated by the Athenians according to his merit, public honours would have been decreed him much rather than a shameful death. And, after all, for whom do the laws appoint this punishment? Is it not for the thief? for the assaulter on the highway? for the underminer of walls, and the committer of sacrilege? But where, among mankind, shall we find any one at so great a distance from any of these crimes as Socrates? Who can accuse him of holding intelligence with the common enemy? of spreading sedition and treason throughout the city? or of having been the cause of any one calamity whatsoever? Where is he who, in private life, can say, "Socrates hath defrauded me of my possessions, or hath injured me in any kind?" Nay, when did he incur even the suspicion of any of these things? And as to the points whereof he stood accused, could he be a denier of those very gods whom in so eminent a manner he worshipped? Could he be a corrupter of youth, whose only employment was to root out of the mind of man every vicious inclination, and plant in their stead a love of that virtue, which is so amiable in itself, and so becoming us as men, and which alone hath the power to make, whether cities or private families, flourishing and happy? This being so, who seeth not how much his country stood indebted to Socrates? and that honours, not ignominy, should have been his reward?

III. Now, as I am persuaded the benefit arising to all those who accompanied with Socrates was not less owing to the irresistible force of his example than to the excellency of his discourses, I will set down whatever occurs to my memory, whether it relates to his words or his actions.

And first, with respect to sacred rites and institutions. In these things it was ever his practice to approve himself a strict observer of the answer the Pythian priestess gives to all who inquire the proper manner of sacrificing to the gods, or paying honours[1] to their deceased ancestors: "Follow," saith the god, "the custom of your country:" and therefore Socrates, in all those exercises of his devotion and piety, confined himself altogether to what he saw practised by the republic; and to his friends he constantly advised the same thing, saying, it only savoured of vanity and superstition in all those who did otherwise.

When he prayed, his petition was only this —"That the gods would give to him those things that were good." And this he did, forasmuch as they alone knew what was good for man. But he who should ask for gold or silver, or increase of dominion, acted not, in his opinion, more wisely than one who should pray for the opportunity to fight, or game, or any thing of the like nature, the consequence whereof being altogether doubtful, might turn, for aught he knew, not a little to his disadvantage. When he sacrificed, he feared not his offering would fail of acceptance in that he was poor; but, giving according to his ability, he doubted not, but, in the sight of the gods, he equalled those men whose gifts and sacrifices overspread the whole altar. And, indeed, he made no scruple to assert, that it would not be agreeable to the nature of the gods to respect the costly offerings of the rich and the great, whilst the poor man's gift was altogether disregarded. For by this means it might happen, nor yet unfrequently, that the sacrifice of the wicked would find the most acceptance: which, if so, he thought life itself would not be desirable to a reasonable creature. But Socrates always reckoned upon it as a most indubitable truth, that the service paid the Deity by the pure and pious soul, was the most grateful sacrifice; and therefore it was, he so much approved that precept of the poet, which bids us "offer to the gods according to our power." And not only on these, but on every other occasion, he thought he had no better advice to give his friends, than "that they should do all things according to their ability." Farther,

<hr>

[1] These honours consisted of sacrifices, libations, and various other rites and ceremonies, and were performed on the 9th and 30th days after burial, and repeated when any of their friends arrived who had been absent from the solemnity; and upon all other occasions which required their surviving relations to have the deceased in memory. On these public days it was the custom to call over the names of their dead relations, one by one, excepting such as died under age, or had forfeited their title to this honour by dissipating their paternal inheritance, or for some other crime.—*Pott. Antiq.*

whenever he supposed any intimation had been given him by the Deity concerning what ought or ought not to be done, it was no more, possible to bring Socrates to act otherwise, than to make him quit the guide, clear sighted and well instructed in the road he was to go, in favour of one not only ignorant but blind. And to this purpose he always condemned the extreme folly of those, who, to avoid the ill opinion and reproach of men, acted not according to the direction of the gods; looking down with contempt on all the little arts of human prudence, when placed in competition with those divine notices and admonitions which it is oftentimes their pleasure to communicate to man.

As to his manner of living, it may be said, that whoever is willing to regulate and discipline his body and his mind after the example of Socrates, can hardly fail, no deity opposing, to procure for himself that degree of health and strength as cannot easily be shaken. Neither shall he want large sums for such a purpose. On the contrary, such was his moderation, that I question whether there ever was any man, if able to work at all, but might have earned sufficient to have supported Socrates. His custom was to eat as long as it gave him any pleasure; and a good appetite was to him what delicious fare is to another: and as he only drank when thirst compelled him, whatever served to allay it could not fail of being grateful. So that it was easy for him, when present at their feasts, to refrain from excess, which other men find so much difficulty in doing. And as to such persons as gave proof how very little they could command themselves, to these he would counsel even the not tasting of those delicacies which might allure them to eat when they were not hungry, and drink when they were not dry; since the fruits (he said) of so doing were not only pains in the head and loss of digestion, but disorder and confusion in the mind of man. And it was frequent with him to say, between jest and earnest, " that he doubted not its being with charms like these that Circe turned the companions of Ulysses into swine; while the hero himself, being admonished by Mercury, and, from his accustomed temperance, refusing to taste the enchanting cup, happily escaped the shameful transformation."

With regard to love, his counsel always was to keep at a distance from beautiful persons; saying, it was difficult to approach any such and not be ensnared. As for himself, his great continence was known to every one; and it was more easy for him to avoid the most beautiful objects, than for others those who were the most disgusting. But although this was the manner in which Socrates lived, yet could he not be persuaded that he enjoyed less of the pleasures of life than the voluptuous man, who employed all his thoughts in the eager pursuit of them; at the same time that he escaped all that vexation and grief so sure to attend on those who too freely indulge in sensual gratifications.

IV. Now, should there be any inclined to believe what some on conjecture have undertaken to advance, both in their conversations and writings, " that Socrates could indeed inflame his hearers with the love of virtue, but could never influence them so far as to bring them to make any great proficiency therein:" let these, I say, consider what his arguments were, not only when his design was to refute such men as pretended to know every thing, but even in his retired and familiar conversation, and then let them judge whether Socrates was not fully qualified for the bringing his followers and his friends to make proficiency in the paths of virtue.

And, for this purpose, I will now relate the manner in which I once heard him discoursing with Aristodemus, surnamed the Little, concerning the Deity. For, observing that he neither prayed nor sacrificed to the gods, nor yet consulted any oracle, but, on the contrary, ridiculed and laughed at those who did, he said to him:

" Tell me, Aristodemus, is there any man whom you admire on account of his merit?"

Aristodemus having answered, " Many."—" Name some of them, I pray you."

" I admire," said Aristodemus, " Homer for his epic poetry, Melanippides for his dithyrambics, Sophocles for tragedy, Polycletes for statuary, and Xeuxis for painting."

" But which seems to you most worthy of admiration, Aristodemus;—the artist who forms images void of motion and intelligence; or one who hath the skill to produce animals that are endued, not only with activity, but understanding?"

" The latter, there can be no doubt," replied Aristodemus, " provided the production was not the effect of chance, but of wisdom and contrivance."

" But since there are many things, some of

which we can easily see the use of, while we cannot say of others to what purpose they were produced; which of these, Aristodemus, do you suppose the work of wisdom?"

" It should seem the most reasonable to affirm it of those, whose fitness and utility is so evidently apparent."

" But it is evidently apparent, that He, who at the beginning made man, endued him with senses because they were good for him; eyes, wherewith to behold whatever was visible; and ears, to hear whatever was to be heard. For say, Aristodemus, to what purpose should odours be prepared, if the sense of smelling had been denied? Or why the distinctions of bitter and sweet, of savoury and unsavoury, unless a palate had been likewise given, conveniently placed, to arbitrate between them, and declare the difference? Is not that Providence, Aristodemus, in a most eminent manner conspicuous, which, because the eye of man is so delicate in its contexture, hath therefore prepared eyelids like doors, whereby to secure it; which extend of themselves whenever it is needful, and again close when sleep approaches? Are not these eyelids provided, as it were, with a fence on the edge of them, to keep off the wind and guard the eye? Even the eyebrow itself is not without its office, but, as a penthouse, is prepared to turn off the sweat, which, falling from the forehead, might enter and annoy that no less tender than astonishing part of us! Is it not to be admired that the ears should take in sounds of every sort, and yet are not too much filled by them? That the fore-teeth of the animal should be formed in such a manner as is evidently best suited for the cutting of its food, as those on the side for grinding it in pieces? That the mouth, through which this food is conveyed, should be placed so near the nose and the eyes, as to prevent the passing, unnoticed, whatever is unfit for nourishment; while nature, on the contrary, hath set at a distance, and concealed from the senses, all that might disgust or any way offend them? And canst thou still doubt, Aristodemus, whether a disposition of parts like this should be the work of chance, or of wisdom and contrivance?"

" I have no longer any doubt," replied Aristodemus: " and, indeed, the more I consider it, the more evident it appears to me, that man must be the masterpiece of some great artificer; carrying along with it infinite marks of the love and favour of Him who hath thus formed it."

" And what thinkest thou, Aristodemus, of that desire in the individual which leads to the continuance of the species? Of that tenderness and affection in the female towards her young, so necessary for its preservation? Of that unremitted love of live, and dread of dissolution, which take such strong possession of us from the moment we begin to be?"

" I think of them," answered Aristodemus, " as so many regular operations of the same great and wise Artist, deliberately determining to preserve what he hath once made."

" But, farther, (unless thou desirest to ask me questions), seeing, Aristodemus, thou thyself art conscious of reason and intelligence, supposest thou there is no intelligence elsewhere? Thou knowest thy body to be a small part of that wide extended earth which thou everywhere beholdest: the moisture contained in it, thou also knowest to be a small portion of that mighty mass of waters whereof seas themselves are but a part, while the rest of the elements contribute, out of their abundance, to thy formation. It is the soul then alone, that intellectual part of us, which is come to thee by some lucky chance, from I know not where. If so be, there is indeed no intelligence elsewhere: and we must be forced to confess, that this stupendous universe, with all the various bodies contained therein—equally amazing, whether we consider their magnitude or number, whatever their use, whatever their order—all have been produced, not by intelligence, but chance!"

" It is with difficulty that I can suppose otherwise," returned Aristodemus; " for I behold none of those gods, whom you speak of, as making and governing all things; whereas I see the artists when at their work here among us."

" Neither yet seest thou thy soul, Aristodemus, which, however, most assuredly governs thy body: although it may well seem, by thy manner of talking, that it is chance, and not reason, which governs thee."

" I do not despise the gods," said Aristodemus: " on the contrary, I conceive so highly of their excellence, as to suppose they stand in no need either of me or of my services."

" Thou mistakest the matter, Aristodemus; the greater magnificence they have shown in their care of thee, so much the more honour and service thou owest them."

" Be assured," said Aristodemus, " if I once

could be persuaded the gods took care of man, I should want no monitor to remind me of my duty."

"And canst thou doubt, Aristodemus, if the gods take care of man? Hath not the glorious privilege of walking upright been alone bestowed on him, whereby he may, with the better advantage, survey what is around him, contemplate with more ease those splendid objects which are above, and avoid the numerous ills and inconveniences which would otherwise befall him? Other animals, indeed, they have provided with feet, by which they may remove from one place to another; but to man they have also given hands, with which he can form many things for his use, and make himself happier than creatures of any other kind. A tongue hath been bestowed on every other animal; but what animal, except man, hath the power of forming words with it, whereby to explain his thoughts, and make them intelligible to others? And to show that the gods have had regard to his very pleasures, they have not limited them, like those of other animals, to times and seasons, but man is left to indulge in them, whenever not hurtful to him.

"But it is not with respect to the body alone that the gods have shown themselves thus bountiful to man; their most excellent gift is that soul they have infused into him, which so far surpasses what is elsewhere to be found. For by what animal, except man, is even the existence of those gods discovered, who have produced, and still uphold, in such regular order, this beautiful and stupendous frame of the universe? What other species of creatures are to be found that can serve, that can adore them? What other animal is able, like man, to provide against the assaults of heat and cold, of thirst and hunger? That can lay up remedies for the time of sickness, and improve the strength nature hath given by a well-proportioned exercise? That can receive, like him, information and instruction; or so happily keep in memory what he hath seen, and heard, and learnt? These things being so, who seeth not that man is, as it were, a god in the midst of this visible creation; so far doth he surpass, whether in the endowments of soul or body, all animals whatsoever that have been produced therein! For, if the body of the ox had been joined to the mind of man, the acuteness of the latter would have stood him in small stead,

while unable to execute the well-designed plan; nor would the human form have been of more use to the brute, so long as it remained destitute of understanding! But in thee, Aristodemus, hath been joined to a wonderful soul, a body no less wonderful: and sayest thou, after this, 'the gods take no thought for me!' What wouldst thou then more to convince thee of their care?"

"I would they should send, and inform me," said Aristodemus, "what things I ought or ought not to do, in like manner as thou sayest they frequently do to thee."

"And what then, Aristodemus? supposest thou, that when the gods give out some oracle to all the Athenians, they mean it not for thee? If, by their prodigies, they declare aloud to all Greece,—to all mankind,—the things which shall befall them, are they dumb to thee alone? And art thou the only person whom they have placed beyond their care? Believest thou they would have wrought into the mind of man a persuasion of their being able to make him happy or miserable, if so be they had no such power? or would not even man himself, long ere this, have seen through the gross delusion? How is it, Aristodemus, thou rememberest, or remarkest not, that the kingdoms and commonwealths most renowned as well for their wisdom as antiquity, are those whose piety and devotion have been the most observable? and that even man himself is never so well disposed to serve the Deity, as in that part of life when reason bears the greatest sway, and his judgment supposed in its full strength and maturity. Consider, my Aristodemus, that the soul which resides in thy body can govern it at pleasure; why then may not the soul of the universe, which pervades and animates every part of it, govern it in like manner? If thine eye hath the power to take in many objects, and these placed at no small distance from it, marvel not if the eye of the Deity can, at one glance, comprehend the whole! And as thou perceivest it not beyond thy ability to extend thy care, at the same time, to the concerns of Athens, Egypt, Sicily; why thinkest thou, my Aristodemus, that the providence of God may not easily extend itself throughout the whole universe? As, therefore, among men, we make best trial of the affection and gratitude of our neighbour, by showing him kindness; and discover his wisdom, by consulting him in our distress; do thou, in like manner, behave towards the gods: and, if thou wouldst experience what their wisdom, and what their love, render thyself deserving the communication of some of those divine secrets which may not be penetrated by man; and are imparted to those alone, who consult, who adore, who obey the Deity. Then shalt thou, my Aristodemus, understand there is a being whose eye pierceth throughout all nature, and whose ear is open to every sound; extended to all places; extending through all time; and whose bounty and care can know no other bounds than those fixed by his own creation!"

By this discourse, and others of the like nature, Socrates taught his friends that they were not only to forbear whatever was impious, unjust, or unbecoming before men; but even, when alone, they ought to have a regard to all their actions; since the gods have their eyes continually upon us; and none of our designs can be concealed from them.

V. And now, if temperance be a virtue conducing to the honour and happiness of man, let us see in what manner Socrates endeavoured to stir up his followers to the practice of it.

"My fellow-citizens! would he say, when war is declared, and it becomes necessary for you to make choice of a general, choose ye the man enslaved to wine or women; luxurious in his diet; intemperate in his sleep; incapable of labour; impatient of fatigue? Can ye, from such a one, expect safety to yourselves; or conquest over your enemies? Or, when death draweth nigh, and no thought remaineth but for the welfare of your children, do ye then inquire for the debauchee wherewith to intrust them? Is it he who must direct in the virtuous education of your sons, and guard the chastity of your virgin daughters; or secure to them the inheritance from the hand of the oppressor? Do ye intrust your flocks or your herds to the conduct of him who is overcharged with drunkenness? or expect from such a one despatch to your affairs? Would even the slave be received, though sent as a gift, who came to us branded with so loathsome a vice? If, therefore, intemperance appears to us so odious when seen only in the slave, how should we dread the being ourselves degraded by it! The rapacious and covetous have the pleasure of growing rich, and add to their own substance what they take from others: but the dissolute man injures his neighbour without profit to himself; nay, he injures every one, and himself most of all, if the ruin of his family, his health, his body, and his mind, may be termed injuries? Neither can such a one add to the pleasures that arise from social conversation: for what pleasure can he give whose only delight is in eating and drinking, and, destitute of shame, prefers the company of the common prostitute to that of his best friend? Hence, therefore, we may see how necessary it is to make temperance our chief study; since, without this as its basis, what other virtue can we attain? How can we learn what is profitable, or practise what is praiseworthy? Neither can we conceive a state more pitiable, whether in respect to body or mind, than the voluptuary, given up to all the drudgery of intemperance. And, certainly, we should wish no worthy man may be encumbered with a slave of this disposition: or, however, we are sure all slaves who abandon themselves to such irregularities ought to entreat the gods that they may fall into the hands of mild and gentle masters,—their only chance to save them from utter ruin."

Thus would Socrates talk concerning temperance; and if the whole tenor of his discourse showed his regard for this virtue, the whole tenor of his life served more abundantly to confirm it. For he was not only superior to the pleasures of sense, but the desire of gain: it being his full persuasion, that the man who received money bought himself a master; whose commands, however humbling, could not honestly be rejected.

VI. It may not be improper, nor yet to the discredit of Socrates, to relate a conversation he had with Antipho the sophist. [1] Now this man, having a design to draw to himself the followers of Socrates, came to him one day, and, in the presence of many of them, accosted him as follows:

"I always thought," said he, "that philo-

---

1 These were a sort of men, who, as Socrates says, pretended to know, and teach every thing: geometry, arithmetic, astronomy, natural philosophy, eloquence, politics, &c. Their promises, however, always ended in giving some slight superficial notions of these several sciences; and they exercised their disciples chiefly in idle disputations, whereby they might learn to defend whatever they had a mind to affirm. Those who studied under them, were filled with pride, and vain conceit of their own abilities; while the sophist, on his side, regarded nothing but his own gain: and it is said, that one Protagoras, although there were at that time many others of them in Greece, accumulated by this profession ten times the sum that Phidias, the famous statuary, could ever gain by his trade.

sophy served to make men happier; but the fruit of your wisdom, Socrates, seems to be the very reverse: for I know not that slave who would tarry with his master a single day, if compelled to live in the manner that you do. You eat and drink the meanest of every thing. Your habit is not only coarser than others, but you make no difference between summer and winter; and your feet are always naked. You will take no money, though we find no little pleasure in accumulating wealth: and besides, when a man hath once made his fortune, he hath nothing more to do than to live nobly, and go on at his ease. Now, if all who attend to your instructions are to follow your example, as is commonly the case of pupils with their masters, may we not well say you only teach men how to be miserable?"

To which Socrates: " I perceive, Antipho, you have formed to yourself so woeful a picture of my manner of life, as shows you had much rather die than live as I do: let us therefore examine what it is you are so much afraid of. You think I am to be pitied for not taking money: is it because those who do, are no longer masters of their own time, but must perform their engagements, however contrary to their inclinations; while I am at liberty to talk or not talk, as best suits my humour? The manner in which I eat may not be to your mind: Doth my dinner afford less nourishment than yours? doth it cost more? or is it, do you think, more difficult to procure? And though I allow the things they provide for your table may be more delicious than those on mine, consider, Antipho, he who sits down with a good appetite hath no want of rich sauce to give a relish to his food: neither will he wish for the high-flavoured wine, who hath already with delight quenched his thirst with water. As to my habit: You know, Antipho, he who changes his dress, doth it on account of the heat or cold; and puts on shoes only that the ruggedness of the road may not prevent his passing it: but tell me, I desire you, when hath the cold kept me within doors? or where did you see me contend for the shade, to avoid the scorching heat of the sun? or, when was I hindered by the anguish of my feet from going wherever my fancy led me? Besides, you cannot but know many, whose constitution being naturally weak, have brought themselves by the force of exercise to bear labour and fatigue far better than those of a more robust make, who through indolence and sloth have shamefully neglected it. Why then should you not suppose that I, who have always accustomed myself to bear with patience whatever might fall to my lot, may do it at present with somewhat more ease than you, Antipho, who, perhaps, have not so much as once thought of the matter? If I am observed to be not over delicate in my diet, if I sleep little, nor once taste of those infamous delights which others indulge in, assign no other cause than my being possessed of pleasures in themselves far more eligible, which delight not alone for the moment in which they are enjoyed, but gladden with the hope of yielding perpetual satisfaction. Now, you must have remarked, Antipho, that people who doubt their affairs go ill, are never cheerful; while those who think they are in the way to succeed, whether in agriculture, traffic, or whatever it may be, are happy as if they had already succeeded. But suppose you there can arise from any of these a pleasure equal to what the mind experiences while it is conscious of improving in the paths of virtue, and sees the wise and the good add to the number of its friends? Yet these are the purposes to which I think I employ myself; and this, the reward I have for my labour! Besides, should we suppose our friends or our country wanting assistance, who would be judged the best able to bestow it; he, Antipho, who lives as I do? or he who engaged in that course of life which seems to you so very delightful? Or, when called on to bear arms, which would you think the most likely to discharge the duty of a good soldier; he who sits down dissatisfied to his table unless loaded with delicacies, however difficult to be obtained; or he who is not only content, but rises well pleased from whatever is set before him? And if the city is besieged, which will be the first to advise the surrendering it up to the enemy? It should seem your opinion, Antipho, that happiness consisted in luxury and profusion; whereas, in truth, I consider it as a perfection in the gods that they want nothing; and consequently, he cometh the nearest to the divine nature, who standeth in want of the fewest things: and seeing there is nothing which can transcend the divine nature, who ever approacheth the nearest thereto, approaches the nearest to sovereign excellence."

At another time, Antipho disputing with him, said, "I am willing to acknowledge you a just man, Socrates, but surely not a man of much knowledge; and of this you seem to be yourself aware, since you refuse to receive any reward for your instructions. Now it is certain you would not give your house, or even your cloak, for nothing; nay, nor for less than the full worth of them; yet you will talk, it is well known, for a whole day gratis;—a plain proof how the case stands with you. Now it is for this very reason I commend your honesty, that will not suffer you, through desire of gain, to deceive any; but then you must give up all pretences to knowledge, since you hereby declare you have none worth purchasing."

To which Socrates:—" You know, Antipho, that among us it is imagined there is no small similarity between beauty and philosophy; for that which is praiseworthy in the one, is so likewise in the other; and the same sort of vices are apt to blemish both. Now, when we see a woman bartering her beauty for gold, we look upon such a one as no other than a common prostitute; but she who rewards the passion of some worthy youth with it, gains at the same time our approbation and esteem. It is the very same with philosophy: he who sets it forth for public sale, to be disposed of to the best bidder, is a sophist, a public prostitute. But he who becomes the instructor of some well-disposed youth, and makes thereby a friend of him, we say of such a one, he discharges as he ought the duty of a good citizen. And besides, Antipho, as there are some who delight in fine horses, others in dogs, and others in other animals, my pleasure is in the company of my friends. If I know any thing whereby they may at all be profited, I communicate it to them, or recommend them to those whom I think better qualified for carrying them on in the paths of virtue. When we are together, we employ ourselves in searching into those treasures of knowledge the ancients have left us: we draw from the same fountains; and running over whatever these sages have left behind them, where we find any thing excellent, we remark it for our use; and think ourselves not to have profited a little, when we see mutual love begin to flourish among us."

Thus did Socrates reply: and truly, when I have heard him talk in this manner, I could not doubt of his being a happy man; nor yet of his kindling in the minds of his hearers an ardent love for that virtue which in him appeared so amiable.

Being asked at another time by the same man, "Why he, who fancied himself so able to make skilful statesmen of others, did not himself engage in state affairs?"—" And by which of these methods," said Socrates, " supposest thou I shall most advantage the commonwealth? taking on me some office, which, however well executed, would only be the service of one man; or, by instructing all I meet, furnish the republic with many good citizens, every one capable of serving it well ?" [1]

VII. And now let us examine, whether, by dissuading his friends from vanity and arrogance, he did not excite them to the practice of virtue. It was his custom to assert, " that the only way to true glory, was for a man to be really excellent, not affect to appear so:" and to show this the more plainly, he would often make use of the following example: " Let us suppose," said he, " that one altogether ignorant in music desires to be thought an excellent musician. To this purpose he takes care to imitate whatever is imitable in those who are the greatest proficients in the art. He is uncommonly curious in the choice of his instruments; and a crowd must follow him, to cry him up for a wonder wherever he goes, as they do the most admired masters; but for all this, he must never venture the public with a specimen of his skill, lest his ignorance, as well as arrogance, should instantly appear, and ridicule, not fame, prove the reward of his ill-judged expenses. The case," he would say, " is the same with the man who endeavours to pass for an able general, or a good pilot, without knowing any thing of the matter. If his word is not taken, he is displeased; if it is, what will become of him when called to preside at the helm, or command the army? what but shame

---

[1] Epictetus talks to the same purpose concerning his cynic philosopher, but in terms somewhat more haughty than the humble Socrates. "Ask me, if you please, too, whether a cynic will engage in the administration of the commonwealth? What commonwealth do you inquire after, blockhead, greater than what he administers? Whether he will harangue among the Athenians about revenues and taxes, whose business is to debate with all mankind; with the Athenians, Corinthians, and Romans equally; not about taxes and revenues, or peace and war, but about happiness and misery, prosperity and adversity, slavery and freedom. Do you ask me, whether a man engages in the administration of the commonwealth who administers such a commonwealth as this ?"—*Carter's Epic.*

to himself, and perhaps ruin to his best friends, can possibly be the result of the vain undertaking? Neither will he who foolishly affects the character of valiant, or rich, or strong, be exposed to less danger. By the help of some false appearance he may be called, indeed, to some honourable employment; but it is an employment exceeding his abilities to perform; and his mistakes will not be pardoned by those whom he imposed on. For as the man can be deemed no other than a cheat who refuseth to return the money, or the cloak, which, through his fair demeanor, hath been lent him by his neighbour, much rather ought he to be stigmatized as such, who, destitute of every talent necessary for the purpose, shall dare impose himself on the state, as one well qualified to direct in the administration."

Thus Socrates endeavoured to make vanity and ostentation the more odious to his followers, by showing clearly how much folly attended the practice of it.

XENOPHON'S

MEMOIRS OF SOCRATES.

BOOK II.

CONTENTS OF BOOK II.

XENOPHON'S

MEMOIRS OF SOCRATES.

BOOK II.

I. It is likewise my opinion that Socrates contributed not a little by his discourses to make his followers more patient of hunger, and thirst, and labour; contemn heat and cold; despise sleep; with every other sensual gratification. For hearing that one of them lived too effeminately, he asked him, saying, "Suppose now, Aristippus, the education of two young men was submitted to your direction; the one intended to bear rule in the state, the other to obey; what method would you take with them? Shall we examine the matter, and begin with their food?"

"It will be right to do this, most certainly," replied Aristippus, "since food seems to be the support of life."

"It is probable then," said Socrates, "that you will accustom them both to eat and drink at certain stated hours?"

"Most probably."

"But which would you teach to relinquish this stated hour of repast when urgent business called him away from it?"

"He whom I intend for sovereignty, most assuredly, that the affairs of the commonwealth may not suffer from delay."

"And the power of enduring thirst patiently, ought not this likewise to be added?"

"Certainly."

"And which of these would you accustom to rise early and go to rest late, or pass, when necessary, whole nights in watching? which to subdue even love itself, with every tender inclination, while fatigue and labour are not shunned, but with cheerfulness submitted to?"

"The same, no doubt of it."

"But if there is an art teaching us in what manner we may best subdue our enemies, which of these young men would you endeavour to make master of it?"

"He whom I intended for rule," replied Aristippus; "since, without this art, all the rest will be useless."

"One should suppose then," said Socrates, "that a man thus educated would not so readily fall into the snares that are laid for him, as those animals, whereof some, we know, are destroyed by their gluttony, while they rush forward, however timorous by nature, to seize the bait thrown out to allure them: others, with equal greediness, swallow down the liquor which has been prepared and set for that very purpose; and, intoxicated therewith, are easily taken; while the partridge and quail find their destruction in running too eagerly after the female's call."

Aristippus assenting to this, Socrates went on: "But is it not then most shameful, Aristippus, when men do fall into the same snares with which those foolish animals are taken? Yet so doth the adulterer. He meanly submits to be shut up like a prisoner in the chamber of the man whom he is seeking to injure. Neither the rigour of the laws, [1] nor the fear of a discovery, though sensible how many evils besides that of infamy must attend it, are sufficient to restrain him; but, regardless of the danger, and neglecting those many ra-

---

1 See Potter's Antiq. b. iv. ch. 12.

tional and creditable amusements which are still within his power, and might serve to divert him from so shameful a passion, he rushes headlong to his ruin? And can any other be said of so wretched a being, but that some fury hath possessed him?"

" So it should seem," said Aristippus.

" But," continued Socrates, " since so many, and those the most important employments of life,—as war, husbandry, and others,—are of necessity to be carried on in the open fields, from under shelter; do you not think, Aristippus, that mankind are much to blame in neglecting to inure themselves to the inclemencies of the air, and the changes of the seasons? Above all, should not he endeavour to bring himself to bear these inconveniences with patience, who expects one day to command others?"

" I believe he should."

" But if he who has thus brought himself to endure pain and inconvenience, is alone qualified for command; they who have not done this, ought never to pretend to it?"

This being granted, Socrates went on:— " Seeing then you so well perceived, Aristippus, the rank to which each of these properly belong; in which would you rather we should place you?"

" Not with those, Socrates, who are intended to command; I envy not these: and, indeed, since men are obliged to take so much pains to provide for their own wants, I see no great wisdom in undertaking to supply the wants of a whole community. For, while he who does this is forced to relinquish many of the things he most ardently desires; it will be held highly criminal, if, during his administration, any one wish of the capricious multitude remains ungratified: these behaving towards their governors exactly in the manner I do to my slaves. I expect them to prepare what I am to eat and drink, and all other necessaries; but suffer them to take no part for themselves. The people likewise require that plenty and abundance should flow in upon them from every quarter; but permit not the person, to whose care they owe this, even to taste of those indulgences he hath so amply provided for others. Such, therefore, Socrates, as are fond of employment, and have been educated in the manner you mentioned, may do very well to make governors; but, as for me, I am for a life of more ease and tranquillity?"

" Let us see then, Aristippus, which of the two leads a life of the greatest tranquillity and ease; those who govern, or they who obey? Among the nations that are known to us; in Asia, the Syrians, Phrygians, and Lydians are subject to the Persians; in Europe, the Meotians to the Scythians; and, in Africa, the Carthaginians lord it over all the rest; which of these do you take to be in the most eligible situation? Or here, in Greece, where you are placed, which seem to you the most happy; they who are possessed of the sovereign power, or those who are compelled to submit to it?"

" I do not desire to be ranked among slaves," returned Aristippus; " but there is a station equally remote from sovereignty and servitude; this is the true path of liberty; and in this I would walk, as the surest road to happiness."

" This path," replied Socrates, " which lieth so equally clear, whether of sovereignty or servitude, might perhaps be supposed to have some existence in nature, could we place it beyond the bounds of human society: But how, Aristippus, to live among men without governing or being governed? Do you not see that the strong will always oppress the weak; and compel them at last, by repeated injuries, both public and private, to fly, as it were, to slavery for refuge! If they refuse to submit willingly, their lands are ravaged, their trees cut down, their corn ruined: till, wearied out at last by oppression of every kind, they are obliged to give up the unequal combat. Also, in private life; see you not how the bold and strong trample upon such as are weak, or want courage to defend themselves?"

" I do see it," said Aristippus: " and to the end it may not fall out so with me, I confine myself to no one commonwealth, but move here and there, and think it best to be a stranger every where."

" Truly," said Socrates, " this method of providing for your safety hath something peculiar in it: and it should seem, Aristippus, that since the days of Sinnis, Sciro, and Procrustes,[1] no man hath dared to molest the traveller. What, then! those who remain continually in their own country have the laws to secure them against violence of every sort; they have their relations, their friends, their dependents, to

---

1 Famous robbers, who infested Greece in the times of Theseus, and were slain by him.

assist them; their cities are fortified; they have arms for their defence: and, to strengthen them still more, they make alliance with their neighbours: yet shall not all this secure them from falling sometimes into the snares of bad men: while you, destitute of all those various advantages; exposed continually to the many dangers, in a manner unavoidable to those who pass from one place to another; nor yet can enter that city whose very meanest inhabitant doth not surpass you in credit: you, who shall then be seen in that situation wherein all the world would wish the man whom they purposed to betray: will they then spare you, Aristippus, because you are a stranger? or, because the public faith hath been given, that neither at your entrance into, or going from the city, you shall meet with any molestation? But perhaps you think yourself of so little worth, that no one will be found willing to purchase you[1]: and in truth, Aristippus, I know not that man who would wish to have such a slave in his family, as would do nothing, and yet expect to live well. But shall we see how masters generally manage such sort of people? If their appetites and passions are very outrageous, fasting is made use of to reduce them to order. If they are inclined to take what does not belong to them, every thing valuable is kept carefully out of their way. If escape is meditated, chains shall secure them: and when inclined to be lazy, stripes are called in, to quicken their motions. And you, Aristippus, if you discovered such a slave among your domestics, in what manner would you treat him?"

"I would certainly leave no sort of severity untried," said Aristippus, "till I had brought him to better manners. But let us return to our first subject, Socrates; and tell me, if you please, wherein the happiness of sovereignty consists, which you make such account of; if pain and fatigue, and hunger and cold, and ten thousand other inconveniences, not only pave the way to it, but are afterwards the chosen portion of the man who undertakes to command others? As to my part, I see no greater difference between the strokes of the whip which we give ourselves, and those laid on by the order of another: for, if my body is to be tortured, it matters not the hand by which it is done: except that folly may also be added to the account, when the pain appears of our own procuring."

"Is it so then, Aristippus, that you perceive no difference between the things we submit to voluntarily, and those we undergo, compelled to it by some other? Now, he who through choice abstains from his food may return to his food whenever he pleases: and he who endures thirst, because he is so minded, may, when minded otherwise, as easily remove it: but the case is not the same when we have constraint to encounter. Besides, he who of his own accord engages in what may be attended with labour, hath the hopes of success to animate him in the way, and the fatigue of the chase never discourages the hunter.

"But, if the prospect of acquiring what he is in pursuit of, however worthless in itself, is sufficient to make him regard neither thirst nor hunger; what may not he, whose aim is to, procure the friendship of the good, conquer his enemies, gain the command over himself, and wisely govern his own family, benefit his friends, serve his country? Will such a one shrink at fatigue and pain? Rather, will he not court them, while they add to the delight arising from his own consciousness, and the united approbation of those who best know him? And, to show still farther how necessary labour and pain are judged for all who would perform any thing laudable; it is a maxim of those who instruct youth, to regard the exercises that are gone through with ease, or give pleasure on their first performance, as of little worth; whether in forming the body or improving the mind: whereas those which require patience, application, and labour, these are they which prepare the man for illustrious deeds and noble undertakings, as many who were excellent judges have told us; and, among the rest, Hesiod, for he speaks somewhere or other after the following manner:

"See Vice, preventing even thy wish, appears
To lead through down-hill paths and gay parterres,
Where Pleasure reigns; while Virtue, decent maid,
Retires from view in yon sequester'd shade.
Craggy and steep the way that to her leads;
Fatigue and pain, by order of the gods,
Stern sentry keep. But, if nor pain, nor toil,
Can check the generous ardour of thy soul,
Exert thy powers, nor doubt thy labour's meed;
Conquest and joy shall crown the glorious deed."[2]

---

[1] Those who fell into the hands of robbers were commonly sold by them for slaves.

[2] These lines were translated by the same hand with those of Theognis, in the first book.

Epicharmus saith likewise,

"Earn thy reward—the gods give nought to sloth."

And again,

"Seek not the sweets of life, in life's first bloom;
They ill prepare us for the pain to come!"

And the wise Prodicus is also of the same opinion; for to him is the allegory given. Now this writer tells us, to the best of my remembrance, "that Hercules having attained to that stage of life when man being left to the government of himself, seldom fails to give certain indications whether he will walk in the paths of virtue or wander through all the intricacies of vice, perplexed and undetermined what course to pursue, retired into a place where silence and solitude might bestow on him that tranquillity and leisure so necessary for deliberation, when two women, of more than ordinary stature, came on towards him. The countenance of the one, open and amiable, and elevated with an air of conscious dignity. Her person was adorned with native elegance, her look with modesty, every gesture with decency, and her garments were altogether of the purest white. The other was comely, but bloated, as from too high living. Affecting softness and delicacy, every look, every action, was studied and constrained; while art contributed all its powers to give those charms to her complexion and shape which nature had denied her. Her look was bold, the blush of modesty she was a stranger to, and her dress was contrived, not to conceal, but display those beauties she supposed herself possessed of. She would look round to see if any observed her; and not only so, but she would frequently stand still to admire her own shadow. Drawing near to the place where the hero sat musing, eager and anxious for the advantage of first accosting him, she hastily ran forward; while the person who accompanied her moved on with her usual pace, equal and majestic. Joining him, she said, ' I know, my Hercules! you have long been deliberating on the course of life you should pursue; engage with me in friendship, and I will lead you through those paths which are smooth and flowery, where every delight shall court your enjoyment, and pain and sorrow shall not once appear. Absolved from all the fatigue of business and the hardships of war, your employment shall be to share in the social plea-sures of the table, or repose on beds of down; no sense shall remain without its gratification; beauty shall delight the eye and melody the ear, and perfumes shall breathe their odours around you. Nor shall your care be once wanted for the procuring of these things: neither be afraid lest time should exhaust your stock of joys, and reduce you to the necessity of purchasing new, either by the labour of body or mind: it is to the toil of others that you alone shall owe them! Scruple not, therefore, to seize whatever seemeth most desirable;[1] for this privilege I bestow on all who are my votaries.'

" Hercules, having heard so flattering an invitation, demanded her name.—' My friends,' said she, ' call me Happiness; but they who do not love me endeavour to make me odious, and therefore brand me with the name of Sensuality.'[2]

" By this time the other person being arrived, thus addressed him in her turn:
' I also, O Hercules! am come to offer you my friendship, for I am no stranger to your high descent; neither was I wanting to remark the goodness of your disposition in all the exercises of your childhood; from whence I gather hopes, if you choose to follow where I lead the way, it will not be long ere you have an opportunity of performing many actions glorious to yourself and honourable to me. But I mean not to allure you with specious promises of pleasure, I will plainly set before you things as they really are, and show you in what manner the gods think proper to dispose them. Know therefore, young man, these wise governors of the universe have decreed, that nothing great, nothing excellent, shall be obtained without care and labour. They give no real good, no true happiness, on other terms. If, therefore, you would secure the favour of these gods, adore them. If you would conciliate to yourself the affection of your friends, be of use to them. If to be honoured and respected of the republic be your aim, show your fellow-citizens how effectually you can serve them. But if it is your ambition that all Greece shall esteem you, let all Greece share

---

1 This is finely imagined, to show how closely injustice and oppression are connected with intemperance.

2 It is hoped the having chosen to denominate this person by the word sensuality, rather than pleasure, hitherto commonly used, may be allowed, as it seemed that pleasure should always be considered, not as contrary to, but a sure attendant on virtue.

the benefits arising from your labours. If you wish for the fruits of the earth, cultivate it. If for the increase of your flocks or your herds, let your flocks and your herds have your attendance and your care. And if your design is to advance yourself by arms, if you wish for the power of defending your friends, and subduing your enemies, learn the art of war under those who are well acquainted with it; and, when learnt, employ it to the best advantage. And if to have a body ready and well able to perform what you wish from it be your desire, subject yours to your reason, and let exercise and hard labour give to it strength and agility.'

"At these words, as Prodicus informs us, the other interrupted her:—'You see,' said she, 'my Hercules, the long, the laborious road the means to lead you; but I can conduct you to happiness by a path more short and easy.'

"'Miserable wretch!' replied Virtue, 'what happiness canst thou boast of? Thou, who wilt not take the least pains to procure it! Doth not satiety always anticipate desire? Wilt thou wait till hunger invites thee to eat, or stay till thou art thirsty before thou drinkest? Or, rather, to give some relish to thy repast, must not art be called in to supply the want of appetite? while thy wines, though costly, can yield no delight, but the ice in summer is sought for to cool and make them grateful to thy palate! Beds of down, or the softest couch, can procure no sleep for thee, whom idleness inclines to seek for repose; not labour and fatigue, which alone prepare for it. Nor dost thou leave it to nature to direct thee in thy pleasures, but all is art and shameless impurity. The night is polluted with riot and crimes, while the day is given up to sloth and inactivity: and, though immortal, thou art become an outcast from the gods, and the contempt and scorn of all good men. Thou boastest of happiness, but what happiness canst thou boast of? Where was it that the sweetest of all sounds, the music of just self-praise, ever reached thine ear? Or when couldst thou view, with complacency and satisfaction, one worthy deed of thy own performing? Is there any one who will trust thy word, or depend upon thy promise; or, if sound in judgment, be of thy society? For, among thy followers, which of them, in youth, are not altogether effeminate and infirm of body? Which of them, in age, not stupid and debilitated in every faculty of the mind? While wasting their prime in thoughtless indulgence, they prepare for themselves all that pain and remorse so sure to attend the close of such a life! Ashamed of the past, afflicted with the present, they weary themselves in bewailing that folly which lavished on youth all the joys of life, and left nothing to old age but pain and imbecility!

"'As for me, my dwelling is alone with the gods and good men; and, without me, nothing great, nothing excellent, can be performed, whether on earth or in the heavens; so that my praise, my esteem, is with all who know me! I make the labour of the artist pleasant, and bring to the father of his family security and joy; while the slave, as his lord, is alike my care. In peace I direct to the most useful councils, in war approve myself a faithful ally; and I only can tie the bond of indissoluble friendship. Nor do my votaries even fail to find pleasure in their repasts, though small cost is wanted to furnish out their table; for hunger, not art, prepares it for them; while their sleep, which follows the labour of the day, is far more sweet than whatever expense can procure for idleness: yet, sweet as it is, they quit it unreluctant when called by their duty, whether to the gods or men. The young enjoy the applause of the aged, the aged are reverenced and respected by the young. Equally delighted with reflecting on the past, or contemplating the present, their attachment to me renders them favoured of the gods, dear to their friends, and honoured by their country. And when the fatal hour is arrived, they sink not, like others, into an inglorious oblivion, but, immortalized by fame, flourish for ever in the grateful remembrance of admiring posterity! Thus, O Hercules! thou great descendant of a glorious race of heroes! thus mayest thou attain that supreme felicity wherewith I have been empowered to reward all those who willingly yield themselves up to my direction.'"

"See here my Aristippus," continued Socrates, "see here the advice which, Prodicus tells us, Virtue gave the young hero. He clothes it, as you may suppose, in more exalted language than I have attempted; but it will be your wisdom if you endeavour to profit from what he hath said, and consider at present what may befall you hereafter."[3]

---

3 One would have thought this single conversation alone sufficient to have reclaimed Aristippus; but the

II. Socrates, seeing his eldest son Lamprocles enraged with his mother, spoke to him in the following manner; "Tell me, my son," said he, "did you ever hear of any who are called ungrateful?"

"Many," replied Lamprocles.

"Did you consider what gained them this appellation?"

"They were called ungrateful, because, having received favours, they refused to make any return."

"Ingratitude, then, should seem one species of injustice!"

"Most certainly."

"Have you ever examined thoroughly what this sort of injustice is? Or do you think, Lamprocles, because we are only said to be unjust when we treat our friends ill, not so when we injure our enemies; therefore we are indeed unjust when we are ungrateful to our friends, but not so when only ungrateful to our enemies?"

"I have considered it thoroughly," replied Lamprocles; "and am convinced, that to be ungrateful, is to be unjust; whether the object of our ingratitude be friend or foe."

"If then," continued Socrates, "ingratitude is injustice, it will follow, that the greater the benefit of which we are unmindful, the more we are unjust?"

"Most assuredly."

"But where shall we find the person who hath received from any one, benefits so great or so many, as children from their parents? To them it is they owe their very existence; and, in consequence of this, the capacity of beholding all the beauties of nature, together with the privilege of partaking of those various blessings which the gods have so bountifully dispensed to all mankind. Now these are advantages universally held so inestimable, that to be deprived of them exciteth our very strongest abhorrence; an abhorrence well understood, when the wisdom of the legislator made death to be the punishment of the most

atrocious crimes: rightly judging, that the terror wherewith every one beheld it, would serve the most powerfully to deter from the commission of such offences, as they saw must bring upon them this greatest of all evils. Neither shouldst thou suppose it sensuality alone which induceth mankind to enter into marriage, since not a street but would furnish with other means for its gratification: but our desire is to find out one wherewith to unite ourselves, from whom we may reasonably expect a numerous and a healthful progeny. The husband then turneth his thoughts in what manner he may best maintain the wife whom he hath thus chosen, and make ample provision for his children yet unborn; while she, on her part, with the utmost danger to herself, bears about with her, for a long time, a most painful burden. To this she imparts life and nourishment, and brings it into the world with inexpressible anguish: nor doth her task end here; she is still to supply the food that must afterward support it. She watches over it with tender affection; attends it continually with unwearied care, although she hath received no benefit from it; neither doth it yet know to whom it is thus indebted. She seeks, as it were, to divine its wants: night or day her solicitude and labour know no intermission; unmindful of what hereafter may be the fruit of all her pain. Afterward, when the children are arrived at an age capable to receive instruction, how doth each parent endeavour to instil into their minds the knowledge which may best conduce to their future well-doing! And if they hear of any better qualified than themselves for this important task, to these they send them, without regard to the expense; so much do they desire the happiness of their children!"

"Certain it is," replied Lamprocles, "although my mother had done this, and a thousand times more, no man could bear with so much ill humour."

"Do not you think it easier to bear the anger of a mother, than that of a wild beast?"

"No, not of such a mother."

"But what harm hath she done you? Hath she kicked you, or bit you, as wild beasts do when they are angry?"

"No, but she utters such things as no one can bear from any body."

"And you, Lamprocles, what have you not made this mother bear, with your continual cries and untoward restlessness! what fatigue

---

badness of his disposition, like to that of Critias and Alcibiades, prevailed over the precepts of Socrates, illustrated as they were by the beautiful picture borrowed from Prodicus. He became afterwards the founder of a sect of philosophers, whose leading tenet was, "that man was born for pleasure, and that virtue is only so far laudable as it conduces thereto." One of his disciples taught publicly, that there were no gods:—a short and easy transition from vice and sensuality to atheism.

in the day! what disturbance in the night! and what pangs when sickness at any time seized you!"

"But, however, I never did or said any thing to make her ashamed of me."

"It is well. But why, Lamprocles, should you be more offended with your mother, than people on the stage are with one another? There is nothing so injurious or reproachful that these do not often say, yet no one becomes outrageous against the man whom he hears threaten and revile him, because he well knows he intends him no real injury: but you, although you as well know that no hurt is designed you, but, on the contrary, every kindness, you fly out into rage against your mother; or, perhaps, you suppose she intended you some harm?"

"Not at all," replied Lamprocles; "I never once suspected any such matter."

"What! a mother who thus loves you! who, when you are sick, spareth no means, no pains for your recovery; whose care is to supply your every want; and whose vows to the gods are so frequent on your behalf! Is she harsh and cruel? Surely the man who cannot bear with such a mother, cannot bear with that which is most for his advantage. But tell me," continued Socrates, "doth it seem to you at all necessary to show respect or submission to any one whatsoever? Or are you indeed conscious of such a degree of self-sufficiency, as makes it needless to pay any regard, whether to magistrate or general?"

"So far from it," said Lamprocles, "I endeavour all I can to recommend myself to my superiors."

"Perhaps, too, you would cultivate the good-will of your neighbour, that he may supply you with fire from his hearth, when you want it; or yield you ready assistance, when any accident befalls you?"

"I would, most surely."

"And if you were to go a journey, or a voyage with any one, it would not be indifferent to you, whether they loved or hated you?"

"No, certainly!"

"Wretch! to think it right to endeavour to gain the good-will of these people; and suppose you are to do nothing for a mother, whose love for you so far exceeds that of any other! Surely you have forgot, that while every other kind of ingratitude is passed over unnoticed by the magistrate, those who refuse to return good offices, in any other case, being only punished with the contempt of their fellow-citizens; the man who is wanting in respect to his parents, for this man public punishments are appointed: [1] the laws yield him no longer their protection; neither is he permitted any share in the administration, since they think no sacrifice offered by a hand so impious, can be acceptable to the gods, or beneficial to man: and conclude the mind so altogether degenerate, equally incapable of undertaking any thing great, or executing any thing justly. For such, too, as neglect to perform the rites of sepulture for their parents, for these, the same punishments have been allotted by the laws: and particular regard is had to these points, when inquiry is made into the lives and behaviour of those who offer themselves candidates for any public employment. You, therefore, O my son! will not delay, if wise, to entreat pardon of the gods; lest they, from whom your ingratitude cannot be hid, should turn away their favour from you: and be you likewise careful to conceal it from the eyes of men, that you find not yourself forsaken by all who know you; for no one will expect a return to his kindness, however considerable, from him who can show himself unmindful of what he oweth to his parents."

III. Socrates having observed that Chærephon and Chærecrates, two brothers, with whom he was acquainted, were at variance, he wished very much to reconcile them to each other. To which end, meeting one of them, he said to him, "What, are you then, Chærecrates, one of those mercenary kind of people, who prefer riches to a brother, and forget that these being only inanimate things, require much vigilance and care to protect them; whereas a brother endued with reason and reflection, is able to give assistance and protection to you? And, besides, brothers are somewhat less plentiful than gold! It is strange a man should think himself injured because he cannot enjoy his brother's fortune! Why not equally complain of injury done him by the rest of his fellow-citizens, because the wealth of the whole community doth not centre in him alone? But in this case they can argue right, and easily see that a moderate fortune secured by the mutual aid of society, is much better than the riches of a whole city

---

[1] Neither was this confined to their immediate parents, but equally understood of their grandfathers, grandmothers, and other progenitors.—*Potter's Antiq.*

attended with the dangers to which solitude would expose them, yet admit not this reasoning in regard to a brother. If rich, they buy slaves in abundance to serve them: they endeavour all they can to gain friends to support them; but make at the same time no account of a brother, as if nearness in blood disqualified for friendship! But surely, to be born of the same parents, and educated in the same house, ought rather to be considered as so many powerful cements, since even wild beasts themselves show some inclination to animals they are brought up with. And besides, Chærecrates, he who hath a brother, is much more regarded than he who hath none; his enemies too will be the less forward to molest him."

"I will not deny," replied Chærecrates, "that a brother, when such as he should be, is, as you say, an inestimable treasure, and therefore we ought to bear long with one another, so far from quarrelling on every slight occasion; but when this brother fails in every particular, and is indeed the very reverse of all he ought to be, to keep on terms with such a one, is next to an impossibility."

"Your brother then, my Chærecrates, is displeasing to every one? Or are there some to whom he can make himself very agreeable?"

"Therefore he the more deserves my hatred," said Chærecrates, "because wherever he comes he fails not to make himself pleasing to others; whereas, he seems to aim at nothing but displeasing me."

"But may not this happen, Chærecrates, from your not knowing how to converse properly with a brother? As the horse, not untractable to others, becomes altogether unmanageable to the unskilful rider."

"And why should I, who well know how to return any kindness shown me either in words or actions, be supposed ignorant in what manner to behave properly to a brother? No: but when I see a man catch at every opportunity to vex and disoblige me, shall I, after this, show kindness to such a one? I cannot, Socrates; nor will I even attempt it!"

"You surprise me, Chærecrates! Suppose you had a dog who watched and defended your sheep diligently; this dog fawns and caresses your shepherds, but snarls at you whenever you come near him. What do you on this occasion? Fly out into rage? Or endeavour, by kindness, to reconcile him to you? You ᵁdge a brother, when such as he ought

to be, an invaluable treasure: you say you are not unacquainted with the arts of conciliating favour and affection, but yet are resolved to employ none of them to gain the love of Chærephon!"

"I do not believe, Socrates, I have arts sufficient to succeed in such an attempt."

"And yet I should imagine," said Socrates, "no new one necessary: practise only those you are already master of, and you will find them sufficient to regain his affection."

"If you know what these are, of favour inform me," replied Chærecrates; "for they are unknown to me."

"Suppose, Chærecrates, you wished some friend to invite you to his feast when he offered sacrifice; what means would you take to induce him thereto."

"Invite him to one of mine."

"And if you wanted him, in your absence, to manage your affairs, what then?"

"I would try what I could to engage his gratitude, by first rendering him the service I wished to receive."

"But, suppose you desired to secure for yourself an hospitable reception in some foreign country, what would you do?"

"When any of that place came to Athens, I would invite them to my house," said Chærecrates; "and would spare no pains to assist them in despatching the business they came for, that they, when I went thither, might help me in return to expedite mine."

"Is it so then!" replied Socrates; "and are you so well skilled in all the arts of conciliating favour and affection, yet know nothing of the matter? But you are afraid, Chærecrates, of making the first advances to your brother, lest it should degrade you in the opinion of those who hear it? Yet surely it ought not to be less glorious for a man to anticipate his friends in courtesy and kind offices, than get the start of his enemies in injuries and annoyance! Had I thought Chærephon as well disposed as you towards a reconciliation, I should have endeavoured to have prevailed on him to make the first advances; but you seemed to me the better leader in this affair; and I fancied success the most likely to ensue from it."

"Nay, now, Socrates," cried out Chærecrates, "you certainly speak not with your usual wisdom. What! would you have me, who am the youngest, make overtures to my brother;

when in all nations it is the undoubted privilege of the first-born to lead the way?"

"How!" replied Socrates; "is it not the custom every where for the younger to yield precedency to the elder? Must not he rise at his approach and give to him the seat which is most honourable; and hold his peace till he hath done speaking? Delay not therefore, my Chærecrates, to do what I advise: use your endeavour to appease your brother; nor doubt his readiness to return your love. He is ambitious of honour: he hath a nobleness of disposition: sordid souls, indeed, are only to be moved by mercenary motives; but the brave and liberal are ever best subdued by courtesy and kindness."

"But suppose, my Socrates, when I have acted as you advise, my brother should behave no better than he has done?"

"Should it prove so, Chærecrates, what other harm can arise to you from it, than that of having shown yourself a good man, and a good brother to one whose badness of temper makes him undeserving of your regard? But I have no apprehension of so unfavourable an issue to this matter: rather, when your brother shall see it your intention to conquer by courtesy, he himself will strive to excel in so noble a contest. As it is, nothing can be more deplorable than your present situation; it being no other than if these hands, ordained of God for mutual assistance, should so far forget their office, as mutually to impede each other: or these feet, designed by Providence for a reciprocal help, should entangle each other to the hinderance of both. But surely, it shows no less our ignorance and folly, than works our harm, when we thus turn those things into evil which were not created but for our good. And, truly, I regard a brother as one of the best blessings that God hath bestowed on us; two brothers being more profitable to each other than two eyes or two feet, or any other of those members which have been given to us in pairs, for partners and helps, as it were, to each other by a bountiful Providence. For, whether we consider the hands or feet, they assist not each other unless placed at no great distance: and even our eyes, whose power evidently appears of the widest extent, are yet unable to take in, at one and the same view, the front and the reverse of any one object whatsoever, though placed ever so near them: but no situation can hinder brothers, who live in amity, from rendering one another the most essential services."

IV. I also remember a discourse that Socrates once held concerning friendship; which I think could not but greatly benefit his hearers; since he not only taught us how we might gain friends, but how to behave towards them when gained. On this occasion he observed, "that although the generality of mankind agreed in esteeming a firm and virtuous friend an invaluable possession, yet were there very few things about which they gave themselves less trouble. They were diligent, he said, to purchase houses and lands, and slaves, and flocks, and household goods; and when purchased, would take no little pains to preserve them; but were no way solicitous either to purchase or preserve a friend, however they might talk of the advantages of having one. Nay, he had seen people, who, if they had a friend and a slave sick at the same time, would send for the physician, and try every means to recover the slave, while the friend was left to take care of himself; and, if both died, it was easy to see how each stood in their estimation. Of all their possessions this alone was neglected: they would even suffer it to be lost for want of a little attention.[1] Their estates here and there they could with readiness point out to you; but ask them of their friends, how many and what they are, and you reduce them to some difficulty. The number, though acknowledged small, is more than they can well make out to you; so little do these people concern themselves about the matter. And yet, what possession shall be placed in competition with a friend? What slave so affectionate to our persons, or studious of our interest? What horse able to render us such service? From whence, or from whom, can we at all times and

---

1 One proof we have of this want of attention, even in Pericles himself; and which possibly Socrates might have in his eye, though, out of respect to his memory, he forbore to mention it; for he suffered Anaxagoras, to whom he stood indebted for so much useful knowledge both in philosophy and politics, to be reduced to such distress, that, partly from want, and partly from vexation, he determined to starve himself to death: and having muffled up his head in his cloak, he threw himself on the ground to expect its coming. Indeed, Pericles no sooner heard of this but he flew to his assistance; begging him to live, and bewailing his own loss, in case he was deprived of so wise a counsellor. When, opening his cloak, the philosopher, in a feeble and low voice, said to him, "Ah, Pericles! they who need a lamp, do not neglect to supply it with oil!" A gentle reproof; but therefore the more piercing to an ingenuous mind.

on every occasion receive so many and such essential benefits ? Are we at a loss in our own private affairs, or in those the public have intrusted to our management ? A friend will supply every deficiency. Do we wish for the pleasure of giving assistance to some other? A friend will furnish us with the power. Are we threatened with danger? He flies to our assistance; for he not only dedicates his fortune to our service, but his life to our defence.— Do we purpose to persuade? His eloquence is ever ready to second all we say.—Are we compelled to contend? His arm is ever found among the foremost to assist us. He doubles the joy which prosperity brings, and makes the load of affliction less heavy. Our hands, our feet, our eyes, can yield us small service in comparison to that we receive from a friend; for what we are not able to do for ourselves: that which we neither see, nor hear, nor think of, when our own interest is the question, a friend will perceive, and perform for us. And yet, this friend, whilst the plant that promiseth us fruit shall be carefully cultivated, this friend we neglect to nourish and improve; though where else the tree from whence such fruit is to be found !"

V. I remember likewise another discourse of his, wherein he exhorteth his hearers to look well into themselves, and see in what estimation they might reasonably hope their friends should hold them. For, having observed one of his followers desert a friend when oppressed with penury, he thus questioned Antisthenes in the presence of the man, together with many others : "Pray, say, Antisthenes, is it allowable to value our friends as we do our slaves : for one of these we perhaps rate at five mina;[1] while we think another dear at two; these again we will give ten for; and for some, it may be, twenty; nay, it is said that Nicias, the son of Nicerates, gave no less than a whole talent[o] for one he intended to set over his mines. May we estimate our friends in the same manner ?"

"I think we may," replied Antisthenes; "for, while I know some whose affection I would purchase at no mean price, there are others whom I would scarcely thank for theirs, if I might have it for nothing. And there are, my Socrates, whose favour and friendship I

should be glad to secure, though at the expense of the last farthing."

"If this is the case," replied Socrates, "it behoves us not a little to consider of how much worth we really are to our friends ; at the same time that we use our diligence to raise our value with them as much as we can, that they may not lay us aside like useless lumber. For when I hear this man cry out, 'My friend hath deserted me;' and another complain, 'that one whom he thought most strongly attached to him, had sold his friendship for some trifling advantage,' I am inclined to ask, Whether, as we are glad to get rid of a bad slave at any rate, so we may not wish to do the same by a worthless friend? since, after all, we seldom hear of the good friend being forsaken, any more than of the good slave wanting a master."

VI. And here, on the other hand, I will relate a conversation Socrates once had with Critobulus; from whence we may learn to try our friends, and find out such as are worthy of our affection.

"Suppose," said he, "Critobulus, we wanted to choose a worthy friend, what should be our method of proceeding in this matter? Should we not beware of one much addicted to high living? to wine or women? or of a lazy disposition? since, enslaved to such vices, no man could be of use either to himself, or any other."

"Certainly."

"Suppose we met with a man whose possessions being small, he is yet most lavish in his expenses; who stands daily in need of his friend's purse, as a necessary supply for his own profusion; with whom, however, all that is lent is lost; yet, whom to refuse is most deadly to offend: Would not such a one prove rather troublesome, think you?"

"No doubt, Socrates."

"And if there was a person, provident indeed enough, but withal so covetous, as never to be content unless he hath the advantage of you on every occasion ?"

"I think of him worse than of the other."

"But what do you say to the man, Critobulus, who is so much bent on making a fortune, as to mind nothing but what serves to that end ?"

"I say, leave him to himself," returned Critobulus; "since it is sure he will never be of use to any other."

" And suppose one of so turbulent a disposition, as to be daily engaging his friends in some quarrel on his account ?"

" I would keep clear of such a one, most certainly, my Socrates."

" But what if the man were free from these defects, and had only such a sort of selfishness belonging to him, as made him always ready to receive favours, not at all solicitous about returning any ?"

" Why certainly," replied Critobulus, " no person would wish to have any thing to say to such a one. But, my Socrates," continued he, " since none of these people will serve our purpose, show me, I desire you, what sort of man he must be whom we should endeavour to make a friend of ?"

" I suppose," said Socrates, " he should be the very reverse of all we have been saying : moderate in his pleasures, a strict observer of his word, fair and open in all his dealings ; and who will not suffer even his friend to surpass him in generosity ; so that all are gainers with whom he hath to do."

" But how shall we find such a one," said Critobulus ; " or make trial of these virtues and vices, without running some hazard by the experiment ?"

" When you are inquiring out the best statuary, Critobulus, you trust not to the pretences of any, but examine the performances of all ; and conclude that he who hath hitherto excelled, gives the best grounded assurance of excelling for the future."

" So you would have us infer, Socrates, that he who hath already discharged the duties of a good friend towards those with whom he hath been formerly connected will not fail to do the same when connected with you ?"

" Undoubtedly," my Critobulus : " just as I should infer, that the groom who hath taken proper care of your horses, will do the same by mine, whenever I send him any."

" But," my Socrates, " when we have found out a man whom we judge proper to make a friend of, what means may we use to engage his affection ?"

" In the first place," returned Socrates, " we must consult the gods, whether it be agreeable to their will that we engage in friendship with him."

" But suppose the gods disapprove not of our choice, what way shall we take to obtain his favour ?"

" Not hunt him down, Critobulus, as we do hares ; nor catch him by stratagem, as we do birds ; neither are we to seize him by force, as we are wont to serve our enemies ; for it would prove an arduous task to make a man your friend in spite of inclination. To shut him up like a criminal might create aversion, but would never conciliate favour and esteem."

" But what must we do then ?"

" I have heard," said Socrates, " of certain words that have all the force in them of the most powerful charms. There are likewise other arts, wherewith such as know them seldom fail to allure to themselves whomsoever they please."

" And where can we learn these words ?" said Critobulus.

" You know the song the Syrens used to charm Ulysses ? It begins with,

" O stay, O pride of Greece, Ulysses stay !"
Pope's Odyssey.

" I do know it, Socrates. But did they not mean to detain others by these charms, as well as Ulysses ?"

" Not at all, Critobulus ; words like these are only designed to allure noble souls, and lovers of virtue."

" I begin to understand you," said Critobulus ; " and perceive the charm which operates so powerfully, is praise : but, in order to make it effectual, we must bestow it with discretion, lest ridicule should seem intended by us, rather than applause. And, indeed, to commend a man for his beauty, his strength, or his stature, who knows himself to be weak, little, and deformed, would be to incur his resentment, not conciliate his affection ; and make mankind not seek but shun our society.—But do you know of no other charms ?"

" No : I have heard, indeed, that Pericles had many, wherewith he charmed the city, and gained the love of all men."

" By what means did Themistocles procure the affection of his fellow-citizens ?"

" By no incantations, most certainly," replied Socrates ; " if you except that of serving the state."

" You would insinuate then, my Socrates, that, in order to obtain a virtuous friend, we must endeavour first of all to be ourselves virtuous ?"

" Why, can you suppose, Critobulus, that a bad man can gain the affection of a good one ?"

" And yet," said Critobulus, " I have seen many a sorry rhetorician live in great harmony with the best orator in Athens : and a general, perfectly well skilled in the art of war, shall admit others to his intimacy, who know nothing of the matter."

" But did you ever see a man, Critobulus, who had no one good quality to recommend him ;—for that is the question ;—did you ever see such a one gain a friend of distinguished abilities ?"

" I do not know I ever did. But if it is so clear, Socrates, that those who have much merit, and they who have none, can never unite together in friendship ; are the virtuous equally sure of being beloved by all the virtuous ?"

" You are led into this inquiry, my Critobulus, from observing that the great and the good, although alike enemies to vice, and equally engaged in the pursuit of glory, are so far from expressing their mutual good-will, that enmity and opposition sometimes prevail among them ; and are with more difficulty reconciled to each other, than even the most worthless and vile of all mankind. This you see, and are concerned at."

" I am so," replied Critobulus ; " and the more, as I observe this not confined to particulars, but communities : those, too, where vice finds its greatest discouragement, and virtue its best reward ; even these shall engage in hostilities against each other ! Now when I see this, my Socrates, I almost despair to find a friend ; for where shall I seek one ? Not among the vicious ; for, how can one who is ungrateful, profuse, avaricious, idle, intemperate, faithless, be a friend ? He may hate, but cannot love. Neither yet is it more possible for the virtuous and the vicious to unite in the bonds of amity ; since, what concord can subsist between those who commit crimes, and they who abhor them ? And if, after this, we are to add the virtuous ; if ambition can sow enmity among the best of men ; if these, desirous all of the highest places, can envy and oppose each other, where can friendship be found ? or where the asylum on earth for fidelity and affection ?"

" My Critobulus," answered Socrates, " we shall find it no easy matter to investigate this point. Man is made up of contrarieties. Inclined to friendship from the want he finds in himself of friends, he compassionates the sufferer ; he relieves the necessitous ; and finds complacency and satisfaction, whether his turn is to receive or confer an obligation. But as one and the same thing may be an object of desire to many ; strife, enmity, and ill-will, become thereby unavoidable : benevolence is extinguished by avarice and ambition ; and envy fills the heart, which till then was all affection ! But friendship can make its way, and surmount every obstacle, to unite the just and good. For virtue will teach these to be contented with their own possessions, how moderate soever : nay, infinitely prefer them to the empire of the world, if not to be had without hatred and contention. Assisted by this, they willingly endure the extreme of thirst and hunger, rather than injure, or bear hard on any ; nor can love itself, even when the most violent, transport them beyond the rules of decency and good order. They are satisfied with whatever the laws have allotted them : and so far from desiring to encroach on the rights of others, they are easily inclined to resign many of their own. If disputes arise, they are soon accommodated, to the contentment of each party : anger never rises so high, as to stand in need of repentance ; nor can envy once find admission into the minds of those who live in a mutual communication of their goods ; and plead a kind of right in whatever a friend possesses. Hence, therefore, we may be very sure, that virtuous men will not oppose, but assist each other in the discharge of the public offices. Those, indeed, who only aim at highest honours, and posts of the greatest power, that they may accumulate wealth, riot in luxury, and oppress the people, are too profligate and unjust to live in concord with any : but he who aspires to an honourable employment, for no other end than to secure himself from oppression, protect his friends, and serve his country ; what should hinder his uniting with those whose intentions are no other ? Would it render him less able to accomplish these designs ? Or would not his power become so much the more extensive, from having the wise and good associate in the same cause with him ? In the public games, continued Socrates, " we permit not the skilful and the strong, to unite themselves together, as knowing that in so doing they must bear away the prize in every contention : but here, in the administration of the public affairs, we have no law to forbid the honest from joining with the honest ; who are generally, too, the most able ; and on that account to be chosen rather for associates than opponents. Besides, since contentions will arise, confederates should be sought for; and the greater number will be necessary, if those who oppose us have courage and ability. For this purpose, and to make those whom we engage the more zealous in serving us, favours and good offices are to be dispensed with a liberal hand: and even prudence will direct us to prefer the virtuous, as not being many: besides, evil men are always found insatiable. But however this may be, my Critobulus, take courage; make yourself, in the first place, a virtuous man, and then boldly set yourself to gain the affection of the virtuous: and this is a chase wherein I may be able to assist you, being myself much inclined to love. Now, whenever I conceive an affection for any, I rest not till it becomes reciprocal; but, borne forward towards them by the most ardent inclination, I strive to make my company equally desirable. And much the same management will you find necessary, my Critobulus, whenever you would gain the friendship of any: conceal not, therefore, from me the person whose affection you most desire. For, as I have made it my study to render myself pleasing to those who are pleasing to me, I believe I am not ignorant of some of the arts best calculated for such a purpose."

"And I," replied Critobulus, "have long been desirous of receiving some instructions herein; and more especially if they will help me to gain the affection of those who are desirable on account of the beauty of their persons as well as the graces of their minds."

"But all compulsion is entirely excluded my scheme," continued Socrates; "and I verily believe," says he, "that the reason why all men fled the wretched Scylla, was, from her employing no other means; since we see them easily detained by the Syren's song; and, forgetful of every thing, yield themselves up to the enchanting harmony."

"Be assured, Socrates," said Critobulus, "I shall never think of taking any man's affection by storm: of favour, therefore, proceed, I beseech you, to your instructions."

"You must promise me, likewise, to keep at a proper distance, and not give way to overmuch fondness."

"I shall make no great difficulty to promise you this, Socrates, provided the people are not very handsome."

"And those who are so will be in less danger, as far less likely to suffer you than those who are more plain."

"Well, I will not transgress in this point," said Critobulus; "only let me know how I may gain a friend."

"You must permit me then," said Socrates, "to tell him how much you esteem him, and how great your desire to become one of his friends."

"Most readily, my Socrates; since I never knew any one displeased with another for thinking well of him."

"And that your observation of his virtue hath raised in you great affection of his person; Would you think I did amiss, and might hurt you in the man's opinion?"

"The very reverse, I should imagine; for I find in myself a more than ordinary affection towards those who express an affection for me."

"I may go then so far in speaking of you to those you love: but will you allow me to proceed, Critobulus, and assure them, that the sweetest pleasure you know is in the conversation of virtuous friends? That you are constant in your care of them? That you behold their honourable achievements with no less satisfaction and complacency than if you yourself had performed them, and rejoice at their prosperity in like manner as at your own? That, in the service of a friend, you can feel no weariness, and esteem it no less honourable to surpass him in generosity than your enemy in arms? By this, or something like this, I doubt not to facilitate your way to the forming of many very excellent friendships."

"But why do you ask my leave, Socrates, as if you were not at liberty to say what you please of me?"

"Not so," returned Socrates; "for I have often heard Aspasia[1] declare, that matchmakers succeed pretty well if they keep to the truth in

---

1 A person well known on the account of her eloquence and her illustrious pupils; for both Pericles and Socrates attended her lectures. Her conversation was not more brilliant than solid; uniting the symmetry arising from art, with the vehemence and warmth which flows from nature. She is generally allowed to have composed the famous Funeral Oration which Pericles pronounced with so much applause, in honour of those who fell in the Samian war. She was likewise well versed in many other parts of useful knowledge; particularly politics and natural philosophy. — *Plutarch's Life of Pericles.*

what they say of each party; whereas, if false-hood is employed, nothing but vexation can en-sue; for they who have been deceived hate one another, and those most of all who brought them together. Now, I hold this observation of Aspasia to be right, and not less to concern the point in question: and, therefore, I think I cannot urge any thing in your behalf, Cri-tobulus, which strict truth will not make good."

"Which is as much as to say," replied Cri-tobulus, "that if I have good qualities sufficient to make myself beloved, I may then have your helping hand: but, otherwise, you are not so very much my friend as to be at the trouble to feign any for me."

"And by which of these methods shall I best serve you, Critobulus? Bestowing on you some praise, which, after all, is not your due, or exhorting you to act in such a manner as may give you a just claim to it, and that from all mankind? Let us examine the matter, if you are still doubtful. Suppose I should re-commend you to the master of a ship, as a skilful pilot, and on this you were admitted to direct at the helm, must not destruction to yourself, as well as the loss of the ship, be the inevitable consequence? Or suppose I spoke of you everywhere as a great general, or able statesman, and you, on the credit of this false representation, were called to determine causes, preside in the council, or command the army, would not your own ruin be involved in that of your country? Nay, were I only to commend you as a good economist to my neighbour, and thereby procure for you the management of his affairs, and the care of his family, would not you expose yourself to much ridicule, at the same time that you were exposing him to ruin? But the surest, as the shortest way, to make yourself beloved and honoured, my Critobulus, is to be indeed the very man you wish to ap-pear. Set yourself, therefore, diligently to the attaining of every virtue, and you will find, on experience, that no one of them whatsoever but will flourish and gain strength when pro-perly exercised. This is the counsel I have to give you, my Critobulus. But, if you are of a contrary opinion, let me know it, I en-treat you."

"Far from it," replied Critobulus; "and I should only bring shame upon myself by con-·····ing you, since thereby I should contra-··· sure principles of truth and virtue."

VII. Socrates had the greatest tenderness for his friends. Had ignorance or imprudence brought them into difficulties, Socrates, by his good advice, would often set them at ease. Or, if sinking under poverty, he would pro-cure to them relief, by pressing upon others the duty of mutual assistance.

I will give some instances of his sentiments on such occasions.

Perceiving on a time a deep melancholy on the countenance of one of his friends, "You seem oppressed," said he, "Aristarchus; but impart the cause of it to your friends; they may be able to relieve you.'

"I am indeed," said Aristarchus, "oppressed with no small difficulty: for since our late troubles, many of our men being fled for shelter to the Piraeus, the women belonging to them have all poured down upon me; so that I have at present no less than fourteen sisters, and aunts, and cousins, all to provide for! Now, you know, my Socrates, we can receive no profit from our lands; for these our enemies have got into their possession: nor yet from our shops and houses in the city; since Athens hath scarcely an inhabitant left in it. Nobody to be found neither to purchase our wares; no-body to lend us money, at what interest so-ever: so that a man may as well hope to find it in the very streets as to borrow it any where. Now, what am I to do, my Socrates, in this case? It would be cruel not to relieve our re-lations in their distress; and yet, in a time of such general desolation, it is impossible for me to provide for so great a number."

Socrates having patiently heard out his com-plaint,—"Whence comes it," said he, "that we see Ceramo not only provide for a large family, but even become the richer by their very means; while you, Aristarchus, are afraid of being starved to death, because some addi-tion hath been lately made to yours?"

"The reason is plain," replied Aristarchus; "Ceramo's people are all slaves; whereas those with me are every one of them free."

"And which, in your opinion, do you rate the highest? Ceramo's slaves, or the free peo-ple your house is filled with?"

"There can be no comparison."

"But is it not then a shame," said Socrates, "that your people, who so far exceed in worth, should reduce you to beggary, whilst those with Ceramo make him a rich man?"

"Not at all," replied Aristarchus: "the

slaves with him have been brought up to trades; but those I speak of had a liberal education."

"May we be said to be masters of some trade when we understand how to make things which are useful?"

"No doubt of it."

"Is flour or bread useful?"

"Certainly."

"And clothes, whether for men or women, are they useful?"

"Who doubts it?" said Aristarchus.

"But the people with you are altogether ignorant of these things?"

"So far from it," replied Aristarchus, "that I question not their being able to perform any one of them."

"But of what are you afraid then, my Aristarchus. Nausycides with one of these can maintain himself and family; and not only so, but buy flocks and herds, and accommodate the republic with a round sum on occasion: Cyribes also supports his household in ease and affluence by making bread: Demeas, the Collytensian, his, by making cassocks: Menon, his, by making of cloaks: and the Megarensians theirs, by making of short jackets."

"That is true," interrupted Aristarchus; "for the way with these is to buy Barbarians, whom they can compel to labour: but I can do no such thing with the women who live with me; they are free, they are my relations, Socrates."

"And so, because they are free, and related to you, they are to do nothing but eat and sleep! Do you suppose, Aristarchus, that such as live in this manner are more content than others? or enjoy more happiness than they, who by their labour earn bread for their families? Suppose you that idleness and inattention can gain any useful knowledge, or preserve in the memory what hath been already gained? That they can keep the man in health, add strength to his body, and gold to his stores, or give security to what he hath already in his possession; and shall labour and industry stand him in no stead? To what purpose, I pray you, did your relations learn any thing? Did they resolve at the time to make no use of their knowledge? Or, rather, did they not intend from it some advantage to themselves, or benefit to others? Surely we give small proof of our wisdom when we thus decline all employment. For, which is most reasonable —procuring to ourselves the things that are useful, by exerting the powers which nature hath bestowed; or, with arms across, sit listless and musing, considering only the means by which others may provide for us? And verily, if I may speak my mind to you freely, I should suppose, Aristarchus, you cannot have any great love for your guests, in your present situation; nor they for you. You think them a burthen; and they perceive you think them so: and it will be well if discontent does not increase daily, till all gratitude and affection are compelled to give way. But show them once in what manner they may become useful; and you will henceforth regard them with complacency and satisfaction; while they, perceiving it, will hardly be wanting in affection to you. They will be able to look back with pleasure, not pain, on all you have done for them: and the sweet familiarity of friendship, together with all the tender charities arising from the sacred ties of consanguinity, will again be restored to your happy society! Were the employments indeed of that nature as would bring shame along with them, death itself were to be chosen rather than a subsistence so obtained: but such as they are skilled in, are, as I suppose, decent and honourable; to be performed with pleasure, since they can perform them with so much ease. Delay not then, my Aristarchus, to propose what may be of so much advantage both to them and you; and doubt not their compliance with what they must perceive to be so very reasonable."

"O heavens!" cried Aristarchus; "what truths have I now heard! But your advice, my Socrates, shall be regarded as it ought: hitherto I have been afraid to borrow money of my neighbour, as not knowing, when spent, by what means to repay it; but my scruples are now over: this moment I will buy such materials as may be wanted."

Nor did he at all cool in his resolutions. Wool, with whatever was necessary for the working of it, were sent in by Aristarchus; and each one was employed from morning to night. Melancholy gave way to continual cheerfulness; and mutual confidence took the place of that mutual suspicion, which, till then, had possessed the minds of Aristarchus and his guests. They consider him now as their generous protector; and his love for them increased in proportion to their usefulness.

Some time afterward, Aristarchus coming to see Socrates, related with much pleasure in what manner they went on : " But my guests," said he, " begin now to reproach me, for being, as they say, the only idle person in the whole family."

" Acquaint them," answered Socrates, " with the fable of the dog. You must know," continued he, " that in the days of yore, when brutes could talk, several of the sheep coming to their master, ' Is it not strange, sir !' say they to him, ' that we, who provide you with milk, and wool, and lambs, have nothing at all given us but what we can get off the ground ourselves ; while the dog there, who cannot so much as help you to one of them, is pampered and fed with the very bread you eat of ?'— ' Peace !' cries the dog, who overheard their complaint ; ' it is not without reason I am taken most care of ; for I secure you from the thief and the wolf ; nor would you, wretches ! dare to eat at all, if I did not stand sentinel, to watch and defend you.' The sheep, saith the fable, on hearing this, withdrew, convinced that the dog had reason on his side : and do you, Aristarchus, convince your guests that it is by your care they are protected from harm ; and enjoy a life of security and pleasure."

VIII. At another time, Socrates meeting his old friend Eutherus, whom he had not seen for many years, asked him, " Where he came from ?"

" From no great distance, at present," replied Eutherus. " Towards the end of our late destructive war, I returned, indeed, from a long journey ; for, being dispossessed of all the estate I had on the frontiers of Attica, and my father dying, and leaving me nothing here, I was obliged to gain a subsistence by my labour wherever I could : and thought it better to do so, than beg of any one ; and borrow I could not, as I had nothing to mortgage."

" And how long," said Socrates, " do you imagine your labour will supply you with necessaries ?"

" Not long."

" And yet age increases the number of our wants, at the same time that it lessens our power of providing for them ?"

" It does so."

" Would it not then be more advisable, my Eutherus, to seek out for some employment, which might enable you to lay up some little for old age ? What if you were to go to some wealthy citizen, who may want such a person, to assist him in gathering in his fruits ; inspect-

ing his affairs ; and overlooking his labourers ; whereby you might become a mutual benefit to each other ?"

" But slavery, my Socrates, is a thing I can ill submit to."

" Yet magistrates, Eutherus, and those who are employed in public affairs, are so far from being considered as slaves on that account, that, on the contrary, they are held in the highest estimation."

" It may be so, Socrates, but I never can bear the being found fault with."

" And yet," saith Socrates, " you will be hard set to do any one thing whose every circumstance is secure from blame. For it is difficult so to act, as to commit no error ; which yet if we could, I know of no security against the censure of ill judges : and truly I should wonder, Eutherus, if what you are at present employed about could be performed in such a manner as to escape all blame. It seems therefore to me, that all you can do, is only to take care, as far as may be, to keep clear of those people who seem glad to find fault ; and seek out such as are more candid. Which done, pursue with steadiness and alacrity whatever you undertake, but beware how you undertake any thing beyond your power. Thus will your indigence find relief, without the hazard of much blame to you. Certainty shall take the place of a precarious subsistence, and leave you to the full enjoyment of all the peaceful pleasures of old age !"

IX. I remember one day Crito complaining how difficult it was at Athens for a man who loved quiet to enjoy his fortune in security : " For," said he, " I have now several lawsuits on my hands, for no other reason, that I can guess at, but because they know I would rather pay my money than involve myself in business and perplexity."

Socrates asked, " If he kept never a dog, to defend his sheep from the wolves ?"

" I keep several," said Crito, " as you may imagine ; and they are of no small use to me."

" Why then," said Socrates, " do you not engage some person in your service, whose vigilance and care might prevent others from molesting you ?"

" So I would, my Socrates, did I not fear that this very man might, at last, turn against me."

" But wherefore should you fear this ? Are you not pretty certain, that it may be more for the interest of people to keep on good terms with you, than have you for an enemy. Believe me, my Crito, there is many a man in Athens who would think himself very much honoured by your friendship." Saying this, Archidemus came immediately into their mind; a man able and eloquent, and, withal, well versed in business; but poor, as being one of those few who are not for having whatever they can lay hands on. He loved honest men; though he would often say, nothing was more easy than to grow rich by calumny. To this man, Crito, in consequence of what Socrates had said to him, would send corn, or wool, or wine or oil, or any other produce of his estate, when they brought him those things from the country: and when he sacrificed to the gods, he sent for him to the feast, nor ever omitted any opportunity of showing respect to him. Archidemus seeing this, began to detach himself from all other dependencies, and consider Crito's house as the place that would shelter him from every want. He therefore gave himself entirely to him: and discovering that Crito's false accusers were guilty of many crimes, and had made themselves many enemies, he undertook to manage them. He therefore summoned one of them to answer for an offence, which, if proved against him, must subject him at least to a pecuniary mulct, if not to corporal punishment. The man, knowing how little he could defend his malepractices, endeavoured by every art to make Archidemus withdraw his prosecution, but to no purpose; for he would never lose sight of him till he had compelled him not only to leave Crito in peace, but purchase his own with no inconsiderable sum of money. Archidemus having conducted this affair, and many others of the same nature, successfully, Crito was thought not a little happy in having his assistance: and as the shepherds ofttimes avail themselves of their neighbour's dog, by sending their sheep to pasture near him, Crito's friends would entreat him to lend Archidemus to them. He, on his side, was glad of an opportunity to oblige his benefactor; and it was observed, that not only Crito himself, but all his friends, lived free, for the future, from any molestation. Likewise, when any reproached him with having made his court to Crito for his own interest: "And which," said he, "do you think the most shameful? serving the good who have already served you, and joining with them in their opposition to the wicked; or, confederating with the bad, assist them the more effectually to oppress the virtuous, and thereby make every honest man your enemy?"

From this time Archidemus lived in the strictest intimacy with Crito; nor did Crito's friends less honour and esteem him.

X. I remember Socrates once saying to Diodorus, "Suppose, Diodorus, one of your slaves ran away from you, would you be at any pains to recover him?"

"Yes, certainly," said the other; "and I would even go so far as to publish a reward for whoever would bring him to me."

"And if any of them were sick, you would take care of them, I imagine, and send for a physician to try to save them?"

"Undoubtedly."

"But what if a friend, something of more worth to you than a thousand slaves, were reduced to want, would it not become you, Diodorus, to relieve him? You know him for a man incapable of ingratitude; nay, one who would even blush to lie under an obligation without endeavouring to return it. You know too, that the service of him who serves from inclination—who not only can execute what you command, but of himself find out many things that may be of use to you—who can deliberate, foresee, and assist you with good counsel—is infinitely of more value than many slaves? Now good economists tell us, it is right to purchase when things are most cheap; and we can scarcely recollect the time, at Athens, when a good friend might be had for such a pennyworth."

"You are in the right," said Diodorus; therefore you may bid Hermogenes come to me."

"Not so neither," returned Socrates; "for, since the benefit will be reciprocal, it seems just as reasonable that you go to him, as he come to you."

In consequence of this discourse, Diodorus went himself to Hermogenes, and, for a small consideration, secured a valuable friend, whose principal care was to approve his gratitude, and return the kindness shown him with many real services.

XENOPHON'S

MEMOIRS OF SOCRATES.

BOOK III.

CONTENTS of BOOK III.

XENOPHON'S

MEMOIRS OF SOCRATES.

BOOK III.

We will now relate in what manner Socrates as useful to such of his friends as aimed at y honourable employment, by stirring them) to the attainment of that knowledge which one could qualify them for discharging it pro-rly.

Being told that one Dionysidorus was come) Athens, and there made public profession ' teaching the military art, Socrates from ience took occasion to address the following scourse to a young man of his acquaintance, hom he knew at that very time soliciting for ie of the principal posts in the army:— "Is not," said he, "a most scandalous thing, for ie who aims at commanding the forces of his untry, to neglect an opportunity of gaining ie instructions necessary for it? And does ; not deserve to be more severely treated, than ? who undertakes to form a statue without iving learnt the statuary's art? In time of ar, no less than the safety of the whole community is intrusted to the general : and it is in is power either to procure to it many and eat advantages, by a prudent discharge of the ities of his station, or involve his country, rough misconduct, in the very deepest distress; id therefore that man must be worthy of no nall punishment, who whilst he is unwearied his endeavours to obtain this honour, takes :tle or no thought about qualifying himself 'operly for executing a trust of such vast im-irtance."

This reasoning wrought so powerfully upon e mind of the young man, that he immediately iplied himself to the gaining of instruction.

And coming a little time after where Socrates was standing with others of his friends, Socrates, on his approach, said to them laughing, "You remember, sirs, that Homer, speaking of Agamemnon, styles him venerable. Do you not think our young man here has acquired new dignity, and looks far more respectable, now he hath learnt the art of commanding? For, as he who is a master of music, will be a master of music, though he touches no instrument; and he who hath the skill of a physician, will be a physician, though not actually employ-ed in the practice of his art: so, no doubt of it, this young man, now that he hath gained the knowledge of a general, is incontestably a general, though he never should be chosen to command the army: whereas it would be to very little purpose for an ignorant pretender to get himself elected, since this could no more make a general of him, than it would make a man a physician, to call him one. But," continued Socrates, turning towards him, "since it may fall out that some of us may command a company, or a cohort under you, inform us, I pray you, with what point your master began his instructions, that we may not be altogether ignorant of the matter?"

"With the very same point with which he ended," replied the other; "the right ordering of an army, whether in marching, fighting, or encamping."

"Surely," answered Socrates, "this is out a small part of the office of a general : for he must likewise take care that none of the ne-cessaries of war be wanting, and that his soldiers are supplied with every thing needful, as well for their health as daily subsistence. He should be diligent, patient, fruitful in expedients, quick of apprehension, unwearied in labour, mildness and severity must each have their place in him : equally able to secure his own, and take away that which belongeth to another. Open, yet reserved ; rapacious, yet profuse ; generous, yet avaricious ; cautious, yet bold ; besides many other talents, both natural and acquired, necessary for him who would discharge properly the duties of a good general. Yet I do not esteem the right disposition of an army a slight thing : on the contrary," said he, " nothing can be of so much importance ; since, without order, no advantage can arise from numbers any more than from stones, and bricks, and tiles, and timber, thrown together at random : but when these are disposed of in their proper places ; when the stones and the tiles, as least perishable, are made use of for the foundation and covering ; the bricks and timber, each likewise in their order ; then we may see a regular edifice arising, which afterward becomes no inconsiderable part of our possessions."

" Your comparison," interrupted the other, " makes me recollect another circumstance, which we were told the general of an army ought to have regard to ; and that is, to place the best of his soldiers in the front and in the rear ; whilst those of a doubtful character being placed in the middle, may be animated by the one, and impelled by the other, to the performance of their duty."

" Your master then," said Socrates, " taught you how to know a good soldier from a bad one ; otherwise this rule could be of no use : for if he ordered you, in the counting of money, to place the good at each end of the table, and that which was adulterated in the middle, without first instructing you by what means to distinguish them, I see not to what purpose his orders could be."

" I cannot say," replied the other ; " but it is very sure my master did no such thing : we must therefore endeavour to find it out ourselves."

" Shall we consider this point then a little farther," said Socrates, " that so we may the better avoid any mistake in this matter ? Suppose," continued he, " the business was to seize some rich booty ; should we not do well to place in the front, those whom we thought the most avaricious ?"

" Certainly."

" But where the undertaking is attended with peril, there, surely, we should be careful to employ the most ambitious, the love of glory being sufficient to make men of this stamp despise all danger : neither shall we be at a loss to find out these people ; since they are always forward enough to make themselves known. But this master of yours," continued Socrates, " when he taught you the different ways of ranging your forces, taught you at the same time the different use you were to make of them."

" Not at all, I do assure you."

" And yet a different disposition of the army should be made, according as different occasions require."

" That may be," replied the other ; " but he said not a word to me of the matter."

" Then return to him," said Socrates, " and question him concerning it ; for if he is not either very ignorant, or very impudent, he will be ashamed of having taken your money, and sent you away so little instructed."

II. Meeting with one who had been newly elected general, Socrates asked him, " Why hath Agamemnon the title of pastor of the people given him by Homer ? Must it not be for this reason, think you, that like as a shepherd looks carefully to the health of his flock, and provides them pasture ; so he, who hath the command of the army, should provide his soldiers with all things necessary ; and procure those advantages to them for which they endure the hardships of war, conquest over their enemies, and to themselves more happiness ? Why also doth the same poet praise Agamemnon for being,

" Great in the war ; and great in arts of sway,"
Pope.

but to show in him, that personal bravery, however remarkable, is not enough to constitute the general, without he animates his whole army with courage, and makes every single soldier brave ? Neither," continued he, " can that prince be celebrated for the arts of sway, however successful he may be in regulating his domestic affairs, who doth not cause felicity and abundance to be diffused throughout his whole dominion. For kings are not elected that their cares should afterwards centre in their own private prosperity ; but to advance the happiness of those who elect them, are they called to the throne. As, therefore, the only motive for submitting to war, is the hope of rendering our future lives more secure and happy; and commanders are chosen for no other purpose, than to lead the way to this desirable end; it is the duty of a general to use his utmost endeavours not to disappoint the people therein: for, as to answer their expectations will bring to him the highest glory; so, to fail through misconduct, must be attended with the greatest shame."

We may here see, from what hath been just said, that Socrates designed to give us his idea of a good prince; passing over every other consideration; confines it to him alone, who diligently promotes the happiness of his people.

III. Meeting at another time with a person who had been chosen general of the horse, Socrates said to him, "As I doubt not, my young man, your being able to give a good reason why you desired the command of the cavalry, I should be glad to hear it: for I cannot suppose you asked it only for an opportunity of riding before the rest of the army, as the archers on horseback must go before you: neither could it be, to make yourself the more taken notice of; for madmen will still have the advantage of you there. But your design, I conclude, was to reform the cavalry, in hopes of making them of more service to the republic."

"I did design this, most certainly."

"A noble intention!" replied Socrates, "if you can but accomplish it. But your station obliges you to have an eye to your horses, as well as men."

"Undoubtedly."

"Pray tell us then," said Socrates, "what method you will take to get good horses?"

"O that," answered the general, "belongs not to me: the rider himself must look to that particular."

"Very well," said Socrates. "But suppose you wanted to lead them on to charge the enemy: and you found some of them lame; and others so weak, from being half-starved, that they could not come up with the rest of the army: while others again were so restive and unruly, as to make it impossible to keep them in their ranks: of what use would such horses be to you? or you to the republic?"

"You are in the right," said the other; "and I will certainly take care what sort of horses are in my troop."

"And what sort of men too, I hope," replied Socrates.

"Certainly."

"Your first endeavour, I suppose then, will be, to make them mount their horses readily?"

"It shall," said the other, "to the end they may stand a better chance to escape, if they are thrown off them."

"You will likewise take care," said Socrates, "to exercise them often: sometimes in one place, and sometimes in another; particularly there where it seems the most like to that in which you expect to meet the enemy, that your troops may be equally dexterous in all: for you cannot, I suppose, when going to engage, order your enemies to come and fight you on the plain, because there alone you were accustomed to exercise your army? You will likewise instruct them in throwing the dart: and if you would indeed make good soldiers, animate them with the love of glory, and resentment against their enemies: but, above all, be careful to establish your authority; since neither the strength of your horses, nor the dexterity of the riders, can be of much use to you without obedience?"

"I know it, Socrates: but what must I do to bring them to this obedience?"

"Have you not observed," said Socrates, "that all men willingly submit to those whom they believe the most skilful; in sickness, to the best physician; in a storm, to the best pilot; and in agriculture, to him whom they consider as the best husbandman?"

"I have," replied the other.

"If so, may we not well conclude, that he who is known to have the most skill in conducting the cavalry, will always find himself the most willingly obeyed?"

"But need I do no more than convince them of my superior abilities?"

"Yes; you must likewise convince them that both their glory and safety depend on their obedience."

"But how shall I be able to convince them of this?

"With less trouble," replied Socrates, "than you can prove to them it is better and more for their advantage to be vicious than virtuous."

"But, at this rate, it will be necessary for a general to add the study of the art of speaking to all his other cares."

"And do you imagine," said Socrates, "he can discharge his office without speaking? It is by the medium of speech the laws are made known to us for the regulation of our conduct;

and whatsoever is useful in any science, we become acquainted with it by the same means; the best method of instruction being in the way, of conversation: and he who is perfectly master of his subject will always be heard with the greatest applause. But have you never observed," continued Socrates, "that, throughout all Greece, the Athenian youth bear away the prize in every contention, from those sent by any other republic? Even a chorus of music going from hence to Delos, exceeds, beyond all comparison, whatever appears from any other places. Now the Athenians have not, naturally, voices more sweet, or bodies more strong, than those of other nations, but they are more ambitious of glory, which always impels to generous deeds and noble undertakings. Why, therefore, may not our cavalry be brought in time to excel any other; whether in the beauty of their horses and arms; whether in their discipline, order, and courage; were they but shown that conquest and glory would almost prove the infallible result of it?"

" I see not why, indeed," answered the other, "if we could but convince them this would be the event.

" Lose no time, then," said Socrates; "but go, excite your soldiers to the performance of their duty; that while you make them of use to you, they may likewise make you of some use to your country."

" I certainly shall make the attempt," replied the general.

IV. Seeing, at another time, Nichomachides return from the assembly of the people, where they had been choosing the magistrates, Socrates asked, whom they had fixed upon to command the army? "Could you have thought it!" said the other, "the Athenians, my Socrates, paid no regard to me, who have spent my whole life in the exercise of arms! passed through every degree, from that of common sentinel to colonel of the horse, covered with these scars (showing them on his bosom), my whole strength wasted with fighting in defence of them! while Antisthenes, one who never served among the infantry, nor ever did any thing remarkable among the horse, him they have elected, though all his merit seems to consist in being able to get money."

" No bad circumstance," replied Socrates; "we may hope, at least, to have our troops well paid."

" But a merchant can get money as well as Antisthenes; doth it follow from thence that a merchant is a fit man to command an army?"

" You overlook, Nichomachides, that Antisthenes is likewise a lover of glory, and seeks to excel in whatever he undertakes;—a quality of some worth in the commander of an army. You know, whenever he led the chorus, he always took care to carry off the prize."

" But, surely, there is some difference between commanding an army and ordering the chorus?"

" And yet," replied Socrates, "Antisthenes has no great knowledge himself either in music or the laws of the theatre? but as he had penetration sufficient to find out those who excelled in them, you see how, by their assistance, he came off conqueror."

" He must have somebody then to fight, and give out his orders, when at the head of his army?"

" Be that as it may," returned Socrates, "it is certain that he who follows the counsel of such as are best skilled in any art, let it be war or music, or any thing else, is pretty sure of surpassing all who are engaged in the same pursuit with him. Neither is it probable that he who so liberally expends his money, when the affair is no more than to amuse the people, and purchase a victory which only brings honour to himself and to his own tribe,[1] will be more sparing when the point is to gain a conquest far more glorious over the enemies of his country, and in which the whole republic are equally concerned."

" We are to conclude, then," returned the other, "that he who knows how to preside properly at a public show, knows in like manner how to command an army."

" It is certain," said Socrates, "so much may be concluded, that he who has judgment enough to find out what things are best for him, and ability to procure them, can hardly fail of success, whether his design be to direct the stage or govern the state,—manage his own house or command the army."

" Truly," replied Nichomachides, "I scarcely expected to hear from you, Socrates, that a good economist and a good commander was the same thing."

" Do you think so?" answered Socrates: "Let us inquire then if you please, into the

---

1 The citizens of Athens were all divided into tribes, which had their peculiar customs and honour.

duty of each; and see what agreement we can find between them. Is it not the business of them both to endeavour to make the people who are placed under them tractable and submissive?"

" It is."

" Must they not see that every person be employed in the business he is most proper for? Are they not, each of them, to punish those who do wrong, and reward those who do right? Must they not gain the love of the people who are placed under their authority, and procure to themselves as many friends as may be, to strengthen and stand by them in time of need? Should they not know how to secure their own? And, in short, should not each of them be diligent and unwearied in the performance of his duty?"

" So far," replied Nichomachides, " it may be as you say; but surely the comparison can scarcely hold, when the case is to engage an enemy."

" Why so?" said Socrates, " have they not each of them enemies to engage?"

" Certainly."

" And would it not be for the advantage of both, to get the better of these enemies?"

" No doubt of it, Socrates! But I still see not of what use economy can be to a general, when the hour is come for his soldiers to fall on."

" The very time," said Socrates, " when it will be the most; for, as economy will show him his greatest gain must arise from conquest, his greatest loss from being overcome; he will for that reason be very careful not to take any one step whatsoever which may hazard a defeat; wisely declining an engagement while in want of any thing; but equally ready to seize the hour, when, provided with all that is necessary, victory seems to him no longer doubtful. Thus you see of what use economy may be to a general: nor do you, Nichomachides, despise those who practise it, since the conduct of the state, and that of a private family, differ no otherwise than as greater and less; in every thing else there is no small similarity. The business is with men in either case: neither do we know of one species of these, whereby to manage the affairs of government, and another for carrying on the common concerns of life; but the prince at the helm, and the head of his family, must serve themselves from the same mass. And, to complete the parallel, be assured, Nichomachides, that whoever hath the skill to use these instruments properly, hath also the best secret for succeeding in his design; whether his aim be to direct the state, or limit his care to the concerns of his own household; while he who is ignorant of this point must commit many errors, and of course meet with nothing but disappointments."

V. Being in company with Pericles, son to the great Pericles, Socrates said to him,—" I hope, my young man, when you come to command the forces of the republic, the war may be carried on with more glory and success than we have lately known it."

" I should be glad if it were so," replied the other; " but how it is to be done I cannot easily see."

" Shall we try," said Socrates, " to get some light into this matter? You know the Bœotians are not more numerous than we."

" I know they are not."

" Neither are they stronger or more valiant."

" They are not."

" But the Bœotians, it may be, are more united among themselves?"

" So far from it," said Pericles, " that the Bœotians hate the Thebans on account of their oppression; whereas we can have nothing of this sort in Athens."

" But then we must own," said Socrates, " that the Bœotians are not only the most courteous of all mankind, but the most ambitious; and they who are so, the love of glory and of their country, will impel to undertake any thing."

" But I knew not," replied Pericles, " that the Athenians are deficient in any of these particulars."

" It must be acknowledged," said Socrates, " if we look back to the actions of our forefathers, and consider either the lustre or the number of their glorious deeds, no nation can exceed us: and having such examples, taken out too from among ourselves, they cannot but inflame our courage, and stir us up to a love of valour and of virtue."

" And yet you see," answered Pericles, " how much the glory of the Athenian name is tarnished since the fatal defeat of Lubea, wherein Tolmides lost more than a thousand men; and that other at Delium, where Hippocrates was slain: for whereas, till then, the Bœotians feared to make head against us, though in defence of their own country, without the assistance of the Lacedæmonians and the rest of Peloponnesus, they now threaten to invade us, and that with their own forces only; while the Athenians, instead of ravaging, as formerly, Bœotia at pleasure, when not defended by foreign troops, are made to tremble in their turn, lest Attica itself should become the scene of slaughter."

"The case," said Socrates, "is, I fear, as you have stated it; but for that reason it seemeth to me, my Pericles, the very time wherein to desire the command of our armies. It is of the nature of security to make men careless, effeminate, and ungovernable; while fear, on the contrary, awakens their diligence, renders them obedient, and reduces them to order. We may see this among our seamen. So long as they are under no apprehension of danger, they give themselves over to riot and disorder; but at the sight of a pirate, or the appearance of a storm, become immediately other men: not only diligent in performing whatever is commanded, but even watching, in silence, the master's eye, ready to execute, as in a well-ordered chorus, whatever part he shall think proper to assign them."

"Supposing," replied Pericles, "the people of Athens were at present in such a state as might dispose them to obedience, what way shall we take to rouse them to an imitation of our ancestors, that, with their virtues, we may restore the happiness and the glory of the times they lived in?"

"Was it our desire," answered Socrates, "to stir up any one to regain an inheritance now in the possession of another, what more should we need than to tell them it was theirs by long descent from their progenitors? If, therefore, my Pericles, you wish our Athenians to hold the foremost rank among the virtuous, tell them it is their right, delivered down to them from the earliest ages; and that, so long as they are careful to maintain this pre-eminence in virtue, pre-eminence in power cannot fail to attend it. You would likewise do well to remind them, how highly the most ancient of their forefathers were esteemed and honoured on account of their virtue."

"You mean when, in the time of Cecrops, the people of Athens were chosen in preference to all others, to arbitrate in the dispute which had arisen among the gods?"[1]

"I do," said Socrates; "and I would have you go on, and relate to them the birth and the education of Erictheus, the wars in his time with all the neighbouring nations; together with that undertaken in favour of the Heraclides against those of Peloponnesus. That also, in the days of Theseus, when our ancestors gained the reputation of surpassing all their contemporaries both in conduct and courage, ought not to be passed over. After which it may not be amiss to recall to their minds what the descendants of these heroes have performed in the ages just before us. Show them the time when, by their own strength alone, they made head against the man who lorded it over all Asia, and whose empire extended even into Europe itself, as far as Macedonia; inheriting from his forefathers a formidable army, as well as wide dominions, that had already made itself famous for many noble undertakings. Tell them at other times of the many victories, both by sea and land, when in league with the Lacedæmonians; men no less famous than themselves on the account of military courage: and, although innumerable have been the revolutions throughout the rest of Greece, whereby many have been compelled to change their habitations, show them the Athenians still in possession of their ancient territories; and not only so, but oftentimes made arbiters of the rights of other people, while the oppressed, on every side, have had recourse to them for protection."

"When I think of these things, my Socrates, I marvel by what means our republic hath sunk so low."

"I suppose," replied Socrates, "the Athenians acted in this respect like men, who, seeing themselves exalted above the fear of a competitor, grow remiss, and neglect discipline, and become thereby more despicable than the people whom they once despised; for, no sooner had our virtue set us above the rest of our contemporaries but we sunk into sloth, which ended, as you see, in a total degeneracy."

"But how shall we recover the lustre of the ancient virtue?"

"Nothing more easy to point out," replied Socrates; "let but our people call to mind what were the virtues and discipline of their forefathers, and diligently endeavour to follow their example, and the glory of the Athenian name may rise again as high as ever! But, if

---

[1] Alluding to the fabled contest between Neptune and Minerva for the patronage of Athens, which was determined by the Athenians in favour of Minerva.

this is too much for them, let them copy at least the people, whom, at present, they are compelled to consider as far above them : let them apply themselves with the same diligence to perform the same things, and let them not doubt of becoming again their equals : their superiors, if so be they will but surpass them in virtue."

" You speak, my Socrates, as if you thought our Athenians at no little distance from it. And, indeed," continued Pericles, " when do we see them, as at Sparta, reverencing old age? Or, rather, do we not see them showing their contempt of it even in the person of a father? Can they be expected to imitate that republic in the exercises which render the body healthful, who make sport of those who do? Will people who even glory in despising their rulers, submit readily to their commands? Or will concord and unanimity subsist among men, who seek not to help, but injure one another, and bear more envy to their fellow-citizens than to any other of mankind? Our assemblies, both public and private, are full of quarrels and contentions, whilst we harass each other with perpetual suits at law ; choosing by that means some trifling advantage, though with the ruin of our neighbour, rather than content ourselves with an honest gain, whereby each party might be equally profited. The magistrate's aim is altogether his own interest, as if the welfare of the community no way concerned him. Hence that eager contention for places and power, that ignorance and mutual hatred among those in the administration, that animosity and intrigue which prevail among private parties. So that I fear, my Socrates, lest the malady should rise to such a height, that Athens itself must, ere long, sink under it."

" Be not afraid, my Pericles, that the distemper is incurable. You see with what readiness and skill our people conduct themselves in all naval engagements : how regular in obeying those who preside over their exercises, lead the dance, or direct the chorus."

" I am sensible of this," said Pericles : " and hence, my Socrates, is the wonder, that, being so complying on all such occasions, our soldiers, who ought to be the choice and flower of this very people, are so frequently disposed to mutiny and disobedience."

" The senate of the Areopagus," said Socrates, " is not this likewise composed of persons of the greatest worth ?"

" Most certainly."

" Where else do we see judges who act in such conformity to the laws, and honour to themselves? Who determine with so much uprightness between man and man ; or discharge, with such integrity, whatever business is brought before them ?"

" I cannot reproach them," said Pericles, " with having failed in any thing."

" Therefore, let us not give up our Athenians, my Pericles, as a people altogether degenerate."

" Yet in war," replied Pericles, " where decency, order, and obedience, are more especially required, they seem to pay no regard to the command of their superiors."

" Perhaps," returned Socrates, " some part of the blame may belong to those who undertake to command them? You hardly know of any man, I believe, pretending to preside over a chorus, directing the dance, or giving rules to the athletics, whilst ignorant of the matter. They who take upon them to do any of these things, must tell you where, and by whom they were instructed in the art they now pretend to teach others ; whereas the greater part of our generals learn the first rudiments of war at the head of their armies. But I know, my Pericles, you are not of that sort of men ; but have made it your employment to study the military art ; and have gone through all the exercises so necessary for a soldier. In the memorials of your father, that great man ! I doubt not your having remarked, for your own advantage, many of those refined stratagems he made use of ; and can show us many more of your own collecting. These you study : and to the end that nothing may be omitted by one who hopes to command our armies, when you find yourself either deficient or doubtful, you are not unwilling to own your ignorance ; but seek out for such as you imagine more knowing ; while neither courtesy of behaviour, nor even gifts, are wanting, whereby to engage them to give you assistance."

" Ah, Socrates !" cried Pericles, interrupting him, " it is not that you think I have done these things, but wish me to do them, that you talk in this manner."

" It may be so," replied Socrates. " But to add a word or two more. You know," continued he, " that Attica is separated from Bœotia by a long chain of mountains, through which the roads are narrow and craggy ; so that all access to our country from that side, is both difficult and dangerous."

" I know it," said Pericles.

" It has been told you too, I imagine, how the Mysians and Pisidians, having seized for themselves several considerable places, and a large tract of land, in the territories of the king of Persia, are able, from the advantages of their situation, not only to secure their own liberty, but with their light-armed horse greatly annoy their enemies, by making perpetual inroads upon them?'

" Yes, I have heard this," replied the other.

" Why then may it not be supposed," said Socrates, " that if we secured those passes on the mountains which divide us from Bœotia, and sent there our youth properly armed for making incursions, we might in our turn give some annoyance to our enemies; while these mountains, as so many ramparts, secured us from their hostilities?"

" I agree with you," said Pericles, " this might turn to our advantage, and that all you have said hath been much to the purpose."

" If you think so," replied Socrates, " and that my observations may be of service, you have nothing more to do than to carry them into execution. Should success be the consequence, you, my friend, will have the honour, and the republic much gain. If you fail through want of power, no great mischief can ensue; Athens will not be endangered; nor shall you, my Pericles, incur either shame or reproach, for having engaged in such an undertaking."

VI. Glauco, the son of Aristo, was so strongly possessed with the desire of governing the republic, that, although not yet twenty, he was continually making orations to the people : neither was it in the power of his relations, however numerous, to prevent his exposing himself to ridicule; though sometimes they would drag him, by very force, from the tribunal. Socrates, who loved him on the account of Plato and Charmidus, had alone the art to succeed with him. For meeting him, he said, " Your design then, my Glauco, is to be at the very head of our republic?"

" It is so," replied the other.

" Believe me," said Socrates, " a noble aim ! For, this once accomplished, and you become, as it were, absolute; you may then serve your friends, aggrandize your family, extend the limits of your country, and make yourself renowned, not only in Athens, but throughout all Greece : nay, it may be, your fame will spread abroad among the most barbarous nations, like another Themistocles : while admiration and applause attend wherever you go !"

Socrates having thus fired the imagination of the young man, and secured himself a favourable hearing, went on : " But if your design is to receive honour from your country, you intend to be of use to it; for nothing but that can secure its applause."

" Undoubtedly," replied Glauco.

" Tell me then, I entreat you, what may be the first service you intend to render the republic ?"

Glauco remaining silent, as not knowing what to answer : " I suppose," said Socrates, " you mean to enrich it ? for that is generally the method we take, when we intend to aggrandise the family of some friend."

" This is indeed my design," returned the other.

" But the way to do this," said Socrates, " is to increase its revenues."

" It is so."

" Tell me then, I pray you, whence the revenues of the republic arise, and what they annually amount to; since I doubt not of your having diligently inquired into each particular, so as to be able to supply every deficiency; and, when one source fails, can easily have recourse to some other."

" I protest to you," said Glauco, " this is a point I never considered."

" Tell me then only its annual expenses ; for I suppose you intend to retrench whatever appears superfluous?"

" I cannot say," replied Glauco, " that I have yet thought of this affair any more than of the other."

" We must postpone then our design of enriching the republic to another time," said Socrates : " for I see not how a person can exert his endeavours to any purpose so long as he continues ignorant both of its income and expenses."

" Yet a state may be enriched by the spoils of its enemies."

" Assuredly," replied Socrates : " But, in order to this, its strength should be superior, otherwise it may be in danger of losing what it hath already. He, therefore, who advises war, ought to be well acquainted not only with the forces of his own country, but those of the enemy ; to the end, that if he finds superiority on his side, he may boldly persist in his first opinion, or recede in time, and dissuade the people from the hazardous undertaking."

"It is very true," returned the other.

"I pray you, then, tell me what are our forces by sea and land; and what the enemy's?"

"In truth, Socrates, I cannot pretend to tell you, at once, either one or the other."

"Possibly you may have a list of them in writing? If so, I should attend to your reading it with pleasure."

"No, nor this," replied Glauco, "for I have not yet begun to make any calculation of the matter."

"I perceive then," said Socrates, "we shall not make war in a short time; since an affair of such moment cannot be duly considered at the beginning of your administration. But I take it for granted," continued he, "that you have carefully attended to the guarding our coasts; and know where it is necessary to place garrisons; and what the number of soldiers to be employed for each: that while you are diligent to keep those complete which are of service to us, you may order such to be withdrawn as appear superfluous."

"It is my opinion," replied Glauco, "that every one of them should be taken away, since they only ravage the country they were appointed to defend."

"But what are we to do then," said Socrates, "if our garrisons are taken away? How shall we prevent the enemy from overrunning Attica at pleasure? And who gave you this intelligence, that our guards discharge their duty in such a manner? Have you been among them?"

"No: but I much suspect it."

"As soon then," said Socrates, "as we can be thoroughly informed of the matter, and have not to proceed on conjecture only, we will speak of it to the senate."

"Perhaps," replied Glauco, "this may be the best way."

"I can scarcely suppose," continued Socrates, "that you have visited our silver mines so frequently, as to assign the cause why they have fallen off so much of late from their once flourishing condition?"

"I have not been at all there," answered Glauco.

"They say, indeed," answered Socrates, "that the air of those places is very unhealthful; and this may serve for your excuse, if the affair at any time should be brought under deliberation."

"You rally me, Socrates, now," said the other.

"However," said Socrates, "I question not but you can easily tell us how much corn our country produces; how long it will serve the city; and what more may be wanted to carry us through the year, that so you may be able to give out your orders in time; that scarcity and want may not come upon us unawares."

"The man," replied Glauco, "will have no little business on his hands, who pretends to take care of such a variety of things."

"Yet so it must be, my Glauco," said Socrates: "you see even here, in our own private families, it is impossible for the master to discharge the duties of his station properly, unless he not only inquires out what is necessary for those who belong to him, but exerts his utmost endeavours to supply whatever is wanted. In the city there are more than ten thousand of these families to provide for; and it is difficult to bestow upon them, at one and the same time, that attention and care which is necessary for each of them. I therefore think you had better have given the first proof of your abilities in restoring the broken fortunes of one in your own family, from whence, if succeeding, you might afterwards have gone on to better those of the whole community; or finding yourself unable to do the one, thought no longer of the other; for surely the absurdity of the man is most apparent, who knowing himself not able to raise fifty pound weight, shall nevertheless attempt the carrying of five thousand."

"But I make no doubt," replied Glauco, "of my having been able to have served my uncle, and that very considerably, if he would have followed my advice."

"Alas!" returned Socrates, "if you could not to this hour prevail on so near a relation as your uncle to follow your counsel, how can you hope that all Athens, this very man too among others, should submit to your direction? Beware then, my Glauco; beware lest a too eager desire of glory should terminate in shame. Consider how much they hazard who undertake things, and talk on subjects of which they are ignorant. Call to mind those of your acquaintance who have thus talked and thus done, and see whether the purchase they made for themselves had not more of censure than applause in it; of contempt than admiration. Consider, on the other hand, with what credit they appear, who have made themselves masters of the point in question: and when you have done this, I doubt not your seeing that approbation and glory are alone the attendants of capacity and true merit; while contempt and shame are the sure reward of ignorance and temerity. If, therefore, you desire to be admired and esteemed by your country beyond all others, you must exceed all others in the knowledge of those things which you are ambitious of undertaking: and thus qualified, I shall not scruple to insure your success, whenever you may think proper to preside over the commonwealth."

VII. On the other hand, having observed that Charmidas, the son of Glauco, and uncle to the young man of whom we have been speaking, industriously declined any office in the government, though otherwise a man of sense, and far greater abilities than many who at that time were employed in the administration; Socrates said to him, "I pray you, Charmidas, what is your opinion of one, who being able to win the prize at the Olympic games, and thereby gain honour to himself and glory to his country, shall nevertheless, decline to make one among the combatants?"

"I should certainly look upon him," said Charmidas, "as a very effeminate and mean-spirited man."

"And suppose there may be one who hath it in his power, by the wisdom of his counsels, to augment the grandeur of the republic, and raise at the same time his own name to no common pitch of glory, yet timorously refusing to engage in business; should not this man be deemed a coward?"

"I believe he should," replied Charmidas: "but wherefore this question to me?"

"Because," said Socrates, "you seem to be this very man; since, able as you are, you avoid all employment; though, as citizen of Athens, you are certainly a member of the commonwealth, and, consequently, ought to take some share in serving it."

"But on what do you ground your opinion of my ability?"

"I never once doubted it," said Socrates, "since I once saw you in conference with some of our leading men: for, when they imparted any of their designs to you, you not only counselled what was best to be done, but expostulated freely and judiciously, when you thought they were mistaken."

"But surely there is some difference," said Charmidas, "between discoursing in private and pleading your own cause before a full assembly."

"And yet," said Socrates, "a good arithmetician will not calculate with less exactness before a multitude than when alone: and he, who is a master of music, not only excels while in his own chamber, but leads the concert with applause in presence of the full audience."

"But you know, Socrates, the bashfulness and timidity nature hath implanted, operates far more powerfully in us when before a large assembly, than in a private conversation."

"And is it possible," said Socrates, "that you, who are under no sort of concern when you speak to men who are in power, and men who have understanding, should stand in awe of such as are possessed of neither? For, after all, Charmidas, who are the people you are most afraid of? Is it the masons, the shoemakers, the fullers, the labourers, the retailers? Yet these are the men who compose our assemblies. But to converse thus at your ease, before people who hold the highest rank in the administration, (some of them, perhaps, not holding you in the highest estimation,) and yet suffer yourself to be intimidated by those who know nothing of the business of the state, neither can be supposed at all likely to despise you, is, certainly, no other than if he, who was perfectly well skilled in the art of fencing, should be afraid of one who never handled a file. But you fear their laughing at you?"

"And do they not often laugh at our very best speakers?"

"They do," replied Socrates; "and so do the others—those great men whom you converse with daily. I therefore the rather marvel, Charmidas, that you who have spirit and eloquence sufficient to reduce even these last to reason, should stand in awe of such stingless ridiculers! But endeavour, my friend, to know yourself better; and be not of the number of those who turn all their thoughts to the affairs of others, and are, the meanwhile, utter strangers at home. Be acquainted with your own talents, and lose no occasion of exerting them in the service of your country; and make Athens, if it may be, more flourishing than it is at present. The returns they bring will be glorious! Neither is it the commonwealth alone that shall be advantaged by them; yourself, my Charmidas, and your best friends, shall share the benefit."

VIII. Aristippus being desirous to retaliate in kind for having been formerly put to silence by Socrates, proposed a question in so artful a manner, as he doubted not would pose him. Socrates, however, was at no loss for an answer; though regardful rather of the improvement of his hearers than the ordering of his speech. The question was, " If he knew any thing that was good?"—Now, had it been said of food, money, health, strength, courage, or any thing else of the like nature, that they were good, Aristippus could with ease have demonstrated the contrary, and shown that each, and all of them, were oftentimes evil: but Socrates was better provided with a reply; for, knowing with what eagerness we wish to be relieved from whatever molests us—" What," said he, " Aristippus, do you ask me if I know any thing good for a fever?"

" No, not so," returned the other.

" For an inflammation in the eye?"

" Nor that, Socrates."

" Do you mean any thing good against a famine?"

" No, nor against a famine."

" Nay, then," replied Socrates, " if you ask me concerning a good, which is good for nothing, I know of none such; nor yet desire it."

Aristippus still urging him: " But do you know," said he, " any thing beautiful?"

" A great many," returned Socrates.

" Are these all like one another?"

" Far from it, Aristippus: there is a very considerable difference between them."

" But how can beauty differ from beauty?"

" We want not many examples of it," replied Socrates; " for the same disposition of the body which is beautiful in him who runs, is not beautiful in the wrestler; and while the beauty of the shield is to cover him well who wears it, that of the dart is to be swift and piercing."

" But you return," said Aristippus, " the same answer to this question as you did to the former."

" And why not, Aristippus? for do you suppose there can be any difference between beautiful and good? Know you not, that whatever is beautiful, is, for the same reason, good? And we cannot say of any thing,—of virtue, for example, —that on this occasion it is good, and on the other, beautiful. Likewise, in describing the virtuous character, say we not of it, " It is fair and good?" Even the bodies of men are said to be fair and good, with respect to the same purposes: and the same we declare of whatever else we meet with, when suited to the use for which it was intended."

" You would, perhaps, then call a dung-cart beautiful?"

" I would," said Socrates, " if made proper for the purpose; as I would call the shield ugly, though made of gold, that answered not the end for which it was designed."

" Possibly you will say too," returned Aristippus, " that the same thing is both handsome and ugly."

" In truth, I will," said Socrate ; " and I will go still farther, and add, that the same thing may be both good and evil: for I can easily suppose, that which is good in the case of hunger, may be evil in a fever; since what would prove a cure for the one, will certainly increase the malignity of other; and in the same manner will beauty, in the wrestler, change to deformity in him who runneth. For whatsoever, continued he, " is suited to the end intended, with respect to that end it is good and fair; and, contrariwise, must be deemed evil and deformed, when it defeats the purpose it was designed to promote."

Thus, when Socrates said that " beautiful houses were ever the most convenient," he showed us plainly in what manner we ought to build: To this end he would ask, " Doth not the man who buildeth a house intend, principally, the making it useful and pleasant?"

This being granted, Socrates went on: " But to make a house pleasant, it should be cool in summer and warm in winter." This also was acknowledged. " Then," said he, " the building which looketh towards the south will best serve this purpose: for the sun, which by that means enters and warms the rooms in winter, will, in summer, pass over its roof. For the same reason, these houses ought to be carried up to a considerable height, the better to admit the winter sun; whilst those to the north should be left much lower, that they may not be exposed to the bleak winds which blow from that quarter: for in short," continued Socrates, " that house is to be regarded as beautiful, where a man may pass pleasantly every season of the year, and lodge with security whatever belongs to him." As for paintings, and other ornaments, he thought they rather impair than improve our happiness.

With regard to temples and altars, Socrates thought the places best fitted for these were such as lay at some distance from the city, and were open to the view; for, when withheld from them, we should pray with more ardour, while in sight of those sacred edifices; and being sequestered from the resort of men, holy souls would approach them with more piety and devotion.

IX. Socrates being once asked, "Whether he took courage to be an acquisition of our own, or the gift of Nature?"—"I think," said he, "that, as in bodies some are more strong, and better able to bear fatigue than others; even so, among minds, may be discerned the same difference; some of these, being by Nature endued with more fortitude, are able to face dangers with greater resolution. For we may observe," continued he, "that all who live under the same laws, and follow the same customs, are not equally valiant. Nevertheless, I doubt not but education and instruction may give strength to that gift Nature hath bestowed on us: for, from hence it is we see the Thracians and the Scythians fearing to meet the Spartans with their long pikes and large bucklers; while, on the contrary, the Spartans are not less afraid of the Scythians with their bows, or of the Thracians with their small shields and short javelins. The same difference is likewise observable in every other instance; and so far as any man exceedeth another in natural endowments, so may he, proportionably, by exercise and meditation, make a swifter progress towards perfection. From whence it follows, that not only the man to whom Nature hath been less kind, but likewise he whom she hath endowed the most liberally, ought constantly to apply himself, with care and assiduity, to whatsoever it may be he wishes to excel in."[1]

Socrates made no distinction between wisdom and a virtuous temperature; for he judged, that he who so discerned what things were laudable and good, as to choose them, what evil and base, as to avoid them, was both wise and virtuously tempered. And being asked,

"Whether those persons who knew their duty but acted contrary to it, were wise and virtuously tempered?" his answer was, "that they ought rather to be ranked among the ignorant and foolish; for that all men whatever do those particular things, which having first selected out of the various things possible, they imagine to be well for their interest. I am of opinion, therefore," added Socrates, "that those who do not act right, are, for that very reason, neither wise nor virtuously tempered."

Agreeable to this, Socrates would often say, "That justice, together with every other virtue, was wisdom; for that all their actions being fair and good, must be preferred as such by all who were possessed of a right discernment; but ignorance and folly could perform nothing fair and good; because, if attempted, it would miscarry in their hands. Whence it follows, that as whatever is just and fair must be the result of sound wisdom; and as nothing can be fair and just where virtue is wanting; therefore, justice, and every other virtue, is wisdom."

And although Socrates asserted that madness was the very reverse of wisdom, yet did he not account all ignorance madness. But for a man to be ignorant of himself, and erect those things into matters of opinion, belief, or judgment, with which he was totally unacquainted, this he accounted a disorder of the mind bordering on madness. He farther said, that "the vulgar never deemed any one mad, for not knowing what was not commonly known; but to be deceived in things wherein no other is deceived, as when he thinks himself too tall to pass upright through the gates of the city, or so strong as to carry the house on his shoulders, in these, and such like cases, they say at once, 'the man is mad;' but pass over, unnoticed, mistakes that are less striking. For, as they only give the name of love to that which is the very excess of the passion, so they confine their idea of madness to the very highest pitch of disorder that can possibly arise in the human mind."

Considering the nature of envy, he said, "It was a grief of mind which did not arise from the prosperity of an enemy, or the misfortunes of a friend; but it was the happiness of the last the envious man mourned at." And when it seemed strange that any one should grieve at the happiness of his friend, Socrates showed them, "It was no uncommon thing

---

1 Though I am sorry to lessen the merit of this excellent philosopher, yet I cannot but wish the reader might see how much more usefully this subject hath been treated by a Christian moralist, in Number 106 of *The Adventurer.*

for the mind of man to be so fantastically disposed, as not to be able to bear either the pains or the pleasures of another; but that while it spared for no labour to remove the first, it would sicken and repine on seeing the other: but this," he said, " was only the punishment of minds ill-formed: the generous soul was above such weaknesses."

As to idleness, Socrates said he had observed very few who had not some employment; for the man who spends his time at the dice, or in playing the buffoon to make others laugh, may be said to do something: but, with Socrates, these, and such as these, were in reality no better than idlers, since they might employ themselves so much more usefully. He added, that no one thought himself at leisure to quit a good occupation for one that was otherwise: if he did, he was so much less excusable, as he could not plead the want of employment.

Socrates likewise observed, that a sceptre in the hand could not make a king; neither were they rulers in whose favour the lot or the voice of the people had decided, or who by force or fraud had secured their election, unless they understood the art of governing. And although he would readily allow it not less the province of the prince to command, than the subjects to obey, yet he would afterwards demonstrate, that the most skilful pilot would always steer the ship; the master, no less than the mariners, submitting to his direction. " The owner of the farm left the management of it," he said, " to the servant whom he thought better acquainted than himself with the affairs of agriculture. The sick man sought the advice of the physician; and he, who engaged in bodily exercises, the instructions of those who had most experience. And whatever there may be," continued Socrates, " requiring either skill or industry to perform it, when the man is able, he doth it himself; but if not, he hath recourse, if prudent, to the assistance of others, since in the management of the distaff a woman may be his instructor: neither will he content himself with what he can have at hand; but inquireth out with care for whoever can best serve him."

It being said by some present, " that an arbitrary prince was under no obligation to obey good counsel."—" And why so," replied Socrates; " must not he himself pay the penalty of not doing it? Whoever rejects good counsel commits a crime; and no crime can pass unpunished." It being farther said, " That an arbitrary prince was at liberty to rid himself even of his ablest ministers."—" He may," returned Socrates : " but do you suppose it no punishment to lose his best supports? or think you it but a slight one? For, which would this be; to establish him in his power, or the most sure way to hasten his destruction?"

Socrates being asked, " What study was the most eligible and best for man?" answered, " To do well." And being asked by the same person, " If good fortune was the effect of study?" " So far from it," returned Socrates, " that I look upon good fortune and study as two things entirely opposite to each other: for that is good fortune, to find what we want, without any previous care or inquiry: while the success which is the effect of study, must always be preceded by long searching and much labour, and is what I call doing well: and I think," added Socrates, " that he who diligently applies himself to this study, cannot fail of success; [1] at the same time that he is securing to himself the favour of the gods and the esteem of men. They, likewise, most commonly excel all others in agriculture, medicine, the business of the state, or whatever else they may engage in; whereas they who will take no pains, neither can know any thing perfectly, or do any thing well, they please not the gods, and are of no use to man."

X. But all the conversations of Socrates were improving. Even to the artists while engaged in their several employments, he had always somewhat to say which might prove instructive. Being on a time in the shop of Parrhasius the painter, he asked him, " Is not painting, Parrhasius, a representation of what we see? By the help of canvass and a few colours, you can easily set before us hills and caves, light and shade, straight and crooked, rough and plain, and bestow youth and age where and when it best pleaseth you; and

1 " Since but to wish more virtue, is to gain :" He has virtually attained his end, at the very time that he seems only busied about the means. As the term Εὐπραξία, which is here translated, to do well, is equivocal, and implies in it rectitude of conduct, as well as prosperity and success, as commonly understood by these words: it seems to be chiefly, in respect to the first of these, viz. rectitude of conduct, that Socrates here promises success to those who diligently make it their study and endeavour; not omitting to point out to us the favourable influence care and industry commonly have on whatever we engage in.

when you would give us perfect beauty, (not being able to find in any one person what answers your idea,) you copy from many what is beautiful in each, in order to produce this perfect form."

" We do so," replied Parrhasius.

" But can you show us, Parrhasius, what is still more charming,—a mind that is gentle, amiable, affable, friendly? Or is this inimitable?"

" And how should it be otherwise than inimitable, my Socrates, when it hath neither colour, proportion, nor any of the qualities of those things you mentioned, whereby it might be brought within the power of the pencil ? In short, when it is by no means visible ?"

" Are men ever observed to regard each other with looks of kindness or hostility?"

" Nothing more frequently observed," replied Parrhasius.

" The eyes, then, discover to us something ?"

" Most undoubtedly."

" And, in the prosperity or adversity of friends, is the countenance of him who is anxiously solicitous, the same with theirs who are indifferent about the matter ?

" Far otherwise, Socrates : for he who is solicitous, hath a countenance all cheerfulness and joy, on the prosperity of a friend ; pensive and dejected, when this friend is in affliction ?"

" And can this also be represented ?"

" Certainly."

" Likewise, where there is any thing noble and liberal ; or illiberal and mean ; honest, prudent, modest ; bold, insolent, or sordid ; are any of these to be discovered in the countenance and demeanour of a man, when he sits, stands, or is in motion ?"

" It may."

" And imitated ?"

" Imitated, no doubt of it."

" And which yields the most pleasure, Parrhasius—the portrait of him on whose countenance the characters of whatever is good, virtuous, and amiable, are impressed ; or his, who wears in his face all the marks of a base, evil, and hateful disposition ?"

" Truly," returned Parrhasius, " the difference is too great, my Socrates, to admit of any comparison."

Entering another time into the shop of Clito the statuary, he said to him : " I marvel not, my Clito, at your being able to mark out to us ----- the difference between the racer and the wrestler, the pancratiast and gladiator ; but your statues are very men ! Tell me, I pray, by what means you effect this ?"

Clito hesitating, as at a loss how to reply ; Socrates went on : " But, perhaps, you are particularly careful to imitate persons who are living ; and that is the reason why your statues are so much alive ?"

" It is," returned Clito.

" Then you have certainly remarked, and that with no little exactness, the natural disposition of all the parts, in all the different postures of the body : for, whilst some of these are extended, others remain bent ; when that is raised above its natural height, this sinks below it ; these are relaxed, and those again contracted, to give the greater force to the meditated blow : and the more these sort of things are attended to, the nearer you approach to human life."

" You are right, my Socrates."

" But it undoubtedly gives us the greatest pleasure, when we see the passions of men, as well as their actions, represented ?"

" Undoubtedly."

" Then the countenance of the combatant going to engage the enemy, must be menacing and full of fire ; that of the conqueror, all complacency and joy ?"

" They must."

" Therefore," concluded Socrates, " he will ever be deemed the best sculptor, whose statues best express the inward workings of the mind."

Socrates entering the shop of Pistias the armourer, was shown some corslets that were thought well made.

" I cannot but admire," said Socrates, " the contrivance of those things which so well cover that part of the body which most wants defending, and yet leave the hands and arms at liberty. But tell us, Pistias, why you sell your armour so much dearer than any other, when it is neither better tempered, stronger, nor the materials of it more costly ?"

" I make it better proportioned," said Pistias ; " and therefore I ought to have a better price."

" But how are we to find out this proportion, Pistias? Not by weight or measure : for as you make for different people, the weight and the size must likewise differ, or they will not fit."

" We must make them to fit," said Pistias ; otherwise the armour would be of little use."

" And are you aware that all bodies are not justly proportioned ?"

" I am."

" How can you make a well-proportioned suit of arms for an ill-proportioned body ?"

" I make it fit; and what fits is well-proportioned."

" Then you are of opinion, that when we declare any thing well-proportioned, it must be in reference to the use for which it was intended: at when we say of this shield, or this cloak, it is well-proportioned, for it fits the person for whom it was made ? But I think," added Socrates, " there is still another advantage, and that no small one, in having arms made to fit the wearer."

" Pray, what is that ?"

" Armour which fits," replied Socrates, " doth not load the wearer so much as that which is ill made, although the weight may be the same: for that which doth not fit hangs altogether upon the shoulders, or bears hard upon some other part of the body ; and becomes, thereby, almost insupportable ; whereas the weight of that which is well made, falls equally on all;—the shoulders, breast, back, loins;—and is worn with ease, not carried as a burthen."

" It is for this very same reason," said Pistias, " that I set such a value on those I make : nevertheless, my Socrates, there are who pay more regard to the gilding and carving of their arms than to any other matter."

" And yet," answered Socrates, " these people will make but a bad bargain with all their gilding and various colours, if they buy such arms as do not sit easy. But," continued Socrates, " since the position of the body is not always the same, being sometimes stooping and sometimes erect, how can the arms, that are made with such exactness, be at all times easy ?"

" Neither can they," replied the other.

" You think then, Pistias, the arms which are well made are not those which are exact, or sit close to the body, but give the least trouble to him who wears them ?"

" You think so," said Pistias ; " and have certainly taken the matter right."

XI. There was a courtezan at Athens, called Theodota, of great fame on the account of her many lovers. It being mentioned in company that her beauty surpassed all description, that painters came from all parts to draw her picture, and that one was now gone to her lodgings for that very purpose,—" We should do well," said Socrates, " to go ourselves and see this wonder, for we may then speak with more certainty when we speak from our own knowledge, and do not depend on the report of others."

The person who first mentioned this seconding the proposal, they went that instant to the lodgings of Theodota, and found her, as was said, sitting for her picture. The painter being gone, Socrates said to those who came along with him : " What say you, sirs, which of the two ought to think themselves the most obliged : we to Theodota, for the sight of so much beauty ; or she to us, for coming to see it ? Now, if the advantages of showing herself are found to be altogether on her side, then certainly is she indebted to us for this visit : if otherwise, indeed, we must thank her."

The reasonableness of what was said being assented to by the rest, Socrates proceeded— " The praises we bestow at present, ought not even these to be had in some estimation by Theodota ? But when we come to blaze abroad the fame of her beauty, what manifold advantages may not arise to her from it ! while all our gain from the sight of so many charms can terminate in nothing but fruitless longing ! We take our leave with hearts full of love and anxiety, and are henceforth no other than so many slaves to Theodota, with whom she has no more to do than to show them her pleasure !"

" If this is the case," replied Theodota, " I am to thank you for coming to see me."

Socrates, during this conversation, had observed how sumptuously she was adorned, and that her mother was the same ; her attendants, of whom there was no small number expensively clothed, and all the furniture of her apartment elegant and costly : he therefore took occasion from thence to ask her concerning her estate in the country ; adding, it must of necessity be very considerable ?

Being answered, " she had not any."

" You have houses then," said he, " in the city, and they yield you a good income ?"

" No, nor houses, Socrates."

" You have certainly many slaves, then, Theodota, who by the labour of their hands supply you with these riches ?"

" So far," replied Theodota, " from having many, that I have not one."

" But whence then," said Socrates, " can all this come ?"

" From my friends," returned Theodota.

" A fair possession, truly !" replied Socrates ; " and a herd of friends we find to be a far better thing than a flock of sheep or a herd of cattle. But tell me, pray, do you trust fortune to bring these friends home to you, as flies fall by chance into the spider's web, or do you employ some art to draw them in ?"

" But where, Socrates, shall I be furnished with this art ?"

" You may procure it," said Socrates, " with far greater ease than the spider her web. You see how this little animal, who lives only upon her prey, hangs her nets in the air, in order to entangle it ?"

" You advise me, then, to weave some artificial nets," said Theodota, " in order to catch friends ?"

" Not so neither," returned Socrates ; " it is necessary to go a little less openly to work in a pursuit of such importance. You see what various arts are employed by men to hunt down hares, which, after all, are of little value. As these are known to feed chiefly in the night, they provide dogs to find them out at that season : and as they lie concealed in the day, the sharp-scented hound is employed to trace them up to their very forms : being swift of foot, the greyhound is let loose upon them, as more swift of foot than they ; and, lest all this should not be sufficient for the purpose, they spread nets in the paths to catch and entangle them."

" Very well," replied Theodota ; " but what art shall I make use of to catch friends ?"

" Instead of the hunter's dog," said Socrates, " you must set somebody to find out those who are rich and well-pleased with beauty, whom afterwards they shall force into your toils."

" And what are my toils ?" replied Theodota.

" You are certainly mistress of many," said Socrates, " and those not a little entangling. What think you of that form of yours, Theodota, accompanied as it is with a wit so piercing, as shows you at once what will be most for your advantage ? It is this which directs the glance, tunes the tongue, and supplies it with all the shows of courtesy and kindness. It is this which teaches you to receive with transport him who assiduously courts your favour, and scorn such as show you no regard.

If your friend is sick, you spare for no pains in your attendance upon him : you rejoice in all his joy, and give every proof of having bestowed your heart on him who seems to have given his to you. In short, I make no doubt of your being well versed in all the arts of allurement, and dare venture to say, the friends you have, if true, were not gained by compliments, but substantial proofs of kindness."

" But," said Theodota, " I never practise any of the arts you mention."

" And yet," answered Socrates, " some management is necessary, since a friend is a sort of prey that is neither to be catched nor kept by force ; a creature no otherwise to be taken and tamed, but by showing it kindness, and communicating to it pleasure."

" You say right, Socrates ; but why will you not help me to gain friends ?"

" And so I will," said Socrates, " if you can find out how to persuade me to it."

" But what way must I take to persuade you ?"

" Do you ask that ?" returned Socrates : " You will find out the way, Theodota, if you want my assistance."

" Then come to me often."

Socrates, still joking with her, said laughing :—" But it is not so easy for me to find leisure : I have much business both in public and private, and have my friends too, as well as you, who will not suffer me to be absent night or day, but employ against me the very charms and incantations that I formerly taught them."

" You are then acquainted with those things ?"

" Verily !" returned Socrates ; " for what else can you suppose, Theodota, engaged Apollodorus and Antisthenes to be always with me ? Or Cebes and Simmias to leave Thebes for my company, but the charms I speak of ?" [1]

---

1 Antisthenes lived at the port Piræus, about five miles from Athens, and came from thence every day to see Socrates. Cebes and Simmias left their native country for his sake ; and almost the whole of what we know of Apollodorus is the violence of his affection for Socrates. But the proof which Euclides gave of his was the most extraordinary ; for, when the hatred of the Megareans was so great, that it was forbidden on pain of death for any one of them to set foot in Attica, and the Athenians obliged their generals to take an oath, when they elected them, to ravage the territories of Megara twice every year, Euclides used to disguise

"Communicate these charms to me," said Theodota, "and the first proof of their power shall be upon you."

"But I would not be attracted to you, Theodota; I would rather you should come to me."

"Give me but a favourable reception," said Theodota, "and I will certainly come."

"So I will," replied Socrates, "provided I have then no one with me whom I love better."

XII. Socrates having taken notice how very awkward Epigenes, one of his followers, was in all his actions, and that he was moreover of a sickly constitution, both which he attributed to a neglect of those exercises which make so large a part of a liberal education,[2] he reproved him for it, saying, "How unbecoming it was in him to go on in such a manner!" Epigenes only answered, "He was under no obligation to do otherwise."

"At least as much," replied Socrates, "as he who hath to prepare for Olympia. Or do you suppose it, Epigenes, a thing of less consequence to fight for your life against the enemies of your country, whenever it shall please our Athenians to command your service, than to contend for a prize at the Olympic games? How many do we see, who, through feebleness and want of strength, lose their lives in battle; or, what is still worse, save themselves by some dishonourable means! How many fall alive into the enemy's hand, endure slavery of the most grievous kind for the remainder of their days, unless redeemed from it by the ruin of their families! Whilst a third procures himself an evil fame; and the charge of cowardice is given to imbecility. But, perhaps, Epigenes, you despise all the ills which attend on bad health, or account them as evils that may easily be borne?"

"Truly," replied the other, "I think them rather to be chosen, than so much fatigue and labour for the purchase of a little health."

"It may be, then," answered Socrates, "you equally contemn all the advantages arising from a contrary complexion; yet, to me, they seem to be many and great; since he who is possessed of a good constitution, is healthful, strong, and hardy, and may acquit himself with honour on every occasion. By the means of this he ofttimes escapes all the dangers of war; he can assist his friends, do much service to his country, and is sure of being well received wherever he shall go. His name becomes illustrious: he makes his way to the highest offices; passes the decline of life in tranquillity and honour; and leaves to his children the fair inheritance of a good example. Neither ought we to neglect the benefits arising from military exercises, though we may not be called upon to perform them in public, since we shall find ourselves not the less fitted for whatever we may engage in, from having a constitution healthful and vigorous: and as the body must bear its part, it imports us much to have it in good order; for who knoweth not," continued Socrates, "that even there—where it seems to have least to do—who knoweth not how much the mind is retarded in its pursuits after knowledge, through indisposition of the body; so that forgetfulness, melancholy, fretfulness, and even madness itself, shall sometimes be the consequence, so far as to destroy even the very traces of all we have ever learned. But he whose constitution is rightly tempered, need fear none of these evils; and, therefore, he who hath a just discernment will choose with pleasure whatever may best secure him from them. Neither doth an inconsiderable shame belong to the man who suffers himself to sink into old age, without exerting to the utmost those faculties nature hath bestowed on him; and trying how far they will carry him towards that perfection, which laziness and despondence can never attain to; for dexterity and strength are not produced spontaneously."

XIII. A certain man being angry with another for not returning his salutation, Socrates asked, "Why was he not enraged when he met one who had less health than himself, since it would not be more ridiculous, than to be angry with one who was less civil?"

Another bemoaning himself because he could not relish his food; "There is an excellent remedy for this complaint," answered Socrates; "fast often. By this means you will not only eat more pleasantly, but likewise better your health, and save your money."

himself in the habit of an old woman, and covering his head with a veil, set out in the evening from Megara; and arriving in the night-time at the house of Socrates, staid till the next evening with him, and then returned in the same manner; so much stronger was his affection than the fear of death. And when, to friends like these, we may still add many others, Plato, Chærephon, Crito, and, to mention no more, our amiable Xenophon—almost all of them the wisest as well as the best men of their age—who can suspect the virtue of Socrates,—who can doubt his being a happy man!

2 No slaves were allowed to anoint, or perform exercises in the Palestra.—Pott. Antiq.

Another complaining that the water which ran by his house was too warm to drink; "You are lucky, however," said Socrates, "in having a bath thus ready prepared for you."

"But it is too cold to bathe in," replied the other.

"Do your domestics complain of it when they drink or bathe?"

"So far from it," answered the man, "that it is often my wonder to see with what pleasure they use it for both these purposes."

"Which do you account," said Socrates, "the warmest; this water you speak of, or that in the temple of Esculapius?"

"O! that in the temple," replied the other.

"And how is it," said Socrates, "that you do not perceive yourself more froward and harder to please, not only than your own servants, but even people who are sick?"

Socrates seeing one beat his servant immoderately, asked him, "What offence the man had committed?"

"I beat him," replied the other, "because he is not only a drunkard and a glutton, but avaricious and idle."

"You do well," said Socrates; "but judge for yourself which deserves the most stripes, your servant, or you?"

Another dreading the length of the way to Olympia; Socrates asked him, "What he was afraid of? For is it not your custom," said he, "to walk up and down in your own chamber, almost the whole day? You need therefore but fancy you are taking your usual exercise between breakfast and dinner, and dinner and supper, and you will find yourself, without much fatigue, at the end of your journey; for you certainly walk more in five or six days, than is sufficient to carry you from Athens to Olympia. And as it is pleasanter to have a day to spare, than to want one, delay not, I advise you; but set out in time, and let your haste appear, not at the end, but the beginning of your journey." [1]

A certain person complaining of being tired with travelling, Socrates asked, "If he had carried any thing?"

"Nothing but my cloak," replied the other.

"Was you alone?" said Socrates.

"No; my servant went along with me."

"And did he carry any thing?"

"Yes, certainly, he carried all I wanted."

"And how did he bear the journey?"

"Much better than I."

"What, if you had carried the burthen; how then?"

"I could not have done it," replied the other.

"What a shame," said Socrates, "for a man who hath gone through all his exercises not to be able to bear as much fatigue as his servant!"

XIV. It being generally the custom, when they met together, for every one to bring his own supper; [2] Socrates observed, that whilst some of them took such care of themselves, as to have more than was sufficient; others were compelled to be content with less. He, therefore, so ordered the matter, that the small portion of him who brought little should be offered about to all the company in such a manner, that no one could, civilly, refuse to partake of it; nor exempt himself from doing the like with what he brought: by which means a greater equality was preserved among them. There was also this farther advantage arising from it; the expenses of the table were considerably abridged: for when they saw, that whatever delicacy they brought thither, the whole company would have their share of it, few chose to be at the cost to procure it: and thus luxury was in some degree put a stop to in these entertainments.

Having observed at one of these meetings,

---

1 Many of the circumstances here mentioned seem as if they should not be so much considered as things spoken by Socrates, as Socrates; but by Socrates whom Xenophon most tenderly loved.

2 The feasts, or entertainments of the Grecians, were of different sorts. In the primitive ages, entertainments were seldom made but on the festivals of their gods; for it was not customary with them to indulge in the free use of wine, or delicacies, unless they did it on a religious account. Afterwards, when a more free way of living was introduced, they had three distinct sorts of entertainments, of which the marriage entertainment was one. Of the other two, one was provided at the sole expense of one person; the other was made at the common expense of all present. Hither also may be referred those entertainments wherein some of the guests contributed more than their proportion; and that other, (which is, I believe, what Socrates had in this place more particularly in his eye,) in which it was the custom for any man, after he had provided his supper (the Grecian's best meal), to put it in a basket, and go and eat it in another man's house.—*Pott. Antiq.*

The Greek name for an entertainment defined by Plutarch, "a mixture of seriousness and mirth, discourses and actions."

They who forced themselves into other men's entertainments were called flies; a general name of reproach for such as insinuated themselves into company where they were not welcome.

a young man who ate his meat without any bread; and the discourse turning at that time on the cause why this or that person had procured to themselves some particular appellation. —" Can you tell me, sirs," said Socrates, "why they call a man a gormandizer, since not one of us here but takes part of whatever is set before him; and therefore we cannot suppose this to be the reason?"

" I suppose it cannot," replied one of the company.

" But," continued Socrates, " when we see any one greedily swallowing down his meat without mixing any bread with it, may we not call this man a gormandizer? For, if otherwise, I know not where we shall meet with one." And being asked by another who was present, What he thought of him who ate a little bread to a great deal of meat? " The same," answered Socrates, " as I did of the other; and while the rest of mankind supplicate the gods to find them plenty of corn, these men must pay for an abundance of the well-mixed ragout."

The young man whom this discourse glanced at, suspecting it was meant for him, thought proper to take a little bread, but, at the same time continued to cram down his meat as formerly; which Socrates observing, called to one who sat near him, to take notice " whether his neighbour ate his meat for the sake of the bread, or his bread for the sake of the meat."

At another time, seeing a person dip a piece of bread into several different sauces, Socrates asked—" Whether it was possible to make a sauce so costly, and at the same time so little good as this person had made for himself? For, as it consisted of a greater variety, there could be no doubt of its costing more; and as he had mixed such things together as no cook

ever once thought of, who could doubt his having spoiled all? Besides," said Socrates, " what folly to be curious in searching after cooks, if a man is to undo at once all they have done for us!" Moreover, he who is accustomed to indulge in variety, will feel dissatisfied when not in his power to procure it; but the man who generally restrains himself to one dish, will rise well satisfied from every table. He used also to say, that the compound verb, which in the Attic dialect signified to feast, or fare well,[1] meant to eat; and that the term WELL was added to express the eating in such a manner as neither to disorder the body nor oppress the mind; and with such plainness that the food could not be difficult to come at : so that this Attic verb was only applicable to such persons as ate with decency and temperance, and agreeably to the nature of social rational beings.

---

1 The verb here mentioned by Socrates is εὐωχεῖσθαι, to feast, or make one at a banquet, which comes from εὐωχία, a feast or banquet. Of this last word we have two etymologies; the first deduces it from εὖ, bene, and ἐχή, cibus, because those who attend feasts are well fed, the second deduces it from εὖ ἔχειν, bene sese habere, because those who attend feasts are well off; they find their advantage in being there, from faring so sumptuously and well. Whichever etymology we admit, the ingenuity of Socrates remains the same; who by transferring the term εὖ in εὐωχεῖσθαι, from its vulgar and gross meaning into a moral and rational one, has the address to transform a verb of luxury and excess into a verb of temperance and decorum. This method of conveying knowledge, by discussing the meanings of words and their etymologies, was much practised by Socrates. Many instances occur in this work; in particular see lib. iv. cap. 2, where διαλέγεσθαι is etymologized. Plato wrote an entire dialogue, called Cratylus, upon this subject. From these early philosophers the Stoics took the practice, as may be seen in Cicero de Natura Deor. and also Arrian, lib. i. cap. 17; where the learned editor, Mr Upton, has fully illustrated his author, and given a multitude of similar passages.—Mr Harris.

XENOPHON'S

MEMOIRS OF SOCRATES.

BOOK IV.

CONTENTS of BOOK IV.

XENOPHON'S

MEMOIRS OF SOCRATES.

BOOK IV.

I. In this manner would Socrates make himself useful to all sorts of men, of whatsoever employment. Indeed no one can doubt the advantages arising from his conversation, to those who associated with him whilst living; since even the remembrance of him, when dead, is still profitable to his friends. Whether serious or gay, whatever he said carried along with it something which was improving. He would frequently assume the character and the language of a lover; but it was easy to perceive it was the charms of the mind, not those of the body, with which he was enamoured, as the objects he sought after were always such as he saw naturally inclining towards virtue. Now he thought an aptness to learn, together with a strength of memory to retain what was already learned, accompanied with a busy inquisitiveness into such things as might be of use for the right conduct of life, whether as head only of a single family or governor of the whole state, indicated a mind well fitted for instruction; which, if duly cultivated, would render the youth in whom they were found not only happy in themselves, and their own families, but give them the power of making many others the same; since the benefits arising from thence would be diffused throughout the whole community. His method, however, was not the same with all; but whenever he found any who thought so highly of themselves on the account of their talents as to despise instruction, he would endeavour to convince them, that of all mankind they stood in the greatest want of it: like to the high-bred horse, which having more strength

and courage than others, might be made for that very reason of so much the more use, if properly managed; but, neglected while young, becomes thereby the more vicious and unruly. Also those dogs which are of the nobler kind: these, being trained to it, are excellent in the chase; but, left to themselves, are good for nothing. And it is the same, would he say, with respect to men; such of them to whom nature hath dealt the most liberally, to whom she hath given strength of body and firmness of mind, as they can execute with greater readiness and facility whatever they engage in, so they become more useful than others, and rise to nobler heights of virtue, if care is taken to give them a right turn: but, this not being done, they excel only in vice; and become, by the means of these very talents, more hurtful to society; for, through ignorance of their duty, they engage in a bad cause, and make themselves parties in evil actions; and, being haughty and impetuous, they are with difficulty restrained and brought back to their duty; so that many and great are the evils they occasion.

As to those men who relied upon their riches, and imagined they stood in no need of instruction, as their wealth would be sufficient to supply all their wants, and procure them every honour: these Socrates would endeavour to reduce to reason, by showing how foolish it was to imagine they could of themselves distinguish between things that were useful, and those which were hurtful, without having first been shown the difference. Or, wanting this power of discriminating, still vainly supposed, that because they could purchase the things they had a mind to, they could therefore perform whatever would be to their advantage; or, if not, could yet live safe and easy, and have all things go well with them. " Neither was it," he said, "less absurd in them to suppose that wealth could supply the want of knowledge, and make the possessor of it pass for a man of abilities; or at least procure for him that esteem which is only acquired by true merit."

II. But, on the other hand, when he met with any who valued themselves on account of their education, concluding they were qualified for every undertaking; we see the method Socrates took to chastise their vanity, from the manner in which he treated Euthedemus, surnamed the Fair.—This young man having collected many of the writings of the most celebrated poets and sophists, was so much elated by it, as to fancy himself superior to any other of the age, both in knowledge and abilities; and doubted not to see himself the very first man in Athens, whatever the business; whether to manage the affairs of the state, or harangue the people. Being, however, as yet too young to be admitted into the public assemblies, his custom was to go into a bridle-cutter's shop, which stood near to the forum, when he had any business depending: which Socrates observing, he also went in thither, accompanied by some of his friends; and one of them asking, in the way of conversation, " Whether Themistocles had been much advantaged by conversing with philosophers; or, whether it were not chiefly the strength of his own natural talents which had raised him so far above the rest of his fellow-citizens, as made them not fail to turn their eyes towards him whenever the state stood in need of a person of uncommon ability?" Socrates, willing to pique Euthedemus, made answer: " It was monstrous folly for any one to imagine, that whilst the knowledge of the very lowest mechanic art was not to be attained without a master; the science of governing the republic, which required for the right discharge of it all that human prudence could perform, was to be had by intuition."

Socrates went no further at that time; but plainly perceiving that Euthedemus cautiously avoided his company, that he might not be taken for one of his followers, he determined to attack him something more openly. To this purpose, when he was next along with

him, Socrates, turning to some who were present, " May we not expect," said he, " from the manner in which this young man pursues his studies, that he will not fail to speak his opinion even the very first time he appears in the assembly, should there be any business of importance then in debate? I should suppose, too, that the proem to his speech, if he begins with letting them know that he hath never received any instruction, must have something in it not unpleasant. ' Be it known to you,' will he say, ' O ye men of Athens! I never learnt any thing of any man: I never associated with persons of parts or experience; never sought out for people who could instruct me: but, on the contrary, have steadily persisted in avoiding all such; as not only holding in abhorrence the being taught by others, but careful to keep clear of every the least suspicion of it: but I am ready, notwithstanding, to give you such advice as chance shall suggest to me.' —Not unlike the man," continued Socrates, " who should tell the people, while soliciting their voices; ' It is true, gentlemen, I never once thought of making physic my study; I never once applied to any one for instruction; and so far was I from desiring to be well versed in this science, I even wished not to have the reputation of it: but, gentlemen, be so kind as to choose me your physician; and I will gain knowledge by making experiments upon you.'"

Every one present laughed at the absurdity of such a preface; and Euthedemus, after this, never avoided the company of Socrates: but still he affected the most profound silence, hoping, by that means, to gain the reputation of a modest man. Socrates, desirous to cure him of his mistake, took an opportunity of saying to some of his friends, Euthedemus being present, " Is it not strange, sirs, that while such as wish to play well on the lute, or mount dexterously on horseback, are not content with practising in private as often as may be, but look out for masters, and submit willingly to their commands, as the only way to become proficients and gain fame; the man whose aim is to govern the republic, or speak before the people, shall deem himself aptly qualified for either without the trouble of any previous instruction? Yet surely the last must be owned the most difficult; since, out of the many who force themselves into office, so few are seen to succeed therein; and therefore it should seem, that diligence and study are here the most needful."

By these and the like discourses, Socrates disposed the young man to enter into farther conference, and give him a patient hearing. Which having observed, he took an opportunity of going on a time alone into the bridle-cutter's shop, where Euthedemus then was; and sitting down by him—" Is it true," said he, " Euthedemus, that you have collected so many of the writings of those men whom we call wise?"

" Most undoubtedly it is true," replied the other ; " neither shall I give over collecting till I have gained as many of them as I well can."

" Truly," said Socrates, " I admire you much for thus endeavouring to accumulate wisdom rather than wealth : for by this, Euthedemus, you plainly discover it to be your opinion, that gold and silver cannot add to our merit ; whereas we furnish ourselves with an inexhaustible fund of virtue, when we thus treasure up the writings of these great men."

Euthedemus was not a little pleased with hearing Socrates speak in such a manner; concluding his method of obtaining wisdom had met with approbation; which Socrates perceiving, he continued the discourse.

" But what employment do you intend to excel in Euthedemus, that you collect so many books ?"

Euthedemus returning no answer, as at a loss what to say :

" You perhaps intend to study physic," said Socrates ; " and no small number of books will be wanting for that purpose."

" Not I, upon my word."

" Architecture, perhaps, then ? and for this too you will find no little knowledge necessary."

" No, nor that," replied Euthedemus.

" You wish to be an astrologer, or a skilful geometrician, like Theo ?"

" Not at all."

" Then you possibly intend to become a rhapsodist, and recite verses ; for I am told you are in possession of all Homer's works ?"

" By no means," replied Euthedemus, " will I do this ; for however ready these men may be with their verses, it doth not prevent their being thought troublesome, wherever they come."

" Perhaps you are desirous of that knowledge, my Euthedemus, which makes the able statesman or good economist ? which qualifies for command, and renders a man useful both to himself and others ?"

" This, indeed, is what I sigh for, and am in search of," replied Euthedemus, with no small emotion.

" Verily !" answered Socrates, " a noble pursuit : for this is what we call the royal science, as it belongeth in a peculiar manner to kings. But have you considered the matter, Euthedemus, whether it will not be necessary for the man to be just, who hopes to make any proficiency therein ?"

" Certainly, Socrates ; for I know very well, he who is not just cannot make even a good citizen."

" Then you are a just man, Euthedemus ?"

" I think I am, as much as any other."

" Pray say, Euthedemus, may one know when a just man is engaged in his proper work, as we can when the artist is employed in his ?"

" Undoubtedly."

" So that—as the architect, for example, can show us what he is doing ; so the just man likewise ?"

" Assuredly, Socrates ; nor should there be any great difficulty in pointing out what is just or unjust, in actions about which we are conversant daily."

" Suppose, Euthedemus, we should make two marks ; an A here, and a D there : under which to set down the things that belong to justice and injustice ?"

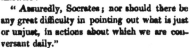

" You may," replied Euthedemus, " if you think there wants any such method."

Socrates having done this, went on.

" Is there any such thing as lying."

" Most certainly."

" And to which side shall we place it ?"

" To injustice, surely."

" Do mankind ever deceive each other ?"

" Frequently."

" And where shall we place this ?"

" To injustice still."

" And injury ?"

" The same."

" Selling those into slavery who were born free ?"

" Still the same, certainly."

" But suppose," said Socrates, " one whom you have elected to command your armies should take a city belonging to your enemies and sell its inhabitants for slaves ?—Shall we say of this man he acts unjustly ?"

" By no means."

" May we say he acteth justly ?"

" We may."

"And what if, while he is carrying on the war, he deceiveth the enemy?"

"He will do right by so doing."

"May he not likewise, when he ravages their country, carry off their corn and their cattle without being guilty of injustice?"

"No doubt, Socrates; and when I seemed to say otherwise, I thought you confined what was spoken to our friends only."

"So then, whatever we have hitherto placed under our letter D, may be carried over, and ranged under A?"

"It may."

"But will it not be necessary to make a further distinction, Euthedemus, and say, that to behave in such a manner to our enemies is just; but, to our friends, unjust: because to these last the utmost simplicity and integrity is due?"

"You are in the right Socrates."

"But how," said Socrates, "if this general, on seeing the courage of his troops begin to fail, should make them believe fresh succours are at hand; and by this means remove their fears? To which side shall we assign this falsehood?"

"I suppose to justice."

"Or if a child refuseth the physic he stands in need of, and the father deceiveth him under the appearance of food—where shall we place the deceit, Euthedemus?"

"With the same, I imagine."

"And suppose a man in the height of despair should attempt to kill himself; and his friend should come and force away his sword; under what head are we to place this act of violence?"

"I should think, where we did the former."

"But take care, Euthedemus, since it seemeth from your answers that we ought not always to treat our friends with candour and integrity, which yet we had before agreed was to be done."

"It is plain we ought not," returned Euthedemus; "and I retract my former opinion, if it is allowable for me so to do."

"Most assuredly," said Socrates; "for it is far better to change our opinion, than to persist in a wrong one. However," continued he, "that we may pass over nothing without duly examining it: which of the two, Euthedemus, appears to you the most unjust; he who deceives his friend wittingly, or he who does it without having any such design?"

"Truly," said Euthedemus, "I am not certain what I should answer, or what I should think; for you have given such a turn to all I have hitherto advanced, as to make it appear very different to what I before thought it: however, I will venture so far as to declare that man the most unjust who deceiveth his friend designedly."

"Is it your opinion, Euthedemus, that a man must learn to be just and good, in like manner as he learneth to write and read?"

"I believe so."

"And which," said Socrates, "do you think the most ignorant, he who writes or reads ill designedly, or he who doth it for want of knowing better?"

"The last, certainly," replied Euthedemus; "since the other can do right whenever he pleases."

"It then follows that he who reads ill, from design, knows how to read well; but the other doth not?"

"It is true."

"Pray tell me," continued Socrates, "which of the two knoweth best what justice is, and what he ought to do; he who offends against the truth and deceives designedly, or he who does it without having any such design?"

"He, no doubt, who deceives designedly," replied Euthedemus.

"But you said, Euthedemus, that he who understands how to read, is more learned than one who does not?"

"I did so, Socrates; and it is certainly true."

"Then he who knows wherein justice consists, is more just than he who knows nothing of the matter?"

"So it seems," said Euthedemus; "and I know not how I came to say otherwise."

"But what would you think of the man, Euthedemus, who, however willing he might be to tell the truth, never tells you twice together the same thing: but if you ask him about the road, will show you to-day to the east, and to-morrow to the west; and make the very same sum amount sometimes to fifty, and sometimes to a hundred; what would you say to this man, Euthedemus?"

"That it was plain he knew nothing of what he pretended to know."

Socrates still went on, and said, "Have you never heard people called base and servile?"

"Frequently."

"And why were they so called? for their ignorance, or knowledge?"

"Not for their knowledge, certainly."

"What then? for their ignorance in the business of a brazier? building a house? or sweeping a chimney?"

"Nor this, nor that," replied Euthedemus; "for the men who are the most expert in employments of this nature, are generally the most abject and servile in their minds."

"It should seem then, Euthedemus, these appellatives only belong to those who are ignorant of what is just and good?"

"So I imagine."

"Doth it not then follow, that we ought to exert our powers to the utmost, to avoid this ignorance, which debases men so low?"

"O Socrates!" cried Euthedemus, with no little emotion, "I will not deny to you that I have hitherto believed I was no stranger to philosophy, but had already gained that knowledge so necessary for the man who aspires after virtue. What then must be my concern to find, after all my labour, I am not able to answer those questions which most importeth me to know? And the more, as I see not what method to pursue whereby I may render myself more capable!"

"Have you ever been at Delphos?"

"I have been there twice."

"Did you observe this inscription somewhere on the front of the temple—KNOW THYSELF?"

"Yes, I read it."

"But it seems scarcely sufficient to have read it, Euthedemus: did you consider it? and, in consequence of the admonition, set yourself diligently to find out what you are?"[1]

"I certainly did not," said Euthedemus; "for I imagined I must know this sufficiently already: and, indeed, it will be difficult for us to know any thing, if we can be supposed at a loss here."

"But for a man to know himself properly," said Socrates, "it is scarcely enough that he knows his own name. He who desires to purchase a horse, doth not imagine he hath made the proper trial of his merit, till by mounting him he hath found out whether he is tractable or unruly, strong or weak, fleet or heavy, with every thing else, either good or bad, in him: so likewise we should not say, he knows himself as he ought, who is ignorant of his own powers; or those duties which, as man, it is incumbent upon him to perform."

"It must be confessed," replied Euthedemus, "that he who knoweth not his own powers cannot be said to know himself."

"And yet, who seeth not," continued Socrates, "how great the advantage arising from this knowledge; and what misery must attend our mistakes concerning it! For he who is possessed of it, not only knoweth himself, but knoweth what is best for him. He perceiveth what he can and what he cannot do; he applieth himself to the one, he gaineth what is necessary, and is happy; he attempts not the other, and therefore incurs neither distress nor disappointment. From knowing himself he is able to form a right judgment of others, and turn them to his advantage, either for the procuring some good or preventing some evil. On the contrary, he who is ignorant of himself, and maketh a wrong estimate of his own powers, will also mistake those of other men: he knows neither what he wants or undertakes, nor yet the means he maketh use of; so that he not only fails of success, but ofttimes falls into many misfortunes; while the man who sees his way before him, most commonly obtains the end he aims at; and not only so, but secures to himself renown and honour. His equals gladly attend to his counsel and follow his advice; and they who, by wrong management, have plunged themselves into difficulties implore his help, and found all their hopes of being restored to their former ease, on the prudence of his administration: while they who blindly engage in business, as they choose ill, so they succeed worse; nor is the damage they then sustain the only misfortune they incur; but they are disgraced for ever; all men ridiculing, despising, or blaming them. Neither doth it fare any thing better with commonwealths themselves," continued Socrates, "when mistaking their own strength, they engage eagerly in war with their more powerful neighbours, which ends either in the ruin of the state, or the loss of their liberty; compelled to receive their laws from the hand of the conqueror."

"Be assured," answered Euthedemus, "that I am now fully convinced of the excellence of the precept which bids us KNOW OURSELVES: but from what point shall the man set out, my Socrates, on so important an inquiry? To inform me of this, is now what I hope from you."

[1] "The subject-matter," said Epictetus, "of a carpenter, is wood; of a statuary, brass; and so of the art of living, the subject-matter is, each person's own life."

3 E

" You know what things are good, what evil, Euthedemus ?"

" Certainly," replied Euthedemus ; " for otherwise I should know less than the very lowest of our slaves."

" Show me then, I pray you, what you think good ; what evil."

" Most willingly," answered Euthedemus ; " and truly, I think, the task will not be difficult.—First, then, I count sound health good, and sickness evil, and whatever conduces to the one, or the other, are to be estimated accordingly ; so that the food and exercise which keeps us in health, we may call good, and that which brings on us sickness and disease, evil."

" But might it not be as well to say, Euthedemus, that health and sickness are both of them good, when they are the cause of good ; and evil, when they are the cause of evil ?"

Reason. " But when do we see," replied Euthedemus, " that health is the cause of evil ; or sickness of good ?"

" It is certainly the case," answered Socrates, " when levies are raising for some unsuccessful expedition ; or embarkations made, which afterwards suffer shipwreck : for the healthy and the strong being selected on these occasions, they are unhappily involved in the same common misfortune ; while the feeble and the infirm remain in safety."

" That is true," replied Euthedemus : " but then, on the other hand, you must own, my Socrates, that the healthful and strong have their share, and that to their no small advantage, in more fortunate undertakings ; while the sickly and infirm are entirely excluded."

" These things being so, as indeed they are, sometimes profitable, and sometimes hurtful, we should not do amiss to set them down," said Socrates, " as being in themselves not more good than evil."

" So indeed it appears," said Euthedemus, " from this way of reasoning : but knowledge, my Socrates, must ever remain an indubitable good ; since he who hath knowledge, whatever the business, may certainly execute it with far greater advantage than he who wants it."

" Have you not heard then," said Socrates, " how it fared with the wretched Dædalus, on the account of his excelling in so many different arts ?[1] This man falling into the hands of

Minos, was detained by him in Crete : at once torn from his country, and deprived of his freedom : and when afterwards attempting to escape with his son, he was the cause of the loss of the miserable youth. Neither was he able to secure himself ; but being seized by the Barbarians, was compelled to return, again to endure all the evil of slavery."

" I have heard this," replied Euthedemus.

" You know too," continued Socrates, " the unhappy fate of Palamedes, whose praises all men celebrated :[2] he fell a sacrifice to the envy of Ulysses ; and miserably perished, through the insidious artifices of his rival : and how many are now languishing in perpetual bondage, whom the king of Persia caused to be carried away, and still keeps near him, merely on the account of their superior talents ?"

" But granting this to be as you say ; yet certainly," replied Euthedemus, " we may esteem happiness an undoubted good ?"

" We may," answered Socrates, " provided this happiness ariseth from such things as are undoubtedly good."

" But how can those things which produce happiness, be otherwise than good ?"

" They cannot," said Socrates," if you admit not of the number, health, strength, beauty, riches, fame, and such like."

" But we certainly do admit such things into the number," replied Euthedemus ; " for how are we to be happy without them ?"

" Rather, how are we to be happy with them," returned Socrates, " seeing they are the source of so many evils ? For how often hath a beautiful form been the cause of defilement ! How often, from a persuasion of their strength, have men been induced to engage in hazardous undertakings which overwhelm them in ruin ! How many have sunk into luxury by means of their riches, or fallen into the snares that were insidiously laid for them, by the people whose

---

1 He was the most ingenious artist in the world ; and hence the proverb *Dædali opera,* when we would com-

mend the curiousness of the workmanship. He invented the saw, the axe, the plummet, the auger, glue, cement, sails, and sail-yards ; and made statues, with a device to make the eyes move as if living.

2 Palamedes invented four Greek letters, and added them to the other sixteen already invented by Cadmus. He was skilful in astrology, and the first who found out the cause of an eclipse ; and brought the year to the course of the sun, and the month to the course of the moon : he was skilful in ordering an army, and introduced the use of the watch-word ; both which he took the hint of, as was said, from the conduct and the flying of cranes.

to examine what things were just or unjust; and have as steadily persisted in practising the one and refraining from the other; and this I take to be the best way of preparing for my trial."—" But know you not," replied Hermogenes, " that here, in Athens, the judges ofttimes condemn those to death who have no way deserved it, only because their manner of speaking was displeasing; while, on the other hand, they not less frequently acquit the guilty ?"

" I do know it," answered Socrates ; " and be assured, my Hermogenes, that I did not neglect to take the matter of my defence under consideration,—but the Genius opposed me."

Hermogenes replying, that he talked marvellously ; " But why," said he, " should it be marvellous that God should think this the very best time for me to die ? Know you not that hitherto I have granted to no man that he hath lived either better, or even more pleasurably, than I ; if, as I think it is, to be alone solicitous after the attainment of virtue be living well ; and the consciousness of making some proficiency therein pleasant : and that I did make some proficiency therein I well perceived, by comparing myself with others, and from the testimony of my own conscience ; my friends also saying the same concerning me. Not for that they love me : since, if so, every friend would think the same of him whom he was a friend to ; but because, as it seemed to them, they themselves became better men from having much conversed with me. But if my life should be still prolonged, it can hardly be but the infirmities of old age will likewise come upon me : my sight will fail, my hearing grow heavy, and my understanding much impaired ; so that I shall find it more difficult to learn, as less easy to retain what I have learnt already ; deprived too of the power of performing many of those things which heretofore I have excelled in. And if, after all, I should become insensible to these decays, still life would not be life, but a wearisome burthen. And if otherwise, if I indeed find and feel them, how unpleasant, how afflicting, must a state like this prove ! If I die wrongfully, the shame must be theirs who put me wrong-

fully to death : since, if injustice is shameful, so likewise every act of it : but no disgrace will it bring on me, that others have not seen that I was innocent. The examples drawn from former ages sufficiently show us, that those who commit wrong, and they who suffer it, stand not alike in the remembrance of men : and I am persuaded, that if I now die, I shall be held in far higher estimation by those who come after me than any of my judges : since posterity will not fail to testify concerning me, that I neither wronged, nor yet, by my discourses, corrupted any man ; but, contrariwise, strove throughout life, to the utmost of my power, to make all those who conversed with me happy."

In this manner did Socrates continue to discourse with Hermogenes and others : nor are there any among those who knew him, if lovers of virtue, who do not daily regret the loss of his conversation ; convinced how much they might have been advantaged thereby.

As to myself, knowing him of a truth to be such a man as I have described ; so pious towards the gods, as never to undertake any thing without having first consulted them : so just towards men, as never to do an injury, even the very slightest, to any one ; whilst many and great were the benefits he conferred on all with whom he had any dealings : so temperate and chaste, as not to indulge any appetite, or inclination, at the expense of whatever was modest or becoming : so prudent, as never to err in judging of good and evil ; nor wanting the assistance of others to discriminate rightly concerning them : so able to discourse upon, and define with the greatest accuracy, not only those points of which we have been speaking, but likewise of every other ; and looking as it were into the minds of men, discover the very moment for reprehending vice, or stimulating to the love of virtue. Experiencing, as I have done, all these excellencies in Socrates, I can never cease considering him as the most virtuous and the most happy of all mankind. But if there is any one who is disposed to think otherwise, let him go and compare Socrates with any other, and afterwards let him determine.

THE

BANQUET OF XENOPHON.

TRANSLATED BY

JAMES WELWOOD, M.D.
FELLOW OF THE ROYAL COLLEGE OF PHYSICIANS, LONDON.

4 G

BANQUET OF XENOPHON.

Sophists

I. I AM of opinion, that as well the sayings as the actions of great men deserve to be recorded, whether they treat of serious subjects with the greatest application of mind, or, giving themselves some respite, unbend their thoughts to diversions worthy of them. You will know by the relation I am going to make, what it was inspired me with this thought, being myself present.

During the festival of Minerva, there was a solemn tournament, whither Callias,[1] who tenderly loved Autolicus, carried him, which was soon after the victory which that youth had obtained at the Olympic games. When the show was over, Callias taking Autolicus and his father with him, went down from the city to his house at the Piræum,[2] with Nicerates the son of Nicias.

But upon the way meeting Socrates, Hermogenes, Critobulus, Antisthenes, and Charmides, discoursing together, he gave orders to one of his people to conduct Autolicus and those of his company to his house; and addressing himself to Socrates, and those who were with him, "I could not," said he, "have met with you more opportunely; I treat to-day Autolicus and his father; and, if I am not deceived, persons who like you have their souls purified[3] by refined contemplations, would do much more honour to our assembly, than your colonels of horse, captains of foot, and other gentlemen of business, who are full of nothing but their offices and employments." —"You are always upon the banter," said Socrates; "for, since you gave so much money to Protagoras, Gorgias, and Prodicas,[4] to be instructed in wisdom, you make but little account of us, who have no other assistance but from ourselves to acquire knowledge."—"'Tis true," said Callias, "hitherto I have concealed from you a thousand fine things I learned in the conversation of those gentlemen; but if you will sup with me this evening, I will teach you all I know, and after that I do not doubt you will say I am a man of consequence."

Socrates and the rest thanked him with the civility that was due to a person of so high a rank, that had invited them in so obliging a manner: and Callias, showing an unwillingness to be refused, they at last accepted the invitation, and went along with him. After they had done bathing and anointing, as was the custom before meals, they all went into the eating-room, where Autolicus was seated by his father's side; and each of the rest took his place according to his age or quality.

The whole company became immediately sensible of the power of beauty, and every one at the same time silently confessed, that by natural right the sovereignty belonged to it, especially when attended with modesty and a virtuous bashfulness. Now Autolicus was one of that kind of beauties; and the effect which the sight of so lovely a person produced was to attract the eyes of the whole company to him, as one would do to flashes of lightning

---

1 Callias was of the noblest families in Athens, and was surnamed the rich.

2 The sea-port town of Athens.

3 Socrates was called the purifying philosopher, because he purified the minds of those he conversed with from vice and errors of education.

4 Three famous pedants that pretended to teach wisdom, alias ophists.

in a dark night. All hearts surrendered to his power, and paid homage to the sweet and noble mien and features of his countenance, and the manly gracefulness of his shape.

It is very certain, that in those who are divinely inspired by some good demon, there appears something which makes them behold with the strictest attention, and a pleasing astonishment: whereas, those who are possessed by some evil genius or power, besides the terror that appears in their looks, they talk in a tone that strikes horror, and have a sort of unbounded vehemence in all they say and do, that comes but little short of madness. Thence it is, as it was in this case, that those who are touched with a just and well regulated love, discover in their eyes a charming sweetness, in the tone of the voice a musical softness, and in their whole deportment something that expresses in dumb show the innate virtue of their soul.

At length they sat down to supper, and a profound silence was observed, as though it had been enjoined: when a certain buffoon, named Philip, knocked at the door, and bade the servant that opened it tell the gentlemen he was there, and that he came to sup with them; adding, there was no occasion to deliberate whether he should let him in, for that he was perfectly well furnished with every thing that could be necessary towards supping well on free cost, his boy being weary with carrying nothing in his belly, and himself extremely fatigued with running about to see where he could fill his own." Callias understanding the arrival of this new guest, ordered him to be let in, saying, " We must not refuse him his dish;" and at the same time turned his eyes towards Autolicus, to discover, probably, the judgment he made of what had passed in the company with relation to him; but Philip coming into the room, " Gentlemen," said he, "you all know I am a buffoon by profession, and therefore am come of my own accord. I choose rather to come uninvited, than put you to the trouble of a formal invitation, having an aversion to ceremony."—" Very well," said Callias, " take a place then Philip; the gentlemen here are full of serious thoughts, and I fancy they will have occasion for somebody to make them laugh."

While supper lasted, Philip failed not to serve them up, now and then, a dish of his profession; he said a thousand ridiculous

things; but not having provoked one smile, he discovered sufficient dissatisfaction. Some time after he fell to it again, and the company heard him again without being moved. Thereupon he got up, and throwing his cloak over his head, [1] laid himself down at his full length on his couch, without eating one bit more. " What is the matter," said Callias; "has any sudden illness taken you?"—" Alas !" cried he, fetching a deep sigh from his heart, "the quickest and most sensible pain that ever I felt in my whole life; for, since there is no more laughing in the world, it is plain my business is at an end, and I have nothing now to do but to make a decent exit. Heretofore I have been called to every jolly entertainment, to divert the company with my buffooneries; but to what purpose should they now invite me? I can as soon become a god as say one serious word; and to imagine any one will give me a meal in hopes of a return in kind, is a mere jest, for my spit was never yet laid down for supper; such a custom never entered my doors."

While Philip talked in this manner, he held his handkerchief to his eyes, and personated to admiration a man grievously afflicted. Upon which every one comforted him, and promised, if he would eat, they would laugh as much as he pleased. The pity which the company showed Philip having made Critobulus [2] almost burst his sides, Philip uncovered his face and fell to his supper again, saying, " Rejoice, my soul, and take courage, this will not be thy last good meal; I see thou wilt yet be good for something."

II. They had now taken away, and made effusion of wine in honour of the gods, when a certain Syracusan entered, leading in a handsome girl, who played on the flute; another, that danced and showed very nimble feats of activity; and a beautiful little boy, who danced and played perfectly well on the guitar. After these had sufficiently diverted the company, Socrates, addressing himself to Callias, " In truth," says he, "you have treated us very handsomely, and have added to the delicacy of eating, other things delightful to our seeing and hearing."

---

1 The Greeks under any disgrace, threw their mantle over their head.

2 It is thought that by Critobulus the author meant himself.

"But we want perfumes [3] to make up the treat," answered Callias : "What say you to that ?"—"Not at all," replied Socrates ; "perfumes, like habits, are to be used according to decency ; some become men, and others women ; but I would not that one man should perfume himself for the sake of another : and for the women, especially such as the wife of Critobulus or Nicerates, they have no occasion for perfumes, their natural sweetness supplying the want of them. But it is otherwise if we talk of the smell of that oil that is used in the Olympic games, or other places of public exercise.[4] This, indeed, is sweeter to the men than perfumes to the women ; and when they have been for some time disused to it, they only think on it with a greater desire. If you perfume a slave and a freeman, the difference of their birth produces none in the smell ; and the scent is perceived as soon in the one as the other : but the odour of honourable toil, as it is acquired with great pains and application, so it is ever sweet, and worthy of a brave man."—"This is agreeable to young men," said Lycon ; "but as for you and me, who are past the age of these public exercises, what perfumes ought we to have ?"—"That of virtue and honour," said Socrates.

Lycon. "And where is this sort of perfume to be had ?"

Soc. "Not in the shops, I assure you."

Lycon. "Where then ?"

Soc. "Theognis sufficiently discovers where, when he tells us in his poem :

"When virtuous thoughts warm the celestial mind
,With generous heat, each sentiment's refin'd :
Th' immortal perfumes breathing from the heart,
With grateful odours sweeten every part.

"But when our vicious passions fire the soul,
The clearest fountains grow corrupt and foul ;
The virgin springs, which should untainted flow,
Run thick, and blacken all the stream below."

"Do you understand this, my son?" said Lycon to Autolicus. "He not only understands it, but will practise it too," said Socrates, "and I am satisfied, when he comes to contend for that noble prize, he will choose a master to instruct him, such as you shall approve of, who will be capable of giving him rules to attain it."

Then they began all to reassume what Socrates had said. One affirmed there was no master to be found that was qualified to instruct others in virtue ; another said it could not be taught : and a third maintained that if virtue could not be taught nothing else could. "Very well," said Socrates ; "but since we cannot agree at present in our opinions about this matter, let us defer the question to another opportunity, and apply ourselves to what is before us ; I see the dancing girl entering at the other end of the hall, and she has brought her cymbals along with her." At the same time the other girl took her flute ; the one played and the other danced to admiration ; the dancing girl throwing up and catching again her cymbals, so as to answer exactly the cadency of the music, and that with a surprising dexterity. Socrates, who observed her with pleasure, thought it deserved some reflection : and therefore, said he, "This young girl has confirmed me in the opinion I have had of a long time, that the female sex are nothing inferior to ours, excepting only in strength of body, or perhaps steadiness of judgment. Now you, gentlemen, that have wives amongst us, may take my word for it they are capable of learning any thing you are willing they should know to make them more useful to you." "If so, sir," said Antisthenes ; "if this be the real sentiment of your heart, how comes it you do not instruct Xantippe, who is, beyond dispute, the most insupportable woman that is, has been, or ever will be ?"—"I do with her," said Socrates, "like those who would learn horsemanship : they do not choose easy tame horses, or such as are manageable at pleasure, but the highest metalled and hardest mouthed ; believing, if they can tame the natural heat and impetuosity of these, there can be none too hard for them to manage. I propose to myself very near the same thing ; for having designed to converse with all sorts of people, I believed I should find nothing to disturb me in their conversation or manners, being once accustomed to bear the unhappy temper of Xantippe."

The company relished what Socrates said, and the thought appeared very reasonable. Then a hoop being brought in, with swords fixed all around it, their points upwards, and placed in the middle of the hall, the dancing

3 It was the custom of the Greeks at great entertainments to perfume their guests, at which they sometimes expended great sums.

4 At the Olympic and other games of Greece they rubbed their joints with hot oils, to make them more supple and active.

girl immediately leaped head foremost into it, through the midst of the points, and then out again, with a wonderful agility. This sight gave the company more surprise and fear than pleasure, every one believing she would wound herself; but she received no harm, and performed her feats with all the courage and assurance imaginable.

" The company may say what they please," said Socrates : " but, if I am not mistaken, nobody will deny but courage may be learned, and that there are masters for this virtue in particular, though they will not allow it in the other virtues we were just now speaking of; since a girl, you see, has the courage to throw herself through the midst of naked swords, which I believe none of us dare venture upon."— " Truly," said Antisthenes, to whom Socrates spoke, " the Syracusan may soon make his fortune, if he would but show this girl in a full theatre, and promise the Athenians that, for a considerable sum of money, he would instruct them to be as little afraid of the Lacedæmonian lances as this girl of her swords."—" Ah !" cries the buffoon, " what pleasure should I take to see Pisander, that grave counsellor of state, taking lessons from this girl; he that is like to swoon away at the sight of a lance, and says it is a barbarous cruel custom to go to war and kill men."

After this the little boy danced, which gave occasion to Socrates to say, " You see this child, who appeared beautiful enough before, is yet much more so now, by his gesture and motion, than when he stood still."—" You talk," said Carmides, " as if you were inclinable to esteem the trade of a dancing-master." —" Without doubt," said Socrates, " when I observe the usefulness of that exercise, and how the feet, the legs, the neck, and indeed the whole body, are all in action, I believe whoever would have his body supple, easy, and healthful, should learn to dance. And, in good earnest, I am resolved to take a lesson of the Syracusan whenever he pleases." But it was replied, " When you have learned to do all this little boy does, what advantage can it be to you?"—" I shall then dance," said Socrates. At which all the company burst out a laughing : but Socrates, with a composed and serious countenance, " Methinks you are pleasant," said he. " What is it tickles you ? Is it because dancing is not a wholesome exercise ? or that after it we do not eat and sleep with

more pleasure ? You know those who accustom themselves to the long foot-race [1] have generally thick legs and narrow shoulders ; and, on the contrary, our gladiators and wrestlers have broad shoulders and small legs. Now, instead of producing such effects, the exercise of dancing occasions in us so many various motions, and agitating all the members of the body with so equal a poise, renders the whole of a just proportion, both with regard to strength and beauty. What reason then can you find to laugh, when I tell you I design to dance ? I hope you would not think it decent for a man of my age to go into a public school, and unrobe myself before all the company to dance ? I need not do that; a parlour, like this we are in, will serve my turn. You may see, by this little boy, that one may sweat as well in a little room as an academy, or a public place ; and in winter you may dance in a warm apartment; in summer, if the heat be excessive, in the shade. When I have told you all this, laugh on, if you please, at my saying I design to dance. Besides, you know I have a belly somewhat larger than I could wish; and are you surprised if I endeavour to bring it down by exercise ? Have you not heard that Carmides, the other morning, when he came to visit me, found me dancing?"—" Very true," said Carmides ; " and I was extremely surprised, and afraid you had lost your senses : but when you had given me the same reasons you have now, I went back to my house ; and, though I cannot dance, I began to move my hands and legs, and practise over some lessons, which I remembered something of when I was young."

" Faith!" said Philip to Socrates, " I believe your thighs and shoulders are exactly of the same weight; so that if you put one into one scale, and the other into the other, as the civil magistrate weighs bread in the market-place, you will not be in danger of being forfeited, for there is not an ounce, no not a grain difference between them."—" Well then," said Callias, " when you have an inclination for a lesson of dancing, Socrates, pray call upon me, that we may learn together."—" With all my heart," answered Socrates.—" And I could wish," said Philip, " that some one would take

---

1 Running was a part of the Olympic and other public games ; and what is here called the Dolic, was the place where they ran, about the length of two English miles.

the flute, and let Socrates and me dance before this good company; for methinks I have a mighty mind that way." With that he jumped up, and took two or three frisks round the hall, in imitation of the dancing boy and girl. Upon which every body took notice, that all those gestures or motions, that were so beautiful and easy in the little boy, appeared awkward and ridiculous in Philip: and when the little girl, bending backwards, touched her heels with her head, and flung herself swiftly round three or four times like a wheel, Philip would needs do the same, but in a manner very different; for, bending himself forward, and endeavouring to turn round, you may imagine with what success he came off. Afterwards, when every one praised the child for keeping her whole body in the exactest and most regular motion in the dance, Philip bade the music strike up a brisker tune, and began to move his head, his arms, and his heels, all at once, till he could hold out no longer: then throwing himself on the couch, he cried out, " I have exercised myself so thoroughly, that I have already one good effect of it, I am plaguy thirsty; boy, bring the great glass that stands on the sideboard, and fill it up to me, for I must drink." — " Very well," said Callias; " the whole company shall drink, if you please, master Philip, for we are thirsty too with laughing at you."—" It is my opinion too," said Socrates, " that we drink; wine moistens and tempers the spirits, and lulls the cares of the mind to rest, as opium does the body: on the other hand, it revives our joys, and is oil to the dying flame of life. It is with our bodies as with seeds sown in the earth; when they are over-watered they cannot shoot forth, and are unable to penetrate the surface of the ground: but when they have just so much moisture as is requisite, we may behold them break through the clod with vigour; and pushing boldly upwards, produce their flowers, and then their fruits. It is much the same thing with us; if we drink too much, the whole man is deluged, his spirits are overwhelmed, and is so far from being able to talk reasonably, or indeed to talk at all, that it is with the utmost pain he draws his breath: but if we drink temperately, and small draughts at a time, the wine distils upon our lungs like sweetest morning dew (to use the words of that noble orator Gorgias). It is then the wine commits no rape upon our reason, but pleasantly invites us to agreeable

mirth." Every one was of his opinion; and Philip said he had something to offer, which was this: " Your servants," said he, " that wait at the sideboard should imitate good coachmen, who are never esteemed such till they can turn dexterously and quick." The advice was immediately put in practice, and the servants went round and filled every man his glass.

III. Then the little boy, tuning his guitar to the flute, sung and played at the same time; which gave mighty satisfaction to all the company. Upon this Carmides spoke: " What Socrates," said he, " just now offered about the effects of wine, may, in my opinion, with little difference, be applied to music and beauty, especially when they are found together: for I begin in good earnest to be sensible that this fine mixture buries sorrow, and is at the same time the parent of love." Whereupon Socrates took occasion to say, " If these people are thus capable of diverting us, I am well assured we are now capable ourselves, and I believe nobody here doubts it. In my judgment, it would be shameful for us, now we are met together, not to endeavour to benefit one another by some agreeable or serious entertainment. What say you, gentlemen?" They generally replied, " Begin then the discourse from which we are to hope so good an effect."—" I hope," said Socrates, " to obtain that favour of Callias, if he would but give us a taste of those fine things he learnt of Prodicus: you know he promised us this when we came to sup with him." — " With all my heart," said Callias, " I am willing, but on condition that you will all please to contribute to the conversation, and every one tell, in his turn, what it is he values himself most upon." —" Be it so," said Socrates.—" I will tell you then," added Callias, " what I esteem most, and value myself chiefly upon: it is this, that I have it in my power to make men better."— " How so," said Antisthenes; " will you teach them to become rich or honest ?"—" Justice is honesty," replied Callias. " You are in the right," said Antisthenes, " I do not dispute it; for though there are some occasions when even courage or wisdom may be hurtful to one's friends or the government, yet justice is ever the same, and can never mix with dishonesty."—" When, therefore, every one of us," says Callias, " has told wherein he chiefly values himself, and is most useful to others, I shall then likewise make no scruple to tell you by what arts I am able to perform what I told you : that is, to make men better."

Soc. " But, Nicerates, what is the thing that you value yourself most upon ?"

[1] *Nic.* " It is that my father, designing to make a virtuous man of me, ordered me to get by heart every verse of Homer ; and I believe I can repeat you at this minute the whole Iliad and Odyssey."—" But you know very well," said Antisthenes, " every public rehearser, [2] or ballad-singer, does the same at all the corners of the streets." " I acknowledge it," said Nicerates ; " nor does a day pass but I go to hear them."

Ant. " I think them a pack of scandalous wretches : What say you ?"

Nic. " I am of your opinion."

Soc. " It is certain they do not know the sense of one verse they recite : but you, [3] who have given so much money to Hesimbrotus, Anaximander, and other wise men, to instruct you in wisdom, you cannot be ignorant of any thing."

" Now it is your turn, Critobulus," continued Socrates : " tell us then, if you please, what it is you value yourself most upon ?"— " On beauty," replied he.—" But will you say, Socrates, that yours is such as will help to make us better ?"

Soc. " I understand you : but if I do not make that out anon, then blame me. What says Antisthenes ? upon what does he value himself ?"

Ant. " I think I can value myself upon nothing in this world equal to that of being rich."

He had scarce done speaking, when Hermogenes took him up, and asked him how much he was worth ? " Faith, not one halfpenny," said Antisthenes.

Her. " But you have a good estate in land ?"

Ant. " I may perhaps have just as much as may afford dust for Autolicus, the next time he has a mind to wrestle." [4]

Soc. " Carmides, will you, in few words, acquaint us with what it is you value yourself most upon ?"

Car. " Poverty."

Soc. " Very well ; you have made an excellent choice : it is indeed in itself of an admirable nature ; nobody will be your rival ; you may preserve it without care, and even negligence is its security. These are not small reasons, you see."

Callias. " But, since you have asked the whole company, may we not inquire of you, Socrates, what it is you value yourself upon ?"

When Socrates, putting on a very grave and solemn air, answered coldly, and without hesitation, " I value myself upon procuring." [5] The gravity of the speaker, and the manner of speaking a word so little expected from Socrates, set the whole company a laughing. " Very well, gentlemen," said he, " I am glad you are pleased ; but I am very certain this profession of mine, if I apply myself closely to it, will bring in money enough if I pleased."

When Lycon, pointing to Philip ; " Well, what say you ?"—" You, I suppose, value yourself upon making men laugh ?"—" Yes, certainly," said Philip ; " and have I not more reason to be proud of myself for this, than that fine spark, Callipides, who is so fond, you know, of making his audience weep, when he recites his verses in the theatre ?"—" But, Lycon," said Antisthenes, " let us know what it is you value yourself most upon ? What gives you greatest content ?"—You know very well," answered he, " what I esteem the most, and which gives me the greatest pleasure, it is to be the father of such a son as Autolicus."

" And for your son," said some of the company, " he, no question, values himself most upon carrying the prize the other day at the Olympic games ?"—" Not so, I assure you," said Autolicus, blushing. And then the whole company turning their eyes with pleasure towards him, one of them asked him, ' What is it, then, Autolicus, you value yourself most upon ?'—" It is," replied he, " that I am the son of such a father ;" and at the same time turned himself lovingly towards him for a kiss. —Callias, who observed it, said to Lycon, " Don't you know yourself to be the richest man in the world ?"—" I cannot tell that," replied Lycon. " And yet it is true," said Callias, " for you would not change this son of yours for the wealth of Persia."

---

1 Nicerates here represents a true pedant.

2 These were people who got their livelihood by singing Homer's verses about the streets of Athens.

3 This is spoken in raillery.

4 The wrestlers at the public games, after they had rubbed themselves with oils, had dust thrown upon them to dry it up.

5 I cannot find a softer word in English for the Greek here. Socrates explains himself afterwards.

Lycon. " Be it so; I am then the richest man in the world; nor will I contradict your opinion."

Then Nicerates addressing himself to Hermogenes: " What is it," said he, " that you value yourself most upon?"—" On virtue," answered he, " and the power of my friends: and that, with these two advantages, I have yet the good fortune to be beloved by these friends."

Then every one looking upon him, began to inquire who were his friends?"—" I will satisfy you," said he, " as you shall see, when it comes to my turn."

IV. Then Socrates resumed the discourse: " Now you have all," said he, " declared your opinions, as to what you value yourselves most upon, it remains that you prove it. Let us now then hear every man's reasons, if you please, for his opinion."

" Hear me first then," said Callias: " for though you have all been inquiring what justice is, I alone have found the secret to make men just and honest."

Soc. " How so?"

Call. " By giving them money."

At these words, Antisthenes rising up, asked him hastily, " Is justice to be found in the heart or the pocket?"

Call. " In the heart."

Ant. " And would you then make us believe, that by filling a bag with money, you can make the heart honest or just?"

Call. " Most assuredly."

Ant. " How?"

Call. " Because when they have all things necessary for life, they will not, for the world, run any hazard by committing evil actions."

Ant. " But do they repay you again what they receive of you?"

Call. " Not at all."

Ant. " Nothing but gratitude, I hope; good thanks for good money."

Call. " Not that neither: for I can tell you something you will hardly believe; I have found some people of so evil a nature, that they love me less for receiving benefits from me." Then Antisthenes replied briskly,

Ant. " That is wonderful: you make men just and honest to others, and they prove unjust and dishonest only to you?"

Call. " Not so wonderful neither!"—" Have we not architects and masons, who build houses for other men, and live in hired lodgings

themselves?"—" Have patience, my master," said he, (turning to Socrates) " and I will prove this beyond dispute."—" You need not," said Socrates; " for, beside what you allege for a proof, there is another that occurs to me: Do you not see there are certain diviners who pretend to foretell every thing to other people, and are entirely ignorant of what is to happen to themselves." Socrates said no more.

" It is now my turn to speak," said Nicerates:[1] " hear then to what I am going to say, attend to a conversation which will necessarily make you better, and more polite. You all know, or I am much mistaken, there is nothing that relates to human life but Homer has spoken of it. Whoever then would learn economy, eloquence, arms; whoever would be master of every qualification that is to be found in Achilles, Ajax, Ulysses, or Nestor; let him but apply himself to me, and he shall become perfect in them, for I am entirely master of all that."—" Very well," said Antisthenes, " you have learned likewise the art of being a king; for you may remember Homer praises Agamemnon for that he was

" A noble warrior and a mighty prince."

Nicer. " I learnt too, from Homer, how a coachman ought to turn at the end of his career. He ought to incline his body to the left, and give the word to the horse that is on the right, and make use at the same time of a very loose rein. I have learnt all this from him, and another secret too, which, if you please, we will make trial of immediately: the same Homer says somewhere, that an onion relishes well with a bottle. Now let some of your servants bring an onion, and you will see with what pleasure you will drink."—" I know very well," said Carmides, " what he means; Nicerates, gentlemen, thinks deeper than you imagine. He would willingly go home with the scent of an onion in his mouth, that his wife may not be jealous, or suspect he has been kissing abroad."—" A very good thought," said Socrates; " but perhaps I have one full as whimsical, and worthy of him: it is, that an onion does not only relish wine, but victuals too, and gives a higher seasoning: but if we should eat them now after supper, they would say we had committed a debauch at Callias's."—" No, no," said Callias, " you can never think so: but on-

---

1 Here Nicerates plays the pedant indeed, as if to repeat Homer was to be truly learned.

4 H

ions, they say, are very good to prepare people for the day of battle, and inspire courage; you know they feed cocks so against they fight: but our business, at present, I presume, is love, not war; and so much for onions."

Then Critobulus began. "I am now," said he, "to give my reasons why I value myself so much upon my beauty. If I am not handsome (and I know very well what I think of the matter), you ought all of you to be accounted imposters, for without being obliged to it upon oath, when you were asked what was your opinion of me, you all swore I was handsome, and I thought myself obliged to believe you, being men of honour that scorned a lie. If, then, I am really handsome, and you feel the same pleasure that I do when I behold another beautiful person, I am ready to call all the gods to witness, that were it in my choice either to reign king of Persia, or be that beauty, I would quit the empire to preserve my form. In truth, nothing in this world touches me so agreeably as the sight of Amandra, and I could willingly be blind to all other objects, if I might but always enjoy the sight of her I so tenderly love.

"I curse my slumbers, doubly curse the night,
That hides the lovely maid from my desiring sight;
But, oh! I bless the cheerful god's return,
And welcome with my praise the ruddy morn;
Light with the morn returns, return my fair,
She is the light, the morn restores my dear."

"There is something more in the matter, besides this, to be considered. A person that is vigorous and strong, cannot attain his designs but by his strength and vigour; a brave man by his courage; a scholar by his learning and conversation: but the beautiful person does all this, without any pains, by being only looked at. I know very well how sweet the possession of wealth is, but I would sacrifice all to Amandra: and I should with more pleasure give all my estate to her, than to receive a thousand times more from any other. I would lay my liberty at her feet if she would accept me for her slave: fatigue would be much more agreeable to me than repose, and dangers than ease, if endured in the service of Amandra. If, then, you boast yourself so much, Callias, that you can make men honester by your wealth, I have much more reason to believe I am able to produce in them all sorts of virtue by the mere force of beauty; for when beauty inspires, it makes its votaries generous and industrious;

they thereby acquire a noble thirst after glory, and a contempt of dangers; and all this attended with an humble and respectful modesty, which makes them blush to ask what they wish most to possess. I think the government is stark mad, that they do not choose for generals the most beautiful persons in the state; for my part, I would go through fire to follow such a commander, and I believe you would all do the same for me. Doubt not then, Socrates, but beauty may do much good to mankind; nor does it avail to say beauty does soon fade; for there is one beauty of a child, another of a boy, another of a man. There is likewise a beauty of old age, as in those who carry the consecrated branches[1] at the feast of Minerva; for you know for that ceremony they make choice always of the handsomest old men. Now, if it is desirable to obtain without trouble what one wishes, I am satisfied that, without speaking one word, I should sooner persuade that little girl to kiss me than any of you, with all the arguments you can use; no, not you yourself, Socrates, with all the strength of your extolled eloquence."—"Why, Critobulus, do you give yourself this air of vanity," said Socrates, "as if you were handsomer that me?"—"Doubtless," replied Critobulus, "if I have not the advantage of you in beauty, I must be uglier than the Sileni,[2] as they are painted by the poets." Now Socrates had some resemblance to those figures.

Soc. "Take notice, if you please, that this article of beauty will be soon decided anon, after every one has taken his turn to speak: nor shall we call Paris to make a judgment for us, as he did in the case of the three goddesses about the apple: and this very young girl, who you would make us believe had much rather kiss you than any of us, she shall determine it?"

Crit. "And why may not Amandra be as good as a judge of this matter?"

Soc. "Amandra must needs have a large possession of your heart, seeing, by your good will, you would never name any other name but hers."

Crit. "True; and yet when I do not speak of her, do you think she lives not in my memory? I assure you, if I were a painter or a

---

1 These were of the olive-tree, kept sacred in the citadel of Athens; and both old men and old women carried them by turns.

2 The Sileni were the fosterfathers of Bacchus, and horridly deformed.

statuary, I could draw her picture or statue by the idea of her in my mind, as well as if she were to sit to it."

Soc. " Since then you have her image in your heart, and that image resembles her so strongly, why is it that you importune me continually to carry you to places where you are sure to meet her ?"

Crit. " It is because the sight of Amandra only gives me real joy.

" The idea does no solid pleasure give;
She must within my sight, as well as fancy, live."

Hermogenes interrupted the discourse; and addressing himself to Socrates, said, " You ought not to abandon Critobulus in the condition he is in, for the violent transport and fury of his passion makes me uneasy for him, and I know not where it may end."

Soc. " What! do you think he is become thus only since he was acquainted with me? You are mightily deceived; for I can assure you this fire has been kindled ever since they were children. Critobulus's father having observed it, begged of me that I would take care of his son, and endeavour, if I could, by all means to cure him of it. He is better now; things were worse formerly: for I have seen, when Amandra appeared in company, Critobulus, poor creature, would stand as one struck dead, without motion, and his eyes so fixed upon her, as if he had beheld Medusa's head; insomuch, that it was impossible almost for me to bring him to himself.

" I remember one day, after certain amorous glances, (this is between ourselves only,) he ran up to her and kissed her; and, Heaven knows, nothing gives more fuel to the fire of love than kisses. For this pleasure is not like others, which either lessen or vanish in the enjoyment : on the contrary, it gathers strength the more it is repeated; and flattering our souls with sweet and favourable hopes, bewitches our minds with a thousand beautiful images. Thence it may be, that to love and to kiss are frequently expressed by the same word in the Greek: and it is for that reason, I think, he that would preserve the liberty of his soul, should abstain from kissing handsome people." " What, then," said Carmides, "must I be afraid of coming near a handsome woman ? Nevertheless, I remember very well, and I believe you do so too, Socrates, that being one day in company with Critobulus's beautiful sister, who resembles him so much, as we were

searching together for a passage in some author, you held your head very close to that beautiful virgin; and I thought you seemed to take pleasure in touching her naked shoulder with yours."—" Good God !" replied Socrates, " I will tell you truly how I was punished for it for five days after: I thought I felt in my shoulder a certain tickling pain, as if I had been bit by gnats, or pricked with nettles : and I must confess too, that during all that time I felt a certain hitherto unknown pain at my heart. But, Critobulus, take notice what I am going to tell you before this good company: it is, that I would not have you come too near me, till you have as many hairs upon your chin as your head, for fear you put me in mind of your handsome sister."

Thus the conversation between these gentlemen was sometimes serious, sometimes in raillery. After this Callias took up the discourse. " It is your turn now," said he, " Carmides, to tell us what reasons you have for valuing yourself so much upon poverty."—" I will," replied Carmides, "and without delay. Is any thing more certain, than that it is better to be brave than a coward; a freeman, than a slave; to be credited, than distrusted; to be inquired after for your conversation, than to court others for theirs? These things, I believe, may be granted me without much difficulty. Now, when I was rich, I was in continual fear of having my house broken open by thieves, and my money stolen, or my throat cut upon the account of it. Besides all this, I was forced to keep in fee with some of these pettyfogging rascals that retain to the law, who swarm all over the town like so many locusts. This I was forced to do, because they were always in a condition to hurt me; and I had no way to retaliate upon them. Then I was obliged to bear public offices at my own charges, and to pay taxes: nor was it permitted me to go abroad for travel, to avoid that expense. But now that my estate, which I had without the frontiers of our republic, is all gone, and my land in Attica brings me in no rent, and all my household goods are exposed to sale, I sleep wonderfully sound, and stretched upon my bed as one altogether fearless of officers. The government is now no more jealous of me, nor I of it; thieves fright me not, and I myself affright others. I travel abroad when I please; and when I please I stay at Athens. What is to be free, if this is not? Besides, rich men pay respect to me ; they run from me, to leave me the chair, or to give me the wall. In a word, I am now perfectly a king; I was then perfectly a slave. I have yet another advantage from my poverty ; I then paid tribute to the republic ; now the republic pays tribute to me; for it maintains me. Then every one snarled at me, because I was often with Socrates. Now that I am poor, I may converse with him, or any other I please, without anybody's being uneasy at it. I have yet another satisfaction : in the days of my estate, either the government or my ill fortune were continually clipping it : now that is all gone, it is impossible to get any thing of me ; he that has nothing, can lose nothing. And I have the continual pleasure of hoping to be worth something again, one time or other."

"Don't you pray heartily against riches ?" says Callias. "And if you should happen to dream you were rich, would you not sacrifice to the gods to avert the ill omen :"— "No, no," replied Carmides : "but when any flattering hope presents, I wait patiently for the success." Then Socrates turning to Antisthenes ; "And what reason have you," said he, "who have very little or no money, to value yourself upon wealth ?"

Ant. "Because I am of opinion, gentlemen, that poverty and wealth are not in the coffers of those we call rich or poor, but in the heart only ; for I see numbers of very rich men, who believe themselves poor ; nor is there any peril or labour they would not expose themselves to, to acquire more wealth. I knew two brothers, the other day, who shared equally their father's estate. The first had enough, and something to spare ; the other wanted every thing. I have heard likewise of some princes so greedy of wealth, that they were more notoriously criminal in the search of it than private men : for though the latter may sometimes steal, break houses, and sell free persons to slavery, to support the necessities of life ; yet those do much worse : they ravage whole countries, put nations to the sword, enslave free states : and all this for the sake of money, and to fill the coffers of their treasury. The truth is, I have a great deal of compassion for these men, when I consider the distemper that afflicts them. Is it not an unhappy condition to have a great deal to eat, to eat a great deal, and yet never be satisfied ? For my part, though I confess I have no money at home, yet I want

none ; because I never eat but just as much as will satisfy my hunger, nor drink but to quench my thirst. I clothe myself in such manner that I am as warm abroad as Callias, with all his great abundance. And when I am at home, the floor and the wall, without mats or tapestry, make my chamber warm enough for me. And as for my bed, such as it is, I find it more difficult to awake than to fall asleep in it. If at any time a natural necessity requires me to converse with women, I part with them as well satisfied as another. For those to whom I make my addresses, having not much practice elsewhere, are as fond of me as if I were a prince. But don't mistake me, gentlemen, for governing my passion in this as in other things : I am so far from desiring to have more pleasure in the enjoyment, that I wish it less ; because, upon due consideration, I find those pleasures that touch us in the most sensible manner deserve not to be esteemed the most worthy of us. But observe the chief advantage I reap from my poverty ; it is, that in case the little I have should be taken entirely from me, there is no occupation so poor, no employment in life so barren, but would maintain me without the least uneasiness, and afford me a dinner without any trouble. For if I have an inclination at any time to regale myself and indulge my appetite, I can do it easily ; it is but going to market, not to buy dainties (they are too dear,) but my temperance gives that quality to the most common food ; and, by that means, the contentedness of my mind supplies me with delicacies, that are wanting in the meat itself. Now, it is not the excessive price of what we eat that gives it a relish, but it is necessity and appetite. Of this I have experience just now, while I am speaking ; for this generous wine of Thasos,[1] that I am now drinking, the exquisite flavour of it is the occasion that I drink it now without thirst, and consequently without pleasure. Besides all this, I find it is necessary to live thus, in order to live honestly. For he that is content with what he has, will never covet what is his neighbour's. Further, it is certain the wealth I am speaking of makes men liberal. For, Socrates, from whom I have all mine, never gave it me by number or weight ; but, whenever I am willing to receive, he loads me

---

1 The noblest vines, that grew in one of the Grecian islands.

always with as much as I can carry. I do the same by my friends; I never conceal my plenty. On the contrary, I show them all I have, and at the same time I let them share with me. It is from this, likewise, I am become master of one of the most delightful things in the world; I mean, that soft and charming leisure, that permits me to see every thing that is worthy to be seen, and to hear every thing that is worthy to be heard. It is, in one word, that which affords me the happiness of hearing Socrates from morning to night; for he having no great veneration for those that can only count vast sums of gold and silver, converses only with them who he finds are agreeable to him, and deserve his company."—" Truly," said Callias, " I admire you, and these your excellent riches, for two reasons: first, that thereby you are no slave to the government; and, secondly, that nobody can take it ill you do not lend them money."— " Pray do not admire him for the last," said Nicerates;[2] " for I am about to borrow of him what he most values, that is, to need nothing; for by reading Homer, and especially that passage where he says,

" Ten golden talents, seven three-legg'd stools,
    Just twenty cisterns, and twelve charging steeds ;"

I have so accustomed myself, from this passage, to be always upon numbering and weighing, that I begin to fear I shall be taken for a miser." Upon this they all laughed heartily; for there was nobody there but believed Nicerates spoke what he really thought, and what were his real inclinations.

After this, one spoke to Hermogenes : "It is yours now," said he, " to tell us who are your friends; and make it appear, that if they have much power, they have equal will to serve you with it, and, consequently, that you have reason to value yourself upon them."

Hermog. "[3] There is one thing, gentlemen, universally received among barbarians as well as Greeks; and that is, that the gods know both the present and what is to come : and for that reason they are consulted and applied to by all mankind, with sacrifices, to know of them what they ought to do. This supposes

that they have the power to do us good or evil; otherwise, why should we pray to them to be delivered from evils that threaten us, or to grant us the good we stand in need of? Now these very gods, who are both all-seeing and all-powerful, they are so much my friends, and have so peculiar a care of me, that be it night, be it day, whether I go any where, or take any thing in hand, they have me ever in their view and under their protection, and never lose me out of their sight. They foreknow all the events and all the thoughts and actions of us poor mortals : they forewarn us by some secret prescience impressed on our minds, or by some good angel or dream, what we ought to avoid, and what we ought to do. For my part, I have never had occasion yet to repent these secret impulses given me by the gods, but have been often punished for neglecting them."—" There is nothing in what you have said," added Socrates, " that should look incredible : but I would willingly hear by what services you oblige the gods to be so much your friends, and to love and take all this care of you?"—" That is done very cheap, and at little or no expense," replied Hermogenes, " for the praises I give them cost me nothing. If I sacrifice to them after I have received a blessing from them, that very sacrifice is at their own charge. I return them thanks on all occasions; and if at any time I call them to witness, it is never to a lie, or against my conscience."—" Truly," said Socrates, " if such men as you have the gods for their friends, and I am sure they have, it is certain those gods take pleasure in good actions and the practice of virtue."

Here ended their serious entertainment. What followed was of another kind; for all of them turning to Philip, asked him, " What it was he found so very valuable in his profession?"—" Have I not reason to be proud of my trade," said he, " all the world knowing me to be a buffoon? If any good fortune happens to them, they cheerfully invite me; but when any misfortune comes, they avoid me like the plague, lest I should make them laugh in spite of themselves." Nicerates, interrupting him, " You have reason indeed," said he, " to boast of your profession, for it is quite otherwise with me: when my friends have no occasion for me, they avoid me like the plague; but in misfortunes they are ever about me, and, by a forged genealogy, will needs claim kindred

---

[2] Nicerates was both very rich and very covetous, being the son of Nicias, whose life is written by Plutarch.

[3] This is one of the noblest periods in all antiquity.

with me, and at the same time carry my family up as high as the gods."—" Very well," said Carmides, " now to the rest of the company."

" Well, Mr Syracusan, What is it which gives you the greatest satisfaction, or that you value yourself most upon? I suppose it is that pretty little girl of yours?"—" Quite contrary," says he; " I have much more pain than pleasure upon her account: I am in constant apprehension and fear when I see certain people so busy about her, and trying all insinuating ways to ruin[1] her."—" Good God!" said Socrates, " What wrong could they pretend to have received from that poor young creature, to do her a mischief? Would they kill her?"

Syr. " I do not speak of killing her; you do not take me, they would willingly get to bed to her."

Soc. " Suppose it were so, why must the girl be ruined therefore?"

Syr. " Ay, doubtless."

Soc. " Do not you lie in bed with her yourself?"

Syr. " Most certainly, all night long."

Soc. " By Juno, thou art a happy fellow to be the only man in the world that do not ruin those you lie with. Well, then, according to your account, what you are proudest of must be, that you are so wholesome and so harmless a bedfellow?"

Syr. " But you are mistaken; it is not her I value myself for neither."

Soc. " What then?"

Syr. " That there are so many fools in the world; for it is these kind of gentlemen, who come to see my children dance and sing, that supply me with the necessaries of life, which otherwise I might want."

" I suppose then," said Philip, " that was the meaning of your prayer you made the other day before the altar, when you asked the gods that there might be plenty of every thing in this world wherever you came, but of judgment and good sense?"

> " Immortal beings, grant my humble prayer;
> Give Athens all the blessings you can spare;
> Let them abound in plenty, peace, and pence,
> But never let them want a dearth of sense."

" All is well hitherto," said Callias: " But, Socrates, what reason have you to make us believe you are fond of the profession you attributed to yourself just now, for really I take it for a scandalous one?"

Soc. " First, let us understand one another; and know in few words what this artist is properly to do, whose very name has made you so merry: but, to be brief, let us, in short, fix upon some one thing that we may all agree in. Shall it be so?"—" Doubtless," answered all the company: and during the thread of his discourse they made him no other answer but " doubtless." Having began so, " Is it not certainly true,"[2] said Socrates, " that the business of an artist of that kind is to manage so as that the person they introduce be perfectly agreeable to one that employs him?"—" Doubtless," they replied. " Is it not certain, too, that a good face and fine clothes do mightily contribute towards the making such a person agreeable?"—" Doubtless."—" Do you not observe that the eyes of the same person look at some times full of pleasure and kindness, and at other times with an air of aversion and scorn?"—" Doubtless."—" What, does not the same voice sometimes express itself with modesty and sweetness, and sometimes with anger and fierceness?"—" Doubtless."—" Are there not some discourses that naturally beget hatred and aversion, and others that conciliate love and affection?"— " Doubtless."—" If, then, this artist be excellent in his profession, ought he not to instruct those that are under his direction which way to make themselves agreeable to others in all these things I have mentioned?"—" Doubtless."—" But who is most to be valued; he who renders them agreeable to one person only, or he that renders them agreeable to many? Are you not for the last?" Some of them answered him as before, with " doubtless;" and the rest said, it was very plain that it was much better to please a great many than a few. " That is very well," said Socrates; " we agree upon every head hitherto: but what if the person we are speaking of can instruct his pupil to gain the hearts of a whole state, will not you say he is excellent in his art?" This, they all agreed, was clear. " And if he can raise his scholars to such perfection, has he not reason to be proud of his profession? And deserves he not to re-

---

1 The word in the original signifies to kill, to ruin, or to corrupt.

2 It was a great advantage that Socrates had in conversation, that his arguments were generally by way of interrogation, by which he argued from the concessions that were made him, what he designed to prove.

ceive a handsome reward?" Every one answered, it was their opinion he did. "Now," said Socrates, "if there is such a man to be found in the world, it is Antisthenes, or I am mistaken."

Ant. "How, Socrates! Will you make me one of your scurvy profession?"

Soc. "Certainly, for I know you are perfectly skilled in what may properly be called an appendix to it."

Ant. "What is that?"

Soc. "Bringing people together."

To this Antisthenes, with some concern, replied, "Did you ever know me guilty of a thing of this kind."

Soc. "Yes, but keep your temper. You procured Callias for Prodicus, finding the one was in love with philosophy, and the other in want of money: you did the same before, in procuring Callias for Hippias, who taught him the art of memory; and he is become such a proficient, that he is more amorous now than ever; for every woman he sees, that is tolerably handsome, he can never forget her, so perfectly has he learnt of Hippias the art of memory. You have done yet more than this, Antisthenes; for lately praising a friend of yours, of Heraclea, to me, it gave me a great desire to be acquainted with him: at the same time you praised me to him, which occasioned his desire to be acquainted with me; for which I am mightily obliged to you, for I find him a very worthy man. Praising likewise in the same manner Esquilius to me, and me to him, did not your discourse inflame us both with such mutual affection, that we searched every day for one another with the utmost impatience till we came acquainted? Now, having observed you capable of bringing about such desirable things, had not I reason to say you are an excellent bringer of people together? I know very well, that one who is capable of being useful to his friend, in fomenting mutual friendship and love between that friend and another he knows to be worthy of him, is likewise capable of begetting the same disposition between towns and states: he is able to make state-marriages; nor has our republic or our allies a subject that may be more useful to them: and yet you were angry with me, as if I had affronted you, when I said you were master of this art."

Ant. "That is true, Socrates; but my anger is now over; and were I really what you say I am, I must have a soul incomparably rich."

Now you have heard in what manner every one spoke, when Callias began again, and said to Critobulus, "Will you not then venture into the lists with Socrates, and dispute beauty with him?"

Soc. "I believe not; for he knows my art gives me some interest with the judges."

Crit. "Come, I will not refuse to enter the lists for once with you; pray then use all your eloquence, and let us know how you prove yourself to be handsomer than I."

Soc. "That shall be done presently; bring but a light, and the thing is done."

Crit. "But, in order to state the question well, you will give me leave to ask a few questions?"

Soc. "I will."

Crit. "But, on second thoughts, I will give you leave to ask what questions you please first."

Soc. "Agreed. Do you believe beauty is no where to be found but in man?"

Crit. "Yes certainly, in other creatures too, whether animate, as a horse or bull, or inanimate things, as we say that is a handsome sword, or a fine shield, &c."

Soc. "But how comes it then, that things so very different as these should yet all of them be handsome?"

Crit. "Because they are well made, either by art or nature, for the purposes they are employed in."

Soc. "Do you know the use of eyes?"

Crit. "To see."

Soc. "Well! it is for that very reason mine are handsomer than yours."

Crit. "Your reason?"

Soc. "Yours see only in a direct line; but, as for mine, I can look not only directly forward, as you, but sideways too, they being seated on a kind of ridge on my face, and staring out."

Crit. "At that rate, a crab has the advantage of all other animals in matter of eyes?"

Soc. "Certainly: for theirs are incomparably more solid, and better situated than any other creature's."

Crit. "Be it so as to eyes; but as to your nose, would you make me believe that yours is better shaped than mine?"

Soc. "There is no room for doubt, if it be granted that God made the nose for the sense of smelling; for your nostrils are turned downward, but mine are wide and turned up towards heaven, to receive smells that come from every part, whether from above or below."

Crit. " What! is a short flat nose, then, more beautiful than another?"

Soc. " Certainly; because being such, it never hinders the sight of both eyes at once; whereas a high nose parts the eyes so much by its rising, that it hinders their seeing both of them in a direct line."

Crit. " As to your mouth, I grant it you; for if God has given us a mouth to eat with, it is certain yours will receive and chew as much at once as mine at thrice."

Soc. " Don't you believe too that my kisses are more luscious and sweet than yours, having my lips so thick and large?"

Crit. " According to your reckoning, then, an ass's lips are more beautiful than mine."

Soc. " And lastly, I must excel you in beauty, for this reason: the Naiades, notwithstanding they are sea-goddesses, are said to have brought forth the Sileni; and sure I am much more like them than you can pretend to be. What say you to that?"

Crit. " I say it is impossible to hold a dispute with you, Socrates; and therefore let us determine this point by ballotting; and so we shall know presently who has the best of it, you or I: but pray let it be done in the dark, lest Antisthenes's riches and your eloquence should corrupt the judges."

Whereupon the little dancing boy and girl brought in the ballotting box, and Socrates called at the same time for a flambeau to be held before Critobulus, that the judges might not be surprised in their judgment. He desired likewise that the conqueror, instead of garters and ribands, as were usual in such victories, should receive a kiss from every one of the company. After this they went to ballotting, and it was carried unanimously for Critobulus. Whereupon Socrates said to him, " Indeed, Critobulus, your money has not the same effect with Callias's, to make men juster; for yours, I see, is able to corrupt a judge upon the bench."

VI. After this, some of the company told Critobulus he ought to demand the kisses due to his victory; and the rest said, it was proper to begin with him who made the proposition. In short, every one was pleasant in his way except Hermogenes, who spoke not one word all the time; which obliged Socrates to ask him, " If he knew the meaning of the word *paroinia* ?"

Her. " If you ask me what it is precisely, I do not know; but if you ask my opinion of it, perhaps I can tell you what it may be."

Soc. " That is enough."

Her. " I believe, then, that *paroinia* signifies the pain and uneasiness we undergo in the company of people that we are not pleased with."—" Be assured then," said Socrates, " this is what has occasioned that prudent silence of yours all this time."

Her. " How my silence! when you were all speaking ?"

Soc. " No, but your silence when we have done speaking and make a full stop."

Her. " Well said, indeed! No sooner one has done but another begins to speak; and I am so far from being able to get in a sentence, that I cannot find room to edge in a syllable."—" Ah, then," said Socrates to Callias, " cannot you assist a man that is thus out of humour?"—" Yes," said Callias; " for I will be bold to say, when the music begins again, every body will be silent as well as Hermogenes."

Her. " You would have me do then as the poet Nicostrates, who used to recite his grand iambics to the sound of his flute: and it would be certainly very pretty if I should talk to you all the time the music played."—" For God's sake do so," said Socrates; " for as the harmony is the more agreeable that the voice and the instrument go together, so your discourse will be more entertaining for the music that accompanies it; and the more delightful still, if you give life to your words by your gesture and motion, as the little girl does with her flute."—" But when Antisthenes," said Callias, " is pleased to be angry in company, what flute will be tunable enough to his voice ?"

Ant. " I do not know what occasion there will be for flutes tuned to my voice; but I know, that when I am angry with any one in dispute, I am loud enough, and I know my own weak side."

As they were talking thus, the Syracusan observing they took no great notice of any thing he could show them, but that they entertained one another on subjects out of his road, was out of all temper with Socrates, who he saw gave occasion at every turn for some new discourse. " Are you," said he to him, " that

Socrates who is sirnamed the *Contempla-tive?*'

Soc. "Yes," said Socrates : " and is it not much more preferable to be called so, than by another name, for some opposite quality?"

Syr. "Let that pass. But they do not only say in general that Socrates is contem-plative, but that he contemplates things that are sublime."

[1] *Soc.* "Know you any thing in the world so sublime and elevated as the gods?"

Syr. "No. But I am told your contempla-tions run not that way. They say they are but trifling ; and that, in searching after things above your reach, your inquiries are good for nothing."

Soc. "It is by this, if I deceive not myself, that I attain to the knowledge of the gods : for it is from above that the gods make us sensible of their assistance ; it is from above they in-spire us with knowledge. But if what I have said appears dry and insipid, you are the cause, for forcing me to answer you."

Syr. "Let us then talk of something else. Tell me then the just measure of the skip of a flea ; for I hear you are a subtle geometrician, and understand the mathematics perfectly well."

But Antisthenes, who was displeased with his discourse, addressing himself to Philip, told him : "You are wonderfully happy, I know, in making comparisons.' Pray who is this Syracusan like, Philip? Does he not resem-ble a man that is apt to give affronts, and say shocking things in company?"—"Faith," said Philip, "he appears so to me, and I believe to every body else."—"Have a care," said So-crates ; "do not affront him, lest you fall under the character yourself that you would give him."

Phil. "Suppose I compare him to a well-bred person : I hope nobody will say I affront him then?"

Soc. "So much the more," said Socrates ; "such a comparison must needs affront him to some purpose."

Phil. "Would you then that I compare him to some one that is neither honest nor good?"

Soc. "By no means."

Phil. "Who must I compare him to then? To "nobody?"

Soc. Nobody."

Phil. "But it is not proper we should be silent at a feast."

Soc. "That is true ; but it is as true we ought rather be silent than say any thing we ought not to say."

Thus ended the dispute between Socrates and Philip.

VII. However, some of the company were for having Philip make his comparisons ; others were against it, as not liking that sort of diversion ; so that there was a great noise about it in the room : which Socrates observing, "Very well," said he, "since you are for speaking all together, it were as well, in my opinion, that we should sing all together ;" and with that he began to sing himself. When he had done, they brought the dancing girl one of those wheels the potters use, with which she was to divert the company in turning herself round it. Upon which So-crates, turning to the Syracusan : "I believe I shall pass for a contemplative person indeed," said he, "as you called me just now, for I am now considering how it comes to pass that those two little actors of yours give us pleasure in seeing them perform their tricks, without any pain to themselves, which is what I know you design. I am sensible that for the little girl to jump head foremost into the hoop of swords, with their points upwards, as she has done just now, must be a very dangerous leap ; but I am not convinced that such a spectacle is proper for a feast. I confess likewise, it is a surprising sight to see a person writing and reading at the same time that she is carried round with the motion of the wheel, as the girl has done ; but yet I must own it gives me no great pleasure. For would it not be much more agreeable to see her in a natural easy pos-ture, than putting her handsome body into an unnatural agitation, merely to imitate the mo-tion of a wheel? Neither is it so rare to meet with surprising and wonderful sights ; for here is one before our eyes, if you please to take notice of it. Why does that lamp, whose flame is pure and bright, give all the light to the room, when that looking-glass gives none at all, and yet represents distinctly all objects in its surface? Why does that oil, which is in its own nature wet, augment the flame ; and that water, which is wet likewise, extinguish it?

---

1 Here Socrates banters the Syracusan ; and in the Greek it is a play of words which cannot be imitated in English.

2 To make biting comparisons was a part of the buf-foons of that age.

But these questions are not proper at this time. And, indeed, if the two children were to dance to the sound of the flute, dressed in the habits of nymphs, the graces, or the four seasons of the year, as they are commonly painted, they might undergo less pain, and we receive more pleasure."—"You are in the right, sir," said the the Syracusan to Socrates; "and I am going to represent something of that kind, that certainly must divert you;" and at the same time went out to make it ready, when Socrates began a new discourse.

VIII. "What then," said he, "must we part without saying a word of the attributes of that great demon, or power, who is present here, and equals in age the immortal gods, though, to look at, he resembles but a child? That demon, who by his mighty power is master of all things, and yet is engrafted into the very essence and constitution of the soul of man; I mean Love. We may indeed with reason extol his empire, as having more experience of it than the vulgar, who are not initiated into the mysteries of that great god as we are. Truly, to speak for one, I never remember I was without being in love: I know, too, that Carmides has had a great many lovers, and being much beloved, has loved again. As for Critobulus, he is still of an age to love, and to be beloved; and Nicerates too, who loves so passionately his wife, at least as report goes, is equally beloved by her. And who of us does not know that the object of that noble passion and love of Hermogenes, is virtue and honesty? Consider, pray, the severity of his brows, his piercing and fixed eyes, his discourse so composed and strong, the sweetness of his voice, the gaiety of his manners. And what is yet more wonderful in him, that, so beloved as he is by his friends the gods, he does not disdain us mortals. But for you, Antisthenes, are you the only person in the company that does not love?"

Ant. "No! for in faith I love you, Socrates, with all my heart."

Then Socrates rallying him, and counterfeiting an angry air, said, "Do not trouble me with it now; you see I have other business upon my hands at present."

Ant. "I confess you must be an expert master of the trade you valued yourself so much upon a while ago; for sometimes you will not be at the pains to speak to me, and at other times you pretend your demon will not permit you, or that you have other business."

Soc. "Spare me a little, Antisthenes; I can bear well enough any other troubles that you give me, and I will always bear them as a friend; but I blush to speak of the passion you have for me, since I fear you are not enamoured with the beauty of my soul, but with that of my body.'

"As for you, Callias,[1] you love, as well as the rest of us: for who is it that is ignorant of your love for Autolicus? It is the town-talk; and foreigners, as well as our citizens, are acquainted with it. The reasons for your loving him, I believe to be, that you are both of you born of illustrious families; and, at the same time, are both possessed of personal qualities that render you yet more illustrious. For me, I always admired the sweetness and evenness of your temper; but much more, when I consider that your passion for Autolicus is placed on a person who has nothing luxurious or affected in him; but in all things shows a vigour and temperance worthy of a virtuous soul; which is a proof, at the same time, that if he is infinitely beloved, he deserves to be so.

"I confess, indeed, I am not firmly persuaded whether there be but one Venus or two, the celestial and the vulgar: and it may be with this goddess, as with Jupiter, who has many different names, though there is still but one Jupiter. But I know very well that both the Venuses have altogether different altars, temples, and sacrifices. The vulgar Venus is worshipped after a common, negligent manner; whereas the celestial one is adored in purity and sanctity of life. The vulgar inspires mankind with the love of the body only, but the celestial fires the mind with the love of the soul, with friendship, and a generous thirst after noble actions. I hope that it is this last kind of love that has touched the heart of Callias. This I believe, because the person he loves is truly virtuous; and whenever he desires to converse with him, it is in the presence of his father, which is a proof his love is perfectly honourable."

Upon which Hermogenes began to speak: "I have always admired you, Socrates, on

---

1 Here Socrates shows a wonderful address in turning the passion of Callias from Autolicus, to something more elevated, and beyond personal beauty.

every occasion, but much more now than ever. You are complaisant to Callias, and indulge his passion. And this your complaisance is agreeable to him; so it is wholesome and instructive, teaching him in what manner he ought to love."—" That is true," said Socrates; "and that my advice may please him yet the more, I will endeavour to prove that the love of the soul is incomparably preferable to that of the body. I say then, and we all feel the truth of it, that no company can be truly agreeable to us without friendship; and we generally say, whoever entertains a great value and esteem for the manners and behaviour of a man, he must necessarily love him. We know, likewise, that among those who love the body only, they many times disapprove the humour of the person they so love, and hate perhaps at the same time the mind and temper, while they endeavour to possess the body. Yet further, let us suppose a mutual passion between two lovers of this kind; it is very certain that the power of beauty, which gives birth to that love, does soon decay and vanish: and how is it possible that love, built on such a weak foundation, should subsist, when the cause that produced it has ceased? But it is otherwise with the soul; for the more she ripens, and the longer she endures, the more lovely she becomes. Besides, as the constant use of the finest delicacies is attended, in progress of time, with disgust: so the constant enjoyment of the finest beauty palls the appetite at last. But that love that terminates on the bright qualities of the soul, becomes still more and more ardent: and, because it is in its nature altogether pure and chaste, it admits of no satiety. Neither let us think, with some people that this passion, so pure and so chaste, is less charming, or less strong than the other. On the contrary, those who love in this manner are possessed of all that we ask in that our common prayer to Venus: ' Grant, O goddess! that we may say nothing but what is agreeable, and do nothing but what does please.' Now, I think it is needless to prove, that a person of a noble mien, generous and polite, modest and well-bred, and in a fair way to rise in the state, ought first to be touched with a just esteem for the good qualities of the person he courts, for this will be granted by all. But I am going to prove, in few words, that the person thus addressed to must infallibly return the love of a man that is thus endued with

such shining accomplishments. For, is it possible for a woman to hate a man, who she believes has infinite merit, and who makes his addresses to her upon the motive of doing justice to her honour and virtue, rather than from a principle of pleasing his appetite? And how great is the contentment we feel, when we are persuaded that no light faults or errors shall ever disturb the course of a friendship so happily begun, or that the diminution of beauty shall never lessen one's affection? How can it ever happen otherwise, but that persons who love one another thus tenderly, and with all the liberties of a pure and sacred friendship, should take the utmost satisfaction in one another's company, in discoursing together with an entire confidence, in mingling their mutual interests, and rejoicing in their good fortune, and bearing a share in their bed? Such lovers must needs partake of one another's joy or grief, be merry and rejoice with one another in health, and pay the closest and tenderest attendance on one another when sick, and express rather a greater concern for them when absent, than present. Does not Venus and the Graces shower down their blessings on those who love thus? For my part, I take such to be perfectly happy; and a friendship like this must necessarily persevere to the end of their lives, uninterrupted and altogether pure. But I confess I cannot see any reason why one that loves only the exterior beauty of the person he courts, should be loved again. Is it because he endeavours to obtain something from her, that gives him pleasure, but her shame? Or is it, because in the conduct of their passion they carefully conceal the knowledge of it from their parents or friends? Somebody, perhaps, may object, that we ought to make a different judgment of those who use violence, and of those who endeavour to gain their point by the force of persuasion; but, I say, these last deserve more hatred than the first. The first appear in their proper colours, for wicked persons; and so every one is on their guard against such open villany; whereas the last, by sly insinuations, insensibly corrupt and defile the mind of the person they pretend to love. Besides, why should they, who barter their beauty for money, be supposed to have a greater affection for the purchasers, than the trader, who sells his goods in the market-place, has for his chapmen that pays him down the price. Do not be surprised, then, if such lovers as these meet often with the contempt they deserve. There is one thing more in this case worthy of your consideration; we shall never find that the love which terminates in the noble qualities of the mind has ever produced any dismal effects. But there are innumerable examples of tragical consequences, which have attended that love which is fixed only on the beauty of the body. Chiron and Phœnix loved Achilles, but after a virtuous manner, without any other design than to render him a more accomplished person. Achilles likewise loved and honoured them in return, and held them both in the highest veneration. And indeed I should wonder, if one that is perfectly accomplished should not entertain the last contempt for those who admire only their personal beauty. Nor is it hard to prove, Callias, that gods and heroes have always had more passion and esteem for the charms of the soul, than those of the body: at least this seems to have been the opinion of our ancient authors. For we may observe in the fables of antiquity, that Jupiter, who loved several mortals upon the account of their personal beauty only, never conferred upon them immortality. Whereas it was otherwise with Hercules, Castor, Pollux, and several others; for having admired and applauded the greatness of their courage, and the beauty of their minds, he enrolled them in the number of the gods. And, whatever some affirm to the contrary of Ganymede, I take it he was carried up to heaven from mount Olympus, not for the beauty of his body, but that of his mind. At least his name seems to confirm my opinion, which in the Greek seems to express as much as, 'to take pleasure in good counsel, and in the practice of wisdom.' When Homer represents Achilles so gloriously revenging the death of Patroclus, it was not properly the passion of love that produced that noble resentment, but that pure friendship and esteem he had for his partner in arms. Why is it, that the memory of Pylades and Orestes, Theseus and Perithous, and other demigods, are to this day so highly celebrated? Was it for the love of the body, think you? No! by no means: it was the particular esteem and friendship they had for one another, and the mutual assistance every one gave to his friend, in those renowned and immortal enterprises, which are to this day the subject of our his- ries and hymns. And, pray, who are they

that performed those glorious actions? Not they that abandoned themselves to pleasure, but they that thirsted after glory; and who, to acquire that glory, underwent the severest toils, and almost insuperable difficulties.

" You are then infinitely obliged to the gods, Callias, who have inspired you with love and friendship for Autolicus, as they have inspired Critobulus with the same for Amandra; for real and pure friendship knows no difference in sexes. It is certain Autolicus has the most ardent passion for glory; since, in order to carry the prize at the Olympic games, and be proclaimed victor by the heralds, with sound of trumpet, as he lately was, he must needs have undergone numberless hardships and the greatest fatigues: for no less was required towards gaining the victory in so many different exercises.[1] But if he proposes to himself, as I am sure he does, to acquire further glory, to become an ornament to his family, beneficent to his friends, to extend the limits of his country by his valour, and by all honest endeavours to gain the esteem of Barbarians as well as Greeks: do not you believe he will always have the greatest value for one who he believes may be useful and assistant to him in so noble a design? If you would then prove acceptable, Callias, to any one you love, you ought to consider and imitate those methods by which Themistocles rose to the first dignities of the state, and acquired the glorious title of The Deliverer of Greece; the methods by which Pericles acquired that consummate wisdom, which proved so beneficial, and brought immortal honour to his native country. You ought to ponder well how it was, that Solon became the lawgiver to this republic of Athens, and by what honourable means the Lacedæmonians have arrived to such wonderful skill in the art of war: and this last you may easily acquire, by entertaining, as you do, at your house, some of the most accomplished Spartans. When you have sufficiently pondered all these things, and imprinted those noble images upon your mind, doubt not but your country will some time or other court you to accept the reins of government, you having already the advantage of a noble birth, and that important office of high priest, which gives you a greater lustre

---

1 There were five exercises, leaping, running, throwing the javelin, fighting with the whirlbat, and wrestling, and the victor was to conquer in them all.

already, than any of your renowned ancestors could ever boast of: and let me add that air of greatness, which shines in your person, and that strength and vigour that is lodged in so handsome a body, capable of the severest toils, and the most difficult enterprises."

Socrates having said all this to Callias, addressed himself to the company, and said: "I know very well this discourse is too serious for a feast, but you will not be surprised, when you consider that our commonwealth has been always fond of those who, to the goodness of their natural temper, have added an indefatigable search after glory and virtue. And in this fondness of mine for such men, I but imitate the genius of my country."

After this the company began to entertain one another, upon the subject of this last discourse of Socrates: when Callias, with a modest blush in his face, addressed himself to him: "You must then lend me," said he, "the assistance of your art, to which you gave such a surprising name [2] a while ago, to render me acceptable to the commonwealth, and that when it shall please my country to intrust me with the care of its affairs, I may so behave myself as to preserve its good opinion, and never do any thing, but what tends to the public good."—"You will certainly succeed; do not doubt it," said Socrates. "You must apply yourself in good earnest to virtue, and not content yourself, as some people do, with the appearance of it only, as if that might suffice. For know, Callias, that false glory can never subsist long. Flattery or dissimulation may for a while varnish over such a rotten structure; but it must tumble down at last. On the contrary, solid glory will always maintain its post; unless God, for some secret reasons, hid from us, think fit to oppose its progress: otherwise, that sublime virtue, which every man of honour should aim at, does naturally reflect back upon him such rays of glory, as grow brighter and brighter every day, in proportion as his virtue rises higher and higher."

IX. The discourse being ended, Autolicus rose to take a walk, and his father following turned towards Socrates, and said, "Socrates, I must declare my opinion, that you are a truly honest man."

After this, there was an elbow chair brought

into the middle of the room, and the Syracusan appearing at the same time; "Gentlemen," said he, "Ariadne is just now entering; and Bacchus, who has made a debauch to day with the gods, is coming down to wait upon her: and I can assure you, they will both divert the company and one another. Immediately Ariadne entered the room, richly dressed, in the habit of a bride, and placed herself in the elbow chair. A little after Bacchus appeared, while at the same time the girl that played on the flute struck up an air that used to be sung at the festival of that god. It was then that the Syracusan was admired for an excellent master in his art: for Ariadne being perfectly well instructed in her part, failed not to show, by her pretty insinuating manner, that she was touched with the air of the music; and that though she rose not from her chair to meet her lover, she yet expressed sufficiently the great desire she had to do it. Bacchus perceiving it, came on dancing toward her, in the most passionate manner, then sat himself down on her lap, and taking her in his arms, kissed her. As for Ariadne, she personated to the life a bride's modesty; and for a while, looking down to the ground, appeared in the greatest confusion; but at length recovering herself, she threw her arms about her lover's neck, and returned his kisses. All the company expressed the great satisfaction the performance gave them; and, indeed nothing could be better acted, nor accompanied with more grace in the acting. But when Bacchus rose, and took Ariadne by the hand to lead her out, they were still more pleased; for the pretty couple appeared to embrace and kiss one another after a much more feeling manner than is generally acted on the stage. Then Bacchus addressing himself to Ariadne, said, "Dost thou love me, my dearest creature?" "Yes, yes," answered she, "let me die if I do not; and will love thee to the last moment of my life." In fine, the performance was so lively and natural that the company came to be fully convinced of what they never dreamt of before; that the little boy and girl were really in love with one another: which occasioned both the married guests, and some of those that were not, to take horse immediately, and ride back full speed to Athens, with the briskest resolutions imaginable. I know not what happened afterwards; but for Socrates, and some who staid behind, they went a-walking with Lycon, Autolicus, and Callias.

HIERO:

ON THE

CONDITION OF ROYALTY.

TRANSLATED BY

THE REV. R. GRAVES.

HIERO:

ON THE

CONDITION OF ROYALTY.

A CONVERSATION BETWEEN HIERO AND SIMONIDES.

I. THE poet Simonides being come to reside at the court of Hiero king of Syracuse, one day as they were conversing at their leisure, "Will you, Hiero," said Simonides, "inform me of some particulars, which, it is reasonable to suppose, you must know much better than I can do?"

"What particulars then do you imagine," said Hiero, "I can possibly know better than so learned and wise a man as you are generally acknowledged to be?"

"Why," replied Simonides, "I have known you, when you were yet a private man, and now see you advanced to royalty. It is probable, therefore, that you, who have experienced both these states, should know better than I can do, wherein the life of a king differs from that of a private man, in regard to the pleasures or inconveniences attendant on each state."

"Well then," said Hiero, "but as you are now in a private station, ought not you first to recall to my remembrance the pleasures and inconveniences of a private life? By which means, I shall be better enabled to show you the difference of the two states in question."

To this Simonides thus replied: "I think then, Hiero, I have observed, that men in private life possess all the genuine feelings of nature. They receive pleasure and pain from the proper objects of their several senses; from visible objects by their eyes; of sounds by their ears; of scents by their nostrils; of food by the palate; and other sensual enjoyments, the source of which every one knows.

"It appears to me likewise," added he, "that we receive agreeable or painful sensations from heat and cold, from things hard and soft, heavy and light, in the whole and in every part of the body. But to perceive pleasure or pain from what is good or evil (in a moral sense), belongs, I think, to the mind alone: yet in some sense, to the mind and body in conjunction. [1]

"I find by experience also, that we receive pleasure from sleep; but, from what source, and from what kind of sleep, and when this pleasure arises, I own myself at a loss to explain. Neither is this at all surprising, as we certainly have less distinct perceptions when asleep, than when we are awake."

To this Hiero answered: "I confess Simonides, I know not any sensations of pleasure or pain that a king can receive, besides those which you have mentioned. And consequently I do not see, hitherto, in what the life of a king differs from that of a private person."

"Yet even in these particulars," answered Simonides, "there is a very material difference. And, in each of these, kings experience infinitely more pleasure and less pain than private persons."

---

1 The meaning here is not very obvious.

" Ah !" cried Hiero, " this is by no means the case : but be assured, that in all these respects, kings taste much less pleasure, and feel much more chagrin, than those individuals who are placed in the middle ranks of life."

" What you say," replied Simonides, " is altogether incredible. For, if it were so, why should such numbers, and those who are esteemed for their sense and wisdom, be so ambitious of royalty? And why do all mankind envy kings ?"

" Because," said Hiero, " they form their opinions without having experienced both these conditions of life. But I will endeavour to convince you of the truth of what I assert, and will proceed in the same order which you have suggested, and begin with the pleasures of sight: for it was thence, I think, that you commenced this discourse.

II. " In the first place, then, if we reason from the objects of sight, I am convinced that kings have the least share of pleasure in that respect.

" Every country has its curiosities ; which deserve to be visited and viewed by strangers. Now men in private stations can come or go to any part of the world without ceremony ; and into whatever cities they please, for the sake of the public spectacles ; and into those general assemblies [1] of all Greece, where are collected together, whatever is thought worthy of the attention and curiosity of mankind.

" As for kings,[2] they can rarely amuse themselves with spectacles of any kind. For neither would it be safe for them to go, where they would not be superior to any force which could be exerted against them ; nor are their affairs usually so firmly established at home, that they could securely trust the administration of them to others, and go out of their kingdoms. They could not do it without the danger of being deprived of their sovereignty ; and, at the same time, of being unable to avenge themselves on those who had injured them.

" Yet you will tell me, perhaps, that spectacles of this kind may be presented to kings, though they remain at home. But I assure you, Simonides, this is the case only with regard to a very few : and even for those, such as they are, kings must generally pay extremely dear. As they who have obliged a king with

any trifling exhibition of this kind, expect to be dismissed at once with a greater reward than they could hope for from any other man after a whole life's attendance."[3]

III. " Well then," said Simonides, " granting that you are in a worse condition, with regard to the objects of sight, yet you have greatly the advantage from the sense of hearing ; as you are incessantly entertained with the most delightful of all music, that of your own praises. For all those who approach you, applaud every thing you say and every thing you do. And, on the contrary, you are never exposed to what is most painful, the hearing yourself censured or reproached. For no one will venture to rebuke a king to his face."

" Alas !" answered Hiero, " what pleasure do you imagine a king can receive from those who do not speak ill of him, when he is convinced that, although they are silent, they think every thing that is bad of him ? Or what delight can they afford, who applaud him when he has so much reason to suspect their praises of adulation ?"

" Why, really," replied Simonides, " I must so far entirely agree with you, that those praises must be most agreeable, which are bestowed on us by men who are entirely free and independent.[4]

IV. " However," added Simonides, " with regard to the sense of taste, you surely cannot convince any one but that you enjoy the pleasures of the table more than the rest of mankind."

" I know," said Hiero, " that most men imagine we must necessarily receive more pleasure in eating and drinking ; because they would do the same, from the variety with which our tables are served, than from what they usually meet with at their own. For whatever is rare, and excels what we are accustomed to, affords a greater pleasure. For which reason all men expect with joy the approach of a feast, except kings ; for their tables being constantly provided to the full, can have no sort of addition on any festival occasions. In this respect then, in the first place, by being deprived of hope, kings are less happy than private men.

---

1 The Olympic games. See the Appendix.
2 The word kings must here mean tyrants.

3 It is probably a common remark, which I often heard from a man of rank and large fortune, that he could not afford to receive presents.
4 Xenophon says of Agesilaus, " That he was much pleased with the praises of those who would have blamed him with equal freedom, if he had acted improperly."— AGESIL. ch. ii. § 5.

" I make no doubt, likewise, but you yourself have experienced that the more superfluous dishes are set before us, the sooner we are cloyed with eating. So that, with regard to the duration of this pleasure, he who is served with such profusion is in a much worse condition than one who lives in a more frugal and less plentiful style."

" But after all," replied Simonides, " as long as the appetite for food continues, those must certainly find more pleasure who feed at a sumptuous table, than those who are confined to cheap and ordinary provisions."

" Do not you imagine then, Simonides," said Hiero, " that in proportion to the delight which any one takes in any thing, the more fondly he is usually attached to it?"

" Undoubtedly," says Simonides.

" Have you then ever remarked, that kings approach with greater delight to the food which is prepared for them, than private persons do to their frugal viands?"

" No, really," answered Simonides, " the very reverse seems to me to be the truth of the case."

" For have you not observed," says Hiero, " those many artificial preparations and variety of sauces, of a sharp and poignant relish, to stimulate the appetite, which are served up at the table of kings?"

" I certainly have," replied Simonides; " and am convinced these high sauces are quite unnatural, and inimical to the health of man."

" Do you think then," said Hiero, " that these unnatural delicacies can afford pleasure to any one, but to those whose palates are vitiated by luxury and indulgence? For my part, I know by experience, and you cannot be ignorant, that those who have a good appetite want no artificial preparations of this kind."

V. " Then as to those expensive perfumes which you make use of," said Simonides, " I really believe that those who approach your persons have more enjoyment of them than you yourselves have. As in respect to those who have eaten any thing of a disagreeable odour, the person himself is not so much incommoded by it, as those who come too near him."

" That is precisely the case," replied Hiero, " with those who have constantly a variety of food set before them. They eat nothing with an appetite: whereas he who but rarely meets with any delicacy, feeds upon it with a true relish, whenever it makes its appearance."

VI. " But, after all," says Simonides, "perhaps the greatest incitement to your aspiring after royalty are the pleasures of love. For in this respect it is in your power to enjoy every object, the most beautiful in its kind."

" Alas!" cries Hiero, " you have now produced an instance, in which you must certainly know we are far less happy than private persons. For, in the first place, those marriages are generally esteemed most honourable, and to confer the greatest dignity, as well as pleasure, which we contract with our superiors in rank and fortune: and in the second place, are those of equals with their equals: but to form an alliance of that kind with an inferior, is disgraceful and injurious to our character. Unless a king marries a stranger, therefore, he must necessarily marry an inferior; so that he can never enjoy what is most agreeable in the married state.

" The attention and respect also which is paid us by a woman of birth and spirit gives a man great pleasure; but, when paid us by a slave, it affords us very little satisfaction. Yet if they fail of that respect which is our due, we are provoked and chagrined.

" In short, with regard to the mere sensual pleasures of love, where marriage is out of the question, kings have still less of that pleasure to boast of: for we all know, that it is love alone which renders fruition so exquisitely delightful; but love is more rarely excited in the breast of kings than of any other men. For we despise easy and obvious pleasures; but the passion is nourished by hope. And as a person who is not thirsty never drinks with pleasure, so he who is not stimulated by love knows not the true pleasure of enjoyment."

Hiero having thus spoken, Simonides, with a smile, replied: " What is this which you assert, O Hiero! that love cannot be excited in the breast of kings? Whence comes it to pass then, that you are so fond of Dailocha, the most beautiful of her sex?"

" Why truly, my Simonides," said he, " it is not for what I could with so much ease obtain of her, but for what it is least of all in the power of kings to effect.

" I own I love Dailocha for what we naturally desire to obtain from a beautiful object. Those favours, however, which I so earnestly wish to receive voluntarily, and with mutual affection, I could no more endure to extort by force, than I could to do violence to my own person.

" To plunder and take by force from an enemy, we consider as a real cause of exultation: but no favours from a beloved object can give us any joy, except those which are voluntarily bestowed. From such an object, who returns our passion, every thing is agreeable: her slightest regards; her trifling questions; her childish answers; and the most agreeable of all, perhaps, and the most alluring, are her struggles and counterfeited resentments. But, to possess by force a woman whom we love, is, in my opinion, to act more like a robber than a lover. A robber indeed receives some gratification from the idea of gain, and perhaps from having done an injury to an adversary; but to take a pleasure in giving pain to a person whom we love, and to treat one for whom we profess a regard, as if we really hated them; and to torment a woman, to whom our caresses are odious and disgusting, is surely most detestable and inhuman.

" In short, if a private person receives favours from a woman whom he loves, it is an unequivocal pledge of her affection; as he knows she is under no necessity to comply with his solicitations.

" But a king has no right to imagine that he is ever sincerely beloved.[1] For we know, that those who submit to our pleasure through fear, counterfeit as much as is in their power the air and manner of those whose compliance is the effect of a sincere affection. Yet never are conspiracies against kings so frequently conducted as by those who affect to love them with the greatest sincerity."

VII. To all this Simonides replied: " Well, my good Hiero, in regard to what you have hitherto alleged, I confess they are but trifles; for I see many men of respectable characters, who voluntarily refrain from the pleasures of the table, and are indifferent to what they eat or drink, and also entirely abstain from all intercourse with the fair sex.

" But in another respect there is certainly a striking superiority of kings over private men; that you conceive and readily execute great projects; that you have a greater abundance of whatever is excellent in its kind; you possess the finest and most spirited horses; the most beautiful arms; the richest ornaments for your women; the most magnificent palaces, and those adorned with the most sumptuous furniture; you are attended with a greater number of domestics, and those of the most expert and dexterous that can be found. Add to this, that you have the most ample means of avenging yourselves on your enemies, and of rewarding your friends."

"'Alas! my Simonides," said Hiero, " that the multitude are dazzled with the splendour of royalty I am not at all surprised; for the vulgar in general seem to me to judge of happiness and misery merely by appearances. Now, as royalty displays to the eyes of the world those possessions which are commonly esteemed the most valuable, so it conceals the evils to which kings are exposed in the inmost recesses of their soul, where alone real happiness or misery resides.

" That these things, therefore, should escape the notice of the multitude, I am not at all surprised, as I said; but, that you should be under the same mistake, who form your judgment from reflection more than external appearances, I own, excites my astonishment. For my part, Simonides, I assure you, from my own experience, that kings have the least share of the greatest goods, and much the largest portion of the greatest evils, incident to human life.

" For instance, if peace is esteemed in the opinion of mankind the greatest good, it is certain, the smallest portion of that good is allotted to kings: and likewise, if war is the greatest evil, the greatest part of that evil is the portion of kings.

" In the first place, then, unless the whole country be engaged in a civil war, private individuals may securely go where they please, without danger to their persons. Whereas kings[2] find it always necessary to march as through an enemy's country; armed themselves, and attended by guards completely armed.

" Moreover, private persons, if they go to make war in an enemy's country, as soon as they return home find themselves again in per-

1 Un roy, qui peut s' assurer de cent mille bras, ne peut guères s' assurer d'un cœur.—*Fontenelle Dialog. des Morts.*

2 The reader must here advert, that in the Attic writers, the word "tyrant" has three distinct senses. Sometimes,—1st, a lawful king, appointed by the constitution of any country: 2dly, one who usurps the sovereign power in a free state, whether he exercise it with moderation, or with cruelty and injustice: 3dly, a despot, or absolute monarch, who rules by force. In the sequel of this discourse it is generally used in the last sense.

fect security; but kings, (I mean arbitrary despots) when they return to their own capitals, find themselves in the midst of the greatest number of enemies. And if a more powerful enemy make war upon any city, those who are attacked may be in danger so long as they are without the walls; but as soon as they have retreated within their intrenchments, they find themselves in perfect security: whereas a tyrant, far from finding himself safe, even within his own palace, has then the greatest cause to be upon his guard.

"Again, when by negotiation peace is restored, private persons find themselves freed from the inconveniences of war: but tyrants never really are at peace with those whom they hold in subjection; nor dares a tyrant rely upon the faith of any treaty which he makes with the rest of mankind.

"In short, there are wars indeed which free states are obliged to carry on with each other, as there are those which kings are forced to wage with those whom they have deprived of their liberty: but whatever inconveniences these states may experience from such wars, the same occur in those which kings are obliged to maintain.

"Both the one and the other are under a necessity of being always armed, and continually upon their guard, and of exposing themselves to great dangers: and if they chance to lose a battle, or meet with any disaster, they are both thrown into equal consternation.

"And thus far wars are nearly upon the same footing, both with kings and free states. But then the agreeable circumstances which those experience from victory who serve under a free state, to these tyrants are entirely strangers. For when the individuals of a free city gain the advantage over their adversaries in a battle, it is not easy to express the pleasure which they feel to see their enemies put to flight; their alacrity in the pursuit, and their delight even in the havoc which they make of their foes: how much they glory in such an exploit; how splendid their triumph; and how much they exult in the idea of having augmented the strength of the commonwealth;[3] every individual gives himself the credit of having had a part in planning the expedition, and of contributing to its success. Nay, you will hardly find a man who does not magnify his own prowess, and pretend to have slain more with his own hand, than perhaps were left dead on the field of battle. So glorious to every individual does the victory appear which was obtained by a free state.[4]

"As for a king, or tyrant, when he suspects and is actually convinced that his subjects are forming dangerous designs against him, if he puts some of them to death, he is certain that he shall not by that means bring over the whole city to his interest; and is sensible at the same time, that he is diminishing the number of his subjects: of course he can neither rejoice (much less can be pride himself) on such an achievement. Nay, he extenuates, as far as is in his power, and makes an apology for what he has done, as having been void of any ill intention.

"And even after the death of those who were the chief objects of his fear, he is so far from being freed from his apprehensions, that he finds it necessary to be still more upon his guard than he was before. And thus does a tyrant live in a continual state of war; as, from experience, I can testify.

VIII. "Observe, in the next place, what kind of friendships kings are capable of enjoying: but let us first consider how great a blessing friendship is to mankind. For when a man is sincerely beloved, his friends are always happy in his presence, and delight in serving and doing him good. When he is absent, they anxiously wish for his return; and when he does return, receive him with transports of joy: they rejoice with him in his good fortune, and are eager to assist him in his adversity.

"Neither has it escaped the attention of several states, that friendship is the greatest and most valuable good that mortals can enjoy. For, under many governments, the laws permit adulterers alone to be slain with impunity. And for this reason; that they suppose them to alienate that affection and friendship which a woman ought to have for her husband. For if a woman, by any extraordinary concurrence of circumstances, should be guilty of an act of infidelity, the husband may not perhaps esteem her the less, if he is convinced that her friendship for him continues inviolate and undiminished.[5]

---

3 Xenophon seems to speak with the feelings of a soldier and a patriotic statesman.

4 We might add here what Rousseau observes, "How many sovereigns have been made unhappy by the loss of countries which they had never seen!"

5 Comfortable doctrine. If a china dish happens to slip out of a poor girl's hand, and is broken, who can blame her?

" For my part, I esteem it so great a happiness to be beloved by our friends, that we can hardly have any thing further to wish for from gods or men. But of this happiness, I am convinced, no one enjoys less than tyrants or kings. That what I assert is true, Simonides, attend to the following particular.

" The firmest friendships then seem to be those which reciprocally subsist between parents and their children; between brothers and brothers; between husbands and their wives; and lastly, those which a daily intercourse produces between companions and acquaintance.

" Now, if you consider the affair attentively, Simonides, you will find that private persons enjoy the greatest share of this affection : but amongst kings or tyrants, how many do you find who have put to death their own children; or, on the contrary, have perished by their own offspring! How many brothers who have slain each other to arrive at the sovereign power! How many tyrants, possessed of that power, have been murdered by their wives, and by their associates who have professed the greatest friendship for them? If, therefore, those who were prompted by natural affection, or obliged by the laws, to show a regard to kings, have nevertheless expressed their detestation of them; how is it probable, do you think, that any others should entertain any friendship for them?

IX. " Again; as mutual confidence among mankind is a very great blessing, is not he who has the least share of this confidence deprived of a very great blessing? For, with what pleasure can men converse familiarly together without mutual confidence ? What happiness can exist between the sexes in marriage, if this confidence is banished? or, how can we bear even a domestic in our family, if we have not an opinion of his fidelity?

" Of this happiness then, I mean, of relying with confidence on those about us, no one partakes less than a tyrant : since he lives in a continual state of suspicion, even when the most delicious food, or the most exquisite liquors, are set before him. Insomuch that, before he makes any offering or libation to the gods, he obliges some domestic first to taste it, lest even in those sacred viands something poisonous should be concealed.

X. " Moreover, to every other mortal, their country is held dear, and the chief object of their affection : and the citizens of the same state protect each other, without stipend, against their slaves, and against other base assassins, that no one may be exposed to any violent death. And this precaution has been carried so far, that many laws have been enacted, declaring those polluted who should associate or converse with a homicide. Thus every private citizen lives in security under the protection procured him by his country ; but even in this respect the very reverse is the case with tyrants. For, so far from punishing those who put a tyrant to death, they usually reward them with distinguished honours. And, instead of excluding them from the religious rites, as they do those who have murdered a private citizen, they generally erect statues to them in the temples of the gods.

" But should you imagine, that a king is more happy, from possessing more wealth, than a private individual, in this, my Simonides, you are extremely mistaken. For as an athlete never prides himself on vanquishing one who is ignorant of the gymnastic exercises, but is sensibly mortified if he is overcome by his antagonist; thus a king takes no pleasure in having larger possessions than a private subject ; but he is greatly chagrined to see other kings more opulent than himself; for these only he considers as his antagonists, or rivals, with regard to riches.

XI. " Neither can a king, in general, gratify his wishes more readily than a private man. For the object of a private man's utmost ambition is, perhaps, no more than a house, a field, or a slave ; but a king usually aims at the acquisition of cities, of extensive provinces, harbours, or fortified citadels ; which are obtained with much more difficulty and danger than those objects which excite the wishes of private individuals.

" Nay, you will find but few that are really poor amongst private persons, in comparison with those who may be called so amongst sovereigns : for an abundance, or a sufficiency, [1] is not to be estimated by the number of our possessions, but by the exigencies of our station : and, according to this idea, whatever exceeds a sufficiency, may be called too much, and what falls short of it, too little. Now, much more ample revenues may not be sufficient for the necessary expenses of a king,

---

1 See this subject elegantly treated by our author, at the beginning of his Economics, infra.

than what would suffice a private person. As for private persons, they are at liberty to contract their daily expenses, as they find it convenient; but kings have not the same privilege: for, as their greatest and most necessary expenses are employed for the maintenance of those who guard their persons, to retrench these expenses, seems to threaten their immediate destruction.

" Then, how can we consider those as poor, and the objects of compassion, who can obtain, by lawful means, whatever they stand in need of? But those who are under a necessity of being guilty of unjust and dishonourable actions, how can we but esteem them really poor and miserable beings? But tyrants are often forced to pillage the temples of the gods, and plunder men, through mere want of their necessary supplies: for when engaged in war, they must either keep on foot a sufficient force, or inevitably perish by their adversaries."

XII. " But give me leave, my Simonides, to mention another difficulty to which kings are exposed. They are equally capable, with private persons, of distinguishing the merit of accomplished, of wise, and of virtuous men. But, instead of viewing them with pleasure and admiration, they behold them with fear. They dread men of courage, lest they should make some bold attempt in favour of liberty. They dread men of great parts, lest they should engage in some dangerous plot; and virtuous men, lest the multitude should wish to raise them to the sovereign power.

" Now when, from suspicion, they have secretly freed themselves from men of this respectable character, whom have they left to employ in their service, but dishonest, or debauched, or slavish wretches? They trust these dishonest miscreants, because men of that character must fear, as much as the tyrant himself, that if a city become free, they will meet with their deserts; the debauched, because from their luxury and sloth they will be attached to the present power; slaves, because, being accustomed to the yoke, they will not wish to be free. This then, in my opinion, is a most mortifying reflection, to behold with approbation men of virtue, and to be under a necessity of employing men of a character entirely the reverse.

XIII. " It is likewise necessary for a tyrant to show a love and regard for the city under his dominion: for he cannot be happy, nor

even safe, independently of the affection of the citizens. And yet the necessity he is under to support his authority, obliges him, in some measure, to treat them with severity. For tyrants do not wish to render their subjects brave, or to see them well armed; but they love to raise the power of a foreign force over their countrymen, and to use them as the guards of their person.

" Neither do they rejoice with their fellow-citizens, when a fruitful year of corn produces every thing in abundance. For the more indigent the people are, the more humble and more submissive they expect to find them.

XIV. " But I will now lay before you, my Simonides," added Hiero, "a true account of those pleasures which I enjoyed, when I was a private man, and which I find myself deprived of since I became a king. I then conversed familiarly with my equals; delighted with their company, as they were with mine: and I conversed also with myself, whenever I chose to indulge in the calm of solitude.

" I frequently spent my time in convivial entertainments, and drinking with my friends, so as to forget the chagrins to which human life is obnoxious; nay, often to a degree of extravagance; to singing, dancing, and every degree of festivity, unrestrained but by our own inclinations. But I am now debarred from the society of those who could afford me any delight, as I have slaves alone for my companions, instead of friends: nor can I converse agreeably with men in whom I cannot discover the least benevolence or attachment to me; and I am forced to guard against intoxication or sleep, as a most dangerous snare.

" But now, to be continually alarmed, either in a crowd, or in solitude; to be in fear when without guards, and to be afraid of the guards themselves; to be unwilling to have them about me without their arms, and to be under apprehensions to see them armed; what a wretched state of existence is this !

" Moreover, to place a greater confidence in strangers than in one's own countrymen; in Barbarians, than in Greeks; to be under a necessity of treating freemen like slaves, and to give slaves their freedom; are not all these things evident symptoms of a mind disturbed and quite deranged by fear? Now this passion of fear not only creates uneasiness, and diffuses a constant gloom over the mind, but, being mixed with all our pleasures, deprives us of all kind of enjoyment.

"But, if you have had any experience of military affairs, Simonides, and have ever been posted near a body of the enemy, only recollect how little you were disposed either to eat or to sleep in that situation. Such as were your uneasy sensations on that occasion, such, or rather more dreadful, are those to which tyrants are continually exposed; for their imagination not only represents their enemies as encamped in their sight, but as surrounding them on every side."

To this Simonides answered, " Your observation is extremely just. War is undoubtedly subject to continual alarms. Nevertheless, even during a campaign, when we have previously disposed our sentinels, we eat and sleep in the utmost security."

"That is very true," said Hiero, "for the laws watch over the guards themselves; so that they are as much in fear on their own account as on yours. But kings have only mercenaries for their guards, whom they pay as they do their labourers in the harvest. And though the principal duty of guards is to be faithful to their trust, yet it is more difficult to find one of that description faithful, than the generality of workmen in any branch of business; especially when these guards enlist themselves for the sake of the stipend, and have it in their power, in a short time, to gain a much larger sum, by assassinating a tyrant, than they would receive from the tyrant by many years' faithful attendance.

XV. "As for what you observed," continued Hiero, "that kings were to be envied for the power which they enjoy, of serving their friends, and of subduing their enemies; neither is this by any means true. As for our friends, how can you suppose that we should be very desirous to serve them, when we are convinced, that he who is under the greatest obligation to us, will be the first to withdraw himself from our sight, and to avoid any further intercourse with us; for no one considers what he has received from a tyrant as his property, till he is escaped from his power.

"Then as for his enemies, how can you say that tyrants can so readily subdue them, when they are sensible that every one is their enemy who is subject to their power. They cannot put them all to death, nor confine them all in prison. For over whom could they, in

that case, exercise their dominion? But although he knows them all to be his enemies, he is under a necessity, at the same time, both to guard himself against them, and yet to make use of their service.

"Be assured of this then, my Simonides, that with regard to their fellow-citizens, whom they thus fear, it is equally painful to tyrants to see them alive, and to put them to death. It is with them as with a spirited horse, which we are afraid to mount, yet are unwilling to put him to death on account of his good qualities, though we dare not make use of him for fear of some fatal accident.

"The same is applicable to other possessions, which are useful, and yet attended with some inconvenience; though we possess them with anxiety, we cannot lose them without pain and vexation."

XVI. Simonides, having listened to Hiero, replied: "Well then, Hiero; but honour and respect appear to me to be objects of so much importance, that men submit to every kind of toil and danger to obtain them. And you yourself, it should seem, notwithstanding the many inconveniences which you say attend on royalty, yet are thus strongly attached to it, that you may be honoured and respected; that all your orders may be implicitly obeyed; that all men may have their eyes upon you; may rise from their seats, or give you the way on your approach: in short, that all who are about you, may testify their respect by their words and their actions; for it is by these, and every other instance of deference, that subjects continually show their respect to their kings.

"For my part, Hiero, I confess that I think this desire of esteem and honour is the distinguishing characteristic of man from other animals; for it appears probable, that the pleasure arising from eating, drinking, sleeping, and other natural functions, are common to all animals. But the love of honour is not discoverable in brutes, nor in all men: insomuch, that those in whom the love of honour or glory is most conspicuous, are usually the furthest removed from mere brutes; and are commonly named men,[1] in its most noble sense, by way of eminence. So that it is not without reason, in my opinion, that you submit to all these inconveniences which attend on royal-

---

1 The Greek has two words to express this: ἀνὴρ, and ἄνθρωπος.

ty, when you are so much more honoured and respected than other men. For, of all the pleasures which mankind can enjoy, no one seems to approach nearer to divine than that which they receive from being honoured and respected."

To this Hiero replied: " But, I assure you, my Simonides, that the honours which are paid to kings are extremely similar to the pleasures which, I have already shown you, they receive from love.[2] For neither are those compliances which are shown us by them who are void of a reciprocal affection, to be esteemed as favours; nor can those which are extorted by force, give us any pleasure. In like manner, we ought not to consider as marks of respect, those honours which are paid us by such as fear us.[3] For how can we suppose, that they who rise from their seats to those who have injured them, or that give the way to those who tyrannise over them, can possibly entertain any real honour or regard for them? We, every day, make presents to those whom we hate: and this at the very time when we are most apprehensive of suffering from their power: but those things ought certainly to be considered as acts of servility; whereas real respect must proceed from quite contrary causes. For when we think a man is capable to do us service, and we really enjoy the effects of his good-will, we then celebrate his praises with pleasure; every one considers him as his benefactor: pays him the utmost deference; rises from his seat on his approach, not from fear, but love; they present him with crowns[4] and other donations, as a tribute to his virtue and public spirit. In this case, in my opinion, both those who bestow these marks of respect on such a man confer substantial honour, and he who is thought worthy of them is truly and effectually honoured; and I cannot but pronounce him a happy man who is thus honoured and respected. For, instead of forming conspiracies against such a man, I observe, that every one is solicitous to prevent his suffering any injury: so that he spends his life happily, free from fears, from envy, and from danger; a tyrant, on the contrary, assure yourself, Simonides, passes every day and night as if all mankind had already condemned him to death for his injustice."

XVII. Having heard all these particulars, " Whence comes it to pass then," cries Simonides, " if the condition of royalty is so wretched, and you are convinced that it is so, that you, Hiero, do not free yourself from so great an evil? Yet neither you, nor any one else, who was in possession of royalty, ever voluntarily resigned it."

" It is for that very reason, my Simonides," replied he, " that the condition of a king is the most wretched state imaginable: for there is really no possibility of resigning it with safety. Indeed, how can a tyrant find sufficient resources, either to restore that wealth which he has extorted from his subjects; or to recompense those whom he has suffered to languish in prison? or how can he restore life to those whom he has put to death?

" In short, my Simonides, if ever any man could be a gainer by hanging[5] himself, a tyrant would be so, for he alone is in a situation to which he can hardly submit, nor yet gain any thing by quitting it.'

XVIII. Simonides, resuming the discourse, thus replied: " Now then, O Hiero! I am no longer surprised, that you speak so disadvantageously of the condition of royalty: since, ambitious as you are to gain the friendship of mankind, you find it an invincible obstacle to your wishes. I think, however, I can convince you, that sovereign power is so far from preventing one who is possessed of it from being beloved, that it gives him a great advantage in that respect over a private individual.

" In considering this subject, however, I will not insist, that, because a king has more power, he therefore can bestow greater favours upon his friends: but, suppose a private person and a king do the same thing, let us inquire which confers the greatest obligation. — To begin with matters of the least importance.

" Suppose a king and a private person to address any one whom they chance to see in an obliging and affectionate manner; to which of the two will such a one listen with the greatest satisfaction? Or, let them proceed to praise or compliment him; whose praises, do you

---

2 See chap. vi. 3 See the Appendix.
4 This is to be taken in its literal sense, as it was a custom among the Athenians to present a crown to any citizen who had signalised himself on any particular occasion. This gave rise to Demosthenes's well-known Oration, " de Corona."

5 Ἀπαγξασθαι : literally so.

4 L

imagine, would affect him the most sensibly? Or, let each of them invite him to an entertainment after the sacrifice ;[1] to which of the two do you think he would esteem himself the most obliged for that honour? Let both of them pay him the same attention when he is sick; is it not evident likewise, that the kind offices of those who have the most power, give him the most sensible pleasure? Lastly, let each of them make him equal presents; is it not visible also, that favours of half the value from a great man have more weight, and impress him with a deeper sense of gratitude, than those of double the value from a private person?

" Nay, there appears to me a certain dignity and grace which the gods have attached to the very person of a king; which not only adds a lustre to his appearance, but makes us really behold the same man with more pleasure, when vested with authority, than when in a private station; and, in general, we certainly take a pride and are more delighted to converse with our superiors than with our equals.[2]

" As for the favours of the fair sex, which supplied you with the principal complaint against the condition of royalty, they are the least disgusted with the old age of a prince, and the reputation of those with whom he has an amour do not suffer any diminution. For the honour which he does them, adds a lustre to their character: so that what is ignominious in such a connexion seems to disappear, and what is honourable appears with more splendour.

" Then, as by equal services you confer greater obligations, why ought not you to be more beloved than private persons, since you have it in your power to be much more useful to mankind, and to bestow more liberal donations than any private individual can possibly do?"

" It is," replied Hiero, with some vivacity, "because, my Simonides, we are under the necessity of doing more invidious and unpopular acts than private persons usually do.· We must raise money by imposing taxes, if we would

have sufficient for our ordinary expenses : we must have persons to guard what is necessary to be guarded: we must punish crimes, and restrain the injurious and petulant ; and when any occasion requires expedition, and an attack is to be made, either by sea or land, we are responsible for the success, and must take care not to give the charge either to negligent or cowardly commanders.

" Moreover, a king is obliged to have mercenary troops, and nothing is more odious or insupportable to a free city, than the burthen of such an expense : for they naturally suppose, that these troops are kept in pay, not merely for state, but to enable him to tyrannise over his subjects."

XIX. To this Simonides again replied : " I do not deny, O Hiero! that all these affairs must be carefully managed. But, amidst this variety of concerns, as there are some which render those who have the charge of them extremely odious, there are others which have a contrary effect.

" Thus, to instruct mankind in things the most excellent, and to honour and applaud those learned men who perform this service with industry and care, is a duty, the performance of which must procure the love of all good men. On the contrary, to be forced to rebuke and treat with severity, to fine and chastise those who do ill, these things must certainly render a king odious and unpopular.

" I should think it advisable, therefore, for a prince, when the occasion requires it, to employ others to inflict punishments, and to reserve to himself the distribution of rewards. And that this conduct is attended with good effects, experience testifies.

" Thus, for instance, at our public solemnities, when the different choirs contend for victory, he that presides over the contest, distributes the prizes, but leaves to the magistrate the care of collecting the bands, and to others, that of instructing them, and of correcting those who are defective in the performance. By this means the agreeable part is executed by the president, and whatever is of a contrary kind is committed to others. What forbids, therefore, to manage other political affairs in the same manner? For all cities are usually divided, some into tribes, others into classes, and others into centuries and the like; and each of these divisions has its proper chief, who presides over them.

---

1 Among the Greeks, they usually invited their friends, after the sacrifice, to partake of what remained of the victims; that is, the best and greatest part, says Mons. Coste.

2 This sentiment will not be relished in this enlightened age; but, perhaps, the philosopher intended it as a delicate compliment to Hiero, who had been a private man.

" If, therefore, we were to propose rewards to these different bodies, as we do in the musical contests to the different choirs, to those who were the best armed, or who kept their ranks best, or showed most skill in horsemanship, or most courage in an engagement, or most justice in their civil transactions, it is reasonable to suppose, that, through emulation, all these several duties would be more strenuously performed; and, animated by the love of glory, they would be more ready to march whenever the service required, and would more cheerfully contribute to the necessities of the public.

" Again : one of the most useful employments in any state, but which it never has been usual to encourage by motives of emulation, is agriculture. Now this would flourish much more, if rewards were publicly established in different parts of the country and the villages, for those who showed the greatest skill in the cultivation of their land ; and from thence great advantages would accrue to those individuals who diligently applied themselves to their occupation : the public revenues would be greatly augmented; temperance and sobriety would attend this laborious occupation, as vice and immorality seldom spring up amongst those who are constantly employed.

" If, likewise, trade or commerce is advantageous to the commonwealth; if he were to be the most honoured, who applied himself with the greatest diligence to trade, the number of merchants would be increased in proportion. And if it were publicly made known, that he who should discover any new method of increasing the public revenue, without detriment to individuals, should be well rewarded ; neither would this kind of speculation be so much neglected.

" In short, if, in every branch of science, it were made manifest, that no one who discovered or introduced any thing useful to the state would be unrewarded, this consideration would excite numbers to apply themselves strenuously to make such discoveries. And when many rival competitors for this honour were thus constantly employed in the service of the public, a greater number of useful discoveries must necessarily be made.

" But if you are apprehensive that all these prizes and rewards should be attended with too great expense, consider, O Hiero ! that there are no commodities that cost less than those which are purchased by this means. Do you not see, every day, to what vast expense, to what cares and toils, men submit, for a very trifling reward, in the chariot-races, the gymnastic exercises, and in the musical contests between the several choirs ?"[3]

XX. " What you observe, my Simonides, is extremely reasonable," said Hiero; " but in regard to the troops which I have in pay, can you give me any advice how to render myself less odious to my subjects on that account ? or, would you say, perhaps, that if a prince could make himself beloved, he would have no longer need of guards ?"

" By no means," replied Simonides, " he certainly would still want guards. For, I am sensible, it is with some men, as with some horses, the more plenty they have, and the better they are fed, the more fierce and unmanageable they are. Now nothing can keep in awe these turbulent spirits, but a strong military force, such as you now employ.

" As for the virtuous and peaceable citizens, you cannot, in my opinion, do them a greater service, than by maintaining these troops in your pay. You maintain these mercenaries, 'tis true, as guards of your own person : but it frequently happens, that the masters have been massacred by their slaves. You ought, therefore, particularly to give it in charge to your guards, to consider themselves as the protectors of the citizens in general : and to give them immediate assistance if ever they perceive them forming any such dangerous designs against them. For there are, as every one knows, in all cities those desperate villains, over whom, if your guards are ordered to keep a watchful eye, the citizens, in this respect, would acknowledge their utility.

" Further yet, your troops may probably give protection and security to the labourers and to the cattle in the country : not only to your own private possessions, but to the proprietors in general. And, likewise, by guarding certain advantageous posts, leave the citizens at leisure to attend their private affairs in the utmost tranquillity.

" Add to this, that to discover and prevent any secret and sudden irruption of enemies to the state, who can be more alert or more ready at hand, than such a standing force, always un-

---

3 At the public festivals and solemnities.

der arms and united in one body? And, in time of war, what can be more useful to the citizens, than these mercenary troops? For it is natural to suppose, that they will be more willing to undergo fatigue, and to expose themselves to danger, and more vigilant for the public good.

" In fine, the neighbouring states must necessarily be more desirous to live in peace with those who have constantly an armed force on foot; for these regular troops have it most in their power to protect their friends, and to annoy their enemies.

" Now, if your subjects are convinced that these forces never injure those who do no injury to others; but, on the contrary, keep in awe the turbulent, and assist those who are unjustly oppressed; watch over and expose themselves to danger for the public good: how can they avoid contributing with pleasure to their support? At least they often maintain guards at their own private expense for things of infinitely less moment.

XXI. " It is necessary likewise, Hiero! that you should contribute cheerfully part of your own revenues for the service of the public. For it appears to me, that what a king lays out for the public, is more usefully bestowed than what he spends on his own private account. Let us consider the affair more minutely. Which of the two, do you imagine, would be most to your credit;—a palace, built in an elegant style, at an enormous expense, for your own use; or to adorn the whole city with public edifices, walls, temples, porticoes, squares, and harbours? Or which would make you more formidable to your enemies;—to be adorned yourself with the most splendid armour, or to have the whole city completely armed?

" Or, which do you think the most probable method of augmenting your revenues;—by managing to advantage your own private property alone, or by contriving by what means the industry of the whole city may turn to the best account?

" As the breeding horses for the chariot race is esteemed one of the most noble and most magnificent amusements for a prince, which do you suppose is most honourable;—that you⁴

alone should provide and send to the public games more chariots than all the rest of Greece; or, that the greatest part of your subjects should breed horses and contend for the prize at those games? Which do you deem the most noble: —the superiority which you gain over others in the managing your chariot; or that which you acquire by making happy the city over which you preside?

" For my part, Hiero! I think it by no means consistent with propriety, or even decent, for a prince to enter the list with private persons; for, if you are victorious, you would be so far from being applauded, that you would incur the odium of the public, as having supplied the expenses of your victory from the substance of many wretched families. And if you were vanquished, you would be exposed to more ridicule than any private individual.

" But, if you would listen to me, Hiero, permit me to advise you to enter the lists against the governors of other states: and if you can render the city over which you preside, more happy than those, you may be assured, that you obtain the victory in the most noble contest in which a mortal can engage.

" And, in the first place, you will succeed immediately in the grand object of your ambition, the gaining the love of your fellow-citizens: and, in the next place, this victory of yours will not merely be proclaimed by a single herald, as at the Olympic games, but all mankind will concur in celebrating your virtue.

" And you will not only attract the respect of a few individuals, but the love of whole cities; and not only be admired privately within the walls of your own palace, but publicly, and by the whole world.

" You may also, if you desire it, either go abroad to see any thing rare or curious, or satisfy your curiosity though you remain at home. For there will always be a crowd of those about you, who will be proud to exhibit whatever they have discovered, either ingenious, beautiful, or useful; and of those who will be ambitious to serve you.

" Every one who is admitted to your presence will be devoted to your person; and those who live at a distance will passionately desire to see you. So that you will not only be respected, but sincerely and cordially beloved by all men. You will be under no necessity of soliciting the favours of the fair sex, but must even suffer yourself to be solicited by

---

4 Hiero, it is well known from the Odes of Pindar, was particularly attached to the Olympic games. See West's and Banister's translations of Pindar.

them. You will not be afraid of any one, but every one will be anxious for your preservation.

" Your subjects will pay you a voluntary obedience, and carefully watch for the safety of your person. And should you be exposed to any danger, you will find them alert, not only to assist you, but to protect you,[2] and avert the danger, at the hazard of their own lives. You will be loaded with presents; nor will you want friends to whom you may have the pleasure of imparting them. All men will rejoice in your prosperity, and will contend for your rights as earnestly as for their own. And you may consider the wealth of your friends[3] as treasure laid up for your use.

" Take courage then, Hiero, enrich your friends with a liberal hand; for by that means you will enrich yourself. Augment the power of the state, for thus you will render yourself more powerful, and secure alliances in time of war.

" In a word, regard your country as your own family; your fellow-citizens, as your friends; your friends, as your own children; and your children as your own life: but endeavour to surpass them all in acts of kindness and beneficence. For if you thus secure the attachment of your friends by acts of beneficence, your enemies will not be able to resist you.

To conclude: if you regulate your conduct according to these maxims, be assured, Hiero, you will obtain the most honourable and most valuable possession which mortals can possibly enjoy; you will be completely happy, yet unenvied by any one."

---

[2] Προμαχων.   3 See Appendix.

APPENDIX.

No. I.

RESPUBLICA, res est populi, cum bene et juste geritur; sive ab uno rege, sive a paucis optimatibus, sive ab universo populo. Cum vero injustus est rex, quem tyrannum voco; aut injusti optimates, quorum consensus factio est; aut injustus est populus, cui nomen usitatum nullum reperio; nisi ut etiam ipsum tyrannum, adpellem; non jam vitiosa sed omnino nulla respublica est: Quoniam non est res populi, cum tyrannus eam factiove capessat; nec ipse populus jam populus est, si sit injustus; quoniam non est multitudo juris consensu et utilitatis communione sociata.

FRAG. l. 3. de Republica.

" A legitimate commonwealth is where the commonweal or good of the whole is consulted; whether under a king, an aristocracy, or a democracy. But if either of these act unjustly, or in defiance of the law, there is no longer a commonwealth; nor are the people properly a people, but a mob; because not united under common laws, or a community of rights and advantages." This is partly the sense, but it cannot well be literally translated.

No. II.

Tully, in his pleadings against Verres, not only calls Syracuse, " maximam Græciæ urbem pulcherrimamque,"—the largest and most beautiful city of Greece,—but is so minute in his description of its harbours, temples, and theatres, and of the statues and pictures of which Verres plundered them, that it seems to have exceeded almost any other city in the world; which is partly confirmed by the ruins yet remaining, as described by Mr Brydone, Watkins, &c.

No. III.

Diodorus Siculus calls him φιλάργυρος καὶ βίαιος, covetous and cruel, &c. But Pindar, who resided much at the court of Hiero, and has celebrated his victories at the Olympic games, speaks of him as a truly virtuous character. And indeed a man that was notorious for any crime or depraved morals, could not be a candidate at those games. And the glory acquired by a victory in the chariot-races, or in the gymnastic exercises, or the more liberal arts, history, poetry, &c. seemed to supersede all other virtues.

The mere English reader, who has taken his ideas of the Olympic and other games of ancient Greece, from what he has seen or heard of our Newmarket sports, or our boxing-matches, which are usually an assembly of gamblers and pickpockets, attended with every species of profligacy and blackguardism, will be astonished at the veneration in which those games were held by all ranks of people, and the almost divine honours which were paid to them who gained the prize on those occasions, who were almost literally exalted to the rank of demigods, as Horace has observed:

> " Palmaque nobilis
> " Terrarum dominos evehit ad deos."
>
> OD. l. b. i.

But these solemn games were originally instituted by the command of the Delphic oracle, to put a stop to a great pestilence, which, with the continual wars between the petty states of Greece, had almost depopulated the country: so that they had partly a religious and partly a political view: as, during these solemnities, even states that were at war with each other were obliged to suspend their hostilities, and join the general assembly of all Greece.

The utility of the gymnastic exercises, to

render the body more hardy and active; and of the chariot races, to encourage the breeding and management of horses,[1] was indeed in time defeated, by their sacrificing the end to the means, and making them mere prize-fighters, instead of good soldiers, &c.[2]

Plutarch has recorded a few wise sayings and anecdotes of Hiero, which seem to indicate this mixed and motley character.

He said, " That no man was impertinent, who told him freely what ought not to be concealed; but that he who told what ought to be concealed, did an injury to the person to whom he told the secret: for we not only hate the man who discovers, but him who has heard what we wish to conceal."

It is a common anecdote of Hiero, that a stranger having hinted to him that his breath was offensive, he expostulated with his wife for having never mentioned that circumstance to him. " I thought," said she, (with great simplicity) " all men's breaths smelled the same." An amiable and artless proof of her fidelity to a suspicious husband!

I am sorry to add, "that Hiero fined the celebrated comic-poet, Epicharmes, for having uttered something indecent when his wife was present." A frown from a king would have been sufficient, and have shown a love of virtue; a fine savoured rather of the love of money.

No. IV.

" Non enim poeta solum suavis, verum etiam ceteroqui doctus sapiensque."

De Nat. Deorum, lib. i.

Simonides seems to have been a very elegant writer, from the fragments which remain of his poetry.

The coarseness of his satire on women must be imputed to the simplicity of the age in which he lived; (about four hundred and fifty years after the Trojan war) and to the low rank of the ladies who were the subject of his satire.

Mr Addison has given the substance of this satire in the third volume of the Spectator,

No. 209. But, in the character of a slut, whom Simonides compares to a sow, Mr A. has, out of delicacy, lost the idea of the original, *σιαίνεται*, " she grows fat amidst the filth of her sty;" which he translates, " her family is no better than a dunghill." He concludes his satire with a description of a good woman, whom he compares to a bee. Solomon concludes his book of Proverbs in the like manner; but as that of Simonides is a mere sketch, it cannot be compared with Solomon's beautiful picture.[3]

Horace has almost literally translated some of his moral sentences, L. ii. Od. 13; and L. iii. Od. 2.

" Mors et fugacem persequitur virum."

Θάνατος ἰχθαι καὶ τὸν φυγόμαχον.

Tully has recorded his answer to Hiero, who asked him " what God was?" Simonides desired a day to consider of it. Being asked the same question the next day, he desired two days for that purpose, and thus often doubled the number.

Hiero, being greatly surprised at this, inquired the reason of his conduct. " Because," said Simonides, " the longer I consider the subject, the more obscure it seems to be."— *De Natura Deor*. lib. i.

The following reflections of human life, though now trite, were not so, probably, three thousand years ago. It appears to have been the received opinion at that time, that Homer was a native of Chios; that, at least, was his chief residence, where the present inhabitants pretend to point out the very place in which he established a school in the latter part of his life.

ON THE BREVITY OF HUMAN LIFE.

FROM SIMONIDES.

How swiftly glide life's transient scenes away!
" Like vernal leaves men flourish and decay."
Thus sung, in days of yore, the Chian bard;
This maxim all have heard, but none regard.
None keep in mind this salutary truth,
Hope still survives, that flatters us in youth.
What fruitless schemes amuse our blooming years!
The man in health, nor age nor sickness fears;
Nay, youth's and life's contracted space forgot,
Scarce thinks that death will ever be his lot.
But thou thy mind's fair bias still obey,
Nor from the paths of virtue ever stray.

---

[1] The Greeks were so ignorant, in the earlier ages, of the management of horses, that the fable of the Centaurs probably took its rise from seeing some Thessalians on their backs at a distance.

[2] See West on the Olympic Games, p. 184.

[3] Proverbs, chap. xxxi.

The original seems to inculcate the Epicurean maxim of "indulge genio," as Buchanan translates it; which would incline one to believe that these lines were of an age subsequent to Simonides.

No. V.

Nothing can give us a more lively idea of the perpetual alarms and anxiety of a tyrant, than Tully's sketch of the elder Dionysius; which, though familiar to every scholar, may not be disagreeable to the English reader.

After describing him as possessed of many natural advantages, and as a man of great abilities, and (as an ingredient of happiness) very temperate in his way of life, he proceeds:—

"Though Dionysius," says he, "had a number of friends and relations, with whom he lived on the most intimate and familiar terms, yet he placed no confidence in any of them; but committed to those slaves whom he had selected from wealthy families, and given them their freedom, and to some foreign mercenaries, the guard of his person. Thus, from an unjustifiable ambition of domineering over other people, he delivered himself up to a kind of voluntary imprisonment.

"Nay, he grew at length so astonishingly suspicious, that he would not trust his throat to a barber, but taught his own daughters to shave: so that these young princesses, like little female barbers,[4] performed the mean and servile offices of shaving and cutting the hair of their own father. And even from them, when they grew up, he took away his razors and every thing of steel, and instructed them to burn off his beard with the inner rinds[5] and shells of the walnut.

"Neither did he ever go to the apartments of his two wives,[6] by night, till it had been first searched and scrutinized with the utmost care. And having his bed-chamber surrounded with a broad ditch, the passage was secured by a narrow wooden bridge, which, after fastening his door, he himself drew up. In short, to such an extreme did his apprehensions carry

him, that he never ventured to harangue the people but from the top of a lofty tower.

"But this tyrant himself has sufficiently shown us what degree of happiness he enjoyed. For when Damocles, one of his flatterers, was enumerating the abundance of his wealth, his grandeur, his power, and the magnificence of his royal palaces; and, in a strain of adulation, insisted upon it, that there never was a more happy man existed. 'Will you then, Damocles,' says the tyrant, 'since you are so delighted with my way of life, have yourself a taste of it, and make the experiment?' As Damocles, of course, answered in the affirmative, he ordered him to be seated on a golden sofa, covered with a fine mattress, and sumptuous carpets, highly wrought in the most elegant taste; the table set out with the most exquisite dainties; the room adorned with cabinets, with gold and silver vases highly embossed; perfumes, garlands of flowers, and incense burning: to crown all, he was served by the most beautiful slaves, who were ordered carefully to watch his eye, and attend his nod. In short, Damocles felt himself the happiest of mortals.

"But, alas! in the midst of these splendid preparations, Dionysius had ordered a glittering naked sword to be suspended from the ceiling, by a single horse hair, immediately over the head of this happy man.

"Now, therefore, the whole visionary scene instantly vanished: he no longer beheld the beautiful attendants, nor the plate, so artificially carved; nor could he touch any of the delicacies on the table; the garlands dropped from his head. In short, he begged of the tyrant to let him depart, for he did not wish to be happy upon such terms." Does not Dionysius himself, then, sufficiently demonstrate, that no one can possibly be happy in a state of continual terror and anxiety, like that of the tyrant?—*Tusc. Quæst.* lib. v. c. xx.

"I cannot forbear mentioning a peculiar source of misery to Dionysius; he unfortunately took it into his head, that he excelled all others in poetry as well as in power; and was so offended with his friend Philoxenus for attempting to undeceive him in that particular, that he in his wrath sent him instantly to that horrible dungeon, called the Latumiæ, or Stone-Quarries. He was set at liberty, however, the very next day, and restored to favour: and the tyrant made a noble entertainment on

---

4 Ut Tonstriculæ.　　5 Putaminibus.
6 It may be worth while to read the account of the magnificence with which he brought home his two wives,—one drawn by four white horses, &c.—*Univer. Hist. from Diod. Sic.*

the occasion. But in the midst of their jollity, the prince was determined to gain the applause of Philoxenus, whose approbation he preferred to that of a thousand flatterers. He desired him, therefore, to divest himself of envy, (for Philoxenus was a poet as well as a critic) and declare his real sentiments. Philoxenus could not dissemble; and therefore, without making any answer to Dionysius, turned to the guards, who always attended, and with a humorous air, desired them to carry him back to the stone-quarries.

Dionysius (though probably piqued) said, the wit of the poet had atoned for his freedom.— *Plut. Moral.*

N. B. It was Dionysius the younger, who, after enduring the miseries of royalty, was condemned to be a schoolmaster.

No. VI.

Montaigne, who has pillaged every ancient classic author, quotes and enlarges upon some of Hiero's sentiments; but gives them the vulgar turn, to prove that kings and beggars, if stripped of their external appendages, are upon a level, which few people now a-day will dispute. The following, however, are put in a striking light.

" The honour we receive from those that fear us does not deserve the name; that respect is paid to my royalty, not to me. Do I not see, that the wicked and the good king, he that is hated, and he that is beloved, has the one as much reverence paid him as the other? My predecessor was, and my successor will be, served with the same ceremony and parade as myself. If my subjects do not injure me, it is no proof of their good-will towards me. It is not in their power, if they were inclined to do it. No one follows me from any friendship which subsists between us: there can be no friendship contracted, where there is so little connection or correspondence. All that they say or do is pretence and show: I see nothing around me but disguise and dissimulation."— Lib. i. c. 42.

No. VII.

I shall conclude these extracts with a short one from Lord Bolingbroke's " Letter on Patriotism." Speaking of superior spirits, whether invested with royalty, or placed in other elevated situations, " They either appear," says he, " like ministers of divine vengeance, and their course through the world is marked by desolation and oppression, by poverty and servitude; or, they are the guardian angels of the country they inhabit; busy to avert even the most distant evil, and to maintain or to procure peace, plenty, and the greatest of human blessings, LIBERTY."

P. S. I have availed myself of Peter Coste's French translation, but have never adopted an expression without having first examined the original with the most scrupulous attention.

THE SCIENCE

OF

GOOD HUSBANDRY;

OR

THE ECONOMICS OF XENOPHON.

TRANSLATED BY

R. BRADLEY, F. R. S.

PROFESSOR OF BOTANY IN THE UNIVERSITY OF CAMBRIDGE.

THE

SCIENCE OF GOOD HUSBANDRY;

OR

THE ECONOMICS OF XENOPHON.

I. I remember once to have heard the learned Socrates reasoning with Critobulus, concerning the management of a house, in the following manner:

Soc. " Tell me, Critobulus, whether the ordering of a house is a science, such as that of physic, or the brasiers, and of the masons?"

Crit. " My opinion is, that the good management of a house is as great a science as either masonry, or physic, or any other; from whence we may infer there is a distinct business or duty belonging to an economist or housekeeper, as well as to any science whatever: a farmer or a master of a family ought to be a good judge of every particular which relates to the good ordering of his farm or house."

Soc. " But may we not find a trusty steward well skilled in this science, who may take the management of the household upon him, and save the master the trouble? for a master mason employs a deputy under him, who will do his work as well as himself; and for the same reason we may expect that a steward well skilled in the management of a house, may be as serviceable to his master as the mason's deputy."

Crit. " I am of the same opinon, good Socrates."

Soc. " Then the man who is well skilled in this science, though he has no property of his own, may gain a comfortable living by directing another man's house. For the man would be worthy of the master's favour, and a good

steward, if in the discharging of his stewardship he could improve his master's house. But what do we mean by the word house, or the economy of it? Is it only the good distribution of the things that are in the house? or is it the good management and improvement of every thing belonging to a house, and the master of it."

Crit. " It is my opinion, that a man's estate, whether it lie in or about the house, or remote from it, yet every branch of that estate may be said to belong to the house; nay every thing that a man has, except his enemies, which some men have in great numbers, but these are not to be reckoned among his goods or substance. It would be ridiculous if we were to say that the man who had been the occasion of making us more enemies than we had before, should be rewarded with favour or money; but a man's enemies, or any thing which he possesses to his hurt or prejudice, must not I suppose, be reckoned among his goods: therefore I conclude, that those things only which contribute to the welfare of a man may be reckoned among his riches, or be properly called his goods."

Soc. " I am of the same mind, that whatever is injurious to a man must not be esteemed a part of his goods; for if a man buy a horse, and for want of skill to manage him, he falls from him and hurts himself, can that horse be reckoned amongst his goods? No, certainly; because those things should be called goods that are beneficial to the master. Neither can those lands be called goods, which by a man's unskilful management put him to more expense than he receives profit by them; nor may those lands be called goods, which do not bring a good farmer such a profit as may give him a good living: so likewise if a man has a flock of sheep, and they come to damage by his unskilful management, he cannot reckon them among his goods."

Crit. "So these may only be called goods which are profitable, and those which are hurtful be deemed the contrary."

Soc. "You distinguish right, that nothing ought to be esteemed goods to any man which he does not receive advantage by; and that those things which bring him disprofit must be esteemed the contrary. A flute, when it is in the hands of a person who can play well upon it, is an advantage, and may be reckoned among his goods; but the same instrument in the possession of one who does not know the use of it, is no better to him than a stone, unless he sells it, and then the price of it may be accounted among his goods; but if he keeps it, when he has no knowledge of its use, it cannot be ranked among them."

Crit. "I agree with you in this point, that those things only which are profitable may be called goods: the flute, while we keep it unemployed, is no part of our goods, for we have no advantage from it; but if we sell it, it is then profitable to us."

Soc. "You say right, if a man has wit enough to sell it well: but when it is sold, and the man has not wisdom enough to use the value of it to his advantage, yet whatever price he gets for it cannot be esteemed to be good."

Crit. "By this you seem to intimate that money itself is not good, if it is in the hands of one who does not know how to use it."

Soc. "Yes, certainly; for we have already agreed that nothing may be esteemed good but what we can get profit by. If a man bestow the money he gets upon harlots, and by continual conversing with them he impairs his health, and abandons the care of his estate, then his money is no profit to him; but, on the contrary, is an errant poison, which will shortly bring him to destruction: therefore, friend Critobulus, money is good only to those who know how to use it; but to those who know not rightly the value of it, it were better for them to cast it away, to avoid the damage it would do them."

Crit. "But what say you of friends? If a man knows how to use them, and make them profitable to him, what shall we esteem them to be?"

Soc. "These may truly be called goods; they ought to be preferred before our houses, our land, our cattle, or our flocks; the profit which may arise by them may be superior to all others."

Crit. "Then by the same rule our enemies may be esteemed goods, if we know how to profit ourselves by them."

Soc. "Undoubtedly they are so; therefore it behoves a master of a house to use his enemies with that discretion that he may make them advantageous to him by any means: for how many instances have we, good Critobulus, of ordinary men, as well as of noblemen and kings, who have increased and amplified their fortunes by law, and warring with their enemies."

Crit. "You reason well, good Socrates, of these matters. But what think you of those who have good learning, and many other good properties, whereby they have every opportunity of improving their estates, and yet never put their minds to it? We have many instances of men with these qualifications, who never regard the advancement of their fortunes; shall we then reckon their learning, or their other properties, among their goods, seeing they make no advantage of them, or ought we to esteem them the contrary?"

Soc. "I imagine you mean bondmen, or such other vile persons."

Crit. "No, good Socrates; but the persons I speak of are young gentlemen, who are expert in affairs of war, as well as peace; and yet they abandon their knowledge for trifles; and such as them I esteem in a worse condition than bondmen; for I suppose they do not employ themselves in the sciences they have been bred to, because they have not masters to direct them or set them to work."

Soc. "How can that be, friend Critobulus, that they are without directors? they have many masters, which, when they would study their felicity and their advantage, lead them away from their virtuous inclinations."

Crit. "These masters then are invisible!"

Soc. "Not so invisible, good Critobulus, but that we may easily discover them to be the most mischievous of any that reign upon earth. What think you of sloth, idleness, negligence, want of public spirit? Where these govern, what can we expect but mischief? But, besides these, there are others which govern under the name of pleasures; as gaming, lewd company, rioting, and such others, which in process of time teach their adherents that pleasures are not without their inconveniences. These rulers keep them so much in servitude, that they do not allow them the least liberty to do any thing for their advantage."

Crit. "But there are others, friend Socrates, who have none of these directors to prevent their welfare, but apply themselves assiduously to business, and give their minds entirely to the advancement of their fortunes, and yet waste their estates, ruin their families, and destroy themselves, without hope of redemption."

Soc. "These also are bondmen, and are rather worse slaves than the others, for these have the most severe masters of the two: some are under the tyranny of drunkenness, others slaves to gluttony, and some to vanity and vain-glory; all which keep their subjects in that severity of servitude, that as long as they find them young, lusty, and able to work, they make them bring all that they can get by any means to bestow upon these lusts and pleasures; but as soon as they perceive them to grow so old, that they can labour no longer for them, they are then turned off to lead the remainder of their days in want and misery, while their quondam masters are contriving to ensnare others in their room. Wherefore, good Critobulus, we ought by all means to resist such invaders of our liberties, even with as much force and resolution as we would oppose an enemy who with sword in hand attempts to bring us into slavery. There are some enemies who have wisdom and goodness enough, when they have brought men into their subjection, to learn them government and moderation, which before were proud and arrogant. But as for the tyrants I have mentioned before, they never cease harassing and tormenting both the bodies and estates of those which fall into their hands, till they have utterly destroyed them."

II. *Crit.* "You have sufficiently spoken to this point; and, now I examine myself, I verily believe I have conduct and courage enough to resist such deceitful invaders; and I now desire your advice concerning the management of my house, that both myself and fortune may be improved; for I am persuaded I

shall not be overcome by those enemies to reason which you have so largely exposed. And therefore, good Socrates, give me your deliberate opinion how I shall act for the good of myself and estate; although perhaps you may think that we are already rich enough."

Soc. "For my own part, if I am one of those you speak of, I want nothing, I have riches enough; but for yourself, Critobulus, I esteem you a very poor man; and, by the faith I owe to the gods, I often pity you."

Crit. "Your discourse makes me laugh! If you are so very rich as you esteem yourself, pray inform me what may be the value of all your estate if it were sold, and what do you imagine is the worth of all my possessions?"

Soc. "Perhaps, if I sell all my possessions at a good market, I may gain five or six pounds for them: but I know very well, that were your whole estate to be sold, the price would be more than a thousand times as much; and yet though you know this, you are still desirous to increase your estate, and upbraid me with my poverty. What I possess is enough to supply me with necessaries; but to support your grandeur, and draw the respect due to your quality and the post you possess, I am of opinion, that were you master of four times as much as you have already, you would still be in want."

Crit. "I do not conceive how that can be."

Soc. "In the first place, your rank requires you to feast and make entertainments for the people, to gain their good-will, and command their respect. In the next place, you must live hospitably, and receive and entertain all strangers, and gain their esteem. And in the third place, you must continually be doing good offices to your fellow citizens, that upon an emergency you may find friends. Besides, I already observe that the city of Athens begins to put you upon expensive works; viz. to furnish them with horses, to raise public buildings, to muster men, to erect theatres, and to treat the citizens with plays. But if this nation should be once involved in war, I am sure their demand upon you in taxes, and other duties, will be as much as your purse will be able to bear. And when that happens, if you are discovered to conceal any of your riches, or do not answer their demands to your full power, you must undergo the same punishment as if you had robbed the common treasury. And besides, I find you possessed with the opinion that you have riches enough, and therefore give yourself up to vain and trifling pleasures, which is the effect of your riches. It is for these reasons, good Critobulus, that I grieve for you lest you fall under misfortunes that may end in the greatest poverty without remedy: and for myself, if I should be necessitous, you know very well that many would relieve me; and if I received but a little of every one, I should have more money than would satisfy my wants: but, as for your friends, though they have more riches in their stations, than you possess in yours, they have yet expectations of preferment from you."

Crit. " I confess I find nothing amiss in your discourse. I so much approve of it, that my greatest desire is, that you will instruct me with such good precepts as may preserve me from the misery you speak of, and that I may never be an object of your compassion, unless it be in a good cause."

Soc. " I suppose then, friend Critobulus, you are not now in the same laughing mind you was in, when I told you I had riches enough; do you now believe I know wherein consists the value of riches? You ridiculed me when you made me confess that I had not by a thousandth part so much as you have, and now you desire my most friendly instructions to keep you from extreme poverty."

Crit. " I perceive, good Socrates, that you have sufficient wisdom to instruct a man how to gain true riches, even in the greatest plenty: and I am persuaded, that the man who knows how to make the most of a little, is no less capable of managing the greatest fortune."

Soc. " You may remember, that towards the beginning of our discourse I told you that horses ought not to be reckoned among the goods of those who know not how to use them, nor land, nor sheep, nor money, or any other thing whatever; and yet every one of these are profitable, when they are used discreetly. As for my own part, I have never had any of these; and how then should I be able to inform you of the use of them? But though a man has neither money nor goods, yet I am persuaded there is such a science as the good ordering of a house. Why then, good Critobulus, should you not be master of this science? For the reason why every man cannot play well upon the flute, is either because he has not a flute of his own, or cannot borrow a flute of another to practise upon. The same impediment have I in the science of ordering a house; for I was never yet master of the implements belonging to housekeeping, neither goods nor money; nor was there ever any who intrusted me with the management of their house, or estate, although you now desire my directions. But you are sensible, that learners of music in the beginning spoil their instruments: so that were I now to begin my practice upon your estate, I should destroy it."

Crit. " Thus you endeavour to evade the business I desire you to undertake, and would shun taking share with me in the management of my affairs."

Soc. " That is not the case. I am willing to serve you in any thing within the bounds of my capacity. But suppose you was in want of fire, and came to me for it, and I had none, but directed you to a place where you might have it: would not that be of the same account? Or if you want water, and I have it not, but direct you where to have it, will not that be as agreeable to you? And if you would be instructed in music, and I directed you to a better judge in music than myself, would not that answer your design? Therefore, since I have no knowledge of myself in the affair you speak of, the best pleasure I can do you, is to recommend you to such persons who are most expert in the business you require; and that, I judge, I am able to do; for I have made it my business to search out the most ingenious of all sorts in every quarter of the city, having observed that among the practisers of the same service, and the same trade, some of the practitioners were hardly capable of subsisting, or getting their bread, while others got estates. This, I confess, made me admire; till at length I discovered that some men ran headlong upon their business without any consideration, and are so rash in their undertakings, that they always come off losers; while, on the other hand, I observed that all those who went about their work deliberately, and advised well upon their business before they set about it, these men accomplished their affairs with more facility, more despatch, and to more advantage. Which observation may serve, as a lesson, to instruct you how your fortune may be advanced upon a sure foundation."

III. *Crit.* " Then I am resolved not to part from you till you have acquainted me with those wise men you speak of, who are capable of informing me of the matters I want."

Soc. " Will it be amiss if I show you some men who have been at vast expenses in building, and set about their work with so little judgment or consideration, that after an immense measure has been spent by them, they have only raised an unprofitable pile to their discredit? And, on the contrary, there are other men, who with much less charge have erected useful and profitable buildings. Will not this be one step towards the good ordering of a house?"

Crit. " You are surely right."

Soc. " Will it then be improper, if I show you, in the next place, that some men have plenty of rich and useful furniture for their houses, and for all uses; and when any part of it should be used, it is out of the way, and to seek, and it is not known whether it be lost, or laid in safety? This, wherever it happens, discomposes the master of the house, and occasions him to be angry with his servants. But there are others, who have no more goods or furniture, or, perhaps, have not half so much, and yet have every thing ready at hand to answer their occasions."

Crit. " The reason is plain, good Socrates; the first have no order in the distribution of their goods, but let them lie in confusion; the others have a regard that every thing should be laid up in its proper place."

Soc. " You are in the right, good Critobulus; but it is not only necessary that every thing should be set in its place, but also, that there should be a proper and convenient place to set it in."

Crit. " This also is necessary towards the good ordering of a house."

Soc. " Suppose I likewise show you, that in some places the slaves and servants are chained and strictly watched, and yet often run away from their masters; while in other places, where they are in freedom, and have their liberty, they work heartily for their masters, and are perpetually striving who shall act most for their advantage. Is not this a point worthy the regard of a housekeeper?"

Crit. " Certainly, it is very worthy the regard of a master."

Soc. " Nor will it be of less use, if I show you that some husbandmen continually complain of want, and are in a starving condition; while others, who practise the same science of husbandry, have every thing necessary about them, and live upon the fat of the land."

Crit. " This will surely be of good use. But perhaps the first you speak of bestow their money and goods improperly; or dispose of what they get to the disadvantage of themselves and their families."

Soc. " There are surely some such husbandmen; but I only speak of those who call themselves husbandmen, and yet can hardly find themselves with a sufficiency of meat and drink."

Crit. " What should be the cause of this?"

Soc. " I will bring you among them, that you may learn by their example."

Crit. " That is my desire, good Socrates."

Soc. " But first you must learn how to distinguish between the good and the bad, when you see them. I have known you rise early in the morning, and travel long journeys to see a comedy, and you have pressed my company with you; but you never invited me to such a sight as this we speak of."

Crit. " Dear Socrates, forbear your banter, and proceed in your good instructions."

Soc. " Suppose I show you some men, who by keeping great stables of horses are reduced to extreme poverty; while others, by the same means, have got great estates, and live splendidly?"

Crit. " I have seen them, and know them both; but I cannot discern what advantage that will be to me."

Soc. " The reason is, that you see them as you do plays, not with a design of becoming a poet, but purely for amusement and recreation; and perhaps you do not amiss in that, if your genius does not lead you to be a poet; but as you are obliged to keep horses, is it not necessary that you should understand what belongs to them, that by your skill you may reap an advantage by them?"

Crit. " You mean that I should breed horses."

Soc. " By no means; for you may have a good servant without the trouble of bringing him up from a child. There are ages both of horses and men wherein they are immediately profitable, and will improve every day upon your hands. Moreover, I can show you some men, who have been so discreet in the management of their wives, that their estates have been greatly advantaged by them; but there are others, and not a few, who by means of their wives have been utterly ruined."

Crit. " But who is to be blamed for this; the husband, or the wife?

4 N

Soc. " If a sheep is out of order, we commonly blame the shepherd ; and if a horse have not his goings as he should, but is skittish and mischievous, we blame the breaker ; and as for a wife, if her husband instruct her well in his affairs, and she neglect them, she is not wise : but if her husband does not his part, in giving her proper instructions for her government, and she behaves herself disorderly, and unbecoming her sex, or herself as a mistress of a house, is not then the man to blame ?"

Crit. " Yes, without doubt ; and it is a subject that I should be glad to discourse with you about ; and, by the friendship we owe one another, tell me sincerely and freely, Is there any one among all your friends whom you intrust with so great a share of your household affairs as your wife ?"

Soc. " It is true, I do not : but tell me likewise, Is there one you converse with seldomer upon that subject than you do with your wife ?"

Crit. " You judge right ; for if there are any, there are very few, who know less of my affairs than my wife."

Soc. " You married her very young, before she had seen or heard much of the world ; therefore it would be more to be admired if she acted as she ought to do, than if she did amiss."

Crit. " Then, good Socrates, do you imagine that those, who bear the character of good housewives, have been taught to be so ?"

Soc. " I will not dispute that with you at present, but refer you to my wife Aspasia, who will inform you better than I can myself. But, to proceed ; I esteem a wife to be a good and necessary companion for the master of a house, and one who ought to bear the next share of government under the master of the house ; there is only a little more power in the husband than in the wife : the substance of the estate is generally increased by the industry and labour of the man ; but the wife, for the most part, has the care upon her to distribute and order those things that are brought into the house ; and if, therefore, the husband and wife agree in their management, the houses and estates improve ; but where there is not this harmony, they must necessarily decay. I could likewise inform you in many other sciences, if the instruction were needful."

Crit. " There is no occasion, good Socrates ; for the richest man has not occasion to employ men of all faculties, nor is there any man who has occasion to practise them all. But such sciences as are honourable and becoming my province to understand, those I desire to learn, as well from the persons you may judge most capable of teaching me, as from yourself, whom principally I shall depend upon to give the finishing stroke."

Soc. " You reason well, friend Critobulus ; for there are many crafts which are not necessary for you to know : those are called handicraft, and are the least regarded in our city and commonwealth ; for they destroy the health of those who practise them, by keeping their bodies in the shade, and confining them to a sedentary habit, or else by employing them all day over the fire, which is yet as unhealthful ; and when once the body is tender and feeble, the stomach and spirits must certainly be weak. And besides, men of such occupations can have no time to bend their minds either to do their friends any good, or can have leisure to assist the commonwealth : therefore such people cannot readily serve their friends, if they should happen to be in distress ; nor are persons fit to serve their country in time of adversity. For which reason, in some cities and commonwealths, especially such as are deeply engaged in war, a citizen is not suffered to practise any handicraft."

Crit. " What faculties then, good Socrates, would you advise me to use ?"

Soc. " The king of Persia, I think, may set us a good example ; for we are told that the sciences which are most esteemed by him are war and husbandry ; these, of all others, he reckons the most honourable as well as the most necessary, and accordingly gives them encouragement."

Crit. " And can you imagine, good Socrates, that the king of Persia has any regard for husbandry ?"

Soc. " I shall endeavour to satisfy you whether he has or not. You will allow with all the world that he delights in war, because of his obligations on the princes under him to furnish him with certain numbers of troops by way of tribute ; either to keep his subjects in awe and prevent rebellion, or to gaurd his country against foreign enemies that may come to invade it. Besides these, he keeps large garrisons in several castles, and appoints a treasurer to pay their wages duly, that they may be kept in good order. His tributary troops are all mustered once in twelve months, that they may be disciplined and ready for an engagement, if any commotion or invasion should happen; but the garrisoned forces and his own guards he reviews himself, and intrusts the inspection of his remoter troops to such a lieutenant as he can best confide in, upon whose report he either rewards or punishes the leaders of the several legions, according as they have acted for his honour in their several stations. Those especially who have their troops in the best order and discipline, he confers on them the greatest honours, and rewards them with such presents as may put them above the world ever after; and for those who have neglected their duty and abused the soldiers under them, he dismisses them from their governments, and loads them with shame. It cannot be doubted but a prince that acts with this conduct must understand war, and is well skilled in the military science.

" On the other hand, he employs great part of his time in riding about his neighbouring part of the country, and observing the state of husbandry, whether the lands are tilled as they ought to be; and for the remote parts, he sends such deputies to examine them as are esteemed to be the properest judges; and when he finds that his governors and deputies have kept their several countries well inhabited, and the ground well cultivated, with such produce as it will best bear, he raises them in honours, loads them with presents, and enlarges their governments; but if he finds the country thin of people, or the ground uncultivated, or that extortions or cruelties have been committed by his governors, he inflicts severe punishments on them, and discharges them from their employments. From these examples, do you believe that the king of Persia has not as great regard to the peopling his country, and the science of husbandry, as he has to keeping an army in such an order as may defend it? But it is to be observed among his high officers, that no one of them has the charge of two commissions at one time; for some are appointed to be overseers of his lands and husbandmen, and to receive his tributes that arise by them, while others are employed to overlook the soldiery and garrisons; so that if the governor of the garrison neglects his duty in keeping good order or defending his country, the lieutenant over the affairs of husbandry accuses him, that his land is not cultivated for want of a sufficient defence against the encroaching parties, which are common enough in those parts. But if the governor of the garrison performs his duty, and keeps the country under his jurisdiction in peace; and the director of affairs of husbandry neglects his business, so that the country is in want of people, and the lands are not ordered as they ought to be, then he is accused by the governor of the garrison; for if the husbandry is neglected, the soldiers must starve, and the king himself must lose his tribute. But in some part of Persia there is a great prince called Satrapa, who takes upon him the office both of soldiery and husbandry."

Crit. " If the king acts as you inform me, he seems to take as much delight in husbandry as he does in war."

Soc. " I have not yet done concerning him; for in every country where he resides, or passes a little time, he takes care to have excellent gardens, filled with every kind of flower or plant that can by any means be collected, and in these places are his chief delight."

Crit. " By your discourse it appears also, that he has a great delight in gardening; for, as you intimate, his gardens are furnished with every tree and plant that the ground is capable of bringing forth."

Soc. " We are told likewise, that when the king distributes any rewards, he first appoints the principal officers of his soldiery, who have the greatest right to his favour, to appear before him, and then bestows on them presents according to their deserts: for the tilling of ground would be of no effect, unless there were forces well managed to defend it. And after the soldiers he next distributes his honours and preferments among those who have taken good care that his lands were well cultivated and the people kept from idleness; observing at the same time that vigilant soldiers could not subsist without the care of the industrious husbandmen. We are told likewise, that Cyrus, a king famed for his wisdom and warlike disposition, was of the same mind with regard to husbandry; and used to distribute rewards to his most deserving soldiers and husbandmen, telling them at the same time, that he himself had deserved the presents he gave away, because he had taken care of the tillage of his country, and had also taken care to defend it."

Crit. "If this is true of Cyrus, it is evident enough that he had as much love for husbandry as he had for war."

Soc. "If Cyrus had lived, he would have proved a very wise prince, for we have many extraordinary proofs of his wisdom and conduct: one passage in particular I may take notice of, which is, when he met his brother in battle to decide the dispute who should be king, from Cyrus no man deserted, but many thousands deserted from the king to Cyrus; which surely must be the effect of his virtue, for there is no greater argument of a prince's goodness, than the love of the people, and especially when they pay him a voluntary obedience, and stand by him in time of distress. In this great contest, the friends of Cyrus stood fighting about him while he was yet alive, and even after his fall, maintained their post till they were all slain by his side, except Ariæus, who was posted in the left wing of the army. When Lysander brought presents to Cyrus from the cities of Greece that were his confederates, he received him with the greatest humanity, and among other things showed him his garden, which was called " the Paradise of Sardis;" which when Lysander beheld, he was struck with admiration of the beauty of the trees, the regularity of their planting, the evenness of their rows, and their making regular angles one to another; or, in a word, the beauty of the quincunx order in which they were planted, and the delightful odours which issued from them. Lysander could no longer refrain from extolling the beauty of their order, but more particularly admired the excellent skill of the hand that had so curiously disposed them; which Cyrus perceiving, answered him: ' All the trees that you here behold are of my own appointment; I it was that contrived, measured, and laid out the ground for planting these trees, and I can even show you some of them that I planted with my own hands.' When Lysander heard this, and saw the richness of his robes, and the splendour of his dress, his chains of gold, and the number and curiosity of the jewels about him, he cried out with astonishment, ' Is it possible, great king, that you could condescend to plant any of these trees with your own hands?'—' Do you wonder at that, Lysander?' answered Cyrus. ' I assure you, that whenever I have leisure from war, or am the most at ease, I never dine till I have either done some exercise in arms, or employed myself in some point of husbandry, till I sweat.' To which Lysander replied: ' You are truly fortunate, great king, in being a wise and good man.'

V. "This, good Critobulus, I thought proper to acquaint you of, that you may know how much the richest and most fortunate among men delight themselves in husbandry: for it is a business of that nature, that at the same time it is delightful and profitable, both to the body and estate, affording such exercise as will increase a man's health and strength, and such advantages as may greatly improve his fortune. By husbandry the ground gives us every thing necessary for our food and nourishment, and such things likewise as afford the greatest pleasures. Moreover, it furnishes us with beautiful flowers, and other excellent materials for the ornament and decoration of the temples and altars, affording the richest gayety, and most fragrant odours. So likewise it produces meats for the use of men; some without much trouble, others with more labour; for the keeping of sheep is a branch of husbandry. But though it gives us plenty of all kinds of things, yet it does not allow us to reap them in sloth and idleness, but excites us to health and strength by the labour it appoints us. In the winter, by reason of the cold; and in summer, by reason of heat; and for them who labour with their hands, it makes them robust and mighty; and those who only oversee their works, are quickened and prompted to act like men; for they must rise early in the morning, and must exercise themselves with walking from one place to another. For, both in the fields and in cities, whatever is undertaken to the purpose, must be done in a proper time and season. Again: if a man is inclined to practise horsemanship, and grow expert in that science for the defence of his country, a horse can be nowhere better kept, than in the country; or if a man choose to exercise himself on foot, or in running, husbandry gives him strength of body, and he may exercise himself in hunting: here is also meat for his dogs, as well as entertainment for wild beasts, and beasts of the game: and the horses and dogs, thus assisted by husbandry, return us good service to the ground; for the horse may carry his master early in the morning to oversee that the workmen and labourers do their duty in the fields, and returns with the master again at night at the latest hour, if his pre-

senee should be required till that time; and
the dogs are a defence against wild beasts,
that they spoil not the fruits of the earth, nor
destroy the sheep, and even keep a man safe
in a wilderness. Again; the practice of husbandry makes men strong and bold enabling
them to defend their country; for in open
countries the husbandmen are not without robbers, who would invade their lands, and carry
off their crops, if they had not strength and
courage enough to resist them. What faculty
will sooner encourage a man to leap, to run, or
draw a bow, than husbandry? and what science
is there that brings a man more advantage for
his labour? What science is more agreeable to
a studious man? for he finds in it every thing
he can have occasion for. Where shall a
stranger be better received and entertained?
or where shall a man live more commodiously
in winter, than in the place where he may be
accommodated with firing enough and hot
baths? Where can we abide with greater
pleasure in summer, than near rivers, springs,
woods, groves, and fields, where gentle breezes
fan the air? Where may a man treat his guests
more agreeably or make more triumphant banquets? What place do servants delight in
more? Or what other place is more agreeable
to the wife? Where do children covet more
to be? Or where are friends better received,
or better satisfied? There is no science, in
my mind, more delightful than this, if a man
has a convenient substance to put him to work;
nor any business more profitable to a man, if
he has skill and industry. Again: the ground
may teach men justice, if they have discretion
enough to observe it; for it rewards those very
liberally, who take care of it and assist it. But
if it should happen that a country, by means of
wars, should be obliged to lie uncultivated;
yet those who have been bred up to husbandry
are hardy and fit for soldiers, and may by that
means get their living; and oftentimes it is
more certain seeking a livelihood with weapons
of war, in time of war, than with instruments
of husbandry.

"The science of husbandry also brings men
to good discipline, and prepares them to go to
war when there is occasion. For the ground
cannot be tilled without men; and a good husbandman will always provide the strongest,
lustiest workmen he can get for that purpose,
and such especially as will readily obey his
commands, and are tractable in their business;

and this is much the same with the business of
a general when he is ordering his army: in
either case those are rewarded that behave
themselves well, or those are punished who are
obstinate and neglect their duty. A good
husbandman must as often call upon his workmen and encourage them, as a general or leader
of an army ought to encourage his soldiers;
for bondmen should be no less encouraged and
fed with hopes by their masters than freemen;
nay, rather more, that their inclinations may
bind them to their masters, and keep them
from running away. He was surely a wise man
who said, that husbandry was the mother and
nurse of all other sciences; for if husbandry
flourish, all other sciences and faculties fare
the better; but whenever the ground lies uncultivated, and brings no crop, all other sciences are at a loss both by sea and land."

Crit. "Good Socrates, you reason well of
this matter; but you are sensible there are
many unforeseen accidents that happen in husbandry, which sometimes will destroy all our
hopes of profit, though a husbandman has
acted with the greatest skill and diligence;
sometimes hail, droughts, mildews, or continual
rains, spoil our crops, or vermin will even eat
up the seed in the ground; and also sheep,
though they never have so good pasture, are
sometimes infected with distempers, which
destroy them."

Soc. "I thought, good Critobulus, that you
allowed the gods to have the direction of husbandry, as well as the battle. We all know
that before our generals lead forth their armies,
they make vows, prayers, and offer sacrifices to
the gods, to bribe them in favour of their enterprise, and consult the oracles what is best to
do. And think you that, in the business of
husbandry, we ought not to implore the favour
of the gods as much as we do in the affair of
war? Be assured, friend Critobulus, that all
virtuous men attend the temples with sacrifices,
prayers, and oblations for the welfare of all
their fruits, their oxen, their sheep, their horses,
and of every thing else that they possess."

VI. *Crit.* "I agree with you, good Socrates,
that in all our undertakings we ought, before we
set about them, to consult and implore the pleasure of the gods, as their power is superior to
all others, as well in war as in peace: but our
purpose is to consult about the well-ordering
of a house; therefore I desire you will resume
your discourse, and proceed to the purport of

our design: for I confess you have already made such an impression on me with regard to the ordering of a house, and how a man ought to live, that I long for your farther instructions."

Soc. "Will it not then be proper to have a respect to our foregoing arguments, and make a recapitulation of those things that we have agreed in, that in the progress of our discourse we may know what has been settled between us?"

Crit. "It will be a great pleasure; for when two men have lent money to one another, there is nothing more agreeable to them both, than to agree in their reckoning: so now in our discourse it will be no less agreeable to know what particulars we have settled betwixt us."

Soc. "We first agreed, that the ordering of a house is the name of a science; and that to act for the increase and welfare of a house, is that science.

"Secondly, we agreed, that by the word house, we mean all a man's possessions, and such goods as are useful to a man's life; and we found that every thing was profitable to a man that he knew how to use with judgment: wherefore we concluded it was impossible for a man to learn all manner of sciences: and as for the handicrafts, we thought proper to exclude them, as many cities and commonwealths do, because they seem to destroy bodily health; and this particularly where there is danger of enemies invading the country, or where there are wars; for were we on that occasion to set the handicraftmen on one side, and the husbandmen on the other, and ask them whether they would rather go out against their enemies, or give up their fields and defend the cities; those who had been used to the labour of the field would rather go out to fight and deliver their country, and the artificers would choose rather to sit still in the way they had been brought up, than put themselves into the least danger: we, moreover, recommended husbandry as a good exercise, and a calling of that profit that will bring its master every thing that is necessary: besides, it is a business soon learned, and extremely pleasant to them who practise it; it also makes the body robust and strong, gives a bloom to the face, and qualifies a man with a generosity of spirit to assist his friends and his country: besides this, we have also joined in opinion, that the practice of husbandry makes men hardy and courageous, and able to defend their country; because, by

the fields lying open and exposed to invaders, they have frequent skirmishes, and therefore know the better how to fight. It is for these reasons that husbandry is esteemed the mother of sciences and the most honourable in all governments: it is healthful, and breeds good men, and occasions generosity of spirit and good will towards one's friends and country."

Crit. "You have fully persuaded me that husbandry is a most pleasant and profitable occupation; but I remember in your discourse you told me of some husbandmen who get plentiful fortunes by their practice, and that there were others who through mismanagement became beggars by it: I desire you would clear up these two things to me, that when I come to practise this science, I may follow that way which will be the most advantageous, and avoid the contrary."

Soc. "But suppose I should first tell you, good Critobulus, of a discourse I once had with a man who might truly be called good and honest; for it will assist in what you desire."

Crit. "I shall be glad to hear that discourse, which may inform me how to gain the worthy name of a truly good and honest man."

Soc. "That which first led me to consider the value of one man more than of another, was by finding among the artificers, such as builders, painters, and statuaries, those were always esteemed the best and most worthy whose works were the most perfect; so that it was their works that gained them the applause of the people. I had likewise heard that there were those among the people, who had so behaved themselves, that they were esteemed good and honest men: these men, above all others, I coveted to converse with, that I might learn how they gained that character; and because I observed that good and honest were companions in their character, I saluted the first man I met that had a goodly presence, expecting to find the character of good and honest in the most comely personage, rather than any other: but I soon found I was far from my aim, and began to recollect myself that there are many fair faces, and personages of graceful appearance, that possess the most sordid dispositions, and ungenerous souls; so that now I was sensible the good and honest man was not to be known by the external appearance, but that the surest way to find what I sought for, was to search for one of those that bore the character. In the course of my inquiries I was recommended to one whose name is Ischomachus, a man esteemed by both the sexes, citizens and strangers, as truly worthy the character I sought for; and I soon made it my business to find him out.

VII. "When I first saw him, I found him sitting in a portico of one of the temples alone; and as I concluded he was then at leisure, I placed myself by him, and addressed myself to him in the following manner:—

"Good Ischomachus, I much wonder to see you thus unemployed, whose industry leads you ever to be stirring for the good of some one or other."—"Nor should you now have found me here, good Socrates," said Ischomachus, "if I had not appointed some strangers to meet me at this place."—"And if you had not been here," said Socrates, "where would you have been? or, I pray you, how would you have employed yourself? for I wish to learn what it is that you do to gain the character from all people of a good and honest man: the good complexion of your features seems to denote, that you do not always confine yourself to home." At this, Ischomachus, smiling, seemed to express a satisfaction in what I had said, and replied; "I know not that people give me the character of a good and honest man, for when I am obliged to pay money either for taxes, subsidies, or on other occasions, the people call me plainly Ischomachus: and for what you say concerning my not being much at home, you conjecture right, for my wife is capable of ordering such things as belong to the house."—"But pray tell me," said Socrates, "did you instruct your wife how to manage your house, or was it her father and mother that gave her sufficient instructions to order a house before she came to you?"—"My wife," answered Ischomachus, "was but fifteen years old when I married her; and till then she had been so negligently brought up, that she hardly knew any thing of worldly affairs."—"I suppose," said Socrates, "she could spin, and card, or set her servants to work."—"As for such things, good Socrates," replied Ischomachus, "she had her share of knowledge."—"And did you teach her all the rest," said Socrates, "which relates to the management of a house?"—"I did," replied Ischomachus, "but not before I had implored the assistance of the gods, to show me what instructions were necessary for her; and that she might have a heart to learn and practise those instructions to the advantage and profit of us both."—"But, good Ischomachus, tell me," said Socrates, "did your wife join with you in your petition to the gods?"—"Yes," replied Ischomachus, "and I looked upon that to be no bad omen of her disposition to receive such instructions as I should give her."—"I pray you, good Ischomachus, tell me," said Socrates, "what was the first thing you began to show her? for to hear that, will be a greater pleasure to me, than if you were to describe the most triumphant feast that had ever been celebrated."—"To begin then, good Socrates, when we were well enough acquainted, and were so familiar that we began to converse freely with one another, I asked her for what reason she thought I had taken her to be my wife, that it was not purely to make her a partner of my bed, for that she knew I had women enough already at my command; but the reason why her father and mother had consented she should be mine, was because we concluded her a proper person to be a partner in my house and children: for this end I informed her it was, that I chose her before all other women; and with the same regard her father and mother chose me for her husband: and if we should be so much favoured by the gods that she should bring me children, it would be our business jointly to consult about their education, and how to bring them up in the virtues becoming mankind; for then we may expect them to be profitable to us, to defend us, and comfort us in our old age. I further added, that our house was now common to us both, as well as our estates; for all that I had I delivered into her care, and the same she did likewise on her part to me; and likewise that all these goods were to be employed to the advantage of us both, without upbraiding one or the other, which of the two had brought the greatest fortune; but let our study be, who shall contribute most to the improvement of the fortunes we have brought together; and accordingly wear the honour they may gain by their good management.

"To this, good Socrates, my wife replied, 'How can I help you in this? or wherein can the little power I have do you any good? for my mother told me, both my fortune, as well as yours, was wholly at your command, and that it must be my chief care to live virtuously and soberly.'—' This is true, good wife,' answered Ischomachus, ' but it is the part of a sober husband and virtuous wife to join in their care, not only to preserve the fortune they are possessed of, but to contribute equally to improve it.'—' And what do you see in me,' said the wife of Ischomachus, ' that you believe me capable of assisting in the improvement of your fortune ?'—' Use your endeavour, good wife,' said Ischomachus, ' to do those things which are acceptable to the gods, and are appointed by the law for you to do.'— ' And what things are those, dear husband ?' said the wife of Ischomachus. ' They are things,' replied he, ' which are of no small concern, unless you think that the bee which remains always in the hive, is unemployed: it is her part to oversee the bees that work in the hive, while the others are abroad to gather wax and honey; and it is, in my opinion, a great favour of the gods to give us such lively examples, by such little creatures, of our duty to assist one another in the good ordering of things; for, by the example of the bees, a husband and wife may see the necessity of being concerned together towards the promoting and advancing of their stock: and this union between the man and woman is no less necessary to prevent the decay and loss of mankind, by producing children which may help to comfort and nourish their parents in their old age. It is ordained also for some creatures to live in houses, while it is as necessary for others to be abroad in the fields: wherefore it is convenient for those who have houses and would furnish them with necessary provisions, to provide men to work in their fields, either for tilling the ground, sowing of grain, planting of trees, or grazing of cattle; nor is it less necessary, when the harvest is brought in, to take care in the laying our corn and fruits up properly, and disposing of them discreetly. Little children must be brought up in the house, bread must be made in the house, and all kinds of meats must be dressed in the house; likewise spinning, carding, and weaving, are all works to be done within doors; so that both the things abroad, and those within the house, require the utmost care and diligence; and it appears plainly, by many natural instances, that the woman was born to look after such things as are to be done within the house: for a man naturally is strong of body, and capable of enduring the fatigue of heat and cold, of travel-

ling and undergoing the harsher exercises; so that it seems as if nature had appointed him to look after the affairs without doors: the woman being also to nurse and bring up children, she is naturally of a more soft and tender nature than the man; and it seems likewise that nature has given the woman a greater share of jealousy and fear than to the man, that she may be more careful and watchful over those things which are intrusted to her care; and it seems likely, that the man is naturally made more hardy and bold than the woman, because his business is abroad in all seasons, and that he may defend himself against all assaults and accidents. But because both the man and the woman are to be together for both their advantages, the man to gather his substance from abroad, and the woman to manage and improve it at home, they are indifferently endowed with memory and diligence. It is natural also to both to refrain from such things as may do them harm, and likewise they are naturally given to improve in every thing they study, by practice and experience; but as they are not equally perfect in all things, they have the more occasion of one another's assistance: for when the man and woman are thus united, what the one has occasion for is supplied by the other: therefore, good wife, seeing this is what the gods have ordained for us, let us endeavour, to the utmost of our powers, to behave ourselves in our several stations to the improvement of our fortune: and the law, which brought us together, exhorts us to the same purpose. And also, as it is natural, when we are thus settled, to expect children, the law exhorts us to live together in unity, and to be partakers of one another's benefits: so nature, and the law which is directed by it, ordains that each severally should regard the business that is appointed for them. From whence it appears, that it is more convenient for a woman to be at home and mind her domestic affairs, than to gad abroad; and it is as shameful for a man to be at home idling, when his business requires him to be abroad: if any man acts in a different capacity from that he is born to, he breaks through the decrees of nature, and will certainly meet his punishment, either because he neglects the business which is appointed for him, or because he invades the property of another. I think that the mistress bee is an excellent example for the wife.'—' And what is the business of the mistress bee,' said the wife of Ischomachus, ' that I may follow the example of that which you so much recommend to me, for it seems you have not yet fully explained it?'—' The mistress bee,' replied Ischomachus, ' keeps always in the hive, taking care that all the bees, which are in the hive with her, are duly employed in their several occupations; and those whose business lies abroad, she sends out to their several works. These bees, when they bring home their burthen, she receives, and appoints them to lay up their harvest, till there is occasion to use it, and in a proper season dispenses it among those of her colony, according to their several offices. The bees who stay at home, she employs in disposing and ordering the combs, with a neatness and regularity becoming the nicest observation and greatest prudence. She takes care likewise of the young bees, that they are well nourished, and educated to the business that belongs to them; and when they are come to such perfection that they are able to go abroad and work for their living, she sends them forth under the direction of a proper leader.'—' And is this my business, dear Ischomachus?' said his wife. —' This example, good wife,' replied Ischomachus, ' is what I give you as a lesson worthy your practice: your case requires your presence at home, to send abroad the servants whose business lies abroad, and to direct those whose business is in the house. You must receive the goods that are brought into the house, and distribute such a part of them as you think necessary for the use of the family, and see that the rest be laid up till there be occasion for it; and especially avoid the extravagance of using that in a month which is appointed for twelve months' service. When the wool is brought home, observe that it be carded and spun for weaving into cloth; and particularly take care that the corn, which is brought in, be not laid up in such a manner that it grow musty and unfit for use. But, above all, that which will gain you the greatest love and affection from our servants, is to help them when they are visited with sickness, and that to the utmost of our power.' Upon which his wife readily answered, ' That is surely an act of charity, and becoming every mistress of good nature; for, I suppose, we cannot oblige people more than to help them when they are sick: this will surely engage the love of our servants to us, and make them doubly diligent upon every occasion.'—This answer, Socrates," said Is-

chomachus, " was to me an argument of a good and honest wife; and I replied to her, ' That by reason of the good care and tenderness of the mistress bee, all the rest of the hive are so affectionate to her, that whenever she is disposed to go abroad, the whole colony belonging to her, accompany, and attend upon her.'—To this the wife replied: ' Dear Ischomachus, tell me sincerely, Is not the business of the mistress bee, you tell me of, rather what you ought to do, than myself; or have you not a share in it? For my keeping at home and directing my servants, will be of little account, unless you send home such provisions as are necessary to employ us.'—' And my providence,' answered Ischomachus, ' would be of little use unless there is one at home who is ready to receive and take care of those goods that I send in. Have you not observed,' said Ischomachus, ' what pity people show to those who are punished by pouring water into sieves till they are full? The occasion of pity is, because those people labour in vain.'—' I esteem these people,' said the wife of Ischomachus, ' to be truly miserable, who have no benefit from their labours.'—' Suppose, dear wife,' replied Ischomachus, ' you take into your service one who can neither card nor spin, and you teach her to do those works, will it not be an honour to you? Or if you take a servant which is negligent, or does not understand how to do her business, or has been subject to pilfering, and you make her diligent, and instruct her in the manners of a good servant, and teach her honesty, will not you rejoice in your success? and will you not be pleased with your action? So again, when you see your servants sober and discreet, you should encourage them and show them favour; but as for those who are incorrigible and will not follow your directions, or prove larcenaries, you must punish them. Consider, how laudable it will be for you to excel others in the well-ordering your house; be therefore diligent, virtuous, and modest, and give your necessary attendance on me, your children, and your house, and your name shall be honourably esteemed, even after your death; for it is not the beauty of your face and shape, but your virtue and goodness, which will bring you honour and esteem, which will last for ever.'—After this manner, good Socrates," cried Ischomachus, " I first discoursed with my wife concerning her duty and care of my house."

4 O

VIII. "And did you perceive,": said Socrates, "that she improved by what you taught her?"—"Yes," replied Ischomachus, "she was as extremely diligent to learn and practise what was under her care, as one of her tender years could be, who knew nothing of her duty before. Once I saw her under a great concern, because she could not readily find a parcel which I had brought home; but when I perceived her grieved, I bid her take no further thought about it, for it was time enough to grieve when we wanted a thing which we could not purchase, but this was not our case; and even though what I asked for was then out of the way, it was not her fault, because I had not yet appointed proper places or repositories for the several things that belonged to the house; but that I would take care to do it, that she might put every thing in proper order, allotting to every particular thing its place, where it might be found when there was occasion for it. 'There is nothing, dear wife,' said Ischomachus, 'which is more commendable or profitable to mankind, than to preserve good order in every thing.

" ' In comedies and other plays, where many people are required to act their parts, if the actors should rashly do or say whatever their fancy led them to, there must of necessity be such confusion as would disgust the audience: but, when every person has his part perfect, and the scenes are regularly performed, it is that order which makes the play agreeable and pleasing to the beholders.

" ' So likewise, good wife, an army, when it is once in disorder, is under the greatest confusion and consternation, if the enemy is at hand; for the enemy has little to do to overcome them; their own hurry and confusion will contribute more to their overthrow than the attacks of the adversary. Here you may imagine waggons, footmen, horsemen, chariots, elephants, and baggage, all intermixed and crowded together: obstructing and hindering one another. If one runs, he is stopped by him that would stand the battle; and he that stands is jostled by every messenger that passes him; the chariots overrun the men of arms; and the elephants and horsemen, which in their proper places would be useful, are intermixed among the foot, trampling on them, and in a great measure doing them as much mischief as their enemies would do. And suppose, while an army is in this confusion, they are attacked by their enemy in good order, what can they expect but destruction? But an army drawn up in good order, how glorious a sight is it to their friends, and how terrible to their enemies! How delightful it is to see the infantry drawn up and exercising in good order, or marching with so much exactness and regularity, that the whole body moves like one man! How agreeable is this to their friends! And to observe an army drawn up in a line of battle, well disciplined, and advancing in good order, have not their enemies reason to fear them? Or what makes a galley, well-furnished with men, so terrible to the enemy, and so pleasant a sight to their friends, but because of its swift passage upon the waters? And what is the reason that the men within it do not hinder one another, but that they sit in order, make their signs in order, lie down in order, rise up in order, and handle their oars in order.

" ' As for confusion and disorder, I can compare it to nothing better, than if a countryman should put together in one heap, oats, wheat, barley, and pease, and when he had occasion to use any one of them, he must be obliged to pick out that sort grain by grain. Wherefore, good wife, by all means avoid confusion as much as possible, and study good order in every thing, for it will be both pleasant and profitable to you. Every thing then, as you have occasion for it, will be ready at hand to use as you please, and what I may happen to ask for will not be to seek; let us therefore fix upon some proper place where our stores may be laid up, not only in security, but where they may be so disposed, that we may presently know where to look for every particular thing. And when once we have done this in the best order we can, then acquaint the steward of it, that when any thing is wanted he may know where to find it; or when any thing is brought into the house, he may at once judge of the proper place to lay it in. By this means we shall know what we gain and what we loose; and, in surveying our storehouses, we shall be able to judge what is necessary to be brought in, and what may want repairing, or what will be impaired by keeping. When we have visited these a few times, we shall grow perfect in the knowledge of all our goods, and readily find what we seek for.'

" I remember, good Socrates," said Ischomachus, " I once went aboard a Phœnician ship, where I observed the best example of good order that I ever met with: and, especially, it was surprising to observe the vast number of implements, which were necessary for the management of such a small vessel.

"What numbers of oars, stretchers, shipbooks, and spikes, were there for bringing the ship in and out of the harbour! What numbers of shrowds, cables, halsers, ropes, and other tackling, for the guiding of the ship! With how many engines of war was it armed for its defence! What variety and what numbers of arms, for the men to use in time of battle! What a vast quantity of provisions were there for the sustenance and support of the sailors! And, besides all these, the loading of the ship was of great bulk, and so rich, that the very freight of it would gain enough to satisfy the captain and his people for their voyage: and all these were stowed so neatly together, that a far larger place would not have contained them, if they had been removed. Here, I took notice, the good order and disposition of every thing was so strictly observed, that, notwithstanding the great variety of materials the ship contained, there was not any thing on board which the sailors could not find in an instant; nor was the captain himself less acquainted with these particulars than his sailors: he was as ready in them, as a man of learning would be to know the letters that composed the name Socrates, and how they stand in that name. Nor did he only know the proper places for every thing on board his ship; but, while he stood upon the deck, he was considering with himself what things might be wanting in his voyage, what things wanted repair, and what length of time his provisions and necessaries would last: for, as he observed to me, it is no proper time, when a storm comes upon us, to have the necessary implements to seek, or to be out of repair, or to want them on board; for the gods are never favourable to those who are negligent or lazy; and it is their goodness that they do not destroy us when we are diligent. When I had observed the good order which was here practised, I informed my wife of it; at the same time admonishing her to observe the great difficulty there must needs be to keep up such a regular decorum on board a ship, where there were such numerous varieties of materials, and such little space to lay them in: 'But how much easier, good wife,' said Ischomachus, 'will it be for us, who have large and convenient storehouses for every thing

to its degree, to keep a good decorum and order, than for those people on board a ship, who yet are bound to remember where, and how, every thing is distributed in the midst of a storm at sea? But we have none of these dangers to disturb and distract our thoughts from the care of our business; therefore we should deserve the greatest shame, and be inexcusable, if we were not diligent enough to preserve as good order in our family as they do on board their vessel. But we have already said enough,' continued Ischomachus, 'concerning the necessity and advantage of good order; nor is it less agreeable to see every thing belonging to the dress, or wearing apparel, laid carefully up in the wardrobe; the things belonging to the kitchen, let them be there; and so those belonging to the dairy, likewise in the dairy; and, in a word, every thing which regards any kind of office belonging to the house, let it be neatly kept and laid up in its proper office. And this is reputable both to the master and mistress of the house; and no one will ridicule such good management, but those who are laughed at for their own ill management. This, good wife,' said Ischomachus, 'you may be sensible of at an easy rate, with little trouble. Nor will it be difficult to find out a steward, who will soon learn from you the proper places or repositories for every thing which belongs to the house; for in the city there is a thousand times more variety of things than ever we shall have occasion for; and yet if we want any thing, and send a servant to buy it for us, he will readily go to the place where it is to be had, from the good disposition of things in the several shops which are proper for them, and from the remembrance he will have of observing them in such and such places. There can be no other reason for this, than the disposing every thing in the market or city in its proper place, as all kinds of fowls at the poulterers', all sorts of fish at the fishmongers', and the like of other things which have places determined for them; but if we go about to seek a man who at the same time is seeking us, how shall we find one another, unless we have beforehand appointed a meeting place? Then, as for setting our household goods in order, I spoke to her in the following manner."—

IX. "But tell me, good Ischomachus," said Socrates, "did your wife understand and practise what you taught her?"—"She promised me," answered Ischomachus, both by words and by her countenance, that she agreed to what I said, and was delighted that method and good order would take off so great a share of her trouble; she rejoiced to think she should be delivered from the perplexed state she was in before, and desired that I would not delay putting my promise in practice as soon as possible, that she might reap the fruits of it."—"And how did you proceed, good Ischomachus?" said Socrates. "I answered her," said Ischomachus, "in such a manner, that she might learn first what a house was properly designed for; that it was not ordained to be filled with curious paintings or carvings, or such unnecessary decorations; but that the house should be built with due consideration, and for the conveniency of the inhabitants; and as a proper repository for those necessaries which properly belong to a family, and, in some measure, directs us to the proper places wherein every particular ought to be placed · the most private and strongest room in the house seems to demand the money, jewels, and those other things that are rich and valuable; the dry places expect the corn; the cooler parts are the most convenient for the wine; and the more lightsome and airy part of the house for such things as require such a situation. I showed her likewise," continued Ischomachus, "which were the most convenient places for parlours and dining-rooms, that they might be cool in summer and warm in winter; and also, that as the front of the house stood to the south, it had the advantage of the winter's sun; and in the summer it rejoiced more in the shade, than it could do in any other situation. Then," said Ischomachus, "I appointed the bed-chambers, and the nursery, and apartments for the women, divided from the men's lodging, that no inconveniency might happen by their meeting without our consent or approbation; for those who behave themselves well, and we allow to come together to have children, they will love us the better for it; but those, who through subtilty will endeavour to gain their ends with any of the women without our consent, will be always contriving and practising ways to our disadvantage, to compass or carry on their lewd designs. When we were come thus far," proceeded Ischomachus, "we began to set our goods in order. In the first place, we assorted all the materails belonging to sacrifices: after that, my wife's · assigned to their proper places;

her richest habits by themselves, and those which were in more common use by themselves. Next to these, we appointed a wardrobe for the master's clothes; one part for his armour and such accoutrements as he used in war, and another for his wearing apparel, to be used upon common occasions: after these, we directed places for the instruments which belong to spinning, and for the bakehouse, the kitchen, and the baths; and took care, in the appointment of all these things, to make a division between those things which are most commonly required to be in use, and such as are only in use now and then: we likewise separated those things which were for a month's service from those which were to serve twelve months; for by this means we might know the better how our stock is employed. When we had done this, we instructed every servant respectively where every thing belonging to his office might be found, and directed them carefully to observe, that every implement under their care should be put into the same place where they took it from, when they had done using it; and as for such things as are but seldom required to be used, either upon festivals, or upon the reception of strangers; those we delivered into the care of a discreet woman, whom we instructed in her province; and when we had made an account with her of the goods delivered into her care, and taken it in writing, we directed her to deliver them out to those under her, as she saw proper occasions, and be careful to remember who were the persons to which she delivered every particular; and that upon receiving again the things which she had delivered out, they should be every one laid up in their proper place. In the next place, we chose a discreet, sober, and judicious woman to be our storekeeper or housekeeper, one who had a good memory, and was diligent enough to avoid faults, studying our pleasure and satisfaction in all her business, and endeavouring to gain our esteem, which we always signified by presents, by which means we gained her love and friendship for us; so that, whenever we had occasion to rejoice, we made her partaker of our mirth; or if any accident happened which brought sorrow with it, we made her acquainted with that likewise, and consulted her in it: this made her bend her mind to the advancement of our fortunes. We instructed her to show more esteem for those servants in the house whom she found were deserving of favour, than the others who neglected their duty; for we took care to observe to her, that those who did well were worthy reward in the world; while those who were deceitful and evil-minded, were rejected of the people. And then, good Socrates," said Ischomachus, " I let my wife know that all this would be of little effect, unless she was careful to observe that every thing was preserved in the good order we had placed it: for in cities, and in other governments that are well ordered, it is not enough to make good laws for their conduct, unless there are proper officers appointed to see them put in execution, either to reward those who deserve well, or punish the malefactors. ' This, dear wife, I chiefly recommend to you,' continued Ischomachus, ' that you may look upon yourself as the principal overseer of the laws within our house.' And I informed her also, that it was within her jurisdiction to overlook, at her own pleasure, every thing belonging to the house, as a governor of a garrison inspects into the condition of his soldiers, or as the senate of Athens review the men of arms, and the condition of their horses; that she had as great power as a queen in her own house, to distribute rewards to the virtuous and diligent, and punish those servants who deserved it. But I further desired her, not to be displeased, if I intrusted her with more things, and more business, than I had done any of our servants; telling her at the same time, that such as were covenant-servants have no more goods under their care and trust, than are delivered to them for the use of the family; and none of those goods may be employed to their own use, without the master's or mistress's consent: for whoever is master or mistress of the house, has the rule of all that is within it, and has the power of using any thing at their pleasure; so that those who have the most profit by goods, have the most loss by them, if they perish or are destroyed. So it is therefore the interest of them that have possessions, to be diligent in the preservation of them."— " Then," said Socrates, " tell me, good Ischomachus, how did your wife receive this lesson?" —" My wife," replied Ischomachus, "received it like a woman ready to learn and practise what might be for the honour and welfare of us both, and seemed to rejoice at the instructions I gave her." ' It would have been a great grief to me,' said she, ' if, instead of those good rules you instruct me in, for the welfare

of our house, you had directed me to have no regard to the possessions I am endowed with; for as it is natural for a good woman to be careful and diligent about her own children, rather than have a disregard for them; so it is no less agreeable and pleasant to a woman, who has any share of sense, to look after the affairs of her family, rather than neglect them.'

X. " When I heard," continued Socrates, " the answer which the wife of Ischomachus gave him, I could not help admiring her wisdom."—" But I shall tell you yet much more of her good understanding," said Ischomachus " there was not one thing I recommended to her, but she was as ready to practise it, as I was willing she should go about it."—" Go on, I pray you, good Ischomachus," said Socrates, " for it is far more delightful to hear the virtues of a good woman described, than if the famous painter Zeuxis was to show me the portrait of the fairest woman in the world."— " Then," continued Ischomachus, " I remember, on a particular day, she had painted her face with a certain cosmetic, attempting to make her skin look fairer than it was; and with another mixture had endeavoured to increase the natural bloom of her cheeks; and also had put on higher shoes than ordinary, to make her look taller than she naturally was. When I perceived this," said Ischomachus, " I saluted her in the following manner: ' Tell me, good wife, which would make me the most acceptable in your eyes, to deal sincerely by you, in delivering into your possession those things which are really my own, without making more of my estate than it is; or for me to deceive you, by producing a thousand falsities which have nothing in them: giving you chains of brass instead of gold, false jewels, false money, and false purple, instead of that which is true and genuine?' To which she presently replied: ' May the gods forbid that you should be such a man! for, should you harbour such deceit in your heart, I should never love you.' —' I tell you then, dear wife,' replied Ischomachus, ' we are come together, to love one another, and to delight in each other's perfections: do you think I should be the more agreeable to you in my person, or should you love me the better, if I was to put a false lustre upon myself, that I might appear better complexioned, more fair in body, or more manly than what nature has made me; or that I should paint and anoint my face, when you receive me to your arms, and give you this deceit instead of my natural person?'—' Surely, dear Ischomachus,' replied his wife, ' your own person, in its natural perfections, is preferable to all the paints and ointments you can use to set it off; nor can all the art you might use be comparable to your natural appearance.'—' Believe then, good wife,' said Ischomachus, ' that I have the same abhorrence of false lustre that you have: can there be any thing more complete in nature than yourself? or would there be any thing less engaging to me than that you should use any means to hide or destroy those perfections in you which I so much admire? The God of nature has appointed beauties in all creatures, as well in the field as among the human race; the magnificence of the male to be admired by the female, and the tender and curious texture of the female to be admired by the male. It is natural for the creatures in the field to distinguish one another by the purity of their beauties; there is no deceit, there is no corruption: so the men always admire that body which is most pure, or the least deformed by art. Such wiles and deceits may, perhaps, deceive strangers, because they will not have opportunities of discovering and laughing at them; but if such things should be practised between those who are daily conversant with one another, how soon will the imposition be discovered! how soon will they be ridiculed! For these deceits appear at the rising out of bed, and from that time till the persons have had opportunity of renewing them; as well as when they sweat, when they shed tears, when they wash, and when they bathe themselves.'

" What answer, good Ischomachus," said Socrates, " did your wife give you to this lecture?"—" The best that could be," replied Ischomachus, " for she has never since attempted any of these false glosses, but has constantly appeared in her natural beauties, and repeated her solicitations to me to instruct her, if there was any natural means of assisting them. I then directed her that she should not sit too much, but exercise herself about the house as a mistress, to examine how her several works went forward; sometimes to go among the spinners or weavers, to see that they did their duty, and to instruct those who were ignorant, and encourage the most deserving among them; sometimes to look into the bake-house, to see the neatness and order of

the woman that looks after it; and sometimes visit her housekeeper, to account with her for the yarn, or other commodities, that are brought into her charge: and now and then to take a turn about her house, to see that every thing is disposed in its proper place. This method, I suppose," said Ischomachus, " would be a means of giving her a healthful exercise, and at the same time of leading her to that business which would be for her advantage, in benefiting our fortune. I also told her, the exercise of bolting, baking, and looking after the furniture of her house, to brush it and keep it clean, when she wanted something to do, would be commendable, and help to employ her; for I recommended exercise to her as a great benefit: ' for exercise,' said Ischomachus, ' will create you an appetite to your meat, and by that means you will be more healthful, and add, if possible, to the bloom of your beauty: and also the clean appearance of the mistress among the servants, and her readiness to set her hand to work, will encourage them to follow her example; for a good example does more than all the compulsion that can be used. Those who study nothing but their dress, may indeed be esteemed by those who understand nothing else; but the outside appearance is deceitful. And now, good Socrates, I have a wife who lives up to the rules given her."

XI. " Then," said Socrates, " good Ischomachus, you have fully satisfied me concerning the duty of a wife, as well as of your wife's good behaviour, and your own management. I beg now you will acquaint me, good Ischomachus," continued Socrates, " what method it is that you have taken on your part towards the management of your fortune, and especially what it is that has gained you the character of a good and honest man; that when I have heard what you have done, I may give my thanks according to your deserts."—" I shall be glad," replied Ischomachus, " to satisfy you in any thing within my power, provided you will correct my errors, if I am guilty of any. " —" But," answered Socrates, " how can I correct you, when you are already possessed of the character of a good and honest man? and especially when I am the man who is taken for the greatest trifler, and who employs himself in nothing but measuring the air; or, which is a far worse character, that I am a poor man, which is a token of the greatest

fully? This, indeed, might have been a trouble to me, if I had not met the other day a horse belonging to Nicias, with a crowd of people about him, admiring his good qualities, and talking abundance in praise of his strength and spirit: this made me ask the question of the master of the horse, Whether his horse was very rich? but he stared upon me, and laughed at me, as if I had been a madman; and only gave me this short answer; ' How should a horse have any money?' When I heard this, I went my way contented, that it was lawful for a poor horse to be good, on the account only of his free heart and generous spirit; and therefore, I conclude, it is likewise possible for a poor man to be good: for which reason, I beseech you, good Ischomachus, tell me your manner of living, that I may endeavour to learn it, and model my life after your example; for that may well be called a good day, when a man begins to grow good and virtuous."—" Good Socrates, you seem to banter me," said Ischomachus: "however, I will tell you, as well as I can, the whole method of my living, which I design constantly to follow till the day of my death. I perceived, that except a man knew well what was necessary to be done, and diligently applied himself to put his knowledge in practice, the gods would not suffer him to prosper. And I also observed, that those who act with wisdom and diligence, the gods reward them with riches. Therefore, first of all, I paid my adoration to the gods, and implored their assistance in all that I had to do, that they would be pleased to give me health, strength of body, honour in my city, good will of my friends, safety in the day of battle, and that I might return home with an increase of riches and honour."—" When I heard that," said Socrates, " I asked him, are riches then so much worthy your esteem, good Ischomachus; seeing that the more riches you have, the more care and trouble you have to order and preserve them?"—Then Ischomachus replied: " I have no small care to provide me with riches, for I have great pleasure in serving the gods honourably with rich sacrifices; and also to serve my friends, if they happen to want; and likewise to help the city in time of danger or distress."—" Truly, what you say, good Ischomachus," said Socrates, "is honourable, and becoming a man of power and substance."—To which Ischomachus answered: " These are my reasons, good Socrates, why I

think riches worth my labour; for there are some degrees of men who cannot subsist without the help of others; and there are also some who think themselves rich enough, if they can get what is barely necessary for their support. But those who order their houses and estates with such discretion and good judgment, that they advance their fortunes and increase their riches; and by that means become serviceable and honourable to the city, and are capable of serving their friends; why should not such men be esteemed wise and generous, and deserve power?"—" You are in the right," replied Socrates; "there are many of us that may well respect such men: but I pray you, good Ischomachus, go on to relate what method you take to support your health and strength of body, and what means you use to return home honourably from the war: and as for the ordering and increasing of the estate, we may hear that by and by."—" I think," said Ischomachus, " these things are so chained together, that they cannot well be separated; for when a man has a sufficient store of meat and drink, and uses a convenient share of exercise, his body must of necessity be healthful and strong; and such a body, when it is well exercised in the affairs of war, is most likely to return home from battle with honour. And he who is diligent and industrious in his business, must as surely improve his estate."—" Good Ischomachus," said Socrates, " all that you have yet said, I grant to be good, that he who uses diligence and exercise will increase his fortune. But tell me, I beseech you, what exercise do you take to maintain your good complexion, and to get strength, and how do you exercise yourself to be expert in war, and what methods do you follow to increase your estate, that enables you to help your friends, and assist the city in honour and strength? These things I desire to learn."—" To tell you freely, good Socrates," said Ischomachus, " I rise so early in the morning, that if I have any one to speak with in the city, I am sure to find him at home; or if I have any other business to do in the city, I do it in my morning's walk: but when I have no matter of importance in the city, my page leads my horse into the fields, and I walk thither, for I esteem the walk into the free air of the country to be more healthful than to walk in the galleries or piazzas of the city; and when I arrive at my ground where my workmen are planting trees, tilling the ground, or sowing, or carrying in of the fruits, I observe how every thing is performed, and study whether any of these works may be mended or improved: and when I have diverted myself enough at my villa, I mount my horse, and make him perform the exercise of the academy, such as is serviceable in war; and then ride him through all the difficult paths, waters, through trenches, and over hedges, to make him acquainted with those difficulties as much as possible, without hurting him: and when I have done this, my page takes my horse, and leads him trotting home, and takes along with him to my house, such things out of the country as are wanted, and walk home myself: then I wash my hands, and go to such a dinner as is prepared for me, eating moderately, and never to excess, or too sparingly."

" Good Ischomachus," said Socrates, " you do your business very pleasantly; and your contrivance is excellent, in performing so many good things at one time, as increase your health, your strength, your exercise in war, your study for the increase of your estate: all these to be done under one exercise is a great token of your wisdom; and the good effect of this exercise is apparent enough to all that know that you are healthful and strong, and every one allows you to be the best horseman in this country, and one of the richest men in the city."—" Alas! good Socrates," answered Ischomachus; " and yet, though I believe this to be true, I cannot escape detraction. You thought, perhaps, I was going to say, that it was these things which gave me the name of an honest and good man." —" It was my thought," said Socrates; " but I have a mind to ask you, how you guard against detractors, and whether you speak in your own cause, or in such causes as relate to your friends?"—" Do you believe," answered Ischomachus, " that I do not sufficiently do my part against my detractors, if I defend myself by my good deeds, in doing no wrong, and acting as much as I can for many men's good? or do you not think I am in the right if I accuse men who are mischievous, and do injustice in private cases, and to the city?"—" I pray you explain yourself," said Socrates. " I must tell you," said Ischomachus, " I am always exercising myself in rhetoric and eloquence, and in the practice of justice; for if I hear one of

my servants complain of another, or justify his own cause, I always endeavour to settle the truth between them; or if I discover any dispute among my friends or acquaintance, I endeavour to make it up, and recover their friendship for one another, by showing them the happiness and profit of friendship, and the distraction and inquietude which attend those who are at variance with one another. I praise and defend those who are accused wrongfully, or are oppressed without a cause; and before the lords of our government I accuse them who are promoted unworthily; I praise them who set about their business with care and deliberation, and blame such who go rashly about their work. But I am now brought to this dilemma, whether I am to bear with faults, or punish them."—" What is your meaning in that," said Socrates, " and who's the person you mean?"—" It is my wife,' said Ischomachus.—" In what manner then are your disputes?" said Socrates.—" We have very little occasion for that," replied Ischomachus, " as yet; nor have we more words in our disputes than, such a thing is not done so carefully as it might have been; and that we may learn by a false step how to guide ourselves for the future: but if she should be unfortunate enough to give her mind to lying and deceit, there is no reforming her." To this Socrates answered: " If she should at any time tell you a lie, you will hardly insist upon the truth of the matter.

XII. " But, perhaps, good Ischomachus, I detain you from your business, and I would by no means hinder a man of your capacity and understanding from proceeding in your affairs." —" You are no hindrance to me," answered Ischomachus, " for I am determined to stay here till the court is up."—" This gives me another token of your justice," said Socrates; " it is an instance of your circumspection, and regard to maintain the noble character the world has given you, of being a good and honest man; for, notwithstanding the many employments you usually engage yourself in, and the delightful method you take in the exercise of them, yet because of your promise to these strangers, to wait for them in this place, you choose to neglect your own business and pleasure, rather than prove worse than your word."—" As for the business you speak of," said Ischomachus, " I have taken care that nothing shall be neglected; and my greatest pleasure is in being punctual with those that I appoint; for in my farm I have my bailiff or steward of husbandry, and deputies who take care of my businesses."—" Since we are fallen into this discourse, pray tell me, good Ischomachus," said Socrates, "when you have occasion for a good bailiff or steward for your country affairs, do you use the same method as if you wanted a good builder, to inquire after one who is best skilled in the science? or do you teach and instruct those you hire into your service, in the business you want to employ them in?"— " Good Socrates," answered Ischomachus, " I endeavour to teach them myself; for he whom I instruct in the management of my affairs, when I am absent, will know the better how to carry on my works agreeable to my liking; rather than if I was to employ one who already had a pretence to knowledge of the business I wanted him for: as I guess I have experience enough to set men to work, and to direct them how they shall go about their business, I therefore suppose I am able to teach a man what I can do myself."—" Then, surely, your bailiff in husbandry," replied Socrates, "must be always ready and willing to serve you; for, without he has a love for you, he will never use the utmost of his diligence for the advancement of your affairs, though he be never so expert in his business."—" You say right," answered Ischomachus: " but the first of my endeavours is to gain his love and affection to me and my family, by which means he has a regard to my welfare."—" And what method do you take, good Ischomachus," said Socrates, " to bring the man to love and respect you and your family? Is it by the benefit you do him, by learning him a profitable business?"—" I do not suppose that," said Ischomachus; " but, whenever the gods are favourable to me in the advancement of my fortune, I always reward my steward."—" So I suppose," said Socrates, "that you mean by this, that such people as you assist with money or goods will bear you the best service and respect."—" Yes, certainly," said Ischomachus, " for there are no instruments in the world so engaging, or that will prevail so much over mankind, as money or profit."—" But is it sufficient for him to love you?" replied Socrates; " for we have instances enough that men love themselves before all others; and we have also some examples of those who are lovers of themselves, and yet

are so negligent to their own profit, that they never reap those things they wish for."—Ischomachus answered: " But, good Socrates, before I choose them among my servants that I have brought to love me, to dignify with the places of stewards or deputies, I teach them the good consequence of diligence and industry." —" Is it possible you can do that?" said Socrates; " for, in my opinion, we can hardly bring men to do another man's business as punctually as he might do it himself."—" That I allow," said Ischomachus: " I mean, that we can never instruct a man to use the same diligence for another that he would do for himself." —" But," replied Socrates, " who are those, then, whom you think worthy of employment, or of receiving your instructions?"—To this Ischomachus answered: " Those, in the first place, who cannot avoid drunkenness, are excluded from this care; for drunkenness drowns the memory, and is the occasion of forgetfulness."—" And is this the only vice," said Socrates, " which is the occasion of negligence?" —" No," replied Ischomachus, " for those who indulge themselves in sleep, are incapable of such employments."—" And are there any more," said Socrates, " whose vices make them unfit for your service?"—" Yes," answered Ischomachus; " for I am persuaded those who are addicted to the flesh, bend their minds so much to that thought, that they neglect all other business; for their whole hope and study is upon those they love: and if one was to order them to business, it would be the greatest punishment that could be inflicted on them; for there can be no greater pain laid upon any creatures in nature, than to prevent them from the object of their desires. For these reasons, when I find people engaged in such affairs, I set them aside, and never take the pains to instruct them in the matters that relate to my estate."—" But what say you," said Socrates, " of those who have a provident thought, and are saving on their own account; do you believe these would not be diligent in the management of your estate?"—" These," replied Ischomachus, " I choose to employ before all others; for they are sooner brought to be diligent than those who have contrary sentiments; and, besides, it is easy to show them the profit of diligence; and if such a man happens to come in my way, I commend him and reward him."—" But how do you treat those servants," said Socrates, " who are ready to obey you in all your commands, and are diligent at your word, and have a moderate share of good order in the management of themselves?"—" These," said Ischomachus, " I have a great regard for; for I carefully reward those who are diligent, and lay as many hardships as I can upon those who are idle and careless."—" But tell me, dear Ischomachus," said Socrates, " is it possible to reform a man who is naturally negligent ?"—" No more" answered Ischomachus, " than it would be for a man who is ignorant in music, to teach and instruct another man in that science; for it is impossible to make a good scholar, if the master does not know his business; and, by the same rule, no servant will be diligent when his master sets him the example of neglect. I have heard often enough, that bad masters made bad servants; and I have often seen a small reproof to a servant put him or her upon their duty. However, the best way to make a good servant, is for the master to set him a good example of industry, and be careful and watchful to oversee and regard, that every one about him is diligent in their respective office, and reward those who are deserving, and punish the negligent. The king of Persia once spoke much to the purpose in a case of this nature. When he was riding upon a fine horse, one of the company asked him what made his horse so fat: his reply was, ' The eye of his master;' and we have many beside, good Socrates, who think that every thing whatever is improved by the same regard of the master."

XIII. " But, good Ischomachus," said Socrates, " when you have trained up your steward to be diligent, and to observe your directions, do you esteem him thoroughly qualified to be your steward or bailiff, or has he then any thing else to be instructed in ?"—" Then," answered Ischomachus, " there is yet more which is necessary for him to understand; for he must learn the particulars of his business, to know when and how he must dispose of every thing; for, without the knowledge of these particulars, a steward is an insignificant person; he is like a physician who has the care of a patient, and is up early and late to attend him, and at last knows nothing of his distemper."— " But when he has learned all this, good Ischomacbus," said Socrates, " is he then perfectly qualified to be your steward, or director of your farm ?"—" There is still more required of him," replied Ischomachus, " for he must learn to rule, as well as direct the workmen."—" And is it possible," said Socrates, " that you can teach a man to govern, or know the great science of command ?"—" I think," said Ischomachus, " there is no difficulty in it; though, perhaps, the reasons I may give for it are ridiculous."—" An affair of this consequence," said Socrates, " is no laughing matter; for the man who can instruct others how to govern, must himself be a person of great wisdom, and deserve the highest character; for he, who can teach men how to rule, may teach them how to become masters: and he who can raise them to that dignity, may teach them those princely virtues, which will make them worthy the command of kingdoms."—" Good Socrates," answered Ischomachus, " let us look into the fields among the beasts for an example of the facility of learning to govern. Those creatures who are restiff and stubborn are beaten into obedience; while, on the other hand, those who obey our directions are treated handsomely, and rewarded. Colts, when they are under the management of the breaker or jockey are caressed when they take their lessons kindly; but when they are restiff or disobedient, they receive the correction of the lash ? and by these means they are brought to make good horses. If we breed spaniels, we treat them in the same manner, to learn them to hunt, to take the water, to fetch and carry, and be watchful; but, as for men, we may persuade them, and bring them to obedience, by setting before them rewards and punishments, and teaching them that it will be for their advantage to obey; but, as for bondmen, or those of the lowest rank, they may be brought to obedience another way; provide well for their bellies and they will do any thing; while those, who have noble spirits, are best encouraged by praise, for praise is no less welcome to them, than meat and drink is to those of the meaner sort. And when I have instructed my steward to govern by my example, I add this, as an instruction to him, that in the bestowing of clothes or apparel among my workmen, he should always give the best to those among them who are most diligent in their business; for industrious men ought always to have better dress, and have the pre-eminence in all things, before the lazy and negligent; for I am of opinion there is nothing more irksome to industrious servants, than to see those who are negligent in their business promoted or encouraged, while they themselves are neglected and overlooked It discourages them from minding their business for the future; therefore I always take care to keep that difference among my servants. And when I observe that my bailiff shows the same regard for those servants under his care, I praise him for it; but when I perceive he has preferred any one unworthily, by means of flattery or some such deceit, I never suffer his award to pass, but blame him and reprimand him."

XIV. "Then," said Socrates, "tell me, good Ischomachus, when you have thus taught your steward to rule, and discipline the workmen and servants under his care, is he then completely qualified for your service? or is there any thing else that you are to instruct him in?" To this Ischomachus replied: "There is yet a very material point, which concerns the business and character of a good steward; and that is, honesty; for if after he has received all my former instructions, he gives his mind to pilfer, and clandestinely to make away with my goods, his diligence in overseeing the management of my lands will be but of little profit to me, or it may be I may happen to be out of pocket by his service, so that I had much better be without the industry of such a man."—" But, good Ischomachus, I pray you tell me," said Socrates, " Are you capable of teaching men justice and honesty?"—" Yes," replied Ischomachus; " but I find that it is not every one I teach or instruct in these ways of truth and equity, who follow my instructions: but, that I may yet make my servants follow the rules of justice which I teach them, I use those laws of Draco and Solon, which say, that little pilferers must be punished, but the great robbers must be imprisoned and put to death. Whereby it appears, that those, who enrich themselves by indirect methods, and amass to themselves fortunes by thievish practices, those goods shall not be profitable to them. And to these laws I likewise add some of the Persian laws: for those of Draco and Solon only inflict punishments on those who do amiss; but those of the king of Persia do not only punish those who do wrong, but reward those who do right. There are some men, who out of covetousness care not what they do, nor what indiscreet means they take, so that they gather riches together; seeing that others can amass great fortunes in an honest way; believing that, so long as riches may be got by honest men, every one who is rich shall be accounted an honest man: but these have never any pleasure or good advantage in their ill-got goods; or it is very rarely that they preserve them: but those who get their riches by industry and honesty, are always prosperous, and have pleasure in what they have got, especially because they have wronged no man. If among my people I discover any such who have that covetous and deceitful temper, and do not receive benefit by my instructions, I discharge them out of my service. And, on the other hand, those who make honesty their rule and study, behave themselves as true and faithful servants, without having so much regard to profit, as honour and praise from me; if they are bondmen, I give them their liberty; and do not only promote them and advance their fortunes, but take every opportunity of recommending them to the world as good and honest men; for I judge, that the man may be esteemed good and honest, who upon the principle of virtue will employ himself for his master's interest, and will not scruple going through a little difficulty for his master's service, when there is occasion, without a design of making his advantage of him by deceitful or indiscreet means.

XV. Such a man, when I have once gained his esteem and affection, by instructing him in the science of making a good advantage of the work he is employed in, and have sufficiently instructed him to rule; I am persuaded he will transact every thing for his master's advantage, as well as if the master was continually to be present: and, with these qualifications, I think a man sufficiently capable of the business of a steward, and worthy of being employed in that office."—" But, methinks," said Socrates, "the principal part of a steward's business you have not yet explained."—" What is that, good Socrates?" said Ischomachus.— " I remember," said Socrates, "in your discourse, you said, that before all things a steward ought to know every particular of his business, and how to order every thing for his master's profit; for, without that, you observed that diligence would be of little use."—" Then, I suppose, good Socrates," answered Ischomachus, "you would have me instruct you in the science of husbandry?"—" That is my desire," said Socrates; "for the science of husbandry is extremely profitable to those who understand it; but it brings the greatest trouble and misery upon those farmers who undertake it without knowledge."—" I shall first of all, good Socrates," said Ischomachus, "acquaint you, that husbandry is an honourable science, and the most pleasant and profitable of any other: it is favoured by the gods, and beloved by mankind, and may be learned with ease. Husbandry, therefore, is becoming a gentleman; for if we were to take a view of all creatures upon earth, those only are esteemed, and worthy our regard, which are docile enough to become profitable to us; while the others, which are wild and fierce in their nature, and are not capable of becoming useful to us, are rejected."—" If I remember right," said Socrates, "you have already instructed me, that a steward or deputy should first love you, then be diligent; in the next place, he should be able to rule, and then be honest; but I am impatient to hear how he must behave himself in the practice of husbandry, with regard to the works, when and how they are to be done; but hitherto you have not explained those particulars, but passed them over as if you imagined I knew as much of the affair as yourself, or understood the business. For my part, I am in the same state, with regard to husbandry, that a man would be who does not understand letters, and you were to show him a writing; he will be never the better for seeing that writing, unless he know the use of the letters that composed it. So I imagine, that it is not enough to be diligent in the science of husbandry, but a man must understand every particular of it. This I suppose you are a master of, but you have not yet acquainted me with the matter. Therefore, if I was now to set about the business of husbandry, I should be like a quack in physic, who went about visiting of sick people, and neither knew their distempers, nor what medicines were proper for them. Therefore, good Ischomachus, I desire you will learn me every particular point of the husbandry you practise."—" Good Socrates," replied Ischomachus, "the science of husbandry is not like other sciences, which require length of time to study them, or a great deal of labour to compass them before a man can get his living by them; for husbandry is easily learned, by observing the workmen now and then, and by consulting those who understand it. By these means you may instruct your friends in it. Again, we may observe, that men of other sciences, which are artificers, will always keep some secret of their business to themselves; but the husbandmen are open and free in their discoveries, that every one may learn from them. The husbandman, who has the greatest knowledge in planting of trees, is proud of being observed, or that any man takes notice of his excellence in that art. And the sower is no less pleased to have any one stop to look upon him. And if you ask him about any thing which has been well done in his way, he will be free enough to inform you how it was done. And so, good Socrates, we may see by this, that husbandry teaches men good manners and good nature."—" This," said Socrates, "is a good beginning: and now you have come thus far, I cannot leave you till you have given me every particular relating to husbandry; and especially I insist upon it, because you say it is a science so easy to learn. You will therefore have the less trouble to instruct me; and it will be the greater shame to me, if I do not learn it by your instructions, particularly since it is so profitable a science."

XVI "I am very willing to answer your desire," said Ischomachus, "and instruct you in every point of husbandry. The principal part, which men dispute about, is the soil. On this account, all the philosophers, who have busied themselves about it, have given us more words than truth; for they throw some occult quality in the way, which leaves us as we were before: and at the best tell us, that he, who designs to be a husbandman, must first know the nature of the soil."—" It is not contrary to my opinion," said Socrates, "that one ought to know the quality of the soil; for those who do not know what the ground will bring forth, how can they appoint either trees, plants, or seeds for it, which are natural to its intent, or are proper for it?'—" Dear Socrates," said Ischomachus, "this is easily discovered, by observing the grounds of other people, where you may see the diversities of plants growing on them, and, by a little observance that way, you will learn what they will produce, and what are contrary to their nature; and when a man has once made his due observation of this, he will see that it will be unprofitable to resist nature or the will of Providence. For when a man plants or sows those things which he accounts necessary for his use, and the soil does not delight in the nourishment or production of them, or has not a will to bring them forth, his expense and rouble is to no purpose. But if he cannot discover the nature of the grounds next about him, which either through idleness, or any other cause, have been mismanaged or neglected, let him consult other lands remoter from him; and if even they happen not to be cultivated, he may learn by the weeds that grow upon them, what they will produce: for those plants, which grow wild, show best the inclination and disposition of the soil; so that husbandmen may even learn their business by observing what the ground will produce of itself."—"Then," replied Socrates, "I perceive that a man need not abstain from husbandry surely because he does not know how to describe the nature of a soil; for, I remember, I have seen fishermen who have employed themselves continually upon the sea, without inquiring what the water is, or its principles, but pass over it, and when they find any thing to their advantage they take it, and leave the rest. The same, I suppose, is the design of the husbandmen; when they look upon soils, it is to observe what they bring forth, that is valuable, and what they will not."—"In what point of husbandry would you have me begin,' said Ischomachus, "dear Socrates, for you talk like an adept in that science? Your reasoning is good, and must proceed from understanding."—"All that I mean by my reasoning with you," replied Socrates, "is to know how I shall till the ground, so as to reap the most profitable crops of corn, or other fruits, from it; for it is becoming a philosopher to inquire into those things which are pleasant and profitable."—"I suppose," said Ischomachus, "you already understand that the stirring or breaking of the ground, which one may call fallowing, is of great advantage."—"This," answered Socrates, 'I believe."—"And suppose we were to fallow or plough the ground in winter?" said Ischomachus.—"That I don't approve of," said Socrates; "for the earth is then too wet, in my opinion."—"And what do you think if we were to turn it up in the summer?" said Ischomachus.—"Then, I doubt," said Socrates, "it would be too dry and hard for the plough."—"Then let us plough," said Ischomachus, "in the spring."—"I think you are much in the right," said Socrates, "for then the ground is most free and ready to open itself to the plough, and also is most ready to distribute its virtue." "It is not only so," answered Ischomachus, "but then whatever weeds are upon the ground, being turned into the earth, enrich the soil as much as dung. And again, these plants are not grown to such a point of maturity or perfection that their seeds are ripe, and therefore cannot fill the ground with weeds; and besides, I suppose you know that both the fallowing and tilling of ground is always the better as the ground has the fewer weeds in it; for, besides the hindrance the weeds may give to corn, or other profitable herbs, they prevent the ground from receiving the benefit of the sun and free air."—"This I agree to," said Socrates.—"Then," replied Ischomachus, "do not you think that often stirring the ground in summer will be the best way for it to enrich itself by the air and sun, as well as to destroy the weeds?"—"I am very sensible," said Socrates, "that weeds will wither and dry quickly in the summer; and the ground can never receive more benefit from the sun, than if it is stirred with the plough, or fallowed in the heat of summer: and if a man dig his ground in summer, he will have the same advantage in destroying of weeds, which will then soon die; or else, by turning them in before they seed, they will enrich the ground: and by the turning up of the earth at that season, the sourness and rawness of that, which is turned up, will be corrected by the sun."

XVII. "So I find," said Ischomachus, "that we are both of one opinion concerning the stirring and fallowing of the ground."—"It is true," said Socrates; "but, to proceed to sowing, do you allow that the old opinion, which is agreed to and followed by the present operators in husbandry, concerning the season of putting the seed into the ground, is agreeable to reason, or are you of another opinion."—To this Ischomachus replied; "When summer is once past, and September is upon us, all men then wait the pleasure of the gods to send rain to moisten the ground and prepare it for the seed; and, as soon as the rains fall, then every one employs himself in sowing, as the gods seem to direct."—"Then," said Socrates, "it seems that all men in the world have determined, by one assent, that it is not convenient to sow when the ground is dry; and those who act against this rule of nature are sufferers by it, as if they had offended the gods, by practising against their laws."

"We agree likewise in this," said Ischomachus."—"Then," Socrates replied, "I perceive that mankind consent to the order of nature, which is the will of the gods; as, for example, every one thinks it convenient to wear furred gowns and warm clothes in the winter, and then also to make a good fire, if he can get wood."—"But there are many," said Ischomachus, "who vary in their opinions concerning the time of sowing; some will sow sooner, others later."—"There is good reason for that," replied Socrates, "for the gods do not always give us the same kind of weather one year as another. Therefore it is sometimes best to sow early, and at other times it is better to sow late."—"I allow what you say," said Ischomachus: "but whether is it best to sow much seed, or little?"—"I am of opinion," answered Socrates, "that it is best to allow seed enough, and distribute it truly and equally upon the ground: but one may sow the seed too thick, as well as employ too small a quantity of it."—"I agree with you," said Ischomachus, "in this point."—"I imagine," said Socrates, "there is a great art in sowing."—"It is surely so," replied Ischomachus; "for there are many sorts of grain, and all of them must be cast upon the ground by a man's hand."—"I have seen that," said Socrates.—"But some men," replied Ischomachus, "can cast it even, and distribute it equally upon the ground, and others cannot."—"Then, I suppose," said Socrates, "that the skill in sowing the seeds depends upon the frequent practice and exercise of the hand; as those who play upon the harp, or other instruments of music, must keep their hands continually in practice, that their fingers may readily follow their mind."—"You reason well," said Ischomachus: "but suppose the ground is light and open, or suppose it is stiff and heavy?"— "What would you have me understand by that?" said Socrates: "do you not take the lighter ground to be the weakest, and the heavy ground to be the strongest?"—"I am of that opinion," said Ischomachus.—"I would then fain know of you," said Socrates, "whether you would allow the same quantity of seed to one kind of ground as you would to another, or whether you make any difference?" —"You know, good Socrates," said Ischomachus, "that it is as natural to put the most water to the strongest wines, and the stronger a man is, the greater burden he may carry; so some men are nourished with a very spare diet, while others require a greater share of nourishment: the same ought to be considered in our present case."—"Will not the ground," said Socrates, "grow more strong by the more use, as horses and mules are thought to do?" —"This I take as a jest," said Ischomachus: "but what I think necessary to acquaint you of, is, that you sow your grain when the ground is moist, and has the best advantage of the air; and when the corn is come up, and is high in the blade, if you then turn it into the ground with a plough, it will greatly enrich the land, and give it as much strength as a good dunging would do: and we must also remark, that if we continue to sow for a long space the same sort of grain upon any ground, but upon that especially which is weak or overcharged with seed, it will impoverish the ground, and wear it out of heart. We may compare this to a sow which suckles many pigs, and sustains them till they grow large; the more pigs she suckles, the more will she be weakened."—"You intimate by this," said Socrates, "that one ought to sow the smaller quantity of grain upon the weakest soil."—"It is true," replied Ischomachus, "and is what we have partly agreed on before, that to overburden ground with seeds or corn, is the ready way to weaken it."—"But for what reason, good Ischomachus, do you make ditches or thorows in the corn fields?"—"You know very well," replied Ischomachus, "the winter is subject to wet weather."—"What mean you by that?" said Socrates.—"When the rains fall in great quantity," replied Ischomachus, "the wet is apt to do great damage to corn; for sometimes our corn fields are incommoded with waters, and the corn, in some of its parts, smothered with mud; and besides, the roots of the corn in other places will be washed bare; the waters also carry the seeds of weeds to the lower parts of the ground, and by that means fill the corn with weeds."—"I presume," said Socrates, "what you say is agreeable to reason."—"And do you think," said Ischomachus, "that corn which is subject to these inconveniences ought not to be assisted?"— "Undoubtedly," answered Socrates.—"Then what shall we do," said Ischomachus, "to prevent the waters from covering the corn with mud?"—"I find then," said Socrates, "it is proper to ease the ground from wet to secure the corn."—"But," said Ischomachus, "if the roots of the corn should be laid bare, and the earth about them worn away?"—"Then I suppose," continued he, "the best way to remedy that, is to find some means of covering the roots with earth, that they may be well nourished."—"But if the weeds, which may come up by this management," replied Socrates, "should suck up, or destroy the nourishment which the corn ought to receive, like the drone-bees in a hive, who are of no value in themselves, and yet live upon the industry of the working bees, and destroy the provisions which they have laid up to be manufactured into wax and honey."—"The weeds," replied Socrates, "should then be plucked up, as the drones in a hive are killed and discharged from it."—"Do you think then," said Ischomachus, "that water-thorows, or trenches in the ground to draw off the water, are not good to save corn?"—"I see now the use of similes," said Socrates; "for there is nothing can instruct me so much as similes; for by them you have learned me to know the disadvantage of weeds among corn, as well as instructed me that drones are not always advantageous to bees.

XVIII. "But now I desire of you, dear Ischomachus, to tell me what is the business of harvest?"—"This," replied Ischomachus, "I shall be ready to do, if you are not already as wise as myself. I suppose," continued he, "you have heard that corn must be reaped?"—"Certainly," said Socrates; "but I am impatient till you proceed to inform me what are your sentiments in the affair of reaping, or getting in the harvest."—"Which do you think, good Socrates, we ought to do;—to stand to reap with the wind, or to reap against it?"—"I suppose," said Socrates, "it would be improper to reap against the wind, for it would increase the labour; it would hurt the eyes, and be likewise more difficult to the hands; for we sometimes meet with corn that is laid or beat down by the wind."—"And then," replied Ischomachus, "how will you cut it? will you cut the tops only? or cut it close to the ground?"—"If the straw is short," replied Socrates, "I would cut it near the ground, for the advantage of the straw; but if the straw is very long, then I would rather cut it about the middle, for two reasons. In the first place, because the corn will be separated more easily from the straw: and in the next place, the remaining straw, if it is burned, will enrich the ground very much; or if it is afterwards cut and mixed with dung, it will increase it."—"Good Socrates, your discourse,"

said Ischomachus, "shows me plainly, that you understand reaping as well as I do."—"As you agree with me," said Socrates, "in what I say concerning reaping, I suppose I am right in my argument; but let me now see if I understand how to separate the corn from the straw."—"You know, undoubtedly," said Ischomachus, "that horses do that work."—"I am sensible," said Socrates, "that it is not only horses that separate corn from the straw, by treading upon it, but asses and oxen also are used on the same occasion."—"But how do you think, good Socrates," said Ischomachus, "that horses, or the other creatures you speak of, can so equally tread the corn as to get it all clear of the straw?"[1]—"The men who have the care of this work," said Socrates, "take care to stir the corn as they see occasion, that it may be all equally separated from the straw, flinging into the way of the cattle's feet such corn as they observe to lie still in the straw."—"I perceive," said Ischomachus, "that you understand this part of husbandry as well as myself."—"In the next place," said Socrates, "let us examine how we ought to clean corn from the husk or chaff."—"I suppose," said Ischomachus, "you know that if you begin to winnow your corn on that side of the winnowing place which is next the wind, the chaff will be scattered all over the winnowing floor?"—"It must certainly be so," said Socrates.—"And it must also fall upon the corn," said Ischomachus.—"This," said Socrates, "is certain; but it is the skill of a good husbandman to winnow his corn in such a manner that the chaff may fly from it, and be carried to its proper place."—"But when you have cleaned the corn," said Ischomachus, "as far as the middle of the winnowing place, will you rather let it remain there, or carry the clean corn to another place where you design to lodge it?"—"When I have a sufficient quantity of corn clean," said Socrates, "I would set that by; lest, in cleaning the rest, the corn I have already cleaned, and lies scattered abroad upon the floor, should partake of the chaff from the corn that is cleaning, and then I shall be obliged to do my work twice over."—"I find, good Socrates," said Ischomachus, "that you are sufficiently skilled in the manage-

---

[2] It was the method among the ancients, to have the corn trodden out by cattle, for the flail is a modern invention.

ment of corn, even to the cleaning of it, for the markets; and I am of opinion, that you are well able to instruct, rather than to be instructed. In my discourse with you on this branch of husbandry, I find that I have yet some remembrance of the management of corn. If there is no more in it than what we have mentioned, I knew as much of it many years ago. And now I recollect that once I could play upon the harp, and the flute, could paint, and carve, and knew many other sciences, and yet I never had a master to teach me any of these sciences, no more than I had one to instruct me in this branch of husbandry: but I have seen men work as well in the sciences I speak of as in husbandry. You are satisfied," said Ischomachus, "that husbandry is a pleasant science, and that it is easy to learn."

XIX. "I am persuaded," said Socrates, "that I now understand, and have long since known, the business of sowing and reaping of corn. But I was not certain in my judgment, till I had the opportunity of conversing with you about it: but I desire you to tell me, whether setting of trees is any part of husbandry?" —" Yes," replied Ischomachus.—" Then," said Socrates, "though I know something relating to sowing and cleaning of corn, yet I doubt I am ignorant in the business of planting of trees." —" I guess," said Ischomachus, "you have as much knowledge in the one as in the other." —" I must certainly be ignorant," said Socrates, "in the art of planting trees, because I do not know what sort of earth a tree should be planted in, nor what depth, nor of what size the tree should be : nor yet, when it is planted, what is the best means to make it grow."—" I am ready to instruct you," said Ischomachus, "in any thing you are ignorant of. Have you observed, good Socrates, what holes or pits are commonly made to plant trees in?"—" I have observed that very often," said Socrates. "Have you ever observed these deeper," said Ischomachus, "than three feet?"—" No," replied Socrates, "nor yet more than two feet and a half."—" And the breadth of the trench which is made for planting a tree, did you ever observe that?" said Ischomachus; "for by such inquiries you may guess at the size of the trees which are fit to be transplanted."—" I never," said Socrates, "saw any wider than two feet and a half."—" And have you ever seen any shallower than two feet?" said Ischomachus.

"I have not observed," said Socrates, "any of those trenches which are dug for planting trees less than two feet and a half deep; for if the trees were to be set shallow, the summer heats would soon make them wither, and scorch the roots."—" Then I suppose," said Ischomachus, "that your opinion is, that the trenches or holes, which are to be dug for planting of trees, ought to be no deeper than two feet and a half, and just as much over?"—" I guess," said Socrates, "they should be so."—" But do you consider the nature of the ground," said Ischomachus, "and make the proper differences—which is dry, and which is wet?"—" The ground," said Socrates, "which lies about Licabectus, I call dry ground; and the ground about Phalericus I call wet ground, for that is a marsh."—" I then desire to know," said Ischomachus, "whether you would plant trees deeper, or shallower, in wet than in dry soil?" —" My opinion is," said Socrates "that in the dry ground we ought to dig the trenches the deeper, for in wet ground we shall soon come to the water, and I do not think it convenient to plant trees deep in such wet places."—" You argue very rightly," said Ischomachus; "but do you know, good Socrates," continued he, "when you have the choice of these grounds, which are those trees which are most proper to plant in them?"—" I think I do," said Socrates. —" And do you think," replied Ischomachus, "that when you set a tree to the best advantage, it will be best to plant it in such earth as has been made very fine by working, or in such as has not been made loose and open by culture?" —" It is my opinion," said Socrates, "that a tree planted in well-loosened earth will prosper much better than in that which has been uncultivated."—" Do you allow, then," said Ischomachus, "that the earth ought to be fine and prepared on this occasion?"—" I guess it should be so," said Socrates.—" But concerning the branch or cutting of a vine, when you plant it," continued Ischomachus, "will it grow better if you set it upright in the ground, or lay it along in the earth?" [1]—" Certainly," said Socrates, "it will grow the stronger if we plant it, or lay it lengthwise in the ground; for the more roots it gains, the greater strength it

---

1 The laying the cuttings of vines lengthwise in the ground, is the French way now practised; for they strike root at every joint; and the more joints they have the more roots they get, and the stronger shoots they make.

will have in its shoots."—"We are both of one opinion," said Ischomachus. "But when you plant one of these cuttings or branches of vines, would you leave it with the earth loose about it, or tread it hard over the part of the cutting which you bury?"—"I am of the opinion," said Socrates, "that it is best to tread down the earth very close about it, for else the ground would lie so hollow all round, that the air and moisture would come unequally to it, and rot and spoil the roots; or else the sun's heat would too soon reach it, and prove of as bad consequence."—"So far we are of one opinion," said Ischomachus.—"And must I plant or raise a fig-tree," answered Socrates, "as I do the vines?"—"I suppose so," said Ischomachus; "for he who is master of the art of raising vines, may as well raise figs, or most sorts of trees."—"But is there not," replied Socrates, "something particular in the propagating of olive-trees?" "You may observe that," said Ischomachus, "on every highway side, when we set a large truncheon of an olive-tree, we dig deep holes, and plant them very deep in the ground, covering the top of the truncheon with clay, and yet we do not find that any other trees or plants are covered in this manner."—"I know this," replied Socrates, "for I have often seen it."—"Surely then," answered Ischomachus, "when you have seen an experiment, you must remember it; and especially in this common case you know that it is not sufficient to put clay over the large top of the olive truncheon, but also to cover the clay close with a shell.[1]"

"All that you have said relating to this, I likewise know perfectly," said Socrates: "but when we began to discourse whether I understood the planting of trees, I was not satisfied whether I was sure of the right method: and when you came to the particulars, I gave you my opinion freely; and it happened to agree with you, who of all men upon the face of the earth are esteemed the most perfect husbandman. I am happy, good Ischomachus," continued Socrates, "in what you have taught me, which by degrees I brought you to do: you have taught me every particular of good husbandry; and have led me, by your instructions in those things I did not understand, to those that I find I have some knowledge in; and, by your easy way of reasoning, I shall be capable of remembering every thing you have laid before me."—"Do you believe," said Ischomachus, "that if I were to discourse with you concerning the goodness and fineness of silver and gold, that you could answer as pertinently as you have done to the affair of husbandry? or if I were to ask you concerning music and painting, do you think that you could reason about them so well as you have done in husbandry?"—"I think so," said Socrates; "for you have satisfied me that I am not ignorant in husbandry, and yet I never had any master to instruct me in it."—"You may remember," said Ischomachus, "that in this discourse I told you that husbandry was easily learned by a little observation and conversation; for the practice of it teaches us many particulars, which no master can ever teach us, or would ever have thought on. In the first place, the vine will, of its own accord, run up trees, if there are any near it. This natural disposition in the vine shows us, that we ought to sustain the vine with props. Again: we observe that it spreads its leaves abroad the most at that time of the year when its fruit is in its growth; which shows us, that the fruit, during its growth, should be shaded from the too scorching rays of the sun. And again, we may observe, that about the time when grapes ripen, the leaves shrink, and lay the fruit more open to the sun, that they may ripen the better: so it appears that shade is necessary to help the growth of fruit, and a full sun is natural to the good ripening of fruit. And also when we see the vine full of clusters, we find some ripe, and others green; then let the ripe clusters be gathered, for otherwise they would spoil and rot, as it is in the fruit of the fig-tree; gather those which you perceive are completely ripe, lest they drop and are lost."

XX. "It is surprising to me," said Socrates, "that seeing husbandry is so easy to learn, we find such a vast difference among the husbandmen: some we may observe to be very rich, while others have hardly bread to eat."—To this Ischomachus replied: "It is not the want of knowledge which makes the poor husbandman, for both the rich and the poor may have the same knowledge in sowing or planting, or in the virtue of the soil, and what is best

---

1 In the modern practice we find it necessary to keep out the air and rain from those large incisions, or places which have suffered amputation, by soft wax, or such vegetable mummies as I have taught Mr Whitmill to make and sell. The shell over the clay is, I suppose, put there to keep out the wet and ill weather.

to plant upon it, and in the ordering of vines, or that ground is improved by fallowing and by manuring: but that which makes some farmers poor and some rich, is because the first are negligent and lazy, and the latter are industrious and thrifty. The poor farmers often lose the profit of a year by neglecting to make proper provision either by fallowing, manuring, or sowing; nor has he any wine through his neglect in planting of vines, or taking care to prune and dress those vines he has already: such a man has neither oil, nor figs, for he neglects the care of his tree. It is for these causes, good Socrates, that you find one farmer richer than another; for the knowledge of farming, or any thing else, is of no service or advantage, if it is not industriously practised. And so among generals of armies, it is likely that they all understand their business, but yet we perceive that some of them gain more honour and more riches than others. Their case is like that of the husbandmen; the industrious are always gainers, while the negligent always come off losers. If a general leads an army through an enemy's country, and be discreet and careful, he will march his forces in good order, and be vigilant; so that upon any occasion he is prepared for battle; and yet there are some generals who know these things, and do not act with that care, which ever brings them either honour or profit. All these are convinced that there is a necessity of keeping watches, and sending out scouts to reconnoitre the enemy, or observe their motion; but yet some neglect this business, and lose themselves by it. So likewise we all know that manuring the ground is necessary; but yet some are negligent, and never employ themselves about it, though it may as well be done by turning of cattle into it, as by other means. Some farmers use all their industry to gather together all the sorts of manures they can find; and others, though they might as well enrich their ground by the same means, yet never set their minds about it. The rain falls in hollow places, and remains there to the injury of the ground; and where this happens, it shows the carelessness of the farmer; the weeds which rise on this occasion are witnesses of his negligence; for the diligent farmer always takes care to lay his ground in good order, and to clear it of weeds; and the very weeds he pulls up reward him for that work; for if he cast these weeds into a pit of water, and let

them rot there, they will produce as good manure as dung itself. For there are no herbs or plants which will rot by lying in water, that will not make good manure for land; nor is there any sort of earth which will not make very rich manure, by being laid a due time in a standing water, till it is fully impregnated with the virtue of the water.[1] We may yet remark further, that if the ground be too wet to sow upon, or too surly or sour to plant in, there is still a remedy for it: if it be wet, we may drain it by ditches or thorows; and if the ground be stiff and sour, mix it with such things as are light and dry, or of a contrary nature to the soil. We find some husbandmen have regard to this, and some have no thought of it, and throw away those things which might prove to their profit. But suppose we were to know nothing of ground, or what it would bring forth, or can see neither tree nor plant upon it; nor have the opportunity of consulting, or learning, from some experienced husbandman, the worth of the ground; may we not satisfy ourselves at a very easy rate, by trying what it will bear or bring forth, in making a few experiments upon it? Is not this more easy than to experience what a horse or a man is? for in all that we can discover by our experiments upon soils, we are sure of the truth of what we see; there is no dissimulation: therefore the ground is the best master or director for the husbandman, in showing him what things are proper for it, and what are the contrary; and it gives us satisfactory proofs who among the farmers are diligent and discerning, and who are not. For the science of husbandry is not like other sciences, or trades or callings; for in them the artificers may excuse themselves by saying they wanted skill in what they wanted to undertake; but husbandry, we know, is within the compass of every man's knowledge; so that whenever we see that the ground is tilled and sown, it will always produce something beneficial, and is the most pleasant of all others; and therefore I suppose it is that husbandry, above all other sciences, encourages men to practise it: and besides,

1 This is a remark very well worthy our observation, especially where manures are scarce. As for the common notion, that weeds will breed weeds, it is an error, unless we suppose that weeds have their seeds ripe when we use them on this occasion; and as for earth being laid in water for a manure, it is much more beneficial to lands than the cleaning of ponds and ditches.

this is preferable to all others, because every man, who has the least regard to himself, must surely know that no man can live without necessaries : and what does not this produce? We may therefore know, that those who will not learn such sciences as they might get their living by, or do not fall into husbandry, are either downright fools, or else propose to get their living by robbery or by begging. But we will suppose that some of the husbandmen we speak of, are such as employ deputies or bailiffs to look over their workmen ; and the overseers of some do right, and the greater part do wrong. Those who do right will take care to see their work done in season ; but the negligent steward will not keep his workmen to their business ; he will let them leave their business when they think convenient, without regard to his master's profit. And to compare the diligent and careless steward, there will be the difference, that he who sets his people to work regularly, and keeps them employed, gains half as much more as the man who is careless of his labourers : it is like two men who are sent out to travel fifty miles, who are both equally strong and in health ; the man who is the most industrious shall perform his day's journey to the utmost of his power, and lose no time ; while the other stops at every spring, at every shade, and at every refreshment he can get, and loses so much in his progress, that though they both run and walk alike, the lazy and negligent man makes two days of the same length that the industrious man makes in one day : so, in all sorts of works, there is a great deal of difference between the man who sets himself heartily about his business, and him who is careless and does not regard his work ; for when these last happen to weed or clean the vines at such an improper season that the weeds spring again, they rather spoil than mend their vineyards : their absolute neglect would have been more excusable. Such errors as these are the occasion why many farmers are sufferers. A man who has a large family, and is at great expenses for the maintenance of his house, if he cannot get enough by his rents and by his husbandry to find him and his people with necessaries, must certainly come to poverty. But such as are diligent, and apply themselves to husbandry, will as certainly increase their substance, and may easily grow rich. I remember my father had an excellent rule, which

he advised me to follow ; that if ever I bought any land, I should by no means purchase that which had been already well improved, but should choose such as had never been tilled ; either through the neglect of the owner, or for want of capacity to do it : for he observed, that if I was to purchase improved grounds, I must pay a high price for them, and then I could not propose to advance their value, and must also lose the pleasure of improving them myself, or seeing them thrive better by my endeavours. It was my father's opinion, that both land and cattle, with good management and industry, would doubly improve, and reward the master, and be no less pleasant than profitable to him. There is nothing which brings us a better return for our care and labour, than such ground as has lain a long time without culture ; nor is there any thing so agreeable and pleasant, as to observe the good use such lands make of the industry and labour we bestow on them. Nothing rewards our labours so much as these ; and I assure you," continued Ischomachus, "that I have often brought such land, as had never produced any thing of value, to bring such crops as were twice as much worth as the price I gave for the ground. This, I suppose, you will remember, and teach to those who fall into the way of your instructions. I may observe to you also, good Socrates, that my father neither learned this, nor any other branch of husbandry, from any one ; his genius led him to study the reason of it, and even to assist in the working part ; for he delighted extremely to see the reward of his own labour and industry, and well knew that he could never expect so great a return from cultivated and improved grounds, as from uncultivated lands, which he took in hand. I believe, good Socrates, that you have heard of my father's excellence in husbandry above all the Athenians, and of his natural bent of fancy towards it."—Then Socrates replied : " Tell me, good Ischomachus, did your father, when he had improved such parcels of land, keep them to himself, or sell them to good advantage ?"—" Now and then," replied Ischomachus, " he sold a parcel of land when he could receive a sufficient advantage for his improvements ; and immediately bought fresh unimproved land in the room of it, that he might enjoy the pleasure of bringing it to his own mind."—" By what I can understand," said Socrates, " your father was wise and diligent in the science of husbandry, and had no less desire towards it, than the corn merchants have to find out where the best wheat is to be had; not even scrupling to pass the roughest seas, or run any other hazard to gain their intent; and when they have bought up as much corn as they can purchase, they then immediately despatch it to their own houses; and reserve it in their warehouses till they see a good opportunity of selling it. I suppose then they do not sell it without consideration, or carelessly dispose of it at low markets; but are first assured where they may sell it at the dearest price."—" You seem to banter," replied Ischomachus; " but can we say the mason is in the wrong who builds houses and sells them, and perhaps has afterwards an advantage in repairing or improving them?"

XXI. " I am very well persuaded," said Socrates, " from what you say, that your opinion is, every man ought to study that thing chiefly which may redound the most to his advantage, with the greatest facility. For, in the discourse we have had, you have insisted that husbandry is the science most easily learnt of any other, and particularly have given proofs of its being the most profitable study a man can pursue: and what you have observed in your discourse relating to it, has convinced me that husbandry is as pleasant and profitable as you represent it."—" It is certain, as I have told you," replied Ischomachus, " that husbandry is a most delightful and beneficial study; and it is as sure that it may be greatly advanced by the application, industry, and good management of the professors of it: we may compare it to a galley upon the sea, which is obliged to make its way as far in a day with oars, as it should with sails. We find that those masters or overseers of the rowers, who keep them encouraged with good words and proper rewards, gain so much upon the good-will of the labourers under their command, that they even outdo themselves, and perform almost as much work as double the number would do of such who are under the discipline of careless or surly masters: for, where such evil masters happen to rule over any sets of people, they never have their work done with a good-will, nor to the purpose: but a generous spirit in a master creates a free, hearty spirit in his servants, which makes them

work merrily and heartily, sweating and pressing upon one another who shall excel in his business: so there are likewise some captains, who are of that ill disposition towards their soldiers, and use them with that vile barbarity, that they can never gain their will to perform any thing for their service either in peace or war; and in time of war especially, rather than assist, will expose their captains to the utmost danger. Nor can such leaders ever bring the men under their commission to be ashamed of any thing they do, even though they commit the worst actions; for the unmerciful or careless officer hardens the soldiers, that they have neither a regard for right or wrong: but there are other captains, who have discretion and prudence enough to manage their soldiers with so much good order, and gain so much upon their affections, that if these were to have the command of the same which we have been speaking of, would bring them to duty, and to act as one man in their officers' defence and service, in time of necessity; and instruct them to be ashamed of every thing that is base or dishonourable; exciting them to diligence, and to work with good will in such things as are becoming them to do, praising their labours, and rewarding them on all occasions. Such rule and management gains the captain victory and honour; for it is not only the business of the soldier to learn to draw the bow, or throw the javelin, but to know how and when to obey the word of command: and nothing will bring them sooner to this, than to gain their love and affection; for the general or captain who has good sense enough to gain the good esteem of the men under his command, may lead them through the greatest dangers. It is, therefore, such generals as have good generosity and discretion, who, in the management of their soldiers, commonly gain the characters of valiant and expert officers: for, though the number of the soldiers contribute to gain the battle, yet without the commanding officer gives them good instructions, and gains their love and affection to him, they never act to the purpose; nor can their captain gain any reputation by them; so that the great name is rather gained by wisdom and prudence, than by labour and strength of body: and it is no less to be observed in the science of husbandry, or other sciences, that those stewards, who have discretion and generosity enough to gain the good-will of the men they employ, such will always d their work well done, and increase their hes. But if a master, or his overseer, be reless, and at the same time has the power rewarding and punishing those under his diction, and, when he views his workmen, does t make them sensible, either one way or her, of his authority; whenever he comes, goes, it is the same thing to them; they ork or play at their discretion. Such a one very little worth the regard of any man: but e man who ought to be admired and valued, be, who, when he comes among his servants, eates in them a pleasant countenance, and akes them rejoice, every one running or riving in their business to serve him, and ing all ways to get his praise and love. Such man as this is worthy the rank of a king. A aster of any science, as well as husbandry, who has good sense enough to bring his family to such affection toward him, and good order, he does not possess this by learning only, but he must receive his good nature and wisdom from the gods; he must be born with a generous nature, which must proceed from the gods; for I have never yet found the true gift of government, but it was attended with generosity. Where these excellent qualities appear, all under that direction are willing to obey, and especially if the power of rule be in the hands of those who are endowed with virtue and temperance: but where a master exercises himself in cruelty, or acts in a tyrannical way, against the good-will and reason of mankind, he can never hope for the least ease or comfort."

DISCOURSE

UPON

IMPROVING THE REVENUE OF THE STATE

OF

ATHENS.

TRANSLATED

By WALTER MOYLE, Esq.

A

DISCOURSE

UPON

IMPROVING THE REVENUE OF THE STATE

OF

ATHENS.

I ALWAYS held it for a certain maxim, that governments resembled their governors, and that the prosperity or declension, the vigour or decay of all states, was derived from the virtues and vices, the abilities or weakness of their rulers : but since it is generally alleged in vindication of the Athenian ministry, that they understand the common principles of justice as well as the rest of mankind, but that they are compelled by the necessities[1] of the common people to oppress their confederate[2] cities with unreasonable tributes and taxes : I have attempted to examine whether this apology is well grounded, and whether they are not capable by native riches, and revenue of the state of Athens, to maintain the whole body of our people, which is the justest and most honourable provision can be thought of : for I imagine if such a design could be compassed, that the wants of the people would be more effectually relieved, and the jealousies and suspicions of our neighbours would be quieted.

Upon a general view of the whole matter, it appeared to me that the Athenian territory is capable of affording a mighty income and revenue, the truth of which assertion may be easily evinced by a brief survey of the state and nature of the country.

The fruits of the earth, and native products of our soil, are a proof of the temperature of our climate and the mildness of our seasons ; for we have plants which bear in great abundance in our country, which will never grow in others ; and our sea, as well as land, abounds in all things necessary for life, or luxury : add to this, that all the blessings which the gods have made peculiar to the different seasons of the year, begin earlier, and end later with us, than in any part of the world.

Besides the vast plenty we enjoy of perishable goods, our soil affords us some staple and permanent commodities, such as our noble quarries of marble, out of which are drawn the best materials for the building and ornamenting of temples, and for the altars and statues of the gods, and which both the Greeks and barbarous nations set a high value upon.

And where the soil is too barren to receive the common improvements of husbandry, it

---

1 Διὰ δὲ τὴν τοῦ πλήθους πενίαν. The state of Athens was at a great charge in maintaining the common people. They were allowed three oboli a man for every cause they judged ; and this pension was called the τριώβολον διακαστικον : Lucian in his accusato. And some days many thousands received this pension.

The Θεωρικον was an allowance of two oboli a-piece, to pay for the sight of public shows. Liban in argu. Olyn. prima.

The ἐκκλησιαστικον was an obolus a-piece, paid them every time they assembled, Jull. Poll. l. 6. c. 9 ; and this pension was afterwards increased to three oboli. Besides, all maimed and disabled citizens had a pension of two oboli a day. Harpocrat. in verbo ἀδύνατοι.

2 Xenophon says only περι τας πόλεις, but the word συμμαχίδας is plainly understood, as appears from the sequel of this discourse, and Xenophon's treatise of the government of Athens. This tax upon the confederates was at first but 460 talents, but it was afterwards advanced to 1300. Plutarc. in vita Aristidis. This tribute was so burdensome, that it provoked the confederates to frequent revolts.

contains hidden treasures, which will feed a much greater number of mouths than any arable lands can do : for the Divine Bounty has bestowed upon us inexhaustible mines of silver, an advantage which we enjoy above all our neighbouring cities by sea and land, who never yet could discover one vein of silver ore in all their dominions.

We have reason likewise to believe that Athens is seated in the centre of Greece, and the habitable world ; for all nations are incommoded with more intense degrees of heat or cold in proportion to their (northern or southern) distance from us ; and that we lie in the heart of Greece is evident, for all travellers, that pass by sea or land, from one extremity of Greece to the other, must take Athens in their way.

And though Attica is no island, yet we have the same benefit of trading with all winds, for we are bounded on two sides by the sea, and by being joined to the continent we have the convenience of driving on an inland traffic.

Other cities lie exposed to the fury of barbarous nations, but we are so far from having so ill a neighbourhood, that the states which border immediately upon us, lie at a remote distance from them.

To all those advantages which conspire to the felicity and greatness of our state, and which we owe to the happy situation, and the native wealth of our country, a mighty improvement might be made by the institution of public laws, in favour of strangers who establish themselves among us ; for besides the general benefits derived to all cities from numbers of people, our strangers would be so far from living on the public, and receiving pensions from the state as our own citizens do, that they would maintain themselves, and be the foundation of the noblest branch of our revenue by the payment of the aliens' duties.[1]

An effectual inducement to the settlement of foreigners among us might be established, by taking off all those public marks of dishonour from them which are of no service, nor advantage to the state, and by excusing them from serving among our heavy-armed troops ; for an exemption from the dangers of war, and from the necessity of being absent from their families, and trades,[2] would be a very powerful encouragement.

It is likewise the interest of the commonwealth, rather to fight our battles with our own troops, than to keep up in our armies, a mixture of Lydians, Phrygians, and Syrians, and all kinds of barbarous nations, out of whom the greatest number of our aliens are composed.

Besides the advantage of avoiding the confusion such a mixture of troops produces, it would be more for our reputation abroad, to trust the fortune of our state to the courage and valour of our own citizens, than in the hands of foreigners.

Besides all other proper encouragement to strangers, the privilege of being enrolled[3] among our horse, would more warmly unite them in our interests, and prove a solid foundation of strength and greatness to the state.

It would be likewise a strong inducement to greater numbers of considerable strangers to plant among us, if we gave the waste ground within our walls to be built on by such of them as deserved and desired it of the public.

The institution of a new magistracy,[5] like the public guardians[6] of our orphans, for protection and security of strangers, with rewards of honours and dignities to those, who, by their

---

some extraordinary service to the state. Demost. oratio contra Neæram.

2 Τέχνων, not τένων. The Basil edition reads it right ; for most part of the mechanic and handicraft trades were carried on by the aliens at Athens. Xenoph. de Polit. Athen.

3 Τοῦ ἱππικοῦ. Xenophon explains this passage in his Hipparchicus, where he advises the state to enrol aliens among their horse. Besides the dignity of the horse-service, there was a considerable pay in peace and war allowed them. Ulpianus in Timocratem. Xenoph. in Hippar.

4 See Thucydides' history of the Peloponnesian war, book 2. chap. 17.

5 Μετοικοφύλακις. Every alien by the laws of Athens, was obliged to choose a private patron among the citizens. Harpocration in verbo ὀψωνιτων. But here Xenophon proposes public patrons for the whole body of the aliens.

6 Ὀρφανοφύλακις. Vide Demosthen. contra Macartatum

---

1 Μετοίκιον, aliens' duties. This was an annual tribute paid by the aliens, of twelve drachmas for every man, and six for every woman. Harpocrat. in verbo μετοίκιον. The number of the aliens amounted generally to 10,000. Originally at Athens there was no distinction between strangers and natives, for all foreigners were naturalised promiscuously, Thucyd. l. 1. c. 2. Thus all the Platæans were naturalized at once, Thucyd. l. 3. c. 55 ; and this custom was the foundation of their future greatness. But as the city grew more populous, they grew more sparing of this favour. Scholi. Thucyd l. 1. c. 2 ; and this privilege was given to such only as had deserved it by

care and industry, procured the most numerous settlements of foreigners among us, would gain the affections of the aliens, and have a very happy effect, in drawing a vast concourse of exiles [7] and strangers to live under the protection of our government, and augment our public revenue.

III. That of all cities, Athens lies the fairest for inviting an extended commerce, is evident from the convenience of our stations and harbours, where ships can ride secure in all weather. And whereas in other trading cities merchants are forced to barter one commodity for another, in regard their coin is not current abroad, we abound not only in manufactures, and products of our own growth, sufficient to answer the demands of all foreign traders, but in case they refused to export our goods, in return for their own, they may trade with us to advantage, by receiving silver in exchange for them, which transported to any other market, would pass for more than they took it for at Athens. [8]

It would be a great encouragement to commerce, if prizes and rewards were allotted to such judges of the court-merchant, [9] as made the quickest and justest determination of all causes relating to trade, that the merchant might not lose the benefit of his market by an attendance upon the courts of justice.

It would be likewise for the honour and advantage of the public, to give the first rank [10]

and precedence in all public places to foreign seamen, and merchants, and to invite to the public feasts of the city, such of them as by their ships or commodities do service to the state; for this distinction of honour, as well as the consideration of their own profit, would invite them to make quick returns from their voyages to so friendly a government.

And it is manifest beyond all contradiction, that our trade and commerce would be extended, our exportations and importations increased, and the standing income and revenue of the state improved, in proportion to the number of foreign seamen, and merchants of all kinds that establish themselves among us.

To the improvement of these articles of our revenue, nothing more is required than a generous lenity and indulgence in our public laws, and a universal encouragement and protection to strangers. But the improvements that may be added by other methods to advance our standing income, will of necessity require a settlement of some public fund. [11]

And I have good grounds to believe that the people will make large contributions in favour of such a public undertaking, when I consider what sums they advanced when we sent succours to the Arcadians under the command of Lysistratus, and likewise of Hegesilaus. [12]

How often have we set out squadrons of galleys by extraordinary subsidies, without any certain prospect of advantage to the state? but this we were all sure of, that no particular contributor would ever be repaid the whole, or any part of his money.

But in the present case no man can possess a more honourable or advantageous revenue, than what he will receive in recompense for his contribution to this public fund: for a contributor of ten minæ, will receive a triobolon [13] a day from the state, which in a year's

---

7 'Aπόλιδις. Men whose cities have been destroyed.
8 Πανταχοῦ πλειον τοῦ ἀρχίου λαμβάνουσιν. The meaning of Xenophon is that the Athenian money was more valuable abroad than the coin of any other nation, because it was of finer silver. For it is impossible that an ounce of Athenian silver should be worth more in specie than an ounce of other silver of the same fineness. 'Sensus moresque repugnant atque ipsa utilitas.'

A table of the Attic coins reduced to the value of English money.

	£	s.	d.
The obolus was equal to	0	0	1¼
The triobolus was three oboli, and made	0	0	3½
The drachma was six oboli, and made	0	0	7¾
The mina was an hundred drachmas, and made	3	2	6
The common Attic talent consisted of 60 minæ, which amounts in our money to	187	10	0

These are the common Attic coins, which are most frequently mentioned by their writers, and which I have reduced to our English money, to make way for the easier understanding of this discourse.
9 Τοῦ ἱμπορίου ἀρχή. This court of judicature was probably the same with the ναυτιδίκαι, mentioned by Suidas and Hesychius, in verbo ναυτιδίκαι.
10 Πρωεδρίαις τιμᾶσθαι. This was a right of prece-

dence in the theatres, senate, assemblies of the people, and in all public places whatsoever. Schol. Aristoph. in equ. This custom was practised by the Spartans, who gave this privilege to the Deceleans. Herodotus, lib. 9. c. 72.
11 'Αφορμή, a fund. Harpoc. Hesychius in verbo ἀφορμή.
12 Hegesilaus commanded the Athenian troops sent to the assistance of the Mantineans at the battle of Mantinea; which is a proof that this discourse was written after that battle. Diog. Laer. in Xenoph. Diodorus Siculus by mistake calls him Hegelochus.
13 Τριώβολον. Salmasius de modo usurarum thinks that this was the τριώβολον δικάστικον which the people

time, amounts to near 20 per cent. This is a running income as high as the produce of Nautic[1] interest : and a contributor of five minæ, will at the year's end receive more than a third[2] part of the capital sum he advanced : as for the body of the people, if they pay in one minæ a piece, they will in a year's time very near double[3] their principal money, and be paid in the city, without any hazard, or contingency, upon the public faith, which is the most certain, and most lasting profit.

I am of opinion likewise, that private strangers, and foreign cities, kings, and governors, if they had the honour of being registered to posterity in our public monuments and records, as benefactors to the state, would mutually vie in emulation who should contribute most largely to the carrying on so generous a design.

The necessary funds being advanced, it would be for the honour and interest of the state, to build a greater number of public inns, and houses of entertainment in our ports, for the use of seamen, in the trading parts of the city for merchants, and in general for the reception of all strangers whatsoever.

And if we build shops, warehouses, and exchanges for common retailers, the rents of the houses would be a great addition to our public revenues, and the magnificence of the buildings would be an ornament to the city.

As the public builds galleys for war, so it might likewise be for the advantage of the state to make a new experiment, and build merchant ships for trade, which might be farmed out, like the other branches of our revenue, upon good security ; for if this design was found practicable, it would prove a considerable article in the increase of our public income.

IV. Our silver mines alone, if rightly managed, besides all the other branches of our revenue, would be an inestimable treasure to the public. But for the benefit of those who are unskilled in inquiries of this nature, I design to premise some general considerations upon the true state and value of our silver-mines, that the public, upon a right information, may proceed to the taking such measures and counsels, as may improve to the best advantage.

No one ever pretended from tradition, or the earliest accounts of time, to determine when these mines first began to be wrought, which is a proof of their antiquity ; and, yet as ancient as they are, the heaps of rubbish which have been dug out of them, and lie above ground, bear no proportion with the vast quantities which still remain below, nor does there appear any sensible decay, or diminution in our mines ; but as we dig on, we still discover fresh veins of silver-ore in all parts, and when we had most

---

received for judging causes. But Xenophon's computation plainly confutes this opinion : he says that a contributor of 10 minæ, or 1000 drachmas, at the rate of a triobolus or half a drachma a day, will in a year's time receive almost the fifth part of the principal money he advanced, which is very true, for reckoning (as Xenophon always does in this discourse) 300 days to the year, the payment of a triobolus a day will amount to 180 drachmas, which is near the fifth part of 1000 drachmas. But the payment of the τριώβολον διασώτικον could never amount to this sum, because the holydays, by the confession of Salmasius, took up two months in the year, and on these days the people never heard causes, so that 30 drachmas must be deducted from 180, which reduces the sum to 150, which is little more than the seventh part of 1000, so that Salmasius is mistaken, or Xenophon was a very loose calculator. The true meaning of the passage I take to be thus : Xenophon in the following part of this discourse, in order to make provision for the citizens, makes a proposal to the state, to buy as many slaves as would treble the number of their own citizens, which slaves were to be let out at the rate of an obolus a day to the adventurers in the mines, which brought in a revenue of three oboli a day to every citizen, because the slaves were thrice as many as the citizens among whom this revenue was to be divided. And this I take to be the triobolus mentioned by Xenophon, which every citizen was to receive in recompense for his contribution.

1 It was the highest interest, and is here opposed to lend interest, which was considerably less ; for in the former the creditor run a greater hazard ; for if the merchant who borrowed the money, employed it in trade, lost his ship, the creditor lost his money, and had no right to demand it of the merchant ; a trade somewhat like our bottomry. This interest generally amounted to 20 per cent, or the fifth part of the principal per annum. It is true it often varied, and was higher or lower according to the plenty and scarcity of money, or the danger and distance of the voyage ; but the general medium may be safely established at 20 per cent. There are several contracts of money lent upon Nautic interest, extant in the orations of Demosth. contra Lacrit. pro Phormi. contra Pant. contra Phormi.

2 Πλέον ἢ ἐπίτριτον. More than a third part of the principal money : for a triobolus a day in a year makes 180 drachmas, which is above the third part of five minæ or 500 drachmas. The τόκος ἐπίτριτος was the highest Nautic interest, and came to above 33 per cent. There is an instance which comes very near this computation, in the Oration of Demosthenes contra Phormi.

3 1800 drachmas is almost double one mina, or 100 dr.

---

4 Foreign cities, &c. Foreign states often contributed to the public buildings of the Greeks. The Rhodians when their Colossus was overturned by an earthquake, received contributions from all the neighbouring states in order to restore it. Polybius, lib. 5. And there are many inscriptions of such public benefactors extant in Gruter, and elsewhere.

labourers at work in the mines, we found that we had still business for more hands than were employed.

Nor do I find that the adventurers in the mines retrench the number of their workmen, but purchase as many new slaves as they can get; for their gains are greater, or less, in proportion to the number of hands they employ. And this is the only profession I know of where the undertakers are never envied, be their stock or profits ever so extraordinary, because their gains never interfere with those of their fellow traders.

Every husbandman knows how many yoke of oxen and servants are necessary to cultivate his farm, and if he employs more than he has occasion for, reckons himself so much a loser; but no dealer in the silver mines ever thought he had hands enow to set to work.

For there is this difference between this, and all other professions; that whereas in other callings, for instance, braziers and blacksmiths, when their trades are overstocked, are undone, because the price of their commodities is lowered of course, by the multitude of sellers; and likewise a good year of corn, and a plentiful vintage, for the same reason does hurt to the farmers, and forces them to quit their employment, and set up public houses, or turn merchants and bankers.

But here the case is quite otherwise, for the more ore is found, and the more silver is wrought, and made, the more adventurers come in, and the more hands are employed in our mines.

A master of a family indeed, when he is well provided with furniture, and household-goods, buys no more, but no man was ever so overstocked with silver, as not to desire a farther increase: if there are any who have more than their occasions require, they hoard up the rest with as much pleasure as if they actually made use of it.

And when a nation is in a flourishing condition, no one is at a loss how to employ his money: the men lay it out in fine armour, in horses, and in magnificent houses and buildings; women lay it out in great equipage, costly habits, and rich clothes.

And in accidents of war, when our lands lie fallow and uncultivated, or in a public dearth and scarcity, what reserve have we left to apply to but silver, to purchase necessaries for our subsistence, or hire auxiliaries for our defence?

If it be objected that gold is as useful as silver, I will not dispute it; but this I am sure of, that plenty of gold always lowered its value, and advanced the price of silver.

I have insisted the longer upon these general reflections, to encourage adventurers of all kinds, to employ as many hands as possible in so advantageous a trade, from these plain considerations, that the mines can never be exhausted,[5] nor can silver ever lose its value.

That the public has known this long before, is evident from our laws, which allow foreigners to work our mines upon the same terms[6] and conditions our own citizens enjoy.

But to draw this discourse more immediately to the subject of my present consideration, which is the maintenance of our citizens, I will begin to propose those ways and means, by which the silver mines may be improved to the highest benefit and advantage to the public. Nor do I set up for the vanity of being admired for an author of new discoveries: for that part of my following discourse, which relates to the examples of the present age, lies obvious to all the world; as for what is past it is matter of fact, and every man might inform himself that would be at the pains of inquiring.

It is very strange, that after so many precedents of private citizens of Athens, who have made their fortunes by the mines, the public should never think of following their example: for we who have heard, that Nicias, the son of Niceratus, had a thousand slaves employed in the mines, whom he let out to Sosias the Thracian, upon condition to receive an obolus a day, clear of all charges, for every head, and

5 'That the mines can never be exhausted.' It is plain from Pausanias that these mines were not worked in his time. Paus. Attic; but this does not destroy the assertion of Xenophon, for the plundering the temple of Delphi brought out two millions of our money, which lay dead before; and the conquest of Persia by the Macedonians brought such a vast quantity of silver into Greece, and consequently made labour so dear, that the silver found in the mines would in all probability scarce countervail the expenses of the working them; or it might proceed from the subjection of Athens to a foreign power, or from other accidents, and not from any decay of the mines.

6 'Ἐπὶ ἰσοτελείᾳ. 'Upon the same terms,' &c. The state was the proprietor of the silver-mines, and strangers or Athenians that worked in them, were obliged to pay the same tribute of the 24th part of the silver found, to the public. Suidas in ἀγράφου μετάλλου δίκη.

that the same complement of workmen should be always kept on foot.

In like manner Hipponicus had 600 slaves let out at the same rate, which yielded him a revenue of a mina a day, and Philemonides 300, which brought him in half a mina a day, and many others made the same advantage, in proportion to the number of slaves they possessed. But what need we to appeal to precedents of an elder date, when at this day we have so many instances of the same nature before our eyes ?

In the proposals which I offer, there is only one thing new, namely, that as private men have a constant revenue coming in from the slaves whom they let out to work in the mines; so the public, in imitation of their example, should purchase as many slaves to be employed in the same manner, as will treble the number of their own citizens.

Let any reasonable man take this whole proposal to pieces, and examine every distinct head apart, and then judge whether the design is feasible or not. It is plain the state can bear the charge of the price of the slaves better than private men; and nothing can be easier than for the senate to make proclamation for all that have slaves to sell, to bring them in, and then buy them up for the public use.

And when they are bought, what should hinder any one from hiring them of the state upon the same terms they hire them from private men; for we see that our revenues are farmed by particular men, and the repair, and the building of our public structures and temples[1] are let out to private undertakers.

And that the public may be no loser by the desertion of slaves, or other accidents, the adventurers in the mines, like the farmers of our revenue, should be obliged to give good security to save the state harmless : though at the same time the commonwealth may be much more easily cheated by the farmers of their revenue, than by the hirers of their slaves.

For how is it possible to discover the frauds that are committed in the management of the public money ? there being no visible distinction between public and private money; the same materials and stamp being common to both. But when our slaves are burned with the public mark of the state, with severe penalties to be inflicted upon all that buy, or sell them; what danger is there of their being stolen ? Thus much of my proposal as relates to the buying and preserving our slaves, appears practicable beyond all contradiction.

If any one questions whether, after we have purchased a great number of workmen, there will be adventurers enow to hire them of the public, let him consider, that the undertakers who have a good stock of slaves will hire more of the state; for the mines are so great, that they will require a vast number of hands to work them; and many of the workmen that are grown old and unserviceable, and many others, Athenians, and strangers whose bodies are not vigorous enough for labour, would yet be willing to get their living by easier callings, would turn adventurers in the mines, and hire our slaves; so that there is little danger of wanting employment for our workmen.

Twelve hundred slaves, when bought, will probably in five or six years' time, produce a revenue sufficient to purchase as many more as will make the number 6000. This number, at the rate of an obolus a day a head, clear of all charges, will afford a yearly revenue of sixty talents.[2]

And if but twenty of these talents are laid out in the purchase of more slaves, the city may employ the overplus as they think convenient; and when the number of slaves is increased to 10,000, it will produce a standing revenue to the public, of a hundred talents a year.

To demonstrate that the mines would take up a greater proportion of slaves to work them, I appeal to the authority of all these living witnesses who remember, what numbers of workmen were employed in them before the taking of Decelea[3] by the Lacedemonians. And

---

1 'The repair of our temples,' &c. Μισθοῦντας ἱερά. It was the custom of the Greeks to let out the building and repair of their temples to private undertakers, Athenæus l. 6. Herod. l. 5. c. 62. where he makes use of the same word, τὸν μισθοῦντας; that is, 'they hired the building of the temple upon such terms.' And the Latins used the word conducunt in the same sense. Conducunt foricas, i. e. repurgandas. Juvenal. Sat. 3.

2 'Revenue of 60 talents.' This computation proves that Xenophon reckoned but 360 days to the year : for 6000 oboli, multiplied by 360, make 2,160,000 oboli; which sum, divided by 600 (for 600 oboli make a mina) makes 3,600 minæ, which divided by 60 (for 60 minæ make a talent) reduces the whole sum to 60 talents. And the following computation of 100 talents a year, produced by 10,000 oboli a day, answers exactly to the former.

3 'The taking of Decelea,' &c. Decelea was taken

our silver mines that have been wrought for so many ages, with such numbers of hands, and continue still so far from being drained, or exhausted, that we can discover no visible difference in their present state from the accounts our ancestors have delivered down to us, are undeniable proofs of my assertion.

And their present condition is a good argument that there never can be more hands at work in the mines than there is employment for: for we dig on still without finding any bottom or end of our mines, or decay of the silver-ore.

And at this day we may open new mines as well as in former ages, and no one can determine whether the new mines may not prove more rich than the old ones.

If any one demands why our miners are not go forward in pursuit of new discoveries, as formerly; I answer, it is not long since that the mines have begun to be wrought afresh, and the present adventurers are not rich enough to run the risk of such an undertaking.

For if they discover a rich mine, their fortunes are made; but if they fail, they lose all the charges they have been at; and this consideration chiefly has discouraged the adventurers from trying so dangerous an experiment.

But in order to remedy this difficulty, I have some proposals [4] to offer to the public. There are ten tribes at Athens, and to each of these I would have the government assign an equal proportion of their public slaves, to be employed in search of new mines, and the gains to be equally divided in common among all the sharers in the ten tribes: for if the mines were once settled upon this establishment, and the whole undertaking carried on by a national stock, the adventurers would run little hazard; and if but one of the ten tribes succeeded in the attempt, the whole community would be gainers; and if two, three, four, or half the tribes had the same good fortune, the profits would be proportionably greater; for it is a wild supposition, and against the experience of

all ages, to imagine that not one in ten should succeed in such an undertaking.

Companies of private adventurers may carry on the same trade in a joint-stock, nor is there any danger that they and the national company will interfere one with another; but as confederates are strengthened by their mutual assistance to each other, so the more adventurers of all kinds are employed in the mines, so much larger will the gains and advantages be to all.

Thus have I briefly proposed some considerations to the public, for establishing the management of the national revenue upon such an institution, as shall make effectual provision for the whole body of our people.

Nor let any man be discouraged from the considerations of the vast expense, which will be necessary for the perfecting so great a work: for there is no necessity that either the whole design must be finished at once, or the public will receive no advantage from it; quite the contrary, every step we advance in our way, the state will gain ground; and by the gradual progress we make in our public buildings in the rigging out our trading-vessels, or in the purchase of our slaves, the commonwealth will be an immediate gainer.

And it is certainly more for the advantage of the public to parcel out the design, and finish it by degrees: for when many houses are building at once, they cost more, and are worse built: in like manner, if we purchase our complement of slaves all at once, we must pay more for them, and buy worse into the bargain.

But if we proceed gradually, according to our abilities, we shall still have the same advantage of continuing any right methods we pitched upon in the beginning, and shall be at liberty to correct the oversights and mistakes we made at our first setting out. And if we perfect some parts of our undertaking, and delay the execution of the rest, the revenue arising from part of our design, which is finished, will be sufficient to answer the whole expense of the remainder; but if we resolve to execute the whole project at once, the whole charge of the enterprise must be raised at once likewise.

And then the great difficulty which will be objected to this whole scheme is, that in case the public purchase so great a number of slaves, the mines may happen to be overstocked; but there can be no grounds for such an apprehen-

---

and fortified by the Lacedemonians in the 19th year of the Peloponnesian war, and lying in the heart of Attica, gave opportunity to 20,000 Athenian slaves to desert to the enemy. Thucyd. l. 7. c. 27.

4 Xenophon in his former proposal would have 10,000 slaves let out at a certain rate to the adventurers in the mines, but in this second proposal he advises the state itself to adventure in search of discoveries of new mines, which work was to be carried on by another set of slaves, and not by the former 10,000.

sion, if we take care every year to employ no more than there is actually occasion for.

Thus I think the easiest methods of finishing this design are the best and most effectual. It may be objected that the immense charges of this war have exhausted our treasure in such a manner, that it will be impossible for the public to raise any new subsidies, much less to advance the necessary funds of such an undertaking. But this difficulty may be easily removed, for let the state employ no more money in the administration of the government the next year after we have a peace, than the annual income of the public produced during the war, and whatever additional improvements of our revenue are made by the peace, from the encouragement of strangers and merchants, from the increase of our exportations and importations, occasioned by the resort of more people, and from a greater vent of commodities in our ports and markets, let all that be appropriated to this particular service in order to advance the national revenue.

If any one imagines that a war will ruin our whole undertaking, let him but consider that the execution of this design will enable us to meet a foreign invasion, with so many advantages on our side, that a war in such a juncture will be less formidable to us, than to our enemies themselves.

For what advantage can better enable us to carry on a vigorous and successful war, than numbers of men? and by such an addition to the stock of our people, as might be made by due care and encouragement; what levies might be raised, what mighty fleets and armies set out to disappoint all the designs of our enemies?

And I have reason to believe that it is possible to work our mines in the conjuncture of a foreign war, for they are covered on the south-sea, by a strong citadel in Anaphlystus, and on the north-sea, by another in Thoricus, and these two fortresses lie at the distance of but 60 furlongs from one another.

But if a third fort was built upon the top of a mountain, in the middle of the two former, the three works would meet together, and other silver mines would be inclosed in a circle, and guarded on all sides, and the workmen at the first notice of an invasion might retire to a place of security.

But if we are invaded with more numerous armies, our enemies may make themselves masters of our corn, wine, and cattle that lie without the works; but if they possess themselves of our silver mines, what can they find to carry off more than a heap of stones and rubbish?

But how is it possible for our enemies to make an inroad upon our mines? for the city Megara, which lies nearest, is above 500 furlongs from them; and Thebes, which is nearer than any but Megara, is more than 600 furlongs distant from them.

If they advance to our mines in a small body from this side, they must leave Athens behind them, and run the hazard of being cut off by our horse and flying parties; and it is a wild notion to imagine that they will invade us with their whole force, and unguard their own country, and leave it exposed to our inroads; for in such a case, Athens would be nearer to their cities than their own army.

But suppose they marched up to our mines with a numerous army, how could they subsist for want of provisions? if they foraged in small parties, they would be in danger of having their convoys intercepted; if they foraged with their whole armies, they must act upon the defensive, and we should be the aggressors.

The revenue arising from our slaves would not only make a considerable article in the charge of maintaining our citizens, but by the vast concourse of people from all parts, the customs of the fairs and markets at the mines, and the rent of our public buildings, and melting-houses, and many other heads, would produce a mighty income to the state.

The state, upon such an establishment, would be peopled with a prodigious number of inhabitants, and the value of lands at the mines would be as high as those that lie near Athens.

A pursuit of such measures and counsels would not only enrich the city, but introduce a habit of obedience in the people: reform their discipline, and revive the courage of the nation.

For if, upon this improvement of our revenue, a larger allowance was established for the maintenance of our youth, they would be trained up to the art of war in our public academies [1] with more exactness, and perform their military

1 There were at Athens, and in other parts of Greece, military academies or gymnasia, where the young men exercised. Theophrastus de Blanditia. Aristoph. et Schol. in Equi. Xenoph. in 1. 2. 3. et 6 lib. de rebus Græc.

exercises with a more regular discipline, than the racers in the torch-course [2] are taught to observe. And our troops in garrison and the standing guards of our coasts, would do their duty in their several posts with more cheerfulness, if any effectual provision was settled for their subsistence.

V. If it be made to appear that the revenue of Athens can never be improved, or advanced to the full height without a peace, it may deserve the public inquiry, whether the establishment of a council of peace [3] would not be for the benefit and advantage of the state.

For the institution of such a magistracy would invite more numerous settlements of foreigners to make Athens the place of their abode.

For it is an absurd supposition to imagine, that peace will weaken our strength, and ruin our authority and reputation abroad; for of all governments, those are happiest who have continued longest without war, and of all commonwealths, Athens lies fairest for flourishing and increasing by the arts of peace.

For Athens in time of peace is the great theatre to which all mankind have occasion to resort: to begin with merchants and commanders of ships, where can the traders in wine, oil, corn, or cattle have a quicker vent, or a better market for their commodities than at Athens? Where can monied men make a better improvement of their wealth; and where is there greater encouragement for those who live by arts of invention and ingenuity?

Where is there better employment for artificers and mechanic trades? Where can the sophists, philosophers, poets, and the lovers of the liberal arts, resort to a more renowned school of learning and humanity? Where is there a nobler scene to gratify the curiosity of all strangers that are delighted with divine rites and institutions, and the celebrations of religious games and festivals? And where

can merchants of all kinds whatsoever find a better market to make quick returns of their money, than Athens?

If my opposers acknowledge all this to be true, but still imagine that we can never recover the dominion of Greece but by a war, I desire them to look back to the Persian invasion, and examine whether it was by force of arms, or our good offices to the Greeks, that we were placed at the head of the naval confederacy, [4] and the common treasury of Greece?

And when by a tyrannical exercise of our power we lost our jurisdiction, by an alteration of our measures, and a milder administration, we were restored [5] to our ancient authority by the joint consent of all the islands.

Did not the Thebans, in acknowledgment of our generous assistance to their state, place us at the head of the common alliance? [6] and our rivals the Lacedemonians, for the same consideration, quitted their old pretensions, and suffered us to give laws to the last treaty, and dispose of the supreme command of Greece at our own discretion.

And at this juncture, in the general confusion of Greece, we have the most favourable opportunity of recovering our ancient dominion without difficulty, hazard, or expense, that ever any nation had: for if we set up to be the common mediators of Greece, and interposed our authority to unite all the divided interests abroad, and reconcile all the factions at home; and if by solemn embassies to all the neighbouring states we declared for the liberty of Delphi, [8]

4 'Ελλωταμίας. After the Persian invasion the Athenians had the command of the confederate fleet, and were made treasurers of the money contributed by the Greeks to the carrying on the war against Persia. Thucydides, lib. 1.

5 The Athenians recovered the command of the Greek islands, (which they lost in the Peloponnesian war,) in the fourth year of the 100th Olymp. Diod. Sicul. lib. 15.

6 This alliance between the Thebans and Athenians was made in the second year of the 96th Olymp'ad. Diod. Siculus, lib. 14. Xenophon, lib. 3. de rebus Græc.

7 This league between the Spartans and Athenians was made in the fourth year of the 102d Olympiad, not long after the battle of Leuctra. Diod. Sic. l. 15. Xenop. l. 7. de. rebus Græc.

8 The Greeks made it a part of their religion, to preserve the liberty of Delphi. Thus the Lacedemonians entered into a war to restore the oracle to the Delphians, Thucyd. lib. l. c. 112. And the first article of their leagues often began with a mutual engagement on both parts, to protect the liberty of Delphi. Thucyd. l. 4. c. 118. l. 5. c. 18. Besides their religion, they had reasons

2 'Εν ταῖς λαμπάσι. Torch-course. There was a festival at Athens, on which a certain number of men ran with lighted torches in their hands. Paus. Attic. To this ceremony Lucretius makes that fine allusion in his second book,

Et quasi cursores vital lampada tradunt.

Ειρηνοφύλακες. "Council of peace." This new magistracy which Xenophon proposes to be instituted for the preservation of the public peace, was to be, in all probability, like the ειρηνοδίκαι or fœciales of the Romans, who were instituted by Numa for the same considerations. Dion. Halicarn. lib. 2.

all Greece would support us at the head of so glorious a cause, and unite in a general confederacy against common enemies, who endeavoured to make themselves masters of Delphi,[1] when the Phocians were reduced to extremity.

And if we afterwards warmly interested ourselves to establish a general peace by sea and land ; all Greece, next to the security of their own governments, would desire the preservation of Athens.

If any man can have so wild a notion, as to imagine that war will contribute more to the increase of the riches of the state than peace, I know no better way to decide the controversy, than by appealing to the experience of former ages, and producing precedents to the contrary out of our own story.

---

of state for this proceeding : for if Delphi were subject to a foreign power, the priestess might be forced to utter whatever oracles the conqueror pleased to impose : nor could the resolutions and sentences of the Amphictyons, who often sat at Delphi, be free and unbiassed so long as Delphi was under a foreign dominion.

1 If we knew who the enemies were that designed to seize upon Delphi, it would be no difficult matter to determine exactly the time when it was written. Jason, the tyrant of Thessaly, had formed a design upon Delphi, but his death prevented the execution of it. Diod. Sic. Xenop. Hist. Græc. Ælian. Frag. But this passage cannot be understood to mean this attempt, for Jason was assassinated in the third year of the 102d Olympiad, some years before the battle of Mantinæa, and this discourse, as I have proved in a former note, was written after that battle. I think that this passage (taking the word ἐκλυσόντων in a neutral sense as I have rendered it, and for which there are a thousand authorities) ought to be understood of a design the Thebans had formed upon Delphi. The story in short is this : the Thebans being engaged in a war with the Phocians, upon some dispute about a frontier, formed a design upon the temple of Delphi. Demost. de falsa Legatione, Ulpianus. And the Phocians at the same time being condemned by the Amphictyons to pay a great fine for ploughing up some consecrated land, the Greeks prepared to execute the sentence by force of arms. The Phocians being unable to resist such an approaching storm, were reduced to great extremities, and compelled, for their own preservation, to seize upon the treasures of Delphi : this gave beginning to the Holy War, and all Greece engaged in the quarrel. The Athenians assisted the Phocians, but Xenophon advises them to break off that alliance, and declare for the liberty of Delphi, and under that plausible pretence, to unite all Greece against the Thebans, who were equally criminal with the Phocians, (as Demosthenes observes,) for having formed the first design upon the temple. This counsel he recommends to the Athenians as the best method to recover the dominion of Greece. I know it will be objected that Diog. Laertius places the death of Xenophon in the first year of the 105th Olympiad, and the Phocian war breaking out some years after, it will be impossible to explain this passage in my sense.

To this I answer, that this account of Laertius is certainly false : for Xenophon, in his Greek history, mentions the death of Alexander the tyrant of Pheræ ; which happened, as Diodorus observes, in the fourth year of the 105th Olymp. so that Xenophon must be a prophet, or be alive at that time, three years after his supposed death. Xenophon likewise in the conclusion of his Greek history affirms, that after the battle of Mantinæa, Greece was in a greater disorder and confusion than ever. But we read of no considerable commotion in

Greece till the breaking out of the Holy War, in the first year of the 106th Olympiad, which engaged all Greece in an intestine division.

To confirm this account of Laertius, it may be urged, that Xenophon lived ninety years, according to Lucian in Macrob. And being present at the battle of Delium, which was fought in the first year of the 89th Olympiad, about sixty-seven years before the Holy War, it is highly improbable that he was living at the time of the Holy War. It is true, Laertius says, that Socrates saved Xenophon's life at that battle : but Athenæus, l. 5, says, that Socrates was not at the battle ; and it is probable that the other part of the story of Xenophon's being there, may be equally fabulous, especially if what Athenæus (according to Casaubon's correction) says be true, that Xenophon was but a boy at the banquet of Callias, which was three years afterwards. Besides he is called a young man in his expedition into Asia ; but at this rate he must have been fifty years old at that time, an age at which a man cannot properly be called young.

But granting that he was present at the battle of Delium, if we allow him to be eighteen years old, the age, if I mistake not, that the Athenians usually made their first campaign, he would be but eighty-one years old on the first year of the 105th Olympiad, and consequently might write of the Holy War, which broke out four years afterwards. Nor does Lucian precisely limit his age to ninety years only, but says he lived above ninety years.

Xenophon in this discourse says, that the Athenians had been engaged in a war by sea and land ; that the war by sea was at an end, but the war by land still continued. This exactly agrees with the Bellum Sociale, or the war of the Athenians against their revolted islands which was carried on by sea, and begun in the third year of the 105th Olympiad, and ended in the second year of the 106th Olympiad, two years after the breaking out of the Holy War, which the Athenians were then engaged in.

By this account Xenophon wrote this discourse about the third year of the 106th Olympiad, a year after the conclusion of the peace with the islands.

If the account of Xenophon's death in Laertius be true, I cannot believe this work to be genuine ; for I think it almost impossible to explain this passage in any other sense. But the authority of all the writers who ascribe this discourse to Xenophon, and the conformity of the style with the rest of his works, and that character of piety which runs through the whole piece, which is so peculiar to the writings of Xenophon, and that particular maxim at the conclusion of this treatise, " of undertaking every thing under the favour and protection of the gods," which he inculcates in all his works, and particularly at the end of his Ἱππαρχικος, are undeniable proofs that this discourse is genuine.

For upon inquiry he may find that the vast treasure we had amassed in peace, was all consumed in our former wars; and to quote instances of a fresher date, in the present war all the branches of our income have been deficient, and what money came in upon the public funds, has been all applied to the pressing occasions of the state; but since the seas have been open, and our trade free, every article of our income is advanced, and the government is at liberty to employ it as they think convenient.

Not that I would advise the commonwealth to sit down tamely by their injuries in case of a foreign invasion; but this I am sure of, that we should be better enabled to revenge the affront, if we are not the aggressors, for our enemies will never be able to form a confederacy to support them in an unjust war.

VI. Upon the whole matter, if nothing in this proposal appears impossible, or difficult, and if a pursuit of these counsels and resolutions will gain the affections of Greece, and establish our security at home, and increase our reputation abroad; if the common people will abound in all things necessary for life, and the rich be eased of their taxes to the wars: if in this universal plenty our temples will be rebuilt, and our religious festivals and solemnities celebrated with more magificence; if our walls, docks, and arsenals will be repaired, and our priests, senate, magistrates, and cavalry, restored to their ancient rights and privileges, is it not fit that all engines should be set at work to promote so glorious an undertaking, that in our days we may see our country established upon a solid foundation of security and happiness?

And if the public, upon due consideration, thinks fit to execute these orders and institutions, I would advise them to send ambassadors to Delphi and Dodona to consult the gods, whether such a reformation of our government would not turn to the advantage of the present age, and the benefit of all posterity.

And if these resolutions are ratified by the divine approbation, to consult the oracle once more, to the protection of what gods we should recommend the success of this enterprise, and then to propitiate those gods we are directed to apply to, in order to engage their assistance; and after this solemn invocation to enter boldly upon the execution of this design: for it is but reason that all undertakings should be attended with more favourable success, that are begun, and carried on, under the immediate care and protection of the Divine Providence.

ON THE

ATHENIAN REPUBLIC.

ATHENIAN REPUBLIC.

I. THE Athenians,[1] in my opinion, are entitled to little commendation for having originally adopted their present political institutions, because they are calculated to give an undue ascendancy to the poor and the bad over the rich and the good : I cannot therefore commend them. These institutions, however, as they have been adopted, can be demonstrated by abundant proofs to be admirably adapted to support the spirit of their constitution, and to enable them to transact public business, though among the rest of the Greeks a contrary opinion is prevalent.

First then, at Athens, the poor and the plebeians are wisely rendered more influential than the nobles and the rich ; because the lower orders man the ships, and extend the power of the republic: for pilots,[2] and pursers, and commanders of fifties, and boatswains, and ship-builders, acquire much more real influence to a republic than the nobility and richer citizens. This being the state of their affairs, it seems a matter of justice that all the citizens should participate in the offices of state, whether they be filled by lot[3] or by open suffrage, and that every citizen who chooses should be allowed to speak publicly at their deliberations.

The people never require a participation in those offices, whether superior or inferior, in which are centred the safety or danger of the whole nation : nor do they expect to be eligible to the offices of generals or masters of horse, as the people know that it is much more advantageous for them not to engage in such offices, but allow them to be possessed by the rich ; but the people lay claim to all those offices to which salaries are attached, and which better the circumstances of their families.[4]

The Athenians invariably give greater advantages to the bad, the poor, and the plebeians, than to the good ; and this circumstance, though it has excited the wonder of many, still proves incontestably their desire to preserve the spirit of a democratical government. For the poor, the plebeians, and the lower orders, when held in consideration, and when their numbers increase, extend the democracy : but when the rich and good are prosperous,

---

1 περὶ δὲ. This treatise, from its abrupt introduction, is generally supposed to have been a fragment of a larger work, in which a comparison was instituted between the different forms of government in ancient Greece.

2 κυβερνῆται, &c. Κυβερνήτης was the master or pilot, who had the care of the ship, and the government of the seamen in it, and who sat at the stern to steer. All things were conducted according to his direction ; and it was therefore necessary that he should possess an exact knowledge of the art of navigation, called κυβερνητικὴ τέχνη, and which chiefly consisted in the proper management of the rudder, sails, and of the several instruments used in navigation ; in the observance of the winds, and of the motions of the celestial bodies ; in the knowledge of commodious harbours, of rocks, and quicksands.— Κελευστὴς, the purser, whom some interpret the boatswain, signified the word of command to the rowers, and distributed to all the crew their daily portion of food.— Πρωρεὺς or πρωράτης, the boatswain, was next under the pilot, and, as the appellation imports, had his station upon the prow, ὁ τοῦ κυβερνήτου διάκονος, ὃς πρωρεὺς τῆς νὼς καλεῖται. To his care were committed the tackle of the ship and the rowers, whose places were assigned by him. He assisted the master at consultation respecting the seasons, and other matters.

3 κλήρῳ. Those who were chosen by lot were στρατηγοὶ, ἵππαρχοι, δικασταὶ, βουλωταὶ, ἐπιστάται τῶν πρυτάνεων, ταμίαι, γραμματεῖς, λογισταὶ, and several others. These were called κλήρῳ λαχόντες, κληρωθέντες, κληρωτοὶ, κυαμωτοί. Those, on the contrary, who were chosen by the suffrages of the people, were called αἱρετοὶ, αἱρεθέντες, χειροτονηθέντες.

4 μισθοφορίας. Judges, senators, and the citizens who frequented the public assemblies, received a certain allowance in money.

then the plebeians are exerting themselves to strengthen a party opposed to them in interest.

In every country the better portion of the people is hostile to a democratical government: for among that class the least petulance and injustice exist, and the most ardent desire of reputation and probity; but among the plebeians the greatest ignorance, insubordination, and wickedness are to be found: for their poverty leads them to crimes, and unskilfulness and ignorance, through want of money to some men [1] . . . .

It might be remarked that they should not have allowed every person without distinction to speak publicly and attend the senate, but should have restricted this right to men of the greatest genius and virtue: yet in this respect they have consulted excellently, by permitting even the bad to speak. For if the higher orders alone had harangued and deliberated, it might be of advantage to men like themselves, but not so to the plebeians: and at present when every one may speak, a bad man is enabled to rise and propose what may be advantageous to himself and his equals.

The question may be asked, What proposal can such a man make, likely to be profitable either to himself or the people? But they know well that his ignorance and wickedness, coupled with good will towards them, are more likely to be beneficial to them than the virtue and wisdom of the good man conjoined with malice.

Such institutions will not produce the best system of government, but they are admirably calculated to preserve the democracy. The people by no means desire a well constituted republic, which would inevitably subject them to slavery; they prefer to be free and to govern. A bad constitution gives them little uneasiness; for what you consider a bad political condition, enlarges their power and preserves their freedom.

If you desire a well constituted republic, you must first procure men of the greatest talents to make the laws; then the good will punish the bad: and consult on what is most beneficial to the commonwealth, and not allow persons like madmen to consult, harangue, and address public assemblies. These advantages would speedily reduce the plebeians to a state of slavery.

The licentiousness of slaves and of aliens at Athens is excessive; none are allowed to strike them; nor will the slave yield to the freeman. I will explain the cause of this practice being indigenous. If it were customary for the slave, or alien, or freedman to be struck by the freeman, the citizen of Athens would frequently be beaten under the supposition of his being a slave; for neither in dress nor personal appearance are the people superior to slaves or aliens.

It may be reckoned a subject of wonder that slaves are there allowed to live luxuriously, some of them even magnificently; yet even in this they appear to have acted with judgment. For where a naval power exists, it is necessary, for pecuniary considerations, to humour the slaves, and allow them a more liberal mode of living, that their masters may receive from them their hire for labour performed in the fleet; for where the slaves are rich, it is no longer expedient that my slave should dread you; but in Lacedæmon my slave dreads you; and where my slave is afraid of you, there is danger lest he should surrender his property to get rid of personal fear.

This consideration urges us to grant an equality of rights to slaves and freemen; and also to aliens and citizens, because the republic requires the aid of aliens on account of the multiplicity of her arts and the exigencies of the naval service. This is the reason that we have justly admitted the aliens to an equality of rights.

The people have here abrogated the gymnastic exercises and profession of music at private expense, as being unsuited to their means, and being deprived of leisure to attend to them. In the public academies [2] and gym-

---

1 Commentators have proposed many alterations of this sentence, so as to produce a meaning somewhat corresponding with the context; but they require to supply many words. We have, therefore, thought it preferable to give a translation of the words as they stand, without attending to the proposed emendations.

2 χορηγίαις, &c. Χορηγοί were at the expense of players, singers, dancers, and musicians, as oft as there was occasion for them at the celebration of public festivals and solemnities.—Γυμνασίαρχοι were at the charge of the oil and other necessaries for the wrestlers and combatants.—Τριέραρχοι were obliged to provide necessaries for the subsistence of the crew belonging to the fleet; for, in general, the republic only furnished the rigging and sailors. They were also to build ships. To this office no certain number of men was appointed; but their number was increased or diminished as the value of their estates, and the exigences of the commonwealth, seemed to require. Commonly, however, there were two to each galley, who served six months each.

nastic exercises, and in serving on ship-board, they know that when the rich act as choregi, the people are instructed and supported ; when the rich command at sea and in military academies, the people labour and are paid. The people, therefore, think it proper to receive money for singing, running, dancing, and serving on ship-board, that they may enjoy themselves, and the rich become poorer.

In deciding cases in courts of justice, equity is less an object with them than advantage.

Those who are deputed from Athens by sea to visit the allies, are reported to abuse and detest the good among them, knowing that the governor must be hated by the governed ; and that, if the rich and the nobles are powerful in these cities, the power of the populace at Athens will be of very short duration. For these considerations, then, they dishonour the good, despoil them of their property, banish, and kill them : but they increase the influence of the bad. On the contrary, the good among the Athenians preserve the good in the allied republics, knowing it to be advantageous for themselves always to preserve the best citizens in these states.

It might be observed that the strength of the Athenians lies in their allies being able to contribute money. But to the plebeians it seems to be a greater advantage that each individual Athenian should possess the property of their allies, and that the allies should have only so much as to enable them to supply themselves with food and to till the fields, without being able to conspire against their masters.

The Athenian people, at first sight, appear to have enacted a bad law, in obliging their allies to resort to Athens for the decision of their lawsuits.[3] The Athenian people, on the other hand, only consider what advantage is likely to accrue to themselves from this practice. First of all, they receive the court dues[4]

throughout the year ; besides, remaining at ease at home, without sailing to foreign lands, they administer the government of the allied states ; preserve their lower orders, and ruin their enemies in the courts of justice : but if each of the allies had the administration of justice at home, as they bear a deadly hatred to the Athenians, they would ruin those among themselves who were most friendly to the Athenian people.

In addition to these, the Athenian people gain these advantages from justice being administered to the allies at Athens ; for first, the city receives the hundredth part of what is landed at the Piræus, and the keepers of lodging-houses gain profit, and those who possess cattle and slaves for hire : heralds, too, are benefitted by the arrival of the allies.

Besides, if the allies did not come for decision in law-suits to Athens, they would only pay their respects to those of the Athenians who were delegated to visit them, such as generals and trierarchs and ambassadors ; but at present each individual of the allies is obliged to flatter the Athenian plebeians, knowing that when he comes to Athens, the decision of his law-suit depends solely and entirely on the people, who are the law at Athens. He is obliged, in courts of justice, to supplicate the people, and even when one enters the court to seize him by the hand. By these means the allies are rendered much more the slaves of the Athenian people.

Moreover, on account of their transmarine[5] possessions, and to avoid giving umbrage to the magistrates of these places, they and their followers are obliged to learn secretly to handle the oar ; for the man who sails frequently must handle the oar, both himself and domestics, and become acquainted with nautical phrases.

Thus they become good pilots by their experience and exercise at sea. Some are trained in piloting small vessels ; some, vessels of burden ; and some are advanced from them to the galleys : many of them are even able to take the charge of ships as soon as they go on

---

3 πλεῖν ἐπὶ δίκας Ἀθήναζε. The great inconvenience which attended the administration of justice to the insular allies of Athens, seems to have been frequently brought forward as a heavy accusation. Isocrates alludes to it in Panath., καὶ τάς τε δίκας καὶ τὰς κρίσεις τὰς ἰνθάδε γιγνομένας τοῖς συμμάχοις—διαβαλοῦσι.

4 τῶν πρυτανίων. Commentators differ as to the amount and appropriation of this money. Aristotle in his Polit. says, τὰ δικαστήρια μισθοφόρα κατέστησε Περικλῆς. The Scholia on the Clouds of Aristophanes, 1134, translate πρυτανεῖα thus: ἀργύριὸ τι, ὅπερ κατετίθεσαι οἱ δικαζόμενοι ἀμφότεροι, καὶ ὁ φεύγων καὶ ὁ διώκων. Pollux VIII. 38. adds, ὁ δὲ ἡττηθεὶς ἀπεδίδου τὸ παρ᾽ ἀμφοτέρων δεθὶν ἐλάμβανον δὲ αὐτὸ οἱ δικασταί. Καὶ οἱ μὲν ἀπὸ

ἑκατὸν δραχμῶν ἄχρι χιλίων δικαζόμενοι τρεῖς δραχμὰς κατετίθεντο· οἱ δὲ ἀπὸ χιλίων μέχρι μυρίων, τριάκοντα. He also subjoins the opinion of others, πρυτανεῖα ἶναι τὸ ἱππόδεκατον τοῦ τιμήματος κατατίθεσθαι δὲ αὐτὸ τοὺς γραψαμένους ἐπὶ μισθοδοσίᾳ τῶν δικαστῶν. Ammonius and Thomas Magister have adopted the latter opinion.

5 ὑπερορίοις. These possessions were in the islands, the Chersonesus, Thrace, and elsewhere.

4 T

board, from having been exercised at sea all their lives.

II. The land army,[1] which is by no means in good condition at Athens, is thus constituted: They reckon themselves inferior by land to such of their enemies as are there reckoned the most powerful; but to the allies who pay tribute they deem themselves superior, and they suppose that they will maintain the sovereignty as long as they are superior to their allies.

I will now enumerate a few of the advantages of their condition as decided by fortune. Those who are governed by land can collect men together from small towns, and fight in great numbers; but those who are governed by a naval power, such as islanders, cannot collect into one place the inhabitants of other towns for mutual aid; for the sea intervenes, and their governors are masters of the sea: and if it were possible secretly to collect the islanders together into one island, they could be reduced by famine.

The cities on the continent,[2] which are governed by the Athenians, are retained in subjection, the larger ones through fear, the smaller through penary. For there is no city which does not require either to import or export. This they cannot do unless they be subject to the masters of the sea. Those who have the ascendancy at sea can do what cannot be done by those who have it on land: they can make a descent on the country of a more powerful nation, and lay it waste with fire and sword; they can land at those places where either there is no enemy at all, or not so many as to dare to encounter them. In doing this by sea the difficulty is less than when attempted with a land army.

Besides, it is possible for those who rule the sea to sail away from their own country on whatever voyage they please; but those who rule on land cannot depart a distance of many days' journey from their own country; for their marches are slow, and they cannot carry provision for a long journey in an overland expedition. He who marches by land, too, must go through a friendly country, or force his way by the sword; but he who goes by sea, wherever he is superior, may make a descent; and where inferior, can sail past that country until he reaches a friendly country or a nation inferior in power.

And then the blight of the crops, which proceeds from heaven, is borne with difficulty by those who rule on land, but with ease by the rulers of the sea. For the crop is never everywhere at the same time deficient; so that from the prosperous and fertile land provisions reach the lords of the sea.

And if we may enumerate small advantages, by the command of the sea, they associate with other nations, and discover their different kinds of good cheer: and whatever is pleasant in Sicily, or in Italy, or in Cyprus, or in Egypt, or in Lydia, or in Pontus, or in Peloponnesus, or any where else, all these may be collected into one spot by having the ascendancy at sea. And, besides, becoming acquainted with the words of many languages, they choose from them the most elegant and useful. The rest of the Greeks have adopted one peculiar language, mode of living, and dress; but the Athenians have adopted a compound from Greeks and Barbarians.

The people knowing that every poor man cannot sacrifice to the gods, enjoy the festivals, possess temples and groves, and inhabit a beautiful and extensive city, devised means for obtaining these. The state, then, publicly

---

1 τὸ δὲ ὁπλιτικόν. So much is lost here that it is difficult to judge of the author's meaning. His intention seems to have been to draw a comparison between the land and naval forces, and to point out by what means the Athenians aimed to obtain and preserve the sovereignty of Greece. Τὸ ὁπλιτικὸν, therefore, which elsewhere signifies the heavy-armed troops in a land army, seems to designate the land army as contradistinguished from the naval power; and we are informed that the latter was in greatest repute. Thucydides, i. 143, and Isocrates Orat. de Pace, state that their ships were formerly manned with slaves and aliens, and that the citizens engaged in the land service. This practice was so much changed in the time of Isocrates, that the land army was composed of foreigners, and the fleet of citizens. The power of the Athenians extended to the islands and often to cities on the continent, and for this reason, our author informs us, the Athenians attached little importance to the land forces, but exerted themselves to increase and support their power at sea. Wherever our author speaks indefinitely of enemies, he refers to the Lacedemonians. Plutarch, in his life of Themistocles, informs us how that general gradually induced the Athenians to turn their attention to gaining an ascendancy at sea: ὃς τὰ πεζὰ μὲν οὐδὲ τοῖς ὁμόροις ἀξιομάχους ὄντας, τῇ δ' ἀπὸ τῶν νεῶν ἀλκῇ καὶ τοὺς βαρβάρους ἀμύνασθαι καὶ τῆς Ἑλλάδος ἄρχειν δυναμένους, ἀντὶ μονίμων ὁπλιτῶν, ὥς φησι Πλάτων, ναύτας καὶ θαλαττίους ἐποίησεν.

2 ἐν τῇ ἠπείρῳ. Ἤπειρα here seems to mean the shore of Asia Minor. Both Isocrates and Xenophon frequently use the word in this sense. In Greece Proper, no cities or states were subject at this period to the authority of the Athenians.

sacrifices all the victims, and the people enjoy the banquets and divide the victims by lot. Some of the rich possess, privately, places for exercising, and baths, and places for undressing before the baths; but the people, for their own private use, build many palæstra, undressing places, and baths, and the mob enjoys a greater number of these than the few and the rich.

The Athenians are the only nation of the Greeks or Barbarians who can possess wealth; for if any state is rich in timber for ship-building, where can they dispose of it, unless they conciliate the favour of the lords of the sea? and if any state is rich in steel, brass, or flax, where can they dispose of it, unless they conciliate the favour of the lords of the sea? and from these very materials our ships are made. From one nation timber is procured; from another, steel; from another, brass; from another, flax; from another, wax.

In addition to these, we will not allow them to be imported by our enemies, who are excluded from the use of the sea. And, without labour, we enjoy all these benefits from the land by means of the sea; no other city has them: nor does the same state abound in timber and flax; for where there is flax, there the country is level and woodless: nor are brass and steel procured from the same state, nor are two or three of the others produced by one state: one state abounds in one; another produces another.

And, in addition to these advantages, near every continent there is either a projecting shore or an island situated before the coast, or a part of the shore, to which there is only a narrow approach from the continent; so that those who rule the sea may there make a descent, and do much injury to those who live on the mainland.

They are destitute of one favourable circumstance; for if the Athenians, while lords of the sea, inhabited an island, they would have had it in their power, when they pleased, to injure others, and suffer no injury in return, as long as they commanded the sea; and their land should not be devastated or invaded by the enemy. At present, the cultivators of the fields, and the rich men of Athens, are much afraid of the enemy; but the people, being well aware that the enemy can commit to the flames or devastate none of their property, live in safety and free from terror. In addition

to this, they would be freed from another fear if they inhabited an island,—that the city would never be betrayed by a few, nor would their gates be opened, nor would the enemy break in upon them. How could these things happen to the inhabitants of an island? Nor would there be seditions among the people if they inhabited an island. At present, if a sedition took place, it would be with the hope that the enemy could be introduced by land: if they inhabited an island, they would not require to dread such an event. But as it was not their fortune to inhabit an island from the beginning, they now act thus,—they deposit their property in islands, trusting in their ascendancy at sea; and they overlook the devastation committed on the territory of Attica, knowing that their commiseration may deprive them of other greater advantages.

It is necessary, in cities governed by an oligarchy, that alliances and leagues should be rigidly observed. If engagements are not strictly formed, from whom can the injury be supposed to have proceeded, except those few by whom they were made. Whatever the people may decide, any one may lay the blame on the proposer of the measure, and those who confirmed it, asserting that he was not present when the decree was passed, and that the proposals by no means pleased him. And if, upon making inquiry, they ascertain that these things were decided in a full meeting of the people, they devise a thousand pretexts not to do what they do not wish to do. And when any harm happens from what the people decree, they complain that a few persons opposed to them have corrupted the whole matter, and if any good, they appropriate the credit to themselves.

They do not allow the people to be traduced or evil spoken of on the stage, as they do not wish to be evil spoken of themselves. But they grant liberty to any one to satirise another individual if he choose, being well aware that one of the people or the rabble is seldom pitched upon for that purpose, but generally either one of the rich, of the nobility, or the powerful. Very few of the poor or the plebeians are traduced on the stage; and not even these, except on account of their officiousness, and of attempting to be more influential than the rest of the people. They do not, therefore, take it amiss that such persons should be satirised.

I assert, then, that the people at Athens

know who are good among the citizens, and who are bad : and as they know this, they love those who are necessary and advantageous to themselves, however bad they may be, and entertain a great hatred at the good; for they do not think that virtue is naturally beneficial to them, but rather injurious. Some, however, on the contrary, who, by birth, really belong to the people, are by no means plebeians.

I can easily excuse the people for choosing a democracy, as every one must be excused for wishing to benefit himself. But whoever is not one of the people, and prefers living under a state subject to democratic rule, rather than one subject to oligarchical, is devising means to do injury; and knows that a scoundrel has much greater facility in escaping notice in a popular republic, than when the government is in the hands of a few.

III. I do not commend the plan of the Athenian republic: but since they have thought it proper to subject themselves to a democracy, they seem to me to be preserving the democracy, by adopting the plans which I have enumerated.

I observe that some blame the Athenians, because the allies sometimes cannot get a response from the senate or the people, after having remained a whole year. This happens at Athens from no other reason than that the multitude of their business prevents them from settling the affairs of the allies, and dismissing them.

For how could they, who must celebrate more festivals than any of the Grecian cities? and while these last, business of the state is at a stand : they must also settle private controversies and public accusations, and actions against public[1] men, so numerous, that all their judges cannot settle them. The senate have also many deliberations about war, and many about procuring money, and many about enacting laws, and many about the usual contingencies in a state, many also about the allies and receiving tribute, and they must pay great attention to naval and sacred affairs. Is it wonderful, then, that, since they have so much business to transact, they cannot give sentence in every lawsuit?

Some say that money is very influential with the senate and the people, in procuring a decision in a court of justice. I agree with them that much can be done with money at Athens, and that much more business would be settled if a greater number used bribes. This, however, I know well, that the state could not transact all their necessary business, even although much more gold and silver were given. It is necessary, also, to give sentence in the event of one refusing to furnish a ship, and when a building is erecting at the public expense. In addition to these, they must decide who ought to undertake the duty of choragus, for the Dionysian,[2] Thargelian,[3] Panathenæan,[4] Promethean,[5] and Hephæstian[6]

---

[1] εὐθύνη, an action against magistrates, ambassadors, and other officers, who had misemployed the public money, or committed any other offence in the discharge of their trusts. The action against ambassadors was sometimes peculiarly called παραπρεσβεία.

[2] Διονύσια were solemnities in honour of Διόνυσος; Bacchus, and were sometimes called by the general name of Ὄργια, which, though sometimes applied to the mysteries of other gods, more particularly belongs to those of Bacchus. They were also sometimes denominated Βακχεῖα. They were observed at Athens with greater splendour, and with more ceremonious superstition, than in any other part of Greece ; for the years were numbered by them, the chief archon had a share in the management of them, and the priests who officiated, were honoured with the first seats at public shows. At first, however, they were celebrated without splendour, being days set apart for public mirth, and observed only with the following ceremonies : a vessel of wine, adorned with a vine branch, was brought forth ; next followed a goat ; then was carried a basket of figs; and, after all, the phalli.

[3] Θαργήλια was an Athenian festival in honour of the sun and his attendants, the hours ; or, as some think, of Delian Apollo, and Diana. It was celebrated on the sixth and seventh of Θαργηλιών, and received its name from Θαργήλια, which was a general word for all the fruits of the earth ; because one of the principal ceremonies was the carrying of first fruits in pots called Θαργήλια. The chief solemnity was on the latter day, the former being employed in preparing for it.

[4] Παναθήναια was an Athenian festival in honour of Minerva, the protectress of Athens. It was first instituted by Erichthonius, who called it Ἀθήναια, and afterwards revived by Theseus, when he had united into one city all the Athenian people, and denominated Παναθήναια. At first, it continued only one day ; but was afterwards prolonged several days, and celebrated with great magnificence. There were two solemnities of this name, one of which was called Μεγάλα Παναθήναια, the Great Panathenæa, and was celebrated once in five years, beginning on the twenty-second of Hecatombæon: the other was denominated Μικρὰ Παναθήναια, the Less Panathenæa, and was observed every third year, or, as some think, every year, beginning on the twentieth or twenty-first of Thargelion.

[5] Προμήθεια was an Athenian solemnity celebrated in honour of Prometheus with torches, in memory of his teaching men the use of fire.

[6] Ἡφαίστια was an Athenian festival in honour of Ἡφαιστος, Vulcan. At this time there was a race with torches, called ἀγὼν λαμπαδούχος, in the academy. The contenders were three young men, one of whom being

games. Four hundred trirarchs are appointed each year; and such of these as wish, must every year exercise themselves in deciding in courts of justice. Besides these, the magistrates must be approved of and decided on, pupils are to be elected, and keepers of prisoners' to be appointed. These must be done every year.

At intervals, also, they must decide on persons refusing to enter the army, and if any unexpected instance of injustice should happen, and if any unusual insolence should be offered or impiety shown. I pass over many things: what is of most consequence has been mentioned, except the settlement of the tribute: this happens generally every fifth year. Do you not think that they must pass judgment on all these cases?

Some one may say that it is not necessary it should be done in their present courts of justice. But if he confesses that all these must be settled, it is necessary that it should be done in the course of the year. So that not even at present are they able, in the course of the year, to pass judgment, to be a check on evil doers, on account of the great number of cases which come before them. But it may be said, that no doubt it is necessary to judge, but that fewer judges should sit together. If they appoint a greater number of courts of justice, there will be fewer in each of them; and it will be much easier to corrupt a few judges, and bribe them, and cause them to decide with less show of justice. It must also be taken into consideration, that the Athenians must attend to festivals, on which days no decisions in courts of justice can be made. They have double the number of holidays that any other state has; but we go on the supposition that they are equal to them who have least. Since this is the state of their affairs, I insist that it is impossible that business at Athens can be otherwise conducted than at present, except that a little alteration may be made on their present institutions by addition or subtraction. A great change cannot be made, for fear of detracting from the democratical influence.

It is possible to devise many plans to better their political state: but it is not easy to propose a plan which will procure a better system of government without endangering the democracy, except as I have already stated, by a little addition or subtraction.

The Athenians seem also not to have consulted well, in always supporting the worst party in revolted cities. Yet, in this respect, they act with judgment; for if they chose the best, they would support a party entertaining notions on political points different from themselves: for in no state are the better class of citizens friendly to the plebeians, though the worst class are friendly to the plebeians; for equals entertain friendly notions of their equals. These reasons induce the Athenians to prefer what is advantageous to themselves.

As often as they have supported the party of the better class, it has been injurious to them; and within a short period the plebeians were inslaved. This happened once in the case of interference with the Bœotians. Again, when they supported the nobility of the Milesians, who, in a short period after, rose up and massacred the plebeians. Again, when they took the part of the Lacedemonians against the Messenians, a very short time intervened until the Lacedemonians overpowered the Messenians, and made war on the Athenians themselves.

---

ppointed by lot to begin the race, took a lighted torch i his hand, and commenced his course: if the torch ras extinguished before he arrived at the goal, he gave to the second; and the second, in like manner to the hird. He who carried the torch lighted to the end of he race, was the victor, and was called λαμπαδηφόρος or νεσσηφόρος.

7 φύλακας δεσμωτῶν. These were also called οἱ ἕνδεκα, ie eleven, from their number, and were elected from ie ten tribes, one from each. To them was added γραμματεὺς, or registrar, to complete the number. sometimes they were called νομοφύλακες, keepers of the iws; and they superintended public prisoners, and onducted criminals to execution. They had power to iize on persons suspected of theft and robbery, and, if iey confessed that they were guilty, to put them to eath; but, if not, they were obliged to prosecute them i a judicial manner.

8 ἀστρατείας, refusing to serve in war was punished ·ith ἀτιμία infamy

9 Βοιωτοῖς. The author is here supposed to allude to the unsuccessful expedition of Tolmides against the Bœotian exiles, mentioned by Thucydides, i. 113.; Diodorus, xii. 6.; Plutarch, in life of Pericles, 24.— Μιλησίων, reference is probably here made to the war which the Athenians undertook against the Samians, when accused by the Milesians, Thucyd. i. 115., Plutarch, Pericles, 24, Diodorus, 12., and Scholia ad Aristoph. Vesp. 283, though we are not aware that the issue of either of these wars corresponded with the allusions in the text.—Μεσσηνίων, the instance here given is referred to the third Messenian war, in which the Athenians, being invited by the Lacedemonians to besiege Ithome, were immediately after dismissed by them, Thucyd. i. 108.

It might be suspected that none are unjustly branded as infamous at Athens: there are however some, though these are few. The popular authority at Athens, however, cannot be shaken by the influence of a few. Besides, we ought to consider that the mind of man is so constituted, that those who have been deservedly deprived of their privileges, pay little attention to their disgrace; those, however, who are unjustly condemned, are easily impelled to revenge, under the consideration of the injury they have received. How can it be supposed that the many can be dishonoured at Athens, where the plebeians have authority over the laws?

At Athens the infamous consist of those who rule unjustly, and who do not speak or act uprightly. He who takes these things into consideration, can never suppose that any danger can spring from those who are branded as infamous at Athens.

ON THE

LACEDEMONIAN REPUBLIC.

LACEDEMONIAN REPUBLIC.[1]

I.   As I was once reflecting how Sparta, which was not a populous city, had rendered herself the most powerful[2] and celebrated in Greece, I wondered how this had happened: when, however, I took into consideration the Spartan mode of living, my wonder ceased.

Lycurgus, the enactor of the laws, which rendered them happy, is a man whom I admire, and whom I consider the wisest of mankind ; for he made his country excel in happiness, not by imitating other states, but by adopting institutions quite contrary to that of the majority.

In the procreation of children—to begin at the beginning—other nations nourished their young women who were pregnant and well-educated, with as moderate a quantity as possible of bread and sauces ; they caused them to refrain from wine, or to use it in a diluted state. And as the greater number of those engaged in arts are sedentary, so the rest of the Greeks required their young women to sit solitary and spin wool.   How can it be

expected that persons thus trained should produce a beautiful and manly offspring?

Lycurgus supposed that female slaves were perfectly competent to supply clothes : and as he reckoned the procreation of children a matter of the greatest consequence to free women, he, first of all, enjoined that the female, as well as the male part of the community, should engage in bodily exercise ; and as he had instituted trials of running and strength with each other among the men, he did the same with the women, imagining that when both parties were robust, more robust children would be produced.

In the connection between man and wife, he adopted a plan different from others : as he observed that men generally at first associated immoderately with their wives, he made a law that it should be deemed disgraceful to be seen going in or coming out from them.   When they associated in this manner, their love to each other was necessarily stronger, and their offspring, if they had any, much more robust than if the parents had been cloyed with each other.

He prevented them, besides, from marrying whenever they wished, and enjoined that marriage should be consummated when the body was in full strength, as he considered this conducive to the procreation of a robust and manly offspring.

And as he observed that when an old man had a young spouse, he watched his wife with jealous care, he devised a law differing from other nations, for he decreed that the old man should bring to his wife whatever man was most deserving of admiration, either for qualifications of body or mind, and should support the children produced by them.

---

1 This treatise is deservedly held in great estimation, as being the work of a man who was trained by a philosopher who διὰ διελέγετο εκατῶν, ... τί πόλις, τί πολιτικός· τί ἀρχὴ ἀνθρώπων, τί ἀρχικὸς ἀνθρώπων· καὶ περὶ τῶν ἄλλων, ἃ τοὺς μὲν εἰδότας ἡγεῖτο καλοὺς κἀγαθοὺς εἶναι, τοὺς δὲ ἀγνοοῦντας ἀνδραποδώδεις ἂν δικαίως κεκλῆσθαι. Mem. 1. 1. 16.   To this may be added Xenophon's great experience in civil and military affairs, his acquaintance with many of the highest in rank of the Lacedemonians, such as Agesilaus, Cheirisophus, and others of that nation with whom he lived on friendly terms when in exile.

2 δυνατωτάτη.   Their superiority first began to appear in the Peloponnesian war, but chiefly about the ninety-third Olympiad, when they conquered the Athenians at Ægospotamos : from which period they held the sovereignty in Greece till the hundred and second Olympiad, that is, till the battle of Leuctra, in which they were so completely defeated by the Thebans that they never afterwards recovered the shock.

If any person, again, should have an aversion to living with a wife, and should be desirous of a fair and robust family, he enacted a law that if he saw a woman of a good disposition, and well fitted for procreating such a progeny, and could persuade her husband to allow it, he should beget children by her. He made many similar concessions. For the women wish to have the charge of two families, and the men to obtain brothers to their children, who have a common origin and power, but are excluded from participating in their property.

In thus differing from other legislators in his enactments regarding the procreation of children, I leave others to judge whether he was instrumental in producing men to Sparta eminently distinguished for size and strength.

II. Having thus treated of the procreation, I will now explain the mode adopted in the education of both sexes. Among the other Greeks, those who take credit to themselves for having their sons best educated, put a servant over them as soon as their children understand what is said to them, and immediately send them to schools to be instructed in literature, music, and wrestling. Moreover, they render their children's feet delicate by sandals, and debilitate their bodies by the variety and change of their clothes: their appetite, too, is the measure of their food.

But Lycurgus, instead of giving each of the children into the charge of slaves, set over them one of those men, from whom the chief officers of state are chosen, and he was called Pædonomus. To him he delegated the authority of collecting the boys, and punishing them severely when they neglected their duty. He also gave him, as assistants, some of the grown lads, furnished with whips, that he might punish whenever it was necessary, and thus infuse into them a great dread of disgrace, and a desire of obedience.

Instead of making their feet delicate with sandals, he enjoined that they should be rendered hardy by going barefooted; as he believed that if they exercised themselves in this state, they would be able to ascend steep places with greater ease, and descend declivities with much more safety: they would skip, leap, and run quicker unshod, if their feet were trained to it, than shod.

And instead of being made effeminate by clothes, he decreed that they should accustom themselves to one dress throughout the year,

supposing that they would be thus better enabled to endure the extremes of cold and heat.

He likewise enjoined that the young men should exert themselves never to take so much food as to be burdened with satiety; and that they should have some experience in enduring hunger, supposing that persons thus trained would be more able to endure fatigue when necessary, without food; persevere in exertion a much longer time on the same food, when they are commanded; stand less in need of sauces; be much more easily satisfied with any kind of food; and spend their lives much more healthily. He also considered that the fare which rendered the body slender, was more conducive to good health, and increasing the stature of the body, than that which expanded it.

But that they might not be too much oppressed by hunger, though he did not permit them to receive what they stood in need of without difficulty, he allowed them to steal what was necessary to satisfy their hunger; and he made it honourable to steal as many cheeses as possible.[1]

I suppose every person is aware that he did not prescribe the laying of schemes for their livelihood, because he had nothing to give them, but because it is evident that he who intends to steal must watch during the night, and cheat during the day, and lay snares, and, if he expects to receive any thing, he must even employ spies. It is plain, then, that the children were thus instructed, because he wished to make them most dextrous in procuring provisions, and well trained for warfare.

It may be said, Why, then, since he reckoned it honourable to steal, did he inflict many strokes on the person apprehended in the fact? because, I assert, that in all other branches in which men receive instructions, they are punished unless they act properly up to them. They are punished, therefore, when detected, because they have stolen in a bungling manner.

These persons are given in charge to others, to be flogged at the altar of Orthian[2] Diana.

---

1 This sentence, in almost all editions, is to be found farther on, in a place where it injures the sense materially. We have followed the recommendation of Schneider in introducing it here.

2 Ορθίας. This festival was called Diamastigosis, because boys were whipped before the altar of the goddess. These boys, called Bomonicæ, were originally free-born Spartans; but, in the more delicate ages, they were of mean birth, and generally of a slavish origin. The parents of the children attended the solemnity, and

By this he wished to prove that, after a short endurance of pain, a person may enjoy pleasure a long period. He also demonstrates by this, that, when speed is required, the indolent man is of least advantage, and occasions most trouble.

And that the children should not be in want of a leader when their pædonomus was absent, he decreed that whatever citizen was present should be master, and enjoin whatever he thought advantageous for the children, and punish them when in the wrong. By this means he rendered the boys much more modest; for neither boys nor men respect any person more than their rulers. And that the boys should not be deprived of a leader when even no man was present, he decreed that the most courageous of the monitors of each class should assume the command: so that the boys of Lacedæmon are never without a leader.[2]

III. As soon as the boys have become youths, then the rest of the Greeks cease to be attended by slaves who have them in charge —cease from attending teachers—no one has then rule over them, but they are left to the freedom of their own will. Lycurgus enacted a different law.

Having observed that nature had infused into persons of their age the greatest exuberance of daring, the greatest excess of insolence, and the most vehement desire of pleasures, he therefore imposed upon them the heaviest toils, and contrived as much occupation for them as possible.

He also added, that whoever should attempt to evade these, should be deprived of all the privileges of the state; and thus brought it about, that not only public characters, but also those who had the charge of individuals, exerted themselves that they might not, through laziness or aversion to labour, become completely contemptible in the state.

Besides, as he was extremely anxious to instil into them the principles of modesty, he directed that, on the road, they should always keep their hands within their robes, walk in silence, look around nowhere, and should only attend to those things which were before their feet. By this, he proved that the male sex can conduct themselves with greater modesty than the female. You would certainly no more hear their voices than if they had been stones, you would have more difficulty in turning their eyes than if they were made of brass, and you would reckon them much more modest than virgins in the bridal-chamber; and whenever they came to the phiition,[4] you would hear nothing from them but what they were asked.

We have now explained the education, both of the Lacedæmonian and the other Grecian states, and by which of them men can be ren-

---

exhorted them not to commit any thing, either by fear or groans, that might be unworthy of Laconian education. These flagellations were so severe, that the blood gushed in profuse torrents, and many expired under the lash of the whip without uttering a groan, or betraying any marks of fear. Such a death was reckoned very honourable, and the corpse was buried with much solemnity, with a garland of flowers on its head. The origin of this festival is unknown. The general supposition is, that Lycurgus first instituted it to inure the youths of Lacedæmon to bear labour and fatigue, and render them insensible to pain and wounds.

3 The rest of this section is περὶ τῶν παιδικῶν ἐρώτων.

4 φιλίτια or φιλίτια, an association of friends. In this assembly, kings, magistrates, and private citizens, met to eat together in certain halls, in which a number of tables were spread, most frequently with fifteen covers each, which were called κάλλω; and hence, when any one was ejected from the rest, he was said ἀπαλλώσθαι. The guests at one table never interfered with those at another, and formed a society of friends, in which no person could be received but by the consent of all those who composed it. They reclined on hard couches of oak, leaning with their elbows on a stone or a block of wood. Black broth was served up to them, and afterwards boiled pork, which was distributed to each guest in equal portions, sometimes so small that they scarcely weighed a quarter of a mina each. They had wine, cakes, and barley-bread in plenty; and at other times fish and different kinds of game were added by way of supplement to their ordinary portion. They, who offered sacrifices, or went out to hunt, might, on their return, eat at home; but it was necessary to send their companions at the same table a part of the game or the victim. Near each cover a small piece of bread was laid to wipe their fingers. The guests were enjoined that their decorum should be accompanied with gaiety, and, with that view, a statue of the god of laughter was placed in the hall. But the pleasantries that excited mirth were to contain nothing offensive; and the too severe sally, if it escaped any one present, was never to be repeated in any other place; the oldest of the company showing the door to those who entered, reminded them that nothing they might hear was to go out there. The different classes of youth were present at these repasts without partaking of them: the youngest carried off adroitly from the table some portion which they shared with their comrades; and the others received lessons of wisdom and pleasantry. These repasts, during peace, produced union, temperance, and equality; and during war, they held forth to the citizens to flee to the succour of another, with whom he had participated in sacrifices and libations. The expense was defrayed by individuals, who were obliged to furnish every month, a certain quantity of barley-meal, wine, cheese, figs, and even money; and, by this contribution, the poorest class were in danger of being excluded from the meal in common.

dered more obedient, more modest, and more temperate, we leave others to decide.

IV. His greatest solicitude was shown towards the young men, as he considered that if they were what they should be, they would have great influence in promoting the happiness and virtue of their fellow-citizens, and the welfare of their country. And observing that, among those who were possessed of an innate desire of emulation, their singing was most deserving of being heard, and their gymnastic contests most deserving of being seen, he thought that if he could excite in young men a contest of virtue, that they would thus become possessed of the greatest manliness of spirit. How he attained this I will explain.

The Ephori choose three men come to the years of maturity, and these are called hippagretæ. Each of these chooses one hundred men, explaining why he prefers some and rejects others. They, then, who have not obtained this honourable preference, fight with those who have rejected them, and those who are chosen in their stead, and they strictly watch each other lest they should do any thing slily, which was not considered honourable.

And this contest is most agreeable to the gods, and most advantageous to the state, in which it is shown what a brave man ought to do: and they each exercise themselves apart, that they may always be most powerful, and, if it should be necessary, that they may defend the city with all their strength. It is necessary for them also to attend to good health, for they must box whenever they encounter in this contest. Every man of authority who is present may stop the contest. And if any one should disobey the person who interrupts the contest, the pædonomus leads him to the ephori, and they fine him heavily, wishing to hinder anger from prevailing so far as to check the due execution of the law.

And with regard to those who exceed the years of puberty, from whom all the higher officers of state are chosen, the other Greeks, though they deprive them of any anxiety to husband their strength, still require them to serve in the army with others; but Lycurgus enacted a law that it should be reckoned honourable for such persons to engage in hunting, unless public business prevented it, that they might be as able as the young men to endure the ~s incident to a soldier's life.

 ⁊e have now nearly explained what mode of life Lycurgus had enjoined by law for each period of life. What mode of living he adopted, I will now attempt to explain.

Lycurgus having found the Spartans, like the other Greeks, taking their meals at home, and knowing that the majority indulged in knavery at them, he caused their meals to be taken publicly, supposing that they would be thus less apt to transgress their orders.

He also ordered food to be given to them that they should neither be exposed to repletion nor want. Many things, also, beyond their apportioned quantity, are procured from the hunters; and the rich sometimes give bread in exchange for this, so that the table is never either expensive or destitute of eatables, as long as they enjoy this common meal.

Moreover, having checked the use of unnecessary drinks, which cause both body and mind to totter, he allowed every man to drink when thirsty; for in this manner he supposed that the drink would be less injurious and much more pleasant. When they lived thus together, how was it possible for any one to ruin himself or family by gluttony or drunkenness?

For in other cities, equals generally associate together,—among these there exists the least modesty; but Lycurgus, in Sparta, mixed those of different ages together, to enable the younger to be instructed by the experience of the elder.

According to the custom of the country, at these public banquets, each one relates what gallant feat he has performed to the state; so that no insolence, no drunken frolic, no foul deed or indecent language, can ever be there introduced.

Public banquets are useful for this, that the citizens are obliged to walk home, and to take care that they do not stagger through wine, knowing that they do not remain where they supped, and they must walk during the night as well as day; for no one not yet freed from military duty is allowed to proceed with a torch.

Lycurgus also having observed that, after meals, those who contended with others in labours, were well coloured, plump, and robust, and those who did not exercise themselves were puffed up, ill coloured, and feeble, turned much of his attention to this subject; but considering that when each individual exerts himself, in his own opinion he appears to have a body fit by exercise for business, he commanded that

...est should always take care on each y of exercising, that they should never in-lge so much in meat as to weaken their body r exercise.

And, in this respect, he seems to me not have been mistaken. You will rarely find en surpassing the Spartans in health or ength of body; for they are equally exer-ied in their legs, in their hands, and their ck.

In this respect also he adopted a plan differ-g from others. For in other cities each indi-dual has authority over his own children, ser-nts, and property. But Lycurgus, wishing enable the citizens to enjoy some common od, without injuring each other, enacted a w, that each individual should have equal athority over his own children and those of thers.

When any one considers that his fellow-citi-ens are fathers of the children over whom he ercises authority, he must do it in such a man-er as he would wish it done to his own; and if ny boy, at any time, should receive blows from nother, and inform his father of it, it is dis-raceful not to inflict additional blows on his ou. Thus they have confidence in each other hat nothing disgraceful will be imposed on heir children.

He enacted also, that if any one stood in eed of servants, he should use his neighbour's. He also introduced the common use of hunt-ng-dogs, so that those who require them invite heir proprietor to hunt, and if he has no lei-ure, be cheerfully surrenders them. They in ike manner use their neighbour's horses; for when one is sick and in want of a chariot, or desirous of reaching some place quickly, when he sees a horse anywhere he takes it, and hav-ing made a proper use of it, restores it.

He did not however wish that done among his people, which is customary with others. For at times persons belated by hunting stand in need of provisions, unless they have been previously prepared. He also enacted this law, that those who had fed should leave the food dressed, and those who needed it should open the seals and take whatever they stood in need of, and leave it sealed. When they thus divide with each other, even those who have little property share in all the products of the coun-try, when they require any thing.

VII. With regard to these things, Lycurgus proposed a law in Sparta different from that of the other Greeks. For in other cities all the citizens are as intent on gain as possible; one engages in farming, another in commerce, another in trade, and another is supported by the arts.

But in Sparta, Lycurgus forbade freemen to have any connection with matters of gain; whatever procures freedom to cities he enjoin-ed them to consider as their only occupation.

Where he caused every man to contribute equally to the necessaries of life, and where all eat together, how could wealth be eagerly sought after for the sake of voluptuousness? But money was not even necessary for clothes, for they are adorned not by costliness of dress but by robust constitution of bodies.

Nor was it necessary to collect money to be at expense in assisting their companions, for he made it more honourable to assist their ac-quaintances with bodily labour than money, having demonstrated that the one depended on the mind, the other on wealth.

He also absolutely forbade the procuring of money by unjust means. For first of all, he instituted such a kind of money, that if only 10 minæ were introduced into a house it could neither escape the notice of masters nor ser-vants, for it would occupy much space and would require a carriage to convey it.

Silver and gold are carefully searched after, and if found anywhere the possessor is punish-ed. What anxious desire could there then be for money, when the possession occasioned more pain than the enjoyment pleasure?

VIII. We all know how very obedient the Spartans were to their rulers and the laws. I however suppose that Lycurgus would not have attempted to settle this sound political consti-tution, before he had converted to his opinions the most powerful men in the state.

I prove it thus, that in other states the most powerful men do not wish to seem to fear ma-gistrates, but deem this unworthy of a free-man; but in Sparta the most powerful pay great respect to the magistrates, and reckon it honourable to demean themselves; and when addressed, not to walk but run to obey. For they suppose that if they lead the way in obe-dience, the rest will follow their example, which was the case.

And it is probable that these same persons assisted Lycurgus in instituting the power of the ephori, because they knew that obedience was the greatest good in a state, in an army, in a family. In proportion to the extent of the power of the magistracy, they supposed that they would inspire in the citizens, and enforce obedience.

The ephori then are enabled to amerce whom they choose, and are empowered to demand the fine instantly; they are empowered to abrogate the authority of the magistrates at times, to incarcerate, and even to institute a trial for life. And having so much authority, they do not, like other states, allow those chosen always to command during the year as they choose, but like kings and presidents in the gymnastic contests, if they perceive any one acting contrary to law, they immediately punish him.

Though there were many other excellent devices which Lycurgus used to inspire in the people a wish to obey the laws, this one seems to me to have been the best, that he did not deliver his laws to the people until he came with some of the nobles to Delphi, and questioned the god whether it would be more desirable and advantageous for Sparta to obey the laws which he had made. When the answer was received that it would on every account be preferable, he then delivered them, decreeing that it was not only against the laws of man but against those of heaven, to disobey the laws sanctioned by the oracle of Apollo.

IX. This also is deserving of admiration in Lycurgus, that he effected this in the state, that an honourable death should be reckoned preferable to a disgraceful life; and if any one examines, he will find fewer of them dying than of those who attempt to escape danger by flight.

So that it may be truly said, that a man is preserved a much longer period by bravery than by cowardice; for it is much easier, pleasanter, more capable of assisting us in difficulty, and stronger; and it is plain that glory is the attendant of bravery, for all men wish to assist the brave.

By what contrivances he attained this object should not be overlooked. His laws wisely entailed happiness on the brave, misery on cowards.

For in other states when any one acts cowardly, he is merely branded with the name of coward; he goes to the same market with the brave man, and sits or exercises himself if he chooses: but at Lacedæmon every one would be ashamed to admit the coward into the same tent, or exercise himself with him in wrestling.

Frequently also such a person, when the two parties who play at ball are divided, has no place assigned for him, and at dances he is expelled into the most dishonourable places; on the road too he must give place to others, and at public meetings he must even rise to his juniors. He must also support his female relations at home, apart from the public games, and they must remain without husbands, in the city: the coward was not allowed to take a wife, and yet a fine was imposed for not having one. He is not allowed to walk about anointed, nor to imitate those whose character is irreproachable, unless he wishes to receive blows from his betters.

When such disgrace was inflicted upon cowards, it cannot be reckoned wonderful that death should be preferred by them, to a life so dishonourable and infamous.

X. Lycurgus also seems to me to have wisely devised a plan for encouraging the practice of virtue throughout life till old age. For to his other institutions he added the making the senate consist entirely of old men distinguished for virtue, and brought it about that honour and virtue were not neglected even in old age.

It is also deserving of admiration, that he gave great authority to the old age of the brave; for having appointed the old men umpires in the contest for superiority of intellect, he rendered their old age more honourable than the strength of those in full bloom.

This contest is deservedly celebrated with highest exertion by men. Gymnastic contests are honourable, but they refer to the body,—but the contest regarding the dignity of an old man, exhibits the deciding on brave souls. In proportion as the soul is better than the body, so the contest of superiority of mind deserves to be more zealously aimed at than that of the body.

Does not this, moreover, deserve distinguished admiration in Lycurgus? When he perceived that those who did not wish to attend to virtue were not able to enlarge their country, he obliged all men publicly in Sparta to practise all the virtues. For as private men excel each other in virtue, those who practise it from those who neglect it, so also Sparta is naturally superior to all states in virtue, as being the only one which enjoins honour and virtue.

Is not this then also deserving of commendation, that when other states punish one who

. had committed an injury upon another, they inflicted not less punishment on him who showed himself regardless of excelling in virtue.

He considered, it appears, that those who made others slaves, or took any plunder, or stole any thing, only injured the individual sufferers, but that by cowards and effeminate men, whole republics had been overturned. So that in my opinion he deservedly imposed heaviest punishments on them.

And he rendered the necessity most inviolable of practising every political virtue. For to all those who performed what was enjoined by law, he gave an equal participation in the benefits of the state, and he took no account either of the weakness of their bodies, or slenderness of their means. If any one through indolence should neglect to toil through what was enjoined by law, he pointed him out as one no longer deserving to be reckoned among the equal-honoured.

But it is very plain that these laws are very ancient; for Lycurgus is said to have lived in the times of the Heraclidæ, and though they are so old they are still reckoned the most recent with other nations, for what is most wonderful, all men praise such institutions, though no state wishes to imitate them.

XI. The advantages of his institutions already enumerated were common both to peace and war,—but we may also explain the peculiar advantages of his plans in military affairs.

He first caused the ephori to announce beforehand to the cavalry, the heavy-armed, and then to the artizans, the years in which they must join the army, that the Lacedæmonians may have in the army abundance of all those things which are necessary in a city; and the instruments which the army require for common use, whatever be the purpose for which they are intended, are commanded to be supplied partly on waggons, partly on beasts of burden; and thus their deficiencies are less likely to escape notice.

In war he enacted that they should wear a purple robe and carry a brazen shield, as he supposed this to have least in common with the female robe, and fittest for war, for it is soonest made splendid and is with difficulty soiled. He also allowed those above the age of youths to wear their hair long, as he supposed them thus to appear taller, genteeler, and sterner.

When they were thus arrayed, he divided them into six regiments of cavalry and heavy-armed. Each of these political regiments[1] has one general officer, four colonels, eight captains, and sixteen subalterns. These regiments are put in battle array by word of command, sometimes each enomotia making only one file, sometimes three files, sometimes six.

In supposing the Lacedæmonian arrangement in arms to be most intricate, the majority of mankind have conceived what is most opposite to fact. For in the Lacedæmonian arrangement in arms there are commanders in the front ranks, and each line has within itself every thing necessary for war.

It is so easy to understand this arrangement, that no one acquainted with military movements can mistake it; for some are enjoined to lead, others to follow. The marching with one of the wings in front is pointed out by the orders of the subaltern, as if by a herald, by which the phalanxes become both narrower and closer; there cannot be the slightest difficulty in understanding this circumstance.

But that the body thus arranged should be able to fight with the enemy when thrown into confusion, is not so easily understood; except by those educated under the laws of Lycurgus.

The Lacedæmonians make these things very easy which seem very difficult to men in arms. For when they march by the wing, the enomotia follows in the rear; and if, in such a position, the enemy's phalanx should appear in front, orders are given to the enomotarch to to arrange his men with front to the left; and in like manner throughout the whole, until the phalanx stands opposite. But if, when in this position, the enemy appear in the rear, each

---

1 πολιτικῶν μερῶν. Thucydides, v. 68. mentions the same division of the Lacedæmonian army. What number of soldiers was contained in each *mora* is uncertain; some make them five, some seven, and others nine hundred; but at the first formation of the commonwealth, they seem not to have exceeded four hundred, who were all foot-men. 'Ενωμοτία was the half of πεντηκοστύς; contained originally twenty-five men, and derived its name from the soldiers in it, being bound by a solemn oath upon a sacrifice to be faithful and loyal to their country. In the course of time the numbers of the ενωμοτίαι were changed and increased, though the ancient name still remained, so that the ενωμοτία consisted of upwards of fifty, and πεντηκοστύς of upwards of one hundred men. From a calculation made on a passage of Thucydides, the ενωμοτία is proved to consist of thirty-two men, which makes up for the whole regiment the number of 512.

rank countermarches[1] until the bravest are opposed to the enemy.

But when the commander is on the left, even then they are not reckoned to be in a worse condition, and they are even sometimes in a better. For if any person should attempt to

1 Ἐξιλίττεται. Ἐξιλιγμὸς, ἰξιλισμὸς, or ἰξίλιξις, was a countermarch, by which every soldier, one marching after another, changed the front for the rear, or one flank for another; whence there were two sorts of countermarches, κατὰ λόχους, and κατὰ ζυγὰ, one by files, the other by ranks.

1 Ἐξιλιγμὸς Μακεδὼν κατὰ λόχους, was as follows: first, the leaders of the files having turned to the right or left, the next rank passed through by them on the same hand, and, occupying the distant spaces, placed themselves behind the leaders of their files, and turned their faces the same way. In like manner the third and fourth ranks, and all the rest, till the bringers-up were last, and had turned about their faces, and again occupied the rear. By this motion the army was removed into the ground before the front, and the faces of the soldiers were turned backward. It appeared so like a retreat, that Philip of Macedon, instead of it, used the following motion. — 2 Ἐξιλιγμὸς Λάκων κατὰ λόχους, was contrary to the last: this motion occupied the ground behind the phalanx, and the soldiers' faces turned the contrary way; it was made from front to rear. This evolution was performed in two ways: one was, when those in the rear first turned about their faces, the next rank also turned theirs and began the countermarch, every man placing himself directly before his bringer-up; the third did the same, and the rest, till the rank of file-leaders was first. The other method was, when the leaders of the files began the countermarch, every one in their files followed them in order: by this means they were brought nearer to the enemy, and represented a charge.—3 Ἐξιλιγμὸς Περσικὸς, or Κρητικὸς, κατὰ λόχους, sometimes termed χορίως, because managed like the Grecian chori, which being ordered into files and ranks, like soldiers in battle-array, and moving forward toward the brink of the stage, when they could pass no farther, retired, one through the ranks of another; the whole chorus keeping all the time the same ground of which they were before possessed.

Ἐξιλιγμὸς κατὰ ζυγὰ, countermarch by rank, was contrary to the countermarch by file: in the counter-march by file, the motion was in the depth of the battalia, the front moving towards the rear, or the rear towards the front, and succeeding into each other's place. In this, the motion was in length of the battalia flankwise, the wing either marching into the midst, or quite through to the opposite wing. In doing this, the soldiers who were last in the flank of the wing, moved first to the contrary wing, the rest following in their order. It was also performed three ways.

1 The Macedonian countermarch began its motion at the corner of the wing nearest the enemy, and removing to the ground on the side of the contrary wing, resembled a flight ..2 The Lacedæmonian counter-march, beginning its motion in the wing farthest distant from the enemy, seized the ground nearest to them, by which an attack was represented.—3 The Chorean counter-march maintained its own ground, only removing one wing into the place of the other.

surround them, he would fall in, not with unarmed, but heavy-armed men. But if at any time it may seem advantageous for some purpose, that the leader should stand on the right wing, turning the troop upon the wing, they deploy the phalanx until the general is on the right and the rear is on the left.

But if again from the right a body of the enemy should appear marching, each cohort makes a central movement of half-turning like a galley, whose prow is wished to be presented to the enemy, and then the rear company comes to the right. And if again the enemy should attempt the left, they do not allow this, but drive them off, or turn the opposing companies to the enemy, and thus again the rear company is placed on the left.

XII. I will also explain how Lycurgus enacted that their camps should be pitched. Because the angles of a quadrangle were useless, the camp was pitched in a circle, unless they were protected by a mountain, or had a wall or river on their rear.

He instituted daily watches which looked inwards to the camp: these are placed, not for the sake of the enemy, but their friends; and cavalry watch the enemy from places where they can see farthest in advance.

But if any one should advance during the night beyond the phalanx, he decreed that he should be watched by the Scyrites: but now this is done by strangers, provided some of them be present.

It ought to be well understood, that they always go about with their spears, and for the same reason, they prevent their slaves from joining the army. And it is not to be wondered at, that those going out for necessary purposes, do not retire so far from each other, or the army, as to excite uneasiness in each other; this is done for self-preservation.

They frequently change their camp, that they may injure their enemy, and assist their friends. And it is enjoined by law, that all Lacedæmonians should exercise themselves wherever they are engaged in war; which adds greatly to their magnanimity and ingenuousness. Their exercises in walking and running take place in front of their own regiment, and no one can proceed beyond it.

And after the exercises the first polemarc issues orders for them to sit down; this serves all the purposes of a review: after this they breakfast, and immediately the advanced centinel is relieved : after that again, conversation and recreation before the evening exercises.

Immediately afterwards, orders are given to sup, and when they have sung to the gods, to whom they have previously sacrificed, they retire to rest in their armour.

No person need wonder that I write so much on this subject, as nothing which requires diligence seems to have been overlooked by the Lacedemonians in warlike matters.

XIII. I will also explain the power and honour which Lycurgus decreed should be given to the king when with the army. First, then, the state supports a king and attendants in the camp: the polemarchs live in the same tent with him, that being always present they may be better enabled to hold a common council when necessary. Other three men, also, of the alike-honoured, live in the same tent with him. These attend to all the necessaries of life, that their minds may not be distracted by minor considerations,from attending to warlike affairs.

I will now explain how the king moves forward to battle with the army. He sacrifices first at home to Jupiter the leader, and the other gods ; and when he has thus sacrificed, the fire-bearing attendant taking fire from the altar, leads the way to the borders of the country: the king then again sacrifices to Jupiter and Minerva.

When they have sacrificed to both these gods, then he passes the boundaries of the country. Fire from these sacrifices leads the way, never to be extinguished ; all kinds of victims are then sacrificed. Whenever he sacrifices he begins this work at daybreak, wishing to anticipate the good-will of the god.

There are present at the sacrifice, the polemarch, lochagi, pentecosteres, commanders of mercenary troops, the commanders of baggage troops, and any one of the generals from the city who chooses.

Two of the ephori are also present, who do not interfere in the conducting of business, unless they are summoned by the king ; but looking on what each did, they naturally render them more modest. When the sacred rites are finished, the king, having called them all forward, prescribes what is to be done ; so that contemplating these things, you would suppose that other nations enter into military affairs with precipitation, but that the Lacedæmonians alone in reality were the artists of war.

But when the king leads, if no enemy appears, no one proceeds before him except the Sciritæ and the cavalry, who march in advance to reconnoitre, and if at any time they suppose a battle likely to ensue, the king takes the troop of the first regiment and leads it, turning aside to the right, until he is in the middle between the two moræ and the two polemarchias.

Whatever instructions in addition to these must be given, are arranged by the eldest of those connected with the public table; and these are the men who live in the same tent with the alike-honoured, the prophets, physicians, musicians, officers of the army, and the volunteers present. So that of the things necessary to be done none is neglected ; for every thing is previously considered.

Lycurgus, in my opinion contrived what was very advantageous with respect to the contest on arms. For when in sight of the enemy the goat is sacrificed, the law is, that all the musicians present should play, and that none of the Lacedæmonians should be uncovered with garlands; and they are enjoined before-hand to clean their arms. The youth are allowed to march to battle combed, and to be sprightly and graceful. . . . And that it may be well done, the polemarch must take care.

The king decides on the proper season and place for pitching the camp. He possesses also the right of dismissing ambassadors whether friendly or hostile. He also commences whatever they wish done.

When any person comes desiring justice, the king refers him to the Hellanodicæ, and if money, to the quæstor, and if bringing in booty, to the dealer in booty. When they do thus no other business is left in battle for the king, than to be priest in what regards the gods and general in what regards men.

XIV. Should the question be asked, do the laws of Lycurgus at present seem to remain unchanged ? to this I certainly would not answer in the affirmative.

For I know that the Lacedæmonians formerly preferred to associate together, in possession of moderate means, than to govern cities and be corrupted by adulation.

And formerly, I know that they were afraid to appear possessed of gold ; but I know some who are at present vain and ostentatious of their possessions.

I know, too, that formerly on this account strangers were expelled, and the citizens were not allowed to reside abroad, lest their morals should be corrupted by strangers. But now I know that they prove the first to exert themselves, that they may never cease to govern a foreign city.

There was a time, too, when they were sedulous to make themselves worthy of governing; but now they study more to obtain rule than deserve it.

The Greeks, formerly, resorted to Lacedæmon, and requested of them to take the lead against those who did an injury—but now, many of the Greeks exhort each other to hinder them from again taking the lead in their affairs.

It is by no means wonderful, that such blame should be attached to them, as they show themselves neither obedient to the deity, nor to the laws of Lycurgus.

XV. I wish also to explain what agreements Lycurgus made between the king and the city; for he is the only magistrate, whose office remains such as it was originally instituted: the other political situations have been changed, and are even now changing.

For he enacted that the king should offer without the city, all the public sacrifices, as he was descended from the deity, and be commander wherever the state should send the army.

He granted also, that he should receive a share of the sacrifices, and be possessed of so much good land in many of the neighbouring cities, as never to be in want of moderate means, and never be possessed of excessive wealth.

He assigned a public tent for the kings, that even they should live in tents, and allowed them a double share at supper, not that they might consume that portion; but that they might have it in their power to honour any one they pleased.

He granted also, that each of them should choose two companions, who were called Pythii. He granted him also, to receive a pig from every litter, that he might never be in want of victims, when it was necessary to consult the gods on any matter. And near his house a pool of water presents abundance: that this is useful for many purposes, those who do not possess one know best. All rise up from their seats to the king, but the ephori do not rise from their chairs of office.

They bind each other by oaths every month, the ephori for the city, and the king for himself. The king's oath is, that he will govern according to the existing laws of the city: the city's oath, that if he does not violate his oath, they will preserve his kingdom unshaken and firm.

And these are the honours which are paid to the king in his native land when living: they do not far exceed those paid to a private individual; for he did not wish to infuse a tyrannical spirit in the kings, nor to excite among the citizens an envy of their power.

But honours are paid to the king when dead: by this, the laws of Lycurgus wish to show, that they have honoured the kings of the Lacedæmonians, not as men, but as heroes.

ON

HORSEMANSHIP.

HORSEMANSHIP.

As it has fallen to our lot, from long practice, to have become experienced in horsemanship, we wish to point out to our younger friends how we think they can use their horses most properly. Simon has indeed written a treatise on horsemanship; he also erected a brazen horse at the temple of Ceres at Athens, and carved on the pedestal his own deeds. We will not expunge from our own writings whatever we find in accordance with his views, but we will give them with much more pleasure, to our friends, reckoning them more deserving of credit, inasmuch as he, who was a horseman, corresponded in opinion with us. Whatever he has omitted, we will attempt to explain.

We will first describe how a man may be least deceived in purchasing a horse. It is evident that we ought to prove the body of the untamed foal, for the horse not yet mounted cannot exhibit very distinct proofs of his spirit.

And, of his body, we assert that the feet should first be examined. For as a house would be useless which had the upper parts beautiful, without having the necessary foundation laid; so also a war-steed would be useless, though every other part of the body were good, if the feet were badly shaped, for none of his advantages could be brought into action.

When we wish to prove the feet, the hoofs must first be examined. Soundness of feet is much influenced by the thickness or thinness of the hoofs. This also must not be lost sight of, whether the hoofs are high before and behind, or low; for the high ones have the hollow of the sole removed from the ground; but the low walk equally on the strongest and softest part of the foot, like in-kneed men. Simon excellently remarks, that good feet are known by the sound; the hollow hoof struck on the ground sounds like a cymbal.

Having begun with the feet we will ascend gradually to the rest of the body. It is necessary then that the upper part of the hoofs and the lower bones of the fetlock should not be too erect, like a goat's; for being very elastic, it fatigues the rider, and such legs are more easily inflamed: nor ought the bones to be too low, for the fetlocks would become hairless and ulcerated, whether the horse rode over clods or stones.

The bones of the leg ought to be thick, for these are the supports of the body; they should not however be covered with fat flesh or large veins. For when driven through rough roads, these must necessarily be filled with blood, hard tumours arise, the legs become fat, and the skin separates. And when the skin becomes loose, the smaller bone of the leg frequently separates, and renders the horse lame.

Moreover, if the foal, when walking, bends his knees pliantly, you may reckon it probable that when ridden he will have pliant legs. For they all in the course of time bend their knees much more pliantly. Flexible knees are justly held in repute; inasmuch as they render the horse less liable to stumble and shake the rider, than stiff legs.

When the arms are fat, horses appear stronger and more elegant, as is the case in the human form. And when the chest is wide, it contributes both to his beauty, to his strength, and bears the legs more gracefully; not close one to the other, but considerably separated. Moreover, from the chest his neck should not fall forward like boar's, but, like a cock's. should rise erect to the head, and be slender at the arch. The head should be bony, and have a small jaw-bone; thus his neck will be before the rider, and his eye see what is before his feet.

A horse thus shaped would be less able to

use violence, even though very spirited; for horses attempt to do injury, not by arching the neck, but by extending the head forward.

It is also necessary to consider, whether the inside of both their jaws be tender or hard, or if only one; for those which have dissimilar jaws are generally unmanageable. When the eyes are prominent, the horse seems more vigilant, and can see much farther than when they are sunk in the socket.

Wide nostrils are also much more convenient for breathing; and render the appearance of the horse more terrible; for when one horse is enraged at another, or is excited in riding, he distends his nostrils exceedingly.

When the head is large at the top, and the ears small, the horse appears much more elegant. When the point of the shoulder is high, the rider has a safer seat, and adheres more closely to the shoulders. The loins, when double, are much more easily sitten upon, than when single, and much more pleasant to the eye.

When the sides are deep, and somewhat protuberant at the belly, the horse is generally more easily ridden; and stronger, and more capable of enjoying food. In proportion as the loins are broader and shorter, so much easier is it for the horse to raise the fore-part of the body and bring forward the hinder; and the belly thus appears smaller, which when large deforms the horse, weakens it, and renders it less capable of carrying burdens.

It is necessary also that the haunches should be broad and fleshy, to correspond with the sides and breast: when all these parts are solid, it renders the horse lighter for the race, and much fleeter.

Moreover, if the hocks be separated by a broad line, then the hind legs in walking will be separated by a proper space, and be brought up so as not to touch each other: when this is the case a great addition is made to the boldness and strength of his look, both in walking and riding. This may be proved from men, for when they wish to raise anything from the earth, they attempt to do so by standing astride rather than with legs close.

A horse, besides, should not have large testicles; this cannot be observed in the foal. With regard to the pastern, the shank bones, the fetlocks, and hoofs of the hind legs, the same may be said as of the fore.

I now explain how a man may run the least risk of being deceived, when conjecturing the future height of a horse. The young horse which, when foaled, has the shank-bones longest, invariably turns out the largest. For as time advances, the shank-bones of all quadrupeds increase but little; but that the rest of the body may be symmetrical, it increases in proportion with them.

Persons who thus prove the form of a foal, seems, in my opinion, most likely to obtain a good-footed, strong, well-fleshed, graceful, and large-sized horse. Though some, when growing, change much, still, in our choice of them, we may confidently follow the above rule; for there are far more deformed foals which turn out beautiful horses, than beautiful foals which prove deformed horses.

II. It seems now necessary to explain how young horses should be trained. Those men in cities are enjoined to ride, who are best enabled from their wealth, and who partake in the honours of the state. It is much better that a young man should be studious of firm habits of body and of horsemanship; or if already skilled in riding, of exercising himself, than be a breaker of horses; and that an old man should be engaged with his family, his friends, political and military affairs, than be engaged in training horses.

Whoever is acquainted with the method of rearing horses, as I am, will give them out to be trained. It is necessary, however, before giving them out, to have a written agreement regarding the manner in which you wish them trained, as is done when a boy is engaged to learn any art; for that will show the breaker what he ought to attend to, in order to receive his reward.

Care must be taken, that when the breaker receives the foal, he be gentle, tractable, and fond of men. For he is generally rendered so at home by the groom, if the foal is made to understand that hunger, thirst, and irritation, are procured by solitude; and that meat, drink, and freedom from irritation, are procured by men. When these things take place, foals not only love, but long for men.

It is necessary also to touch those parts which, when touched, give greatest pleasure to the horse; and these are the hairiest, and those parts in which, when he feels any pain, he cannot relieve himself.

The groom should be enjoined to lead him through a crowd, and cause him to approach all kinds of sights and sounds. Whichever of these the foal may dread, it is necessary to teach him not by harshness, but gentleness, that they are not dangerous. Regarding the training of horses, it seems to me sufficient, to tell the unskilled to follow the above instructions.

III. We will now suggest a few things which ought to be attended to, by the purchaser of a riding horse, if he wishes to avoid being cheated in the bargain. First, then, let it not escape his notice what his age is; for if he has not the foal-teeth, he can neither give us pleasure with anticipated exertion, nor can he be easily disposed of again.

When his youth is manifest, it is necessary again to observe narrowly how he receives the bit in his mouth, and the bridle about his ears; there is least chance of this escaping notice, if the bridle be put on and off before the purchaser.

Then we must also observe, how he receives the rider on his back. For many horses are with difficulty approached, as they know, if they allow it, they will be obliged to labour.

This must also be considered, if when mounted he desires to withdraw from other horses, or if when they chance to be near, he advances to them without the will of his rider. There are some, who on account of bad training, fly homewards from the race ground.[1]

Fetlock riding, as it is called, shows the intractable horse, and much more the sudden change of the riding. For many do not attempt to run against the will of their rider, unless the hard jaw which does not feel the force of the bit, and the horse's speed directed homewards, coincide. It is necessary also to know, if when forced to full speed he is drawn up quickly, and if he wishes to be turned.

It is good also not to be inexperienced, if the horse, when roused with blows, is equally willing to obey as formerly. For a disobedient servant and army, are equally useless: but a disobedient horse is not only useless, but frequently acts traitorously.

When we wish to purchase a war-steed, we must try him in all those things of which experience are required in war: these are, to leap across ditches, scale walls, spring up ascents,

and dash down descents, and to be experienced in charging on slopes, declivities, and transverse ways. For all these things prove the strength of his spirit, and health of his body. The horse, however, which does not excel in these things, is not to be rejected. For many fail, not for want of ability, but want of experience in these things: but if instructed, accustomed, and trained, they would excel in them, if otherwise healthy and not vicious.

We must also guard against naturally timid horses. For the excessively timorous, do not allow the enemy to be injured, and they frequently deceive their rider, and bring him into the greatest difficulties.

It is necessary also to learn if the horse is fierce, either towards other horses, or towards men, and if sullen and peevish; for all these things become difficulties to the purchaser.

The refusing to be reined and mounted, and other tricks, may be much more easily learned, if when the horse has already been toiled, he should attempt again to do the same things as before he began to ride. Such as have toiled, and are willing again to undergo labour, show sufficient proofs of a strong spirit.

In short, that horse which has good feet, is gentle, fleet enough, is willing and able to endure labour, and is very obedient, is most likely to occasion least uneasiness, and be the author of most safety to his rider in warfare. But those which require much driving on account of laziness, or much coaxing and care, on account of being high mettled, occasion much employment to the rider, and despondence in dangers.

IV. When a man has purchased a horse which he admires, and brings him home, it is proper that the stall should be in a part of the house where the master could oftenest see the horse: and it is good, that the stable should be so situated, that it would be as difficult to steal provisions out of the manger, as out of the master's cellar. He who is negligent of this, seems to me to be heedless of his own interest; for it is evident, that in dangers the master entrusts his body to his horse.

A secure stable is not only good for preventing the stealing of the horse's provender, but also, because it shows when he disdains his food, and throws it out of the stall. When this is perceived, it is known that the body through abundance of blood, requires curing, or having toiled hard needs repose, or broken

---

1 Riding in a circle when tied by a rope to the centre.

windedness, or some other malady is creeping upon him. It is with a horse as with a man, diseases are all much more easily cured at the beginning, than when they have become inveterate, and errors have been committed in attempting their cure.

And as attention must be paid to a horse's provisions and exercises, that the body may be strong, so also his feet must be exercised. Moist and smooth stalls injure hoofs which are naturally good. It is also necessary, that they be not moist, be sloping, and have sewers: and not to be smooth, to have large stones against each other, almost equal in size to their hoofs; for such stalls at the same time consolidate the hoofs of those standing on them.

After that, the horse must be led by the groom where he may be rubbed: he must be untied after breakfast from the manger, that he may go with greater pleasure to the evening meal. The outside of the stall should be as good as possible, and would strengthen the feet, if there were strewed here and there four or five cart loads of tapering stones, measuring a hand breadth, and about a mina in weight, encompassed with iron braces, that they may not be scattered. When he stands on these, he always goes some part of the day, as if on a stony road.

It is necessary also, when taken out to be rubbed or driven by the spur, that he should use his hoofs as when he walks. Stones thus strewn, strengthen the hollow of the horse's hoof. It is necessary to be careful about the strength of their hoofs, and the softness of their mouths. For the same things soften a man's flesh and a horse's mouth.

V. It seems to me to be the duty of a horseman, to have his groom instructed in what is necessary to be done about a horse. And first, he ought to know never to make the knot of the manger headstall where the reins round the head are put: for the horse frequently moves his head in the manger, and if the headstall hurts his ears, it frequently occasions ulcers; and when these are ulcered, it is a necessary consequence, that the horse is more difficult to rein and to rub.

It is good also to enjoin the groom to carry out to one place, every day, the dung and straw from under the horse. When he does this, he will remove it with greatest ease, and at the same time do a benefit to the horse.

The groom should also be accustomed to put the breaking bridle upon the horse, when he leads him out for rubbing or for weltering. It is necessary that he should be always cavessoned when led out unbridled. For the cavesson does not prevent his breathing, and does not allow him to bite; and when thrown around the horse, prevents him from laying snares for other horses.

The horse should be bound by suspending the reins from the upper part of the head. For whatever troublesome object affects his face, he instinctively attempts to remove it by throwing up his head. When thus bound, it rather loosens the halter than draws it tight.

He who uses the currycomb should commence with the head and mane; for it would be vain to clean the lower parts, when the upper are not yet cleaned. And then the hair of the rest of the body should be raised with all the instruments of cleaning, to brush off the dust, not according to the grain of the hair. The hairs on the spine of the back should not be touched by any instrument, but be merely rubbed by the hands, and softly touched in the manner in which they lie naturally, and the seat on the horse's back would thus be least injured.

The head ought to be washed by water, for being bony, if it were cleaned with iron or wood, it would pain the horse. The forelock also should be moistened; for when these hairs are long, they do not hinder the horse from seeing, and they dash away from his eyes whatever gives pain. It is natural enough to suppose that the gods gave these locks to the horse instead of large ears, which they have given to asses and mules to protect their eyes from injury.

It is proper also to wash the tail and mane, as the hair should be caused to grow, that on the tail, that the horse extending it at its full length, may switch off whatever pains him, and that on the main, that the mounter may have the most abundant quantity to take in his grasp. The mane, forelock, and tail are given by the gods as an ornament. In proof of this, those horses kept for breeding, do not allow asses to mount them as long as they have long hair: wherefore, all those who take the charge of connecting mares with asses, cut off their hair that they may copulate.

Moreover, we exempt the legs from washing; for it is of no advantage, and a daily washing injures the hoofs. It is necessary also to be moderate in washing the parts under the belly; for it pains the horse excessively, and the cleaner these parts are, they are the more apt to collect what occasions pain under the belly.

And even though great pains be spent upon them, the horse is no sooner led out, than he is immediately as dirty as ever. These parts must therefore be let alone, as rubbing the legs with the hands is sufficient.

VI. We will show also this, how a person with least injury to himself, and most advantage to the horse, can rub him down; for if he cleans him looking the same way as the horse, there is danger that he should be struck in the face with the knee or hoof.

But if he looks the contrary way to the horse, and to the outer part of the leg when he cleans, and comes gradually down from the shoulder blade to the hoofs, thus he can suffer no injury, and will be enabled to cure the hollow of the horse's hoof, by opening up the hoof. The hind legs must be cleaned in a similar manner.

The person engaged about the horse should know, that these and all other things which must be done, ought to be done by approaching the horse neither in front nor rear; for if the horse attempts to injure by either of these ways, he is superior to the man. But whoever approaches laterally, does so with least injury to himself, and he can injure the horse materially.

When it is necessary to lead a horse, I do not commend, that the leader should go before the horse; because the leader cannot be upon his guard, and the horse has thus the power of doing what he pleases.

We reprehend also the allowing the horse to precede the groom with a long halter, because the horse can work mischief on whichever side he chooses; he may also turn back and rush against his leader.

How could horses when in crowds be kept separate when thus led? But the horse accustomed to be led by the side, can do least injury either to horses or men, and would be most excellently prepared for his rider, if it should at any time be necessary to mount with speed.

And that the groom should put on the reins correctly, he should approach the horse on the left side, and then throwing the reins upon his head, let him place them upon the point of the shoulder, seize the headstall in his right hand, and bring forward the bit in his left.

And if he does not receive it, then the throat band of the bridle must be put on; and if he does not open his mouth, the bridle must be held near the teeth, and the middle finger of the left hand inserted within the horse's jaw. Many horses when this is done open their mouth. And if he does not receive it then, let the lip be pressed to the eye-tooth: there are very few which do not receive it when they suffer this.

The groom must also be instructed in the following points. First, never to lead the horse by the reins, for this renders one side of the mouth harder than the other. He must also keep the reins as much as possible apart from the jaws. For when it is brought too close, it renders the mouth callous and consequently insensible; when, however, the bit hangs too far out of the mouth, it enables the horse to hold the bit in his teeth and refuse obedience to his rider.

The groom must also pay the closest attention to this, if his exertions are anywhere necessary; for it is a matter of so much consequence that the horse should be willing to take the bridle, that the one which does not receive it is altogether useless.

But if the horse is bridled not only when about to labour, but also when led to be fed, and when led from riding into the house, it would not be wonderful if he should seize the bridle of his own accord when stretched out to him.

It is proper also that the groom should understand the Persian mode of assisting in mounting,[1] that the master himself, if he should be at any time sick, or become advanced in years, should have at hand a person who can so assist him, and enable him to gratify another who wishes that assistance.

This precept and practise is best on treating a horse, never to ill use him through anger. For anger frequently excites to such rash and inconsiderate deeds, that they must be followed by repentance.

When a horse sees any thing suspicious, and does not wish to approach it, he should be made to see that there is nothing fearful in it, more especially a high mettled horse: but if that cannot be done, the horseman himself must touch the object exciting terror, and lead the horse gently to it.

---

1 See note, p. 343.

Those who drive horses forward with blows, inspire them with greater terror. For they suppose that, when they suffer any injury in such a situation, the suspected object is the cause of it.

When the groom presents the horse to the rider, we would recommend that he should be acquainted with the manner of causing the horse to bend down, to enable the rider to mount easily. We are of opinion, however, that the rider should exercise himself in mounting, even when the horse does not assist him. For sometimes a different horse falls in our way, and sometimes the same horse acts in a manner different from that to which he is accustomed.

VII. When a horse has been received for the purpose of being mounted, we will explain what the horseman should do, to be most advantageous to himself and the horse in riding. He should first hold the reins easily turning in his left hand, and fitted to the under part of the bridle or the curb, and so loose as not to draw back the horse, whether he mounts by seizing hold of the mane near the ears, or jumps on horseback with the assistance of his spear. And with his right hand let him seize the reins near the point of the shoulder along with the mane, so that he may not in any manner, when mounting, draw the horse's mouth with the bridle.

When he has prepared himself for the ascent, let him support his body with his left hand, and stretching forth his right hand, let him leap on horseback, and when he mounts thus, he will not present an uncomely spectacle from behind. This should be done with the leg bent, and without touching the horse's backbone with the knee, but by throwing the leg over to the horse's right side. And when he has thrown his leg across, he should then take his seat on the horse's back.

But if the horseman should happen to lead the horse with his left hand, and have his spear in the right, it seems to us proper, that he should exercise himself in mounting on the right side. This can be learned in no other manner, than merely doing with the left side, what he otherwise did with the right, and with the right what he did with the left.

For this reason we commend the latter mode of mounting, because as soon as the rider is on horseback, he is prepared for every event, if it should be necessary suddenly to encounter the enemy.

As soon as he is mounted, whether on the horse's bare back or on a saddle, we do not approve of the same bearing a man has in a carriage, but that an upright posture be observed with the legs apart. His thighs will thus have a firmer hold of the horse, and being erect, he will be enabled when necessary, to hurl the javelin or strike a blow from horseback much more vigorously.

The shank bone and foot should be pliant and loose at the joint under the knee; for when the leg is rigid, it is apt to be broken when struck against any thing. When the leg is moist at the joint, if any thing should befall it, it would yield, and not dislocate the thigh.

The horseman should by exercise accustom himself to keep the parts of his body above the thigh bone as agile as possible. He will thus be better fitted for labour, and if any person should drag or push him, he would be less likely to tumble.

When he has mounted, he should first train the horse to stand still till he has put his mantle in order, when necessary, and adjusted the reins, and taken the most convenient grasp of his spear. Let him then hold his left arm by his side, which attitude is most graceful in the rider, and gives greatest power to the hand.

We commend those reins which are equal in length, not weak, nor slippery, nor thick, that the spear may be held in the same hand when necessary.

When the horse receives the signal to advance, he should be made to commence slowly, as this causes least alarm. If the horse stoops somewhat, let the reins be managed higher up in the hands, but if he walk with his head erect, they must be held lower down. The carriage of the horse will be thus more graceful.

Besides, when he drives in his natural course and pace, he relaxes the body with greatest ease, and advances with greatest pleasure when the rod is held over the head to point out the way. As it is the most approved practice to begin with the left feet, this would be best done, if, when the horse is running on the right after being mounted, a signal should be given with the rod.

For when he is about to lift the left side, he

will commence the gallop with it ; and when he turns to the left, he could then commence the inclination. For a horse is accustomed when turned to the right, to commence with the right, and when turned to the left, with the left.

We commend that riding which is directed straight forwards, for it accustoms the horse to be turned by both jaws. It is good also to change the course of the horse, that both jaws may be made equal by both modes of riding.

We commend the oblong riding in preference to the circular: as the horse will thus turn with greater ease, being satisfied with the straight line, and he will thus be exercised both in running in a straight line, and in turning suddenly.

In these turns, the reins must be held in. For it is not easy or safe for the horse to turn speedily in a small compass, more especially if the ground be rugged or slippery.

When the reins are held in, the horse must not by any means be turned sideways by the reins, and the rider himself must not sit obliquely; for he ought to be well aware, that the slightest impulse in that situation, will be sufficient to overthrow both himself and the horse.

When the horse after having turned, has a straight forward course, then he must be spurred to full speed; for it is plain, that in warfare, there must be sudden turns either for pursuit or retreat: it is proper therefore, to train the horse to exert his utmost speed after having turned.

When the horse seems to have been sufficiently exercised, it will be proper to spur him suddenly after he has rested, to full gallop, both away from other horses, and directly against them; and after full speed to halt as near them as possible, and after having stood, he should be turned, and driven forward again. For it is evident that occasions will occur in which both these modes will be necessary.

When it is time to dismount, this ought not to be done among other horses, nor near an assembly of men, nor beyond the race ground, but in whatever place the horse is obliged to labour, there he ought to enjoy ease.

VIII. As occasions will occur in which it will be necessary for the horse to run over declivous, mountainous, and transverse roads, and also to leap across, jump out, and rush down; he ought to instruct and train both himself and his horse completely in these mat-

ters, and they will thus prove most salutary and advantageous to each other.

It may be supposed that we are now repeating what we have already explained—this is not the case.—When a man purchased a horse, we exhorted him to prove if the horse could do these things: but now we insist upon the necessity of instructing the horse in these matters, and explain how it may be done.

He who has got a horse completely unacquainted with leaping ditches, should slacken the halter, and leap over first, and then draw the reins tight to urge him to leap.

And if he is unwilling, let some person take a whip or rod and apply it lustily; he will then not only leap over the proper space, but much more than necessary. There will be no occasion afterwards to strike him; for if he only observes any one approaching behind him, he will take the leap.

When he has been thus accustomed to leap, let him be gradually induced to leap when mounted, first over small ditches, and then gradually over broader. When he is about to leap, let him be urged forward with the spur. He should be treated in the same manner when to leap up and down; for when the horse's whole body assists in the leap, both horse and rider are much safer than when the hinder parts fag, either in leaping across a ditch, springing up, or dashing down a declivity.

In training a horse to mount declivities, he must first be tried on soft ground : and finally, when accustomed to this, he will run with greater pleasure on acclivities, than declivities. Those who are afraid lest the horse's shoulder should be dislocated by driving up steep places, should take courage when they consider, that the Persians and Odrysians, who are accustomed to fight on declivities, have their horses as sound as the Greeks.

We will not omit to explain how the rider ought to accommodate himself to all these situations. When the horse commences a gallop suddenly, he should stoop forward, for the horse will thus be less depressed with his weight, and less able to throw back the rider by rearing, and immediately when he pulls in the reins, let him bend back and he will be thus less jolted.

In crossing a ditch and ascending an acclivity, it is proper to seize the mane, lest the horse should be oppressed both by the difficulty of the ground and the bridle. In descending a declivity, the rider's head must be kept up, and the horse checked by the bridle, lest horse and rider be borne precipitately down the declivity.

It is proper frequently to change the place and extent of the race ground : for this is more agreeable to the horse, than being always trained in the same places and in the same manner.

Since it is necessary, that he who drives his horse rapidly through all sorts of places, should be able to sit firmly on his back, and use his arms dexterously; we much commend the exercise of horsemanship in hunting, where the situation is convenient, and wild beasts to be found. When that is not the case, it is a useful exercise for two horsemen to agree between themselves, that the one shall retire on horseback through all sorts of places, and retreat, often turning about with his spear presented : and the other shall pursue, having javelins blunted with balls, and a spear of the same description, and whenever he comes within a javelin throw, that he hurl the blunted weapons at the person retreating, and whenever he comes within the stroke of a spear, that he strike him with it.

It is good also when they encounter, that he drag his enemy to himself, and suddenly repel him : for this is apt to unhorse him. It is also advisable that the person dragged should spur on his steed : for when he does this, he is more likely to overthrow his antagonist than be overthrown.

And if at any time, when one camp is pitched opposite another, a charge should take place, and they should pursue the enemy to the hostile ranks, and then retreat to their own lines, it is good even here to know, that as long as he is near his friends, he will act bravely and safely, by advancing among the first, and pressing closely and vigorously on the enemy. When he comes near the enemy, he should tighten the reins and check the horse, that he may be able to retreat suddenly : when he acts thus, it is natural to suppose that he will injure the enemy, and receive no injury in return.

The gods have granted the ability to men, to inform others by speech what they wish done. A horse, however, cannot be instructed by speech : but if when he does what you wish, you grant a favour in return, and when he is disobedient, punish him, he will be thus trained to obey when necessary.

This rule has been given in few words, but it is advantageous in every branch of horsemanship. For he will endure the bridle more willingly, if when he does so, something good happens to him, and he will leap across ditches, spring forward and obey in all other occasions, if he expects some indulgence after having performed what he is ordered.

IX. We have now explained how a person may be least deceived in purchasing a foal or horse, and how he may be least injured in using them, more especially if it be necessary to exhibit a horse, as possessed of all the qualities a horseman requires in war. It is perhaps time to explain how we should use correctly a horse, which is either too spirited or too lazy.

First, then, he ought to know that spirit is to a horse, what anger is to a man. And as there is little likelihood of a man being put in a passion, who has nothing unpleasant either said or done to him, so also a high-mettled steed cannot be exasperated, when he suffers nothing disagreeable.

In mounting a horse we must be careful not to occasion any pain. When we have mounted, we ought to remain quiet a longer time than usual, and then move him forward by the gentlest signs : we should commence very slowly, and gradually induce him to quicken his step, that even he may not observe when he is forced to full speed.

A spirited horse, like a man, when he sees, or hears, or feels any thing suddenly, is thrown into confusion : this circumstance ought always to be kept in view when managing him.

If we require to rein in a spirited horse when running quicker than required, we should not draw in the reins suddenly, but pull back the bridle gently, and thus coax not force him to stand still.

Long continued rides are more apt to tame horses than frequent short turns; and long gentle rides soften, and tame, and do not exasperate the high-mettled horse.

If any person imagines, that by fatiguing the horse with a swift and long race he will tame him, he is greatly deceived. For in such circumstances, the spirited horse attempts to use violence, and when enraged, like a passionate man, frequently does irreparable injury both to himself and rider.

It is proper also to check the high-mettled horses from galloping at full speed, and restrain them altogether from contending with other horses; for if permitted, they generally become most fond of contention and refractory.

A smooth bridle is much more suitable than a rough one. But, if a rough one be put on, it must be rendered similar to a smooth one by being held slackly. It is good also to accustom one's self to sit quiet, especially on a spirited horse, and to touch no other part than what is necessary to preserve a firm seat.

A horseman should also know, that it is a received precept to soothe him by whistling, and rouse him by a sharp sound made between the tongue and the palate. But, if the rider commence by accustoming the horse to the latter sound when receiving soothing treatment, and to whistling when roughly used, he will soon learn to be roused by whistling, and pacified by the sharp sound made between the tongue and the palate.

So also when a shout is raised, or at the sound of a trumpet, the rider should not approach the horse as if he were dismayed, nor exhibit any thing to the horse exciting consternation, but in such circumstances soothe him as much as possible, and present to him his dinner or supper if it can be conveniently done.

Never to procure a very high-spirited horse for war, is a most excellent advice. I consider it sufficient to recommend, that the lazy horse should be treated in a manner directly contrary to that in which we advised the high-mettled to be used.

X. If a horseman desires to possess a horse useful for war, and very magnificent and conspicuous to ride upon, he ought to refrain from drawing his mouth with the bridle, and from spurring and flogging him, which when the majority of people do, they suppose that they cause him to act splendidly. Such persons produce an effect contrary to what they intend. For when they draw up the horse's head, instead of allowing him to look forward, they blind him, and when they spur and strike him, they agitate him so much as to terrify him, and cause him to expose himself to dangers. Horses which act thus, are those which have taken a dislike to riding, and conduct themselves shamefully.

But, if the horse should be trained to ride with a slack rein, and to rear his head, and arch his neck, he will thus be impelled to do what he rejoices and exults in.

As a proof that they delight in such gestures, when they come among other horses, but more especially mares, spirited fiery horses rear their heads, arch their necks, elevate their limbs pliantly, and erect their tails.

When the horse is excited to assume that artificial air which he adopts when he is proud, he then delights in riding, becomes magnificent, terrific, and attracts attention. How that gait can be obtained, we shall now attempt to explain.

First, then, it is necessary to have no fewer than two reins. Let one of these be smooth, having large olive bits, and the other have heavy and small olive bits, with sharp small globes: that, as soon as they seize it and feel its roughness intolerable, they may let it go: and when they have exchanged it for the smooth one with which they are pleased, they will perform the same actions when urged by the smooth, which they were trained to do with the rough.

But, if again they despise its smoothness, and frequently press against it, we must then add a few larger rollers to the smooth rein, that being obliged to open his mouth by them, they may admit the bit. It is possible also, to diversify the rough bridle by coiling it up and extending it.

Whatever number of bridles there be, they should all be flexible and soft. When they are not pliant, the horse wherever he seizes it, holds it all close to the jaws. He raises the whole like a spit whenever he seizes it.

The other description of bridle is like a chain; for wherever it is held, that alone remains unmoved, the rest hangs loose: as he is always catching at it while it is escaping out of his mouth, he drops the bit out of his jaws. For this reason little rings are suspended at the middle from the axles called players, that while he aims at these with his tongue and his teeth, he may neglect to seize the bridle at the jaws.

If it should not be known what we mean by a flexible and soft bridle, and what by a hard one, we will explain it. It is called flexible when the axles have broad and smooth junctures, so as to be easily bent: and every thing which encircles the axles, if it be large and not compact is flexible.

But, if each of these parts of the bridle run with difficulty on their axles, then we call it a hard bridle. Whatever kind of bridle it be, all the following directions must be attended to, by him who wishes to render the horse's form such as we have explained above.

The horse's mouth must not be too severely drawn back, lest he should refuse obedience by declining his head; nor too gently, lest he should not feel it. When he raises his neck by throwing his head upwards, the rein must be immediately given him, and even in other respects, as we are always recommending, when he has performed his duty properly, we must humour him.

When the rider perceives that the horse is well pleased by holding his neck high, and by the laxity of his reins, then nothing disagreeable must be offered, as forcing him to labour, but he must be coaxed, as if it were desired that he should cease from toil. By these means he will advance more cheerfully to his quickest speed.

It is a sufficient proof, that horses delight in running, that when set free, none of them proceeds slowly, but at a gallop. Of this they are naturally fond, unless they are forced to run to an immoderate distance. Nothing immoderate is agreeable either to horse or man.

When we wish our horses trained to ride with pomp and magnificence, they must previously have been accustomed in riding, to proceed at full speed after being turned. And should the rider, having previously trained his horse to this, at the same time rein him in, and give him the signal to advance rapidly, the horse is stimulated by being checked with the bridle, and incited to proceed rapidly, and he throws forward his chest, and raises his legs furiously though not pliantly : for when horses are hurt or offended, their legs are no longer pliant.

If the reins be given to a horse thus rendered fiery by being checked, then for joy that he supposes himself set free, on account of the slackness of the bit, he is borne along prancingly, with a triumphant gait and pliant limbs, and in every respect imitating the graceful motion assumed by horses approaching each other.

Persons beholding such a horse pronounce him generous, free in his motions, fit for military exercise, high-mettled, haughty, and both pleasant and terrible to look on. To those who desire a horse trained to the above attitudes, we consider the precepts now given to be satisfactory.

XI. If any one should desire to be possessed of a horse fit for show, erectly walking, and splendid, he cannot indeed expect these qualities in every horse, but only in those which nature has endowed with a high spirit and a robust body.

It is generally supposed that those horses which have soft pliant legs, have the greatest facility in lifting them : this is not the case; this quality is to be found in those which have soft, short, and robust loins. We do not at present allude to the loins near the tail, but at the belly between the sides and the hips. Horses thus shaped will be able to throw their hinder legs considerably in advance of their fore legs when running.

When the horse is in this position, if the rider should pull back the reins, he falls back on the pasterns of his hind legs, raises the fore part of his body, and exhibits to those in front his belly and privy parts. When in this position, therefore, the reins should be given to him, that he may of his own accord assume the most graceful attitude, and seem to the spectators to do so.

Some train their horses to these things, one party by striking them under the pasterns with a rod, and another by causing a man to run by their side and strike them on the thigh.

But we consider it the best method of training, as we have always said, if upon every occasion that he performs readily and gracefully what his rider requires, he should enjoy ease.

For whatever a horse does when forced to it, as Simon also remarks, he does not understand, nor is it more comely, than if we were to flog and spur on a dancer to his duty. For either a horse or man when thus treated would act much more ungracefully than otherwise. A horse should be excited by signs, of his own accord to assume all the most graceful and splendid attitudes.

But if after riding and a copious sweat, and when he has reared gracefully, he should be immediately relieved of his rider and reins, there is little doubt but that he will of his own accord advance to rear when necessary.

In this attitude gods and heroes are painted as seated on horseback; and men who manage their horses gracefully appear magnificent.

A steed which rears gracefully is an object

of so much comeliness, wonder, and astonishment, that he attracts the attention of all spectators whether young or old. No person leaves him or grows tired of seeing him, until he has exhibited all his splendour.

If a person possessed of such a steed should happen to lead and command a troop of cavalry, it is not proper that he should individually be ostentatiously splendid, but rather that the whole of the line which follows him should be gratifying to the sight.

And if one of these horses, so much commended, should take the lead, which rears very high and frequently, and advances with quick short steps, it is evident that the other horses must follow him with a slow and gentle pace. In what consists the splendour of such a spectacle?

But if he excites his steed and leads the van neither with too great speed, nor too great slowness, he will cause the horses which follow to exhibit themselves as very high-spirited, fiery, and graceful': there will then be an uninterrupted noise, and a universal snorting and panting throughout the troop, so that not only the leader but the whole line will exhibit a gratifying spectacle.

If a person be fortunate in the purchase of a horse, and feed him so as to enable him to endure labour, and train him properly for martial exercises, and ostentatious exhibitions of horsemanship, and contests in the field of battle, what can be an obstacle to his rendering horses more valuable than when he received them, and to his possessing approved horses, and obtaining renown as a horseman, unless some heavenly power prevent it?

XII. We will also explain how he should be armed who intends to encounter danger on horseback. First, then, we assert that the breastplate should be made to fit the body: when it fits well, the body supports it; when it is too loose, the shoulders alone sustain the weight; when it is too strait, it becomes a prison, not armour.

And as the neck is one of the vital parts, we recommend that a covering be made similar to the neck out of the breastplate; for this is at the same time ornamental, and if properly made, will receive within it, when necessary, the rider's face as high as his nose.

Moreover, we consider the helmet of Bœotian manufacture as by far the best: because it completely protects all above the breastplate.

and does not prevent our seeing. Let the breastplate be so made that it may not hinder either our sitting down or stooping.

About the lower extremity of the belly, the genitals, and the parts around, let extremities of the mail of such a description and size be so placed as to defend the limbs.

When the left hand suffers any injury it proves destructive to the rider, we therefore recommend the defensive armour invented for it, called gauntlets. For it both protects the shoulder, and the arm above and below the elbow, and the contiguous parts of the reins, and may be extended and contracted at pleasure; and, besides, it covers up the vacant space of the breastplate under the armpit.

The right hand must also be raised, whether the rider wishes to hurl the javelin or strike a blow. Whatever part of the breastplate hinders this must be removed, and instead of it, let there be artificial extremities on the joints, that when the hand is raised, they may be unfolded, and when it is drawn back, they may be closed.

It seems to us much preferable to have a covering of the arms similar to greaves for the legs, than to have it connected with the rest of the armour. That part which is bared by raising the right hand, must be protected near the breastplate by a piece of leather or brass, otherwise a most vital part is left unguarded.

And since, when an accident befals a horse, the rider is also brought into the greatest danger, the horse must be armed with a plate of brass on the forehead, another on the breast, and another on the side: for these also prove coverings for the rider's thighs. Above every thing, the horse's belly must be protected; for it is the most fatal and infirm part of his body and it may be defended by the saddle.

The saddle should be formed of such materials as to enable the rider to sit with greatest safety, and not injure the seat on the horse's back. On the other parts of the body let horse and horseman be thus armed.

The rider's legs and feet will naturally hang down below the covering of the horse's thighs; these would be armed, if covered with boots made of the same leather as the military shoes; and they would thus serve as defensive armour to the legs, and shoes to the feet.

The above is the equestrian armour, by which, with the assistance of the gods, injury may be warded off. But in injuring the enemy, we give a decided preference to the poniard over the sword: for as the horseman is elevated, the stroke of a falchion is more effectual than that of a sword.

Instead of a spear made of a pole, as it is fragile and incommodious to carry, we give a preference to two spears made of the cornel tree. For the one can be hurled by the person skilled in throwing it, and the remaining one can be used in front, laterally, and in rear: they are besides stronger and lighter than a spear.

We commend that hurling of javelins which takes place at the greatest distance; for by this means more time is granted to turn aside and to change the missile weapon. We will now briefly explain the best mode of hurling the javelin. If we throw forward the left hand, draw back the right, rise from our thighs, and hurl the javelin slightly pointed upwards, it will be thus carried most impetuously to the greatest distance, and with unerring aim, provided the point of the lance when thrown is directed towards the mark.

The above are our admonitions, instructions, and exercises, which we recommend to the unskilled rider: what the general of the horse should understand and practise is explained in another treatise.

THE

EPISTLES OF XENOPHON.

TRANSLATED BY

THOMAS STANLEY, ESQ.

EPISTLES OF XENOPHON.

EPISTLE I.

TO ÆSCHINES.

MEETING with Hermogenes, amongst other things I asked him what philosophy you followed, he answered, the same as Socrates. For this inclination I admired you, when you lived at Athens, and now continue the same admiration for your constancy above other students of wisdom; the greatest argument to me of your virtue, is your being taken with that man, if we may call the life of Socrates mortal. That there are divine beings over us, all know: we worship them as exceeding us in power; what they are is neither easy to find, nor lawful to inquire. It concerns not servants to examine the nature and actions of their masters, their duty is only to obey them, and which is most considerable, the more admiration they deserve who busy themselves in those things which belong to man; the more trouble this brings them, who affect glory in vain unseasonable objects: For when, Æschines, did any man hear Socrates discourse of the heavens, or advise his scholars to mathematical demonstrations? we know he understood music no farther than the ear; but was always discoursing to his friends of something excellent; what is fortitude and justice and other virtues. These he called the proper good of mankind; other things he said men could not arrive at; or they were of kin to fables, such ridiculous things as are taught by the supercilious professors of wisdom. Nor did he only teach this, his practice was answerable; of which I have written at large elsewhere, what I hope will not be unpleasing to you, though you know it already, to peruse.

Let those who are not satisfied with what Socrates delivered, give over upon this conviction, or confine themselves to what is probable. Living, he was attested wise by the deity; dead, his murderers could find no expiation by repentance. But these extraordinary persons affect Egypt, and the prodigious learning of Pythagoras, which unnecessary study argueth them of inconstancy towards Socrates, as doth also their love of tyrants, and preferring the luxury of a Sicilian table before a frugal life.

EPISTLE II.

TO CRITO.

Socrates often told us, that they who provide much wealth for their children, but neglected to improve them by virtue, do like those that feed their horses high, and never train them to the manage; by this means their horses are the better in case, but the worse for service, whereas the commendations of a horse consists not in his being fat, but serviceable in war. In the same kind err they who purchase lands for their children, but neglect their persons; their possessions will be of great value, themselves of none, whereas the owner ought to be more honourable than his estate. Whosoever therefore breeds his son well, though he leave him little, gives him much: it is the mind which makes him great or small: whatsoever they have, to the good seems sufficient, to the rude too little. You leave your children no more than necessity requires, which they, being well educated, will esteem plentiful. The ignorant, though free from present trouble, have nothing the less fear for the future.

EPISTLE III.

TO SOTIRA.

Death in my opinion is neither good nor ill, but the end of the life, not alike to all, for as stronger or weaker from their birth, their years are unequal; sometimes death is hastened by good or evil causes: and again, neither is it fitting to grieve so much for death, knowing that birth is the beginning of man's pilgrimage, death the end. He died as all men, though never so unwilling, must do: but to die well, is the part of a willing and well educated person. Happy was Gryllus, and whosoever else chooseth not the longest life, but the most virtuous· though his, it pleased God, was short.

EPISTLE IV.

TO LAMPROCLES.

You must first approve the excellent assertion of Socrates, that riches are to be measured by their use. He called not large possessions riches, but so much only as is necessary, in the judgment whereof he advised us not to be deceived, these he called truly rich, the rest poor, labouring under an incurable poverty of mind, not estate.

EPISTLE V.

They who write in praise of my son Gryllus, did as they ought, and you likewise do well in writing to us the actions of Socrates; we ought not only to endeavour to be good ourselves, but to praise him who lived chastely, piously, and justly, and to blame fortune, and those who plotted against him, who ere long will receive the punishment thereof. The Lacedæmonians are much incensed at it, for the ill news is come hither already, and reproach our people, saying, they are mad again, in that they could be wrought upon to put him to death, whom Pythia declared the wisest of men. If any of Socrates's friends want those things which I sent, give me notice, and I will help them, for it is just and honest; you do well in keeping Æschines with you, as you send me word. I have a design to collect the sayings and actions of Socrates, which will be his best

apology, both now and for the future, not in the court where the Athenians are judges, but to all who consider the virtue of the man. If we should not write this freely, it were a sin against friendship; and the truth. Even now there fell into my hands a piece of Plato's to that effect, wherein is the name of Socrates, and some discourses of his not unpleasant. But we must profess that we heard not, nor can commit to writing any in that kind, for we are not poets as he is, though he renounce poetry; for amidst his entertainments with beautiful persons, he affirmed that there was not any poem of his extant, but one of Socrates, young and handsome. Farewell, both, dearest to me.

EPISTLE VI.

Intending to celebrate the feast of Diana, to whom we have erected a temple, we sent to invite you hither; if all of you would come, it were much the best, otherwise, if you send such as you can conviently spare to assist at our sacrifice, you will do us a favour. Aristippus was here, and before him, Phædo, who were much pleased with the situation and structure, but above all, with the plantation which I have made with my own hands. The place is stored with beasts convenient for hunting, which the goddess affects; let us rejoice and give thanks to her who preserved me from the king of the Barbarians, and afterwards in Pontus and Thrace from greater evils, even when we thought we were out of the enemies' reach. Though you come not, yet am I obliged to write to you. I have composed some memorials of Socrates, when they are perfect you shall have them. Aristippus and Phædo did not disapprove of them; salute in my name Simon the leather-dresser, and commend him that he continueth Socratic discourses, not diverted by want, or his trade, from philosophy, as some others, who decline to know and admire such discourses and their effects.

EPISTLE VII.

Come to us, dear friend, for we have now finished the temple of Diana, a magnificent structure, the place set with trees, and consecrated, what remains will be sufficient to maintain us; for, as Socrates said, if they are not fit for us, we will fit ourselves to them; I write to Gryllus my son and your friend, to supply your occasions; I write to Gryllus, because, of a little one you have professed a kindness for him.

EPISTLE VIII.

TO XANTIPPE.

To Euphron of Megara, I delivered six measures of meal, eight drachms, and a new raiment for your use this winter; accept them, and know, that Euclid and Terpsion are exceeding good, honest persons, very affectionate to you and Socrates; if your sons have a desire to come to me, hinder them not, for the journey to Megara is neither long nor incommodious; pray forbear to weep any more, it may do hurt, but cannot help. Remember what Socrates said, follow his practice and precepts; in grieving you will but wrong yourself and children; they are the young ones of Socrates, whom we are obliged not only to maintain, but to preserve ourselves for their sakes; lest, if you or I, or any other, who, after the death of Socrates, ought to look to his children, should fail, they might want a guardian to maintain and protect them. I study to live for them, which you will not do unless you cherish yourself. Grief is one of those things which are opposite to life, for by it the living are prejudiced. Apollodorus surnamed the Soft, and Dion, praise you, that you will accept nothing from any, professing you are rich; it is well done, for as long as I and other friends are able, to maintain you, you shall need none else. Be of good courage, Xantippe, lose nothing of Socrates, knowing how great that man was, think upon his life, not upon his death; yet, that to those who consider, it will appear noble and excellent. Farewell.

EPISTLE IX.

TO CEBES AND SIMMIAS.

It is commonly said, nothing is richer than a poor man. This I find true in myself, who have not so much, but whilst you my friends take care of me, seem to possess much; and it is well done of you to supply me as often as I write: as concerning my commentaries, there is none of them but I fear should be seen by any in my absence, as I professed in your hearing, at the house where Euclid lay. I know, dear friends, a writing once communicated to many is irrecoverable. Plato, though absent, is much admired throughout Italy and Sicily for his treatises; but we cannot be persuaded they deserve any study; I am not only careful of losing the honour due to learning, but tender also of Socrates, lest his virtue should incur any prejudice by my ill relation of it. I conceive it the same thing to calumniate, or not praise to the full those of whom we write; this is my fear, Cebes and Simmias, at present, until my judgment shall be otherwise informed. Fare ye well.

INDEX.

I & J

K

L

THE END.

GLASGOW:
HUTCHISON & BROOKMAN, PRINTERS TO THE UNIVERSITY.